Fodor's

ESSENTIAL
GREECE

D0017087

Welcome to Greece

A visit to the land of Homer, Aristotle, and Sophocles is a journey to the dawn of classical civilization, with archaeological splendors from Athens to Crete. The monasteries of Meteora and Mount Olympus inspire awe, while islands like Corfu and Santorini invite a taste of the good life on the Aegean Sea. The Greek countryside presents the perfect coda with landscapes of cypress groves, vineyards, and olive trees. This book was created in the middle of the COVID-19 pandemic. As you plan your upcoming travels to Greece, please confirm that places are still open and let us know when we need to make updates by writing to us at: editors@fodors.com.

TOP REASONS TO GO

★ **Athens.** Spread out below the towering Acropolis, Greece's capital pulses with excitement.

★ **Islands.** Spiritual Patmos, peaceful Naxos, medieval Rhodes, sylvan Skopelos, and more.

★ **Stunning Beaches.** Some 9,000 miles of shoreline means a beach for every interest.

★ **Ancient Splendors.** Sacred Delphi, ancient Olympia, and the Minoan palaces of Crete.

★ **Food and Drink.** Succulent lamb, freshly grilled fish, fiery ouzo, and flavorful wines.

★ **Nightlife.** The world parties at the beaches of Mykonos and seaside clubs of Glyfada.

Contents

Fodor's Features

MAPS

Chapter 1

EXPERIENCE GREECE

22 ULTIMATE EXPERIENCES

Greece offers terrific experiences that should be on every traveler's list. Here are Fodor's top picks for a memorable trip.

1 Sunset in Santorini

The crescent-shaped Cycladic island offers dramatic views over the Aegean Sea. The town of Ia, perched on an 1,100-foot cliff, provides some spectacular—and wildly popular—sunset-watching opportunities across the caldera. *(Ch. 8)*

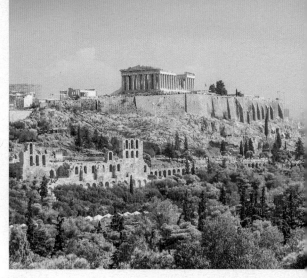

2 The Acropolis of Athens

Every city-state in ancient Greece had a fortress on a hill. But there is only one Acropolis, built in 5 BC and rightly considered the jewel of Athenian civilization. *(Ch. 3)*

3 The Palace of Knossos, Crete

The palace of King Minos reveals a gentrified people some 5,000 years ago in possession of advanced technology, a written language, and intellectual prowess. *(Ch. 9)*

4 Pine-Covered Skopelos

One of the greenest Greek islands offers aquamarine waters and a church for every day of the year, including one that was the setting for the *Mamma Mia!* films. *(Ch. 5)*

5 Greece's First Capital

Nafplion, the first capital of Greece in 1821, retains its picturesque, Venetian-era historic center and is ideal for exploring the Peloponnese. *(Ch. 15)*

6 Greece's Second City

Historic sites such as the medieval White Tower have made Thessaloniki a UNESCO World Heritage Site, while vibrant nightlife draws partiers. *(Ch. 14)*

7 Low-Key Folegandros

With one of the prettiest towns in the Cyclades perched upon a windswept cliff, the archetypal island is rocky and tiny and still largely untouched by mass tourism. *(Ch. 8)*

8 A Treasure Trove

The National Archaeological Museum in Athens holds the most important findings from excavations around Greece. It's a must-see for first-time visitors. *(Ch. 3)*

9 Mountain of the Gods

The tallest mountain in Greece is the mythical sanctuary of the Olympian Gods. These days it's an impressive national park with numerous hiking trails. *(Ch. 14)*

10 Keep the Flame Alive

Olympia is a must-do day trip when touring the Peloponnese. The sanctuary dedicated to Zeus will forever be associated with the Olympic Games, which began here. *(Ch. 15)*

11 Partying in Mykonos

Greece's quintessential party paradise attracts jet-setters and A-listers, but the island also has a quieter side and a magical old town. *(Ch. 7)*

12 Delos, the Sacred Island

A short boat trip from Mykonos lies the abandoned birthplace of Apollo, once a religious capital and a safe port for incoming vessels, now an archaeological site. *(Ch. 7)*

13 Live the Middle Ages

The narrow alleyways of Monemvasia transport you five centuries back in time to the clashes between the Byzantine empire and the Franks. *(Ch. 15)*

14 Rhodes Town

The oldest populated medieval town in the world draws you into its mazelike, traffic-free streets with beautiful restored buildings and cobbled lanes. *(Ch. 10)*

15 Beaches Everywhere

With 8,498 miles of coastline, you are never too far away from a beach in Greece. Several of the most beautiful white-sand beaches, including Elafonissi, are in Crete. *(Ch. 9)*

16 Get Closer to Heaven

There is something out-of-this-world about Meteora and the determination of the human spirit, which willed that there would be monasteries atop these massive rocks. *(Ch. 13)*

17 Places of Worship

Thousands of churches are scattered around Greece, ranging in style from the Cycladic (with blue and white domes) to the Venetian style of Panayia Evangelistria on Tinos. *(Ch. 7, 8)*

18 Italianate Style in Corfu

The lush green slopes, protected coves, and mild climate lured Ulysses, but also a string of Byzantine, Venetian, and British settlers (including the literary Durrells). *(Ch. 6)*

19 Island of the Apocalypse

It is not easy to get to Patmos, so the atmosphere remains serene, sophisticated, and relaxed, as transporting as when St. John wrote the Revelation here in AD 95. *(Ch. 10)*

20 Enter Warrior Country

The Mani is the land of warriors, from where many Greek heroes hail, an isolated, barren land dotted with stone towers and fortresses that is still strangely beautiful. *(Ch. 15)*

21 Car-Free Hydra

The approach to the harbor is spectacular as the crescent-shaped, hilly settlement is slowly revealed. Life on this simply beautiful island follows a relaxed, slow pace. *(Ch. 4)*

22 Respect the Oracle

For ancient Greeks, Delphi, with its oracles, was the center of the world. Today, it has a high concentration of ancient ruins and a wonderful museum. *(Ch. 12)*

WHAT'S WHERE

1 Athens. Contemporary Athens has a sleek subway, a brand new culture center, a thriving arts scene, and happening nightlife. But for 5 million Athenians, it's still the tried-and-true pleasures that put the spin on urban life here: the endless parade of cafés, the Plaka and other spirited neighborhoods, and, of course, the Acropolis.

2 The Saronic Gulf Islands. When Athenians want a break, they often make a quick crossing to the idyllic islands of the Saronic Gulf. The most popular of these destinations are Aegina, Hydra, and Spetses.

3 The Sporades. The northern Sporades deliver quintessential Greek-island pleasures: villages spilling down hillsides like giant sugar cubes and Byzantine monasteries. Weekenders savor Skiathos, but Skopelos has great beaches, and Skyros is washed by some of the clearest waters in Greece.

4 The Ionian Islands. On temperate, multi-hued Corfu, turquoise waters lap rocky coves, but first stop, of course, is Corfu town, a stage set for a Verdi opera

with colorful landmarks from the Venetian, French, and British past. Kefalonia is dotted with enchanting villages, while exotic Zakynthos is ringed with dazzling white sands.

5 The Northern Cyclades. With its sexy jet-set lifestyle, Mykonos takes the prize for hedonism, while church-studded Tinos is a pilgrimage island, and ancient Delos is sacred ground, the birthplace of Apollo.

6 The Southern Cyclades. Santorini, with its ravishing caldera, is the most picturesque island in Greece, with millions of selfies to prove the claim. Mountainous, cliff-ringed Folegandros, verdant Naxos, and beach-lined Paros, with its getaway islet of Antiparos, all have their own distinct charms.

7 Crete. Crete is Greece's southernmost and largest island, and its claims to superlatives don't stop there. Here, too, are some of Greece's tallest mountains, its deepest gorge, many of the best beaches, and a wealth of Venetian and Byzantine wonders.

WHAT'S WHERE

8 Rhodes and the Dodecanese. Wrapped enticingly around the shores of Turkey, the Dodecanese ("Twelve Islands") have attracted some notable visitors. St. John the Divine received his *Revelation* on quiet, refined Patmos, Hippocrates established a healing center on Kos, now a beacon for beach-goers, and the Crusader Knights of St. John lavished their wealth on palaces in Rhodes.

9 Northern Aegean Islands. Flung like puzzle pieces into the Aegean, each of these islands is distinct: Chios retains an eerie beauty amid its fortified villages and Byzantine monasteries; Lesvos is a getaway favored by artists and writers, and has lent a helping hand to high numbers of war-torn Middle East refugees; and lush, mountainous Samos whispers of the classical wonders of antiquity.

10 Attica. Some of the most important remains of ancient Greece are only an hour away from Athens. Delphi was the center of the universe for the ancients; at Marathon, the Athenians defeated the Persians; and the Temple of Poseidon hovers between sea and sky at Sounion.

11 Epirus and Thessaly.
Epirus is a land of stark
mountains and swift
rivers, where Ali Pasha
ruled an 18th-century
kingdom from Ioannina.
The route east to
Thessaly leads into the
Byzantine mountaintop
monasteries of Meteora.

**12 Thessaloniki and
Central Macedonia.** This
northern region includes
two sacred places, Mount
Olympus, where Zeus
reigned, and Mount
Athos, a male-only
sanctuary dedicated,
ironically, to the Virgin
Mary. The hub of the
region is Thessaloniki,
Greece's second-largest
city—a cosmopolitan
crossroads leading to
remnants of Alexander
the Great's Macedonian
empire.

13 The Peloponnese. The
mountains that loom here
cradle some of Greece's
most important ancient
sites—Olympia, Corinth,
Mycenae, and Ancient
Messene. Gorgeous
Nafplion is the work of
later empire builders—
Byzantines, Venetians,
and Turks—and is as
mellow as wines from the
region's vineyards. Southward lies the hauntingly
beautiful Mani
Peninsula.

Greece Today

RESPONDING TO CRISIS

You don't need us to tell you that times have been tough in the cradle of democracy. COVID-19 took it's toll here, as elsewhere. While government action helped keep infection and death rates relatively low compared to other European nations and the U.S., the effects on travel have been hard-felt in this country where one-fifth of the population works in tourism. This comes as the country is slowly climbing out of the economic crisis that erupted a decade ago, when public debt topped €350 billion and Greece found itself in need of a bailout. The nation is also coping with an ongoing immigration crisis, and more than a million refugees, many fleeing the civil war in Syria, have arrived in the country, often coming ashore on the Northern Aegean island of Levbos. More than 30,000 have remained on the island, but most were left homeless when the Moria camp burned in September 2020. Other arrivals have moved on to Athens, other Greek islands, and to Western Europe. But as the rest of the Europen Union tightens immigration quotas and the U.S. more or less turns it back on the situation, Greece is left to house and care for these many stateless men, women, and children.

FAMILY AND FORWARD THINKING

All this said, don't be spooked by the headlines. The Acropolis is not for sale, and life goes on, often in colorful Greek style. While the struggling economy and high unemployment rates, especially among young people, have forced some Greeks to seek opportunities abroad, a strong sense of family has helped others to weather the storm. Families work together to provide child care and help to their elders. With less income, trips abroad are often out of reach, but many city dwellers tap their family networks to head out to a cousin's house by the sea or spend time in a traditional village where they have roots.

In fact, many Greeks have begun to appreciate their villages in a new way. Some young Athenians have shipped off to their "home" islands and opened businesses. Others have learned that local agricultural products that provide cheap, healthful, and delicious sustenance at home can be marketed with success abroad. While Greece remains the world's top olive oil consumer, the country has fallen behind competing producers, Spain and Italy. So, instead of packaging their oil in bulk, some producers have begun to bottle and market their quality extra virgin olive oil abroad for the first time. Greek wine makers are moving into international markets, too, with crisp dry whites from Crete, the Peloponnese, and Macedonia leading the way, and some excellent reds are increasingly available as well.

STARTING UP

Greece has always shown strong entrepreneurship, and cosmetics companies Apivita and Korres, with products based on native-Greek botanicals and other natural ingredients, continue to establish a worldwide presence, as do Bug Sense and other Greece-based high-tech firms. Tourists are benefitting from startups like Beat, an app to summon yellow cabs in Athens and Thessaloniki, and Coco-Mat, the eco-minded furniture company that very likely makes the supercomfortable mattress in your Greek hotel room and has also opened a chain of chicly luxurious inns of their own. Agribusiness, one of Greece's most promising sectors, moves forward with companies like Fage, producer of yogurt, and Mastihashop, with foods and other products from the island of Chios.

THE FUTURE OF TOURISM?

Despite the political, social, and economic upheaval around them, Greeks remain optimistic by nature and are hospitable hosts. No matter what challenges they face, they're warm-hearted and outgoing and proud to showcase their country's beautiful landscapes and islands. Even in downtrodden Athens, restaurant, bar, and café owners are bringing new life to once-abandoned squares and streets in the commercial center, including the Psirri district. Steady as ever above the modern city, the Acropolis continues to undergo seemingly endless renovations. The oracles have yet to portend what the future holds, and no one really knows how tourism will fare in the coming seasons. That depends on such factors as the world economy, the course of COVID-19, and the emergence of vaccines and therapeutics. What's certain is that those sandy beaches and blue seas will continue to send out a siren call, and Greeks will extend a warm welcome to those who answer.

Greece's Best Beaches

CANAL D'AMOUR, CORFU
Legend has it that if you swim the length of this cove wedged between tall rock formations you will meet the love of your life at the other end—if you've already done so, settle for watching young divers take daring plunges from the cliff tops into the turquoise waters.

LALARIA, SKIATHOS
A majestic arch frames a sparkling expanse of shimmering marble and limestone pebbles, and adjacent sea grottos enhance the otherworldly ambiance. A boat trip around the coast—the only way to reach this idyllic hideaway—adds to the romance of a visit.

PSILI AMMOS, PATMOS
A boat ride from the port in Skala or a half-hour hike are the only ways to reach the island's most beautiful stretch of sand (aptly, the name means "fine sand") where some stands of fragrant pines provide scented and coveted shade.

MYRTOS BEACH, KELAFONIA
One of the most beautiful beaches in all of Greece (and that's saying a lot) passed its screen test as a setting in the film *Captain Corelli's Mandolin,* and the cinematic inlet washing onto perfect sands backed by dramatically steep, forested mountainsides is also the star of countless vacation pics. Around the bend is postcard worthy Fiskardo, a port and fishing village straddling an isthmus.

MAVRA VOLIA, CHIOS
Homer's "wine-dark sea" washes onto the dark volcanic shores of a cove nestled beneath sheltering cliffs. Little wonder the name of this hauntingly appealing spot means "Black Pebbles." The beach is located in the southern part of the island near the traditional village of Pirgi.

PANORMOS BEACH, MYKONOS
On an island famous (or is that infamous?) for fun in the sun and the paradise-for-partygoers beaches of Paradise and Superparadise, this seductive North Coast strand is a relative wall flower and all the more lovely for it—just a long and beautiful stretch of sand where you will find peace, quiet, and your own place in the sun.

VAI, CRETE
The largest natural palm grove in Europe provides an MGM-worthy backdrop to fine sands and crystalline waters. How the palm trees grew here is a mystery though it's been said that Phoenician merchants docked their ships at the port and threw the seeds of the date palms they were eating on the ground, hence giving rise to this majestic forest. But certainly this lovely stretch of sand was a beach that even the ancients raved about. Speaking of which, a swim at adjacent Itanos comes with views of a submerged Greek and Roman harbor.

Lemonakia, Kokkari, Samos

LEMONAKIA, KOKKARI, SAMOS

Rocky promontories carpeted with pine forests frame this perfect half-moon crescent of sand that fringes calm, warm waters sheltered by two headlands, known appropriately as the Dydimi, the Twins.

NEO ITILO, PELOPONNESE

The colorful little port on a beautiful bay is just a small collection of waterside houses strung out along a white-pebble beach, but the scene seems downright cosmopolitan amid the stark and brooding foothills of the Taygettus mountain range. Beachgoers here mingle with fishermen who mend their nets and show off their catch.

SCHINIAS, MARATHON, ATTICA

Many beaches near Athens are noisy party scenes, but this long, sandy stretch is positively pristine by comparison, with some simple tavernas and beach bars and backed by an enchanting pine forest. Combine some beach time with a visit to the sights at Marathon, of race fame, and Rhamnous, an ancient sacred precinct.

PLAKA, NAXOS

The most beautiful of them all, on an island of beautiful, soft-sand beaches, is backed by more than two miles of dunes and bamboo groves, an exotic setting enhanced by spectacular sunsets almost every evening.

AGIOS GEORGIOS, RHODES

The most paradisaical beach on an island noted for its sands is a hideaway from more cosmopolitan stretches of coastline, shaded with heavenly scented cedars, and well worth the adventurous drive down a cypress-shaded dirt track. The name comes from the little chapel standing by itself in the scrubby wilderness.

What to Eat and Drink

OUZO

Savor the good life in Greece in an *ouzeri*, a bar where the star of the show is the anise-flavored liquor made from grape must and served with a small plate of mezedes. The clear, potent liquid is sipped from a tall glass, a *konokia*.

COFFEE

Elderly gents pack into village *kafeneia* (coffeehouses), while students sip in city *kafeterias* (cafes). However old-fashioned or chic the shop, the choices are the same: *elliniko*, thick traditional coffee; *frappe*, a blend of instant Nescafe, water, evaporated milk, and sugar; and *freddo*, an iced cappuccino or espresso.

GRANDMA'S CASSEROLES

Staples from any Greek kitchen are *moussaka*, a casserole of spiced beef and eggplant topped with bechamel, and *pastitsio*, tube-shaped pasta baked with spiced beef, bechamel, and cheese. Any self-respecting cook follows a secret recipe handed down from *yiayia* (grandma).

MEZEDES

Greek meals kick off with small plates meant to be shared. Tzaziki (yogurt with garlic and dill), taramosalata (creamy fish roe dip), fava (pureed yellow split peas), dolmades (grape leaves stuffed with ground beef or lamb)—try a few and order more to make a meal of them.

HORIATIKI

What the rest of the world knows as Greek salad is best in the homeland, bursting with flavorful tomatoes, onions, olives, and cucumbers, fresh from the home garden in even the fanciest city restaurants, and topped with a generous slab of creamy feta cheese.

AMYGDALOTA

You've probably had baklava, the honey-and-sweet syrup soaked, nut-rich dessert, but on your travels in Greece you're likely to discover another favorite sweet: almond cookies, often served alongside coffee. There's usually a plate in the kitchen at the ready to bring out to guests.

GYROS AND SOUVLAKI

They taste sort of the same, and both are delicious. Gyro: shaved from meat, often chicken or lamb, that's roasted on a vertical spit. Souvlaki: the same meat, that's been skewered then grilled. They're the street food of choice everywhere in Greece and often stuffed inside pitas alongside vegetables and fries for a portable feast.

Horiatiki

SAGANAKI

If you think *saganaki* is one those dishes that come out of the kitchen of your local Greek place in flames with everyone screaming "oopa," you have to come to Greece for the real thing: slabs of *graviera* cheese dredged in flour, fried to golden perfection in a pan called a *saganaki*, and drizzled with lemon. In addition to graviera cheese, other cheeses that can be used include *kefalograviera, halloumi, kasseri, manouri,* and *kefalotyri.* Cut it into bite-sized pieces and serve it for all to enjoy. So simple yet so tasty, you might want to shout "oopa"!

TOMATOKEFTEDES

Among Santorini's great gifts to the world, aside from stunning scenery and legendary sunsets, are tomatokeftedes, one of the most traditional dishes on the island and often served as an appetizer at restaurants. These incredibly delicious fried tomato fritters are best when topped with tzatziki or another dip and served with a crisp glass of wine or a glass of ouzo. *Kolokithokeftedes,* zucchini fritters, are also a vegetarian-pleasing starter on Greek menus, and among many meatless main courses is *briam,* a casserole of roasted vegetables.

SPANIKOPITA

Leave those notions of being as American as apple pie at home. Because in Greece, pies aren't fruity and sweet but burst with savory fillings, like the classic, *spanakopita,* light-as-a-feather phyllo layered with feta cheese and spinach and flavored with dill.

Under the Radar

TEMPLE OF APOLLO AT BASSAE, PELOPONNESE
Even the presence of a protective shed can't detract from the majesty of this beautifully preserved monument of classical antiquity, surrounded by crags on a high perch.

SYMI, DODECANESE
The quiet island is a retreat from cosmopolitan Rhodes. Once you've explored the colorful port of Yialos, lined with neoclassical mansions, slip even farther away by boarding one of the little boats that chug to Aghios Nikolas.

LEKES, PAROS, SOUTHERN CYCLADES
Long ago, residents of this beautiful village hidden in the folds of the protective mountains would make their way to and from the sea on Byzantine mule tracks. Find one of these paths of well-worn stones just off a village square and make a scenic descent through olive groves to Piso Livadi, an ancient port.

VOULIAGMENI LAKE, ATTICA
These spring-fed waters south of central Athens are said to have curative powers. A dip beneath picturesque cliffs and a nap on the pretty terraces are certainly restorative and well worth the detour off the usual sightseeing circuit.

CAPE TENARO, PELOPONNESE

The farther down the isolated Mani peninsula you travel, the starker the landscapes become. Beyond Vathia, a ghost town of tower houses, the road winds through barren terrain to land's end, where an underwater cave was thought to be the entrance to the underworld. The views over the gulfs of Messina and Laconia are timeless.

TEMPLE OF DEMETER, NAXOS, SOUTHERN CYCLADES

No wonder this remote and splendidly restored temple of Naxian marble is dedicated to the goddess of grain, so bountiful is the surrounding countryside. Fields, lemon groves, and gardens full of roses enhance a journey to this out-of-the-way and enchanting spot.

GALAXIDI, DELPHI, AND ENVIRONS

Combine a visit to the ruins at Delphi with a side trip down the mountainside to seaside Galaxidi, a frozen-in-time port town where the beautifully restored homes of 19th-century sea captains line quiet lanes. A walk around the colorful harbor leads to coves that are ideal for a swim.

Mt. Tsiknias, Tinos

AYIOS NIKOLAOS MONASTERY, METSOVO, EPIRUS

Stone, slate-roofed houses huddling in a deep ravine seem a world removed, and a hike from town out to this remote 14th-century monastery takes you even farther from modern life. Colorful wall paintings are as transporting as the lush grounds on the banks of the Metsovo River.

FOLEGANDROS, SOUTHERN CYCLADES

The stark, cliff-ringed island is out of the way, quiet (no discos here), and a treasure for travelers who want a dose of Greek authenticity. The best way to soak in the isolated beauty while basking in the heavenly scent of wild oregano and thyme is on a hike on one of many well-marked paths that often end at a beach.

MT. TSIKNIAS, TINOS, NORTHERN CYCLADES

These uplands were the domain of Borealis, the god of winds, and you can breeze around them on a circuit of monasteries and mountain villages. Arnados is especially atmospheric and always shady, because many of the little lanes are arcaded.

The Most Beautiful Cities and Towns

PIRGI, CHIOS, NORTHERN AEGEAN

The maze of lanes twisting beneath towers and houses piled one atop the other to fend off marauding pirates seem like the work of a madman, or an Escher drawing. For a final flourish of fantasy, walls are adorned with stencils of animals, flowers, and geometric designs, and the effect is bedazzling.

KALAMBAKA, THESSALY

Talk about heavenly neighbors! The monastery-topped pinnacles of the Meteora loom right over town. Especially old-world-atmospheric is outlying Kastraki, a hamlet where flowers cascade from balconies and houses are set in gardens around a pretty square.

ARGOSTOLI, KEFALONIA

In a country where older is often better (i.e., the Acropolis), this beautiful island capital breaks the rule, rebuilt around spacious and leafy Plateia Vallianou after a 1953 earthquake. The most popular pastime is watching loggerhead turtles swimming beneath one of the few remaining historic landmarks, the stone-arched De Bosset bridge.

MYKONOS TOWN, MYKONOS

Maybe it's jaded beauty, but this bar-filled, scene-crazed, way-too-popular island capital is still lovely. White-washed lanes, laid out to thwart pirates, are as enticing as ever, and waterfront Little Venice never fails to thrill, especially when sea foam drenches the café tables. The town's iconic windmills are not just scenic, but also comforting reminders of a simpler time.

DELPHI

The famous oracle seems to be a positive influence on this mountainside, where well-tended, handsome stone houses are nestled beneath cliffs next to the ruins of temples and treasuries. The haunting setting and the homey inns overlooking groves sweeping down toward the distant sea are as soul-soothing as the ancient sanctuary.

CHANIA, CRETE

A harbor front lined with Venetian-era houses and *arsenali* is so photogenic, especially with the mosque of the Janissaries to one side, that it's tempting to stay put. But savor this beautiful and exotic city to the fullest by wandering through the Turkish and Venetian quarters.

DIMITSANA, PELOPONNESE

This lovely procession of stone houses clings to a ridge above a gorge of the Lousios River, and dense forests of chestnut and fir carpet a backdrop of mountains. Water mills attest to centuries-old enterprise and the ruins of an acropolis evoke an ancient presence.

Corfu Town

MONEMVASIA, PELOPONNESE

Castellated walls and a narrow gate put this unique and haunting fortress town at a remove from the rest of the world, as does an improbable setting high on a massive rock face rising from the sea. Narrow, rough-hewn lanes and tiny squares appear to be a labyrinth—until they suddenly open to remarkable vistas of blue sky melding with blue sea.

NAFPLION, PELOPONNESE

Rambling fortresses guard the heights above this beautiful assemblage of Venetian houses and neoclassical mansions on wisteria-scented lanes and marble-paved squares, all wedged onto a narrow promontory in the Gulf of Argos. Café-sitting and strolling along a promenade that skirts sea cliffs at the edge of town are popular pastimes.

CORFU TOWN, IONIAN ISLANDS

The gardens of the Esplanade are French inspired, the Campiello quarter is Venetian, and the Palace of St. Michael and St.George is decidedly British.

Cruising in Greece

Travelers have been sailing Greek waters at least since 3500 BC, when according to some historians, Odysseus, the world's first tourist and hero of Homer's *Odyssey*, was journeying around the Greek islands—1,425 geological jewels thickly scattered over the Aegean Sea like stepping-stones between East and West. Today's pleasure cruisers have an easier time of it.

ITINERARIES

Most itineraries that focus on Greece last 7 to 10 days. They may be round-trip cruises that begin and end in Piraeus, or they may begin in Venice (usually ending in Piraeus) or Piraeus (usually ending in Istanbul). Some cruises concentrate on covering an area that includes the Greek islands, Turkish coast, Cyprus, Israel, and Egypt, while others reach from Gibraltar to the Ionian isles, the western Peloponnese, and Athens.

For an overview of Greece's top sights, choose an itinerary that includes port calls in Piraeus for a shore excursion to the Acropolis and other sights in Athens; Mykonos, a sparkling Cycladic isle with a warren of whitewashed passages, followed by neighboring Delos, with its Pompeii-like ruins; Santorini, a stunning harbor that's actually a partially submerged volcano; Rhodes, where the Knights of St. John built their first walled city before being forced to retreat to Malta; and Heraklion, Crete, where you'll be whisked through a medieval harbor to the reconstructed Bronze Age palace at Knossos. Port calls at Katakolon and Itea mean excursions to Olympia and the Temple of Apollo at Delphi. Some cruises call at Epidavros and Nafplion, offering an opportunity for visits to the ancient theater and the citadel of Mycenae, or at Byzantine Monemvasia or Patmos, the island where St. John wrote the *Book of Revelation*.

Some lines allow you to spend extra time (even stay overnight) in Mykonos to experience the party scene, or Santorini, so that you can see the island after the crush of cruise-ship tourists leaves for the day.

WHEN TO GO

When to go is as important as where to go. The Greek cruising season is lengthy, starting in March and ending in November. In July or August, some islands, especially Santorini and Mykonos, are jammed with Greek and foreign vacationers. High temperatures might also limit time spent on deck. May, June, September, and October are the best months—warm enough for sunbathing and swimming, yet not so uncomfortably hot as to make you regret the trek up Lindos. Cruising in the low seasons provides plenty of advantages besides discounted fares. Availability of ships and particular cabins is greater in the low and shoulder seasons, and the ports are almost completely free of tourists.

MAJOR PORTS

The cruise ports of Greece vary in size and popularity, and some require passengers on larger ships to take a smaller tender to go ashore. In some ports, the main sights may be an hour or more away by car or bus, so plan your day appropriately. At virtually every port listed, a beach stop can be found nearby if you prefer to relax by the sea instead of exploring a village or archaeological site.

Ayios Nikolaos, Crete. This animated port town is built around the "bottomless" Lake Voulismeni (shallower than romantic myths suggest) and hilly streets lined with Venetian and Byzantine houses offer fantastic views over Mirabello Bay and a backdrop of bare mountains. Some pleasant strips of sand fringe bays right in town, while the beaches of the Elounda peninsula are a cab or bus ride away.

Chania, Crete. This elegant city of eucalyptus-lined avenues has miles of waterfront promenades and shady, cobbled alleyways lined with Venetian and Ottoman houses. A lighthouse guides the way into the Venetian outer and inner harbors, where the waterfront Firka Fortress was once a Turkish prison and is now a maritime museum and a converted Turkish mosque hosts art exhibitions. A short walk west of the harbor takes you to Chania's main beach, while others are east of town on the Agia Triada peninsula, where several beautiful monasteries are surrounded by miles of olive groves. Buses and tours depart for the Samaria Gorge, a deep cleft through Crete's soaring mountains.

Corfu. Strolling along the narrow, winding streets and up and down steep stairways is a magical experience, taking you through the medieval Campiello, where seven- and eight-story Venetian houses block the sun, and into what might be the most beautiful square in Greece, the arcade- and cafe-lined Esplanade. The sea laps against the thick walls of the New Fortress, built by the Venetians, and the Old Fortress, a town in itself that once housed the entire population. Churches—St. George, St. Spyridon Cathedral, and Antivouniotissa church among them—are filled with treasures that provided Corfiots with comfort through many centuries of occupation. Close to town is the royal palace of Mon Repos, with splendid gardens.

Delos. During a stop in Mykonos, a short boat ride takes you to this tiny uninhabited island, a well-preserved archaeological site that was a holy sanctuary for a thousand years, the fabled birthplace of Apollo and Artemis. Luxurious villas, including the House of Cleopatra and the House of Dionysus, show off 2,500-year-old mosaic floors and remnants of magnificent marble sculptures. The splendidly monumental Sacred Way leads to the Temple of Apollo, and the marbled and imposing Avenue of Lions is flanked by reproductions of the namesake guardians. Smaller cruise ships can anchor nearby and tender their passengers ashore.

Gythion. A position at the top of the Mani peninsula in the Peloponnese makes this small port a good jumping off point for touring. Sights amid the intriguingly barren landscapes of the Mani include the Diros caves, accessible by underground boat tours and 37 km (22 miles) southwest of Gythion. The Byzantine towns of Mystras and Monemvasia are within easy reach, too, as is Sparta, no longer the formidable stronghold it once was. It's a pleasure to wander along the harbor in Gythion, where octopi dry in the sun and café tables face a fleet of fishing boats. Sandy beaches flank the town.

Heraklion, Crete. The outlying Palace of Knossos, residence of the Minoan kings, is the big draw, and a mandatory follow-up is a visit to the outstanding Archaeological Museum on Platia Elefthrias, where artifacts from Minoan culture discovered during the Knossos excavations include exquisite frescoes and jewelry. The hectic city is more appealing than it might at first appear, with Venetian and Ottoman landmarks, leafy promenades and shady squares filled with outdoor cafés, and the waterfront Koules, a massive fortress.

Katakolon. The so-called "door to Olympia" is just below the ancient city known for sanctuaries to the gods and as the birthplace of the ancient Olympic Games. A 20,000-spectator stadium and other venues remain, and the archaeological museum is a treasure trove of classical statues. Katakolon is a nice place for a leisurely Greek lunch and nearby beaches stretch along the Olympic Riviera.

Kos. Ships dock in Kos Town, putting you within walking distance of the impressive 15th-century Castle of the Knights and other sights in the birthplace of Hippocrates, father of modern medicine. Roman houses, the Greek agora (marketplace), and other ancient ruins are scattered around the pleasant town and shaded by palms and plane trees. The Asklepieion, the ruins of an ancient Greek hospital, are just outside of town, as are many fine beaches.

Monemvasia. Cruise ships tender you close to this medieval Byzantine town, a natural fortress that's been carved out of the rock and has been inhabited since AD 583. Once inside the single gate the only way to get around is on two feet or the back of a donkey. Narrow streets of rough stone (this is not a place for visitors with mobility issues) open to enchanting squares and sea vistas, and the higher you climb, past Ayia Sofia and other wonderful old churches, the better the views.

Mykonos. Cruise ships drop anchor at Tourlos, from where a small boat shuttles you to Mykonos Town, or at a modern cruise port from where connections are by bus. Famous, infamous even, as the haunt of jet-setters and partiers, this well-preserved whitewashed maze is intrguing and it's a pleasure to wander through waterfront Little Venice and along quiet back lanes. At night Mykonos ramps up to full volume in many bars and beach clubs, but amid it all is Panagia Paraportiani, an extremely photogenic church.

Mytilini, Lesvos. Greece's third-largest island is famous as the birthplace of the ancient Greek poet Sappho and renowned for the natural beauty of its lush forests, mountains, deep bays, hot springs, sweeping coastlines, and seemingly endless groves of olive trees. From these landscapes come fine olive oil and ouzo, available from the many shops and eateries on the bustling streets of Mytilini, where ships dock beneath the vast Fortress of Mytilini. The most charming of many museums is one dedicated to Theophilos, a local artist whose primitve works capture the details of everyday life in the late-19th and early-20th centuries.

Nafplion. Ships sail past the picturesque Bourtzi islet, where a tower fortress seems to stand in the center of the sea, and it soon becomes apparent how attractive the first capital of Greece is. The old town of neoclassical houses is wedged onto a peninsula in the Gulf of Argos, with the Palamidi Fortress commanding the inland heights. Narrow streets open into shaded squares, long promenades skirt the seafront, and nearby are Mycenae, Ancient Nemea, Ancient Corinth, and other monumental sights.

Patmos. Smaller ships only can dock on the pretty, mountainous island where St. John the Divine was once exiled and wrote his *Book of Revelation* and where many Europeans spend summer months enjoying laidback island life. St. John lived for two years in what has come to be known as the Sacred Grotto, just below the walls of the fortified medieval complex of the Monastery of St. John the Theologian, in hilltop Chora. These religious associations attract many pilgrims to the island, along with others who enjoy an abundance of charm and some excellent beaches.

Piraeus. The port of Piraeus is located 11 km (7 miles) southwest of Central Athens, easy to reach by metro, bus, or taxi. And oh, Athens—exhilarating and exhausting, beautiful and gritty, and endlessly fascinating. Rising above the fray is the Acropolis, the greatest monument of the anicent world and visible from just about anywhere you wander in the capital. Once you descend from the temples you needn't walk far to take in more ancient sights: on the slopes you'll see the Odeon of Herodes Atticus and the Acropolis Museum, with its impressively displayed panels from the Parthenon Frieze, and within easy reach are the Agora and the National Archaeological Museum, filled with treasures from tombs and temples throughout Greece. Then there's the rest: the jam-packed alleyways of the Plaka, the bazaars of Monastiraki, stately Syntagma Square, with the parliament and Changing of the Evzone Guards, the Benaki and other fine museums, and, proof that this ancient city is always on the move, Psyri and other once-derelict neighborhoods that are vital once again.

Rhodes. Ships dock at the cruise port east of St. Catherine's Gate, not far from where the Knights of St. John stepped ashore in 1291 after fleeing Palestine—over the next two centuries they bestowed enormous wealth on their island stronghold. Their 4-km (2½-mile) fortress walls and magnificent palaces still stand, alongside the monuments of later conquerors. The minaret of the Mosque of Süleyman, dedicated to a Turkish sultan, rises high above the old city, and a palm-shaded avenue of arcaded, early-20th-century Italian landmarks follows the harbor. Then there are ancient wonders, too. Most impressive of them is in medieval Lindos, 48 km (30 mile) south, where a glorious hilltop acropolis rises above the whitewashed town.

Santorini. One of the most photographed scenes in the world greets you upon docking beneath the cliffs of Fira, where cubic, whitewashed houses seem about to tumble right into the blue sea. The scene stealer is the volcanic caldera rimmed with white villages that look like snow from a distance, but the island has a lot else to show off, too. The top three of many memorbale sights: Akrotiri, a remarkably well-preserved town destroyed by a volcanic eruption some 3,500 years ago; Ancient Thira, a magnificently perched ancient city; and the black sand beaches at Kamari and Perissa. Yes, and Ia, another stunning white village tottering on the edge of the caldera.

What to Read and Watch

No other country can claim such a long literary heritage. After all, the *Iliad* and the *Odyssey* are the oldest works of Western literature, and with their descriptions of travels across the "wine dark seas" are riveting travelogues. By the 6th century B.C. Greeks were staging plays, and the works of Sophocles, Aristophanes, and others are the foundation of Western theater. When in Greece, you can still enjoy these classics in such evocative settings as the Odeon Theater, where the floodlit Acropolis forms the backdrop, and the theater at Epidaurus. Other, more recent works of literature also make ample use of Greece's transporting landscapes as the setting for dramas, musings, tragedies, love stories, and the other business of humanity, and filmmakers find similarly fertile ground in these sea-washed landscapes. Here are just a few of the works that might whet your appetite for a trip to Greece.

On Screen

BEFORE MIDNIGHT

In director Richard Linklater's *Before* trilogy, Celine and Jesse met in Vienna and reunited in Paris, and now the chatty, no longer starry-eyed couple travels to the southern Peloponnese to resurrect their on-the-rocks marriage. The moonlight twinkling off the water is one surefire tonic.

CAPTAIN CORELLI'S MANDOLIN

A World War II Italian army officer stationed on Kefalonia (the real star of this shot-on-location romance) meets a beautiful island girl and their love survives the Nazis, a devastating earthquake, and years'-long separation. It's based on a superior and transporting 1994 novel of the same name by Louis de Bernieres.

THE DURRELLS IN CORFU

A genteel, impoverished widow relocates her eccentric family to a ramshackle seaside villa on Corfu, where stunning landscapes and many zany adventures await. The engaging PBS series is adapted from naturalist Gerald Durrell's autobiographical *The Corfu Trilogy*.

MAMA MIA! AND MAMA MIA! HERE WE GO AGAIN

A star ensemble, an iconic sea-girt chapel on Skopelos, and music by ABBA all dazzle. Open-air, sing- and dance-along screenings are a summer staple throughout Greece.

TRIP TO GREECE

In the final installment of their road-trip movies, British actors Steve Coogan and Rob Brydon follow in the footsteps of Odysseus from island to island and onto the sun-drenched mainland. When the guys' quips and imitations start to get on your nerves just look over their shoulders and take in those shimmering blue seas and transporting ruins.

THE TWO FACES OF JANUARY

An adaption of the dark, same-named novel by Patricia Highsmith takes us from Athens to Crete, as all sorts of sinister doings unfold against the splendid backdrops of the Acropolis and Minoan city of Knossos. You may want to take a sartorial cue from these stylish-though-jaded voyagers and pack some crumpled linen and cool vintage shades for you next trip to Greece.

ZORBA THE GREEK

The landscapes are as harsh as the hardscrabble villagers, but when the title character (Anthony Quinn in a tour de force) ventures to Crete with a studious sidekick to open a mine, he proves that the human spirit can overcome all odds and a dance on a beach brighten the bleakest of times. This film is a worthy adaptation of the same-named novel by Nikos Kazantzakis (1883–1957), a master of modern Greek literature.

In Print

THE COLOSSUS OF MAROUSSI
On the eve of World War II the novelist Henry Miller quits Paris to explore a then-undiscovered Greece, where he is swept away, even transfixed by the landscapes and light that "is not the light of the Mediterranean alone, it is something more, something unfathomable, something holy." May we all approach our Greek travels with such enthusiasm and record them so evocatively.

ELENI
The *New York Times* investigative reporter Nicholas Gage recounts his Greek mother's struggles through World War II and the subsequent communist takeover, plus his search for the rebels who executed her. In *North of Ithaka,* Gage's daughter returns to northern Greece and rebuilds her grandmother's home.

THE GREEK WAY
The classicist Edith Hamilton gracefully puts into insightful perspective the Golden Age of the 5th century B.C., when Greek art and writing reached their greatest achievements, changing the course of Western civilization.

THE ISLAND
Perfect beach reading while soaking up the sun, this romance by Victoria Hislop is filled with family drama, doomed love affairs, village life, and the courage of the doomed souls banished to Spinalonga, the island and onetime leper colony just off Crete's Elounda Peninsula.

MANI: TRAVELS IN THE SOUTHERN PELOPONNESE
The British author and adventurer Patrick Leigh Fermor has been called the greatest British travel writer of his time and a mix of Indiana Jones, James Bond, and Graham Greene. In this engagingly colorful narrative he travels down the Mani peninsula, where he lived for more than half a century.

OUTLINE
In this book by Rachel Cusk, a novelist teaches a summer writing course in Athens, where she does not do much but go out to dinner, take the occasional boat ride, and mostly listen as students and acquaintances talk about relationships, careers, goals, and other things. One of the lessons here is that the power of observation is an asset for any traveler.

PROSPERO'S CELL
The novelist and essayist Lawrence Durrell richly draws from his diaries to evoke Corfu, where he and his family lived from 1935 to 1939. His brother, Gerald Durrell, wrote *The Corfu Trilogy,* from which much of the delightful PBS series *The Durrells in Corfu* is drawn (see above).

THE ROAD TO ITHACA
In this installment by Ben Pastor of the well-crafted Lumen war drama/detective series, German officer Martin Bora makes an almost mythical journey across sun-baked, Nazi-occupied Crete to investigate a massacre.

Greece With Kids

Children are treated like honored citizens in Greece. They can elicit smiles from the sternest faces, and shopkeepers, waiters, and hotel staff will probably dote on the little guests. Many cities and towns seem tailormade for young visitors, with traffic-free streets and squares where they can walk and romp in relative safety. When booking a hotel, remember that those universal kid pleasers, swimming pools, are plentiful in Greece (see our listings). Don't underestimate the mood-changing effects of some pool time after a day of sightseeing.

ATHENS

The capital can be a lot of fun for young visitors. Top stop, of course, is the Acropolis, with its dramatic temples and eye-popping views, and the action-filled friezes in the nearby Acropolis Museum are attention grabbers, provided you point out what's happening in the scenes and don't drag out the visit for too long. A walk through shop-lined lanes in the Plaka into Monastiraki provides plenty of diversion, though you might emerge from the maze with a Spartan helmet or tacky T-shirt—on the other hand, evil-eye pendants and *komboloi* (worry beads) are souvenirs with lasting value. The shady arbors and ponds of the National Gardens provide an escape from the swirl of traffic outside the gates, and a visit should include a stop at the adjacent Parliament Building to see the soldiers in colorful traditional garb guarding the tomb of the unknown soldier. Another fun urban activity is a trip aboard the Telefirik to the top of Lycabettus Hill, where a café serves ice cream to accompany the remarkable views over the city.

ELSEWHERE ON THE MAINLAND

Ruins can be a challenge for youngsters, though Delphi, with its dramatic, pine-scented setting and captivating oracle associations, is pretty mesmerizing, and at the bottom of the mountain is pretty, seaside Galaxioli, surrounded by beaches. In the Peloponnese, young visitors enjoy scrambling around the theater of Epidaurus and can take a bow in front of the rows of beautifully preserved stone seats. Nearby Nafplion is Greece's most beautiful town and maybe also the kid-friendliest, with car-free squares, hilltop fortresses to explore, and seaside promenades leading to a town beach with shallow waters. Olympia, with its stadium, gymnasium, baths, and association with the modern Olympic Games, can bring ancient history to life. In the Meteora, monasteries cling to the sides of rocky outcroppings, and the magical atmosphere will mesmerize young sightseers.

THE ISLANDS

Getting there is part of the fun, provided you opt for the slower-moving ferry boats, with outside decks (on fast boats, passengers are confined to airplane-like cabins). On just about any island you will find beaches (many attended by lifeguards), old towns, natural attractions, and boat trips and other attractions to amuse kids. Rhodes is especially well-suited to young visitors. The beautifully preserved medieval Old Town fires up the imagination, with walks atop a circuit of walls and down the transporting Street of Knights. Lindos is another Disney-worthy town on Rhodes, with a remarkable hilltop castle, and the island offers a lot of modern attractions, too, including an aquarium and a water/amusement park at Faliraki Beach. Europeans with kids often head to Kos, where dozens of family-oriented resorts are packed with water slides and loads of other amenities for young travelers.

Chapter 2

TRAVEL SMART GREECE

Updated by
Stephen Brewer

★ **CAPITAL:**
Athens

♔ **POPULATION:**
10, 423, 054

💬 **LANGUAGE:**
Greek

$ **CURRENCY:**
Euro

☎ **COUNTRY CODE:**
30

⚠ **EMERGENCIES:**
166

🚗 **DRIVING:**
On the right

⚡ **ELECTRICITY:**
200v/50 cycles; electrical
plugs have two round prongs

🕐 **TIME:**
Seven hours ahead of New
York

🌐 **WEB RESOURCES:**
www.visitgreece.gr
www.breathtakingathens.com
www.culture.gr

✈ **AIRPORT:**
ATH

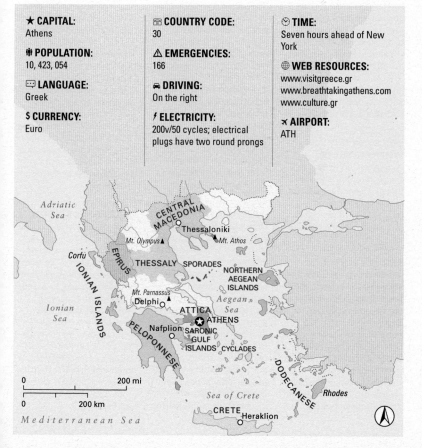

Know Before You Go

So many islands, so many sights, so many beaches. Greece is one of the most rewarding places on the planet to travel, and from staying safe to dining well to getting along with the locals, here are some ways to get the most out of a trip.

CALL A TAXI IF YOU'VE BEEN DRINKING

That's a good idea wherever you are, and an especially wise plan in Greece. The admissible blood alcohol level while driving is 0.05 percent, the equivalent of just two drinks, compared to 0.08 percent levels in the United States. Fines for driving under the influence run from 200 to 2,000 euros, and a DUI usually comes with loss of your license and often some jail time.

DON'T LEAVE HOME WITHOUT THESE

As long as COVID-19 is in the picture, you'll need to fill out a Passenger Locator Form (PLF) online no later than 24 hours before arriving in Greece, proving a local address and other information; you'll be sent a QR code to present at passport control. Chances are you'll also need to show proof of a vaccine, when one becomes available. Beginning in late 2022, non-EU travelers (and that includes post-Brexit Brits) will have to supplement their passports (required, of course) with an electronic ETIAS (European Travel Information and Authorization System) visa waiver. Everyone needs a valid driver's license to rent a car, obviously, but Americans also need an International Driving Permit (IDP). Even if you manage to talk someone into letting you get behind the wheel without an IDP, you can get a stiff fine for driving without one and insurance will not be valid if you have an accident. Get the permit before you leave home from the American Automobile Association (AAA) or the American Automobile Touring Alliance (AATA). You just need to fill out a form, have a photo taken, and pay a small fee.

A PRIVATE FUNCTION

Especially outside big cities, some toilets in public restrooms are squatters (an enamel basin in the floor, the use of which requires some deft maneuvering). Toilets often are not equipped with seats, a good reason to carry some disinfecting wipes to swab the equipment before use, and in most places, pipes and septic systems cannot handle toilet paper, so you'll be asked to dispose of tissue in a bin (takes some getting used to). Better restaurants and major attractions are likely to have well-maintained restrooms, and bathrooms in hotels are usually well fitted-out and often quite deluxe.

HYDRATE, WITH ECO-AWARENESS

Summertime temps in Greece can top 100 degrees, so it's important to drink plenty of water. You can do so right from the tap in Athens and Thessaloniki, but on the islands and in other rural areas bottled water is usually a safer bet. The natural springs that you'll come across all over Greece, often by the sides of mountain roads, are healthful and refreshing sources. They're easy to spot—just look for the locals filling up containers. You'll want to carry a reusable water bottle wherever you go, because Greece banned the use of single-use plastics as of July 2021. These products (including coffee cups, straws, and plastic bags) often end up in the sea, wreaking havoc on marine life.

SHOW SOME RESPECT

Many monasteries impose a dress code for visitors, usually no shorts and no bare shoulders. That goes for both women and men, and women may be asked to wear skirts as well. Sometimes the monks bring out a basket filled with scarves for covering up. Churches also request a degree of modesty from their visitors. Street attire is fine, swimsuits, tank tops, and other beachwear is are not.

WATCH OUT FOR THE EVIL EYE

Forward thinking as Greeks are, they hold on to many age-old superstitions. Follow their lead and wear a pendant with an eye embedded in blue glass to ward off the evil eye, the mati, the bad vibes a jealous person sends your way. For a little extra protection, spit out "ftou, ftou, ftou" any time you hear bad news, to chase the devil away. Speaking of possible misfortune, Tuesday the 13th is an unlucky day in Greece, the equivalent of our Friday the 13th. But since Greeks greet each other with "kalo mino" (good month) every time the first rolls around, bad luck should never befall anyone.

PACK A PAIR OF GOOD WALKING SHOES

You will probably walk a lot in Greece. Much of central Athens and town centers across the country are pedestrian-only zones. Ruins are spread out, often along rough paths. Many beaches, often the best ones, can be reached only with a scramble down a hillside. Hydra, Naxos Town, Monemvasia, Ia, Lindos, and many other beautiful old towns are full of steep ups and downs and rough cobbles. Comfortable, sturdy shoes will make the going easier, while flip-flops and open-toed sandals provide little support and leave feet prone to injury. Some hotels in old towns can only be reached on foot, so check when booking about the practicalities of arriving with luggage.

IT WON'T ALL BE GREEK TO YOU

Many younger people, who start studying English in grade school, are fluent, and many older Greeks have picked up English from relatives in America or Australia or have lived there themselves. English is the lingua franca of the tourist industry, and road signs are usually in Greek and English. You'll probably get by easily without knowing Greek, but you'll get more smiles if you can at least say *kalimera* (good morning) and *efcharisto* (thank you; this one's easy to pronounce—just think "fairy's toe"). *Milate anglika?* (Do you speak English?) is handy, too.

LINGER OVER DINNER

Greeks usually show up at restaurants around nine or ten for a long, drawn-out evening meal, a happy occasion to be savored with family and friends, along with enjoying food that is one of the great pleasures of being in Greece. For a Greek, good means fresh, and you might be taken into the kitchen and shown fish that's usually been caught that day, along with *mayirefta*, one-pot casseroles simmering on the stove. Plates are shared and passed around the table (always to the left). Service tends to be casual but attentive, and you will never be rushed—only the most touristic places adhere to the American practice of turning a table several times in an evening. The bill will include a 13 percent service charge, but it's customary to leave a tip by rounding up (say, from 45 euros to 50), and doing so in cash, even if you're paying by credit card. Service is usually so pleasant that you'll be inclined to tip generoulsy, especially since wages for servers are low in Greece, and in many places the work is seasonal.

GET OFF THE TOURIST TRACK TO SAVE MONEY

Basking in the buzz on Mykonos and soaking up the scene on Santorini can put a big dent in the travel budget. But beyond these popular places, and some other pricey tourist meccas, costs for food and lodging in Greece tend to be much lower than they are in the United States and Western Europe. Even in Athens, you can find a hotel room for a fraction of what you'd pay in New York. Along with travel bargains, spending time in the gorges on Crete, little port towns on Lesvos, villages in the Mani, and other less-trammeled spots comes with the chance to experience authentic Greek life, and that's priceless.

Getting Here and Around

Air

Flying time to Athens is 3½ hours from London, 10½ hours from New York, 12 hours from Chicago, 16½ hours from Los Angeles, and 19 hours from Sydney.

In the days before COVID-19, Delta and other carriers operated a few nonstop flights from the Unitedt States to Athens, and Air Canada had some nonstop routes from Canada. Airlines may reinstate these nonstops as travel returns to normal, but most travelers from North America will need to connect in an airport in Europe to reach Athens and need to transfer in Athens to reach any other destination in Greece. Delta and Air Canada are among airlines that offer one-stop connections through European hubs to Athens. Most of the larger European airlines also offer code-share flights with U.S. partners. Some European budget carriers, including EasyJet and Ryanair, offer flights to a wide range of destinations throughout Greece. A large number of charter flights, especially from Northern Europe, fly directly to resort destinations in Greece during the high season.

Strikes, either for several hours or days, can be a sporadic problem in Greece, so it's always a good idea to keep your eyes on the local headlines while traveling. Athens International Airport (Eleftherios Venizelos) posts real-time flight information on its website.

FLIGHTS WITHIN GREECE

When faced with a boat journey of six hours or more, a domestic flight can be a time-saving option. The frequency of flights varies according to the time of year (with an increase between Greek Easter and November), and it is essential to book well in advance for summer or for festivals and holidays, especially on three-day weekends. There is usually a fee to check bags; only hand luggage (with strictly enforced limits) is free.

Scheduled domestic air travel in Greece is provided by Aegean Airlines and its subsidiary Olympic Air (both of which operate out of Athens International Airport in Spata), Astra Airlines and Ellinair (which fly from Thessaloniki), and Sky Express (which has a network of flights around Greece). Aegean Airlines and Olympic Air have the largest route network around Greece, with flights to virtually every destination you might need, and the best connections through Athens. If you fly into Athens, you'll be able to transfer quite easily to a domestic flight.

AIRPORTS

Athens International Airport at Spata, 33 km (20 miles) southeast of the city center, is the country's main airport. Officially named Eleftherios Venizelos, after Greece's first prime minister, the airport is modern and quite user-friendly (there's also a very nice, albeit expensive, Sofitel if you need to stay over). The main terminal building has two levels: upper for departures, ground level for arrivals. It's quite easy to switch from international to domestic flights or get to Greece's main harbor, Piraeus, about a one-hour bus or train ride south of the airport. Thessaloniki Makedonia Airport handles both international and domestic flights, too. So does the airport on Rhodes (in the Dodecanese islands). Heraklion and Chania, on Crete, and Corfu also handle international flights. Airports on many smaller islands (Santorini, Mykonos, Karpathos, Kos, Skiathos, and Paros among them) receive international charter flights during the busier summer months.

AIRPORT TRANSFERS

*See the respective destination chapters for detailed information on airport transfers.*While both Athens and Thessaloniki are well-conected by public transportation, other places in Greece, especially the islands, are not, and the only way from the airport into town will be by taxi.

Boat

Ferries, catamarans, and hydrofoils make up an essential part of the national transport system of Greece, reaching every inhabited island. There are fast and slow boats and ferries that are more modern than others. When choosing a ferry, take into account the number of stops and the estimated arrival time. Sometimes a ferry that leaves an hour later gets you there faster than an earlier boat. On the other hand, so-called fast boats are often delayed, and a slower boat will get you to your port earlier.

Ferry timetables change frequently, and special sailings are often added in summer and around holiday weekends when demand is high. With so many private companies operating, so many islands to choose from, and complicated timetables—and with departures changing not just by season but also by day of the week—the most sensible way to arrange island-hopping is to select the islands you would like to visit, then consult a travel agent to ask how your journey can be put together. Dolphin Hellas, a full-service tour and travel company based in Athens *(see Travel Agents)*, has a unique online portal to view various schedules and purchase ferry tickets. The websites ⊕ *www.gtp.gr*, ⊕ *www.ferries.gr*, ⊕ *www.ferryhopper.com*, and ⊕ *www.greekferries.gr* are helpful tools for planning routes.

Greek fast-food franchises operate on most ferries. On longer trips ferries have both cafeteria-style and full-service restaurants, and these can be excellent. Overnight ferries usually have a couple of decks of cabins, and these are quite comfortable, with two to four bunks and bathrooms with showers.

Ferries may be delayed by weather conditions, especially when the northern winds called *meltemia* hit in August, so stay flexible—one advantage of not buying a ticket too far in advance. Fast hydrofoils cannot operate in high seas and are often delayed or canceled in windy conditions. If your ship's departure is delayed for any reason (and this may include weather), you may be entitled to a refund. If you miss your ship, you forfeit your ticket; if you cancel in advance, you receive a partial or full refund, depending on how far in advance you cancel.

MAJOR FERRY PORTS

Of the major ferry ports in Greece, Piraeus, Rafina, and Lavrion are fairly well connected to Athens by bus, and the latter two are close enough to the Athens airport in Spata to be reached by taxi and KTEL buses. Within the Cycladic, Dodecanese, and Ionian islands, small ferry companies operate local routes that are not published nationally; passage can be booked through travel agents on the islands served.

PIRAEUS

Greece's largest and busiest port is Piraeus, 10 km (6 miles) south of Central Athens, at the end of metro Line 1, which is close to gates E5 and E6. The train ride from Central Athens takes about 25 minutes, and you can board at Thisseion, Monastiraki, or Omonia; change at Monastiraki for trains to and from Syntagma.

Getting Here and Around

A taxi can take longer than the metro and will cost around €20. Often, drivers heading from Piraeus to Athens wait until they fill their taxi with debarking passengers headed in roughly the same direction, which leads to a longer, more circuitous route to accommodate everyone's destination. It's often faster to walk to the main street and hail a passing cab than to join the long lines at the port. Taxi apps, such as Uber and Beat, usually offer better rates (about €15 from Central Athens to the port of Piraeus).

From the airport, bus X96 runs 24 hours and the trip takes about 40 minutes, much longer in traffic. Buses leave from outside the arrivals area every 20 minutes between 5 am and 10:30 pm, less frequently during the night, and the cost is €3. Suburban trains also make the trip, in about an hour, and leave hourly from the airport metro station; the fare is €10.

From Piraeus you can reach the Saronic islands (Aegina, Hydra, Poros, Angistri, and Spetses); Peloponnesian ports (Hermioni and Porto Heli); the Cyclades (Amorgos, Folegandros, Anafi, Ios, Milos, Mykonos, Naxos, Paros, Santorini, Serifos, Sifnos, Syros, and Tinos); and the northern Aegean islands (Samos, Ikaria, Mytileni, and Chios).

Be aware that Piraeus port is so vast that you may need to travel some distance to your gate (quay) of departure once you arrive, so be sure to leave yourself plenty of time to spare. Free bus service connects the main port entrances with the departure gates. Gate changes may occur at the last moment, so confirm at an information kiosk. Usually, the gates serve the following destinations:

E1 the Dodecanese

E2 Crete, Chios, Mytilini (Lesvos), Ikaria, Samos

E3 Crete, Kithira

E4 Kithira

E5 Main pedestrian entrance

E6 Cyclades, Rethymnon (Crete)

E7 Cyclades, Rethymnon (Crete)

E8 Saronic islands

E9 Cyclades, Samos, Ikaria

E10 Cyclades, Samos, Ikaria

RAFINA

From Greece's second-busiest port, 35 km (22 miles) northeast of Athens, you can reach Evia (Euboea) daily, as well as some of the Cyclades (Mykonos, Paros, Tinos, Santorini, Naxos, Ios, and Andros).

KTEL buses to the Rafina port leave approximately every half hour (or every 15 minutes during rush hour; inquire about their schedule before your departure). Usually KTEL buses run from 5:30 am to 9:30 pm from Mavrommateon terminal near Pedion Areos park, which is within walking distance from the Viktoria (green line) station. The KTEL bus takes about an hour to get to Rafina and the cost of the trip is €3; the port is slightly downhill from the bus station. A KTEL bus also connects the port of Rafina to the airport, about 20 km (12 miles) away, and runs between 4:30 am and 8:45 pm. The journey takes about 30 minutes and the trip costs €6. Buses depart from the airport every hour and the bus stop is located between exits 2 and 3 at the Arrivals level (opposite the Sofitel hotel).

From Athens, it's also possible to take a taxi (a 40-minute trip), but it is fairly expensive.

LAVRION

From the port of Lavrion, 61 km (38 miles) southeast of Athens and close to Sounion, you can reach Kea (Tzia) and Kythnos, and (less regularly) Syros,

Mykonos, Paros, Naxos, Anafi, Ios, Sikinos, Folegandros, Kimolos, Milos, Tinos, Andros, Ag, Efstratios, Limnos, Kavala, and Alexandroupolis. There are hourly buses from the Athens airport directly to Lavrion (bus change at Markopoulo), or it's about 35 to 40 minutes by taxi.

PATRAS
From Patras, on the western coast of the Peloponnese, 210 km (130 miles) west of Athens, you can reach Italy (Ancona, Bari, Brindisi, Ravenna, Trieste, and Venice). The drive or bus trip from Athens takes about three hours.

KILLINI
From Killini, 73 km (45 miles) south of Patras, you can reach the Ionian islands of Kefalonia and Zakynthos. Buses connect Killini with Athens, and passengers can purchase a combined bus and ferry ticket.

IGOUMENITSA
From Igoumenitsa, on Greece's northwest coast 482 km (300 miles), you can reach Italy (Ancona, Bari, Brindisi, Ravenna, Trieste, and Venice) and Corfu (several ferries daily), with connecting bus service for Corfu-bound passengers from Athens. Given the distance from Athens, it is generally more realistic to fly to Corfu.

OTHER PORTS
From the northern mainland towns of **Kavala** and **Alexandroupolis** you can reach the Dodecanese islands of Limnos, Samothrace (Samothraki), Lesvos, Samos, and Thassos.

From **Agios Konstantinos, Volos,** or **Thessaloniki** you can reach the Sporades islands of Alonissos, Skiathos, and Skopelos. Thessaloniki also has frequent seasonal connections to Mykonos and Santorini.

From **Kimi,** on the east coast of Evia, you can reach Skyros, Skopelos, and Alonissos.

From **Heraklion** you can reach the islands of Mykonos, Paros, Naxos, Ios, Santorini, Karpathos, Rhodes, Kasos, Anafi, Chalki, and Milos (summer only).

BUYING FERRY TICKETS
It's best to buy your ticket at least two or three days ahead if you are traveling between July 15 and August 30, when most Greeks vacation, if you need a cabin (good for long trips), or if you are taking a car. If possible, don't travel by boat around August 15, when most ferries are very crowded. The ferry schedule systems are fairly seasonal, so by the end of April it is usually possible to book tickets for the busy summer months.

You can buy tickets from a travel agency or ticket office *praktoreio* at the port, online through travel websites (popular sites include ⊕ *www.directferries.gr*, ⊕ *www.greekferries.gr*, and ⊕ *www. ferries.gr*). It's usually easier to buy tickets from a travel agent, who can explain schedules and options. Last-minute tickets can be purchased from a ferry company kiosk at every port.

Generally you can pay with either credit card or cash. On islands the local office of each shipping line posts a board with departure times.

FERRY TYPES
Greek ferries can be either slow or fast. On longer trips on slower boats, the experience is a bit like a minicruise. You can relax on board, dine, enjoy the sea views, snap photos from the deck at ports of call (there may be multiple calls on some routes), and rent a berth or a private cabin on overnight trips. Some popular long ferry routes are those between Piraeus and Lesvos (Mytilini), Samos, Chios, Rhodes, Kos, Patmos,

Getting Here and Around

Crete, and Santorini and can last twelve hours or more.

High-speed ferries, catamarans, and hydrofoils (sea jets)—or in Greek *iptamena delphinia* (flying dolphins)—are a pricier option that cuts travel time in half. Catamarans are the larger of these fast ferries, with more space to move around, although passengers are not allowed outside when the boat is not docked. If the sea is choppy, these boats often cannot travel and often run very late. They usually make shorter trips, between islands in the Cyclades or Dodecanese, for instance, and between Piraeus or Rafina and Mykonos. Although they are faster, they lack the flavor of the older ferries and do not have open decks.

INTERNATIONAL FERRIES

From Greece you can travel to neighboring Italy and Turkey. Travel time to Turkey from many Greek islands in the Dodecanese and Northern Aegean is relatively short, usually less than 90 minutes. Travel from Patras to various stops in Italy, including Brindisi, Bari, and Venice, can take from 9 to 21 hours.

TRAVEL TO TURKEY

You can cross to Turkey from the northeastern Aegean islands. The journey takes anywhere from one hour to 90 minutes, depending on the destination. Ferries sail between the Greek islands of Rhodes, Kos, Samos, Simi, Chios, and Lesvos to the Turkish destinations of Bodrum, Marmaris, Kusadasi, Turgutreis, Datca, Fethiye, Dikely, Ayvalik, and Cesme.

Note that American, Canadian, and Australian passport holders must pay $60 or €50 to obtain an Electronic Visa for visiting Turkey. British subjects and New Zealanders don't need a visa, though this may change as details of Brexit evolve. The Electronic Visa (e-Visa) Application

System was launched in 2013 by the Turkish Ministry of Foreign Affairs and has now become mandatory for port entry (some airports still provide sticker visas at border crossings). This system allows visitors traveling to Turkey to obtain their e-Visas online in advance (⊕ *www.evisa. gov.tr*). The online application process takes approximately three minutes. Just be aware that visa rules can change, so you should always verify the current requirements before you decide to make a last-minute trip to Turkey from Greece.

Ferry lines that sail between Greece and Turkey include the following: Erturk, Turyol, Marmaris Ferry, Meander Travel, SeaDreams, Bodrum Ferryboat, Dodecanese Flying Dolphins, Tuana Maritime, Dodecanisos Seaways, and Yesil Marmaris Lines.

TRAVEL TO ITALY

There are also frequent ferries between Greece and Italy. From Igoumenitsa, Patras, Zante, and Corfu you can find ferries that head to Ancona, Bari, Brindisi, Trieste, and Venice. The fastest ferry crossing is from Corfu to Otranto in Italy, which takes about 2½ hours with Liberty Lines.

Many routes are operated by Minoan Lines (which is now a subsidiary of Italy's Grimaldi Lines). Modern, well-maintained vessels are outfitted with bars, restaurants, pools, spas, gyms, casinos, and shops.

Prices depend on the season and your class of service (deck, seat, or cabin). High season runs from mid-July to late August; prices drop considerably in low and middle season. Some companies offer special family or group discounts, while others charge extra for pets or offer deep discounts on return tickets, so comparing rates does pay. When booking, also consider when you will be traveling;

an overnight trip can be offset against hotel costs, and you will spend more on incidentals like food and drink when traveling during the day.

Ferry lines that sail between Greece and Italy include the following: Anek, Blue Star Ferries, European Seaways, Minoan Lines, Superfast Ferries, Grimaldi Lines, Liberty Lines, and Ventouris.

Bus

For information on guided bus tours, see Tours in the Planning section of individual chapters.

Greece's nationwide bus network is extensive, with routes to even the most far-flung villages. A fairly reliable regional bus system (KTEL) is made up of local operators throughout the mainland and on the islands. Buses from Athens travel throughout Greece, with connections through regional hubs to smaller towns and villages. Buses from Athens also serve the islands of Corfu and Kefalnia, via ferry connections. KTEL does not have a centralized website, though most regional operators in the system do, and in English. You'll find a list at ⊕ *www. greeka.com/greece-travel/buses.*

BUYING TICKETS

It's possible to purchase tickets on many of the websites of regional KTEL networks, but it's easiest to purchase your bus tickets in person at the KTEL station or on the bus. Reservations are unnecessary on most routes, especially those with several trips a day. If you are traveling on holiday weekends, it's best to go to the station and buy your ticket a couple of days in advance. To give you a sense of costs and schedules, buses from Athens to Corinth costs €16, run every half hour from 5:30 am to 10:30 pm, and the ride takes about 1 hour

(⊕ *www.ktelkorinthias.gr*); to Nafplion, €14.40, with service every 2 hours for the 2-hour trip, often with a change in Corinth (⊕ *www.ktelargolida.gr*); to Patras, €12, with hourly service for the trip of 2½–3 hours (⊕ *www.ktelachaias. gr*); and to Thessaloniki, €35, with service every 2 hours for the trip of 5 hours and 45 minutes (⊕ *www.ktelmacedonia.gr*).

CATCH YOUR BUS

Athens has three bus stations. KTEL's Terminal A, better known as Kiffisou, is the arrival and departure point for bus lines to northern Greece, including Thessaloniki, and to the Peloponnese destinations of Epidauros, Mycenae, Nafplion, and Corinth. Terminal B, better known as Liossion, serves Evia, most of Thrace, and central Greece, including Delphi. Most KTEL buses to the east Attica coast—including those for Sounion, Marathon, and the ports of Lavrion and Rafina—leave from the KTEL stops grouped around Pedion Areos park and known as Mavrommateon terminal.

The buses, which are punctual, are comfortable and air-conditioned, with upholstered seats and, usually, Wi-Fi. There is just one class of ticket. Board early, because Greeks have a loose attitude about assigned seating, and ownership counts here. Although smoking is forbidden on KTEL buses, the driver will stop every two and a half hours at a roadside establishment for a smoking and refreshment break.

PUBLIC TRANSPORTATION BUSES

In Athens, you can buy tickets for urban buses and trams at booths and machines in metro and tram stations. If you are planning on getting around by bus and don't have a pass, carry an extra ticket or two with you, because you may find yourself at a stop some distance from one of these dispensers. *See our Athens chapter Getting Here and Around section*

Getting Here and Around

for information on the city's convenient multiday transportation passes (good for buses, trolleys, and the metro).

Car

Road conditions in Greece have improved in the last decade or so, yet driving in Greece still presents some challenges. In Athens, traffic is mind-boggling most of the time and parking is scarce, so public transportation or taxis are much better options than a rental car. If you are island hopping, taking a car on ferries will increase your ticket costs substantially and limit your ease in hopping onto any boat (fast ferries do not accommodate cars). It's far easier and cheaper to rent a car on the islands you wish to visit, or to tour them by bus or taxi.

DOCUMENTS

International driving permits (IDPs), required for nonresident drivers who are not citizens of many EU countries (including the United States and Canada), are available from the American, Australian, Canadian, and New Zealand automobile associations. These international permits are valid only in conjunction with your regular driver's license.

GASOLINE

Service stations are everywhere, and lead-free gas is widely available. Nevertheless, away from the main towns, especially at night, open gas stations can be very far apart. Don't let your gas supply drop to less than a quarter tank when driving through rural areas. Gas costs about €1.50 a liter for unleaded ("ah- *mo*-lee-vdee"), €1.25 a liter for diesel ("*dee*-zel"). Prices may vary by as much as €0.50 per liter from one region to another, but a price ceiling has been imposed on gas prices during the busy summer months in popular tourist

destinations. You aren't usually allowed to pump your own gas. If you ask the attendant to give you extra service (check oil, air, and water or clean the windows), leave a small tip. Gas stations are now required by law to issue receipts, so make sure you pick up yours from the attendant. The word is *apodiksi*. Credit cards are usually accepted. During off hours, some stations have self-service pumps that you can use by inserting cash or a credit card.

INSURANCE

You must have third-party car insurance to drive in Greece. Check with your insurance company about international coverage before arriving. You can also buy a policy from your car-rental company or a booking site, such as Expedia; keep the papers handy. Most rental-car insurance policies specify deductibles: minimum amounts you will be required to pay in the event of damage or theft (often €500 for damage, €2,000 for theft). You will usually be offered the opportunity to waive deductibles by paying an extra fee, and your insurance or credit card may cover deductibles as well. Deductibles can be a tricky business, so be sure to check with your insurance and credit-card company before renting. The advantge of a zero-deductible policy is peace of mind, and you won't incur extra charges for such minor damage as broken side mirrors (a common occurence in Greece) or dents and scratches. The disadvantage, of course, is the added cost.

PARKING

The scarcity of parking spaces in Athens is one good reason not to drive in the city. Although a number of carparks operate in the city center and near suburban metro stations, these aren't enough to accommodate demand. They can also be quite expensive, with prices starting at €6 for an hour, usually about €20 a day.

Pedestrians are often frustrated by cars parked on sidewalks, and police have become stricter about ticketing. "Controlled parking" zones in some downtown districts like Kolonaki, Pangrati, and Acropolis have introduced some order to the chaotic system; a one-hour card costs €1, with a maximum of three hours permitted for a total cost of €6. Buy a parking card from the kiosk and display it inside your windshield. Be careful not to park in the spots reserved for residents.

Many villages, towns, and islands have designated free parking areas just outside the center where you can leave your car. Do be mindful of signs, though, as parking is often restricted around ports and other high-density areas, and standard practice is for police to remove plates and return them only on payment of fines.

ROAD CONDITIONS

Driving defensively is the key to safety in Greece, one of the most hazardous European countries for motorists. In the cities and on the highways, the streets can be riddled with potholes; motorcyclists seem to come out of nowhere, often passing on the right; and cars may even go the wrong way down a one-way street. In the countryside and on islands, you must watch for livestock crossing the road, as well as for tourists shakily learning to use rented motorcycles.

The many motorcycles and scooters weaving through traffic and the aggressive attitude of fellow motorists can make driving in Greece's large cities especially unpleasant—and the life of a pedestrian dangerous. Greeks often run red lights or ignore stop signs on side streets, or round corners fast without stopping. It's a good idea at night at city intersections and at any time on curvy country lanes to beep your horn to warn errant drivers.

In cities, you will find pedestrians have no qualms about standing in the middle of a busy boulevard, waiting to dart between cars. Make eye contact so you can both determine who's going to slow. Rush hour in the cities is roughly weekdays from 7 to 10 am, 1:30 to 3:30 pm (lunch) and 8 to 10 pm (evening). Saturday morning brings bumper-to-bumper traffic in shopping districts, and weekend nights guarantee crowding around nightlife hubs. In Athens, the only time you won't find traffic is very early morning and most of Sunday (unless you're foolish enough to stay at a local beach until Sunday evening in summer, which means heavy end-of-weekend traffic when you return). Finally, perhaps because they are untrained, drivers seldom pull over for wailing ambulances; the most they'll do is slow down and slightly move over in different directions.

Highways are color-coded: green for the new toll roads and blue for old national roads. Tolls are usually €2.50–€4. The older routes are slower, but they follow more scenic routes, so driving is more enjoyable. The national roads can be very slick in places when wet—avoid driving in rain. It's also wise to avoid the days preceding or following major holidays, when traffic is at its worst as urban dwellers leave for villages.

ROADSIDE EMERGENCIES

You must put out a triangular danger sign if you have a breakdown. Roving repair trucks, owned by the major road assistance companies, such as Interamerican, Intersalonica, Mondial, Europ Assistance, etc., patrol the major highways; summon them by calling ☎ 1154. On the Attiki Odos, the privately owned network of toll roads around Athens, a contracted road assistance company provides assistance for free, so long as it is something that can be fairly easily repaired roadside; call

Getting Here and Around

them on ☎ *1024*. Your rental-car company may also provide a roadside assistance number. ᵺou may call the emergency telephone line provided by the Greek Animal Friends Society ☎ *210 602–0202* if you spot a dead or wounded animal on a national road.

RULES OF THE ROAD

You have to be at least 18 to be able to drive in Greece. Remember to always buckle your seat belt here, as fines are very costly if you don't. Children 10 years old or younger are required to sit in the backseat. Motorcycle helmets are compulsory, though Greeks tend to ignore these rules, or comply with them by "wearing" the helmet strapped to their arms.

International road signs are in use throughout Greece. You drive on the right, pass on the left, and yield right-of-way to all vehicles approaching from the right at intersections (except on posted main highways). This applies to roundabouts, too; cars in the roundabout are required to stop for cars entering the roundabout from the right (this is the opposite of roundabout etiquette in most other countries and the cause of many accidents). Cars may not make a right turn on a red light. The speed limits are 120 kph (74 mph) on a national road, 90 kph (56 mph) outside urban areas, and 50 kph (31 mph) in cities, unless lower limits are posted. But limits are often not posted, and signs indicating a lower limit may not always be visible, so if you see Greek drivers slowing down, take the cue to avoid speed traps.

In Central Athens there is an odd-even rule to avoid traffic congestion (vehicles with license plates ending in even numbers can only enter the city center on even days of the month, vehicles with license plates ending in odd numbers on odd days). This rule does not apply

to rental cars, provided the renter has a foreign passport. If you are renting a car, ask the rental agency about any special parking or circulation regulations in force. Although sidewalk parking is illegal, it is common. And although it's tempting as a visitor to ignore parking tickets, keep in mind that rental agenies will pass your information onto police to persue, and charge a hefty administration fee for doing so. You can pay your ticket at local police stations, and sometimes at city halls and post offices as well. Under a driving code aimed at cracking down on violations, fines start at €50 (for illegal parking in places reserved for the disabled) and can go as high as €1,200 if you fail an alcohol test; fines for running a red light or speeding are now €700, plus you can have your license revoked for 60 days and your plates revoked for 20 days. If fines are paid in cash within 10 days, there is a 50 percent discount.

If you are involved in an accident, don't drive away. Accidents must be reported (something Greek motorists often fail to do) before the insurance companies consider claims. Try to get the other driver's details as soon as possible; hit-and-run is all too common in Greece. If the police take you in (they can hold you for 24 hours if there is a fatality, regardless of fault), you have the right to call your local embassy or consulate for help getting a lawyer.

DRIVING IN AND OUT OF ATHENS

Greece's two main highways, the newly redesigned Athens–Corinth and Athens–Thessaloniki (connecting through national road *Ethniki Odos* and the Attiki Odos), circulate traffic around the metropolis. Avoid using them during periods of mass exodus, such as Friday afternoons and Sunday evenings. These highways and the Egnatia Odos, which runs east to west across northern Greece, along with the secondary roads, cover most of the mainland. In remote rural areas and on islands, some places (beaches, for example) are accessible via dirt or gravel paths. With the exception of main highways and a few flat areas like the Thessalian plain, you will average about 60 km (37 miles) an hour: expect some badly paved or disintegrating roads, stray flocks of goats, slow farm vehicles, detours, curves, and, near Athens and Thessaloniki, traffic jams. At the Athens city limits, signs in English mark the way to Syntagma and Omonia squares in the center. When you exit Athens, signs are well marked for the National Road, usually naming Lamia and Thessaloniki for the north and Corinth or Patras for the southwest.

CAR RENTAL

When you reserve a car, ask about cancellation penalties, taxes, drop-off charges (if you're planning to pick up the car in one city and leave it in another), and surcharges (for being under or over a certain age, for additional drivers, or for driving across state or country borders or beyond a specific distance from your point of rental). Don't forget to check if the rental price includes unlimited mileage and what the cost of additional insurance is. All these things can add substantially to your costs. Reserve extras, such as car seats, when renting, as these items may not otherwise be available at time of pickup, or to ensure that you get certain types of cars (vans, SUVs, exotic sports cars).

■ TIP→ Make sure that a confirmed reservation guarantees you a car. Agencies sometimes overbook, particularly for busy weekends and holiday periods.

Car rental prices can be higher than they are in the United States, but rates during high season (July–September) are much cheaper if you rent through local

agents rather than the large international companies. You might want to reserve with them in advance though, through websites or the accommodation you've arranged, since cars can be hard to come by on some islands during high season. These local agencies provide good service, and prices are at the owner's discretion. Don't be afraid to bargain for a price. It helps if you have shopped around and can mention another agency's offer. If you're visiting several islands or destinations, larger agencies may be able to negotiate a better total package through their local offices or franchises. Some hotels also have partner agencies that offer discounts to guests.

In summer, renting a small car with standard transmission will cost you about €230 to €340 for a week's rental (including tax, insurance, and unlimited mileage). Four-wheel-drives can cost anywhere from €100 to €180 a day, depending on availability and the season. Luxury cars are available at some agencies, such as Europcar, but renting a BMW or a Mercedes can be expensive—anywhere from €100 per day in low season to €300 a day in high season. This does include the 24% V.A.T. (V.A.T. is 17% on the islands). Convertibles and minibuses are also available. Probably the most difficult car to rent is an automatic, rarely available. Note that car rental fees really follow laws of supply/demand, so there can be huge fluctuations and, in low season, lots of room for bargaining. Off-season, rental agencies are often closed on islands and in less-populated areas.

Moped rentals are available through local agents.

North Americans and citizens of many other non-EU countries must have an international driver's permit (IDP) as well as a driver's license that's been valid for one year. Renters must be at least

Getting Here and Around

21 years of age and with some companies at least 23 years old to rent (or you face additional insurance surcharges); for some car categories and for some agencies, you must be 25. A credit card is required for the pre-authorization of the renter's liability. You need the agency's permission to ferry the car or cross the border (some agencies do not allow across-the-border rentals). A valid driver's license is usually acceptable for renting a moped, but you will need a motorcycle driver's license if you want to rent a larger bike.

Most major car-rental agencies have several offices in Athens and also at the Athens airport, in major cities like Thessaloniki, and often throughout the country. Some apply a surcharge for delivering the vehicle at the Athens airport, where there is also usually an additional surcharge for delivering your vehicle between 11 pm and 6 am. Read the General Terms and Conditions carefully to see what particular surcharges might apply to you.

If you are planning to rent a car in Athens, to explore the Peloponnese, for instance, plan to pick up and drop off at an airport location. This will save you the considerable hassle of driving in and out of the city center, and worse, finding a specific address when you drive back in. From the airport, you will have easy access to the beltways that circle the capital and provide links to major roadways.

🚗 Taxi

In Greece, as everywhere, unscrupulous taxi drivers sometimes try to take advantage of out-of-towners. All taxis must display the rate card; it's usually on the dashboard, though taxis outside the big cities often don't bother. Before engaging a taxi ask what the fare to your destination ought to be. It should cost between €35 and €50 from the airport (depending on whether day or night charges apply) to the Athens city center (this includes tolls) and about €10 to €20 from Piraeus port to the center. It does not matter how many are in your party (the driver isn't supposed to squeeze in more than four); the metered price remains the same. Taxis must give passengers a receipt (*apodiksi*) if requested.

Taxi rates in Athens and Thessalonika are inexpensive compared to fares in American and other European cities. The meter starts at €1.29 and the minimum is €3.47 in Athens and Thessaloniki. Daytime rates are €.74 a kilometer, €1.30 at night. A surcharge applies when taking a taxi to and from the airport (€4.72 in Athens, €3.47 in Thessalonika) and from (but not to) ports and bus and train stations (€1.18). There is also a surcharge of €0.43 for each item of baggage that's over 10 kilograms (22 pounds). If you suspect a driver is overcharging, demand to be taken to the police station; this usually brings them around. Complaints about service or overcharging should be directed to the tourist police; at the Athens airport, contact the Taxi Syndicate information desk. The taxi complaint number, with English sometimes spoken by the operator who happens to be on duty, is ☎ *1019* and operates weekdays between 8 am and 10 pm and Saturdays between 8:30 am and 8 pm.

Taxis operate on the jitney system, indicating willingness to pick up others by blinking their headlights or slowing down. Would-be passengers shout their destination as the driver cruises past. Don't be alarmed if your driver picks up other passengers this way (although he should ask your permission first). Drivers rarely pick up additional passengers if you are a woman traveling alone at night. Each new party pays full fare for the distance he or she is traveling.

A taxi is available when a white-and-red sign (*elefthero*) is up or the light is on at night. Once the driver indicates he is free, he cannot refuse your destination, so get in the taxi before you give an address. He also must wait for you up to 15 minutes, if requested, although most drivers would be unhappy with such a demand. Drivers are familiar with the major hotels, but it's good to know a landmark near your hotel and to have the address and phone number written in Greek.

You can download the popular Beat app from home, which lets you order a nearby taxi that is equipped with GPS (to easily find your destination), and choose your taxi driver based on languages spoken and customer rating. The driver will come right to your destination, recognizable by his license plates. The service is at no extra cost and is available in Athens and Thessaloniki.

On islands and in the countryside, the meter may often apply higher rates outside city limits. Do not assume taxis will be waiting at smaller island airports when your flight lands; often, they have all been booked by arriving locals. If you get stuck, try to join a passenger going in your direction, or call your hotel to arrange transportation.

When you're taking an early-morning flight, it's a good idea to reserve a radio taxi the night before, for an additional charge of €3 to €5 (depending on whether it is daytime or night tariff). These taxis are usually quite reliable and punctual; if you're not staying in a hotel, the local tourist police can give you some phone numbers for companies. Taxis charge €9.60 per hour of waiting.

Train

Traveling by train is a convenient, cost-effective (train travel is usually cheaper than bus travel), and scenic way to reach certain destinations in Greece. The problem is, the train network in Greece is *extremely* limited, and buses are usually the only link between cities. The Greek Railway Organization (TrainOSE) runs the national train network and the *proastiakos* light-rail line is part of the it. In Athens, the main train station is Larissis Station, off Diliyianni Street, west of Omonia Square. In Thessaloniki the station is located on Monastiriou Avenue, which is a 15-minute drive from Aristotle Square.

ABOUT TRAVEL IN GREECE

Trains are generally on time. At smaller stations, allow about 15–20 minutes for changing trains; on some routes, connecting routes are coordinated with the main line.

All trains have first- and second-class seating. On any train, during high season, around holidays, or for long distances it is best to travel first class, with a reserved seat, as the difference between the first- and second-class coaches can be significant: the cars are cleaner, the seats are wider and plusher, and, most important, the cars are emptier. On some trains, such as high-speed service from Athens to Thessalonki, you need to book seats ahead even if you are using a rail pass *(see Rail Passes, below)*.

You can get train schedules in stations and online.

POPULAR TRAIN ROUTES

Within Greece, some popular routes include Athens to Thessaloniki and Alexandroupoli (Dikaia), Athens to Kalambaka, and Athens to Corinth. There is also a fast InterCity Express service from Athens to

Getting Here and Around

Thessaloniki that takes four hours instead of six. The cost is €45 for a standard seat, €55 for premium.

A few historic train lines have been kept up and continue to be popular with travelers. The one-hour journey from Diakofto to Kalavryta in the northern Peloponnese travels up a pine-crested gorge in the Peloponnese mountains. It is one of the oldest rail lines in Greece, assigned by PM Harilaos Trikoupis in 1889. The 90-minute trip aboard the steam train of Pelion departs from Ano Lehonia, stops in Ano Gatzea, and arrives in Milies, crossing breathtaking landscapes in central and northern Greece. Finally, the 45-minute journey from Katakolo to Ancient Olympia passes through Pirgos.

BUYING TICKETS

You can pay for all train tickets with cash (euros) or with credit cards (Visa and MasterCard only). The online system is available up to 24 hours before departure. You can also book and pay by telephone, but given the quirks of the online booking system and complexities of the train network, you will probably find it easiest to purchase tickets in Greece from a station or the OSE sales office in Athens. Note that any ticket issued on the train costs 50% more.

RAIL PASSES

Greece is one of 28 countries in which you can use Eurail passes, which provide unlimited travel. With few exceptions (such as the Greek Islands Pass for boat travel, see below) you probably won't need a pass if you will be spending most of your time in Greece, since train travel is so limited. If you plan to rack up miles in several other countries as well, you might consider getting a standard Eurail Global Pass. These are available for 15 days of second-class travel in multiple countries within two months ($440), 15 days continuous ($395), and in many other combinations.

The Greece Pass allows unlimited first-class rail travel throughout Greece for three days, while the Eurail Greek Island Pass allows a certain number of ferry trips within a month, for instance, five trips for $107. The Greece–Italy Pass gives you four days' travel time over a span of two months and includes ferry travel between the two countries; the cost is $325 for first class, $260 for second. Youths (18–25 years of age) pay about 50% less, and there are special rates for groups and families.

You can't buy a Eurail pass in Europe; it has to be purchased through Eurail or another agency before you leave. Passes can be shipped to anywhere you are in Europe, as well as worldwide. Shipping is by registered mail.

Essentials

Addresses

To make finding your way around as easy as possible, it's wise to learn to recognize letters in the Greek alphabet. Most areas have few street signs in English, and even those that *are* in English don't necessarily follow the official standardized transliteration code (⊕ *www.elot.gr*), resulting in some odd spellings of foreign names. Sometimes there are several spelling variations in English for the same place: Agios, Aghios, or Ayios; Georgios or Yiorgos. Also, the English version may be quite different from the Greek, or even what locals use informally: Corfu is known as Kerkyra, Lesvos as Mytilini, and Santorini as Thira: island capitals are often just called Chora or Hora (town), no matter what their formal title; and streets are often known by informal names (Panepistimiou, a main Athens boulevard, is officially named Eleftheriou Venizelou, but if you ask for that, no one will know what you're talking about). A long street may change names several times, and a city may have more than one street with the same name. Know the district you're headed for, or a major landmark nearby, especially if you're taking a taxi. Also ask for a cross street, since odd- and even-numbered addresses fall on opposite sides of the streets, but No. 124 could be several blocks from No. 125. In this guide, street numbers appear after the street name.

Dining

PAYING

For restaurant price categories, see the Planning section in every regional chapter. For guidelines on tipping, see Tipping below.

RESERVATIONS AND DRESS

Regardless of where you are, it's a good idea to make a reservation in the most popular restaurants during high season. In some places (especially the more upmarket restaurants), it's expected. We only mention reservations specifically when they are essential (there's no other way you'll ever get a table) or when they are not accepted. For the most popular restaurants, book as far ahead as you can and reconfirm on the day of your reservation. (Large parties should always call ahead to check the reservations policy.) We mention dress only when men are required to wear a jacket or a jacket and tie, which is extremely rare in Greece and almost unheard of on the islands.

MEALS AND MEALTIMES

Greeks don't really sit down for breakfast, so with the exception of hotels, few places serve this meal. You can pick up a cheese pie, a baguette sandwich, and rolls at a bakery or a sesame-coated bread ring called a *koulouri* sold by city vendors; order a *tost* ("toast"), a sort of dry grilled sandwich, usually with cheese or paper-thin ham slices, at a café; or dig into a plate of yogurt with honey. Local bakeries may offer fresh doughnuts in the morning. On the islands in summer, cafés serve breakfast, from Continental to combinations that might include Spanish omelets and French coffee. So-called "English breakfast" is popular on many islands, and usually includes eggs, bacon, and toast. Caffeine junkies can get a cup of coffee practically anywhere.

Greeks eat their main meal at either lunch or dinner, so the offerings are the same. For lunch, heavyweight meat-and-potato dishes can be had, but you might prefer a real Greek salad (no lettuce, a slice of feta with a pinch of oregano, and ripe tomatoes, cucumber, onions, olives, and green peppers) or

Essentials

souvlaki or grilled chicken from a taverna. For a light bite you can also try one of the popular Greek chain eateries such as Everest or Grigori's for grilled sandwiches or spanakopita and *tiropita* (cheese pie); or Goody's Burger House, the local equivalent of McDonald's, where you'll find good-quality burgers, pasta dishes, and salads.

Coffee and pastries are eaten in the afternoon, usually at a café or *zaharoplastio* (pastry shop). The hour or so before restaurants open for dinner—around 7—is a time to have an ouzo or glass of wine and try Greek hors d'oeuvres, called *mezedes,* in a bar, *ouzeri,* or *mezedopoleio* (Greek tapas place, a good option for a light dinner). Dinner is often the main meal of the day, and is usually a festive occasion, enjoyed outdoors whenever possible. A typical dinner for a couple might be two or three shared appetizers, a shared entrée and salad, and wine. Starters include dips such as taramosalata (made from fish roe), *melitzanosalata* (made from smoked eggplant, lemon, oil, and garlic), and the well-known yogurt, cucumber, and garlic tzatziki. If a Greek eats dessert at all, it will be fruit or a modest wedge of a syrup-drenched cake like *ravani* or semolina halvah, often shared between two or three diners and often served compliments of the house. Only in fancier restaurants might diners order a tiramisu or crème brûleé with an espresso.

In most places, the menu is broken down into appetizers (*orektika*) and entrées (*kiria piata*), with additional headings for salads (Greek salad or *horta,* boiled wild greens; this also includes dips like tzatziki) and vegetable side plates. But this doesn't mean there is any sense of a first or second "course," as in France. Often the food arrives all at the same time, or as it becomes ready, and it's often shared with the whole table.

Breakfast is usually available until 10:30 or 11 at many hotels and until early afternoon in beach cafés. Lunch is between 1 and even as late as 6, especially during summer months, and dinner is served from about 8 to midnight, or even later in the big cities and resort islands. Most Greeks dine very late, around 10 or 11 pm. Unless otherwise noted, the restaurants listed in this guide are open daily for lunch and dinner, and uness noted otherwise, are open seven days a week.

SMOKING

Smoking is banned in all restaurants and bars, though the rule is often not enforced.

RESTAURANT PRICES

What It Costs in euros			
$	$$	$$$	$$$$
AT DINNER			
under €15	€15–$25	€26–€40	over €40

✚ Health and Safety

Greece is generally a safe country in which to travel, and crime against visitors is a fairly rare occurence. Pickpockets are the biggest menace, especially in Athens, so be careful when touring the major attractions and use the basic precautions. Never carry wallets in back pockets, keep handbags close to the body and zipped shut, and keep a close eye on phones and cameras. Carry as few credit cards as possible, so you won't be without one in case of a theft, and avoid carrying your passport and other important documents around with you. If possible, stash them in a hotel safe. Other minor theft is rare in most other places.

Falls and stumbles are probably the major risk for injury, as pavements are often uneven and broken, curbs can be high, potholes are common, and streets are sometimes poorly lit. In towns in Santorini and elsewhere, many passages are a series of steep steps that are hard to navigate, even when stone sober and in bright daylight. So, mind your step, wear sturdy shoes, and carry a flashlight or use the one on your phone as necessary when walking at night.

Greece's strong summer sun and low humidity can lead to sunburn or sunstroke if you're not careful. A hat, a light-colored long-sleeve shirt, and long pants or a sarong are advised for spending a day at the beach or visiting archaeological sites. Sunglasses, a hat, and sunscreen are necessities, and be sure to drink plenty of water. Most beaches present few dangers, but keep a lookout for the occasional jellyfish and, on rocky coves, sea urchins. Should you step on one, don't break off the embedded spines, which may lead to infection, but instead remove them with heated olive oil and a needle. Tap water is safe to drink in Athens and Thessaloniki, but many residents prefer bottled spring water. Avoid drinking tap water in rural areas and on islands.

In greener, wetter areas, mosquitoes may be a problem. In addition to wearing insect repellent, you can burn coils ("spee- *rahl*") or buy plug-in devices that burn medicated tabs ("pah- *steel*-ya"). Hotels usually provide these. Lemon eucalyptus sprays are a more natural way to keep insects away. The only poisonous snakes in Greece are the adder and the sand viper, which are brown or red, with dark zigzags. The adder has a V or X behind its head, and the sand viper sports a small horn on its nose. When hiking, wear high tops and hiking socks and don't put your feet or hands in crevices without looking first. If bitten, try to slow the spread of the venom until a doctor comes: Lie still with the affected limb lower than the rest of your body. Apply a tourniquet, releasing it every few minutes, and cut the wound a bit in case the venom can bleed out. Do NOT suck on the bite. Whereas snakes like to lie in the sun, the scorpion (rare) likes cool, wet places, in woodpiles and under stones. Apply Benadryl or Phenergan to minor stings, but if you have nausea or fever, see a doctor at once.

For minor ailments, go to a local pharmacy first, where the licensed staff can make recommendations for over-the-counter drugs. Pharmacies are open in the morning (8–2) and three evenings per week (Tuesday, Thursday, and Friday 5–8), and each posts the name of the nearest pharmacy open off-hours and on weekends. Most state hospitals and rural clinics won't charge you for tending to minor ailments, even if you're not an EU citizen; at most, you'll pay a minimal fee. For a doctor or dentist, check with your hotel, embassy, or the tourist police.

Do not fly within 24 hours of scuba diving.

COVID-19

A new novel coronavirus brought travel to a virtual standstill in 2020. Although the illness is mild in most people, some experience severe and even life-threatening complications. Once travel started up again, albeit slowly and cautiously, travelers were asked to be particularly careful about hygiene and to avoid any unnecessary travel, especially if they are sick.

Older adults, especially those over 65, have a greater chance of having severe complications from COVID-19. The same is true for people with weaker immune systems or those living with some types

Essentials

of medical conditions, including diabetes, asthma, heart disease, cancer, HIV/AIDS, kidney disease, and liver disease.

Starting two weeks before a trip, anyone planning to travel should be on the look-out for some of the following symptoms: cough, fever, chills, trouble breathing, muscle pain, sore throat, new loss of smell or taste. If you experience any of these symptoms, you should not travel.

To protect yourself during travel, do your best to avoid contact with people showing symptoms. Wash your hands often with soap and water. Limit your time in public places, especially enclosed ones, and when you are out and about, wear a cloth face mask that covers your nose and mouth. Indeed, a mask may be required in some places, such as on an airplane or in a confined space like a theater, where you share the space with a lot of people.

You may wish to bring extra supplies, such as disenfecting wipes, hand sani-tizer (12-ounce bottles were allowed in carry-on luggage at this writing), and a first-aid kit with a thermometer.

For the time being, the Greek govern-ment is asking travelers to complete a Passenger Locator Form (PLF) no later than 24 hours before entering the country to provide an address in Greece and other information that is stored in a database. Travelers will then recieve a QR code they must present upon entering the country. Forms and instructions are on the Visit Greece app and at ⊕ *travel.gov.gr.*

Given how abruptly travel was curtailed in March 2020, it is wise to consider protecting yourself by purchasing a travel insurance policy that will reimburse you for any costs related to COVID-19 related cancellations. Not all travel insurance policies protect against pandemic-related cancellations, so always read the fine print.

 Immunizations

At this time, there are no immunization requirements for visitors traveling to Greece for tourism, but it is possible that a vaccination requirement will be issued for COVID-19 when a vaccine is available.

Internet

Just about all accommodations, even the most basic rooms for rent are equipped with Wi-Fi. Many places also have a ter-minal in the lounge for guests' use.

The city of Athens offers free Wi-Fi access in Syntagma Square and many other public spaces, as well as on most buses and in many metro sta-tions. Cafés and bars usually offer free Wi-Fi to guests, and there is also free Wi-Fi inside the Acropolis Museum, the Onassis Cultural Center, and other tourist destinations. Wi-Fi is available at the bigger airports (Athens, Thessaloniki, Mykonos, etc.), some shopping centers, and elsewhere.

Computer parts, batteries, and adaptors of any brand are expensive in Greece and may not be in stock when you need them, so carry spares for your laptop. Also note that many upscale hotels will lend you a laptop or tablet. Be sure to pack a converter to plug in your devices to recharge them.

Lodging

The first thing to know is that Greeks are gracious hosts, and they take pride in keeeping even modest establishments in top form and in welcoming guests. When it comes to making reservations, it is wise to book several months in advance for the high season, from June through

August, especially at top-end hotels in high-profile destinations like Mykonos, Santorini, and Hydra. Accommodations may be hard to find in smaller summer resort towns in winter (when many hotels close for repairs) and at the beginning of spring.

Many hotels have reduced their prices to remain competitive in the face of the country's ongoing economic crisis, exacerbated by the restrictions COVID-19 has imposed. Sometimes, especially during off-season, you can bargain down the official prices even further (rumor has it to as much as a quarter of the officially quoted price). The response you get will depend largely on the length of your stay, the hotel's policy, and the demand at the time of your stay. Booking websites and local travel agencies also offer competitive prices, particularly for larger hotels on major islands and in Athens and Thessaloniki. However, if you do find a good price from one of these sources, contact the property to see if they can match the price and do better, or maybe throw in some extras. However you book, check to see if a hotel provides transportation from the airport/port as part of their services; this is a real blessing when arriving on an island. A 13% (9% in the islands) government Value-Added Tax and 0.5% municipality tax are added to all hotel bills, though usually the rate quoted includes the tax; be sure to ask. You will also be required to pay a tourism tax of €0.50 and €4 per room per night, based on the official rating of the accommodation, and you are required to pay the tax at check-in.

In even upscale hotels on the islands and in rural ares, you will probably be asked to put toilet paper in a wastebasket rather than flush it.

The lodgings we list are the cream of the crop in each price category. When pricing

accommodations, always ask what's included and what's not. Common items that may add to your basic room rate are breakfast, parking, and use of certain facilities such as tennis courts, the spa or gym, Wi-Fi, etc.

Note that some resort hotels also offer half- and full-board arrangements for part of the year, and these kinds of all-inclusive resorts are mushrooming. Avoid these plans if you can, as being forced to dine at a resort means missing out on experiencing authentic Greek restaurants and cuisine, and that would be a shame. Plus, all-inclusive resorts tend to charge a lot for drinks and other extras, and the so-called reasonable rates may not be such a savings after all. Quite likely, you will find yoruself in a remote location isolated from real Greek life.

HOTELS

The EOT (GNTO) authorizes the construction and classification of hotels throughout Greece. Five categories, A–E, govern the rates that can be charged, with hotels in the A category being the most expensive. Ratings are based on considerations such as room size, hotel services, and amenities that include the furnishing of the room. Within each category, quality varies greatly, but prices don't, so the classifications can be misleading. Also, you may come across an A-category hotel that charges less than a B-class, and a C-rated hotel in one town might qualify as a B in another. Plus, the classifications do not take into consideration such important factors as charm, location, ambiance, and friendliness of the staff, so you won't want to rely on them too heavily.

For category A expect the equivalent of a five-star hotel in the United States, although the room will probably be somewhat smaller. A room in a C-class hotel can be perfectly acceptable; with a D the

Essentials

bathroom may or may not be shared. Ask to see any room before checking in.

Official prices are posted in each room, usually on the back of the door or inside the wardrobe. The room charge varies over the course of the year, peaking in the high season when breakfast or half-board (at hotel complexes) may also be obligatory.

A hotel may ask for a deposit of the first night's stay or up to 25% of the room rate. If you cancel your reservation at least 21 days in advance, you are entitled to a full refund of your deposit. Online booking sites, meanwhile, often require nonrefundable payment in full at time of booking, or offer fairly stringent cancellation terms. Be careful when locking yourself into a room. Greece is best enjoyed at leisure, and you may well decide to stay on an island longer than planned, or a ferry may not be operating when you need to get from Point A to Point B.

Unless otherwise noted in this guide, hotels have air-conditioning (*klimatismo*), room TVs, and private bathrooms (*banio*). Bathrooms are usually equipped with showers, though some older or more luxurious hotels may have tubs. Beds are usually twins (*diklina*). If you want a double bed, ask for a *diplo krevati*. In upper-end hotels, the mattresses are full- or queen-size. One amenity that many Greek hotels offer is a balcony, and always ask for one when booking a warm-weather stay.

Use the following as a guide to making accommodations inquiries: to reserve a double room, *thelo na kleiso ena diklino*; with a bath, *me banio*; without a bath, *horis banio*; or a room with a view, *domatio me thea*. If you need a quiet room (*isiho domatio*), get one with double-glazed windows (*dipla parathyra*) and air-conditioning, away from the elevator and public areas, as high up (*psila*) as possible, and off the street.

RENTAL ROOMS

For low-cost accommodations, consider Greece's ubiquitous "rooms to rent": bed-and-breakfasts without the breakfast. You can count on a clean room, often with such amenities as a terrace, air-conditioning, and a private bath, at a very reasonable price, in the range of €40–€50 for two. Look for signs in any Greek town or village; or, let the proprietors find you—they have a knack for spotting strangers who look like they might need a bed for the night. When renting a room, take a good look first and be sure to check the bathroom before you commit. If there are extra beds in the room, clarify in advance that the amount agreed on is for the entire room—owners occasionally try to put another person in the same room.

When approached by one of the touts who meet the island ferries, make sure he or she tells you the location of the rooms being pushed, and look before you commit. Avoid places on main roads or near all-night discos. Around August 15 (an important religious holiday of the Greek Orthodox Church, commemorating the Assumption of the Virgin Mary), when it seems all Greeks go on vacation, even the most basic rooms are almost impossible to locate, although you can query the tourist police or the municipal tourist office. On some islands, the local rental room owners' association sets up an information booth.

AIRBNB IN GREECE

Renting out spare rooms and empty apartments and homes on Airbnb (⊕ *www.airbnb.com*) has become a favorite practice of many Greek home owners, who amidst a tough and persistent economic climate are looking for ways to increase their income. In addition, the notion of letting out, for a limited period of time, one's home or summer house agrees with the Greek notion of hospitality, *philoxenia*, hence Airbnb's popularity with Greek hosts. The range of accommodation on offer varies from affordable basic to high-end luxury. Popular as Airbnb is in Greece, these rentals have been harmful to many Greeks. They cut into hotel business, and for Greek residents they remove rental units from the market, making it much more difficult to find an affordable place to live in central Athens and elsewhere. Plus, a stay in someone's empty apartment or house deprives you of the chance to interact with Greeks as you would in a hotel and enjoying Greek hospitality.

HOTEL PRICES

What it Costs in euros

$	$$	$$$	$$$$
FOR TWO PEOPLE			
under €125	€125–€225	€226–€275	over €275

💲 Money

Although costs have risen since Greece switched to the euro currency in 2002, the country will seem reasonably priced to travelers from the United States and Great Britain. Popular tourist resorts (including Mykonos, Santorini, and some of the other islands) and Athens are more expensive than elsewhere, though you can find bargains. Though restaurant prices have increased in recent years, you will still be pleasantly surprised at how affordable it is to dine out here; if you're not, you've probably chosen an overpriced restaurant. Hotels are generally moderately priced, even in the major cities.

Other typical costs: soft drink (can) €1, in a café €2; spinach pie, €1.80; souvlaki, €2.20; local bus, €1.30; foreign newspaper, €3–€5.30.

Item	Average Cost
Cup of Coffee	€2–€5 (in a central-city café; Greek coffee is a bit cheaper)
Glass of Wine	€3–€6
Glass of Beer	€3; €4–€9 in a bar
Sandwich	€2.50–€4
1-mile (1 ½-km) Taxi Ride in Capital City	€1
Archaeological Site Admission	€2–€12

Prices throughout this guide are given for adults. Discounts are almost always available for children, students, and senior citizens.

ATMS AND BANKS

Your own bank will probably charge a fee for using ATMs abroad; the foreign bank you use may also charge a fee. Nevertheless, you'll usually get a better rate of exchange at an ATM than you will at a currency-exchange office or even when changing money in a bank. Not only are ATMs convenient, but extracting funds as you need them is a significantly safer option than carrying around a large amount of cash for your entire trip. However, it's normally a bad idea to use your debit card to make purchases abroad; if there's any kind of fraud or problem, that money is gone from your bank account until you can contact the bank and dispute the transaction. Save your debit card for cash withdrawals, and use a credit card for purchases.

■TIP➔ PIN numbers with more than four digits are not recognized at ATMs in Greece. If yours has five or more, remember to change it before you leave. Letters do not generally appear on Greek ATM keypads.

ATMs are widely available throughout the country. Virtually all banks, including the

Essentials

National Bank of Greece (known as *Eth-niki*), as well as many post offices, have machines that dispense money to Cirrus or Plus cardholders. ATMs at Greek post offices (Hellenic Post) often have the most favorable exchange rates for withdrawals. You may find bank-sponsored ATMs at harbors and in airports as well. Other systems accepted include Visa, MasterCard, and, less often, American Express, Diners Club, and Eurocard. The farther away from larger towns you go, the less likely you are to encounter card machines and ATMs, so make sure you always carry some cash with you, particularly when traveling to smaller islands or rural parts of the mainland. The word for PIN is pronounced "peen," and ATMs are called *Ei Ti Em* after the letters, or just *to mihanima,* "the machine." Machines usually let you complete the transaction in English, French, or German and seldom create problems, except Sunday night, when they sometimes run out of cash. For most machines, the minimum amount dispensed is €20. Sometimes an ATM may refuse to "read" your card. Don't panic; it's probably the machine. Try another bank.

■TIP➔ At some ATMs in Greece you may not have a choice of drawing from a specific account. If you have linked savings and checking accounts, make sure there's money in both before you depart.

CREDIT CARDS

It's a good idea to inform your credit-card company before you travel, especially if you don't travel internationally very often. Otherwise, the credit-card company might put a hold on your card owing to unusual activity—not a good thing to happen halfway through your trip. Record all your credit-card numbers—as well as the phone numbers to call if your cards are lost or stolen—in a safe place, so you're prepared should something go wrong.

Most credit-card transactions in Europe now require a chip-and-PIN or chip-and-signature card, and most credit cards in the United States now have these; if not, you can sometimes get a PIN from your bank to make transactions abroad easier. If you plan to use your credit card for cash advances from an ATM (which we strongly advise against), you'll certainly need to apply for a PIN at least two weeks before your trip. Some credit-card companies and the banks that issue them add substantial percentages to all foreign transactions, whether they're in a foreign currency or not. Check on these fees before leaving home, so there won't be any surprises when you get the bill.

■TIP➔ Before you charge something, ask the merchant whether or not he or she plans to do a dynamic currency conversion (DCC). In such a transaction the credit-card processor (shop, restaurant, or hotel, not Visa or MasterCard) converts the currency from euros to dollars. It's an expensive transaction since in most cases you'll pay the merchant an additional 3% fee for this service on top of any credit-card company and issuing-bank foreign-transaction surcharges.

It's always safer to use a credit card for purchases while traveling. A credit card allows you to delay payment and gives you certain rights as a consumer, including the right to dispute a fraudulent charge before you have to make a payment on your account and a limit of $50 for fraudulent charges to a lost or stolen card (provided you report the loss as soon as you discover it). A debit card deducts funds directly from your checking account and helps you stay within your budget, but you may not receive an automatic credit if you dispute a charge. You will almost always need a credit card to rent a car.

Shop owners and many hotels in Greece often give you a lower price if you pay with cash rather than credit, because they want to avoid the credit-card bank fees.

CURRENCY AND EXCHANGE

Greece uses the euro. Under the euro system, there are eight coins: 1 and 2 euros, plus 1, 2, 5, 10, 20, and 50 euro cents. Euros are pronounced "evros" in Greek; cents are known as "lepta." All coins have the euro value on one side; the other side has each country's unique national symbol. Greece's images range from triremes to a depiction of the mythological Europa being abducted by Zeus, who is in the form of a bull. Bills (banknotes) come in six denominations: 5, 10, 20, 50, 100, and 200 euros. Bills are the same for all EU countries.

Off Syntagma Square in Athens, the National Bank of Greece, Alpha Bank, and Pireos Bank have automated machines that change your foreign currency into euros. When you shop, remember that it's always easier to bargain on prices when paying in cash instead of by credit card.

If you use an exchange service, good options are American Express and OneX-change (formerly Eurochange). Watch daily fluctuations and shop around. Daily exchange rates are prominently displayed in banks and you can find current rates online at such sites as XE ⊕ *www. xe.com*. In Athens, Syntagma Square is the best place to look. In some tourist resorts you might be able to change money at the post office, where commissions may be lower than at banks. For peace of mind, you may want to get a bit of local currency before you leave home, though it's probably easier and less expensive to use airport ATMs upon arrival.

■TIP➔ **Even if a currency-exchange booth has a sign promising no commission, rest assured that there's some kind of substantial, hidden fee that can be as much as 8%, often in the form of a bad rate. And as for rates, you will always get a better exchange rate for euros at an ATM.**

🖥 Packing

Travel light. That's the best packing advice you'll get for Greece. For starters, you won't need much, since dress is informal, especially in summer, and even for dinner in a good restaurant nice casual attire is fine. Men can easily get by without a sports jacket, and putting one on in the summer heat will almost be unthinkable. Also, if you'll be moving around by boat, you won't want to be hindered by more than one easy-to-handle rollerbag as you climb up and down gangplanks and stairs and maneuver ports. (Even if you plan to fly to islands, remember that planes are usually small and you'll be charged for anything more than small cabin luggage.) Town centers are ofen closed to cars, so you may well be walking to your accommodation and pulling your bag along narrow cobbled lanes and up steps. Pack clothing that lends itself to hand washing and easy drip dry, as laundromats are expensive and scarce outside of Athens and big towns, and hotels usually charge exorbinant fees for laundry. Bring shorts, for comfort (they're everyday wear on the islands) and for women, a skirt or pants, and for men, one pair of light troursers, for cool nights, nicer restaurants, and occasions such as monastery visits; for women, a light pashmina or other cover up for sun protection and to wear as a wrap; comfortable walking shoes; and a hat, sunglasses, and sunscreen (though these are widely available in Greece).

Essentials

Passports and Visas

All citizens (even infants) of the United States, Canada, Australia, and New Zealand need a valid passport to enter Greece, which is a party to the Schengen Agreement, for stays of up to 90 days. As of late 2022, these ctizens will also need an ETIAS (European Travel Information and Authorization System) visa waiver. As of 2022, British subjects will also need a passport and an ETIAS waiver, though these requirements are still being hammered out as details of Brexit are finalized. You must apply for ETIAS online and pay a €7 application fee; the waivers will be entered into a database and be valid for three years of multiple entries and allow you a stay of 90 days per entry. You'll find more information on the ETIAS website. Your passport should be valid for at least three months beyond the period of your stay (the U.S. Department of State recommends six months). If you leave after 90 days and don't have a visa extension, you will be fined anywhere from €600 to €1,300 (depending on how long you overstay) by Greek airport officials, who are not flexible on this issue. If you want to extend your stay beyond 90 days, there is heavy bureaucracy involved but eventually you will be able to do it for a cost of about €150. Inquire at your local police station for details.

$ Taxes

Taxes are typically included in all quoted prices.

Value-Added Tax in Greece is 6% for books and 24% for almost everything else, including most groceries. In Greece the tax is called FPA (pronounced "fee-pee-ah"). If you are a citizen of a non-EU country, you may get a V.A.T. refund on products (except alcohol, cigarettes, or toiletries) worth €120 or more bought at one time from participating stores that usually display a Tax-Free Shopping sticker in their window. Merchants participate in the program by choice, and many choose not to, so check when making a large purchase. To be clear, you can get V.A.T. refunds for multiple purchases, but each receipt you present must be for €120 or more. The merchant will ask to see your passport, and should then issue a completed V.A.T. refund form (called a Tax-Free Check receipt) along with the receipt for your purchases. You must have both to get the refund, so don't leave the store without them. Note that the V.A.T. refund may also apply to some portions of hotel bills, package tours, car rentals, and other services, so be sure to ask in advance. Maximum refunded V.A.T. per transaction is up to the equivalent of €1,500.

At the airport, have the form stamped by customs officials (if you're visiting several European Union countries, do this when leaving the EU). Be ready to show customs officials what you've bought (pack purchases together, in your carry-on luggage); budget extra time for this. After you're through passport control, take the form to a refund-service counter for an on-the-spot refund, or mail it back in the pre-addressed envelope given to you at the store. The processing time for a mail refund can be long, especially if you request a credit-card adjustment.

If you are leaving from the Athens airport for a country outside the EU, after your Tax-Free Check form has been stamped, you can go directly to the OneXchange bureau de change (extra-Schengen area, Gates 1–4, opening hours 6 am–10 pm) and get your refund cash.

Many stores only participate in the VAT-refund program through firms such as Global Blue, a Europe-wide service with 300,000 affiliated stores; you'll see the logo in the window. The process at the aiport is the same as with other V.A.T. refund plans, and OneXchange issues Global Blue refunds in the form of cash, check, or credit-card adjustment, minus a processing fee. If you don't have time to wait at the refund counter, you can mail in the form instead.

☎ Telephones

Most travelers prefer to connect through their own mobile phones, making use of Wi-Fi or cellular connectivity and such apps as Skype, Facetime, Facebook Messenger, or What'sApp. In fact, many hotel rooms no longer have telephones, though you'll still find public card phones (steadily declining in numbers).

The country code for Greece is 30. When dialing Greece from the United States, Canada, or Australia, first dial 011, then 30, the country code, before punching in the area code and local number. From continental Europe, the United Kingdom, or New Zealand, start with 0030.

CALLING WITHIN GREECE
For Greek directory information, dial 11888. The people behind 11888 also operate the website ⊕ *www.vrisko.gr*, which is a Greece-based online directory inquiries resource.

Pronunciations for the numbers in Greek are: one ("*eh*-na"); two ("*dthee*-oh"); three ("*tree*-a"); four ("*tess*-ehr-a"); five ("*pen*-de"); six ("*eh*-ksee"); seven ("ef-*ta*"); eight ("och- *toh*"); nine ("eh- *nay*-ah"); ten ("*dtheh*-ka").

All telephone numbers in Greece have 10 digits and include the area code. For cell phones, dial both the cell prefix (a four-digit number beginning with 69) and

the telephone number, which can vary in the number of digits it contains.

CALLING OUTSIDE GREECE
To place an international call from Greece, dial 00 to connect to an international network, then dial the country code (for the United States and Canada, it's 1), and then the area code and number. If you need assistance, call 13888. Your cellular carrier may have its own protocol. With Wi-Fi calling, available from most carriers, you may call anywhere outside Greece for free as long as you have a Wi-Fi connection. All four major U.S. carriers (T-Mobile, Sprint, AT&T, and Verizon) provide built-in Wi-Fi calling, but check to make sure there are no additional costs involved in using it. From a Greek landline, you may also call internationally through plans with AT&T, Verizon, and other networks.

MOBILE PHONES
If you have a multiband phone (some countries use different frequencies from what's used in the United States) and your service provider uses the world-standard GSM network (as do T-Mobile, AT&T, Sprint, and Verizon), you can probably use your phone abroad. Before traveling call your provider for specific info, and ask also if the provider has a connection agreement with a Greek mobile carrier. If so, manually switch your phone to that network's settings as soon as you arrive to avoid international roaming fees, which can be steep (however, they are on the decline at about 30¢ a minute, but overseas you normally pay the toll charges for incoming calls as well). It's almost always cheaper to send a text message than to make a call, since text messages have a very low set fee (often less than 2¢). Many mobile networks now offer international plans with daily rates of about $10 for unlimited calling and data usage; fees only apply on

Essentials

days you use the phone, so you needn't commit to a plan in advance.

If you want to make a lot of local calls, consider buying a SIM card (note that your provider may have to unlock your phone for you to use a different SIM card) and a prepaid service plan in Greece. You'll then have a local number and can make local calls at local rates. If your trip is extensive, you can also buy a Greek cell phone, and the initial cost will be offset over time.

■ TIP → **If you travel internationally frequently, save one of your old mobile phones or buy a cheap one on the Internet; ask your cell phone company to unlock it for you, and take it with you as a travel phone, buying a new SIM card with pay-as-you-go service in each destination.**

🔘 Tipping

How much you tip in Greece is up to you, but please do tip. Wages in Greece are low, the person serving you may well be supporting others who are not able to find work, and employment is often seasonal and uncertain for most of the year. So, if service is pleasant, and it most often is, be generous.

📍 Travel Agents

Many travel arrangements in Greece are still made (and indeed better made) through travel agencies. There are countless travel agents in Greece, and as is the case anywhere, the service you get makes a difference. Some agents simply want to confirm as many bookings as

Tipping Guidelines for Greece

Bartender	10% maximum
Bellhop	€1 per bag
Hotel Concierge	€3–€5, if he or she performs a service for you
Hotel Maid	Up to €10 per stay
Hotel Room-Service Waiter	€2–€3 per delivery, even if a service charge has been added
Porter at Airport or Train Station	€1 per bag
WSW Skycap Services at Airport	€1–€3 per bag checked
Taxi Driver	Round up the fare to the nearest €0.50 or €1
Tour Guide	5% of fee
Waiter	By law a 13% service charge is figured into the price of a meal; however, it is customary to round up the bill if the service was satisfactory. During the Christmas and Greek Easter holiday periods, restaurants tack on an obligatory 18% holiday bonus to your bill for the waiters.
Others	For restroom attendants €1–€2 is appropriate. People dispensing programs at theaters get about €2.

possible then move on, but when you find an agent who understands that personalized attention is great for you and for future business, you'll find no more helpful professional. Greek travel agents who do the job right can take the headache out of figuring out the logistics behind your dream Greek itinerary. They know the ins and outs of the ferry systems from timetables to schedules, they can suggest which accommodations suit your style, and they can propose tours that interest you. They can often get you better prices than you can find on your own, even through popular online discounters.

If you are traveling in July and August, travel agencies can come to the rescue with preset packages for the islands you want to visit or suggest other options from archaeological sites, mountain trips, or coastal villages. *See the individual destination chapters for more local recommendations.*

🖥 U.S. Embassy

The U..S. Embassy in Athens is at the edge of Kolonaki, in a neighborhood of embassies. This is the place to go to replace a lost passport, or to seek advice if you need medical or legal assistance. While the embassy is open to the public on weekdays 8:30 am to 5 pm, it closes for all the Greek and American holidays, so check opening times before making the trek. You may call the main number during off hours with emergencies. The only U.S. consulate in Greece is in Thessaloniki; you will be referred to the embassy in Athens for passport services and most other matters.

📍 Visitor Information

Tourist police, often stationed near ports and the most-popular tourist sites, can answer questions in English about transportation, steer you to an open pharmacy or doctor, and locate phone numbers of hotels, rooms, and restaurants. Official tourist offices are a fairly rare commodity in Greece, though some municipalities operate them. The many, many private travel agencies can usually provide a wealth of information about a destination along with providing tours, booking accommodation, selling boat and train tickets, and renting cars. You can download maps, brochures, and guides from Visit Greece, the website of the Greek National Tourism Organization. The complete *Greek Travel Pages* is available online and is a valuable resource for all travel in Greece, with a handy tool for planning ferry travel. Among other info-filled resources are the popular online *Greece Guides* by knowledgeable and entertaining ex-pat Matt Barrett.

📅 When to Go

High Season: June through August is the most popular time to visit Greece, though June is still relatively quiet. Some islands, including Mykonos and Santorini, can seem uncomfortably overcrowded and ridiculously expensive from mid-July through August, when many hotels charge their highest rates. Athens is fairly empty in August, except for tourists and those who remain to cater to them.

Essentials

Low Season: Most island hotels are closed in the low season, from mid-October to at least the middle of April, although this is a good time to discover the Peloponnese and other mountainous regions of the mainland. Some islands, including Crete and Rhodes, with their large resident populations, are open for business in the winter, as are Lesvos and other islands that are never that heavily reliant on tourism. This is the season to enjoy everyday life in these places, but you'll forgo beach time and some other outdoor activities. Spring comes early to much of Greece, and with it a profusion of wildflowers in the countryside, so March and April are good hiking months. Though Athens can be cold and humid for much of the winter, the city is lively, entertainment is in full gear, and museums and attractions are not nearly as crowded as they are at other times.

Value Season: With May, September, and October comes a pleasant combination of mild Mediterranean weather and good value. The Aegean may still be too cold for swimming in May but the water remains warm enough for a swim well into October. Island hotels usually open at Easter or in early May; some remain open until the start of November, but many close by mid-October. Spring visits come with the advantage of lengthening hours of sunlight, while earlier sunsets in the fall can curtail sightseeing and beach time.

Contacts

Air

AIRLINES Aegean Airlines. ☎ 801/112–0000 toll-free in Greece, 210/626–1000 from abroad ⊕ en. aegeanair.com. **Air Canada.** ☎ 888/247–2262 toll-free for U.S. and Canada ⊕ www.aircanada.com. **Air France.** ☎ 800/237–2747 in the U.S. ⊕ www. airfrance.us. **Air Transat.** ☎ 877/872–6728 ⊕ www. airtransat.com. **Alitalia.** ☎ 800/223–5730 ⊕ www. alitalia.com. **American Airlines.** ☎ 800/433–7300 in U.S. and Canada ⊕ www.aa.com. **Astra Airlines.** ☎ 801/7007466 (within Greece) ⊕ www. astra-airlines.gr. **British Airways.** ☎ 800/247–9297 in the U.S. ⊕ www. britishairways.com. **Delta Airlines.** ☎ 800/241–4141 international reservations in the U.S. and Canada, 210/998–0090 in Greece, 210/353–0116 office at El. Venizelos Airport ⊕ www. delta.com. **easyJet.** ☎ 0033/365–5454 in the U.K., 211/198–0013 in Athens ⊕ www.easyjet. com. **Ellinair.** ☎ 2311/224–700 international calls and calls from mobiles, 801/100–8182 in Greece ⊕ www.ellinair.com. **Emirates.** ☎ 800/777–3999 toll-free reservations in the U.S. (24 hrs) ⊕ www. emirates.com. **Iberia Airlines.** ☎ 800/772–4642, 211/198–0095 in Athens

⊕ www.iberia.com. **Jet2. com.** ☎ 203/059–8336 in the U.K. ⊕ www.jet2.com. **KLM Royal Dutch Airlines.** ☎ 800/618–0141 in the U.S. ⊕ www.klm.com. **LOT.** ☎ 212/789–0970 in the U.S. ⊕ www.lot.com. **Lufthansa.** ☎ 800/645–3880 in the U.S., 210/617–5225 in Athens ⊕ www.lufthansa.com. **Norwegian.** ☎ 800/357–4159 in the U.S. ⊕ www. norwegian.com. **Olympic Air.** ☎ 210/355–0500 in Athens, 210/355–0500 El. Venizelos Airport desk ⊕ www.olympicair.com. **Ryanair.** ☎ 0330/1007–838 fee per min. ⊕ www.rya-nair.com. **SAS Scandinavian Airlines.** ☎ 211/211–1542 in Greece, 800/221–2350 from U.S. and Canada ⊕ www.flysas.com. **Sky Express.** ☎ 801/112–8288 toll-free in Greece, 212/215–6510 ⊕ www. skyexpress.gr. **Swiss International Airlines.** ☎ 877/359–7947 in the U.S., 210/300–4339 in Athens, 210/353–0382 in Athens airport ⊕ www. swiss.com. **United Airlines.** ☎ 800/864–3331 ⊕ www. united.com.

AIRPORTS
CONTACTS Athens International Airport–Eleftherios Venizelos. (ATH). ✉ End of Attiki Odos, Spata ☎ 210/353–0000 flight information and customer service, 210/353–0515 lost and found ⊕ www.aia.

gr. **Heraklion International Airport–Nikos Kazantzakis.** (HER). ☎ 2810/397129 ⊕ www.heraklion-airport. info. **Kerkyra Airport–Ioannis Kapodistrias.** (CFU). ✉ Anapafseos 1, Corfu Town ☎ 26610/89602 ⊕ www. cfu-airport.gr. **Rhodes International Airport Diagoras.** (RHO). ☎ 22410/88700 ⊕ www.rhodes-airport. org. **Thessaloniki International Airport–Makedonia.** (SKG). ✉ Kalamaria ☎ 2310/985000 ⊕ www. thessalonikiairport.com.

⛵ Boat
REGIONAL PORT AUTHORITIES Agios Konstantinos Port Authority. ☎ 22350/31759. **Igoumenitsa Port Authority.** ☎ 26650/99300. **Kimi Port Authority.** ☎ 22220/22161 ⊕ olne.gr. **Lavrion Port Authority.** ☎ 22920/27711, 22920/22089. **Patras Port Authority.** ☎ 2610/365113 ⊕ www.patrasport. gr. **Piraeus Port Authority.** ☎ 14541 in Greece ⊕ www.olp.gr. **Rafina Port Authority.** ☎ 22940/23605, 22940/22840 ⊕ www.rafinaport.gr. **Thessaloniki Port Authority.** ☎ 2310/593130 ⊕ www.thpa.gr. **Volos Port Authority.** ☎ 24210/31888, 2410/31226 ⊕ www. port-volos.gr.

FERRY LINES Aegean Flying Dolphins. ☎ 210/412–1654 in Athens ⊕ www.

Contacts

aegeanflyingdolphins.
gr. **Aegean Speed Lines.**
210/969–0959 in
Athens www.aegean-
speedlines.gr. **Anek Lines.**
210/419–7400 phone
bookings, 210/419–7470
customer service www.
anek.gr. **ANEM Ferries.**
22420/59124 www.
anemferries.gr. **ANEN
Lines.** 2810/346185
www.ferries.gr/
anen-lines. **Anes Ferries.**
210/523–7613 www.
anes.gr. **Blue Star Ferries.**
210/891–9800 www.
bluestarferries.gr. **Bodrum
Ferryboat.** 252/316–0882
in Bodrum www.
bodrumferryboat.
com. **Dodecanese Flying
Dolphins.** 22413/04030
in Rhodes www.12fd.
eu. **Dodecanisos Seaways.**
22410/304030 in Rho-
des www.12ne.gr. **Erturk
Lines.** 232/712–6768 in
Cesme, Turkey www.
erturk.com.tr. **European
Seaways.** 210/956–1630
in Athens www.euro-
peanseaways.com. **Fast
Ferries.** 210/418–2005 in
Piraeus www.fastfer-
ries.com.gr. **Golden Star
Ferries.** 212/222–4000
www.goldenstarfer-
ries.gr. **Grimaldi Lines.**
081/496444 in Naples
www.grimaldi-lines.
com. **Hellenic Seaways.**
210/891–9800 in Athens
hellenicseaways.gr.

Levante Ferries. 210/949–
9400 in Athens www.
levanteferries.com. **Liberty
Lines.** 0923/022–022
in Trapani, Italy www.
libertylines.it. **Marmaris
Ferry.** 252/413–0230 in
Marmaris, Turkey www.
marmarisferry.com. **Meander Travel.** 256/612–
8888 in Turkey www.
meandertravel.com. **Minoan Lines.** 2810/399899 in
Heraklion, Crete www.
minoan.gr. **SAOS Ferries.**
22510/28186 www.
saos.gr. **Saronic Ferries.**
210/411–7341 in Athens
www.saronicferries.
gr. **Sea Dreams–Aege-
an Shipping Company.**
22410/74535 in Rhodes
www.seadreams.gr.
Seajets. 210/710–7710 in
Piraeus www.seajets.gr.
Skyros Shipping Company.
22220/92164 www.
sne.gr. **Superfast Ferries.**
210/891–9010 www.
superfast.com. **Turyol.**
266/331–67000 in
Turkey www.turyolon-
line.com. **2 Way Ferries.**
210/625–0131 www.
2wayferries.gr. **Ventouris
Ferries.** 210/482–8001 in
Piraeus www.ventouris-
ferries.com. **Yesil Marmaris
Lines.** 252/413–2323 in
Turkey www.yesilmar-
marislines.com.

Bus

ATHENS BUS STATIONS
**Athens Mavromatteon
Terminal.** Aigyptou
Sq., Mavromateon and
Leoforos Alexandras,
near Pedion Areos park,
Athens 210/880–8000
ktelattikis.gr. **Terminal
A–KTEL Kifissou.** Kifissou
100, Kolonos . **Terminal
B–KTEL Liossion.** Rikaki
6 and Liosion 216, Kato
Patissia 210/512–9140
www.ktel-fokidas.gr,
www.ktel-trikala.gr.

Car

CAR RENTAL COMPANIES
Avis. 210/322–4951
in Athens www.avis.
gr. **Budget Rent a Car.**
210/353–0553 in
Athens www.budget.
gr. **Enterprise Rent a Car.**
210/349–3418 in Athens
www.enterprise.
gr. **Europcar Car Rental.**
210/973–5000 in Ath-
ens www.europcar.com.
Hertz. 210/626–4000 in
Athens www.hertz.gr.
Sixt Car Rental. 210/922–
0171 in Athens www.
sixt.com.

🚕 Taxi

TAXI COMPLAINTS IN ATHENS Taxi Complaint Line. ☎ *1091 for Attica (incl. Athens).*

🚃 Train

TRAIN CONTACTS Train-OSE Office of Tourism and Travel. ✉ *Sina 6, Athens* ☎ *210/362–1039* ⊕ *www.trainose.gr.* **TrainOSE Customer Service.** ✉ *Karolou 1–3, Omonia Sq.* ☎ *14511 customer phone service (6 am–11 pm)* ⊕ *www.trainose.gr.*

💲 Taxes

V.A.T. REFUNDS Global Blue. ☎ ⊕ *www.globalblue.com.*

☎ Telephones

CELL PHONE RENTALS Cellular Abroad. ☎ *800/287–5072 U.S. toll free, 310/862–7100 International* ⊕ *www.cellularabroad.com.* **Mobal.** ☎ ⊕ *www.mobal.com.*

📍 Travel Agents

CONTACTS Dolphin Hellas Travel. ✉ *Syngrou 16, Athens* ☎ *210/922–7772 in Athens* ⊕ *www.dolphin-hellas.gr.* **Fantasy Travel.** ✉ *Filillenon 19, Central Athens* ☎ *210/331–0530* ⊕ *www.fantasy.gr.* **Navigator.** ✉ *Akadimias 32, Athens* ☎ *211/234–1004 in Athens* ⊕ *www.navigator.gr.*

🇺🇸 U.S. Embassy

CONTACTS U.S. Embassy. ✉ *Vassilissis Sophias 91, Central Athens* ☎ *210/7212951* ⊕ *gr.usembassy.gov/embassy-consulate* Ⓜ *Evangelismos.* **U.S. Consulate General Thessaloniki.** ✉ *Tsimiski 43, 7th fl., Thessaloniki* ☎ *2310/242905* ⊕ *gr.usembassy.gov/embassy-consulate/thessaloniki.*

📍 Visitor Information

CONTACTS ETIAS. ⊕ *www.etiasvisa.com.* **Greece Guides.** ⊕ *www.greecetravel.com.* **Greek National Tourism Organization.** (*GNTO*). ✉ *800 3rd Ave., 23rd floor, New York* ☎ *212/421–5777* ⊕ *www.visitgreece.gr.* **Greek Travel Pages.** ✉ *International Publications Ltd., Psylla 6, at Filellinon, Athens* ☎ *210/324–7511* ⊕ *www.gtp.gr.* **Tourist Police.** ☎ *1571.*

Helpful Greek Phrases

BASICS

Hello	Yia	Yeah
Yes/No	Nai/Ohi	Neh/O-hee ('eh' as in n'e'gative)
Please	Parakalo	Para-ka-loh ('oh' as in odyssey)
Thank you	Efharisto	Eff-ha-ree-stoh
You're welcome	Parakalo	Pa-ra-ka-loh
I'm Sorry (apology)	Signomi	Sea-gnow-me
Sorry (Excuse me)	Me Sinhorite	Me Seen-ho-reet-eh
Good morning	Kalimera	Kali-me-rah
Good day	Kalimera	Kali-me-rah
Good evening	Kalispera	Kali-spe-rah
Goodbye	Yiasou (singular) / Yiasas (plural)	Yeah-sue / Yeah-sass
Mr. (Sir)	Kirios	Key-ree-oss
Mrs.	Kiria	Key-ree-ah
Miss	Despinis	Des-pea-knees
Pleased to meet you	Harika	Harry-kah
How are you?	Pos Eise (singular)/ Pos eiste (plu)	Paws Ease-eh / Paws-ease-teh

NUMBERS

one-half	Miso	Meas-oh
one	Ena	Eh-na
two	Dyo	Dee-oh
three	Tria	Tree-ah
four	Tessera	Tesser-ah
five	Pende	Pen-day
six	Exi	Ex-ee
seven	Efta	Eff-tah
eight	Okto	Oak-toe
nine	Ennia	En-yeah
ten	Deka	Deck-ah
eleven	Endeka	End-deck-ah
twelve	Dodeka	Doe-deck-ah
thirteen	Dekatria	Deck-ah-tree-ah
fourteen	Dekatessera	Deck-ah-tess-erah
fifteen	Dekapende	Deck-ah-pen-day
sixteen	Dekaexi	Deck-ah-ex-ee
seventeen	Dekaefta	Deck-ah-eftah ('ah' as in 'a'fter)
eighteen	Dekaokto	Deck-ah-ok-toh ('o' as in odyssey)
nineteen	Dekaennia	Deck-ah-en-yeah
twenty	Ikosi	Ee-koss-ee
twenty-one	kosi-ena	Ee-koss-ee eh-na
thirty	Trianda	Tree-and-ah
forty	Saranda	Sar-and-ah
fifty	Pendinda	Pen-een-dah
sixty	Exinda	Ex-een-dah
seventy	Evdominda	Ev-doe-mean-dah
eighty	Ogdonda	Og-thon-dah ('th' as in the')
ninety	Eneninda	En-en-een-dah

one hundred	Ekato	Eck-ah-toe
one thousand	Hilia	Heal-yeah
one million	Ena ekatomirio	En-ah eckat-toe-mere-ee-oh

COLORS

black	Mavro	Mav-roe
blue	Ble	Bl-e ('e' as in ever)
brown	Kafe	Caff-e ('e' as in ever)
green	Prasino	Prass-ee-no
orange	Portokali	Port-oh-kalee
red	Kokkino	Cock-ee-no
white	Aspro	Ass-pro
yellow	Kitrino	Key-tree-no

DAYS OF THE WEEK

Sunday	Kiriaki	Key-ree-ah-key
Monday	Deftera	Deaf-terra
Tuesday	Triti	Tree-tea
Wednesday	Tetarti	Tet-arty
Thursday	Pempti	Pem-tea
Friday	Paraskevi	Para-skev-ee
Saturday	Savato	Savva-toe

MONTHS

January	Ianouarios	Yen-wah-ri-oss ('oss' as in toss)
February	Fevrouarios	Fev-wah-ri-oss
March	Martios	Marty-oss
April	Aprilios	Ap-real-ee-oss
May	Maios	M-ee-oss
June	Iounios	Ee-oon-ee-oss
July	Ioulios	Ee-oo-lee-oss
August	Avgoustos	Av-goos-toss
September	Septemvrios	Septem-vree-oss
October	Octovrios	Ock-to-vree-oss
November	Noemvios	N-emm-vree-oss
December	Dekemvrios	De-kem-vree-oss

USEFUL WORDS AND PHRASES

Do you speak English?	Milate Anglika	Me-latte Ang-leak-ah
I don't speak Greek.	Den Milao Ellinika	Den Meal-ow Elly-knee-ka
I don't understand.	Den Katalavaino	Den Cat-allah-veno
I don't know.	Den Xero	Den Xe-roe
I understand.	Katalavaino	Cat-allah-veno
I'm American.	Eimai Amerikanos(M)/ Amerikanitha(F) Amerikanos(M)/ Amerikanitha(F)	Ee-may American-oss / American-ee-the
I'm British.	Eimai Anglos (M) /Anglitha (F)	Ee-may Angloss(M)/ Ang-lee-the
What's your name.	Pos sas (plur)/ se (singular) Lene?	Pos sas(plur)/se (singular) len-eh
My name is ...	Me lene...	May len-eh
What time is it?	Ti ora einai?	Tea oar-ah ee-neh ('eh' as in 'e'ver)

w?	Pos?	Poss
en?	Pote	Pot-ay ('eh' as in ever)
terday	Ehtes	E-h-tess (pronopunce 'h' as in 'has')
ay	Simera	Seam-era
norrow	Avrio	Av-ree-oh
s morning	Simera to proi	Seam-era toe pro-ee
s afternoon	Simera to apogevma	Seam-era toe apo-gev-ma
ight	Apopse	A-pop-say
at?	Ti	Tea
at is it?	Ti einai	Tea ee-nay
y?	Yiati	Yeah-tea
o?	Pios	Pea-oss
ere is ...	Pou einai...	Poo- ee-nay
he train tion?	...o stathmos tou trainou	...oh stath-moss too tren-oo
he subway tion?	...o stathmos tou metro	...oh stath-moss too met-roe
he bus stop?	...o stathmos tou leoforiou	...oh stath-moss too leo-for-ee-oo
he airport?	... to aerodromio	...tow aero-drom-ee-oh
the post ice?	... to tahidromio	...tow ta-he'd-row-me-owe
the bank?	... I trapeza	...Ee trap-eh-zah
the hotel?	...to xenondoheio	...tow xenon-doe-he-owe
the museum?	... to mouseio	...tow mousse-ee-oh
the hospital?	...to nosokomeio	...tow noss-o-com-ee-oh
the elevator?	...to asanser	...tow ass-an-ser
here are the strooms?	Pou einai to banio	Poo ee-nay tow ban-ee-oh
re/there	Edo/ekei	Ed-oh/Eh-key
t/right	Aristera/dexia	Arr-ee-stair-ah/dex-ee-ah
t near/far?	Einai konda/makria	Ee-nay con-dah/mack-ree-ah
like ...	Tha ithela	Tha ('th' as in 'thistle') ee-thell-ah
a room	...ena domatio	En-ah dom-a-tea-oh
the key	...to kleidi	Tow klee-thee
a newspaper	...mia efimerida	Mia eff-ee-mer-ee-the
a stamp	...ena grammatosimo	Ena gram-ah-tow-sea-moe
like to buy ...	Tha ithela na agoraso...	Tha ('th' as in 'thistle') ee-thell-ah na agor-ah-sew
a city map	...enan harti tis polis	...en-ah harty teas polly's
a road map	...enan odiko harti	...en-an o-thee-co harty
a magazine	... ena periodiko	...en-ah per-ee-oh-thee-co
envelopes	...fakelous	...fack-elle-oos
writing paper	...harti yia grafi	...har-tea yeah graff-ee
a postcard	...mia carte postale	...mia carte postale
a ticket	...ena eisitirio	...en-ah ees-ee-tea-ree-owe

How much is it?	Poso kanei	Poss-oh can-ee
It's expensive/cheap	Einai akrivo/fthino	Ee-nay ack-ree-voh/fthee-no ('th' as in thistle)
A little/a lot	Ligo/poly	Lee-go/poll-ee
More/less	Pio poly/Ligotero	Pee-oh poll-ee/Lee-go-terro
Enough/too (much)	Ftanei/einai poli	F-tanny/ee-nay poll-ee
I am ill/sick	Eimai arosti (F)/arostos (M)	Ee-may a-ross-tea (F)/a-ross-toss (M)
Call a doctor	Kaleste giatro	Call-ess-tay yeah-trow
Help!	Voitheia	Vo-ee-thee-ah ('th' as in thistle)
Stop!	Stamata	Stam-at-ah

DINING OUT

A bottle of ...	Ena boukali...	En-ah book-all-ee
A cup of ...	Ena flytzani	En-ah flea-tzan-ee
A glass of ...	Ena potiri...	En-ah poh-tea-ree
Beer	Bira	Beer-ah
Bill/check	Logariasmos	Log-are-ee-as-moss
Bread	Psomi	Pss-om-ee
Breakfast	Proino	Pro-ee-no
Butter	Voutyro	Vou-tea-roe
Cocktail/aperatif	Coktail/apertif	Cock-tail/aper-itif
Coffee	Kafe	Café
Dinner	Vradyno	Vra-thee-noh
Fixed-price menu	Menu statheris timis	Kata-log-oss sta-ther-iss team-ease
Fork	Pirouni	Peer-uni
I am a vegetarian/I don't eat meat	Eimai hortofagos/den troo kreas	Ee-may horto-fagos/then tro (last 'o' as in odyssey) cray-ass
I cannot eat ...	Den boro na fao...	Then borrow na fa-oh...
I'd like to order ...	Tha ithela na parangeilo	Tha eeth-ella na par-an-ghee-low (('th' as in thistle)
Is service included?	Perilamvanete I ypiresia	Per-ee-lamva-nay-te ee eep-ee-ray-sea-ah
I'm hungry/thirsty	Peinao/deipsao	Pea-now/thee-p-sow
It's good/bad	Einai kalo/kako	Ee-nay kall-oh/kak-oh
It's hot/cold	Einai zesto/kryo	Ee-nay zest-oh/kree-oh
Knife	Mahairi	Ma-her-ee
Lunch	Mesimeriano	Messy-meh-ree-ano
Menu	Katalogos	Kata-log-oss
Napkin	Hartopetseta	Heart-oh-pet-set-ah
Pepper	Piperi	Peep-err-ee
Plate	Piato	Pea-at-oh
Please give me ...	Sas parakalo doste mou...	Sass para-ka-loh doss-tay moo...
Salt	Alati	Ah-la-tea
Spoon	Koutali	Koo-tally
Tea	Tsai	Tsa-ee
Water	Nero	Ner-oh
Wine	Krasi	Crass-ee

Great Itineraries

Classical Sites

Lovers of art, antiquity, and mythology journey to Greece to make a pilgrimage to the great archaeological sites. Here, at Delphi, Olympia, and Epidauros, the gods of Olympus were revered, Euripides's plays were first presented, and some of the greatest temples ever built still evoke the genial atmosphere of Greece's golden age (in spite of 2,500 years of wear and tear). Take this tour and you'll learn that it's not necessary to be a scholar of history to feel the proximity of ancient Greece.

DAYS 1–2: ATHENS

Begin at the beginning—the Acropolis plateau—where you can explore the greatest temple of Periclean Greece, the Parthenon, while drinking in heart-stopping views over the modern metropolis. After touring the Acropolis Museum and the Odeon of Herod Atticus at the base of the plateau, and the nearby ancient Agora and Monument of Lysikrates, finish up at the National Archaeological Museum.

Logistics: *Your Acropolis ticket also gets you into the other archaeological sites in Athens. Use the efficient Metro to avoid constant traffic slowdowns.*

DAY 3: SOUNION

Sun, sand, art, and antiquity all lie southeast of Athens in Sounion. Here, the spectacular Temple of Poseidon sits atop a cliff 195 feet over the Saronic Gulf. Pay your own respects to the god of the sea at the beach directly below or enjoy the coves of the Apollo coast as you head back west to the seaside resort of Vouliagmeni for an overnight.

Logistics: *If you don't want to go on your own, most travel agencies offer tours to Sounion, and then you can spend another night in Athens.*

DAY 4: ELEUSIS AND CORINTH

Heading west of Athens, make a stop at Eleusis (*Elefsina* in modern Greek), home of the Sanctuary of Demeter and the haunted grotto of Hades, god of the Underworld. Past the isthmus of Corinth—gateway to the Peloponnese—Ancient Corinth and its sublime Temple of Apollo beckon. Head south to the coast and Nafplion; en route, stop at a roadside stand for some tasty Nemean wine.

Logistics: *Stopping briefly at Eleusis is easier if you have a car. Otherwise, you are at the mercy of bus schedules.*

DAYS 5–6: NAFPLION, TIRYNS, MYCENAE, EPIDAUROS

Nafplion is a stage set of spectacular Venetian fortresses, Greek churches, and neoclassical mansions, and you can explore the mysteries of forgotten civilizations in nearby Tiryns (*Tiryntha* in modern Greek), Mycenae, and Epidauros. North is Tiryns, where Bronze Age ramparts bear witness to Homer's "well-girt city." Farther north is Agamemnon's blood-soaked realm, the royal citadel of Mycenae, destroyed in 468 BC. Then take a day trip east to the famous ancient Theater at Epidauros, where a summer drama festival still presents the great tragedies of Euripides.

Logistics: *Set up base in Nafplion and visit the nearby sights at your leisure. It's obviously easier to do this if you have a car.*

Anitrion · Rion · Patras · Galaxidi · Delphi · Gulf of Corinth · Eleusis · Athens · Corinth · Vouliagmeni · Mycenae · Argos · Epidauros · Nafplion · Tiryns · Sounion · Olympia · Tripoli · Bassae · Aegean Sea · Ionian Sea · Sea of Crete

DAYS 7–8: OLYMPIA AND BASSAE

After your third overnight in Nafplion, head west to Olympia—holiest site of the ancient Greek religion, home to the Sanctuary of Zeus, and birthplace of the Olympics. Walk through the olive groves of the sacred precinct; then get acquainted with Praxiteles' *Hermes* in the museum. Overnight in this pleasant mountain town then make a trip south to the remote Temple of Apollo at Bassae (if traveling by car, look for road signs to *Vasses*).

Logistics: *From Nafplion, you can get to Olympia via Argos by train or Tripoli by car (on the E65).*

DAY 9: DELPHI

Set aside a day to discover Delphi, whose noble dust and ancient ruins are theatrically set amid cliffs. Despite the tour buses, it is still possible to imagine the power of the most famous oracle of antiquity. From here, head back to Athens.

Logistics: *From Olympia, head north through verdant forests of the Elis (Ilieia) region to Patras or nearby Rion for the ferry or bridge across the Corinthian gulf; travel east along the coast and overnight in chic Galaxidi, with its elegant stone seafarers' mansions.*

Tips

KTEL buses leave from Mavromateon, Liossion, and Kifissou stations in downtown Athens and connect to most of the major sites: southeast to Sounion along the coast, northwest to Delphi, and west to the Peloponnese. In some cases you will need to take the bus to the provincial capital (Corinth, Argos, Tripoli), then change to a local bus.

Daily trains connect Athens to Corinth and Kiato, with bus connections to Nafplion and Olympia.

These are popular destinations and can also be seen on guided tours arranged through almost any travel agent in Athens.

Great Itineraries

Marvels of Central Greece

With a rich wilderness of mountains, rocky gorges, and white-water rivers crossed by stone-arch bridges, Epirus is the antithesis of what most people think about Greece. Take a tour of the region that sweeps down from the borders of Albania, and drive south into Central Greece almost to the Gulf of Corinth to discover a stunning landscape that shows off Greece's mountainous character at its best.

DAY 1: IOANNINA

Ioannina, which was a crossroads of trading, is the handsome capital of Epirus and reflects its Balkan, Ottoman, and Byzantine roots that are preserved in its Old Town. You can soak in the panoramic view of the city from its castle walls that date back to AD 528 and visit the Byzantine Museum within the city's citadel. Take a boat ride and glide across the city's landmark, Lake Pamvotis, for a stop at Nissi Island and its little village free of most vehicular traffic. Then head to the museum that unveils the historical details of enigmatic Ottoman ruler Ali Pasha during his dramatic reign of the region from 1788 until he was deposed by the Turks in 1821. It's housed in the 16th-century-era Pandelimonos Monastery, where Ali Pasha lived until he was killed.

Logistics: *A bus from Athens to Ioannina can take 7 hours; it's much easier to fly.*

DAY 2: ZAGOROHORIA

In the Zagorohoria region north of Ioannina, numerous traditional villages defined by stone, wood, and slate rock hug the mountain slopes. Admire the handicrafts in Monodendri village, altitude 3,400 feet, where you can also enter the depths of the Vikos Gorge, the deepest in the world, and walk the cobblestone trail to the 15th-century Aghia Paraskevi Monastery.

Logistics: *Drive from Ioannina to Zagorohoria (1 hour), or take a bus. There are just a few places to stay in Zagorohoria, so you may want to remain for a second night in Ioannina and visit on a day trip, especially if you have a car. The area can be especially busy during summer weekends in July and August, so plan ahead if visiting during that time.*

DAY 3: METSOVO

Metsovo is a traditional village cascading down a mountainside in the heart of the Pindos mountain range (below the Katara pass marking the highest point in Greece and the border between Epirus and Thessaly), where outdoor aficionados can hike and raft. Even during the summer, the temperatures at this altitude will be considerably cooler than in other parts of Greece, with highs in the 70s F. Wind down in the village and walk through its stone-paved streets. Be sure to see the Tositsa Museum, once the home of one of the village's most prominent families. Stop to sample local wines and cheeses; the Katogi-Averoff Winery produces fine reds.

Logistics: *Metsovo is another 1½ hours from Zagorohoria; drive to Kalambaka (1 hour farther), just outside Meteora, for an overnight stay.*

DAY 4: METEORA

Wake up ready to spend the day exploring Meteora's sky-high monasteries built on seemingly inaccessible sandstone peaks. In an awe-inspiring effort, Byzantine emperors funded the construction of these aeries, and monks settled on

these rock towers from the 11th century onwards. At one point there were 16 monasteries. Today six remain, and they are on the UNESCO World Heritage list.

Logistics: *Two or three monasteries are usually enough for anyone. After your visit, drive to the next stop, Delphi (3½ hours), in the early afternoon.*

DAYS 5–6: DELPHI AND ENVIRONS

Wake up in the land that was once regarded as the center of the world by Ancient Greeks. Spend the day touring the archaeological site of Delphi. Positioned on the slopes of Mt. Parnassos the site housed the ancients' most famous oracle. Next, visit Arachova, also perched on the slopes of Mt. Parnassos, then stop at the monastic complex of Osios Loukas before heading back to Delphi or dropping down to beautiful seaside Galaxidi for the night.

Logistics: *It's 3 to 4 hours back to Athens by car, longer if you are going by bus.*

Tips

■ Points in Epirus may be quite high in altitude, and those who are sensitive to heights may be affected. Mountain roads may have numerous blind curves and they can be steep. Drive with caution.

■ The preferred route back to Athens takes you through Levadia; if you want a short detour, follow the signs for the ancient springs of Lethe and Mnemosyne.

■ Guided tours can get you to Delphi and back, but to do this full itinerary, you will need to rent a car or take multiple buses.

Great Itineraries

Greece's Great North

Northern Greece sparkles with the sights, sounds, and aromas of a melting-pot history and crossroads geography. The region's seaside capital, Thessaloniki, impresses with its stylish young people, hip nightlife, diverse culture, and easy-going nature. Just east of the metropolis is the trident-shaped arch of Halkidiki, the summer playground for northern Greeks and southeastern Europeans. The landmass juts out into the Aegean, offering spectacular beaches lined with aquamarine waters and green rolling hills and mountains. The Sporadic island chain including its southernmost island, Skyros, matches that nature with the same loveliness and charm only a Greek island can offer. To get the most out of your trip around northern Greece's coast and on Skyros island, plan your flights in advance and consider the drive times between each destination.

DAYS 1–3: SKYROS

Fly from Athens directly to Skyros. Once your flight gets in, rent a car and get settled in. Time your next few days to explore the sights of this island of the Sporades chain that resembles a Cycladic island due to its whitewashed architecture, and a Dodecanese island due to its rugged landscape. Its main town was built like an amphitheater around the Byzantine-era Monastery of St. George, where an ancient acropolis remains on the highest point of the Old Town. Weave in through its alleyways, where much of the island's population lives, and be sure to visit the outstanding Faltaits Historical and Folklore Museum. Choose one of the golden sandy beaches, typically surrounded by green hills covered by lush pine trees. Take a day trip to the tiny Sarakino island and feel calmly isolated on its white-sand beach, Glyfada.

Logistics: *If you don't want to fly, you can get a ferry to Skyros from Evia, but that requires a bus ride from Athens. Should you want a more worldly island experience, begin this itineraey in Skiathos, another Sporades island with many sandy beaches and a lot of nightlife and air connections to Athens and Thessloniki.*

DAYS 4–5: THESSALONIKI

Wake up early and take a flight to Greece's second-largest city, Thessaloniki. Walk around the port where the icon of the city, a 15th-century White Tower stands by the sea. Stop at the city's grand monuments including the 5th-century Church of Agios Dimitrios, the impressive Roman Rotunda, and the 3rd-century palace ruins of Roman emperor Galerius. Much of the city's charm lies in its ever-changing character, since it's been conquered and rebuilt so many times. The modern appeal lies in part in its warmth, accessibility, and languid pace, making this a place to slow down and relax for a couple of days. In the evening, enjoy the city's vibrant nightlife and great restaurants.

Logistics: *You'll need to fly from Skyros to Thessaloniki; there's just no other way to do the trip in a reasonable amount of time.*

DAY 6: ALEXANDER THE GREAT COUNTRY

After enjoying Greece's second city, rent a car and explore some of the fascinating sights in Central Macedonia. These include Pella, Alexander the Great's birthplace; the royal tombs of Vergina, where his father was buried after his assassination; and Dion at the base of Mount Olympus, an underrated temple city named after Zeus that is not widely visited.

Logistics: *If you want to see everything here, you must have a car. If you want to rely on buses, choose either Vergina or Dion, not both, but keep your hotel base in Thessaloniki; there are not very many places to stay in this area.*

DAYS 7–8: HALKIDIKI AND MT. ATHOS

Reserve some time to explore Halkidiki's Mt. Athos. Drive from Thessaloniki to Ouranoupolis, which will be your base, and give yourself some time to simply wind down. That's why the Greeks come here. The village, which is on the final point of land that separates the secular world from the sacred sanctuaries of Mt. Athos, is noted for its tapestry and rug weaving. On the second day, the men in your group can make a pilgrimage to the monastery of Mt. Athos, which is open only to men who seek advance permission to enter. But anyone can enjoy a scenic boat ride around the peninsula, which is like no other in the world. All boats depart from the docks in Ouranoupolis.

Logistics: *Drive back to Thessaloniki (2 hours) in the afternoon, and take a 1-hour flight or a train back to Athens.*

Tips

Athens to Skyros flights leave at least three times per week and more frequently (currently six times daily) during peak season. Skyros to Thessaloniki flights depart at least two times per week, but schedules change all the time so plan carefully.

You'll have a choice of many daily flights between Athens and Thessaloniki, and a fast train travels the route as well.

Great Itineraries

Wonders of the Peloponnese Coast

The Peloponnese remains generally unknown to most Americans, but for those who take the leap to explore it the rewards are great. The coastline is divine, showcasing the natural and rural beauty of Greece from rugged cliffs that meet the sparkling seas swirling in bright shades of turquoise. Peloponnese port cities also give off a special Greek island–like charm with their small village atmosphere, beautiful architecture, and expansive views of the sea. If you have time, an excursion here will be well rewarded.

DAY 1: EPIDAVROS

Epidavros has Greece's best-preserved ancient theater, which still amazes audiences with its perfect acoustics. You can literally hear a pin drop on the stage from 55 rows up. Seating 14,000 people, with a breathtaking view of the mountains and valleys directly behind its stage, the venue gets packed each summer (June through August) for the Athens Epidauros Festival, which features notable actors from all over the world. Also visit the Sanctuary of Asklepios, the supposed birthplace of Apollo's son, the world's greatest healer, which has been a major place of healing since the 4th century. Take a break with an orange juice, freshly squeezed from oranges grown in the area's famous orange groves, or for that matter, with a glass of wine from the Nemea vineyards.

Logistics: *This itinerary really needs to be done by car; it's 1½ hours from Athens to Epidauros. During the festival, however, buses run to and from Nafplion especially for the performances, and that's where you should base yourself for the night.*

DAY 2: NAFPLION

The first capital of Greece is a cultured, historic, and romantic port city, and beautiful as well. Discover its Old Town, a peninsula that juts out into the Gulf of Argos and where Greek, Venetian, and Turkish architecture melds in harmony in little streets and tree-shaded plazas. The city, and neabry ruins at Mycenae, deserves at least a day of your undivided attention, but you could certainly spend more time if you have it.

Logistics: *The drive from Epidauros to Nafplion is just 40 minutes, but if you are staying the night, you'll likely want to start this itinerary in Nafplion, which is 2 hours from Athens by toll road.*

DAY 3: MONEMVASIA

From afar it's incredible to think people live in the massive rock, towering at 1,148 feet, just ahead of you. One narrow bridge connects the Peloponnese landmass to Monemvasia, where a smallwalled community has thrived since AD 600. The name translates as *one entrance,* and the perfectly preserved medieval town beyond the gate is filled with shops, small hotels, and restaurants. Alleyways lined with traditional homes are a delight to explore, with viewing spots, including at Agia Sofia Church, that offer sweeping views over the town and sea.

Logistics: *An overnight here allows you to enjoy this strange place when the tour groups have departed. Just be aware that cars are not allowed, so you will have to carry your luggage in over rough paving stones and up and down steps (have your hotel's staff meet you to help).*

DAY 4: MYSTRAS AND SPARTA

While modern Sparta may be disappointing to many because of its paucity of ruins, not so for Mystras, which has the most impressive ruins in the

Peloponnese, albeit from the 14th century rather than from ancient times. The abandoned palaces, churches, and monasteries are well worth the detour, and on a stopover in Sparta, you can pay homage at a statue to the stern warrior Leonidas.

Logistics: *You'll find several nice places to stay and dine in the countryside around Mystras, and Sparta is a pleasant and bustling town where you can enjoy an evening stroll through the animated squares.*

DAYS 5–6: MANI

Mani is one of the most unique areas of Greece. Byzantine chapels, towered houses, and stories of lawless locals are connected with a rocky, wild, and dry yet strikingly handsome landscape. Walk to the mythical gate to the end of the world and the southernmost point of mainland Greece, Cape Tenaro. Then explore seaside villages of Gerolimenas, Areopolis, and Kardamyli, trying Mani's famous local olive oils and honey along the way.

Logistics: *You'll have a choice of some distinctive places to stay in the Mani, along with many places to swim. It's a 3-hour drive back to Athens from here.*

Tips

Driving through the Peloponnese is pleasant, scenic, and easy. Roads are typically traffic-free and safe, and exits are marked with the Latin alphabet.

An overnight stay at one of the small hotels situated within "the rock" of Monemvasia is a unique experience, so be sure to book in advance in July and August, and remember, they can only be reached on foot.

If you are up for a scenic, rocky but easy-to-follow hike, head toward the lighthouse at the tip of Cape Tenaro. The amazing views from the very tip of mainland Greece will be your reward. Some more strenuous hiking routes lead into the mountains from Kardamyli.

Great Itineraries

Island-Hopping: Cyclades to Crete

There is no bad itinerary for the Greek islands, whether you choose the Sporades, the Dodecanese, or any of those other getaways floating in the Aegean. Greek isles differ remarkably, but just about all of them are all beautiful. The needle flies off the beauty-measuring gauge when it comes to the Cyclades. It might be possible to "see" any of these famous islands in a day. Still, it is best to take a slower pace and enjoy a sumptuous, idyllic 14-day tour.

DAYS 1–2: MYKONOS

One of the world's most famous islands manages to retain its seductive charm, despite an onslaught of visitors and the presence of some annoyingly tireless partiers. Spend the first day and evening enjoying appealing Mykonos Town, where a maze of beautiful little lanes is lined with shops, bars, restaurants, and clubs; laze on one of the splendid beaches; and, if you want to indulge in some hedonism, partake of the wild nightlife that doesn't slow down until dawn. The next morning take the local boat to nearby Delos for one of the great classical sites in the Aegean.

Logistics: *Mykonos is one of the main transport hubs of the Greek islands, with many ferries, boats, and planes connecting to Athens and its port of Piraeus. For a short stay like this, it's best to be in or near Mykonos Town.*

DAYS 3–4: NAXOS

Sail into the Southern Cyclades, to Naxos, arriving from Mykonos in the late afternoon or evening, and begin with a pre-dinner stroll around Naxos town, enjoying the Portara (the doorway of an ancient temple), the castle, and other sights in the old quarter. The next morning, drive through the island's mountainous center through welcoming countryside. Along the way, visit such sights as the Panayia Drosiani, a church near Moni noted for its frescoes; the village of Apeiranthos; and the Temple of Demeter. Stop for a swim at one of the beaches facing Paros, say Mikri Vigla.

Logistics: *During high season in summer, there are many ferries to Naxos from Mykonos, but there are fewer in the off-season. The fast-ferry trip (by sea jet) takes less than an hour.*

DAYS 5–7: PAROS

Go west, but not far, to Paros, another delightful stop in the Southern Cyclades. Paros town has delights profane—buzzing bars—and sacred, such as the legendary Hundred Doors Church. A highlight will be a meal in the impossibly pretty little fishing harbor of Naousa or, on a morning drive around the island, a visit to the lovely mountain village of Lefkes. Then spend an extra night of magic on the neighboring isle of Antiparos, where off-duty Hollywood celebs bliss out with all the white sands, pink bougainvillea, and blue seas.

Logistics: *It's a very short hop from Naxos to Paros.*

DAYS 8–9: FOLEGANDROS

This smaller isle is not only beautiful but, rarer in these parts, authentic. It boasts one of the most stunning Chora towns, deliberately downplayed touristic development, several good beaches, quiet evenings, traditional local food, and respectful visitors. The high point, literally and figuratively, is the main town—on a towering cliff over the sea, a scenic perch that almost rivals the spectacle of Santorini.

Gulf of Corinth

Aegean Sea

TURKEY

✪ Athens

Mykonos

Delos

Paros Naxos

Antiparos
CYCLADES

Folegandros

Ia
Santorini Fira

DODECANESE

Sea of Crete

Hania
Crete Heraklion

Ionian Sea

Palace of
Knossos

DAYS 10–11: SANTORINI

Take a ferry from Folegandros south to the spectacle of all spectacles. Yes, in summer the crowds will remind you of the running of the bulls in Pamplona, but even they won't stop you from gasping at the vistas, the seaside cliffs, and the stunning Cycladic Cubist architecture. Once you've settled in, have a sunset drink on a terrace overlooking the volcanic caldera. You can also find many view-providing watering holes in Fira, the capital, or Ia, Greece's most photographed village. The next day, visit the the Akrotiri excavation and enjoy the black-sand beaches at Kamari or Perissa.

DAYS 12–14: CRETE

The mystery surrounding Europe's first civilization and empire is what draws many travelers to Crete. Like them, you can discover stunning testimony to the island's mysterious Minoan civilization, particularly at the legendary Palace of Knossos. Along these shores are also many blissful beaches as well as the enchanting Venetian-Turkish cities of Hania and Rethymnon; in fact, try to arrange a late afternoon ferry from Santorini so your first experience on Greece's largest island will be an enchanting evening spent in one of these remarkable ports. As you explore the rest of the island, best done by car, you'll discover stunning mountain and gorge scenery, out-of-the-way villages on the Lasithi Plateau, isolated monasteries, and a lively resort scene in places like Ayios Nikolaos. From Heraklion, Crete's main port and also a fascinating place with Ventian landmarks and an outstanding antiquities museum, there are frequent flights and ferries back to Athens.

Tips

■ High-speed catamarans have halved travel time between Piraeus and Santorini. If you have more time, you can take a slower car ferry all the way to Crete and work your way back to Athens on quicker, high-speed ferries.

■ Be sure to make advance reservations in August, when ferries sell out; days on and around the August 15 holiday are especially busy.

■ Mykonos, Naxos, Paros, and Santorini have airports, with daily service to and from Athens in season, and Crete has two busy airports.

On the Calendar

Many celebrations throughout the year revolve around Greek Orthodox holidays and saint days. But Greeks also love any good excuse to dance and feast, and they love to celebrate the arts, including film, dance, and drama. Some of these events may be curtailed until the COVID-19 pandemic is under control.

January

Epiphany, January 6. To commemorate the day of Christ's baptism, a sizable gathering in Athens takes place at the port of Piraeus (and every other port nearby). A priest throws a large crucifix into the water, and young men brave the cold to recover it. The finder is rewarded with a blessing.

February

Apokries. Thousands take to the streets, prancing and dancing in costume, drinking, and just being merry during the country's three-week pre-Lenten Carnival season. The islands of Skyros and Crete attract some of the largest crowds, but the Greek Carnival capital is Patras in the northern Peloponnese. ⊕ *www.rethymnocarnival.gr* or ⊕ *www.carnivalpatras.gr*

March

Thessaloniki International Documentary Festival. Documentary filmmakers from all over the world screen their work at this March festival that's gaining a name for itself in the industry. ⊕ *tdf.filmfestival.gr.*

Greek Independence Day, March 25. A military parade that commemorates the start of the War of Greek Independence of 1821 is held with pomp and circumstance. It marches straight through the heart of Athens.

Feast of the Annunciation, March 25. While Greece celebrates its independence, the islands of Tinos and Hydra hold special religious festivities to honor the news that Mary would be the mother of Christ.

April—May

Holy Easter Week Celebrations, April or May. Throughout the country, church services and processions are scheduled during the most important holiday in Greece. On Easter midnight, families gather at local churches, candles in hand. The rest of the day is dedicated to feasting on roasted lamb and other traditional food. On Holy Thursday, "The Last Supper" is reenacted at the Monastery of St. John the Divine on the island of Patmos.

May

Dora Stratou Dance Troupe in Athens. The 75-member dance troupe performs a full repertoire of Greek folk dances wearing traditional costumes and jewelry beginning in May. Frequent performances light the stage at the group's open-air theater near the Acropolis. The season continues through September. ⊕ *www.grdance.org.*

International Museums Day, May 18. A day established by the International Council of Museums encourages public awareness of the importance of museums in today's society. Some of the best museums in Greece, including the Acropolis Museum, the Benaki Museum, and the National Archaeological Museum, offer free admission. ⊕ *imd.icom.museum*

Art Athina Festival. One of the longest-lasting contemporary art fairs in Europe takes place in Athens each May. International artists gather to collaborate and present their work to more than 30,000 visitors over a four-day period.

Anastenaria Fire Walking Festival, May 21–23. Outside of Thessaloniki, in the northern Greek villages of Agia Eleni and Langadas, the pagan ritual of walking over fire still goes on. Today, however, it is dedicated and attached to the Christian faith and always begins on St. Constantine Day, lasting for three days.

June

Athens and Epidavros Festival, June to October. A full schedule of classical Greek dramas, opera, orchestra, and dance performances fills venues across Athens, including the ancient Odeon of Herodes Atticus next to the Acropolis. Over the years a roster of famous actors, including Helen Mirren and Ethan Hawke, have graced the stage at the magnificent ancient Theatre of Epidauros in the Peloponnese. ⊕ www.greekfestival.gr.

Nafplion Festival. Established as one of the most successful classical music events in Greece, the festival is set in various venues in the beautiful seaside Peloponnese city and attracts the brightest ensembles and artists from around the world. ⊕ www.nafplionfestival.gr.

Rockwave Festival. The Black Eyed Peas, Megadeth, Oasis, and Guns N' Roses are just a few headliners that have taken the stage at Terravibe Park, north of Athens, since this festival began in 1995. Crowds pack the outdoor venues for four days of performances, rocking on to established and upandcoming bands. ⊕ www.rockwavefestival.gr.

July

Medieval Rose Festival. The gorgeous medieval town of Rhodes is the perfect backdrop for well-rehearsed reenactments from Byzantine and medieval times. Musical and art events add to the program with the aim to educate and entertain. ⊕ www.medievalfestival.gr.

Festival of the Aegean. Hundreds of singers and dancers from all over the world, including more than a dozen choirs, gather in Syros, the capital of the Cyclades, each summer. Their inspiring performances pack audiences at beautiful venues including the elegant Apollo Theatre and St. Nicholas Church. ⊕ www.festivaloftheaegean.com.

Sani Festival. Artists from around the world gather for a jam-packed program of concerts in the Halkidiki Peninsula of northern Greece. Performances take place at various venues, including Sani Hill, a small islet surrounded by the lapping waves of the Aegean and run through mid-August. ⊕ sanifestival.gr.

August

Feast of the Assumption of the Virgin, August 15. On this national holiday, thousands of pilgrims crowd Tinos to ask for a special blessing or a miracle. In crowds, they crawl on their hands and knees to the cathedral of Panagia Evangelistria. Throughout the country, the less devout kick back and have a good time.

On the Calendar

Megaro Gyzi Festival. A combination of classical music, traditional Greek performances, and art exhibitions add to the already beautiful atmosphere on Santorini. A 17th-century mansion called Megaro Gyzi, located in the cliff-hugging village of Fira, houses each event. ⊕ *www.megarogyzi.gr.*

Renaissance Festival at Rethymnon. In a celebration of art, theater, and music, hundreds of artists from around the globe act, sing, and dance in venues throughout the most picturesque Cretan town in performances that begin in August and continue through September. Each performance aims to honor the spirit of the Renaissance era. ⊕ *www.rfr.gr.*

September

Aegina Pistachio Festival. Dance, sing, and enjoy your share of delicious pistachio products as you learn about the Aegina's appreciation for the nut that has helped their island thrive. ⊕ *hwww.aeginagreece.com/aegina-island/greece/aegina-fistiki-festival.*

Dionysia Wine Festival. One of Naxos island's key events, with music, theater, and art exhibitions, celebrates the island's ties to the Ancient Greek God of Wine, Dionysus, during the first week of September.

October

Spetses Mini Marathon. The biggest island sporting event in Greece features running and swimming races and a children's run. Social events are also open for those who want to feel the energetic vibe of the island during the action-packed weekend. Get a welcoming taste of the savory homemade pies baked and handed out by local women. ⊕ *spetsesmarathon.com.*

Ochi Day, October 28. *Ochi* means *no* in Greek, a word that sums up Greece's defiance to the Italian invasion of 1940. The day is a national holiday that's widely celebrated and honored. Major cities like Athens and Thessaloniki hold military parades, and coastal villages schedule naval parades.

November

Thessaloniki International Film Festival. For more than 50 years, the sophisticated city has hosted independent filmmakers from all over the world, who compete for the event's highest award, the Golden Alexander. ⊕ *www.filmfestival.gr.*

Athens Marathon. Tens of thousands of runners head to Greece in early November to run the route based on the original marathon from Ancient Greek times. The 26.2-mile course begins in Marathon and finishes at the grand marble Panathenaic Stadium in Athens. ⊕ *www.athensauthenticmarathon.gr.*

November 17th. The widely observed anniversary commemorates the 1973 uprising by Athens Polytechnic University students, who were killed for protesting the Greek military junta. Metro stations close down, and protests typically take to the streets, making it a difficult day for travel and sightseeing.

December

Christmas. Athens gets festive, especially for kids. The National Gardens and Syntagma Square are transformed into a Christmas village, where activities are scheduled during school vacation. Additional city venues and public spaces hold events as well. ⊕ *www.cityofathens.gr.*

Chapter 3

ATHENS

Updated by
Alexia Amvrazi

⊙ Sights	🍴 Restaurants	🛏 Hotels	👜 Shopping	🍸 Nightlife
★★★★★	★★★★★	★★★★★	★★★★☆	★★★★☆

WELCOME TO ATHENS

TOP REASONS TO GO

★ **The Acropolis:** A beacon of classical glory rising above Athens's architectural mishmash, this iconic citadel represents everything the Athenians were and still aspire to be.

★ **Evzones on Syntagma Square:** Evzones guards act out a changing of the guard that falls somewhere between discipline and performance art.

★ **The Ancient Agora and Monastiraki:** Socrates and Plato once philosophized at the Agora, and today you can do the same, perambulating around the nearby Monastiraki marketplace.

★ **Opa!:** Whether drinking cocktails til dawn around Syntagma or dirty dancing on the tables at live-bouzouki clubs, Athenians party like no one else.

★ **Thriving Culture:** Galleries, cooperatives, artistic events, performances, museums, and the new Stavros Niarchos Cultural Center have put Athens on the road to being the new Berlin.

1 Acropolis, Makriyianni, and Koukaki. The massive citadel and its architecturally sophisticated structures rise majestically above the city. Just below is Makriyianni, a trendy neighborhood with the New Acropolis Museum. Koukaki is officially one of the city's hippest districts.

2 Plaka and Anafiotika. Touristy and tranquil at once, old-fashioned Plaka is dotted by Byzantine churches, neoclassical mansions, ancient Greek monuments, and souvenir shops. Above it is the whitewashed mini-village of Anafiotika, with Cycladic-inspired architecture and splendid city views.

3 Monastiraki and Psirri. Adjacent to the ancient Agora is where you'll find Athens's Central Market, not to mention flea markets, specialty shops, and a chaotic buzz. To the south, Psirri is a diverse area of low-key eateries, traditional and ethnic grocery shops, and artisanal workshops.

4 Thissio. Graced by classical ruins, Thissio is lined with pretty cafés, street stalls selling jewelry, restaurants, and galleries.

5 Syntagma. The heart of modern Athens is surrounded by the Parliament House, the city's top restaurants and bars, the most grandiose hotels, and Ermou shopping boulevard.

6 Gazi-Kerameikos. This area is home to the city's Technopolis gasworks and a buzzy arts and nightlife hub.

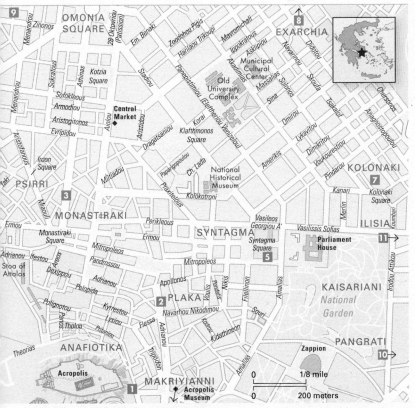

7 Kolonaki. East of Syntagma Square lies this fashionable residential area loaded with see-and-be-seen restaurant-bars and cafés, glossy boutiques, galleries, and top museums.

8 Exarchia. In the northern reaches of the city, the offbeat area known as the "anarchic neighborhood" is home to the famed National Archaeological Museum.

9 Omonia and Metaxourgeio. Omonia is an important transport hub with good hotels but can be sketchy at night; edgy Metaxourgeio is popular for its arts scene and nightlife.

10 Pangrati. The mostly residential neighborhood of Pangrati has become one of the hippest neighborhoods, 24/7.

11 Ilisia. Home to the Athens Concert Hall, the U.S. Embassy, some high-end restaurants and hotels, and nearby nightlife spot Mavili Square.

12 Neos Kosmos. This former refugee neighborhood is transforming into a hip, trendy area.

13 Piraeus. Athens's busy port also has some recommendable restaurants, mainly in scenic Mikrolimano.

It's no wonder that all roads lead to the fascinating and paradoxical metropolis of Athens. Lift your eyes 200 feet above the city to the Parthenon, its honey-colored marble columns rising from a massive limestone base, and you'll behold architectural perfection that has not been surpassed in 2,500 years. Today, this shrine of classical form dominates a 21st-century boomtown.

One of the world's oldest cities, Athens is home to 4.5 million souls, many of whom spend the day discussing the city's faults, including budget woes, red tape, overcrowding, transport strikes, immigration problems, and unemployment. These analysis sessions are usually accompanied by excellent coffee, food, or cocktails since Athenians refuse to stay indoors in any weather or mood. But while Athens is a difficult city to love, it's also a difficult city to leave, and many temporary visitors end up settling here for years or consistently returning without ever having expected to. As damaging as it has been to the Greek psyche and businesses alike, the financial crisis also served to inspire Greeks to try out new jobs and start innovative and sophisticated entrepreneurial pursuits, while the blossoming urban arts scene has earned the Greek capital the title of being "the new Berlin." Over the last five years it has undergone a huge transformation, and almost every day an innovative new shop, gallery, or eatery pops up.

To experience Athens—Athìna in Greek—fully is to understand the essence of Greece: ancient monuments surviving in a sea of cement, startling beauty amid the squalor, folkish tradition and vintage kitsch juxtaposed with ultramodern concepts. To appreciate Athens is to appreciate life with all its refreshing surprises and paradoxical complexities.

THE NEW ATHENS
Many splendid features were created for the city's 2004 Olympics. In 2000, Athens opened its still-expanding metro, many of whose gleaming stations display ancient artifacts and modern artworks and installations by famous artists. High-tech Eleftherios Venizelos International Airport serves as the country's efficient entry point. New infrastructure blessings also include a (somewhat slow) tram line running from the city center to the south-coast beaches; an express train running to the airport and far-flung suburbs; and a ring-road beltway and the repaving and expansion of most of the city's potholed highways.

Within the city, beautification projects took priority. The most successful has been the completion of Athens's Archaeological Park, which links the capital's ancient sites in a pedestrian network that includes the Panathenaic stadium, the Temple of Olympian Zeus, the Acropolis, Filopappou Hill, the ancient Greek and Roman agoras, Hadrian's Library, and Kerameikos. The capital is now seeing the creation of "The Great Walk of Athens," which is unifying historical spaces, better showcasing landmarks from the palimsest of Athenian history, creating bike lanes and car-free zones, and offering pedestrians an entirely new experience of the city.

Two major projects include the National Museum of Contemporary Art (EMST) on Syngrou Avenue, housed in a massive, 19th-century beer factory, and the Stavros Niarchos Foundation Cultural Center (SNFCC) in the southern suburbs, housing the National Opera House of Greece and the National Library.

While various museums have received renovations, such as the National Archaeological Museum and the Benaki Museum, one museum garnered headlines around the world when it finally opened in June 2009: the spectacularly modern New Acropolis Museum, which showcases some of the most venerated ancient statues and artifacts in the world. Right under the Acropolis and excellently maintained, the museum has reignited and amplified the argument for Greece to get its "marbles" back from The British Museum. The invigorating buzz that seized Athens pre-2004 also helped transform entire neighborhoods like Gazi-Kerameikos, Thissio, Metaxourgeio, and Psirri from industrial warehouse districts to hot spots of hip art spaces, restaurants, and happening nightclubs.

THE AGELESS CITY

Happily, you can still wander into less-touristy areas to discover pockets of timeless charm. Here, in the lovelier Athenian neighborhoods, you can delight in the pleasures of strolling—*Peripatos,* the Athenians call it, and it's as old as Aristotle, whose students learned as they roamed about in his Peripatetic school. This ancient practice survives in the modern custom of the evening *volta,* or stroll, especially charming when taken along the pedestrianized Dionyssiou Areopagitou Street skirting the base of the Acropolis or the cobblestone road leading to deeply historical Pnyx and Filopappou Hills.

Along your way, be sure to stop in a taverna to observe Athenians in their element, usually sharing several dishes in the middle of the table. They are lively and expressive, often gesturing excitedly and speaking loudly. Although often expansively friendly and good humored, they can behave somewhat dramatically when threatened, but they're also passionate about discovering other nationalities and cultures.

Amid the ancient treasures and the 19th-century delights of neighborhoods such as Anafiotika and Plaka, are countless office buildings and modern apartments. Hardly a monument of importance, apart from certain churches and mansions, attests to the city's history between the completion of the Temple of Olympian Zeus 19 centuries ago and the present day. That is the tragedy of Athens: the long vacuum in its history, the centuries of decay, neglect, and even oblivion. But within the last 150 years the Greeks have created a modern capital out of a village centered on a group of ruined marble columns and have gone far in transforming Athens into a vibrant and multifaceted modern metropolis that the ancients would strain to recognize but would heartily endorse. Its ebullient spirit remains unscathed even in the face of financial adversity and shrinking public coffers.

3

Athens

Planning

When to Go

Athens often feels like a furnace in summer, due to the capital's millions of circulating cars and shortage of parks. Mornings between 7 am and 9 am or evenings after 8 pm are often pleasant, but temperatures can still hover in the 90s during heat waves. The capital is far more pleasant in spring and fall, when the air is crisp and the sunlight bearable. Winters are moody but generally mild here, just as they are in all of Greece: it rains but rarely snows, but in deep winter the cold can cut to the bone.

Getting Here and Around

Many major sights, as well as hotels, cafés, and restaurants, are within a fairly small central area of Athens. It's easy to walk everywhere, though sometimes cars and bikes obstruct sidewalks. Most far-flung sights, such as beaches, are reachable by metro, bus, and tram.

AIR

Athens's sleek Eleftherios Venizelos International Airport has made air travel around the country much easier. Greece is so small that few in-country flights take longer than an hour or cost more than €200 round-trip. Aegean Airlines and Olympic Airways have regular flights between Athens, Thessaloniki, and most major cities and islands in Greece. *For further information, see Air in Travel Smart.*

AIRPORT TRANSFERS

The best way to get to or from the airport and Athens is by metro or light-rail. Single tickets cost €10 and include transfers to bus, trolley, or tram within 90 minutes of the ticket's initial validation. Multi-passenger tickets for groups of two (€18) or three (€24) passengers are also available; if you're just making a stopover in Athens, opt for a round-trip ticket (€18), valid for trips to and from the airport made within a week.

In Athens four reliable express buses connect the airport with the metro (Nomismatokopeio, Ethniki Amyna, and Dafni stations), Syntagma Square, Kifissos Bus Station, and Piraeus. Express buses leave the arrivals level of the airport every 15 minutes and operate 24 hours a day. Bus X95 will take you to Syntagma Square (Amalias Avenue); Bus X96 takes the Vari–Koropi road inland and links with the coastal road, passing through Voula, Glyfada, and Alimos; it then goes on to Piraeus (opposite Karaiskaki Square), and this is the best option if you are getting directly on a cruise ship. Bus X97 goes to the Dafni metro stop, while X93 brings voyagers to the dusty Kifissos intercity bus station. The Attiki Odos ring road and the expansion of the city's network of bus lanes have made travel times more predictable.

Bus tickets to and from the airport cost €5 and are valid on all forms of transportation in Athens for 24 hours from the time of validation. Purchase tickets (and get bus schedules) from the airport terminal, kiosks, metro stations, or even on the express buses.

Taxis are readily available at the arrivals level of the Athens airport; it costs an average of €35 to get into downtown Athens. (If you fear you have been overcharged, insist on a receipt with the driver's details and contact the tourist police.) Prestige Limousine Service and Central VIP Services provide service; an evening surcharge of up to 50% often applies, and you should call in advance. Prices range between €60 and €90 one-way from the airport to a central hotel for four people.

CONTACTS Central VIP Services. ⊠ *25 Ethnarchou Makariou str* ☎ *210/9249–500* ⊕ *www.centralvip.gr.* **Prestige Limousine Service.** ⊠ *Korai 3* ☎ *210/3254–151* ⊕ *www.prestigegreece.com.*

BOAT AND FERRY

Boat travel in Greece is common and reasonably priced. Every weekend thousands of Athenians set off on one- and two-hour trips to islands like Aegina, Hydra, and Andros, while in summer ferries are weighed down with merrymakers on their way to Mykonos, Rhodes, and Crete. Cruise ships, ferries, and hydrofoils from the Aegean and most other Greek islands dock and depart every day from Athens's main port, Piraeus, 10 km (6 miles) southwest of Central Athens. Ships for Corfu sail from ports nearer to it, such as Patras and Igoumenitsa. Connections from Piraeus to the main island groups are good, as are those from main islands to smaller ones within a group, although in some cases less regular.

Boat schedules are published in *Kathimerini*, an insert in *The New York Times International Edition*, but it's often more convenient to book tickets through a travel agent; it's what Greeks do as well. Schedules can be found online or by calling the Piraeus Port Authority, and ferry bookings (including details like the type of seat or cabin you desire) can also be done online by going directly to the site of the ferry company you're interested in traveling with, or just Googling "boat tickets, Greece." Just realize that timetables change according to seasonal demand, and boats may be delayed by weather conditions or occasional strikes, so your plans should be flexible. Ideally, buy your tickets at least two or three days in advance, especially if you are traveling in summer or taking a car. If there's no time, get to the port an hour earlier to buy tickets from travel agents there, but in high season you're unlikely to find any. Reserve your return journey or continuation soon after you arrive. *For further information, see Boat in Travel Smart.*

To get to and from Piraeus, you can take the Green Line metro (Line 1) from Central Athens directly to the station at the main port. The trip takes 25 to 30 minutes, but there may be a rather long walk to your dock from there, depending on your destination and ferry company. A taxi from the center can take longer because of traffic and costs around €15–€18. Express bus line X80 links the OLP cruise terminal to the Acropolis and Syntagma Square in the center of Athens and runs daily every 30 minutes from 7 am until 9:30 pm.

Athens's other main port is Rafina, which serves some of the closer Cyclades (like Andros, Tinos, and Mykonos) and Evia. KTEL buses run every 45 minutes between the Mavromateon bus terminal in Central Athens and the port, from 5:40 am until 10:30 pm, and cost €2.40 At Rafina, the buses arrive and depart from an area slightly uphill from the port. The trip takes about one hour depending on traffic. *(See Bus and Tram Travel.)*

CONTACTS Rafina KTEL Buses. ☎ *210/ 880–8000* ⊕ *www.ktelattikis.gr.*

BUS AND TRAM WITHIN ATHENS

Athens and its suburbs are covered by a good network of buses, with express buses running between Central Athens and major neighborhoods, including nearby beaches. During the day, buses tend to run every 15 to 30 minutes, with reduced service at night and on weekends. Buses run daily from about 5 am to midnight.

A tram link between downtown Athens and the coastal southern suburbs features two main lines. Line A runs from Syntagma to Glyfada; Line B traces the shoreline from Glyfada to the Peace & Friendship Stadium on the outskirts of Piraeus. Single tickets cost €1.40 and are sold at machines on the tram platforms.

Main bus stations are at Akadimias and Sina and at Kaningos Square. Bus and trolley tickets cost €1.20 for one ride. A more expensive €1.40 ticket is valid for 90 minutes of travel on all modes of public transport (bus, trolley, tram, and metro). Remember to validate the ticket (insert it in the ticket machine in the ticket area of the metro or aboard the train or bus) when you begin your journey and keep it until you've exited the bus or tram station. Day passes for €4.50, and five-day tickets for €9 are also popular with tourists, but they don't include airport transport; a three-day tourist ticket costs €22 and does include one round-trip for the airport train. Monthly passes are also sold at special booths at the main terminals on the first and last week of each month.

Maps of bus routes are available at terminal booths or from EOT. The website of the Organization for Urban Public Transportation (OASA) has a helpful English-language section.

CONTACTS City Tram. ⊕ *www.stasy.gr.* **Organization for Urban Public Transportation (OASA).** ☎ *11185 Call center* ⊕ *www.oasa. gr.*

BUS BEYOND ATHENS
Travel around Greece by bus is inexpensive and usually comfortable; most buses are now air-conditioned. Make reservations at least one day before your planned trip, earlier for holiday weekends.

Most buses to the east Attica coast, including those for Sounion (€6.50 for inland route, €7 on coastal road) and Marathon (€4.50), leave from the KTEL terminal in Pedion Areos.

The journey from Athens to Thessaloniki takes roughly the same time as the regular train (around 6 hours), though the InterCity Express train covers the distance 1¼ hours faster. Make reservations at least one day before your planned trip, earlier for holiday weekends. To reach the Peloponnese, buses are as fast as trains thanks to Proastiakos, the high-speed suburban rail to Corinth and beyond. Information and timetables are available at tourist information offices and metro stations.

Terminal A—aka Kifissos Station—is the arrival and departure point for bus lines that serve parts of northern Greece, including Thessaloniki, and the Peloponnese destinations of Epidauros, Mycenae, Nafplion, Olympia, and Corinth. Terminal B serves Evia, most of Thrace, and central Greece, including Delphi. Tickets for these buses are sold only at this terminal, so you should call to book seats well in advance in high season or holidays. *For more detailed bus information, see Bus in Travel Smart.*

CONTACTS KTEL Attica. ⊠ *Patission 68 and Kotsika 2, Aigyptou Sq., at corner of Mavromateon and Leoforos Alexandras near Pedion Areos Park, Pedion Areos* ☎ *210/880–8000 all information* ⊕ *ktelattikis.gr.*

CAR IN ATHENS
Greek drivers can be feisty, but standards today are the closest they've ever been to typical European style—except on the coastal roads late at night. Locals have welcomed the accessible, affordable, and generally reliable public transport, while taxi fares also remain affordable. Driving is on the right, and although the vehicle on the right has the right of way, don't always expect this to be obeyed; in fact, be prepared to discover how creatively the rules can be bent. Drivers have priority over pedestrians here, so if you are walking and the light is green, stay fully aware of cars.

The speed limit is 50 kph (31 mph) in town. Seat belts are compulsory, as are helmets for motorcyclists, though many flagrantly ignore the laws. In the downtown sectors of the city do not drive in the bus lanes marked by a yellow divider; if caught, you may be fined. You're better off leaving your car in the hotel garage and walking or taking a cab. Gas pumps and service stations are everywhere, but be aware that all-night stations are few and far between.

CAR BEYOND ATHENS

Greece's main highways to the north and the south link up in Athens; both are called Ethniki Odos (National Road). Take the Attiki Odos, a beltway around Athens that also accesses Eleftherios Venizelos International Airport, to speed your travel time entering and exiting the city. The toll is €2.80 for cars, payable upon entering this privately owned highway. At the city limits, signs in English clearly mark the way to both Syntagma Square and Omonia Square in the city center. Leaving Athens, routes to the highways and Attiki Odos are well marked; green signs usually name Lamia for points north, and Corinth or Patras for points southwest. From Athens to Thessaloniki, the distance is 515 km (319 miles); to Kalamata, 257 km (159 miles); to Corinth, 84 km (52 miles); to Patras, 218 km (135 miles); to Igoumenitsa, 472 km (293 miles).

Most car rental offices are around Syngrou and Syntagma Square in Central Athens, but it can be cheaper to book from your home country; small-car rentals start at around €20/day. *For more information, see Car Rental in the Travel Smart chapter.*

CRUISE

Chinese-owned Piraeus is the main port of Athens, 11 km (7 miles) southwest of the city center, and is itself the third-largest city in Greece, with a population of about 500,000. In anticipation of a flood of visitors during the 2004 Olympics, the harbor district was given a general sprucing up. The cruise port has 12 berths, and the cruise terminal has duty-free shops, information, and refreshments.

The cheapest (and often fastest) way to get to Athens from Piraeus is to take the metro. Line 1 (Green Line) reaches the downtown Athens stops most useful to tourists, including Platia Victorias, near the National Archaeological Museum; Omonia Square; Monastiraki, in the old Turkish bazaar; and Thission, near the ancient Agora. The trip takes 25 to 30 minutes. The Piraeus metro station for Line 1 (Piraeus-Kifissia) is off Akti Kallimasioti on the main harbor, a 20-minute walk from the cruise port, and you must walk all the way around the harbor to reach these piers.

You can also take the express X80 bus line, leaving the OLP cruise terminal for Acropolis and Syntagma Square (for info, visit ⊕ *www.oasa.gr*).

Taxis wait outside the terminal entrance. Taxis into the city are not always quicker than public transport because of traffic, and cost around €15 to €18. Make sure the meter is running from the moment you start your ride (the starting fee is set at €3.20). If a driver wishes to pick up other passengers if there is room in the cab, you have the right to refuse. Taxis are also readily available at the port to get you to the airport for around €45.

METRO (SUBWAY)

The best magic carpet ride in town is the polished metro, which is fast, cheap, and convenient; its three lines go to all the major spots in Athens. Line 1, or the Green Line, of the city's metro system is often called the *ilektrikos* (or the electrical train) and runs from Piraeus to the northern suburb of Kifissia, with several downtown stops (including Victoria Square, near the National Archaeological Museum; Omonia Square; Monastiraki, in the old Turkish bazaar; Thissio, near Kerameikos; the ancient Agora; and a 5–10 minute walking distance from the nightlife districts of Psirri, Gazi-Kerameikos, and Thissio).

The other two lines are newer and more modern. Line 2, or the Red Line, cuts northwest across the city, starting from suburban Anthoupoli and passing through such useful stops as Syntagma Square, opposite the Greek Parliament; Panepistimiou (near the Old University complex and the Numismatic Museum); Omonia Square; Metaxourgeio; the Stathmos Larissis stop next to Athens's central train station; Acropolis, at the foot of the famous site; and finishing off at the south suburb of Elliniko.

Line 3, or the Blue Line, runs from the suburb of Ayia Varvara (the Ayia Marina terminal station) through Kerameikos (the stop for bustling Gazi-Kerameikos) and Monastiraki; some trains on this line go all the way to the airport, but they only pass about every half hour and require a special ticket. The stops of most interest for visitors are Evangelismos, near the Byzantine and Christian Museum, Hilton Hotel, National Gallery of Art, and Mega-ron Mousikis, next to the U.S. Embassy and the concert hall.

Since 2018, the transportation system has transitioned to using the ATHENA cards, similar to the London Oyster cards or those used on the Washington, DC Metro. These can be bought in plastic, rechargable form (using ticket machines at the stations, which also accept credit cards although this doesn't always work), or card form. The fare for a 90-minute ticket is €1.20. A 24-hour travel pass, valid for use on all forms of public transportation, is €4.10, while a three-day ticket for all transport costs €20. Tickets to the airport are €9, or €16 for a return ticket used within 48 hours. Tickets need to be swiped at the machines with bars in metro stations before heading to the platform and at machines in buses and trams (if you're caught without a valid ticket you will be fined 60 times the price of your ticket, so retain your ticket until you reach your final destination). Trains run between 5:30 am and 12:30 am, and every Friday and Saturday night lines 2 and 3 stay open until 2:30 am. Maps of the metro are available in stations and online at ⊕ *www.athenstransport.com*.

CONTACTS Athens Transport. ⊕ *www. athenstransport.com*.

TAXI

Most drivers in Athens speak at least basic English. Make sure the driver turns on the meter and that the rate listed in the lower corner is 1, the normal rate before midnight; after midnight, the rate listed is 2.

Most taxi drivers use a GPS system and know the major central hotels, but make sure you have the address and phone number of your destination written down in case you need to look up the street or make a call to get directions. Neither tipping nor bargaining is generally practiced; if your driver has gone out of the way for you, a small gratuity (10% or less) is appreciated.

The local ride-hailing app is BEAT, allowing you to choose your driver and follow your ride on your phone. Uber operates (only) regular taxis in Athens and can also be downloadeed on your phone, with choices for Economy, Premium, Accessibility (for wheelchair users), and Pool rides. BEAT offers pet-friendly taxi options, displayed in the individual driver's profile via a paw-print.

The Athens taximeter starts at €1.19 and, even if you join other passengers, you must add this amount to your final charge. The minimum fare is €3.20. The basic charge is €0.70 per kilometer (½ mile); this increases to €1.19 between midnight and 5 am or if you go outside city limits. There are surcharges for holidays (€1), trips to and from the airport (€3.84), and rides to (but not from) the port, train stations, and bus terminals (€1.07). There is also a €0.40 charge for each suitcase over 10 kilos (22 pounds), but drivers expect €0.40 for each bag anyway. Waiting time is €10.85 per hour. Radio taxis charge an additional €2 to €5.65 for the pickup, depending on time of day requested.

CONTACTS Athens 1 Intertaxi. ☏ *210/9212800, 210 /9210417* ⊕ *www. athens1.gr*. **Beat.** ⊕ *thebeat.co/gr*. **Ermis**

Taxi Service. ☎ *210/4115200* ⊕ *www. radiotaxiermis.gr.* **Radio Taxi Hellas.** ☎ *210/6457000, 18189* ⊕ *www.radiotaxi-hellas.gr.* **Uber.** ⊕ *www.uber.com.*

TRAIN

The *Proastiakos* ("suburban"), a light-rail network offering travelers a direct link from Athens Eleftherios Venizelos Airport to Kiato (en route to Patras for €13), has introduced Athenians to the concept of commuting. The trains now serve the city's northern and eastern suburbs as well as western Attica. The Athens-to-Corinth fare is €8.50; lower fares apply for points in between. If you plan on taking the train while in Athens, call the Greek Railway Organization (OSE) to find out which station your train leaves from, and how to get there. Trains from the north and international trains arrive at, and depart from, Stathmos Larissis, which is connected to the metro. If you want to buy tickets ahead of time, it's easier to visit a downtown railway office. *For further information, see Train in the Travel Smart chapter.*

CONTACTS Stathmos Larissis Train Station. ☎ *14511 customer service (daily 6 am–11 pm)* ⊕ *www.trainose.gr/en/contact-us.*

Hotels

Greeks pride themselves on their *philoxenia,* or hospitality. Even in antiquity, many of them referred to Zeus as Xenios Zeus—the God in charge of protecting travelers. Today, Greek philoxenia is alive and well in the capital city, whether displayed in the kindness of strangers you ask for directions or in the thoroughness of your hotel receptionist's care. With 18.5% of the small country's GDP derived from tourism, philoxenia is vital, and since the advent of the financial crisis almost a decade ago, Greeks have woken up to a whole new level of awareness when it comes to quality service and customer satisfaction.

The city is full of hotels, many of which were built in Greek tourism's heyday in the 1960s and '70s. In the years prior to the 2004 Athens Olympic Games, financial incentives were provided to hoteliers to upgrade and renovate their facilities, to the effect that many hotels—such as the Athens Hilton—completely renovated themselves inside and out as they increased their range of services.

But while prices have increased since the Olympics, accommodations are still available at all price levels. In Athens you can find everything from boutique hotels dreamed up by prestigious designers and decorated by well-known artists to no-fuss youth hostels. Airbnb has shaken the waters for the hotel industry, with many visitors now preferring plush and idyllically located apartment and studio rentals over hotels, and this has also catalyzed the hotel industry to raise its standards. Athens's budget hotels—once little better than dorms—now almost always have air-conditioning and a TV in all rooms, along with more stylish public spaces and Wi-Fi. In the post-Olympics years, there was a notable increase in the number of good-quality, middle-rank family hotels, and over a decade later the newest trend is the so-called "micro hotel," a style of accommodation that throws standard hotel features like an entrance lobby, set breakfast hours, and standard hotel layouts to the wind, offering guests the feeling of staying in a beautiful, homelike space (often a restored mansion or building) with exquisite furnishings and modern facilities. At the same time, the city's classic luxury hotels, such as the Grande Bretagne, Hilton Athens, and the King George, continue to be considered the cream of the crop for anyone seeking the full package in hotel pampering, and not least because of their impressive spas, restaurants, and bars.

The most convenient hotels for travelers are in the heart of the city center. Some of the older hotels in charming Plaka and near less charming Omonia

Square are comfortable and clean, their appeal inherent in their age, while there's also an enticing range of choices in Syntagma, an ideally central location for exploring the city. Makriyianni, the area directly beneath the Acropolis, makes for a perfect location for those seeking elegant tranquility away from the hubbub of the city and tree-lined pedestrianized roads ideal for morning jogs. Beware that as charming as some of the smaller, cheaper hotels may have become, you're bound to come across some lapses in the details—take a good look at the room before you register. The thick stone walls of neoclassical buildings keep them cool in summer, but few of the budget hotels have reliable central heating, and Athens can be devilishly cold in winter.

HOTEL PRICES

Along with higher quality have come higher hotel prices: room rates in Athens are not much less than in many European cities. Still, there are bargains to be had. It's also a good idea to bargain in person at smaller hotels, especially off-season. When negotiating a rate, note that the longer the stay, the lower the nightly rate, so it may be less expensive to spend six consecutive nights in Athens than to stay two or three nights at either end of your trip through Greece.

Bear in mind that usually hotels will charge extra for a view of the Acropolis, and that breakfast is not always included. It is sometimes best to book through an agent for better bulk rates (this can lead to cost savings of up to 20%). Often it is also well worth checking the websites of hotels for special seasonal offers or bargain packages. In the off-season months (October to April) it is possible to negotiate for, and achieve, better rates.

Hotel reviews have been shortened. For full information, visit Fodors.com.

What it Costs in euros			
$	$$	$$$	$$$$
HOTELS			
under €125	€125– €225	€226– €275	over €275

Nightlife

Despite demanding working hours, significantly tighter budgets, and family obligations, Athenians don't like staying home, and will always find good reasons to sit out with friends at a bar until the latest hours. Athens's heady nightlife starts late. Most bars and clubs don't get hopping until 10 pm and stay open at the very least until 3 am. Drink prices can be rather steep (about €9–€13), but the pours are generous, and in recent years cocktail-mixing has become a widespread, sophisticated, and sometimes globally-awarded art. Often there is a cover charge on weekends at the largest and most popular clubs, which also have bouncers (aptly called "face-control" by Greeks because they tend to let only the "lookers" or personalities in). For a uniquely Greek evening, visit a club featuring *rembetika* music, a type of underground blues of the 1920s, or the popular *bouzoukia* (clubs with live bouzouki, a stringed instrument, music and singing). Credit cards are accepted almost everywhere.

Nightclubs in Greece migrate with the seasons. From October through May, they're in vast, throbbing venues in Central Athens and the northern suburbs; from June through September, many relocate to luxurious digs on the south coast for moonlit beach and pool views. The same spaces are used from year to year, but owners and names tend to bounce around. Before heading out, check local listings or talk to your hotel concierge, especially during the summer. One way to avoid both lines and cover charges—since the real party doesn't start until after midnight—is to make an earlier dinner reservation at one of the many clubs that have restaurants as well, or somewhere nearby.

BOUZOUKIA

Many tourists think Greek social life centers on large clubs where live bouzouki music plays while patrons smash up the plates. Plate-smashing has been prohibited since 1976, but plates of flowers (at high prices) are sold for scattering over the performer or your companions when they take to the dance floor. At these thriving clubs, you can catch a glimpse of Greek social life and even join the dances (but remember, it's considered extremely rude to interrupt a solo dance). The two most common dances are the *zeimbekiko,* in which the man improvises in circular movements that become ever more complicated, and the belly dance–like *tsifteteli.* Upscale bouzoukia clubs line the middle section of Pireos Avenue and stretch out to the south coast, where top entertainers command top prices. There is a per-person minimum (around €25) or a prix-fixe menu. Drink prices range from €10 to €15, a bottle of whiskey from €70 to €100, and the food is often expensive and unexceptional; it's wisest to order a fruit platter or a bottle of wine. For those who choose to stand at the bar, a drink runs about €15 to €20 at a good bouzoukia place.

REMBETIKA

The Greek equivalent of the urban, underground blues, rembetika music is rooted in the traditions of Asia Minor and was brought to Greece by refugees from Smyrna in the 1920s. It filtered up from the lowest economic levels to become one of the most enduring genres of Greek popular music, still enthralling clubgoers today. The scene at these usually small bars is richly atmospheric because of the lyrical sounds made by singers and their instruments, and usually people don't get up to dance,

but just listen or chat. At rembetika bars you'll usually find wine (even house wine served in carafes, in old fashioned Greek taverna style), beer, and simple cocktails, as well as meze dishes.

Performing Arts

Athens's energetic year-round performing arts scene kicks into a higher gear from June through September, when numerous stunning outdoor theaters host everything from classical Greek drama (in both Greek and English), opera, symphony, and ballet, to rock, pop, and hip-hop concerts, many of them as part of the annual Athens-Epidaurus Festival. In general, dress for summer performances is fairly casual, though the city's glitterati get decked out for events such as a world premiere opera at the Odeon of Herodes Atticus. From October through May, when the arts move indoors, the Megaron Mousikis/Athens Concert Hall is the biggest venue, but there are literally hundreds of theaters and performance venues catering to all cultural tastes and ages around the city. Performances at outdoor summer venues, stadiums, and the Megaron tend to be priced between €15 to €120 for tickets, depending on the location of seats and popularity of performers.

LISTINGS

The Greek weekly *Athinorama* (also online) covers current performances, gallery openings, and films, as does English-language *Kathimerini,* inserted in the *International New York Times* (available Monday through Saturday and online as ⊕ *www.ekathimerini.com*).

You can also find out everything that's going on in the city by visiting English-language websites like ⊕ *www.thisisathens.org*, ⊕ *www.elculture.gr*, and ⊕ *www.insightsgreece.com*, while websites like ⊕ *www.athensvoice.gr* and ⊕ *www.popaganda.gr* (all translatable via Google) offer an in-depth look at events, places, and people.

TICKETS

It's easiest to buy tickets through ticket vendors like Ticket House or at Public (an electronics store that sells music CDs).

Hunter Agency

TICKETS | Like Ticketmaster in the United States, Hunter Agency sells all sorts of performing arts and popular music concert tickets. ⊠ *Panepistimiou 42, Kolonaki* ☎ *210/360–8366* ⊕ *www.hunteragency.gr.*

Public

TICKETS | You can buy tickets for popular concerts and performing arts events at this electronics store chain with convenient locations in Central Athens. ⊠ *Karageorgi Servias 1, Syntagma* ☎ *80111/40000* ⊕ *tickets.public.gr.*

Viva

TICKETS | Viva is a good, reliable online ticket service. ⊠ *Athens* ☎ *11876* ⊕ *www.viva.gr/tickets/en.*

FESTIVALS

Every summer, the city center is covered with posters for a host of big-name music festivals.

★ Athens and Epidaurus Festival

MUSIC FESTIVALS | The city's primary artistic event (formerly known as the Hellenic Festival) runs from June through August at more than 50 venues, from ancient sites and museums to abandoned but renovated factories and public spaces. The most beloved and enchanting venue is the millennia-old theater Odeon of Herodes Atticus at the foot of the Acropolis. The festival has showcased performers such as Maria Callas, Norah Jones, Dame Kiri Te Kanawa, Luciano Pavarotti, and Diana Ross; such dance troupes as the Royal London Ballet, the Joaquin Cortes Ballet, and Maurice Béjart; symphony orchestras; and the best of local groups performing ancient Greek drama. Usually a major world premiere is staged during the festival. Starting in 2006, the then creative director Yiorgos Loukos rejuvenated the festival, adding more youthful venues and bringing a wider gamut of performances, including world musicians, modern dance, and multimedia artists. The Odeon makes a delightful backdrop, with the floodlit Acropolis looming behind the audience and the Roman arches behind the performers. The upper-level seats have no cushions, so bring something to sit on, and wear low shoes, since the marble steps are steep. For viewing most performances, the *Gamma* zone is the best seat choice. Tickets go on sale three weeks before performances but sell out quickly for popular shows. They are available from the festival box office in Syntagma Square, at the box office outside the Odeon theater, and at major bookshops in Athens (for a full list, check the website). Prices range from €15 to as high as €120 for the big names; student and youth discounts are available. ⊠ *Athens* ☎ *210/928–2900 general information* ⊕ *www.greekfestival.gr.*

Ejekt Festival

CONCERTS | The Ejekt Festival, which brings together global pop, rock, and electronica bands, usually takes place every June in one of the Olympic venues in the southern suburb of Faliro. ☎ *210/9636–489* ⊕ *www.ejekt.gr.*

Festival Vrahon "In the Shadow of the Rocks"

THEATER | Performances by well-known Greek performers and ancient Greek theater classics are staged in an attractively remodeled old quarry, now known as the Theatro Vrahon *Melina Merkouri* (and its sister stage nearby, the *Anna Synodinou*). The festival begins in early June and lasts until the end of September every year; most performances start at 9 pm. Buy tickets (€20–€100) at the theater before the show. ☎ *210/760–9340, 210/760–9350* ⊕ *www.festivalvrahon.gr.*

FILM

One of the most delightful aspects of summer in Athens is sitting al fresco to watch a film on the silver screen at an old outdoor cinema. Sipping a homemade *vyssinada* (sour cherry drink) or an icy beer, munching on popcorn, and occasionally diverting your eyes off-screen only to see the gold-lighted Acropolis in the distance is a precious experience. Films are shown in original-language versions with Greek subtitles (except for major animated films), a definite boon for foreigners. Tickets run about €8. To see what's playing, walk past the cinema during the day or check their websites.

Restaurants

Doesn't anybody eat at home anymore? When you're on vacation, travelers don't have much choice in the matter, but these days Athenians are going out to restaurants (many of which have lowered their prices since the years of the economic crisis) in record numbers. And it's easy for visitors to the capital to become a part of the clatter, chatter, and song, especially at the city's neighborhood tavernas.

These Athenian landmarks were famous for their wicker chairs that inevitably pinched your bottom, wobbly tables that needed coins under one leg, and *hima* wine drawn from the barrel. There are still some of them around, but today most of their clientele has moved up to a popular new restaurant hybrid: the "gastro-taverna," which serves traditional fare in surroundings that are more modern and creative. Most are located in the up-and-coming industrial-cum-arty districts of Central Athens, such as Gazi-Kerameikos and Metaxourgeio and attract youths who stay nibbling, sipping *tsipouro* (a distilled grape spirit), and laughing for hours. At the same time, enduring in popularity are the traditional *magereia* ("cookeries"): humble, no-frills eateries where the food, usually displayed behind glass windows, is cooked in grandma's style—it's simple, honest, time-tested, filling comfort food. Some noteworthy magereia are located around the bustling Ayias Irinis Square in the heart of Monastiraki. Of course cheap, filling, and delicious souvlaki is more popular than ever, and local favorites still have queues. Meanwhile, Athenians' evolving taste for exotic foods, combined with a tighter budget, has led to the opening of numerous ethnic street food restaurants—some just holes in the wall—serving expertly made, authentic options.

Trends? Athens has them. Health-centric restaurants and cafés specializing in vegan, vegetarian, and raw food seem to be blossoming more, as well as sophisticated juice bars. These would have stood out just a few years ago; now they have competitors. Organic health-food stores can be found in every neighborhood, selling Greek-grown concoctions made in the traditional style by small producers, many of whom returned to the rural homeland after facing unemployment; look for local truffle oils, unpasteurized craft beer, and even gold leaf honey. Most Greeks value pure, high-quality, and easily accessible staples like the seasonal vegetables and fruit, medicinal handpicked herb teas, and nuts that they hunt for at the weekly neighborhood open-air *laiki* market, as well as the multitude of Greek product stores. With less money to spend, Athenians now order more discerningly and in smaller quantities, but they resolutely linger outside, which never seems to be a problem for restaurant owners.

But some things remain eternal. Athenian dining is seasonal. In August, when residents scatter to the hills and seaside, many restaurants and tavernas close, with the hippest bar-restaurants reopening at choice seaside positions. And visitors remain shocked by how late Greeks dine. It's normal (even on a weekday) to show up for a meal at 9 or 10 and to leave after midnight, only to head off for drinks. Hotel restaurants, seafood places, and tavernas keep very late hours. Most places serve lunch from about noon to 4 (and sometimes as late as 6) and dinner from about 8 or 9 until at least midnight. When in Athens, don't hesitate to adopt this Zorbaesque lifestyle. Eat, drink, party, and enjoy life—knowing full well that, as a traveler, there can always be a siesta the next day.

ATHENIAN DINING STYLE

Taverna culture is all about sharing. People often order their own main meat, fish, or vegetable courses, but often start by sharing a plethora of salads and appetizers, which may be placed in the middle of the table for easy access by the entire dinner party. It's a nice alternative to being stuck with just one choice. Vegetarians at classic Greek eateries will find plenty of options, including rice-stuffed dolmades or tomatoes, tomato-and-garlic-baked aubergines, fried zucchini, and tomato-stewed okra, as well as several bean dishes—and of course the classic Greek salad, although now almost every taverna will have at least three salad options. Tipping is less strict than in many countries. There is a service charge on the bill, but it doesn't necessarily go to the staff, so Athenians usually leave a tip of 10%. Feel free to request tap water in a pitcher (it's good in Athens) as opposed to bottled water. Although Athens is informal (and none of the restaurants listed here requires a jacket or tie), locals usually dress up when out on the town, so you may feel more comfortable following suit, especially at more expensive places. Children are welcome in most places, but it's best to check in advance for upscale establishments.

RESTAURANT PRICES

What it Costs in euros			
$	$$	$$$	$$$$
RESTAURANTS			
under €15	€15–€25	€26–€40	over €40

Shopping

For serious retail therapy, most Athenians head to the shopping streets that branch off central Syntagma and Kolonaki Squares. Syntagma is the starting point for popular Ermou, a pedestrian zone where large, international chains like Zara, Sephora, H&M, Massimo Dutti, Mothercare, Replay, Nike, Accessorize, and Marks & Spencer have edged out small, independent retailers. You'll find local shops on streets parallel and perpendicular to Ermou: Mitropoleos, Voulis, Nikis, Perikleous, and Praxitelous among them. Poke around here for real bargains, like strings of freshwater pearls, loose semiprecious stones, or made-to-fit hats. Much ritzier is the Kolonaki quarter, with boutiques and designer shops on fashionable streets like Anagnostopoulou, Tsakalof, Skoufa, Solonos, and Kanari. Voukourestiou, the pedestrianized link between Kolonaki and Syntagma, is where you'll find the best luxury boutiques: Louis Vuitton, Hermes, Polo Ralph Lauren, and similar brands. In Monastiraki Flea Market on Pandrossou (which also operates on Sundays) there's a mishmash of tourist trinkets, clothing, footwear, jewelry, and rugs; in Psirri you'll find coppersmiths selling wine jugs, candlesticks, cookware, and more at generally low prices. Athinas Street is loaded with stores selling everything from homewear to DIY tools, leather goods, plastic flowers, incense, desserts, and foods, and if you walk down "the spice street" of Evripidou and turn into Menandrou, you'll discover an area where migrants mainly from India and Pakistan have set up a whole different style of stores, barbershops, and authentic restaurants (only venture there by day). Meanwhile, to get a feel rrr the local shopping lifestyle of Athens it's well worth getting lost in the mazelike backstreets of Monastiraki (start from Aiolou and turn anywhere). This area has flourished over recent years and is packed with quirky stores, eateries, bars, and yoga studios.

Many stores in Athens are open from 9 am to 3 pm on Monday, Wednesday, and Saturday, while on Tuesday shops on Ermou Street remain open until 5 pm. On Thursday and Friday, shops operate from 9 to 2 and then again from 5:30 to 9.

WHAT TO BUY

Antiques are always in vogue, so the prices of these items can be high. On Sunday mornings, antique hunters gather at Avyssinias Square from the crack of dawn to grab the best offers. Shops on Pandrossou sell small antiques and icons, but always check for authenticity. You must have government permission to export genuine objects from the ancient Greek, Roman, or Byzantine periods.

Greece is known for its well-made shoes (most shops are clustered around the Ermou pedestrian zone and in Kolonaki), its furs (Mitropoleos near Syntagma), its jewelry (Voukourestiou and Panepistimiou), and its durable leather items (Pandrossou in Monastiraki). In Plaka shops you can find sandals (currently making a fashionable comeback), fishermen's caps, and the wool, hand-knit sweaters worn by Greek fishermen; across the United States these can sell at triple the Athens prices. Mainly organic and almost completely chemical-free Greek skin-care lines, which include Korres and Apivita, are also much more affordable in Athens than abroad, and most pharmacies sell Korres products at excellent prices.

Discover touristy treasures in the numerous souvenir shops along the streets of Plaka and Monastiraki—in particular, look for them in the Monastiraki flea market and the shops along Adrianou Street, behind the Monastiraki train station.

Prices are much lower for gold and silver in Greece than in many Western countries, and the jewelry is of high quality. Many shops in Plaka carry original pieces available at a good price. For those with more expensive tastes, the Voukourestiou pedestrian mall off Syntagma Square has a number of the city's leading jewelry shops.

If you're looking for a cheap and iconic gift to take back home, pick up a string of *komboloi* (worry beads)—made of wood, semiprecious gems, or stone—which have had a comeback, especially among stressed-out youths and ex-smokers, who wish to keep their hands busy and their nerves in check. You can pick them up very cheaply in Monastiraki, or look in antiques shops for more expensive versions, with amber, silver, or black onyx beads (each stone is said to have its own healing properties). Another popular gift option is the *mati,* the good-luck charm (usually turquoise or cobalt blue) depicting a symbol that wards off the evil eye.

Tours

Most travel agencies offer excursions at about the same prices, but CHAT is reputed to have the best service and guides. You can take traditional day or night tours of Athens by bus and be picked up at your hotel. Full- and half-day tours go to many destinations in Attica, including Sounion, Corinth, Delphi; longer tours go to Meteora, Nafplion, and the Peloponnese. It's best to reserve a few days in advance. *For a full list of agencies that offer tours—including CHAT—see Travel Agents in Travel Smart.*

BICYCLE TOURS

★ **Solebike**

BICYCLE TOURS | FAMILY | Let the eco-friendly bike do all the work and enjoy the breeze, choosing between the Athens Grand City Tour, Old City Tour, and City to Coast Tour. ✉ *11 Lempessi, Makri-yianni* ☎ *210/921–5620* ⊕ *www.solebike. eu* Ⓜ *Acropolis.*

BUS TOURS

City Sightseeing

BUS TOURS | The easiest way to get quickly acquainted with Athens is to opt for a ride on the Athens City Sightseeing Bus, a typical tourist double-decker with open top levels that stops at all the city's main sights. Those buses run by City Sightseeing run every 15 minutes and tickets cost €18. The full tour takes 90 minutes, but you can hop on and off as you please at any of the stops throughout the day. There are also combined tours of Piraeus and Athens, and Athens and the beach riviera. Book online for discounted fares. ✉ *Athens* ☎ *210/922–0604* ⊕ *www. citysightseeing.gr.*

GUIDED TOURS

Alternative Athens

GUIDED TOURS | FAMILY | Tours are centered on food, nightlife, local experiences, and kid-friendly locations, presented in a fresh, colorful way. ✉ *28 Karaiskaki* ☎ *211/012–6544* ⊕ *www.alternativea-thens.com* Ⓜ *Monastiraki.*

Union of Certified Guides

GUIDED TOURS | The Union of Official Guides provides licensed guides for individual or group tours, for a four-hour tour of the Acropolis and its museum. Prices start at around €200 for this tour. ✉ *Apollonos 9a* ☎ *210/322–9705, 210/322–0090* ⊕ *www.tourist-guides.gr* Ⓜ *Syntagma.*

WALKING TOURS

It's easy to arrange for a private or small-group tour in Athens.

Athens Walking Tours

WALKING TOURS | The certified guides of the Athens Walking Tours company offer walking tours of the Acropolis and other sites, as well as a culinary Food Tour around the city's central food market. ✉ *2 Heiden St., Central Athens* ☎ *210/884–7269, 69458/59662* ⊕ *www.athenswalk-ingtours.gr* Ⓜ *Victoria.*

Personality Journeys

WALKING TOURS | The company offers walking tours in the historical center, Anafiotika, and the Athenian Riviera as well as food and wine tours. ✉ *1 Orfeos* ☎ *215/215–1629* ⊕ *www.personalityjour-neys.com* Ⓜ *Kerameikos.*

Visitor Information

The Greek National Tourism Organization has a new information center in Central Athens near the Acropolis Museum. The website of the city of Athens has a growing section in English. The English-speaking tourist police can handle complaints, steer you to an open pharmacy or doctor, and locate phone numbers of hotels and restaurants.

CONTACTS City of Athens. ⊕ *www. cityofathens.gr/en* Ⓜ *Monastiraki.* **Greek National Tourism Organisation.** ✉ *18–20 Dionyssiou Aeropagitou Street, Plaka* ☎ *210/331–0529* ⊕ *www.visitgreece.gr* Ⓜ *Acropolis.*

The Acropolis, Makriyianni, and Koukaki Ακρόπολη, Μακρυγιάννη, Κουκάκι

Although Athens, together with its suburbs and port, sprawls across the plain for more than 240 square km (150 square miles), most of its ancient monuments cluster around the Acropolis, which rises like a massive sentinel, white and beautiful, out of the center of the city. In mountainous Greece, most ancient towns were backed up by an acropolis, an easily defensible upper town (which is what the word means), but when spelled with a capital *A* it can only refer to antiquity's most famously splendid group of buildings.

Towering over the modern metropolis of 4.5 million as it once stood over the ancient capital of 50,000, it has remained Athens's most spectacular attraction ever since its first settlement around 5000 BC. It had been a religious center long before Athens became a major city-state in the 6th century BC. It has been associated with Athena ever since the city's mythical founding, but virtually all of the city's other religious cults had temples or shrines here as well. As Athens became the dominant city-state in the 5th century BC, Pericles led the city in making the Acropolis the crowning symbol of Athenian power and successful democracy.

An elegant and tranquil neighborhood on the foothills of the Acropolis, Makriyianni was really put on the map by the opening of the nearby Acropolis Museum and is one of the most coveted residential areas of the city, both for its exclusive ambience and beautiful examples of neoclassical architecture; indeed, it is now considered one of the most

up-and-coming districts of the capital. Explore the streets south of the museum to discover artsy new shops like Athena Design Workshop, Greek delis like Ellinika Kaoudia and Pelasgea, galleries (the Eleni Marnieri Galerie is a treasure trove of modern jewelry designs to ogle at or buy), the classic Ilias Lalaounis Jewelry Museum, and hip "third-wave" coffee shops like Coffee Dive. Stop for lunch at Strofi, Peloponnesian cuisine–centered Mani Mani or Attalos Greek House Restaurant.

Adjacent, and serviced by Fix and Acropolis metro stations, Koukaki is one of the most sought-after residential areas of Athens. In recent years it has become one of the most fashionable places for seeing and being seen (also recently eulogized by *Vogue*), at bars like Bobo Winebar and Bel Ray Cafe in popular Faliron Square. A resurgence of the area, also inspired by the spanking-new National Museum of Contemporary Art (EMST), a massive structure that was once a beer factory, has followed the pedestrianization of G. Olympiou Street on Koukaki Square.

Sights

★ Acropolis

ARCHAEOLOGICAL SITE | You don't have to look far in Athens to encounter perfection. Towering above all—both physically and spiritually—stands the Acropolis, a millennia-old survivor. The Greek term *Akropolis* means High City, and today's traveler who climbs this table-like hill is paying tribute to the prime source of Western civilization. As of September 2020, this amazing monument has been lit up in a new way by the Onassis Cultural Center in collaboration with the Greek state; using 690 LED lights, every monument on the Acropolis can now be relished in a new light.

Continued on page 114

THE ACROPOLIS
ASCENT TO GLORY

One of the wonders of the world, the Acropolis symbolizes Greece's Golden Age. Its stunning centerpiece, the Parthenon, was commissioned in the 5th century BC by the great Athenian leader Pericles as part of an elaborate building program designed to epitomize the apex of an iconic culture. Thousands of years later, the Acropolis pulls the patriotic heartstrings of modern Greeks and lulls millions of annual visitors back to an ancient time.

You don't have to look far in Athens to encounter perfection. Towering above all—both physically and spiritually—is the Acropolis, the ancient city of upper Athens and womb of Western civilization. Raising your eyes to the crest of this *ieros vrachos* (sacred rock), the sight of the Parthenon will stop you in your tracks. The term Akropolis (to use the Greek spelling) means "High City," and today's traveler who climbs this table-like hill is paying tribute to the prime source of civilization as we know it.

A TITANIC TEMPLE

Described by the 19th-century French poet Alphonse de Lamartine as "the most perfect poem in stone," the Acropolis is a true testament to the Golden Age of Greece. While archaeological evidence has shown that the flat-top limestone outcrop, 512 feet high, attracted settlers as early as Neolithic times, most of its most imposing structures were built from 461 to 429 BC, when the intellectual and artistic life of Athens flowered under the influence of the Athenian statesman, Pericles.

Even in its bleached and silent state, the Parthenon—the Panathenaic temple that crowns the rise—has the power to stir the heart as few other ancient relics do.

PERICLES TO POLLUTION

Since the Periclean Age, the buildings of the Acropolis have been inflicted with the damages of war, as well as unscrupulous transformations into, at various times, a Florentine palace, an Islamic mosque, a Turkish harem, and a World War II sentry. Since then, a more insidious enemy—pollution—has emerged. The site is presently undergoing conservation measures as part of an ambitious rescue plan. Today, the Erechtheion temple and Temple of Athena Nike have been completely restored, and work on the Parthenon and the Propylaea is due for completion by the end of 2014. A final phase, involving massive landscaping works, will last through 2020. Despite the ongoing restoration work, a visit to the Acropolis today can evoke the spirit of the ancient heroes and gods who were once worshiped here.

THE PARTHENON

PINNACLE OF THE PERICLEAN AGE

DEDICATED TO ATHENA

At the loftiest point of the Acropolis stands the Parthenon, the architectural masterpiece conceived by Pericles and executed between 447 and 438 BC by the brilliant sculptor Pheidias, who supervised the architects Iktinos and Kallikrates in its construction. It not only raised the bar in terms of sheer size, but also in the perfection of its proportions.

Dedicated to the goddess Athena (the name Parthenon comes from the Athena Parthenos, or the virgin Athena) and inaugurated at the Panathenaic Festival of 438 BC, the Parthenon served primarily as the treasury of the Delian League, an ancient alliance of cities formed to defeat the Persian incursion. In fact, the Parthenon was built as much to honor the city's power as to venerate Athena. Its foundations, laid after the victory at Marathon in 490 BC, were destroyed by the Persian army in 480–479 BC. In turn, the city-state of Athens banded together with Sparta to rout the Persians by 449 BC.

To proclaim its hegemony over all Greece, Athens envisioned a grand new Acropolis. After a 30-year building moratorium, the titanic-scale project of reconstructing the temple was initiated by Pericles around 448 BC.

490 BC
Foundation for Acropolis laid

447–438 BC
The Parthenon is constructed

420 BC
Temple of Athena Nike is complete

TIMELINE

EDIFICE REX: PERICLES

His name means "surrounded by glory." Some scholars consider this extraordinary, enigmatic Athenian general to be the architect of the destiny of Greece at its height, while others consider him a megalomaniac who bankrupted the coffers of an empire and an elitist who catered to the privileged few at the expense of the masses.

Indeed, Pericles (460–429 BC) plundered the treasury of the Athenian alliance for the Acropolis building program. One academic has even called the Periclean building program the largest embezzlement in human history.

MYTH IN MARBLE

But Pericles's masterstroke becomes more comprehensible when studied against the conundrum that was Athenian democracy.

In truth an aristocracy that was the watchdog of private property and public order, this political system financed athletic games and drama festivals; it constructed exquisite buildings. Its motto was not only to live, but to live well. Surrounded by barbarians, the Age of Pericles was the more striking for its high level of civilization, its qualities of proportion, reason, clarity, and harmony, all of which are epitomized nowhere else as beautifully as in the Parthenon.

To their credit, the Athenians rallied around Pericles' vision: the respect for the individualistic character of men and women could be revealed through art and architecture.

Even jaded Athenians, when overwhelmed by the city, feel renewed when they lift their eyes to this great monument.

TRICK OF THE TRADE

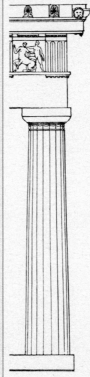

One of the Parthenon's features, or "refinements," is the way it uses meiosis (tapering of columns) and entasis (a slight swelling so that the column can hold the weight of the entablature), deviations from strict mathematics that breathed movement into the rigid marble. Architects knew that a straight line looks curved, and vice versa, so they cleverly built the temple with all the horizontal lines somewhat curved. The columns, it has been calculated, lean toward the center of the temple; if they were to continue into space, they would eventually converge to create a huge pyramid.

The Acropolis in Pericles's Time

RAISING A HUE
"Just my color—beige!" So proclaimed Elsie de Wolfe, celebrated decorator to J. Pierpont Morgan, when she first saw the Parthenon. As it turns out, the original Parthenon was anything but beige. Especially ornate, it had been covered with a tile roof, decorated with statuary and marble friezes, adorned with gilded wooden doors and ceilings, and walls and columns so brightly hued that the people protested, "We are adorning our city like a wanton woman" (Plutarch). The finishing touch was provided by the legendary sculptor Pheidias, who created some of the sculpted friezes—these were also brightly colored.

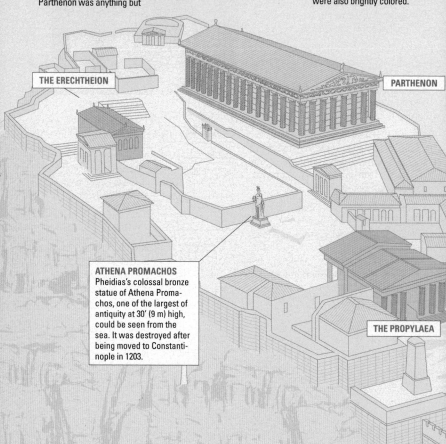

THE ERECHTHEION

PARTHENON

ATHENA PROMACHOS
Pheidias's colossal bronze statue of Athena Promachos, one of the largest of antiquity at 30' (9 m) high, could be seen from the sea. It was destroyed after being moved to Constantinople in 1203.

THE PROPYLAEA

TOURING THE ACROPOLIS

Most people take the metro to the Acropolis station, where the New Acropolis Museum opened in 2009. They then follow the pedestrianized street Dionyssiou Areopagitou, which traces the foothill of the Acropolis to its entrance at the Beulé Gate. Another entrance is along the rock's northern face via the Peripatos, a paved path from the Plaka district.

THE BEULÉ GATE

You enter the Acropolis complex through this late-Roman structure named for the French archaeologist Ernest Beulé, who discovered the gate in 1852. Made of marble fragments from the destroyed monument of Nikias on the south slope of the Acropolis, it has an inscription above the lintel dated 320 BC, dedicated by "Nikias son of Nikodemos of Xypete." Before Roman times, the entrance to the Acropolis was a steep processional ramp below the Temple of Athena Nike. This Sacred Way was used every fourth year for the Panathenaic procession, a spectacle that honored Athena's remarkable birth (she sprang from the head of her father, Zeus).

THE PROPYLAEA

This imposing structure was designed to instill the proper reverence in worshipers as they crossed from the temporal world into the spiritual world of the sanctuary, for this was the main function of the Acropolis. Conceived by Pericles, the Propylaea was the masterwork of the architect Mnesicles. Conceived to be the same size as the Parthenon, it was to have been the grandest secular building in Greece. Construction was suspended during the Peloponnesian War, and it was never finished. The struc-ture shows the first use of both Doric and Ionic columns together, a style that can be called Attic. Six of the sturdier fluted Doric columns, made from Pendelic marble, correspond with the gateways of the portal. Processions with priests, chariots, and sacrificial animals entered via a marble ramp in the center (now protected by a wooden stairway), while ordinary visitors on foot entered via the side doors. The slender Ionic columns had elegant capitals, some of which have been restored along with a section of the famed paneled ceiling, originally decorated with gold eight-pointed stars on a blue background. Adjacent to the Pinakotheke, or art gallery (with paintings of scenes from Homer's epics and mythological tableaux), the south wing is a decorative portico. The view from the inner porch of the Propylaea is stunning: the Parthenon is suddenly revealed in its full glory, framed by the columns.

THE TEMPLE OF ATHENA NIKE

The 2nd-century traveler Pausanias referred to this fabled temple as the Temple of Nike Apteros, or Wingless Victory, for "in Athens they believe Victory will stay forever because she has no wings." Designed by Kallikrates, the mini-temple was built in 427–424 BC to celebrate peace with Persia. The bas-reliefs on the surrounding parapet depicting the Victories leading heifers to be sacrificed must have been of exceptional quality, judging from the section called "Nike Unfastening Her Sandal" in the New Acropolis Museum. In 1998, Greek archaeologists began dismantling the entire temple for conservation. After laser-cleaning the marble to remove generations of soot, the team reconstructed the temple on its original site.

TEMPLE OF ATHENA NIKE

THE BEULÉ GATE

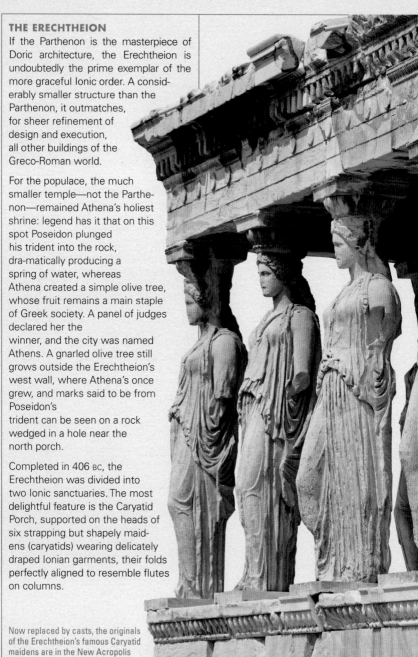

THE ERECHTHEION

If the Parthenon is the masterpiece of Doric architecture, the Erechtheion is undoubtedly the prime exemplar of the more graceful Ionic order. A considerably smaller structure than the Parthenon, it outmatches, for sheer refinement of design and execution, all other buildings of the Greco-Roman world.

For the populace, the much smaller temple—not the Parthenon—remained Athena's holiest shrine: legend has it that on this spot Poseidon plunged his trident into the rock, dra-matically producing a spring of water, whereas Athena created a simple olive tree, whose fruit remains a main staple of Greek society. A panel of judges declared her the winner, and the city was named Athens. A gnarled olive tree still grows outside the Erechtheion's west wall, where Athena's once grew, and marks said to be from Poseidon's trident can be seen on a rock wedged in a hole near the north porch.

Completed in 406 BC, the Erechtheion was divided into two Ionic sanctuaries. The most delightful feature is the Caryatid Porch, supported on the heads of six strapping but shapely maidens (caryatids) wearing delicately draped Ionian garments, their folds perfectly aligned to resemble flutes on columns.

Now replaced by casts, the originals of the Erechtheion's famous Caryatid maidens are in the New Acropolis Museum.

PLANNING YOUR VISIT

When exploring the Acropolis, keep the below pointers in mind. As the hill's stones are slippery and steep, it is best to wear rubber-soled shoes.

What Are the Best Times to Go? Such is the beauty of the Acropolis and the grandeur of the setting that a visit in all seasons and at all hours is rewarding. In general, the earlier you start out the better. In summer, by noon the heat is blistering and the reflection of the light thrown back by the rock and the marble ruins is almost blinding. An alternative, in summer, is to visit after 5 PM, when the light is best for taking photographs. In any season the ideal time might be the two hours before sunset, when occasionally the fabled violet light spreads from the crest of Mt. Hymettus (which the ancients called "violet-crowned") and gradually embraces the Acropolis. After dark the hill is spectacularly floodlighted, creating a scene visible from many parts of the capital. A moonlight visit—sometimes scheduled by the authorities during full moons in summer—is highly evocative. In winter, if there are clouds trailing across the mountains, and shafts of sun lighting up the marble columns, the setting takes on an even more dramatic quality.

How Long Does a Visit Usually Run? Depending on the crowds, the walk takes about three hours, plus several more spent in the nearby Acropolis Museum.

Are Tour Guides Available? The Union of Official Guides (Apollonos 9A, Syntagma, 210/322-9705, 210/322-0090) offers licensed guides for tours of archaeological sites within Athens. However, most tour companies and travel agents can set up group or private tours. Guides will also help kids understand the site better.

What's the Handiest Place to Refuel? The Tourist Pavilion (Filoppappou Hill), a landscaped, tree-shaded spot soundtracked by chirping birds is just outside the Beulé Gate. It serves drinks, snacks, and a few hot dishes.

Dionysiou Areopagitou, Acropolis

☎ 210/321–4172 or 210/321–0219

🌐 www.culture.gr

🎫 Joint ticket for all Unification of Archaeological Sites €12. Good for five days—and for free admission—to the Ancient Agora, Theatre of Dionysus, Kerameikos cemetery, Temple of Olympian Zeus, and the Roman Forum.

🕐 Apr.–Oct., daily 8–6:30; Nov.–Mar., daily 8–3

Ⓜ Acropolis

DON'T FORGET:

■ If it's hot, remember to bring water, sunscreen, and a hat to protect yourself from the sun.

■ Get a free bilingual pamphlet guide (in English and Greek) at the entrance gate. It is packed with information, but staffers usually don't bother to give it out unless asked.

■ An elevator now ascends to the summit of the Acropolis, once inaccessible to people with disabilities.

■ All large bags, backpacks, and shopping bags will have to be checked in the site cloakroom.

Temple of Olympian Zeus

Most of the notable structures on this flat-top limestone outcrop, 512 feet high, were built from 461 to 429 BC, when the intellectual and artistic life of Athens flowered under the influence of the Athenian statesman Pericles. Since then, the buildings of the Acropolis have undergone transformations into, at various times, a Florentine palace, an Islamic mosque, and a Turkish harem. They have also weathered the hazards of wars, right up to 1944, when British paratroopers positioned their bazookas between the Parthenon's columns. Today, the Erechtheion temple has been completely restored, and conservation work on the Parthenon is ongoing, focusing now on the western side. With most of the major restoration work now completed, a visit to the Acropolis evokes the spirit of the ancient heroes and gods who were once worshiped here. The sight of the Parthenon—the Panathenaic temple at the crest of this *ieros vrachos* (sacred rock)—has the power to stir the heart as few other ancient relics do.

The walk through the Acropolis takes about four hours, depending on the crowds, including an hour spent in the New Acropolis Museum. In general, the earlier you start out the better—in summer the heat is blistering by noon and the light's reflection off the rock and marble ruins is almost blinding. Remember to bring water, sunscreen, nonslip footwear, and a hat to protect yourself from the sun. An alternative, in summer, is to visit after 5 pm, when the light is best for taking photographs. The two hours before sunset, when the fabled violet light occasionally spreads from the crest of Mt. Hymettus and embraces the Acropolis, is an ideal time to visit in any season. After dark the hill is spectacularly floodlighted, creating a scene visible from many parts of the capital.

You enter the Acropolis complex through the **Beulé Gate,** a late-Roman structure named for the French archaeologist who

Full-Moon Festival in Athens

On the night of August's full moon, the Ministry of Culture celebrates by offering free, nighttime access to various museums and ancient sites in and around the city. Venues including the Acropolis, Roman Agora, and the Odeon of Herodes Atticus have been open for free, with music and dance performances held amid the ancient columns by moonlight. Check ⊕ *www.culture. gr* to see if you're lucky enough to be there when this is happening.

discovered the gate in 1852. Before Roman times, the entrance to the Acropolis was a steep ramp below the Temple of Athena Nike that was used every fourth year for the Panathenaic procession, a spectacle that honored Athena's remarkable birth (she sprang from the head of her father, Zeus). When you enter the gate, ask for the free, information-packed bilingual (in English and Greek) pamphlet guide.

At the loftiest point of the Acropolis stands the **Parthenon,** the architectural masterpiece conceived by Pericles and executed between 447 and 438 BC. It not only raised the bar in terms of sheer size, but also in the perfection of its proportions. Dedicated to the goddess Athena (the name comes from the Athena *Parthenos*, the virgin Athena), the Parthenon served primarily as the treasury of the Delian League, an ancient alliance of cities formed to defeat the Persian incursion. In fact, the Parthenon was built as much to honor the city's power as to venerate the goddess. After the Persian army sacked Athens in 480–479 BC, the city-state banded with Sparta, and together they routed the Persians by 449 BC. To proclaim its hegemony over all Greece, Athens then set about constructing its Acropolis, ending a 30-year building moratorium.

Once you pass through the Beulé Gate you will find the **Temple of Athena Nike.** Designed by Kallikrates, the mini-temple was built in 427–424 BC to celebrate peace with Persia. The bas-reliefs on the surrounding parapet depict the Victories leading heifers to be sacrificed.

Past the temple, the imposing **Propylaea** structure was designed to instill the proper reverence in worshippers as they crossed from the temporal world into the spiritual world of the sanctuary, for this was the main function of the Acropolis. The Propylaea was intended to have been the same size as the Parthenon, and thus the grandest secular building in Greece, but construction was suspended during the Peloponnesian War, and it was never finished. The structure shows the first use of the Attic style, which combines both Doric and Ionic columns. The building's slender Ionic columns had elegant capitals, some of which have been restored along with a section of the famed paneled ceiling, originally decorated with gold, eight-pointed stars on a blue background. Adjacent to the Pinakotheke, or art gallery (which has paintings of scenes from Homer's epics and mythological tableaux), the south wing is a decorative portico (row of columns). The view from the inner porch of the Propylaea is stunning: the Parthenon is suddenly revealed in its full glory, framed by the columns.

If the Parthenon is the masterpiece of Doric architecture, the **Erechtheion** is undoubtedly the prime exemplar of the more graceful Ionic order. A considerably smaller structure than the Parthenon, it outmatches, for sheer elegance and refinement of design, all other buildings of the Greco-Roman world. For the populace, the Erechtheion, completed in 406 BC, remained Athena's holiest shrine, for legend has it that Poseidon plunged

his trident into the rock on this spot, dramatically producing a spring of water, while Athena created a simple olive tree, whose produce remains a main staple of Greek society. A panel of judges declared the goddess the winner, and the city was named Athena. The most delightful feature is the south portico, known as the Caryatid Porch. It is supported on the heads of six maidens (caryatids) wearing delicately draped Ionian garments. What you see at the site today are copies; the originals are in the New Acropolis Museum.

Most people take the metro to the Acropolis station, where the Acropolis Museum is just across the main exit. They then follow the Dionyssiou Aeropagitou, the pedestrianized street that traces the foothill of the Acropolis to its entrance at the Beulé Gate. Another entrance is along the rock's northern face via the pretty Peripatos, a paved path from the Plaka district. The summit of the Acropolis can also now be reached by people with disabilities via an elevator.

Don't throw away your Acropolis ticket after your tour. It will get you into all the other sites in the Unification of Archaeological Sites for five days—at no extra cost. Guides to the Acropolis are quite informative and will also help kids understand the site better. ✉ *Dionyssiou Areopagitou, Acropolis* ☎ *210/321–4172 ticket information* ⊕ *odysseus.culture.gr* 🎫 *€20 Acropolis and Theater of Dionysus; €30 joint ticket for all Unification of Archaeological Sites* Ⓜ *Acropolis.*

★ **Acropolis Museum**
ARCHAEOLOGICAL SITE | Designed by the celebrated Swiss architect Bernard Tschumi in collaboration with Greek architect Michalis Fotiadis, the Acropolis Museum made world headlines when it opened in June 2009. If some buildings define an entire city in a particular era, Athens's monumental museum boldly sets the tone of Greece's modern aspirations. Occupying a large plot of the city's

most prized real estate, the Acropolis Museum nods to the fabled ancient hill above it but speaks—thanks to a building that looks spectacular from its every angle—in a contemporary architectural language.

The museum drew 90,000 visitors in its first month and proved it is spacious enough to accommodate such crowds (a whopping 14½ million visitors had entered the doors of the ingenious, airy structure by the end of its first decade). Unlike its crammed, dusty predecessor, there is lots of elbow room, from the museum's olive tree–dotted grounds to its prized, top-floor Parthenon Gallery.

Regal glass walkways, very high ceilings, and panoramic views are all part of the experience. In the five-level museum, every shade of marble is on display and bathed in abundant, UV-safe natural light. Visitors pass into the museum through a broad entrance and move ever upward.

The ground-floor exhibit, "The Acropolis Slopes," features objects found in the sanctuaries and settlements around the Acropolis—a highlight is the collection of theatrical masks and vases from the sanctuary of the matrimonial deity Nymphe. The next floor is devoted to the Archaic period (650 BC–480 BC), with rows of precious statues mounted for 360-degree viewing. The floor includes sculptural figures from the Hekatompedon—the temple that may have predated the classical Parthenon—such as the noted group of stone lions gorging on a bull from 570 BC. The legendary five Caryatids (or Korai)—the female figures supporting the Acropolis's Erectheion building—symbolically leave a space for their sister, who resides in London's British Museum.

The second floor is devoted to the terrace and a restaurant/coffee shop with a wonderful view of the Acropolis, which starts by serving a traditional Greek breakfast every day except Monday,

before moving on to more delicious Greek dishes (every Friday the restaurant remains open until midnight).

Drifting into the top-floor atrium, the visitor can watch a video on the Parthenon before entering the star gallery devoted to the temple's Pentelic marble decorations, many of which depict a grand procession in the goddess Athena's honor. Frieze pieces (originals and copies), metopes, and pediments are all laid out in their original orientation. This is made remarkably apparent because the gallery consists of a magnificent, rectangle-shaped room tilted to align with the Parthenon itself. Floor-to-ceiling windows provide magnificent vistas of the temple just a few hundred feet away.

Museum politics are unavoidable here. This gallery was designed—as Greek officials have made obvious—to hold the Parthenon Marbles in their *entirety*. This includes the sculptures Lord Elgin brought to London two centuries ago. Currently, 50 meters of the frieze are in Athens, 80 meters in London's British Museum, and another 30 meters scattered in museums around the world. The spectacular and sumptuous new museum challenges the British claim that there is no suitable home for the Parthenon treasures in Greece. Pointedly, the museum avoids replicas, as the top-floor gallery makes a point of highlighting the abundant missing original pieces with empty space and outlines.

Elsewhere on view are other fabled works of art, including the *Rampin Horseman* and the compelling *Hound*, both by the sculptor Phaidimos; the noted pediment sculpted into a calf being devoured by a lioness—a 6th-century BC treasure that brings to mind Picasso's *Guernica*; striking pedimental figures from the Old Temple of Athena (525 BC) depicting the battle between *Athena and the Giants*; and the great *Nike Unfastening Her Sandal*, taken from the parapet of the Acropolis's famous Temple of

Athena Nike. ✉ *Dionyssiou Areopagitou 15, Acropolis* 🕾 *210/900–0900* ⊕ *www.theacropolismuseum.gr* 🖃 *€10, reduced to €5 Nov.–Mar.* Ⓜ *Acropolis.*

★ **Filopappou**

ARCHAEOLOGICAL SITE | This summit includes **Lofos Mousson** (Hill of the Muses), whose peak offers the city's best view of the Parthenon. Also there is the **Monument of Filopappus,** depicting a Syrian prince who was such a generous benefactor that the people accepted him as a distinguished Athenian. The marble monument is a tomb decorated by a frieze showing Filopappus driving his chariot. In 294 BC a fort strategic to Athens's defense was built here, overlooking the road to the sea. On the hill of the **Pnyx** (meaning "crowded"), the all-male general assembly (Ecclesia) met during the time of Pericles. Originally, citizens of the Ecclesia faced the Acropolis while listening to speeches, but they tended to lose their concentration as they gazed upon the monuments, so the positions of the speaker and the audience were reversed. The speaker's platform is still visible on the semicircular terrace. Farther north is the **Hill of the Nymphs,** with a 19th-century observatory designed by Theophilos Hansen. He was so satisfied with his work, he had *servare intaminatum* ("to remain intact") inscribed over the entrance. ✉ *Acropolis* ⬧ *Enter from Dionyssiou Areopagitou or Apostolou Pavlou* Ⓜ *Acropolis.*

Hadrian's Arch

ARCHAEOLOGICAL SITE | One of the most important Roman monuments surviving in Athens, Hadrian's Arch has become, for many, one of the city's most iconic landmarks. This marble gateway, built in AD 131 with Corinthian details, was intended both to honor the Hellenophile emperor Hadrian and to separate the ancient and imperial sections of Athens. ✉ *Vasilissis Amalias at Dionyssiou Areopagitou, Makriyianni* 🖃 *Free* Ⓜ *Acropolis.*

★ **Ilias Lalaounis Jewelry Museum**

MUSEUM | Housing the creations of internationally renowned artist-jeweler Ilias Lalaounis, this private foundation also operates as an international center for the study of decorative arts. The collection includes 4,000 pieces inspired by subjects as diverse as the Treasure of Priam of Troy to the wildflowers of Greece. Many of the works are eye-catching, especially the massive necklaces evoking the Minoan and Byzantine periods. Besides the well-made videos that explain jewelry making, craftspeople in the workshop demonstrate ancient and modern techniques, such as chain weaving and hammering. The company also operates several jewelry stores in Athens. ✉ *Kallisperi 12, at Karyatidon, Makriyianni* 🕾 *210/922–1044* ⊕ *www.lalaounis-jewelrymuseum.gr* 🖃 *€5* ⊙ *Closed Mon.* Ⓜ *Acropolis.*

★ **Odeon of Herodes Atticus**

ARTS VENUE | Hauntingly beautiful, this ancient theater was built in AD 160 by the affluent Herodes Atticus in memory of his wife, Regilla. Known as the Irodion and visited throughout the summer by culture vultures, it is nestled Greek-style into the hillside, but with typically Roman arches in its three-story stage building and barrel-vaulted entrances. The circular orchestra has now become a semicircle, and the long-vanished cedar roof probably covered only the stage and dressing rooms, not the 34 rows of seats. The theater, which holds 5,000, was restored and reopened in 1955 for the Athens and Epidaurus Festival. To enter you must hold a ticket to one of the summer performances, which range from the Royal Ballet to ancient tragedies usually performed in Modern Greek. Contact the festival's box office for ticket information. Children under six are not allowed except at some special performances. ✉ *Dionyssiou Areopagitou, Acropolis* ⬧ *Near Propylaion* 🕾 *210/928–2900 box office, 210/322–1897 persons with disabilities* ⊕ *www.greekfestival.gr* Ⓜ *Acropolis.*

Temple of Olympian Zeus

ARCHAEOLOGICAL SITE | Begun in the 6th century BC, this gigantic temple was completed in AD 132 by Hadrian, who also commissioned a huge gold-and-ivory statue of Zeus for the inner chamber and another, only slightly smaller, of himself. Only 15 of the original Corinthian columns remain, but standing next to them may inspire a sense of awe at their bulk, which is softened by the graceful carving on the acanthus-leaf capitals. The site is floodlit on summer evenings, creating a majestic scene when you turn round the bend from Syngrou Avenue. On the outskirts of the site to the north are remains of Roman houses, the city walls, and a Roman bath. Hadrian's Arch lies just outside the enclosed archaeological site. ✉ Vasilissis Olgas 1, Makriyianni ☎ 210/922–6330 ⊕ odysseus.culture.gr ≊ €6; €30 joint ticket for all Unification of Archaeological Sites Ⓜ Acropolis.

Theater of Dionysus

ARTS VENUE | It was on this spot in the 6th century BC that the Dionysia festivals took place; a century later, dramas such as Sophocles's Oedipus Rex and Euripides's Medea were performed for the entire population of the city. Visible are foundations of a stage dating from about 330 BC, when it was built for 15,000 spectators as well as the assemblies formerly held on Pnyx. In the middle of the orchestra stood the altar to Dionysus; a fantastic throne in the center was reserved for the priest of Dionysus. On the hillside above the theater stand two columns, vestiges of the little temple erected in the 4th century BC by Thrasyllus the Choragus. ✉ Dionyssiou Areopagitou, Acropolis ✛ Across from Mitsaion St. ☎ 210/322–4625 ≊ €20 Acropolis and Theater of Dionysus; €30 joint ticket for all Unification of Archaeological Sites Ⓜ Acropolis.

🍽 Restaurants

Makriyianni eateries have the distinct advantage of a prestigious location with an exclusive vibe and unbeatable views of the Acropolis; the food is also highly recommended by the locals.

Dionysos Zonars

$$$ | MEDITERRANEAN | This famous, historic restaurant just happens to be the spot where movies are often filmed because of its astounding location, looking out to exquisite views of the Acropolis, and it has been an idyllic dining spot for the world's glitterati for decades. Today's plush, renovated establishment serves high-quality, traditional Greek and international dishes with a creative twist. You'll be able to choose from sea bass fillet with fennel risotto, zucchini, and lemon; slow-cooked lamb with orzo; or mousaka with goat milk béchamel. You can still get traditional Greek appetizers like stuffed vine leaves and grilled octopus, but you can also get greater amberjack carpaccio or a mixed salad with goji berries, pistachios, strawberry, and talagani cheese from Messinia. Desserts are similarly international in scope, from baklava to chocolate souffleé. **Known for:** exclusive ambience; magnificent Acropolis views; a mix of Greek and international food. Ⓢ Average main: €30 ✉ Rovertou Galli 43, Makriyianni ☎ 210/923–3182 ⊕ www. dionysoszonars.gr Ⓜ Acropolis.

★ Manhmanh

$$ | GREEK | Pronounced Manimani this creative restaurant features inspired recipes—and many ingredients—from the southern Peloponnese's Mani region, and it strikes the perfect balance between sophistication and heartiness. The food and extensive regional wine list take center stage, and its comforting dishes sweetly scream "village," with the chef adding delicate new fruity or spicy touches and embracing organic products.

Grand Promenade

One of the most popular features created in Athens for the 2004 Olympics was the Grand Promenade, a pedestrian walkway meant to beautify some of the traffic-choked streets much favored by tourists. Part of the city's Archaeological Unification Project, the promenade connects fabled ancient sites along a landscaped walkway paved with gneiss cobblestones from Naxos and marble slabs from Tinos. It stretches through several neighborhoods but is often accessed near the Acropolis since its pedestrian ribbon includes the roads around its southern end.

Start out at the Acropolis metro stop, and walk north and then left to find Dionyssiou Areopagitou, the famed road running below the hill. You'll first pass the Acropolis Museum on your left and the Theater of Dionysus and Odeon of Herodes Atticus on your right. You can begin your climb here up to the Beulé Gate entrance to the Acropolis but, instead, take the marble walkway up Filopappou Hill—its summit flaunts Cinerama views of the Acropolis and Lycabettus hill side by side. Head back down to Apostolou Pavlou to find some of the best café real estate in the world.

Farther down the road is the Thissio metro station, Ayion Asomaton Square, and Ermou Street, which heads down to the great ancient cemetery of Kerameikos, and ends on Pireus Street and the Technopolis and the Gazi-Kerameikos district across the road.

Keep the following restaurants and cafés in mind if you want to enjoy food with a view, and not just any old view, but the Acropolis itself: Dionysos Zonars; Filistron mezedopoleio-restaurant (especially the rooftop on summer nights); Strofi restaurant (perfect for a summer post-performance dinner at the ancient Odeon of Herodes Atticus); Kuzina (for a wonderful view from its rooftop); and Orizontes Lycabettus (seen from another angle, this one from Lycabettus Hill). Last but not least, the café and restaurant of the Acropolis Museum, which can be visited without a museum entry ticket, with its huge glass windows and extensive verandas, is a definite must for spectacular photo ops of the ancient landmark. Some hotels in the area, for example Herodion Hotel, Athens Was, and the Grande Bretagne in Syntagma, also have rooftop restaurants with mouthwatering views.

Located in a converted neoclassical residence, the decor has the relaxed precision of an upscale home-decor catalog (a gauzy drape or rag rug here, a beautiful glass vase there). **Known for:** authentic Peloponnesian cuisine; farm-to-table ingredients; good wine list. $ *Average main: €23* ✉ *Falirou 10, Makriyianni* ☎ *210/921–8180* ⊕ *www.manimani.com. gr* Ⓜ *Acropolis.*

★ **Strofi**

$$ | GREEK | It's the place where the likes of Rudolph Nureyev, Maria Callas, and Elizabeth Taylor dined after performances at the Odeon of Herodes Atticus nearby, and its walls are lined with images attesting to its glamorous past. Once a humble taverna with a fantastic Acropolis view, its current modernist renovated version and simple traditional Greek menu are still pleasing to tourists and politicians alike. The amazing views come close to

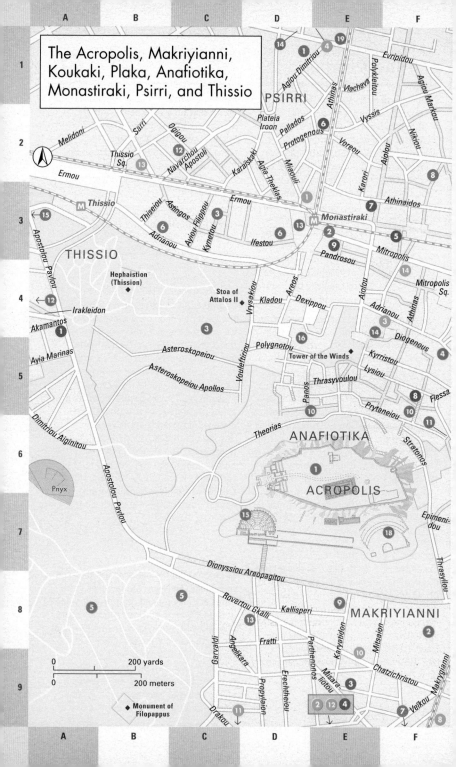

Sights ▼

1 Acropolis **E6**
2 Acropolis Museum **F8**
3 Ancient Agora **C4**
4 Benizelos Mansion **F5**
5 Filopappou **A8**
6 Flea Market **D3**
7 Greek Folk Art
   Museum **G6**
8 Hadrian's Arch **H7**
9 Ilias Lalaounis
   Jewelry Museum **E8**
10 Kanellopoulos
   Museum **D5**
11 Little Mitropolis **G4**
12 Melina Mercouri
   Cultural Centre **A4**
13 Monastiraki Square **D3**
14 Museum of Greek
   Popular Musical
   Instruments **E4**
15 Odeon of Herodes
   Atticus **D7**
16 Roman Agora **D4**
17 Temple of Olympian
   Zeus **I8**
18 Theater of Dionysus **F7**
19 Varvakeios Agora **E1**

Restaurants ▼

1 Avli Psirri **D1**
2 Bairaktaris **E3**
3 Café Avissinia **C3**
4 Daphne's **G7**
5 Dionysos Zonars **C8**
6 Kuzina **B3**
7 Manhmanh **F9**
8 Melilotos **F2**
9 O Platanos **H5**
10 The Old Taverna
   of Psarra **F5**
11 Scholarhio **F6**
12 Spiti Mas **C2**
13 Strofi **D8**
14 Ta Karamanlidika
   Tou Fani **D1**
15 To Steki tou Ilia **A3**

Quick Bites ▼

1 Athinaion Politeia **A4**
2 Cafe Oionos **H6**
3 Drupes & Drips **E9**
4 Guarantee Sandwich **E9**
5 Kapnikarea **F3**
6 Kokkion **E2**
7 Lukumades **E3**
8 Melina Cafe **F5**
9 Thanasis **E3**
10 Vyzantino **G6**

Hotels ▼

1 A for Athens **D3**
2 Acropolis Select **E9**
3 Adrian Hotel **F4**
4 Athens Center
   Square **E1**
5 Athens Was **G8**
6 AVA Hotel & Suites **G7**
7 Electra Palace **H5**
8 Hera Hotel **F9**
9 Hermes Hotel **G4**
10 Herodion Hotel **E9**
11 Marble House **C9**
12 NLH FIX –
   Neighborhood
   Lifestyle Hotels **E9**
13 O&B Athens
   Boutique Hotel **B2**
14 Plaka Hotel **F4**

stealing the show, although the cuisine comes a very close second. Start with some *mezedes,* including the smoked eggplant salad or a velvety tzatziki, which perfectly complements the baked zucchini. For the main course, there's roast lamb wrapped in vine leaves and stuffed with cheese, rooster served with Greek pasta, or a variety platter of specially grilled meats. **Known for:** a magnificent view of the Parthenon; a reliable Greek menu; grilled meats. $ *Average main: €25* ⊠ *Rovertou Galli 25, Makriyianni* ☎ *210/921–4130* ⊕ *www.strofi.gr* ☉ *No lunch weekdays* Ⓜ *Acropolis.*

Coffee and Quick Bites

Drupes & Drips

$ | CAFÉ | On a tiny street, across from Takis Bakery, one of Athens's best, is a small spot with outside seats that serves coffee and fresh juices in the morning and turns into something quite different from noon. As the clock strikes 12, you'll hear bubbles and the chatter intensify as drinks (especially Spudorato and other Buglioni wines from Italy, Aperol spritzes, and craft beer from Tinos island) are poured into glasses. These are happily paired with premium cold cuts and cheeses from Greece and around the world. The charcuterie is served until midnight. **Known for:** high quality wines; cozy, buzzy ambience; Takis bakery across the road (owned by the same people). $ *Average main: €5* ⊠ *Zitrou 20, Makriyianni* ☎ *697/030–0404* Ⓜ *Acropolis.*

Guarantee Sandwich

$ | FAST FOOD | In-the-know locals will patiently queue here to get their fill of a fantastic, freshly made sandwich stuffed with deli ingredients of their choice. This small, family-run 1980s place is both vintage and progressive, and despite its huge fan-base remains completely unpretentious. Choose among ingredients like cheeses, chutneys, cold cuts, pickled or marinated vegetables, and seafood to create the sandwich of your dreams,

made with fresh artisanal bread. You can also buy fresh salads and freshly-pressed fruit and vegetable juices. **Known for:** an excellent variety of deli ingredients; friendly, personalized service; freshly baked, artisanal bread. $ *Average main: €6* ⊠ *Veikou 41, Koukaki* ☎ *210/922–6924* ⊕ *www.toguarantee.gr* ☉ *Closed Sunday* Ⓜ *Syngrou Fix.*

★ Lukumades

$ | FAST FOOD | Try (and probably get addicted to) one of Greece's most popular and traditional desserts—*loukoumades.* These doughnut-like balls are deep fried, then stuffed and slathered with an impressively enormous variety of delicious fillings and toppings. You can sit at the bench outside to feast on your selected sweets, or take them to go. The dough is freshly prepared every day using quality ingredients, as are the sauces and toppings that are sprinkled over them. **Known for:** top quality ingredients; great variety of toppings and fillings; excellent flavor every time. $ *Average main: €6* ⊠ *Aiolou 21 & Aghias Eirinis St., Acropolis* ☎ *210/321–0880* ⊕ *www.lukumades. com* Ⓜ *Monastiraki.*

Hotels

Acropolis Select

$ | HOTEL | For not significantly more per night than many basic budget options, you get to stay in a slick-looking hotel with an artfully modernized lobby full of designer furniture in the residential and newly fashionable neighborhood of Koukaki, a 10-minute walk from the Acropolis (and literally around the corner from the Acropolis Museum). **Pros:** comfortable rooms; friendly staff; good value for money. **Cons:** no Acropolis views from rooms; small elevator; some noise from the street at night. $ *Rooms from: €105* ⊠ *Falirou 37–39, Koukaki* ☎ *210/921–1610* ⊕ *www.acropoliselect.gr* ⇗ *72 rooms* ‖⊙‖ *No meals* Ⓜ *Acropolis.*

Athens Was

$$ | HOTEL | FAMILY | Idyllically located at the border between Makriyanni and Plaka, this modern, luxurious, and trendy hotel is walking distance away from all the best parts of town—Plaka, the ancient monuments, Syntagma for shopping, dining, and nightlife, and Kolonaki for boutiques and museums. **Pros:** great location; fantastic views; sophisticated dining. **Cons:** service could do with improvement; high prices; can be noisy especially during the weekend. $ *Rooms from: €200* ✉ *Dyionissiou Aeropagitou St 5, Plaka* ☎ *210/924–9954* ⊕ *www.athenswas.gr* ⤴ *21 rooms* ⦿ *Free breakfast* Ⓜ *Acropolis.*

Hera Hotel

$$ | HOTEL | Attention to elegant detail— the lobby's marble floors, dark wood paneling, and leather sofas—reigns at this small and elegant hotel, a good value that is perfectly located just down the street from the Acropolis Museum. **Pros:** unbeatable location; the Acropolis view from the dreamy roof garden; cleanliness and service. **Cons:** some of the rooms are small; rooms at the back have no views; lofty restaurant prices. $ *Rooms from: €130* ✉ *Falirou 9, Makriyanni* ☎ *210/923–6682, 210/923–5618* ⊕ *www.herahotel.gr* ⤴ *38 rooms* ⦿ *Free breakfast* Ⓜ *Acropolis.*

Herodion Hotel

$$ | HOTEL | A good compromise between the area's budget venues and deluxe digs, this hospitable hotel is down the street from the Odeon of Herodes Atticus, where Athens Festival performances are held in summer, and a few minutes from the Acropolis. **Pros:** tastefully designed rooms; wide choice at buffet breakfast; great Acropolis views from some rooms. **Cons:** rooms a bit small; barely justifies 4 star status; a little pricey if you're on a budget. $ *Rooms from: €150* ✉ *Rovertou Galli 4, Makriyanni* ☎ *210/923–6832* ⊕ *www.herodion.gr* ⤴ *90 rooms* ⦿ *Free breakfast* Ⓜ *Acropolis.*

Marble House

$ | B&B/INN | This welcoming guesthouse has a steady clientele who don't mind the basic accommodations and facilities in return for gracious, welcoming service, a convenient location, and unbeatable prices. **Pros:** unbeatable price for the budget traveler; quiet neighborhood ideally located for sightseeing; friendly staff. **Cons:** a bit outdated, no-frills interiors; breakfast costs extra; cramped bathrooms (not en suite). $ *Rooms from: €50* ✉ *Anastassiou Zinni 35, Koukaki* ☎ *210/923–4058, 210/922–8294* ⊕ *www.marblehouse.gr* ⤴ *16 rooms, 11 with bath* ⦿ *No meals* Ⓜ *Fix.*

★ NLH Fix - Neighborhood Lifestyle Hotels

$$ | HOTEL | FAMILY | Right behind the brand-new National Museum of Contemporary Art (EMST), this new seven-story hotel opened in 2017 and has already received rave reviews for its large, light-filled, and modern rooms that are ideal for families or small groups of friends (up to four). **Pros:** wonderfully spacious, airy, and light-filled rooms; staff offer exceptional insider tips; excellent value for families. **Cons:** breakfast not included in price (and only in-room); no hotel restaurant; rooms don't have Acropolis views. $ *Rooms from: €150* ✉ *Syggrou 64, Koukaki* ⚓ *At Stratigou Kontouli* ☎ *210/920–0170* ⊕ *nlh.gr* ⤴ *13 rooms* ⦿ *No meals* Ⓜ *Fix.*

Shopping

GIFTS

Athena Design Workshop

CRAFTS | One of the neighborhood's most original stores is a design shop run by artist Krina Vronti, from whom you can buy original printed T-shirts, home decor items, and cloth bags— all handmade, with traditional Greek themes, sometimes with a quirkily droll take on the area's classic, kitschy tourist shops. ✉ *Parthenonos 30, Makriyanni* ☎ *210/924–5713* Ⓜ *Acropolis.*

Most restaurants in the heart of Athens offer tables out on the street, where you can dine under an umbrella or a spreading plane tree. Few sections of the city are as picturesque as the Plaka district.

JEWELRY

★ Eleni Marnieri Galerie

JEWELRY/ACCESSORIES | Greece's only contemporary jewelry museum and shop features creations by more than 50 Greek and foreign designers. Original, handmade jewelry and home decor items as well as perfumes and cosmetics by hand-picked quality brands can be admired at a distance or bought. The gallery also presents themed seasonal exhibitions and video installations. ✉ *Lebessi 5–7 ✛ At Porniou 16* ☎ *210/866–8195* ⊕ *www.elenimarneri.com* ☾ *Closed Mon.* Ⓜ *Acropolis.*

SHOES

★ Melissinos Art Sandals

SHOES/LUGGAGE/LEATHER GOODS | **FAMILY** | Multi-talented Pantelis follows in the steps of his father, Stavros, aka "the poet sandalmaker," a legendary cultural figure in his own right, gentle soul, and internationally acclaimed shoemaker. His father's shop, where he worked throughout his life, was once visited by the Beatles, Elizabeth Taylor, Maria Callas, and Jackie O—and numerous TV crews thereafter. Pantelis is also a poet, composer, sculptor, and painter, and although he continues to create his father's classic sandal and bag designs he now also makes magnificently artistic sandals of his own. Visitors continue to arrive from around the world for their custom-made footwear, often with cameras in hand and happy to listen to Pantelis play the piano as they wait, admiring his artworks. ✉ *Tzireon 16* ☎ *210/321–9247, 694/4597–307* ⊕ *melissinos-art.com* Ⓜ *Acropolis.*

Plaka and Anafiotika
Πλάκα Αναφιώτικα

Fanning north from the slopes of the Acropolis, picturesque Plaka is the last corner of 19th-century Athens. Set with Byzantine accents provided by churches, the Old Town district extends north to Ermou Street and eastward to the Leofóros Amalias. During the 1950s and '60s, the area became garish with neon as nightclubs moved in and residents moved out, but locals, architects, and academicians joined forces in the early 1980s to transform a decaying neighborhood. Noisy discos and tacky pensions were closed, streets were changed into pedestrian zones, and old buildings were restored. At night merrymakers crowd the old tavernas, which feature traditional music and dancing; many have rooftops facing the Acropolis.

Set in the shadow of the Acropolis and often compared to the whitewashed villages of the rural Greek islands, the Anafiotika section of the Plaka is populated by many descendants of the Anafi stonemasons who arrived from that small Cycladic island in the 19th century to work in the expanding capital. It remains an enchanting area of simple stone houses, many nestled right into the bedrock, most little changed over the years, others stunningly restored. Cascades of bougainvillea and pots of geraniums and marigolds enliven the balconies and rooftops, and the prevailing serenity is in blissful contrast to the cacophony of modern Athens. In classical times, this district was abandoned because the Delphic Oracle claimed it as sacred ground. The original residents erected their homes overnight, as they took advantage of an Ottoman law decreeing that if you could put up a structure between sunset and sunrise, the property was yours.

Today, the residents are seldom seen—only a line of wash hung out to dry, the lace curtains on the tiny houses, or the curl of smoke from a wood-burning fireplace indicates human presence. Perched on the bedrock of the Acropolis is **Ayios Georgios tou Vrachou** (St. George of the Rock), which marks the southeast edge of the district. One of the most beautiful churches of Athens, it is still in use today. **Ayios Simeon,** a neoclassical church built in 1847 by the settlers, marks the western boundary and contains a copy of a famous miracle-working

icon from Anafi, Our Lady of the Reeds. The **Church of the Metamorphosis Sotiros** (Transfiguration), a high-dome 14th-century stone chapel, has a rear grotto carved right into the Acropolis.

Sights

★ Benizelos Mansion

HISTORIC SITE | Known as "the oldest house in Athens," this Byzantine mansion was once the home of the prestigious Benizelos Paleologou family, and Athens' patron saint Aghia Filothei (1522–1589). Filothei dynamically sought to protect and secretly educate women and the poor, while engaging in diplomatic affairs in her effort to oust the occupying Ottomans, who eventually killed her. Dating back to the 16th and 17th centuries, the space with its lovely marble-arched courtyard, a fountain, and remains of a Roman wall is now a folk museum of sorts, presenting visitors with how people of that caliber lived. There is also a screening room to watch a short documentary about the family and the Byzantine era. ✉ Adrianou 96, Plaka ☎ 210/324–8861 ⊕ archontiko-mpenizelon.gr ⊗ Closed Mon. Ⓜ Monastiraki.

Greek Folk Art Museum

MUSEUM | **FAMILY** | The Greek Folk Art Museum (also known as the Modern Greek Culture Museum) encompasses numerous buildings and focuses on folk art from 1650 to the present, with especially interesting embroideries, stone and wood carvings, carnival costumes, and Karaghiozis (shadow player figures). After an impressive expansion, it now incorporates the beautiful 19th-century neoclassical Bath-House of the Winds in Kyrristou Street, a spectacularly vast mosque (now deconsecrated and given over to museum displays) located in Areos Street, and exhibitions at nearby 22 Panos Street, which handles the vast overflow of objects on view. The permanent exhibition at the museum is entitled "Man and Tools" and presents

Step-by-Step: A Walk through Plaka

Begin your stroll at the ancient, jewel-like **Monument of Lysikrates**, one of the few remaining supports (334 BC) for tripods (vessels that served as prizes) awarded to the producer of the best play in the ancient Dionyssia festival. Take Herefondos to Plaka's central square, Filomoussou Eterias (or Kidathineon Square), a great place to people-watch.

The **Greek Folk Art Museum**, one of Athens's most rewarding cultural stops, has been renovated and is soon to open to the public in the form of an ultramodern museum presenting artifacts from 1650 until the present day. Across from the former museum on Kidathineos Street is the 11th- to 12th-century church of Metamorfosi Sotira Tou Kottaki, in a tidy garden with a fountain that was the main source of water for the neighborhood until sometime after Turkish rule. Down the block and around the corner on Angelikis Hatzimichali is the **Center of Folk Art and Tradition**. Continue west to the end of that street, crossing Adrianou to Hill, then right on Epimarchou to the striking Church House (on the corner of Scholeiou), once a Turkish police post and home to Richard Church, who led Greek forces in the War of Independence.

At the top of Epimarchou is Ayios Nikolaos Rangavas, an 11th-century church built with fragments of ancient columns. The church marks the edge of the **Anafiotika** quarter, a

village smack-dab in the middle of the metropolis. Wind your way through the narrow lanes off Stratonos, visiting the churches Ayios Georgios tou Vrachou, Ayios Simeon, and Metamorphosis Sotiros. Another interesting church is 8th-century Ayioi Anargyroi, at the top of Erechtheos. From the church, make your way to Theorias, which parallels the ancient *peripatos* (public roadway) that ran around the Acropolis. The collection at the **Kanellopoulos Museum** spans Athens's history; nearby on Panos you'll pass the Athens University Museum (Old University, otherwise known as the Kleanthis Residence), the city's first higher-learning institution. Walk down Panos to the **Roman Agora**, which includes the Tower of the Winds and the Fethiye Mosque. Nearby visit the engaging **Museum of Greek Popular Musical Instruments**, where recordings will take you back to the age of *rembetika* (Greek blues). Also next to the Agora is Athens's only remaining Turkish bathhouse, providing a glimpse into a daily social ritual of Ottoman times. On your way back to Syntagma Square, cut across to Mitropoleos Square to see the newly renovated cathedral and the beautiful 12th-century church of **Little Mitropolis**. From there, walk the tiny Benizelou Paleologou Street (recently opened to the public) to admire the **Benizelou Mansion**, among the city's oldest abodes and once the home of the city's patron saint, Aghia Filothei on Adrianou Street.

utilitarian objects that have served a purpose in the evolution of culture. Don't miss the room of uniquely fanciful landscapes by beloved Greek folk painter Theophilos Hatzimichalis, from Mytilini. ⊠ *Main building, Thespidos 4–8, Plaka* ☎ *210/324–5957* ⊕ *www.mnep. gr* ⊠ *€3, valid for each of the 4 buildings* Ⓜ *Acropolis.*

★ **Kanellopoulos Museum**

MUSEUM | FAMILY | The stately Michaleas Mansion, built in 1884, now showcases the Kanellopoulos family collection. It spans Athens's history from the 3rd century BC to the 19th century, with an emphasis on Byzantine icons, jewelry, and Mycenaean and Geometric vases and bronzes. Note the painted ceiling gracing the first floor. ⊠ *Theorias 12 and Panos, Plaka* ☎ *210/331–8873, 210/321–2313* ⊕ *pacf.gr/en* ⊠ *€4* ⊙ *Closed Tues.* Ⓜ *Monastiraki.*

Little Mitropolis

RELIGIOUS SITE | This church snuggles up to the pompous Mitropolis (on the northern edge of Plaka), the ornate Cathedral of Athens. Also called Panayia Gorgoepikoos ("the virgin who answers prayers quickly"), the chapel dates to the 12th century; its most interesting features are its outer walls, covered with reliefs of animals and allegorical figures dating from the classical to the Byzantine period. Light a candle for a loved one and then look for the ancient frieze with zodiac signs and a calendar of festivals in Attica. Most of the paintings inside were destroyed, but the famous 13th- to 14th-century Virgin, said to perform miracles, remains. ⊠ *Mitropolis Sq., Plaka* Ⓜ *Syntagma.*

Museum of Greek Popular Musical Instruments

MUSEUM | FAMILY | An entertaining crash course in the development of Greek music, from regional *dimotika* (folk) to rembetika (blues), this museum has three floors of instruments. Headphones are available so you can appreciate the sounds made by such unusual delights as goatskin bagpipes and discern the differences in tone between the Pontian lyra and Cretan lyra, string instruments often featured on world-music compilations. ⊠ *Diogenous 1–3, Plaka* ☎ *210/325–0198, 210/325–4119* ⊕ *www.mnep.gr/* ⊠ *€2* ⊙ *Closed Mon.* Ⓜ *Monastiraki.*

★ **Roman Agora**

ARCHAEOLOGICAL SITE | The city's commercial center from the 1st century BC to the 4th century AD, the Roman Market was a large rectangular courtyard with a peristyle that provided shade for the arcades of shops. Its most notable feature is the west entrance's Bazaar Gate, or **Gate of Athena Archegetis,** completed around AD 2; the inscription records that it was erected with funds from Julius Caesar and Augustus. Halfway up one solitary square pillar behind the gate's north side, an edict inscribed by Hadrian regulates the sale of oil, a reminder that this was the site of the annual bazaar where wheat, salt, and oil were sold. On the north side of the Roman Agora stands one of the few remains of the Turkish occupation, the **Fethiye (Victory) Mosque.** The eerily beautiful mosque was built in the late 15th century on the site of a Christian church to celebrate the Turkish conquest of Athens and to honor Mehmet II (the Conqueror). During the few months of Venetian rule in the 17th century, the mosque was converted to a Roman Catholic church; it is now closed to the public.

Surrounded by a cluster of old houses on the western slope of the Acropolis, the world-famous **Tower of the Winds** (Aerides) is now open to the public for visits. Located inside the Roman Agora, it is the most appealing and well preserved of the Roman monuments of Athens, keeping time since the 1st century BC. It was originally a sundial, water clock, and weather vane topped by a bronze Triton with a metal rod in his hand, which

Did You Know?

Looming over the ancient Agora, the Hephaistion is the best-preserved ancient Greek temple in the world. Unlike the Parthenon, it has retained all of its columns and pediments intact.

followed the direction of the wind. Its eight sides face the direction of the eight winds into which the compass was divided; expressive reliefs around the tower personify these eight winds, called *I Aerides* (the Windy Ones) by Athenians. Note the north wind, Boreas, blowing on a conch, and the beneficent west wind, Zephyros, scattering blossoms. ✉ *Pelopidas and Aiolou, Plaka* ☎ *210/324–5220* 🌐 *odysseus.culture.gr* 🎫 *€8; €30 joint ticket for all Unification of Archaeological Sites* [M] *Monastiraki.*

🍴 Restaurants

Popular Plaka delights in its traditional homes, winding alleys, and bustling cafés and gift shops.

Daphne's

$$ | **GREEK** | Daphne's is one of the most exclusive (and at times priciest) destinations in Plaka. The Pompeian frescoes on the walls, the fragments of an ancient Greek building in the garden, and the tasteful restoration of the neoclassical building in terra-cotta and ocher hues also contribute to a pleasant and romantic evening. The refined Mediterranean and Greek dishes (such as pork with celery and egg lemon sauce, fricassee of melt-off-the-bone lamb with greens, rabbit *stifado* and the traditional moussaka) help make this one of Athens's better restaurants. **Known for:** refined Greek cuisine based on quality produce; exclusive surroundings; excellent Greek wine list. [$] *Average main: €25* ✉ *Lysikratous 4, Plaka* ☎ *210/322–7991* 🌐 *www.daphnes-restaurant.gr* [M] *Acropolis.*

The Old Taverna of Psarra

$$ | **GREEK** | Founded way back in 1898, this is one of the few remaining Plaka tavernas serving reliably good food with excellent Acropolis views. It doesn't draw the same crowd of locals as in the past, and it doesn't just serve fish, as the name suggests, rather, you'll find simple, tasty entrées such as rooster in wine sauce, *arnaki pilino* (lamb baked in clay pots), and pork chops with ouzo. Can't make up your mind? Try the *ouzokatastasi* ("ouzo situation"), a plate of tidbits to nibble while you decide. **Known for:** scenic Plaka location; classic Greek fare; shaded outdoor terrace for summer, big fireplace for winter. [$] *Average main: €20* ✉ *Erechtheos 16, Plaka* ☎ *210/321–8733* 🌐 *www.psaras-taverna.gr* [M] *Syntagma.*

O Platanos

$$ | **GREEK** | On a picturesque pedestrianized square, this is one of the oldest tavernas in Plaka (established 1932). Although not as good as it was during its glory years when intellectuals and artists sat here sipping retsina until the early hours, it's still worth a stop. It is a district landmark—set midway between the Tower of the Winds and the Museum of Greek Popular Musical Instruments. Most of the crowds prefer to relax under the courtyard's plane trees (which give the place its name) rather than dine inside the cozy dining room, at least when the weather is pleasant. Locals come here because the food is good Greek home cooking. Don't miss the oven-baked potatoes, lamb or veal casserole with spinach or eggplant, the stuffed squid, and the cheap but delicious barrel retsina. It's also open for lunch. **Known for:** beautiful setting under plane trees; traditional Greek cooking like stuffed squid and lamb casserole; pitchers of the house retsina. [$] *Average main: €17* ✉ *Diogenous 4, Plaka* ☎ *210/322–0666* 🌐 *eleinitsa.wixsite.com/platanos* 💳 *No credit cards* 🕒 *Closed Sun. June–Aug. No dinner Sun.* [M] *Syntagma.*

Scholarhio

$ | **GREEK** | A favorite with university students and tourists, this open-hearted ouzo taverna offers a tasty daily platter of all the best in home-cooked Greek cuisine. Waiters bring a giant tray of the day's offerings, which include such favorites as taramosalata, Smyrna-style tzatziki, cuttlefish stewed with onions, *lahanodolmades* (cabbage rolls), eggplant dip, fried calamari, moussaka, and *bekri mezedes* (wine-marinated pork cutlets). You can choose between one of six menus, based on the number of people dining and the number of dishes desired. Dessert (traditional Greek halva) is on the house. **Known for:** tasty mezedes; fun, relaxed atmosphere; friendly service. [$] *Average main: €14* ✉ *Tripodon 14, Plaka* ☎ *210/324–7605* 🌐 *www.scholarhio.gr* [M] *Monastiraki.*

Coffee and Quick Bites

Cafe Oionos

$ | **CAFÉ** | Stop for an ice-cold frappé (Nescafé instant coffee frothed with sugar and condensed milk) and a game of backgammon at Cafe Oionos. Have a light lunch and watch the world go by on buzzy Kydathinaeon square. **Known for:** freshly made salads; pastas and sandwiches; relaxing atmosphere. [$] *Average main: €5* ✉ *Kydathinaion and Geronta 7, Plaka* ☎ *210/322–3139* 🌐 *www.facebook.com/oionoscafe* [M] *Acropolis.*

★ **Kapnikarea**

$ | **GREEK** | A perfect stop while exploring Ermou Street's shops and the Monastiraki area, Kapnikarea serves up tasty meze with a live soundtrack of the Greek blues (*rembetika*), especially between 6 and 11 pm, in a relaxed, authentic setup reflective of the owner's heritage from "longevity island," Ikaria. **Known for:** rembetika music played by skilled musicians; great location; favorite local hang-out. [$] *Average main: €8* ✉ *Hristopoulou 2, at Ermou 57, Monastiraki* ✣ *Behind Kapnikarea church* ☎ *210/322–7394* [M] *Monastiraki.*

Melina Cafe

$$ | **CAFÉ** | Melina is dedicated to its namesake, the dynamic *Never on Sunday* actress turned Minister of Culture, Melina Mercouri. Set on a scenic, village-style Plaka street framed by pink bougainvillea, the tables are always packed. On a hot afternoon try the delectable club sandwich on crisp sourdough bread, creamy egg salad, or seafood salad; at night try the peppered fillet or "Melina chicken." The desserts here are great, too, including a rich chocolate *sokolatina* (pudding cake) and a syrupy orange *portokalopita* cake (made from shredded phyllo), with a strong Greek coffee. **Known for:** buzzy atmosphere; good food you can linger over; traditional desserts. [$] *Average main: €15* ✉ *Lysiou 22, Plaka* ☎ *210/324–6501* 🌐 *cafemelina.gr* [M] *Acropolis.*

Vyzantino

$ | **GREEK** | **FAMILY** | A favorite of tourists and locals alike, Vyzantino is directly on Plaka's main square—good for a reasonably priced, flavorsome, and traditional bite to eat with a front seat to all the action. **Known for:** creamy pastitsio; friendly service; central location. [$] *Average main: €5* ✉ *Kidathineon 18, Plaka* ☎ *210/322–7368* 🌐 *www.vyzantinorestaurant.gr* 💳 *No credit cards* [M] *Acropolis.*

Hotels

Adrian Hotel

$ | **HOTEL** | This comfortable pension offers friendly service and an excellent location in the heart of Plaka—incurable romantics should ask for one of just three rooms looking toward the Acropolis. **Pros:** great central location; friendly staff; excellent value for the money. **Cons:** Adrianou Street can be noisy during the summer months; need to book well in advance; small bathrooms. [$] *Rooms from: €98* ✉ *Adrianou 74, Plaka* ☎ *210/322–1553* 🌐 *adrian-hotel-athens.hotel-ds.com/en/* 🛏 *22 rooms* 🍴 *Free breakfast* [M] *Monastiraki.*

★ **AVA Hotel & Suites**

$$$ | **HOTEL** | On a quiet side street in the Plaka, this lovely small hotel (fully renovated in 2016) is ideally located for all the major Athens attractions and has become a firm favorite among leisure and business travelers alike. **Pros:**

spacious rooms; elegant furnishings; impeccable service. **Cons:** lacks big-hotel amenities and a restaurant; small elevator; the breakfast could be richer. $ *Rooms from: €250* ⊠ *Lyssicratous 9–11, Plaka* ☎ *210/325–9000* ⊕ *www.ava-hotel.gr* ⇆ *16 rooms* ⦿ *Free breakfast* Ⓜ *Acropolis.*

★ Electra Palace

$$$ | **HOTEL** | If you want luxurious elegance, good service, and a great location, this is the hotel for you: rooms from the fifth floor up have a view of the Acropolis, and, in summer, you can bask in the sunshine at the outdoor swimming pool (taking in the view of Athens's greatest monument) or catch the sunset from the rooftop garden—if you're not enjoying some serious pampering in the spa. **Pros:** gorgeous rooms; great location; shady garden and rooftop pool. **Cons:** air-conditioning can be problematic; pool is small and gets busy; traffic jams on road in front. $ *Rooms from: €250* ⊠ *Nikodimou 18–20, Plaka* ☎ *210/337–0000* ⊕ *www.electrahotels.gr* ⇆ *175 rooms* ⦿ *Free breakfast* Ⓜ *Syntagma.*

★ Hermes Hotel

$$ | **HOTEL** | **FAMILY** | Athens's small, modestly priced establishments have generally relied on little more than convenient central locations to draw visitors, but the Hermes goes further, with sunny guest rooms with brightly colored decorative details that feel warm and welcoming and marble bathrooms. **Pros:** great staff; sleek, clean decor; free Wi-Fi. **Cons:** some smallish rooms, some without a balcony (check availability); on a sometimes noisy street; room walls are thin. $ *Rooms from: €135* ⊠ *Apollonos 19, Plaka* ☎ *210/323–5514, 210/322–2706 reservations* ⊕ *www.hermeshotel.gr* ⇆ *45 rooms* ⦿ *Free breakfast* Ⓜ *Syntagma.*

Plaka Hotel

$$ | **HOTEL** | The guest rooms in this charming, centrally located hotel offer a comfortable place to rest your head while in the heart of old Athens. **Pros:** view of the Acropolis from the roof garden; diligent staff; good breakfast and lounge areas. **Cons:** small and sometimes stuffy rooms; no pets allowed; cleanliness standards could be higher. $ *Rooms from: €130* ⊠ *Kapnikareas 7 and Mitropoleos, Plaka* ☎ *210/322–2706* ⊕ *www.plakahotel.gr* ⇆ *67 rooms* ⦿ *Free breakfast* Ⓜ *Monastiraki.*

 ## Nightlife

BARS

Brettos

BARS/PUBS | With walls adorned with brightly lit bottles in all colors of the spectrum, Brettos is mainly popular among tourists who have seen photos of it over the years. Locals who still choose to come here do so to relish the memories of the oldest distillery in town (going strong since 1909) and the second-oldest bar in the whole of Europe. The huge barrels store head-spinning spirits produced on the premises even today—ouzo, cognac, liqueurs (like top picks cinnamon or mango), tsipouro, and more. Order a *mezedes* platter to accompany your beverage of choice. ⊠ *Kydathinaion 41, Plaka* ☎ *210/323–2110* ⊕ *www.brettosplaka.com* Ⓜ *Acropolis.*

TAVERNAS WITH MUSIC

Palia Taverna (*Old Tavern of Stamatopoulos*)

MUSIC CLUBS | **FAMILY** | This taverna has everything: good food, barrel wine, and an acoustic duo with guitar and bouzouki playing old Athenian songs in an 1882 house. In summer, the show moves to the garden. Whatever the season, Greeks will often get up and dance, beckoning you to join them (don't be shy). Live music starts at about 8:30 and goes on until 1 am. ⊠ *Lysiou 26, Plaka* ☎ *210/322–8722* ⊕ *www.stamatopoulo-stavern.gr* Ⓜ *Monastiraki.*

For food with a view, the Plaka district is famed for its lovely garden restaurants with front-row seats to the Acropolis Hill.

Performing Arts

DANCE

★ Dora Stratou Dance Theater

DANCE | The country's leading folk dance company performs exhilarating and sublime Greek folk dances (from all regions) in eye-catching, authentic costumes in programs that change every two weeks. Performances are held Wednesday through Sunday from the end of May through September. ✉ Arakinthou and Voutie, Filopappou ☎ 210/324–4395 office, 210/921–4650 theater ⊕ www. grdance.org Ⓜ Acropolis.

FILM

★ Cine Paris

FILM | This rooftop-garden movie theater, which offers Dolby Digital sound, is the oldest (dating from 1920) and most romantic in Athens. It's located on pedestrianized Kydathinaion Street, which also means it's close to many hotels and tavernas. In the lobby there's a store selling vintage film posters. It is open from May to October. Most films are in English (with Greek subtitles). ✉ Kidathineon 22, Plaka ☎ 210/322–2071 ⊕ www.cineparis. gr Ⓜ Monastiraki.

Shopping

ANTIQUES AND ICONS

Elliniko Spiti

ANTIQUES/COLLECTIBLES | For more than 40 years, art restorer Dimitris Koutelieris has been inspired by his home island of Naxos. He salvages most of his materials from houses under restoration, then fashions them into picture frames, little wooden boats, small chairs, and other decorative objects. In his hands objects like cabin doors or window shutters gain a magical second life. ✉ Kekropos 14, Plaka ☎ 694/ 576–7643 Ⓜ Acropolis.

FOOD

Malotira

FOOD/CANDY | Named after an herb that grows in the higher reaches of Crete, this deli has expanded to include authentic, pure products of the traditional as well as modern variety, from aromatic soaps and homemade jams to herb infused spirits. The friendly staff will be happy to offer you various foods to taste as you explore the shelves. ⊠ *Apollonos 30, Plaka* ☎ *210/324–6008* ⊕ *www.malotira. gr* Ⓜ *Syntagma.*

GIFTS
Fine Wine
WINE/SPIRITS | Elegant wine gift packs are available at this old-fashioned wineshop, where you can browse a broad selection of Greek wines and liqueurs. The couple who own this place are wine lovers themselves and will be eager to offer any advice you need. ⊠ *Thespidos 12, Plaka* ☎ *210/323–0350* ⊕ *www.finewine.gr* Ⓜ *Acropolis.*

★ Forget Me Not
CERAMICS/GLASSWARE | This inspirational "cultural goods" shop has gained a loyal following for its unique souvenirs. Here, you can buy gifts with a contemporary Greek design twist and a sense of humor, created by local designers Greece is for Lovers, Beetroot, Zeus + Dione, Studiolav, AC Design, and more. From a leather skateboard made in sandal style to unique bags that look like they're made from fishmonger's paper to Plexiglass evil-eye charms, this is contemporary Greek design at its best. ⊠ *Adrianou 100, Plaka* ☎ *210/325–3740* ⊕ *www. forgetmenotathens.gr* Ⓜ *Syntagma.*

HANDICRAFTS
Amorgos
ANTIQUES/COLLECTIBLES | Wood furniture and ceramics, all hand-carved and hand-painted by the shop's owners—a creative couple specializing in antique furniture restoration and interior design—beautifully feature motifs from regional Greek designs. Needlework, hanging ceiling lamps, shadow puppets, and other decorative accessories like cushions, fabrics, wooden carved chests, and traditional low tables called *sofras,* are also for sale. ⊠ *Kodrou 3, Plaka* ☎ *210/324–3836* ⊕ *www.amorgosart.gr* Ⓜ *Acropolis.*

The Loom
TEXTILES/SEWING | A cornucopia of fantastically embroidered cushion covers, blankets, and tapestries as well as beautiful carpets, and rugs (including vintage, stone-washed rugs). This is the kind of shop where you can browse at your leisure. The store can ship your merchandise home to you as well. ⊠ *Adrianou 94, Plaka* ☎ *210/323–8540* Ⓜ *Monastiraki.*

The Olive Tree Store
GIFTS/SOUVENIRS | This unique shop sells items made exclusively of olive wood, such as salad bowls and tongs, wall clocks, jewelry, and even backgammon sets. Alas, the beautiful specially made olive wood Gibson-style guitar is not for sale. ⊠ *Adrianou 67, Plaka* ☎ *210/323–3002* ⊕ *www.theolivetree. com* Ⓜ *Monastiraki.*

 Activities

SPAS
Al Hammam
FITNESS/HEALTH CLUBS | Sumptuous massages are offered here with Greek olive oil and raki or with Eastern ingredients. And the option of overlooking the Acropolis during your treatment, which can be carried out by two skilled therapists, is all part of the Al Hammam experience. And that's after relaxing in an Ottoman-style, circular marble steam room. It's a relaxing ritual that's ideal after a day of shopping and sightseeing. The Hammam also offers mani-pedis and beauty treatments. ⊠ *Tripodon 10, at Ragava, Plaka* ☎ *211/012–9099* ⊕ *alhammam.gr* Ⓜ *Acropolis.*

Monastiraki and Psirri
Μοναστηράκι Ψυρή

The Agora was once the focal point of urban life. All the principal urban roads and country highways traversed it; the procession of the great Panathenaea Festival, composed of chariots, magistrates, virgins, priests, and sacrificial animals crossed it on the way to the Acropolis; the Assembly met here first, before moving to the Pnyx; it was where merchants squabbled over the price of olive oil; the forum where Socrates met with his students; and centuries later, where St. Paul went about his missionary task. Lying just under the citadel of the Acropolis, it was indeed the heart of the ancient city and a general meeting place, where news was exchanged and bargains transacted, alive with all the rumors and gossip of the marketplace. The Agora became important under Solon (6th century BC), founder of Athenian democracy; construction continued for almost a millennium. Today, the site's sprawling confusion of stones, slabs, and foundations is dominated by the best-preserved Doric temple in Greece, the Hephaistion, built during the 5th century BC, and the impressive reconstructed Stoa of Attalos II, which houses the Museum of the Agora Excavations.

You can still experience the sights and sounds of the marketplace in Monastiraki, which retains vestiges of the 400-year period when Greece was subject to the Ottoman Empire. The Varvakeios Agora (Central Market) in the heart of Athinas Street sells fish, meat, and produce from all over Greece and is the major supplier for the city. Not for the squeamish, the bustling market is where you'll see every variety of fish, skinned goats, and cow's tongues. It is a bustling and colorful complex of both indoor and outdoor stalls and shops scattered around the back streets.

For anyone who may have explored the city even only a few years ago, Monastiraki today is unrecognizable, especially at night. Cool, artsy bars, some managed by savvy mixologists, tiny street food eateries, dessert places, third-generation cafés making designer coffee, restaurants, yoga schools, and vintage or design stores have mushroomed across the area in the true style of a European capital. It's a great idea to head down Ermou and cross into the heart of Monastiraki's mazelike streets without any map or any plan, just a thirst for adventure and to gain a new understanding of what Athens's real center is all about.

During his stint in Athens, Lord Byron stayed in Psirri, adjacent to Monastiraki, and this is where he supposedly met Thiresia-Tereza Makri, who inspired him to write "The Maid of Athens." Over the last 20 years an influx of artists, designers, bakers, and organic grocers took advantage of the available rental opportunities, changing the area's profile and bringing the rents up considerably.

Defined by Ermou, Kerameikou, Athinas, Evripidou, Epikourou, and Pireos streets, Psirri has many buildings older than those in picturesque Plaka. Although nowhere near as fashionable as it was in the late 1990s–early 2000s, it still draws the crowds for its plethora of tavernas, *mezedopoleio* (Greek tapas bars), nightspots, and cafés, while a small number of artsy shops and modern hotels, including the O&B Athens Boutique Hotel, can be found in the area. Peek over the wrought-iron gates of the old houses on the narrow side streets between Ermou and Kerameikou to see the pretty courtyards bordered by long, low buildings, whose many small rooms were rented out to different families. Linger on into the evening if you want to dance on tabletops to live Greek music or sing along with a soulful accordion player. The classic old Athens eatery Diporto is well hidden in the corner basement of an olive shop (with no sign) on Platia Theatrou. The regulars know where it is, and that's good enough (you can ask). Just follow your nose to Evripidou Street, where the city's best spice and herb shops are. If you're feeling adventurous (during the day only) get lost in the border between Psirri and Omonia to discover the immigrant zone brimming with Indian and Pakistani restaurants and grocers, Chinese clothes shops, and Middle Eastern barbers.

Sights

★ Ancient Agora

ARCHAEOLOGICAL SITE | FAMILY | The commercial hub of ancient Athens, the Agora was once lined with statues and expensive shops, the favorite strolling ground of fashionable Athenians and a mecca for merchants and students. The long colonnades offered shade in summer and protection from rain in winter to the throng of people who transacted the day-to-day business of the city, and, under their arches, Socrates discussed matters with Plato, and Zeno expounded the philosophy of the Stoics (whose name comes from the six *stoas,* or colonnades of the Agora). Besides administrative buildings, the schools, theaters, workshops, houses, stores, and market stalls of a thriving town surrounded it. The foundations of some of the main buildings that may be most easily distinguished include the circular **Tholos,** the principal seat of executive power in the city; the Mitroon, shrine to Rhea, the mother of gods, which included the vast state archives and registry office (*mitroon* is still used today to mean registry); the Vouleuterion, where the council met; the Monument of Eponymous Heroes, the Agora's information center, where announcements such as the list of military recruits were hung; and the Sanctuary of the Twelve Gods, a shelter for refugees and the point from which all distances were measured.

The Agora's showpiece was the **Stoa of Attalos II,** where Socrates once lectured and incited the youth of Athens to adopt his progressive ideas on mortality and morality. Today the Museum of Agora Excavations, this two-story building was first designed as a retail complex and erected in the 2nd century BC by Attalos, a king of Pergamum. The reconstruction in 1953–56 used Pendelic marble and creamy limestone from the original structure. The colonnade, designed for promenades, is protected from the blistering sun and cooled by breezes. The most notable sculptures, of historical and mythological figures from the 3rd and 4th centuries BC, are at ground level outside the museum.

Take a walk around the site and speculate on the location of Simon the Cobbler's house and shop, which was a meeting place for Socrates and his pupils. The carefully landscaped grounds display a number of plants known in antiquity, such as almond, myrtle, and pomegranate. By standing in the center, you have a glorious view up to the Acropolis. **Ayii Apostoloi** is the only one of the Agora's nine churches to survive, saved because of its location and beauty. A quirky ruin to visit here is the 1st Century AD latrine in the northeastern corner.

On the low hill called Kolonos Agoraios in the Agora's northwest corner stands the best-preserved Doric temple in all Greece, the **Hephaistion,** sometimes called the Thission because of its friezes showing the exploits of Theseus. Like the other monuments, it is roped off, but you can walk around it to admire its preservation. A little older than the Parthenon, it is surrounded by 34 columns and is 104 feet in length, and was once filled with sculptures (the only remnant of which is the mutilated frieze, once brightly colored). It never quite makes the impact of the Parthenon, in large part due to the fact that it lacks a noble site and can never be seen from below, its sun-matured columns towering heavenward. The Hephaistion was originally dedicated to Hephaistos, god of metalworkers, and it is interesting to note that metal workshops still exist in this area near Ifestou Street. ✉ *3 entrances: from Monastiraki on Adrianou; from Thission on Apostolou Pavlou; and descending from Acropolis on Polygnotou St. (near the church of Ayion Apostolon), Monastiraki* ☎ *210/321–0185* ⊕ *odysseus.culture.gr* 🎫 *€10; €30 joint ticket for all Unification of Archaeological Sites* Ⓜ *Monastiraki.*

Flea Market

MARKET | Here is where the chaos, spirit, and charm of Athens turn into a feast for the senses. The Sunday morning market has combined sight, sound, and scent into a strangely alluring little world where everything is for sale: 1950s-era scuba masks, old tea sets, antique sewing machines, old tobacco tins, gramophone needles, old matchboxes, army uniforms, and lacquered eggs. Get there before the crowd becomes a throng at 11 am, and practice your haggling skills. ✉ *Along Ifestou, Kynetou, and Adrianou Sts., Monastiraki* Ⓜ *Monastiraki.*

Monastiraki Square

PLAZA | One of Athens's most popular meeting places, the square is always alive with fruit sellers, bunches of youths hanging out, and street dance performances. If you are coming by metro, look for the special glassed-in view revealing the ancient Iridanos riverbed, where the water still flows. The square takes its name from the small Panayia Pantanassa Church, commonly called Monastiraki ("Little Monastery"). It once flourished as an extensive convent, perhaps dating to the 10th century, and once stretched from Athinas to Aiolou. The nuns took in poor people, who earned their keep weaving the thick textiles known as *abas*. The buildings were destroyed during excavations, and the train (and later metro) line construction that started in 1896. The convent's basic basilica form, now

recessed a few steps below street level, was altered through a poor restoration in 1911, when the bell tower was added. ✉ *Monastiraki* ✛ *South of Ermou and Athinas junction* Ⓜ *Monastiraki.*

★ **Varvakeios Agora** (*Central Market*)
MARKET | Athens's cacophonous Central Market runs along Athinas Street: on one side are open-air stalls selling fruit and vegetables, with a few stores selling mainly eastern European foods tucked at the back. Across the street, in the huge neoclassical covered market, built between 1870 and 1884 (and renovated in 1996), are the meat market next to the fish market, juxtaposing the surrealistic composition of suspended carcasses and shimmering fish on marble counters. The shops at the north end of the market, to the right on Sofokleous, sell the best cheese, olives, halvah, bread, spices, and cold cuts—including *pastourma* (spicy cured beef)—available in Athens. Nearby is Evripidou Street, lined with herb and spice shops all the way down. Small restaurants serving traditional fare and *patsa* (tripe soup), dot the market; these stay open until almost dawn and are popular stops with weary clubbers trying to ease their hangovers. ✉ *Athinas Street, Monastiraki* ⊙ *Closed Sun.* Ⓜ *Monastiraki.*

🍴 Restaurants

Avli Psirri

$ | GREEK | A very well-kept secret until a couple of years ago, Avli remains well under the radar even today. But if you walk past its inconspicuous entrance, you'd be missing out on uniquely satisfying small plates and bottomless carafes of barrel wine. Dining here remains a unique experience in a village-like backyard that is nothing like the rest of Athens. Foreign artists and Greek businesspeople alike find refuge here, especially when they want to take the afternoon off and indulge a little.
Known for: basic grills, from fried liver to

One of the hearts of the city center, Monastiraki Square is presided over by the 18th-century Tzistarakis Mosque.

meatballs; simple authenticity; completely original village atmosphere. $ *Average main: €6* ✉ *Aghiou Dimitriou 12, Psirri* ☎ *210/324–4117* Ⓜ *Monastiraki.*

Bairaktaris

$ | GREEK | Run by the same family since 1879, this is an almost legendary souvlaki eatery in Monastiraki Square. After admiring the painted wine barrels and the black-and-white stills of Greek film stars and politicians who have lunched here, go to the window case to view the day's *magirefta* (stove-top-cooked dish, usually made earlier)—possibly a delicious *pastitsio*. Or sit down and order a popular gyro or kebab platter. **Known for:** traditional kebabs and gyros; historic setting; simple food for reasonable prices. $ *Average main: €10* ✉ *Monastiraki Sq. 2, Monastiraki* ☎ *210/321–3036* ⊕ *www.bairaktaris.gr* Ⓜ *Monastiraki.*

★ Café Avissinia

$$ | GREEK | Facing hoary and merchant-packed Abyssinia Square, this timeworn but exceptional eatery is popular with locals who want home-cooked traditional food with heavy Asia Minor influences and endless servings of the excellent barrel wine and ouzo. Diners love to settle within the elegant glass-and-wood interior to sample mussels and rice pilaf, wine-marinated octopus with pasta, fresh garden salad, or any of the dips. Little wonder so many head here to relax after a day of shopping at the nearby flea market. A newer rooftop addition offers spectacular Acropolis views. Another plus: during the winter months, music is often in the air—on weekend afternoons, you can enjoy live accordion performances sometimes accompanied by the piano. **Known for:** delicious spinach-enriched moussaka and Soutzoukakia; an air of nostalgia but with style; live music on weekend afternoons.

$ *Average main: €18* ⊠ *Abyssinia Sq., Kinetou 7, Psirri* ☎ *210/321–7047* ⊕ *www.cafeavissinia.net* ⏱ *Closed Mon.* Ⓜ *Thissio, Monastiraki.*

Melilotos

$$ | GREEK | In the city's main shopping district, the compact but modern Melilotos offers a large variety of refreshing, quick-bite options based on traditional Greek dishes with influences from other cuisines. The menu offers a large array of dishes at reasonable prices. Grilled meats, wholesome salads, Greek pastas, macrobiotic and vegetarian options, as well as quality coffee and dessert are all on the menu. **Known for:** a modern take on traditional Greek; healthy options; reasonable prices. $ *Average main: €15* ⊠ *Kalamiotou 19, Monastiraki* ☎ *210/322–2458* ⊕ *www.melilotos.gr* Ⓜ *Monastiraki.*

Spiti Mas

$ | MEDITERRANEAN | With a name that means "our house" in Greek, Spiti Mas is designed like the interior of a home, with a bed, a dining area, a "balcony" out on the street, a nice homey bathroom, and a living room. The menu changes by the day, as it would at home, and light meals (omelets, sandwiches, etc.) are prepared according to the day's fresh groceries. Guests can bring a laptop and work while they sip coffee or even have breakfast in bed. **Known for:** breakfast and brunch; spinach pie; friendly, homelike setting. $ *Average main: €12* ⊠ *Navarchou Apostoli 10, Psirri* ☎ *210/331–4751* ⊕ *www.facebook.com/spitimas.net* Ⓜ *Monastiraki.*

Ta Karamanlidika Tou Fani

$$ | GREEK FUSION | A deli-cum-meze restaurant serving the authentic cuisine of the Karamanlides, who were once inhabitants of Cappadocia and Cilicia in Asia Minor. Huge hams, salamis, smoked camel meat, and cheeses hang in abundance over the counter and are displayed through a glass counter. Try the homemade pies baked in a stone oven with *sujuk* spiced sausage, minced meat, or various cheeses and vegetables. Salad dishes include Maria's spicy cheese salad, tabbouleh, creamy chickpeas with avocado, and eggplant salad. **Known for:** authentic Asia Minor–inspired meze dishes; traditional setting and good service; rare ingredients like smoked camel meat and regional cheeses. $ *Average main: €15* ⊠ *Ermou 119, Monastiraki* ☎ *210/321–9119* ⊕ *karamanlidika.gr* ⏱ *Cosed Sun.* Ⓜ *Monastiraki.*

☕ Coffee and Quick Bites

★ Kokkion

$ | FAST FOOD | FAMILY | An ice cream workshop (dare we say laboratory) and store, Kokkion is the brainchild of a Cordon Bleu patissiere and serves ice cream like no other in Athens. The parlor uses only super-fresh ingredients like cow's milk from a small farm in northern Greece, high quality French chocolate, and homemade caramel, seasonings, and flavorings. Most exciting of all are the unique flavors, like milk chocolate with orange and pepper and coconut sorbet with chocolate steamed biscuit and chocolate pieces, as well as classics like bitter chocolate, salted caramel, and vanilla. Vegan options are available, too. **Known for:** fresh ingredients—no ice cream mixes here; unique flavors; homemade flavorings. $ *Average main: €6* ⊠ *Protogenous 2, Psirri* ☎ *698/1563–511* ⊕ *en.kokkion.com* Ⓜ *Monastiraki.*

Thanasis

$ | GREEK | With the hands-down best kebab (especially the traditional *yiaourtlou,* i.e., with yogurt sauce) in town, and open since 1950, Thanasis is always crowded with hungry Greeks who crave the specially spiced ground meat, along with a nicely oiled pita bread, yogurt, onions, and tomatoes. **Known for:** kebabs with all the trimmings; popular with both locals and visitors; reasonable prices. $ *Average main: €7* ⊠ *Mitropoleos 69, Monastiraki* ☎ *210/324–4705* ⊕ *www.othanasis.gr* ⊟ *No credit cards* Ⓜ *Monastiraki.*

Hotels

★ A for Athens

$$ | HOTEL | One of Athens's hippest hotels, in a restored 1960s building with minimalist rooms, has wooden floors and all the modern amenities (including both air-conditioning and free Wi-Fi). **Pros:** central location next to a metro stop; comfortable rooms with a contemporary design; breathtaking views. **Cons:** some noise from the street and the bar; no gym or pool; small elevator and steep stairs. $ *Rooms from: €130* ✉ *Miaouli 2–4, Monastiraki* ☎ *210/324–4244* ⊕ *aforathens.com* ⬎ *35 rooms* ⧉ *Free breakfast* Ⓜ *Monastiraki.*

Athens Center Square

$ | HOTEL | This surprisingly peaceful, modern hotel nevertheless blends nicely into the iconic, bustling landscape of the Athens Central Market. **Pros:** knowledgeable, friendly staff; rooftop with Acropolis views; excellent price-to-quality ratio. **Cons:** a safe, albeit inner-city, location that may not be to everyone's taste; free Wi-Fi can be slow in rooms; cheapest rooms rather small. $ *Rooms from: €100* ✉ *Aristogeitonos 15, Psirri* ⊹ *At Athinas* ☎ *210/321–1770, 210/322–2706 reservations* ⊕ *www. athenscentersquarehotel.gr* ⬎ *54 rooms* ⧉ *Free breakfast* Ⓜ *Omonia.*

★ O&B Athens Boutique Hotel

$$$ | HOTEL | Each room in this boutique hotel with a sleek design and an outstanding restaurant-bar is a little haven of urban cool, thanks to flat-screen TVs, personal stereo/DVD systems, Molton Brown bath products, high-drama high-design color schemes, black minimalistic headboards, and soft, white Egyptian cotton sheets. **Pros:** beautiful rooms; excellent food; personalized service. **Cons:** all rooms but the penthouse have limited views; street not very attractive; pricey. $ *Rooms from: €260* ✉ *Leokoriou 7, Psirri* ☎ *210/331–2940* ⊕ *www.oandbhotel.com* ⬎ *27 rooms* ⧉ *Free breakfast* Ⓜ *Monastiraki.*

▽ Nightlife

BARS
★ Baba Au Rum

BARS/PUBS | Rum is the star at this trendy, popular bar in the heart of Monastiraki. All the liqueurs, syrups, and essences to flavor highly original and delicious cocktails are made in-house. The vibe is buzzy both indoors—where the decor has stylish yet quirky vintage touches like stained-glass lamps and antique drinking glasses—and out, where crowds gather especially on weekends. From tiki-inspired beverages to dark rum, chocolate, and lemon creations, you can spend hours experimenting here. Voted as one of the top 50 bars worldwide. ✉ *Klitiou 6, Monastiraki* ☎ *211/710–9140* ⊕ *babaaurum.com* Ⓜ *Monastiraki.*

Couleur Locale

BARS/PUBS | This youthful, scenic, and modish bar offers a different kind of local color than the usual walk-in or street-level place, as you'll have to enter an arcade selling antiques and take the elevator to the top floor of an old building to reach it. As you step out onto the roof, you'll come face to face with a stunning view of the Acropolis, the National Observatory, and the Anafiotika area—and after sunset all of them beautifully lit up. The cocktails are creative, the finger foods tasty, the music loud (there are regular DJ sets hosted), and the service friendly. ✉ *Normanou 3, Monastiraki* ☎ *216/700–4917* ⊕ *www.couleurlocaleathens.com* Ⓜ *Monastiraki.*

Six d.o.g.s

MUSIC CLUBS | You can choose to lounge at the bar or squeeze yourself into a bopping crowd to watch a top DJ or alternative electronica band do their thing. Or if you're the quiet-loving type, simply walk down the stairs to find yourself in a huge urban garden, where you can sip a cold beer and chat until late into the night. Since it opened in the early 2000s, this bar/club has never for a moment lost its edge, or popularity. ✉ *Avramiotou 6–8, Monastiraki* ☎ *210/321–0510* ⊕ *sixdogs. gr* Ⓜ *Monastiraki.*

360 Cocktail Bar

BARS/PUBS | With a menu of more than 70 cocktails and an extensive wine list, there is something for everyone at this rooftop bar in the heart of lively Monastiraki Square. An unexpected bonus is the magical view of the Acropolis. ✉ *Ifaistou 2, Monastiraki Sq., Monastiraki* ☎ *210/321–0006* ⊕ *www.three-sixty.gr* Ⓜ *Monastiraki.*

BREWERIES
Beertime

BREWPUBS/BEER GARDENS | Over the last few years Greece has exploded with microbreweries, with even ordinary supermarkets now selling at least a handful of exceptionally fresh, sometimes unpasteurized and always interestingly flavored beers. The ideal place for choosing among hundreds of labels of Greek craft beers is this pub in Psirri, where you can relax for hours watching the world go by. ✉ *Iroon Sq. 1, Psirri* ☎ *210/322–8443* ⊕ *www.beertime.gr* Ⓜ *Monastiraki.*

TAVERNAS WITH MUSIC
Cinque Wine Bar

BARS/PUBS | With wine-obsessed and highly knowledgeable owners, Cinque is a deli/wine bar where you can get to know some of the most unknown and fascinating Greek wines from around the country. The ambience is friendly, intimate, and warm and the staff is always happy to help you find the ideal label for your palate or to suggest pairings with the cheeses and cold cuts they serve. As this is a small place, book your table in advance. ✉ *Voreou 10, Psirri* ☎ *215/501–7853, 694/8496–002* ⊕ *www.cinque.gr* Ⓜ *Monastiraki.*

The Clumsies

BARS/PUBS | Located between Syntagma and Psirri, this innovative bar-restaurant is among the most popular in Athens and its barmen/owners have received several global mixology awards. The impressively decorated, multilevel venue even has a private room (for 10, which must be prebooked), where clients can order bespoke drinks. Despite its appeal to people of all ages and styles, The Clumsies is generally unpretentious, and the unique cocktails (there's a degustation menu that offers the chance of tasting four to five smaller versions) are top quality. Don't expect to find somewhere to sit on a weekend night. ✉ *Praxitelous 30, Monastiraki* ☎ *210/323–2682* ⊕ *www. theclumsies.gr* Ⓜ *Monastiraki, Syntagma.*

Klimataria

BARS/PUBS | FAMILY | On Wednesdays, Fridays, and Saturday evenings, a rembetika or traditional *laiko* band plays sing-along favorites much appreciated by the largely Greek crowd., and the price of the old-style Greek entertainment at this century-old taverna is surprisingly reasonable. Meanwhile, the food at this all-day taverna is displayed on big trays, which allows you to choose the dish of your choice with help from owners Mario and Pericles (the latter is also a noted rembetika singer). ✉ *Platia Theatrou 2, Psirri* ☎ *210/321–6629* ⊕ *www.klimataria. gr* Ⓜ *Monastiraki, Omonia.*

🛍 Shopping

ANTIQUES AND ICONS
Old Market

ANTIQUES/COLLECTIBLES | Old coins, from Greece and around the world, are for sale at this antiques shop, along with stamps, engravings, antique toys and radios, musical instruments, and medals. ✉ *Normanou 7, Monastiraki* ☎ *210/331–1638* ⊕ *www.oldmarket.gr* Ⓜ *Monastiraki.*

CLOTHING
★ Athens Remember Fashion

CLOTHING | A concept store with cult status since it opened in the 1970s, this is where you'll find everything from the perfect rockstar outfit to S&M-style punk accessories and hand-painted T-shirts with bold messages. Created by fashion designer Dimitris Tsaounatos and now run by his son, the rebelliously-natured shop has everything from original, hand-made, as well as vintage clothes and accessories. Hollywood A-listers and music legends come here from around the world to get decked out in outfits that they know they won't find any-where else. ⊠ *Eschilou 28, Monastiraki* ☎ *210/321–6409* Ⓜ *Monastiraki.*

Capelo Shop

JEWELRY/ACCESSORIES | FAMILY | What started as a small business in the 1940s has now become the Karfil hat empire, and this shop is the main storefront for the company's great creations, sold at outlets around the country. Whether you're a man, woman, or child you're sure to find the perfect stylish headgear at affordable prices. Select among fedoras, berets, trilbies, visors, floppies, caps, and straw creations in all shades and of premium quality. ⊠ *Aghias Eirinis 12, Psirri* ☎ *211/189–4189* ⊕ *www.capelo. shop* Ⓜ *Monastiraki.*

Thissio Θησείο

On the opposite side of the Agora is another meeting place of sorts: Thissio, a former red-light district that has been one of the most sought-after residential neighborhoods since the early 1990s. Easily accessible by metro and offering a lovely view of the Acropolis, it has become one of the liveliest café and restaurant districts in Athens. Mainly on Adrianou Street along the rail track, you'll find excellent *rakadika* and *ouzeri*—publike eateries that offer plates of appetizers to go with *raki,* a fiery spirit made from grape must; *rakomelo,* a mix of raki and honey heated to boiling; the ever-appealing ouzo; as well as barrels of homemade wine. On a summer evening, walk to the main strip on the Nileos pedestrian zone to sit at an outdoor table in summer in local style, or perch yourself under the Acropolis on Apostolou

Pavlou Street. The rest of the neighborhood is quiet, an odd mix of mom-and-pop stores and dilapidated houses that are slowly being renovated.

◉ Sights

Melina Mercouri Cultural Centre

MUSEUM | Named in honor of the famous *Never on Sunday* Greek actress who became a political figure in the 1980s, this center is installed in the former Poulopoulos hat factory built in 1886. Throughout the year the center has a calendar of temporary exhibitions, usually featuring contemporary Greek art. But the permanent collection is interesting, too. Several rooms give a rare glimpse of Athens during the 19th century. You can walk through a reconstructed Athens street with facades of neoclassical homes that evoke the civilized elegance of the past, along with a pharmacy, printing press, tailor's, *kafeneio* (coffeehouse), a mayor's home, and hairdressers, all painstakingly fitted out with authentic objects collected by the Greek Literary and Historical Archives. The other permanent exhibition showcases the shadow theater puppets of the traditional Greek shadow theater (*Karagiozis*), thanks to a vast collection amassed by the Haridimos performing family. ⊠ *Iraklidon 66a, at Thessalonikis, Thissio* ☎ *210/345–2150* 🎫 *Free* ⊗ *Closed Mon.* Ⓜ *Thissio.*

🍴 Restaurants

Thissio's pedestrianized streets are perfect meeting points for coffee lovers, but the mezedopoleia here are also of a high caliber and offer beautiful Acropolis views.

★ Kuzina

$$$ | GREEK FUSION | Kuzina may be sleek, dazzlingly decorated, and moodily lit, but it's not just a pretty face. The food—especially the inventive seafood and pasta dishes—is among the best in Athens, standing out on touristy

Adrianou. The main room soars skyward, glittering with birdcage chandeliers and factory ducts, with a vast oak-covered gray bar set below a spotlit wall lined with hundreds of wine bottles. The menu showcases newfangled and alternative Greek dishes with traditional touches as well as some Asian influences such as salmon with ponzu sauce and spicy tuna with ginger-soy sauce. Cocktails are to be relished on the rooftop terrace, blessed by very drinkable views of the Acropolis. If you can tear yourself away from that, visit the Porta art gallery on the second floor. **Known for:** 12-hour pork with pineapple salad; great pedestrianized location; scenic rooftop for delicious drinks. $ Average main: €30 ⊠ Adrianou 9, Thissio ☎ 210/324–0133 ⊕ www.kuzina.gr Ⓜ Thissio.

To Steki tou Ilia
$$ | STEAKHOUSE | FAMILY | Unpretentious and overall unremarkable, this restaurant is justifiably famous for its freshly grilled *paidakia* (lamb chops), to be eaten with unabashed gusto by hand. It's always busy and always a great escape from an increasingly modernized city, but avoid the *hima* wine, which almost certainly leads to a headache. Enjoy your lamb with thick-cut fried potatoes that might have come from your yiayia's kitchen and perhaps some tzatziki or fava bean spread. The meat taverna's popularity led to the opening of a second branch farther down the same road and an extension across the pedestrianized Eptahalkou Street into a garden area. **Known for:** lamb chops with thick fries and tzatziki; a relaxed village vibe in the heart of the city; lovely garden. $ Average main: €17 ⊠ Eptachalkou 5, Thissio ☎ 210/345–8052 ▭ No credit cards ⊙ No dinner Sun. Ⓜ Thissio.

☕ Coffee and Quick Bites

Athinaion Politeia
$ | CAFÉ | For a fancy coffee (think espresso mixed with Sambuca), sweet crêpes, or an impromptu meal, stop at this restored neoclassical-style mansion and watch the crowds on Apostolou Pavlou. The seating in the square in front of the restaurant bordering the ancient agora has one of the best views of the Acropolis in town. **Known for:** people-watching; good coffee; Acropolis view. $ Average main: €8 ⊠ Akamantos 1, at Apostolou Pavlou 33, Thissio ☎ 210/341–3795 Ⓜ Thissio.

🎭 Performing Arts

FILM
★ **Cine Thisio**
FILM | Films at this open-air theater, among the oldest in Athens (dating from 1935), come complete with a view of the Acropolis. It's on the Unification of Archaeological Sites walkway and conveniently offers tables among the seating, for your film-munchies spread. In fact, the bar sells homemade cheese pie, sour cherry juice, and *tsipouro* accompanied with bottarga fish roe from Messolonghi. ⊠ Apostolou Pavlou 7, Thissio ☎ 210/342–0864, 210/347–0980 ⊕ www.cine-thisio.gr Ⓜ Thissio.

🏃 Activities

SPAS
★ **Hammam Baths**
FITNESS/HEALTH CLUBS | For an ancient-modern steam bath experience head to Hammam Baths, a gorgeous neoclassical house that has been converted into a full-amenities day spa with Eastern decorative undertones and excellent service. Prices start at €25. ⊠ Ayion Asomaton 17, Thissio ☎ 210/323-1073 ⊕ www.hammam.gr Ⓜ Thissio.

Syntagma Συντάγματος

From the Tomb of the Unknown Soldier to Queen Amalia's National Garden, to the top of Mt. Lycabettus, to a cluster of top museums, this center-city sector is packed with cultural marvels and wonders of old. Paradoxically, in crisis-hit Athens it has also blossomed into a newly stylish and popular hangout for coffee, dinner, and drinks. Sooner or later, everyone passes through the capital's heart, the spacious Syntagma (Constitution) Square, which is surrounded by remnants of Athens's history from the days of the Roman emperors to King Otto's reign after the 1821 War of Independence. Some may have likened his palace (now the Parliament) to a barracks, but things could have been much worse: Otto's father, King Ludwig I of Bavaria, vetoed plans for a royal residence atop the Acropolis itself, a plan that would have used one end of the Parthenon as the entrance and blown up the rest. The palace was finished just in time for Otto to grant the constitution of 1843, which gave the square its name. Besides culture-hopping, you can spend time window-shopping and people-watching; nursing a single coffee for hours remains not only socially acceptable but a vital survival tactic in frequently stressful modern Greek life.

Sights

★ National Garden

BUILDING | FAMILY | When you can't take the city noise anymore, step into this oasis completed in 1860 as part of King Otto and Queen Amalia's royal holdings. Here old men on the benches argue politics, children run free among lush nature, runners count early-morning jog laps, and animal lovers feed the stray cats that roam among the more than 500 species of trees and plants, many labeled. At the east end is the neoclassical **Zappeion Hall,** built in 1888 as an Olympic building (with funds from Greek benefactor Evangelos Zappas). Since then it has been used for major political and cultural events: it was here that Greece signed its accession to what was then the European Community. Next door, the leafy Aegli Zappiou café and open-air cinema attract Athenians year-round. Cross the road to the nearby Panathenaic Stadium, which was built on the very site of an ancient stadium for the revived Olympic Games in 1896. You can look at the stadium only from the outside, but there is an elevated dirt running track behind it (free entrance through a big gate on Archimidous Street, which runs directly behind the stadium). The tree-lined track area and adjacent Ardittos hill constitute one of the most pleasant, quiet public spaces in the city—they also offer some stunning vantage points. Children appreciate the playground, duck pond, and small zoo at the east end of the National Garden. ⊠ Syntagma ☎ 210/323–7830 ⊕ www.zappeion.gr ☉ Gates shut at sunset Ⓜ Syntagma.

National Historical Museum

MUSEUM | After making the rounds of the ancient sites, you might think that Greek history ground to a halt when the Byzantine Empire collapsed. A visit to this gem of a museum, housed in the spectacularly majestic Old Parliament mansion (used by parliamentarians from 1875 to 1932), will fill in the gaps, often vividly, as with Lazaros Koyevina's copy of Eugene Delacroix's *Massacre of Chios*, to name but one example. Paintings, costumes, and assorted artifacts from small arms to flags and ships' figureheads are arranged in a chronological display tracing Greek history from the mid-16th century and the Battle of Lepanto through World War II and the Battle of Crete. A small gift shop near the main entrance—framed by a very grand neoclassical portico of columns—has unusual souvenirs, like a deck of cards featuring Greece's revolutionary heroes. ⊠ Old Parliament

Syntagma, Kolonaki, Exarchia, Pangrati, and Ilisia

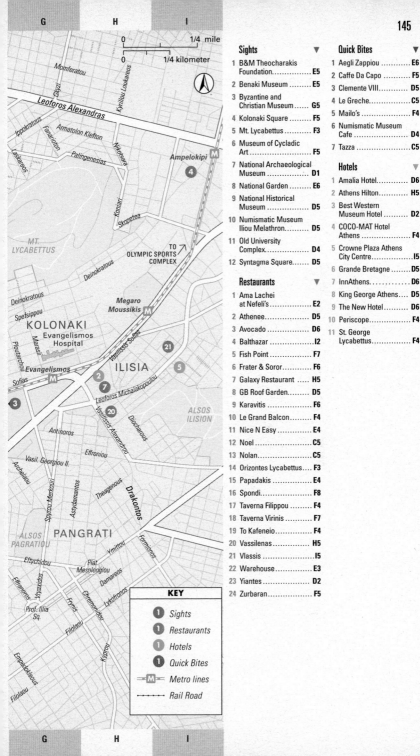

0   1/4 mile
0   1/4 kilometer

Momferatou
Leoforos Alexandras
Ippokratous
Armatolon Klefton
Fanarioton
Patingenesias
Lastareos
Kyrillou Loukareos
Niketara
Komari
Skopetea
Ampelokipi **M**
④

MT. LYCABETTUS
TO
OLYMPIC SPORTS COMPLEX

Deinokratous
Deinokratous
Spefsippou
Megaro Moussikis **M**
KOLONAKI
Evangelismos Hospital
Vasilissis Sofias
Marasli
Ploutarchou
Evangelismos M
Sofias
ILISIA
Leoforos Michalakopoulou
②⑤
⑦
③
⑳
Vasilissis Alexandrou
Diocharous
ALSOS ILISION
Antinoros
Effroniou
Vasil. Georgiou II.
Archelaou
Spirou Merkouri
Astydamantos
Theagenous
Drakontos
Eftychidou
Plat. Mesolongiou
Damareos
Ymittou
Formionos
ALSOS PANGRATI
PANGRATI
Vryzaxidos
Efthenoros
Chremonidou
Lykofronos
Prof. Illia Sq.
Filolaou
Frynis
Kiprou
Filolaou
Empedokleous
Filolaou

Sights ▼
1 B&M Theocharakis Foundation................. **E5**
2 Benaki Museum **E5**
3 Byzantine and Christian Museum **G5**
4 Kolonaki Square **F5**
5 Mt. Lycabettus **F3**
6 Museum of Cycladic Art **F5**
7 National Archaeological Museum **D1**
8 National Garden **E6**
9 National Historical Museum **D5**
10 Numismatic Museum Iliou Melathron.......... **D5**
11 Old University Complex................. **D4**
12 Syntagma Square....... **D5**

Restaurants ▼
1 Ama Lachei at Nefeli's................. **E2**
2 Athenee................. **D5**
3 Avocado **D6**
4 Balthazar **I2**
5 Fish Point **F7**
6 Frater & Soror............ **F6**
7 Galaxy Restaurant **H5**
8 GB Roof Garden......... **D5**
9 Karavitis **F6**
10 Le Grand Balcon.......... **F4**
11 Nice N Easy **E4**
12 Noel **C5**
13 Nolan..................... **C5**
14 Orizontes Lycabettus.... **F3**
15 Papadakis **E4**
16 Spondi..................... **F8**
17 Taverna Filippou **F4**
18 Taverna Virinis **F7**
19 To Kafeneio.............. **F4**
20 Vassilenas............... **H5**
21 Vlassis **I5**
22 Warehouse............... **E3**
23 Yiantes **D2**
24 Zurbaran................. **F5**

Quick Bites ▼
1 Aegli Zappiou **E6**
2 Caffe Da Capo **F5**
3 Clemente VIII............. **D5**
4 Le Greche................. **C5**
5 Mailo's **F4**
6 Numismatic Museum Cafe **D4**
7 Tazza **C5**

Hotels ▼
1 Amalia Hotel............. **D6**
2 Athens Hilton............ **H5**
3 Best Western Museum Hotel **D2**
4 COCO-MAT Hotel Athens **F4**
5 Crowne Plaza Athens City Centre................ **I5**
6 Grande Bretagne **D5**
7 InnAthens............... **D6**
8 King George Athens..... **D5**
9 The New Hotel **D6**
10 Periscope................. **F4**
11 St. George Lycabettus................ **F4**

KEY
① Sights
① Restaurants
① Hotels
① Quick Bites
M Metro lines
Rail Road

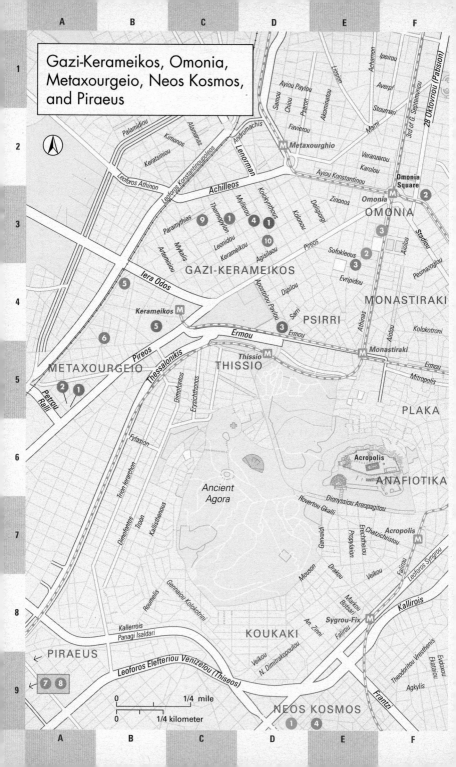

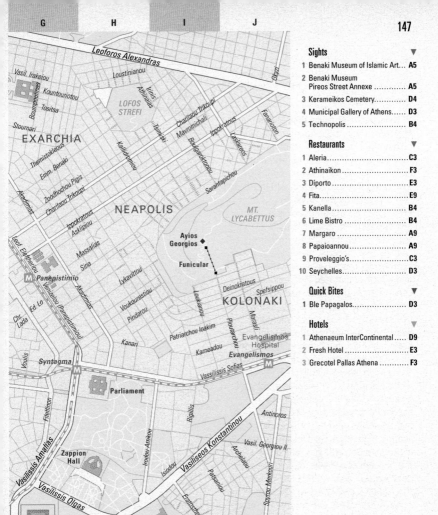

Sights ▼

1 Benaki Museum of Islamic Art... **A5**
2 Benaki Museum
  Pireos Street Annexe **A5**
3 Kerameikos Cemetery............. **D4**
4 Municipal Gallery of Athens...... **D3**
5 Technopolis **B4**

Restaurants ▼

1 Aleria.................................**C3**
2 Athinaikon **F3**
3 Díporto **E3**
4 Fita...................................**E9**
5 Kanella **B4**
6 Lime Bistro **B4**
7 Margaro **A9**
8 Papaioannou......................**A9**
9 Proveleggio's......................**C3**
10 Seychelles.........................**D3**

Quick Bites ▼

1 Ble Papagalos.....................**D3**

Hotels ▼

1 Athenaeum InterContinental **D9**
2 Fresh Hotel **E3**
3 Grecotel Pallas Athena **F3**

Building, Stadiou 13, Syntagma ☎ *210/323–7617, 210/323–7315* ⊕ *www. nhmuseum.gr* 🎫 *€3* ⊙ *Closed Mon.* Ⓜ *Syntagma.*

★ **Numismatic Museum Iliou Melathron**

MUSEUM | Even those uninterested in coins might want to visit this museum for a glimpse of the former home of Heinrich Schliemann, who famously excavated Troy and Mycenae in the 19th century. Built by the Bavarian architect Ernst Ziller for the archaeologist's family and baptized the "Iliou Melathron" (or Palace of Troy), it flaunts an imposing neo-Venetian facade. Inside are some spectacular rooms, including the vast and floridly decorated Hesperides Hall, a shimmer with colored marbles and neo-Pompeian wall paintings. Today, in this exquisite Neoclassical mansion, seemingly haunted by the spirit of the great historian, you can see more than 600,000 coins, including those from the archaeologist's own collection, as well as 4th-century BC measures employed against forgers and coins grouped according to what they depict—animals, plants, myths, and famous buildings like the Lighthouse of Alexandria. The museum's peaceful garden café is a tranquil and cozy oasis ideal for a rendezvous. ✉ *Panepistimiou 12, Syntagma* ☎ *210/363–2057, 210/361–2834* ⊕ *www. nummus.gr* 🎫 *€6; €15 for unified museum ticket (includes National Archaeological Museum, Epigraphical Museu, Byzantine and Christian Museum)* ⊙ *Closed Tues.* Ⓜ *Syntagma or Panepistimiou.*

Syntagma Square (*Constitution Square*)

PLAZA | At the top of the city's main square stands the **Greek Parliament,** formerly King Otto's royal palace, completed in 1838 for the new monarchy. It seems a bit austere and heavy for a southern landscape, but it was proof of progress, the symbol of the new ruling power. The building's saving grace is the stone's magical change of color from off-white to gold to rosy-mauve as the

Changing of the Guards

Near the Parliament, you can watch the **Changing of the Evzones Guards** at the Tomb of the Unknown Soldier—in front of Parliament on a lower level—which takes place at intervals throughout the day. On Sunday the honor guard of tall young men don a dress costume—a short white and very heavy *foustanella* (kilt) with 400 neat pleats, one for each year of the Ottoman occupation, and red shoes with pom-poms—and still manage to look brawny rather than silly. A band accompanies them.

day progresses. Here you can watch the **Changing of the Evzones Guards** at the **Tomb of the Unknown Soldier**—in front of Parliament on a lower level—which takes place at intervals throughout the day. On a wall behind the Tomb of the Unknown Soldier, the bas-relief of a dying soldier is modeled after a sculpture on the Temple of Aphaia in Aegina; the text is from the funeral oration said to have been given by Pericles.

Pop into the gleaming Syntagma metro station to examine artfully displayed artifacts uncovered during subway excavations. A floor-to-ceiling cross section of earth behind glass shows finds in chronological layers, ranging from a skeleton in its ancient grave to traces of the 4th-century BC road to Mesogeia to an Ottoman cistern.

This is the capital's key zone for mass demonstrations and protests, Christmas celebrations (the city's tree is set up here), and political speeches. It is increasingly a hot spot for shopping or a rendezvous at the many nearby trendy cafés, top notch restaurants, and a

For patriotic Greeks, the Changing of the Guard in front of the Tomb of the Unknown Soldier is always a heart-stirring ceremony.

growing number of ethnic street food places. ⊠ *Vasilissis Amalias and Vasilissis Sofias, Syntagma* Ⓜ *Syntagma.*

🍴 Restaurants

Syntagma, a bustling central square between Parliament and Ermou Street, is also popular with tourists.

Athenee

$$$ | MODERN GREEK | FAMILY | Famously known as Zonars until falling into new ownership recently, Athenee is one of Athens's most established and elegant restaurant-cafés, where a multitude of international film stars, academics, and politicians have sipped their coffee since 1939. The plush decor, elegant atmosphere and sophisticated crowd create a feeling of nostalgic old-style luxury combined with modern urban liveliness. Throughout the day Athenee caters to all culinary desires, offering plush brunches, modern Greek dishes, exciting varieties of sushi, mouth-watering pastries, and perfectly mixed cocktails. **Known for:** a long and glamorous history; it's a cultural institution; delicious pastries; a perfect location for business chats. $ *Average main: €25* ⊠ *Voukourestiou 9 & Panepistimiou, Syntagma* ☎ *210/325–1430* ⊕ *www.atheneeathens.gr* ⊙ *Closed Sunday* Ⓜ *Syntagma.*

Avocado

$ | VEGETARIAN | FAMILY | For such a tiny spot in a narrow street just off Syntagma Square, this small but stylish vegetarian favorite has many devoted fans. The veg and vegan comfort food appeals to health-conscious diners who appreciate the friendly atmosphere and internationally focused menu. Options include mock burgers, pizza, and heartwarming curries. Its nutritious juices, teas, and smoothies helped start a juice bar trend in the capital. Big hits are the Margherita pizza, vegetable curries and stir-frys, and the forest mushroom burger. **Known for:** vegan and vegetarian cuisine; delicious smoothies and juices; macrobiotic and gluten-free options. $ *Average main: €12* ⊠ *Nikis 30, Syntagma* ☎ *210/323–7878* ⊕ *www.avocadoathens. com* ⊙ *No dinner Sun.* Ⓜ *Syntagma.*

★ GB Roof Garden

$$$$ | **MODERN GREEK** | With a skillfully-curated modern Greek-Mediterranean menu of haute cuisine dishes and an excellent wine list, this classic restaurant on the rooftop of the legendary Grand Bretagne hotel makes for an idyllic fine dining experience. Premium meats, hand-picked seasonal ingredients, and the freshest fish are served. Add to that some of the most stunning 360-degree views of the city under the twinkling sky and abundant greenery all around and you're sure to enjoy a stellar dinner. **Known for:** fantastic city views, including the Acropolis; creative and flavorsome gourmet dishes; a stylish VIP crowd. [$] *Average main: €50* ✉ *Vas. Georgiou 1A, Syntagma Square, Syntagma* ☎ *210/333–0766* 🌐 *www.gbroofgarden.gr* [M] *Syntagma.*

Noel

$$ | **MEDITERRANEAN** | A recent addition to the trendy Syntagma nightlife scene, Noel is the kind of bar-restaurant that people talk about with a smile on their face. The casual and modern Mediterranean menu is wide-ranging and internationally oriented, including everything from pizzas to pastas to chicken curry. Its bold "holiday" theme is bolstered by a high-ceilinged interior decorated with exotically dark Italian Renaissance art juxtaposed with in-your-face Christmas-inspired glee in the form of twinkling lights and feel-good tunes. The avant-garde cocktail menu is inspired by dramatic figures like the Lord of Lombardy. **Known for:** cheerful holiday theme; excellent and innovative cocktails; brunch. [$] *Average main: €20* ✉ *Kolokotroni 59B, Syntagma* ☎ *211/215–9534* 🌐 *noelbar.gr* [M] *Syntagma.*

Nolan

$$ | **MODERN GREEK** | With a near-cultish following since it opened a few years ago, Nolan is the only restaurant in town serving original Greek-Asian cuisine, creatively prepared with Michelin-style attention by its Greek-Japanese executive chef/owner. The dishes here are designed to be shared, so diners can taste as many of the intriguing combinations of fusion ingredients as possible. The food is sophisticated, sometimes complex, yet always comforting and fun. **Known for:** original, playful recipes; unique, comforting flavors; uplifting vibe. [$] *Average main: €20* ✉ *Voulis 31–33, Syntagma* ☎ *210/324–3545* 🌐 *www.nolanrestaurant.gr* 🕒 *Closed Sun.* [M] *Syntagma.*

☕ Coffee and Quick Bites

★ Aeglí Zappiou

$$ | **MEDITERRANEAN** | Visit the elegant Aeglí Zappiou, an excellent spot for a classic Greek coffee experience. Nestled among fountains and flowering trees next to the Zappio Exhibition Hall in the National Garden, it's an ideal spot to sample a fresh dessert or some haute cuisine, or watch a movie at the open-air Cine Aegli next door. Adjacent to this café is the noted Cibus restaurant, which offers a special *degustation* menu of modern Greek cuisine every Wednesday evening (reservations recommended). **Known for:** good desserts; great coffee; views of open-air Cine Aegli next door. [$] *Average main: €15* ✉ *Zappio Megaro, Syntagma* ☎ *210/336–9300* 🌐 *www.aeglizappiou.gr* [M] *Syntagma.*

Le Greche

$ | **ITALIAN** | There's nothing like an ice cream to revive flailing, sweaty spirits on a hot day of touring the city. Le Greche serves fresh, handmade ice cream made with pure ingredients and inspired by Italian gelato, as well as cakes and sorbets. **Known for:** high-quality ice cream and sorbet; central location; good coffee. [$] *Average main: €5* ✉ *16 Mitropoleos, Syntagma* ☎ *216/700–6458* 💳 *No credit cards* [M] *Syntagma.*

Numismatic Museum Cafe

$ | **CAFÉ** | Sip quality coffee in the pretty garden setting of a neoclassical mansion-turned-museum. Whether you want to see the country's most extensive collection of coins spanning through the ages or just head for the café to meet a friend, the experience is always pleasant. The menu includes salads, light snacks, and desserts as well as wine and soft drinks. **Known for:** live jazz music every Thursday night; sophisticated and scenic ambience; good coffee. ⓢ *Average main: €5* ✉ *Panepistimiou 12, Syntagma* ☎ *210/363-2057* ⊕ *www.nummus.gr* Ⓜ *Syntagma.*

Tazza

$ | **CAFÉ** | Colorful vintage lampshades, flowers, and romantic-style crockery make this corner cafe-bistro a delightful spot to stop for coffee and cake or wine and salad. Located on a small pedestrianized street a few minutes' walk from Syntagma square it's also ideal for a break from shopping on Ermou Street. In the colder months customers sitting outdoors are warmed by foor heater lamps and blankets, while indoors you can enjoy the elaborate 17th-century decor. **Known for:** pretty, vintage decor; cozy atmosphere; good coffee and desserts. ⓢ *Average main: €10* ✉ *Petraki 5 & Pentelis 9, Syntagma* ☎ *210/331–1999* Ⓜ *Syntagma.*

 Hotels

Amalia Hotel

$$ | **HOTEL** | **FAMILY** | The central location and competitive prices are the main attractions here for most visitors—it's right on one of Athens's biggest, busiest streets, directly across from Parliament, but double-glazed windows (fortunately) and a view to the pretty National Garden keep things peaceful inside. **Pros:** perfect central location; easy access to transport, to Plaka, and to the pretty National Garden; free Wi-Fi. **Cons:** on a busy thoroughfare; no restaurant at the hotel, just a snack bar; front rooms can be a bit noisy. ⓢ *Rooms from: €160* ✉ *Amalias 10, Syntagma* ☎ *210/323–7300* ⊕ *www.amalia.gr* ⟿ *97 rooms* ⦿ *Free breakfast* Ⓜ *Syntagma.*

★ Grande Bretagne

$$$$ | **HOTEL** | **FAMILY** | With a guest list that includes more than a century's worth of royals, rock stars, and heads of state, the landmark Grande Bretagne remains the most exclusive hotel in Athens. **Pros:** all-out luxury; exquisite rooms; excellent café, spa, and pool lounge. **Cons:** expensive; decor may not suit all tastes; demonstrations take place at Syntagma Square. ⓢ *Rooms from: €450* ✉ *Vasileos Georgiou A'1 at Syntagma Sq., Syntagma* ☎ *210/333–0000, 210/331–5555 through 210/331–5559 reservations* ⊕ *www.grandebretagne.gr* ⟿ *320 rooms* ⦿ *Free breakfast* Ⓜ *Syntagma.*

★ InnAthens

$$ | **HOTEL** | **FAMILY** | Five minutes' walk from Syntagma Square is this homey 20-room boutique hotel built from a renovated neoclassical building with minimalist decor, that draws travelers with its helpful, friendly service and great, included breakfast. **Pros:** excellent service; great location; delicious breakfast made with fresh, seasonal ingredients. **Cons:** some rooms a bit boxy; not ideal for wheelchair users; water pressure is low. ⓢ *Rooms from: €165* ✉ *Georgiou Sourri 3, Syntagma* ✛ *At Filellinon* ☎ *210/325–8555* ⊕ *www.innathens.com* ⟿ *22 rooms* ⦿ *Free breakfast* Ⓜ *Syntagma.*

★ King George Athens

$$$$ | **HOTEL** | One of the most historic and luxurious hotels in Athens, the King George is where numerous celebrities stay (often in the Royal Penthouse suite), and first impressions tell you why: a spacious lobby done in marble, mahogany, velvet, leather, and gold trim lures you into a world where antique crystal lamps and frosted glass shower stalls with mother-of-pearl tiles raise standards of luxury to dizzying heights. **Pros:**

outstanding food; luxurious rooms; attentive service. **Cons:** slow elevators; thin walls in some rooms; no pool. $ *Rooms from: €401* ✉ *3 Vasileos Georgiou A, Syntagma* ☎ *210/322–2210* ⊕ *www.king-georgeathens.com* ⮡ *102 rooms* ⦿| *Free breakfast* Ⓜ *Syntagma.*

★ The New Hotel

$$ | HOTEL | The cutting-edge New Hotel was heralded as an aesthetic triumph in the inner city's ever-changing landscape when it opened in 2011, and it has maintained its edge, attracting guests who still prefer something avant-garde. **Pros:** helpful staff; sumptuous breakfast; great spa. **Cons:** pricey pay-per-view TV; front-facing rooms can be noisy; may be a bit too avant-garde for some. $ *Rooms from: €200* ✉ *Filellinon 16, Syntagma* ☎ *210/327–3000* ⊕ *www.yeshotels. gr* ⮡ *79 rooms* ⦿| *Free breakfast* Ⓜ *Syntagma.*

Nightlife

BARS

Heteroclito

WINE BARS—NIGHTLIFE | This small and elegant wine bar focuses exclusively on Greek wines, and has knowledgeable owners who will help you navigate their extensive wine list. The vibe is breezy and relaxed, somewhat reminiscent of a Parisian street café, where you can dawdle for hours sipping a perfect glass of wine. ✉ *Fokionos 2, at Petraki 30, Syntagma* ☎ *210/323–9406* ⊕ *www. heteroclito.gr* Ⓜ *Syntagma.*

★ Oinoscent

WINE BARS—NIGHTLIFE | If you'd like to learn about Greek wine using both your mind and your taste buds, this modern bar with bold yellow walls and high stools is the place for you. Serving some 50 Greek labels by the glass among a selection of 500, this wine cellar–turned–wine bar/restaurant is popular for its high-quality wines, educationally minded staff (it is run by a team of wine experts),

and foods that pair well with what you choose to drink. ✉ *Voulis 45–47, Syntagma* ☎ *210/322–9374* Ⓜ *Syntagma.*

Shopping

ACCESSORIES

Attica City Link

CLOTHING | At Attica you'll find everything and anything you need from top designer brands (mainly foreign but also some Greek). From cosmetics to clothes and accessories, you can pop by for a look or hours of shopping therapy. ✉ *Panepistimiou 9, Syntagma* ☎ *211/180–2600* ⊕ *www.atticadps.gr* Ⓜ *Syntagma.*

Ippolito

SHOES/LUGGAGE/LEATHER GOODS | Luxurious bags, handcrafted in Athens using Italian leather, are sold here in addition to elegant straw and linen backpacks (with men's designs thrown into the mix) and even a back-friendly maternity range. Prices are as high as the quality. ✉ *Voulis 38, Syntagma* ☎ *210/331–5051* ⊕ *www.facebook.com/IppolitoWorld/* Ⓜ *Syntagma.*

ANTIQUES AND ICONS

Roussos Antiques

ANTIQUES/COLLECTIBLES | Here you will find a wide array of carefully selected Greek, European, and Asian antiques ranging from as far as ancient Greece to the Byzantium to the 18th and 19th centuries. Artworks, jewelry, statuettes, antiquities, Greek Orthodox religious icons, and home decor objects are among the store's tasteful selection. The store has existed since 1920. ✉ *Stadiou 3, Syntagma* ☎ *210/322–2815* ⊕ *www.roussosantiques.gr/en/homeen* Ⓜ *Syntagma.*

CLOTHING

Anamesa Concept Store

CLOTHING | You'll first hear the music coming from down the stairs, where the store is quirkily located. The originality and surprise of its location is expanded upon entering and observing the designer items, including clothes and accessories for men, women, and children created by Greek and foreign new fashion visionaries. Simple home decor items, cosmetics, hair accessories, and jewelry are also sold here, always obeying the store's minimal, modern, and "funky" styleguide. And there's coffee "with a twist," too. ⊠ *Nikis 24, Syntagma* ☎ *210/325–4930* ⊕ *anamesaspot.com* Ⓜ *Syntagma.*

GIFTS

★ Diplous Pelekys

GIFTS/SOUVENIRS | A large variety of hand-woven articles, genuine folk art, ceramics from all over Greece, and traditional and modern jewelry all on show here make excellent, and affordable, gifts. The cozy and tasteful shop is run by third-generation weavers and is the oldest folk-art shop in Athens (established 1925). ⊠ *Bolani Arcade, Voulis 7 and Kolokotroni 3, Syntagma* ☎ *210/322–3783* ⊕ *www. diplouspelekis.gr* Ⓜ *Syntagma.*

Fresh Line

GIFTS/SOUVENIRS | Among the solid shampoo cakes, body oils, lotions, and face masks sold here are a tremendous number of organic Greek-made soaps, most sliced from big blocks or wheels, which you pay for by weight. Try the watermelon soap, shimmering fizzing ball, and the soothing body soufflé. ⊠ *Ermou 30, Syntagma* ☎ *210/324–6500* ⊕ *www. freshline.gr* Ⓜ *Syntagma.*

Korres

GIFTS/SOUVENIRS | The flagship store of this cosmetics line sells a broad variety of the company's popular namesake cosmetics, from body lotions and soaps to shower gels and makeup. ⊠ *Ermou 4, Syntagma* ☎ *210/321–0054* Ⓜ *Syntagma.*

Mastiha Shop

FOOD/CANDY | Medical research lauding the healing properties of gum mastic, a resin from trees found only on the Greek island of Chios, has spawned a range of exciting wellness products, from chewing gum and cookies to liqueurs and cosmetics. The chain was originally founded by the Chios Mastiha Growers Association. ⊠ *Panepistimiou 6, at Kriezotou, Syntagma* ☎ *210/363–2750* Ⓜ *Syntagma.*

Tanagrea

GIFTS/SOUVENIRS | Hand-painted ceramic pomegranates—a symbol of fertility and good fortune—are one of the most popular of the multitude of Greek decor items in one of the city's oldest gift shops. ⊠ *Petraki 3, Syntagma* ⊹ *Enter from Ermou 11* ☎ *210/321–6783* ⊕ *tanagrea.gr* Ⓜ *Syntagma.*

JEWELRY

★ Lalaounis

ANTIQUES/COLLECTIBLES | This world-famous Greek jewelry house experiments with its designs, taking ideas from nature, biology, African art, and ancient Greek pieces—the last are sometimes so close to the original that they're mistaken for museum artifacts. The pieces are mainly in gold, some in silver—look out for the decorative objects inspired by ancient Greek housewares. ⊠ *Panepistimiou 6, at Voukourestiou, Syntagma* ☎ *210/361–1371* ⊕ *www.lalaounis.gr* Ⓜ *Syntagma.*

Zolotas

JEWELRY/ACCESSORIES | Since it opened in 1895, this jewelry boutique has been favored by Athens's crème de la crème, visiting dignitaries, and grateful receivers of magnificent gold gifts. Designs inspired by ancient Greece and Byzantium are as stunning as the modern ones. ⊠ *Panepistimiou 10, Kolonaki* ☎ *210/360–1272* ⊕ *www.zolotas.gr* Ⓜ *Syntagma.*

Gazi-Kerameikos
Γκάζι-Κεραμεικός

Gazi-Kerameikos takes its name from the industrial gas works that even today dominate the neighborhood's landscape. The plant that used to provide gas for lighting and power throughout the city (called Technopolis) is now a cultural center offering festivals, temporary exhibitions, and open-air concerts. A slew of bars, clubs (with a zone popular among the LGBT community), and restaurants have made the neighborhood a lively nightlife area conveniently served by the sleek Kerameikos metro station.

Sights

Benaki Museum of Islamic Art

MUSEUM | FAMILY | Housed in a gleaming white neoclassical mansion with a sweeping view of the Kerameikos cemetery (that can be relished over coffee at the rooftop café), this annex of the Benaki Museum provides a welcoming home to its extensive Islamic art collection (which is considered among the most important in the world). More than 8,000 pieces of art hail from regions as widely spread geographically as North Africa, India, Persia, Asia Minor, Arabia, Mesopotamia, and even Sicily and Spain. ⊠ Dipilou 12, at Ag. Asomaton 22, Gazi-Kerameikos ☎ 210/325–1311 ⊕ www.benaki.gr ⊠ Permanent collection €9; temporary exhibitions €7 ⊗ Closed Mon.–Wed ⓂKerameikos.

Benaki Museum Pireos Street Annexe

MUSEUM | The eye-knocking Benaki Museum Annexe is located at one of the busiest and most industrially developed points in the city. The minimalist exterior is covered in smooth pink stone—a kind of beacon of modernity—with creatively designed clean lines on the dusty, loud avenue. Inside, all is high-ceilinged atriums, transparent walkway ascents, and multiple levels, a dramatic setting for the museum's temporary exhibitions (many of which are far more avant-garde in character than those housed in the main building). ⊠ Pireos 138, Gazi-Kerameikos ⊹ At Andronikou St. ☎ 210/345–3111 ⊕ www.benaki.gr ⊠ €5–€8 (varies by special exhibit) ⊗ Closed Mon.–Wed. and Aug. Ⓜ Kerameikos.

★ Kerameikos Cemetery

ARCHAEOLOGICAL SITE | At the western edge of the modern Gazi district lies the wide, ancient green expanse of Kerameikos, the main cemetery in ancient Athens until Sulla destroyed the city in 86 BC. The name is associated with the modern word "ceramic": in the 12th century BC the district was populated by potters who used the abundant clay from the languid Iridanos River to make funerary urns and grave decorations. From the 7th century BC onward, Kerameikos was the fashionable cemetery of ancient Athens. During succeeding ages cemeteries were superimposed on the ancient one until the latter was discovered in 1861. From the main entrance, you can still see remains of the **Makra Teixi** (Long Walls) of Themistocles, which ran to Piraeus, and the largest gate in the ancient world, the **Dipylon Gate,** where visitors entered Athens. The walls rise to 10 feet, a fraction of their original height (up to 45 feet). Here was also the **Sacred Gate,** used by pilgrims headed to the mysterious rites in Eleusis and by those who participated in the Panathenaic procession, which followed the Sacred Way. Between the two gates are the foundations of the **Pompeion,** the starting point of the Panathenaic procession. It is said the courtyard was large enough to fit the ship used in the procession. On the **Street of Tombs,** which branches off the Sacred Way, plots were reserved for affluent Athenians. A number of the distinctive *stelae* (funerary monuments) remain, including a replica of the marble relief of Dexilios, a knight who died in the war against Corinth (394 BC); he is shown on horseback preparing to spear a fallen foe. To the left of the site's entrance is the **Oberlaender Museum,** also known as the Kerameikos Museum, whose displays include sculpture, terra-cotta figures, and some striking red-and-black-figured pottery. The extensive grounds of Kerameikos are marshy in some spots; in spring, frogs exuberantly croak their mating songs near magnificent stands of lilies. ✉ *Ermou 148, Gazi-Kerameikos* ☎ *210/346–3552* 🌐 *odysseus.culture.gr* 🎫 *Full: €8 site and museum; €30 joint ticket for all Unification of Archaeological Sites* [M] *Kerameikos.*

Technopolis

FESTIVAL | Gazi, the neighborhood surrounding this former 19th-century-gas-works-turned-arts-complex, takes its name from the toxic gas fumes that used to spew from the factory's smokestacks. Today Gazi district is synonymous with an intellectual gallery scene and buzzy nightlife, with a special LGBT-friendly zone to boot. The smokestacks are now glowing crimson referential landmarks anchoring a burgeoning stretch that runs from the central neighborhood of Kerameikos to the once-decrepit neighborhood of Rouf. Since the city of Athens bought the disused gasworks in the late 1990s, it was converted, retaining the original brick architecture, into Technopolis, where large art exhibitions and events centered on gastronomy, social history, lifestyle, and culture (like the annual European Jazz Festival) regularly take place, and where the Industrial Gas Museum is housed. ✉ *Pireos 100, Gazi-Kerameikos* ☎ *213/010–9300* 🌐 *www.technopolis-athens.com* 🎫 *Technopolis free, Gas Museum €1* 🕒 *Closed Mon.* [M] *Kerameikos.*

🍴 Restaurants

West of Psirri, Gazi-Kerameikos has turned into the city's hottest art, culture, and nightlife zone. The Kerameikos metro station has also made it ultraconvenient.

Kanella

$$ | MODERN GREEK | FAMILY | Housed in a cool, airy building with modern and traditional touches, this lively example of a neo-taverna serves mama's cooking but infused with Gazi's creative energy. Regional specialties, great barrel wine served in lovely carafes, and a familial atmosphere make dining here a pleasure. Warning: when the neutral-tone interior gets busy, it gets almost psychedelically loud. Thankfully, there are outside tables on the street where you can dine in good weather. **Known for:** traditional home-style favorites like slow-cooked lamb and stuffed grape leaves; lively atmosphere great for groups of friends; excellent house wine. [$] *Average main: €25* ✉ *Konstantinoupoleos 70, at Evmolpidon, Gazi-Kerameikos* ☎ *210/347–6320* 🌐 *www.kanellagazi.gr* [M] *Kerameikos.*

Lime Bistro

$ | VEGETARIAN | FAMILY | Athenians have been known historically as meat lovers, but they are beginning to discover the merits of creative, sophisticated, and delicious vegetarian cuisine. The popularity of this bistro attests to the fact with a modern and playful layout that includes a charming back garden and a seasonal menu packed with guilt-free, nutritious vegan and vegetarian choices. The food here offers a wealth of taste bud-pleasing flavors. Try the Greek salad on a rusk made from carob, topped with almond "goat" cheese, and sip the lemonade with turmeric, agave, and cayenne pepper. The restaurant eagerly explores all avenues in healthy, trendy cuisine. **Known for:** raw vegan homemade cheeses;

fresh, crispy salads and vegan burgers; gluten-free and raw options. $ *Average main: €10* ⊠ *Dekeleon 23, Gazi-Kerameikos* ☎ *210/347–4423* Ⓜ *Kerameikos.*

Proveleggio's

$$ | MEDITERRANEAN | This is a fresh and hip arrival in the Athenian dinner scene, with a refreshing attitude of improvising the menu according to which top quality ingredients are available at the time, what the chef and his team feel like experimenting with and, of course, the season they're in. **Known for:** top quality ingredients and dishes; modern, trendy decor; memorable cocktails. $ *Average main: €18* ⊠ *Paramithias 11, Gazi-Kerameikos* ☎ *210/523–4749* Ⓜ *Metaxourgeio.*

 ## Nightlife

BARS

Intrepid Fox

BARS/PUBS | Rockers and metal-heads look no further. With walls splattered with album cover posters from bands like AC/DC and Metallica, the Intrepid Fox will satiate any yearning you may have for this genre of thunderous compositions. Pride of place in the center of this large, grungy bar is a pool table facing the main live stage, and tucked away in a corner is a boxing machine. For a less intense but no less sanguine experience head up to the rooftop bar to take in the view of this post-industrial quarter of central Athens. ⊠ *Triptolemou 30, Gazi-Kerameikos* ☎ *210/346–6055* Ⓜ *Kerameikos.*

Sodade2

BARS/PUBS | Now in its twentieth year, this gay-friendly bar-club-lounge attracts a standing-room-only crowd every weekend. The draw is the great music, the joyous vibe, and the very fact that it's in Gazi, where a number of LGBT-friendly spots are located. ⊠ *Triptolemou 10, Gazi-Kerameikos* ☎ *210/346–8657* Ⓜ *Kerameikos.*

CLUBS

Afrikana

BARS/PUBS | Get here before 9 pm for a drink and a chat, but after that be prepared for a fun night of bopping along to live jazz, funk, or blues performances as you sip your drink and maybe even sing along. There's always a happy atmosphere here, plus fresh talent, good drinks, and friendly service. ⊠ *Ierofandon 13, Gazi-Kerameikos* Ⓜ *Kerameikos.*

Bios

CAFES—NIGHTLIFE | Cool architects and graphic designers, arty students and hipster DJs, revolutionaries and experimental philosophers: they all hang out in the cavernous basement of this Bauhaus building in the Kerameikos neighborhood, part of the greater Gazi district. Expect to hear the best electronica music in town. In summer, relish the view of the Acropolis from the postmodern, neon-lighted roof terrace. A handful of "multispace" imitators have emerged, offering offbeat film/video and music events in painfully hip industrial spaces—but Bios remains the standard. ⊠ *Pireos 84, Gazi-Kerameikos* ☎ *210/342–5335* ⊕ *www.bios.gr* Ⓜ *Kerameikos.*

Shamone

CABARET | This live music venue for well-known singers as well as a broad host of drag show artists is usually busy, lively, and full of movement. ⊠ *Konstantinoupoleos Ave. 46, Gazi-Kerameikos* ☎ *210/345–0144, 694/720–4020* ⊕ *www.shamone.gr* Ⓜ *Kerameikos.*

Kolonaki Κολωνάκι

Kolonaki was named after a marble column dating from the Middle Ages, probably a memento of a religious procession, that was discovered in Dexameni Square, on the foot of Mt. Lycabettus. On its southwestern edge is Syntagma Square and the Parliament building; the neighborhood extends all the way to

Lycabettus and beyond. It is a posh area with lots of upmarket boutiques, glossy cafés, and upscale restaurants, galleries, and museums. At the bottom edge of Kolonaki on Vas. Sophias Avenue, you can pay homage to the power of movement and clean lines of the impressive *Runner,* a glass sculpture of impressive proportions by local artist Kostas Varotsos across from the Hilton Hotel.

Sights

B&M Theocharakis Foundation

ARTS VENUE | A key reference point for Athens's culture vultures, this private nonprofit foundation focuses on the visual arts and music, with a special interest in modernism. The driving force behind the imposing cultural center, housed in a neoclassical building beside the Greek Parliament, is Basil Theocharakis, a prominent businessman who is also an avid and talented painter, and his wife, Marina. Temporary exhibitions, classical concerts, and educational workshops are held here on a regular basis, while Cafe Merlin, the elegant first-floor café, offers a welcome respite from the city's hustle and bustle. On the mezzanine floor you'll also find a lovely café-bistro, and on the ground floor a charming gift shop. ⊠ *Vassilissis Sofias 9, at Merlin 1, Kolonaki* ☎ *210/361–1206* ⊕ *www.thf. gr* ⌨ *€7* ⊘ *Closed Aug.* Ⓜ *Syntagma.*

★ Benaki Museum

LIBRARY | Greece's oldest private museum received a spectacular addition in 2004, with a hypermodern new branch that looks like it was airlifted in from New York City. The imposing neoclassical mansion in the posh Kolonaki neighborhood was turned into a museum in 1926 by an illustrious Athenian family and was one of the first to place emphasis on Greece's later heritage at a time when many archaeologists were destroying Byzantine artifacts to access ancient objects. The permanent collection (more than 20,000 items are on display in 36 rooms, and that's only a sample of the holdings) moves chronologically from the ground floor upward, from prehistory to the formation of the modern Greek state. You might see anything from a 5,000-year-old hammered-gold bowl to an austere Byzantine icon of the Virgin Mary to Lord Byron's pistols to the Nobel medals awarded to poets George Seferis and Odysseus Elytis. Some exhibits are just plain fun—the re-creation of a Kozani (Macedonian town) living room; a Karaghiozi shadow puppet piloting a toy plane—all contrasted against the marble and crystal-chandelier grandeur of the Benaki home. The mansion that serves as the main building of the museum was designed by Anastassios Metaxas, the architect who helped restore the Panathenaic Stadium. The Benaki's gift shop, a destination in itself, tempts with exquisitely reproduced ceramics and jewelry, some with exciting contemporary design twists. The second-floor café is on a generous veranda overlooking the National Garden. A couple of blocks away is the Benaki Ghika Gallery, at 3 Krietzou Street, dedicated to the painter Nikos Hadjikyriakos-Ghika. The annex at 138 Pireos Street in the Gazi-Keremeikos neighborhood displays avant-garde temporary exhibitions, while behind Kerameikos Cemetery stands the Benaki Museum of Islamic Art. ⊠ *Koumbari 1, Kolonaki* ☎ *210/367–1000* ⊕ *www.benaki. gr* ⌨ *€12* ⊘ *Closed Tues.* Ⓜ *Syntagma, Evangelismos.*

Byzantine and Christian Museum

MUSEUM | One of the few museums in Europe focusing exclusively on Byzantine art displays an outstanding collection of icons, mosaics, tapestries, and sculptural fragments (the latter provides an excellent introduction to the architecture of the period). The permanent collection is divided into two main parts: the first is devoted to Byzantium (4th through 15th century AD) and contains 1,200 artifacts, while the second is entitled "From Byzantium to the Modern Era" and presents

Try to catch the purple glow of sundown from atop Mt. Lycabettus, Athens's highest hill.

1,500 artworks dating from the 15th to the 21st century. ⊠ *Vasilissis Sofias 22, Kolonaki* ☎ *213/213–9572* ⊕ *www.byzantinemuseum.gr* 🎟 *€8; €30 for unified museum ticket (includes National Archaeological Museum, Epigraphical Museum, Numismatic Museum)* Ⓜ *Evangelismos.*

Kolonaki Square

PLAZA | To see and be seen, Athenians gather not on Kolonaki Square—hub of the chic Kolonaki district—but at the cafés on its periphery and along the Tsakalof and Milioni pedestrian zones. Clothespin-thin models, slick talk-show hosts, middle-aged executives, elegant pensioners, university students, and expatriate teen queens can be spotted lounging at the square (officially known as Filikis Eterias). ⊠ *Intersection of Patriarchou Ioakeim and Kanari, Kolonaki* Ⓜ *Syntagma, Evangelismos.*

★ Mt. Lycabettus

VIEWPOINT/SCENIC OVERLOOK | **FAMILY** | Myth claims that Athens's highest hill came into existence when Athena removed a piece of Mt. Pendeli, intending to boost the height of her temple on the Acropolis. While she was en route, a crone brought her bad tidings, and the flustered goddess dropped the rock in the middle of the city. Dog-walkers and joggers have made it their daily stomping grounds, and kids love the ride up the steeply inclined *teleferique* (funicular) to the summit (one ride every 30 minutes), crowned by whitewashed **Ayios Georgios** chapel with a bell tower donated by Queen Olga. On a clear day, you can see Piraeus port and as far as Aegina island. Built into a cave on the side of the hill is a small shrine to **Ayios Isidoros.** Cars park up at the top at sunset for swoon-inducing magic-hour views of the city lights going on, as the moon rises over "violet-crowned" Mt. Hymettus. Refreshments are available from the modest kiosk popular with concertgoers, who flock to events at the hill's open-air theater during summer months. Diners should also note that Lycabettus is home to Orizontes Lyka-vittou, an excellent fish restaurant (by day this establishment also houses the relaxing Café Lycabettus). ⊠ *Kolonaki* ⊹ *The base is a 15-min walk northeast of Syntagma Sq.; funicular runs every 30 min (10 min during rush hr) from corner of Ploutarchou and Aristippou (take Minibus 060 from Kanari or Kolonaki Sq.); the terminal is on Aristippou St. (walk all the way up Ploutarchou St., right to the top of the stairs).* ☏ *210/721–0701 funicular information* ⊕ *www.lycabettushill.com* ☐ *Funicular €7.50 (round-trip) €5 one way* Ⓜ *Evangelismos.*

★ **Museum of Cycladic Art**

MUSEUM | FAMILY | Funded by one of Greece's richest families, this museum has an outstanding collection of 350 Cycladic artifacts dating from the Bronze Age, including many of the enigmatic marble figurines whose slender shapes fascinated such artists as Picasso, Modigliani, and Brancusi. The main building is an imposing glass-and-steel design dating from 1985 and built to convey "the sense of austerity and the diffusion of refracted light that predominate in the Cycladic landscape," as the museum puts it. Along with Cycladic masterpieces, a wide array from other eras is also on view, ranging from the Bronze Age through the 6th century AD. The third floor is devoted to Cypriot art, while the fourth floor showcases a fascinating exhibition on "scenes from daily life in antiquity." To handle the overflow, a new wing opened in 2005. A glass corridor connects the main building to the gorgeous, 19th-century, neoclassical Stathatos Mansion, where temporary exhibits are mounted. There is also a lovely skylighted café in an enclosed courtyard around a Cycladic-inspired fountain, a charming art shop, and many children-oriented activities all year-round. ⊠ *Neofitou*

Douka 4, Kolonaki ☏ *210/722–83215* ⊕ *www.cycladic.gr* ☐ *€7* ⊙ *Closed Tues.* Ⓜ *Evangelismos.*

Old University Complex

BUILDING | In the sea of concrete that is Central Athens, this imposing group of white marble buildings, known as the Athenian Trilogy, gleams majestically under perfect azure skies like an illusion of classical antiquity. The three dramatic buildings belonging to the University of Athens were designed by the Hansen brothers in the period after independence in the 19th century and are built of Pendelic marble, with tall columns and decorative friezes. In the center is the **University**, after which Panepistimiou (*panepistimio* means university) Street is named, with its huge colorful mural. To the right is the **Academy,** flanked by two slim columns topped by statues of Athena and Apollo; paid for by the Austro-Greek Baron Sina, it is a copy of the Parliament in Vienna. Frescoes in the reception hall depict the myth of Prometheus. At the left end of the complex is a griffin-flanked staircase leading to the **National Library,** which has been housed in the building since 1903 and contains more than 2 million Greek and foreign-language volumes; the books are now being transferred to their new home, the Stavros Niarchos Foundation Cultural Center. ⊠ *Panepistimiou, between Ippokratous and Sina, Kolonaki* ☏ *210/368–9765 Senate, 210/366–4700 Academy, 210/360–8185 Library* ⊕ *www.nlg.gr* ⊙ *Closed Sun. and Aug.* Ⓜ *Panepistimiou.*

Restaurants

Located east of Plaka, Kolonaki is an old-money neighborhood that's a haunt for politicians, businesspeople, and high-maintenance ladies who lunch (and shop). Options for quality (and pricey) dining and coffee are more than satisfying.

Le Grand Balcon

$$$ | **MEDITERRANEAN** | **FAMILY** | Located on the rooftop of the St. George Lycabettuys hotel, this restaurant offers some of the most jaw-dropping panoramic vistas of the city as well as high quality dishes. Upon enetering the restaurant guests are immediately faced with a wall of photos presenting all the celebrity guests who have dined here. Arrive at sunset and start with a cocktail as you look out to the Acropolis and the sea behind it, a truly breathtaking view. The menu is based on Greek-Mediterranean ingredients, recipes, and tastes and the food is sophisticated and generally pleasing but not as remarkable as what your eyes will feast on. **Known for:** stunning panoramic views; fine dining with good service; elegant ambience. ⓢ *Average main: €40* ✉ *Kleomenous 2, Kolonaki* ☎ *210/741–6000* ⊕ *www.sglycabettus.gr* Ⓜ *Evangelismos.*

★ Nice N Easy

$$ | **MEDITERRANEAN** | **FAMILY** | Inspired in its decor and the names of the dishes on the menu by old Hollywood glamour, this was Athens's first farm-to-table restaurant. Having received several awards over the years for its top quality ingredients—mainly organic and sourced from small producers—as well as its great service and many healthy comfort-food options, it's also set up in Kifissia and Mykonos. The all-day restaurant has an easy-going and upbeat urban ambience and serves creative as well as classic modern Greek, Mediterranean, and North American-inspired cuisine to suit all tastes, moods and dietary requirements. You can head here for a full brunch, lunch, or dinner or order a great bottle of wine accompanied by several appetizers to share with friends. If you have a sweet tooth, don't miss out on the dairy and sugar-free olive oil ice cream, which comes in several indulgent flavors. **Known for:** top quality ingredients put together in a flavorsome way; many healthy, tasty choices for vegans and vegetarians; excellent brunch

menu. ⓢ *Average main: €20* ✉ *Omirou 60, Kolonaki* ☎ *210/361–7201* ⊕ *www. niceneasy.gr* Ⓜ *Evangelismos.*

Orizontes Lycabettus

$$$ | **MEDITERRANEAN** | As you are handed the menu, you'll find it nearly impossible to avert your eyes from the stunning view from the very top of verdant Lycabettus Hill, the highest point in Athens; the Acropolis glitters below, and beyond it, the metropolis unfolds like a map out to the Saronic Gulf. The restaurant centers on gourmet Mediterranean cuisine with bold French elements, but the chef also cooks up playful renditions of classic Greek dishes. The restaurant is reached by cable car or by foot only. Every season Orizontes offers very reasonably priced set menus for two. **Known for:** quirky updates on Mediterranean classics; high-quality service; some of the most romantic views in Athens. ⓢ *Average main: €35* ✉ *Lycabettus Hill, Kolonaki* ☎ *210/721–0701* ⊕ *www.orizonteslycabettus.gr* Ⓜ *Evangelismos.*

Papadakis

$$$ | **SEAFOOD** | Picture this: it's twilight and you're sitting under bitter-orange trees at one of Athens's best fish restaurants, in the heart of Kolonaki, overlooking the Parthenon as you sip a perfectly chilled glass of wine and wait for your order of succulent seafood to arrive. There's muted conversation at the gleaming white-tableclothed tables around you, where opinion makers, theater directors, and loyal customers relax. You may start with a bowl of thick and flavorsome *kakavia* fish soup that the elegant and attentive waitress pours out of a large silver teapot, and then progress to steamed mussels and chili-fried shrimp with feta, before digging into a beautifully baked fish like white grouper with summer truffles. Indoors, the cool-in-summer and cozy-in-winter interiors have walls covered by giant, colorful paintings and a silver wall sculpture of fish. **Known for:**

high-profile dining at high quality; fresh, artfully prepared seafood; great wine list. $ *Average main: €35* ⊠ *Voukourestiou 47, at Fokylidou 15, Kolonaki* ☎ *210/360–8621* ⊕ *www.papadakisrestaurant.com* Ⓜ *Evangelismos.*

Taverna Filippou

$$ | GREEK | FAMILY | This unassuming urban taverna is hardly the sort of place you'd expect to find in chic Kolonaki, yet its devotees (since 1923) have included cabinet ministers, diplomats, actresses, and film directors. The appeal is simple: well-prepared Greek classics, mostly *ladera* (casseroles cooked in an olive oil and tomato sauce), *moussaka* (layered eggplant and ground beef in béchamel sauce), and delicious side dishes like shrimp in a mayonnaise sauce. The menu adapts to what's fresh at the open-air produce market. **Known for:** best moussaka in town; familial atmosphere; sophisticated clientele. $ *Average main: €20* ⊠ *Xenokratous 19, Kolonaki* ☎ *210/721–6390* ⊕ *www.filippou.gr/en* ⊘ *Closed Sun. and mid-Aug. No dinner Sat.* Ⓜ *Evangelismos.*

To Kafeneio

$$ | GREEK | A Kolonaki institution, this bistro-style traditional restaurant is slightly fancier and more costly than the normal mezedopoleio, with cloth napkins, candles on the tables, and walls decorated with writings by its famous patrons. The menu centers on delicate Greek classics (such as lamb with lemon or roast suckling pig) but also some international fare. The service is warm and professional andhe clientele includes politicians and diplomats on their lunch break. For the freshest dishes, ask the waiter for the day's specials. **Known for:** reliably good Greek classics; an excellent location in the heart of Kolonaki; sophisticated setting. $ *Average main: €25* ⊠ *Loukianou 26, Kolonaki* ☎ *210/723–9600* ⊘ *Closed Sun. and 3 wks in Aug.* Ⓜ *Evangelismos.*

Zurbaran

$$$ | MEDITERRANEAN | This new, ultra-modern spot just minutes from Kolonaki Square draws the city's fashionistas and moneyed good-timers like bees to honey. A solid, modern Greek and Mediterranean menu, funky decor, and high-resonance sound track set the right mood. The chef's culinary style leans toward light, healthy gourmet dishes with some surprises, but the menu has many classics. From raw seafood to Chateaubriand, there is a lot of choice for all tastes, but it's the ambience that makes everything work. The downside is that the service doesn't always live up to the standards. **Known for:** trendy, modern setting; innovative cuisine and good cocktails; uneven service. $ *Average main: €30* ⊠ *Patriarchou Ioakeim 38, Kolonaki* ☎ *210/723–8334* ⊕ *zurbaranathens.gr* Ⓜ *Evangelismos.*

☕ Coffee and Quick Bites

Caffe Da Capo

$ | CAFÉ | Enjoy a cappuccino and an Italian panini standing inside Caffe Da Capo, or if you have more time, watch the world go by. at an outside table. This place is usually packed with trendsetters and stern policy makers. **Known for:** people-watching; hangout for Greek movers and shakers; excellent cappuccino. $ *Average main: €8* ⊠ *Tsakalof 1, Kolonaki* ☎ *210/360–2497* ▭ *No credit cards* Ⓜ *Syntagma.*

Clemente VIII

$ | CAFÉ | Located on pedestrian Voukourestiou Street, where all the most luxurious fashion boutiques are, the Italian-style café serves freshly ground, high-quality espresso and cappuccino and a fresh daily platter of sandwiches and sweets. It is named after the 16th-century pope who gave his blessing to the then-exotic coffee bean. **Known for:** chichi coffee drinking; elegant location; good, albeit expensive, sandwiches and desserts. $ *Average main: €10* ⊠ *City Link Mall, Voukourestiou 3, Kolonaki* ☎ *210/321–9340* Ⓜ *Syntagma.*

Mailo's

$ | FAST FOOD | FAMILY | Fresh pasta cooked to order and made to go make. Mailo's, recently opened and super-popular, a great option for anyone craving a quick, hot meal without the fuss. This place is especially ideal for families or shoppers wanting to stop for a quick bite that's nutritious, packed with flavor, and prepared. There are a few seats outside if you'd rather sit. **Known for:** fresh pasta; great variety of recipes; freshly made food. *$ Average main: €7 ⊠ Patriarchou Ioakim 39, Kolonaki* ☎ *210/721–0177* Ⓜ *Evangelismos.*

 # Hotels

COCO-MAT Hotel Athens

$$ | HOTEL | In a first, a manufacturer of luxury mattresses has opened up its own boutique hotel right above the company's mattress showroom, offering chic, minimalist rooms centered on the bed. **Pros:** blissfully comfortable beds; just off Kolonaki Square; friendly, helpful service. **Cons:** breakfast could be better; some rooms have little natural light; bathroom lighting can be low. *$ Rooms from: €180 ⊠ Patriarchou Ioakeim 36, Kolonaki* ☎ *210/723–0000* ⊕ *www. cocomatathens.com ↴ 39 rooms* Ⓧ *Free breakfast* Ⓜ *Syntagma.*

Periscope

$$ | HOTEL | This sleek concept hotel combines minimalist urban-chic design, amenity-filled rooms, and exceptional service for a truly relaxing experience. **Pros:** outstanding service; right at the heart of cool Kolonaki; great breakfast. **Cons:** rooms are a bit on small side and have limited views; only suites have balconies; no parking. *$ Rooms from: €160 ⊠ Charitos 22, Kolonaki* ☎ *210/729–7200* ⊕ *www.yeshotels.gr ↴ 22 rooms* Ⓧ *Free breakfast* Ⓜ *Evagelismos.*

St. George Lycabettus

$ | HOTEL | FAMILY | At the foothills of Lycabettus Hill, this elegant hotel is considered one of the most elegant in central Athens. **Pros:** astounding Acropolis and city views from some rooms; scenic rooftop restaurant and swimming pool; right above Dexameni Square, ideal for coffee and meze. **Cons:** a 15-minute walk from Kolonaki Square and taxi ride from most sites; service could be friendlier and more efficient; Wi-Fi in rooms available for a charge. *$ Rooms from: €115 ⊠ Kleomenous 2, Kolonaki* ☎ *210/729–0711 through 210/729–0719* ⊕ *www.sglycabettus.gr ↴ 153 rooms, 5 suites* Ⓧ *No meals* Ⓜ *Syntagma.*

 # Nightlife

CLUBS

Ippopotamos

BARS/PUBS | A lively bar with tables sprawled out onto the pedestrianized street outside during summer and a colorful, vibrant interior in the ground-floor space it occupies in a neoclassical building. Fairy-lights, plants and trees, friendly service, and artsy "hidden" rooms make this a fun place to enjoy a few artfully mixed cocktails. It's open from 9 am until midnight so you can also visit for coffee. *⊠ Delfon 3B, Kolonaki* ☎ *210/036–34583* Ⓜ *Syntagma.*

★ Minnie the Moocher

BARS/PUBS | Just two minutes walk from Kolonaki Square, on the buzzy Tsakalof street packed with bars, this sleek, Pro-hibition-era-themed bar is always kicking with a mixed crowd sipping excellently mixed cocktails. Chesterfield-style sofas, high padded stools, and elaborately tiled floors as well as a vibrant soundtrack keep customers here until the late hours. *⊠ Tsakalof 6, Kolonaki* ☎ *210/364–1686* Ⓜ *Syntagma.*

Rock n' Roll

BARS/PUBS | This legendary bar from the 1980s and '90s has reopened its doors a couple of hundred meters from its original location. Athens's party crowd comes to this club/restaurant to groove mostly to rock music (with some dance and Greek pop hits subtly making their way into the playlist). Saturday is very busy, so your best bet is to book a table and enjoy the Mediterranean menu before moving on to cocktails and a bit of dancing. From May to September, Rock n' Roll goes on holiday. ⊠ *Loukianou 6, Kolonaki* ☎ *210/722–0649* ⊕ *www.rocknroll.gr* Ⓜ *Evagelismos.*

Shopping

ANTIQUES AND ICONS
★ Martinos

ANTIQUES/COLLECTIBLES | Antiques collectors should head here to look for items such as exquisite dowry chests, old swords, precious fabrics, and Venetian glass. You will certainly discover something you like in the four floors of this renovated antiques shop that has been an Athens landmark for the past 100 years. There's another branch in Monastiraki, at Pandrossou 50. ⊠ *Pindarou 24, Kolonaki* ☎ *210/360–9449* ⊕ *www.martinosart.gr* Ⓜ *Syntagma.*

ART GALLERIES
Kalfayan

ART GALLERIES | The gallery presents some of Greece's most acknowledged contemporary artists as well as new talent in temporary solo and group exhibitions. In the shape of a large glass box, it's impressive to look at both from the outside and from within. Armenian relics and artifacts dating to a century ago and collected by the Armenian-origin owners are also on show. ⊠ *Charitos 11, Kolonaki* ☎ *210/721–7679* ⊕ *www.kalfayangalleries.com* Ⓜ *Evagelismos.*

Zoumboulakis Art-Design-Antiques

GIFTS/SOUVENIRS | The art shop of this respected private art gallery stocks some beautiful objets d'art, including candlesticks and other decor, in addition to gifts like limited-edition silkscreens by famous Greek painters Yiannis Moralis, Nikos Xatzikyriakos-Gikas, Yiannis Tsarouchis, and many more. ⊠ *Kriezotou 6, Kolonaki* ☎ *210/363–4454* ⊕ *www.zoumboulakis. gr* Ⓜ *Syntagma.*

CLOTHING
★ Aesthet

CLOTHING | If you're looking for the best from Greece's top fashion designers, this is the place for you. Aesthet is the only store where you can find a collection of many different Greek luxury brands like Lalaounis, Zeus+Dione, Ancient Greek Sandals, Ioanna Kourbella, Ancient Kallos, Yiorgos Eleftheriades, and many more. From clothing to accessories like footwear, hangbags, and swimwear, the store constantly updates its collection and does seasonal clearances, too. ⊠ *Valaoritou 15, Kolonaki* ☎ *210/363–8573* ⊕ *www.aesthet.com* Ⓜ *Evangelismos.*

Parthenis

CLOTHING | Fashion designer Dimitris Parthenis opened his first boutique in 1970. Today his daughter Orsalia continues the family tradition of creating urban chic fashion with a Bohemian hint. Natural fibers such as wool, silk, and cotton are used to create relaxed, body-hugging silhouettes. There is an eyewear line and a wedding collection, too. ⊠ *Dimokritou 20, at Tsakalof, Kolonaki* ☎ *210/363–3158* ⊕ *www.orsalia-parthenis.gr* Ⓜ *Syntagma.*

GIFTS
★ Apivita Experience Store

LOCAL SPECIALTIES | On the 4th floor of this store you'll find the Beehive Spa; on the 3rd floor a hair salon that uses only natural, chemical-free dyes; on the 2nd floor a lecture hall for events; and the ground floor is where you can check out all the Apivita products. Here at the flagship store of Apivita, a Greek brand that has become globally respected for its use of pure, organic, and scientifically manufactured cosmetic and pharmaceutical concoctions, you can create your own products. Guided by experts, choose among a plethora of wonderful natural Greek ingredients to create the ideal cosmetics or alternative medicines for you. Of course, you can also find all the ranges of ready-made products—from makeup and shampoos to face creams and essential oils—as well. ✉ Solonos 6 and Kanari, Kolonaki ☎ 210/364–0560 ⊕ www.apivita.com/hellas/apivita-experience-store Ⓜ Syntagma.

★ **Benaki Museum Gift Shop**
GIFTS/SOUVENIRS | The airy museum shop has excellent copies of Greek icons, jewelry, and folk art—at fair prices. You will also find embroideries, ceramics, stationery, art books, small reliefs, and sculpture pieces. The new Benaki Museum Annex on Pireos Street has its own shop with an interesting collection of modern Greek jewelry. The gift shop is also open on Monday (even though the museum is closed). ✉ Benaki Museum, Koumbari 1, at Vasilissis Sofias, Kolonaki ☎ 210/367–1045 ⊕ www.benaki.gr Ⓜ Syntagma.

★ **Kombologadiko**
GIFTS/SOUVENIRS | From real amber, or pinhead-size "evil eyes," to 2-inch-diameter wood, sugarcane, or shell beads, you'll find a dizzying selection of beads and styles to string your own komboloi (worry beads). You'll admire the variety of this unique Greek version of a rosary, which can be made from traditional amber, but also from coral root, camel bone, semiprecious stones, and many more materials. ✉ Amerikis 9, Kolonaki ☎ 212/700–0500 ⊕ www.kombologadiko.gr Ⓜ Syntagma.

JEWELRY
Elena Votsi
JEWELRY/ACCESSORIES | Elena Votsi designed jewelry for Gucci and Ralph Lauren before opening her own boutiques, where she sells exquisite, larger-than-life creations in coral, amethyst, aquamarine, and turquoise. In 2003 she designed the Athens 2004 Olympic Games gold medal; in 2009 her handmade 18-karat gold ring with diamonds won a Couture Design Award in the Best in Haute Couture category in Las Vegas. Brava! ✉ Xanthou 7, Kolonaki ☎ 210/360–0936 ⊕ www.elenavotsi.com. Ⓜ Syntagma.

Fanourakis
JEWELRY/ACCESSORIES | Original gold masterpieces can be had at these shops, where Athenian masters, prompted by jewelry designer Lina Fanouraki, use gold almost like a fabric—creasing, scoring, and fluting it. There's another branch at Panagitsas 6 (210/623–2334) in the Kifissia neighborhood. ✉ Patriarchou Ioakeim 23, Kolonaki ☎ 210/721–1762 ⊕ www.fanourakis.gr Ⓜ Evangelismos.

★ **Museum of Cycladic Art Shop**
JEWELRY/ACCESSORIES | Exceptional modern versions of ancient jewelry designs are available in the gift shop of this museum, where you can also find museum replicas and inspired ceramics. ✉ Museum of Cycladic Art, Neofitou Douka 4, Kolonaki ☎ 210/722–8321 ⊕ www.cycladic.gr Ⓜ Syntagma.

Pentheroudakis
JEWELRY/ACCESSORIES | Browse among the classic designs in gold, diamond, and gemstones but, happily, there are less expensive trinkets, like silver worry beads that can be personalized with cubed letters in Greek or Latin and with the stone of your choice. ✉ Voukourestiou 19, Kolonaki ☎ 210/361–3187 ⊕ www. pentheroudakis.com Ⓜ Syntagma.

Continued on page 168

GREEK BY DESIGN

Shopping is now considered an Olympic sport in Greece. Many get the urge to splurge in the chic shops of Mykonos, Rhodes, and Crete, the islands that launched a thousand gifts. But if you really want to bag the best in Greek style, Athens is where to get the goods.

The Greeks had a word for it: *tropos*. Style. You would expect nothing less from the folks who gave us the Venus de Milo, the Doric column, and the lyre-back chair. To say that they have had a long tradition as artisans and craftsmen is, of course, an understatement. Even back in ancient Rome, Greece was the word. The Romans may have engineered the stone vault and perfected the toilet, but when it came to style and culture, they were perfectly content to knock off Grecian dress, sculpture, décor, and architecture, then considered the height of fashion. Fast-forward 2,500 years and little has changed. Many works of modern art were conceived as an Aegean paean, including the statues of Brancusi and Le Corbusier's minimalistic skyscrapers—both artists were deeply influenced by ancient Cycladic art. Today, the goddess dress struts the runways of Michael Kors and Valentino while Homer has made the leap to Hollywood in such box-office blockbusters as *300* and *Troy*.

Speaking of which, those ancient Trojans may have once tut-tutted about Greeks bearing gifts but would have second thoughts these days. Aunt Ethel has now traded in those plastic souvenir models of the Parthenon for a new Athenian bounty: pieces of Byzantine-style gold jewelry; hand-woven bedspreads from Hydra; strands of amber *komboloi* worry beads; and reproductions of red-figure ceramic vases. These are gifts you cannot resist and will be forever be glad you didn't.

(above) Byzantine design jewelry

BEARING GIFTS?

Seeing some of the glories of Aegean craftsmanship is probably one of the reasons you've come to Greece. The eggshell-thin pottery Minoans were fashioning more than 3,500 years ago, Byzantine jewelry and icons, colorful rugs that were woven in front of the fire as part of a dowry, not to mention all those bits of ancient masonry—these comprise a magnificent legacy of arts and crafts.

LEATHER SANDALS

Ancient Greek women with means and a sense of style wore sandals with straps that wrapped around the ankles—what today's fashion mags call "strappy sandals," proof that some classics are always in vogue. The most legendary maker is Athens's very own Stavros Melissinos, whose creations were once sported by the Beatles and Sophia Loren. He has been crafting sandals for more than 50 years.

TAVLÍ BOARDS

No matter where you are in Greece, follow the sound of clicking dice and you'll probably find yourself in a kafenion. There, enthusiasts will be huddled over Greece's favorite game, a close cousin to backgammon. Tavlí boards are sold everywhere in Greece, but the most magnificent board you'll ever see is not for sale—a marble square inlaid with gold and ivory, crafted sometime before 1500 BC for the amusement of Minoan kings and now on display at the archaeological museum in Heraklion, Crete.

WORRY BEADS

Feeling fidgety? Partake of a Greek custom and fiddle with your worry beads, or komboloi. The amber or coral beads are loosely strung on a long strand and look like prayer beads, yet they have no religious significance. Even so, on a stressful day the relaxing effect can seem like divine intervention. Particularly potent are beads painted with the "evil eye."

ICONS

Icon painting flourished in Greece as the Renaissance took hold of Western Europe, and panels of saints and other heavenly creatures are among the country's greatest artistic treasures. Some, like many of those in the 799 churches on the island of Tinos, are said to possess miraculous healing powers, attracting thousands of cure-seeking believers each year. Icons attract art buyers too, but if you can easily afford one, it's almost certainly a modern reproduction.

WEAVING

Even goddesses spent their idle hours weaving (remember Arachne, so proud of her skills at the loom that Athena turned her into a spider?). From the mountains of Arcadia to such worldly enclaves as Mykonos, mortals sit behind handlooms to clack out folkloric rugs, bedspreads, and tablecloths.

BARGAINING FOR BEGINNERS

In Greece there is often the "first price" and the "last price." Bargaining is still par for the course (except in the fanciest stores). And if you're planning a shopping day, leave those Versace shoes at home—shopkeepers often decide on a price after sizing up the prospective buyer's income bracket.

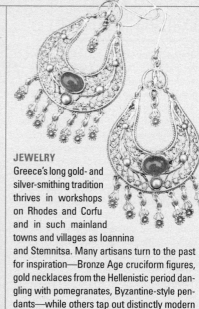

JEWELRY

Greece's long gold- and silver-smithing tradition thrives in workshops on Rhodes and Corfu and in such mainland towns and villages as Ioannina and Stemnitsa. Many artisans turn to the past for inspiration—Bronze Age cruciform figures, gold necklaces from the Hellenistic period dangling with pomegranates, Byzantine-style pendants—while others tap out distinctly modern creations using age-old techniques.

CERAMICS

Ancient Greek pottery was a black-and-red medium: the Spartans and Corinthians painted glossy black figures on a reddish-orange background; later ceramists switched the effect with stunning results, reddish-hued figures on a black background. Artisans still create both, and potters on Crete and elsewhere in Greece throw huge terracotta storage jars, pithoi, that are appealing, if no longer practical, additions to any household.

Exarchia Εξάρχεια

The neighborhood of Exarchia is full of life and largely student-central, as the National Technical University of Athens (Polytechneio) is located just a few hundred yards away from Exarchia Square down tech-friendly Stournari Street. The area is also infamous for the anarchist groups that use it as a base for their demonstrations, although in recent years peace and quiet have largely prevailed. The National Archaeological Museum (the neighborhood's biggest draw) is next to the Athens Polytechnic, where the historic student uprising of 1973, which led to the ousting of the junta, took place. Look for the "Blue" building in Exarchia Square, which is a prime example of the modernist movement in Greek architecture. Rembetika music clubs, vintage record shops, comic-book shops, musical instrument stores, quaint little bars, traditional tavernas, and cheap souvlaki corners all coexist in the area, which is always buzzing with creative—one might dare say revolutionary—energy.

 Sights

★ **National Archaeological Museum**
MUSEUM | FAMILY | Many of the greatest achievements in ancient Greek sculpture and painting are housed here in the most important museum in Greece. Artistic highlights from every period of its ancient civilization, from Neolithic to Roman times, make this a treasure trove beyond compare. With a massive renovation completed, works (more than 11,000 of them) that have languished in storage for decades are now on view, reorganized displays are accompanied by enriched English-language information, and the panoply of ancient Greek art appears more spectacular than ever.

While the classic culture that was the grandeur of the Greek world no longer exists—it died, for civilizations are mortal—it left indelible markers in all domains, most particularly in art, and many of its masterpieces are on show here. The museum's most celebrated display is the **Mycenaean Antiquities.** Here are the stunning gold treasures from Heinrich Schliemann's 1876 excavations of Mycenae's royal tombs: the funeral mask of a bearded king, once thought to be the image of Agamemnon but now believed to be much older, from about the 15th century BC; a splendid silver bull's-head libation cup; and the 15th-century BC Vapheio Goblets, masterworks in embossed gold. Mycenaeans were famed for their carving in miniature, and an exquisite example is the ivory statuette of two curvaceous mother goddesses, each with a child nestled on her lap.

Withheld from the public since they were damaged in the 1999 earthquakes, but not to be missed, are the beautifully restored **frescoes from Santorini,** delightful murals depicting daily life in Minoan Santorini. Along with the treasures from Mycenae, these wall paintings are part of the museum's Prehistoric Collection.

Other stars of the museum include the works of Geometric and Archaic art (10th to 6th century BC), and **kouroi** and **funerary stelae** (8th to 5th century BC), among them the stelae of the warrior Aristion signed by Aristokles, and the unusual *Running Hoplite* (a hoplite was a Greek infantry soldier). The collection of Classical art (5th to 3rd century BC) contains some of the most renowned surviving ancient statues: the bareback *Jockey of Artemision,* a 2nd-century BC Hellenistic bronze salvaged from the sea; from the same excavation, the bronze *Artemision Poseidon* (some say Zeus), poised and ready to fling a trident (or thunderbolt?); and the *Varvakios Athena,* a half-size marble version of the gigantic gold-and-ivory cult statue that Pheidias erected in the Parthenon.

Light refreshments are served in a lower ground-floor café, which opens out to a patio and sculpture garden. Don't forget to also check the museum's temporary exhibitions. ⊠ *28 Oktovriou (Patission) 44, Exarcheia* ☎ *213/214–4800* ⊕ *www.namuseum.gr* ⊠ *€12; €15 for unified museum ticket (includes Byzantine and Christian Museum, Epigraphical Museum, Numismatic Museum)* Ⓜ *Omonia, Victoria.*

🍽 Restaurants

The student district of Exarcheia offers some casual and more adventurous dining options.

Ama Lachei at Nefeli's

$ | MODERN GREEK | FAMILY | Step out of Kallidromiou Street in edgy Exarcheia and find yourself in a large, lovely courtyard full of little tables and abundant greenery. Ama Lachei has gained a loyal following for its decently priced, delectable Greek dishes always made with a fanciful flourish and with bona fide ingredients. You'll find scrumptious regional cheeses; seafood appetizers such as orzo pasta with Kozani saffron and tiny shrimps; succulent meats and sausages; and plenty of vegetarian options such as the *makarounes Karpathou* (a traditional handmade pasta from Karpathos island) with rocket and *myzithra* cheese. Do like the Greeks, and accompany them with a gratifying choice of regional wines and *tsipouro* (the local firewater), then linger on with your *parea* (group of friends) until late at night. Every day there are five to nine new daily specials. **Known for:** large selection of fish, meat, and vegetable mezedes (small plates); a good choice of regional wines; verdant courtyard setting. Ⓢ *Average main: €13* ⊠ *Kallidromiou 69, Exarcheia* ☎ *210/384–5978* Ⓜ *Omonia.*

Warehouse

$$ | MEDITERRANEAN | What started as a small café and then moved on to be a wine bar, has now become a popular wine restaurant that is busy almost every night of the week. With a list of more than 500 labels from Greece and around the world, the restaurant's focus is still very much on wine, but has also developed a menu with plenty of starters that are especially great for pairing with wine—from bruschettas and salads to carpaccio and ceviche, as well as hot meals like pasta and burgers. The in-house sommelier is always happy to suggest the ideal wine for you. In summer, tables are spread out along the long sidewalk while in winter it's a cozier affair. The restaurant also prides itself on its excellent quality of coffee, so pop by during the day, too. **Known for:** a wonderful selection of Greek and foreign wines and spritzes; a wide and tasty selection of appetizers; friendly service and a lively buzz. Ⓢ *Average main: €15* ⊠ *Mavromichali and Valtetsiou 21, Exarcheia* ☎ *215/ 540–8002* ⊕ *www.warehouseproject.gr* Ⓜ *Panepistimio.*

★ Yiantes

$$ | GREEK | FAMILY | In a flower-filled courtyard—fashionably green and framed by wisteria and jasmine—you peruse a menu that, despite some modern influences, reads like an honest culinary journey through the far reaches of Greece. Almost everything is fresh and delicious, as the chef estimates that about 90% of the ingredients he uses are organic (the owners are organic farmers), including the house wine. And there are plenty of healthy, vegetarian choices, too. Although a little pricier than the norm, this neo-taverna and urban oasis, which attracts a high-brow clientele, is located right next to a charming open-air Riviera cinema. The bargain prix-fixe menu offers excellent value for money. **Known for:** mainly organic ingredients; beautiful garden setting; bargain prix-fixe menu. $ *Average main: €20* ☒ *Valtetsiou 44, Exarcheia* ☎ *210/330–1369* ⏱ *Closed Mon.* Ⓜ *Panepistimio.*

Hotels

Best Western Museum Hotel

$ | HOTEL | FAMILY | If you'd like to stay just a few blocks from the National Archaeological Museum, this reliable hotel offers elegant rooms in good, clean condition, as well as friendly, helpful service, free Wi-Fi, and a satisfying breakfast. **Pros:** clean, well-maintained rooms; pleasant, central location; a good breakfast included. **Cons:** unexciting in terms of ambience and decor; a little dated; not near the ancient sites. $ *Rooms from: €70* ☒ *Bouboulinas 16, Exarcheia* ☎ *210/380–5611* ⊕ *www.museum-hotel.gr* ⇆ *93 rooms* ⏸ *Free breakfast* Ⓜ *Omonia.*

Nightlife

BARS
Alexandrino

BARS/PUBS | This elegant Parisian-style bar and café is frequented by fashion personalities, academics, and thespians alike, who come to unwind over a few cocktails. During the day you'll find a great range of teas and coffees served in porcelain cups. Bistro-style food is also served. ☒ *Benaki 69A, Exarcheia* ☎ *210/382–7780* Ⓜ *Omonia.*

★ Santaroza

BARS/PUBS | Dark, moody, and very atmospheric, with a long bar lined with leather stools upon which the city's hip and glamorous people sip their cocktails, this newish spot can easily become a favorite hangout. Drinks are accompanied by small cold cut meze instead of the usual bowl of nuts, and cocktails are expertly crafted. Music is very important to both the owners and customers here, and every Wednesday and Sunday DJs play vinyl-record sessions, while on other nights you'll hear everything from German B-movie soundtracks to

Leave the Driving to Them

Looking for some summer nightlife? Most of the popular clubs (and even some restaurants) relocate to the beach for the long, hot days and nights of Greek summer. The best way to get to Athens's seaside nightclubs is by taxi—driving on the coastal road can be a nightmare. Just tell the taxi the name of the club; drivers quickly learn the location of the major spots once they open each year.

spiritual jazz. To experience the bar in its full stylish glory, head here between 6–8 pm and sprawl out. After that it gets extremely busy on most nights. ☒ *Asklipiou 69, Exarcheia* ☎ *215/510–1784* Ⓜ *Panepistimio.*

Tralala

BARS/PUBS | An all-day bar that's always bouncing at night, Tralala is especially charming for its variety in music choices, which makes it open to all kinds of punters, and for its happy hour cocktail prices on Saturday night. It also hosts parties throughout the year, the most amusing possibly being the back-to-school night when customers arrive dressed as kids. There are simple chairs and tables and a mosaic tiled floor, all of which contribute to a playful, laid back and cozy vibe. ☒ *Asklipiou 45, Exarcheia* ☎ *210/362–8066* Ⓜ *Panepistimio.*

Shopping

GIFTS
Eftychia

CERAMICS/GLASSWARE | Mainly nature-inspired ceramics (representing birds, flowers, trees, and the sea) are created and sold by artist Eftychia Barzou in her pretty shop. The top seller is a pomegranate, considered a good luck charm for abundance and fertility in Greece. ✉ *Ippokratous 32, Exarcheia* ☎ *210/363–9110* Ⓜ *Panepistimio.*

Plastikourgeio

CRAFTS | Everything in this charming store is recycled, recyclable, reusable, and compostable. The variety of 100% eco-friendly products from Greece and around the world include decor items, table-wear, jewelry and accessories, toys, books, and bags. The store also has a visitable lab in the back where the owners create recycled items, 3D printed designs, and more. They also collaborate with neighborhood cafés, who bring them used plastic to recycle and organize various awareness-raising initiatives throughout the year. Apart from helping the environment by shopping here, you're sure to find some unique pieces to give as gifts. ✉ *Asklipiou 51, Exarcheia* ☎ *213/044–3356* ⊕ *plastikourgeio.com* Ⓜ *Panepistimio.*

Omonia and Metaxourgeio Ομονοίας Μεταξουργείο

Omonia is the meeting point of several vital avenues: Stadiou, Panepistimiou, Ayiou Konstantinou, 3rd September, Pireos, and Athinas. The commercial hot spots of the pedestrianized Aiolou Street and Patission Avenue are also within walking distance. It's a major transport hub, the meeting place of lines 1 (from Kifissia to Piraeus) and 2 (the red metro line). Omonia Square was built at the request of King Otto in 1846, and it quickly became one of the busiest meeting points in the young capital. Soon, however, the low and elegant neoclassical buildings gave way to the gray concrete blocks that dominate the urban horizon today. In recent years, the economic crisis has meant that the once-lively commercial square (a symbol of the economic development of the 1960s) is struggling to find its character after the dramatic influx of illegal immigrants and rise in drug addiction and petty crime.

In Kotzia Square, one can admire the imposing Old Town Hall (now the city's registry office), an ongoing archaeological excavation in the middle of the square, and some lovely neoclassical buildings scattered around (one of them is the National Bank of Greece's Cultural Centre). The Grecotel Pallas Athena hotel is right here, and Omonia Square is just a couple of hundred yards away.

Once ignored as simply a transient neighborhood, Metaxourgeio has acquired its own character as an emerging artist hub. The Municipal Gallery of Athens set up shop here. The surrounding urban grid is an assorted collection of crumbling buildings and renovated houses that pays equal tribute to the glorious past and the hopeful future. But this is definitely a transitional neighborhood filled with recent immigrants (a small Chinatown of grocery and clothing shops is located between Kolonou and Kolokynthous streets), so always be mindful of your surroundings. You may wish to see the Metaxourgeio metro station even if you don't have to go anywhere in particular, if only to admire the wall mural "The myth of my neighborhood" by renowned Greek painter Yiannis Moralis. Just up the road from traffic-ladden Metaxourgeio Square, on Ayiou Konstantinou Street, is the headquarters of the Greek National Theatre.

 Sights

Municipal Gallery of Athens

MUSEUM | One of Athens's oldest neoclassical buildings became the new home of the city's Municipal Art Collection in 2010. The former silk factory, designed in 1833 by Danish architect Hans Christian

Hansen, now houses almost 3,000 important art works from leading 19th- and 20th-century mainly Greek artists (most of the works were acquired during the 1930s and '40s). The museum also hosts archaeological and cultural tours. ✉ *Leonidou and Myllerou, Metaxourgeio* ☎ *210/323–1841* 🎫 *Free* ⏲ *Closed Mon.* [M] *Metaxourgeio.*

🍴 Restaurants

North of Monastiraki, Omonia, the city's main square, is busy by day and seedy by night, but its side streets burst with cultural diversity from the huge influx of immigrants, and trendy art spaces and galleries are scattered around. To the west, the former red-light district of Metaxourgeio gets the green light when it comes to award-winning and avant-garde dining.

★ Aleria

$$$ | **MEDITERRANEAN** | Restaurants, including this award-winning gem of neoclassical design and inventive Mediterranean cuisine, are one reason Metaxourgeio's star is rising. Chef Gikas Xenakis's cooking is a serious candidate for notoriety. Currently there are two types of tasting menus, "earth & sea" or "garden & nature," with a choice of four, five, or six dishes all paired with wine. If you prefer to choose your own there is a wide-ranging wine list. **Known for:** elaborate tasting menus; elegant setting but reasonable prices; deconstructed Greek classics. [$] *Average main: €40* ✉ *Megalou Alexandrou 57, Metaxourgeio* ☎ *210/522–2633* 🌐 *www.aleria.gr* ⏲ *Closed Sun. No lunch* [M] *Metaxourgeio.*

Athinaikon

$$ | **GREEK** | Choose among classic specialties at this old-fashioned mezedopoleio founded in 1932: grilled octopus, shrimp croquettes with white sauce, broad beans simmered in thick tomato sauce, fresh grilled calamari, and *ameletita* (sautéed lamb testicles). All goes well with the light barrel red or ouzo. The decor is no-nonsense ouzeri, with marble tables, dark wood, and framed memorabilia. It's a favorite of attorneys, politicians, and local office workers. A new branch of this eatery has recently opened at Mitropoleos 34, in Central Athens (10563), with the same menu but a more modern interior. **Known for:** small-plates menu; old-fashioned charm and decor; good house-made wine. [$] *Average main: €20* ✉ *Themistokleous 2, Omonia Sq.* ☎ *210/383–8485, 210/383–5905* 🌐 *www.athinaikon.gr* ⏲ *Closed Sun. and Aug.* [M] *Omonia.*

Diporto

$ | **GREEK** | It's the savvy locals' treasured secret—and one of Athens's oldest tavernas—where everyone wandering around Omonia Square has been welcomed through the years. Owner-chef Barba Mitsos keeps everyone happy with his handful of simple, delicious, and dirt-cheap homemade dishes, from the always exceptional *horiatiki* (Greek salad) and buttery *gigantes* (giant beans in tomato sauce) to saucy boiled meats with vegetables and tiny fried fish. Wine is drawn directly from the barrels lining the walls. As for decor, the feeling is authentic 1950s Athens. There is no sign on the door: just walk down the staircase of this corner neoclassical building. **Known for:** an authentic, legendary old-school taverna; wine barrels and the wine in them; dirt-cheap prices (and cash only) for excellent food. [$] *Average main: €10* ✉ *Platia Theatrou, Socratous 9, Omonia Sq.* ☎ *210/321–1463* 💳 *No credit cards* ⏲ *Closed Sun. No dinner* [M] *Omonia.*

Seychelles

$$ | **GREEK** | Although it's named after one of the world's most exotic destinations, this restaurant is almost provincially Greek in its ingredients and culinary attitude. You may experience some exciting moments of surprise, however, when scanning the menu and spotting

Greek Fast Food

Souvlaki is the original Greek fast food: spit-roasted or grilled meat (mainly pork or chicken) on a *kalamaki* stick, with tomatoes, onions, and garlicky tzatziki, all wrapped in a pita. The financial crisis made this cheap, filling, and not terribly unhealthy food even more accessible with souvlaki restaurants popping up almost around every corner. Greeks on the go have always eaten street food, such as the endless variations of *tiropita* cheese pie, *koulouri* (sesame-covered bread rings), roasted chestnuts or ears of grilled corn, and palm-size paper bags of nuts. But modern lifestyles and the arrival of foreign pizza, sandwich, and burger chains, and in more recent years ethnic street food from Asia and South America (mainly located around Syntagma, with falafel shops being the latest rage), have made busy Athenians particularly reliant on fast food. In almost every neighborhood you'll come across a handful of Greek fast-food chains. **Goody's** serves burgers and spaghetti as well as some salads and sandwiches. **Everest** is tops when it comes to *tost*—oval-shaped toasted sandwich buns with any combination of fillings, from omelets to smoked turkey breast, and various spreads (it also sells sweet and savory pies, coffee, and desserts). **Grigoris**, the main rival to Everest, is a chain of sandwich and pie shops that also serves freshly squeezed orange juice and *cappuccino freddo*, which is so beloved to Greeks. If you want to sit down while you eat your fast food, look for a **Flocafe**, where you can find a great choice of coffees as well as a selection of pastries, cookies, and sandwiches.

old favorites like smoked swordfish, hot and sweet little steaks, baked beetroot stuffed with garlicky *skordalia* sauce, and pappardelle with *kavourmas* (terrine). In a neighborhood that's especially à la mode amongst artists from all over, the neotraditional element is played up for its unpretentious and familial charm, but don't fool yourself, this place is decidedly "in." **Known for:** home-style cooking with contemporary flair; an excellent assortment of regional cheeses; artistic following. $ *Average main: €15* ⊠ *Kerameikou 49, Metaxourgeio* ☎ *211/183–4789* ⊕ *www.facebook.com/seychellesrestaurant* Ⓜ *Metaxourgeio*.

🍵 Coffee and Quick Bites

Ble Papagalos

$$ | MEDITERRANEAN | The trendiest and most happening spot for coffee, snacks, and cocktails in Metaxourgeio, Ble Papagalos (Blue Parrot in Greek) is an all-day social destination. Always abuzz mainly with local youth but also people of varying ages, the charming hangout reflects the up-and-coming area's aspirations as an artsy, hip, green, and friendly locale. Try a fresh homemade dessert with your coffee by day or a light snack and drink by night as you watch the world go by. At night it also hosts swing parties and jazz-themed DJ sets. **Known for:** hip, vibrant crowd; funky decor and ambience; great coffee and cocktails. $ *Average main: €15* ⊠ *Leonidou 31, Metaxourgeio* ☎ *211/012–1099* Ⓜ *Metaxourgeio*.

Hotels

★ Fresh Hotel

$$ | HOTEL | Reveling in minimalist glam, this attractive and unconventional boutique hotel has relaxing and expertly decorated rooms, a plugged-in staff, and two restaurants that feature nouvelle-Mediterranean cuisine—in a centrally located, albeit somewhat dodgy neighborhood (by night, at least). **Pros:** Air Lounge Bar restaurant has great food and views; central location; plugged-in staff. **Cons:** surrounding neighborhood is a bit dodgy at night; only a few rooms have great views; noisy if you keep your window open. $ *Rooms from: €150 ⊠ Sofokleous 26, Omonia Sq.* ☎ *210/524–8511 ⊕ www. freshhotel.gr* ⤳ *133 rooms* ⦿ *Free breakfast* Ⓜ *Omonia.*

Grecotel Pallas Athena

$$ | HOTEL | FAMILY | Fun yet posh, this is a crazy/cool boutique art hotel in a slightly sketchy but strategic location near City Hall, Omonia, and the Central Market. **Pros:** reliable Wi-Fi; attentive staff; excellent in-house food. **Cons:** many rooms have poor views; run-down neighborhood that is especially unpleasant at night; some rooms are poorly decorated. $ *Rooms from: €140 ⊠ Athinas 65, at Lykourgou, Omonia Sq.* ☎ *210/325–0900 ⊕ www.grecotelpallasathena.com* ⤳ *63 rooms* ⦿ *Free breakfast* Ⓜ *Omonia.*

 Performing Arts

SHOWS

Rex Music Theatre

THEATER | Over-the-top is the way to describe a performance at Rex Music Theatre—it's a laser-light show, multi-costume-change extravaganza, with headlining pop and bouzouki stars. Programs and performances change every season, so check out the local press for the most current listings. ⊠ *Panepistimiou 48, Omonia Sq.* ☎ *210/382–3269* Ⓜ *Omonia.*

Pangrati Παγκράτι

Just behind the marble Panathenaic Stadium, which hosted the first Olympic Games of modern times, in 1896, Pangrati is filled with concrete apartment blocks as well as such leafy squares as Platia Proskopon and Platia Varnava. Unfortunately, only a few neoclassical buildings from the turn of the 20th century survived the building boom of the 1960s. This is a safe and quiet neighborhood, with Central Athens a comfortable half-hour walk (there is also good bus service). The First Cemetery of Athens is located in Mets, which borders Pangrati, and notable politicians and personalities in recent Greek history are buried here; the artful marble statues and tombs made in their memory are worth a visit. The neighborhood also has a few noteworthy tavernas and restaurants. In recent years its nightlife scene has sprung up, too.

Restaurants

Urbane without being snobby or expensive, mostly residential Pangrati is a haven for academics, artists, and expats who bask in the homey if somewhat shabby warmth of this neighborhood in the southeastern quarter of the city.

Fish Point

$$ | SEAFOOD | At first glance you may think this is just an ordinary fishmonger, with all its glistening goods laid out in ice boxes like jewels, unless you look to the right and see that next to the display of the day's catch is a modern, polished restaurant. You'll find wonderful seafood at very reasonable prices in an increasingly exciting neighborhood spot just off Plastira Square. The menu includes playful and mouthwatering appetizers (including ceviches and tartares), traditional Greek cooked and grilled dishes, perfect seafood pastas (unsurprising, as the chef is Roman), and even an excellent selection of sushi. A deli sells rare fish products from around Greece. It's obvious that everyone involved here knows and loves fish dearly; after all, they own two quality fish farms in the country. **Known for:** superfresh fish and many raw fish choices (ceviche, sushi, etc.); attached fish market and seafood deli; seafood pastas. [$] *Average main: €20* ✉ *Archimidous 8, Pangrati* ☎ *210/756–5321* 🌐 *www.fishpoint.gr* [M] *Evangelismos.*

Frater & Soror

$$ | **ECLECTIC** | With stylish designer decor and a menu to match its eclectic approach, this all-day restaurant-bar serves scrumptious feel-good fusion foods until midnight. Having set up a wood oven in its basement, used to lend smoky flavors and rustic textures to original dishes, the chef plays with a combination of American street-food favorites with Middle Eastern and Italian touches as well as creative modern Greek twists.The music is loud and the bar, which specializes in gin cocktails, can get a little raucous on weekend nights—after all, one of the restaurant's mottos is "everything boring is strictly forbidden." **Known for:** original recipes; a lively bar with gin specials; sophisticated culinary strokes. [$] *Average main: €15* ✉ *Amynta 6, Pangrati* ☎ *210/721–3720* 🌐 *www.fraterandsoror.com* 🕒 *Closed Mon.* [M] *Evangelismos.*

Karavitis

$$ | **GREEK** | This very traditional taverna has been around since 1926 and doesn't seem to have changed a bit in that span, serving classic, well-prepared Greek cuisine. Pungent *tirokafteri* (a peppery cheese dip), *stamnaki* (beef baked in a clay pot), and *bekri mezes* (lamb in a zesty tomato sauce) are among the taverna's specialty. The winter dining room maintains its prewar ambience and is insulated with huge wine casks; in summer there is garden seating in a patio across the street (get there early so you don't end up at the noisy sidewalk tables). **Known for:** plenty of prewar charm; beef baked in a clay pot and lamb cooked in zesty tomato sauce; cash only. [$] *Average main: €15* ✉ *Arktinou 35, at Pausaniou, Pangrati* ☎ *210/721–5155* 🌐 *www.facebook.com/karavitistavern* 💳 *No credit cards* 🕒 *Closed 1 wk mid-Aug. No lunch Mon.–Sat.* [M] *Evangelismos.*

★ Spondi

$$$$ | **MODERN FRENCH** | What is perhaps the capital's top restaurant is justly celebrated as a feast for both the eyes and the taste buds, and eating here is a serious affair. Chef Anghelos Lantos uses French techniques to create his inspired culinary art. Both à la carte and prix-fixe offerings convey why Michelin has awarded the restaurant two coveted stars. The wine list contains both Greek and international options, all carefully chosen. You will pay dearly to dine here, but it's worth the splurge. **Known for:** langoustines served with caviar and citrus sauce; lamb with eggplant; elaborate prix-fixe menus with wine pairings. [$] *Average main: €50* ✉ *Pirronos 5, at Varnava Sq., Pangrati* ☎ *210/756–4021* 🌐 *www.spondi.gr* 🕒 *No lunch* [M] *Evangelismos.*

Taverna Virinis

$$ | **GREEK** | **FAMILY** | In summer, Athenian couples, families, and groups of all ages find refuge in the pleasant, open-air garden of this taverna, as they chomp on grilled meats, tasty homemade *ladera*, salads, and dips. Run by the third generation of the same family, who provide you with very friendly service, the taverna has an effervescent atmosphere and sees a lot of excellent house wine flowing with every meal. **Known for:** good lamb; friendly service and laid-back atmosphere; excellent housemade wine. [$] *Average main: €20* ✉ *Archimidou 11, Pangrati* ☎ *210/701–2153* 🕒 *No dinner Sun.* [M] *Evangelismos.*

The Greek Fish Taverna

Enjoying the bounty of the seas that wash against Greek shores can be a fishy business. The waters have been overfished for decades and much "Greek" fish served today is often frozen from other waters. Take heart, though. You can still feast on delicious fish in Greece—it's just a question of what you order, and where.

Patrons of fish restaurants are usually greeted with iced displays of the catch of the day. Proprietors will often spout some mumbo-jumbo about the fish being caught only an hour earlier— allow the shills some poetic license and go for the operative word here: *fresco*, fresh, as opposed to *katepsigmeno*, frozen.

The fish you choose will be sold by the portion, *merida*, and priced by the kilo. Expect to pay at least €55 a kilo for such popular fish as *xifia*, swordfish; *lavraki*, sea bass; *tsipoura*, sea bream; and *barbounia*, red mullet.

Yes, fish is expensive in Greece, but remember: that price is per kilo, and the portion you order may well weigh, and cost, less.

What to Order

Garides, shrimp, are often served deliciously as *saganaki*: baked with fresh tomatoes and feta cheese and brought to the table sizzling.

Sardelles, sardines, are grilled, fried, or eaten salt-baked and marinated.

Papalina are small sardines, and *atherina* are very small sardines, usually fried crisp.

Gavros, anchovies, are almost always marinated in lemon and vinegar or deep-fried.

Kalamari, squid, are often fried, but they are sometimes grilled on the fire. A tasty relative is the *soupia*, cuttlefish, usually cooked in its own ink and wine.

Htapodi, octopus, is grilled, marinated in vinegar and oil, or stewed with tomatoes and onions.

Mydia, mussels, are usually steamed, and are often taken out of their shells and served in risotto, seafood pasta, or salads.

Old-Time Favorites

In addition to fresh fish, keep an eye out for these old standards. *Taramosalata*, fish roe salad, is a tasty spread, a poor man's caviar made from carp eggs, blended with olive oil, lemon juice, and garlic.

Kakavia and *psarosoupa* are velvety variations of fish soup, usually made from pieces of whatever fish is available, simmered in broth with vegetables.

Bakaliaros, cod, is often served as *bakaliaros skordalia*, dipped in batter, deep-fried, and drizzled with garlic sauce.

⬤ Shopping

CLOTHING

Juju de Kokimo

CLOTHING | Billowy silks, soft cotton, and fluffy wool are the raw materials for the designer's luxuriantly abstract, handmade creations. Kimono-style tops and asymmetrical dresses, coats inspired by 1920s-era Japan, leather bags, and jewelry made from a variety of materials. All pieces are limited editions and unique. ✉ *Archelaou 20, Pangrati* ☎ *210/723–3870* Ⓜ *Evangelismos*.

Ilisia Ιλίσια

Nearly on the outskirts of Central Athens (just 15 minutes' walk from Syntagma Square), this densely populated neighborhood takes its name from the river Ilisos, which once flowed here (between the streets Michalakopoulou and Kalirrois) before it was drained in the 1960s to create space for the construction of apartment blocks and the expansion of the city's road network. It is also known for its many hospitals built early in the 20th century. It is still within easy reach of the main sights (via Megaron Mousikis metro station) and a tiny bit closer to the Eleftherios Venizelos Airport than more central neighborhoods like Monastiraki and Plaka, and offers some excellent accommodation and dining options. The most important museum in the area is the National Gallery of Art, which is closed for seemingly never-ending renovation until at least 2021. The area also encompasses the mostly residential neighborhood of Ambelokipi, which is bounded by Kifissias, Vassilissis Sofias, and Alexandras avenues, and has the dubious honor of being the second most densely populated district (after Kypseli) in Athens. The United States Embassy is here, while lively Mavili Square is a popular nightlife haunt.

🍴 Restaurants

Ilisia is close to the center, and its open spaces are an excellent base for some easily accessible restaurants offering tastes of Greek regional cuisine.

Balthazar

$$ | CONTEMPORARY | In an airy neoclassical mansion with a leafy, minimalist courtyard—paved with original painted tiles, canopied by huge date palms, and illuminated by colored lanterns—Balthazar truly feels like a summer oasis in the middle of Athens. Acclaimed chef Christophoros Peskias keeps the quality and flavor high on the up-to-the-minute Mediterranean menu, adding exotic touches from Asia in menus of finger food, summer dishes, and sushi—all of which go brilliantly with a few well-mixed cocktails. The crowd is fun and hip, moneyed, cosmopolitan, and beautiful, and this place has miraculously managed to remain as fresh and trendy today as when it first opened in 1973. **Known for:** glamorous garden setting; sophisticated, Asian-influenced dishes; fashionable clientele. $ *Average main: €18* ✉ *Tsocha 27, Ilisia* ✛ *At Vournazou* ☎ *210/644–1215* ⊕ *www.balthazar.gr* ⊘ *Closed Sun. No lunch* Ⓜ *Ampelokoipi.*

Galaxy Restaurant

$$$$ | MEDITERRANEAN | On the rooftop of Hilton Athens you can drink and dine on a long, curving white terrace that overlooks one of the city's most mesmerizing views. From VIPs to lovers, since the '60s diners have come here to take in the stunning, starlit vistas of Athens's most notable landmarks in a tranquil, glamorous atmosphere. There are two menus here, one featuring modern Mediterranean dishes like shrimp carbonara with crispy Iberico guanciale or beef burger with pulled duck confit and *mimolette* cheese and the other offering a wide selection of classic as well as creative sushi dishes. The wine list is well curated and the cocktail (and mocktail) options very generous—while you wait you can also ask the barman to create a cocktail to suit your tastes. **Known for:** rooftop setting; modern Mediterranean dishes; glamorous setting. $ *Average main: €50* ✉ *Vas. Sofias 46, Ilisia* ☎ *210/728–1000* ⊕ *www.hiltonathens.gr* Ⓜ *Evangelismos.*

★ Vassilenas

$$ | MODERN GREEK | With a 100-year history, Vassilenas was once a humble fish tavern in Piraeus that gained cult status among Greece's leading intelligensia and the world's glitterati for its 18-course set menu of small but delectable dishes. Today it has moved on to a new location

and a new conceptual direction, but remains true to the authentic value of its dishes. Its modern, beautifully lit interior decor mirrors the unique facade of the nearby Hilton, an iconic '60s building, and its set menu is now made up of eight courses, from amuse-bouche to dessert, paired with three different wines. Indeed, excellent wine is a strong point at this establishment, as is the quality of the ingredients and the gourmet preparation of the dishes. There is also an à la carte menu. Dress up a little and look forward to a delightful experience in a warm yet sophisticated ambience with accommodating service, whether you're sitting in the garden or indoors. **Known for:** fresh fish and authentic flavors in modern renditions; an excellent wine list; designer decor. [$] *Average main: €25* ✉ *Vrasida 16, Ilisia* ☎ *210/721–0501* 🌐 *www.vassilenas.gr* [M] *Evangelismos.*

Vlassis

$$ | GREEK | FAMILY | Relying on traditional recipes from northern Greece and the islands, as well as gourmet Mediterranean creations, the chefs here whip up some noteworthy home-style cooking in the heart of the city. With a menu that changes every winter and summer, this family-run restaurant, which opened in 1983, always centers on fresh regional ingredients such as fish, seafood, vegetables, cheeses, and meats. In winter, head inside, where large windows look out, and authentic works of art by well-known Greek painters decorate the walls. In summer book a table outdoors and watch the world go by. **Known for:** well-prepared fresh fish; garbanzo bean soup starter; seasonally changing menu. [$] *Average main: €25* ✉ *Maiandrou 15, Ilisia* ☎ *210/725–6335* 🌐 *www.vlassisrestaurant.gr* 🕓 *Closed Aug.–mid-Sept. No dinner Sun.* [M] *Megaro Mousikis.*

Hotels

★ Hilton Athens

$$ | HOTEL | FAMILY | Although the impressive Hilton is one of the city's venerable architectural landmarks, characteristically covered in Egyptian-style hieroglyphics, it's also been kept up to date with modern, glossy, and minimalist design. **Pros:** outstanding service; the city's largest pool surrounded by greenery; fantastic rooftop restaurant and bar. **Cons:** very expensive restaurant; extra fee to use the pool, spa, and gym, unless you are staying in one of the suites; high extra charge for Internet access. [$] *Rooms from: €170* ✉ *Vasilissis Sofias 46, Ilisia* ☎ *210/728–1000* 🌐 *www.hiltonathens.gr* 🛏 *517 rooms* 🍴 *No meals* [M] *Evangelismos.*

Crowne Plaza Athens City Centre

$$ | HOTEL | FAMILY | On the site of the city's former Holiday Inn (it opened its doors in mid-2008), this is among the most technology-friendly Athens hotels. **Pros:** high-tech infrastructure; outdoor swimming pool (closes at 7 pm); spacious rooms and bathrooms. **Cons:** costly breakfast; not central, so you'll need to take taxis; the pool is on the small side. [$] *Rooms from: €130* ✉ *Michalakopoulou 50, Ilisia* ☎ *210/727–8000* 🌐 *www.cpathens.com* 🛏 *193 rooms* 🍴 *No meals* [M] *Megaro Mousikis.*

Nightlife

BARS

Balthazar

BARS/PUBS | Athenians of all ages come to escape the summer heat at this stylish, upscale bar-restaurant in a neoclassical house with a lush garden courtyard and subdued music. Reservations are essential for the popular restaurant. ✉ *Tsoha 27, at Vournazou, Ilisia* ☎ *210/644–1215* 🌐 *www.balthazar.gr* [M] *Ambelokipi.*

Briki

BARS/PUBS | On hot summer nights the fountain in Mavili Square, spreads coolness over the tables of café-bars like this one, enjoyed by the most flirtatious of urban night owls until the morning's wee hours. Funk and jazz music is usually on the playlist. In the morning Briki—really anyplace in Mavili Square—is ideal for a coffee break. ⊠ *Dorilaiou 6, Ilisia* ☎ *210/645–2380* Ⓜ *Megaro Mousikis.*

★ O Kyrios

BARS/PUBS | Unlike Briki next door, where the younger generations go to flirt and down shots, O Kyrios caters to a more mature and glamorous crowd seeking sophisticated cocktails and finger foods to match. Dress up, perch yourself on a gold stool, and order a bottle of Prosecco or a potent martini in a tiny glass. ⊠ *Dorileou 4, Ilisia* ☎ *210/640–0615* ⊕ *kyriosathens.com* Ⓜ *Megaro Mousikis.*

🎭 Performing Arts

PERFORMANCE VENUES
★ Megaron Mousikis/Athens Concert Hall

CONCERTS | World-class Greek and international artists take the stage at the Megaron Mousikis to perform in concerts and opera from September through June. Information and tickets are available weekdays 10–6 and Saturday 10–2. Prices range from €12 to €90; there's a substantial discount for students and those 8 to 18 years old. Tickets go on sale a few weeks in advance, and many events sell out within hours. ⊠ *Vasilissis Sofias and Kokkali, Ilisia* ☎ *210/728–2000* ⊕ *www. megaron.gr* Ⓜ *Megaro Mousikis.*

Neos Kosmos
Νέος Κόσμος

Not too far from Athens's historic center lies another neighborhood, which was created in order to accommodate Greek refugees who arrived by the thousands after the Smyrna catastrophe of 1922. Its name means "New World" in Greek. Opposite the main entrance of the Athenaeum Intercontinental Hotel, it is still possible today to see some of the original surviving refugee buildings, built in the Bauhaus style of the 1930s and still occupied by immigrants who moved into the area in the 1980s. Since the arrival of the Onassis Cultural Centre, Neos Kosmos has been developing into a trendy area—and not least because it's also across Koukaki, one of Athens's most "in" neighborhoods.

🍽 Restaurants

Fita

$$$ | **MODERN GREEK** | When it opened quite recently, this place became the talk of the town both for its constantly (as in, daily) changing menu and for its interesting approach to classic Greek ingredients and culinary culture. Using the freshest ingredients, chiefly sourced from small producers in Athens and around Greece, this place honors Greek cooking principles and flavors but the chef doesn't hesitate to add his own quirky twists. Expect clean, enjoyable, and authentic Greek flavors with a modern perspective. **Known for:** a menu that changes daily; fresh, regional ingredients; regional tastes with a modern twist. Ⓢ *Average main: €30* ⊠ *Dourm 1, Neos Kosmos* ⊹ *Kasomoule Tram Stop* ☎ *211/414–8624.*

🛏 Hotels

Athenaeum InterContinental

$$ | **HOTEL** | **FAMILY** | With a marble atrium lobby, highlighted by the "Blue Man" by George Lappas, as well as a private art collection, Athens's largest hotel is like a world unto itself. **Pros:** beautiful, spacious rooms; excellent restaurants with Acropolis view; top conference facilities. **Cons:** located along a busy thoroughfare; a long walk to city center (10-minute taxi ride); no free Wi-Fi in rooms. Ⓢ *Rooms from:*

€160 ✉ Syngrou 89–93, Neos Kosmos ☎ 210/920–6000 🌐 www.ichotelsgroup.com 🛏 553 rooms 🍴 No meals [M] Neos Kosmos.

Piraeus Πειραιάς

When you think of Piraeus, you'll most likely visualize a massive (Europe's largest) passenger port with every kind of ship and thousands of bag-pulling travelers scurrying about. It's Greece's main gateway to its many islands. But it's also a city within a city (locals don't consider themselves Athenians) that has charming pockets with traditional eateries and attractive architecture.

🍴 Restaurants

Athenians enjoy going to Piraeus for a change of scene and fresh fish, usually to be enjoyed at tavernas by the sea. Urban explorers can also discover small, rustic tavernas reminiscent of the one created for the hit film *Never on Sunday,* in which Melina Mercouri sang "Ta Paidia Tou Pirea" (to the boys of Piraeus) in one of the town's little pockets.

★ Margaro

$ | SEAFOOD | With one of the most refreshingly simple menus in Athens (it's limited to fresh, fried sea bream, red mullet, and shrimps with a side of Greek salad and house wine), this taverna is always busy. On weekends lines form, as there is a no-reservation policy. Although located next to the seafront Naval Academy, there is no view to speak of—all the more reason to focus on the seafood. Eating the shrimps with your hands will only add to the pleasure. **Known for:** basic yet rewarding menu; very fresh fish, fried to a perfect crisp; delicious Greek salad. *[$] Average main: €10 ✉ Marias Chatzikiriakou 126, Piraeus ☎ 210/451–4226 ⏲ No dinner Sun.*

Papaioannou

$$ | SEAFOOD | FAMILY | Elegant but unpretentious and located in Piraeus's prettiest spot—the Mikrolimano (little port) marina where sailboats, fishing boats, and yachts bob up and down in the sea—Papaioannou is a classic fish restaurant for those craving every kind of seafood (from mouthwatering razor clams, crawfish with spinach, and sea urchin, to marinated, grilled calamari and fried giant shrimp). For romantics, the ideal time to visit is sunset, although this is a great place to take your family for a fish feast or even have a stylish and tasty business lunch. **Known for:** daily-changing menu according to what's available and fresh; beautiful seafront setting; good service. *[$] Average main: €20 ✉ Akti Koumoundourou 42, Piraeus ☎ 210/422–5059 ⏲ No dinner Sun.*

Chapter 4

THE SARONIC GULF ISLANDS

4

Updated by
Adrian Vrettos

⊙ Sights	🍴 Restaurants	🛏 Hotels	🛍 Shopping	🍸 Nightlife
★★★★☆	★★★☆☆	★★☆☆☆	★☆☆☆☆	★★☆☆☆

WELCOME TO THE SARONIC GULF ISLANDS

TOP REASONS TO GO

★ **Handsome Hydra:** The place for the jet-setter who appreciates walking more than showing off new wheels, Hydra offers both tranquility and sociability—a bustling main town and abundant walking trails. What's here (stone houses set above a welcoming harbor) and what's not (cars) provide a relaxing retreat.

★ **Ship-Shape Spetses:** A fine jumping-off point for the Peloponnesian shore, cosmopolitan Spetses is famed for its Spetsiot seafaring tradition—not surprisingly, the Old Town harbor is car-free and picture-perfect.

★ **Ancient Aegina:** Not far from this vast island's medieval Paliachora—with nearly 20 churches—is the Temple of Aphaia, one of Greece's best-preserved Archaic sites. Aegina's isle is the closest Saronic island to Athens's port of Piraeus.

★ **Pistachio Perfection:** You can already taste them—salty, sweet, mellow—and the best pistachio nuts anywhere may come from Aegina.

Bounded on three sides by sea, Attiki (Attica) has an indented, sun-gilded coastline fringed with innumerable sandy beaches and rocky inlets. Just to the south of Athens, straddling the gulf between its bustling port of Piraeus and the Peloponnese, are the Saronic Gulf islands, the aristocracy of the Greek isles. Riddled with coves and natural harbors ideal for seafaring, the islands of Aegina, Hydra, and Spetses are enveloped in a patrician aura that is the combined result of history and their more recent cachet as the playgrounds of wealthy Athenians. Owing to their proximity and beauty, they can get swamped with vacationers during the summer, yet they retain their distinct cultural traditions, perhaps best appreciated out of season.

1 Aegina. The largest of the Saronic islands, Aegina is a land of contrasts—from its crowded beach towns to its isolated, rugged mountain peaks, scattered ruins, and forgotten monasteries. Take in the main town's famous fish market, visit the pre-Hellenic Temple of Aphaia, and then explore the ghost town of Palia-chora, still spirit-warm thanks to its 20 chapels.

2 Hydra. Noted for its 19th-century *archontika* (mansions), its crescent-shaped waterfront, and fashionable boutiques, Hydra has been catnip to writers and artists for decades—visit the isle's galleries or bring along your easel and let your own creative juices flow. For Hydriot splendor in excelsis, visit the 1780 Lazaros Koundouriotis Mansion or buy a glittering jewel or two at Elena Votsi's harbor-front jewelry shop.

3 Spetses. The island, with regular boat service to pine-lined beaches, is perfect for beach-hopping. It's also top contender for the most dining and night-life offerings of the Saronic isles. As for sights, Bouboulina's museum in the main town offers fascinating details about the island's storied history.

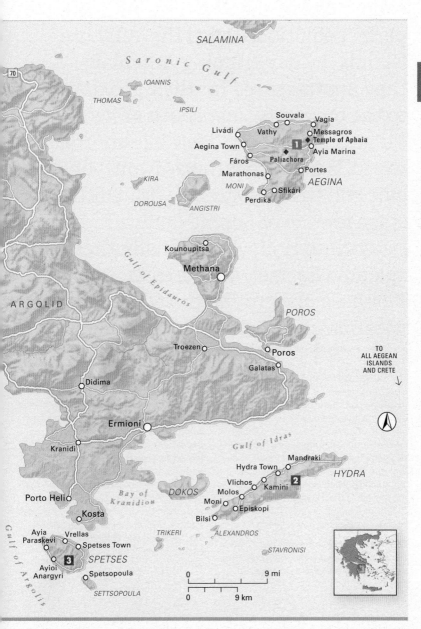

SALAMINA

Saronic Gulf

IOANNIS

THOMAS

IPSILI

70

Souvala
Vagia
Livádi
Vathy
Messagros
Temple of Aphaia
Aegina Town
1
Ayia Marina
Fáros
Paliachora
KIRA
Marathonas
Portes
MONI
AEGINA
Sfikári
DOROUSA
Perdika
ANGISTRI

Kounoupitsa

Gulf of Epidauros

Methana

ARGOLID

POROS

Troezen
Poros
Galatas

TO
ALL AEGEAN
ISLANDS
AND CRETE
↓

Didima

N

Ermioni

Gulf of Idras

Kranidi

Mandraki
Hydra Town
2
HYDRA
Vlichos
Kamini
Molos
Porto Heli
DOKOS
Moni
Episkopi
Bay of
Kranidíou
Bilsi
Kosta
TRIKERI
ALEXANDROS
Ayia
Paraskevi
Vrellas
STAVRONISI
Spetses Town
3
SPETSES
Ayioi
Anargyri
Spetsopoula
SETTSOPOULA

Gulf of Argolis

0   9 mi
0   9 km

Only have a few days in Greece but need a taste of island life? Hopping over to one of the Saronic isles is the perfect solution. Called the "offshore islands" by day-tripping Athenians, they are treasured for their proximity to the burly city. Just south of hectic Piraeus, Aegina still feels like another world. Heading southward you'll find chic and cosmopolitan Hydra, a fitting stage for one of Sophia Loren's first forays into Hollywood. Finally, there is splendid Spetses, anchored off mainland Kosta—a playground prized by carefree vacationing Greeks.

The Saronic Gulf islands, whose ancient city-states rivaled Athens, are now virtually a part of the capital. Aegina, one of the most-visited islands in Greece because of its proximity to the capital, is 30 minutes from Piraeus by hydrofoil, while Spetses, the most "remote" and the greenest of the Saronic islands, is 120 minutes away. South of the Argolid, the peninsula that divides the Saronic Gulf from the Gulf of Argolis, rests Hydra, poor in beaches but rich in charm.

Aegina's pretty country villas have drawn shipping executives, who often commute daily from the island to their offices in Piraeus. Here pine forests mix with groves of pistachio trees, a product for which Aegina is justly famous. Hydra and Spetses are farther south and both ban automobiles. Hydra's stately mansions, restaurants, and boutiques cater to the sophisticated traveler and art lover. Spetses has both broad forests and regal, neoclassical buildings. Rather than being spoiled by tourism, all four islands have managed to preserve their laid-back attitude, well suited to the hedonistic lifestyle of weekend pleasure-seekers arriving by yacht and hydrofoil.

Planning

When to Go

The weather on the islands tends to be the same as in Athens, though the heat can feel more intense on the arid peaks of Aegina and Hydra. The island breeze—felt on all the Saronic isles, particularly later in the day—makes these vacation destinations more refreshing than the mainland on summer evenings (and in winter, more bitter, due to the lower humidity). There is a risk of summer fires, so do not wander into forested areas in the hot-weather months. Check the forecast before heading to Aegina, Hydra, or Spetses at any time of year—bad weather in the off-season or strong August winds (*meltemia*) may strand you on the island you only intended to visit briefly.

Planning Your Time

The Saronic isles make fabulous day trips, though an overnight stay—or hop to a second isle—is recommended if you have the time. To ease into the pace of island life probably requires at least two days per island; however, you can visit all the islands in as few as four days. Aegina—the closest to Piraeus—is the easiest to do in a day since it has the most regular traffic to and fro, especially if your time is very limited. Although all the Saronic islands have swimming beaches, those on Spetses are the best, so you may want to linger. In three days you can explore most of Hydra or Spetses, or really get to know Aegina. Is island-hopping on your agenda? Devote the first two days to the small main town and beautiful beaches of Spetses. In the next two, wander Hydra's port town, and if you're ambitious (and in shape), hike to a monastery. Then give Aegina its day's due. One no-sweat tip to keep in mind: In July and August visit Saronic island archaeological sites like the Temple of Aphaia as early in the day as possible. There is little shade at such sites, and the midday heat can be withering. And, of course, an early start may help you avoid crowds.

Getting Here and Around

A car is only truly useful on Aegina, as cars are prohibited on the islands of Hydra and (except by special permit) Spetses. Renting scooters, mopeds, and bicycles is popular with tourists on Aegina and Spetses. But extreme caution is advised: roads can be narrow, winding, and treacherous, and some drivers are scornful of your safety. Always wear a helmet! If braving the road isn't part of your plan, never fear: on Aegina, there is regular bus service between towns and beaches. But on Hydra, you can famously travel only by water taxi, mule, bike, horse, or donkey—no cars or buses allowed. On Spetses, get around by buggy, bike, scooter, boat, and two buses. But, as with any personal transportation in Greece, it's best to confirm prices first, so you don't get taken for a different kind of ride.

BOAT AND FERRY

Spetses is so close to the Peloponnese mainland that you can drive there from Athens, park, and cross the channel in any of a number of caïques (price negotiable) at the ports, but to get to any of the other Saronic Gulf islands, you must take to the sea in a ferry. You can get a weekly boat schedule from the Greek National Tourism Organization (⊕ www.visitgreece.gr). You can get detailed info about ferry schedules at ⊕ www.ferries.gr, ⊕ ferriesingreece. com, or the handy app ⊕ www.nisea.co, and you can also reserve through a travel agent. Large ferries are the leisurely and least expensive way to travel; however, most people prefer the speedier passenger-only "flying dolphins" (and be aware that there's also a ferry company called "Aegean Flying Dolphins") and hydrofoils.

Saronic Gulf Islands

○ Elefsis

E94

Megara

Peramos

ATHENS ★

Perama

Xeno ○ Paloukia

Perama

Isthmus ○

Salamina

Eandio ○ ○ Selinia

70

SALAMINA

Saronic Gulf

IOANNIS

IPSILI

THOMAS

Korfos ○

AEGINA

Souvala **Souvala** *Vagia Beach*

Livádi ○ Vathy ○ Vagia

KIRA

Aegina Town ○ Fáros ○ Messagros

Kolona Beach Hellenic **Temple of Aphaia**

Marathonas Beach Wildlife **Ayia Marina**

Aeginitissa Beach Hospital

Ayia Marina Beach

Galaneika ○

ANGISTRI ○ Portes

DOROUSA **Marathonas**

Moni Beach Sfikári

MONI **Perdika**

Ligourio ○

70

Klima **TO ALL AEGEAN ISLANDS AND CRETE** ↓

ARGOLID

Kounoupitsa ○

Gulf of Epidauros **Methana** ○

Trahia ○

POROS

Troezen ○

Didima ○

Poros ●

Galatas ○

Ermioni ○

Piepi ○ ○ Metochi

Kranidi ○

Gulf of Idras Mandraki Beach

Zourvas Monastery

Mikro Kamini **Mandraki**

Porto Heli ○ *Vlichos Beach* **Hydra Town** **HYDRA**

Bay of Kranidiou **Kamini**

Molos ○ Ayios Nikolaos Monastery

Zogeria Beach *DOKOS* **Vlichos**

Gulf of Argolis Kosta ○ Moni ○ Profitis Ilias Monastery

Zogeria Bisti ○ Episkopi ○

Ayia Vrellas *Kaiki* *Bisti Beach* Ayios Nikolaos Beach

Paraskevi **Spetses Town**

TRIKERI

Ayioi **Ayia Marina**

Anargyroi Ayia Marina

SPETSES *ALEXANDROS*

○ Spetsopoula *STAVRONISI*

Ayia Paraskevi *SETTSOPOULA*

Ayioi Anargyroi

0   9 mi

0   9 km

Hellenic Seaways, ANES Ferries, and Nova Ferries will carry you and your car from the main port in Piraeus (Gate E8), about a thousand feet from the metro, to Aegina (1 hour). There are approximately a half dozen daily departures, and boat fares begin at about €8 per person for Aegina, from €20 for cars (there are no slow ferries to Hydra or Spetses). Speedier Hellenic Seaways and Aegean Flying Dolphins ferries and hydrofoils also depart from Piraeus (Gate E8 or E9). These faster ferries can get you to Aegina in 40 minutes (€13), to Hydra in 90 minutes (€28), and to Spetses in just under two hours (€38.50). There are about a half dozen departures daily to each island, but make reservations ahead of time—boats fill quickly.

What about boats and ferries between the various Saronic Gulf islands? Hellenic Seaways fast-ferry routes connect Piraeus to Hydra and Spetses year-round. There are about five daily round-trips from October to April, more the rest of the year. In summer, Saronic Ferries offers daily service that connects Aegina with the tiny islands of Angistri, Poros, and Methana. But plan your Argo-Saronic island-hopping carefully in the off-season. During that time, boats between the islands are much less frequent, and you may have to combine several ferries to reach your destination, some fast and some slow. And connecting service is not available every day; on some days (and in some seasons), you will have to backtrack to the main port at Piraeus to catch another boat. *For information regarding specific ferry companies, see Boat and Ferry in Travel Smart.*

CAR

On Aegina, there is a good network of mostly narrow rural roads (two lanes at best). Drivers should be prepared for occasional abrupt turns; major towns and sites are well marked. Cars are not allowed on Hydra. Unlike on Hydra, cars are not banned outright on Spetses:

residents are permitted to ferry their autos to the island. Sadly, the presence of cars seems to be getting more pronounced every year, despite the wishes of many inhabitants. Karagiannis Klimi Travel, on Aegina, rents both cars and motorcycles. *(See Tour Options, below.)*

Hotels

Accommodations on the Saronic Gulf islands range from elegant 19th-century mansions—usually labeled as "traditional settlements"—to boutique-style hotels to spare rental rooms overlooking a noisy waterfront. Rented rooms can be less expensive than hotels and offer an easy option for fly-by-the-seaters: just follow signs, or solicitors who show up when boats come in. (And note that it's okay to check out the room before committing.) From June to September, book far in advance. Off-season (October–April), you'll have fewer hotels to choose from, as many close during the colder months. Souvala and Ayia Marina are suitable lodging alternatives to Aegina's main town, but on the other islands it's best to stay in or around the main ports, the hubs of these islands. If you want to plan a great off-season trip with minimum hassle, putting your itinerary in the hands of a professional is your best bet. On Aegina we recommend Karagiannis Klimi Travel *(see Tour Options, below)*. Also note that during certain times of the year (most notably summer), you may get better deals on weekdays than on Athenian-heavy weekends.

Restaurants

The cuisine of the Saronic islands resembles that of Athens, Attica, and the Peloponnese. Local ingredients predominate, with fresh fish perhaps the greatest (and most expensive) delicacy. Because much of Attica's vegetation is used to support herds of grazing sheep and the omnivorous goat, the meat of both animals is also a staple in many country tavernas. Although it is becoming increasingly difficult to find the traditional Greek taverna with large stew pots full of the day's hot meal, or big *tapsi* (pans) of *pastitsio* (layers of pasta, meat, and cheese laced with cinnamon) or *papoutsakia* (eggplant slices filled with minced meat), market towns still harbor the occasional rustic haunt, offering tasty, inexpensive meals. Always ask to see the *kouzina* (kitchen) to look at the day's offerings, or to even peer inside the pots. Informal dress is appropriate at all but the very fanciest restaurants and, unless noted, reservations are not necessary.

Restaurant and hotel reviews have been shortened. For full information, visit Fodors.com.

What it Costs in euros			
$	$$	$$$	$$$$
RESTAURANTS			
under €15	€15–€25	€26–€40	over €40
HOTELS			
under €125	€125–€225	€226–€275	over €275

Tour Options

Most agencies run tour excursions at about the same prices, but CHAT and Key Tours have the best service and guides. A full-day cruise from Piraeus, with either CHAT or Key Tours, visits Aegina, Poros, and Hydra, and costs around €98 (including buffet lunch on the ship). Karagiannis Klimi Travel on Aegina and Hydreoniki Travel on Hydra also offer local tours.

CONTACTS Karagiannis Klimi Travel. ✉ *Panayi Irioti 44, Aegina Town* ☎ *22970/28780, 6944116863.* **Key Tours.** ✉ *Athanasiou Diakou 26, Athens* ☎ *210/923-3166, 210/923-3266* ⊕ *www.*

keytours.gr. **Personality Journeys.** ✉ *1 Orfeos str, Vouliagmeni* ☎ *2152/151629, 69324/44427* ⊕ *www.personalityjourneys.com.*

Visitor Information

There are few main official tourist offices for the Saronic Gulf islands, though you'll find an information center on Aegina that is operated by the Aegina Municipality. Keep in mind that in lieu of official agencies, there is an array of private travel agencies (usually based in offices near each island's harbor port), and these offer myriad services, tickets, car rentals, and guided tours. Top agencies include Key Tours based in Athens, Karagiannis Klimi Travel on Aegina, and Hydreoniki Travel on Hydra.

Aegina Αίγινα

30 km (19 miles) south of Piraeus by ferry.

The eastern side of Aegina is rugged and sparsely inhabited today, except for Ayia Marina, a former fishing hamlet now studded with hotels. The western side of the island, where Aegina Town lies, is more fertile and less mountainous than the east; fields are blessed with grapes, olives, figs, almonds, and, above all, the treasured pistachio trees. Idyllic seascapes, quaint backstreets, and a number of beautiful courtyard gardens make Aegina Town attractive.

Although it may seem hard to imagine, by the Archaic period (7th to 6th centuries BC), Aegina was a mighty maritime power. At that time it introduced the first silver coinage (marked with a tortoise), the first proper coins of the "western world." By the 6th century BC, Egina—to use its alternative spelling—had become a major art center, known in particular for its bronze foundries (worked by such sculptors as Kallon, Onatas, and

Anaxagoras) and its ceramics, which were exported throughout the Mediterranean. Testimony to its great glory is the Temple of Aphaia, one of the most extant of the great Greek temples and famed for its spectacular Doric columns.

As it turns out, this powerful island, lying so close to the Attica coast, could not fail to come into conflict with Athens. As Athens's imperial ambitions grew, Aegina became a thorn in its side. In 458 BC Athens laid siege to the city, eventually conquering the island. In 455 BC the islanders were forced to migrate, and Aegina never again regained its former power.

From the 13th to the 19th century, Aegina ping-ponged between nations. A personal fiefdom of Venice and Spain after 1204, it was fully claimed by Venice in 1451. Less than a century later, in 1537, it was devastated and captured by the pirate Barbarossa and repopulated with Albanians. Morosini recaptured Aegina for Venice in 1654, but Italian dominance was short-lived: the island was ceded to Turkey in 1718. Its Greek roots flourished again in the early 19th century, when it experienced a rebirth as an important base in the 1821 War of Independence, briefly holding the fledgling Greek nation's government (1826–28). By happenstance the first modern Greek coins were minted here. At this time many people from the Peloponnese, plus refugees from Chios and Psara, immigrated to Aegina, and many of the present-day inhabitants are descended from them.

GETTING HERE AND AROUND

Aegina is so close to the port of Piraeus (less than an hour) that some Athenians live on the island and commute. Two well-known companies that offer boat service to Aegina are Hellenic Seaways and Aegean Flying Dolphins.

To get around while in Aegina, use the KTEL buses that leave from the main bus station on Ethneyersias Square (⊠ *Platia Ethneyersias* ☎ *22970/22787*), just left

of the main port; purchase tickets here, not on the bus. Routes stop at many spots, including Ayia Marina and Perdika; a popular destination is the Temple of Aphaia, with departures roughly every hour in summer (€1.80). Service on the island becomes infrequent from late October to early May.

VISITOR INFORMATION

CONTACTS Aegina Municipality. ⊠ *Town hall, Xristou Lada 1, Aegina Town* ☎ *22973/20026.*

Aegina Town ΑΙΓΙΝΑ ΠΟΛΗ

84 km (52 miles) southwest of Piraeus by ferry.

As you approach from the sea, your first view of Aegina Town takes in the sweep of the harbor, punctuated by the tiny white chapel of Ayios Nikolaos. A large population of fishermen adds character to the many waterfront café-taverna hybrids serving ouzo and beer with pieces of grilled octopus, home-cured olives, and other *mezedes* (appetizers).

Much of the ancient city lies under the modern, although the world-famous ancient Temple of Aphaia looms over the entire island from its hilltop perch. Although some unattractive contemporary buildings (and some less well-preserved older ones) mar the harborscape, a number of well-preserved neoclassical buildings and village houses are found on the backstreets.

⊙ Sights

Aegina Archaeological Museum

MUSEUM | This small but choice collection of archaeological artifacts was the first ever to be established in Greece (1829). Finds from the famed Temple of Aphaia and excavations throughout the island, including early and middle Bronze Age pottery, are on display. Among the Archaic and classical works of art is the distinctive Ram Jug, which depicts Odysseus and his crew fleeing the Cyclops, and a 5th-century BC sphinx, a votive monument with the head of a woman and a body that is half-eagle, half-lion.

Aegina was one of the best schools of pottery and sculpture in antiquity and the exhibits here prove it. Just above the Archaeological Museum is the ancient site of the **Acropolis of Aegina**, the island's religious and political center. The settlement was first established in the Copper Age (early Bronze Age), and was renamed Kolona, or "column," in the Venetian era, after the only remaining pillar of the Temple of Apollo that once stood there. While in great disarray—11 successive cities once stood here—it remains a true treat for those into archaeology. Examine ruins and walls dating back to 1600–1300 BC, as well as Byzantine-era buildings. ⊠ *Harbor front, 350 feet from ferry dock* ☎ *22970/22248* 🖃 *€4, Reduced: €2* ☉ *Closed Tues.*

Aegina Museum of History and Folklore

MUSEUM | FAMILY | Within an 1828 neoclassical house endowed to the municipality of Aegina, this museum colorfully allows you to experience home and working life in a traditional Aegina house. On the second floor discover exhibits of authentic old furniture, paintings, costumes, and lace in a typical island setting. On the first floor, the Fisherman's house features fishery and sponge-fishing equipment, while the Cottage house displays farm tools of the old days. The first-floor hall regularly hosts temporary exhibitions. ⊠ *Spyrou Rodi 16* ✛ *Behind the harbor road* ☎ *22970/26401* ⊕ *laografiko.gr* 🖃 *2€* ☉ *Closed Mon.–Thurs.*

Ayios Nikolaos

RELIGIOUS SITE | As you approach from the sea, your first view of Aegina Town takes in the sweep of the harbor, with quaint neoclassical buildings in the background, the lovely vista punctuated by the gleaming white chapel of Ayios Nikolaos Thalassinos (St. Nicholas the Seafarer). ⊠ *Harbor front*.

Psaragora

HISTORIC SITE | A trip to (not to mention a bite to eat at) the covered fish market is a must in Aegina Town. A small dish of grilled octopus or sea urchin salad at the World War II–era Tavernas Agora or To Steki is perfect with an ouzo—if you aren't averse to the smell of raw fish wafting over. Fishermen gather mid-afternoon and early evening on the pedestrian-only street, worrying their beads while seated beside glistening octopus hung up to dry—as close to a scene from the movie *Zorba the Greek* as you are likely to see in modern Greece. ⊠ *Panayi Irioti* ☎ *22970/27308*.

Tower of Markellos

BUILDING | During the negotiations for Greece during the War of Independence, Ioannis Kapodistrias, the first president of the country, conducted meetings in the Markelon Tower, which dates back to the late 17th century. Today, the pink-and ocher-hued tower is being looked after by the municipality and occasionally houses cultural events and exhibitions. ⊠ *Corner of Thomaidou and Pileos*.

 Beaches

Kolona Beach

BEACH—SIGHT | Aegina Town's beaches, notably the pine-surrounded Kolona, are pleasant enough with their shallow waters—and crowds—for a refreshing dip after a hot day. This largely undeveloped beach is within easy walking distance to a few tavernas and the archaeological site of Kolona (hotel Rastoni is also not too far away); you can find some precious shade in the adjacent pine forest. **Amenities:** none. **Best for:** swimming. ⊠ *Aegina Town* ✛ *Near Kolona site*.

🍴 Restaurants

O Skotadis

$$ | SEAFOOD | Since 1945 O Skotadis has been serving a large selection of *mezedes* for starters and mostly fresh fish mains (a good option is the fried katsoula fish, cleaver wrasse), usually to be accompanied by ouzo, the classic Greek anise drink. See if you can snag a table (reservations are best) on the second-floor terrace with its panoramic view of Aegina's harbor. **Known for:** super fresh local fish; prime harbor-front location; great views. $ *Average main: €20* ⊠ *Dimokratias Ave. 46* ⊕ *Across from the floating grocers at the harbor* ☎ *22970/24014.*

Pelaisos

$$ | SEAFOOD | One of the oldest tavernas on the busy harbor strip of Aegina Town, Pelaisos is now in the capable hands of Vagelis, the third generation. His father still cooks in the morning, preparing such homey dishes of the day as stuffed zucchini, usually locally sourced, but fresh fish is the mainstay of this old-school establishment, from affordable grilled sardines to the more expensive sea bass or mullet priced by the kilo. **Known for:** great fish and seafood; popular with locals and Athenians alike; homegrown vegetables. $ *Average main: €17* ⊠ *Dimokratias Ave. 41* ⊕ *Opposite the 2 landmark floating grocers* ☎ *22970/23897* ⊕ *pelaisos.gr.*

Tsias

$$ | SEAFOOD | For a light bite, try this harborside *ouzeri* restaurant, a hangout for locals as well as tourists, where warm yellow walls are decorated with stencils. Except for the 30 varieties of ouzo, everything is homemade, including palate-pleasing Vouta Vouta (Dip Dip), a dish of shrimp and spicy sauce, and the real don't-miss dishes: custom omelets for breakfast and baked apple in cognac. **Known for:** good friendly service; tasty and inventive Greek fare; harbor view. $ *Average main: €15* ⊠ *Dimokratias Ave. 47* ☎ *22970/23529.*

★ Vatzoulias

$$ | GREEK | Ask a local to name the best restaurant in Aegina, and the response is invariably Vatzoulias. In summer the garden is a pleasant oasis, scented with jasmine and honeysuckle; in winter, nestle inside the cozy dining room to dine on expertly prepared taverna classics. **Known for:** rustic dishes; a favorite with locals; wholesome village feel. $ *Average main: €20* ⊠ *Aphaias 75, Ayioi Asomatoi* ☎ *22970/22711* ▤ *No credit cards* ☉ *Closed Mon., Tues., and Thurs. No lunch.*

☕ Coffee and Quick Bites

Pitsi's Coffee & Food

$ | BURGER | Burgers, club sandwiches, wraps, and fresh salads are the headliners on Pitsi's simple menu, all of which can be eaten in or taken away as you continue your meandering exploration around Aegina Town. You can also pop in for a quick coffee, smoothie, or freshly sqeezed juice. **Known for:** fast food; great coffee; quick, friendly service. $ *Average main: €6* ⊠ *2, Aiantos* ☎ *22970/25250.*

Rodi Coffee Shop

$ | CAFÉ | This lovely little establishment whips up a mean *freddo* (iced) cappuccino. They serve large and satisfying made-to-order sandwiches and creamy ice cream. **Known for:** central location; big sandwiches; ice cream. $ *Average main: €6* ⊠ *Ioulias Katsa and Agion Theodoron 7* ☎ *22970/29064.*

Tenekedakia

$ | GREEK | Fast food all over Greece usually consists of souvlaki or gyro wrapped in a pita and that is available at Tenekdakia, but this spot also has the added draw of being in a superb harbor-front location. The pork gyro is crispy yet juicy and the pita is also stuffed full with fries, onion, tomato, and cooling tzatziki. **Known for:** great location; good service; high quality for low prices. $ *Average main: €5* ⊠ *Dimocratias Ave. 39* ☎ *22970/28944.*

An often overlooked wonder of ancient Greece, Aegina's Temple of Aphaia boasts more than 25 of its original 32 columns and spectacularly perches atop a promontory.

Hotels

Aegina Hotel

$ | **HOTEL** | The family-run Hotel Aegina, only 100 meters from the port, offers clean yet basic comfort for visitors who prefer to be out and about, exploring the island and lounging on one of the many beaches. **Pros:** central location; good budget option; welcoming staff. **Cons:** many rooms don't have good views; books up quickly; no pool. *$ Rooms from: €55 ⊠ Stratigou Dim. Petriti 23 ⊕ www.aeginahotel.gr/en/ ⇗ 19 rooms ⊚ Free breakfast.*

★ Rastoni

$$ | **B&B/INN** | Quiet and secluded, this boutique hotel's peaceful quality is heightened by the landscaped mature Mediterranean garden filled with aromatic herbs, wild flowers, and pistachio trees. **Pros:** views of the garden, the pistachio groves and beyond; beautiful four-poster beds; excellent and restrained service. **Cons:** few hotel amenities; best hotel on the island fills in summer, so book early; 10-minute walk to the beach. *$ Rooms from: €150 ⊠ Dimitriou Petriti 31 ☎ 22970/27039 ⊕ www.rastoni.gr ⇗ 12 rooms ⊚ Free breakfast.*

Nightlife

Greek bars and clubs frequently change names, so it's sometimes hard to keep up with the trends.

Avli

BARS/PUBS | The ever-popular Avli, which goes from café-bistro by day to bar (playing Latin rhythms) by night, serves delicious appetizers in a small courtyard, crowned by an impressively tall palm tree. Free Wi-Fi is available. *⊠ Panayi Irioti 17 ☎ 22970/26438.*

Caps Love

BARS/PUBS | This is probably the coolest bar on Aegina, on the southern edge of the main town. Enjoy the lounge vibe with a gourmet pizza or burger downstairs in this creatively restored old town house with exposed stonework, and then head upstairs where most of the action is after dark. ✉ *Achilleas 4* ✛ *Past Panagitsa church* ☎ *22970/29418.*

Inn on the Beach

BARS/PUBS | On the outskirts of Aegina Town, this multilevel venue draws an early crowd with its sunset seafront cocktails and chill-out music, before notching up the music to a beach-party tempo. ✉ *Akti Toti Hatzi* ☎ *22970/25116.*

🛍 Shopping

Aegina's famous pistachios, much coveted by Greeks, can be bought from stands along the town harbor. At Fistikato, one of the better vendors, you can get these Moorish nuts, along with a whole host of other pistachio products like pesto, honey-nut balls, and pistachio butter; gifts your loved ones will be eternally grateful for, if indeed these hellishly addictive snacks make it all the way home (best buy a couple of pistachio shower gels, just in case). Another treat found at some of the Aegean Town bakeries behind the harbor is *amygdalota,* rich almond macaroons sprinkled with orange flower water and powdered sugar. If you want to have a picnic lunch on the island or on the ferryboat while en route to another Saronic island, check out the luscious fruit displayed on several boats that double as picturesque floating groceries, in the center of the harbor.

Ceramics Art Lab

CERAMICS/GLASSWARE | Sisters Martha and Maria Kottaki are talented examples of the new generation of Aegina potters (following in the footsteps of their equally talented mother, Triantafyllia). They create utilitarian yet elegant household items such as colorful salad bowls and country-chic fruit platters. ✉ *P. Irioti Str., 22* ☎ *22974/ 01005 shop, 6980/72–4558 workshop.*

Beach Bummed?

If Aegina's beaches don't wow you, climb aboard one of the many daily boats from Aegina's harbor to the smaller nearby isle of **Angistri**. Without cars, but with food, drink, and small coves to swim in, Angistri has a relaxed, out-of-the-way feel, and more than its share of lovely beaches. A closer alternative is the tiny **Moni island**, which can be reached in less than 10 minutes from the fishing village of Perdika.

Cool Soap

PERFUME/COSMETICS | The locally created handmade natural soaps here are all made from the finest extra virgin olive oil and scented with expertly blended Mediterranean essential oils. The workshop, just beyond town, also doubles as a selling point. Check out the fun and colorful mood-of-the-day boxes. ✉ *Ag. Paraskevis Av.* ☎ *22970/29359* ⊕ *www. thecoolprojects.gr.*

Fistiki

CLOTHING | Flip-flops, shoes, bikinis, jewelry, papier-mâché figures, dangling Turkish charms, and kitchenware form the rainbow of items available at Fistiki. The shop's small entrance opens into a maze of boxy rooms filled with everything you could possibly need to stay stylish on your trip. ✉ *Panayi Irioti 15* ☎ *22970/28327.*

Tria-Aegina Arts and Crafts

CERAMICS/GLASSWARE | You can find handmade jewelry for all ages and to suit all pockets, as well as printed T-shirts, paintings, and pottery in this magical little shop. Located on an alley behind the harbor, you can also pick up chic beachwear here. ✉ *Ioulias Katsa 7* ☎ *22975/00206, 69721/90796* ⊕ *aegina-tria.gr.*

Activities

BOATING AND SAILING

Aegean Sailing School
SAILING | Learn to sail a yacht, try power boating, or join this lively international group of sailors on one of their day trips to the nearby islands of Moni and Angistri. ✉ *Martyros Leontiou 8* ☎ *22970/25852* 🌐 *www.aegeansailing-school.com.*

Souvala ΣΟΥΒΑΛΑ

10 km (6 miles) northeast of Aegina Town.

Souvala is a sleepy fishing village that comes to life in summer, as it is a favorite resort of many Athenians. The tamarisks and pine trees offer natural shade on the beach, or you can head to Vagia Beach, 3 km (2 miles) farther down the seaside road.

Beaches

Souvala
BEACH—SIGHT | **FAMILY** | The sandy and pebbled beach of Souvala is one the nicest on the island and used to be famous for its therapeutic hot and cold springs (which dried up a while back). Close to the Souvala village, it offers umbrellas, sun beds, and a beach bar. Elsewhere along the coastline here are many other spots where you can sunbathe and swim off the rocks. Windsurfing is available near the hotel Irides. **Amenities:** food and drink; lifeguards; showers; water sports. **Best for:** swimming; windsurfing. ✉ *Souvala* ☎.

Vagia Beach
BEACH—SIGHT | This is a sandy beach next to a picturesque little harbor. There is a coffee shop next to the beach that rents sun beds and umbrellas, and serves coffee, drinks, and bites all day long. A few pine trees provide much-needed shade, and there's easy parking nearby. The taverna is also open during winter weekends, with lunch and dinner served by a fireplace. Look for an even quieter stretch of beach at the right side of the little harbor. **Amenities:** food and drink. **Best for:** solitude; swimming; walking. ✉ *Vagia* ✣ *13 km (8 miles) northeast of Aegina Town* ☎.

Hotels

Aethrio Guesthouse
$ | **B&B/INN** | About 9 km (5½ miles) from Aegina Town, at the small port of Souvala, this modern bed-and-breakfast is popular with Athenians seeking relaxing weekends away from the city, and its studios (including one larger suite) can accommodate two to five people each. **Pros:** homey; clean and modern; decent breakfast. **Cons:** few hotel-type facilities; no in-room Wi-Fi; small rooms. [$] *Rooms from: €60* ✉ *Souvala Beach, Aliprantі 154* ☎ *22970/52030* 🌐 *www.aethrioguest-house.gr* 💳 *No credit cards* 🛏 *10 rooms* 🍴 *Free breakfast.*

★ Irides Luxury Apartments Hotel
$ | **B&B/INN** | **FAMILY** | Irides Luxury Studios is housed in a slightly quirky building, just 100 feet from the seafront, so all guest rooms and studios here get a sea view. **Pros:** great for families; excellent breakfast; friendly owners. **Cons:** rocky beach; somewhat isolated; patchy Wi-Fi in some of the rooms. [$] *Rooms from: €110* ✉ *Agii, Odos Thermopilon* ☎ *22970/52215, 6937/129896* 🌐 *www.irides.gr* 🕓 *Closed Nov.–Feb.* 🛏 *25 rooms* 🍴 *Free breakfast.*

Vagia Hotel
$ | **B&B/INN** | The well-sized and simply decorated white rooms of this quaint little hotel have cool stone floors and king-size beds, and the balconies have either sea views or views of the forested mountain, home to the temple of Afaia, rising behind the building. **Pros:** only a five-minute walk from the beach; quiet and laid-back; excellent breakfast. **Cons:**

Vagia is a little off the beaten track; bathrooms are a little dated; difficult to find a room in high season. $ *Rooms from: €55* ✉ *Vagia* ✛ *On main village road leading to the beach* ☎ *22970 /71179* ⊕ *www.vagia-hotel.gr* ⇆ *21 rooms* |○| *Free breakfast.*

Performing Arts

FESTIVALS
Aegina Music Festival
MUSIC FESTIVALS | Taking place from the second week in August until the end of the month, Aegina town hosts local and international classical musicians who perform on Avra Beach right in front of the ancient site of Kolona and at the church of Sotiras. The event is directed by the renowned pianist Dora Bakopoulou. Tickets are available at Aiakeion café (Aegina Port) or at the venues. ✉ *Aegina Town* ⊕ *www.aeginamusicfestival.com* ⊡ *€10.*

Ayios Nektarios Monastery
FESTIVALS | Two of the most important festivals held at Ayios Nektarios Monastery are Whit Monday, or the day after Pentecost (the seventh Sunday after Easter), and the November 9th Saint's nameday, when the remains of Ayios Nektarios are brought down from the monastery and carried in a procession through the streets of town, which are covered in carpets and strewn with flowers. ✛ *7 km (4½ miles) southeast of Aegina Town* ☎ *22970/53806 monastery.*

Panayia Chrysoleontissa
FESTIVALS | On the Assumption of the Virgin Mary, August 15th—the biggest holiday of the Christian summer throughout Europe—a celebration is held at Panayia Chrysoleontissa, a mountain monastery built between 1403 and 1614. ✛ *6 km (4 miles) east of Aegina Town* ☎ *22970/62100.*

Ayia Marina ΑΓΙΑ ΜΑΡΙΝΑ

13 km (8 miles) east of Aegina Town, via a small paved road below Temple of Aphaia.

The small, somewhat-overrun port of Ayia Marina has many hotels, cafés, restaurants, and a family-friendly beach with shallow waters. On the opposite side of the Ayia Marina harbor, you'll find small bays with deeper waters, ideal for diving. Ayia Marina is easily accessible by regular KTEL bus service from Aegina Town (about a 25-minute trip).

◉ Sights

★ Temple of Aphaia
ARCHAEOLOGICAL SITE | One of the great glories of ancient Greek art, the Temple of Aphaia is among the most extant examples of classical Doric architecture. Once adorned with an exquisite group of pedimental sculptures (now in the Munich Glyptothek) it still proudly bears 25 of its original 32 columns, which were either left standing or have been reconstructed. The structure is perched on a pine-clad promontory, offering superb views of Athens and Piraeus across the water—with binoculars you can see both the Parthenon and the Temple of Poseidon at Sounion. The saying goes that the Ancient Greeks built the Temple of Aphaia in Aegina, the Parthenon in Athens, and the Temple of Poseidon at Sounion as the tips of a perfect equidistant triangle (called Antiquity's Perfect Triangle). This site has been occupied by many sanctuaries to Aphaia; the ruins visible today are those of the temple built in the early 5th century BC. Aphaia was apparently a pre-Hellenic deity, whose worship eventually converged with that of Athena.

You can visit the museum for no extra fee. The exhibit has a reconstructed section of the pediment of the temple, many fragments from the once brilliantly colored temple interior, and the votive tablet (560 BC) on which is written that the temple is dedicated to the goddess Aphaia. From Aegina Town, catch the KTEL bus for Ayia Marina on Ethneyersias Square, the main Aegina Town bus station; ask the driver to let you off at the temple. A gift and snack bar across the road is a comfortable place to have a drink and wait for the return bus to Aegina Town or for the bus bound for Ayia Marina and its pebbled beach. ✉ *Ayia Marina* ✥ *15 km (9 miles) east of Aegina Town* ☎ *22970/32398* 🌐 *www.culture.gr* 🎟 *€6.*

Beaches

Ayia Marina Beach

BEACH—SIGHT | **FAMILY** | The best sandy beach on the island, Ayia Marina is popular with the parenting set, as the shallow water is ideal for playing children. A more rocky beach lies to the north of the marina that is good for diving and snorkeling. There are plenty of tavernas and cafés along the bay, while Hotel Apollo is not too far away. **Amenities:** food and drink; lifeguards; toilets; water sports. **Best for:** snorkeling; swimming; walking. ✉ *Ayia Marina.*

Restaurants

Kiriakakis

$$ | **GREEK** | This seafront taverna, the oldest and most established one in Ayia Marina, has been here since 1950, when Kyriakos Haldaios brought out a gas stove and started frying fish and fries under the pine trees for local sunbathers. Today, it is owned by his grandson, also named Kyriakos, and offers traditional Greek specialties like *moussaka*, the famous dish of layered eggplant and ground meat, and plenty of fresh fish, especially gilthead and sea bass. **Known for:** fresh fish; dinner overlooking the sea; vegetarian dishes. [$] *Average main: €18* ✉ *Ayia Marina* ☎ *22970/32165* 🌐 *kiriakakis-aegina.gr.*

Tholos

$ | **GREEK** | The go-to taverna for the islanders, Tholos is nestled in the pine forest spilling down from the temple of Afaia on the road down to Ayia Marina. The wonderful views through the trees down to the sea are complemented by the flavorsome rustic dishes served at this establishment. **Known for:** authentic Greek village fare; warm friendly service; family run. [$] *Average main: €13* ✉ *Ayia Marina* ✥ *On the road from Afaia to Ayia Marina* ☎ *22970/32129.*

Thymari

$ | **SEAFOOD** | **FAMILY** | On the main road behind the port, the location is the only minor drawback of this traditional Greek taverna. But balancing this out, you can also dine in the pretty courtyard at the back (if you find a table). **Known for:** fresh seafood; great service; kids' menu. [$] *Average main: €12* ✉ *Afaias Ave* ☎ *22970/32859.*

Hotels

★ Hotel Apollo

$ | **HOTEL** | Take advantage of this hotel's beautiful hillside location over a beach by relaxing on the restaurant terrace or renting a boat to water-ski in the clear blue waters; not surprisingly, guest rooms at this gracefully aging hotel, built in a typical 1970s style, have balconies and most of them sea views. **Pros:** refurbishment in 2019; pool with saltwater; crystal sea waters set against a dramatic volcanic backdrop. **Cons:** room decor a bit on the spartan side; rocky beach; Wi-Fi doesn't cover all the hotel. [$] *Rooms from: €87* ✉ *Ayia Marina Beach* ☎ *22970/32271, 210/323–4292 Nov.–Mar.* ⏲ *Closed Nov.–Mar.* 🛏 *107 rooms* 🍴 *Free breakfast.*

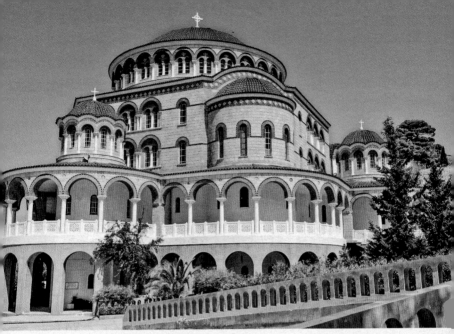

Be at the regal Ayios Nektarios Monastery on November 9 to see the saint's day celebration, when the streets are covered with carpets and strewn with flowers.

Marathonas ΜΑΡΑΘΩΝΑΣ

6 km (4 miles) south of Aegina Town.

This small village a few miles south of Aegina Town is reachable by bicycle or bus. The beach is just beyond.

Beaches

Aeginitissa Beach

BEACH—SIGHT | After Marathonas, Aeginitissa is a small, sandy bay with crystalline green waters surrounded by huge eucalyptus trees. The shallow water makes it accessible to novice swimmers. There's a bar, a beach volleyball court, and umbrellas and lounge chairs are available for rent. **Amenities:** food and drink; showers; water sports. **Best for:** sunset; swimming. ⊠ *Paliachora* ⊹ *7 km (4½ miles) south of Aegina Town.*

Marathonas Beach

BEACH—SIGHT | FAMILY | There's a good swimming spot at the sandy Marathonas A beach on the west side of the island. Beyond the village lies another nice beach, Marathonas B; both beaches get very busy during the summer months, and both have sun beds and umbrellas for rent, so be sure to arrive early if you want to beat the crowds (and pick the perfect spot!). **Amenities:** food and drink; lifeguards. **Best for:** sunset; swimming. ⊠ *Marathon* ☎ *22970/28160 Ammos Taverna, 22970/27682 Ostria Taverna.*

Perdika ΠΕΡΔΙΚΑ

9 km (5½ miles) south of Aegina Town.

Follow the lead of the locals and visiting Athenians and, for an excursion, take a bus (a 25-minute ride from Ethneyersias Square) to the pretty port village of Perdika to unwind and eat lunch at a seaside taverna. Places to eat in Perdika have multiplied over the years but are still low-key and have a strong island flavor, transporting you light-years away from the bustle of much of modern Greece. Try O Nontas, the first fish taverna after the bus station, for a meal on the canopied terrace overlooking the little bay, the sailing boats, and the islet of Moni. Antonis, the famous fish tavern, draws big-name Athenians year-round. Across the bay, and only a short walk away, stands the sole modern building of a camera obscura. Inside, the cylindrical chamber allows the light to enter and projects an inverted image of the landscape outside—a technique that is now thought to have been used by many celebrated artists, including Leonardo and Vermeer. It is definitely worth a visit.

Beaches

Klima

BEACH—SIGHT | FAMILY | A semisecluded sandy beach, Klima (aka Keithi), which is just south of Perdika, has a finely pebbled bay of crystal-clear waters that rarely kicks up any waves. To reach it, turn left at the intersection toward Sfentouri before entering Perdika, and then go right at the crossroads and continue until you reach Klima. It is also a popular destination for yachts. There's a beach bar that rents sun beds and umbrellas during the summer months. **Amenities:** food and drink. **Best for:** snorkeling; swimming. ✉ *Perdika* ✣ *10 km (6 miles) south of Aegina Town.*

★ Moni Beach

BEACH—SIGHT | In summer, caïques make frequent 10-minute trips from the fishing port of Perdika to the little island of Moni, a real heaven-on-earth inhabited only by peacocks, wild deer, relocated *kri-kri* (Cretan goats), and some remains of a 1960s campground. Shadowed by pine trees, hiking trails wind their way through the island's pristine landscape. Once the property of the Monastery of Chrysoleontissa, it is now a nature preserve. After your hike, take a most refreshing swim off the little sandy beach in the marvelously clear green waters by the quay. Note that the boatmen come back every hour, allowing you to leave whenever you wish (the round-trip ticket costs €5). A small beach bar operates in summer, offering cool drinks and toasted sandwiches, but if you plan to spend the day here, you would be better off bringing a full picnic lunch. In crowded peak season, Moni is a lovely way to escape the madding crowds. **Amenities:** food and drink. **Best for:** swimming; walking. ✉ *Moni.*

Restaurants

Antonis

$$ | SEAFOOD | Seafood is the word at this famed taverna run by Antonis and his sons, and the octopus grilled in front of the establishment lures bathers and other visitors who tuck into options ranging from teeny fried smelt to enormous lobsters. People-watching is as much of a draw as the food, since the tables afford a view of all the comings and goings of the harbor's small boats as well as some sleek yachts. **Known for:** catch of the day from local fishermen; great harbor-front location; friendly service. [$] *Average main: €15* ✉ *Perdika* ✣ *Waterfront* ☎ *22970/61443, 69329/23749* 🌐 *www.antonisperdika.gr.*

Nightlife

Muzik Café Bar

BARS/PUBS | In Perdika, Muzik Café Bar is popular with the yachting crowd, who appreciate the food and relaxed atmosphere, as well as the great music and cocktails (try the lemon mojito) served until late at night. ✉ *Waterfront* ☎ *22970/29888* 🌐 *www.muzikaegina.gr.*

 **Performing Arts**

FESTIVALS

Ayios Sostis

FESTIVALS | On September 6 and 7, the feast of the martyr Sozon is observed with a two-day *paniyiri* (saint's day festival), celebrated at the church of Ayios Sostis in Perdika. The revelry spills over into town especially the local tavernas. ✉ *Perdika ✛ 9 km (5½ miles) south of Aegina Town.*

Hydra Ύδρα

139 km (86 miles) south of Aegina by ferry.

As the full length of Hydra stretches before you when you round the easternmost finger of the northern Peloponnese, your first reaction might not, in fact, be a joyful one. Gray, mountainous, and barren, Idra (to use its alternative spelling) has the gaunt look of a saintly figure in a Byzantine icon. But as the island's curved harbor—one of the most picturesque in all of Greece—comes into view, delight will no doubt take over. Because of the nearly round harbor, the town is only visible from a perpendicular angle, a quirk in the island's geography that often saved the island from attack, since passing ships completely missed the port. Although there are traces of an ancient settlement, the island was sparsely inhabited until the Ottoman period. Hydra took part in the Greek War of Independence, begun in 1821, by which time the island had developed an impressive merchant fleet, creating a surge in wealth and exposing traders to foreign cultures. Their trade routes stretched from the mainland to Asia Minor and even America.

In the middle of the 20th century the island became a haven for artists and writers like Arthur Miller, Canadian singer-songwriter Leonard Cohen, and the Norwegian novelist Axel Jensen. In the early 1960s, an Italian starlet named Sophia Loren emerged from Hydra's harbor waters in the Hollywood flick *Boy on a Dolphin*. The site of an annex of Athens's Fine Arts School, today Hydra remains a favorite haunt of new and established artists.

The arrival of world-famous contemporary art collector Dakis Joannou (who set up an exhibition space at the island's former slaughterhouse in 2009 for his DESTE Foundation) means that Hydra is now a magnet for today's chic art crowd. Every summer, the opening night of the Slaughterhouse is one of the art world's most coveted invitations; modern-art lovers flock here to catch a glimpse of the most avant-garde artworks, refreshed by the Hydriot breeze. In summer there are ongoing art exhibitions in many venues around the island, from the town's schools (where curator Dimitrios Antonitsis organizes his annual collaborative Hydra School Projects) to the Melina Mercouri exhibition space right by the Hydra harbor, opposite the hydrofoil dock. The Hydra Workshop is a waterfront art space that puts together an annual exhibition inspired by the collection of London-based art patron Pauline Karpidas.

There are many reasons to love Hydra, not the least of which is the fact that all motor traffic is banned from the island (except for several rather noisy garbage trucks). After the racket of inner Athens and ear-splitting assaults on the eardrums by motorbikes in Aegina and Spetses, Hydra's blissful tranquility, especially off-season, is a cause for rejoicing.

GETTING HERE AND AROUND

At this writing the only ferry company that travels to Hydra is Hellenic Seaways. Due to high-season demand, it is essential to make reservations for boat tickets on weekends. It takes about 90 minutes to get to Hydra. These depart from Gate E8 or E9 in the port of Piraeus. There are eight departures per day during high season. Scheduled itineraries become scarcer during the winter months. The price of the ticket starts at €28.50 for economy class. You can get detailed information about departures on the websites ⊕ *hellenicseaways.gr* or ⊕ *www.ferries.gr.*

Famously, cars are not allowed on Hydra—and that means there are no public buses either. Mules are the time-honored and most practical mode of transportation up to the crest; you may see mules patiently hauling anything from armchairs and building materials to cases of beer. When you arrive, mule tenders in the port will rent you one of their fleet to carry your baggage—or better yet, you—to your hotel, for around €10 (be sure to agree on a price before you leave).

Other modes of transportation include water taxis (⊕ *www.hydraislandgreece. com*) and bicycles for rent—hotel concierges can give you information.

VISITOR INFORMATION
CONTACTS Hydra Tourist Information.
✉ *Town Hall, Hydra Harbor, Hydra Town* ☏ *22980/53003, 22980/52210* ⊕ *www. hydra.gr.*

Hydra Town ΥΔΡΑ ΠΟΛΗ

Even though Hydra's beautiful harbor is flush with bars and boutiques, Hydra Town seems as fresh and innocent as when it was "discovered." The two- and three-story gray-and-white houses with red tile roofs, many built from 1770 to 1821, climb the steep slopes around Hydra Town harbor. The noble port and houses have been rescued and placed on the Council of Europe's list of protected monuments, with strict ordinances regulating construction and renovation. Although Hydra has a landmass twice the size of Spetses, only a fraction is habitable, and after a day or so on the island, faces begin to look familiar—and not just because you saw them in last month's *Vanity Fair.*

Hydra's Taste Treat

Before departing Hydra, be sure to enjoy some *amygdalota*, the island's famed sweet almond macaroons. They can be purchased in many bakeries and candy stores on the island. Especially scrumptious are the amygdalota from Tsangaris, a candy store near the port (☏ 22980/52314).

👁 Sights

Church of the Dormition
RELIGIOUS SITE | Founded in 1643 as a monastery, the Church of the Dormition has since been dissolved and the monks' cells are now used to house municipal offices and the small ecclesiastical museum "Ayios Makarios Notaras." The church's most noticeable feature is an ornate, triple-tier bell tower made of Tinos marble, likely carved in the early 19th century by traveling artisans. There's also an exquisite marble iconostasis. ✉ *Hydra Town* ✛ *Along central section of harbor front* ☏ *22980/54071 museum* 🎫 *Church free (donations accepted), museum €2* ⊙ *Museum closed Nov. 16– Mar. 31 and every Mon.*

★ Hydra Historical Archives and Museum
MUSEUM | Housed in an impressive mansion, this collection of historical artifacts and paintings has exhibits that date back to the 18th century. Heirlooms from the Balkan wars as well as from World War I and II are exhibited in the lobby. A small upstairs room contains figureheads from ships that fought in the 1821 War of Independence. There are old pistols and navigation aids, as well as portraits of the island's heroes and a section devoted to traditional local costume, including the dark *karamani* pantaloons worn by Hydriot men. Temporary art exhibits

are also showcased from time to time. ⊠ *Hydra Town* ✛ *On east end of harbor* ☎ *22980/52355* ⊕ *www.iamy.gr* 🎫 *€5*.

Lazaros Koundouriotis Mansion

HOUSE | Impressed by the architecture they saw abroad, shipowners incorporated many of the foreign influences into their *archontika*, old, gray-stone mansions facing the harbor. The forbidding, fortresslike exteriors are deliberately austere, the combined result of the steeply angled terrain and the need for buildings to blend into the gray landscape. One of the finest examples of this Hydriot architecture is the Lazaros Koundouriotis Mansion, built in 1780 and beautifully restored in the 1990s as a branch of Greece's National Historical Museum. The interior is lavish, with hand-painted ceiling borders, gilt moldings, marquetry, and floors of black-and-white marble tiles. Some rooms have pieces that belonged to the Koundouriotis family, who played an important role in the War of Independence; other rooms have exhibits of costumes, jewelry, wood carvings, and pottery from the National Museum of Folk History. The basement level has three rooms full of paintings by Periklis Vyzantinos and his son, friends of the Koundouriotis family ⊠ *Hydra Town* ✛ *On a graded slope above the port, on west headland* ☎ *22980/52421* ⊕ *www. nhmuseum.gr* 🎫 *€3* ⊘ *Closed Nov.–Feb. and Mon. Mar.–Oct.*

Slaughterhouse/DESTE Foundation Project Space

ARTS VENUE | Internationally renowned modern art collector Dakis Joannou acquired this former Hydra slaughterhouse, a leisurely 10-minute walk from the town (toward Mandraki), in 2009 to host artistic events and projects organized by his budding DESTE Foundation. Surprisingly, this is not what one might expect a chic and modern art gallery to look like: housed in an unassuming small building on a cliff by the sea, it can be missed if you don't actively look for it. But perhaps that is exactly the point that Joannou wanted to make with the Slaughterhouse, which has already acquired a leading role in Hydra's cultural life. Starting with the 2009 multimedia project "Blood of Two" by Matthew Barney and Elizabeth Peyton (which paid homage to the space's morbid past), every summer the space is now assigned to a different artist who is invited to stage a site-specific exhibition. Since then Doug Aitken, Urs Fischer, Paul Chan, Pawel Althamer, and Kara Walker, among others, have had works and installations exhibited there. Jeff Koons' new project is slated for June 2021. ⊠ *Hydra Town* ✛ *10-min walk east of the port, toward Mandraki* ☎ *210/2758490* ⊕ *www.deste.gr*.

🔆 Beaches

Beaches are not the island's main attraction; the only sandy beach on Hydra is at Mandraki, east of Hydra Town. There are small, shallow coves at Kamini and Vlichos, both west of the harbor. And a few mostly pebble beaches are found on the southern coast, also reachable by water taxi.

At Hydroneta beach bar and café, just underneath the Hydriot cannons, the gray crags have been blasted and laid with cement to form sundecks. Sunbathing, socializing at the cocktail bar, and the views of the harbor may take priority over swimming, but old-timers can attest to the fact that diving off the rocks into the deep water is truly exhilarating, and it's the closest spot to Hydra Town where you can take a refreshing dip.

Seeing Hydra's Monasteries

If you're staying for more than a day, you have time to explore Hydra's monasteries. Hire a mule (the donkey rank is located just outside the Alpha Bank in the western corner of Hydra's harbor; be sure to check prices with the muleteers first, as these can soar to more than €70 for some routes) for the ascent up Mt. Klimaki, where you can visit the **Profitis Ilias Monastery** (about two hours by mule from Hydra Town) and view the embroidery work of an inhabitant of the nearby nunnery of **Ayia Efpraxia**. Experienced hikers might be tempted to set off for the **Zourvas Monastery** at Hydra's tip. It's a long and difficult hike, but compensation comes in the form of spectacular views and a secluded cove for a refreshing dip.

An alternative: hire a water taxi to Zourvas.

The convent of **Ayios Nikolaos Monastery** is to the southeast of Hydra Town, after you pass between the monasteries of Ayios Triadas and Ayias Matronis (the latter can be visited). Stop here for a drink and a sweet (a donation is appropriate), and to see the beautiful 16th-century icons and frescoes in the sanctuary. When hiking, wear sturdy walking shoes, and in summer start out early in the morning—even when traveling by mule—to minimize exposure to the midday sun. Your reward: stunning vistas over the island (resplendent with wildflowers and herbs in spring), the western and eastern coasts, and nearby islets on the way to area monasteries.

★ **Ayios Nikolaos**

BEACH—SIGHT | Boats ferry bathers from Hydra Town harbor near the Mitropolis church to pebble beaches on the island's southern coast, the best of which is Ayios Nikolaos, where there are sun beds and umbrellas for a charge (starting at €3) and you can also rent canoes. Ayios Nikolaos is located on the south side of the island, facing the Aegean Sea, and it is the largest organized beach on the island. It is mostly pebbled with some small sandy stretches that are ideal for children's play. The large boats heading to and from here have set fees (to Ayios Nikolaos from Hydra Town is €8; water taxis, max 8 passengers, charge around €150 for the round trip. **Amenities:** food and drink; water sports. **Best for:** snorkeling; swimming.

🍴 Restaurants

Kryfo Limani (Secret Port)

$ | **GREEK** | This familly-run taverna, passed from father to son, is set in a typical Hydriot walled garden, down one of the anonymous winding alleyways in town. Adding to the allure, Andreas, who runs the show, has a double life as a fisherman, and the cook expertly serves up his catch of the day. **Known for:** fresh fish; lovely garden setting; reasonable prices. $ *Average main: €8* ✉ *Tompazi 8* 📞 *22980/52585.*

★ Omilos

$$$ | **MEDITERRANEAN** | This spot where Aristotle Onassis and Maria Callas once danced is a vision in minimalist island stone and white. The restaurant/bar is set in the high-ceilinged Hydra Nautical Club and the deck outside, which affords an

Hydra is a shore thing—who needs a beach when you have waters as electric-blue as this?

exquisite sea view. **Known for:** excellent service; popular with visiting high society; great views. $ Average main: €35 ⊠ Hydra port ✛ On the way to Hydronetta ☎ 22980/53800 ⊗ Closed Mon.–Thurs. Oct.–Apr.

To Geitoniko

$$ | GREEK | Christina and Manolis, the former owners, have now passed the baton to their son Constantinos, who has modernized the home-style Greek dishes served here, in his traditional old Hydriot house with stone floors and wooden ceilings, where time seems to have been standing still since the 1950s. If it's available, try the fresh fish that is prepared to perfection. **Known for:** popular with the discerning locals; cool roof terrace dining; tasty Greek food. $ Average main: €15 ⊠ Spiliou Harami ✛ Opposite Pension Antonis ☎ 22980/53615 ⊕ geitonikon. gr ⊗ No lunch Sept.–June; no dinner Dec.–mid-Apr.

☕ Coffee and Quick Bites

Isalos Cafe

$ | INTERNATIONAL | This harbor-front establishment has something for everyone. Service starts in the morning with coffee, juices, and breakfast, then on to brunch, lunch, and snacks, extending into the evening and night time with easy dining, drinks, and cocktails. **Known for:** harbor view; people-watching; homemade ice cream. $ Average main: €10 ⊠ Harbor Front ☎ 22980/29661 ⊕ www.isaloshydra.gr.

Kai Kremmidi (And Onion)

$ | GREEK | No Greek experience is complete without a quick gyro pita on the hoof. And if that's what you're after pop into Kai Kremmidi for the best of that ilk on Hydra. **Known for:** souvlaki; quick service; good location. $ Average main: €5 ⊠ Andrea Papandreou & Topazi Street ☎ 22980/53099.

Continued on page 208

EAT LIKE A GREEK

Hailed for its healthfulness, heartiness, and eclectic spicing, Greek cuisine remains one of the country's greatest gifts to visitors. From gyros to galaktoboureko, moussaka to myzthira, and soutzoukakia to snails, food in Greece is rich, exotic, and revelatory.

To really enjoy communal meals of fresh fish, mama's casseroles, flavorful salads, house wine, and great conversation, keep two ground rules in mind.

ORDER LIKE A NATIVE
Go for *tis oras* (grilled fish and meat "made to order") or *piato tis imeras* (or "plate of the day," often stews, casseroles, and pastas). Remember that fish is always expensive, but avoid frozen selections and go for the freshest variety by asking the waitstaff what the day's catch is (you can often inspect it in the kitchen). Note that waiters in Greece tend to be impatient—so don't waffle while you're ordering.

DINE LIKE A FAMILY
Greeks share big plates of food, often piling bites of *mezedes*, salads, and main dishes on small dishes. It's okay to stick your fork into communal platters but not in each other's personal dishes (unless you're family or dear friends).

(top) lunching alfresco; (bottom)
Kadalee with cinnamon

GRECIAN BOUNTY

Can't understand the menu? Just point!

Greece is a country of serious eaters, which is why there are so many different kinds of eateries here. Here is a list of types to seek out.

Estiatorio: You'll often find fine tablecloths, carefully placed silverware, candles, and multipage menus at an *estiatorio*, or restaurant; menus range from traditional to modern gastronomy.

Oinomageirio: Now enjoying a retro resurgence, these simple eateries were often packed with blue-collar workers filling up on casseroles and listening to *rembetika*, Greece's version of the blues.

Taverna: This is vintage Greece—family-style eateries noted for great spreads of grilled meat *tis oras* (of the hour), thick-cut fried potatoes, dips, salads, and wine—all shared around a big table and often with a soundtrack of *bouzouki* music.

Psarotaverna: Every bit like a regular taverna, except the star of the menu is fresh fish. Remember that fish usually comes whole; if you want it filleted, ask "*Mporo na exo fileto?*" Typical fish varieties include *barbounia* (red mullet), *perka* (perch), *sardella* (sardine), *bakaliaros* (cod), *lavraki* (sea bass), and *tsipoura* (sea bream).

Mezedopoleia: In this Greek version of tapas bars, you can graze on a limited menu of dips, salads, and hot and cold mezedes. Wildly popular with the pre-nightclub crowd.

Ouzeri and Rakadiko: *Ouzo* and the Cretan firewater *raki* (also known as *tsikoudia*) are the main attractions here, but there's always a generous plate of hot or cold mezedes to go with the spirits. A mix of old-timers and young scenesters make for great people-watching.

Kafeneio (café): Coffee rules here—but the food menu is usually limited to sandwiches, crepes, *tiropites* (cheese pies), and *spanakopites* (spinach pies).

Zacharoplasteio (patisserie): Most dessert shops are "to go," but some old-style spots have a small klatch of tables to enjoy coffee and that fresh slice of *galaktoboureko* (custard in phyllo dough).

FOR THOSE ON THE GO

Greeks are increasingly eating on the run, since they're working longer (right through the afternoon siesta that used to be a mainstay) and happy that eateries have adapted to this lifestyle change. *Souvlatsidika* (grill shops) have the most popular takeaway food: the wrapped-in-pita *souvlaki* (pork, lamb, or chicken chunks), *gyros* (slow-roasted slabs of pork and lamb, or chicken), or *kebabs* (spiced, grilled ground meat). *Tzatziki*, onions, tomatoes, and fried potatoes are also tucked into the pita. Toasted sandwiches and tasty hot dogs are other satisfying options.

Gyros: a take-away treat

ON THE GREEK TABLE

Mezedes Μεζέδες **(appetizers):** Eaten either as a first course or as full meals, they can be hot (pickled octopus, chickpea fritters, dolmades, fried squid) or cold (dips like *tzatziki*; *taramosalata*, puree of salted mullet roe and potato; or the spicy whipped feta called *htipiti*). Start with two or three, then keep ordering to your heart's content.

Tzatziki (cucumber in yogurt)

Salata Σαλάτα **(salad):** No one skips salads here since the vegetables burst with flavor, texture, and aroma. The most popular is the *horiatiki*, or what the rest of the world calls a "Greek salad"—this country-style salad has tomato, onion, cucumber, feta, and Kalamata olives. Other popular combos include *maroulosalata* (lettuce tossed with fresh dill and fennel) and the Cretan *dakos* (bread rusks topped with minced tomato, feta, and onion), and *lahanocaroto*, cabbage and carrot salad with olive oil and lemon.

Horiatiki (Greek salad)

Kyrios Piato Κύριο Πιάτο **(main course):** Main dishes were once served family-style, like mezedes, but the plates are now offered as single servings at many restaurants. Some places serve the dishes as they are ready while more Westernized eateries bring all the plates out together. Order all your food at the same time, but be sure to tell the waiter if you want your main dishes to come after the salads and mezedes. Most grilled meat dishes come with a side of thick-cut fried potatoes, while seafood and casseroles such as *moussaka* are served alone. *Horta*, or boiled greens, drenched in lemon, are the ideal side for grilled or fried fish.

Sardines with rice, potatoes, and salad

Epidorpio Επιδόρπιο **(dessert):** Most restaurants give diners who have finished their meals a free plate of fresh seasonal fruit or some homemade *halva* (a cinnamony semolina pudding-cake with raisins).

Krassi Κρασί **(wine):** Greeks almost always have wine with a meal, usually sharing a carafe or two of *hima* (barrel or house wine) with friends. Bitter resinated wine, or *retsina*, has become less common in restaurants. Instead, the choice is often a dry Greek white wine that goes well with seafood or poultry.

Moussaka

Psomi Ψωμί **(bread):** Bread, often pita-fashion, always comes with a meal and usually costs 1 to 2 euros—a *kouver* (cover) charge—regardless of whether you eat it.

Nero Νερό **(water):** If you ask for water, waitstaff will usually bring you a big bottle of it—and charge you, of course. If you simply want tap water (free and safe to drink) ask for a *kanata*—or a pitcher.

Galaktoboureko (custard-filled phyllo pastry)

LIKE MAMA USED TO MAKE

Nearly all Greek restaurants have the same homey dishes that have graced family dinner tables here for years. However, some of these dishes are hardly ever ordered by locals, who prefer to eat them at home—most Greeks just avoid moussaka and pastitsio unless they're made fresh that day. So if you order the following foods at restaurants, make sure to ask if they're fresh ("*tis imeras*").

■ **DOLMADES**—grape leaves stuffed with rice and herbs

■ **KOTOPOULO LEMONATO**—whole chicken roasted with thickly sliced potatoes, lemon, and oregano

■ **MOUSSAKA**—a casserole of eggplant and spiced beef topped with béchamel

■ **PASTITSIO**—tube-shaped pasta baked with spiced beef, béchamel, and cheese

Best bet: Grape leaves

■ **PSARI PLAKI**—whole fish baked with tomato, onions, garlic, and olive oil

■ **SOUPA AVGOLEMONO**—an egg-lemon soup with a chicken stock base

COFFEE CULTURE

Greek coffee: tiny but strong

A kafeneio coffeehouse

Frappé

Greeks go out for coffee not because of caffeine addiction but because they like to spend at least two hours mulling the world with their friends. *Kafeneia*, or old-style coffeehouses, are usually full of courtly old men playing backgammon and sipping tiny but strong cups of *elliniko* (Greek coffee). Trendy cafés often run by hipsters, brewing up a range of coffees in a multitude of styles are packed with frappé-loving office workers, freddo-swilling students, and arty types nursing espressos.

Frappé—a frothy blend of instant coffee (always Nescafé), cold water, sugar, and evaporated milk

■ **Elliniko**—the strong traditional coffee made from Brazilian beans ground into a fine powder

■ **Freddo**—an iced cappuccino or espresso

■ **Nes**—instant coffee, often served with froth

★ Tsagkaris Hydriot Macaroons

$ | **GREEK** | Don't leave Hydra without some traditional almond macaroons in your suitcase. The Tsagkaris family, led by octogenarian matriarch Anna Tsagkari, have been lovingly making them in their workshop for more than 70 years. **Known for:** traditional Greek sweets; cakes and deserts; almond macaroons. [$] *Average main: €6* ✉ *Miaouli* ✥ *100 feet from the harbor front* ☎ *22980/52314.*

Hotels

Angelica Hotel

$$ | **HOTEL** | A three-minute walk from Hydra's bustling port, this alluring place is composed of two villas in Hydra stone, with red barrel-tile roofs and garden areas; both have been restored and renovated to a high standard. **Pros:** the Jacuzzi on the veranda (free use for VIP Villa rooms); generously sized rooms; friendly owners. **Cons:** no elevator; limited variety of breakfast options; slow Wi-Fi. [$] *Rooms from: €130* ✉ *Andrea Miaouli 43* ☎ *22980/53202* 🌐 *www.angelica.gr* 🛏 *21 rooms* 🍴 *Free breakfast.*

Bratsera Hotel

$$$ | **HOTEL** | An 1860 sponge factory was transformed into this charming character hotel (doors made out of old packing crates still bearing the "Piraeus sponge" stamp, etc.), which has a bevy of alluring delights, including guest-room decor accented with framed portraits, old engravings, four-poster ironwork beds, and cozy natural wood lofts, and the hotel restaurant—considered one of the island's best—which is set in the oleander-and-bougainvillea-graced courtyard. **Pros:** excellent restaurant; the relaxing-by-the-pool experience; free Wi-Fi. **Cons:** fitness room is small; some small dark bathrooms; patchy Wi-Fi in some of the rooms. [$] *Rooms from: €250* ✉ *Hydra Town* ✥ *On left of port up Tompazi, then follow the alley straight ahead as Tompazi veers to the right* ☎ *22980/53971, 22980/52794 restaurant* 🌐 *bratserahotel.com* ⏲ *Closed mid-Oct.–Mar.* 🛏 *25 rooms* 🍴 *Free breakfast.*

★ Cotommatae 1810 Guesthouse

$$ | **B&B/INN** | This old mansion has been refurbished into a lovely boutique hotel by a descendant of the original owners, a wealthy and well-known Hydriot shipping family, without losing its original charm. **Pros:** relaxing, elegant atmosphere; easy walking distance from the port; welcoming staff. **Cons:** no swimming pool, just a small plunge pool in the garden; no sea views; slow Internet at times. [$] *Rooms from: €200* ✉ *Votsi* ☎ *22980/53873* 🌐 *www.cotommatae.gr* 🛏 *7 rooms* 🍴 *Free breakfast.*

Hotel Hydra

$$ | **HOTEL** | In an idyllic setting, this boutique hotel with eight relaxing, modern, and beautifully decorated guest suites offers panoramic views of the port and separate living and bedroom areas (as well as a small kitchenette). **Pros:** suites feel more like small apartments rather than rooms; friendly host; fast Wi-Fi. **Cons:** about 150 steps to get to the hotel from the port; not all rooms have great panoramic views of the harbor; need to book far in advance to get a room with the best view. [$] *Rooms from: €200* ✉ *Petrou Voulgari 8* ✥ *Close to the Lazaros Koundouriotis mansion* ☎ *22980/53420* 🌐 *www.hydra-hotel.gr* ⏲ *Closed Nov.–late Mar.* 🛏 *8 rooms* 🍴 *Free breakfast.*

Hotel Leto Hydra

$$ | **HOTEL** | Right in the middle of Hydra Town, this small upscale hotel has sparkling interiors with an elegant "old Greece" touch provided by an array of antique Hydriot rugs, mirrors, and lanterns—and some modern artworks by well-known Greek painters (Papanikolaou and Akrithakis to name two) thrown in to liven things up. **Pros:** the distinguished feel of an old mansion; spacious, shady rooms; marble bathrooms. **Cons:** could do

with a bit of an upgrade; no views and no significant outside spaces; can be difficult to find on your own (ask for directions at the port). [$] *Rooms from: €150* ✉ *Corner of Miaouli and Mandrakiou-Molou* ☎ *22980/53385* ⊕ *www.letohydra.gr* ⊘ *Closed Nov.–mid-Mar.* ⇨ *30 rooms* ⦿❘ *Free breakfast.*

Miranda Hotel

$$ | B&B/INN | Antiques lovers might feel right at home among the 18th- and 19th-century furniture and decor (Oriental rugs, wooden chests, nautical engravings, ceilings painted in detailed Venetian motifs) decorating this traditional Hydriot home, now a gracious small hotel. **Pros:** peaceful garden; precious artworks on display; close to ferry. **Cons:** somewhat dated and small rooms; thin doors do not provide enough sound insulation; the cramped bathrooms could do with a makeover. [$] *Rooms from: €140* ✉ *Miaouli* ⊹ *2 blocks inland from port center* ☎ *22980/53510* ⊕ *www.miranda-hotel.gr* ⊘ *Closed Nov.–Feb.* ⇨ *14 rooms* ⦿❘ *Free breakfast.*

★ Orloff Boutique Hotel

$$ | B&B/INN | Commissioned in 1796 by Catherine the Great for her lover Count Orloff—who came to Greece with a Russian fleet to try to dislodge the Turks—this *archontiko* mansion regained its former splendor when it was turned into a small boutique hotel. **Pros:** homey feeling with lovely decor; friendly owners; excellent breakfast. **Cons:** slightly noisy air-conditioning; no balconies; minimum two-night stay. [$] *Rooms from: €165* ✉ *Rafalia 9 and Votsi* ⊹ *350 feet from the port* ☎ *22980/52564, 22980/52495* ⊕ *www.orloff.gr* ⊘ *Closed Nov.–Mar.* ⇨ *9 rooms* ⦿❘ *Free breakfast.*

 Nightlife

Bars often change names, ownership, and music—if not location—so check with your hotel for what's in vogue.

Amalour

BARS/PUBS | On the ground floor of an early 19th-century whitewashed mansion and spilling out onto the cobble Tombazi street, Amalour attracts youthful crowds who sip expertly made and reasonably priced cocktails (especially the exquisite daiquiris), socializing and dancing to ethnic, jazz, soul, and funk music. ✉ *Tombazi* ⊹ *Behind the port* ☎ *22980/53775.*

Beach Club Spilia

BARS/PUBS | Tucked into the coastal rocks just below the Hydroneta bar, Spilia provides a nice escape from the midday sun and is a popular nocturnal haunt, too. The view toward the port is impressive and the deck chairs are comfortable. The steps down to the refreshing sea are especially inviting on hot summer days, which means you can end up spending a whole day here without realizing it, enjoying coffee, nibbles, and then drinks. ✉ *Hydra Town* ⊹ *After Omilos, on the way to the Cannons* ☎ *22980/52240.*

Hydronetta

BARS/PUBS | The minuscule Hydroneta bar-restaurant has an enchanting view from its perch above the harbor. Embraced by rocks and surrounded by water, it is jam-packed during the day, and it is *the* place to enjoy a glass of chilled beer or fruity long drink at sunset. Hydroneta's trademark events are its "Full Moon" parties, fun-filled affairs under Hydra's starlit skies. ✉ *Hydroneta Beach* ⊹ *West of Hydra Town, on the way to Kamini, past the Canons* ☎ *22980/54160.*

Papagalos

BARS/PUBS | On the western tip of the harbor toward Mandraki, where the first disco club of the island used to be, Papagalos is a cocktail and tapas bar doubling up as a daytime port-side coffee spot, with a panoramic view of the harbor action. Rock and ethnic music are the staples on the decks, while live events are held here on a regular basis. Free Wi-Fi is available. ✉ *Harbor front* ☎ *22980/52626.*

★ The Pirate Bar

BARS/PUBS | Ahoy mateys! Café-bar Pirate has been a fixture of the island's nightlife since the mid-1970s. Over the years, it's gotten face-lifts, added some mainstream dance hits to its onetime rock music–only playlist, and remains popular and raucous. The spot is actually open all day with delicious home-cooked dishes (burgers, salads, and lemon pies) but it is at night that the fun really takes off, often with the help of one of the popular rum-based house drinks, such as the fruity Tropical Sun. ⊠ *Hydra Town* ✧ *South end of harbor* ☎ *22980/52711* ⊕ *www.thepiratebar.gr.*

🅽 Performing Arts

FESTIVALS

Its image as a weekend destination has made Hydra a popular venue for all sorts of events, from trail races and art exhibitions to sailing events and regattas. Exhibitions, concerts, and performances are usually held from June through August to coincide with the busy summer season. The international *rembetika* (Greek blues) music festival takes place here in October. Plus the new and ever-growing contemporary art scene here is sure to be highlighted with happenings that will draw an international art crowd.

★ Hydra's Trail Event

RUNNING | FAMILY | Wisely taking place during a cool, long weekend in April the whole of Hydra lives and breathes trail running. The locals have embraced the vertical trail race that sees runners starting at the top of the mountain by the monastery of Profitis Hlias (individual starts every minute ensure their safety) and finishing after a steep downhill 3.2 km (2 miles) later, in the heart of the harbor. Other trail races, including a 38 km "marathon," and plenty of side activities take place, too, as well as many that are aimed for kids (no doubt some of which will be deemed as punishment for past misdemeanors against their parents). ⊠ *Hydra Town* ☎ *6932/271106* ⊕ *www.hydrastrail.gr.*

★ Miaoulia

FESTIVALS | The island celebrates its crucial role in the War of Independence with the Miaoulia, which takes place the last weekend of June. At around 10 o'clock on Saturday night, Hydra's small port goes dark, and a journey into history commences as the day's festivities culminate in a reenactment of the night Admiral Miaoulis loaded a vessel with explosives and sent it upwind to the Turkish fleet back in 1821. Naturally, the model enemy's ship goes down in flames. Fireworks, music, traditional dancing, treasure hunts, and sports competitions all accompany the burning of the fleet, a glorious part of Hydra's Naval Week. ⊠ *Hydra Town.*

🛍 Shopping

A number of elegant shops (some of them offshoots of Athens stores) sell fashionable and amusing clothing and jewelry, though you won't save much by shopping here.

Donkeycat Gallery Shop

CERAMICS/GLASSWARE | Run by Catherine Tsimogianni and her partner, actor Sokratis Patsikas, Donkeycat, as the name suggests, is a quirky art gift shop. Pick up handcrafted memorabilia in the form of ceramics, paintings, jewelery, Greek-themed board games, and limited edition T-shirts among other things. ⊠ *Hydra Town* ☎ *22980/29789.*

Elena Votsi

JEWELRY/ACCESSORIES | Worth a visit, the stylish store of local jewelry designer Elena Votsi showcases her exquisite handmade pieces—more works of art than accessories—which sell well in Europe and New York. She was the creator of the 2004 Athens Olympic medals and the design has been used in all subsequent games. ⊠ *Ikonomou 3* ☎ *22980/52637.*

Speak Out Hydra

CLOTHING | This boutique is so hip the owners run an art and fashion blog (⊕ *speakouthydra.blogspot.com*). Most of the stock is by up-and-coming Greek designers. ✉ *Harbor front* ☎ *22980/52099* ⊕ *www.speakout-hydra. com.*

Studio Hydra

CLOTHING | Not simply your typical tourist gift shop, this is a treasure trove of stylish fashion finds, chic mementos, and even dreamy Hydra watercolors. There's something for everyone. ✉ *Harbor front* ☎ *22980/52132.*

Activities

HORSEBACK RIDING
★ Harriet's Hydra Horses

HORSEBACK RIDING | Discover Hydra by riding one of Harriet's good-natured horses; the friendly Hydra native leads rides over the island's brown/gray arid mountains to mysterious monasteries and gorgeous beaches. Prices start at €25 (plus tax) for a 60-minute clip to Kaminia village, suitable for all levels. ✉ *Hydra Town ⊹ 300 feet from harbor, past Phaedra Hotel* ☎ *6980/323347.*

SCUBA DIVING
Hydra Diving Center

DIVING/SNORKELING | For those who love the great outdoors, snorkeling and scuba diving in the rocky seabeds of Hydra, especially around the Bay of Bisti, could be a highlight of a Greek vacation. Diving instruction is available, too. The center is located at the back of Taverna Enalion, in Vlichos, whose owner, Yiannis Kitsos, also passionately runs the dive school. His boat can also pick up aspiring divers from Hydra's port. ✉ *Taverna Enalion* ☎ *6977/792493* ⊕ *www.hydra.com.gr/ diving-center.*

Kamini

1 km (mile) west of Hydra Town.

A small fishing hamlet built around a shallow inlet, Kamini has much of Hydra Town's charm but none of its bustle—except on Orthodox Good Friday, when the entire island gathers here to follow the funerary procession of Christ. On a clear day, the Peloponnese coast is plainly visible across the water, and spectacular at sunset. Take the 20-minute stroll from Hydra Town west; a paved coastal track gives way to a staggered, white path lined with fish tavernas; Kamini's small beach also has restaurants nearby, which you can spot arriving by boat or sea taxi.

Beaches

Mikro Kamini

BEACH—SIGHT | FAMILY | Kamini's small gray-pebbled beach, known as Mikro Kamini, is about 1,000 feet beyond the sleepy fishing port, just in front of the Castello Bar & Restaurant, where you can rent sun beds and umbrellas. There are more tavernas nearby where you can spot arriving boats and water taxis. The water here is calm and shallow, so the beach is good for families with small children. **Amenities:** food and drink. **Best for:** swimming; walking. ☎ *22980/54101 sun lounger reservation.*

Restaurants

★ Castello Bar and Restaurant

$$$ | MEDITERRANEAN | Set right on Mikro Kamini, a leisurely 15-minute walk from the port (or 5 minutes by mule or couple of minutes by water taxi), this fully renovated 18th-century fortress is a popular bar-restaurant offering some of the most fortifying dining on the island. Castello is the only place where you can find sushi, or if you are craving a snack, try the catch of the day served with wild greens and saffron. **Known for:** gourmet Mediterranean food; stunning views from the old fortress; sophisticated yet laid-back atmosphere. $ *Average main: €29* ☎ 22980/54101 ⊕ *www.castellohydra.gr* ⊗ *Closed Dec.–Feb.*

Kodylenia's Taverna

$$$ | SEAFOOD | Kodylenia's Taverna looks like a whitewashed fisherman's cottage on a promontory overlooking the little harbor of Kamini, with a veranda terrace charmingly set with folkloric pennants and communal tables—it's the perfect perch to catch some sublime sunsets. It is also an irresistibly alluring (if a little pricey) place that has enraptured town folk and off-duty billionaires alike. **Known for:** gleaming fresh fish; kritamos (rock samphire); eccentric service. $ *Average main: €26* ⊕ *On the headland above Kamini harbor* ☎ 22980/53520 ⊕ *www. hydra-kodylenia.gr* ⊗ *Closed Nov.–Feb.*

Pirofani

$$ | MEDITERRANEAN | The half-Greek, half-Danish host of this taverna in Kamini, the second-largest village in Hydra, likes to cook for and entertain all his visitors himself. Being the life of the party that he is, by the time you leave after a heartening dinner, you will feel as if you've made a new friend. **Known for:** hangout for island's artists; good-humored eccentricities of the owner; spontaneous outbreaks of live music and dance. $ *Average main: €15* ☎ 22980/53175 ⊕ *www.pirofani.com* ⊗ *Closed Mon. and Tues. and Oct.–Apr.*

Vlichos ΒΛΥΧΟΣ

6 km (4 miles) west of Hydra Town.

From Kamini, the coastal track continues to Vlichos, another pretty village with tavernas, a historic bridge, and a gray-pebbled beach on a bay. It's a 5-minute water-taxi ride from the Hydra Town port or a 40-minute walk (25 minutes past Kamini).

Beaches

Vlichos Beach

BEACH—SIGHT | FAMILY | This scenic little gray-pebble beach west of Kamini is a good dive destination (ask at Enalion taverna) as well as a nice swimming spot for families due to its shallow waters. Sun beds and umbrellas can be rented from the beachfront tavernas. **Amenities:** food and drink. **Best for:** swimming; walking. ⊠ *Vlichos.*

Restaurants

★ Enalion

$$ | MEDITERRANEAN | The charming young trio of owners—Yiannis, Kostas, and Alexandros—have imbued this beach taverna just 100 feet from Vlichos Beach with energy and attentive service. The traditional taverna fare includes favorite Greek dishes like *ntakos*, prawn linguine, and lively salads, which all go perfectly with a glass of house wine or a cold beer. **Known for:** tasty Greek fare; beachfront location; friendly service. $ *Average main: €18* ⊠ *Vlichos* ☎ 22980/53455 ⊕ *www.enalion-hydra.gr* ⊗ *Closed Dec.–Mar.*

Hotels

Four Seasons Luxury Suites

$$$$ | HOTEL | No, this is not one of the famous chain's hotels but rather a tiny hotel inspired by the magical colors of the four seasons (the Sun Suite is the cream of the crop) sweetly set in an atmospheric, fully renovated 150-year-old stone mansion. **Pros:** alluring interiors; next to the beach; excellent à la carte breakfast. **Cons:** challenging distance from town; slightly expensive for Hydra; limited number of suites. $ *Rooms from: €380* ⊠ *Vlichos Beach* ☎ 22980/53698 ⊕ *www.fourseasonshydra.gr* ⊗ *Closed Nov.–late Mar.* ⌁ *8 rooms* ⦿⦿ *Free breakfast.*

Mandraki ΜΑΝΔΡΑΚΙ

4 km (1 miles) east of Hydra Town.

The only sandy beach on Hydra is an activity-centered beach by the Miramare Hotel, near Mandraki, which is currently closed (but you can still visit the beach with one of the boats or water taxis that regularly depart from Hydra Town; the nearby taverna is also open).

Beaches

Mandraki Beach

BEACH—SIGHT | One of the few sandy beaches of Hydra, the ever popular Mandraki is a leisurely 2-km (1-mile) walk west of the town, but you can also come here by small boat or water taxi from the main port. You can enjoy the fine sand and the comfy sun beds (€10). **Amenities:** food and drink. **Best for:** swimming; walking. ✉ *Mandraki, Hydra Town.*

Spetses Σπέτσες

24 km (15 miles) southwest of Hydra.

Spetses shows evidence of continuous habitation through all of antiquity. From the 16th century BC, settlers came over from the mainland and, as on Hydra, they soon began to look to the sea, building their own boats. They became master sailors, successful merchants, and fearsome pirates, and later, during the Napoleonic Wars, they were skilled blockade runners, earning fortunes that they poured into building larger boats and grander houses. With the outbreak of the War of Independence in 1821, the Spetsiots dedicated their best ships and brave men (and women) to the cause.

In the years leading up to the revolution, Hydra's great rival and ally was the island of Spetses. Lying at the entrance to the Argolic Gulf, off the mainland, Spetses was known even in antiquity for its hospitable soil and verdant pine tree–covered slopes. The pines on the island today, however, were planted by a Spetsiot philanthropist dedicated to restoring the beauty stripped by the shipbuilding industry in the 18th and 19th centuries. There are far fewer trees than there were in antiquity, but the island is still well watered, and prosperous Athenians who have made Spetses their second home compete to have the prettiest gardens and terraces. Today's visitor can enjoy spotting this verdant beauty all over the island.

GETTING HERE AND AROUND

Hellenic Seaways' Flying Dolphins hydrofoils and catamarans travel regularly, year-round, from Piraeus (Gate E8 or E9) to Spetses (usually stopping at Poros and Hydra as well). There are half a dozen such daily rounds from April to October, and fewer the rest of the year. You can get to Spetses (€38.50 economy) in just under two hours. Make reservations ahead of time—boats fill quickly. You can get detailed info about departure times on ⊕ *hellenicseaways.gr.*

The island of Spetses is so close to the Peloponnese mainland that you also can drive to the small port of Kosta (200 km [124 miles] from Athens), park your car, and ferry across the channel in any of a number of caïques (price at around €5 per person, but you have to wait for the boat to fill up before it leaves for the 20-minute crossing). You can also take a water taxi on demand 24 hours a day (€23 for the five-minute crossing). For water taxi information, call ☎ *22980/72072.*

Only homeowners are usually allowed to bring cars onto the island. Visitors must rent bikes, scooters, or mopeds, hire water taxis or carriages, or use one of the two high-season-only (June 15–September) municipal buses: one bus line goes from Ayios Mamas Beach to Ayioi Anargyroi and Ayia Paraskevi; the other, with regular departures during the day, from Poseidonion Grand Hotel to Ligoneri and Vrellos beach. Tickets range from €1 to €3. For bus schedule information you can contact the two bus drivers directly on their cell phones (for Ayios Mamas and Ayioi Anargyroi, call Anargyros Kotzias at ☎ 69/4480–2536; for Ligoneri and Vrellos, call Konstantinos Mouratis at ☎ 69/7894–9722). It is worth going on one of the buses if only for the scenic route, but rather quaintly, the vehicles morph into school buses in early September, when they also stop serving as public transport.

Spetses Town
ΣΠΕΤΣΕΣ ΠΟΛΗ

91 km (56 miles) southwest of Hydra.

By most visitors' standards, Spetses Town is small—no larger than most city neighborhoods—yet it's nevertheless divided into districts populated with many well-to-do neoclassical mansions and 19th-century villas. You will arrive in Dapia, the modern harbor. Kastelli, the oldest quarter, extends toward Profitis Ilias and is marked by the 18th-century Ayia Triada Church, the town's highest point. The area along the coast to the north is known as Kounoupitsa, a residential district of pretty cottages and gardens with pebble mosaics in mostly nautical motifs.

 Sights

Anargyrios and Korgialenios School
COLLEGE | Known as the inspiration for the school in John Fowles's *The Magus*, this institution was established in 1927 as an English-style boarding school for the children of Greece's Anglophile wealthy elite. Until 2010, tourism management students studied amid the elegant amphitheaters, black-and-white-tile floors, and huge windows. Today, the buildings are used for conferences, private seminars, and summer schools. Nevertheless, visitors can still take a peek (free) inside the school and stroll around the fabulous gardens throughout the year. ⊠ *Spetses Town* ✛ *½ km (¼ mile) west of Dapia* ☎ *22980/74306* ⊕ *www.akss.gr.*

Ayios Mamas
RELIGIOUS SITE | The town's stone promontory is the site of the little 19th-century church, Ayios Mamas—take your photos from a distance as the church is privately owned and often locked. Bring a swimsuit, as the beach here is great for a dip. ⊠ *Spetses Town* ✛ *Above the harbor.*

★ Bouboulina's Museum
HOUSE | In front of a small park is Bouboulina's House, now a museum, where you can take a 45-minute guided tour (available in English) and learn about this interesting heroine's life. Laskarina Bouboulina was the bravest of all Spetsiot revolutionaries, the daughter of a Hydriot sea captain, and the wife—then widow—of two more sea captains. Left with a considerable inheritance and nine children, she dedicated herself to increasing her already substantial fleet and fortune. On her flagship, the *Agamemnon,* the largest in the Greek fleet at the time, she sailed into war against the Ottomans at the head of the Spetsiot ships. Her fiery temper led to her death in a family feud many years later. It's worth visiting the mansion, which is run by her fourth-generation grandson, just for the architectural details, like the carved-wood Florentine ceiling in the main salon. Tour times (in groups of up to 35 visitors) are posted on the museum website, in front of the museum, and in announcement boards at the port of Dapia. The museum closes for maintenance during winter. ⊠ *Spetses Town* ✛ *Behind Dapia* ☎ *22980/72077* ⊠ *€6* ☉ *Closed Nov.–late Mar.*

Dapia

HISTORIC SITE | Ships dock at the modern harbor, Dapia, in Spetses Town. This is where the island's seafaring chieftains met in the 1820s to plot their revolt against the Ottoman Turks. A protective jetty is still fortified with cannons dating from the War of Independence. Today, the town's waterfront strip is packed with cafés, and the navy-blue-and-white color scheme adopted by Dapia's merchants hints of former maritime glory. The harbormaster's offices, to the right as you face the sea, occupy a building designed in the simple two-story, center-hall architecture typical of the period and this place. ⊠ *Dapia.*

Ekklisia Ayios Nikolaos

RELIGIOUS SITE | On the headland sits Ayios Nikolaos, the current cathedral of Spetses, and a former fortified abbey. Its lacy white-marble bell tower recalls that of Hydra's port monastery. It was here that the islanders first raised their flag of independence. ⊠ *Spetses Town* ✛ *On road southeast on waterfront* ☏ *22980/72423.*

Palio Limani (*Balitiza*)

HISTORIC SITE | Take a horse and carriage or stroll the seafront promenade to the old harbor, Palio Limani, from the bustling new harbor, Dapia. As you wander by the waterfront, you might imagine it as it was in its 18th- and 19th-century heyday: the walls of the mansions resounding with the noise of shipbuilding and the streets humming with discreet whisperings of revolution and piracy. Today, the wood keels in the few remaining boatyards are the backdrop for cosmopolitan bars, cafés, and restaurants; the sailing boats linger lazily in the bay. Walk up the hill to the ocher-hued chapel of Panayia Armata for unforgettable sunset views. ⊠ *Spetses Town* ✛ *Waterfront, 1½ km (1 mile) southeast of Dapia.*

Poseidonion Grand Hotel

HOTEL—SIGHT | This 1914 waterfront landmark, a fitting backdrop to the defiant bronze statue of Bouboulina, was the scene of glamorous Athenian society parties and balls in the era between the two world wars. It was once the largest resort in the Balkans and southeastern Europe. The hotel was the brainchild of Sotirios Anargyros, a visionary benefactor who was responsible for much of the development of Spetses. After extensive renovations were completed in 2009, it recaptured its former glory and is once again the focal point of most Spetsiot cultural and social events. ⊠ *Spetses Town* ✛ *West side of Dapia* ☏ *22980/74553* ⊕ *www.poseidonion.com.*

★ Spetses Museum

MUSEUM | A fine and impressive late 18th-century *archontiko*, owned by the locally renowned Hatziyianni-Mexi family and built in a style that might be termed Turko-Venetian, contains the town's municipal museum. It holds articles from the period of Spetses's greatness during the War of Independence, including the bones of the town's heroine, Bouboulina, and a revolutionary flag. A small collection of ancient artifacts consists mostly of ceramics and coins. Also on display are representative pieces of furniture and household items from the period of the Greek revolution. ⊠ *Archontiko Hatziyianni-Mexi* ✛ *600 feet south of harbor* ☏ *22980/72994* ⊠ *€4* ⊙ *Closed Tues.*

🟢 Beaches

Spetses's best beaches are on the west side of the island, and most easily reached by water taxi or the daily boats from Spetses Town. You can ask for caïques information directly at the port. Water taxis at Dapia (the New Port) make scheduled runs to the most popular outlying beaches but can also be hired for trips to more remote coves. The rides can be pricey, ranging from €7 to go from Dapia to the Old Port, up to €30 to the Ayia Paraskevi Beach, and €60 for a tour of the island—but the experience is unique. There are currently seven water taxis serving Spetses.

Kaiki

BEACH—SIGHT | Trendy Kaiki Beach (otherwise known as Scholes or College beach due to its proximity to the Anargyros School) is a triangular patch of sandy beach that draws a young crowd with its beach volleyball court, water-sports activities (about €40 for 20 minutes of Jet Skiing), and the Kaiki Beach bars (yes, there are two of them!) and restaurant, the hippest on the beach in Spetses. It will cost you about €10 for a huge umbrella, two bamboo sun beds, two beach towels, and a bottle of water for a relaxing day on the beach. **Amenities:** food and drink; lifeguards; toilets; water sports. **Best for:** swimming; walking. ✉ *Spetses Town* ✣ *Opposite Anargyrios and Korgialenios School* ☎ *22980/74507 Kaiki Beach Bar Restaurant.*

🍴 Restaurants

Akrogialia

$$ | **SEAFOOD** | Enjoy a meal at this down-to-earth—well, almost in the sea—Greek taverna. As the beach location would suggest, seafood dominates the simple menu, and it is prepared to perfection by the chef. **Known for:** fresh fish; superb location; sea views. [$] *Average main: €16* ✉ *Anargirou, Kounoupitsa* ✣ *10-min walk from the new harbor* ☎ *22980/74749.*

★ Liotrivi Restaurant

$$$ | **MEDITERRANEAN** | Spetses's best restaurant has been morphing and evolving since it first opened 25 years ago, and the owner, Giorgos—a local who grew up on the island working in his father's taverna—still loves what he does and it shows! Everyone from fishermen to Hollywood headliners know him by his first name, and a meal here is not to be missed, not only for the innovative upscale Mediterranean dishes and thoughtful wine list, but also for the dreamy seafront setting and candlelit tables on a little pier jutting into the bay. **Known for:** mayiatiko à la spetsiota, a variation of the local fish specialty made with yellowtail tuna; live Latin music; excellent service. [$] *Average main: €26* ✉ *Palio Limani* ☎ *22980/72269* 🌐 *www.facebook.com/liotrivi.restaurant.spetses/* 🕒 *Closed Nov.–Mar.*

Mourayo

$$ | **MEDITERRANEAN** | This highly regarded restaurant and music "boit" is right on the water in Dapia and is *the* all-time classic bar and nightclub of Spetses (running since 1975). The food in the restaurant is pretty decent, too, and it's probably one of the better choices on the island. **Known for:** live music (piano) every night; very good service; dining alfresco on a seafront terrace. [$] *Average main: €22* ✉ *Palio Limani* ☎ *22980/73700.*

On the Veranda

$$$ | **GREEK FUSION** | Dine in style at the iconic Poseidonion Grand Hotel, where this award-winning restaurant serves local island dishes that have been inventively redefined. Many ingredients come straight from the hotel's own organic farm, harmoniously complementing the headlining fresh seafood. **Known for:** silver service; organic home-grown produce; fresh seafood. [$] *Average main: €35* ✉ *Poseidonion Grand Hotel, Dapia* ☎ *22980 /74553.*

★ Patralis

$$ | **SEAFOOD** | Sit on the waterside veranda and savor seafood mezedes and fresh fish right from the sea in one of the more affordable restaurants on this sometimes overpriced (for Greece) island. As the very friendly waiters will tell you, the house specialties are the fish soup, *astakomakaronada* (lobster with spaghetti), and a kind of paella with mussels, shrimp, and crayfish. *Magirefta*

The Poseidonion Grand Hotel, with its elegant neoclassical facade, takes pride of place on the waterfront in Spetses Town.

(oven-baked dishes) include stuffed aubergines; oven-baked lamb; and roast *scarpine* fish with tomato and garlic. **Known for:** superbly prepared fresh fish; great service; sea view. [$] *Average main: €25* ✉ *Kounoupitsa* ✣ *Near Spetses Hotel* ☎ *22980/72134, 22980/75380* 🌐 *www.patralis.gr* ⏲ *Closed Nov. and Dec.*

Stelios Restaurant

$ | **GREEK** | You don't get the swish, trendy, and inventive modern island styles here, what you do get though is a traditional Greek taverna with swift service and good value for your money, which more than make up for a lack of atmosphere. Pass up the grilled dishes for the goat slowly cooked in a clay pot and oven-roasted potatoes lightly flavored with lemon and oregano. **Known for:** inexpensive and decent food; great location, in the heart of Spetses's buzzy waterfront strip; Greek cuisine. [$] *Average main: €10* ✉ *Dapia* ☎ *22980/73748* ⏲ *Closed mid-Nov.–mid-Mar.*

☕ Coffee and Quick Bites

Souvlucky

$ | **GREEK** | The owners of this spot are as unapologetic about the bad pun in their name as they are about the super tasty souvlaki they dish out. Order traditional gyro or souvlaki wrapped in a lighly grilled pita bread, to eat in or take out. **Known for:** delivery; souvlaki; ice cold beers. [$] *Average main: €5* ✉ *Spetses Town* ☎ *22980/29473.*

★ Vanilia

$ | **BAKERY** | Delightful patisserie-cum-coffee shop in Dapia serving fresh cakes, chocolates, and the quintesentially Greek island almond macaroons. **Known for:** fresh cakes; almond macaroons; friendly service. [$] *Average main: €5* ✉ *Dapia* ☎ *22980/77170.*

Hotels

Niriides Guesthouse

$ | **B&B/INN** | With cheerful, renovated exteriors surrounded by myriad flowers, this charming boutique-style B&B is only a few minutes' walk from the main harbor and offers decent value, especially in the off-season. **Pros:** on a central, quiet side street; hospitable owners; nice breakfast served in pretty, cool courtyard. **Cons:** bathrooms a bit on the small side; aside from breakfast, offers few hotel-style amenities; no 24-hour reception. $ *Rooms from: €100* ⊠ *Dapia ✛ Near the clock tower square* ☎ *22980/73392, 69446/37031* ⊕ *www.niriides-spetses.gr* ⤸ *7 rooms* �î○î *Free breakfast.*

Orloff Resort

$$$ | **RESORT** | A complex of renovated early-20th-century-listed buildings, set around a garden courtyard with a 72-foot swimming pool, comprise these lodgings. **Pros:** friendly down-to-earth staff; architectural splendor of aristocratic Spetses; pickup from the harbor on arrival. **Cons:** the double rooms are on the small side; Wi-Fi doesn't reach all spaces; a 20-minute trek to Dapia, the main part of town. $ *Rooms from: €230* ⊠ *Spetses Old Town* ☎ *22980/75444* ⊕ *www.orloffresort.com* ⤸ *31 rooms* �î○î *Free breakfast.*

★ Poseidonion Grand Hotel

$$$ | **HOTEL** | Set with fin-de-siècle cupolas, an imposing mansard roof, and elegant neoclassical facade, this iconic mansion was acclaimed as the Saronic gulf's own Hotel Negrescu in 1914—like that Nice landmark, this hotel was built to attract the cosmopolitan ocean-liner set and, today, the Poseidonion has been hailed as the most elegant hotel in all the Greek islands. **Pros:** the beautiful landmark building is "the place to stay"; impeccable service; simple but elegant guest rooms with high ceilings. **Cons:** not all rooms have a sea view; occasional hot-water issues in the grand old building; fills quickly in high season, so book early. $ *Rooms from: €280* ⊠ *Dapia* ☎ *22980/74553* ⊕ *www.poseidonion.com* ⤸ *52 rooms* �î○î *Free breakfast.*

Spetses Hotel

$$ | **HOTEL** | Enjoy both privacy—surrounded by greenery, beach, and water—and proximity (about a 20-minute walk) to town at this spot, which dates back to the 1970s. **Pros:** free Wi-Fi in common areas; nice café on the beach; view of the harbor and Spetses Town. **Cons:** rooms quite basic and dated; not the most charming building and dated; a little bit of a hike to and from town. $ *Rooms from: €130* ⊠ *Kounoupitsa beachfront ✛ 1 km (½ mile) west of Dapia* ☎ *22980/72602, 22980/72603, 22980/72604* ⊕ *www.spetses-hotel.gr* ☉ *Closed Nov.–Mar.* ⤸ *77 rooms* �î○î *Free breakfast.*

 Nightlife

For the newest "in" bars, ask at your hotel or, even better, take a stroll on the seafront promenade to the old harbor or Kounoupitsa; you'll be sure to find the spot with the right vibes for you.

Bikini Cocktails & Snacks

BARS/PUBS | This bar in a redesigned neoclassical building stands out for its romantic surroundings. Sip one of the imaginative cocktails, with names like Oki Monkey and Inferno, while sitting at a candlelit table right by the water. Things get more lively later in the evening, as this is one of *the* happening places on the island. ⊠ *Palio Limani* ☎ *22980/74888.*

Mosquito Bar

BARS/PUBS | Spetses's take on the gastro pub serves tasty grub that can be washed down by one (or more) of the many cool craft beers sourced from microbreweries throughout Greece. The sunset views from the roof garden, overlooking the sea, are magical. ⊠ *Kounoupitsa, Anargirou* ☎ *22980/29572.*

Spetsa Bar

BARS/PUBS | The island's all-time-classic hangout, where Kostas likes to play music from the 1960s and '70s. It's a perfect choice for a pre-dinner drink (bar opens at 8 pm). ⊠ *Platia Ag. Mamas* ☎ *22980/74131* ⊕ *www.barspetsa.org* ⊙ *Closed Nov.–Mar.*

Stavento Club

DANCE CLUBS | This club is a latey (opens 11 pm), where you can savor a cool cocktail on the breezey veranda overlooking the old harbor, which many patrons take advantage of to take a break from the steamy dance floor indoors. ⊠ *Old Harbor* ☎ *22980/75245.*

Throubi

NIGHTLIFE OVERVIEW | DJ sets from little-known, creative young Athenian talent set this little bar on the seafront promenade abuzz. The down-to-earth prices attract a less flashy crowd of nighttime fun seekers. ⊠ *Spetses Town* ⊹ *At the entrance of the old harbor* ☎ *69489/57398.*

Votsalo

BARS/PUBS | Tiny, cozy, and cute, Votsalo is a great meeting point for breakfast (it serves excellent espresso), but is equally popular after sunset, when you can order dreamy cocktails and listen to cool acid jazz tunes. ⊠ *Stavrou Niarchou 79, Dapia* ☎ *22980/73031.*

 Performing Arts

FESTIVALS

★ **Armata Festival**

FESTIVALS | Thousands flock in from all over Greece to attend the Armata Festival celebrations on Spetses, held in honor of Panayia Armata (Virgin Mary "of the Army"), in what is probably the most glorious weekend on the island's calendar. During the second week of September, Spetses mounts an enormous harbor-front reenactment of a War of Independence naval battle (the epic battle took place on September 8, 1822), complete with costumed fighters and burning ships. Book your hotel well in advance if you wish to see this popular event. There are also concerts and exhibitions during the week leading up to it. ⊠ *Spetses Town.*

Saronic Chamber Festival

FESTIVALS | The Saronic Chamber Music Festival features the excellent Leondari ensemble, an international group of world-class musicians who perform on the island of Spetses in August. There are also concerts in Galatas, Hydra, Poros, and Kythera. All performances start at 9 pm. ⊠ *Kapodistrian Cultural Hall* ⊹ *Near Ag. Mamas* ⊕ *www.saronicfestival.com.*

Shopping

Nord Ceramics Art & Design

ART GALLERIES | This lovely little gallery has hand-picked paintings and ceramics from local Greek artists and artisans. As well as mainly oil portrait paintings, you can pick up handy gifts like quirky Greek coffee sets, salad bowls and plates, and handmade boho jewelry. ⊠ *Plateia Rologiou, Dapia* ⊹ *close to the clock tower* ☎ *694 44/43534* ⊕ *nord-spetses.gr.*

Rota

CRAFTS | Locally sourced objects, from silver jewelry and kitchen bowls to souvenirs and decorative gifts, some of them handmade by the owner himself, are showcased here. ⊠ *High At., Dapia* ☎ *22980/74013.*

Spetza

CLOTHING | A classic boutique, stocking stylish clothes and accessories by top Greek designers, this is a great place to top up your trending chic island look. ⊠ *Dapia* ☎ *22980/73353* ⊕ *www.spetza-spetses.gr.*

White Boutique

CLOTHING | For a healthy dose of retail therapy, head to this clothing boutique, which offers a wide selection of caftans, bikinis, sandals, and other casual island-chic clothing. ✉ *Dapia* ☎ *22980/73308*.

 Activities

BIKING

The lack of cars and the predominantly level roads make Spetses ideal for cycling. One good trip is along the coastal road that circles the island, going from the main town to Ayia Paraskevi Beach.

Ilias Rent-A-Bike

BICYCLING | Head here to rent well-maintained mountain bikes (from €7 per day), motorbikes, and other equipment. A handy drop-off and pick-up service is available. ✉ *Ayia Marina* ☎ *6973/86407* ⊕ *www.facebook.com/ iliasrentacarskiathos*.

Trails Beyond

BICYCLING | Exploring Spetses on two wheels is a must, and for those with limited time, having a guided tour gets you to all of the island's sweets spots. Prices start at €75. ✉ *Ilia Iliou 57, Athens* ☎ *211/1157114* ⊕ *www.trailsbeyond.gr/ explorations/spetses-bike-tour/*.

BOATING
Artemis Marine

BOATING | For adept seafarers, renting a boat to zip round, at your own pace, to the beaches of your choice is highly desirable. Boat rentals start at €250 per day and rise dramatically depending on the class of boat and whether or not a skipper is included. ✉ *Porto Heli* ✥ *on the mainland a few km from the island (boats are delivered to anywhere on Spetses)* ☎ *69775/80511* ⊕ *www.artemismarine.gr*.

★ Spetses Classic Yacht Race

SAILING | For a long weekend in late June, Spetses fills with skippers and sailors who participate in this popular regatta celebrating the island's seafaring tradition. ✉ *Spetses Town* ☎ *210/4220506 race organizers, in Piraeus* ⊕ *spetsesclassicregatta.com*.

RUNNING
★ Spetses Mini Marathon

RUNNING | At this mid-October running event, you can choose between a 5K (3.1-mile) and 10K (6.2) fun run or a more demanding 25K (15½ miles), though the latter is also more scenic, taking in a whole lap around the island. You can also take part in the demanding endurance swimming competitions taking place over the same weekend: a 3-km (1.8-mile) race from Kosta to Spetses and a 5-km (3.1-mile) round-trip to Kosta and back. There are also runs and other activities for the young members of any group or family. ✉ *Spetses Town* ☎ *22980/72244* ⊕ *www.spetsesmarathon.com*.

Ayia Marina ΑΓΙΑ ΜΑΡΙΝΑ

2 km (1 mile) southeast of Spetses Town.

Ayia Marina is the most cosmopolitan beach on the island, so head here if you want to see and be seen.

 Beaches

Ayia Marina

BEACH—SIGHT | Favored by fashionable Greek socialites, the mostly sandy beach at Ayia Marina is the home of the elegant Paradise Beach Bar, tavernas, and many water-sports activities. Sun beds and umbrellas are available for a fee. You can hire a horse-drawn buggy from town to arrive in style, or you can come by caïque. Warning: this beach can get pretty busy during the summer months with a younger, party-loving crowd. **Amenities:** food and drink; showers; toilets; water sports. **Best for:** partiers; swimming; walking. ✉ *Ayia Marina* ☎ *22980/72195 Paradise Beach Bar*.

Ayia Marina Beach is one of the sizzling reasons why people love Spetses.

Ayioi Anargyroi
ΑΓΙΟΙ ΑΝΑΡΓΥΡΟΙ

6 km (4 miles) west of Spetses Town.

With plenty of water-sports options, this popular beach is set against a luscious green backdrop, offering the added prospect of seeing the nearby Bekiris cave at your own pace.

 Beaches

Ayioi Anargyroi
BEACH—SIGHT | A clean and cosmopolitan beach, Ayioi Anargyroi has a gently sloped seabed with deep waters suitable for snorkeling, waterskiing, and other water sports (rentals are available on-site). It is the island's best-known beach, 6 km (4 miles) away from town. You can also swim (or take a path) to beautiful Bekiris cave, a famous historical spot used by Greek revolutionaries as a hiding place during the 1821 revolution. Look for Taverna Manolis by the beach; nearby you can rent two sun beds and an umbrella for about €10 a day. There is also a pretty hotel (Acrogiali) right on the beach. **Amenities:** lifeguards; showers; water sports. **Best for:** snorkeling; swimming; walking; windsurfing.

Zogeria ΖΟΓΕΡΙΑ

7 km (4½ miles) west of Spetses Town.

A pine-edged cove with deep sapphire waters, Zogeria has a gorgeous natural setting that more than makes up for the lack of amenities—there's just a tiny church and the modest Loula taverna, where you can taste an incredible chicken stew in tomato sauce.

Beaches

Zogeria

BEACH—SIGHT | This is, in fact, two beaches split by a verdurous little peninsula. On the right, the larger beach offers a day of relaxation away from the cosmopolitan crowds, with few amenities other than the beautiful water. You can rent sun beds and umbrellas from Taverna Loula (June–September). On a clear day you can see all the way to Nafplion. **Amenities:** food and drink. **Best for:** solitude; swimming. ☎ *69446/27851 Taverna Loula.*

Ayia Paraskevi ΑΓΙΑ ΠΑΡΑΣΚΕΥΗ

10 km (6 miles) west of Spetses Town.

In a sheltered cove and easily accessible by bus or water taxi, this is a favorite with locals and visitors alike. In the height of summer the pine trees offer some much needed natural shade.

Beaches

Ayia Paraskevi

BEACH—SIGHT | Pine trees, a canteen, sun beds, and umbrellas line Ayia Paraskevi, a sheltered and popular beach with a mostly sandy shore (and coarse pebbles in other parts). Look for the cubic Ayia Paraskevi chapel at the back—it has given its name to the bay. Many locals consider this beach the most beautiful on the island; it can be reached either via road or with a caïque. The beach gets fairly busy during the summer months, and if you don't manage to snag a sun bed (€10 for a pair), you can sun yourself on the red rocks bordering the sandy beach. **Amenities:** food and drink. **Best for:** snorkeling; swimming; walking. ✉ *Ayia Paraskevi.*

THE SPORADES

SKIATHOS, SKOPELOS, AND SKYROS

Updated by
Nora Wallaya

⊙ **Sights**
★★★☆☆

🍴 **Restaurants**
★★★☆☆

🛏 **Hotels**
★★☆☆☆

🛍 **Shopping**
★★☆☆☆

🍸 **Nightlife**
★☆☆☆☆

WELCOME TO THE SPORADES

TOP REASONS TO GO

★ **Ritzy Shores of Skiathos:** Thousands of sunseekers head here to luxuriate on its idyllic beaches, dine in stylish seafront restaurants, explore surrounding coves by sailboat, and sip cocktails in late-night bars.

★ **Nature Filled Skopelos:** A network of hiking trails traverse hills and mountains carpeted with pine and fig trees, olive groves, and citrus orchards; dotted with picturesque churches and monasteries.

★ **Unspoiled Beach Life:** Clear, clean turquoise ocean laps the picture-perfect beaches on all the islands, but the most famous are those on Skiathos—and namely, the sparkling white sand of Koukounaries.

★ **Skyros's Style:** Set against a dramatic rock, the main town of Skyros is a showstopper of Cycladic houses colorfully set with wood carvings and embroideries.

★ **Silver Screen:** Fans of *Mamma Mia!* flock to Skopelos to see first-hand the locations used in the film.

This small cluster of islands off the coast of central Greece is just a short hop from the mainland and, consequently, often busy in high season. Obviously, the Cyclades aren't the only Greek islands that serve up a cup of culture and a gallon of hedonism to travelers. Each of the Sporades is very individual in character. Due east of tourism-oriented Skiathos are lesser-visited Skopelos and Skyros, both greener and quieter.

1 Skiathos. The relatively few residents are eclipsed by the 50,000 visitors who come here each year for clear blue waters and scores of sandy beaches, including the well-known favorite, Koukounaries. Close to the mainland, this island has some of the aura of the Pelion Peninsula, with red-roof villages and picturesque hills. Beauty spots include the Monastery of Evangelistria and Lalaria Beach.

2 Skopelos. Second largest of the Sporades, this island is lushly forested and more prized by nature lovers than fun seekers. The steep streets of Skopelos Town need some negotiating skills, but the charming alleys are irresistible, as are the island's monasteries, the famous cheese pies, and the traditional *kalivia* farmhouses around Panormos Bay. Legend has it that Skopelos was settled by Peparethos and Staphylos, colonists from Minoan Crete, said to be the sons of Dionysus and Ariadne, King Minos's daughter. They brought with them the lore of the grape and the olive.

SKIATHOS
Lalaria
Skiath
Tow
Koukounarie
Troullos

Strait of Skiathos

Agriovotano

EVIA

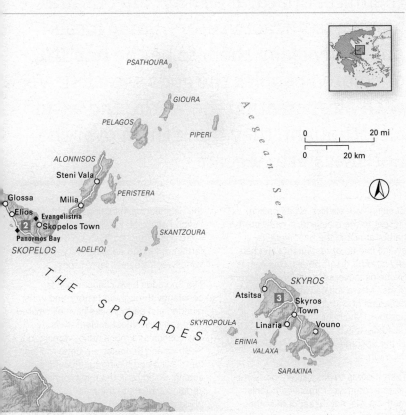

PSATHOURA

GIOURA

PELAGOS

PIPERI

A e g e a n   S e a

ALONNISOS

Steni Vala

PERISTERA

Glossa

Milia

Elios

Evangelistria

2 Skopelos Town

Panormos Bay

SKOPELOS   ADELFOI

SKANTZOURA

T H E   S P O R A D E S

SKYROS

Atsitsa

3 Skyros Town

SKYROPOULA   Linaria   Vouno

ERINIA

VALAXA

SARAKINA

0 ——————— 20 mi

0 ——————— 20 km

3 Skyros. Located at the virtual center of the Aegean Sea, this Sporades Shangri-la is the southernmost of the island group. The top half is covered with pine forests and is home to Skyros Town, a cubic masterpiece that climbs a spectacular rock peak and is a tangle of lanes, whitewashed houses, and Byzantine churches. The arid southern half is the site of noted Edwardian poet Rupert Brooke's grave, at Vouno. The Skyrians have not had a seafaring tradition, and have looked to the land for their living. Their isolation has brought about notable cultural differences from the other Greek islands, such as pre-Christian Carnival rituals

Little mentioned in mythology or history, the Sporades confidently rely on their great natural beauty and cultural history to attract visitors. Some locals poetically claim them to be the handful of colored pebbles the gods were left with after creating the world, and as an afterthought, they flung them over the northwestern Aegean.

Bustling with visitors, Skiathos sits closest to the mainland; it has a pretty harbor area and the best nightlife, a stylish line-up of restaurants and bars, and tasetful resort hotels. Due east is Skopelos, covered with dense, fragrant pines, where you can visit scenic villages, hundreds of churches, and neat pebbled beaches. Much less contemporary than Skiathos, it is the most naturally beautiful of the Sporades and has a fascinating old hill town.

Then there is traditional Skyros. Some visitors return year after year to this mythical isle, southeast of the other islands, for its quiet fishing villages, expansive beaches, and stunning cubist eagle's nest of a town that seems to spill down a hill. This remote island is hard to reach, so a visit is all the more rewarding for those with some extra time to make the journey.

Like emerald beads placed on sapphire satin, the aptly named Sporades ("scattered ones") are resplendent with pines, citrus orchards, pomegranate trees, and olive groves. The verdant countryside, marked with sloping slate roofs and wooden balconies, reflects the aura of

the neighboring, hauntingly beautiful Pelion Peninsula, to which the islands were once attached. Only on Skyros, farther out in the Aegean, will you see windswept, treeless landscapes.

The Sporades have changed hands constantly throughout history, and wars, plunder, and earthquakes have eliminated all but the strongest ancient walls. A few castles and monasteries remain, but Skiathos and Skopelos are better suited for relaxing and having fun than for sight-seeing. Skiathos is the most touristed, in certain locations to the point of overkill, while less-developed Skopelos has fewer beaches, a less contrived nightlife, and a main town that, while being the hot spot for most of the island's tourist stores, is hailed as being the most beautiful in the Sporades. Late to attract tourists, Skyros is the least traveled of the Sporades (probably because it is by far the hardest to reach). It's also the quirkiest, and the most traditional, with its distinct ways and customs.

Quintessential Greek-island delights beckon on all three islands: sun, sand, and surf, along with hazy, fragrant evenings and starlit al fresco dinners. Almost all restaurants have outside seating, often under the shade of trees, where you can watch the passing of ubiquitous Greek life.

Planning

When to Go

Winter is least desirable, as the weather turns cold and rainy; most hotels, rooms, and restaurants are closed, and ferry service is minimal. If you do go from November through April, book in advance and leave nothing to chance. The same advice applies to July and August peak season, when everything is open but often overcrowded, except on Skyros. The *meltemi*, the brisk northeasterly summer wind of the Aegean, keeps things cooler than on the mainland even on the hottest days. Late spring and early summer are ideal, as most hotels are open, crowds have not yet arrived, the air is warm, and the wildflowers filling roadsides and fields are an incredible sight; September is also mild.

If you want to catch one of the famous religious and cultural festivals on your visit, keep the following dates in mind. The lively Carnival (February) traditions of Skopelos, although not as exotic as those of Skyros, parody the expulsion of the once-terrifying Barbary pirates. August 15 is the day of the *Panayia* (Festival of the Virgin), celebrated on Skyros at Magazia Beach and on Skopelos in the main town; cultural events there continue to late August. Skiathos hosts several cultural events in summer, including a dance festival in July. Feast days? Skiathos: July 26, for St. Paraskevi; Skopelos: February 25, for St. Riginosi.

Planning Your Time

You can hop between Skiathos and Skopelos easily, since there are several-times-a-day ferry connections between them, and they are relatively near each other. Traveling between these islands and Skyros, however, requires advance planning, since there are no direct ferries to Skyros but instead boats leave from Kimi, on the island of Evia. Four days can be just enough for touching down on Skiathos and Skopelos, but you need more days if you want to include Skyros, since reaching it means a flight through Athens or a drive or bus trip to the port of Kimi.

How to choose if you're only visiting one of the Sporades? If you're the can't-sit-still type and think crowds add to the fun, Skiathos is your island. By day you can take in the beautiful, thronged beaches and Evangelistria Monastery or the fortress-turned-cultural-center, and at night stroll the port to find the most hopping nightclub. Day people with a historical bent should explore Skopelos's many monasteries and churches and its 18th-century Folk Art Museum. Skyros should be at the top of your list if you're a handicraft collector, as the island's furniture, embroidery, and pottery are admired throughout the country and can be bought and sent abroad from several shops.

Getting Here and Around

AIR

During the summer, Aegean and Olympic fly daily—or even twice a day, depending on the period—to Skiathos from Athens International Airport. The trip takes 45 minutes. In summer there are also weekly flights from Athens and Thessaloniki to Skyros Airport; the flights take 40 minutes. Fares vary dramatically depending on how far in advance you book.

Skiathos Airport also has direct flights from many European cities.

BOAT AND FERRY

Ferry travel to Skiathos and Skopelos requires that you drive or take a bus to Agios Konstantinos, about two hours north of Athens; if arriving from central or northern Greece, however, it's easiest to board a ferry at Volos or Thessaloniki. For all ferries, it's best to call a travel agency ahead of time to check schedules and prices and to book your ferry in advance—especially if you are bringing a car—as boat times change seasonally; to check schedules, go to the Greek Travel Pages (⊕ www.gtp.gr). Tickets are also available from several travel agents on the dock.

There are at least three to four ferries per day in the summer from Agios Konstantinos to Skiathos, often continuing on to Skopelos (these may be regular ferries or the so-called Flying Dolphin and Flyingcat ferries, which are smaller, faster, and more expensive but do not take cars). There are significantly fewer departures in winter.

Fast ferries from Agios Konstantinos to Skiathos take approximately 90 minutes and cost €32–€37; many continue to Skopelos in another 60 minutes and cost €40–€49.50. Regular ferries from Agios Konstantinos to Skiathos take about three hours and cost €30.50; they continue to Skopelos in another hour and 45 minutes and cost €38. From Volos, the travel time is slightly less and has similar pricing. On Skopelos, ferries usually make two stops, at Loutraki (port for the town of Glossa) and in Skopelos Town.

Getting to Skyros from Athens or elsewhere on the mainland requires driving or taking a bus to Kimi—on the giant island of Evia, connected by bridges to the mainland—and then catching one of the two daily ferries (or less-frequent hydrofoils) to Skyros. You can buy ferry tickets at the Kimi dock when you get off the bus; the trip to Skyros takes two hours and costs €9.

In summer only, there are three ferries weekly between Skopelos and Skyros; the trip takes about five hours and the ticket price is €22. *For information on ferry companies, see Boat and Ferry in Travel Smart.*

CONTACTS Port Authority. ☎ *22350/31759 in Agios Konstantinos, 22220/22522 in Kimi, 24270/22017 in Skiathos Town, 24240/22180 in Skopelos Town, 22220/93475 in Skyros Town.*

BUS

From Central Athens, buses leave every hour to Agios Konstantinos, the main port for the Sporades (except Skyros, for which ferries leave from Kimi on the island of Evia). Fares are about €15.70, and travel time is about 2½ hours. Buses from Athens to Kimi, on Evia island (the only port from which boats depart for Skyros) cost €15.30 and take 2½ hours. Schedules and fares change, so be sure to verify them with KTEL or a travel agent.

Bus service is available throughout the Sporades, although on some islands buses run more frequently than on others.

CAR

To get to Skiathos and Skopelos by car, you must drive to the port of Agios Konstantinos (Agios), and from there, take the ferry. The drive to Agios from Athens takes about two hours. For high-season travel you should reserve a place on the car ferry well in advance. Boats for Skyros leave from the port of Kimi on the big island of Evia. From Athens, take Athens–Lamia National Road to Skala Oropou, and make the 30-minute ferry crossing to Eretria on Evia (every half hour in the daytime). No reservations are needed. You can drive directly to Evia over a short land bridge connecting Agios Minas on the mainland with Halkidha, about 80 km (50 miles) from Athens (take National Road 1 to the Schimatari exit, and then follow the signs to Halkidha). From Halkidha it's another 80 km (50 miles) to Kimi;

total driving time from Athens is about 2½ hours, but on weekends crowds can slow traffic across the bridge.

The best way to get around the islands is by renting a car, but in the busy summer months, parking can be hard to come by in the main towns and villages. Car rentals cost €30–€70 per day, while scooters cost €14–€30 (with insurance). Scooters are ubiquitous, but if you rent a scooter, be extra cautious: scooter accidents provide the island clinics with 80% of their summer business.

See the individual island sections for detailed contact information.

TAXI

Taxis throughout the Sporades are unmetered, so be sure to negotiate your fare in advance or (better) check with your hotel for correct fares. You will find "Piatsa" taxi ranks next to all the harbor ports and airports, and taxis will be lined up even late at night if there is a boat or flight coming in. On the other hand, your hotel can usually arrange a taxi for you, but if you need one in the wee hours of the morning make sure you book it in advance. The prices on the islands are not cheap (compared to Athens or Thessaloniki), and can be as much as €10 to €20 for a 10-minute drive.

Hotels

Skopelos has a fair number of hotels, Skiathos a huge number, and Skyros has relatively few. Most hotels close from October or November to April or May. Reservations are a good idea, though you may learn about rooms in pensions and private homes when you arrive at the airport or ferry landing. The best bet, especially for those on a budget, is to rent a room in a private house—look for the Greek National Tourism Organization (EOT or GNTO) license displayed in windows. Owners meet incoming ferries to tout their location, offer rooms,

and negotiate the price. In Skyros most people take lodgings in town or along the beach at Magazia and Molos; accommodations are basic, and not generally equipped with TVs. Always negotiate rates off-season.

Restaurants

Most restaurants facing the ports open early for breakfast, while most others open from midday until just past midnight, and welcome guests to stay as long as they like. Traditional recipes such as *mageirefta* (home cooked) dishes based on local meat and vegetables, and a variety of fresh fish, reign supreme. Look for local specialties such as the *Skopelitiki tiropita,* or cheese pie (a spiral of tubed filo pastry filled with creamy white feta and fried to a crispy texture), or the fluffy *avgato* yellow plums in light syrup that can be savored as a dressing for fresh yogurt or on a small plate as *glyko koutaliou* (literally "spoon sweet"). Be sure to ask the waiter what fresh fish they serve and what the dishes of the day are, and don't hesitate to go inside and see the food for yourself before ordering. As with everywhere in Greece, the *hima* (homemade) house wine is usually good enough, sometimes excellent; the waiter will not mind if you order a taste before deciding.

Restaurant and hotel reviews have been shortened. For full information, visit Fodors.com.

What it Costs in euros			
$	$$	$$$	$$$$
RESTAURANTS			
under €15	€15–€25	€26–€40	over €40
HOTELS			
under €125	€125–€225	€226–€275	over €275

Visitor Information

There are few official tourist offices for the Sporades. The closest you'll come is the Skiathos Municipality agency, and most will only offer useful advice about boat or ferry travel. In lieu of official agencies, however, there is an array of private travel agencies, and these offer myriad services, tickets, car rentals, and guided tours. *See the individual islands sections for specific recommendations.*

Skiathos ΣΚΙΑΘΟΣ

Part sacred (scores of churches), part sin (lots of nightlife), the hilly, wooded island of Skiathos is the closest of the Sporades to the Pelion Peninsula. The island covers an area of only 42 square km (16 square miles) but has some 70 beaches and sandy coves. A jet-set island 25 years ago, today Skiathos teems with European—mostly British and Dutch—tourists and promising sun, sea, and late-night revelry. Higher prices and a bit of Mykonos's attitude are part of the deal, too.

In winter most of the island's 5,000 or so inhabitants live in its main city, Skiathos Town, built after the War of Independence on the site of the colony founded in the 8th century BC by the Euboean city-state of Chalkis. Skiathos was on good terms with the Athenians, prized by the Macedonians, and treated gently by the Romans. Saracen and Slav raids left the island virtually deserted during the early Middle Ages, but it started to prosper during the later Byzantine years.

When the Crusaders deposed their fellow Christians from the throne of Constantinople in 1204, Skiathos and the other Sporades became the fief of the Ghisi, knights of Venice. One of their first acts was to fortify the hills on the islet separating the two bays of Skiathos harbor. Now connected to the shore, the Bourtzi castle-fortress still has a few stout walls and buttresses shaded by some graceful pine trees.

GETTING HERE AND AROUND
AIR
The island airport is located just 1 km (½ mile) northeast of Skiathos Town; buses to town are very infrequent so plan on walking the short distance or jumping in a taxi to get to your hotel.

CONTACTS Skiathos Airport. ⊹ *1 km (½ mile) northeast of Skiathos Town* ☎ *24270/29105* ⊕ *jsi-airport.gr.*

BOAT
Ferries run regularly to Skiathos from both Agios Konstantinos and Volos, and these generally continue to Skopelos. There is also a daily hydrofoil to Thessaloniki.

Caïques leave from the main port for the most popular beaches; captains have signs of their destinations and departure times posted.

BUS
The main bus route follows the southern coast and makes 25 stops between Skiathos Town and the famed beach at Koukounaries (Maratha), a 30-minute ride. Fares are €1.50 to €3, with service from 7:30 am to 1 am in high season. This widely used service provides an easy and hassle-free way to get to towns and beaches along the southern side of the island.

CAR TRAVEL
Many companies, most of them local businesses, operate on Skiathos. To ensure a car is available in July and August, it's best to book in advance. *For information on international car-rental firms, see Car in Travel Smart.*

CONTACTS The First. ✉ *Papadiamantis St., Skiathos Town* ☎ *24270/22810, 69424/43165 mobile* ⊕ *www.skiathoshire.com.* **Skiathos Cheap Car Rental.** ✉ *Port of Skiathos, Skiathos Town* ☎ *24270/21246* ⊕ *www.skiathoscheapcarrental.gr.*

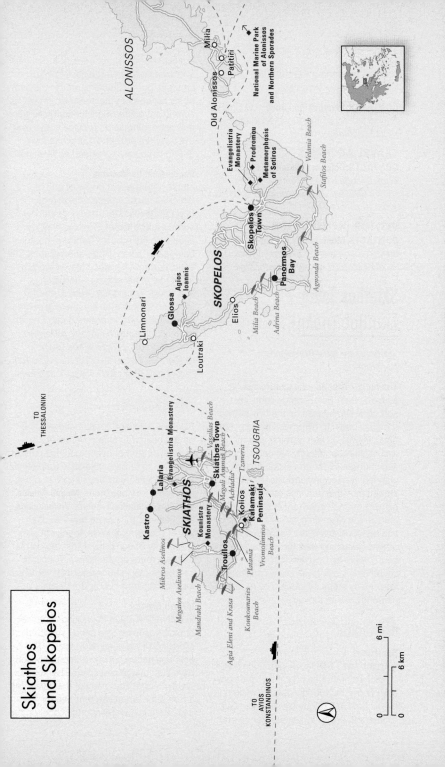

Skiathos and Skopelos

TAXI

Arrange taxis through your hotel, or you can call operators directly.

CONTACTS Skiathos Taxi Rank. (*Skiathos Piasta*) ⊠ *Port of Skiathos, Skiathos Town* ☎ *24270/24461.*

TRAVEL AGENCIES

CONTACTS Dolphin of Skiathos. ⊠ *Parodos Evaggelistrias, Skiathos Town* ☎ *24270/21910* ⊕ *www.dolphin-skiathos. gr.*

VISITOR INFORMATION

CONTACTS Municipality of Skiathos. ⊠ *Nikotsara 12, Skiathos Town* ☎ *24273/22022* ⊕ *www.skiathos.gr.*

Skiathos Town
Σκιάθος (πόλη)

2½ hours by ferry from Agios Konstantinos.

The harbor is especially picturesque at sunset, when violet-orange lights cast a soft glow and houses on the hills behind the quay begin to glimmer. Onshore, pink bougainvillea, sweet jasmine, and the casual charm of brightly painted balconies and shutters add to the experience of wandering through narrow lanes and up steep steps that serve as streets. Activity centers on the waterfront or on Papadiamantis, the main drag, while shops, bars, and restaurants line the cobbled side streets. Watching over the east side of the port (known as the New Port) is the little church and clock tower of Ayios Nikolaos, reached by steps so steep they're almost perpendicular to the earth.

 Sights

Bourtzihos

HISTORIC SITE | This lovely presence on Skiathos harbor stands on a small, pine-covered peninsula that divides the main port. It was built in 1207 by the Venetian Gyzi brothers to protect Skiathos from pirate attacks. Not much remains of the original fortress (also called the castle of St. George), but a cultural center at the site hosts concerts in the summer, as well as art and antiquities exhibitions. Many tranquil, refreshing spots provide views over the busy waterfront. ⊠ *Skiathos Town* ✛ *End of causeway extending from port.*

Papadiamantis Museum

HOUSE | The modest home of one of Greece's finest writers, Alexandros Papadiamantis (1851–1911), lauded by some as "the Greek Dostoyevsky," is filled with his modest furniture, personal belongings, and vintage photographs. The author's native Skiathos played a prominent role in his essays, short stories, and novels, as did his Greek Orthodox faith and simple rural life. Several of his novels have been translated into English, including the internationally acclaimed *The Murderess.* ⊠ *Skiathos Town* ✛ *Right off Papadiamantis St. at the fork* ☎ *24270/23843* ⊠ *€1.50* ☉ *Closed Tues.*

 Beaches

Skiathos is known for its beaches, and on the beautiful, pine-covered 14-km (9-mile) stretch of coast running south of the town to famed, gold-sand Koukounaries, one beach succeeds another. Along this coast, the beaches—**Megali Ammos, Vassilias, Achladia, Tzaneria, Vromolimnos,** and **Platania,** to name a few—all offer water sports, umbrellas, lounge chairs, and plenty of company. Most are on the one bus route on the island so a car or scooter rental is unnecessary if you are just looking for a day at the beach.

Megali Ammos

BEACH—SIGHT | Within walking distance of Skiathos Town, the sandy stretch of Megali Ammos is an easy option. The bars and eating options lining the beach have sun lounges reaching down to the water's edge, and many of the bars offer a free drink when you rent one for the day. There is a water-sports school on the

On Skiathos, the coast is always clear.

busier, right side of the beach where you can enjoy white-knuckle rides on giant inflatable bananas and doughnuts pulled at high speeds by little motorboats. **Amenities:** food and drink; lifeguard; showers; toilets; water sports. **Best for:** swimming. ⊠ *Skiathos Town* ✛ *Walk west over the hill then on the coastal road* Ⓜ *Bus Stop 5.*

Vassilias Beach

BEACH—SIGHT | One of the better beaches close to Skiathos Town, Vassilias is lined by pine trees that lean thirstily toward the shallow seashore, providing shade under their aromatic branches. A rustic canteen and some beachside restaurants serve refreshments, outfitters offer all sorts of sea-based adventures, and rows of shaded sun lounges are lined up for rent. **Amenities:** food and drink; parking (no fee); showers; toilets; water sports. **Best for:** snorkeling; swimming; walking. ⊠ *Skiathos Town* ✛ *2 km (1 mile) from Skiathos Town* Ⓜ *Bus Stop 8.*

Vromolimnos

BEACH—SIGHT | One of the most popular and busiest beaches on Skiathos has a party vibe, along with waterskiing, which is especially good in the afternoon when the sea usually calms to a lakelike smoothness. On the far end of the beach, away from the pulsating tunes and rumbling boat engines, there's space to lay out a towel and soak up the sun. There's also a decent little taverna. **Amenities:** food and drink; lifeguard; parking (no fee); showers; toilets; water sports. **Best for:** partiers; sunset; swimming. ✛ *Kolios, 8 km (5 miles) southwest of Skiathos Town* Ⓜ *Bus Stop 13.*

🍴 Restaurants

Amfiliki

$ | SEAFOOD | The balcony pairs inviting breezes and sprawling views, a perfect setting in which to enjoy fresh local fish. Owner Christos also takes pride in the organic vegetables he serves, all from his own garden. **Known for:** views; fresh fish; ekmek (custard cake) with mastic ice cream. $ *Average main: €12* ✉ *Agia Triada* ✛ *Opposite the health center* ☎ *24270/22839* ⊕ *www.amfiliki.gr* ⊘ *Closed Oct.–May.*

Kahlua

$$ | GREEK | Situated on Skiathos's exceptionally stylish run of seafront restaurants, the recently renovated Kahlua draws in restaurant-goers for its distinctly bohemian style, ample open-air seating, ambient mood lighting, and effervescent energy. Book well ahead of visiting for a spot by the sea, where you'll have the best views of bobbing boats and glorious sunsets. **Known for:** sunset views; fresh seafood; bohemian decor. $ *Average main: €15* ✉ *Paraliakos* ☎ *69733/88294* ⊕ *kahluarestaurant.com.*

★ Marmita

$$ | GREEK | Enclosed within a leafy, serene courtyard, this restaurant serves possibly the highest quality food on the island. Traditional Greek fare is on the menu, with local specialties like Mastelo cheese. **Known for:** verdant setting; eclectic menu; local delicacies. $ *Average main: €20* ✉ *Odos Eyaggelistrías 30* ☎ *24270/21701* ⊕ *marmitaskiathos.com* ⊘ *evening only.*

Coffee and Quick Bites

Ergon

$ | GREEK | Egron is a restaurant, Greek deli, and specialty coffee shop rolled into one stylish, contemporary spot on the main run of Papadiamanti. It serves exceptional fresh fish and a range of meze, with immaculate presentation and great care given to the dishes. **Known for:** specialty coffee; deli ingredients; fish of the day. $ *Average main: €10* ✉ *Papadiamanti* ☎ *24270/21441* ⊕ *ergonfoods.com.*

Hotels

Aegean Suites

$$$$ | RESORT | Romantically inclined twosomes who settle into this couples-only hideaway on a hillside outside town will be excused for thinking they've landed in their own grand Mediterranean villa, since that's what the large, comfortable suites, lovely gardens, and pampering are all meant to do. **Pros:** outstanding service; luxurious amenities; very attractive surroundings. **Cons:** no elevator and lots of stairs; walk into town is along busy road; not on the beach. $ *Rooms from: €450* ✉ *Megali Ammos Beach* ☎ *24270/24066* ⊕ *santikoscollection.com* ⊘ *Closed Nov.–Apr.* ⇗ *20 suites* ⦿ *Free breakfast* Ⓜ *Bus Stop 5.*

Bourtzi Hotel

$$ | HOTEL | Contemporary style and relaxing, luxurious ambience comes to the fore in the island's bastion of chic, with a snazzy cocktail lounge and public rooms, crisp, cool, spotless accommodations, and a laid-back courtyard pool that could hold its own in South Beach. **Pros:** stylish sophistication; restful and quiet accommodations; convenient town center location. **Cons:** not on the beach; pool area is often in shade; minimum-stay requirement some periods. $ *Rooms from: €189* ✉ *Moraitou 8* ☎ *24270/21304* ⊕ *www.hotelbourtzi.gr* ⇗ *38 rooms* ⦿ *Free breakfast.*

Mouria Hotel

$ | HOTEL | A big dose of Greek hospitality comes with a provenance in these simple but cheerful rooms surrounding a bougainvillea-filled courtyard and downstairs taverna that have been a bastion of the Skiathos holiday scene since 1830. **Pros:** delightful atmosphere; immaculate surroundings; hospitable owners and staff. **Cons:** rooms overlooking Papadiamantis can be noisy; more charm than luxury; no sea views. $ *Rooms from: €50* ✉ *Papadiamantis* ✛ *Behind the National Bank* ☎ *24270/021193* ⊕ *www.mouriahotel.com* ⊘ *Closed Oct.–May* ⇗ *12 rooms* ⦿ *Free breakfast.*

★ Skiathos Luxury Living

$$ | RENTAL | Extending up the side of a hill at a quiet end of Skiathos Town (but just a few minutes' walk to the center) each of the property's luxurious open-plan apartments benefit from glittering views of the port and sea beyond. **Pros:** brand-new residences; sea views and balconies with every room; design-conscious interiors. **Cons:** bathrooms dark and a little small; negotiating elevators is awkward, lots of stairs otherwise; surrounding area a bit shabby. $ *Rooms from: €110* ⊠ *Periferiakos Skiathou* 🕾 *24270/22574* ⊕ *skiathosliving.com* ⤶ *24* ❘◯❘ *Free breakfast.*

Nightlife

Skiathos is filled with night owls, and bars for all tastes line main and side streets, from pubs run by Brits to quintessential Greek bouzouki joints in beach tavernas. Most of the nightlife in Skiathos Town is centered along the waterfront and on Papadiamanti, Politechniou, and Evangelistrias streets.

MUSIC AND NIGHTCLUBS

Bourtzi Café

BARS/PUBS | The tip of the promontory beneath the fortress (Bourtzi) is an atmospheric spot for sundowners, and for starlit, sophisticated drinks by night. ⊠ *Bourtzi* 🕾 *24270/23900* ⊕ *www.bourtzi-skiathos.gr.*

Kahlua

MUSIC CLUBS | It's a restaurant by day, and a nightclub after hours where, sooner or later, clubbers will head for cocktails and dancing. The fun gets started at 11 pm—but the action doesn't usually get going till after midnight—and it goes until at least 3 am. ⊠ *Paraliakos* 🕾 *69780/388294* ⊕ *kahluarestaurant.com* ◔ *Closed Sept.–June.*

Kentavros Bar

MUSIC CLUBS | A young, professional crowd gathers here for rhythm and blues, funk, soul, and classic rock starting at 10 pm. ⊠ *Papadiamantis Sq.* 🕾 *24270/22980* ◔ *Closed Oct.–Apr.*

Shopping

ANTIQUES AND CRAFTS

Galerie Varsakis

ANTIQUES/COLLECTIBLES | Kilims, embroideries, jewelry, icons, and hundreds of antiques from around the world are available here, all set off by proprietor Charalambos Varsaki's impressive surrealistic paintings and prints. Also noteworthy is his collection of guns and swords dating from 1780–1820 and used in the Greek War of Independence. ⊠ *Trion Hierarchon Sq.* 🕾 *24270/22255* ⊕ *www.varsakis.com.*

JEWELRY

Phaedra

JEWELRY/ACCESSORIES | Silver and gold pieces that are part of collections by noteworthy Greek designers celebrate jewelry-making with an artsy twist. ⊠ *Papadiamantis 23* 🕾 *24270/21233.*

Activities

SAILING

Active Yachts

SAILING | The way to explore the Sporades in style is aboard these weekly sailboat charters. ⊠ *Skiathos Town* ⚓ *Portside* 🕾 *69722/45391* ⊕ *activeyachts. gr* ⛵ *From €2,000 per wk* ◔ *Closed Oct.–Apr.*

SCUBA DIVING

Dolphin Diving Center

SCUBA DIVING | Several popular beaches have diving-equipment rentals and instructors on hand. Dolphin offers single or multiple dives, as well as full-certification programs. ⊠ *Hotel Nostos, Tzaneria Beach* 🕾 *69449/99181* ⊕ *www.ddiving.gr* ⛵ *Diving courses from €60* ◔ *Closed Nov.–Apr.*

Kalamaki Peninsula Καλαμάκι (χερσόνησος)

6 km (4 miles) south of Skiathos Town.

On the least-developed part of the south coast, villas are tucked above tiny, isolated coves. Access to most of the shoreline is by boat only. Motor launches run at regular intervals to the most popular beaches from Skiathos Town, and you can also hire a boat and find your own private beach.

Hotels

★ Atrium Hotel
$$$ | **HOTEL** | This stunning hillside retreat tucked away in gardens and pine groves above the south coast seems like a private villa, with lots of wood and stone enhancing the airy public spaces, a beautiful pool terrace, and sharply decorated rooms and suites—all with balconies and patios, some with private pools, and most with extensive sea views. **Pros:** beautiful design by architect-owners; attractive and comfortable guest rooms; pleasant lounges and pool area. **Cons:** beach is nearby but across the busy road; stairs on property may be difficult for some guests; not all rooms have sea views. [$] *Rooms from: €230* ✉ *Ayia Paraskevi Platanias* ✣ *On the coastal road 8 km (5 miles) from Skiathos Town* ☎ *24270/49345* 🌐 *atriumhotel.gr* ⏲ *Closed Nov.–Apr.* 🛏 *75 rooms* 🍴 *Free breakfast* [M] *Bus Stop 16.*

Princess Resort
$$ | **RESORT** | **FAMILY** | Understated glamour and polished island chic rule at this luxurious getaway spreading above Ayia Paraskevi Beach. **Pros:** beautiful grounds and facilities; wonderful views; five-star service. **Cons:** some rooms are in need of renovation; bathrooms tend to be small; not all rooms have sea views. [$] *Rooms from: €155* ✉ *Ayia Paraskevi Platanias* ✣ *On the coastal road 8 km (5 miles) from Skiathos Town* ☎ *24270/49731* 🌐 *santikoscollection.com* ⏲ *Closed Nov.–Apr.* 🛏 *158 rooms* 🍴 *Free breakfast* [M] *Bus Stop 16.*

Troullos Τρούλλος

4 km (2½ miles) west of Kalamaki Peninsula, 8 km (5 miles) west of Skiathos Town.

West of the Kalamaki Peninsula the coast road rounds Troullos Bay and comes to Koukounaries Beach—famous and beautiful but not a remote hideaway.

Sights

Kounistra Monastery
HISTORIC SITE | The dirt road north of Troullos leads to beaches and to the small, now deserted, Kounistra Monastery. It was built in 1655 on the spot where a monk discovered an icon of the Virgin "miraculously" dangling from a pine tree. The icon spends most of the year in the church of Trion Hierarchon, in Skiathos Town, but on November 20 the townspeople parade it to its former home for the celebration of the Presentation of the Virgin the following day. You can enter the deserted monastery church any time, though its interior has been blackened by fire and its 18th-century frescoes are difficult to see. ✉ *Troullos* ✣ *4 km (2½ miles) north of Troullos* [M] *Bus Stop 21.*

Beaches

Agia Eleni and Krasa
BEACH—SIGHT | Around the island's western tip are Ayia Eleni and Krasa, facing the nearby Pelion Peninsula. The beaches are also known as Big and Little Banana on account of their crescent shapes. At the latter, sun worshippers often peel their clothes off—it's a popular naturist beach. Its rocky coves provide some privacy. **Amenities:** food and drink; parking

(free); showers; toilets; water sports. **Best for:** nudists; partiers; sunset; swimming. ✉ *Troullos* ✣ *1 km (½ mile) west of Koukounaries Beach, 13 km (8 miles) west of Skiathos Town* [M] *Bus Stop 26.*

Koukounaries

BEACH—SIGHT | Some fans call this scenic slice of shoreline "Golden Coast," after its fine, sparkling golden sand, but in high season, when sunseekers land by the boatload, you'll be lucky to find a free patch. The name, Greek for stone pines, comes from the forest that is almost watered by the waves. Enjoy a leisurely stroll behind the beach to Strofilia Lake, an impressive biotope where rare species of birds find shelter. **Amenities:** food and drink; lifeguard; parking (free); showers; toilets; water sports. **Best for:** partiers; snorkeling; sunrise; swimming; walking. ✣ *4 km (2½ miles) northwest of Troullos, 12 km (8 miles) west of Skiathos Town* [M] *Bus Stop 26.*

★ Mandraki

BEACH—SIGHT | Located in a nature reserve, it's just a 3 km walk from busy Koukounaries. Make the journey on foot to walk through a heady, scented pine forest that rises from terra-cotta-red sand before reaching this "secret" beach that's a haven for those seeking silence and solitude. There are no watersports businesses in operation and the sea is a little rough, so it's frequented by swimmers and surfers rather than families and noisy youths. Sometimes called Xerxes' harbor, the bay is where the notorious Persian king stopped on his way to ultimate defeat at the battles of Artemisium and Salamis. The reefs opposite are the site of a monument Xerxes allegedly erected as a warning to ships, the first such marker known in history. **Amenities:** food and drink; parking (free). **Best for:** swimming; walking; solitude. ✉ *Troullos* ✣ *5 km (3 miles) northwest of Troullos Bay, 12 km (7½ miles) west of Skiathos Town* [M] *Bus Stop 23.*

Megalos Aselinos and Mikros Aselinos

BEACH—SIGHT | At these side-by-side options, separated by a forested headland, expansive and laid-back Megalos Aselinos is a favorite of locals and tourists visiting by boat, while Mikros Aselinos is quieter and can be reached by car or bike. Neither, however, can be reached by bus. **Amenities:** food and drink; parking (free); toilets. **Best for:** snorkeling; solitude; sunset; swimming. ✉ *Troullos Bay* ✣ *7 km (4½ miles) north of Troullos, 12 km (7 miles) west of Skiathos Town* [M] *No Bus.*

🍴 Restaurants

Under The Pine Tree

$ | GREEK | Loved by the locals, this traditional Greek restaurant serves belly-busting portions of gyros, souvlaki, and grilled meats to queues of hungry diners. With plenty of outdoor seating shaded by the immense canopies of fragrant pine trees, and with pretty pendant mood lighting, it's a harmonious space to eat after a scorching day at the beach. **Known for:** gyros and souvlaki; excellent value; nature-filled setting. [$] *Average main: €10* ✉ *Koukounaries* ☎ *24270/49710* 🌐 *underthepinetreeskiathos.com* [M] *Bus Stop 23.*

🛏 Hotels

★ Mandraki Village

$ | HOTEL | FAMILY | Easy luxury and designer charm pervade these soothing accommodations done in warm, summery shades nestled in a "village" of eight buildings, surrounded by an expansive garden of lemon trees and Mediterranean plants. **Pros:** three restaurants; attractive decor; garden setting. **Cons:** some noise from room to room; not on the beach, but within walking distance to several; some rooms and bathrooms are small. [$] *Rooms from: €120* ✉ *Koukounaries* ☎ *24270/49301* 🌐 *www.mandraki-skiathos.gr* 🛏 *38 rooms* 🍽 *Free breakfast* [M] *Bus Stop 21.*

Kastro Κάστρο

13 km (8 miles) northeast of Troullos, 9 km (5½ miles) northeast of Skiathos Town.

The ruins that are also known as the Old Town perch on a forbidding promontory high above the water, accessible only by steps. Skiathians founded this former capital in the 16th century when they fled from the pirates and the turmoil on the coast to the security of this remote cliff—staying until 1829. Its landward side was additionally protected by a moat and drawbridge, and inside the stout walls they erected 300 houses and 22 churches, of which only 2 remain. The little Church of the Nativity has some icons and must have heard many prayers for deliverance from the sieges that left the Skiathians close to starvation.

You can drive or take a taxi or bus to within 325 feet of the Old Town, or wear comfortable shoes for a walk that's mostly uphill. Better, take the downhill walk back to Skiathos Town; the trek takes about three hours and goes through orchards, fields, and forests on the well-marked paths of the interior, with dramatic views of the sea and surrounding islands.

 Sights

Kechria Monastery
RELIGIOUS SITE | Just southwest of Kastro is this romantic, deserted monastic compound, where the 18th-century church is embellished with frescoes and surrounded by olive and pine trees. Be warned: the road to Kechria from Skiathos Town and to the beach below is tough going; stick to a four-wheel-drive vehicle or a sturdy motorbike. ✛ *4 km (2½ miles) southwest of Kastro.*

Lalaria Λαλάρια

2 km (1 miles) east of Kastro, 7 km (4½ miles) north of Skiathos Town.

The much-photographed, lovely Lalaria Beach, on the north coast, is flanked by a majestic, arched limestone promontory. The polished limestone and marble add extra sparkle to the already shimmering Aegean. There's no lodging here, and you can only reach Lalaria by taking an excursion boat or water taxi from the Old Port in Skiathos Town (the buses don't serve this beach). In the same area lie **Skoteini (Dark) cave, Galazia (Azure) cave,** and **Halkini (Copper) cave.** If taking a tour boat, you can stop for an hour or two here to swim and frolic. Bring along a flashlight to turn the water inside these grottoes an incandescent blue.

 Sights

★ **Evangelistria Monastery**
HISTORIC SITE | The island's best-known and most beautiful monastery sits on Skiathos's highest point and was dedicated in the late-18th century to the Annunciation of the Virgin by the monks of Mt. Athos. It encouraged education and gave a base to revolutionaries, who pledged an oath to freedom and first hoisted the flag of Greece here in 1807. Looming above a gorge, and surrounded by fragrant pines and cypresses, the monastery has a high wall that once kept pirates out; today it encloses a ruined refectory kitchen, the cells, a small museum library, and a magnificent church with three domes. Fascinating still, it houses the wooden loom that wove the very first Greek flag. A gift shop sells the monastery's own Alypiakos wine, olive oil, locally made preserves, and Orthodox icons. A café on a hill next to the monastery serves drinks and snacks, with stupendous views of the surrounding mountains and ocean. In summer, a bus goes to and from the monastery from the main bus station

in Skiathos Town, where the bus times are advertised. ⊠ *Lalaria* ✛ *2 km (1 mile) south of Lalaria, 5 km (3 miles) north of Skiathos Town* ✉ *Donations accepted.*

Skopelos ΣΚΟΠΕΛΟΣ

This triangular island's name means "a sharp rock" or "a reef"—a fitting description for the dramatic terrain on the northern shore. It's an hour and a half away from Skiathos by ferry and is the second largest of the Sporades. Most of its 122 square km (47 square miles), up to its highest peak on Mt. Delfi, are covered with dense pine forests, olive groves, and orchards. On the south coast, villages overlook the shores, and pines line the pebbly beaches, casting jade shadows on turquoise water.

Legend has it that Skopelos was settled by Peparethos and Staphylos, colonists from Minoan Crete, said to be the sons of Dionysus and Ariadne, King Minos's daughter. They brought with them the lore of the grape and the olive. The island was called Peparethos until Hellenistic times, and its most popular beach still bears the name Stafilos. In the 1930s a tomb believed to be Staphylos's was unearthed, filled with weapons and golden treasures (now in the Volos museum on the Pelion Peninsula).

The Byzantines were exiled here, and the Venetians ruled for 300 years, until 1204. In times past, Skopelos was known for its wine, but today its plums and almonds are eaten rather than drunk, and incorporated into the simple cuisine. Many artists and photographers have settled on the island and throughout summer are part of an extensive cultural program. Little by little, Skopelos is cementing an image as a green and artsy island, still unspoiled by success.

Although this is the most populated island of the Sporades, with two major towns, Skopelos remains peaceful and absorbs tourists into its life rather than giving itself up to their sun-and-fun desires. It's not surprising that ecologists claim it's the greenest island in the region.

GETTING HERE AND AROUND
AIR
There's no airport on Skopelos, but you can take an Athens–Skiathos flight, and then take a ferry from Skopelos Port (just 2 km from the airport) to Skopelos.

BOAT AND FERRY
Ferries from the mainland leave from Agios Konstantinos or Volos, and ferries back to the mainland stop in Skiathos. Skopelos has two main ports: Skopelos Town and, at the northwestern end of the island, Loutraki (beneath the hilltop village of Glossa). In summer there are weekly ferries between Skopelos and Skyros; the trip takes about five hours.

Caïques (small boats) leave from the docks in Skopelos Town and Loutraki for the most popular beaches. A lot of excursion boats also head over to Skiathos, as well as to nearby Alonissos; just walk along the docks, where captains post their destinations and departure times.

BUS
The main bus station on Skopelos is opposite a children's playground to the right of the main port area, and housed beneath a large white shelter. Buses make trips along various routes on the island several times a day, more often in summer (hotels usually have schedules on hand). From Skopelos Town, buses cross the island to Stafilos then follow the west coast up to Glossa, with stops along the way in Panormos, Elios, and other popular towns. The full journey from Skopelos Town to Glossa costs €4.80

CAR

The only easy way to visit many beaches and see the forested interior is by car, and you'll probably want to rent one for at least part of your stay. The Local Route is a reliable car-rental company on Skopelos, and many international firms also have outlets. *See also Car in Travel Smart.*

CONTACTS The Local Route. ⊹ *50 meters to the right of the port* ☎ *24240/23682* ⊕ *www.thelocalroute.gr.*

TAXI

Taxis can be arranged through your hotel, or you can call operators directly.

CONTACTS Giannis Stamoulos. ☎ *69724/29568 mobile.* **Zahos Stamoulis.** ☎ *69728/41329 mobile.*

TOURS

★ Skopelos Walks

WALKING TOURS | To gain a unique perspective on Skopelos, take one of the walking tours offered by Heather Parsons. She offers an informative two-hour town walk plus half and full-day walking tours of the island, all year round. Tours cost between €10 and €25. Advance reservations online or by phone are required. Heather also organizes a program in which volunteers from all over the world come to help maintain the trails and cobbled *calderimia*—stone paths that criss-cross the island. Lodging and food are provided in exchange for labor. ⊠ *Skopelos Town* ☎ *69452/49328* ⊕ *skopelos-walks.com.*

TRAVEL AGENCIES

Thalpos Holidays

Apart from providing the standard travel services, Thalpos can also arrange hiking, biking, cooking lessons, and other more personalized and alternative activities. ⊠ *Paralia Skopelou, Skopelos Town* ☎ *24240/29036* ⊕ *www.holidayislands. com.*

VISITOR INFORMATION

CONTACTS Skopelos Tourist Office. ☎ *69850/15215* ⊕ *www.skopelosweb.gr.*

Skopelos Town
Σκόπελος (πόλη)

3 hrs from Agios Konstantinos, ½ hr from Skiathos Town by ferry.

Idyllic Skopelos Town, the administrative center of the Sporades, overlooks a sparkling turquoise bay on the north coast. Three- and four-story white-washed houses rise virtually straight up a hillside that's a labyrinth of steps and pebble-studded lanes. The houses look prosperous (18th-century Skopelos society was highly cultured and influential) and cared for, their facades enlivened by brightly painted or brown timber balconies, doors, and shutters, along with vibrant bougainvillea, wisteria, and scatterings of potted plants. Interspersed among the red-tile roofs are several with traditional gray fish-scale slate—too heavy and expensive to be used much nowadays. At the town's summit you're standing within the walls of the ruined 13th-century castle erected by the Venetian Ghisi lords who held all the Sporades as their fief. It in turn rests on polygonal masonry of the 5th century BC, as this was the site of one of the island's three ancient acropoli.

You will encounter many churches here—the island has more than 360, of which 123 are in the town, and their exteriors incorporate ancient artifacts, Byzantine plates or early Christian elements, and slate-capped domes. The uppermost, the 11th-century Ayios Athanasios, is said to be situated on the ruins of the ancient temple of Minerva and has a typically whitewashed exterior and an interior that includes 17th-century Byzantine murals.

◉ Sights

★ Evangelistria Monastery

MOUNTAIN—SIGHT | A perch on Palouki Mountain provides views of the sea and the town. The impressive complex was founded in 1676 and completely rebuilt in 1712 by Ioannis Grammatikos, who believed he was saved from execution by an 11th-century icon of the Virgin. The miraculous object is housed in the church, with an intricately carved iconostasis. It's a short drive from Skopelos Town, but a walk up the quiet, pine-fringed roads and across mountains patched with olive groves offers a serene excursion. Stop by a stone fountain midway for refreshment—the mineral mountain water is safe to drink. ⊠ *Skopelos Town* ✚ *On the mountainside opposite Skopelos Town, 1½ km (1 mile) northeast of town* 🏛 🌐 *Free.*

Folklore Museum

MUSEUM | For an impression of how upper-class Skopelians lived 200 years ago, step into this 18th-century mansion (1795) with hand-carved period furniture, decorative items, paintings, and embroideries. Don't miss the display of the elaborately sewn wedding dress in the bridal chamber. ⊠ *Hatzistamati* 🕾 *24240/23494* 🌐 *€3* 🕙 *Closed weekends Oct.–May.*

Metamorphosis of Sotiros

RELIGIOUS SITE | One of the oldest monasteries (circa 1700) on the island is now occupied by a sole monk. It features iconography in the old basilica, painted by renowned Byzantine painter Agorastos. ⊠ *Skopelos Town* ✚ *Follow the signs east of Skopelos Town, past Ayia Varvara* 🕙 *Closed Dec.–Mar.*

National Marine Park of Alonissos and Northern Sporades

NATURE PRESERVE | Skopelos is at the edge of the largest swath of protected waters in the Mediterranean, covering 2,200 square km (849 square miles). Within the park, only neighboring Alonissos is inhabited; other islands and islets are the domain of goats and falcons, while dolphins and highly endangered Mediterranean monk seals swim in the pristine waters. Boats ply the waters of the park on day excursions from Skopelos, stopping at remote beaches and such outposts of civilization as the islet monastery of Megistis Lavras. Travel agencies and eager captains advertise the trips, easily arranged with a walk along the port. ⊠ *Skopelos Town harbor.*

Timiou Prodromou (*Forerunner*)

RELIGIOUS SITE | Dedicated to St. John the Baptist, Prodromou now operates as a convent. Besides being unusual in design, its church contains some outstanding 14th-century triptychs, an enamel tile floor, and an iconostasis spanning four centuries (half was carved in the 14th century, half in the 18th century). The nuns sell elaborate woven and embroidered handiwork. Opening days and hours vary. ⊠ *Skopelos Town* ✚ *2½ km (1½ miles) east of Skopelos Town.*

Vakratsa Mansion

HOUSE | In this 19th-century mansion, furnishings, precious icons, and quotidian antiques from around the world make this a fine showcase of the life and traditions of a local family of high standing from a time when Skopelos was a hub for a well-traveled, politically influential, and highly cultured society. Andigoni Vakratsa and her father were doctors who offered free medical services to the poor. Head upstairs to view the living room (it was used only for very special occasions) where you can admire a traditional island engagement dress with its 4,000-pleat skirt. Opening hours vary. ⊠ *Skopelos Town* ✚ *A short walk up from Ambrosia sweet shop* 🌐 *€3.*

The Evangelistria Monastery, perched on Palouki Mountain, has beautiful views of the sea and nearby Skopelos Town.

Beaches

Agnonda Beach

BEACH—SIGHT | FAMILY | This little seaside settlement fronts exceptionally clean waters and has numerous tavernas along its pebbled beach serving fresh seafood. Agnonda is named after a local boy who returned here victorious from Olympia in 569 BC brandishing the victor's wreath. **Amenities:** food and drink; parking (no fee); showers; toilets; water sports. **Best for:** snorkeling; solitude; swimming. ⊠ *Agnonda* ✛ *8 km (5 miles) south of Skopelos Town.*

Stafilos Beach

BEACH—SIGHT | Scattered farms and two tavernas, small houses with rooms for rent, and one or two pleasant hotels line the road to the seaside, where fragrant pines meet the cool, crystal-clear, calm waters. There's a simple canteen that serves snacks and refreshments (and even mojitos at sunset), and a lifeguard stand. Nearby, prehistoric walls, a watchtower, and an unplundered grave suggest that this was the site of an important prehistoric settlement. **Amenities:** food and drink; lifeguard; parking (no fee); showers. **Best for:** snorkeling; sunrise; swimming; walking. ⊠ *Stafilos* ✛ *3 km (2 miles) southeast of Agnonda, 4 km (2½ miles) south of Skopelos Town.*

Velania

BEACH—SIGHT | The name comes from the *valanium* (Roman bath) that once stood here on the coast due south of Skopelos Town. The bath has long since disintegrated under the waves, but the fresh spring water used for the baths still trickles out from a cave at the far end of the beach. To get here, follow the footpath that starts at Stafilos Beach, over the forested hill. This extra hike is seemingly off-putting to many beachgoers, keeping Velania isolated and quiet. Today it's broadly favored by nudists. **Amenities:** none. **Best for:** nudists; snorkeling; solitude; sunrise; swimming; walking. ✛ *5 km (3 miles) south of Skopelos Town, 1 km (½ mile) east of Stafilos Beach.*

🍴 Restaurants

Alexander's Garden Restaurant

$ | GREEK | At this little garden restaurant on the hillside, a 200-year-old well in the center of the elegant, leafy terrace produces its own natural spring water, a perfect addition to a traditional meal. Everything that comes from the kitchen is an old-time classic—including bell peppers stuffed with cheese, garlic, and tomato, and the restaurant's *keftedakia,* meatballs made with a secret recipe. **Known for:** home cooking; lovely garden; island institution. $ *Average main: €10* ✉ *Manolaki St.* ✛ *Turn inland after the corner shop Armoloi* ☎ *24240/22324* ⊘ *Closed Nov.–Mar. No lunch.*

★ Anatoli

$ | GREEK | Crowning the Venetian Castle, the picture-perfect blue-and-white painted restaurant—a converted barn—enjoys probably the most breathtaking views in Skopelos Town, overlooking the glittering Aegean and the Panagitsa Church below. Traditional Greek fare like baked aubergines, souvlaki, and stuffed peppers are on the menu, plus plenty of local liqueurs. **Known for:** exceptional views; local liqueurs; live rembetika music. $ *Average main: €12* ✉ *Kastro, Skopelos Town* ☎ *24240/22851* ⊘ *No lunch.*

Anna's Restaurant

$$ | GREEK | You'll spot many signs for this restaurant around Skopelos Town, but don't let that put you off. The jasmine-scented garden setting here offers an escape from the hubub of the busy port, with a neat layout, low lighting, and gracious hosting by owner, Anna. **Known for:** serene garden setting; family-run environment; local specialties. $ *Average main: €15* ✉ *Palia Hora Skopelos, Skopelos Town* ☎ *24240/24730* ⊘ *No lunch.*

Mamma Mia!

The 2008 blockbuster musical *Mamma Mia!* featured Skopelos throughout as the paradise setting for fictional island "Kalokairi"—something many locals take great pride in. Film locations included the tiny Kastani Bay—where they constructed Meryl Streep's taverna (and then dismantled it after the film)—Milia Beach, and the breathtaking (literally) hilltop chapel, Agios Ioannis for Sophie's wedding scene.

Molos

$ | GREEK | A favorite among the cluster of tavernas near the far end at the old port serves quality *magirefta* (dishes cooked ahead in the oven), along with a big dose of hospitality. Chef/owner Panayiotis sometimes takes time to liven things up with live music, stepping out from serving seafood pastas and such Skopelos specialties as stuffed courgette flowers. **Known for:** friendly atmosphere; traditional favorites; live music. $ *Average main: €12* ✉ *Waterfront* ☎ *24240/22551* ⊘ *Closed Nov.–Mar.*

Muses

$ | GREEK | This eminently romantic spot serves seafood and traditional Greek fare at a quiet edge of the seafront, with the sea caressing the beach just a few feet from the tables as classical music tinkles in the background. Fresh fish is grilled with a blend of mountain herbs and the succulent lamb *lemonato* (slow-roasted with garlic, salt, and lemon) falls off the bone. **Known for:** beachfront setting; traditional cuisine; good service. $ *Average main: €12* ✉ *Skopelos Beach* ✛ *Southeast of the port, 350 feet along the beach road* ☎ *24240/24414* ⊕ *www.skopelosmuses.com.*

Ta Kymata

$ | **GREEK** | Spirited brothers Andreas, Riginos, and Christophoros enthusiastically run the seafront taverna that has belonged to their family since 1896, serving traditional Skopelos recipes. The signature dish is *Tis Maharas*, an intense, pungent, yet surprisingly light mix of vegetables and cheeses with a creamy sauce, dedicated to the brothers' grandmother, whose name *Mahi* means battle and whose physical strength and towering height was said to ensure there was never any trouble at the taverna. **Known for:** fresh seafood; nice harborside setting; traditional cooking. $ *Average main: €10* ✉ *Skopelos Town* ✛ *North end of the harbor* ☎ *24240/22381* 🚫 *No credit cards.*

Coffee and Quick Bites

★ Ambrosia

$ | **GREEK** | Confections oozing syrup, loukoumades, and a tantalizing assortment of gelato flavors make a pit-stop at this old-fashioned sweet shop a must in the late afternoon. **Known for:** traditional confectionery; delicious gelato; friendly staff. $ *Average main: €5* ✉ *Skopelos harbor, Skopelos Town* ☎ *24240/24363.*

🛏 Hotels

Alkistis

$ | **RENTAL** | **FAMILY** | These simple but bright and airy apartments offer a feeling of a stay at a friend's summerhouse, with such idyllic touches as a beautifully maintained garden, filled with bougainvillea and lemon trees, and an enormous swimming pool, with a retro swim-up bar. **Pros:** restful atmosphere; nearby supermarket; friendly staff. **Cons:** isolated, although the hotel minibus takes guests to town; basic furnishings and amenities; not in town center. $ *Rooms from: €115* ✉ *Skopelos Town* ✛ *2 km (1 mile) southeast of town on road to Stafilos* ☎ *24240/23006* ⊘ *Closed Oct.–May* ↝ *25 rooms* ⦿ *Free breakfast.*

Pension Kyr Sotos

$ | **HOTEL** | This cozy, restored old Skopelete house on the waterfront is inexpensive and casual, with tiny rooms looking onto one of the hotel's two courtyard terraces. **Pros:** low prices and good value; nice harborfront location; loads of character. **Cons:** no breakfast; few creature comforts; some stairs to climb. $ *Rooms from: €40* ✉ *Skopelos Town* ✛ *On the waterfront* ☎ *24240/22549* ↝ *12 rooms* ⦿ *No meals.*

Skopelos Village

$ | **RESORT** | **FAMILY** | A chic, contemporary take on traditional Greek island charm comes with lots of breezy peacefulness, understated luxury, and comfort in delightful suites with plenty of outdoor space and, in many, sea views. **Pros:** stylish comfort; great views; steps away from the beach. **Cons:** a 10-minute walk from the center of town; neighborhood is quiet but not central; some bathrooms are small. $ *Rooms from: €100* ✉ *Skopelos Town* ✛ *1 km (½ mile) east of the town center* ☎ *24240/22517* ⊕ *skopelosvillagehotel.com* ⊘ *Closed Nov.–Apr.* ↝ *35 suites* ⦿ *Free breakfast.*

★ Thea Home Hotel

$ | **HOTEL** | A wonderful choice for budget travelers, these clean, cozy, and graceful studios and maisonettes are a short walk up from the harbor—and come with a beautiful vista of the town from the large, living-room-like terrace. **Pros:** airy terraces; great views; swimming pool. **Cons:** steep uphill trek to reach the property (though free transport from port is provided); furnishings are fairly basic; some bathrooms are small and outdated. $ *Rooms from: €45* ✉ *Ring road* ✛ *10-min walk up from the harbor* ☎ *24240/22859* ⊕ *www.theahomehotel.com* ↝ *13 rooms* ⦿ *Free breakfast.*

Forget all those worries back home with one delicious dinner on the town square in Skopelos Town.

Nightlife

Nightlife on Skopelos is more relaxed than it is on Skiathos. A smattering of cozy bars play music of all kinds, and the *kefi* (good mood) is to be found at the western end of the waterfront in Skopelos Town. Take an evening *volta* (stroll); most bars have tables outside, so you really can't miss them.

MUSIC CLUBS

Anemos

BARS/PUBS | It's one of the best cocktail bars on the island, serving impeccably mixed concoctions not often found anywhere else. Try the fragrant, sophisticated Paris Martini, or ask the mixologist to create an inspired drink to suit—or perfectly alter—your mood. The large stone terrace opens at 8 am for coffee and snacks. ⊠ *Skopelos Town* ✛ *On the harbor front* ☎ *24240/23564.*

Mercurius

BARS/PUBS | This perch just above the waterfront is ideal for a leisurely breakfast or invigorating sunset drinks with a stunning view and a soundtrack of world music. ⊠ *Skopelos Town* ✛ *5-min walk up from the harbor* ☎ *24240/24593* ⊕ *www. mercurius.gr.*

Shopping

LOCAL CRAFTS

Ploumisti

CRAFTS | Kilims, bags, hand-painted T-shirts, ceramics, and jewelry are among the antique and new wares. ⊠ *Paralia St., opposite the National Bank* ☎ *24240/22059.*

Panormos Bay
Όρμος Πανόρμου

6 km (4 miles) west of Skopelos Town.

With a long beach and sheltered inner cove ideal for yachts, Panormos is fast becoming a holiday village, although so far this stretch of the coast retains a quiet charm. The little town has a long provenance and was founded in the 8th century BC by colonists from Chalkis; a few well-concealed walls are visible among the pinewoods on the acropolis above the bay. Inland, the interior of Skopelos is green and lush; not far from Panormos Bay, traditional farmhouses called *kalivia* stand in plum orchards. Some are occupied; others are used only for family holidays and feast-day celebrations. Look for the outdoor ovens, which baked the fresh plums when Skopelos was turning out prunes galore. This rural area is charming, but the lack of signposts makes it easy to get lost, so pay attention.

 Beaches

Adrina Beach

BEACH—SIGHT | This strand of small pebbles has crystal-clear, turquoise water and, despite some sun beds and umbrellas, a feeling of seclusion. Dassia, the thickly forested islet across the bay, was named after a female pirate who (legend has it) was drowned there—but not before hiding her treasure. ■ TIP→ Access to the beach is somewhat difficult since you now have to go through the new resort to get to the shore—follow the path near the restaurant. **Amenities:** food and drink; showers; toilets; water sports. **Best for:** snorkeling; sunset; swimming. ⊠ *Panormos Bay ⊹ 1 km (½ mile) west of Panormos Bay.*

★ Milia Beach

BEACH—SIGHT | Skopelos's longest beach is considered by many to be its best, with white sands, clear turquoise waters, and vibrant green trees. Though still secluded, the bay is up-and-coming—parasols and recliners are lined halfway across the beach and there's a large taverna tucked into the pine trees. **Amenities:** food and drink; parking (no fee); showers; toilets. **Best for:** snorkeling; sunset; swimming; walking; windsurfing. ⊠ *Panormos Bay ⊹ 2 km (1 mile) north of Panormos Bay.*

 Hotels

Afrodite

$ | HOTEL | FAMILY | Airy, light-filled rooms are steps from a lovely beach and have views of the turquoise sea and lush mountains, all providing the essentials for a laid-back getaway. **Pros:** friendly service; just steps from the beach; tavernas and shops a walk away. **Cons:** some nice amenities but few luxuries; holiday-village atmosphere; away from Skopelos Town. $ *Rooms from: €50* ⊠ *Panormos Bay* ☎ *24240/23150* ⊕ *www.afroditehotel.gr* ⊅ *38 rooms* |O| *Free breakfast.*

Panormos Beach Hotel

$ | HOTEL | The owner's attention to detail shows in the beautifully tended flower garden, the immaculate, attractive rooms with pine furniture and handwoven linens, the country dining room, and the museum-like lobby decorated with antiques and traditional costumes. **Pros:** welcoming environment; excellent hospitality; beautiful grounds. **Cons:** not all rooms have sea views; no elevator; no pool, but beach is nearby. $ *Rooms from: €60* ⊠ *Panormos Bay ⊹ 1 block from the beachfront* ☎ *24240/22711* ⊕ *www.panormos-beach.com* ⊗ *Closed Nov.–Apr.* ⊅ *32 rooms* |O| *Free breakfast.*

Glossa Γλώσσα

38 km (23 miles) northwest of Skopelos Town, 24 km (14 miles) northwest of Panormos Bay, 3 km (1½ miles) northwest of Klima.

Delightful Glossa is the island's second-largest settlement, where whitewashed, red-roof houses are clustered on the steep hillside above the harbor of Loutraki. Venetian towers and traces of Turkish influence remain; the center is closed to traffic. This is a place to relax, dine, and enjoy the quieter beaches. Just to the east, have a look at Agios Ioannis Monastery, dramatically perched on a rock jutting out from the mountains. Walk over a rocky outcrop on the right to reach a small but pretty white-pebble beach.

🍽 Restaurants

★ Agnanti

$$ | MODERN GREEK | This long-established landmark entices with its playful and innovative takes on classic Greek dishes. While the awe-inspiring panoramic vista of the Aegean Sea would be enough to please customers, owner Nikos Stamatakis and his chef father, Stamatis, wow diners with the island's most exciting cuisine, like chicken in geranium sauce, or moussaka with tuna instead of beef. **Known for:** amazing views; gracious ambience; innovative twists on traditional fare. 💲 *Average main: €17* ⊠ *Street of Tastes 3* ☎ *24240/33306* ⊕ *agnanti.com. gr* 🕑 *Closed Nov.–Apr.*

Skyros ΣΚΥΡΟΣ

Even among these unique isles, Skyros stands out. The rugged terrain resembles that of an island in the Dodecanese, and the spectacularly situated main town—occupied on and off for the last 3,300 years and haunted by mythical ghosts—looks Cycladic. Surprisingly beguiling, this southernmost of the Sporades is the largest (209 square km [81 square miles]). A narrow, flat isthmus connects Skyros's two almost-equal parts, whose names reflect their characters—*Meri* or *Imero* ("tame") for the north, and *Vouno* (literally, "mountain," meaning tough or stony) for the south. The heavily populated north is virtually all farmland and forests. The southern half of the island is forbidding, barren, and mountainous, with Mt. Kochilas its highest peak (2,598 feet). The western coast is outlined with coves and deep bays dotted with a series of islets.

Until Greece won independence in 1831, the population of Skyros squeezed sardine-fashion into the area under the castle on the inland face of the rock. Not a single house was visible from the sea. Though the islanders could survey any movement in the Aegean for miles, they kept a low profile, living in dread of the pirates based at Treis Boukes Bay on Vouno.

The Skyrians have not had a seafaring tradition, and have looked to the land for their living. Their isolation has brought about notable cultural differences from the other Greek islands, such as pre-Christian Carnival rituals. Today there are more than 300 churches on the island, many of them private and owned by local families. An almost-extinct breed of pony resides on Skyros, and exceptional crafts—carpentry, pottery, embroidery—are practiced by dedicated artisans whose creations include unique furniture and decorative linens. There are no luxury accommodations or swank restaurants: this idiosyncratic island makes no provisions for mass tourism, but if you've a taste for the offbeat, you may feel right at home.

Did You Know?

In the hit movie *Mamma Mia!*, starring Meryl Streep and Pierce Brosnan, Glossa's church of Agios Ioannis was the backdrop for the spectacular wedding scene, but the interior was totally made up.

GETTING HERE AND AROUND

AIR

You can get to Skyros from Athens by air on Aegean Airlines in about 40 minutes. The airport is on the north of the island 15 km (9 miles) from Skyros Town, but a shuttle bus always meets the plane. Tickets on the bus cost €3 to €6; the trip takes 20 minutes.

CONTACTS **Skyros Airport.** ⚓ *11 km (7 miles) northwest of Skyros Town* ☎ *22220/91684.*

BOAT

Ferries to Skyros are operated by the Skyros Shipping Company (*see Boat and Ferry in Travel Smart*) and leave from Kimi on the large island of Evia (connected to the mainland by bridges) and take 2½ hours; there are several ferries a day on weekends, and usually two daily ferries during the week. All boats dock at Linaria, far from Skyros Town. A shuttle bus always meets the boat; bus tickets cost €2 to €3. Taxis also meet the boats, but settle the fee before setting out. In summer only there are three ferries weekly between Skopelos and Skyros; the trip takes about five hours.

BUS

CONTACTS **Skyros Bus Information.** ☎ *22220/91600.*

CAR

Martina's is one of several reliable local agencies that rent cars on Skyros.

CONTACTS **Martina's.** ✉ *Machairas 1, Skyros Town* ☎ *22220/92022.*

TAXI

Arrange taxis through your hotel, or find them at the ports and town centers.

FESTIVALS

Apokries

FESTIVAL | This pre-Lenten Carnival revelry relates to pre-Christian Dyonisian fertility rites and is famous throughout Greece. Young men dressed as old men, maidens, or "Europeans" roam the streets teasing and tormenting onlookers with ribald songs and clanging bells. The "old men" wear elaborate shepherd's outfits, with masks made of baby-goat hides and belts dangling with as many as 40 sheep bells.

TRAVEL AGENCIES

CONTACTS **Skyros Travel.** ✉ *Agora, Skyros Town* ☎ *22220/91600.*

VISITOR INFORMATION

CONTACTS **Greek National Tourism Organization (GNTO or EOT).** ⊕ *www.visitgreece. gr.* **Skyros Municipality.** ☎ *22223/50300* ⊕ *www.skyros.gr.*

Skyros Town
Σκύρος (Χωριό)

1 hr and 40 mins from Kimi to Linaria by boat, 30 mins from Linaria by car.

From the southern landscapes, amid brown, desolate outcrops with only an occasional goat as a sign of life, Skyros Town suddenly looms around a bend. Blazing white, cubist, dense, and otherworldly, clinging, precariously it seems, to the precipitous rock and topped gloriously by a fortress-monastery, this town more closely resembles a village in the Cyclades than any other you'll find in the Sporades.

Called *Chora* ("village") by the locals, Skyros Town is home to 90% of the island's 3,000 inhabitants. The impression as you get closer is of stark, simple buildings creeping up the hillside, with a tangle of labyrinthine lanes steeply winding up, down, and around the tiny houses, Byzantine churches, and big squares. As you explore the alleyways off the main street, try to peek discreetly into the houses. Skyrians are houseproud and often leave their windows and doors open to show off. In fact, since the houses all have the same exteriors, the only way for families to distinguish themselves has been through interior design. Walls and conical mantelpieces are richly

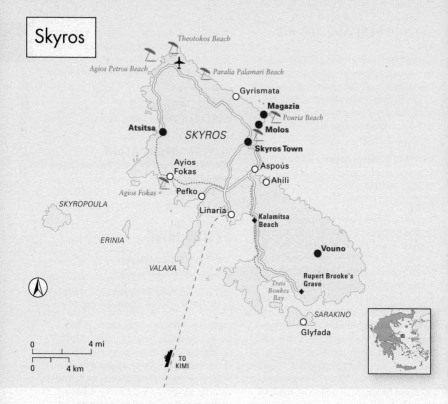

Skyros

Theotokos Beach

Agios Petros Beach

Paralia Palamari Beach

Gyrismata

Magazia

Pouria Beach

Atsitsa

SKYROS

Molos

Skyros Town

Ayios Fokas

Aspoús

Ahíli

SKYROPOULA

Agios Fokas

Pefko

Linariá

Kalamitsa Beach

ERINIA

Vouno

VALAXA

Rupert Brooke's Grave

Treis Boukes Bay

SARAKINO

Glyfada

0   4 mi

0   4 km

TO KIMI

decorated with European- and Asian-style porcelain, copper cooking utensils, wood carvings, and embroideries. Wealthy families originally obtained much of the porcelain from the pirates in exchange for grain and food, and its possession was a measure of social standing. Then enterprising potters started making exact copies, along with the traditional local ware, leading to the unique Skyrian style of pottery. The furniture is equally beautiful, and often miniature in order to conserve interior space.

The summit of the hill is crowned with three tiny cubelike churches with blue-and-pink interiors, and the ruined Venetian cistern, once used as a dungeon. From there you have a spectacular view of the town and surrounding hills. The roofs are flat, the older ones covered with a dark gray shale that has splendid insulating properties. The house walls and roofs are interconnected, forming a pattern that from above looks like a magnified form of cuneiform writing. Here and there the shieldlike roof of a church stands out from the cubist composition of white houses that fills the hillside—with not an inch to spare.

Sights

Most commercial activity takes place in or near the Agora (the market street), familiarly known as Sisifos, as in the myth, because of its frustrating steepness. Found here are the town's pharmacies, travel agencies, shops with wonderful Skyrian pottery, and an extraordinary number of tiny bars and tavernas, but few boutiques and even less kitsch. In the summer heat, all shops and restaurants close from 2 pm to 6 pm, but the town comes alive at night.

Archeological Museum of Skyros

MUSEUM | These two small rooms (on the way to Magazia Beach as you begin to descend from the town) contain rare weapons, pottery, and jewelry, mostly from graves dating from Neolithic to Roman times. Especially alluring are the pony motifs and the vase in the shape of a horse. ⊠ *Rupert Brooke Sq.* ☎ *2220/91327* 🎫 *€2* 🕐 *Closed Tues.*

Episkopi Church

RELIGIOUS SITE | Take the vaulted passageway from St. George's Monastery courtyard to this ruined church, the former seat of the bishop of Skyros, built in AD 895 on the ruins of a temple of Athena. The complex was the center of Skyros's religious life from 1453 to 1837. You can continue up to the summit from here. ⊠ *Skyros Town* ✛ *Above St. George's Monastery.*

★ Faltaits Museum

MUSEUM | Built after Greek Independence by a wealthy family (who still owns the museum), this house is one of the most impressive in Skyros Town and is nearly overflowing with rare books, costumes, photographs, paintings, ceramics, local embroideries, Greek statues, and other heirlooms. Of particular note are the embroideries, which are famed for their flamboyant colors and vivacious renderings of mermaids, *hoopoes* (the Skyrians' favorite bird), and mythical human figures whose clothes and limbs sprout flowers. Top treasure among the museum's historical documents is a handwritten copy of the Proclamation of the Greek Revolution against the Ottoman Empire. The informative guided tour is well worth the extra euros. ⊠ *Palaiopyrgos* ☎ *22220/91232* ⊕ *www.faltaits.gr* 🎫 *€4, tour €7.*

Mythic Skyros

In the legends of *The Iliad*, before the Trojan War, Theseus, the deposed hero-king of Athens, sought refuge in his ancestral estate on Skyros. King Lykomedes, afraid of the power and prestige of Theseus, took him up to the acropolis one evening, pretending to show him the island, and pushed him over the cliff—an ignominious end. In ancient times, Timon of Athens unearthed what he said were Theseus's bones and sword, and placed them in the Theseion—more commonly called the Temple of Hephaistion—in Athens, in what must be one of the earliest recorded archaeological investigations.

★ Monastery of St. George

RELIGIOUS SITE | The best way to get an idea of the town and its history is to follow the sinuous cobbled lanes past the mansions of the Old Town to the Kastro, the highest point, and this fortified monastery founded in AD 962 and radically rebuilt in 1600. Today it is inhabited by a sole monk. A white marble lion, which may be left over from the Venetian occupation, is in the wall above the entrance to the monastery. The once splendid frescoes of the Monastery of St. George are now mostly covered by layers of whitewash, but look for the charming St. George and startled dragon outside to the left of the church door and, within, the ornate iconostasis. An icon of St. George on the right is said to have been brought by settlers from Constantinople, who came in waves during the iconoclast controversy of the 9th century. The icon has a black face and is familiarly known as Ayios Georgis o Arapis ("the Negro");

the Skyrians view him as the patron saint not only of their island but of lovers as well. ⊠ *Skyros Town* ⊹ *1 km (½ mile) above waterfront* ☎ *22220/91216.*

Rupert Brooke Memorial Statue

PUBLIC ART | It'd be hard to miss the classical bronze statue, "To Brooke," an honorary tribute to the heroic Edwardian-era English poet Rupert Brooke, whose nude and very masculine depiction created quite a stir when unveiled in 1931. Every street seems to lead to the statue, with a 180-degree view of the sea as a backdrop. In 1915, aged 28, Brooke was on his way to the Dardanelles to fight in World War I when he died of septicemia in a French hospital ship off Skyros. Brooke was a socialist, but he became something of a paragon for war leaders such as Winston Churchill. ⊠ *Rupert Brooke Sq.* ⊕ *www.rupertbrookeonskyros.com.*

Beaches

Theotokos Beach

BEACH—SIGHT | At the northwest side of Skyros, above Ayios Petros, this is a relatively secluded beach reachable by dirt road followed by a little stroll down a goat path. Nearby is the off-limits military base. **Amenities:** none. **Best for:** nudists; snorkeling; solitude; swimming; windsurfing. ⊹ *15 km (9 miles) northwest of Skyros Town.*

Restaurants

Skyros is especially noted for spiny lobster, almost as sweet as the North Atlantic variety.

O Pappous Ke Ego

$$ | **GREEK** | "My Grandfather and I," as the name translates in English, serves terrific Greek cuisine in an eclectic dining room decorated with hanging spoons, bottles of wine and ouzo, and whole heads of garlic. The proud grandson suggests that diners order a selection of *mezedes* (small plates) and share with others at the table. **Known for:** dishes based on local recipes; homey atmosphere; excellent mezedes. **$** *Average main: €18* ⊠ *Agora* ☎ *22220/93200* ⊗ *Closed Nov. and Dec.*

Coffee and Quick Bites

Juicy

$ | **GREEK** | With white furniture and rattan accoutrements, this swanky retreat on Magazia Beach benefits from sweeping sea views. Take a break to delight in its sweet and savory pastries, fresh Greek salads, or fruity cocktails. **Known for:** restful atmosphere; board games free to play; sun loungers available. **$** *Average main: €7* ⊠ *Magazia Beach* ☎ *22220/93337.*

Hotels

★ Nefeli Hotel

$ | **HOTEL** | It's a bastion of taste and comfort, with soothing Cycladic whites and soft green trim, a dazzling seawater pool, elegant bar terrace, and handsome furnishings in the sophisticated guest rooms. **Pros:** stylish and comfortable; a vast library; easy walk to town and beach. **Cons:** often booked (reserve in advance); pricey by island standards; not on the water. **$** *Rooms from: €100* ⊠ *Plageiá* ☎ *22220/91964* ⊕ *www. skyros-nefeli.gr* ⇥ *100 rooms* ⊙| *Free breakfast.*

Nightlife

Skyros Town's bars are seasonal affairs, offering loud music in summer.

Rodon Music Cafe

DANCE CLUBS | Takis, the owner, is also the DJ here, and he loves spinning the best tunes in town. ⊠ *Agora* ☎ *22220/092387.*

Shopping

Want to buy something really unusual for a shoe lover? Check out the multi-thong *trohadia,* worn with pantaloons by Skyrian men as part of their traditional costume. Just as unique, elaborate Skyrian pottery and furniture are famous around the country. The pottery is both useful and decorative, and the distinctive wooden furniture is easily recognizable by its traditionally carved style. The best places to shop are on the Agora. Skyrian furniture can be shipped anywhere. Don't try to shop between 2 and 6 pm, as all stores close for siesta.

FURNITURE

Thesis Wood

HOUSEHOLD ITEMS/FURNITURE | The workshop of Lefteris Avgoklouris and Emmanouela Toliou, carpenters with flair, is open to visitors. They will show off their chairs and other pieces and tell you about other master carpenters and craftspeople on the island who make original Skyrian furniture, famous around Greece for its intricate technique. They ship their distinctive pieces abroad. ✉ *Lino* ✣ *On the beach south of Skyros Town* ☎ *22220/91106* 🌐 *www.thesiswood.com.*

Magazia and Molos Μαγαζιά και Μώλος

1 km (½ mile) northeast of Skyros Town.

Coastal expansions of the main town, these two resort areas are the places to stay if you love to swim. Magazia, where the residents of Skyros Town used to have their storehouses and wine presses, and Molos, a bit farther north, where the small fishing fleet anchors, are both growing fast. You can sunbathe, explore the isolated coastline, and stop at sea caves for a swim. Nearby are rooms to rent and tavernas serving the day's catch and local wine. From here, Skyros Town is 15 to 20 minutes away on foot, up the steps that lead past the archaeological museum to Rupert Brooke Square.

Beaches

The coastline from **Molos** to **Magazia** is one long, sandy beach.

Paralia Palamari Beach

BEACH—SIGHT | North of Molos, past low hills, fertile fields, and the odd farmhouse, a dirt road leads to this historical beach where ruins from a Neolithic fortress and settlement have been discovered. The beach has cool, crystal waters and sandy shores that offer a sense of privacy. **Amenities:** none. **Best for:** nudists; snorkeling; solitude; sunrise; swimming; walking. ✣ *North of Skyros Town.*

Pouria Beach

BEACH—SIGHT | A short walk south of Magazia, Pouria offers good snorkeling, and nearby on the cape is a small treasure: a sea cave that has been transformed into a chapel. There may be no amenities on the beach itself, but there is a little hotel nearby where one can get refreshments. **Amenities:** none. **Best for:** snorkeling; solitude; swimming; walking. ✉ *Magazia* ✣ *Just south of town.*

Hotels

Perigiali Hotel

$ | **RESORT** | Simply decorated, tasteful rooms and apartments come with many comforts—private terraces, a pretty, lush garden with plenty of shade, and a refreshing pool, all just steps from the beach and a 15-minute walk to Skyros Town. **Pros:** near Magazia Beach; nice outdoor spaces; friendly staff. **Cons:** no parking (but free parking two-minute walk away); no sea views; access difficult for travelers with limited mobility. [$] *Rooms from: €100* ✉ *Magazia* ✣ *On beachfront at foot of Skyros Town* ☎ *22220/92075* 🌐 *www.perigiali.com* 🛏 *27 rooms* 🍴 *Free breakfast.*

Skiros Palace

$ | **RESORT** | With a big pool and near a gorgeous, isolated beach, this cluster of white, cubist houses is a water lover's dream, though the simple, traditionally furnished guest rooms are pleasant, they don't quite live up to the hotel's name. **Pros:** very attractive grounds and pool; great views; Skyros Town is only a 20-minute walk away. **Cons:** half board required at some times; somewhat compoundlike in feeling; can be overrun with groups. $ *Rooms from: €70* ⚓ *North of Molos Town center* ☎ *22220/91994* ⊕ *skirospalace.gr* ⊘ *Closed Oct.–May* 🚪 *104 rooms* 🍴 *Free breakfast.*

 **Performing Arts**

Panagia (*Festival of the Virgin*)

FESTIVAL | On the major Greek Orthodox celebration of August 15 (Dormition of the Virgin), children gather at Magazia Beach to race on the island's domesticated small ponies, similar to Shetland ponies. ⊠ *Magazia Beach, Magazia.*

Atsitsa Ατσίτσα

14 km (9 miles) west of Molos.

On the northwest coast, pine forests grow down the rocky shore at Atsitsa. The beaches north of town—Kalogriá and Kyra Panayia—are sheltered from the strong northern winds called the *meltemi.*

 Sights

Skyros Centre

COLLEGE | The first major center in Europe for holistic vacations has been bringing visitors to Skyros for more than 40 years. Participants come for a two-week session, staying in straw huts or in the main building, in a peaceful environment surrounded by pines and facing the sea. Studies and courses include windsurfing, creative writing with well-known authors, art, tai chi, yoga, massage, dance, drama, and sound-healing. Courses also take place in Skyros Town, where participants live in villagers' traditional houses. Skyros Centre's courses are highly reputed. Contact the UK office well in advance of leaving for Greece. ⊠ *Atsitsa* ☎ *1983/865566 in the UK* ⊕ *www.skyros.com.*

 Beaches

Agios Fokas

BEACH—SIGHT | The road south from Atsitsa deteriorates into a rutted track, nerve-racking even for experienced motorbike riders. If you're feeling fit and the weather's good, however, consider the challenging 6-km (4-mile) trek around the headland to Agios Fokas. There are three lovely white-pebbled beaches and a small taverna. **Amenities:** food and drink; toilets. **Best for:** snorkeling; solitude; sunset; swimming; walking. ⊠ *Atsitsa* ⚓ *5 km (3 miles) south of Atsitsa.*

Agios Petros Beach

BEACH—SIGHT | Close to the airport, this wonderful beach of white sand and pebbles is surrounded by lush greenery, with the little chapel of Agios Petrosa on a hill above as a serene backdrop. Don't be put off by the 4 km (2½ miles) of dirt road leading to the beach, it's definitely worth the effort. **Amenities:** none. **Best for:** snorkeling; swimming; walking; windsurfing. ⊠ *Atsitsa* ⚓ *8 km (5 miles) north of Atsitsa, 15 km (9 miles) north of Skyros Town.*

Vouno Βουνό

Via Loutro, 5 km (3 miles) northwest of Linaria; access to southern territory starts at Ahilli, 4 km (2½ miles) south of Skyros Town and 25 km (15½ miles) from Atsitsa.

In the mountainous southern half of Skyros, a passable dirt road heads south at the eastern end of the isthmus, from Aspous to Ahilli. The little bay of Ahilli (from where legendary Achilles set sail with Odysseus) is a yacht marina. Some

Did You Know?

Many of the remarkable cliff-face churches of Greece were originally caves colonized by ascetic hermits. This tiny example is the Ayios Nikolaos church near Pouria.

beautiful, practically untouched beaches and sea caves are well worth the trip for hard-core explorers.

Thorny bushes warped into weird shapes, oleander, and rivulets running between sharp rocks make up the landscape; only goats and Skyrian ponies can survive this desolate environment. Many scholars consider the beautifully proportioned, diminutive horses to be the same breed as the horses sculpted on the Parthenon frieze. They are, alas, an endangered species, and only about 150 survive.

Sights

Rupert Brooke's Grave

HISTORIC SITE | Pilgrims to the poet's grave should follow the wide dirt road through the Vouno wilderness down toward the shore. As you reach the valley, you catch sight of the grave on your left. Brooke was buried here in 1915 after dying of sepsis from an infected mosquito bite while aboard a French hospital ship anchored off Skyros. His marble grave in an olive grove was immortalized with his prescient words, "If I should die think only this of me: That there's some corner of a foreign field / That is forever England." Restored by the British Royal Navy in 1961, the grave site is surrounded by a stout wrought-iron and cement railing. You can also arrange for a visit by taxi or caïque in Skyros Town. ⊠ *Kalamitsa* ⊕ *Southwest end of the island* ⊕ *www. rupertbrookeonskyros.com.*

Beaches

Kalamitsa

BEACH—SIGHT | The windy beach of Kalamitsa is 4 km (2½ miles) along the road south from Ahilli, and popular with windsurfers for obvious reasons. Nevertheless, this also means that the sands can be whipped up into a skin-cleansing frenzy on certain days, so whether you're a surfer or bather, check the winds first. There are three decent tavernas at this old harbor. **Amenities:** food and drink; parking (free); showers; toilets; water sports. **Best for:** snorkeling; sunset; surfing; swimming; windsurfing. ⊠ *Kalamitsa.*

Chapter 6

IONIAN ISLANDS

CORFU, KEFALONIA, ZAKYNTHOS

Updated by
Hilary Whitton Paipeti
and Gareth Clark

👁 Sights   🍴 Restaurants   🛏 Hotels   🛍 Shopping   🍸 Nightlife

★★★★☆   ★★★★☆   ★★★★☆   ★★☆☆☆   ★★★☆☆

WELCOME TO THE IONIAN ISLANDS

TOP REASONS TO GO

★ **Corfu Town, Corfu:** Recognized by UNESCO as a World Heritage site, this sophisticated little gem of a city glows with a profusion of picturesque reminders of its Venetian, French, and British past.

★ **Pontikonisi, Corfu:** As they savor the famous panorama of Corfu's Pontikonisi, from the patio of the viewpoint in suburban Kanoni, how many of today's visitors know that tiny "Mouse island" was thought by the ancients to be Odysseus's ship turned to stone by Poseidon?

★ **Mount Ainos, Kefalonia:** Few realize this forested mountain lies within the only national park on a Greek island, created in 1962 to protect the island's endemic black firs. Watch out for wild horses as you wander trails up to the 1,628-meter summit, the highest peak in the island chain.

★ **Beaches:** The Ionion islands are famed for their shores. Myrtos (Kefalonia) and Shipwreck Cove (Zakynthos) are among Greece's most dazzling.

The islands of the Ionian Sea, off the western coast of Greece, have had many occupiers over the millennia, but none made a greater impact than the Venetians. Corfu, in particular, was greatly influenced by their ruler's urban lifestyles, as well as that of the French and British "protectors" that followed. Their legacies are still writ large across the capital, while other islands haven't fared as well. After major earthquakes in 1953, much of Kefalonia and Zakynthos was robbed of its historic color, but what remains is arguably as rich: a wealth of rugged mountains, dreamy beaches, and vine-draped countryside make these islands ripe for exploration.

1 Corfu. Along the east coast, mid-island Corfu Town occupies a small peninsula anchored at its eastern tip by the massive Old Fortress and to the north by the New Fortress. The Old Town is crammed with Venetian and English Georgian houses, narrow alleyways, and tiny squres. South of Corfu Town is Mon Repos, a region that royals once called home. Head into the interior and along the western and northeastern coastline to discover the island's natural beauty and charm, especially around Paleokastritsa, home to one of Greece's best beaches.

2 Kefalonia. The legacy of Louis de Bernières' Kefalonia-set novel *Captain Corelli's Mandolin* has done much to solidify the island's idyllic reputation. But while its Venetian charms were largely shook loose in 1953's earthquakes, Assos and Fiskardo, high in the the wild, mountainous north, have retained their colorful architecture. Elsewhere, Argostoli is a short hop to the cliffs of the Paliki Peninsula and the vineyards of the Robola Valley.

3 Zakynthos. With its eastern and southern coasts sacrificed to the resort gods, more adventurous travelers take to the sea on boat trips, setting foot on idyllic shores cut off from land, snorkeling sea caves, and glimpsing protected islands. Yet surprises abound here, and even among the hedonistic south, important loggerhead-turtle-nesting grounds can be found clinging on, while the half-wild beaches and countryside of the Vasilikos Peninsula remains the island's most satisfying escape.

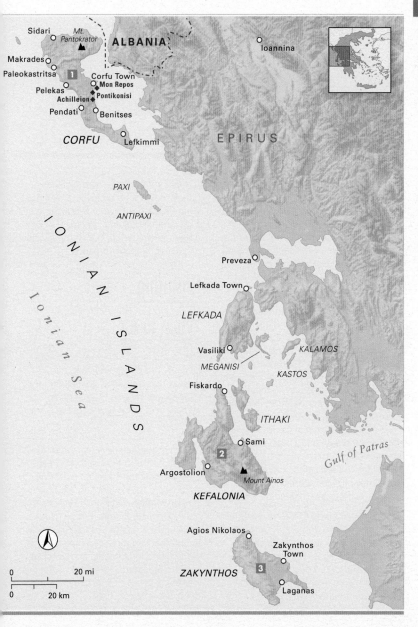

Sidari
Mt. Pantokrator
ALBANIA
Ioannina
Makrades
Paleokastritsa
1
Corfu Town
Mon Repos
Pelekas
Achilleion
Pontikonisi
Pendati
Benitses
CORFU
Lefkimmi
EPIRUS
PAXI
ANTIPAXI
IONIAN ISLANDS
Ionian Sea
Preveza
Lefkada Town
LEFKADA
Vasiliki
KALAMOS
MEGANISI
KASTOS
Fiskardo
ITHAKI
Sami
2
Argostolion
Mount Ainos
KEFALONIA
Gulf of Patras
Agios Nikolaos
Zakynthos Town
ZAKYNTHOS
3
Laganas

0   20 mi
0   20 km

The Ionian Islands—a string of seven pearls clinging to Greece's west-coast décolletage—have always been the most desirable of hand-me-downs. Four-thousand years of invasions saw Romans, Byzantines, Franks, Venetians, Turks, French, and British all clutch them in triumph.

Many left an indelible mark on the islands' culture, by way of Parisian arcades, Italianate palazzos, Venetian fortresses, and a rustic cuisine more in common with Italy than Greece. But this has always been a landscape to conjure with, and it's no coincidence it was from here that Homer's Odysseus sailed into myth.

The islands didn't fall back into Greek hands until 1864, and even then occupation during the Second World War and a series of devastating earthquakes were around the corner. By the time package tourism arrived in the 1960s, it was embraced as a lifeline and so followed the last of the big invaders. Yet the story doesn't end there, and while resorts claim a chunk of each of Corfu, Kefalonia, and Zakynthos, its three most popular islands, you can still easily find yourself bumping into herds of wandering goats on a lonely hillside or strolling pastel-colored hill towns in peace.

Earthquakes insured that Corfu remains the more cultured of the trio; Corfu Town in particular is a lively patchwork of historic flourishes. The more southerly Kefalonia and Zakynthos had to be rebuilt post-1953, though small pockets of Venetian architecture can still be found in the former's northern tip. These islands are better known for their idyllic coastlines, where secretive coves, whittled into dazzling white limestone, and magical sea caves remain the stuff of Homeric asides and Instagram fever dreams.

Planning

When to Go

The Ionian Islands enjoy a temperate climate, with a relatively long rainy season that lasts from late fall through early spring, making them a rather verdant alternative to the rest of Greece. Winter showers bring spring flowers, and the countryside goes into floral overdrive starting in March, when the air is perfumed with the heady fragrance of orange blossoms and jasmine. By May, wildflowers have overtaken the hillsides as the weather clears and it starts to get warm enough for swimming. July and August are peak season; these are the hottest and most crowded months, when the resorts, roads, and beaches swell to bursting. September is gloriously warm and dry, with light evenings and the occasional cool breeze. Swimming is often possible through mid-October. Late September through late October is good for hiking and exploring the countryside, as is the spring. During winter (Nov.–Mar.), much of the islands shut down and public transport is minimal.

Planning Your Time

Corfu is often explored in a day; many people pass through quickly as part of a cruise of the Greek islands. Two days allows enough time to visit Corfu Town and its nearby famous sites. With four days you can spend time exploring the island's other historic sites and natural attractions and make day trips to outlying villages. Six days allows you time to get a closer look at the museums, churches, and forts and perhaps even take a day trip to Albania. To really get off the beaten path, take the coast road northeast from Corfu Town and around Daphnila Bay to Agni and from there into the most mountainous part of the island, or head west from Corfu Town into the mountains and ancient olive groves to stay near Kato Korakiana, home to Etrusco, the best restaurant on Corfu, and many would say Greece itself.

Kefalonia may be the largest of the Ionian Islands, but that rather makes it the tallest pixie. As long as you have a car, the island's big sights are all easily visited in a day or two, whether you want to set your towel on Myrtos beach, stroll the peaceful harbour of Fiskardo, slake your thirst in its famous vineyards, or float the viridescent waters of Melissani Cave (a kind of Greek cenote). But that's not really the point; idyllic beaches, isolated villages, and goat-invaded clifftop roads require time to soak in. Three or four days lets you explore the untouched Peliki Peninsula, wander mountaintops, explore Venetian fortresses, and still get your beach time in.

For Zakynthos, read Kefalonia. Away from the resorts of the south, the pace of life is not fast here and there aren't so many sights that you'll be overwhelmed. Two days is enough to soak up the shimmering Blue Caves or the white sands of Shipwreck Cove (Navagio), take a turtle-spotting tour, and stroll from the likeable Zakynthos Town up to its castle. Stay a little longer and cultural tours of the wooded hills, hidden coves, and quiet villages of the northern coast await, as well as plenty of time on the half-wild beaches of the Vasilikos Peninsula.

Getting Here and Around

AIR

Olympic Air (owned by Aegean Air) and Sky Express offer regular flights from Athens to Corfu, Kefalonia, and Zakynthos (all 1 hour), starting at around €42 one-way. Sky Express even flies daily during summer and also offers a Kefalonia–Zakynthos connection (25 mins). Direct flights from Thessaloniki to Corfu, and from Preveza to Corfu and Kefalonia are also available; all other routes within Greece go through Athens. Many seasonal (Mar.–Oct.) connections link the three islands to the rest of Europe, with the major cities of the UK, Germany, and Italy in particular offering multiple nonstop connections via EasyJet, Ryanair, Volotea, and Jet2. *For information on all airlines, see Air in Travel Smart.*

Corfu's Ioannis Kapodistrias International Airport is just south of Corfu Town, about a mile from the city center. A taxi from the airport to the center costs around €10; an airport bus runs hourly to the New Port via the Green Bus station and the town center. Taxi rates are on display in the arrivals hall.

Zakynthos's Dionysios Solomos International Airport lies 4km (2.5 miles) south of Zakynthos Town. A taxi from the airport to the center costs around €13. Airport buses (€1.60) also run 4 times daily (except Sat. and Sun.) to Zakynthos bus station; tickets can be bought from the driver.

Kefalonia's Pollatou International Airport is 8.5 km (5 miles) south of island capital Argostoli. Pre-booked taxis offer a fixed-fee fare of €20 to Argostoli. An airport bus (€2) also connects to the town center 6–7 times a day during summer; tickets can be bought from the driver.

CONTACTS Corfu International Airport. *(CFU)* ⊕ *www.cfu-airport.gr.* **Kefalonia International Airport.** *(EFL)* ⊕ *www.efl-airport.gr/en.* **Zakynthos International Airport.** *(ZTH)* ⊕ *www.zth-airport.gr/en.*

BOAT AND FERRY

There are no ferries from Piraeus to Corfu. Corfu's gateway to mainland Greece is the city of Igoumenitsa, from which ferries operated by the Kerkyra-Igoumenitsa-Paxi Consortium run almost hourly to Corfu Town throughout the day. Ferries four to five times daily also link Igoumenitsa with the port of Lefkimmi near Corfu's southern tip. Direct ferries from Italy (Brindisi, Bari, and Ancona) run only during July and August; outside of those months, you must change ferries in Igoumenitsa.

Most ferries dock at the New Port, in the northeast part of Corfu Town; from the ferry terminal you can easily walk into town or take a cab to your hotel. You can buy ferry tickets at the ports or book in advance through the ferry lines or travel agents. For the most up-to-date information on boat schedules (which change regularly and seasonally), call the port authority in the city of departure or check the Greek ferry information website.

One-way tickets for the ferry between Igoumenitsa and Corfu Town (1¼ to 2 hours) are about €11 per person and €40 per car.

Hydrofoils zip between Corfu and Paxos between one and three times daily. There is also a hydrofoil service to Saranda in Albania.

Kefalonia has four major ferry ports: Sami and Poros, which both provide links to the mainland, and Fiskardo and Pessada. Passenger fees start from €8 per person and €32 per car for all but the shortest of hops. Tickets are available at ports, agencies, and, in the case of Levante Ferries, directly from the ferry provider's website as e-tickets. As with most of the Ionian islands, these services run regularly during the summer months (May.–Sept.), when there can be as many as five return trips a day on major routes, then drop off considerably in the off-season.

Sami, in the east of Kefalonia, is the busiest port, linking neighboring islands Lefkada (Vasiliki; 2 hours) and Ithaki (Pisaetos, 20 mins) as well as the Greek mainland cities of Astakos (2½ hours) and Patras (3 hours). A Ventouris Ferries connection also runs from here via Igoumenitsa to Corfu Town and Bari (Italy) once a week during summer (Jul.–Sept.).

South of Sami, Poros has ferry connections to mainland Kyllini (1¼ hours) and Ithaki's Pisaetos (55 mins), while the genteel northern outpost of Fiskardo offers an additional seasonal route to Lefkada, stopping at Nidri (1¾ hours).

The fourth and final Kefalonian port is Pessada, nestled in the far south of the island, which has regular ferry links to Agios Nikolaos (1½ hours) on Zakynthos during the summer months (May.–Oct.). The only other regular ferry connection on Zakynthos is to the Greek mainland via a service from its capital to the Peloponnese city of Kyllini (1¼ hours).

CONTACTS Greek Ferry Info. ⊕ *www.greekferries.gr* . **Levante Ferries.** ✉ *18–22 Kon. Lomvardou, Argostolion* ☎ ⊕ *www.levanteferries.com.* **Ionion Pelagos Lines.** ✉ *Akti Miaouli 29, Kefalonia* ☎ *267/4022–111 (Kefalonia), 269/5023–984 (Zakynthos)* ⊕ *www.ionionpelagos.com/en.* **West Ferry.** ✉ *Nautilus Travel, Fiskardo* ☎ *267/4041–440 Nautilus Travel, 264/5093–278 for phone bookings* ⊕ *westferry.gr.*

BUS

KTEL buses leave Athens Terminal A for Igoumenitsa, where there's a ferry to Corfu (11 hours, around €48 one-way, plus ferry fares). For Kefalonia and Zakynthos, you will need to go from the city center. The X93 bus (€5) runs every 30–40 minutes from Athens International Airport to Kifisos Bus Terminal in Athens and takes 1 hour; from there, multiple KTEL services run to Kefalonia's Argostoli (6–7 hours; €30 one-way, plus ferry fare) either via Patras (arriving in Sami) or Kyllini (arriving in Poros). To reach Zakynthos's main town, a similar service runs from Kifisos Bus Terminal via Kyllini (5 hours; €26 one-way, plus ferry fares). Buses are timed to run in tandem with ferries, and tickets can be booked in advance on the various regional KTEL websites.

CONTACTS KTEL Kefalonia. ⊠ *Antoni Tritsi 5, Argostolion* ☎ *267/1022–281* ⊕ *www. ktelkefalonias.gr/en.* **KTEL Zakynthos.** ⊠ *Iatrou Mothonaiou* ☎ *269/5022255* ⊕ *ktel-zakynthos.gr/en.*

CAR AND SCOOTER

For those driving from Athens, take the National Road (8a) via Corinth and cross the Rion Antirion Bridge on the A5, before turning east (A2) to Igoumenitsa (472 km [274 miles]), where the car ferry to Corfu departs. Alternatively, the National Road will also take you to Patras (241 km [150 miles]), where you can catch a ferry to Kefalonia (Sami) or continue west along the E55 to the port of Kyllini (317km [197 miles]), which has services to both Kefalonia (Poros) and Zakynthos.

Bus service is limited in the islands and, with just a handful of daily routes operating largely during summer, can be constrictive. Resorts also typically lie away from the main towns. A car or scooter is vital for exploring remote villages and wilder spots, such as the surprisingly rugged north of Zakynthos or the trails of Kefalonia's Ainos mountain range. As on all Greek islands, exercise caution with regard to steep, winding roads, and fellow drivers equally unfamiliar with the terrain.

Hotels

Corfu has the best variety of accommodation in the islands, with bed-and-breakfast hotels in renovated Venetian town houses, sleek resorts with children's programs and spas, and, outside Corfu Town, simple rooms and studio apartments that can be rented out on the spot. Kefalonia and especially Zakynthos don't have any shortage of resorts, but you won't find quite as many boutique stays. The explosion of tourism in recent years has led to prepaid, low-price package tours, and the largest hotels often cater to groups. These can be offputting and noisy, but are easily avoided as they are usually confined to specific areas, such as Lassi on Kefalonia, Laganas and the entire eastern side of Zakynthos, and along Corfu's southeast and northwest coast. Budget accommodations can be found for €30 and upward, usually in towns and villages. Villas and apartments for rent—some luxurious, others more basic—are increasingly common owing to a government scheme to subsidize 50% of the building costs for local entrepreneurs, and usually require a three-day minimum stay. The islands are popular from Easter (when they are crammed with Greek tourists) through September, and reservations are strongly recommended during that period. Many hotels and restaurants are closed from the end of October to Easter.

Restaurants

Eating habits across the Ionian archipelago are similar. Islanders tend to prefer their main meal at midday, with simpler food in the evening. Given the meat-heavy nature of the local fare, it's no surprise. Many of the more popular tavernas veer away from home-style cooking, preferring generic Greek dishes like moussaka and *stifado* (beef or rabbit cooked in a spicy sauce with onions) alongside grilled meats and pizzas. Main courses are preceded by a meze of dips and small salads, and perhaps some *keftedes* (meatballs). Vegetarians may find themselves living on cheese.

There are plenty of island specialties to seek out. Corfu is synonymous with the Sunday-lunch staple of *pastitsada* (beef or rooster in a spicy tomato sauce served with pasta), as well as *bourdetto* (fish cooked in paprika, sometimes curry-hot) and the more refined *sofrito*, a veal stew that speaks to its Venetian heritage. The southern isles play more to their pastoral settings, and are famed for their cheeses; look out for Kefalonia's briney feta and the tangy oil-preserved *ladotyri* of Zakynthos, typically served crumbled atop a dish of *skordostoubi melitzana*, a local veggie twist on a Greek staple, made with garlicky, mushy aubergine. But meat is ubiquitous here, especially in Kefalonian classic *kreatopita* (three animals in pie form), which requires a good "walking off."

Speaking of meat, restaurants often take the form of *psistaria*, or grillrooms, filled with the aroma of charcoal. Most of these places also run a takeaway service, and you may see neighborhood families waiting in line for souvlaki or whole spit-roasted chicken while you dine. Desserts are not a strong suit on the islands, although Corfiots love *karidopitta* (walnut cake drenched in syrup), and Zakynthos's spongey, syrupy, cream-topped take on *frigania* is worth a try. Wine is the big winner here, however, and differs from that found on the mainland thanks to the islands' Italian roots. Kefalonia is the star of the oenological show with its three PDO (protected designation of origin) wines, made from *Robola, Muscat,* and *Mavrodaphne* grapes. Wherever you go, most tavernas have their own house wine, served in carafes or jugs, and usually this is a good choice. *Kali oreksi*! (Bon appetit!)

Restaurant and hotel reviews have been shortened. For full information, visit Fodors.com.

What it Costs in euros			
$	$$	$$$	$$$$
RESTAURANTS			
under €15	€15–€25	€26–€40	over €40
HOTELS			
under €125	€125–€225	€226–€275	over €275

Corfu

Temperate, multihued Corfu—of emerald mountains; turquoise waters lapping rocky coves; ocher and pink buildings; shimmering silver olive leaves; puffed red, yellow, and orange parasails; scarlet roses, bougainvillea, and lavender wisteria and jacaranda spread over cottages—could have inspired Impressionism.

Kerkyra (Corfu) is certainly the lushest and, quite possibly, the loveliest of all Greek islands. Breathlessly blue waters lap rocky, pine-rimmed coves, and plants like bougainvillea, wisteria, and sweet-smelling jasmine spread over the countryside. Homer's "well-watered gardens" and "beautiful and rich land" were Odysseus's last stop on his journey home. Corfu is also said to be the inspiration for Prospero's island in Shakespeare's *The Tempest*. This northernmost of the major Ionian islands has, through the centuries, inspired other artists, as well as conquerors, royalty, and, of course, tourists.

Today more than a million—mainly British—tourists visit every year, and in summer they crowd the evocative capital city of Corfu Town (population 40,000). As a result, the town has a number of stylish restaurants and hotels and a sophisticated European atmosphere. The interior of Corfu, however, remains largely unspoiled, and the island has absorbed many layers of architectural history, offering an alluring mix of neoclassical villas, Venetian palazzo, pastel-painted hill towns, old farmhouses, and classy, city-sized resorts. You'll find all this plus ancient olive groves, pine-covered cliffs, and heart-stopping, beautiful vistas of sea and sky. Corfu remains an enchanting mixture of simplicity and sophistication.

The classical remains have suffered from the island's tempestuous history; architecture from the centuries of Venetian, French, and British rule is most evident, leaving Corfu and especially Corfu Town with a pleasant combination of contrasting design elements. And although it was bombed during the Italian and Nazi occupation in World War II, the town of Corfu remains one of the most charming in all of Greece.

GETTING HERE AND AROUND

You don't need or want a car in Corfu Town, which is compact and easily walkable. Buses run to the island's main towns and beaches, but if you want to visit some of Corfu's loveliest and most inaccessible places, all of them within an hour of Corfu Town, you'll need your own transportation. Corfu's gentle climate and rolling hills make it ideal motorbike country. You can rent cars and motorbikes at the airport or near the harbor in Corfu Town. If you plan to visit only a few of the major towns, the inexpensive local bus system will do. Taxis can be hired for day trips from Corfu Town.

BUS

On Corfu, bus services run from Corfu Town to the main towns and villages on the island; schedules and prices can change seasonally and yearly. There are two bus lines. The Green KTEL buses leave for distant towns from the Corfu Town terminal between the town center and the airport. Blue suburban buses (with stops including Kanoni and Gastouri) leave from in and around San Rocco Square. Get timetables at both bus depots. Tickets—farthest rides are just under €5—can be bought at the depots or on the bus.

CONTACTS Corfu Surburban (Blue) Buses. ✉ San Rocco Sq., Corfu Town ☎ 26610/31595 ⊕ www.corfucitybus. com. **Corfu KTEL (Green) Buses.** ✉ Between Corfu Town and airport, Corfu Town ☎ 26610/28900 ⊕ www.greenbuses.gr.

CAR AND SCOOTER

Corfu Town has several car-rental agencies, most of them clustered around the port, ranging from international chains to local agencies offering cheap deals; there is also an agency in Ermones. Depending on the season, prices can range from €35 a day to €230 a week for a compact, all insurance included. Chains have a bigger selection, but the locals will usually give a cheaper price. Don't be afraid to bargain, especially if you want to rent a car for several days. You can generally make arrangements to pick up your car at the airport.

A 50cc motorbike can be rented for about €15 a day or €100 a week, but you can bargain, especially if you want it for longer. Helmets are required by law. Check the lights, brakes, and other mechanics before you accept a machine.

CONTACTS Ansa International Rent a Car. ✉ Eleftheriou Venizelou 20, Corfu Town ☎ 26610/21930. **1Car Rental.** ✉ Ermones, Ermones ☎ 26610/71032 ⊕ 1carental. com. **Ocean Car Hire.** ✉ Gouvia Marina, Gouvia ☎ 26610/44017 ⊕ www.oceancar. gr. **Top Cars.** ✉ Donzelot 25, Corfu Town ☎ 26610/35237 ⊕ www.carrentalcorfu. com.

TAXI

Taxis rates are reasonable—when adhered to. If you want to hire a cab on an hourly or daily basis, negotiate the price before you travel. In Corfu Town, taxis wait at San Rocco Square, the Esplanade, the airport, the Old Port Square, and the

New Port. Many drivers speak English. Of course, long-distance trips on the island will pack a hefty price tag.

CONTACTS Radiotaxi Corfu.
☎ 26610/33811.

TOURS

From May through September, local travel agencies run half-day tours of Corfu's Old Town, and tour buses go daily to all the main sights on the island.

All-Ways Travel

GUIDED TOURS | One of the oldest travel agencies on the island, Greek-and-English-run All-Ways Travel is reliable for accommodation reservations, and especially helpful for any flight booking, including complicated connections. ✉ G. Theotoki Sq. 34, San Rocco ☎ 26610/33955 ⊕ www.allwaystravel. com.

Anna Aperghi Travel

ADVENTURE TOURS | Aperghi Travel is an expert on hiking holidays and is a designated agent for accommodation and ground arrangements along the Corfu Trail (⊕ www.thecorfutrail.com), a bottom-to-top-of-the-island hike that offers lovely sections easily worth an hour or two of your time. ✉ Dimokratias Ave. and Polyla St. 1, Corfu Town ☎ 26610/48713 ⊕ www.aperghitravel.gr.

Corfu Sunspots Travel

BUS TOURS | Sunspots runs a variety of coach tours, including the popular Grand Island Tour, as well as half-day trips to the north and south of the island. They specialize in Jeep safaris. ✉ National Paleokastritsa Hwy. 24, Corfu Town ☎ 26610/39707 ⊕ www.corfusunspots.gr.

Ionian Cruises

BOAT TOURS | Ionian Cruises offers boat day trips to other islands in the Ionian group, to mainland Greece, and to Albania. ✉ Eth. Antistaseos 4, Corfu Town ☎ 26610/31649 ⊕ www.ionian-cruises.com.

Corfu Town ΠΟΛΗ ΤΗΣ ΚΕΡΚΥΡΑΣ

34 km (21 miles) west of Igoumenitsa, 41 km (26 miles) north of Lefkimmi.

Corfu Town today is a vivid tapestry of cultures—a sophisticated weave, where charm, history, and natural beauty blend. Located about midway along the island's east coast, this spectacularly lively capital is the cultural heart of Corfu and has a remarkable historic center that UNESCO designated as a World Heritage site in 2007. All ships and planes dock or land near Corfu Town, which occupies a small peninsula jutting into the Ionian Sea.

Whether arriving by ferry from mainland Greece or Italy, from another island, or directly by plane, catch your breath by first relaxing with a coffee or a gelato in Corfu Town's shaded Liston Arcade, then stroll the narrow lanes of its pedestrians-only quarter. For an overview of the immediate area, and a quick tour of Mon Repos palace, hop on the little tourist train that runs from May to September. Corfu Town has a different feel at night, so book a table at one of its famed tavernas to savor the island's unique cuisine.

The best way to get around Corfu Town is on foot. The town is small enough so that you can easily walk to every sight. There are local buses, but they do not thread their way into the streets (many now car-free) of the historic center. If you are arriving by ferry or plane, it's best to take a taxi to your hotel. Expect to pay about €10 from the airport or ferry terminal to a hotel in Corfu Town. If there are no taxis waiting, you can call for one *(see Taxi)*.

Sights

Though beguilingly Greek, much of Corfu's Old Town displays the architectural styles of its conquerors—*molto* of Italy's Venice, a *soupçon* of France, and more than a tad of England; it may remind you of Venice or Bath. Many visitors will want to invest in the multi-attraction ticket, available at any of the sights, which includes admission to the Old Fortress, the Corfu Museum of Asian Art, the Antivouniotissa Museum, and Mon Repos palace.

Antivouniotissa Museum

MUSEUM | Panagia Antivouniotissa, an ornate church dating from the late 15th century, houses an outstanding collection of Byzantine religious art. More than 50 icons from the 13th to the 17th century hang on the walls. Look for works by the celebrated icon painters Tzanes and Damaskinos; they are perhaps the best-known artists of the Cretan style of icon painting. ⊠ *Arseniou St. 25* ☎ *26610/38313* ⊕ *www.antivouniotissamuseum.gr* 🎫 *€4* ⊘ *Closed Tues.*

★ Archaeological Museum

MUSEUM | A makeover and extensive remodelling have brought the island's flagship museum into modern times. Partly using interpretive panels and video screens, the lower floor takes you through the ancient history of mankind in Corfu and how it is revealed by way of the various finds, from stone-age culture through the development of society and skills. This area also tells the story of archaeological discoveries, with contemporary photographs and documents from a succession of digs, including the one that uncovered the museum's star attraction, the Medusa, on display as the centerpiece of the upper floor. This massive bas-relief once formed the pediment of the 6th-century BC Temple of Artemis at Kanoni, but nowadays, the snake-coiffed figure—one of the largest and best-preserved pieces of Archaic sculpture in Greece—is housed in a vast open-plan area that affords visitors a dramatic encounter. Other exhibits are arrayed thematically and stylishly throughout the four main spaces, each one focusing on a distinct aspect of life in ancient times. ⊠ *Vraila 1, off Leoforos Dimokratias, past Corfu Palace hotel* ⊹ *Just off Garitsa Promenade, near the Corfu Palace Hotel* ☎ *26610/30680* 🎫 *€5.*

★ Campiello

NEIGHBORHOOD | This medieval quarter, part of a UNESCO-designated World Heritage site, is an atmospheric labyrinth of narrow, winding streets, steep stairways, and secretive little squares. Laundry lines connect balconied Venetian palazzi engraved with the original occupant's coat of arms to neoclassical 19th-century buildings constructed by the British. Small cobbled squares with central wells, watched over by old churches, add to the quiet, mysterious, and utterly charming urban space. If you enter, you're almost sure to get lost, but the area is small enough that eventually you'll come out on one of Corfu Town's major streets, or on the sea wall. ⊠ *Corfu Town* ⊹ *West of the Esplanade, northeast of New Fortress.*

Casa Parlante

MUSEUM | FAMILY | A highly educational experience as well as an entertaining one, a visit to this living history museum allows you to meet three generations of a noble Corfiot family and their servants. The Count and his kin are not flesh and blood but realistic animated figures who occupy an old town house, fitted out with authentic 19th-century furniture and artifacts. A guided tour of the apartment, with intelligent and informative commentary that includes each character's backstory, brings Corfu's urban past to life, some of it rather graphically. ⊠ *N. Theotoki 16* ☎ *26610/49190* ⊕ *www.casaparlante.gr* 🎫 *€8.*

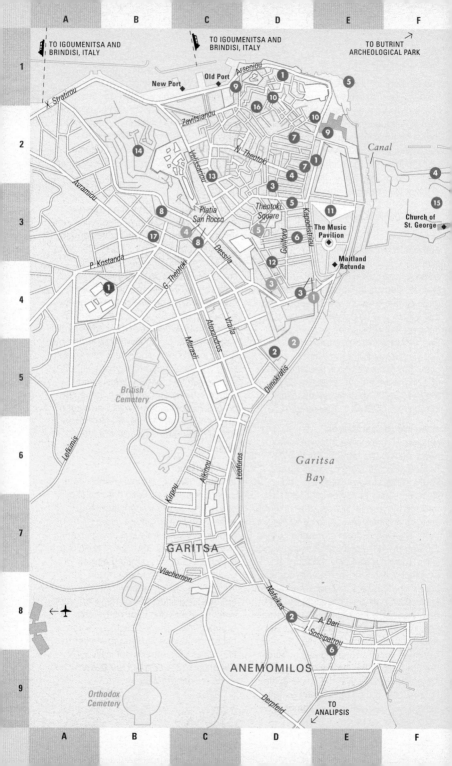

Corfu Town

Ayios Nikolaos Bay

Sights ▼

1 Antivouniotissa Museum D1
2 Archaeological Museum D5
3 Campiello D2
4 Casa Parlante D2
5 Catholic Church of Ayios Iakovos............................. D3
6 Church of Ayios Iason and Ayios Sosipater............... E8
7 Church of St. Spyridon D2
8 Corfu Market........................ B3
9 Corfu Museum of Asian Art E2
10 Corfu Reading Society E2
11 The Esplanade E3
12 Holy Trinity Church D3
13 Jewish Quarter C2
14 New Fortress....................... B2
15 Old Fortress F3
16 Orthodox Cathedral................ D2
17 Patounis Soap Factory........... B3

Restaurants ▼

1 Aegli................................. E2
2 Avli D8
3 Cavalieri Rooftop Restaurant..... D4
4 Corfu Sailing Club Restaurant..... F2
5 En Plo E1
6 La Cucina D3
7 Rex D2
8 Rouvas C3
9 Salto................................. C1
10 Venetian Well D1

Quick Bites ▼

1 Lunatico............................. B4

Hotels ▼

1 Cavalieri Hotel D4
2 Corfu Palace D5
3 Hotel Bella Venezia................ D4
4 Hotel Hermes....................... C3
5 Siorra Vittoria Boutique Hotel..... D3

KEY

1 Sights
1 Restaurants
1 Hotels
1 Quick Bites
✈ Airport

0 — 300 yards
0 — 300 meters

Catholic Church of Ayios Iakovos

RELIGIOUS SITE | Built in 1588 and consecrated 50 years later, this elegant cathedral was erected to provide a grand place of worship for Corfu Town's Catholic occupiers. If you use the Italian name, San Giacomo, locals will know it. When it was bombed by the Nazis in 1943, the cathedral's original neoclassical facade of pediments, friezes, and columns was practically destroyed; only the bell tower remained intact. It's now been restored. Mass takes place daily at 7 pm in high summer and at 10:30 am on Sunday. Across the road is a former Venetian-built theater. Note the carvings and bas-reliefs on the walls. ⊠ Dimarcheiou Sq.

Church of Ayios Iason and Ayios Sosipater

RELIGIOUS SITE | The suburb of Anemomilos is crowned by the ruins of the Paleopolis church and by the 11th-century Church of Ayios Iason and Ayios Sosipater. It was named after two of St. Paul's disciples, St. Jason and St. Sosipater, who brought Christianity to the island in the 1st century. The frescoes are faded, but the icons are beautiful, and the exterior is dramatic among the unspoiled greenery. It's open most mornings. This is one of only two Byzantine churches on the island; the other is in the northern coastal village of Ayios Markos. ⊠ Anemomilos ✛ At south end of Garitsa Bay 🕾 Donations accepted.

★ Church of St. Spyridon

RELIGIOUS SITE | Built in 1596, this church is the tallest on the island, thanks to its distinctive red-domed bell tower, and it's filled with silver treasures. The patron saint's remains—smuggled here after the fall of Constantinople—are contained in a silver reliquary in a small chapel; devout Corfiots visit to kiss the reliquary and pray to the saint. The silver casket is carried in procession through the town four times a year. Spyridon was not a Corfiot but a shepherd from Cyprus, who became a bishop before his death in AD 350. His miracles are said to have saved the island four times: once from famine, twice from the plague, and once from the hated Turks. During World War II, a bomb fell on this holiest place on the island but didn't explode. Maybe these events explain why it seems every other man on Corfu is named Spiros. If you keep the church tower in sight, you can wander as you wish without getting lost around this fascinating section of town. Agiou Spyridonos, the street in front of the church, is crammed with shops selling religious trinkets and souvenirs. ⊠ Agiou Spyridon ☎ 26610/33059 ⊕ www.imcorfu.gr.

★ Corfu Market

MARKET | Picturesquely located in the dry-moat outer defenses of the New Fortress, Corfu's public market is laid out in an attractive, traditional design. The stalls showcase local produce, specifically fruits and vegetables (some of it ecologically grown), fresh fish, and local foodstuffs like olives, dry pulses, wine, and packaged goods. Two coffee bars in the central "square" provide refreshment at very low cost. It's a far cry from the supermarket! ⊠ San Rocco ⊗ Closed Sun.

★ Corfu Museum of Asian Art

CASTLE/PALACE | It may seem a bit incongruous to admire Ming pottery in an ornate British colonial palace as the Ionian Sea shimmers outside the windows, but this elegant, colonnaded, 19th-century Regency structure houses the Museum of Asian Art, a notable collection of Asian porcelains, Japanese ukiyo-e prints, Indian sculpture, and Tibetan temple art. The building was constructed as a residence for the lord high commissioner and headquarters for the order of St. Michael and St. George; it was abandoned after the British left in 1864 and renovated about a hundred years later by the British ambassador to Greece. After visiting the galleries, wander in the shady courtyard behind the palace, where you may have trouble tearing yourself away from the fairy-tale view of the lush islet of Vido and the mountainous coast of Albania. Don't miss the **Municipal Gallery**. ⊠ *Palace of St. Michael and St. George, Palaia Anaktora* ✛ *At north end of Esplanade* ☎ *26610/30443* ⊕ *www.matk.gr* 🎟 *€6.*

★ **Corfu Reading Society**
LIBRARY | The oldest cultural institution in modern Greece, the Corfu Reading Society was founded in 1836. The building, filled with books and archives relating to the Ionian islands, is only open in the morning, stands behind the Palace of Saint Michael and Saint George and has an impressive exterior staircase leading up to a loggia. Inside is a book lover's delight, with 19th-century decor that is evocative testimony to the "English age" that gave Corfu so much of its character. ⊠ *Kapodistriou 120* ☎ *26610/39528* 🎟 *Free for scholars* ⊗ *Closed Sat. and Sun.*

★ **The Esplanade**
MEMORIAL | FAMILY | Central to the life of the town, this huge, open parade ground and park just west of the Old Fortress is, many say, the most beautiful *spianada* (esplanade) in Greece. It is bordered on the west by a street lined with Venetian and English Georgian houses and a famous arcaded building called the **Liston,** built by the French under Napoléon and meant to resemble the Rue du Rivoli in Paris. Cafés spill out onto the passing scene, and Corfiot celebrations, games, and concerts take place here; at night, lovers promenade and children play in this festive public space. Sunday cricket matches, a holdover from British rule, are occasionally played on the northern half of the Esplanade, which was once a Venetian firing range. Standing in the center is an ornate **Victorian bandstand** and, just south of it, the **Maitland Rotunda,** a circular Ionic memorial built in honor of Sir Thomas Maitland, the not-much-loved first British lord high commissioner who was appointed in 1814 when the island became a protectorate of Britain. At the southernmost tip of the Esplanade a **statue of Ioannis Kapodistrias,** a Corfu resident and the first president of modern Greece, looks out over Garitsa Bay. Kapodistrias was also, unfortunately, the first Greek president to be assassinated, in 1831. ⊠ *Corfu Town* ✛ *Between Old Fortress and Old Town.*

Holy Trinity Church
RELIGIOUS SITE | Established in 1870 after the end of the British Protectorate (1815–1864), this Anglican church continues to serve the needs of the English-speaking community. All denominations are welcome to services and to other religious events and social activities in its sphere. Sunday morning service takes place at 10:30. ⊠ *L. Mavili 21* ☎ *26610/31467* ⊕ *www.holytrinitycorfu.net* 🎟 *Donations accepted* ⊗ *Closed Mon.*

Jewish Quarter
NEIGHBORHOOD | This maze of streets was home to the area's Jewish population from the 1600s until 1944, when the community was decimated, most sent to Auschwitz by the occupying Nazis. Fewer than 100 of 3,000 Jews survived. At the southern edge of the ghetto, a 300-year-old synagogue with an interior in Sephardic style still stands. ⊠ *Parados 4, Off Velissariou, 2 blocks from New Fortress.*

New Fortress
BUILDING | FAMILY | Built during the period 1577–78 by the Venetians, the so-called "New" Fortress was constructed to strengthen town defenses—only three decades after the construction of Venetian fortifications on the "Old" Fortress. The French and the British subsequently expanded the complex to protect Corfu Town from a possible Turkish invasion. You can wander through the maze of tunnels and fortifications; the dry moat is the site of the town's fish-and-vegetable marketplace. A classic British citadel stands at its heart. The summit offers a fantastic view over the rooftops of the Old Town. ⊠ *Solomou* ✛ *On promontory overlooking New Port* 🎟 *Free.*

Old Fortress

BUILDING | FAMILY | Corfu's entire population once lived within the walls of the Old Fortress, or Citadel, built by the Venetians in 1546 on the site of a Byzantine castle. Separated from the rest of the town by a moat, the fort is on a promontory mentioned by Thucydides. Its two heights, or *korypha* ("peaks"), gave the island its name. Standing on the peaks, you have a gorgeous view west over the town and east to the mountainous coast of Albania. A statue of Count Schulenburg, an Austrian mercenary who became a local hero in 1716 when he helped to defeat the invading Turks, stands at the fort's entrance; a plaque beside the statue tells Schulenburg's story. Inside, there's an exhibition of Byzantine art and a shop with museum copies, while a second hall hosts changing events. Most of the old Venetian fortifications inside the fortress were destroyed by the British, who replaced them with their own structures. The most notable of these is the **Church of St. George,** built to look like an ancient Doric temple. Near it, overlooking Garitsa Bay, there is a shaded café where you can sit and enjoy the splendid view. ✉ *Corfu Town* ✣ *On eastern point of Corfu Town peninsula* ☎ *266/104–8310* 🌐 *odysseus.culture.gr* 🎟 *€6.*

Orthodox Cathedral

RELIGIOUS SITE | This small, icon-rich cathedral, called Panagia Spiliotissa, was built in 1577. It is sacred to St. Theodora, the island's second patron saint. Her headless body lies in a silver coffin by the altar; it was brought to Corfu at the same time as St. Spyridon's remains. Steps lead down to the harbor from here. ✉ *Corfu Town* ✣ *Southwest corner of Campiello, east of St. Spyridon.*

Patounis Soap Factory

LOCAL INTEREST | A Patounis has been producing olive oil soap by the traditional stamped method since 1850, and the family's factory—the only one left in Corfu—is listed as an Industrial Heritage site. It is also inscribed on the National Inventory of the Intangible Cultural Heritage of Greece. Every weekday at noon, the current (fifth-generation) Patounis, Apostolos, runs an informative guided tour of the premises, during which you will see a demonstration of the traditional stamping and cutting process. You can also buy the merchandise, which is additive-free and hypoallergenic. ✉ *Ioannou Theotoki St. 9* ☎ *26610/39806* 🌐 *www.patounis.gr* 🕒 *Closed Sun.*

🍴 Restaurants

Aegli

$$ | MODERN GREEK | Both local and international dishes are on the menu at this long-established and casually elegant restaurant on the Liston arcade. Start with a plate of steamed mussels or a salad, then move on to hearty Greek and Corfiot classics. **Known for:** home-baked sourdough bread; pastitsada, Corfu's rich beef stew; spectacular view of the Esplanade. [$] *Average main: €15* ✉ *Kapodistriou 23, Liston* ☎ *26610/31949* 🌐 *aeglirestaurant.gr.*

Avli

$ | GREEK | Avli specializes in *mezedes,* so you order a selection of these small dishes for sharing rather than your own main course. The young proprietors, Vasilis (front of house) and Christos (chef) source ingredients locally whenever possible and combine them in inventive and innovative ways, such as with the pork fillet, which comes accompanied by a sauce made from Corfu-grown kumquats. **Known for:** bread baked in-house daily; grilled Talagani cheese garnished with the unique local fig preserve; interesting fresh seafood dishes. [$] *Average main: €13* ✉ *Alk. Dari and Ath. Kavvada, Garitsa* ☎ *26610/31291* 🌐 *www.avlicorfu.com.*

Did You Know?

Corfu's Church of St. Spyridon—its beautiful bell tower is a handy landmark to get your bearings—honors its patron saint with festive processions on Palm Sunday, Holy Saturday, August 11, and the first Sunday in November.

Corfu's Changing Allegiances

It may be hard to believe that an island as small as Corfu could have [undertaken a] noteworthy role in the region's history, but it's proximity to Europe—72 km (45 miles) from Italy and 2 km (1 mile) or so from Albania—and its position on an ancient trade route at the mouth of the Adriatic, assured a lively series of conquests and counter-conquests. In classical times, Corinth colonized the northern Ionian islands, but Corfu, growing powerful, revolted and allied itself with Athens, a fateful move that triggered the Peloponnesian War. Subjection followed: to the tyrants of Syracuse, the kings of Epirus and of Macedonia, in the 2nd century BC to Rome, and from the 11th to the 14th century to Norman and Angevin kings. Then came the Venetians, who protected Corfu from Turkish occupation and provided a 411-year period of development. Napoléon Bonaparte took the islands after the fall of Venice. "The greatest misfortune which could befall me is the loss of Corfu," he wrote to Talleyrand, his foreign minister. Within two years he'd lost it to a Russo-Turkish fleet.

For a short time the French regained and fortified Corfu from the Russians, and their occupation influenced the island's educational system, architecture, and cuisine. Theirs was a Greek-run republic—the first for modern Greece—which whetted local appetites for the independence that arrived later in the 19th century. In 1814 the islands came under British rule and were administered by a series of British lord high commissioners; under their watch, roads, schools, and hospitals were constructed, and commercialism developed. The fight for national independence finally prevailed, and the islands were ceded to Greece in 1864.

Cavalieri Rooftop Restaurant

$$ | ECLECTIC | Recently established and already in receipt of awards, this sophisticated eatery is located on the roof of the prestigious Cavalieri Hotel, overlooking the Historic Center and the sea. The menu is bijou but eclectic, incorporating international classics as well as select Greek dishes; it ranges from imaginative pastas, through seafood like swordfish with grilled vegetables, to USA Black Angus steaks, among other dishes. **Known for:** peerless views; open to non-residents; stylish service. $ *Average main: €20* ✉ *Kapodistriou 4* ☎ *26610/39041* ⊕ *www.cavalieri-hotel. com* ☾ *Closed Nov.–Apr.*

★ Corfu Sailing Club Restaurant

$$ | MODERN GREEK | Everyone—not just sailors—will appreciate the spectacular location of this classy restaurant, tucked under the northern wall of the Venetian-era Old Fortress beside the yacht club harbor. The food is Greek but offers twists on traditional concepts, such as a cheese pie topped with honey, in a dish straight out of ancient times. **Known for:** wide-ranging wine list; excellent seafood combinations; location-appropriate Venetian calves liver. $ *Average main: €15* ✉ *Old Fortress, Mandraki* ☎ *26610/38763* ⊕ *www.corfu-sailing-restaurant.com* ☾ *Closed Nov.–Apr.*

En Plo

$ | GREEK | Blessed with a startlingly wonderful location by a wave-lapped jetty in the little waterfront Faliraki area north of the Old Fortress, En Plo offers everything from snacks and pizzas to a full meal. Enjoy mezedes, a big variety of salads, and interesting pastas. **Known for:** unique location, where you can combine a swim with good food; spectacular view of the Old Fortress and the sea; very relaxed atmosphere. ⓢ *Average main: €13* ✉ *Faliraki* ✛ *On waterfront just north of Old Fortress* ☎ *26610/81813* ☾ *Closed Dec.–Mar.*

La Cucina

$$ | INTERNATIONAL | To describe a restaurant's cuisine as "international" can imply that it is bland, but no one would ever say that about La Cucina. Renowned for its Italian cooking—and particularly handmade pasta—the menu also incorporates Thai curries, a raw fish bar, quirky takes on Corfiot staples, and even nods to British cuisine. **Known for:** handmade pasta and pizza; black Angus strip loin and Florentine T-bone steak on the grill; comprehensive and eclectic wine list. ⓢ *Average main: €20* ✉ *Moustoxidi 13 at Guilford* ☎ *26610/45799* ☾ *No lunch.*

★ Rex

$$ | GREEK | A friendly Corfiot restaurant housed in a classic early-19th-century building just behind the famous Liston arcade, Rex has been a favorite of the locals since the early 20th century. Hearty stews are on the menu alongside examples of modern regional fare such as slow-cooked lamb shank with couscous and Corfu-style rooster. **Known for:** signature dish of duck with kumquat sauce; wonderful location for people-watching; elegant surroundings and service. ⓢ *Average main: €15* ✉ *Kapodistriou 66* ✛ *Behind the Liston arcade* ☎ *26610/39649* ⊕ *www.rexrestaurant.gr.*

Rouvas

$ | GREEK | A local favorite for lunch in town is located near San Rocco Square in the center of Corfu's commercial district. It caters particularly to residents—many of them discerning civil servants and lawyers from local offices—who savor the chef's tasty and filling traditional dishes of the day, like fried fish with garlic sauce. **Known for:** superb pastitsio and rabbit stifado; bustling location near the market; classic taverna style, with food cooked on a traditional range in view of customers. ⓢ *Average main: €10* ✉ *Stamatis Desyllas 13* ✛ *Near the outdoor market* ☎ *26610/31182* ☾ *No dinner, closed Sun.*

Salto

$$ | MEDITERRANEAN | This wine bar-and-bistro is as famous for its food as for a very extensive wine list and a magnificent outlook across the Old Port to the massive walls of the New Fortress. Using pure ingredients from small producers all over Greece, the menu takes traditional Mediterranean dishes and moves them into trendsetting territory. **Known for:** exclusively Greek wine list, featuring the country's best vintages; crunchy cod bites with garlic mousse; creative and beautifully presented salads. ⓢ *Average main: €16* ✉ *Donzelot 23* ☎ *26613/02325* ☾ *Closed Nov.*

★ Venetian Well

$$ | MEDITERRANEAN | The scene is as delicious as the food in this wonderfully romantic restaurant arranged around a 17th-century well on the most beautiful little square in the Old Town. Expect creative Greek and Mediterranean cuisine, with a menu that changes regularly according to the availability of the always fresh ingredients. **Known for:** sous vide lamb cooked for 24 hours; list of some 700 wines from all over the world; exquisite presentation and service. ⓢ *Average main: €18* ✉ *Kremasti Sq., Campiello* ✛ *Across from Church of the Panagia* ☎ *26615/50955* ⊕ *www.venetianwell.gr* ☾ *No lunch.*

Coffee and Quick Bites

Lunatico

$ | **CAFÉ** | Lunatico is set in a secluded park-like garden, in the grounds of a former psychiatric hospital, hence the name. It's popular among Corfiots for good coffee and decent baguette sandwiches. **Known for:** quiet location at town center; tables under shady trees; good value prices. [$] *Average main: €3* ✉ *Plateia Palio Psychiatriou* ✥ *off Dimoulitsa Street, near San Rocco Square* ☎ *26613/61107.*

Hotels

★ Cavalieri Hotel

$ | **HOTEL** | This hotel occupies a landmark 18th-century building with a wonderful location equidistant between the Liston and the sea; it's one of the few hotels here to remain open year-round (and therefore caters to a lot of business travelers). **Pros:** beautiful historic building; great views over the Esplanade and the sea; short walk to the sights of the historic center. **Cons:** small public rooms; the area can be noisy; no dedicated parking. [$] *Rooms from: €100* ✉ *Kapodistriou 4* ☎ *26610/39041* 🌐 *www.cavalieri-hotel.com* 🛏 *50 rooms* 🍴 *Free breakfast.*

Corfu Palace

$$ | **HOTEL** | Built in 1950 as the island's first resort hotel—and these days showing it—the Corfu Palace is a grande dame in bad need of a face-lift, albeit in an unbeatable location and with some lingering grace notes. **Pros:** gorgeous garden and pool area; great breakfast buffet; has Corfu's only casino, open 24 hours a day. **Cons:** decor shows its age; no beach or sea swimming; limited parking space. [$] *Rooms from: €220* ✉ *Leoforos Dimokratias 2* ☎ *26610/39485* 🌐 *www.corfupalace.com* 🛏 *112 rooms* 🍴 *Free breakfast.*

Hotel Bella Venezia

$$ | **HOTEL** | This elegant two-story Venetian town house centrally located has been used as a hotel since the 1800s and remains one of the nicest small hotels in town. **Pros:** very friendly service; short walk to the sights of the historic center; lovely garden breakfast area. **Cons:** some rooms have small windows; views are urban rather than maritime; nearby parking hard to find. [$] *Rooms from: €140* ✉ *Zambelli 4* ☎ *26610/20707, 26610/44290* 🌐 *www.bellaveneziahotel.com* 🛏 *31 rooms* 🍴 *Free breakfast.*

Hotel Hermes

$ | **HOTEL** | The old, no-frills Hermes was always popular with backpackers, but since an upgrade it has more appeal for budget travelers in general. **Pros:** affordable rates; very helpful staff; plenty of restaurants nearby. **Cons:** adjacent market and main road are noisy in early morning; breakfast is not included; no parking nearby. [$] *Rooms from: €75* ✉ *San Rocco, G. Markora 12–14* ☎ *26610/39268* 🛏 *30 rooms* 🍴 *No meals.*

★ Siora Vittoria Boutique Hotel

$$ | **B&B/INN** | Right in the heart of Corfu's historic center and just a minute's walk away from the Liston, this grand mansion was built in 1823 by the aristocratic Metaxas clan and, happily, its conversion to a hotel succeeded in preserving its lovely and authentic Venetian style. **Pros:** exquisite accommodation with a real flavor of old Corfu; close to all the town's best facilities, yet tranquil; open all year. **Cons:** some rooms are small; most rooms lack balconies; not suitable for young children. [$] *Rooms from: €180* ✉ *Stefanou Padova 36* ☎ *26610/36300* 🌐 *www.sioravittoria.com* 🛏 *9 rooms* 🍴 *Free breakfast.*

Nightlife

Corfu Town is a late-night, café-crowded, club-happy city. During the summer months, the Greeks dine very late, often at 10 pm. The nightly *volta*, a pre- or post-dinner promenade along the Esplanade and the Liston, starts at about 9 pm. Couples stroll, families gather, kids play, and the cafés and restaurants fill up. The club and disco scene heats up much later, around midnight. Party Central lies about 2 km (1 mile) north of the town center, near the New Port, on Ethnikis Antistaseos (also known as "Bar Street"). This is where you'll find a string of plush lounge-bars (many with outdoor pools) and discos that really don't start swinging until after midnight. Clubs on Corfu come and go like tourists, with many featuring incredibly loud sound systems that throb with the latest Euro-pop and dance hits. Most clubs have a cover charge, which includes the first drink.

★ Cavalieri Hotel Bar

BARS/PUBS | The rooftop bar and restaurant at the Cavalieri Hotel are hard to beat for views. Hotel guests happily mingle with locals as the scene slowly enlivens from a mellow, early-evening cocktail crowd to a more-energetic party atmosphere. ⊠ *Cavlieri Hotel, Kapodistriou 4* ☎ *26610/39041* ⊕ *www.cavalieri-hotel-corfu-town.com.*

Josephine Bar

BARS/PUBS | FAMILY | Hip but relaxed Josephine Bar on the Liston has chairs out on the flagstones and a good view of decked-out promenade strollers. ⊠ *Liston, Esplanade Square* ☎ *26610/27275.*

Nautilas

BARS/PUBS | Anchored at Anemomylos ("Windmill"), where Garitsa meets Kanoni, Nautilas marks the southern terminus of the long seafront promenade that stretches from the Corfu Palace hotel to Mon Repos, and presides over what is possibly the best distant view of the Old Fortress. Around sundown it buzzes with locals and visitors enjoying the scene as the last rays of the sun blush the waters of the bay and the walls of the castle. To accompany drinks, the seafood platter is celebrated—it's an extravagance, but ample for six or eight people. ⊠ *Anemomylos ⊕ Southern end of Garitsa Bay* ☎ *26610/20033.*

Shopping

Corfu Town has myriad tiny shops, and half of them seem to be selling jewelry. Designer boutiques, shoe shops, and accessory stores can be found in every nook and cranny of the town. The major tourist shopping streets are Nikiphorou Theotoki (designer boutiques, jewelry) and Agios Spyridonos (local souvenirs). The local fish-and-vegetable market is open Monday through Saturday from very early in the morning until around 2 pm. For traditional goods, head for the narrow streets of the historic center, where olive wood, lace, jewelry, and wineshops abound. For perishable products such as liqueurs and candies, you may do better checking out the supermarkets than buying in the Old Town. Most of the shops listed here are in the historic center and are open May to October, from 8 am until late (whenever the last tourist leaves); they're generally closed during winter. Stores in outlying shopping areas tend to close Monday, Wednesday, and Saturday afternoons at 2:30 pm, and all day Sunday.

Ceramic Art

CERAMICS/GLASSWARE | The award-winning ceramic artists Kostas Panaretos and Klio Brenner create beautiful and unique pieces of ceramic art using the ancient Greek technique called Terra Sigillata. To achieve their striking orange colors, they make glazes from Greek soil and then proceed to fire the pieces with wood, imprinting the design through the action of the smoke. In their gallery in the Jewish Quarter and at their atelier near the Old Port you'll find everything from

Fantasy island: Legend has it that Pontikonisi—here pictured behind Vlacherena Monastery—is really Odysseus's ship turned to stone by an enraged Poseidon.

brightly colored bowls to remarkably sophisticated plates and pieces based on ancient Greek forms. ✉ *Ayia Sophia 23 / El. Venizelos 38, Old Port* ☎ *26610/34631.*

Fos tis Anatolis

GIFTS/SOUVENIRS | All goods in the "Light of the Orient" shop—including rugs, lamps, clothes, clay ornaments, and jewelry—have a traditional Eastern style. ✉ *Solomou 5* ☎ *26610/45273.*

Lazari Fine Jewellers

JEWELRY/ACCESSORIES | Kostas Lazaris uses 18- and 22-carat yellow gold and white gold to encapsulate precious stones in his original designs. He will endeavor to create anything you request. ✉ *E. Voulgareos 40* ☎ *26610/20259.*

Rolandos

CRAFTS | Visit the talented artist Rolandos Xanthopoulos and watch him at work on his jewelry. ✉ *N. Theotoki 95-99* ☎ *26610/45004.*

Stella

CERAMICS/GLASSWARE | This shop sells ceramics, religious icons, stone sculptures, and dolls in traditional costume, all handmade and sourced from Greece. ✉ *Kapodistriou 62* ☎ *26610/24012.*

Terracotta

CERAMICS/GLASSWARE | Contemporary Greek jewelry, ceramics, small sculptures, and one-of-a-kind art and craft objects are sold in this appealing shop. ✉ *N. Theotoki 70* ☎ *26610/45260.*

Workshop ... by Tom

CRAFTS | Located right in the heart of the Old Town, this is a genuine olive-wood workshop, where everything is made on the premises by Tom and his son. Salad servers, huge bowls, and various decorative items are among the goods on display next to the machines and tools—and outside in the tiny square. The shop is just off the main street, and you'll have to look carefully to discover it. ✉ *3rd Parados, N. Theotoki 8* ☎ *26610/46683.*

Kanoni Κανόνι

5 km (3 miles) south of Corfu Town.

The suburb of Kanoni was once one of the world's great beauty spots, made famous by countless pictures. Today the landscape has been engulfed by development and a coffee bar has laid claim to the best spot to take in the legendary and still-lovely view, which looks out over two beautiful islets. If you truly want to commune with nature, visit the lush and lovely seaside gardens surrounding the country palace of Mon Repos.

Kanoni's famed vistas encompass the open sea separated by a long, narrow causeway that defines the lagoon of Halikiopoulou, with the intensely green slopes of Mt. Agii Deka as a backdrop. A shorter breakwater leads to the white convent of Moni Vlaherena on a tiny islet—one of the most picturesque islets in all of Greece and the one pictured on nearly all postcards of Mouse Island. Nonetheless, it is the tiny island beyond that islet—the one in the middle of the lake with the tall cypresses—that is **Pontikonisi,** or Mouse Island, a rock rising dramatically from the clear water and topped by a tiny 13th-century chapel. Legend has it that the island is really Odysseus's ship, which an enraged Poseidon turned to stone: the reason why Homer's much-traveled hero was shipwrecked on Phaeacia (Corfu) in *The Odyssey.* From June through August a boat service runs out to Pontikonisi. Keep in mind, though, that while the view *of* the islets has sold a thousand postcards, the view *from* the islets (looking back at Corfu) is that of a hilly landscape built up with resort hotels and summer homes and of the adjacent airport, where planes take off directly over the churches.

GETTING HERE AND AROUND
The local blue bus (line 2) offers frequent daily service (every 20 minutes Monday through Saturday, every 40 minutes on Sunday) to Kanoni from Plateia San Rocco in Corfu Town; the fare is about €1.50. A taxi to Kanoni costs approximately €15. The islet of Pontikonisi can be reached by a short boat trip from the dock at Vlaherena, 2 km (1 mile) below Kanoni and costs €2.50 round trip. The best way to reach Mon Repos from Corfu Town is by walking; it takes about 30 minutes and you follow the seafront most of the way.

Sights

★ Mon Repos

ARCHAEOLOGICAL SITE | FAMILY | The compact neoclassical palace (really a villa) was built in 1831 by Sir Frederic Adam for his wife, and it was later the summer residence of the British lord high commissioners. After Greece won independence from Britain in 1864, Mon Repos was used as a summer palace for the royal family of Greece. Queen Elizabeth II's husband, Prince Philip, was born here in 1921. The Greek government opened the fully restored palace as a museum dedicated to the area's archaeological history. Displays of items found in the area—as well as interpretive displays, rooms showcasing Regency design, contemporary antiques, and botanical paintings—make for a truly eclectic museum collection. The room where Prince Philip was born (on the kitchen table, it is said) houses a 3-D interactive map of Corfu Town and its environs. ⊠ *Dairpfela 16, Paleopolis* ⊹ *2 km (1 mile) south of the Old Fortress, following oceanfront walk* 🚇 *Grounds free; museum €4* 🕙 *Museum closed Tues.*

Restaurants

Flisvos Seaside Cafe Restaurant
$ | CAFÉ | "Flisvos" is the Greek word for the sound of wavelets lapping on the shore, and this low-key bar's seafront setting makes it a perfect location to relax and be lulled—in between the roar of airplanes landing and taking

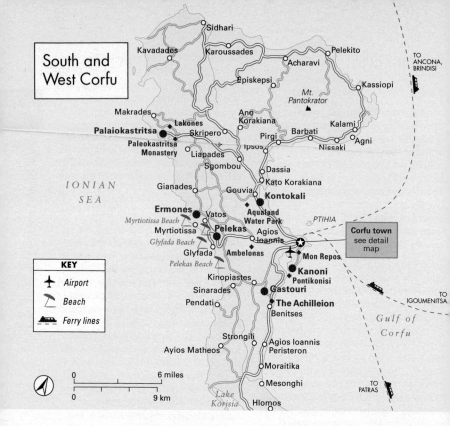

South and West Corfu

KEY

✈ Airport

⛱ Beach

🚢 Ferry lines

---

off, for the runway's end is just a few yards away from the tables. In between refreshments and seafood nibbles you can lounge on the adjacent beach, watch the activity among the small boats in the harbor, visit the Vlacherena Monastery, take a caïque to Mouse Island, or even stroll across the causeway (directly under the flightpath!) to the far shore. **Known for:** airplane watching; seaside setting; good selection of Greek and international wines. $ *Average main: €12* ✉ *Vlacherena* ☎ *26610/46191.*

The Achilleion and Gastouri
Αχιλλείον και Γαστούρι

19 km (12 miles) southwest of Corfu Town.

GETTING HERE AND AROUND
The local blue bus (line No. 10) departs daily from Platia San Rocco in Corfu Town for Gastouri and the Achilleion about every two hours (check with the ticket window at Platia San Rocco for the exact schedule). Return times are approximately 20 minutes after arrival times; round-trip fare is €3—buy your return ticket at the same time as your outgoing one. A taxi costs about €20 (ask the driver for an approximate fare before entering the taxi).

Sights

Achilleion

CASTLE/PALACE | Built in the late 19th century as a retreat for Empress Elizabeth of Austria, this is the most popular tourist attraction in Corfu and remains a monument of 19th-century historicism. After she was assassinated in 1898, Kaiser Wilhelm II bought the villa and lived in it until the outbreak of World War I, during which time the Achilleion was used by French and Serbian troops as a military hospital. After the armistice, the Greek government received it as a spoil of war. For a time it was a casino. Today it's a museum, but not a terribly inspiring one. The vulgar fresco called *Achilles in His Chariot,* behind a window on the upper level, tells you all you need to know about the empress's taste in pseudo-classical art. More appealing is the terrace, with a number of 19th-century statues, the best of which is *The Dying Achilles.* ✉ *Gastouri* ☎ *2661/56210* 🌐 *www.achillion-corfu.gr* 🎟 *€10.*

Restaurants

Klimataria

$$ | **SEAFOOD** | Just steps from the quayside of Benitses harbor, where fishermen land their daily catch, Klimataria is naturally the village favorite for seafood. Diners may kick off with marinated anchovy filets and white taramosalata, continue with fried squid, sardines, or prawns, or choose a fish cooked in a casserole, like spicy local speciality *bourdeto.* **Known for:** its location in Benitses' loveliest traditional building; locally sourced fresh produce; bianco, a casserole unique to the island, made here with the catch of the day. [$] *Average main: €15* ✉ *Harbour Square, Benitses* ☎ *26610/71201* 🌐 *www.klimataria-restaurant.gr.*

★ **Taverna Tripa**

$$$ | **GREEK** | **FAMILY** | This famous taverna (touristy but very quaint) in the charming hill village of Kinopiastes has been in business since 1936 and is still run by the same family. The fixed-price menu includes all the food and wine. **Known for:** gargantuan quantities of food and unlimited house wine; outstanding Greek nights with live music; popular with famous visitors. [$] *Average main: €35* ✉ *Kinopiastes* ✥ *2 km (1 mile) west of Gastouri* ☎ *26610/56333* 🌐 *tripas.gr* ⏰ *No lunch.*

Hotels

San Stefano Archontiko

$ | **RENTAL** | To stay in this family house is to experience the lifestyle of Corfu's Venetian aristocracy. **Pros:** secluded off-road location; sizeable infinity pool in lovely surroundings; a short drive to the stylish coffee bars and quality restaurants around Benitses Harbor. **Cons:** bathrooms are not en-suite so only suitable for a block booking of family or friends; no air conditioning due to heritage status (fans supplied instead); nearby beaches are narrow and shingly. [$] *Rooms from: €120* ✉ *San Stefano, Benitses* ☎ *6985/030290* 🌐 *www.sanstefanoestate.com* ⏰ *Closed Nov.–Apr.* 🛏 *5 rooms* 🍴 *No meals.*

Pelekas Πέλεκας

11 km (7 miles) northwest of Gastouri, 13 km (8 miles) west of Corfu Town.

Inland from the coast at Glyfada is Pelekas, an attractive hilltop village that overflows with tourists because of its much-touted lookout point, called **Kaiser's Throne,** a rocky hilltop with spectacular views of the entire island and sea beyond. German Kaiser Wilhelm II enjoyed the sunset here when not relaxing at Achilleion Palace.

GETTING HERE AND AROUND

The local blue bus (line No. 11) has a regular all-day service from San Rocco Square for Pelekas, starting at 7 am, with the last bus at 10 pm (reduced services on weekends). In high season, the green

KTEL bus has two morning departures for Glyfada, at 9 and 11 am, from the bus terminal between the town center and the airport. A taxi from Corfu Town to the Kaiser's Throne costs about €40 and will save you about 20 minutes' travel time.

Sights

Aqualand Water Park

AMUSEMENT PARK/WATER PARK | FAMILY | This giant, overpriced water theme park could be viewed as yet another example of how tourist-related developments are spoiling Corfu's lovely old landscapes, or you might see it as a great place to let your kids have a few hours of fun in the third-largest wave pool in the world. There are slides, rides, pools, playgrounds, restaurants and snack stands (food is mediocre in both), and stores everywhere you look, plus lots of noise. It's located mid-island, on the main road to Glyfada, near Ayios Ioannis and can be reached by a number of different bus services, the easiest being the No. 8 Afra-Ayios Ioannis Blue Bus from San Rocco Square. ⊠ *National Pelekas highway, Agios Ioannis* ☎ *26610/58351* ⊕ *www.aqualand-corfu.com* ⊠ *€24* ⊘ *Closed Nov.–May.*

Beaches

Glyfada Beach

BEACH—SIGHT | Greeks have voted Glyfada Beach one of the top 10 in the country, and it's easy to see why when you visit this wide stretch of fine, golden sand. The central area, which is dominated by the giant Grand Glyfada hotel, has a number of funky beach bars that are more places to see and be seen. Here, the beach is highly organized, with rows of sun beds and umbrellas, sometimes rented from the nearest establishment. The northern end is more laid-back and has a small hotel, the Glyfada Beach hotel. If you've had enough of the sun, you can find shade among the trees that back the beach. A choice of water sports is available for the active, but swimmers should be aware of the strong undertow. **Amenities:** food and drink; lifeguards; parking; showers; water sports. **Best for:** partiers; swimming. ⊠ *Glyfada* ✛ *3 km (2 miles) west of Pelekas.*

Myrtiotissa Beach

BEACH—SIGHT | The writer Lawrence Durrell described Myrtiotissa as "the loveliest beach in the world." This statement may be hyperbolic, but few would argue that the strand is right up there with the best in Greece. Today, the beach is little changed from Durrell's time on Corfu in the 1930s, due to poor access keeping development at bay—there is a small kiosk for snacks and drinks and umbrellas to rent. Most visitors park and walk down the steep road. The southern end of the beach, sheltered from view by rocks, is designated for nudists only, while at the more open northern end swimsuits are the norm. The sand is fine and golden. The sea can be rough with currents—it's only for experienced snorkelers. A small rustic restaurant stands a few minutes' walk from the far end of the beach. Another minute's walk takes you to a monastery, dedicated to the Virgin of the Myrtles, hence the name. **Amenities:** food and drink **Best for:** nudists; snorkeling. ⊠ *Pelekas* ✛ *5 km (3 miles) north of Pelekas.*

Pelekas Beach

BEACH—SIGHT | FAMILY | Pelekas Beach could be two separate strands, and indeed there are two access roads down the long, steep hill. The busy southern section is overlooked by the huge Mayor Pelekas Monastery hotel complex with its satellite bars and restaurants. As you walk north, the development dwindles, and at the far northern end, the beach still possesses an atmosphere of the 1970s when it was the haunt of hippies. Most amenities, such as sun beds and water sports, are clustered in the vicinity of the hotel. **Amenities:** food and drink;

lifeguards; showers; water sports. **Best for:** sunset; walking. ⊠ *Pelekas*.

🍽 Restaurants

Pink Panther

$ | PIZZA | FAMILY | Don't be put off by the name—this is the real deal for Italian and Greek cuisine. It's most famous for pizza, hand-made in front of you from the base up, and cooked in a traditional wood-fired oven. **Known for:** exquisite pizza; vertiginous sea view; dining on airy terraces. Ⓢ *Average main: €12* ⊠ *Main Street* ✛ *At the west side of the village, on the Glyfada road* ☎ *26610/94360*.

Spiros and Vasilis

$$ | FRENCH | This restaurant, hidden from the road on farmland belonging to the Polymeris family, is something of a surprise because the menu is not Greek but classically French. The owner/chef, born in Corfu, worked for many years in Paris restaurants and is particularly adept with steaks. **Known for:** exceptional steaks, sourced from organic local meat; classic frogs' legs; stylish and sophisticated dining in lovely country garden. Ⓢ *Average main: €18* ⊠ *Agios Ioannis* ✛ *9 km (6 miles) west of Corfu Town on road to Pelekas* ☎ *26610/52552*, ⊕ *www.facebook.com/spirosvasilisrestaurant* ⊘ *Closed Nov.–Apr.*

🛏 Hotels

Levant Hotel

$ | B&B/INN | Located at the top of Pelekas Hill, next to the Kaiser's Throne lookout, this small hotel offers balconied guest rooms with breathtaking views (and sunsets) across silver-green olive groves to the shimmering Ionian Sea. Built in 1989, the Levant has a subdued, neoclassical look enlivened with touches of traditional Corfiot style. **Pros:** great views; personable service; good in-house restaurant with terrace. **Cons:** area particularly busy with tour groups; restaurant is open to nonresidents; quite a long

walk to reach Pelekas village. Ⓢ *Rooms from: €75* ⊠ *Pelekas* ✛ *Near Kaiser's Throne* ☎ *26610/94230* ⊕ *levantcorfu.com* ⊘ *Closed Oct.–Easter* ⇆ *27 rooms* ⊙❙ *Free breakfast*.

★ Pelecas Country Club

$$ | B&B/INN | Some say this small, luxury hotel can be a bit snobbish; others insist that it lets you experience true Corfiot tradition in a unique setting: an old family mansion. **Pros:** lovely rooms and flower gardens; all rooms have a kitchen or kitchenette; quiet and traffic-free location. **Cons:** you need a car to get anywhere; country rather than seashore location; not for visitors who like modern, snazzy decor. Ⓢ *Rooms from: €150* ⊠ *Pelekas* ☎ *26610/52918* ⊕ *www.country-club.gr* ⇆ *10 rooms* ⊙❙ *Free breakfast*.

🛍 Shopping

The Witch House

CRAFTS | Harry Potter would feel right at home in The Witch House, where every single item is made by multitalented sisters Katerina and Lakshen. Artifacts range from stoneware sculptures to "Phos" jewelry, which combines crystals with precious metals, and from witch-motif key rings to hand-sculpted ceramics glazed in subtle turquoise. ⊠ *Main St.*

Ermones Έρμονες

8 km (5 miles) north of Pelekas.

On the coast, 8 km (5 miles) north of Pelekas lies the small, low-key resort of Ermones, with pebbly sand beaches, heavily wooded cliffs, and a backdrop of green mountains. The Ropa River, which drains the vast central plain, flows into the Ionian Sea here; according to local legend, Nausicaa was rinsing her laundry at the river mouth when Odysseus came ashore, as told by Homer in *The Odyssey*. A short walk inland you find the island's only golf course; beyond that, the vast Ropa plain extends, a paradise for hikers, bird-watchers, and botanists. Also to the rear of the resort is the mountain village of Vatos, with its stunning views and traditional, picturesque neighborhoods.

Sights

★ Theotoky Estate

TOUR—SIGHT | The Theotoky Estate stretches over a long saddleback hill covered with pines and olives, while its vineyards and pastures blanket the adjacent valley floor. The boutique winery produces its own cold-pressed olive oil from over 4,000 ecologically managed trees, as well as the famed Theotoky wine, made from the farm's own grapes—it's one of the oldest and most respected estate-bottled vintages in Greece. Visit for a guided tour and tasting in the beautiful Venetian building where the wine is made and stored. Organic snacks are an optional extra, and the products are also for sale. You may book your tour in advance through the website. ✉ *Ropa* ✣ *Near Ermones* ☎ *6945/593016* 🌐 *www.theotoky.com.*

Restaurants

★ Ladokolo

$ | **GREEK** | **FAMILY** | Located in the depths of the countryside, Ladokolo is a magnet for locals and visitors in search of an authentic dining experience. Expect first-class charcoal grills, with mushrooms and vegetables on the menu if you don't eat meat. **Known for:** grills served in a grease-proof paper parcel rather than on a plate; lamb chops; peaceful environment in a characterful hamlet overlooking the Ropa Valley. [$] *Average main: €9* ✉ *Temploni Village Square* ✣ *6 km (4 miles) northeast of Ermones* ☎ *26610/94195* ⏲ *Closed weekdays in winter.*

Navsika

$ | **GREEK** | **FAMILY** | On a shady terrace above Ermones Beach, Navsika showcases home-cooked Corfiot dishes such as pastitsada and rice-and-herb-stuffed tomatoes and peppers, as part of a very extensive Greek and international menu. The stunning outlook takes in the full sweep of Ermones Bay with its forest-cloaked rocky hillsides. **Known for:** stupendous sunsets; perfectly cooked steaks; local ice cream in a variety of flavors. [$] *Average main: €12* ✉ *Ermones Beach* ☎ *6970/859096* ⏲ *Closed Nov.–Apr.*

Tristrato

$ | **GREEK** | Set at a tree-shaded crossroads in the depths of the countryside, Tristrato was formerly an old wayhouse and still retains many of the building's original features. It now functions as a contemporary Greek gastropub where the proprietor brings you a variety of whatever they've got cooking, generally a choice between meat or fish mezes with salads and dips. **Known for:** food that quirkily combines local cooking style with exotic flavors; soothing rural outdoor dining with nice country view; cozy, publike interior. [$] *Average main: €8* ✉ *Giannades–Marmaro crossroads, Giannades* ✣ *3 km (2 miles) north of Ermones* ☎ *26610/51580.*

Hotels

★ Atlantic Grand Mediterraneo Resort

$$ | **RESORT** | This beachside resort, made up of low-rise buildings and bungalows cascading down a hillside, is now one of the most luxurious on Corfu's west coast. **Pros:** gorgeous scenery combining mountain and sea; very spacious rooms; luxurious spa for the use of guests. **Cons:** the beach is not Corfu's finest; the unfit and physically challenged may have difficulties with the terrain; no children under 16. [$] *Rooms from: €175* ✉ *Ermones* ☎ *26610/95381* 🌐 *www.atlanticahotels.com* ⏲ *Closed Nov.–Apr.* 🛏 *279 rooms* 🍴 *Free breakfast.*

🎭 Nightlife

Dizi Bar

BARS/PUBS | With its extensive shady deck terrace, Dizi Bar is a favorite summer rendezvous for locals. Many nights feature live music or DJ-led dancing until late. Call owner Kostas to find out what's happening and when. ✉ *Ermones* ☎ *26610/95080.*

🏃 Activities

Corfu Golf Club

GOLF | It's been called golf's best-kept secret, and, indeed, Corfu Golf Club combines a superb test of a golfer's skills with an outstanding natural environment. The course, in the delightfully rural Ropa valley and surrounded by lushly wooded mountains, was designed in the 1970s by the famous Swiss-based architect Donald Harradine, who blended the natural features of the landscape with man-made hazards to create a course that can be enjoyed by all categories of golfers. Players enter on footbridges crossing the Ropa River, and walk among lakes and streams and between copses and avenues of indigenous trees. Nature lovers may spot otters, turtles, wild birds such as herons and kingfishers, and other native creatures. Back at the clubhouse, attractively built of local stone, the atmosphere is laid-back and welcoming, and the pro shop well stocked. A restaurant serves snacks and meals at reasonable prices. ✉ *Ermones* ☎ *26610/94220* ⊕ *www.corfugolfclub. com* 🅔 *€35 for 9 holes, €55 for 18 holes* 🏌 *18 holes. 6802 yards. Par 72.*

Kontokali Κοντόκαλι

6 km (4 miles) north of Corfu Town.

Kontokali is best known for providing the main entry point to Corfu's biggest marina, a delightful place to stroll and admire the yachts, especially in the evening.

Behind the marina stands a large roofless structure, built by the Venetians in the early 18th century as part of their shipyards. To the south of the marina lies the island's main cricket ground, incorporating a croquet field. The northern arm of the bay comprises the promontory of Kommeno, where expensive villas and large hotels are set among the trees. Tucked in the corner of the bay, on a tiny island at the approach to Kommeno, is the church of Ipapanti, one of Corfu's most picturesque spots.

GETTING HERE AND AROUND

A few kilometers north of Corfu Town, the village of Kontokali squeezes between the main road and the shoreline of Govino Bay. The area is heavily commercialized, but the village, which stretches along its own road parallel with the main one, is quiet and residential.

🍴 Restaurants

★ Etrusco

$$$ | **ECLECTIC** | The Botrini family restaurant is considered one of the best in Greece (the Athens branch has a Michelin star), and it certainly can be classed as among the most inventive, offering a menu of Italian- and Greek-inspired dishes. Chef Ettore Botrini demonstrates his flawless technique with a big blast of creativity on the molecular gastronomy front. **Known for:** elaborate tasting menus with wine pairings; homemade pappardelle with duck; desserts, including upside-down orange pie. 🅢 *Average main: €40* ✉ *Kato Korakiana ⊹ 1 km (½ mile) west of Dassia* ☎ *26610/93342* ⊕ *www.etrusco.gr* 🕙 *Closed Oct.–Apr.*

Fish Taverna Roula

$$ | **SEAFOOD** | Choose from whatever fish is fresh that day—it could be sea bream, mullet, sole, squid, or snapper—or choose a steak or chicken filet. Sit on the waterfront terrace and watch the boats heading in and out of the marina. **Known for:** seafood from their own fishing boats;

traditional fish stews bourdetto and bianco; magical marina view. $ *Average main: €16* ✉ *Kontokali* ☎ *26610/91832* ⊕ *www.facebook.com/roula.fishtaverna.*

Gerekos

$$ | SEAFOOD | One of the island's longest-established and most famous fish restaurants, Gerekos pulls its catch daily from the family's own boats. The choice varies each day according to the season, but the friendly staff will show you what's available and guide your choice. **Known for:** octopus and other fish grilled on charcoal; secret-recipe fish soup; father-son team continuing a family tradition. $ *Average main: €20* ✉ *Kontokali* ☎ *26610/91281.*

Taverna Limeri

$ | GREEK | Sitting in the "V" formed by the two streets in the village of Kato Korakiana, this taverna is where locals come to dine on wonderfully prepared local dishes. It's a good place to order several small plates and share a variety of tastes, like *gigantes* (giant beans stewed with tomato) or pork croquettes in cranberry sauce. **Known for:** exceptional house wines; beautiful steaks with a choice of classic sauces; village atmosphere off the tourist trail. $ *Average main: €10* ✉ *Kato Korakiana* ✛ *1 km (½ mile) west of Dassia* ☎ *26610/97576* ⊘ *No lunch.*

 Hotels

Kontokali Bay Resort and Spa

$$ | HOTEL | This hotel-bungalow complex opened its doors in 1971 with a clean, modern look on a smallish sandy beach with a more relaxed feel than its primary competitor a few miles to the north. **Pros:** great spa; lovely grounds on seafront; contemporary decor. **Cons:** the surrounding area is rather bland; large and somewhat anonymous; the beach is not Corfu's finest. $ *Rooms from: €200* ✉ *Nissi Gerekou* ☎ *26610/90500, 26610/99000* ⊕ *www.kontokalibay.com*

⊘ *Closed mid-Oct.–Easter* ⇥ *261 rooms* ⏐◯⏐ *Free breakfast.*

Paleokastritsa
Παλαιοκαστρίτσα

21 km (13 miles) north of Pelekas, 25 km (16 miles) northwest of Corfu Town.

To quote one recent traveler: "I'd rather go to Paleokastritsa than to Heaven." Considered by many to be the site of Homer's city of the Phaeacians, this truly spectacular territory of grottoes, cliffs, and turquoise waters has a big rock named Kolovri, which the ancient Greeks said resembled the ship that brought Ulysses home. The jaw-dropping natural beauty of Paleo, as Corfiots call it, has brought hotels, tavernas, bars, and shops to the hillsides above the bays, and the beaches swarm with hordes of people on day trips from Corfu Town. You can explore the idyllic coves in peace with a pedal boat or small motorboat rented at the crowded main beach. There are also boat operators that go around to the prettiest surrounding beaches, especially those to the south, mostly inaccessible except from the sea; ask the skipper to let you off at a beach that appeals to you and to pick you up on a subsequent trip. Many visitors also enjoy a trip on the "Yellow Submarine," a glass-bottom boat that also runs night excursions (reservations are recommended—you can book at the Corfu Aquarium).

In the Paleokastritsa region, look for La Grotta bar, built grottolike into the rocks of a tiny cove. A mini-Acapulco, the high cliffs here tempt local youths to dive into the turquoise waters—great entertainment as you sip your cold beer or cocktail.

GETTING HERE AND AROUND

Depending on the day and the season, the green KTEL bus has four to six daily departures for Paleokastritsa from Corfu

Barely changed from the days of Homer, the Paleokastritsa region of Corfu is one of the most achingly beautiful landscapes in Greece.

Town's bus terminal on Avramiou near the New Port (the daily 9 am departure is the fastest and most convenient). The trip takes about 45 minutes. A taxi from Corfu Town to Paleokastritsa costs about €50.

👁 Sights

Corfu Aquarium

ZOO | FAMILY | Although you might spot fish and other sea life when swimming in one of Paleokastritsa's stunning coves, you won't see the diversity of aquatic creatures and assortment of reptiles as on display at the Corfu Aquarium. Located on the seashore at the foot of Paleokastritsa's monastery headland, the aquarium is home to a large number of species—crustaceans, starfish, and sea snails as well as fish—indigenous to Corfu's waters and the wider Mediterranean. The thrilling reptile room boasts boas, pythons, iguanas, and even a crocodile. The ticket price includes a very informative guided tour lasting around 30 minutes. You can book a concessionary dual ticket to the aquarium and on the Yellow Submarine tours at this location. The aquarium has its own beachside café for a drink after the tour. ☎ *26630/41339* ⊕ *www.corfuaquarium.com* ✉ *€6* ⏱ *Closed Nov.–Feb.*

Lakones

ARCHAEOLOGICAL SITE | The village of Lakones, built on the steep mountain behind the Paleokastritsa Monastery, looks rather forbidding, but tourists flock there for the view. Kaiser Wilhelm was among many famous people who would make the ascent to enjoy the magnificent panorama of Paleokastritsa's coves from the cafés at Bella Vista, just beyond the village. In the village center is a small folk museum showcasing old photographs of the village. From nearby Krini you can climb up to the ruins of the 13th-century **Angelokastro**, a fortress built by a despot of Epirus during his brief rule over Corfu. On many occasions during the medieval period, the fort sheltered Corfiots from attack by Turkish invaders. Look for the chapel and caves, which served as

The Corfu Trail

The Corfu Trail is a 220-km (137-mile) trekking route that begins at the island's southern tip and takes a winding course to its northernmost point. Though a relatively small island, Corfu possesses a diversity of scenery that astounds, and the walk—which requires around 10 days to complete in full—takes in many of its varied landscapes. Not only does each day offer a distinctive character, but even on a single day's walk the terrain changes constantly. At every corner, a new scene pleases the eye: a stunning view, a little church, a grove of ancient olive trees, a meadow carpeted with wild flowers. The trail takes in wild beaches, juniper-forested dunes, dense oak woodland, a karst plateau where nomad cattle roam, deep gorges, wetlands, mountain summits, and bucolic plains. The hand of modern man hardly encroaches, and only old monasteries, ruined olive presses, picturesque villages, and ancient fortresses intrude on nature. On-trail accommodation and daily luggage transfer may be booked through Aperghi Travel *(see Tours)*. For more information on the trail, see ⊕ *www. thecorfutrail.com.*

sanctuaries and hiding places. ✛ *5 km (3 miles) northeast of Paleokastritsa.*

Paleokastritsa Monastery
HISTORIC SITE | Paleokastritsa Monastery, a 17th-century structure, is built on the site of an earlier monastery, among terraced gardens overlooking the Ionian Sea. Its treasure is a 12th-century icon of the Virgin Mary, to whom the establishment is dedicated, and there's a small museum with some other early icons. Note the Tree of Life motif on the ceiling. Be sure to visit the inner courtyard (go through the church), built on the edge of the cliff and looking down a precipitous cliff to the placid green coves and coastline to the south. There's a small gift shop on the premises. ✉ *On northern headland* 🖙 *Donations accepted.*

Restaurants

Taverna Elizabeth
$ | **GREEK** | **FAMILY** | Established in 1960 as one of the island's first out-of-town tavernas, this traditional village eatery offers food that is still cooked according to Grandmother Elizabeth's original recipes, by her granddaughter … Elizabeth. **Known for:** hearty and generously portioned local casserole dishes; rooster pastitsada; burly in-house red wine. $ *Average main: €11* ✉ *Doukades Village Square* ✛ *4 km (3 miles) east of Paleokastritsa* 📞 *26630/41728.*

Vrachos
$ | **GREEK** | The stunning view from this restaurant overlooking the cliff-enclosed bay at Paleokastrisa will make you want to linger. The menu offers a bit of everything, though lobster with linguine id the signature house dish. **Known for:** lobster linguine; prime location on Corfu's most famous bay; very polished service. $ *Average main: €14* ✉ *Paleokastritsa* 📞 *26630/41233* ⊕ *www.vrachosp.gr* 🕐 *Closed Nov.–Easter.*

☕ Coffee and Quick Bites

Corfu Dolce
$ | **CAFÉ** | If Dolce is not the top patisserie-gelateria in Corfu, it's certainly among the very best. The store distributes its own brand of ice cream islandwide, and its cakes are made on the premises. **Known for:** more than 40 flavors of ice

cream; overlooks one of the island's best views; cool mood music. $ Average main: €5 ⊠ Lakones Main St. ☎ 26630/49278 ⊕ www.corfudolce.com ▤ No credit cards.

Emeral Café and Pastry Shop

$ | CAFÉ | FAMILY | Directly on the busy national road that connects Corfu Town with Paleokastritsa, Emeral is a very popular place to stop for coffee, a sweet or savory pastry, or an ice cream. You'll have a hard time choosing from the variety of cream cakes, chocolate delicacies, and cookies in the display cases, to eat in or take away. **Known for:** fantastic cakes; variety of breads baked on the premises; great coffee. $ Average main: €3 ⊠ Km 10, Paleokastritsa National Rd., Korakiana ☎ 26610/91780 ⊕ www.emeral.gr.

Veatriki's Bar

$ | CAFÉ | FAMILY | It's rare these days to be able to share the proprietors' lunch, but this is what you get if you order Veatriki's "Dish of the Day." Alternatively, you may choose from an extensive menu of snacks and light meals, along with cakes and ice cream from local producer Corfu Dolce. The tiny shop doubles as village store and post office, while the outdoor tables adorn the settlement's lovely main alleyway. **Known for:** authentic home cooking; gorgeous traffic-free location; at the center of one of Corfu's prettiest villages. $ Average main: €5 ⊠ Makrades Village Square ☎ 26630/49301.

 Hotels

★ Akrotiri Beach Hotel

$ | HOTEL | Few hotels in Corfu are so superbly positioned to take in its natural splendor the way the Akrotiri is, which lords it over a paradisical little peninsula. **Pros:** the location could not be better; wonderful swimming in the bay below; fabulous view from all of of the rooms. **Cons:** public areas look a bit tired; road outside carries heavy traffic; a long walk to the main beach of Paleokastritsa.

$ Rooms from: €120 ☎ 26630/41237 ⊕ www.akrotiri-beach.com ⊗ Closed Nov.–Apr. ⤳ 125 rooms ⫶⊘⫶ Free breakfast.

★ Casa Lucia

$ | RENTAL | FAMILY | There are far grander places to stay on Corfu but few with as much quiet, unpretentious charm as Casa Lucia, where the stone buildings of an old olive press have been converted into guest cottages and smaller studios. **Pros:** gorgeous gardens and pool; all units have a kitchen and terrace; family-friendly with no traffic. **Cons:** fairly basic bathrooms in studios; not by the sea; while two tavernas are a short walk away, you need a car for shops and sights. $ Rooms from: €60 ⊠ Corfu–Paleokastritsa road ⊹ 13 km (8 miles) northwest of Corfu Town ☎ 26610/91419 ⊕ www.casa-lucia-corfu.com ⤳ 8 cottages ⫶⊘⫶ No meals.

Fundana Villas

$ | RENTAL | The charming suites and bungalows at this small hilltop lodging are built into and around a 17th-century stone-and-mortar Venetian storehouse; each has been turned into a comfortable hideaway. **Pros:** surrounded by lovely gardens and olive and orange groves; very quiet, traffic-free location; beautiful pool. **Cons:** short on in-room facilities; you need transport to access restaurants and shops; not by the sea. $ Rooms from: €75 ⊠ Km 15, Paleokastritsa National Rd. ⊹ 3 km (2 miles) east of Paleokastritsa ☎ 26630/22532 ⊕ www.fundanavillas. com ⊗ Closed Nov.–Mar. ⤳ 12 rooms ⫶⊘⫶ Free breakfast.

★ The Merchant's House

$$ | B&B/INN | Owners Mark and Saskia have created their luxurious B&B from one of Perithia's former ruins, with a sensitive and stylish renovation of the old stone structure. **Pros:** perfect for lovers of nature; warm and helpful personal service; homemade sourdough bread and jams for breakfast. **Cons:** no swimming pool due to heritage surroundings; the

Kefalonia and Zakynthos

LEFKADA

Vasiliki ○

KALAMOS

MEGANISI

ARKOUDI   KASTOS

Dafnoudi Beach   **Fiskardo** ●   ATOKOS

Assos ◆

Myrtos Beach

Paliki Peninsula ◆   ITHAKI

Petani Bay Beach

Ammos Beach   **Sami** ●   *Antisamos Beach*

Lixouri ●

Argostolion ●   *Gulf of Patras*

Xi Beach   **Lassi** ◆   **Mount**

Vardiani Island ◆   **Omala**   **Ainos**

Makris Gialos   **Valley**

Beach   **KEFALONIA**

I O N I A N   I S L A N D S

Ionian Sea

Blue Caves ◆   *Agios Nikolaos Beach*

Agios Nikolaos ●   *Makris Gialos Beach*

Navagio Beach   ◆   *Tsilivi Beach*

(Shipwreck Beach)   **The North**

Porto Vromi   ○ **Exo Chora**   **Zakynthos Town** ●

Vasilikos Peninsula

Laganas ●

Kiliomenos ○   **Vasilikos** ○   *Banana Beach*

ZAKYNTHOS   **Vasilikos** ◆   *Lagana*

Marathonisi Island   *Bay*

0 ————— 20 mi
0 ————— 20 km

---

village, though isolated, can be busy with day-trippers; hair-raising drive to get here. ⓢ *Rooms from: €150* ☎ *26630/98444* ⊕ *www.merchantshousecorfu.com* ⊘ *Closed Nov.–Mar.* ⇥ *5 rooms* ⦿ *Free breakfast.*

Kefalonia

65 miles (106 km) south of Corfu.

What saved lush, mountainous Kefalonia, the largest of the Ionian islands, from the first waves of package tourism in the 1960s is likely that which drove the need for it in the first place. When the earthquakes of 1953 ripped through its lands, destroying almost every home, four-fifths of the island's population migrated, leaving behind just 25,000 people. Even today there aren't that many more here.

Money came in to rebuild the island, but in place of Venetian mansions and baroque flourishes, what arose from the ruins were neoclassical imposters, functional and modern. That is to say Kefalonia is not Corfu. It is rougher and readier, yet some would say more charming for it. To explore its mountainous spine or drive the corkscrew roads of the northern and far-western coasts, curving past untouched beaches, lonely monasteries, and picturesque villages, is a delight to match any found in this island chain.

History here dates back long before the Venetians arrived to bring culture, color, and their distinctive architecture to the island in 1500. The first settlers are thought to have arrived in the 10th century BC. Just five centuries later, Kefalonia was divided into city states, each with their own currency and culture.

The acropolis at Sami (though mostly built over by the Romans) is a fantastic relic of this period, while the calling cards of successive rulers, including the Cyclopean walls of the Mycenean era, Roman graves, and Byzantine monasteries, still scatter the island.

After the Venetians, who were ousted by the French, it was the turn of the British to leave their mark here, in the roads and bridges that still exist today. Even the Second World War, with its occupiers and atrocities, couldn't take away what makes this land special. Then, just as the island was emerging from the darkness, the earth gave way beneath it. Kefalonia took decades to bounce back, heralding with it the belated arrival of the resorts, mushrooming along the island's southwest shores in a tidy cluster below capital Argostoli, well confined and easily ignored.

In truth, Kefalonia still flies under the radar a little when compared with the other Ionian islands. The beaches may be packed in summer but mass tourism just isn't as pervasive here as in Corfu or Zakynthos. Sometimes, when gazing out from the cliffs of the Paliki, or tasting the wines of the Omala Valley, or strolling the fir-covered slopes of Greece's only island national park, it's even hard to remember it ever arrived at all.

GETTING HERE AND AROUND
BUS
Island capital Argostoli is the main KTEL bus depot, but you're missing out if you rely solely on public transportation. Only the airport, the resort-heavy Lassi, and the main port towns (Sami, Poros) have daily services in summer; other lines, including Fiskardo, Skala, Agia Efemia, Katelios, Divarata, and Svoronata, run maybe once or twice a day, with no buses usually operating on Sundays. Tickets can be bought on board and start at €2.

BOAT
Two in-island car-ferry companies operate between Argostoli and Lixouri (30 mins), on the western Paliki Peninsula. They typically depart every half-hour during summer (7 am–10:30 pm; May–Sept.) and less frequently across the rest of the year. Tickets (from €2.60 per passenger; €5.30 per car, including driver) can be purchased on board.

CONTACTS Kefalonia Ferries. ☎ 267/1029–514 ⊕ vikentiosdamodos.gr. **Ioniansea Ferries.** ☎ 267/1091–280 ⊕ www.ionian-seaferries.gr/en.

CAR AND SCOOTER
Because of the limited bus services, it's wise to rent your own car or scooter, though be aware that scooter hire (even for a 50cc bike) in Greece requires a specialist license; a regular car driving license is insufficient. Driving here is pretty laid-back, certainly when compared with Athens. The main dangers are from other rental-car drivers, who increase a hundredfold in July and August, and the odd rock slide caused by minor earth tremors. Coastal roads, especially, can be narrow and winding, with rogue goats an occasional menace, but go slow, use your horn, and you'll be fine. Argostoli is the busiest center and is best avoided at rush hour. Cars drive on the right-hand side.

Motorcyclists and scooter drivers will be fined if caught riding without a helmet.

CONTACTS Hertz. ☎ 210/6264–000 ⊕ www.hertz.com/p/car-rental/greece. **Kefalonia2Ride.** ✉ 29 Miaouli St., Sami ☎ 26740/22970 ⊕ www.kefalonia2ride. rentals.

TAXI
Taxis aren't cheap on the island, and with little use of taxi meters it's best to book ahead to confirm the lowest price. Fares soon mount up. A ride from Argostoli to the northern tip of Fiskardo (50 km) might cost as much as €75, while the 8 km journey to the airport is €20. Expect

to pay from around €6 for a short 2 km hop.

TOURS

Outdoor Kefalonia

EXCURSIONS | This outfitter has hiking, coasteering, abseiling, SUP, kite-surfing, and canyoning tours. They also have their own hiking refuge near Mount Ainos. ✉ *Ampatielou 4, Argostolion* ☎ *69799/87611* ⊕ *outdoorkefalonia.com.*

Argostolion and Lassi

26 km (16 miles) from Sami.

As both the island's capital and the setting for Louis de Bernières' wildly successful novel, *Captain Corelli's Mandolin*, Argostolion's name carries more weight than most on Kefalonia. Those expecting lemon-coloured Venetian *archondiká* mansions glimmering in the crystal-blue waterfront will be disappointed however. These met the same fate as the rest of the island during the earthquakes of 1953, and what replaced them is decidedly pragmatic: blockish cement replicas better able to resist the aftershocks.

Yet the town is not without a life of its own. The vast palazzo of Platia Vallianou, named after a Kefalonia-born 19th-century shipping magnate, is a particularly lively spot. Its café-bar terraces fill quickly in the evening and sway to the strains of wandering *kantadoroi*, while by day it offers respite from the bustle of Lithostroto shopping street, to the south. At the far end of Lithostroto stands the city's bell tower, which has fantastic views but is sadly closed to visitors these days.

Many drift through Argostolion for the use of its port. This has regular car ferries connecting it to Lixouri and the beaches and wilderness of the Paliki Peninsula across the bay. The coast south of the city is well known for its shoreline, with the majority of the island's ever-growing resorts confined to the sands around the village of Lassi and below.

Sights

★ Agios Georgios Castle

CASTLE/PALACE | Fortifications have stood atop this hill since the Byzantine era, though the ruins of this castle date from the early 16th century. When the Venetians finally prized it from Turkish control in 1500, after a wearying three-month siege, they levelled the building in the process. Reconstruction took some 40 years, whereupon it became the administrative center for the island until the mid-1800s. By then, the rise of Argostolion had made the port town a better option. Shortly after, the castle was abandoned entirely when earthquakes tore the region apart. Little was done to rebuild it and subsequent historic tremors have all contributed to its current state. While the sprawling grounds offer incredible views over the island, there is little to explain what you're seeing, leaving visitors to pick over its bones largely unguided. A tiny village filled with a cluster of good tavernas lies at the foot of the hill. ✉ *Livathou, Agios Georgios Hill, Argostolion* ☎ *26710/27546* 💶 *€3* 🕙 *Closed Tues.*

Botanic Garden

MUSEUM | Created by the Focas-Cosmetatos Foundation, the Cephalonica Botanica lies a couple of kilometers south of the city center and offers a peaceful opportunity to study the island's rarer flora, which is at constant risk from forest fires and development. Like all attractions in town, it shuts early (2 pm). ✉ *South of Argostolion city center, Argostolion* ☎ *26710/26595* ⊕ *www.focas-cosmetatos.gr/main_en.html* 💶 *€5 (includes entry to Focas-Cosmetatos Foundation)* 🕙 *Closed Sun.*

Cave Hermitage of Agios Gerasimos

MUSEUM | Set on a hill above the nearby village of Lassi, this small chapel hides a

An aerial view of Agios Georgios Castle, which dates from the early 16th century; a series of earthquakes helped ensure, sadly, that it was never rebuilt.

narrow cave that is filled with offerings. This is said to be where Saint Gerasimos, patron saint of the island, lived in the mid-16th century before traveling to the nearby valley of Omala to rebuild its monastery. ⊠ *Lassi, Argostolion.*

De Bosset Bridge

BRIDGE/TUNNEL | The British occupation (1809–64) of Kefalonia transformed Argostolion, rebuilding its streets and beefing up the island's infrastructure. The crowning achievement of this is the bridge built in 1813 by Charles Philip De Bosset, a Swiss engineer in the employ of the British Army. Created to connect Argostoli to the village of Drapano, it reaches out across what was the Kouvatos Lagoon, a swampy area of land once rife with mosquitoes and malaria, that separates the Fanari Peninsula from the mainland. Its original wooden structure was recreated in stone in 1842 and has been reinforced over the years due to earthquake damage, yet it remains in service today. Part way across, look out for the "Kolona" obelisk rising out of the water, a gesture of thanks to the British erected in 1813 by the Kefalonian Parliament. Its inscription, "To the glory of the British Empire," was symbolically erased when the Greeks took back control of the island in 1865 and has repeatedly changed over the years according to who controls the island. The walk makes for a bracing, and now record-breaking, stroll since this was named the world's longest (690 m) stone sea bridge in 2018. ⊠ *Argostolion.*

Focas-Cosmetatos Foundation

MUSEUM | Established by three wealthy brothers in 1984, who turned their family home into a museum to display their personal collections of art, lithographs, coins, and furniture, this tiny museum is as eclectic as any hoarder's pile. Subjects veer from landscapes of the island by 19th-century British painters to an exhibition of photos documenting the effects of the 1953 earthquake. It's a worthy modern history of the island. ⊠ *1 Platia*

Vallianou, Argostolion ☎ *26710/26595* ⊕ *www.focas-cosmetatos.gr/main_ en.html* ✉ *€5 (includes admission to Botanic Garden)* ☾ *Closed Sun.*

Korgialenio History & Folklore Museum

MUSEUM | Squirrelled away to the right of stairs leading to the city library, what this small museum lacks in explanation it makes up for in diversity. Life-sized dioramas of 17th- and 18th-century island life, religious art, wood carvings rescued from derelict churches, embroidery, lithographs, furniture, and some rather excellent photographic studies of Argostolion pre- and post-earthquake make a visit worthwhile experience. ✉ *12 Ilia Zervou, Argostolion* ☎ *26710/28221* ✉ *€4* ☾ *Closed Sun.*

War Memorial & Museum for Acqui Division

MEMORIAL | In 1941, at the height of the Second World War, Greece was occupied by the Axis Powers. During this period Kefalonia was given over to the Italian Acqui Division to run. Two years later, when Italy surrendered to the Allies, German troops moved in to seize control and one of the great atrocities of this era played out. Italian general Antonio Gandin offered his troops a vote on whether to join or fight the Germans; they chose the latter, aided by local resistance, but quickly ran out of ammunition. A recorded 1,315 Italians fell in battle, but the worst was to come. The Italian troops had previously been placed under German command, so all soldiers that had resisted were considered deserters and ordered to be shot on sight. Those that had surrendered were ruthlessly executed, killed eight at a time in Argostolion's main square, though some escaped by being hidden by sympathetic islanders. A further 5,155 Italians died in the massacre, and 3,000 later perished when the German ship taking the island's Italian POWs to a concentration camp sank. Yet few outside Italy and Greece had heard of this atrocity until the publishing of Louis de Bernieres' novel *Captain Corelli's Mandolin*, whose tale touches upon the events—though it is widely disliked on Kefalonia for its portrayal of the Greek partisans. A memorial dedicated to the Italian soldiers that fell lies north of the city, near to the lighthouse. A tiny but moving exhibition-museum run by the Italo-Greco Association can also be found next to the St. Nikolaos Church (free; open 9 am–10:30 pm) in the center. ✉ *Argostolion* ☎ *69361/63802 (museum)* ☾ *Closed Oct.–May.*

Beaches

Makris Gialos Beach

BEACH—SIGHT | The golden-sand beaches surrounding Lassi can be notoriously busy. Access is easy and buses even run here from nearby Argostoli. It's the reason most of the island's resorts are clustered along this stretch of coast, meaning there will always be crowds. Makris Gialos is undeniably beautiful: a rocky collar of tall pine trees encloses the shore, which fades into pale, shallow azure waters ideal for families. Near its southern end, only a few rocks separates the near-identical adjacent beach of Platis Gialos, so you also get two for one. The facilities here are among the best on the island, and phalanxes of sun beds cover most areas not taken up by a volleyball court or bar. It can be quite noisy, though, and when the sun goes down a party atmosphere takes over. **Amenities:** sun beds and umbrellas; food and drink; lifeguard; showers; toilets; volleyball. **Best for:** families; watersports; parties; beach cocktails. ✉ *Lassi.*

Restaurants

Casa Grec

$ | **GREEK** | A charming garden terrace sets the mood here, with its warm terra-cotta tiles and white beams lit by glowing lanterns. Everything is just right. **Known for:** signature pork shanks that just melt off the bone; a nice outdoor terrace; friendly staff. $ *Average main: €14* ✉ *Stavrou Metaxa 12, Argostolion* ☎ *26710/24091.*

★ Il Borgo

$ | GREEK | As is the case with much of Kefalonia, many of its dining gems are found outside of the larger towns. Il Borgo lies in the lee of St. George's Castle, 15 minutes' drive south of Argostoli, and makes for a dramatic pit-stop. **Known for:** sweeping views down to the coast; amiable service; a memorable spot at sunset. $ *Average main: €14* ✉ *Travliata, Around 100m from the entrance to St. George's Castle* ☎ *26710/69800* ⊕ *ilborgo.gr.*

To Arxontiko (Το Αρχοντικό)

$ | GREEK | A stone-walled interior sets the scene for this family-run slice of traditional taverna cooking. The friendly owner is good for a suggestion or two, though the Kefalonian *kreatopita* (three-meat pie) is well worth sinking your teeth into. **Known for:** Greek comfort food at a good price; charming owners and service; a good people-watching spot. $ *Average main: €10* ✉ *Rizospaston 5, Argostolion* ☎ *26710/27213* ⊕ *www.facebook.com/arxontikokefalonia.*

☕ Coffee and Quick Bites

Farmout Vitamin Bar

$ | VEGETARIAN | This small organic market-cum-café sources from local farms across Kefalonia and dishes out tasty wraps, vegan burgers, and excellent homemade smoothies to those in the know. **Known for:** vegan and vegetarian snacks; gluten- and dairy-free options; heavenly veggie burgers. $ *Average main: €5* ✉ *Antoni Tritsi 37, Argostolion* ☎ *26710/26513* ⊕ *www.farmout.gr.*

🛏 Hotels

★ Kefalonia Grand Hotel

$$ | HOTEL | The city's starring boutique hotel has lost none of its power to charm. **Pros:** slickly appointed rooms and great service; nice views over the waterfront; good on-site restaurant. **Cons:** no parking on-site; the street below can be noisy; the tiny lift fills up fast. $ *Rooms from: €140* ✉ *Antoni Tritsi 82, Argostolion* ☎ *26710/24981* ⊕ *kefaloniagrand.gr* ☾ *Closed Nov.–Mar.* ⇄ *42 rooms (4 suites)* ⦿⃒ *Free breakfast.*

Thalassa Boutique Hotel Kefalonia

$$ | RESORT | Despite its name, this is more a resort than a boutique, though its small size (just 32 rooms) means it's a world away from many of the noisy affairs you'll find on this stretch of coast. **Pros:** good facilities and service; recent renovations have spruced up the garden and pool area; fine cocktails at the pool bar. **Cons:** Lassi is the most tourist-heavy part of the island; ten-minute walk to the beach; it's more a resort than a boutique hotel. $ *Rooms from: €145* ✉ *Lassi, Argostolion* ☎ *26710/27081* ⊕ *www.thalassahotel.gr* ☾ *Closed Nov.–Mar.* ⇄ *32 rooms (6 suites)* ⦿⃒ *Free breakfast.*

▽ Nightlife

Bee's Knees

BARS/PUBS | A gloriously friendly cocktail bar with an innovative list of ever-changing creations (from around €8.50), a penchant for prohibition-era slang, and good music. The terrace fills up quickly, so get there early, ask the waiter for their recommendation, and while away the evening people-watching on the square. ✉ *Rizospaston 8, Argostolion* ☎ *26710/28059* ⊕ *beeskneesthebar.com.*

Draught Grill & Beer House

BREWPUBS/BEER GARDENS | In truth, the selection here is nothing more than you'd find in most bars on mainland Europe, with a standard mix of familar Belgian brews by the bottle and a half-dozen mass-market lagers and German pilsners on tap. But in Kefalonia, where the ubiquitous (and tasteless) Mythos beer represents the sum of most bar owner's ambitions, it makes for an exotic find. The burgers aren't bad, either. ✉ *Rizospaston 12, Argostolion* ☎ *26710/28190* ⊕ *www. facebook.com/Draught.BeerHouse.*

Shopping

Down the Rabbit Hole

JEWELRY/ACCESSORIES | Alice would be proud of this wonderland of handmade jewelery, prints, art, bags, and bric-a-brac. ✉ *Kabanas Square, Argostolion* ✛ *Off Lithostrato Street* ☎ *2671/40274* ⊕ *www. down-the-rabbit-hole-kefalonia.com.*

Eros Deli

FOOD/CANDY | Ignore the bunch of loofahs pinned outside, this shop is packed with edible gems, including olive oils, jams, liqueurs, and all manner of herbs and delicacies from the islands. ✉ *Diadochou Konstantinou, Argostolion* ☎ *26710/87639.*

★ Voskopoula

LOCAL SPECIALTIES | A glorious tradition-al sweet and cake shop stood at the entrance to Lithostroto street. Blood-red almond *mandoles*, macaroons, squishy nougat, vanilla puddings, and *galaktoboureko* milk pies accompany honeys from across the island. You'll find their workshop a few doors down for tastings. ✉ *Lithostroto 3* ☎ *26710/26186* ⊕ *voskopoula.gr.*

Activities

BOAT TRIPS

Dreamy Cruises

BOAT TOURS | Cruises typically head out to the southern (Xi, Magas Lakkas) and western (Ammos) coastal beaches of the Paliki Peninsula as well as the island of Vardiani, with snorkeling stops along the way. ✉ *Argostoli Harbour, Argostolion* ☎ *69749/48385* ⊕ *www.dreamycruises. gr.*

Paliki Peninsula

35 km (21 miles) from Argostoli (by land).

Beaches rather than history is what this peninsula is known for. There is a theory, however, that it was here, and not the nearby island of Ithaki, that the poet Homer had in mind when he described Ithaca, the land from which Odysseus set sail. All of which may be mischief making, but if there was ever a shore-line you'd risk monsters, sirens, and the wrath of the Gods to see again, it's that of the Paliki.

The low-rise port town of Lixiouri is the rather underwhelming gateway to the otherworldly coast and gloriously cracked landscape of this peninsula. The car ferry from Argostoli typically cuts some 40 minutes off the drive looping north of the capital and back down to the popular red shores of Xi and Megas Lakkos beaches, where the region's only large resorts lie. But that rather misses the point. The Pali-ki remains gloriously under explored and suprisingly wild, making for an excellent road trip.

Car, scooter, or boat are the only ways to get around here. Breezing west along coastal roads past tiny villages, craggy hillsides, open vineyards, and even wetlands to the blissful shore of Petani Bay is one of the simplest joys you can find on Kefalonia. Such exploration even reveals a few hard-won secrets, such as the heavenly Ammos beach, access to which was cut off from the mainland by a tremor in 2014 and can only now be reached by boat. Or perhaps you'll discover the peninsula's many brilliant rural tavernas. These are rarer since the financial crash of 2007, but you can still find incredible dining among the inland villages, while the seafood in Xi is some of the best on the island.

Sights

Kipouria Monastery

RELIGIOUS SITE | Perched on the far west coast and famed for its clifftop views, this 18th-century monastery is home to just a solitary monk, named Efsevios. He took it upon himself to restore the entire building in the 1990s, after only the church had been rebuilt following the 1953 earthquakes. It wasn't the first time the monastery had been razed. In 1915, during some bad weather, a passing French destroyer was said to have mistaken the smoke from its chimney for an enemy ship; the hail of its canonfire leveled the outer walls. Today, the many empty cells recall how busy it once must have been. Contained within its church are the skulls of its three founders as well as a piece of the "Holy Wood" donated by a Russian prince in the mid-19th century. Its resident monk offically welcomes visitors on March 25 and September 14, though he's not shy and you can usually find him here. A short trail nearby the monastery leads to some fine views over the cliffs. ⊠ *North of Gilaskari Beach, Paliki.*

Lixouri

TOWN | Kefalonia's second-largest town is less businesslike than Argostoli, and its post-quake rebuilding more in line with the old Venetian style, but there's little here to hold the imagination. One of a few buildings in the city to have survived 1953 intact is the Lakovatios library, a grand neoclassical affair that hosts a small free museum. Otherwise, it's a colorful enough port town, mostly used as a jumping off point by tourists en-route to the southern beaches of Xi and Lepeda, or for picking up a boat tour. ⊠ *Lixouri, Paliki.*

Vardiani Island

ISLAND | This T-shaped isle is easily glimpsed from the mainland but may only be visited by boat. A lighthouse, built to replace the old 19th-century tower that was destroyed by Italian bombing in 1942, still stands here along with the ruins of two monasteries dating back to the 17th and 18th centuries. Trips usually stop to snorkle in the surrounding waters, where the odd turtle can sometimes be spotted, while a rough path on the island also makes for a fine walk. Boats here can be found in Lixiouri and Argostoli. ⊠ *Off the coast of Xi, Paliki.*

 # Beaches

★ Ammos Beach

BEACH—SIGHT | Some 280 steps were carved into the cliff face to enable access to this beach, which had previously only been reachable by boat. But in 2014 a tremor caused those steps to crumble. They're now very dangerous and should not be attempted, so sea access has once again become the only way to reach this magical shore. It's worth the trip. A semi-circular amphitheater of cliffs and sand mirrors that of Myrtos and Petani Bay, only without any vestiges of tourist interference. There are no facilities, just nature and you, so caution is advised, especially since the water deepens very quicky. Boat trips to the beach may be organized in Lixiouri and Argostoli. **Amenities:** none. **Best for:** empty shores; adventure; Robinson Crusoe–style Instagam shots. ⊠ *Paliki.*

Petani Bay Beach

BEACH—SIGHT | **FAMILY** | For many this is the best beach on the island. Its setting is Caribbean-esque: a semi-circular ring of lush, green-stubbled cliffs wrapping a white pebble-sand shore that gives way to waters that veer from emerald to cobalt blue. Umbrellas and sundecks fill only part of the beach, so there's room in the corners just to spread out. Its remoteness ensures this remains one of few big shorelines yet to be overwhelmed on the island. Access is impossible without your own transport, so it's worth getting there early as parking is limited. Facilities do exist, however, in the form of a beach bar and a few restaurants. **Amenities:** food and drink; parking (free); showers; toilets. **Best for:** quiet, beautiful views; swimming. ✉ *West coast of Paliki, Paliki.*

Xi Beach

BEACH—SIGHT | FAMILY | Kilometer-long Mars-red sands sheltered by bright-white cliffs make this one of the most distinctive shores on the island. It's also the most popular, in part due to shallow waters that make it especially good for familes. Its popularity also means that it's well catered for, with a number of excellent restaurants and bars having sprouted on its fringes. Umbrellas and sun beds dot the shore. Good access and a mix of watersports and plenty of families ensure this is one of the noisier shores on the island. It can even be reached by bus from Lixiouri. **Amenities:** food and drink; lifeguards; parking (free); showers; toilets; water sports. **Best for:** families; after-bathing drinks. ✉ *South of Lixiouri, Paliki.*

🍴 Restaurants

★ Ladokolla Stin Plagia

$ | GREEK | This inventive taverna, run by a pair of local twins, is well-loved by islanders. The atmosphere is never less than bouncing, with the dying light accompanied by the old-world strains of Greek guitar and the husky accompaniment of moist-eyed diners. **Known for:** a great atmosphere with lively late-night dining; imaginative cooking—try the delicious pork in beer sauce; the owner is a character. [$] *Average main: €8* ✉ *Damoulianata Village, Paliki* ☎ *26710/97493.*

Nisoi Vardianoi

$ | SEAFOOD | FAMILY | A firmly established favorite. Garden terrace views gazing out to Xi Beach and across to the island of Vardinoi offer a feast for the eyes. **Known for:** great seafood; views out over the coast; occasional music nights. [$] *Average main: €14* ✉ *Xi Beach, Paliki* ☎ *69869/48528.*

Sparos Bistrot

$$ | SEAFOOD | Perched on the cusp of Megas Lakkos Beach, with a garden terrace running to the shore, you couldn't get much closer to the water. The seafood is excellent, though demand often curtails the menu, so it pays to get there early. **Known for:** sea views so close you can taste the salt water; some creative cooking using the excellent local seafood; pleasant garden setting. [$] *Average main: €15* ✉ *Megas Lakkos Beach, Paliki* ☎ *69447/18080.*

🛏 Hotels

★ Petani Bay Hotel

$$$ | HOTEL | There probably isn't a better view found in all the Ionian islands than at this secluded, adults-only boutique hotel. **Pros:** unfettered access to the best beach on the island; a great pool and laid-back bar; perfect privacy with mind-altering views. **Cons:** families can look elsewhere as under 16s are banned; it's a long, hot winding walk to Petani Beach; you'll need a car to get here. [$] *Rooms from: €240* ✉ *Agia Thekli, Paliki* ☎ *26710/97701* 🌐 *petanibayhotel.gr* 🕒 *Closed Mid-Oct.–Apr.* 🔑 *16 rooms (2 suites)* 🍴 *Free breakfast.*

Volidiera Guesthouse

$ | B&B/INN | FAMILY | This charming mother-and-daughter-run B&B lies in the green heart of the Paliki. **Pros:** wonderful garden with plenty of shade; a quiet and scenic escape; homemade treats at breakfast. **Cons:** you will need your own transport; there's not much within walking distance; wasps are a bit of menace. [$] *Rooms from: €80* ✉ *Near Favatata, Paliki* ✥ *1 km south of Favatata, along the Lixiouri-Vilatorion Road* ☎ *26710/95158* 🌐 *www.volidieraguesthouse.com* 🔑 *8 rooms* 🍴 *Free breakfast.*

While the cliffside steps to Ammos Beach are no longer safe for use, you can still enjoy this secluded stunner by catching a boat in Lixouri.

Mount Ainos and the Omala Valley

26 km (16 miles) from Argostoli.

The center of Kefalonia is dominated by Mount Ainos, the highest point in the Ionian archipelago and home to a 30-square-kilometer national park. Its upper slopes are blanketed by well-shaded forests of protected fir trees, with trails picking their way through to revealnative wild ponies and endemic wildflowers. If visiting in peak summer, it's best to call ahead as the heat and high winds often see the park closed to visitors for fear of forest fires.

To the north, in the foothills of Mount Ainos, lies the Omala Valley, a tiny community of villages living off the hundreds of vineyards that scatter the plain. It is here, and only here, that the island's famous Robola grapes are cultivated, a vine uniquely adapted to the thin, chalky soils of this mountainous valley. The area is also a famous pilgrim spot, with visitors flocking to the monastery, near Valsamata, where the mummified remains of Kefalonia's patron saint, Gerasimos, still lies in state.

While here, take a moment to stroll the land south of the village, where you can still spy "Old Valsamata." This is one of a number of ghost towns on the island, abandoned and left to ruin after the 1953 earthquakes shattered foundations and lives, leading to newer namesake settlements springing up in their wake. In its crumbling remains you can see why four-fifths of the island left for a brighter future, and perhaps appreciate better the struggle of those who stayed.

TOURS
Kefalonia Wine Tour

SPECIAL-INTEREST | You can go from winery to winery yourself, but for a bit of context (and to avoid driving) these tours include a trip to a traditional cottage winemaker as well as cellar-door visits. ⊠ *Omala* ☎ *69772/45503* ⊕ *www.kefaloniawine-tour.com* ✉ *from €65.*

Sights

★ Mount Ainos National Park

NATIONAL/STATE PARK | As the setting for the only national park on a Greek island (founded in 1962), Mount Ainos doesn't disappoint. Huge swathes of endemic Abies Cephalonica firs wrap the upper reaches of the mountain where tiny wild ponies can be spied on its south-eastern slopes. Five trails wind through the forests and around the mountain top, with a pair of easy 1½-hour hikes circling out from the Environmental Center of Ainos, where information can also be found. A pair of more tricky 4½-hour hikes can be found to Megas Soros, the highest summit, via the circular Kissos trail and from the village of Digaleto, outside the park. If you're coming to walk, do so early in the morning or pick one of the cooler seasons, such as late spring or autumn. May is the perfect month to spy another of the mountain's natural beauties, the native viola Kefallonica flowers that carpet the forest floor in a sea of purple. If you prefers views to hiking, a road stops close to the summit, where you can park and walk ten minutes to the top. ⊠ *Mount Ainos* ☎ *26710/29258* ⊕ *aenos-nationalpark.gr/en.*

Robola Winery

WINERY/DISTILLERY | The Robola Winery is a cooperative that sources grapes from some 300 vineyards across the area to produce, among others, its famously dry namesake white wine. Free guided tours include generous tastings; wine flights start at €4. ⊠ *Near Valsamata, Follow the Mousaton-Valsamata Rd. south from the village for 1 km* ☎ *26710/86430* ⊕ *www. orealios.gr* ⊠ *Free* ⊘ *Closed Sat. and Sun. Nov.–Apr.*

Saint Gerasimos Monastery

CAVE | This monastery, run by nuns, was founded in 1560 by Saint Gerasimos, patron saint of the island. He spent his final years here secluded in a cave, atop which now sits a richly decorated chapel that contains the silver casket where his body lies. He is associated with a number of miracles, and was said to be undecayed when exhumed, smelling of a pleasant, flowery scent that some claim lingers around his casket. The cave itself is reached via a small hole, descending a ladder to its twin chambers below. On his feast day (August 16), Gerasmios's casket is paraded and laid beneath the nearby plane tree said to have been planted by the saint. ■**TIP**➔ **Modest dress (no shorts) is required if you want to enter the chapel; some coverings are available.** ⊠ *Near Valsamata, Omala* ✚ *Follow the Mousaton-Valsamata Rd. south from the village for 1 km* ☎ *26710/86385* ⊠ *Free.*

 Restaurants

Mpotsolos

$ | GREEK | Meat is the order of the day here, typically served in huge portions, at decent prices, and with fries on the side. This robust grillhouse is a favorite with village locals, who make invariably friendly dining companions as you tuck into succulent lamb chops, great heaving hunks of pork, and local-style sausage, all with a glass of chilled Robola wine to hand. **Known for:** the lamb chops are raved about for good reason; friendly local dining companions; cheap local wines. **$** *Average main: €8* ⊠ *Mousaton-Valsamaton Road, Omala* ✚ *800 meters south of Valsamata* ☎ *26710/86155.*

Fiskardo and Assos

49 km (30 miles) from Argostoli.

The two towns of Fiskardo and Assos, sitting high in Kefalonia's wild northern tip, offer a glimpse of how the island used to look. Even the coastal drive up is among the most dramatic in the Greek islands, stubbled with great tumbling forests of cypress trees and rogue stretches of pristine shoreline. But its location also hides a geological secret.

The earthquakes of 1953 that devasted much of the island never reached the northernmost point where Fiskardo stands. A thick crust of solid limestone protected the town, whose intact Venetian architecture and bougainvillea-filled streets now make it especially popular with day-trippers and the mega-yacht owners who drift into the harbor. Yet it's more than just a boho village of waterfront café-bars and pastel-coloured houses. The area is filled with 18 km of sign-posted trails known as the Footpaths of Erissos ⊕ *footpaths-of-erisos.gr/en*. These offer a marvelous potted history of the area, striding out past an early Christian basilica, a Venetian lighthouse, Roman ruins, a German battery, and endless forests of rustling cypress trees. Afterward, you can rest up on some of the most secluded shores on the island.

Assos, just a few miles south, wasn't nearly as lucky as its neighbor when it came to earthquakes and was completely leveled in 1953. But such is its charm that it had a little help. French tourists had long taken a shine to the village and, following the disaster, quickly set about raising the money needed to faithfully rebuild it in its old image. Today, it's immensely popular with both locals and visitors, in no small part owing to its glorious setting and a shallow bay that doubles as a giant paddling pool. From here, a narrow ithmus leads to the hilltop ruins of a 16th-century Venetian castle that still watches over the bay. It's a good hour's walk to the top and well worth it for the views.

Lastly, a short drive south of Assos takes you to the shores of Myrtos, arguably one of the most striking beaches in all Greece and a popular day-trip destination for visitors. It's no secret, but its white shores wrapped by lush cliffs are undeniably captivating.

Sights

Assos

TOWN | FAMILY | There's little to see within the village of Assos, yet it's still a dazzling sight. It is largely made up of a single steep road that plummets down to the harbor and then up past pebble shores to a parking lot, for those wanting to continue on to the castle. En route, pinkish-purple bougainvillea bloom from every crevice; vine-like roots wrap the ruins of hollowed out buildings; pretty townhouses painted vibrant pastels glimmer in the sunlight; and the view from on-high over the turquoise waters below is magnificent. By the village square, which bears a plaque commemorating the "Parisiens" whose money rebuilt Assos after its destruction in 1953, are a string of cafés and tavernas swarming the edges of a pebble beach. Here, visitors swap dips in the knee-deep water of the bay for cooling drinks. It's worth resting a while here after climbing to the castle, which can be a sweaty task. ✉ *Assos, Assos.*

★ Assos Castle

CASTLE/PALACE | Construction of Assos Castle began in 1593. At the time the island's fortified center, Agios Georgios, was deemed too central by its Venetian rulers, so this was built to provide backup against pirate raids to the north. Sadly, very little survives today of the original structure except 2 km of outer walls, remnants of the old barracks, and two of its original gates. Earthquakes have destroyed much of it. The clamber up to the ruins is best done in the morning. It's a steep climb with a choice of two routes: a shorter stony path that wraps the northern coast of the peninsula, and a winding paved trail that faces back toward the village. The former has the better views but is less shaded, so is best done on the way up if setting off early. Set aside at least two hours for the whole endeavor. If you want to explore farther, follow the path to the peninsula's northernmost tip, passing an old prison farm that was built in the 1920s and was still in use until 1953. Part of it was renovated into a conference center in the early 2000s and, bafflingly, hasn't been used since, its courtyards quickly overtaken by foliage. The exhibition hall is still scattered with leaflets for its 2005 event. Just as amazingly, a small village also used to exist within the castle walls up until the 1960s, cultivating olive trees and living off the land. The last resident was said to have left in 1968. ⊠ *Assos* 🖾 *Free.*

Fiskardo

TOWN | Fiskardo derives its name from a Norman Duke and adventurer, Robert Guiscard, who attempted to occupy Kefalonia in 1084. He failed, yet the town rather passively took his name anyway. Today, invaders still arrive in Fiskardo by ship, only these days they're called yachts. Summer sees their ilk far outnumber the traditional fishing boats in the harbor, lending an air of boho chic to the little village and its bustling waterfront of eateries and café-bars. Still, it deserves the attention. Fiskardo remains one of the prettiest stays on the island, with its narrow streets winding past colorful Venetian houses. There's little in the way of museums here, but history surrounds the village. As recently as 2006, a Roman cemetery of 27 tombs was discovered on the edge of the harbor, with its open-air site now easily visited and well-signed. Hiking trails into the hills and forests reveal even more historic relics worth exploring. The town is also a useful port, with ferries to the island of Lefkhada leaving daily during the summer months. ⊠ *Fiskardo.*

Beaches

Dafnoudi Beach

BEACH—SIGHT | While most sun worshippers head to Emblisi Beach, the real find of this area lies a short stroll from the village of Antipata, just a few kilometers from Fiskardo. From there, park your car and follow the signs 800 m to the shore, strolling through sun-dappled cypress forests. This leads to a tiny white-pebbled inlet crested by trees. In the corner lies a small cave in which monk seals have been known to rest, and you'll only ever see a few other people here at most. There aren't any facilities, but that's the point: a wild beach escape away from the masses. Savor it. **Facilities:** none. **Best for:** peace and quiet; a great forest walk; swimming. ⊠ *Antipata, Fiskardo.*

Myrtos Beach

BEACH—SIGHT | Myrtos is the poster child for Kefalonia's shores, and frequently named among the top beaches in Greece. Wrapped in high scrubby cliffs, its semi-circular bowl of white pebbly sand is larger than most others on the island, meaning the huge swathe of umbrellas and deck chairs that dominate its spine still leaves room in the corners for what passes for "isolation" here. Yet, for all its photogenic qualities, with a big reputation comes crowds. There is a canteen on the shore, but queues mean it's often best to pack your own drinks and snacks. The water can also get a little rough, and there is a steep drop off from the shore, so it's not perfect for little ones. **Amenities:** food and drink; lifeguard; showers; umbrellas and sun beds; parking (free). **Best for:** sunset views; panoramic shots from the clifftop. ⊠ *Pylaros, Pylaros.*

🍽 Restaurants

★ Irida Restaurant

$ | GREEK | Fiskardo's harbor is lined with restaurant terraces, but Irida's is the pick of the bunch. Reliably good seafood is the difference-maker, with comforting staples such as shrimp *saganaki* (in a spicy tomato sauce laced with cheese) supplemented by the odd culinary gem like the sole in champagne sauce. **Known**

Earthquakes have destroyed much of Assos Castle save for bits of outer walls, old barracks, and two of the original gates, one of which is seen here.

for: reliably good seafood; a delightful dining terrace on the waterfront; excellent service. $ *Average main: €14 ✉ Akti Panormou, Fiskardo ☎ 26740/23803 ⊕ www.irida-restaurant.com.*

Picnic

$ | **INTERNATIONAL** | **FAMILY** | This delightful mother-and-daughter-run café-restaurant lies a couple of miles outside Fiskardo, on the road to Assos and Myrtos. It's a welcoming restaurant that makes for a great breakfast and brunch spot, and even wraps up picnic lunches for those wanting to drop by and pick up a meal for the beach. **Known for:** healthy, tasty takeaway lunches; open-minded, friendly owners; nice breakfasts. $ *Average main: €6 ✉ Main Road, Magganos ☎ 2674 /041039.*

Platanos

$ | **GREEK** | **FAMILY** | This venerable taverna stands apart from the needy café-bars that ring the waterside of Assos village. It's a solid old-stager with a menu of classic Greek *mezedes,* grills, seafood, souvlakis, and a far larger than usual range of vegetarian dishes. **Known for:** rustic Greek favorites with stews and seafood; peaceful, shaded dining spot; good selection of veggie options. $ *Average main: €10 ✉ Assos Main Road, Assos ☎ 26740/51381.*

Tassia

$ | **GREEK** | Owner Tassia Dendrinou has become something of a local culinary celeb in recent years, with a couple of cookbooks to his name. His menu is creative, with dishes such as octopus and chickpea puree and a fulsome Robola chicken that makes fine use of the island's specialty wine. **Known for:** great use of local produce, especially the island's cheeses; good seafood dishes; waterside terrace. $ *Average main: €14 ✉ Fiskardo Harbor ☎ 26740 /41205 ⊕ www.tassia.gr.*

☕ Coffee and Quick Bites

Melina Patisserie

$ | **CAFÉ** | Yogurt-thick smoothies and scrumptious homemade cakes make this the perfect spot for a breather. Gaze out over the yachts in the harbor and indulge your sweet tooth—the syrup-drenched baklava here is the size of a doorstop and every bit as satisfying as it looks. **Known for:** luxurious cakes; delicious shakes and smoothies; nice views over the harbor. $ *Average main: €5* ⊠ *Akti Panormou, Fiskardo* ☎ *26740/41501.*

 ## Hotels

Emelisse Nature Resort
$$$$ | **RESORT** | **FAMILY** | This sprawling village-style resort crowns the scenic hills above Fiskardo, with a grand panorama of the coast and the best facilities on the island. **Pros:** incredible facilities mean you won't get bored; unmatched views over the northerly tip of the island; restaurant Votsalo is one of the best in Fiskardo. **Cons:** it's a sweaty walk from the gate, let alone Fiskardo; like most hotels, it's only open during the summer season; service can be a little impersonal. $ *Rooms from: €300* ⊠ *Emblisi Bay, Fiskardo* ☎ *26740 /41200* ⊕ *www.emelisseresort. com* ⊗ *Closed Nov.–Apr.* ⌘ *64 rooms (24 suites)* ⦅◎⦆ *Free breakfast.*

Forest Villas
$$$$ | **RENTAL** | Run by mother and son Vaso and Theo, this pair of newly built two-bedroom villas are perfectly placed for Myrtos Beach and road trips to Fiskardo or Sami. **Pros:** secluded setting for a quiet getaway; it's a ten-minute drive to Myrtos beach; 20 minutes to Assos; amazing private pool. **Cons:** you need a car to get anywhere; the road outside can be noisy during the day; two-night minimum stay. $ *Rooms from: €330* ⊠ *Potamianata, Pylaros* ☎ *69747/72984* ⊕ *www.forestvillaskefalonia.com* ⌘ *2 villas* ⦅◎⦆ *Free breakfast.*

★ North Point Rooms 1953
$$ | **B&B/INN** | This sumptuous boutique stay in the village of Antipata, just outside Fiskado, consists of three stone cottages nestled around a walled garden bristling with lemon and lime trees. **Pros:** a daily minibus runs to (7 pm) and from (11 pm) Fiskardo; you can rent bikes and e-bikes from the hotel; free bar, coffee, and snacks in the breakfast area. **Cons:** you really need a car to get here and explore; the pretty pool is really only good for cooling off; early morning church bells make for an unwanted weekend alarm. $ *Rooms from: €160* ⊠ *Markandonata, Fiskardo* ✛ *4 km east of Fiskardo* ☎ *69070/55556* ⊕ *www.northpoint.gr* ⌘ *6 rooms (1 duplex)* ⦅◎⦆ *Free breakfast.*

 ## Nightlife

Le Passage
BARS/PUBS | A breezily good waterside cocktail bar that doubles as a café during the day. Fine coffees and light breakfasts lure the brunch crowd, but the cocktails (from €9), mixed with consumate skill, are the star. ⊠ *Fiskardo Harbor, Fiskardo* ☎ *26740/41505.*

 ## Shopping

Small shops are scattered along the harbor, though most sell an unedifying selection of hats, scarves, and designer wear, as well as touristy Greek souvenirs that you'll find across the island. Few are worth a look, with only a handful of womenswear boutiques in the village rising above the melee.

AnnaMaria's
JEWELRY/ACCESSORIES | This small boutique has collections of beachwear, jewelery, and accessories sourced by its owner, and has become an enduring hit with visitors. ⊠ *Cat Square* ☎ *26740/41270.*

 ## Activities

DIVING
Diving is popular in Kefalonia but facilities aren't as widespread as you'd expect. There are only a handful of dive centers on the island, mostly based up north in Fiskardo and Agia Efimia, though Lassi

and Skala have facilities, too. Dive sites around the area include a number of large caves and catacombs. For more skilled divers there are some wrecks, too, including a few traditional Greek boats within Fiskardo's harbor itself. Farther south, in Myrtos Bay, you can dive the wreck of a 50-meter-long ferry that sank in 2011.

Fiskardo Divers

DIVING/SNORKELING | This is an eco dive resort and center that runs PADI training courses and programs for kids and adults as well as dive trips around the island. ✉ *Fiskardo Harbor, Fiskardo* ☎ *69702/06172* ⊕ *www.fiskardo-divers. com.*

Sami

90 km (45 miles) from Patras (mainland Greece).

There isn't all that much to recommend the town of Sami, the island's busiest port. Mainland ferries dock here and at the similarly anonymous Poros, but connecting buses and taxis swiftly shepherd foot passengers to Argostoli, so most barely set foot on its waterfront. They're not missing much. It's telling that when large parts of the film version of *Captain Corelli's Mandolin* were shot here, the set was constructed *over* the existing buildings.

Go back 2,000 or 3,000 years, however, and Sami was a major power on the island, as both an independent Kefalonian state and then as a Roman port of great renown. Ruins of its old acropolis show a whole other side to the port and are well worth visiting. These days, the main town is best treated as a waterfront coffee stop in between visits to nearby caves, beaches, and the prettier fishing village of Agia Efimia, to the north, whose sheltered marina is the departure point for many scenic boat and dive trips along the east coast.

Sights

Acropolis of Sami

ARCHAEOLOGICAL SITE | Little in modern Sami points to the power this area once held. Its exploits during the Trojan War (1260–1180 BC) were once sung of by Homer, and by the 5th century BC it had become an independent state, controling the entire east coast of the island. It only lost its autonomy when the Romans invaded in 188 BC but thereafter flourished for three centuries as a trading link between Greece and Rome, before the twin threats of pirates and earthquakes quickened its demise. What few relics of its heyday remain are found today at the end of a pleasant 2 km walk uphill from the town. Here, past the ruined monastery of St. Fanentes and sloping pine forests, you'll eventually reach the skeleton of the old acropolis (Kyatis), where anonymous clusters of fallen stone only hint at its past. If you don't fancy the walk, you can also drive there. ✉ *Lapitha Mountain, Sami.*

Drogarati Cave

CAVE | A 4-km drive from Sami, this 150-million-year-old cave was only discovered after a land collapse revealed its entrance. Earthquakes and trophy-seeking tourists have since damaged its more impressive stalactites but it remains a compelling sight, especially its 900-square-meter Chamber of Exaltation, which has also been known to double as a concert venue on occasion. ✉ *Chaliotata-Sami Road* ☎ *26740/23302* 🎟 *€3* ⊘ *Closed Nov.–Mar.*

Melissani Cave

CAVE | An atmospheric Greek-style cenote, the collapsed roof of this limestone cave lake creates a magical setting, albeit one firmly capitalized on by mass tourism. Discovered in the 1950s, it is thought to have been a place of worship during antiquity. In recent years a tunnel has been burrowed down to reach the water, and now rowboats await at the bottom to drift sets of visitors across its cool, cobalt blue, briny waters, said to originate 31 km away. ⊠ *Karavomylos, Sami* ☎ *26740/22997* 💳 *€6* ⏲ *Closed Nov.–Apr.*

 Beaches

Antisamos Beach

BEACH—SIGHT | FAMILY | A few kilometers' walk or drive from Sami lies one of the island's more famous beaches: a forested bay wrapping narrow white-pebble shores and glistening emerald-blue waters. It got a boost in popularity after featuring in the film *Captain Corelli's Mandolin*, though it's a tad more active than the usual beauty spots, with a range of watersports on offer. Toward the end of the bay, a rock provides enough seclusion that naturism is generally considered acceptable. How that goes down with those who run the 18th-century-built Agrillion Monastery, atop a nearby hill, is anyone's guess. **Amenities:** canoes and paddleboats for rent; food and drink; sun beds and umbrellas; parking (free). **Best for:** watersports; nudists; swimming; families. ⊠ *2 km south of Sami, Sami.*

Zakynthos

15 km (9 miles) south of Kefalonia.

Zakynthos is the island that launched a million "I thought it was this, but it was that …" travel articles. Its appeal is obvious. The most southerly isle in the Ionian chain battles Rhodes for the title of Greece's sunniest flop spot, and even when it does rain here (Nov.–Feb.) only locals see it—few visitors arrive outside of package tourism season. The downside is that its eastern and southern shores are now given over entirely to the waves of tourists that crash upon their shores every summer. Yet that's just one side of the island.

Away from the beaches, Zakynthos has a long history that began around the 16th century BC, when it was first colonized. Later, during the Peloponnesian War (431–404 BC), the island sided with Athens, only to be invaded by Sparta. It set a worrying trend. Roman replaced Macedonian rule in the late 3rd century BC, and when the Empire fragmented, the Byzantine era afforded little more protection. During this time the islanders suffered great poverty, weighed down by attacks from Arabs and Goths.

Three centuries of Neapolitan rule brought stability but little security. Turkish assaults dogged its reign, culminating in the soldiers of Sultan Mehmet II brutally laying waste to the island in 1479. The Venetian era (1484–1797) that followed withstood constant Turkish raids but also saw the island grow culturally. Under their influence the sons of newly wealthy locals were sent to Italy to be educated, and the two cultures became inextricably entwined. Not for nothing is Zakynthos still known to many by its Italian name of Zante.

The island largely remained out of Turkish hands. After the Venetians, the British arguably had the second-most-lasting effect here. It was they who first ceded control of the island to Greece in 1864, and it is the legions of excitable young Brits that flood the island today that have done as much as anyone to cement its modern reputation. That doesn't tell the whole story, though, as visitors will discover.

A car lets you escape the noisy ATVs and overdevelopment of the south for the quiet, rocky grandeur of the northwest coast. The central wooded hill country hides retreats such as the hilltop villages of Kiliomeno and Exo Chora. Even in the busy south, a marine park encompassing islands and the half-wild shores of the Vasilikos Peninsula harbors glimpses of wildlife during summer's loggerhead turtle nesting season. Meanwhile, in the charmingly rebuilt capital of Zakynthos Town, the strains of traditional *kantádhes*—Italian-style ballads that originated here—still drift from tavernas, evoking a time before the island ever needed tourists at all.

GETTING HERE AND AROUND
BUS
Zakynthos Town is the main hub for all bus transportation, but the network is very limited. Resort areas on the east and south coast, including Leganes, Kalamaki, and Tsilivi, are well catered to, as are the sandier areas of the Vasilikos Peninsula, with a few routes even running at weekends. Summer weekday services also run four times a day to and from the airport, but that's it; the rest of the island is woefully underserved. Tickets cost €1.60–€1.80 and can be bought from the driver.

CAR AND SCOOTER
Unless you're content to roast on a beach (or at bus stops), a car or scooter is essential. Without one, the whole western and northern parts of the island are inaccessible, and taxi fees soon mount up. Roads are fewer and less developed outside the resort areas, with little street lighting after dark and some rough surfacing, so be careful at night. Minimal signage means a GPS is useful, though the island really isn't large enough to get badly lost. All the usual car-rental agencies are found at the airport and in Zakynthos Town, including Avia, Goldcar, Dollar, and Sixt, with prices from around €30 a day for a three-day hire.

Scooter hire requires a specialist license, which is why many tourists opt for the incredibly noisy four-wheel ATVs instead. These only require a regular driver's license but are, quite simply, the Jet Skis of land: loud, obnoxious, and pretty dangerous.

CONTACTS George & Nick Rentals.
✉ *Laganas Main Road, Laganas*

☎ *69958/07419* ⊕ *www.georgenickrentals.com/en.*

TAXI
Fixed-rate prices are set for most destinations on the island if you book in advance, with trips from Zakynthos Town to the farthest points, such as Shipwreck Cove or the ferry port of Agios Nikolaos, in the far north of the island, costing around €45 one-way. Shorter journeys to the beaches of the Vasilikos, 15 km away, are set at around €23. There are no meters, so book ahead if you can. Note that if coming from Kefalonia by ferry, there is no bus service from the port of Agios Nikolaos, so book a taxi ahead of your arrival.

CONTACTS Zante Taxi. ☎ *26950/48400* ⊕ *www.zantetaxi.gr.*

Zakynthos Town

31 km (20 miles) from Agios Nikolaos.

Zakynthos's main town is often skipped over by visitors. The island attracts a beach-loving crowd, for whom the café-drenched squares, churches, museums, and convenience of the capital is little more than background to its main role as a port and transit hub. It's a shame, though perhaps also a blessing. It allows the city to operate at its own pace, not one dictated by the moods and drinking habits of visitors.

Few would argue Zakynthos Town was beautiful, but it does have charm. Like most of the southern Ionian islands, it was shaken to pieces in the 1953 earthquakes. The rebuild created an airy, laidback center with backstreets revealing splashes of pretty pastel houses wreathed in character and pink bougainvillea. From above, the island's old fortified castle still glares down on its successor. Today it's little more than a likeable forest park scratched with ruins, but the views reveal sharp, lush ridges slashing away from town. It's a surprisingly dramatic setting.

There aren't any notable beaches within the city limits. To the south stretch thin, sandy shores down to Argassi and on to the lush beaches of the Vasilikos Peninsula, where day trips are a must. The narrow, pebbly shores leading north-east to Akrotiri are quiet but rather narrow. The closest major beaches lies six kilometers north of the city, where the coast curls up to the wide-open sands of Tsilivi. The more grown-up crowds tend to gravitate here, but little else of interest exists in this glorified tourist village dominated by increasingly luxurious resorts.

 Sights

Museum of D. Solomos & Kalvos

MUSEUM | A museum dedicated to the life of the island's literary greats, the poets Dhionysios Solomos and Andreas Kalvos. The former, in particular, is considered the father of modern Greek literature, championing the use of demotic Greek, a more colloquial form that had become the language of the people by the early 19th century, as opposed to the more conservative *katharevousa* form. Both are cherished sons of Zakynthos, whose bones are kept within the museum in a ground-floor mausoleum. Many of their letters and writings are on display, along with photographs and paintings, but little is explained or translated into English, so along with the rest of the local scholars and benefactors celebrated here, viewers without the benefit of a guided tour will gain little. ⊠ *Platia Agios Markou, Zakynthos Town* ☎ *26950 /48982* 🖂 *€4.*

St Dionysios Church

MUSEUM | The largest and most impressive church on Zakynthos is named after the island's patron saint and bedecked in impressive frescoes and giltwork. It was completed in 1948 yet miraculously escaped significant damage during the earthquakes of a few years later. Locals

naturally saw this as a sign. Its namesake saint, Dionysios, was born on Zakynthos but spent much of his life on a monastery on Strofades, some 40 km off its coast, where he was first buried. He is considered the saint of forgiveness, after lying to save his brother's murderer from retribution. His body is displayed here in the church and a procession of his relics is held on August 23 and December 17. Many other items rescued from the original Strofades monastery, ranging from paintings to muskets, can also be seen in a small, well-explained Ecclesiastical Museum to the rear (open 9 am–1 pm and 6 pm–10 pm). ⊠ *Voulgareos 2-1, Zakynthos Town* 🖂 *Free (church); €1 museum.*

★ Venetian Castle

ARCHAEOLOGICAL SITE | A steep 30-minute walk from downtown leads to a world utterly removed from the bustle below. This ruined 15th-century Venetian Castle sits high in the quiet hamlet of Bohali, built atop the site where the island's acropolis is thought to have stood. In 1514, invading Turks destroyed it only for its walls to be later rebuilt. It set the tone for the earthquake-stricken years that followed. Attempts by the British to conserve the building in 1812 stopped the rot, though today it's more like a quiet forest park, with only a few vestiges of its past still visible in its dungeons, armory, and fortifications. Views from the top are worth the climb alone. ■ TIP➔ Be warned: while the castle shuts at 4 pm, last entrance is at 3 pm, which catches out a lot of visitors. ⊠ *Anastasiou Street, Bohali, Zakynthos Town* ☎ *26950 /48099* 🖂 *€4* 🕙 *Closed Sun. and Tue.*

★ Zakynthos Museum (Byzantine Museum)

MUSEUM | This remarkable two-floor museum is a testament to the resilience of the island. Most of the ecclesiastical artworks here date from the 17th, 18th, and 19th centuries, and were rescued from more than 100 churches across the island after the 1953 earthquakes tore through the land. Entire frescoes, woodcarvings, iconostases, and religious artworks by key artists from the Ionian School of painters (Doxaras, Koutouzis), who flourished in the post-Renaissance, all survive here. The only tragedy is the lack of English translation to give context to their past. Last entry is 3:30 pm. ✉ *Platia Solomou, Zakynthos Town* ☎ *26950/42714* 🎟 *€4* 🕐 *Closed Sun. and Tues.*

Beaches

Tsilivi Beach

BEACH—SIGHT | FAMILY | For an island that doesn't really do public transport, Zakynthos makes a rare exception for its resort areas. There are regular buses between Tsilivi and Zakynthos Town, around 6 km away, during summer. That helps to make this one of the busiest stretches on the island, and you'll struggle to find an inch of its golden sands not subsumed by a sun bed or lobster-red British tourist. It also means it's well catered to, with umpteen bars, tavernas, and cafés surrounding the shore. Its waters accommodate Jet Skis, kayaks, banana boats, and paragliders. It's busy but you know what you're getting, and it's a good spot for those with little children, who will want for nothing. **Amenities:** food and drink; toilet; lifeguard; showers. **Good for:** families; watersports; resorts. ✉ *Tsilivi.*

Restaurants

★ Bassia

$ | GREEK | Nestled a couple of kilometers up the coast in the quiet village of Akrotiri, where the breezes offer welcome respite from the humidity back in town, is the best-value dining experience on the island. The raised views here are spectacular, and best enjoyed as the sun melts over the sea. **Known for:** incredible views out over the coast; good value for the quality of food; the perfect sunset spot. [$] *Average main: €14* ✉ *Akrotiri* ☎ *26950/25554* 🌐 *www.bassia.gr.*

Komis Fish Tavern

$$ | SEAFOOD | Zakynthos port might not look to be the most appealing setting at first, but you'd be surprised. Nestled in a corner of its own, lapped by sapphire waters, this small quayside eatery is a well-hidden delight. **Known for:** a picture-perfect quayside setting; best seafood on the island; good choice of local wines. [$] *Average main: €24* ✉ *Limani, Zakynthos Town* ☎ *26950/26915* 🌐 *komis-tavern.gr.*

★ Prosilio

$$ | GREEK FUSION | The entrance to this well-hidden fine-dining restaurant nestles discreetly between two bars, but it's worth finding. A courtyard terrace so hip you can taste it in the air is the setting for an adventurous Greek-fusion affair with a superb wine list and dazzling cocktails (from €12). **Known for:** imaginative, modern fine-dining; wonderful cocktails; the best wine list on the island by a mile. [$] *Average main: €24* ✉ *Agios Panton 15, Zakynthos Town* ☎ *26950/22040* 🌐 *www.prosiliozakynthos.gr.*

Yard of Taste

$$ | GREEK | The slightly chintzy Cath Kidston-meets-seaside-beach-hut vibe belies a stylish menu filled with organic, gluten-free, and vegan goodies. Its popular brunch perhaps explains away the peppy decor, but in the evening it comes into its own with a delicious feta in an oat crust whetting the appetite for a wealth of excellent Greek pasta dishes and succulent chops. **Known for:** good brunch options; imaginative array of Greek-style pasta dishes; likeable courtyard dining terrace. [$] *Average main: €18* ✉ *Rizospaston 15, Zakynthos Town* ☎ *26950/29815* 🌐 *www.avlizante.gr.*

Hotels

Few travelers make Zakynthos Town their base of choice, despite the convenience of the islands' best restaurants on your doorstep. They come to Zakynthos for

Take in the postcard-perfect view of the Ionian Sea from the ruined 15th-century Venetian Castle high above Zakynthos Town.

the beaches, and the pebbly strip running east to Akrotiri may be nice but it's of niche appeal (mainly to elderly Italians), which is why the selection of stays in town are mostly small, functional, and at a good price. Venture north a few miles up the coast, however, and you'll reach the sands of Tsilivi, which has seen a wave of plush new boutique stays in recent years to counter the noisy family resorts that once dominated here. Each looks like that one Instagram photo your friend reposts every summer. They are pricey and typically adults-only.

Contessina Suites & Spa

$$$$ | HOTEL | This stylish boutique stay strikes an elegant pose. **Pros:** great food and an impressive restaurant; huge rooms and extra-comfy beds; magnificent spa and pool. **Cons:** the area of Tsilivi sadly doesn't live up to its boutique stays; the gym is pretty small and ill-equipped; the pool area can get a little crowded, with not enough sun beds. $ *Rooms from: €280* ⊠ *Planos, Tsilivi* ☎ *26950/22700*

⊕ *contessinacollection.com* ⊙ *Closed Nov.–Apr.* ⬎ *64 suites* ⦿ *Free breakfast.*

Diana Hotel

$ | HOTEL | The Diana chain has four luxury hotels on the island, with this being their most functional. **Pros:** a rooftop pool and bar is rare here; great location within easy stroll of the city's best bars and restaurants; there is even a babysitting service (on request). **Cons:** some rooms are a little worn in places these days; it's a commute to reach any of the beaches; the noisy city bars make it especially loud at night. $ *Rooms from: €80* ⊠ *Platia Agios Markos, Zakynthos Town* ☎ *26950/28547* ⊕ *www.dianahotels.gr* ⬎ *45 rooms* ⦿ *Free breakfast.*

Zante Maris Suites

$$$ | HOTEL | Zante Maris is among a growing wave of luxury small boutique stays that has taken over Tsilivi. **Pros:** open-air massages on your ocean-view sun deck; ground-floor rooms have their own pool; the communal pool is huge and has double sun beds. **Cons:** it comes with a hefty price tag; the hill to the hotel

is a pain to walk in the heat; the non-pool rooms are a little bland. $ *Rooms from: €270* ✉ *Planos, Tsilivi* ☎ *26950/48689* ⊕ *zantemarissuites.gr* ⊘ *Closed Nov.– Apr.* ⇄ *45 suites* ◯ *Free breakfast.*

Nightlife

Base

MUSIC CLUBS | By day its ground-floor terrace makes for a fine people-watching spot on Platia Agios Markos to sip your coffee; come nightfall the café's rooftop bar and DJs take over as the cocktails flow at this slick local favorite. ✉ *Platia Agios Markos, Zakynthos Town* ☎ *26950/42409* ⊕ *basecafe.gr.*

Bitters

WINE BARS—NIGHTLIFE | A welcome escape from the noisier café-bars in the city. This hip new effort—all red-brick and polished wood floors—caters to a more refined palate, with an excellent selection of well-mixed cocktails (from €9) and 300+ Greek wines. It's worth stopping by for brunch, too. ✉ *Agios Eleftheriou 5, Zakynthos Town* ☎ *26950/44479* ⊕ *www.thebitters.gr.*

🆕 Performing Arts

Cine Negas: Open Air Cinema

ARTS VENUE | This waterfront open-air cinema, on the road to Akrotiri, sees crashing waves and flittering bats compete with the roar of Hollywood blockbusters. It makes for an incredible setting. Films are usually screened in English with Greek subtitles (kids' cartoons are dubbed), and late-night, post–11 pm screenings turn up everything from little-known early Agatha Christie adaptations to the latest thrillers. Expect comfy deckchairs, cheap prices (€5), and a good snack shop. ✉ *Paraliaki Avenue, Zakynthos Town* ☎ *26950/25950* ⊕ *www.facebook.com/Cinema.Negas/.*

The Vasilikos Peninsula and Laganas

10 km (8 miles) from Zakynthos Town

The area south of the main town bears witness to two very different sides of the island. The first is the gloriously lush, hilly peninsula that tumbles into the Ionian Sea. It's a surprisingly rural escape, speckled with countryside tavernas, pottery studios, local cafés, and farms. Around its ragged edges are some of the finest beaches on Zakynthos, defended by thick jungly fringes. Most visitors make straight for these and stay there, leaving the quiet villages and grassy trails to the lucky few.

Big resorts have yet to fully invade the Vasilikos Peninsuaa, and while it's far from untouched, it still feels like an escape. Much of the area's southern shores, stretching west over to Laganas, are part of the National Marine Park, which protects, among other things, the visiting loggerhead turtles that arrive on the island to breed in summer. Eco-conscious turtle cruises are a fantastic reward.

West of the peninsula, Laganas sprawls the southern coast like a sweaty teen with a hangover. Its beach and bar strip are an acquired taste, and where Europe's young men and women (mostly Brits) let loose their inner monster, fueled by cheap shots and the sea air. Neighboring Kalamaki offers a far more relaxing atmosphere, with some nice bars and a smattering of the island's better restaurants. To the far west lies the rugged coast of Keri, a beautiful stretch of coastline usually seen from the deck of a boat, with seabound trips from Agios Sostis and Laganas typically stopping at its majestic caves for snorkeling.

Sights

★ Marathonisi Island

ISLAND | "Turtle Island," as it's known, is one of the most important breeding areas for the Caretta caretta loggerhead turtle in Zakynthos. It lies off the shores of Keri, west of Laganas, and is made up of two small islets, with a pine-speckled hump and a thin sandy outcrop that even makes it look like a turtle. It falls within the boundaries of the National Marine Park. Trips may only be made during daylight, though the chances of spotting a turtle are high. If you do go with a local company, try to book with **Nefis Travel,** which is authorized by the marine park and works in tandem with sea turtle conservation organization Archelon. Boats can be boarded at Agios Sostis, 2 km east of Laganas. ⊠ *Marathonisi, Laganas.*

Oil Press Museum

TOUR—SIGHT | **FAMILY** | A charming tour run by the most famous olive-oil brand on Zakynthos. Many of the island's famed *dopia* olive trees are thought to be more than 2,000 years old, and this deep dive into local oil production in Zakynthos follows the process from branch to bottle. ■**TIP**➔ **If you want to see an ancient dopia in real life, head to the village of Exo Chora, on the northwest coast. At its center grows what's known locally as the "elephant tree," a truly venerable gnarled wonder.** ⊠ *Lithakia* ☎ *26950/52888* ⊕ *www.ariste-on.gr* ☜ *Free.*

Sea Turtle Rescue Center

NATURE PRESERVE | **FAMILY** | The Caretta caretta loggerhead sea turtle is a common visitor to Zakynthos. Every summer, hundreds return to its shores to lay their eggs, and yet their survival remains in the balance. The IUCN still classify this species as vulnerable. The problems caused by encroaching development, uneducated tourists, and unscrupulous boat tours is a major threat to the welfare of a species that, when hatched, already has just a one in 1,000 chance of surviving until adulthood. This center, run by volunteers, does its part to help those that stumble along the way. It should be noted that you aren't guaranteed to see any sea turtles (there are usually a few turtles); that's the nature of a rescue center. Daily feedings (10 am, 2 pm, and 6 pm) do take place, however, when there is something to feed. The center runs on minimal staff and looks a little shabby these days, but still offers good information. ⊠ *Gerakas Beach, Vasilikos* ⊕ *earth-sea-sky-global.org.*

🏖 Beaches

Both the Vasilikos Peninsula and Laganas are home to some incredible stretches of sand. And while the latter doesn't have the best reputation, Vasilikos offers a comparatively peaceful escape, with its tree-lined shores and long stretches of golden sands.

The area is also home to the breeding grounds of the rare Caretta caretta loggerhead turtle, which has, sadly, caused a headache for the island. The breeding season coincides with the busy summer, and for years environmentalists and tourism authorities have been (pardon the expression) at loggerheads.

In 1999, a National Marine Park was created along the south-west coast. It covers 135 square kilometers and includes the six main breeding beaches: **East Laganas, Gerakas, Dafni, Kalamaki,** the island of **Marathonisi,** and **Sekania.** Only the last of these, which has one of the highest concentrations of loggerhead nests in the world, is off-limits to visitors. The others have an uneasy truce with tourists, who are allowed on their sands from 30 minutes after sunrise until 30 minutes before sunset (the turtles only come ashore at night).

Agios Nikolaos Beach

BEACH—SIGHT | This beach owes its name to the small chapel that stands to its western end. Its shores are hardly pious though. This is the sportiest of the sands lining the Vasilikos, with the thwack of volleyballs accompanying loud music, the roar of Jet Skis, and a mostly younger crowd. It's also very pretty, with a thick ring of pines fringing the white-pebble shore and twinkling sapphire waters. There's every variety of watersport here, but it's an especially good spot for diving and snorkeling. **Amenities:** sun beds; umbrellas; food and drink; watersports; showers. **Best for:** snorkeling and diving; sea kayaking; volleyball. ⊠ *North-east Vasilikos, Zakynthos Town.*

Banana Beach
BEACH—SIGHT | FAMILY | Not nearly as unknown as it used to be, though the same could be said for the entire peninsula, Banana Beach's golden sands are still impressive. It is the largest beach on the island, with rocky, wooded fringes and clear, shallow waters perfect for families. It has a few bars, restaurants, and services. Sun beds occupy a good chunk of the shoreline, but its size means you can always find a quieter corner. Around four bus services a day run here from Zakynthos Town, if you don't want to drive. **Amenities:** sun beds; showers; food and drink. **Good for:** families; sunworshippers; swimming. ⊠ *Zakinthos-Vasilikos Road, Zakynthos Town.*

Restaurants

Essence
$$ | TAPAS | The best dining in the south is found around Kalamaki. Essence is the pick of the bunch, with a creative tapas menu that goes its own way, skipping from Gallicia-style octopus to goat's cheese pimped with chorizo. **Known for:** playful cooking that's big on flavors; imaginative tapas with a Greek twist; a good wine list. $ *Average main: €19* ⊠ *Kalamaki* ☎ *69785/65232* ⊕ *www. restaurant-essence.com.*

★ Lithies Taverna
$ | GREEK | A leafy family-run taverna in the countryside of Vasilikos that hits every comfort-food sweet spot. You'll need a car to get there, though it's just a 15-minute walk from the peninsula's namesake village. **Known for:** countryside cooking with the freshest of produce; great value; traditional Greek desserts. $ *Average main: €10* ⊠ *Vasilikos Village, Vasilikos* ☎ *26950/35290* ⊕ *www.lithieshouses.gr.*

Coffee and Quick Bites

Dopia's House
$ | GREEK | This friendly family-run spot is named for the 2,000-year-old *dopia* olive tree that grows in the front yard. It's the perfect retreat for a cool drink or a home-cooked meal in a nicely shaded garden terrace. **Known for:** a useful waiting spot near to the Vasilikos bus stop; a tasty selection of Greek mezedes; pretty garden-terrace setting beneath its famed dopia. $ *Average main: €8* ⊠ *Vasilikos Village, Vasilikos* ☎ *69462/11227.*

Hotels

★ Lithies Organic Farm & Houses
$ | B&B/INN | A charming collection of seven colorful guesthouses that lies off the main road just north of Vasilikos village. **Pros:** a remote rural setting far from the beach-loving masses; the family's great taverna is just a short stroll away; there are nice walking trails (with maps for guests) leading out from the farm. **Cons:** you'll need a car to get there; the nearest village is a 15-minute walk; there is a three-night minimum stay. $ *Rooms from: €82* ⊠ *Vasilikos Village, Vasilikos* ☎ *26950 /35290* ⊕ *www.lithieshouses.gr* ⇥ *7 houses* ⧫⊙⧫ *No meals.*

Did You Know?

While uninhabited Marathonisi Island, off the southern coast of Zakynthos, is popular with sun and sea worshippers, it serves a more important purpose—it's a breeding place for loggerhead turtles, an endangered species of sea turtle that reproduce here each summer.

Nightlife

Cave Bar

BARS/PUBS | Far removed from the hot mess of the Laganas Strip, this cliff-cut bar offers a leafy hideaway in quieter Kalamaki. Visitors unwilling to climb the 100 yards to the bar are picked up by the roadside in a tiny pink buggy. Quiet cocktails in a garden setting await. ⊠ *Kalamaki, Zakynthos Town* ✛ *Just off the eastern end of Kalamaki Main Road* ☎ *26950/41044* ⊕ *cavebar.tripod.com.*

SpeakEasy

BARS/PUBS | A likeably snug and atmospheric gin bar off the main drag of Kalamaki's main road. Great cocktails and an enviably select choice of gins make this a rare find on the south side of the island. ⊠ *Kalamaki Main Road, Kalamaki* ☎ *69784/87761* ⊕ *www.facebook.com/ SpeakEasyZakynthos.*

Shopping

Pottery Studio & Cafe

CERAMICS/GLASSWARE | There is no shortage of ceramic studios on Zakynthos, where pottery classes and cafés go together like feta and honey. This charming spot, run by sisters Andriani and Sisi Kladi, combines the pair's ceramist and baking skills to great effect, while the former's jewelery and colorful creations are highly browsable. ⊠ *Agios Sostis, Laganas* ☎ *26950/52748* ⊕ *potterystudiocafe.com.*

Activities

WILDLIFE BOAT TRIPS

A number of companies operating on the southern coast promise turtle tours, typically with glass-bottomed boats. Most have little oversight. Unscrupulous boat drivers have been known to chase down turtles and crowd around them in five or six boats at a time, causing the creatures great stress. Eco-tourism is perhaps the best chance of ensuring sea turtles can live in harmony with visitors, but it's best done in tandem with conservation organizations and the National Marine Park. Bear this in mind when booking turtle-watching excursions.

Nefis Travel

WILDLIFE-WATCHING | **FAMILY** | Turtle-watching trips run four days a week (Tuesday, Wednesday, Friday, and Sunday) in high season from Agios Sostis Harbor. These visit Marathonisi and the Keri caves, and are run in tandem with Archelon, the Sea Turtle Protection Society, who also provide guides, and with the authorization of the National Marine Park. ⊠ *Tsilivi Planos, Tsilivi* ☎ *26950/48004* ⊕ *nefis-travel.com.*

Agios Nikoloas and the North

15 km (9 miles) from Kefalonia.

The northern half of Zakynthos is day-trip country. Resorts on the east coast of the island pitter out above Alikes Beach, and to the west there's little but a series of wild beaches and quiet, pretty mountain villages and monasteries. Few explore this rocky corner except to peer over the viewpoint at Shipwreck Beach. It's here that those longing to escape the loud beach bars and convoys of ATVs should head.

Take time to stop by the hilltop villages of Exo Chora and Kiliomenos, which are said to have escaped much of the damage of the 1953 earthquakes. Their scattering of old buildings and churches dating back to the 17th century offer rare glimpses of how the island used to look before it took the tourist dollar. In between are verdant forests of cypress, pine, oak, and olive trees. It really is another world.

Up in the north-east, things get a little busier. Here you'll encounter Cape Skinari, from where dozens of small boats skim to the white arches and twinkling waters of the Blue Caves. The

A highlight of a visit to Zakynthos is a boat ride to the Blue Caves, where you can get out and swim or snorkel in and around the caves.

coast here is rocky and impressive as it narrows to the tip. Nearby, the small, anonymous port town of Agios Nikolaos is where ferries run to and from Kefalonia, making this the first sight of the island for many day-trippers. There's not much to see here but you'll find a few decent tavernas hidden in the outskirts.

 Sights

Anafonitria Monastery
RELIGIOUS SITE | This pretty, yellow-walled Venetian-era monastery lies within a pine forest and has some of the oldest and finest frescoes on the island. It was founded in the 15th century and takes its name from an icon smuggled away from Constantinople after it was captured by the Turks. Its complex spans several buildings, including a belfry converted from an old defensive tower. Zakynthos's patron saint Dionysios was said to have lived his final few years here. ⊠ Anafonitria.

Blue Caves
CAVE | Boats cast off from almost every harbor along the eastern side of the island to reach the twinkling waters of the Blue Caves. These trips typically combine a visit to Shipwreck Beach, but you'll find cheaper, faster there-and-back commutes (€10 per person) from Cape Skinari on the northern tip of the island. Once there, the glinting reflections seen within the tall white archways are best witnessed in the morning or before noon, when the sunlight refracts off the water at just the right angle. Many trips include the opportunity to get out and swim or snorkel in and around the caves. ⊠ Cape Skinari.

 Beaches

Makris Gialos Beach
BEACH—SIGHT | One of the better options for those allergic to crowds. Makris Gialos, on the northeast coast, lacks the facilities of many of the larger beaches, so rarely fills up. Limited parking means it isn't the most accessible, though most

just park by the road. A few more sun beds and umbrellas have cropped up in recent years, but it's easy to find your own spot. There's a bar and shop a short hop from the shore. Aside from that, all you have is sunshine and deep waters perfect for swimming and snorkeling. Boats also go from here to the Blue Caves. **Amenities:** bar a short walk away; sun beds and umbrellas. **Best for:** snorkeling; swimming; adults; escaping the crowds. ✉ *Northeast coast, Zakynthos Town.*

Navagio Beach (Shipwreck Beach)
BEACH—SIGHT | **FAMILY** | Most beaches accessible only by boat tend to be remote affairs; their shores little trod. Navagio is the exception. It somehow manages to be impossible to reach yet simultaneously overrun. The reason is simply that every ship on the island heads here—though if you don't want to spend all day on a tour at sea, you can grab a quick boat (30 minutes) there and back at nearby Port Vromi. The beach gets its nickname from the *MV Panagiotis*, a cargo vessel that fell foul of the rocks here in 1983 while smuggling contraband cigarettes. It has been rusting on this shore ever since. Some have theorized it was placed there to attract visitors, but only the most devout of cynics would deny this cove its serendipitous beauty. From above, a curve of white cliffs bristling with green stubble frames its subject and sands perfectly. Strangely, it's perhaps the only beach you can best appreciate from afar. The viewpoint (with nearby parking) is a good hour's drive from Zakynthos Town and just as packed as below. Only from there does its geometry truly sing. **Amenities:** none. **Best for:** boat trips; viewpoints; Instagram photos. ✉ *Northwest Zakynthos, Near the turnoff by the Monastery of Agios Georgios Kremnon, Anafonitria.*

Porto Vromi
BEACH—SIGHT | Porto Vromi is another gem found on the far northwestern coast. Its narrow shore isn't very large and doesn't attract that many visitors. A pebbly shore drops off quickly to reveal deep waters, so it's not much good for families with small children. Most use it as a departure point for boats to Shipwreck Beach and the Blue Caves, but it's worth a visit in its own right. The cove is riddled with small caves and surrounded by quiet mountain villages. A great escape from the masses. **Amenities:** a beach bar; tavernas in the villages; a couple of sun beds. **Best for:** boat trips; mountain trails; rural villages. ✉ *Northwest Zakynthos, Zakynthos Town.*

🛏 Hotels

Potamitis Windmills
$ | **B&B/INN** | The entreprenurial Potamitis brothers (who also own a restaurant and boat company) have converted two old windmills on the clifftop of Skinari into a pair of stays right next to the Blue Caves viewpoint. **Pros:** there's nothing else quite like it on the island; great views from your own private windmill; you're well placed for trips to the Blue Caves (the owners can also arrange boat trips). **Cons:** things are pretty cozy inside; the adjacent taverna can be noisy; there's not all that much to do in this part of the island. [$] *Rooms from: €120* ✉ *Cape Skinari* ☎ *26950/31241* 🌐 *potamitisbros.gr* 🛏 *2 windmill rooms* 🍴 *Free breakfast.*

🛍 Shopping

★ Melissiotises
LOCAL SPECIALTIES | The Women's Agricultural Cooperative runs this little shop selling olive oil, local wines, aromatic herbs, candles, jams, honeys, and a few select cheeses. ✉ *Kiliomenos* ☎ *26950/42872.*

Chapter 7

NORTHERN CYCLADES

TINOS, SYROS, MYKONOS, DELOS

7

Updated by
Liam McCaffrey

Sights	Restaurants	Hotels	Shopping	Nightlife
★★★★★	★★★★★	★★★★☆	★★★★☆	★★★★☆

WELCOME TO THE NORTHERN CYCLADES

TOP REASONS TO GO

★ **Marvelous Mykonos:** The rich arrive by yacht, the middle class by plane, the backpackers by boat— but everyone is out to enjoy the golden sands and Dionysian nightlife.

★ **Breathtaking beaches:** With sweeping blonde strands and cute coves lapped by turquoise seas, the Northern Cyclades have some of the great Greek beaches.

★ **Divine destinations:** From Ancient Delos, birthplace of Apollo and Artemis, to the Holy Island of Tinos, gods of all forms have made their mark on these isles.

★ **Foodie fantasy:** The wild shores, windswept hills, and barren valleys have shaped the culinary landscape, aided and abetted by some of the best chefs in Greece.

★ **Top towns:** Stately and serene Ermoupoli, hectic and maze-like Mykonos Town, and the peaceful mountain villages of Tinos all reward explorers generously.

1 Tinos. Among the most beautiful of the Cyclades, Tinos's charms remain largely unheralded but include the "Greek Lourdes"—the Panayia Evangelistria church— 1,300 traditional stone dovecotes, and idyllic villages like Pirgos.

2 Syros. Elegant and beautiful, Syros is the official legal and administrative capital of the Cyclades. Through its dramatic history, both Roman Catholicism and the Greek Orthodox Church have played major roles. The main town, Ermoupoli, with its ocher color, marble streets, and neoclassical grandeur, is one of the most impressive towns in the island chain.

3 Mykonos. Party central because of its nonstop nightlife, Mykonos Town is the Cyclades' best preserved *chora*—a maze of flat-stone streets lined with white houses and flower-filled balconies.

4 Delos. A short boat ride away from Mykonos is hallowed Delos, sacred to Apollo and now one of the great classical archaeological sites of the Mediterranean.

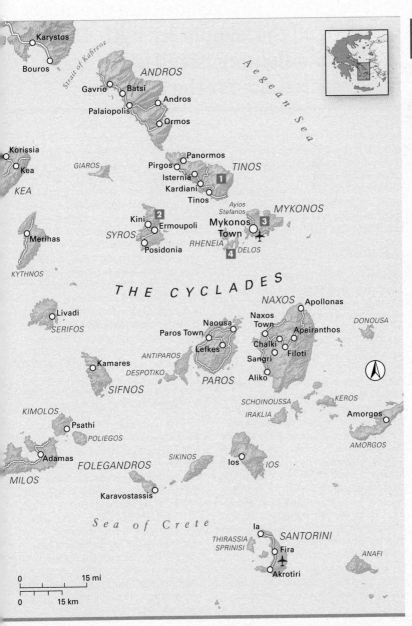

Named after the circle they form around the sacred isle of Delos, the two hundred and twenty or so Cyclades are the most Greek of all the islands. In myth, Delos itself was a floating island and it was a major sacred site for the ancients.

Positioned in the middle of the Aegean by Poseidon and fastened by four diamond chains attached to granite columns, Delos—meaning brilliant, visible—was where Leto, after nine days of labor, gave birth to Artemis and Apollo. The moment Apollo was born, the place was filled full of light and nature flourished, and Leto promised that the island would become rich and well-known.

Nowadays, those attributes seem to have been taken by its near neighbor, Mykonos. A member of the Delian alliance, it benefited greatly from the prosperity of Delos but sank back into obscurity once Delos fell. Romans, Venetians, Turks, even Russians controlled the island until the Greek revolution. Discovered again in the middle of the 20th century by artists drawn to its scenic harbor, sandy beaches, proximity to the archaeological site next door, and a tolerant attitude, it courted celebrities and the monied, bon viveurs of international society. It still retains an egalitarian spirit despite the best efforts of some, but the days of supermodels and film stars mixing with the hoi-polloi have sadly gone. It has become more exclusive in the last ten years, more so than in the preceding fifty, but it pays to remember that the view of Little Venice and the windmills is the same sat on the waterfront with a beer from the kiosk as it is from the stateroom of an oligarch's superyacht.

Farther up the island chain is Tinos, spiritual center of modern Greece, outshining even Patmos for its pilgrim pulling power. Notably quieter than many of its more feted neighbors, it attracts mainly Greek visitors and has a different feel from other islands—timetables and menus may be printed only in Greek outside of the major centers, and Tinos Town is set up for the faithful rather than tourists. Venture out and you will be rewarded by lovely Tinos, though; slowly, the island is unraveling itself to an audience thirsting for authenticity and a pristine, natural landscape. The beaches are numerous and good and the island specialities of dovecotes and mountain villages are impressively attractive. There is also a rich cultural life, with striking architecture and a marble carving tradition dating back through the ages.

Syros is unlike anywhere else in the North Cyclades. If you are imagining little white houses you will be very disappointed. Neoclassical masterpieces rub shoulders with Venetian and Genoese-influenced mansions. In the Apollon theater, a tiny replica of Milan's La Scala, Aeschylus, Homer, and Euripides look down from the ceiling as Rossini and Verdi play below. Two cathedrals stand watch in the town; the Orthodox Church of the Resurrection and the Catholic Church of San Tzortis in Ano Syros, the enchanting district with many preserved alleys and countless stairs.

The Roman Catholic community was protected by the patronage of the King of France, and thus the island escaped much of the chaos and destruction of other islands. As the main port of the Aegean in the 19th century, it grew rich and in its prime it had its own currency, worth more than the drachma. Today, as the capital of the Cyclades, and center of its administrative duties, it has only a fleeting history of tourism and visitors are seen as guests, not as an industry. It makes for a pointed contrast to the rest of the island group.

If Zeus shook and threw the isles like dice across the Aegean, the islands of the north Cyclades were particularly blessed. Countless classical sites, monasteries, churches, and villages wait to be explored, as do some of the most varied beaches in Greece. The best reason to visit the islands may simply be the enjoyment of the evening walk, the beauty of the surroundings, and the hospitality shown to strangers. Do remember, though, that the prevailing wind is the northern *vorias,* known as the *meltemi* in summer, and these islands can suffer from it the most. Tableware and beach umbrellas can go flying during the day, so choose your beaches wisely, and the summer nights can be noticeably cooler—bring a light cashmere sweater for the ultimate Mykonos chic.

Planning

When to Go

The Northern Cycladic experience is different in summer compared to winter, however, it is not as noticeable as in other island groups. Mykonos, Tinos, and Syros are, to differing degrees, self-sufficient and are not completely reliant on a couple of months of tourism in summer to survive. Mykonos's shoulder seasons, in particular, are stretching so

Information, Please

The Cyclades remain among the most popular tourist destinations in Europe, so it is all the more surprising to learn that most islands do not have an official government tourist agency. This role is often filled by private companies, and they are noted as such under each island heading.

that only November through to March is relatively quiet. Nature-lovers, hikers, and cultural travelers are best served by coming in spring and fall, when the temperatures are lower and tourist numbers fewer. May and June can be especially rewarding with flower-filled fields, warming seas, long bright days, and deserted beaches. The workers are not burnt-out either and service can be better than in the packed summer. Be aware that out of season ferry and air travel may be curtailed and that many hotels, restaurants, shops, and museums are closed, but your reward can be to see the natural beauty of the islands without the madding crowds.

Planning Your Time

The Northern Cyclades are places to follow your nose, rather than being bound to a rigid itinerary. Tinos and Syros have natural rhythms based on relaxing days pottering by the water and gentle evenings lingering over dinner, with a little cultural exploration thrown in. There is joy here in stumbling upon the unexpected.

The hardest thing in Mykonos can be the fear of missing out; there is always a better, bigger, and generally more expensive thing happening elsewhere. Do remember to take time out rather than ticking

Getting There: Boat vs. Plane

To get to the Cyclades, you either fly or take a boat. Flights from Athens are short and convenient, but if you want to understand what it means to be in the archipelago, and why an island has a special feeling, take the boat—after all, these are islands in the fabled Aegean, inhabited 5,000 years before Homer. There is always something magical about arriving on an island by ferry, however nondescript the harbor.

Flights may cost three times the price of the slower ferries. Nevertheless, if you fly into Athens in time to make a flight connection, and especially if you don't want to visit the big city, it may be worth it. Seats are booked much in advance, and even in winter you need reservations. High rollers can also hire a helicopter for €4,000 for a flight to Mykonos, and you would be surprised how many travelers do this.

off endless lists, though, as the spontaneous is often the most memorable part of any trip. Plus, do get up and go on that Delos trip, you won't be disappointed.

The Northern Cyclades work well in conjunction with Athens as the ferry trips are relatively short. Consider flying in or out of Mykonos or Syros to save time, and also combine the islands with another group; for example, the Southern Cyclades or Crete work well as a contrast.

Getting Here and Around

Transportation to the islands is constantly improving and the high-speed ferry service between Athens and the islands seems to increase with each season. Do remember, though, that boat schedules depend on Poseidon's weather whims, and service might be canceled when seas are rough. No matter how you travel, it's best to buy tickets well in advance of major spring and summer holidays.

AIR
There are daily flights into Mykonos and Syros from Athens. Moreover, direct flights and charters arrive daily in Mykonos from Europe.

CONTACTS Mykonos Airport. (JMK) ✛ 4 km (2½ miles) southeast of Mykonos Town ☎ 22890/79000 ⊕ www. jmk-airport.gr. **Syros Airport.** (JSY) ☎ 22810/79545.

BOAT AND FERRY
Most boats leave from Athens's port of Piraeus and also from Rafina (accessible by KTEL bus from Athens); a few leave from Lavrio. The larger ferries are more stable; some fast boats are small, and can roll uncomfortably in high seas. Also, high-speeds have little or no deck space; you are closed in. Blue Star will give you a seat number for a small extra fee, and the fast boats have reserved seats only. In summer, you should always reserve seats in advance. All ferries run less frequently in winter, and some fast ferries don't run at all. At Easter and around August 15, seats are hard to come by, especially to the religious island of Tinos, and boat schedules change for the holidays.

For schedules (not too far in advance, please), check ⊕ www.openseas.gr or ⊕ www.gtp.gr.

CONTACTS Blue Star Ferries. ☎ 21089/19800 ⊕ www.bluestarferries. com. **Piraeus Port Authority Departures/ Arrivals.** ☎ ⊕ www.olp.gr. **Rafina KTEL Buses.** ☎ 210/ 880–8000 ⊕ www.

ktelattikis.gr. **Seajets.** ☎ *21071/07710*
⊕ *www.seajets.gr.*

BUS

For information about Bus travel, consult the Getting Here and Around sections listed under each island.

CAR AND SCOOTER

To take cars on ferries, you must make reservations. Though there is bus service on all islands, you may find it more convenient to travel by car, especially on a larger island like Tinos. Although islanders tend to acknowledge rules, many roads on the islands are poorly maintained, and tourists sometimes lapse into vacation inattentiveness. Drive with caution, especially at night, and most especially in Mykonos where people can over-estimate their operational skills. All the major islands have car- and bike-rental agencies at the ports and in the main towns. Car rentals in summer cost about €25–€50 per day, with unlimited mileage and third-party liability insurance. Full insurance costs about €15 per day more.

Often travelers opt for scooters or four-wheel ATV's (quads), but be careful—island hospitals get filled with people with serious-looking injuries due to poor roads, slipshod maintenance, careless drivers, and excessive partying. Choose a dealer that offers 24-hour service and a change of vehicle in case of a breakdown. Most will take you from and to your plane or boat.

FOOT

The Northern Cyclades are great places to head off the beaten track. Tinos has a network of 150 kilometres of trails that follow old footpaths around the island, while Syros has a series of hikes that are rewarding, especially in the wilder and less populated north. Spring and fall are the best times due to the lower temperatures and vivid vegetation. Mykonos isn't known for walks, being relatively flat and developed; nevertheless, traversing the narrow paths that snake along the coastline can be a pleasure.

Hotels

Overall, the quality of accommodations in the North Cyclades is high, whether they be tiny pensions, private houses, or luxury hotels. The best rooms, and and noticeably higher prices, are on Mykonos, where luxury hotels now rank among the world's favorites. Wherever you stay in the Northern Cyclades, make a room with a view and a balcony a priority. If you're not interested in staying at luxury hotels and unless you're traveling at the very height of the season (July 15–August 30), you're unlikely to need advance reservations on Syros and Tinos.

Restaurants

The rocky and arid soils of the Northern Cyclades may not seem ideal growing conditions for plentiful food stuffs but the islanders are nothing if not resourceful. In 1842 French travel writer Alexis de Valon noted about Tinos, "the whole island is cultivated with great determination, almost in defiance of nature; in the absence of soil, the inhabitants even plough rocks." In older times, fruit and grains were grown; mainly summer fruit such as figs and grapes, which could be sold to boats that passed through the ports. Indeed, Mykonos was so barren that it was thought only fit for growing barley to make rusks and to rear pigs that would scratch an existence out of the earth. The long, summer days meant that foods were often dried so that they would keep longer and gain more flavor. The people of the islands sought their livelihood at sea as fishermen, and to this day, fish and seafood play a large role in the local cuisine. The contact with outsiders in maritime trade shaped the culinary traditions, while influences from Venetian and Ottoman occupiers also helped to mold the food as we know it today. Vegetables do well in the tough climate and along with legumes are the base of most meals. Meat was scarce and prized, often slowly cooked in earthenware overnight in wood-fired ovens.

'Today, the food of the islands is unrecognizable at first glance—Indian delicacies on the beach in Mykonos, sushi by the sea in Syros, or pizza in the shadow of the Cathedral in Tinos—but scratch below the surface and the true island food culture is revealed. The best chefs are mixing up their influences and showing off their traditional ingredients. In Mykonos, try *kopanisti*, a rock-star cheese, all punky attitude and tangy flavors, and Louza, a cured pork fillet scented with spices and a genuine alternative to prosciutto. Syros has wild capers, thyme honey and San Michali, a hard, salty parmesan-style cheese. Tinos is a real foodie-heaven with dill-strewn omelets and T-Oinos, a heavyweight winery that competes with the best in Greece. Settle down in a restaurant on any of the islands and you will be fed well, whether you choose a sleepy taverna in a hilltop village or a Michelin-star-chasing show pony. Some of the best food in the whole of Greece is served here, food that tastes of the sunshine, of the scorched rock, and of the moody seas.

Restaurant and hotel reviews have been shortened. For full information, visit Fodors.com.

What it Costs in euros			
$	$$	$$$	$$$$
RESTAURANTS			
under €15	€15–€25	€26–€40	over €40
HOTELS			
under €125	€125–€225	€226–€275	over €275

Shopping

Mykonos is the best island in the Northern Cyclades for shopping. Designer stores rub shoulders with chi-chi boutiques selling Greek designers and individual jewelry pieces. On all of the islands, though, search out the quirky shops—coral jewelry and semi-precious stones look great against tanned skin, traditional Greek sandals are perfect for cobbled streets, and religious paraphenalia can be an unconventional keepsake of your travels. Traditional sweets travel well and the wines of Tinos can be international class. Embroiderers and weavers continue centuries-old traditions and make intricate and beautiful fabrics to grace interiors back home.

Visitor Information

Despite their popularity, most of the Cycladic islands do not have tourist offices. Instead, turn to local travel agencies, who can help you book tours, ferry tickets, and accommodations. General brochures and information about the Cyclades are available through the website and offices of the Greek National Tourism Organization (GNTO; EOT in Greece ⊕ *www.gnto.gr*).

Tinos ΤΗΝΟΣ

160 km (85 nautical miles) southeast of Piraeus harbor in Athens.

Tinos is among the most beautiful and most fascinating of the major Cyclades. The third largest of the island group after Naxos and Andros, with an area of 195 square km (121 square miles), it is inhabited by nearly 9,000 people, many of whom still live the traditional life of farmers or craftspeople. Its long, mountainous spine, rearing between Andros and Mykonos, makes it seem forbidding, and in a way it is. It is not popular among tourists for a few reasons: the main village, Tinos Town (Chora), lacks charm; the beaches are undeveloped; there is no airport; and the prevailing north winds are the Aegean's fiercest (passing mariners used to sacrifice a calf to Poseidon, ancient Tinos's chief deity, in hopes of avoiding shipwreck). On the other hand, Tinos is dotted with possibly the loveliest villages in the Cyclades.

Whether travelers head to Tinos or not, a visit here is essential for Greeks: its great Church of Panayia Evangelistria is the Greek Lourdes, a holy place of pilgrimage and miraculous cures; 799 other churches adorn the countryside. Encroaching development here is to accommodate those in search of their religious elixir and not, as on the other islands, the beach-and-bar crowd.

Tinos's magnificently rustic villages are, for some welcome reason, not being abandoned. The dark arcades of Arnados, the vine-shaded sea views of Isternia, the gleaming marble squares of Pirgos: these, finally, are what make Tinos unique. A map, available at kiosks or rental agencies, will make touring these villages by car or bike somewhat less confusing, as there are nearly 50 of them.

GETTING HERE AND AROUND

In high season many boats stop at Tinos, since it is on the Mykonos line, and consequently it becomes crowded with travelers. Moreover, owing to the famous church, it is also hugely popular with Greeks who arrive on Friday night and leave in time to get to work on Monday. The boats vary from big ferries to fast passengers-only boats, and it takes four to five hours, depending mostly on route and weather. Especially notice, as your boat rounds the point into the harbor, the high peak of Exambourgos with its acropolis and Venetian fort. For August

Lovey-Dovey McMansions

Tinos is renowned for its 1,300 dovecotes (*peristerines*), which, unlike those on Mykonos or Andros, are mostly well maintained; in fact, new ones are being built. Two stories high, with intricate stone-work, carved-dove finials, and thin schist slabs arranged in intricate patterns resembling traditional stitchery, the dovecotes have been much written about—and are much visited by doves.

weekends, reservations are recommended. For Easter and August 15, they are absolutely necessary, and the boats will be packed (the many cars in transit don't help). For these holidays, boat schedules do change; information much in advance is not trustworthy. Tinos has daily ferry connections with Andros, Mykonos, Paros, and Syros. Returning boats go either to Piraeus or to Rafina. When buying tickets at the quayside agencies, remember that not every office handles every boat, so check at more than one.

On Tinos, buses (📞 *22830/22440*) run several times daily from the quay of Chora (Tinos Town) to nearly all the many villages in Tinos, including Kionia (15 minutes) and Panormos (1 hour); in summer buses are added for beaches. Prices range from €2 to €5 and service stops around 7 pm. The bus depot is near the new dock.

VISITOR INFORMATION
CONTACTS Malliaris Travel.
📞 *22830/24241* ⊕ *www.malliaristravel.gr.*

ANDROS

Aegean Sea

Cape Firi Mithi
Cape Skali
Cape Anghanistis
Cape Ahinos

TO
ANDROS

Panormos Bay
Panormos Bay
Panormos Beach
Rohari Beach
Pirgos

Isternia

Ormos
Isternion
Isternia Beach
Kardiani

Aetofolia
Kalloni

Kolympithra
Beach
Cape Halara

Kolimbithra
Wetland

Komi Agapi
Exomvourgo
Volax
Loutra
Livada

0   2 mi
0   2 km

Cape Ayios Petros

Kambos
Xynara
Kechrovouni
Birdemiaros

Mesi
Potamia
Arnados
Dio Horia

Cape Vorni
Kionia
Sanctuary
of Poseidon
*Stavros
Beach*
*Kionia
Beach*
Tinos Town

Triandaros
**Ayios
Ioannis
Bay**
Pachia
Ammos
Beach
Cape
Ayios Ioann.

Ayios Fokas
Beach
Ayios Sostis
Beach
Ayios Ioannis
Porto Beach

TO
SIROS
TO
MYKONOS

Tinos Town Τήνος (Χώρα)

14 km (9 miles) northwest of Mykonos Town.

Civilization on Tinos is a millennium older than Tinos Town, or Chora, founded in the 5th century BC. On weekends and during festivals, Chora is thronged with Greeks attending church, and restaurants and hotels cater to them. As the well-known story goes, in 1822, just as the War of Independence was getting underway, and Tinos the first of the islands to sign up, the Virgin sent the nun Pelagia a dream about a buried icon of the Annunciation. On January 30, 1823, such an icon was unearthed amid the foundations of a Byzantine church, and it started to heal people immediately.

A timely intervention, perhaps, that served to secure the links between the Orthodox Church and Greek nationalism. Today, there are two major pilgrimage days—March 25th (Annunciation) and August 15th (Assumption)—when the icon is carried around the island.

◎ Sights

Archaeological Museum of Tinos

MUSEUM | On the main street, near the church, is the small Archaeological Museum; its collection includes a sundial by Andronicus of Cyrrhus, who in the 1st century BC also designed Athens's Tower of the Winds. Here, too, are Tinos's famous huge, red storage vases, from the 8th century BC. ⊠ *Megalohari* ☎ *22830/29063* ⊠ *€2* ⊘ *Closed Tues.*

Cultural Foundation of Tinos

MUSEUM | Founded in 2002, the Cultural Foundation of Tinos, housed in a large and splendid neoclassical building at the south end of the quay, remains active in promoting the fantastic art, history, and culture of the island. The center revolves around a full schedule of traveling exhibitions, lectures, performances, and other events. It has a permanent exhibit of work by Tinian sculptor, Iannoulis Chalepas. There's also a nice café with harborfront views. ⊠ *Paralia Tinos* ☎ *22830/29070* ⊕ *www.itip.gr* 🎫 *€3* 🕙 *Closed Sun.*

★ Panayia Evangelistria

RELIGIOUS SITE | The Tinians built the splended Church of the Annunciate Virgin on this site in 1823 to commemorate finding a buried icon of the Annunciation in the foundations of an old Byzantine church that once stood here. Imposing and beautiful, framed in gleaming yellow and white, it stands atop the town's main hill ("hora"), which is linked to the harbor via Megalochari, a steeply inclined avenue lined with votive shops. Half Venetian, half Cypriot in style, the facade (illuminated at night) has a distinctive two-story arcade and bookend staircases. Lined with the most costly stones from Tinos, Paros, and Delos, the church's **marble courtyards** (note the green-veined Tinian stone) are paved with pebble mosaics and surrounded by offices, chapels, a health station, and **seven museums.** Inside the **upper three-aisle church** dozens of beeswax candles and precious tin- and silver-work votives—don't miss the golden orange tree near the door donated by a blind man who was granted sight—dazzle the eye. You must often wait in line to see the little icon, encrusted with jewels, that is said to have curative powers. To beseech the icon's aid, a sick person sends a young female relative or a mother brings her sick infant. As the pilgrim descends from the boat, she falls to her knees, with traffic indifferently whizzing about her, and crawls painfully up the faded red carpet lane on the main street—1 km (½ mile)—to the church. In the church's courtyards, she and her family camp for several days, praying to the magical icon for a cure, which sometimes comes. This procedure is very similar to the ancient one observed in Tinos's temple of Poseidon. The **lower church,** called the Evresis, celebrates the finding of the icon; in one room a baptismal font is filled with silver and gold votives. The chapel to the left commemorates the torpedoing by the Italians, on Dormition Day, 1940, of the Greek ship *Elli*; in the early stages of the war, the roused Greeks amazingly overpowered the Italians. ⊠ *Evangelistrias 1* ☎ *22830/22256* ⊕ *www.panagiatinou.gr.*

🏖 Beaches

There is a series of beaches between Chora and Kionia (and beyond, for walkers).

Ayios Fokas Beach

BEACH—SIGHT | This long sandy beach is the closest organized beach to Tinos Town, and it's also the island's largest beach overall. The coastline is marked with natural shade from tamarisk trees, but beach chairs and umbrellas are readily available for rent during the summer. The main road behind the beach has a gathering of beach hotels, rooms, and tavernas. There are also a few beach bars and cafés along its 1½-km (1-mile) stretch. **Amenities:** food and drink. **Best for:** swimming; walking. ⊠ *Ayios Fokas* ⊹ *3 km (2 miles) from Tinos Town.*

Stavros Beach

BEACH—SIGHT | Within walking distance of Tinos Town, this beach is a peaceful little corner of Tinos. One or two tavernas are nearby, but Stavros beach is really known for its fine sand and its beautiful surroundings. The turquoise waters remain clear, and shady green trees dot the area surrounding Ayios Stavros, the pretty whitewashed church that gave the beach

To seek help for a sick relative from the icon within, pilgrims must crawl a full kilometer from the harbor, the up these steps to the breathtaking Panayia Evangelistria.

its name. ■ **TIP→ Come during sunset, as it makes for one of the most romantic settings on Tinos.** **Amenities:** food and drink. **Best for:** sunset; swimming. ✉ *Stavros Beach* ✣ *1 km (½ mile) from Tinos Town.*

🍴 Restaurants

★ Itan Ena Mikro Karavi

$$ | **GREEK** | The old open-air cinema, steps away from the main street, has been lovingly reimagined as the island's gastronomic hot spot. A romantic pastel-painted courtyard festooned with greenery fronts the clearest expression of Tinos's outstanding produce, where clever contemporary trends are married to traditional techniques and recipes. **Known for:** confident and creative cuisine; Cycladic-led wine list is a treat; warm and inviting ambience. [$] *Average main: €20* ✉ *Trion Ierarchon* ☎ *22830/22818* ⏲ *Closed Nov.–Apr.*

San To Alati

$ | **GREEK** | On the corner at the end of Agios Fokas beach, San to Alati—"like salt"—looks over the water and seven different islands are visible on a clear day from this whitewashed little taverna. The menu is wrapped in a fairy tale book cover and magic continues in the kitchen as the gifts of the sea are transformed into crowd pleasing local cuisine with modern touches and super presentation. **Known for:** fairytale menu takes you on a journey; salty sea-breeze setting; husband and wife team offer caring service. [$] *Average main: €14* ✉ *Ir. Politechniou, Ayios Fokas* ☎ *22830/29266.*

Tarsanas

$$ | **GREEK** | The queues that sneak around the block tell you who cooks the best fish in Tinos. At the far east of the harbor—Tarsanas means boatyard—a stylish wood interior and two outside areas are the setting for distinctive dishes prepared with the finest ingredients. **Known for:** reservations needed at busy

Traditional Festivals in the Cyclades

All over Greece, villages, towns, and cities have traditional celebrations that vary from joyous to deeply serious, and the Cyclades are no exception. In Tinos Town, the healing icon from Panayia Evangelistria church is paraded with much pomp on Annunciation Day, March 25, and especially Dormition Day, August 15. As it is carried on poles over the heads of the faithful, cures are effected, and religious emotion runs high. On July 23, in honor of St. Pelagia, the icon is paraded from Kechrovouni Nunnery, and afterward the festivities continue long into the night, with music and fireworks.

If you're on Santorini on July 20, you can partake in the celebration of St. Elias's name day, when a traditional pea-and-onion soup is served, followed by walnut and honey desserts and folk dancing.

Naxos has its share of festivals to discover and enjoy. Naxos Town celebrates the Dionysia festival during the first week of August, with concerts, costumed folk dancers, and free food and wine on the square. During Carnival, preceding Lent, "bell wearers" take to the streets in Apeiranthos and Filoti, running from house to house making as much noise as possible with strings of bells tied around their waists. They're a disconcerting sight in their hooded cloaks,

as they escort a man dressed as a woman from house to house to collect eggs. In Apeiranthos, villagers square off in rhyming-verse contests: on the last Sunday of Lent, the *paliomaskari*, their faces blackened, challenge each other in improvising *kotsakia* (satirical couplets). On July 14, Ayios Nikodemos Day is celebrated in Chora with a procession of the patron saint's icon through town, but the Dormition of the Virgin on August 15 is, after Easter and Christmas, the festival most widely celebrated, especially in Sangri, Filoti (where festivities take place on August 4), and Apeiranthos.

On Paros each year on August 23, eight days after the huge festival in Parikia at the Church of a Hundred Doors, Naousa celebrates the heroic naval battle against the Turks, with children dressed in native costume, great feasts, and traditional dancing. The day ends with 100 boats illuminated by torches converging on the harbor. On June 2, there is much feasting in Lefkes for the Holy Trinity.

On Syros, the International Festival of the Aegean takes place every summer attracting those who simply love the arts. Ermoupoli's historic neoclassical venues, including the Apollo Theater, are the elegant backdrop for opera, concerts, theater, and cultural events featuring artists from around the world.

times; best fish in town; cute family of ducks that waddle around the outdoor tables. $ *Average main: €16* ✉ *kazanova 5* ☎ *22830/24667.*

To Koutouki Tis Elenis

$ | GREEK | On a small alley off the Panagias road is a brightly decorated eatery, run by the even more brightly decorated Eleni, that dates back to 1812. Once a wineshop-cum-hangout for artists and writers, it now serves the most memorable of classic Tinian dishes in a homely environment. **Known for:** kakavia (fish soup) from whatever the nets have brought in; warbling goldfinch that guards the entrance; open all year. $ *Average main: €14* ⊠ *Gafou 5* ☎ *22830/24857* ⊕ *www.koutouki-elenis.gr.*

Coffee and Quick Bites

Halaris

$ | **BAKERY** | This shop and bakery is the local go-to for anything traditional and sweet. It's known for Tinian specialties such as almond paste candies called *psarakia tinou,* and cheesecake bites made with Tinian cheese called *gliko tiropitaki tsibiti.* **Known for:** Tinian handmade specialities; inventive ice cream; beautifully packaged souvenirs. $ *Average main: €5* ⊠ *Tinos Town* ☎ *22830/25087* ⊕ *www.halarisgroup.com.*

🛏 Hotels

Favie Suzanne Hotel

$ | **HOTEL** | Tinos Town hotels generally cater to the pilgrim crowd but Favie Suzanne makes a fair stab at a holiday lodging. **Pros:** great value; good size swimming pool; on-site parking makes it a good base for exploration. **Cons:** near the busy port; not on the waterfront; some rooms lack views from the balconies. $ *Rooms from: €70* ⊠ *Antoniou Sochou 22* ☎ *22830/25992* ⊕ *www.faviesuzanne.gr* ⊗ *Closed Dec.–Feb.* ⤵ *49 rooms* ⊚ *Free breakfast.*

Golden Beach Hotel and Apartments

$ | **HOTEL** | This small village-like complex of sheltered gardens, white pergolas, geranium pots, and spacious terraces is a handful of steps from Aghios Fokas beach. **Pros:** beach bar is a very popular meeting point; all rooms with lovely garden or sea views; free beach beds and umbrellas for guests. **Cons:** outside of Tinos Town; Wi-Fi problems in some rooms; traditional room decor. $ *Rooms from: €80* ⊠ *Ayios Fokas* ☎ *22830/24579*

Calling All Faithful

Evangelistria, the street parallel to Panayia Evangelistria, the legendary church of Tinos Town, is closed to traffic and is a kind of religious flea market, lined with stores hawking immense candles, chunks of incense, tacky souvenirs, tin votives, and sweets. There are several good jewelers' stores on the market street, where, as always on Tinos, the religious note is supreme.

⊕ *www.goldenbeachtinos.gr* ⤵ *26* ⊚ *Free breakfast.*

Vincenzo Family Rooms

$ | **B&B/INN** | Wishes came true as Tinos got what it needs—a central, convenient, comfortable hotel. **Pros:** walking distance to Tinos Town sights and a beach; good value hotel; breakfast ingredients from the family farm. **Cons:** town can feel busy in high season; not on the harborfront; street views from the balconies. $ *Rooms from: €90* ⊠ *25is Martiou 15* ☎ *22830/25888* ⊕ *www.vincenzo.gr* ⤵ *14 rooms* ⊚ *Free breakfast.*

🍸 Nightlife

Tinos has fewer bars and discos than the other big islands, but there's a lively late-night bar scene come summer. The action is behind the waterfront between the two boat docks.

Kaktos Bar

BARS/PUBS | Jutting up next to a restored 16th-century Cycladic windmill, Kaktos is an open-air terrace bar on the edge of town where locals and visitors alike can sit back and enjoy a cocktail while taking in the view of Tinos Town and the Aegean Sea—perfect for a pre-dinner drink or a nightcap. ⊠ *Leof. Tripotamou* ☎ *22830/25930* ⊘ *Closed Oct.–May.*

Koursaros Bar

BARS/PUBS | *Koursaros*, which translates to "Pirate," gets its share of summer party crowds each year. Its decor is a soft mix of dark wood and stone with vintage maps and seafaring artifacts that play into the bar's nautical theme. Its location, at the very corner by the harbor, has made it one of the most visible landmark nightlife spots in Tinos since 1987. Café by day, a DJ turns up the music at night, spinning rock, funk, or jazz. ⊠ *Akti Ellis 1* ☎ *22830/23963.*

Sivilla

BARS/PUBS | Tinos Town has a nightlife district, but it only comes to life in the heat of the summer. Sivilla, located on one of the area's alleyways, churns out both Greek pop and international mainstream dance hits. ⊠ *Taxiarchon 17* ☎ *6977010665* ⊕ *sivilla.business.site.*

🛍 Shopping

Due to the island's landmark church, you'll find a wide variety of stores selling religious icons of every size and style, handmade from all types of material, including gold, silver, and wood. Tinos is still a rural island in many ways, so locally produced honey, cheese, and foodstuffs are of top quality and simply delicious. Finally, the island is particularly known for its marble arts and sculptures. If you're looking for something that may not be found anywhere else, beautiful Tinian artwork may be just the thing.

FOOD

Agricultural Co-operative of Tinos

LOCAL SPECIALTIES | Tinos produces a lot of milk. A short way up from the harbor, on the right, this little store sells milk, butter, and cheeses, including sharp *kopanistí*, a Cycladic specialty that pairs perfectly with ouzo; local jams and honeys are for sale, too. ⊠ *Megalochori 16* ⊹ *The main street up from the harbor* ☎ *22830/23289.*

INTERIORS

Anna Maria Art Gallery

ART GALLERIES | Draped in blue morning-glory vines, this gallery showcases jewelry by Greek craftsmen with bold ancient and Byzantine motifs, but the bulk of the shop is taken over by statuary and island-made marble pieces and other objet d'art. The crowded shop is a delight. ⊠ *Tinou 3* ☎ *22830/23456.*

Trela Tinos

ANTIQUES/COLLECTIBLES | In an old coffee-shop overlooking the sea, Trela is an eclectic collection of antiques and contemporary design pieces where modern ceramics, furniture, and jewelry vie for space with clothing and table linen. ⊠ *25is Martiou 41* ☎ *22830/26897* ⊕ *www.trelatinos.com* ⊘ *Closed Nov.–Mar.*

Marianna Petridi

JEWELRY/ACCESSORIES | An old ceramic store with a beautiful mosaic floor has been transformed into a modern concept store showcasing the best of Greek jewelry designers. Accessories and some household items round out the collection. ⊠ *Nikolaou Gizi 13* ☎ *22830/26626.*

Ostria

JEWELRY/ACCESSORIES | The selection here is especially good; in addition to delicate silver jewelry, Ostria sells silver icon covers, silver plate, and 22-karat gold. ⊠ *Evangelistria 20* ☎ *22830/23893.*

MARKETS

Farmers' Market

OUTDOOR/FLEA/GREEN MARKETS | Tinos is a rich farming island, and every day but Sunday, farmers from all the far-flung villages fill the square with vegetables, herbs, and *kritamos* (pickled sea-plant leaves). ⊠ *Tinos Town* ⊹ *Between two docks* ⊘ *Closed Sun.*

Ayios Ioannis Bay
Άγιος Ιωάννης

7 km (4½ miles) east of Tinos Town.

Heading east from Tinos Town, you'll travel on a winding road surrounded by bare, rocky Cycladic island landscapes. It eventually slopes down into Ayios Ioannis Bay (*O ormos tou Ayiou Ioanni* in Greek). The quiet beaches here offer clear seas that curve into picturesque bays. Around Ayios Ioannis Bay, several hotels, rooms for rent, and tavernas open each summer to cater to the season's travelers.

Beaches

Ayios Ioannis Porto Beach

BEACH—SIGHT | FAMILY | Since it's secluded from the summer's temperamental gusty island winds, the sands that fill up the pretty curved beach of Ayios Ioannis Porto Beach stay put. Here you can spend the day under tamarisk trees for natural shade or rent beach chairs and umbrellas during peak season. Its shallow waters and calm nature make it a choice beach for families. Several beach hotels are in close proximity. A few tavernas are nearby for a beach break. **Amenities:** food and drink. **Best for:** swimming. ✉ *Ayios Ioannis.*

Ayios Sostis Beach

BEACH—SIGHT | FAMILY | Known for its shallow turquoise waters and excellent, clear view of Mykonos, the yellow sand-filled Ayios Sostis Beach is said to be a continuation of Ayios Kyriaki Beach. In the summer, beach chairs and umbrellas are available to rent. A few tavernas and cafés are within walking distance for a meal break or refreshments. There are several ways to get to the beach, including a few small roads lined with bougainvillea and tall reeds, and the beach is served by bus. **Amenities:** food and drink. **Best for:** swimming. ✉ *Ayios Sostis.*

Pachia Ammos Beach

BEACH—SIGHT | Secluded in a cove east of Tinos Town, Pachia Ammos is named for its thick sand, which has a unique green hue that complements the surrounding short shrub hills that roll into the turquoise blue sea. It is undeveloped, and getting to the beach requires a 10 minute walk on an unmarked path. The effort, however, is rewarded in basking in one of the prettiest and most peaceful places on the island, with views across to Mykonos and a giant sand dune to explore. To get there, drive 10 km (6 miles) on the main road east toward Ayios Ioannis Beach and turn off at the signs for Pachia Ammos. Park in the car park at the top, walk through the country club that overlooks the beach, and then descend on one of the paths. **Amenities:** none. **Best for:** solitude; swimming. ✉ *Ayios Ioannis.*

Hotels

Mr and Mrs White

$$ | HOTEL | On a narrow lane above Aghios Ioannis beach, Mr and Mrs White looks over the bay to the twinkling lights of Mykonos. **Pros:** attentive staff are keen to please; a couple of nice beaches in walking distance; good tavernas nearby. **Cons:** scruffy surroundings; a drive to other beaches on the island; elevated position is very windy. [$] *Rooms from: €130* ✉ *Ayios Ioannis* ☎ *22830/29057* 🌐 *www.mrandmrswhitetinos.com* 🕑 *Closed Nov.–Mar.* 🛏 *52* 🍴 *Free breakfast.*

Porto Raphael

$ | HOTEL | FAMILY | This authentic resort-hotel strives for the best in appearance and service with modular Cycladic architecture lending the air of a small village. **Pros:** on a bus route to Tinos Town; good restaurant; friendly and family-run. **Cons:** simple decor; no pool; not much within walking distance. [$] *Rooms from: €110* ✉ *Ayios Ioannis* ☎ *22830/23913* 🌐 *www.portoraphael.gr* 🕑 *Closed Nov.–Mar.* 🛏 *26 rooms* 🍴 *Free breakfast.*

Kionia Κιόνια

2 km (1 miles) northwest of Tinos Town.

The little seaside town of Kionia is a short scenic drive, bike ride, or hike west of Tinos Town. A few simple tavernas and rooms are set off the main beach road, and on the main road the landmark Tinos Beach Hotel directly overlooks Kionia beach. Kionia's main attraction is the Sanctuary of Poseidon, which dates back to the 4th century BC.

Sights

Sanctuary of Poseidon

ARCHAEOLOGICAL SITE | The main reason to come to this small community northwest of Tinos Town, apart from the beach, is to visit the large, untended Sanctuary of Poseidon, also dedicated to the bearded sea god's sea-nymph consort, Amphitrite. The present remains are from the 4th century BC and later, though the sanctuary itself is much older. It was a kind of hospital, where the ailing came to camp and solicit the god's help. The marble dolphins in the Tinos archaeological museum were discovered here. According to the Roman historian Pliny, Tinos was once infested with serpents (goddess symbols) and named Ophiousa (Serpent town), until supermasculine Poseidon sent storks to clean them out. The sanctuary functioned well into Roman times. ⊠ *Kionia.*

Beaches

Kionia Beach

BEACH—SIGHT | Just 3 km (2 miles) west of Tinos Town, Kionia Beach remains one of the island's most visited beaches. It has both pebbles and sand, but the long stretch of sand dominates, and a section of it fronts the archaeological site of the Sanctuary of Poseidon. Kionia's beachfront road is lined with cafés, tavernas, rooms for rent, and the Tinos Beach Hotel, which are all within walking distance of the beach. Beach chairs and umbrellas are available for rent during the summer. **Amenities:** food and drink. **Best for:** swimming; walking. ⊠ *Kionia.*

Restaurants

Tsambia

$ | GREEK | Abutting the Sanctuary of Poseidon and facing the sea, this multi-level taverna offers traditional Greek taverna fare. Open all day, a stone's throw from the beach, and away from the wind that blights much of Tinos, the art of the grill is key here. **Known for:** very hospitable owner; calm, garden setting; sea-views from higher levels. $ *Average main: €10* ⊠ *Epar. Od. Tinou-Kallonis* ☎ *22830/23142.*

🛏 Hotels

Tinos Beach Hotel

$ | HOTEL | FAMILY | Sixties-style architecture is the vintage frame for this large hotel that offers modern beach amenities. **Pros:** good hotel for families; shuttle bus to Tinos Town; in front of the beach. **Cons:** not convenient walking distance from town; busy road between hotel and beach; not much to do at night in Kionia. $ *Rooms from: €100* ⊠ *Kionia* ☎ *22830/22626* ⊕ *www.tinosbeach.gr* ⇥ *165 rooms* ❍ *Free breakfast.*

Exomvourgo

15 km (10 miles) northwest of Tinos Town.

The ring of villages around the mountain of Exomvourgo are worth a visit. The fortified summit has the ruins of Venetian churches and it served as the island's capital in the 16th century. It can be climbed by some steep steps from Xinara.

Sights

Costas Tsoclis Museum

MUSEUM | Little Kambos (population 222) is the unlikely setting for a contemporary art gallery. A giant steel dragon snakes its body around the former schoolhouse-turned-museum next to the childhood home of Costas Tsoclis, a renowned international artist. The museum operates as a living space for culture and creativity and hosts performances throughout the summer months. ☎ *22830/51009* 🌐 *www.tsoclismuseum.gr* 🕓 *Closed Tues.*

Volax

MOUNTAIN—SIGHT | Tiny Volax is the most spectacular village with a landscape that seems to be straight out of *Lord of the Rings*. Windswept and remote, Volax is surrounded by hundreds of giant, granite boulders. Smooth and weatherworn, geologists are still undecided as to their origin—are they the result of volcanic eruption, or meteorites that landed in prehistoric times?.

Restaurants

Tereza

$ | GREEK | They don't make them like this anymore. A handful of tables sit under lilac bushes outside this grocery store/café/ *mezzotaverna* in the mountain village of Myrsini. **Known for:** simple, traditional, delicious food; sweetest, kindest service; sublime, peaceful village setting. [$] *Average main: €10* ☎ *22830/41320.*

Drink the Islands

Daughter of Costas Tsoclis, Maya, started the Cyclades Microbrewery in 2012 and it has now blossomed into an award winning business that supplies many of the best bars and restaurants. Try Nissos—the name means islands—next time you settle down to watch the sunset.

Isternia Ιστέρνια

24 km (15 miles) northwest of Tinos Town.

The village of Isternia (Cisterns); lofty on the slopes of Mount Meroviglia, is verdant with lush gardens. Many of the marble plaques hung here over doorways—a specialty of Tinos—indicate the owner's profession, for example, a sailing ship for a fisherman or sea captain. A long, paved road winds down to a little port, Ayios Nikitas, with a beach and a couple of fish tavernas. North of the village is Mylon, an abandoned settlement with ruined windmills and views across to Pirgos.

Beaches

Isternia Beach

BEACH—SIGHT | The beach, located right at the foot of the little fishing village of Isternia Bay, is actually two beaches—one a pebbled area and one a sandy cove—but both are known for their peaceful seclusion, although two tavernas and a café are nearby. You can also take some time out to visit the inland village of Isternia about 5 km (3 miles) away. Whether you're lying on the beach or having a meal by the sea, you can look forward to enjoying one of the nicest sunset views in Tinos. **Amenities:** food and drink. **Best for:** solitude; swimming. ✉ *Isternia.*

Restaurants

★ To Thalassaki

$$ | MODERN GREEK | Set on a platform on Ormos Isternion Bay, right up against the Aegean Sea with views of Syros, chef and owner Antonia Zarpa produces

innovative, well-thought-out dishes that capture the local flavorsof her beloved island. Just as pilgrims visit the Cathedral, so do foodie-worshippers head to Thalassaki for its ephemeral works of art—the restaurant has such a cult following that speedboats zip over from Mykonos for lunch. **Known for:** fantastic sea views—not next to the sea but actually on it; excellent Greek-inspired cuisine with Tinian influences; Greek wine list is a perfect fit. $ *Average main: €18* ⊠ *Ornos* ⊗ *Closed Nov.–Mar.*

☕ Coffee and Quick Bites

Mayou

$ | **CAFÉ** | A short walk through Isternia's maze-like streets leads to an unexpected terrace in the shade of a plane tree that overlooks the Aegean. Sitting here makes you understand how the Gods must have felt, idly toying with the people below. **Known for:** relaxed, spiritual air; short, delicious brunch menu; concerts and recitals in summer. $ *Average main: €8* ⊠ *Isternia* ☎ *22830/31882.*

Pirgos Πύργος

32 km (20 miles) northwest of Tinos Town, 8 km (5 miles) north of Isternia.

The village of Pirgos, second in importance to Chora, is inland and up from the little harbor of Panormos. Tinos is famous for its marble carving, and Pirgos, a prosperous town, is noted for its sculpture school and marble workshops, where artisans make fanlights, fountains, tomb monuments, and small objects for tourists; they also take orders. The village's main square is aptly crafted of all marble; the cafés, noted for *galaktoboureko* (custard pastry), and tavernas are all shaded by an ancient plane tree. Whitewashed narrow alleys and flower-festooned balconies make it a pleasant place to wander of an afternoon. The quarries for the green-vein marble are north of here,

reachable by car. The cemetery here is, appropriately, a showplace of marble sculpture.

👁 Sights

Museum Iannoulis Chalepas

MUSEUM | The marble-working tradition of Tinos survives here from the 19th century and is going strong, as seen in the two adjacent museums: Museum Iannoulis Chalepas is the renowned sculptor's former house and his tragic story is narrated here along with artifacts from his life, and the Museum of Tinos Artists next door houses some of his work. ⊠ *Pirgos* ✛ *One block from bus stop* ☎ *22830/31262* 🖾 *3€* ⊗ *Closed Oct.–Mar.*

★ Museum of Marble Crafts

MUSEUM | At the highest point on Pirgos hill, the Museum of Marble Crafts is a strikingly modern building where exhibits show the process of quarrying and carving the world famous stone. The tools and techniques are described in detail, as are the social and economic contexts in which the craft developed. The master artists' drawings for altarpieces and tomb sculptures are also on display, as are some of their works. ⊠ *Pirgos* ✛ *Take the staircase up from the main square of Pirgos* ☎ *22830/31290* ⊕ *www.piop.gr* 🖾 *€4* ⊗ *Closed Tues.*

👜 Shopping

The House of Honey

FOOD/CANDY | A quaint little shop dedicated to all things honey. In hives high up in the mountains of Tinos, the bees make their delicious nectar from the wildflowers and herbs. Bee pollen, royal jelly, honey liqueur, candles, and wine from the owner's fields are also offered. ⊠ *Pirgos* ☎ *22830/31407* ⊕ *www.tospititoumeliou. com.gr.*

Panormos Bay
Όρμος Πανόρμου

35 km (22 miles) northwest of Tinos Town, 3 km (2 miles) north of Pirgos.

Panormos Bay, an unpretentious port once used for marble export, has ducks and geese, a row of seafood restaurants, and a good beach with a collapsed sea cave. More coves with secluded swimming are beyond, as is the islet of Panormos. Check the weather before your visit as this coast bears the brunt of the summer winds.

Beaches

Kolimpithra Beach

BEACH—SIGHT | Kolimpithira is made up of two beaches; the smaller is more organized and sheltered with sun beds and a taverna up on the headland, the second is a larger stretch of sand much favored by surfers when the weather is right. A small scene has developed around a VW camper van converted into a cool beach bar, with driftwood furniture and umbrellas disguised as giant mushrooms. **Amenities:** food and drink, water sports. **Best for:** surfing, swimming. ⊠ *Panormos.*

Panormos Beach

BEACH—SIGHT | The sandy beach fronts the lovely fishing village of Panormos, which at one point was the island's main harbor. Located north of Tinos Town, most visitors also make it a point to visit the nearby inland village of Pirgos or beach-hop to little beaches to the east and west of Panormos Beach. When the island winds are right, windsurfers may take on the waters. **Amenities:** food and drink. **Best for:** swimming; windsurfing. ⊠ *Panormos.*

Rohari Beach

BEACH—SIGHT | **FAMILY** | Located in the next cove southeast of Panormos Beach, Rohari remains just as popular in the summer as a favorite northern beach destination. Fully organized, the beachfront cantinas are the perfect spot for a cool drink; there are beach umbrellas and chairs for rent. It's within close proximity to the village of Panormos, which has a wide selection of tavernas and cafés for a beach-day break. **Amenities:** food and drink. **Best for:** swimming. ⊠ *Panormos.*

Syros Σύρος

153 km (96 miles) southeast of Piraeus.

The mercantile bustle of modern Ermoupoli—Syros's port, capital, and the archipelago's business hub since the 18th century—often makes people do a double take. Seen from a distance out at sea, the city looks like a Cycladic village—one, however, raised to the nth dimension, with thousands of houses climbing their way up twin conical hills. The closer you get, the more impressive things look. As you pull into the harbor, lined with big mansions and towering churches, you see that Hermesopolis—the city was originally named after Hermes, the god of trade—is a 19th-century neoclassical jewel. A palatial marble town hall, a grand city square that looks airlifted from Paris, an opera house modeled after La Scala, and a gambling casino: these are just a few of the flourishes that announce Ermoupoli as the centuries-old administrative hub of the Cyclades. Partly colonized by one of Greece's largest Catholic populations, Syros is home to more than half the residents of the island chain.

Though it seems arid, Homer praised the island in Book XV of *The Odyssey*. Markos Vamvakaris, the great Syrian *rebetis* (performer of rembetika music), wrote a song celebrating the beauty of its women of Venetian and Frankish descent, the "Frankosyriani," perhaps the most popular of all *bouzouki* songs. Herman Melville, writing in 1856–57, gave the men equal time: "Lithe fellows tall with gold-shot eyes, Sunning themselves as leopards may."

Near the center of the Cyclades, due east of Kythnos and west of Mykonos, rocky Syros covers an area of 135 square km (52 square miles). Some might say that Ermoupoli is the only real reason for a stopover on Syros—but it is so architecturally rich that it should not be missed. Also, the island's untouristy urbanity and long, exciting history, much of it visible, make it worthwhile.

GETTING HERE AND AROUND

Olympic Air flies to Syros daily (40 minutes), and up to four ferries leave from Piraeus (4 hours), usually stopping at Tinos and/or Mykonos en route; seats book up fast during the summer season, so advance reservations are essential. As Syros is the administrative hub for the Cyclades, you can find daily ferry connections back and forth to any of the islands in the chain, including Paros, Naxos, Tinos, and Mykonos. Several ferry companies timetable regular runs, including Blue Star Ferries, Seajets, and Hellenic Seaways. The Syros Port Authority can answer questions about ferry schedules.

Syros has an organized bus system that offers service every half hour from Ermoupoli. Fares are less than €2 each way. The bus stops at the villages located on the ring road, including Galissas, Finikas, Poseidonia, Megas Yialos, and Vari. Another bus goes toward Kini. There are also taxi stands at the harbor, right where the ferries unload passengers. It costs about €5 to get from the port to Ano Syros.

Rental cars offer you more freedom to get to the beaches and other villages out of Ermoupoli. Compact car rentals start at €25 a day, and motorbike rentals start at €15 per day.

AIRPORT CONTACTS Syros Airport.
☎ 22810/79545.

FERRY CONTACTS Syros Port Authority.
☎ 22810/88888.

TOURS
Galera Travel

EXCURSIONS | Right on the waterfront, Galera has tickets for all the boats and offers accommodation, tours around the island, and car hire. ✉ 16 Papagou Str, Ermoupoli ☎ 22810/87666 ⊕ www. go2syros.gr.

Ermoupoli Ερμούπολη

35 km (22 miles) west of Mykonos, 135 km (84 miles) northwest of Santorini, 154 km (96 miles) southeast of Athens.

Ermoupoli spills like multicolored lava from the twin colonial hills of Ano Syros and Vrodado, topped respectively by churches—Roman Catholic (St. George) on the left-hand peak, when viewed from the harbor, and Greek Orthodox (Resurrection) on the right. Capital not only of the island but of the entire Cycladic island group, Ermoupoli was the main port of Greece for half a century after its conception in 1822, during the War of Independence. During the struggle, refugees fleeing from the Turkish massacres chose the site of the ancient "town of Hermes," god of travelers and merchants, on which to raise their new city, and crowned it with Vrodado's blue-dome Resurrection church. Following the war, Syros became so important it was seriously considered as a site for the fledgling nation's first capital. Starting at that time, waves of rich immigrants from Smyrna, Chios, Hydra, Psara, and Crete made the island into a cultural and commercial center.

◉ Sights

Apollo Theater

ARTS VENUE | Built in 1864 as a small-scale version of Milan's La Scala, the Apollo Theater is another example of Syros's wealth. Severely damaged during WWII, the theater was finally restored and reopened in 2000. Today, operas and other cultural events fill the summer schedule, including the world famous Festival of the Aegean, which takes place every July. ⊠ *Miaoúli Sq., across from the Municipal Palace* ☎ *22810/85192* ⊕ *www.apollontheater.gr.*

Archaeological Museum

MUSEUM | Syros's Archaeological Museum is located on the left side of the town hall. The small space features artifacts from the island's rich history. The collection stretches back to the Neolithic era and includes artifacts taken from the prehistoric acropolis at Kastri to the north. Particularly illustrious are the Early Cycladic objects from Chalandriani (just south of Kastri), which indicate an advanced culture in the 3rd millennium BC. The museum, while not extensive, is one of the oldest in Greece and also has finds from Paros and Amorgos ⊠ *Miaoúli Sq., Left side of Municipal Palace, separate entrance* ☎ *22810/88487* ⌁ *€2* ◷ *Closed Tues.*

Industrial Museum

MUSEUM | Suitably housed in refurbished factories that helped establish the island's wealth and industrial supremacy in the 19th century, the Industrial Museum walks you through the commercial district's rise and fall. The three buildings once belonged to Katsimantis Paint, the Aneroussis Lead Factory, and the Kornilakis Tannery. A tour gives insight into how employees worked, who they worked for, and how their collective skills made Syros a bustling harbor and key European trading zone, all contributing to the island's prosperity and influence on Greece as a fledgling nation. Vintage photographs, various tools, and an exhibit of two-dozen large machines that were used until the mid-20th century also give insight into a thriving industrial center that once was. ⊠ *Georgiou Papandreou 11* ☎ *22810/81243* ⊕ *www.ketepo.gr* ⌁ *€2.*

I Love the Nightlife

Syros is known for its *rembetika* music—the noted songster Markos Vamvakaris was a native. The best places to hear traditional songs are the cafés way up on the Ano Syros hill but you'll also find fine cafés down by the harbor where, late at night, the music begins to wail. Other night-time options: the open-air Pallas movie theater (east of Miaoúli Square), concerts at Apollo Theater, or the elegant casino on the quay.

Miaoúli Square

LOCAL INTEREST | Like the Municipal Palace behind it, this expansive palm-ringed marble square was designed by famed Bavarian architect Ernst Ziller and includes a grand statue of revolutionary war hero Admiral Andreas Miaoúlis. Families and couples fill the length of marbled pavement on summer evenings for their evening *volta* or walk as skateboarding children skid around them. The island's other architectural landmark, the Apollo Theater, is a short walk away. ⊠ *Miaoúli Sq.*

Municipal Palace/Town Hall

GOVERNMENT BUILDING | The Municipal Palace, also known as the Town Hall, was built in 1876 by Ernst Ziller whose credits include Athens's famous Grande Bretagne hotel and the nearby Miaoúli Square. The building is an impeccably maintained neoclassical landmark of Ermoupoli. During working hours, you can stroll in and take in the elegantly designed marble rooms. Local town officials still hold meetings here in the presence of grand oil paintings of King George I and Queen Olga. The building also houses the municipal courts, which deal with legal cases from all the Cycladic islands, since Syros is the administrative capital. A traditional marble floor café, popular with the locals, is situated in the center, surrounded by high marble balconies. ✉ *Miaoúli Square* ☎ *22810/86300.*

Beaches

Although its beaches don't equal those of Mykonos or Tinos, Syros has plenty of pleasant stretches of sand. The most popular are located on the southern side of the island, while the caïque from Kini will take you to the inaccessible beaches on the Northern Coast. If you are in the city and fancy a dip, head down to Asteria in the Vaporia district which has concrete jetties that jut out into the sea.

Azolimnos Beach

BEACH—SIGHT | As one of the closest organized beaches to Ermoupoli, Azolimnos attracts its share of crowds in the height of summer. The coast is a mixture of small rocks and sand with a picturesque little dock that juts out into the bay. Tamarisk trees offer natural shade, and lounge chairs and umbrellas are available for rent. The small road set in the background is lined with various options for food, coffee, drinks, and supplies. **Amenities:** food and drink. **Best for:** swimming. ✉ *Azolimnos.*

Restaurants

Kouzina

$$ | MEDITERRANEAN | FAMILY | The colorful taverna-style restaurant is set in a bougainvillea-laced courtyard at the end of the "Dining Mile" in Ermoupoli. Local Cycladic ingredients are fused with modern techniques and cooking styles to good effect on the menu, with influences from Thessaloniki and the further Mediterranean. **Known for:** daring flavor combinations; burgers are the best in town; homemade breads and organic, slow-food mentality. [$] *Average main: €16* ✉ *Androu 5* ☎ *22810/89150.*

★ Mazi

$$ | GREEK FUSION | An old ceramics factory with a jewel of a courtyard—all stone arches and climbing greenery—is the theater set for the most beautiful restaurant in Ermoupoli. With inspiration from around the globe, this is a very modern iteration of Greek food; ceviches and tartares feature, and some dishes are deconstructed to their constituent parts. **Known for:** desserts are pretty as a picture; all-Greek wine card and inventive cocktails; impressive, artful, and innovative cooking. [$] *Average main: €21* ✉ *2 Leotsakou* ☎ *22810/88811* 🌐 *www.mazi-syros.com.*

To Kastri

$ | GREEK | Located in the central market, To Kastri is run by the Women's Union of Syros, a group of 28 women who cook 10 dishes a day—home cooking so good that local housewives secretly buy food for their midday meals here. Open all year, this cafeteria often sells out by early afternoon. **Known for:** local specialties change daily; no-frills interior; truly home-cooked food. [$] *Average main: €5* ✉ *Parou 13* ✣ *A small side street off El. Venizelou* ☎ *22810/83140* 🌐 *www.tokastri.blogspot.gr.*

Coffee and Quick Bites

★ Daidadi Gelato

$ | FAST FOOD | The lifesize black and white cow outside tells you that you have arrived at the best ice cream shop on the island. Made from Syros milk by an Italian ice cream maker, funky flavors exist alongside the classics. **Known for:** experimental flavors; high-quality ingredients; shaded tables outside. [$] *Average main: €3* ✉ *Papagou Square* ☎ *22810/85953.*

Hotels

Diogenis Hotel

$ | HOTEL | Situated right on the harbor-front where the ferries dock in Syros, the Diogenis Hotel took over a 19th-century neoclassical building that was once used as a warehouse, lumber yard, and, during the Italian occupation, housed the military police. **Pros:** centrally located; good value; friendly, helpful staff. **Cons:** the port can be a busy, noisy place; rooms are a little snug; inferior view in rooms at the rear. $ *Rooms from:* €80 ✉ *Ermoupoli* ☎ *22810/86301* ⊕ *www.diogenishotel. com* ➥ *40 rooms* ¶⊙¶ *Free breakfast.*

★ Hotel Ploes

$$ | HOTEL | Once a private 19th-century estate in the upscale district of Ermoupoli, Hotel Ploes has been completely renovated to luxury hotel status. **Pros:** direct access to the sea; centrally located; beautiful views. **Cons:** no swimming pool; no on-site restaurant; expensive for Syros. $ *Rooms from:* €200 ✉ *Apollonos 2* ☎ *22810/79360* ⊕ *www.hotelploes. com* ➥ *8 rooms* ¶⊙¶ *Free breakfast.*

Nisaki

$ | HOTEL | Convenient and comfortable, this modern three-story building is set amid neoclassical buildings and is within walking distance of Ermoupoli's most visited sites. **Pros:** ideal location for ferries; on-site car parking; views across to Didimi Island. **Cons:** small bathrooms; harborfront location can be noisy; uninspired '70s architecture. $ *Rooms from:* €65 ✉ *E. Padadam 1* ☎ *22810/88200* ⊕ *www.hotelnisaki.gr* ➥ *42 rooms* ¶⊙¶ *Free breakfast.*

Syrou Melathron

$ | HOTEL | Located behind the St. Nicholas Cathedral and just a five-minute walk from Miaoúli Square, this neoclassical building, which was completed in 1857, sits off a paved sea road in the upscale neighborhood of Vaporia. **Pros:** centrally located; great service; fantastic views. **Cons:** rooms can be on the small side; parking not on-site; not all rooms have sea views. $ *Rooms from:* €100 ✉ *Babagiotou 5* ☎ *22810/86495* ⊕ *www. syroumelathron.gr* ⊘ *Closed Nov.–Feb.* ➥ *22 rooms* ¶⊙¶ *Free breakfast.*

 Nightlife

Baba Bar

BARS/PUBS | A few steps away from the nightlife bustle of Petrou Ralli's row of music-pumping bars, Baba Bar is still in the heart of the action, just slightly tucked away in a pretty little street that's lit by strings of soft white light bulbs. The bar's small, Cycladic-style interior can get packed with regulars that come back for their eclectic selection of cocktails with names like Pirate Martini, Rosemary Melon, Pina Rosa, and the signature rum Baba. ✉ *Ermoupoli* ✛ *Near Petrou Ralli* ☎ *6978506207.*

Liquid Gastropub

DANCE CLUBS | Located across the street from the quiet marbled Miaoúli Square, this corner bar gets busy and loud around midnight, when the bouncer is securely in place and a line to get in may start forming. During the day, it's rustic interior is a calming place to have a coffee and sample their international menu. ✉ *El. Venizelou, Across the street from Miaoúli Square* ☎ *22810/83974.*

Mammo Wine and Food Bar

WINE BARS—NIGHTLIFE | Nightlife in Syros revolves around the eastern part of the harbor, along Petrou Ralli, where you may find people dancing in the street; Mammo Wine Bar is at the center of it. Café and restaurant by day—serving bruschettas, gourmet salads, and a variety of international and Mediterranean plates—the energy heightens when the sun sets. Its sleek, dark, and modern space gets packed and comes alive once a DJ is called in to play mainstream dance music, and colorful creative cocktails and shots make the rounds. ✉ *Akti Petrou Ralli 38* ☎ *22810/76416.*

Kini

7 km (4 miles) west of Ermoupoli.

This small village on the island's west coast has a couple of good beaches, a selection of tavernas and cafés, and a few places to stay. Since it has one of the better beaches on the island, it's a popular stop for tourists.

Beaches

Kini Beach

BEACH—SIGHT | If you're looking for the best sunset on the island, head where the locals head—Kini. The beach, long and sandy, features a little picturesque port that's flanked by a line of shady trees and the lovely little whitewashed village it gets its name from. It's big enough to accommodate all beach-going types including families, strolling couples, and water-sports lovers. The selection of taverns, restaurants, and cafés is plentiful and if you need a beach umbrella and chair rental, show up early during peak season. **Amenities:** food and drink. **Best for:** swimming; sunset; walking. ⊠ *Kini.*

Lotos Beach

BEACH—SIGHT | Small, quiet, and secluded, this sand-and-pebble beach is flanked by shady tamarisk trees. There are no amenities here, but it's within walking distance of the well-organized and popular Kini Beach and Kini Village where everything can be found. **Amenities:** none. **Best for:** solitude. ⊠ *Lotos Beach.*

Restaurants

Allou Yialou

$$ | GREEK | Located right off the beach in Kini, on a raised, whitewashed dining space lined with pretty white curtains, Allou Yialou is known for its spectacular sunset dining. It's also where everyone goes for Greek dishes that take on a delightful and delicious gourmet twist. **Known for:** beachfront location and views; fresh seafood plates; attentive staff. $ *Average main: €20* ⊠ *Kini* ☎ *22810/71196* ⊗ *Closed Nov.–Apr.*

Ano Syros Άνω Σύρος

9 km (5½ miles) northwest of Ermoupoli.

One of the two towering peaks that rise over town, Ano Syros was greatly expanded in the 13th century by Venetians, who erected a walled town over the ancient acropolis to protect themselves from pirates. It's now the second city of Syros. From the Roman Catholic bishopric of the church of St. George crowning the hill, this lofty retreat maintains its 13th-century integrity. High atop the hill is the looming Capuchin Monastery (1633), where visitors on official religious business may enjoy a sojourn in the jasmine-scented garden overlooking all of Ermoupoli. Not far away is a belvedere—the town's high point—where a bronze bust of Pherecydes of Syros commemorates that imaginative 6th-century-BC philosopher, Pythagoras's teacher, who reputedly invented the sundial and was the first to write Greek prose. The bishopric, where bishops have presided since the time of Irenaios (343 AD), is downhill from the monastery. Farther down is the Jesuit Monastery, founded in 1747, and the adjacent church of the Virgin of Carmel. As you can see, the hill of Ano Syros remains mostly Catholic, but just across the townscape is the hill of Vrodado, which reminds us that Syros is now two-thirds Greek Orthodox (happily, relations remain cordial). The Catholic-flavored Venetian influence has given the island's culture and architecture a distinct flavor; having welcomed so many religious refugees to its shores, Syros came under the protection of Louis XIII in 1640, which accounts for the French-flavored influence. ■**TIP→ Take a taxi up, but walk down so you can explore Omiros, a handy thoroughfare through this picturesque quarter that's dotted with castle walls and stone alleyways.**

Sights

Vamvakaris Museum

MUSEUM | One of Greece's most prestigious *rembetika* (urban Greek folk music) artists, Markos Vamvakaris hails from Syros, making this a fitting location for a museum in his honor. The composer is a legend in Greek folklore music hailing from the 1930s and is widely known for his *rembetika* songs, especially the Frangosyriani. In the little museum you'll see many of his personal items, vintage photographs, and a passport he never managed to use, all donated by his family. ✉ *Agiou Sevastianou street* ☎ *22813/610655.*

☕ Coffee and Quick Bites

Maison de Meze

$ | **GREEK** | Winding whitewashed streets lead to this little beauty serving superlative local products at great prices. A tiny courtyard with a treasure trove of a shop behind it awaits in Ano Syros—small plates of delicious homemade joy are your reward. **Known for:** small menu of Syros delicacies; products also for sale in cave-like shop behind; just three tables. **$** *Average main: €8* ✉ *Ano Syros* ☎ *22810/76209* ⊕ *www.maisondemeze. gr.*

Galissas ΓΑΛΗΣΣΑΣ

4 km (2½ miles) southwest of Ermoupoli.

The village of Galissas has a selection of tavernas and beach bar-cafés as well as room rentals and the Dolphin Bay Family Beach Resort. Since it has one of the island's longest sandy beaches, it's a popular destination for anyone stopping over on the island.

Sights

St. Stefanos Chapel

RELIGIOUS SITE | Beautiful and picturesque, Aghios Stefanos is a tiny chapel built into a cave right above the sea. A 15-minute walk from Galissas with views to Finikas and beyond, it was built by a fisherman who prayed to the saint to help him after being entangled in the tentacles of a giant octopus. Twice a year—August 19th and December 26th—celebrations are held and after the liturgy attendees are offered *loukoumi*, the local sweet. ✉ *Galissas.*

Beaches

Galissas Beach

BEACH—SIGHT | Competing with Kini for the most magical sunset, the long curve of sand and clear coastline of water at Galissas is a local favorite. It's also won the coveted EU Blue Flag award for being one of the island's cleanest in Europe. As one of the island's largest beaches, it's well organized with beach umbrella and chair rentals available in peak season. When the island winds roar, windsurfers show up. ■**TIP**➔ **There's a separate area for nudists. Amenities:** food and drink. **Best for:** nudists; swimming; windsurfing. ✉ *Galissas.*

Restaurants

★ Iliovasilema

$$ | **MODERN GREEK** | French-trained chef Kostas Bougiouris lends his expertise to this waterside restaurant. Almost on the beach, the setting is elegant and the cooking focuses on seafood and local Syros products, presented in a modern, creative style. **Known for:** reservations needed; superlative sunset dining; recipes inspired by the Aegean. **$** *Average main: €18* ✉ *Galissas* ☎ *22810/43325* ⊕ *www.chefbougiouris.gr/en.*

Poseidonia Ποσειδωνία

6 km (4 miles) southwest of Ermoupoli.

This small village has a few whitewashed taverns, cafés, and churches, which serve as a backdrop to a popular beach. Other good beaches are to the north and south of the village.

Beaches

Agathopes Beach
BEACH—SIGHT | FAMILY | Considered one of Syros's most beautiful beaches, Agathopes gets packed in peak season due to its shallow waters and fine sand. If you're there at the right time, you'll find a unique small islet where white sea lilies blossom. The sea view is also dotted with the uninhabited islands called Schinonissi and Stroggilo. Beachgoers can rent lounge chairs and umbrellas, and there's a local taverna within walking distance. **Amenities:** food and drink. **Best for:** swimming. ⊠ *Agathopes Beach.*

Finikas Beach
BEACH—SIGHT | Sheltered by the summer island winds, Finikas Beach is the perfect spot for those seeking a calm beach day southwest of Ermoupoli. Boasting the island's second largest port, yachts often dock here and there's typically a picturesque scene of fishing boats bobbing on the calm waters. Tamarisk trees dot the beach providing natural shade, although beach umbrella and chair rentals are available during peak season. There are plenty of eateries to choose from as well. **Amenities:** food and drink. **Best for:** swimming. ⊠ *Finikas.*

Poseidonia Beach (*Dellagrazia Beach*)
BEACH—SIGHT | This beach may have two names, but its known for one thing: being pretty. Located in the southwest part of Syros, it features smooth, yellow sand with scatterings of small pebbles. It shares the same views of Schinonissi and Stroggilo as neighboring Agathopes

Strong Greek Flavoring

When Athenians want *real* Greek food, they often head to Syros, which has long been known for its culinary brio. Not only was Greece's first cookbook published here in 1828, famed foodie Elizabeth David earned her toque in Mediterranean cooking here. Flavors are strong and accented with cheese, tomato, and fennel. Check out the lemon-and-anise-flavored *loukanika* sausages; the cured-pork *louza* tenderloin soaked in wine and cloves; the *marathopita*, lemon-herb and fennel pie; and the *kopanisti*, the island's tangy cheese.

beach. Small boats and yachts often park here adding to the quaint views. **Amenities:** food and drink. **Best for:** swimming. ⊠ *Poseidonia.*

Megas Yialos ΜΕΓΑ ΓΙΑΛΟ

9 km (5½ miles) south of Ermoupoli.

Megas Yialos has slowly grown into one of the island's more popular beach towns and is accessible by bus from Ermoupoli. Its nearby beaches, including the favored Megas Yialos beach, are within easy walking distance for those staying at area hotels and rooms. Restaurants and cafés also cater to summer crowds.

Beaches

Megas Yialos Beach
BEACH—SIGHT | One of the largest beaches on Syros, Megas Yialos is also one of the most frequented and organized. Located on the island's southeast corner, the beach is known for its transparent waters and fine sand. The village is

populated with room rentals and small hotels as well as restaurants and beach cafés. Some large shady trees dot the beach, but in peak season chairs and umbrellas are for rent. **Amenities:** food and drink. **Best for:** swimming. ⊠ *Megas Gialos.*

Vari ΒΑΡΗ

6 km (4 miles) southeast of Ermoupoli.

Vari is a small beach town on a sheltered bay on the south side of the island. Its location attracts visitors who seek the low-key, quiet calm of the nearby beaches.

 Beaches

Vari Beach

BEACH—SIGHT | The small beach's fine sand is protected from the sometimes harsh summer Cycladic winds, making its calm water a favorite with local families. Considered an organized beach, beach chair and umbrella rentals are available, and a street lined with tavernas and cafés is within walking distance for any visitors that need a good meal after a day of beach lounging. **Amenities:** food and drink. **Best for:** sunsets; swimming. ⊠ *Vari.*

Mykonos ΜΥΚΟΝΟΣ

From backpackers to the super-rich, from day-trippers to yachties, from Joe Average to celebrities who head here by helicopter, Mykonos has become one of the most popular of the Aegean islands. Today's scene is a weird but attractive cocktail of tradition, beauty, and glitz, but travelers from all over the world have long been drawn to this dry, rugged island—at 16 km (10 miles) by 11 km (7 miles), one of the smaller Cyclades—thanks to its many stretches of sandy

beach, its thatched windmills, and its picturesque port town. One thing is certain: Mykonos knows how to maintain its attractiveness, how to develop it, and how to sell it. Complain as you will that it is touristy, noisy, and overdeveloped but you will be back.

In the 1950s, a few tourists began trickling into Mykonos on their way to see the ancient marvels on the nearby islet of Delos, the sacred isle. For almost 1,000 years Delos was the religious and political center of the Aegean and host every four years to the Delian games, the region's greatest festival. The population of Delos actually reached 20,000 at the peak of its commercial period, and throughout antiquity Mykonos, eclipsed by its holy neighbor, depended on this proximity for income (it has been memorably described as Delos's "bordello"), as it partly does today. Anyone interested in antiquity should plan to spend at least one morning on Delos, which has some of the most striking sights preserved from antiquity, including the beautiful Avenue of the Lions and the startling, enormous stone phalli in the Sanctuary of Dionysus.

Today, the natives of Mykonos have happily welcomed cosmopolitan New Yorkers, Londoners, and Athenians gracefully into their way of life. You may see, for example, an old island woman leading a donkey laden with vegetables through the town's narrow streets, greeting the suntanned vacationers walking by. The truth is, Mykonians regard a good tourist season the way a fisherman inspects a calm morning's catch; for many, the money earned in July and August will support them for the rest of the year. Not long ago Mykonians had to rely on what they could scratch out of the island's arid land for sustenance, and some remember suffering from starvation under Axis occupation during World War II. How things have changed.

GETTING HERE AND AROUND

Mykonos is superpopular and easy to get to. It is totally jammed in season, in part thanks to 6 or more daily 45-minute flights from Athens in summer (there are almost as many in winter); there are also direct flights from Europe. The trip by ferry takes from two to five hours depending on your route, the boat, and Poseidon's weather ways. There are six or more boats a day. For Easter and August 15, book early. In summer, reservations are necessary; off-season, you won't need one, but cars always need them. The boats usually pull in at the huge new dock area, from which you must take a bus or taxi, or get your hotel to pick you up—better hotels do this, and often charge you for it.

In Mykonos Town, the Ayios Loukas bus depot in the Fabrika quarter at the south end of town has buses to Ornos, Ayios Ioannis, Platis Gialos, Psarou, Paradise Beach, the airport, and Kalamopodi. Another depot near the Old Port is for Ayios Stefanos, Tourlos, Ano Mera, Elia, Kalafatis, and Kalo Livadi. Schedules are posted (hotel concierges also should have this info); fares run from €1.80 to €3. Regular taxis line up at Plateia Manto Mavrogenous, while scooter-taxis greet new arrivals at the harbor; use them to get to your Mykonos Town hotel, usually hidden away on a pedestrian- and scooter-only street. Meters are not used on Mykonos; instead, standard fares for each destination are posted on a notice bulletin board; note there are only 34 regular cabs here even in August!

TOURS

Mykonos Accommodation Center

GUIDED TOURS | This center, up a steep staircase in a picturesque old building, has grown to offer just about every service a visitor may need on Mykonos, including a wide variety of group tours. A guide takes a group every morning for a day tour of Delos (€50). The company also has half-day guided tours of the Mykonos beach towns, with a stop in Ano Mera for the Panayia Tourliani Monastery (€50). You can also take an excursion to nearby Tinos (€70), arrange private tours of Delos and Mykonos and off-road jeep trips (€70), charter yachts, and more. ✉ *Enoplon Dynameon 10, upper fl., Mykonos Town* ☎ *22890/23160* ⊕ *www.mykonos-accommodation.com.*

Mykonos Town
Μύκονος (Χώρα)

177 km (110 miles) southeast of Piraeus harbor in Athens.

Although the fishing boats still go out in good weather, Mykonos largely makes its living from tourism these days. The summer crowds have turned one of the poorest islands in Greece into one of the richest. Old Mykonians complain that their young, who have inherited stores where their grandfathers once sold eggs or wine, get so much rent that they have lost ambition, and in summer sit around pool bars at night with their friends, and hang out in Athens in winter when island life is less scintillating.

Put firmly on the map by Jackie Kennedy Onassis in the 1960s, Mykonos Town—called Hora by the locals—remains the Saint-Tropez of the Greek islands. The scenery is memorable, with its white-washed streets, Little Venice, the Kato Myli ridge of windmills, and Kastro, the town's medieval quarter. Its cubical two- or three-story houses and the churches, with their red or blue doors, domes, and wooden balconies, have been long cele-brated as some of the best examples of classic Cycladic architecture. Luckily, the Greek Archaeological Service decided to protect the town, even when the Mykoni-ans would have preferred to rebuild, and so the Old Town has been impressively preserved. Pink oleander, scarlet hibis-cus, and trailing green pepper trees form a contrast amid the dazzling whiteness, whose frequent renewal with whitewash is required by law.

Any visitor who has the pleasure of getting lost in its narrow streets (made all the narrower by the many outdoor stone staircases, which maximize housing space in the crowded village) will appreciate how its confusing layout was designed to foil pirates—if it was designed at all. After Mykonos fell under Turkish rule in 1537, the Ottomans allowed the islanders to arm their vessels against pirates, which had a contradictory effect: many of them found that raiding other islands was more profitable than tilling arid land. At the height of Aegean piracy, Mykonos was the principal headquarters of the corsair fleets—the place where pirates met their fellows, found willing women, and filled out their crews. Eventually the illicit activity evolved into a legitimate and thriving trade network.

Morning on Mykonos Town's main quay is busy with deliveries, visitors for the Delos boats, lazy breakfasters, and street cleaners dealing with the previous night's mess. In late morning the cruise-boat people arrive, and the shops are all open. In early afternoon, shaded outdoor tavernas are full of diners eating salads (Mykonos's produce is mostly imported); music is absent or kept low. In mid- and late afternoon, the town feels sleepy, since so many people are at the beach, on excursions, or sleeping in their air-conditioned rooms; even some tourist shops close for siesta. By sunset, people have come back from the beach, taken their showers, and rested. At night, the atmosphere in Mykonos ramps up. The cruise-boat people are mostly gone, coughing three-wheelers have finished their deliveries in the narrow streets, and everyone is dressed in their sexy summer best and starting to shimmy with the scene. Many shops stay open past midnight, the restaurants fill up, and the bars and discos make ice cubes as fast as they can.

Ready to dive in? Begin your tour of Mykonos Town (Hora) by starting out at its heart: Manto Mavrogenous Square.

 # Sights

Aegean Maritime Museum
MUSEUM | The charming Aegean Maritime Museum contains a collection of model ships, navigational instruments, old maps, prints, coins, and nautical memorabilia. The backyard garden displays some old anchors and ship wheels and a reconstructed 1890 lighthouse, once lit by oil. ✉ *Enoplon Dynameon 10* ☎ *22890/22700* ⊕ *www.aegean-maritime-museum.gr* 🎫 *€4* ⊙ *Closed Nov.–Apr.*

Archaeological Museum of Mykonos
MUSEUM | Before setting out on the mandatory boat excursion to the isle of Delos, check out the Archaeological Museum, which affords insight into the intriguing history of its ancient shrines. The museum houses Delian funerary sculptures, many with scenes of mourning. Most were moved to Rineia when the Athenians cleansed Delos in the 6th century, during the sixth year of the Peloponnesian War, and, under instruction from the Delphic Oracle, the entire island was purged of all dead bodies. The most significant work from Mykonos is a 7th-century BC *pithos* (storage jar), showing the Greeks in the Trojan horse and the sacking of the city. ✉ *Mykonos Town* ⚓ *Old Port* ☎ *22890/22325* ⊕ *odysseus. culture.gr* 🎫 *€4* ⊙ *Closed Tues.*

★ Church of Paraportiani
(*Our Lady of the Postern Gate*)
RELIGIOUS SITE | Mykonians claim that exactly 365 churches and chapels dot their landscape, one for each day of the year. The most famous of these is the Church of Paraportiani. The sloping, whitewashed conglomeration of four chapels, mixing Byzantine and vernacular idioms, looks fantastic. Solid and ultimately sober, its position on a

promontory facing the sea sets off the unique architecture. It's said to be one of the most photographed churches in the world. ⊠ *Ayion Anargyron.*

Folk Museum

MUSEUM | Housed in an 18th-century house originally built for Captain Nikolaos Malouchos, this museum exhibits a bedroom furnished and decorated in the fashion of that period. On display are looms and lace-making devices, Cycladic costumes, old photographs, and Mykoniot musical instruments that are still played at festivals. ⊠ *Kastro* ✛ *Old Port, near Paraportiani church* ☎ *22890/22591* ⊕ *www.mykonosfolkloremuseum.gr* ☉ *Closed Oct.–Apr.*

Lena's House

HOUSE | Take a peek into Lena's House, an annex of the local Folk Museum, and experience an accurate restoration of a middle-class Mykonos house from the 19th century. The name refers to its last inhabitant, Lena Skrivanou. ⊠ *Enoplon Dynameon* ☎ *22890/22390* ☉ *Closed Nov.–Mar.*

★ Little Venice

NEIGHBORHOOD | Many of the early ships' captains built distinguished houses directly on the seafront here, with elaborate buttressed wooden balconies hanging over the water, which is how this neighborhood earned its name. Architecturally unique, it is one of the most attractive areas in all the islands, and many of these fine old houses now host elegant bars. A sunset drink here to the sound of the waves is a Mykonos must-do. ⊠ *Mykonos Town.*

Manto Mavrogenous Square

PLAZA | Start a tour of Mykonos Town (Hora) on the main square, Manto Mavrogenous Square (sometimes called Taxi Square). Pride of place goes to a bust of Manto Mavrogenous, the island heroine, atop a pedestal. In the 1821 War of Independence the Mykonians, known for their seafaring skills, volunteered an armada of 24 ships, and in 1822, when the Ottomans landed a force on the island, Manto and her soldiers forced them back to their ships. After independence, a scandalous love affair caused the heroine's exile to Paros, where she died. An aristocratic beauty who becomes a great revolutionary war leader and then dies for love may seem straight out of Hollywood, but it is all true. ⊠ *Mykonos Town.*

Matoyanni

NEIGHBORHOOD | The main shopping street, Matoyanni, is lined with jewelry stores, clothing boutiques, chic cafés, and candy shops. Owing to the many cruise ships that disgorge thousands of shoppers daily in season—some unload 3,000 jostling tourists—the rents here rival 5th Avenue's, and the more-interesting shops have skedaddled to less-prominent side streets. ⊠ *Mykonos Town* ✛ *Perpendicular to harbor.*

Municipal Art Gallery of Mykonos

MUSEUM | Located on Manto Mavrogenous Square, the Public Art Gallery of Mykonos changes exhibitions often, giving Greek and international artists a great place to showcase their work. ⊠ *Matoyanni* ☎ *22890/27190.*

Mykonos Agricultural Museum

MUSEUM | This museum displays a 16th-century windmill, outdoor oven, waterwheel, wine press, and dovecote, with the intention of illustrating and preserving the traditional rural life of the island. ⊠ *Petassos* ✛ *At top of Mykonos Town* ☉ *Closed Oct.–May.*

Mykonos Windmills

WINDMILL | Across the water from Little Venice, set on a high hill, are the famous Mykonos windmills, echoes of a time when wind power was used to grind the island's grain. The area from Little Venice to the windmills is called Alefkandra, which means "whitening": women once hung their laundry here. A little farther toward the windmills, the bars that teeter

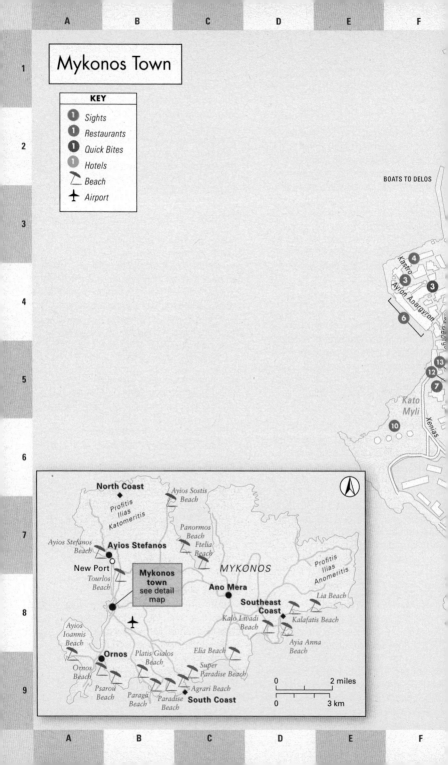

Mykonos Town

KEY
- ① Sights
- ① Restaurants
- ① Quick Bites
- ① Hotels
- Beach
- ✈ Airport

BOATS TO DELOS

Kastro
Ayíon Anárgyron
Kato Myli
Xenías

North Coast
Profitis Ilias Katomeritis
Ayios Sostis Beach
Panormos Beach
Ftelia Beach

Ayios Stefanos Beach
Ayios Stefanos
New Port
Tourlos Beach

Mykonos town see detail map

MYKONOS

Ano Mera

Profitis Ilias Anomeritis

Lia Beach

Southeast Coast
Kalo Livadi Beach
Kalafatis Beach

Ayia Anna Beach

Ayios Ioannis Beach

Ornos
Ornos Beach
Psaroú Beach
Platis Gialos Beach
Paragá Beach
Paradise Beach

Elia Beach
Super Paradise Beach
Agrari Beach
South Coast

0 ——— 2 miles
0 ——— 3 km

Sights ▼

1 Aegean Maritime Museum....... **G5**
2 Archaeological Museum of Mykonos.......................... **H1**
3 Church of Paraportiani **F4**
4 Folk Museum...................... **F3**
5 Lena's House...................... **H5**
6 Little Venice **F4**
7 Manto Mavrogenous Square **H3**
8 Matoyanni.......................... **H5**
9 Mykonos Agricultural Museum... **I4**
10 Mykonos Windmills **F6**
11 Municipal Art Gallery of Mykonos......................... **H5**
12 Roman Catholic Cathedral......... **F5**
13 Zoodochos Pigi, Orthodox Cathedral................ **F5**

Restaurants ▼

1 Avra **H5**
2 Bill and Coo........................ **H9**
3 Funky Kitchen **G6**
4 Kounelas........................... **G4**
5 La Maison de Katrin.............. **G4**
6 M-eating........................... **H5**
7 Nice n Easy........................ **F5**

Quick Bites ▼

1 Cosmo Cafe........................ **G7**
2 Gioras Bakery...................... **G6**
3 Pepper **F4**

Hotels ▼

1 Belvedere........................... **I7**
2 Bill and Coo Suites and Lounge........................ **H9**
3 Leto Hotel.......................... **I2**
4 Livin' Mykonos Boutique Hotel....**J9**
5 Myconian Korali **H9**
6 Poseidon Hotel Suite.............. **G8**
7 Semeli.............................. **I6**
8 Villa Konstantin **J1**

on shoreside decks are barely above sea level, and as the north wind gets up, surf splashes the tables. Farther on, the shore spreads into an unprepossessing beach, and tables are placed on sand or pebbles. ✉ *Alefkandra.*

Roman Catholic Cathedral

RELIGIOUS SITE | Next to the Greek Orthodox Cathedral is the Roman Catholic Cathedral, the Virgin of St. Rosary, from the Venetian period. The name and coat of arms of the Ghisi family, which took over Mykonos in 1207, are inscribed in the entrance hall. ✉ *Platia Alefkandra.*

Zoodochos Pigi, Orthodox Cathedral

RELIGIOUS SITE | The Orthodox cathedral of Mykonos is dedicated to the life-giving spring of the Virgin Mary, as its icon was found inside a well ("pigadi"). The church is also known as Angelohtismeni—built by angels; however, more prosaically, it was probably founded in the 1600s. ✉ *Alefkandra Sq.*

Beaches

Swimming in quiet Aegean bays with clean blue water enclosed by rugged hills cannot be overpraised—so it is little wonder some of Greece's finest strands of sand are found on Mykonos. Mostly protected from the prevailing north winds, they can be conveniently grouped. In general the beaches charge from €15 for an umbrella and sun bed, but the trendiest strips of sand are extorting €150 and you have to have a reservation beforehand. Most of the island's beaches lie along Mykonos's southern coast; from Mykonos Town, Ornos Beach is about 10 minutes, Kalafati is less than an hour. Mykonos Town does have a little beach that attracts local children or townies who just want a quick dip, but it's not going to be your beach of choice. All the others require transportation.

The Prance of the Pelican

By the time morning's open-air fish market picks up steam in Mykonos Town, Petros the Pelican—the town mascot—is preening and cadgeing breakfast. In the 1950s a group of migrating pelicans passed over Mykonos, leaving behind a single exhausted bird; Vassilis the fisherman nursed it back to health, and locals say that the pelican in the harbor is the original Petros, although, in fact, the original bird died back in 1985, and there is now a small colony on the island.

Restaurants

Avra

$$$ | **INTERNATIONAL** | Comforting and friendly, Avra is a long-standing favorite in the heart of town, with a picturesque, bougainvillea-strewn, private garden perfect for balmy summer nights. Avra offers mostly Greek classics but also has a strong international selection with Asian influences. **Known for:** reassuring classic dishes from all over the world; crisp linen and candles promise romance; relaxed and friendly vibe. [$] *Average main: €26* ✉ *Kalogera 27* ☎ *22890/22298* 🌐 *www.avra-mykonos.com* 🕒 *Closed Nov.–Apr.*

★ Bill and Coo

$$$$ | **GREEK FUSION** | Alongside the infinity pool at the Bill and Coo Hotel, complete with shining stars that twinkle from the bottom, is served some of the finest food in Mykonos. A futuristic glass box or the outdoor terrace on balmier nights is the setting, for a master class in modern Mediterranean cooking. **Known for:** stunning setting; staff are pitch-perfect—unstuffy and fun; wine pairings are spot on. [$] *Average main: €50* ✉ *Mykonos Town* ☎ *22890/26292* 🌐 *www.bill-coo-hotel.com.*

The little church of Agios Nikolakis sits right on the Mykonos waterfront near the ferry to Delos and is one of the most photographed sights in Mykonos Town, whether it's in the background or the foreground.

★ Funky Kitchen

$$$ | MEDITERRANEAN | Tucked in a quiet corner of Mykonos Town, on a picturesque whitewashed street lined with bougainvillea, you'll find talented chef Pavlos Grivas at work in his modern, open kitchen perfecting his innovative Mediterranean fusion dishes. Starters delight, reflecting the traditional products of Mykonos, including a uniquely flavorful panna cotta with *kopanisti* cheese, dried figs, and Greek prosciutto. **Known for:** witty, wonderful, welcoming; well-selected Greek wines; genuine, passionate owners give memorable service. $ *Average main: €26* ⊠ *Ignatiou Basoula 40* ☎ *22890/27272* ⊕ *www.funkykitchen.gr* ⊗ *Closed Apr.–Oct.*

Kounelas

$$ | SEAFOOD | This long-established fresh-fish taverna is where many fishermen themselves come for solid, no-frills food. There are a handful of meat dishes but the best choice is the catch of the day—you can pick your own fish—and ask for it to be simply grilled. **Known for:** fresh seafood and meats by the kilo, all grilled outside on a wood grill; cozy, alleyway tables; casual, friendly atmosphere. $ *Average main: €25* ⊠ *Odos Svoronou* ⊹ *Off the port, near Delos boats* ☎ *22890/28220.*

★ La Maison de Katrin

$$$$ | FRENCH | Hidden away in the Dilou quarter, this is one of the most reputable restaurants on the island, featuring the best of both French and Greek cuisine, which makes it well worth the search to find it. Once you're here you'll see a handful of linen-laden tables sit under a canopy of brilliant bougainvillea in an iconic Mykonos photo pose, while the lovely whitewashed candle-lit interior features Cycladic arches and a faded 16th-century tapestry from Constantinople. **Known for:** quality traditional Greek and French cuisine; excellent and professional service; charming, romantic, intimate atmosphere. $ *Average main: €60* ⊠ *Ayios Gerasimos and Nikou, Dilou* ☎ *22890/22169* ⊗ *Closed Nov.–Apr.*

★ M-eating

$$$$ | **MODERN GREEK** | A century old building on a tiny cobbled street hosts white linen tables on a candle-lit veranda. Chef and owner Panagiotis Menardos has worked in top kitchens across the Mediterranean, gathering techniques and ingredients to produce artful, contemporary interpretations of local dishes using the best produce from small suppliers. **Known for:** show-stopping presentation; flawless, knowledgeable service; good value compared to competitors. $ *Average main: €40* ✉ *10 Kalogera* ☎ *22890/78550* ⊕ *www.m-eating.gr* ⊘ *Closed Nov.–Mar.*

Nice n Easy

$$ | **INTERNATIONAL** | At one of the best seafront locations on the island, with Little Venice on one side and the windmills on the other, farm-to-table Mediterranean cuisine is the scene stealer. The menu is plentiful, with diverse choices, but the philosophy is simple—the best organic ingredients from Greek producers cooked simply and with respect. **Known for:** organic, local produce; prime location with waves lapping feet away; vegan and gluten-free options. $ *Average main: €25* ✉ *Platia Alefkandra* ☎ *22890/25421* ⊕ *www.niceneasy.gr.*

☕ Coffee and Quick Bites

Cosmo Cafe

$ | **CAFÉ** | On the road to the windmills, this is the prettiest place to relax over breakfast. Under a bougainvillea shade, healthy plates of yogurt, muesli, and fruits are perfect pick-me-ups to start the day. **Known for:** great coffee, awesome omelets; market-fresh produce; friendly staff love to please. $ *Average main: €8* ✉ *Mykonos Town* ☎ *22890/22215.*

★ Gioras Bakery

$ | **BAKERY** | Descend into the rustic interior of this bakery and you will feel like you have stepped back in time; Gioras dates back to the 18th century and is the

A Seaside Milky Way

The best time to visit Mykonos's central harbor is in the cool of the evening, when the islanders promenade along the esplanade to meet friends and visit the numerous cafés. Mykonians, when they see the array of harbor lights from offshore, call it the String of Pearls, though more and more lights are fuzzing the dazzle.

oldest working wood-fired bakery in the Cyclades. Take a couple of pies for the beach, or sit with a coffee and a slice of *baklava* and breathe in the history. **Known for:** time capsule interior; run by the Varmvakourides family for two centuries; astonishing range of sweets and breads. $ *Average main: €3* ✉ *Aghiou Efthimiou* ☎ *22890/27784.*

Pepper

$ | **FAST FOOD** | Food fashions come and go in Mykonos, but one thing that never goes out of style is souvlaki. Get the cleanest, tastiest in town at Pepper—tiny, with just a few tables outside, this is the answer to all your street-food needs. **Known for:** food cooked to order in front of you; open until late for post-midnight munchies; hidden back seating area to try the rest of the great grill menu. $ *Average main: €5* ✉ *18 Kouzi Georgouli* ☎ *22890/27019* ⊕ *www.pepper-mykonos. com.*

🛏 Hotels

Belvedere

$$$$ | **HOTEL** | This is the hotel for those who seek stylish surroundings and hip fellow guests and who like to know that every detail is just right. **Pros:** still one of Mykonos's best hotels; beautifully stylish minimalist general areas; top restaurants and bars on premises. **Cons:** you can pay plenty for a small room with no view; off a busy back road so can be noisy; no direct beach access. $ *Rooms from: €700 ⊠ Lakka Rohari ⊹ School of Fine Arts District ☎ 22890/25122 ⊕ www. belvederehotel.com ⊗ Closed Nov.–Mar. ⇆ 44 rooms ⯑ Free breakfast.*

★ Bill and Coo Suites and Lounge

$$$$ | HOTEL | From afar, Bill and Coo may look like any whitewashed Cycladic hotel, but inside a world of polished contemporary design and high-level service awaits. **Pros:** excellent service; beautiful infinity pool; one of the top restaurants on Mykonos is here. **Cons:** pricey summer suite rates; not in easy reach of the beach or party scene; not in easy walking distance to Mykonos Town sights. $ *Rooms from: €600 ⊠ Mykonos Town ⊹ Megali Ammos ☎ 22890/26292 ⊕ www.bill-coo-hotel.com ⊗ Closed Nov.–Apr. ⇆ 32 rooms ⯑ Free breakfast.*

Leto Hotel

$$$$ | HOTEL | Originally built in 1953, Leto Hotel is the grande dame of the Mykonos hotel scene and has seen off many an interloper. **Pros:** old fashioned discrete service; the most convenient location; palm-lined pool is large and inviting. **Cons:** classic decoration in need of a spruce-up; some rooms experience noise from the pool area; pricey extras mount up. $ *Rooms from: €350 ⊠ Mykonos Town ☎ 22890/22207 ⊕ www.letohotel. com ⇆ 25 ⯑ Free breakfast.*

Livin' Mykonos Boutique Hotel

$$$$ | HOTEL | Located on the outskirts of Mykonos Town, Livin Mykonos is a small boutique hotel where a trendy pool area enjoys an unexpectedly fantastic sunset view. **Pros:** excellent friendly service; beautiful pool area; minimalist cool design. **Cons:** no hotel shuttle to town; isolated location; not in easy walking distance to sights, with uphill hike back to the hotel. $ *Rooms from:*

€340 ⊠ *Mykonos Town ☎ 22890/ 23474 ⊕ www.livinmykonos.gr ⊗ Closed Oct.– Apr. ⇆ 26 rooms ⯑ Free breakfast.*

Myconian Korali

$$$ | HOTEL | This five-star member of Relais & Châteaux is a chic, modern option for a luxury stay with inspiring views, private pools, and fine service from smartly dressed, hospitable staff. **Pros:** beautiful design with a smart contemporary touch; BAOS restaurant is one of the best on the island; sea views throughout the property. **Cons:** steep uphill walk back from Mykonos Town; pricey standard rooms in high season; a bit isolated, surrounded by other hotels. $ *Rooms from: €250 ⊠ Mykonos Town ☎ 22890/22107 ⊕ www.myconianko-rali.gr ⊗ Closed Nov.–Apr. ⇆ 40 rooms ⯑ Free breakfast.*

Poseidon Hotel Suites

$$ | HOTEL | This quiet, no-frills hotel is conveniently located near Megali Ammos Beach and Mykonos Town. **Pros:** very good value—particularly off season; handy for the beach and town; free airport shuttle. **Cons:** steps throughout and no elevator; poolside menu is snacks only—no restaurant; local beach is a little small and scruffy. $ *Rooms from: €210 ⊠ Mykonos Town ☎ 22890/22437 ⊕ www.poseidonhotel-mykonos.com ⊗ Closed Nov.–Mar. ⇆ 58 ⯑ Free breakfast.*

Semeli

$$$$ | HOTEL | Location is everything at this centrally located hotel. **Pros:** cool and relaxing pool; conveniently in walking distance to town's sights; on-site restaurant and spa. **Cons:** stiff room rates; pool area can get busy; location can feel crowded in high season. $ *Rooms from: €460 ⊠ Mykonos Town ⊹ Below ring road ☎ 22890/27466 ⊕ www.semelihotel. gr ⊗ Closed Dec. and Jan. ⇆ 65 rooms ⯑ Free breakfast.*

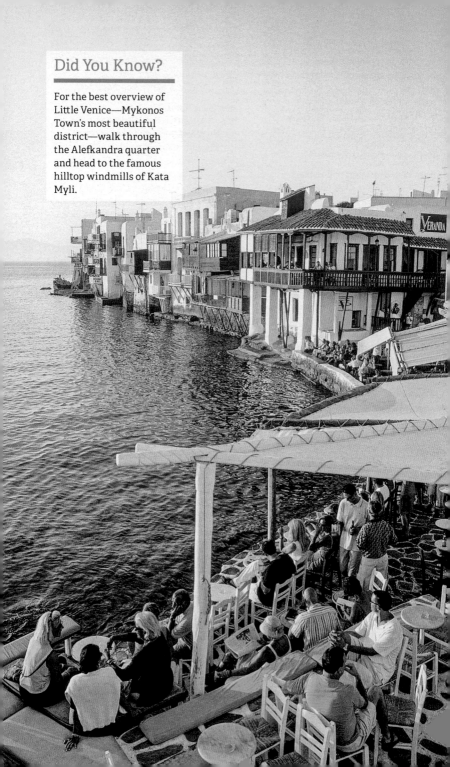

Did You Know?

For the best overview of Little Venice—Mykonos Town's most beautiful district—walk through the Alefkandra quarter and head to the famous hilltop windmills of Kata Myli.

★ Villa Konstantin

$$ | **B&B/INN** | **FAMILY** | With traditional whitewashed Mykonian architecture and cozy lounging areas, this property's quiet apartments and studios are a refuge from the bustle of Mykonos Town yet are still close enough to enjoy it. **Pros:** great pool area; inexpensive for Mykonos; laid-back and relaxed atmosphere. **Cons:** 10 minute walk to Mykonos Town; the walk back from town is uphill; not all rooms have sea views. [$] *Rooms from: €160* ✉ *Agios Vassilios* ☎ *22890/26204* 🌐 *www.villakonstantin-mykonos.gr* 🕑 *Closed Nov.–Mar.* 🛏 *20 rooms* 🍴 *Free breakfast.*

Nightlife

Whether it's bouzouki, jazz, mainstream dance, or techno, the nightlife on Mykonos beats to an obsessive rhythm until undetermined hours—little wonder the world's gilded youth comes here *just* to enjoy the night scene. That scene centers around two places: Mykonos Town and the southern beaches.

Nightlife begins in the late afternoon at the beach bars that dot Paradise, Super Paradise, and Paranga, whereas the bars and clubs along Little Venice and throughout Mykonos Town start to fill up after 11 pm, as patrons sip their first drinks of the night. The gay scene is still alive on Mykonos, but things are very mixed now, to the regret of some. Those who prefer a quieter lounge-type experience remain seated outside a sea-view café with a glass of wine, watching it all go by.

For the true night owls, much happens after midnight. You can either choose to club-hop around town or head south to the glamorous, outdoor arena–style clubs along Paradise and Super Paradise beaches. In the summer, posters and leaflets flung throughout Mykonos Town advertise which of the hottest international DJs are booked to spin each night. That and the promise of a packed, friendly, flirtatious young crowd gets the international partygoers ready for the beach well into the night. What is "the" place of the moment? The scene is ever-changing, so you'll need to track the buzz once you arrive but there are some ever-popular options.

ASTRA

BARS/PUBS | Small and perfectly formed, since 1986 ASTRA has kept up its exclusive, somewhat mature elegance. The clientele is upscale, and the drinks are pretty and expensive. Supermodels, rock stars, and royalty swing by when they're in town. The DJ spins house and funk, which is danceable, and not unbearably loud. ✉ *Tria Pigadia, Enoplon Dynameon* ☎ *22890/24767* 🌐 *www.astra-mykonos.com.*

★ Caprice

DANCE CLUBS | Caprice is a classic Mykonos bar in the heart of scenic sea-hugging Little Venice. Its simple whitewashed Cycladic interior has three rooms, but the two outer rooms are overflow seating areas for the typically jam packed, long and narrow bar room where all the action happens. It attracts a happy party crowd of both foreigners and Greeks that love to drink and dance to music hits that pump into the early morning hours. ✉ *Little Venice* ☎ *22890/23541* 🌐 *www.caprice.gr.*

Galleraki

BARS/PUBS | For more than 30 years, Galleraki has attracted happy, stylish, summer crowds. A compelling reason is its prime location, so close to the water in picturesque Little Venice that you may get sprayed when a boat passes, but it also serves some of the best cocktails on the island. ✉ *Mykonos Town* ☎ *22890/27188* 🌐 *www.galleraki.gr.*

Interni

BARS/PUBS | This sleek and chic garden setting in the heart of town is shaded by large trees and greenery, adding some color to the monochromatic design. A restaurant in the early evening hours, after 11 pm it fills with glamorous drinkers who appreciate the cool surroundings, subdued music, and the fact that they can actually speak to each other. Sister beach club at Ftelia is the chosen boho hangout for the same crowd during the day. ⊠ *Matogianni* ☎ *22890/26333* ⊕ *www.internirestaurant.com.*

JackieO'

BARS/PUBS | A small empire has grown out of this bar just below Paraportiani church. Nicely decorated, it is a great spot to watch the sunset and drinkers remain to catch the nightly drag shows. Less LGBT than it used to be, it is still a fun place to be. If you have not had enough, visit their beach club on Super Paradise with a super restaurant, stay in their hotel, even take a ride on their private boat. ⊠ *Waterfront* ☎ *22890/77298* ⊕ *www.jackieomykonos.com.*

Old Customs Cafe

BARS/PUBS | If the relentless boom and beat of dance music on Mykonos begins to wear you down, head down to this small but perfectly formed bar that plays a good mix of classic and modern rock. The friendliest of staff make this a world away from the cookie-cutter identical bars found all over town. ⊠ *Mykonos Town* ☎ *22890/22460.*

Rhapsody

BARS/PUBS | Rhapsody is a cozy bar on Little Venice that never seems to get as packed as its neighbors, but still benefits from the same windmill views. Popular with locals, Greek music is often mixed in with the international hits. ⊠ *22 Agios Anargiron* ✛ *Little Venice* ☎ *22890/23412.*

Skandinavian Bar

BARS/PUBS | A staple of the Mykonos bar scene since 1978, the renowned Skandinavian encompasses two buildings and an outside seating area. The music in the three bars ranges from classic rock to pop to dance, but it is always rowdy, crowded, and great fun. Dancing on the

All Clubbed Out?

Had enough of the endless merry-go-round of Mykonos's late nights and hungover days? Give your body a rest and head to **Cine Manto**, a unique garden in the center of town. Like an oasis of calm after the thronged cobbled streets, this outdoor haven hosts fish-filled ponds, giant cacti, a funky little café worth a visit on its own, and the icing on the cake, an open-air cinema. Grab some popcorn and a soda, you can always go out tomorrow. ⊛ *www.cinemanto.gr* ☎ *22890 26165*

bar at 3 am is a Mykonos rite-of-passage. ⊠ *K. Georgouli* ☎ *22890/22669.*

🛍 Shopping

Most stores are to be found in Mykonos Town, one right after the other among the warren of streets. In the peak of summer, many are open until midnight. The jet set is catered to well with an abundance of boutiques selling precious gems, fine jewelry, pricey fashion, swimwear, and shoes bearing top international labels. Then there are great local items that you'd only find in Greece—or in Mykonos—including handmade leather sandals, belts, and purses, and a selection of handicrafts and paintings created by local artists. Local food products and all-natural Greek cosmetics and soaps round out the best souvenirs options.

FASHION

Kampanas

SHOES/LUGGAGE/LEATHER GOODS | For a wide selection of handmade leather goods, head to Kampanas. It will be hard to choose from the array of sandals, purses and belts for both men and women that line the walls. The color choices are wide, and the leather is top quality. ✉ *Mitropoleos 3* ☎ *22890/22638*.

Parthenis

CLOTHING | Opened by Dimitris Parthenis in 1978, Parthenis now features designs by his daughter Orsalia, all showcased in a large Mykonian-style building on the up side of Alefkandra Square in Little Venice. The collection of cotton and silk garments, mostly in neutral colors, is very popular for their soft draping and clinging wrap effect. ✉ *Platia Alefkandra* ☎ *22890/22448* ⊕ *www.orsalia-parthenis.gr.*

Salachas

CLOTHING | The small Salachas store is filled with linen and cotton garments of all-Greek materials and manufacture. Grandfather Joseph Salachas was a tailor in the 1930s, and once made clothes for Christian Dior and other celebrities. Today, his grandchildren keep up the tradition. ✉ *K. Georgouli 58* ☎ *22890/22710* ⊕ *www.salachas.gr.*

★ Savvas Traditional Greek Products

FOOD/CANDY | The best place to pick up edible mementos of your trip—a taste of sunshine for back home. Greek delicacies from independent producers are featured, from olive oil to wine, from honey to cheeses, and all are very securely packed for safe transport home. ✉ *Xenias* ☎ *22890/28336* ⊕ *www.savvasmykonos. gr.*

The Workshop

JEWELRY/ACCESSORIES | Walking into The Workshop you'll immediately realize that the owner, Christos Xenitidis, loves two things: music and jewelry. His handiwork is responsible for the lovely gold and silver necklaces, rings, and earrings behind the simple glass displays. Look above his jewelry workbench to see a line of the guitarlike *bouzoukias* that he fixes and collects. Sometimes, his musician Mykonian friends stop by and an impromptu concert will form before your eyes. ✉ *Panachrantou 12* ☎ *22890/26455*.

Zonadiko

CLOTHING | Head up the stairs off one of Mykonos's busiest pedestrian walkways to find Michalis Pavlos at work in his little leather workshop, where he creates leather belts, sandals, and purses. Since the late 1980s, Pavlos has been making his own goods and distributing them all over Greece, but he opened his own shop in 2014 to show and sell his work directly on his favorite island. The quality of the leather he uses is second to none and he takes bespoke orders, too. ✉ *Matoyianni* ☎ *6972512737*.

FINE AND DECORATIVE ART

Galatis Gallery

CLOTHING | Designer Yiannis Galatis has outfitted such famous women as Julie Christie, Elizabeth Taylor, Ingrid Bergman, and Jackie Onassis, but now he focuses on his art gallery with many pieces made out of driftwood. ✉ *Platia Manto Mavrogenous* ☎ *22890/22255*.

Nikoleta

CRAFTS | Mykonos used to be a weaver's island, where 500 looms clacked away. Only two active weavers remain today and Nikoleta Xidakis is one of them. She sells skirts, shawls, and bedspreads made of local wool, as she has for more than 50 years. ✉ *Venetias, Little Venice* ☎ *22890/27503*.

Ninemia

CRAFTS | Maria Kouniou is a local artist and displays her own handmade and hand-painted woodcraft wall hangings in her little whitewashed shop. She's also proud to support other Greek artists and sells their fun, colorful jewelry and T-shirts that reflect the style and beauty of Greece. ✉ *M. Axioti 51* ☎ *6973046501* ⊕ *www.ninemia-jewellery.com.*

JEWELRY

Ilias Lalaounis

JEWELRY/ACCESSORIES | Known internationally, this fine jewelry collection is based on ancient Greek and other designs but reinterpreted for the modern woman.

With many of their earrings and necklaces as lovingly worked as art pieces, the shop is as elegant as a museum. New collections are introduced every year. ✉ *Polykandrioti 14* ✣ *Near taxis* ☎ *22890/22444.*

Activities

WATER SPORTS

Water-sports facilities can be found at many beaches. The main hub for windsurfing in the southern part of the island is at Kalafati Beach. The north side of the island is also a wind lover's haven; Panormos and Ftelia is where they all head.

Ayios Stefanos ΑΓΙΟΣ ΣΤΕΦΑΝΟΣ

6 km (4 miles) north of Mykonos Town.

About a 45-minute walk north from Mykonos Town, Ayios Stefanos has water sports, restaurants, and umbrellas and lounge chairs for rent; kids love it, and you can watch the yachts and enormous cruise ships slide by. The south coast's many beaches include this one fit for families.

Beaches

Ayios Stefanos Beach

BEACH—SIGHT | **FAMILY** | Like many beaches in Greece, Ayios Stefanos takes its name from the little chapel built on it. Just north of Mykonos Town and next to the new harbor, this sandy stretch attracts its share of families for its shallow waters and array of eating, lodging, and café options within reach. Protected from northern winds, it's always been an ideal beach to view the sunsets of Mykonos. **Amenities:** food and drink; lifeguards; parking, water sports **Best for:** sunset; swimming. ✉ *Ayios Stefanos* ✣ *Less than 2 km (1 mile) north from Mykonos Town.*

Hotels

★ Cavo Tagoo

$$$$ | **HOTEL** | Top of the pile of the luxury boutique hotels on the island for style and comfort, Cavo Tagoo is a whitewashed property climbing the hill over the bay in sensuous curves. **Pros:** beautiful views from hotel; alluring Mykonos style—classic and classy; on-site spa and well-reputed restaurant, Zuma. **Cons:** a 15-minute walk to town; high prices; loud music at pool bar at night. [$] *Rooms from: €750* ✉ *Ayios Stefanos* ✣ *Follow coast road, north of Old Port* ☎ *22890/20100* 🌐 *www.cavotagoo.com* 🕒 *Closed Nov.–Apr.* 🛏 *83 rooms* 🍴 *Free breakfast.*

★ Grace Mykonos

$$$$ | **HOTEL** | Small, charming, luxurious, and set above the beach of Ayios Stefanos, the Mykonos Grace is blessed with a truly impressive setting, enjoying an encompassing view of Mykonos harbor. **Pros:** impressive vistas from hillside location; intimate atmosphere; professional service with nice on-site restaurant. **Cons:** a distance to Mykonos Town; not all rooms have direct access to elevator; lowest category rooms are a little snug. [$] *Rooms from: €460* ✉ *Ayios Stefanos* ☎ *22890/20000* 🌐 *www.ariahotels.gr* 🕒 *Closed Nov.–Mar.* 🛏 *32 rooms* 🍴 *Free breakfast.*

Ornos ΟΡΝΟΣ

3 km (2 miles) south of Mykonos Town.

Ornos has always been more popular with Mykonians than tourists. The locals like its relaxed atmosphere for a family swim and beachside dining. There are several good restaurants, two fine hotels above the bay and several cheaper ones lower down, and chairs and umbrellas for rent. In calm weather, boats start here for the other southern beaches, so that they are all connected (45 minutes to the farthest southern beach, Elia), and you can beach-hop easily.

TOURS

★ Mykonos On Board Sailing Tours

BOAT TOURS | Another side to enjoying Mykonos is getting off the island to dive into the surreal aqua waters off the coast of its neighboring islands, which are best experienced by private sailing cruises. The hospitable captain, Artemis, and his team take up to ten guests on a comfortable, scenic, and sun-filled half-day journey to secluded secret swimming coves off Delos and Rhenia islands for swimming, relaxation, and his fresh and tasty Greek barbecue. The tour sets off from Ayios Ioannis Bay. ✉ *Ayios Ioannis* ☎ *6932471055* 🌐 *www.mykonosonboard.com* 🎟 *From €100 per person.*

Beaches

Ayios Ioannis Beach

BEACH—SIGHT | **FAMILY** | One of the best places on Mykonos to catch the sunset is the pebble-and-sand beach of Ayios Ioannis. Divided into two sections by large rocks, the waters usually remain calm but the summer winds can take their hold. The shallow bay is popular with families, and dining and lodging options are plenty, thanks to the white-washed beach town that grew around it. **■ TIP➜ The beach is also referred to as Shirley Valentine Beach, because the 1989 British movie of the same name was filmed here.** **Amenities:** food and drink. **Best for:** sunset; swimming. ✉ *Ayios Ioannis.*

Ornos Beach

BEACH—SIGHT | **FAMILY** | A community has grown around this beach, which is now considered one of the most family-friendly on the island. It's pretty and sandy and there are umbrella and lounge chair rentals. A good selection of beach hotels, tavernas, restaurants, cafés, and shops make up Ornos Bay, and there's bus service from Mykonos Town. It's also the launch point to take a boat to other beaches. **Amenities:** food and drink. **Best for:** swimming. ✉ *Ornos.*

Restaurants

Apaggio

$$ | **GREEK** | Tucked in a quieter corner of Ornos Bay, Apaggio is sparsely decorated and lined with large open windows for a perfect, unobstructed view of the sea. Romantic fairy lights twinkle overhead as you peruse the menu of Greek classics but it is probably wiser to ask about the selection of local fish. **Known for:** views across the bay; a short walk away from the rattle and hum; generous service. [$] *Average main: €20* ✉ *Ornos Beach* ☎ *22890/24344* 🌐 *www.apaggio.gr.*

Buddha Bar Beach

$$$ | **ASIAN FUSION** | Set above the private beach at the exclusive Santa Marina Hotel, Buddha Bar shows off its Greek-island incarnation as part of the renowned upscale chain known for world music, celebrity DJs and chefs, and inspired cocktails. A Japanese, Chinese, Thai, and Peruvian-inspired menu may seem out of place in Greece, but the immaculately presented food is popular with the chic and well-heeled crowd who love the boho atmosphere. **Known for:** lovely beach and sea views; cosmopolitan and stylish crowd; Asian cuisine and fusion dishes. [$] *Average main: €30* ✉ *Ornos* ☎ *22890/23220* 🌐 *buddhabarbeachmykonos.gr* 🕒 *Closed Nov.–Mar.*

★ Hippie Fish

$$ | **INTERNATIONAL** | Fronted by beautiful Ayios Ioannis Beach, Hippie Fish is one of the liveliest on-the-beach restaurants—an institution since the 1970s, it has continuously updated and moved with the times, but what it will always be famous for is making the big screen as the 1989 setting for the movie *Shirley Valentine*, about a dissatisfied housewife "finding herself" on Mykonos. Now offering private dining on the beach with the waves underfoot, visitors can recreate their own cinematic experience. **Known for:** hip cocktail bar for sundowners; sushi and Mediterranean dishes; relaxed and scenic on-the-beach location with views to Delos. $ *Average main: €20* ✉ *Ayios Ioannis* ☎ *22890/23547* ⊕ *www.hippief-ish-mykonos.com.*

 Hotels

Deliades

$$$ | HOTEL | Blessed with a great position overlooking Ornos bay, Deliades—the Delian nymphs—is a budget friendly introduction to Mykonos beach life. **Pros:** Ornos Bay views; large rooms and bath-tubs are good value; relaxed atmosphere backed by friendly staff. **Cons:** awful lot of steps to top-floor rooms; not all rooms enjoy a sea view; transport needed to get to Mykonos Town. $ *Rooms from: €200* ✉ *Ornos Bay* ⚓ *Far end of Ornos Beach, follow road up 30 yards* ☎ *22890/79430, 22890/79470* ⊕ *www.deliades.com* ⊗ *Closed Oct.–Apr.* ⇨ *30 rooms* ⦿ *Free breakfast.*

Kivotos

$$$$ | HOTEL | The Kivotos is a deluxe, architecturally ambitious hotel, stylishly arrayed around an impressive pool, and lovingly tended gardens. **Pros:** exquisite design; quiet ambience; private section for guests on Ornos Beach. **Cons:** isolated location; some rooms are small and lack views; high room rates. $ *Rooms from: €680* ✉ *Ornos* ⚓ *2 km (1 mile) from Mykonos Town* ☎ *22890/24094* ⊕ *www.kivotoshotels.com* ⊗ *Closed Nov.–Apr.* ⇨ *40 rooms* ⦿ *Free breakfast.*

★ Santa Marina

$$$$ | HOTEL | With a sandy private beach, Santa Marina is one of the most exclu-sive hotels on Mykonos. **Pros:** top luxury amenities, services, and restaurants; sheltered peninsula with beautiful views; excellent spa offerings. **Cons:** pricey food and drink; steep steps to some rooms; transportation necessary to get to other sights around the island. $ *Rooms from: €860* ✉ *Ornos* ☎ *22890/23220* ⊕ *www.marriott.com* ⇨ *114 rooms* ⦿ *Free breakfast.*

South Coast NOTIA AKTH

The first beach is Psarou, 4 km (2½ miles) southeast of Mykonos Town; the last beach is Elia, 12 km (7 miles) south-east of Mykonos Town.

The popular south coast beaches stand on their own; hotels, restaurants, cafés, and beach bars have sprung up around them, drawn to their turquoise seas. This is the home of Psarou Beach, where yachts are always moored in the distance and expen-sive sun beds are reserved in advance. Platis Gialos is popular with families and has its own little village behind it. But it's truly known for what the international party crowd loves: the beach bar and club scene that revolves around Paraga, Para-dise, and Super Paradise beaches. Agrari and Elia are less developed, have more nudity, and are quieter.

 Beaches

The south coast is where you'll find the famous party beaches of Mykonos. Psarou draws the jet set while nearby Platis Yialos is popular with families. The young and sexy crowd heads to Paraga, Paradise, and Super Paradise. While they used to be primarily nude beaches, that is not the case any longer, but they are still busy and popular and have parties starting almost every afternoon. Paradise draws the sexy straight crowd, Super Paradise the sexy LGBT crowd, though in truth there's a lot of overlap. The rocky path between Paradise and Super Paradise is a half an hour's dusty walk. Farther along, Little Agrari and Elia are less developed, more nudist, and quieter, though they, too, are becoming more organized.

Agrari Beach

BEACH—SIGHT | Agrari is a low-key beach with yellow pebble sand flanked by a low hill of small whitewashed buildings to the left and a rocky island hill to the right. Umbrellas and sun beds are available for rent. You can grab a snack, drinks, or a full meal at the beach's own bar and restaurant, but there are more options just a walk away. Boats leave from Platis Gialos and Ornos Bay. It's also walkable via a footpath from neighboring Elia Beach, attracting nudists who stay in certain areas. ■TIP➜ **Driving east from Mykonos Town, watch out for a stunning view of the turquoise blue as you make that final turn to the beach. Amenities:** food and drink; water sports. **Best for:** swimming. ⊠ *Agrari.*

Elia Beach

BEACH—SIGHT | Long, tranquil, and beautiful, Elia is a popular option for those who seek beach relaxation. Attracting a predominantly LGBT crowd, this southern beach is also popular with those who want to relax on a soft sand beach that's protected from the north winds that sweep through the island from time to time. Umbrellas and sun beds are for rent and water-sports facilities pop up during the peak summer months. Dining options are plentiful with several cafés and tavernas close by. **Amenities:** food and drink; parking (free); showers; toilets. **Best for:** nudists; swimming. ⊠ *Elia.*

Paradise Beach

BEACH—SIGHT | Famous the world over for its party scene, young, fun, international crowds hop straight to Paradise Beach. There's music, dancing, clubbing, and drinking at most hours of the day, but beach parties typically pick up around 4 pm and go on well into the next morning when everyone is dancing on tabletops, including sexy male and female models hired to get things moving. When partiers take a break, sun beds and umbrellas are available for lounging, and a full line of restaurants and fast-food options provide nourishment. Scuba diving and water-sport rental shops are open for business. The bus from Mykonos Town frequents the beach often in the peak of summer. **Amenities:** food and drink; lifeguards; parking (free); showers; toilets; water sports. **Best for:** partiers. ⊠ *Paradise.*

Paraga Beach

BEACH—SIGHT | Small and stunning, and surrounded by a picturesque rocky coastline that juts out against a sparkling turquoise bay, Paraga Beach—sometimes also spelled Paranga—is not only pretty, it's also one of Mykonos's liveliest party beaches. Several bars and beach clubs organize events every summer attracting a young, international crowd that gathers to mingle, dance, and drink. Hotels, rooms, and a large campground surround the beach. Umbrellas and chairs are available to rent at any of the beachside tavernas and cafés. A footpath to the east leads to neighboring party beach, Paradise, or offers you another view of the sea; it's about a 10-minute walk. **Amenities:** food and drink; lifeguards; toilets. **Best for:** partiers. ⊠ *Paraga* ⊹ *6 km (4 miles) southeast of Mykonos Town.*

Platis Gialos Beach

BEACH—SIGHT | **FAMILY** | Spacious, sandy, and pleasant, Platis Gialos is a popular southern beach that's protected from the island's strong summer winds. Kids enjoy playing in the shallow waters, while adults head to deeper waters to try out the numerous water-sports rental options. The array of taverns, restaurants, and cafés is perfect for any food break. The beach is lined with rental umbrellas and chairs, and getting to it is easy by Mykonos Town beach boat and bus service. ■TIP➜ **You can drive here, too, but parking spaces may be hard to find. Amenities:** food and drink; water sports. **Best for:** swimming. ⊠ *Platis Gialos.*

Psarou Beach

BEACH—SIGHT | With shiny yachts moored in its clear, pretty waters, sandy Psarou attracts vacationing international VIPs, Greek TV stars and singers, and the rich and famous. There are a couple of very expensive restaurants that host afternoon and evening parties that are fun but not crazy. If you drive from Mykonos Town, a steep scenic road leads to the beach, but once you get there you'll notice parking options are slim. Many opt for valet parking run by private companies. You can also reach Psarou by taking a short walk from nearby Platis Gialos or hopping on a boat one stop away at Ornos Bay. **Amenities:** food and drink; parking (paid); water sports **Best for:** partiers; swimming. ✉ *Psarou* ✣ *4 km (2½ miles) south of Mykonos Town.*

Super Paradise Beach

BEACH—SIGHT | Young and wild, gay and straight: All head to Super Paradise to let loose, though the more sedate LGBT crowd now head to Elia. The stunning sandy beach is one plus, but the beach bars and clubs truly dominate the scene. Summer months mean daily late-afternoon beach parties, where drinks and dancing rule. Hired bikini-clad models move to the beat of the music to encourage a crazy party atmosphere that includes people dancing everywhere and anywhere they can. For those not in the party mood (yet), umbrellas and sun beds can be rented and dining options are available for a meal; Super Paradise Rooms is right on the beach for those who need a place to crash. **Amenities:** food and drink; toilets; showers; lifeguards; water sports. **Best for:** partiers. ✉ *Super Paradise* 🌐 *www.superparadise.com.gr.*

🍴 Restaurants

Avli tou Thodori

$$ | MEDITERRANEAN | Overlooking pretty Platis Gialos Beach, Avli tou Thodori offers beachfront dining in an elegant Cycladic setting. More of a taverna than banging beach bar, the focus is on an eclectic Greek-centered menu and excellent presentation.The name of the restaurant translates to Thodori's yard, a dedication to owner Thanassis Kousathanas's late father, a Mykonian fisherman whose black-and-white portraits are hung with pride. **Known for:** bare-foot dining on the sand; good value compared to neighbors; loukamades—fresh donuts—are island-wide famous. [$] *Average main: €20* ✉ *Platis Gialos* ☎ *22890/78100* 🌐 *www.avlitouthodori.gr* ⏲ *Closed Nov.–Mar.*

Indian Palace

$ | INDIAN | If the thought of another Greek salad fills you with dread, turn to this exotic offering on a headland near Cavo Paradiso. Very popular, Indian Palace is a breezy take on Indian classics with great beach views. **Known for:** many vegan and vegetarian options; friendly, family service; large parking area—unusual in Mykonos. [$] *Average main: €14* ✉ *Paradise* ☎ *6955023488* 🌐 *www.jaipur-palace.gr.*

Nammos

$$$$ | GREEKINTERNATIONAL | Legendary Psarou beach restaurant that is the place to go on the island for a healthy dose of excess—super-bling, self-conscious, and selfie-central, Nammos is the spot for late lunches next to the sea with the jet-set. The eye-poppingly expensive Mediterranean fusion cuisine is good, but it's not really about the food and drink: tables are for dancing on rather than eating at, and Champagne is for spraying over your fellow diners, racing-driver style. **Known for:** late and indulgent lunch; fresh sushi; huge bills. [$] *Average main: €50* ✉ *Psarou Beach, Psarou* ☎ *22890/22440* 🌐 *www.nammos.gr.*

🛏 Hotels

Soho Roc House

$$$$ | HOTEL | The former San Giorgio has been remodeled by achingly hip private members brand Soho House. **Pros:** very cool and private; busy neighborhood beach scene a short walk away; individual design with spot-on sea views. **Cons:** more creature comforts would be appreciated; fellow guests can be off-puttingly cool; noise from beach clubs. [$] *Rooms from: €600* ✉ *Paraga* ☎ *22890/27474* 🌐 *www.sohohouse.com* 🛏 *45 rooms* 🍴 *Free breakfast.*

Nightlife

Cavo Paradiso

DANCE CLUBS | This famous mega-club on the rocks above Paradise Beach is classic Mykonos. The huge dance space is spread over two levels, and in the peak of summer every inch is occupied. Famous international DJs spin and you can even moor your superyacht upto their floating platform for true VIP entry. ⊠ *Paradise* ☎ *22890/26124* ⊕ *www.cavoparadiso.gr.*

Paradise Club

DANCE CLUBS | The international, young party people that flock to Mykonos have packed this glamorous open-air club every summer season for fifty years. It has three stages that are designed to feature the world's best DJs who fill its lineup each year. The club also operates a shuttle bus that runs from the bus terminal at Fabrika. ⊠ *Paradise Beach, Paradise* ☎ *6973016311* ⊕ *www.paradiseclubmykonos.com.*

Scorpios

GATHERING PLACES | Legendary beachside lair that has inspired a legion of copies. Self-styled as a "lifestyle commune" there are a lot of carefully staged ethnic rituals and spiritual encounters. It's a bit hippie, a bit glamorous, and very successful—its Sunday gatherings attract 3,500 people. The sassy and eclectic food menu is very well presented, if expensive, but really this is a grown-up chilled-out beach bar for the bright and beautiful. ⊠ *Paraga* ☎ *22890/29250* ⊕ *www.scorpiosmykonos.com.*

Tropicana Beach Bar

BARS/PUBS | One of the most popular beach bars in Mykonos is set on Paradise Beach, where the party starts every afternoon in the peak summer season. The international, young, and looking-for-fun crowd heads to the outdoor bar to dance in the sand, on tables, and by the sea. The music is loud, mainstream, and fun, the people are happy, and the watermelon cocktail is famously strong. ⊠ *Paradise Beach, Paradise* ☎ *22890/23582* ⊕ *www.tropicanamykonos.com.*

Activities

DIVING

Mykonos Diving Center

SCUBA DIVING | Located on Paradise Beach, the Mykonos Dive Center offers a range of excursions for certified divers and training for all levels and experiences. They lead excursions from 30 different points on the island. ⊠ *Paradise Beach, Paradise* ☎ *22890/24808* ⊕ *www.dive.gr.*

Southeast Coast
ΝΟΤΙΟΑΝΑΤΟΛΙΚΗ ΑΚΤΗ

The first beach is Kalo Livadi, 11 km (7 miles) southeast of Mykonos Town; the last beach is Kalafatis Beach, 12 km (7½ miles) southeast of Mykonos Town.

The southeastern beaches, the farthest beaches from Mykonos Town, are favorites for those looking for something calm, yet organized, such as Kalo Livadi. Water sports lovers head to Kalafatis, which is well set up for aquatic adventures.

Beaches

Ayia Anna Beach

BEACH—SIGHT | Somewhat hidden in the shadow of Kalafatis Beach, Ayia Anna is a low-key beach, named after a little whitewashed chapel nearby. It's a place where you can observe windsurfers in the distance as fishing boats bob calmly in the wind-protected waters. Two hills protect the bay—the locals lovingly call them *divounia*, or Aphrodite's breasts. Summer beach chair and umbrella rentals are available and there is a handful of tavernas and cafés. There are also two easy hiking paths to neighboring Platis

Gialos and Paraga beaches. **Amenities:** food and drink. **Best for:** swimming. ✉ *Ayia Anna.*

Kalafatis Beach

BEACH—SIGHT | This long stretch of picturesque beach with a line of shady trees is known for the water-sports and windsurfing crowds it attracts. The back road has an array of hotels, rooms-for-rent, tavernas, and beach bars, as well as a well-known windsurfing school and water-sports rental shop. A small dock to the left side of the beach houses a tavern, beach bar, and a diving center office that leads excursions out to nearby uninhabited islands. **Amenities:** food and drink; lifeguards; water sports. **Best for:** swimming; walking; windsurfing. ✉ *Kalafati.*

Kalo Livadi Beach

BEACH—SIGHT | **FAMILY** | Mykonos's characteristic rocky hills surround Kalo Livadi's long sandy beach, at the edge of the island valley from which it got its name, meaning "good valley." Families head here to spend the day playing with their kids in the shallow waters and take a break at one of the many restaurants surrounding the beach. In summer, paddlers and kayakers criss-cross the bay. **Amenities:** food and drink; water sports **Best for:** swimming. ✉ *Kalo Livadi.*

Lia Beach

BEACH—SIGHT | By Mykonos standards, Lia Beach is considered tranquil and quiet, perhaps because it's one of the farthest organized beaches from Mykonos Town, but it is not as isolated as in the past, mainly due to the popularity of the Italian-influenced beach bar, Liasti. You can drive to the beach or get off at the last stop on the Mykonos Town boat that brings people to the beaches. Rows of beach chairs and umbrellas line the pebble-and-sand beach, which is surrounded on both sides by a rocky coastline and the typical bare yet beautiful hills of the island. Divers and snorkelers head here to explore the turquoise waters. **■ TIP→ Once you're set up, see if you can spot Naxos and Paros in the distance.** **Amenities:** food and drink. **Best for:** snorkeling; swimming. ✉ *Lia Beach* ✣ *14 km (8½ miles) east of Mykonos Town.*

Hotels

Pietra e Mare

$$$$ | **HOTEL** | Overlooking picturesque Kalo Livadi beach, this adults-only resort has a chic, sophisticated atmosphere tempered with splashes of bohemia. **Pros:** relaxed and responsive service; a combination of traditional and chic design; pool with a view. **Cons:** 20-minute drive fron Mykonos Town; not much in Kalo Livadi compared to other beach resort towns; noise from beach clubs in high season. [$] *Rooms from: €500* ✉ *Kalo Livadi* ☎ *22890/71152* 🌐 *www.pietraemaremykonos.com* ⏲ *Closed Nov.–Apr.* 🛏 *31 rooms* 🍴 *Free breakfast.*

Activities

SCUBA DIVING

Kalafati Dive Center

BOATING | Since 1993 the Kalafati Dive Center has offered diving excursions in the clear waters around Mykonos's shores. Wreck dives are a favorite but they offer courses for beginners through to advanced divers. Snorkeling trips are also available, as are equipment rental, children's courses, and private boat excursions. ✉ *Kalafati* ☎ *6945243928* 🌐 *www.mykonos-diving.com.*

WATER SPORTS

Water-sports facilities can be found at many beaches. The main hub for windsurfing in the southern part of the island is at Kalafati Beach.

Kalafatis Water Sports

WATER SPORTS | Water ski, Jet Ski, wakeboard, and banana boat excursions are available, as are speedboat island tours from this established operator just in front of the Aphrodite Beach

Hotel. ⊠ *Kalafati* ☎ *6945261242* ⊕ *www. mykonoswatersports.com.*

WINDSURFING
Pezi Huber Windsurfing
WINDSURFING | Located right on the famed water-sports beach of Kalafati, where the meltemi winds blow "loyal and faithful," Pezi Huber runs his own windsurfing shop. He offers rentals for windsurfing and individual and group lessons for beginners. Rentals for stand-up paddleboards and other surf gear are also available. ⊠ *Kalafati Beach, Kalafati* ☎ *6944139656* ⊕ *www.pezi-huber.com.*

Ano Mera Άνω Μερά

8 km (5 miles) east of Mykonos Town.

Inland, the little town of Ano Mera has a couple of quiet tavernas and a monastery. The town only lights up during the monastery's festival day on August 15.

Sights

Monastery of the Panayia Tourliani
RELIGIOUS SITE | Monastery buffs should head to Ano Mera, a village in the central part of the island, where the Monastery of the Panayia Tourliani, founded in 1580 and dedicated to the protectress of Mykonos, stands in the central square. Its massive baroque iconostasis (altar screen), made in 1775 by Florentine artists, has small icons carefully placed amid the wooden structure's painted green, red, and gold-leaf flowers. At the top are carved figures of the apostles and large icons depicting New Testament scenes. The hanging incense holders with silver molded dragons holding red eggs in their mouths show an Eastern influence. In the hall of the monastery, an interesting museum displays embroideries, liturgical vestments, and wood carvings. A good taverna is across the street. The monastery's big festival—hundreds attend—is on August 15. ⊠ *On central square* ☎ *22890/71249.*

North Coast ΒΟΡΕΙΑ ΑΚΤΗ

The first beach is Ftelia, 7 km (4½ miles) southeast of Mykonos Town; the last beach is Ayios Sostis, 8 km (5 miles) northeast of Mykonos Town.

The beaches along the north coast are blessed with consistent winds suitable for windsurfing, and Ftelia is the island's center for the sport. Yet on calm days Panormos and Ayios Sostis are worth a trip; both offer beautiful beach vistas without the crowds. If you are looking for uncrowded beaches (even in the busy summer season), these are your best bets.

Beaches

Ayios Sostis Beach
BEACH—SIGHT | All you'll find at Ayios Sostis is turquoise waters lapping against the sand and a small-pebble coast. Without natural shade, or any touristic development whatsoever, beachgoers who need shade should come prepared. This is a beach with hidden elements though, so be sure to go in search of the small unnamed beach, accessible by footpath and tucked in between it and neighboring Panormos. Off another path that leads to the main road, you'll find the small church that this beach is named after. **Amenities:** food and drink. **Best for:** solitude; swimming. ⊠ *Ayios Sostis ⊹ 12 km (7½ miles) north of Mykonos Town.*

Ftelia Beach
BEACH—SIGHT | Ftelia is famous for its winds, which attract windsurfers who love to test out the turquoise waters. The beach's smooth sand is mostly free of sun beds or umbrellas, so when you approach it, all you'll see is a wide-open stretch of yellow sand—if the wind isn't blowing it all about. There is a good beach club built into the rocks at the far left-hand side. **Amenities:** food and drink; water sports. **Best for:** windsurfing. ⊠ *Ftelia.*

Panormos Beach

BEACH—SIGHT | FAMILY | A fine golden-sand beach with turquoise waters, Panormos caters to all kinds of beachgoers. Nudists head to the far right for peace and quiet, but there's an all-day beach bar and restaurant that offers music, food, and drinks to the left; it's popular with families, couples, and singles. This is a great spot when the southern winds attack; otherwise it's positioned to get the full brunt of the northern island winds. Watersports equipment, umbrellas, and chairs are available for rent. **Amenities:** food and drink; water sports **Best for:** nudists; swimming. ✉ *Panormos Beach.*

🍴 Restaurants

Kiki's Taverna

$$ | GREEK | With no telephone number or signs, this simple little family-run garden taverna would likely be missed if there wasn't a constant line of people waiting to grab a table—in the summer, expect to wait up to an hour. The sea views of Ayios Sostis Beach are relaxing, and the perfect thing to gaze at as you wait for your meat and fish dishes that will be expertly grilled on a barbecue. **Known for:** simple grill cooking; salad bar specials; glass of wine given to those waiting in line. [$] *Average main: €25* ✉ *Ayios Sostis* 💳 *No credit cards.*

Delos Δήλος

10 km (6 miles) southwest of Mykonos.

Arrive at the mythical, magical, and magnificent site of Delos and you might wonder how this barren islet, which has virtually no natural resources, became the religious and political center of the Aegean. One answer is that Delos provided the safest anchorage for vessels sailing between the mainland and the shores of Asia; another answer is that it was the alleged bithplace of Apollo and Artemis, two of the most important deities of the Greek pantheon. A third is provided if you climb Mt. Kynthos to see that the isle, no more than 5 km (3 miles) long and 1 km (½ mile) wide, is shielded on three sides by other islands. Indeed, this is how the Cyclades—the word means "circling ones"—got their name: they circle around the sacred island. Delos is "the hearth of the islands" as Callimachus wrote in the 3rd century BC.

Delos's amazing saga begins back in the times of myth: Zeus fell in love with gentle Leto, the Titaness, who became pregnant. When Hera discovered this infidelity, she forbade Mother Earth to give Leto refuge and ordered the Python to pursue her. Finally Poseidon, taking pity on her, anchored the poor floating island of Delos with four diamond columns to give her a place to rest. Leto gave birth first to the virgin huntress Artemis on Rineia and then, clasping a sacred palm on a slope of Delos's Mt. Kynthos, to Apollo, god of music and light.

By 1000 BC the Ionians, who inhabited the Cyclades, had made Delos their religious capital. Homeric Hymn 3 tells of the cult of Apollo in the 7th century BC. One can imagine the elegant Ionians, whose central festival was here, enjoying the choruses of temple girls—Delian *korai*, who serve the "Far-Shooter"—singing and dancing their hymn and displaying their graceful tunics and jewelry. However, a difficult period began for the Delians when Athens rose to power and assumed Ionian leadership. In 543 BC an oracle at Delphi conveniently decreed that the Athenians purify the island by removing all the graves to Rineia, a dictate designed to alienate the Delians from their past.

After the defeat of the Persians in 478 BC, the Athenians organized the Delian League, with its treasury and headquarters at Delos (in 454 BC the funds were transferred to the Acropolis in Athens). Delos had its most prosperous period in late Hellenistic and Roman times, when it was declared a free port and quickly became the financial center of the Mediterranean, the focal point of trade, where 10,000 slaves were sold daily. Foreigners from as far as Rome, Syria, and Egypt lived in this cosmopolitan port, in complete tolerance of one another's religious beliefs, and each group built its various shrines. But in 88 BC Mithridates, the king of Pontus, in a revolt against Roman rule, ordered an attack on the unfortified island. The entire population of 20,000 was killed or sold into slavery. Delos never fully recovered, and later Roman attempts to revive the island failed because of pirate raids. After a second attack in 69 BC, Delos was gradually abandoned.

In 1872, the French School of Archaeology began excavating on Delos—a massive project, considering that much of the island's 4 square km (1½ square miles) is covered in ruins. The work continues today. Delos remains dry and shadeless and most guards leave on the last boat to Mykonos in the early afternoon, but if on the way to Mykonos you see dolphins leaping, you'll know Apollo is about and approves.

GETTING HERE AND AROUND

Most visitors arrive from Mykonos on one of the excursions helpfully organized by tour companies whose offices are located at the west end of the old harbor in Mykonos Town (tour boats also leave from Tinos, Paros, and Naxos). These boats leave around 9 am every day. If the sea is too rough, boats are cancelled. There are generally four departures but the last boat returning from Delos can be as early as 3 pm. Ferries cost €20 return and the entrance fee to the island is €12.

 Sights

★ Delos Archaeological Site

ARCHAEOLOGICAL SITE | This tiny 3-mile-long island was once considered the most sacred place in the known world and is now a UNESCO World Heritage Site. Fabled as the birthplace of Apollo and his twin sister Artemis, it is a testament to Greece's glorious ancient civilization and home to one of its most important archaeological sites. First settled in the 3rd millennium BC, the sanctuary reached its glory in the Classical period as pilgrims from all over paid tribute to Apollo. To preserve its sacred importance, births and deaths on the island were forbidden and yet a population of 30,000 crammed on to the island as it became the main trading center of the eastern Mediterranean. Today the island is uninhabited, but it is easy to imagine the ancient society that once ruled here. You will find ruins of ancient temples, houses, an amphitheater, elaborate mosaics, and, of course, the acclaimed Terrace of the Lions statues. Hike to the summit of Mt. Kynthos (370 feet) and you will be blessed with views of the surrounding islands that circle Delos. The boat from Mykonos takes 30 minutes and overnight stays are not allowed.
⚠ **The island has no shade, so don't forget to bring a hat, sunscreen, and plenty of water.**
✛ *Accessible only by boat* ☎ *22890/22259 archaeological museum, 22890/22218 ferry information* ⊕ *odysseus.culture.gr* ▦ *€12* ⊙ *Closed Nov.–Mar.*

Agora of the Competialists

ARCHAEOLOGICAL SITE | The first monument you'll see, on the left from the harbor, is the Agora of the Competialists (circa 150 BC). The competialists were members of Roman guilds, mostly freedmen and slaves from Sicily who worked for Italian traders. They worshipped the *Lares Competales*, the Roman "crossroads" gods; in Greek they were known as *Hermaistai*, after the god Hermes, protector of

As if posing for your camera, the ancient sculpted beasts of the Avenue of the Lions are Delos's most unforgettable photo op. They are copies; the originals are in Delos's museum.

merchants and the crossroads. ⊹ *West of the Archaeological Museum of Delos.*

Ancient Theater and Residential Quarter

ARCHAEOLOGICAL SITE | Beyond the path that leads to the southern part of the island is this ancient theater, built in the early 3rd century BC. It once sat 5,500 people. Close by was the elegant residential quarter inhabited by Roman bankers and Egyptian and Phoenician merchants. Their one- and two-story houses were typically built around a central courtyard, sometimes with columns on all sides. Floor mosaics of snakes, panthers, birds, dolphins, and Dionysus channeled rainwater into cisterns below; the best-preserved can be seen in the House of the Dolphins, the House of the Masks, and the House of the Trident. ⊹ *South of the Archaeological Museum of Delos.*

Archaeological Museum of Delos

MUSEUM | This museum is on the road south of the Gymnasium. It contains most of the antiquities found during excavations on the island: monumental statues of young men and women, stelae, reliefs, masks, mosaics, and ancient jewelry. A spectacular futuristic new structure has been designed to replace the neoclassical existing building to better display the treasures of Delos but as of yet it remains a speculative venture. ☎ *22890/22259* ⊙ *Closed Mon., Nov.–Mar.*

Avenue of the Lions

ARCHAEOLOGICAL SITE | One of the most evocative and recognizable sights of Delos is the 164-foot-long Avenue of the Lions. The five marble beasts, which were carved in Naxos, crouch on their haunches, their forelegs stiffly upright, vigilant guardians of the Sacred Lake. They are the survivors of a line of at

Continued on page 377

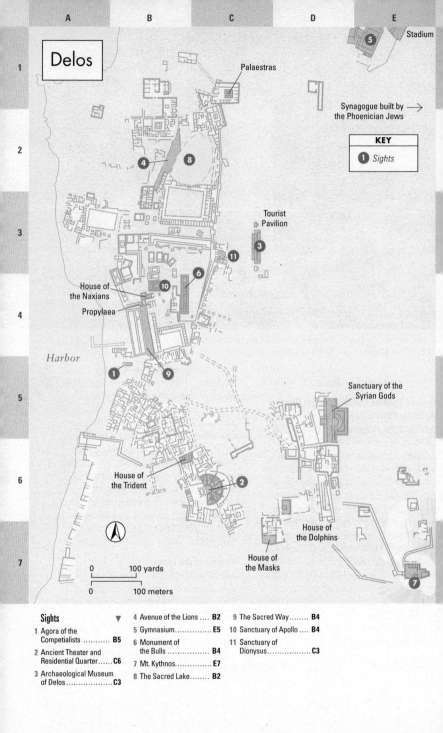

Delos

Palaestras

Stadium

Synagogue built by
the Phoenician Jews →

KEY

❶ *Sights*

Tourist
Pavilion

House of
the Naxians

Propylaea

Harbor

Sanctuary of the
Syrian Gods

House of
the Trident

House of
the Dolphins

House of
the Masks

0	100 yards
0	100 meters

Greece's Gods and Heroes

Superheroes, sex, adventure: it's no wonder Greek myths have reverberated throughout Western civilization. Today, as you wander ancient Greece's most sacred sites—such as Delos, island birthplace of the sun god Apollo—these ageless tales will come alive to thrill and perhaps haunt you.

Whether you are looking at 5th-century BC pedimental sculptures in Olympia or ancient red-figure vase paintings in Athens, whether you are reading the epics of Homer or the tragedies of Euripides, you are in the presence of the Greek mythopoetic mind. Peopled with emblems of hope, fear, yearning, and personifications of melting beauty or of petrifying ugliness, these ancient myths helped early Greeks make sense of a chaotic, primitive universe that yielded no secrets.

Frightened by the murder and mayhem that surrounded them, the Greeks set up gods in whom power, wisdom, and eternal youth could not perish. These gods lived, under the rule of Zeus, on Mount Olympus. Their rivalries and intrigues were a primeval, superhuman version of *Dynasty* and *Dallas*. These astounding collections of stories not only pervaded all ancient Greek society but have influenced the course of Western civilization: How could we imagine our culture—from Homer's *Iliad* to Joyce's *Ulysses*—without them?

Apollo, the sun god

ZEUS

Latin Name: Jupiter
God of: Sky, Supreme God
Attribute: Scepter, Thunder
Roving Eye: Zeus was the ruler of Mount Olympus but often went AWOL pursuing love affairs down on earth with nymphs and beautiful ladies; his children were legion, including Hercules.

HERA

Latin Name: Juno
Goddess of: Sky, Marriage
Attribute: Peacock
His Cheating Heart: Hera married her brother Zeus, wound up having a 300-year honeymoon with him on Samos, and was repaid for her fidelity to marriage by the many love affairs of her hubby.

APHRODITE

Latin Name: Venus
Goddess of: Love, Beauty
Attribute: Dove
And the Winner Is: Born out of the foam rising off of Cyprus, she was given the Golden Apple by Paris in the famous beauty contest between her, Athena, and Hera, and bestowed the love of Helen on him as thanks.

ATHENA

Latin Name: Minerva
Goddess of: Wisdom
Attribute: Owl, Olive
Top Billing: The goddess of reason, she gave the olive tree to the Greeks; her uncle was Poseidon, and the Parthenon in Athens was built in her honor.

APOLLO

Latin Name: Phoebus
God of: Sun, Music, and Poetry
Attribute: Bow, Lyre
Confirmed Bachelor: Born at Delos, his main temple was at Delphi; his love affairs included Cassandra, to whom he gave the gift of prophecy; Calliope, with whom he had Orpheus; and Daphne, who, fleeing from his embrace, changed into a tree.

ARTEMIS

Latin Name: Diana
Goddess of: Chastity, Moon
Attribute: Stag
Early Feminist: Sister of Apollo, she enjoyed living in the forest with her court, frowned on marriage, and most notoriously, had men torn apart by her hounds if they peeked at her bathing.

YE GODS!

WHO'S WHO IN GREEK MYTHOLOGY

The twelve chief gods formed the elite of Olympus. Each represented one of the forces of nature and also a human characteristic. They also had attributes by which they can often be identified. The Romans, influenced by the arts and letters of Greece, largely identified their own gods with those of Greece, with the result that Greek gods have Latin names as well. Here are the divine I.D.s of the Olympians.

EMETER

atin Name: Ceres

oddess of: Earth, ecundity

ttribute: Sheaf, Sickle

ost Dramatic Moment: fter her daughter Persephone was kidnapped by eus, Demeter decided to ake all plants of the earth ither and die.

HERMES

Latin Name: Mercury

God of: Trade, Eloquence

Attribute: Wings

Messenger Service: Father of Pan, Hermes was known as a luck-bringer, harbinger of dreams, and the messenger of Olympus; he was also worshipped as the god of commerce and music.

POSEIDON

Latin Name: Neptune

God of: Sea, Earthquakes

Attribute: Trident

Water Boy: To win the affection of Athenians, Poseidon and Athena were both charged with giving them the most useful gift, with his invention of the bubbling spring losing out to Athena's creation of the olive.

RES

atin Name: Mars

od of: Tumult, War

ttribute: Spear, Helmet

ntisocial: The most famous ale progeny of Zeus and era, he was an irritable man; onsidering his violent mper, few temples ere erected in s honor in reece.

HESTIA

Latin Name: Vesta

Goddess of: Hearth, Domestic Values

Attribute: Eternal Fire

Hausfrau: A famous virgin, she was charged with maintaining the eternal flame atop Olympus; the Vestal Virgins of ancient Romans followed in her footsteps.

HEPHAESTOS

Latin Name: Vulcan

God of: Fire, Industry

Attribute: Hammer, Anvil

Pumping Iron: The best-preserved Doric style temple in Athens, the Hephaestaion, was erected to this god in the ancient agora marketplace; today, ironmongers still have shops in the district there.

HERCULES

THE FIRST ACTION HERO

Greece's most popular mythological personage was probably Heracles, a hero who became a god, and had to work hard to do it. This paragon of masculinity was so admired by the Romans that they vulgarized him as Hercules, and modern entrepreneurs have capitalized on his popularity in silly sandal epics and sillier Saturday morning cartoons. His name means "glory of Hera," although the goddess hated him because he was the son of Zeus and the Theban princess Alcmene. The Incredible Bulk proved his strength and courage while still in the cradle, and his sexual prowess when he impregnated King Thespius' fifty daughters in as many nights. But the twelve labors are his most famous achievement. To expiate the mad murder of his wife and his three children, he was ordered to:

1. Slay the Nemean Lion
2. Kill the Lernaean Hydra
3. Capture the Ceryneian Hind
4. Trap the Erymanthian Boar
5. Flush the Augean stables of manure
6. Kill the obnoxious Stymphalian Birds
7. Capture the Cretan Bull, a Minoan story
8. Steal the man-eating Mares of Diomedes
9. Abscond with the Amazon Hippolyta's girdle
10. Obtain six-armed Geryon's Cattle
11. Fetch the Golden Apples of the Hesperides, which bestowed immortality
12. Capture three-headed Cerberus, watchdog of Hades

In other words, he had to rid the world of primitive terrors and primeval horrors. Today, some revisionist Hellenistic historians considered him to be a historical king of Argos or Tiryns and his main stomping ground was the Argolid, basically the northern and southern Peloponnese. Travelers can today still trace his journeys through the region, including Lerna (near the modern village of Myli), not far from Nafplion, where the big guy battled the Hydra, now seen by some historians as a symbol for the malarial mosquitoes that once ravaged the area. Herc pops up in the myths of many other heroes, including Jason, who stole the Golden Fleece; Perseus, who killed Medusa; and Theseus, who established Athens' dominance. And his constellation is part of the regularly whirling Zodiac that is the mythological dome over all our actions and today's astrology.

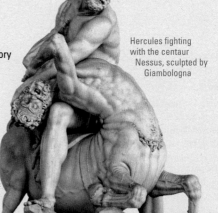

Hercules fighting with the centaur Nessus, sculpted by Giambologna

least nine lions that were erected in the second half of the 7th century BC by the Naxians. One statue, removed in the 17th century, now guards the Arsenal of Venice (though with a refurbished head); the remaining originals are in the Delos Archaeological Museum on the island. ✛ *West of the Agora of the Italians.*

Gymnasium

ARCHAEOLOGICAL SITE | Northeast of the palaestras is the Gymnasium, a square courtyard nearly 131 feet long on each side. Scratched into the rock are early graffiti of the local boys names and the girls they ogled. The long, narrow structure farther northeast is the stadium, the site of the athletic events of the Delian Games. East of the stadium site, by the seashore, are the remains of a synagogue built by Phoenician Jews in the 2nd century BC. ✛ *North of the Archaeological Museum of Delos.*

Monument of the Bulls

ARCHAEOLOGICAL SITE | Southeast of the Sanctuary of Apollo are the ruins of the Monument of the Bulls, also known as the Neorion, an extremely long and narrow structure built, it is thought, to display a *trireme* (an ancient boat with three banks of oars) that was dedicated to Apollo by Antigonas Gonatas thankful for a naval victory over the Ptolemies. Maritime symbols were found in the decorative relief of the main halls, and the head and shoulders of a pair of bulls were part of the design of an interior entrance. ✛ *Southeast of the Sanctuary of Apollo.*

Mt. Kythnos

ARCHAEOLOGICAL SITE | A dirt path leads up the base of Mt. Kynthos, which is the highest point on the island. Here lie the remains of many Middle Eastern shrines, including the Sanctuary of the Syrian Gods, which was built in 100 BC. A flight of steps goes up 113 m (368 feet) to the summit of Mt. Kynthos—from which the name "Cynthia" was derived—where Greek mythology says Zeus watched

the birth of his son, Apollo, on the slope. There are amazing views of Mykonos, Naxos, Paros, and Syros from the top of the mountain. The path is completely unshaded, so be prepared for the heat and the top is usually very windy. ✛ *Near the Sacred Way.*

The Sacred Lake

ARCHAEOLOGICAL SITE | A short distance north of the Monument of the Bulls is an oval indentation in the earth where the Sacred Lake once sparkled. It is surrounded by a stone wall that reveals the original periphery. According to islanders, the lake was fed by the river Inopos from its source high on Mt. Kynthos until 1925, when the water stopped flowing and the lake dried up. Along the shores are two ancient *palaestras* (buildings for physical exercise and debate). ✛ *North of the Agora of the Italians.*

The Sacred Way

ARCHAEOLOGICAL SITE | East of the Agora of the Competialists you'll find the entrance to the Sacred Way, which leads north to the temple of Apollo. The Way was once bordered by beautiful marbled statues and monuments created by various kingdoms and city states of Ancient Greece. It was also the route used by pilgrims during the holy Delian festival. ✛ *Just east of the harbor.*

Sanctuary of Apollo

ARCHAEOLOGICAL SITE | Beyond the Sacred Way is one of the most important sites on the island, the Sanctuary of Apollo. Three separate temples originally stood here flanked by altars, monuments, and statues, although not much remains of them. The main temple was grand, fittingly called the Great Temple of Apollo (circa 480 BC). Inside the sanctuary and to the right is the House of the Naxians, a 7th- to 6th-century BC structure with a central colonnade. Dedications to Apollo were stored in this shrine. Outside the north wall a massive rectangular pedestal once supported a colossal statue of Apollo (one of the hands is in Delos's

Archaeological Museum, and a piece of a foot is in the British Museum in London). Near the pedestal a bronze palm tree was erected in 417 BC by the Athenian general Nikias to commemorate the palm tree under which Leto gave birth. According to Plutarch, the palm tree toppled in a storm and brought the statue of Apollo down with it. In *The Odyssey,* Odysseus compares the Phaeacian princess Nausicaa to a palm he saw on Delos, when the island was wetter. ✛ *West of the Archaeological Museum of Delos.*

Sanctuary of Dionysus

ARCHAEOLOGICAL SITE | Immediately to the right of the Archaeological Museum is the small Sanctuary of Dionysus, which was erected in about 300 BC. Outside the sanctuary you'll find one of the more boggling sights of ancient Greece: several monuments dedicated to Apollo by the winners of the choral competitions of the Delian festivals, each decorated with a huge phallus, emblematic of the orgiastic rites that took place during the Dionysian festivals. Around the base of one of them is carved a lighthearted representation of a bride being carried to her new husband's home. A marble phallic bird, symbol of the body's immortality, also adorns this corner of the sanctuary. ✛ *East of the Sanctuary of the Bulls.*

Chapter 8

SOUTHERN CYCLADES

PAROS, ANTIPAROS, NAXOS, MILOS, FOLEGANDROS, SANTORINI

8

Updated by
Liam McCaffrey

 Sights
★★★★★

 Restaurants
★★★★★

 Hotels
★★★★★

 Shopping
★★★☆☆

 Nightlife
★★★☆☆

WELCOME TO THE SOUTHERN CYCLADES

TOP REASONS TO GO

★ **Invading incomers:** The Venetians, Byzantines, and Ottoman occupiers all left their mark; trace their unique cultural heritage in the architecture, art, and lifestyles of the islanders.

★ **Caldera culture:** Smell the sulfur in the air as you explore landscapes wrought by the hands of Hephaestos, the God of fire and brimstone.

★ **Hotel highlife:** Some of the most luxurious and most individual dwellings in the Aegean are found here—cliff-top aeries are the speciality—with soothing views over the blue-green seas.

★ **Brilliant beaches:** The variety is endless—black, brooding volcanic pebbles contrast with sandy strips that stretch to the horizon—and there is a beach here for all tastes.

★ **Water-sport wonderland:** If the life aquatic is your thing, you will be spoiled for choice. Regular winds and clement conditions make the southern Cyclades the hot-spot for water sports in the area.

1 Paros. West of Naxos and with a little bit of everything—fishing villages, fine beaches, varied nightlife, and gentle interior—Paros is the quintessential Greek island experience.

2 Antiparos. Sandy shores, a picturesque port, discreet nightlife, and a chic atmosphere make Antiparos a slice of heaven for its devotees.

3 Naxos. Presided over by the historic castle of Naxos Town, the island wears its history proudly but it is some of the best beaches in the Aegean that draw most visitors.

4 Milos. Volcanic Milos, with sensational views, hot springs, beautiful beaches, and unearthly topography, is like no other island in Greece.

5 Folegandros. Tides of travelers have yet to discover this stark island, which means it is all the more alluring to Cyclades lovers, particularly those who prize its stunning cliff scenery.

6 Santorini. The main towns of Fira and Ia cling inside a volcanic rim in dazzling white contrast to its somber cliffs. South lies the "Greek Pompeii" that is ancient Akrotiri.

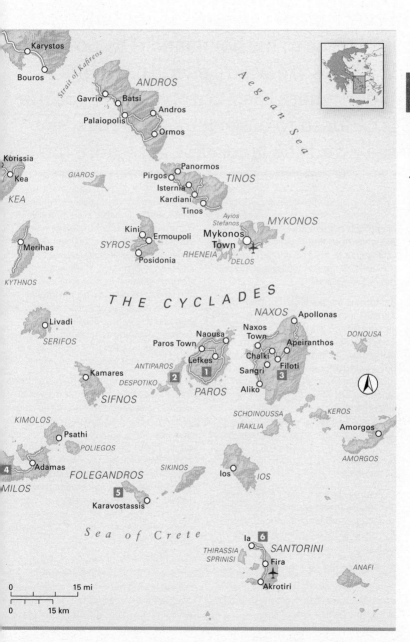

Karystos

Bouros

Strait of Kafireos

ANDROS

Gavrio   Batsi

Palaiopolis   Andros

Ormos

Aegean Sea

Korissia

Kea

KEA

GIAROS

Panormos

Pirgos

Isternia   *TINOS*

Kardiani

Tinos

Ayios Stefanos

MYKONOS

Kini   Ermoupoli

Mykonos Town

SYROS   *RHENEIA*

Posidonia   *DELOS*

Merihas

KYTHNOS

THE CYCLADES

Livadi   *NAXOS*   Apollonas

SERIFOS   Naousa   Naxos Town   Apeiranthos   *DONOUSA*

Paros Town   Chalki

Lefkes   Filoti

ANTIPAROS   Sangri   **3**

Kamares   **2**   Aliko

DESPOTIKO   *PAROS*

SIFNOS   *SCHOINOUSSA*   *KEROS*

KIMOLOS   *IRAKLIA*

Psathi   Amorgos

POLIEGOS   *AMORGOS*

4   Adamas   *SIKINOS*   Ios

MILOS   *FOLEGANDROS*   Ios   *IOS*

5

Karavostassis

Sea of Crete   Ia   **6**   *SANTORINI*

THIRASSIA

SPRINISI   Fira

ANAFI

Akrotiri

0 ___ 15 mi

0 ___ 15 km

"My God, how much blue you spend, so we cannot see you," wrote Nobel Poetry Prize winner Odysseas Elytis with reference to his homeland. The Southern Cyclades are where everything gets bluer, where the horizon gets bigger, life is reduced to bare elements—rock, sky, sea—and the landscape gets more binary.

When you close your eyes and imagine a Greek island, this is what you see; the blue of the sky, the green of the sea, and the white houses that cling to the rock as if scared to fall. This is the Southern Cyclades, the most quintessential of all the Aegean islands.

Santorini is the poster girl of the Mediterranean, the pin-up star. Born of might and power, the island was wrenched from the center of the earth. Pouty and passionate, it has the Hollywood looks but twelve major eruptions over the past million years have shaped its character—it broods, it waits, it is inscrutable and unforgiving, a life made mineral. As recent as 1950, the volcano blew a 3,000-foot column of ash into the sky. Never forget, this is a caldera, a cauldron of flames, the fire breathing mouth of the underworld.

Over-run, expensive, and hectic it may be, but, if you can scratch beneath the surface you will find the other Santorini, the island of filoxenia and friendship. Look into the island, rather than outward, away from the private pools and selfie sticks, toward the coastal plain and the views to neighboring Anafi, past the fields of tomatoes and ground-crawling vines, to a gentler way of life.

A wild blend of geological formations, Milos wears its battle scars proudly. Three million years of undersea eruptions have piled lava upon layer of lava, creating this fascinating landscape, still bubbling and spitting nowadays. Unusual colors and kaleidoscopic striations mark the land, but man has left his imprint here more than on any other island. Giant open craters with toy-like bulldozers working down below attest to the reach mining has held here for millennia, and the subsequent wealth of the island.

Visitors to Milos come to marvel at those multi-hued rocks, to wander the varied shores, to scramble through caves and to swim from boats moored off secret beaches. There are only a handful of bars on the island, scant villages to get lost in, and few cultural diversions, so visitors take their excitement and inspiration from nature, they want stories to tell and to take home with them; stories of bone-white rock beaches, of hidden pirate caves, and of dinner cooked in a volcanic sand pit.

Less brash than its neighbors, Folegandros hides its beauty like a shy child behind his mother's skirt. It was a place of exile for many years and the towering cliffs and the rocky and arid landscape can seem forbidding at first. Persevere, though, and you will be rewarded with one of the most attractive of the traditional Cubist whitewashed villages. The pleasures of life are simple here—geraniums in old olive-oil tins, slumbering cats stretching in the sun, and a plate of flour-and-salt-dusted anchovies on a checked tablecloth. Despite its lofty position on the top of the cliffs, unlike Santorini it doesn't stare at the sea defiantly, rather it wraps its arms around itself and looks inward, maybe as a result of having to hide from marauders for hundreds of years.

Outside of the Chora, the landscape is of an unspoilt rural idyll. Steep and hard, there is a scattering of houses, farmsteads, derelict windmills, and churches. Rough roads and tracks lead down to beaches, either deserted or more popular, and most days merge into each other without excitement. It is just how the people who return here year after year like it.

Naxos and Paros to the north are the smiling twins of plenty. Endless beaches back gentle hills on Paros; photographer Cecil Beaton wrote while staying in Parikia, "We have lived in a timeless haze of repetition. Life is nothing but sleep, swim, eat, and read." Six decades later, little much has changed. Daybreak at the Venetian port of Naoussa may find still-partying revellers crossing paths with returning fishermen, but the majority of visitors seek to spend their days on the sand, with beaches seemingly stacked up one after another. Tiny Antiparos is happy to stay in the shadow of its bigger brother, confident in its combination of a picturesque port, cozy nightlife, and excellent sandy beaches.

Naxos, green and lovely, has an interior of lush valleys and mountainous highlands that sets it apart, as does its unique architecture. The Venetian Duchy of the Archipelago was centered here from 1207 to 1537 and left watchtowers

and mansions scattered across the skyline. Running for miles, the marvellous sandy beaches in the southwest are the primary pull and they are without equal, but you don't have to venture far to discover that agriculture is still the mainstay of the island and an attractive rural atmosphere prevails. The meandering mountain roads take you through silvery olive groves, past fragrant lemon trees to reveal endless rows of vines. Rich, fruitful, benign, and less stark than their southern cousins, nature has been kinder here.

"The islands with their drinkable blue vocanoes," as our poet imagines are the brightest stars in the constellation of the Aegean,.These are the island archetypes we know and dream of—lone trees bent over by the wind, gorges and gaping ravines only scaled by goats, plunging cliffs, and all around the fusion of sunlight and aqua sparkle. Find your favorite and abandon yourself to the rhythm of their days.

Planning

When to Go

The experience of the Cyclades is radically different in summer compared to winter. In summer all services are operating on overload, the beaches are crowded, the clubs noisy, the restaurants packed, and the scene hopping. Walkers, nature lovers, and devotees of classical and Byzantine Greece would do better to come in spring and fall, ideally in late-April–June or September–October, when temperatures are lower and tourists are fewer. However, off-season travel means less-frequent boat service when stormy weather can make the seas too rough for sailing. In winter, many shops, hotels, and restaurants are closed, and the open cafés are full of locals recuperating from summer's intensity. The villages can feel shuttered and the nightlife evaporates. Cultural organizations, film clubs, concerts of island music, and religious festivals become more important. The temperature will often seem colder than the thermometer indicates: if it is in the low 50s, cloudy, drizzling, and windy, you will feel chilled and want to stay indoors, and these islands are at their best outdoors.

Planning Your Time

The Southern Cyclades are more for lazing around than for book-nosed tourism. Although it is true that feverish partying can overwhelm the young in summer, in other seasons the temptations are fewer, gentler, and more profound. If you move fast, you will see little, and the beauty is in the general impression of sea, sky, mountain, and village, and in the details that catch your eye: an ancient column used as a building block, an octopus hung to dry in the sun, a wedding or baptism in a small church you stopped by, a shepherd's mountain hut with a flagstone roof—they are endless. There are important sites but just enjoying the island rhythms often proves as soul-satisfying.

Getting Here and Around

Transportation to the islands is constantly improving. Six of the Cyclades have airports, and high-speed ferry service between Athens and the islands—and among the islands—seems to increase with each season. Do remember, though, that boat schedules depend on Poseidon's weather whims, and service might be canceled when seas are rough. No matter how you travel, it's best to buy tickets well in advance of major spring and summer holidays.

AIR

Flying can save much needed time, though fares are generally higher than those for ferries. Olympic Air and Aegean Airlines have several daily flights to Milos, Naxos, Paros, and Santorini. Many European airlines offer nonstop flights to both Mykonos and Santorini, and charter flights come from the Middle East and around Europe.

CONTACTS Milos Airport. (*MLO*) ⊠ *5 km (3 miles) Southeast of Adamas* ☎ *22870/28410.* **Naxos Airport.** (*JNX*) ⊠ *1 km (½ mile) south of Naxos Town* ☎ *22850/24816.* **Paros Airport.** (*PAS*) ✢ *Near Alyki village, 9 km (5½ miles) south of Paros Town* ☎ *22840/92030.* **Santorini Airport.** (*JTR*) ✢ *On east coast, 6 km (4 miles) from Fira* ☎ *22860/28400* ⊕ *www.santoriniairport.com.*

BOAT AND FERRY

Most boats for the Southern Cyclades leave from Athens's port of Piraeus and also from Rafina (accessible by KTEL bus from Athens); a few leave from Lavrio. The larger ferries are more stable, while some fast boats are small and can roll uncomfortably in high seas. Also, high-speeds have little or no deck space; you are closed in. Blue Star Ferries will give you a seat number for a small extra fee, and the fast boats have reserved seats only. Cabins are also available on larger ferries and are useful for overnight journeys. In summer, you should always reserve seats in advance.

All ferries run much less frequently in winter, and many fast ferries don't run at all. Off-season you don't need reservations, and you can purchase tickets just before departure at offices at the port. Ferries can be canceled owing to gales, and then schedules go haywire and hundreds of people and cars have to fight for new tickets.

For schedules, check ⊕ *www.openseas. gr* or ⊕ *www.gtp.gr.*

CONTACTS Blue Star Ferries. ☎ *21089/19800* ⊕ *www.bluestarferries. com.* **Piraeus Port Authority Departures/ Arrivals.** ☎ ⊕ *www.olp.gr.* **Rafina KTEL Buses.** ☎ *210/ 880–8000* ⊕ *www.ktelattikis.gr.* **Seajets.** ☎ *21071/07710* ⊕ *www. seajets.gr.*

BUS

For information about Bus travel, consult the Getting Here and Around sections listed under each island.

CAR AND SCOOTER

To take cars on ferries, you must make reservations. Though there is bus service on all islands, you may find it more convenient to travel by car, especially on a larger island like Naxos. Although islanders tend to acknowledge rules, many roads on the islands are poorly maintained and tourists sometimes lapse into vacation inattentiveness. Drive with caution, especially at night, when you may well be sharing the roads with motorists returning from an evening of drinking. All the major islands have car- and bike-rental agencies at the ports and in the business districts. Car rentals in summer cost about €20–€60 per day, with unlimited mileage and third-party liability insurance. Full insurance costs about €15 per day more. The roads in Santorini are thin, twisty, and perilous, and demand total attention; consider a tour of the island where somebody else does the driving and you get to watch the scenery from the back seat.

Often travelers opt for scooters or four-wheel ATV's (quads), but be careful—island hospitals get filled with people with serious-looking injuries due to poor roads, slipshod maintenance, careless drivers, and excessive partying. Quads, which Greeks call *gourounia* (piggies), look safer than scooters but in fact turn over easily. Choose a dealer that offers 24-hour service and a change of vehicle in case of a breakdown. Most will take you from and to your plane or boat.

FOOT

The Cyclades are justly famous for their hiking. Ancient goat and donkey trails go everywhere—through fields, over mountains, and along untrodden coasts. Since tourists flock to beaches and town promenades, hiking can be uncrowded even in July and August. Prime hiking months, though, are April and May, when temperatures are reasonable, wildflowers seem to cover every surface, and birds migrate overhead.

Hotels

Overall, the quality of accommodations in the Southern Cyclades is high, whether they be tiny pensions, private houses, or luxury hotels. The best rooms and service (and noticeably higher prices) are on Santorini, where luxury resort hotels now rank among the world's favorites. Wherever you stay, make a room with a view and a balcony a priority. If you're not interested in staying at luxury hotels and unless you're traveling at the very height of the season (July 15–August 30), you're unlikely to need advance reservations on some islands. Sometimes the easiest way to find something, in fact, is to head for a tourist office and describe your needs and price range or talk to the room owners who meet every boat. Do be aware that few hotels have elevators, and even Santorini's best often have breathlessly picturesque cliff-side staircases (though most have porters to carry your bags).

Restaurants

Eating is a lively social activity in the Southern Cyclades, and the friendliness of most taverna owners compensates for the lack of formal service. Unless you ask specifically, the food comes all at once or in the order it is ready. Restaurant schedules on the Cyclades vary; some places close for lunch, most close for siesta, and all are open late. Reservations are not usually required but are recommended in the height of the season if you want to visit a particular place.

Greece produces top-quality vegetables, fish, olive oil, and dairy products. The Southern Cyclades are proud of the foods that reflect their harsh environment; fava (yellow split peas), capers, tiny tomatoes, and small white aubergines—all miniature, minerally bombs of flavor from the volcanic soil. When Greeks go out to eat, they expect good, simple food culled from these elements; do likewise, and you will dine with much pleasure. Naxos is famed for its agriculture, Milos offers dinner cooked in geothermal springs, and Santorini hosts some of the most inventive modern cooking in Greece, often in spectacular settings, but all of the islands can lay claim to having a lively food culture—even plucky little Folegandros with just a handful of permanent residents.

Greek wines have tripled in quality in the last decade. The volcanic soil of Santorini is especially hospitable to the grape, and it is worth seeking out the crisp, bright variety Assyrtiko. Santorini and Paros now proudly produce officially recognized "origin" wines, which are sought throughout Greece.

Restaurant and hotel reviews have been shortened. For full information, visit Fodors.com.

What it Costs in euros			
$	$$	$$$	$$$$
RESTAURANTS			
under €15	€15–€25	€26–€40	over €40
HOTELS			
under €125	€125–€225	€226–€275	over €275

Shopping

Santorini is the best island in the Southern Cyclades for shopping. There are a lot of tourist trinkets still for sale but look beyond and you will find interesting souvenirs. Each island has a unique pottery style that reflects its individuality. Santorini potters like the bright shades of the setting sun, though the best pottery island is Paros. Island specialties are icons hand-painted after Byzantine originals; weavings and embroideries; local wines; and gold jewelry worked in ancient and Byzantine designs. Don't be surprised when the stores close between 2 and 5:30 in the afternoon and reopen in the evenings; even on the chic islands everybody takes a siesta.

Paros ΠΑΡΟΣ

168 km (104 miles) southeast of Piraeus harbor in Athens.

In the classical age, the great sculptor Praxiteles prized the incomparably snowy marble that came from the quarries at Paros; his chief rival was the Parian Scopas. Between them they developed the first true female nude, and gentle voluptuousness seems a good description of this historic island. Today, Paros is favored by people for its cafés by the sea, golden sandy beaches, and charming fishing villages. The island is large enough to accommodate the traveler in search of peace and quiet, yet the lovely port towns of Paroikía (Paros Town), the capital, and Naousa also have an active nightlife. Paros is a focal point of the Cyclades ferry network, and many people stay here for a night or two while waiting for a connection. Paros Town has a good share of bars and discos, though Naousa has a chicer island atmosphere. Moreover, none of the islands has a richer cultural life, with concerts, exhibitions, and readings, than Paros.

Paros is an island favorite among Greeks and visitors alike. The overflow of tourists is such that it has now washed up on Paros's sister, Antiparos: this island "forgetaway" still has an off-the-beaten-track vibe, even though the rich and famous—Tom Hanks is most prominent of them—have discovered it.

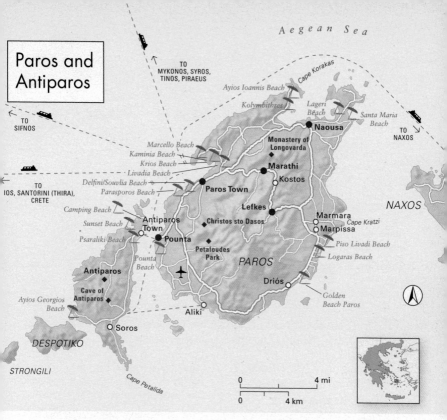

Paros and Antiparos

Aegean Sea

TO MYKONOS, SYROS, TINOS, PIRAEUS

Ayios Ioannis Beach

Cape Korakas

Kolymbithras

Lageri Beach

Santa Maria Beach

TO SIFNOS

Marcello Beach

Kaminia Beach

Krios Beach

Livadia Beach

Delfini/Souvlia Beach

Parasporos Beach

TO IOS, SANTORINI (THIRA), CRETE

Camping Beach

Sunset Beach

Psaraliki Beach

Antiparos Town

Pounta

Pounta Beach

Antiparos

Cave of Antiparos

Ayios Georgios Beach

Soros

DESPOTIKO

STRONGILI

Cape Petalida

Naousa

Monastery of Longovarda

Marathi

Kostos

Paros Town

Lefkes

Christos sto Dasos

Petaloudes Park

PAROS

Marmara

Cape Kratzi

Marpissa

Piso Livadi Beach

Logaras Beach

Driós

Golden Beach Paros

Aliki

TO NAXOS

NAXOS

0 ____ 4 mi

0 ____ 4 km

GETTING HERE AND AROUND

There are seven Olympic Air flights a day from Athens in summer, fewer in winter. Early reservations are essential. Paros is well served by ferries—there are at least 15 of them daily—many connecting Paros to other islands. All the Athens ports—Piraeus, Rafina, and Lavrio—have direct sailings. There are also regular connections to Amorgos, Andros, Anafi, Astypalea, Crete, Donousa, Folegandros, Iraklia, Ios, Kalymnos, Kastelorizo, Kea, Kimolos, Kos, Koufonisi, Serifos, Milos, Mykonos, Naxos, Nisyros, Rhodes, Santorini, Schinousa, Serifos, Sifnos, Sikinos, Syros, and Tinos. For boat schedules check ⊕ *www.openseas.gr* and ⊕ *www. bluestarferries.com.*

From the Paros Town bus depot, just west of the dock, there is service at least every hour to Naousa and less-frequent service to Aliki, Pounta (about 15 buses a day to this departure point for Antiparos), and the beaches at Piso Livadi, Chrissi Akti, and Drios. Schedules are posted. Buy tickets at the booth; fares run from €2 to €3.50. There is a taxi stand across from the windmill on the harbor (☎ *22840/21500*).

TOURS

Erkyna Travel

EXCURSIONS | Many excursions by boat, bus, and foot are offered here including day trips to neighboring islands ✉ *Paros Town ✛ Off the main harbor road where the ferries dock* ☎ *22840/22654, 22840/22655* ⊕ *www.erkynatravel.com.*

Polos Tours

EXCURSIONS | This agency handles all travel arrangements, from boat tickets to car rentals to excursions, with great efficiency. ✉ *Parikia, Paros Town ✛ Next*

Architecture buffs love the great Church of Our Lady of the Hundred Doors, a proto-Byzantine landmark.

to dockside OTE office ☎ 22840/22333 ⊕ www.polostoursparos.com.

VISITOR INFORMATION
The most useful Paros website is ⊕ www.parosweb.com.

Paros Town Πáρος (Παροικιά)

168 km (104 miles) southeast of Piraeus, 35 km (22 miles) west of Naxos.

First impressions of Paroikía (Paros Town. sometimes spelt Parikia), pretty as it is, may not necessarily be positive. The port flashes too much concrete, too many boats dock, and the traffic problem is seemingly insoluble. The waterfront is lined with travel agencies, a multitude of car and motorbike rental agencies, and fast-food outlets. Then, if you head east on the harbor road, you'll see a lineup of bars, tourist shops, and coffee shops. Past them are the fishing-boat dock, a partially excavated ancient graveyard,

and the post office; farther on start the beaches, mostly shaded and over-popular, with their hotels and tavernas.

Yet, go the other way straight into town and you'll find it easy to get lost in the maze of narrow, stone-paved lanes that intersect with the streets of the quiet residential areas. The marble plaza at the town's entrance is full of people strolling and children playing in the evening. Walk along the market street chockablock with tourist shops and you'll begin to traverse the centuries: ahead of you looms the seaside Kastro, the ancient acropolis. In 1207 the Venetians conquered Paros, which joined the Duchy of Naxos, and built their huge marble castle wall out of blocks and columns pillaged from three earlier temples. At the crest, next to the church of Saints Constantine and Helen (built in 1689), are the visible foundations of a late-Archaic temple to Athena—the area remains Paros's favorite sunset spot.

Sights

Archaeological Museum of Paros

MUSEUM | The Archaeological Museum contains a large chunk of the famed Parian chronicle, which recorded cultural events in Greece from about 1500 BC until 260 BC (another chunk is in Oxford's Ashmolean Museum). It interests scholars that the historian inscribed detailed information about artists, poets, and playwrights, completely ignoring wars and shifts in government. Some primitive pieces from the Aegean's oldest settlement, Saliagos (an islet between Paros and Antiparos), are exhibited in the same room, on the left. A small room contains archaic finds from the ongoing excavation at Despotiko—and they are finding a lot. In the large room to the right rests a marble slab depicting the poet Archilochus in a banquet scene, lying on a couch, his weapons nearby. The ancients ranked Archilochus, who invented iambic meter and wrote the first signed love lyric, second only to Homer. When he died in battle against the Naxians, his conqueror was cursed by the oracle of Apollo for putting to rest one of the faithful servants of the muse. Also there are a monumental Nike and three superb pieces found in the last decade: a waist-down kouros, a gorgon with intact wings, and a dancing-girl relief. ⊠ *Paros Town* ⊹ *Behind Hundred Doors Church* ☎ *22840/21231* 🎫 *€2* ⊘ *Closed Mon.*

Folklore Art Museum of Cycladic Civilization

MUSEUM | The Folklore Museum is set in a garden full of large models of traditional windmills, dovecotes, churches, and other such famous Cycladian monuments, making for an utterly charming setting. It also showcases the lifetime hobby of fisherman Benetos Skiadas, who loves to make detailed models of ships and his scrupulous craftsmanship is on view here. ⊠ *On road to Aliki* ☎ *22840/91129* 🎫 *€3* ⊘ *Closed Oct.–Apr.*

Monastery of Longovarda

RELIGIOUS SITE | Halfway from Paros Town to Naousa, on the right, the 17th-century Monastery of Longovarda shines on its mountainside. The monastic community farms the local land and makes honey, wine, and olive oil. Only men, dressed in conservative clothing, are allowed inside, where there are post-Byzantine icons, 17th-century frescoes depicting the Twelve Feasts in the Life of Christ, and a library of rare books; it is usually open mornings. ⊹ *3 km (2 miles) northeast of Paros Town* ☎ *22840/21202.*

★ Panagia Ekatontapyliani
(*Hundred Doors Church*)

RELIGIOUS SITE | The square above the port, to the northwest, was built to celebrate the church's 1,700th anniversary. From there note a white wall with two belfries, the front of the former monastic quarters that surround the magnificent Panagia Ekatontapyliani, the earliest remaining proto-Byzantine church in Greece and one of the oldest unaltered churches in the world. As such, it is a renowned pilgrimage church of the Aegean, second only to Megalochari on nearby Tinos.

The story began in 326, when St. Helen—the mother of Emperor Constantine the Great—set out on a ship for the Holy Land to find the True Cross. Stopping on Paros, she had a vision of success and vowed to build a church there. Though she died before it was built, her son built the church in 328 as a wooden-roof basilica. Two centuries later, Justinian the Great (who ruled the Byzantine Empire in 527–65) commissioned the splendid dome.

According to legend, 99 doors have been found in the church and the 100th will be discovered only after Constantinople is Greek again—but the name is actually older than the legend. Inside, the subdued light mixes with the dun, reddish, and green tufa (porous volcanic rock). The columns are classical and their capitals

Byzantine. At the corners of the dome are two fading Byzantine frescoes depicting six-winged seraphim. The 4th-century iconostasis (with ornate later additions) is divided into five frames by marble columns. One panel contains the 14th-century icon of the Virgin, with a silver covering from 1777. The Virgin is carried in procession on the church's crowded feast day, August 15, the Dormition. During Easter services, thousands of rose petals are dropped from the dome upon the singing celebrant. The adjacent **Baptistery,** nearly unique in Greece, also built from the 4th to the 6th century, has a marble font and bits of mosaic floor. The church **museum,** at the right, contains post-Byzantine icons. ⊠ *Paros Town* ⚓ *750 feet east of dock* ☎ *22840/21243* ⊕ *www.ekatontapyliani.gr.*

Beaches

From Paros Town, boats leave throughout the day for beaches across the bay: to sandy Marcellos and Krios and the quieter Kaminia. Livadia, a five-minute walk, is very developed but has shade. In the other direction, Delfini has a beach bar with music, and Parasporos has a few beach bars. Sun lovers note: Paros is ringed with beaches.

Delfini/Souvlia Beach

BEACH—SIGHT | This small beach is known for its pretty water and relaxed atmosphere. It's also known around the island for Magaya, a colorful beach bar set right in front of the beach. In the summer, beach chairs and umbrellas are available for rent, so grab one and settle in to enjoy the view of Paroikía Bay. ■TIP➔ **There's a small rocky islet with an underwater cave in the near distance, popular for swimmers to head to, but it's often full of sea urchins.** **Amenities:** food and drink. **Best for:** swimming. ⊠ *Paros Town.*

Pride Goeth Before a Fall

At one point, Justinian the Great (who ruled the Byzantine Empire in 527–65) had the Hundred Doors Church rebuilt. He appointed Isidorus, one of the two architects of Constantinople's famed Hagia Sophia, to design it, but Isidorus sent his apprentice, Ignatius, in his place. Upon inspection, Isidorus discovered the dome to be so magnificent that, consumed by jealousy, he pushed the apprentice off the roof. Ignatius grasped his master's foot and the two tumbled to their death together.

Kaminia Beach

BEACH—SIGHT | Sandy, long, and unorganized, Kaminia sits to the north of Paroikía Bay. Beachgoers seeking more solitude can head here, even though it's right next to the popular Krios Beach. See if you can find the cave of Archilochos, which is a small opening on the rock along the coast. The famous Ancient Greek poet was said to visit the cave for inspiration and wrote poetry there. **Amenities:** none. **Best for:** solitude; swimming. ⊠ *Paros Town.*

Krios Beach

BEACH—SIGHT | Close to Paroikía, this sandy beach is a popular summer destination. Cliffs jut into the sand line, parting the coastline and providing protection from the summer island winds. From under a rented umbrella you can watch the boats and ferries slowly sail into the harbor. If you need to take a break, there's a selection of nearby tavernas. ■TIP➔ **To get here, you can hike the half-hour-long cliff-top trail, take a small boat from the harbor, or drive to the nearby** parking area. **Amenities:** food and drink; parking (free). **Best for:** swimming; walking. ✉ *Paros Town.*

Livadia Beach

BEACH—SIGHT | FAMILY | Considered the closest authentic Parian beach near Paroikía, Livadia is the first wide bay north of the harbor that's comprised of a series of smaller, white-sand beaches. Some areas are organized with beach chair and umbrella rentals while others are untouched by tourism, and only trees provide shade. Just a 10-minute walk from the town and harbor and near campgrounds, it can get crowded. **Amenities:** food and drink. **Best for:** swimming. ✉ *Paros Town.*

Marcello Beach

BEACH—SIGHT | FAMILY | Marcello's famously cool waters attract Parians on the hottest summer days. You can spend the entire day eating, drinking, swimming, or watching the calm water lap against this long, sandy stretch of coastline, as the beach is well equipped with beach bars and cafés, tavernas, and umbrellaed lounge-chair rentals. Next to Krios Beach, it's accessible by car, boat, or a 40-minute hike from Paroikía. **Amenities:** food and drink, parking (free). **Best for:** swimming; walking. ✉ *Paros Town.*

Parasporos Beach

BEACH—SIGHT | This large sandy beach is surrounded by a few shady trees, but umbrellas are available for rent in the summer season. The clear turquoise water gets deep fast, making it ideal for swimming. There are a few bars on-site that add a little beach-party fun. **Amenities:** food and drink. **Best for:** partiers; swimming; water sports. ✉ *Paros Town.*

🍴 Restaurants

★ Levantis

$$ | MODERN GREEK | Chef George Mavridis is an expert at merging the flavors of traditional Greek dishes with contemporary tastes to offer an exciting menu that is beautifully presented. The dining space, a whitewashed indoor room and garden dining area shrouded by vines, is inviting. **Known for:** contemporary and stylish modern Greek cooking; polished service; intriguing all-Greek wine list. $ *Average main: €18 ✉ Paros Town ⊹ Off Lochagou Kourtinou* ☎ *22840/23613* ⊕ *www.levantisrestaurant.com* ⊗ *Closed Nov.–Apr.*

★ Stou Fred

$$$$ | FRENCH FUSION | Globe-trotting chef Fred Chesneau finally set down roots in Paros, bringing French-influenced dining to the island. A romantic flower-filled garden with white ironwork furniture is a pretty match for the weekly changing fixed menu that features the best locally sourced seasonal produce. Just twenty-two lucky diners each night get to experience a food journey that may take them from Paros to Paris via Bangkok and Tokyo. **Known for:** genial host Fred guides you through his creations; intriguing wine list of small French producers; five-course cosmopolitan fixed price menu. $ *Average main: €45 ✉ Paros Town* ☎ *6970448763.*

☕ Coffee and Quick Bites

Hellas

$ | GREEK | Bright, multicolored decor sets this apart from your average grill shop as does the freshest of food. Family-run, the owners take a real pride in their establishment. **Known for:** the classic grill shop you have been looking for; menu that suits any time of the day; great position on the port. $ *Average main: €8 ✉ Paros Town* ☎ *22840/28008.*

Hotels

Yria Boutique Hotel and Spa
$$$ | **HOTEL** | **FAMILY** | Palm trees and topiaried conifers and hedges give the air of a glamorous retreat to this Small Luxury Hotel, a few minutes from pretty Parosporos beach. **Pros:** great facilities—super spa, large freshwater pool, and tennis court; beautifully landscaped grounds; a short walk from Parasporos beach. **Cons:** sea views for only the most expensive rooms; reasonable rather than great value, especially for food and beverages; a long 2-mile walk from town. [$] *Rooms from: €270* ✉ *Paros Town* ☎ *22840/24154–8* 🌐 *www.yriahotel.gr* 🕒 *Closed Nov.–Mar.* 🛏 *67 rooms* 🍴 *Free breakfast.*

Nightlife

BARS

Turn right along the waterfront from the port in Paros Town to find the town's famous bars; then follow your ears. At the far end of the *paralia* is the laser-light-and-disco section of town, which you may want to avoid. In the younger bars, cheap alcohol, as everywhere in tourist Greece, is often added to the more-colorful drinks.

Pirate Bar
BARS/PUBS | One of the oldest bars on the island, this cozy hideaway combines whitewashed walls with a stone-and-wood design and soft lighting. Great cocktails made from local ingredients should be taken on one of the handful of tables on the cobbled street outside. ✉ *Old Town.*

Performing Arts

Of all the Southern Cyclades, Paros has the liveliest art scene, with dozens of galleries and public spaces presenting exhibitions. Many artists, Greek and foreign, live on the island or visit regularly. Check the local press and posters for details of forthcoming events and the Aegean Center has proved a strong stimulant.

The Aegean Center for the Fine Arts
ART GALLERIES—ARTS | A small American arts college, the Aegean Center for the Fine Arts hosts readings, concerts, lectures, and exhibitions in its splendidly restored neoclassical mansion. Since 1966 the center has offered courses (two three-month semesters as well as intensive summer workshops) in writing, painting, art history, photography, and classical voice training. ✉ *Main cross street to Market St.* ☎ *22840/23287* 🌐 *www.aegeancenter.com.*

Shopping

CERAMICS

★ Yria Ceramics and Interior Design
CERAMICS/GLASSWARE | On Market Street, look for the house with the beautifully carved Parian marble facade to find Paros's most elegantly designed shop. Here, Stelios Ghikas, Monique Mailloux, and daughter Ramona display their pottery from Studio Yria, as well as a carefully chosen range of stylish household items. You can also visit their workshop, perched on a slope in the village of Kostos, and see the beautiful and stunning original designs being made. ✉ *Market St.* ☎ *22840/24359* 🌐 *www.yriaparos.com.*

JEWELRY

Phaedra's Handmade Jewellery
JEWELRY/ACCESSORIES | Local Phaidra Apostolopoulou, who studied jewelry in Athens, has this tiny shop, where she shows her sophisticated silver and gold designs, and a line of punky and funky pieces for summer. ✉ *Paros Town* ✥ *Between Zoodochos Pyghi and Agios Nikolaos churches* ☎ *22840/23626.*

🏃 Activities

WATER SPORTS

Many beaches offer water sports, especially windsurfing, kayaking and stand-up paddleboarding

Naousa Νάουσα

10 km (6 miles) northeast of Paros Town.

Quaint fishing village no longer, Naousa (also Niaoussa) long ago discovered the benefits of tourism, and its outskirts are mushrooming with villas and hotels that exploit it further. Thankfully, the pretty little harbor is still in use as a fishing port, and red and blue boats rub gently together as fishermen repair their nets. The taverna-filled waterfront is the big draw, charmingly backed by Venetian townhouses. Navies of the ancient Persians, flotillas from medieval Venice, and the imperial Russian fleet have anchored in this harbor. The half-submerged ruins of the Venetian fortifications still remain; they are a pretty sight when lit up at night. Compared to Paros Town, the scene in Naousa is somewhat chicer, with a more intimate array of shops, bars, and restaurants, but although the nightlife is on a par with Paroikia, many people are here for the local beaches.

In 1537 legendary corsair Barbarossa kidnapped the womenfolk of Naousa and the locals engaged in a naval battle to ensure their return. Nowadays, on August 23rd, every year the Festival of the Pirates is enthusiastically celebrated with a re-enactment of the fighting followed by a firework display.

🏖 Beaches

Ayios Ioannis

BEACH—SIGHT | Served by the Kolymbithres boat, Ayios Ioannis's golden, sandy beach is peaceful, clean, and quiet. Also known by locals as Monastiri Beach, it is protected by a rocky cove and has a snack bar and numerous amenities. Nice, gently shelving waters are perfect for kids. The blue-domed, whitewashed Ayios Ioannis Monastery sits to the right side of the beach, a short walk away. **Amenities:** food and drink; showers; toilets; water sports. **Best for:** swimming. ✉ Naousa ✛ In front of Paros Park.

Kolymbithres

BEACH—SIGHT | FAMILY | The beach, which is noted for its anfractuous rock formations, is also considered to be one of Paros's best, attracting its share of crowds to the small, sandy cove. The granite formations create shallow pools of water popular with the kids. It's within walking distance of two tavernas that overlook the region. Lounge chairs and umbrellas are available for rent from a seasonal café. Head to the top of nearby Koukounaries Hill to view the remains of an ancient site. You can get there by car, and there is designated parking for the beach. ■TIP→ **A water-taxi crosses the bay to Kolymbithres from Naousa.** **Amenities**: food and drink; parking (free). **Best for:** swimming. ✉ Naousa ✛ Directly across bay from Naousa.

Lageri

BEACH—SIGHT | A boat from Naousa regularly heads to Lageri, a long beach known for its fine sand, dunes, and calm, quiet atmosphere. These are just a few of the reasons it attracts its share of nudists, who prefer the less crowded Paros beaches. It's also accessible via a small footpath from the main road. **Amenities:** none. **Best for:** nudists; solitude; walking. ✉ Naousa ✛ North of Naousa.

Santa Maria

BEACH—SIGHT | FAMILY | Several sandy footpaths from the main road lead you to one of Paros's most popular family-friendly beaches; the boat that travels to nearby Lageri also makes a stop in Santa Maria. Little fishing boats dock in the distance from the sandy cove, which is filled with sand dunes and lined with green brush. There's no natural shade, but in peak season it's well equipped with beach-chair and umbrella rentals from seasonal cafés. Several tavernas are within walking distance. **Amenities:** food and drink; showers; water sports **Best for:** swimming. ✉ *Naousa* ✣ *Northeastern shore of Paros.*

🍴 Restaurants

Mediterraneo Taverna Ouzerie
$$ | **GREEK** | For a calming view of Naousa harbor and a taste of Greek seafood specialties done to perfection, head to Mediterraneo. Here's the place to try traditional Greek taverna appetizers, including fresh grilled octopus and marinated anchovies, and dips like *taramosalata* (fish roe dip) and fava dip topped with caramelized onion, before mains that add a bit of contemporary creativity. **Known for:** view of Naousa harbor; excellent, fresh Greek-style seafood dishes; friendly family favorite. [$] *Average main: €20* ✉ *On the dock* ☎ *22840/53176.*

★ **Siparos**
$$ | **MEDITERRANEAN** | For many repeat visitors a trip to Paros is unthinkable without a visit to Siparos. This storied eatery is along the coast of Naousa Bay in the beach town of Santa Maria and well deserves its reputation as one of the island's finest. **Known for:** romantic sunset views; attentive, knowledgeable service; reservations essential. [$] *Average main: €25* ✉ *Xifara, Santa Maria* ☎ *22840/52785* 🌐 *www.siparos.gr.*

☕ Coffee and Quick Bites

Pizza Slice
$ | **ITALIAN** | Sicilian owners ensure this pizza joint is the real deal—a thin crust topped by choice ingredients is the best value on the island. Grab a cocktail at the equally super **I Tria** bar next door while you wait (it's owned by the same people). **Known for:** pizza by the pie or by the slice; takeaway or eat in; authentic Italian style. [$] *Average main: €8* ✉ *Naousa* ☎ *6898031215.*

🛏 Hotels

Astir of Paros
$$$$ | **RESORT** | Peaceful views of Kolymbithres Bay are part of the experience at this graceful deluxe resort hotel, where green lawns, tall palm trees, subtropical gardens, and a private beach contribute to its superlative reputation. **Pros:** highly personal service; private beach and a beautiful pool; superlative restaurants in romantic settings. **Cons:** you need a vehicle to get anywhere, including Naousa; not the cheapest option in town; not much in the locale except the beach. [$] *Rooms from: €350* ✉ *Naousa* ✣ *Take Kolymbithres Rd. from Naousa* ☎ *22840/51976, 22840/51984* 🌐 *www.astirofparos.gr* ⏲ *Closed Nov.–Mar.* 🛏 *5 rooms* 🍽 *Free breakfast.*

Mr and Mrs White Paros
$$ | **HOTEL** | This contemporary Cycladic-style hotel sits on a small hill overlooking Naousa, all white cubes and gray and natural woodwork, the better to reflect the blue pool water and bright pink bougainvillea that festoon the walls. **Pros:** great breakfast with lots of local specialities; two pools have plenty of room to chill; relaxed, sincere service. **Cons:** dusty 1/2 mile walk into town; some rooms view the local streets; large and a little impersonal. [$] *Rooms from: €170* ✉ *Naousa* ☎ *22840/55207* 🌐 *www.mrandmrswhiteparos.com* ⏲ *Oct.–May* 🛏 *59 rooms* 🍽 *Free breakfast.*

★ **Parilio Hotel**
$$$ | **HOTEL** | Parilio—from Paros and Helios the sun—is the new face of hotels on the island; modern and yet reflecting the timeless Cycladic style. **Pros:** chicest stay on the island; Mr. E restaurant uses local cuisine to great effect; on-site Elios Spa. **Cons:** nearest beach is a 15-minute walk away; not a lot to do or see in the local area; cool vibes come at a cool price. [$] *Rooms from: €250* ✉ *Naousa* ☎ *22840/51000* 🌐 *www.pariliohotelparos.com* ⏲ *Closed Oct.–Mar.* 🛏 *33 rooms* 🍽 *Free breakfast.*

⅋ Nightlife

BARS

Linardo

BARS/PUBS | You can't miss this place; fuschia bougainvillea on the 400-year-old whitewashed building is mirrored by bright pink doors. Inside, Linardo's interior is impeccably maintained and cooly decorated—it has to be, considering that it's one of Naousa's top hot spots, where crowds gather until the early morning to listen to the coolest music on the isle. ⊠ *Liminaki.*

★ Sommaripa Consolato

CAFES—NIGHTLIFE | A prime spot above idyllic Naousa harbor is where you'll find Sommaripa Consolato, which infuses Paros tradition in its drinks. Instead of a mojito, try their creation—a sumito, which replaces rum with the local homemade island liquor called *suma.* A cool open space with picture-perfect views of the bay, it's a great place to watch the world strolling past, especially from the coveted balcony seat. During the day, stop by for a coffee accompanied by a homemade Greek cookie or a slice of cake. ⊠ *Limanaki.*

🎭 Performing Arts

PERFORMANCE VENUES

Environmental and Cultural Park of Paros

CONCERTS | Set on almost 800 acres of the beautiful Agios Ioannis Detis Peninsula, the Environmental and Cultural Park of Paros offers a full summer program of concerts in its outdoor theater, while Cine Enastron is an open-air movie venue for watching films under the stars. ⊠ *Paros Park* ☎ 22840/53573 ⊕ *www.parospark.com.*

🛍 Shopping

CLOTHES

Bit of Salt

CLOTHING | Paros's favorite surf shop sells its own-brand clothing range of hoodies, T-shirts, beanies, and rash vests, which make great souvenirs. ⊠ *Naousa* ☎ 22840/28625 ⊕ *www.bitofsalt.gr.*

Marathi Μαράθι

10 km (6 miles) east of Paros Town.

During the classical period, the island of Paros had an estimated 150,000 residents, many of them slaves who worked the ancient marble quarries in Marathi. The island grew rich from the export of this white, granular marble known among ancient architects and sculptors for its ability to absorb light. They called it *lychnites* ("won by lamplight").

👁 Sights

Three Caverns

MINE | A short walk from the main road, marked by a sign, three caverns are bored into the hillside. The largest of them, the Cave of the Nymphs, is 300 feet deep. This is where the world-famed Parian marble was mined—the marble of the Acropolis, of the Temple of Poseidon, of Venetian palaces, and of monuments all over the world. The Venus de Milo, Nike of Samothrace, and countless other masterpieces all began here. ⊠ *Marathi.*

Lefkes Λεύκες

6 km (4 miles) south of Marathi, 10 km (6 miles) southeast of Paros Town.

Rampant piracy in the 17th century forced thousands of people to move inland from the coastal regions; thus, for many years the scenic village of Lefkes, built on a hillside in the protective mountains, was the island's capital. It remains the largest village in the interior and has maintained a peaceful island feeling, with narrow streets fragrant with jasmine and honeysuckle. These days, the old houses are being restored, and in summer the town is full of people. Farming is the major source of income, evidenced by the well-kept stone walls and olive groves. For one of the best walks on Paros, take the ancient Byzantine road from the main lower square to the lower villages.

Two 17th-century churches of interest are **Ayia Varvara** (St. Barbara) and **Ayios Sotiris** (Holy Savior). The big 1830 neo-Renaissance **Ayia Triada** (Holy Trinity) is the pride of the village.

Beaches

Beyond Lefkes, the road continues on to Piso Livadi and a string of popular beaches.

Golden Beach

BEACH—SIGHT | Golden Beach (or Chrysi Akti in Greek) is a series of tree-fringed sandy beaches that are well organized and in close proximity to an array of taverns, restaurants, and cafés. The area is famous for its water-sports activities and several centers are based here offering diving excursions, kayaking, and windsurfing lessons. The Windsurfing World Cup has held events here. **Amenities:** food and drink. **Best for:** swimming; water sports; windsurfing. ✉ *Golden Beach.*

Logaras Beach

BEACH—SIGHT | Just around the bend from Piso Livadi is the long stretch of yellow sand known as Logaras Beach. A few tavernas are nearby, and in the distance the little whitewashed church of Ayios Georgios Thalassites, or St. George of the Sea, stands where it has since the 13th century. This quiet beach has chairs and umbrellas available for rent in the summer season. **Amenities:** food and drink. **Best for:** swimming; walking. ✉ *Logaras Beach.*

Piso Livadi Beach

BEACH—SIGHT | **FAMILY** | One of the most popular beaches on Paros's southeastern coast, Piso Livadi has trees offering natural shade, but lounge chairs and umbrellas are also available to rent. The small resort town of Piso Livadi, once an ancient port for the marble quarries, surrounds the sandy stretch of well-developed beach and is filled with lodging options, tavernas, restaurants, and cafés Boats depart from this port for Mykonos, Naxos, Amorgos, Ios, and Santorini. **Amenities:** food and drink. **Best for:** swimming. ✉ *Piso Livadi* ✣ *On road past Lefkes* 🌐 *www.pissolivadi.com.*

Restaurants

Chrisoula - Geuseis Tis Sintrofias

$ | **GREEK** | A breezy verandah at the edge of the village looks down to the sea and across to Naxos. You'll come for the views, but stay for the food—the terraced fields all around supply the raw ingredients that go into the traditional regional cooking. **Known for:** fabulous pies are a must—check the specials board; edge of the village location gives great views; family owned with sweet, friendly service. [$] *Average main: €10* ✉ *Lefkes* ☎ *22840/43144.*

Taverna Klarinos

$ | **GREEK** | Tradition counts for everything at this family-run taverna. Like his parents who ran Klarinos before him, Andreas Ragoussis only uses homegrown vegetables and local meat in his dishes. **Known for:** grilled meat; traditional local vegetable dishes; serviceable homemade wine. [$] *Average main: €12* ✉ *Central Square, 2nd Fl.* ☎ *22840/41608* 🕓 *Closed Oct.–Apr.*

Hotels

Saint George Hotel

$$ | **HOTEL** | **FAMILY** | A step away from Golden Beach, the Saint George does everything it promises at first sight—providing stylish accommodation in a great location away from the hustle and bustle of the busier resorts. **Pros:** cliffside location right on top of the beach; nice breakfast and dinner menu; super clean, well thought-out rooms. **Cons:** little bit out on a limb; this corner of the island can get windy; better for families than couples in search of romance. $ *Rooms from: €150* ✉ *New Golden Beach, Golden Beach* ☎ *22840/43400* ⊕ *www.saintgeorgehotel.gr* ⤳ *56 rooms* ♦︎⊙ *Free breakfast.*

 ## Shopping

ART GALLERIES

Angelika Vaxevanidou Art Studio

ART GALLERIES | A visit to the whitewashed studio and gallery of award-winning sculptor, mosaicist, and portrait artist Angelika Vaxevanidou is a glimpse into the world of a successful, internationally commissioned artist. The longtime local artist and resident is recognized for her impressive, sensitive, and emotional large-scale colored-pencil portraiture, and on display are works past and present. The studio is open year-round. ✉ *Lefkes* ☎ *22840/44076* ⊕ *www.angelikavaxevanidou.com* ⊗ *Closed Sun.*

Pounta ΠΟΥΝΤΑ

4 km (2½ miles) south of Paros Town.

Pounta is not even a village, just a few houses, a handful of restaurants, and a tiny harbor from which ferries leave for Antiparos. The road that turns left just before you get there continues on to a string of beaches; beyond are noisy Pounta beach itself, sleepy Aliki and Drysos, and the busy little bay of Faragas. If it is too windy on the rest of the island, look down here for shelter.

 ## Sights

Christos sto Dasos (*Christ in the Wood*)

RELIGIOUS SITE | A 15-minute walk or 2-minute drive back toward Paros Town from the Valley of Butterflies leads to the convent known as Christos sto Dasos, from where there's a marvelous view of the Aegean. The convent contains the tomb of St. Arsenios (1800–77), who was a schoolteacher, an abbot, and a prophet. He was also a reputed rainmaker, whose prayers were believed to have ended a long drought, saving Paros from starvation. If you want to go in, be sure to wear long pants or skirt, and a shirt that covers your shoulders or the sisters will turn you away. ✛ *Between the Valley of Butterflies and Paros Town.*

Petaloudes Park

NATURE PRESERVE | The Jersey tiger moth returns year after year to mate in Petaloudes (Butterflies Valley), a lush oasis of greenery in the middle of this dry island. In May, June, and perhaps July, you can watch them as they lie dormant during the day, their chocolate-brown wings with yellow stripes still against the ivy leaves. In the evening they flutter upward to the cooler air, flashing the coral-red undersides of their wings as they rise. A notice at the entrance asks visitors not to disturb them by taking photographs or shaking the leaves. ✉ *Petaloudes Park* ☎ *22840/91211* ⊕ *www.parosbutterflies.gr* 🎫 *€2* ⊗ *Closed mid-Sept.–mid-May.*

Beaches

Pounta Beach

BEACH—SIGHT | Boom! Boom! Boom! You will hear it as you approach—Pounta is the party beach of Paros. Beach bars throb with teens and twenty-somethings doing their best to get noticed. The beach itself is lovely but has got lost under a sea of umbrellas and chairs. The winds here are good and consistent and make it a haven for windsurfers, kitesurfers,

8

Southern Cyclades PAROS

and other sport enthusiasts. **Amenities:** food and drink; toilets. **Best for:** partiers; surfing; windsurfing. ✉ *Pounda*.

☕ Coffee and Quick Bites

Kaitas

$ | FAST FOOD | Run by the Paros Kite Pro Center and EuroDivers crew, this is the best place to recuperate after a session on the waves. Great omelets and breakfasts are offered along with pizza and super-fresh juices. **Known for:** relaxed surfer vibes; best burger for miles; will deliver to you on the beach. Ⓢ *Average main: €8* ✉ *Pounta* ☎ *22840/92071* ⊕ *www.paroskite-procenter.com.*

🏃 Activities

SCUBA DIVING

Eurodivers

DIVING/SNORKELING | A proud Professional Association of Diving Instructors (PADI) 5-Star Resort, Eurodivers offers courses from snorkeling tours to professional levels. ✉ *Pounta* ☎ *22840/92071* ⊕ *www. eurodivers.gr.*

WINDSURFING

Paros Kite Pro Center

SURFING | On the island's west coast, where turquoise waters meet windy conditions perfect for kitesurfing, the Paros Kite Pro Center offers International Kiteboarding Organization–certified lessons, equipment, and rentals. ✉ *Pounta* ⊕ *www.paroskite-procenter.com.*

Antiparos Αντίπαρος

5 km (3 miles) southwest of Paros Town.

This smaller sister isle to Paros may have once been a well-kept secret, but thanks to celebrity resident Tom Hanks and his wife Rita Wilson, everybody now knows about this pretty little bolthole—it's certainly a secret no more but it still teeters on the right side of development. Two or three decades ago you would have gone to the Paros hamlet of Pounta, made you way to the church, opened its door as a signal, and waited for a fishing caïque to chug over. Now, 30-car ferries ply the channel all day and a lovely 7-minute ride wafts you over to Antiparos (or you can take a 20-minute ferry ride from Paros Town). A causeway once crossed the Antiparos strait, which would be swimmable but for the current, and on one of its still-emergent islets, Saliagos, habitations and objects have been found dating back almost to 5000 BC.

Antiparos's one town, also called Antiparos, has a main street and two centers of activity: the quay area and the main square, a block or two in. At both are restaurants and cafés. To the right of the square are houses and the Kastro's 15th-century wall. At the other end of the quay from the ferry dock, a road goes to an idyllic sandy beach (it is 10 minutes by foot); you can wade across to the islet opposite, Fira, where sheep and goats graze.

It is pleasant to go around to the other side of Antiparos on the good road to Ayios Georgios, where there are three excellent taverns, perfect after a swim. On request a boat will take you to the nearby islet of **Despotiko,** uninhabited except for seasonal archaeologists excavating a late-Archaic marble temple complex to Apollo, and there are plans to open a museum here in the near future. In autumn the hills are fragrant with purple flowering heather.

👁 Sights

Cave of Antiparos

CAVE | In the 19th century the most famous sight in the Aegean was the cave of Antiparos, and it still draws many visitors every year. Greece's oldest known cave sits on the southeastern part of Antiparos. It's filled with shapely stalactites and stalagmites of which the oldest is said to be 45 million years old. The natural wonder was first discovered by a French ambassador in the 16th century and myths, legends, and stories have been associated with it along the way. You'll need to take exactly 411 steps down into the cave's 100-meter-deep core to explore. Look for Lord Byron's autograph. Outside is the church of Agios Ioánnis Spiliótis, built in 1774. Audio tours are available. ⊠ *Agios Ioannis* 🔒 *€6* ⏲ *Closed Nov.–Mar.*

Venetian Kastro
CASTLE/PALACE | Close to the port you'll find yourself walking into the pedestrian paths of Antiparos Town, lined with whitewashed shops, restaurants, and cafés. Farther up, the arched stonework entrance to the historical center, known as the *camara*, leads to the centuries-old Venetian *kastro,* or castle, of Antiparos. Like other Cycladic islands, this architecture reflects the construction of fortresses built between the 13th and 16th century when Venetian and Ottoman influences took over the islands. You can walk the whitewashed streets of this small village, where Antiparians still live in small homes built on top of each other as one continuous block construction within the stone walls. There are also four churches within the settlement. ⊠ *Antiparos Town* ✛ *Northern tip of the island.*

🏖 Beaches

Ayios Georgios Beach
BEACH—SIGHT | Head 11 km (7 miles) south of Antiparos Town to the calm, southeastern beaches of Ayios Georgios. This series of small, fine-sand coves has a view of the uninhabited island of Despotiko. Here, three small fish tavernas sit on the edge of the tiny village road, overlooking the sea. Otherwise, what you see is what you get—a serene untouched landscape. **Amenities:** food and drink. **Best for:** solitude; swimming; walking. ⊠ *Ayios Georgios.*

Camping Beach
BEACH—SIGHT | This long, quiet sandy stretch of beach is located off a small path leading from the Antiparos Camping campground and just north of Antiparos Town. The view is peaceful: just the neighboring inlet of Diplos and a turquoise sea. On one section of the beach, umbrellas and lounge chairs can be rented and another area is frequented by nudists—it's one of Greece's recognized naturist beaches. **Amenities:** food and drink. **Best for:** nudists; solitude; walking. ⊠ *Antiparos Town.*

Psaraliki Beach
BEACH—SIGHT | FAMILY | Within walking distance of Antiparos Town, this beach has two parts, referred to by locals as Psaraliki One and Psaraliki Two. Yellow, soft sand fills both and each is dotted with natural shade trees; lounge chairs and umbrellas are available during the summer months. The shallow waters make it a favorite for families, and its southeasterly placement on the island keeps it sheltered from gusty Cycladic winds. Several tavernas are close by. **Amenities**: food and drink. **Best for:** swimming; walking. ⊠ *Antiparos Town.*

Sunset Beach
BEACH—SIGHT | As its name implies, this is where Antiparians head to watch their island's fantastic sunsets. Clear water and golden sand are guaranteed, but ideal beach weather is not—located on the west coast, the beach isn't sheltered from the Cycladic winds that can stir things up. When the winds do die down, the conditions are ideal for snorkeling and swimming. ■ **TIP➜ The beach is also known as Sifneiko, because the neighboring island of Sifnos can be seen in the distance. Amenities:** food and drink. **Best for:** snorkeling; sunset; swimming. ⊠ *Antiparos Town.*

Restaurants

★ Captain Pipinos

$$ | SEAFOOD | Dining here is on an elevated veranda right above the calm blue waters of Ayios Georgios Bay. The line of drying octopus may be out, evidence of Captain Pipinos's pride in serving the freshest seafood on the island. **Known for:** fresh seafood from the family fishing boats; great location; bus from Antiparos town stops right outside. $ *Average main: €15* ⊠ *Ayios Georgios* ⊕ *www. captainpipinos.com.*

★ Kalokeri

$$ | MODERN GREEK | A bright and fresh room, wistfully painted with sea creatures and cacti, is the backdrop to this bijou establishment on the main street. Refined Aegean cuisine with jewel-like presentation is the order of the day—this is food that you devour with your eyes first. **Known for:** the gourmet spot on the island; delightful staff; reservations a must. $ *Average main: €18* ⊠ *Main Street, Antiparos Town* ☎ *22840/63037.*

Hotels

Kastro Antiparos

$$ | RESORT | FAMILY | On a small hill and within comfortable walking distance to town and Psariliki Beach, this bright, open, whitewashed property has been consistently upgraded and expanded over the last 20 or so years by Antiparian couple Magda Kritsantoni and Markos Maouni. **Pros:** walking distance to town and beach; sea views from its open spaces; nice and refreshing pool. **Cons:** books up early; may be busy with kids; pool is small. $ *Rooms from: €150* ⊠ *Antiparos Town* ☎ *22840/61011* ⊕ *www.antiparos-greece.com* ⊗ *Closed Nov.–Apr.* 🛏 *12 rooms* ⊗ *Free breakfast.*

Kouros Village Hotel

$$ | HOTEL | The hotels on Antiparos tend to be simple, pleasant places to stay, and this two-story building, which offers a series of rooms, apartments, and suites, most overlooking a pool and beautiful Antiparos Bay, nicely fits the bill. **Pros:** attractive, convenient option; nice restaurant attached; balconies and terraces have fine sea views. **Cons:** in a busy port; pool can feel crowded in high season; patchy Wi-Fi in rooms. $ *Rooms from: €130* ⊠ *Antiparos harbor, Antiparos Town* ☎ *22840/61084* ⊕ *www. kouros-village.gr* ⊗ *Closed mid-Oct.–mid-Apr.* 🛏 *30 rooms* ⊗ *No meals.*

🛍 Shopping

Mariliza

CLOTHING | Antiparos's trendiest concept boutique features a hip selection of clothing, purses, T-shirts, and accessories crafted by Greek designers. You can also browse through creations made with care by the talented owner, Mariliza Dimakou, including stylish Greek leather sandals and handmade Greek-inspired jewelry. ⊠ *Antiparos Town* ⊕ *www. marilizashop.gr.*

Naxos ΝΑΞΟΣ

190 km (118 miles) southeast of Piraeus harbor in Athens.

"Great sweetness and tranquility" is how Nikos Kazantzakis, premier novelist of Greece, described Naxos, and indeed a tour of the island leaves you with an impression of abundance, prosperity, and serenity. The greenest, largest, and most fertile of the Southern Cyclades, Naxos, with its many potato fields, its livestock, its thriving cheese industry, and its fruit and olive groves framed by the pyramid of Mt. Zas (at 3,295 feet, the Cyclades's highest), is practically self-sufficient. Inhabited for 6,000 years, the island has memorable landscapes—abrupt ravines, hidden valleys, long and sandy beaches—and towns that vary from a Cretan mountain stronghold to the seaside capital that strongly evokes its Venetian past.

Naxos's most famous landmark is its "doorway to nowhere." The Portara is the sole remnant of a gigantic ancient Temple to Apollo.

Naxos is full of history and monuments—classical temples, medieval monasteries, Byzantine churches, Venetian towers—and its huge interior offers endless magnificent hikes, not much pursued by summer tourists, who cling to the lively capital and the developed western beaches, the best in the Cyclades.

GETTING HERE AND AROUND

Olympic Air flies from Athens to Naxos up to four times a day, and it takes 35 minutes. Sky Express has a similar schedule throughout the day.

Naxos acts as one of the major ferry hubs and it is very well connected. Ferrries from Piraeus and Lavrio take from 4–6 hours depending on the route, boat, and pelagic happenstance. Boats seem to dock almost continuously in summer and direct connections are available with Amorgos, Anafi, Andros, Astypaleia, Crete, Donoussa, Folegandros, Ios, Iraklia, Kea, Kimilos, Kos, Koufonisi, Kythnos, Leros, Milos, Mykonos, Paros, Patmos, Santorini, Serifos, Sifnos, Schinoussa,

Syros, and Tinos. The Naxos Port Authority can give you information on ferries.

On Naxos, the bus system is reliable and fairly extensive. Daily buses go from Naxos Town, called Chora (near the boat dock) to Apeiranthos, Apollonas, Engares, Filoti, Koronida, Melanes, and Sangri. In summer there is added daily service to the beaches, including Abram, Ayia Anna, Ayiassos, Pachi Ammos, and Pyrgaki. Other villages have bus service but with much less frequency. Schedules are posted and timetables can be found online at ⊕ www.naxosdestinations.com. Fares run from €1.80 to €6.40. There is also a taxi stand near the harbor.

Renting a car is a good idea and brings the better beaches within reach. However, bear in mind that many hotels within Naxos Town have no parking due to the narrow streets.

CONTACTS Auto Tour Rent A Car.
☎ 22850/25480 ⊕ www.naxos-rentacar.com. **Naxos Port Authority.**
☎ 22850/22300.

TOURS

Zas Travel

GUIDED TOURS | This agency runs several one-day tours of the island sights with different itineraries, each costing about €50, and one-day trips to Delos and Mykonos, as well as to Santorini (about €70). ✉ *At harbor, Naxos Town* ☎ *22850/23330, 22850/23331.*

Naxos Town Νάξος (Χώρα)

140 km (87 miles) southeast of Piraeus, 33 km (21 miles) southeast of Mykonos, 35 km (22 miles) east of Paros.

As your ferry sweeps into the harbor, you see before you the white houses of Naxos Town (Chora) on a hill crowned by the one remaining tower of the Venetian castle, a reminder that Naxos was once the proud capital of the Venetian semi-independent Duchy of the Archipelago.

The most ancient settlements of Naxos were directly on the square in front of the Greek Orthodox cathedral. You'll note that several of the churches on this square, including the cathedral itself, hint at Naxos's venerable history, as they are made of ancient materials. In fact, this square was, in succession, the seat of a flourishing Mycenaean town (1300–1050 BC), a classical agora (when it was a 167-foot-by-156-foot square closed on three sides by Doric stoas, so that it looked like the letter "G"; a shorter fourth stoa bordered the east side, leaving room at each end for an entrance), a Roman town, and an Early Christian church complex. City, cemetery, tumulus, hero shrine: no wonder the Early Christians built here. For more of ancient Naxos, explore the nearby precinct of Grotta.

 Sights

Catholic Cathedral of Naxos

RELIGIOUS SITE | Built by Marco Sanudo, Venetian founder of the Duchy of the Aegean, in the 13th century, this grand cathedral was restored by Catholic families in the 16th and 17th centuries. The marble floor is paved with tombstones bearing the coats of arms of the noble families. Venetian wealth is evident in the many gold and silver icon frames. The icons reflect a mix of Byzantine and Western influences: the one of the Virgin Mary is unusual because it shows a Byzantine Virgin and Child in the presence of a bishop, a cathedral benefactor. Another 17th-century icon shows the Virgin of the Rosary surrounded by members of the Sommaripa family, whose house is nearby. ✉ *Kastro.*

Domus Venetian Museum

MUSEUM | Located in the 800-year-old Dellarocca-Barozzi house, the Domus Venetian Museum lets you into one of the historic Venetian residences. The house, enclosed within the soaring walls of Chora's castle, adjacent to the "Traini," or Great Gate, was first erected in 1207. Inside, the house is like an Naxian attic filled with fascinating objects ranging from the Cycadic period to Victorian times. The house's idyllic garden, built into the Kastro wall, provides a regular venue in season for a concert series, from classical to jazz to island music, known as the Domus festival. ✉ *Naxos Town* ✛ *At Kastro north gate* ☎ *22850/22387* ⊕ *www.naxosfestival. com* ✉ *€5* ☉ *Closed Sept.–May.*

Greek Orthodox Cathedral

RELIGIOUS SITE | The Greek Orthodox cathedral was built in 1789 on the site of a church called Zoodochos Pigis (Life-giving Source). The cathedral was built from the materials of ancient temples: the solid granite pillars are said to be from the ruins of Delos. Amid the gold and the carved wood, there is a vividly colored iconostasis painted by a well-known iconographer of the Cretan school, Dimitrios Valvis, and the Gospel Book is believed to be a gift from Catherine the Great of Russia. ✉ *Bourgos.*

Kastro

CASTLE/PALACE | You won't miss the gates of the castle. The south gate is called the **Paraporti** (side gate), but it's more interesting to enter through the northern gate, or **Trani** (strong), via Apollonos Street. Note the vertical incision in the gate's marble column—it is the Venetian yard against which drapers measured the bolts of cloth they brought to the noblewomen. Step through the Trani into the citadel and enter another age, where sedate Venetian houses still stand around silent courtyards, their exteriors emblazoned with coats of arms and bedecked with flowers. Half are still owned by the original families; romantic Greeks and foreigners have bought up the rest.

The entire citadel was built in 1207 by Marco Sanudo, a Venetian who, three years after the fall of Constantinople, landed on Naxos as part of the Fourth Crusade. When in 1210 Venice refused to grant him independent status, Sanudo switched allegiance to the Latin emperor in Constantinople, becoming duke of the archipelago. Under the Byzantines, "archipelago" had meant "chief sea," but after Sanudo and his successors, it came to mean "group of islands," that is, the Cyclades. For three centuries Naxos was held by Venetian families, who resisted pirate attacks, introduced Roman Catholicism, and later rebuilt the castle in its present form. In 1564 Naxos came under Turkish rule but, even then, the Venetians ran the island, while the Turks only collected taxes. The rust-color Glezos tower was home to the last dukes; it displays the coat of arms: a pen and sword crossed under a crown. ⊠ *Naxos Town.*

Metropolis Site Museum

MUSEUM | Built in the square in front of the Metropolitan Cathedral is a small museum that showcases the history of Naxos beginning with the Mycenean era. Displays include pottery, artifacts, and even a tomb from ancient times used to cover the graves of prosperous Naxians. ⊠ *Naxos Town* ☎ *22850/24151* ⊗ *Closed Mon.*

Naxos Folklore Museum

MUSEUM | This little museum shows costumes, ceramics, farming implements, and other items from Naxos's far-flung villages, giving insight into how life was on the island beginning in the 18th century. ⊠ *Old Market St.* ☎ *22850/25531* ⊠ *€3* ⊗ *Closed Oct.–Apr.*

★ Old Town

NEIGHBORHOOD | A bewildering maze of twisting cobblestone streets, arched porticoes, and towering doorways, the Old Town plunges you alternatively into cool darkness and then suddenly into pockets of dazzling sunshine. The Old Town is divided into the lower section, **Bourgos,** where the Greeks lived during Venetian times, and the upper part, called **Kastro** (castle), still inhabited by the Venetian Catholic nobility. ⊠ *Naxos Town* ✛ *Along quay, left at first big square.*

Portara

ARCHAEOLOGICAL SITE | Although the capital town is primarily beloved for its Venetian elegance and picturesque blind alleys, Naxos's most famous landmark is ancient: the Portara, a massive doorway that leads to nowhere. The Portara stands on the islet of **Palatia,** which was once a hill (since antiquity the Mediterranean has risen quite a bit) and in the 3rd millennium BC was the acropolis for a nearby Cycladic settlement. The Portara, an entrance to an unfinished Temple of Apollo that faces exactly toward Delos, Apollo's birthplace, was begun about 530 BC by the tyrant Lygdamis, who said he would make Naxos's buildings the highest and most glorious in Greece. He was overthrown in 506 BC, and the temple was never completed; by the 5th and 6th centuries AD it had been converted into a church; and under Venetian and Turkish rule it was slowly dismembered, so the marble could be used to build the castle. The gate, built with four blocks of marble, each 16 feet long and weighing 20 tons, was so large it couldn't be demolished, so it remains today, along

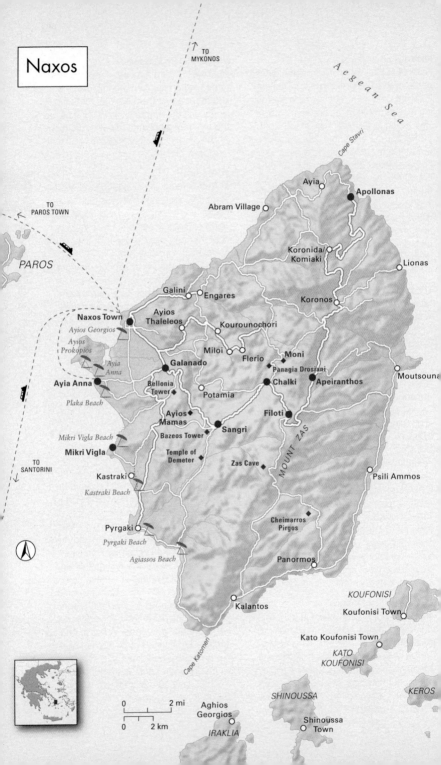

with the temple floor. Palatia itself has come to be associated with the tragic myth of Ariadne, princess of Crete.

Ariadne, daughter of Crete's King Minos, helped Theseus thread the labyrinth of Knossos and slay the monstrous Minotaur. In exchange, he promised to marry her. Sailing for Athens, the couple stopped in Naxos, where Theseus abandoned her. Jilted Ariadne's curse made Theseus forget to change the ship's sails from black to white, and so his grieving father Aegeus, believing his son dead, plunged into the Aegean. Seeing Ariadne's tears, smitten Dionysus descended in a leopard-drawn chariot to marry her, and set her bridal wreath, the Corona Borealis, in the sky, an eternal token of his love.

The myth inspired one of Titian's best-known paintings, as well as Strauss's opera *Ariadne auf Naxos*.

North of Palatia, **underwater remains of Cycladic buildings** are strewn along an area called **Grotta**. Here are a series of large worked stones, the remains of the waterfront quayside mole, and a few steps that locals say go to a tunnel leading to the islet of Palatia; these remains are Cycladic (before 2000 BC). ⊠ *Naxos Town* ✥ *At harbor's far edge.*

Beaches

The southwest coast of Naxos, facing Paros and the sunset, offers the Cyclades's longest stretches of sandy beaches. All the beaches have tavernas in case you get hungry or thirsty, and those directly on the beach may have chairs and umbrellas for rent. The water around Naxos is some of the clearest in Greece.

Ayios Georgios Beach
BEACH—SIGHT | FAMILY | Essentially an extension of Naxos Town, the easily accessible Ayios Georgios Beach is a popular, developed destination that sees its throng of crowds during the peak

Scholarly Imprints

The Convent and School of the Ursulines, a few steps beyond Naxos's cathedral, in the Kastro, was begun in 1739. In a 1713 document, a general of the Jesuits, Francis Tarillon, mentions that the proposed girls' school should be simple; grandeur would expose it to the Turks' covetousness. While it has now been recycled as part of the island's archaeological museum, wealthier Naxian women of a certain age still recall the good education the Ursulines provided.

summer months. Protected from summer winds, the sandy coastline edges up against shallow waters that make it ideal for kids. The bustle of the main town extends here; restaurants, tavernas, and café-bars are all within easy walking distance, with views of the sea. It's also an ideal beach scene to take in the sunset. **Amenities:** food and drink. **Best for:** sunset; swimming; walking. ⊠ *Ayios Georgios.*

🍴 Restaurants

Metaxi Mas
$$ | GREEK | In the winding alleys of the Palia Agora in Naxos Town, Metaxi Mas is the local favorite for home-cooked taverna specialties year-round, making the meaning of its name, "just between us," very appropriate. For more than a decade the Flerianos family has focused on the local flavors that Naxos has to offer—fresh vegetables, meats, cheeses, and seafood cooked in the traditional ways. **Known for:** hearty Naxian specialties; local taverna favorite; alleyway tables tucked away from the wind. Ⓢ *Average main: €18* ⊠ *Naxos Town* ☎ *22850/26425.*

Did You Know?

Many tavernas, often featuring festive and colorful outdoor dining setups, are still family-owned and are known for offering authentic Greek dishes using local vegetables, meat, cheese, and seafood.

Osteria - Le Nuove Storie

$$ | **ITALIAN** | A walk up from the harbor, tucked underneath the Old Town walls, Osteria offers authentic Italian dishes served up in a cute little courtyard. A taste of Umbria, with Naxian diversions, includes interesting variations on classic flavors and this is much better than the faux-Italian dishes on other menus. **Known for:** authentic Italian tastes; semi-hidden gem worth seeking out; well chosen wine list. [$] *Average main: €20* ✉ *Kastro road* ☎ *22850/24080* ⏲ *Closed Nov.–Mar.*

★ **Popi's Grill**

$ | **GREEK** | The oldest family tavern in Naxos, established in 1948, remains true to the Margartis family traditions of cooking authentic Greek dishes with homegrown vegetables and local products. With wonderful views across the harbor to Paros, be sure to check out the historic black-and-white photos inside of Naxos Town as it grew around the taverna over the decades. **Known for:** old-fashioned charm; three generations of family running the show; complimentary yogurt with honey and lemon for dessert. [$] *Average main: €12* ✉ *Naxos Town* ✣ *On the harbor* ☎ *22850/22389* ⏲ *Closed Nov.–Mar.*

Coffee and Quick Bites

Caramella Naxos

$ | **FAST FOOD** | **FAMILY** | Candy lovers of all ages will adore this bright little shop, wheremulti-colored lollipops and sweets are made before your eyes. **Known for:** all flavors under the sun; super frozen yogurts and ice creams; cooking classes available. [$] *Average main: €3* ✉ *Naxos Town* ☎ *22850/26607* 🌐 *www.caramella-naxos.gr.*

Waffle House

$ | **FAST FOOD** | Offering a variety of creamy rich homemade ice cream, fresh waffles, and mini-sized "waffins," Waffle House has expanded since it opened in Naxos Town to the country's capital in Athens. Nevertheless, the Naxos original is a local favorite, and tables get packed here. **Known for:** dessert waffles; house-made ice cream; all day breakfasts. [$] *Average main: €6* ✉ *Pigadakia* ✣ *500 meters up from harbor* ☎ *22850/23007.*

Hotels

Chateau Zevgoli

$ | **B&B/INN** | If you stay in Chora, try to settle in to Despina Kitini's fairy-tale pension, in a comfortable Venetian house that offers distinctive guest rooms and a lovingly appointed salon filled with dark antique furniture, gilded mirrors, old family photographs, and locally woven curtains and tablecloths. **Pros:** great views over to the Portara; in a fetching neighborhood; traditional feel and individual decor. **Cons:** it is uphill and you must walk to it; no parking or access by car; breakfast is extra. [$] *Rooms from: €75* ✉ *Naxos Town* ✣ *Follow the signs stenciled on walls* ☎ *22850/22993, 22850/26123* 🌐 *www.chateau-zevgoli.gr* 🛏 *11 rooms* 🍴 *No meals.*

★ **Galaxy Hotel**

$$ | **HOTEL** | All whitewash and stone, this is the perfect hotel for beach lovers. **Pros:** spacious grounds and gardens; great wheelchair accessibility throughout; right on the beach. **Cons:** rooms without balconies can feel stuffy; pool can get crowded; a walk into Naxos Town. [$] *Rooms from: €180* ✉ *Ayios Georgios Beach* ☎ *22850/22422, 22850/22423* 🌐 *www.hotel-galaxy.com* ⏲ *Closed Nov.–Mar.* 🛏 *54 rooms* 🍴 *Free breakfast.*

★ **Grotta Hotel**

$ | **HOTEL** | Atop a rocky cliff with views across to the Portara, the Grotta Hotel has an enviable position on the edge of Naxos town, within walking distance of the shops, restaurants, and sights. **Pros:** thoughtful staff; locally sourced food; free transfers from and to port. **Cons:** some noise from streets nearby; some rooms lack a sea view; walk to the port is along a dusty track. [$] *Rooms from: €120* ✉ *7 Iakomos Kampanellis* ☎ *22850/22101* 🌐 *www.hotelgrotta.gr* 🛏 *37* 🍴 *Free breakfast.*

Nightlife

During the busy summer season, there are numerous cultural events in Naxos Town and also around the island. Important venues include the Catholic Cultural Center, the Domus Venetian Museum, and the Town Hall.

BARS

520

BARS/PUBS | This cool, whitewashed Cycladic-style space features a rooftop veranda perfect for sipping eclectic cocktails and admiring the view over to Paros. Siblings Argiro and Manos Fotis named this spot 520 for the bar code automatically marked on any products that are made in Greece. ✉ *Naxos Town* ✣ *On the harbor* ☎ *22850/27271* 🌐 *520naxos.gr.*

Meli and Kanela

BARS/PUBS | The Kioulafis family paid attention to every detail when renovating this family treasure, a simple Cycladic dwelling built more than a century ago. Tucked in the walls of Old Town, Meli and Kanela—honey and cinnamon—has a bright turquoise door that beckons you into its bar-lounge and café space that's enhanced by soft lighting, creamy beige-and-white walls, and traditional charm. Outside is a pretty courtyard, perfect for idling the afternoon and evening away. ✉ *Naxos Town* ✣ *On road to Kastro* ☎ *22850/26565* 🌐 *www.melikaikanela.com.*

Ocean Club

BARS/PUBS | A lively chunk of Naxos nightlife is set on the south end of the Old Town, where happening bars face the waterfront and gather packed crowds of party people. The evening starts with cocktails at sunset and continues through to sunrise with a soundtrack of funk, disco, and house. ✉ *Naxos Town* ☎ *22850/26766.*

Shopping

The population of Naxos pours into Naxos Town to get their shopping done, so visitors can be sure to find what they are looking for, whether it's fashionable clothing or souvenirs. Naxians are especially proud of what their land gives them, and many shops sell local products, including honey, liqueurs, sweets, and more. Meanwhile, the streets are filled with myriad stores and galleries run by local artists who showcase artwork, including sculptures and handicrafts. Jewelry stores are also in abundance, selling traditional and more modern Greek designs in gold and silver.

JEWELRY

Nassos Papakonstantinou

JEWELRY/ACCESSORIES | The workshop of Nassos Papakonstantinou, on Old Town's main square, sells one-of-a-kind pieces both sculptural and delicate. His father was a wood-carver; Nassos has inherited his talent. **■TIP→ The shop has no sign—that is Nassos's style.** ✉ *Ayiou Nikodemou* ☎ *6973338234* 🌐 *www.jewelrynassos.com.*

TRADITIONAL CRAFTS AND FOODS

Pocket Gallery

ART GALLERIES | Anglo-Australian expat artist Tim Elkington's small craft and art shop in the Old Town showcases Greek and other expat artists who are inspired by the beauty and culture of Greece. Elkington is a painter, but also sells traditional and modern pottery, cards, ceramics, drawings, jewelry, and clothing that have a connection to Greece. ✉ *Dimitriou Kokkou and Alexinoros* ☎ *22850/27106.*

Promponas Wines and Liquors

LOCAL SPECIALTIES | A large selection of their famous *kitro* (citron liqueur), as well as Naxos wines, thyme honey, and preserves, can be found at Promponas Wines and Liquors, near the Naxos Town waterfront. It has been around since 1915, and free glasses of *kitro* are offered. ✉ *Dimitris Prombona 1* ☎ *22850/22258.*

Techni

CRAFTS | *Techni* translates to "art" in Greek and that's what the shop show-cases—locally and traditionally inspired handmade arts and crafts. The collections include jewelry in traditional designs, as well as embroidery and knitted items created by women in Greece's mountain villages. Handmade carpets and linens are also for sale. ⊠ *Old Market* ☎ *22850/24767* ⊕ *www.naxos-art.gr.*

 Activities

WATER SPORTS
Naxos-Surf Club

WATER SPORTS | On Ayios Georgios Beach, just south of the Chora, the Naxos-Surf Club offers windsurfing lessons, equipment rentals, and other water-sports packages. No-wind alternatives such as catamaran sailing, trekking, mountain biking, and kayaking are also available. ⊠ *Ayios Georgios* ✛ *15-min walk south of Naxos Town* ☎ *22850/29170* ⊕ *www. naxos-surf.com.*

Ayia Anna ΑΓΙΑ ΑΝΝΑ

7 km (4½ miles) south of Naxos Town.

Ayia Anna is one of the island's ideal beach towns, where long stretches of sand front a main road lined with tavernas, restaurants, and cafés. Development along the road has meant that communities have blended into each other in one long strip, but these lines of sand dotted with lagoons are regularly voted as being among the best in Greece.

 Beaches

Ayia Anna Beach

BEACH—SIGHT | South of Naxos Town, Ayia Anna is a sandy-smooth extension of Ayios Prokopios Beach. A small port, with connections to Paros, it often has picturesque little boats docked here. At one point considered a main commercial harbor of the island, today it's a popular beach for water sports and those who want to enjoy the simplicity of its turquoise waters. The small village behind it is filled with restaurants, cafés, and beach bars. Beach chair and umbrella rentals are abundant. **Amenities:** food and drink; water sports. **Best for:** swimming; walking. ⊠ *Ayia Anna.*

★ **Ayios Prokopios Beach**

BEACH—SIGHT | This is one of the most popular beaches on the island due to its close proximity to Naxos Town and its long stretch of pure, fine white sand. It features a small leeward harbor with a unique view of small lagoons where herons find refuge. Its position protects it from island winds, so swimming is a calm experience that you don't always find on neighboring beaches. The small village surrounding it is lined with tavernas and cafés. Nudity is allowed in designated areas. **Amenities:** food and drink. **Best for:** nudists; swimming; walking. ⊠ *Ayios Prokopios.*

Plaka Beach

BEACH—SIGHT | **FAMILY** | South of town, Plaka Beach is a natural extension of Ayia Anna Beach. It's a gorgeous two-and-a-half-mile stretch of sand filled with dunes and bamboo groves. Most of the beach is undeveloped, but you can still find sun beds to rent in organized areas. Come early to grab one in the peak season. There is a range of tavernas, restaurants, and café-bars within walking distance. At the southern end is **Orkos**, haven to wind- and kitesurfers. **Amenities:** food and drink; water sports. **Best for:** swimming; walking. ⊠ *Ayia Anna.*

Restaurants

Gorgona

$$ | **GREEK** | Dimitris and Koula Kapris's beachfront taverna is popular both with sun worshippers on Ayia Anna Beach and locals from Chora, who come here year-round to get away and sometimes to dance until the late hours, often to live music. The daily-changing menu is extensive and the fresh fish comes from the caïques that pull up at the dock right in front every morning. **Known for:** shoreside location since 1970; traditional home cooking; Hotel Agia Anna next door owned by same family. $ *Average main: €16* ✉ *Ayia Anna* ☎ *22850/41007* ⊕ *www. agiaannastudios.com.*

★ Palatia

$$ | GREEK | Fancy dining with the sand between your toes and the waves lapping nearby? Palatia on Ayia Anna Beach fits the bill with traditional fare and a stunning view. **Known for:** scenic beach dining; Naxian specialties and fresh seafood; great vegetarian options. $ *Average main: €18* ✉ *Ayia Anna* ☎ *22850/41591* ⊕ *www.palatiarestaurant.com* ⊘ *Closed Nov.–Apr.*

Hotels

★ Medusa Beach Resort and Suites

$$ | HOTEL | Rooms and suites here are arranged around a Zen-like garden, and some have sea views, but all guests are just a stone's throw away from diving into the sea. **Pros:** secluded private beachfront; lovely garden areas; good on-site restaurant and bar. **Cons:** far from Naxos Town; not much within walking distance; car necessary to get to island sights. $ *Rooms from: €190* ✉ *Ayia Anna* ☎ *22850/75555* ⊕ *www.medusaresort.gr* ⊘ *Closed Oct.–May* 🛏 *21 rooms* ⟨⟩ *Free breakfast.*

Santana Beach Luxury Suites

$$ | HOTEL | This intimate complex of suites and apartments sits right on one of Naxos's most beautiful sandy beaches, Ayia Anna. **Pros:** right on a very nice beach; good service; busy beach scene at the bar downstairs. **Cons:** beach is popular, so can be noisy; rooms could be bigger for the money; car needed to get around the island. $ *Rooms from: €200* ✉ *Ayia Anna Beach* ☎ *22850/42841*

⊕ *www.santanabeach.gr* ⊘ *Closed Oct.– May* 🛏 *5 rooms* ⟨⟩ *Free breakfast.*

Activities

WINDSURFING

Plaka Water Sports

BICYCLING | The paradise that is Plaka Beach is the summer playground for Plaka Water Sports. The well-equipped water ski, wakeboard, SUP, canoeing, and sailing outfitter also organizes beginner and expert bike-riding tours throughout the most scenic areas of Naxos, and their cute little beach bar serves good food all day. ✉ *Ayia Anna* ☎ *22850/41158* ⊕ *www. plaka-watersports.com.*

Mikri Vigla ΜΙΚΡΗ ΒΙΓΛΑ

18 km (11 miles) south of Naxos Town.

Mikri Vigla is a small village known for its nearby pristine beaches. Several small room rentals and a few cafés and beach bars dot the area. Windy days offer the ideal conditions for the windsurfing set.

Beaches

South of Mikri Vigla are the three beaches farthest from Naxos Town: Agiassos, Kastraki, and Pyrgaki

Agiassos

BEACH—SIGHT | FAMILY | The last beach on the eastern coast, this is where Marco Sanudo landed in 1207 to conquer the island from the Byzantines, burning his fleet so that there could be no way back. Sheltered from the winds and with a gently sloping seashore, today it is a paradise for families with small children. There are no facilities but two tavernas are close by. **Amenities:** parking (free). **Best for:** swimming; walking. ✉ *Pyrgaki.*

Kastraki Beach

BEACH—SIGHT | Although close to the popular beach destinations, Kastraki Beach has kept its tranquil, quiet, and low-key status in place. The long, sandy stretch of beach is essentially a continuation of Mikri Vigla but attracts those who prefer the experience of undeveloped and untouched Greek island beaches. There are several designated areas popular with nudists. **Amenities:** none. **Best for:** nudists; solitude; swimming; walking. ⊠ *Mikri Vigla.*

Mikri Vigla Beach

BEACH—SIGHT | The pure white sand here is beautifully offset by a rocky hill, turquoise waters, and large, gentle sand dunes. The beach itself is edged by cedar trees. Here, the fierce island winds are welcome to kitesurfers and windsurfers; Flisvos Kite Centre offers equipment rentals and lessons. It's not as developed as other beaches, but a scattering of tavernas and cafés that mostly service sports aficionados can be found nearby. **Amenities:** food and drink. **Best for:** surfing; swimming; walking; windsurfing. ⊠ *Mikri Vigla.*

Pyrgaki Beach

BEACH—SIGHT | One of the island's quietest beaches is a stunning, wide cove of fine sand bordered by green cedar trees. Its name comes from a nearby hill that was used to scout for pirates back in the day. Today, its beauty remains untouched by development. Only a few tavernas and restaurants surround this corner of beach, which rarely gets crowded. **Amenities:** none. **Best for:** solitude; swimming. ⊠ *Pyrgaki* ✛ *18 km (11 miles) south of Naxos Town.*

 Activities

WINDSURFING
Flisvos Kite Centre
SURFING | Right behind Mikri Vigla Beach, the Flisvos Kite Centre takes advantage of the reliably windy days that bless this beach and offer International Kiteboarding Organization–certified lessons, windsurfing lessons, and equipment rentals. ⊠ *next*

to Orkos Beach Hotel ☎ 22850/75490 ⊕ *www.flisvos-kitecentre.com.*

Galanado Πύργος του Μπελόνια

5 km (3 miles) south of Naxos Town.

On a hill, Galando's village streets offer a pretty view toward Naxos Town. It's an agricultural village that is famous for the landmark Tower of Bellonia that faces the eastern side of the island.

 Sights

Bellonia Tower

CASTLE/PALACE | The graceful Bellonia Tower (Pirgos Bellonia) belonged to the area's ruling Venetian family, and like other fortified houses, it was built as a refuge from pirates and as part of the island's alarm system. The towers were located strategically throughout the island; if there was an attack, a large fire would be lighted on the nearest tower's roof, setting off a chain reaction from tower to tower and alerting the islanders. Bellonia's thick stone walls, its Lion of St. Mark emblem, and flat roofs with zigzag chimneys are typical of these towers. ⊠ *Galanado.*

"Double Church" of St. John

RELIGIOUS SITE | The unusual 13th-century "double church" of St. John exemplifies Venetian tolerance. On the left side is the Catholic chapel, on the right the Orthodox church, separated only by a double arch. A family lives in the tower, and the church is often open. From here, take a moment to gaze across the peaceful fields to Chora and imagine what the islanders must have felt when they saw pirate ships on the horizon. ⊠ *Galanado* ✛ *In front of Bellonia tower.*

Ayios Mamas Άγιος Μάμας

3 km (2 miles) south of Galanado, 8 km (5 miles) south of Naxos Town.

South of Galanado, and a kilometer (½ mile) past a valley with unsurpassed views is one of the island's oldest churches (9th century), Ayios Mamas.

Sights

Ayios Mamas

RELIGIOUS SITE | St. Mamas is the protector of shepherds and is regarded as a patron saint in Naxos, Cyprus, and Asia Minor. Built in the 8th century, the stone church was the island's cathedral under the Byzantines. Though it was converted into a Catholic church in 1207, it was neglected under the Venetians and is now falling apart. You can also get to it from the Potamia villages. ⊠ *Ayios Mamas.*

Sangri Σαγκρί

3 km (2 miles) south of Ayios Mamas, 11 km (7 miles) south of Naxos Town.

Sangri is the center of an area with so many monuments and ruins spanning the Archaic to the Venetian periods it is sometimes called little Mystras, a reference to the famous abandoned Byzantine city in the Peloponnese. The name Sangri is a corruption of Sainte Croix, which is what the French called the town's 16th-century monastery of Timios Stavros. The town is actually three small villages spread across a plateau.

Sights

Bazeos Tower

ART GALLERIES—ARTS | This 17th-century stonework tower, considered one of Naxos's most beautiful Venetian-era monuments, dominates the landscape as you approach the center of the island from Naxos Town. Functioning as the Monastery of the True Cross (Timios Stavros), during the Turkish occupation it served as an illegal school, where children met secretly to learn the Greek language and culture. It was abandoned in 1834 and later bought by the Bassegio family, whence its modern name derives. It has been renovated into a museum and cultural space, and a full calendar of exhibitions, concerts, and events takes place under the aegis of the Naxos Festival. ⊠ *Sangri* ☎ *22850/31402* ⊕ *www.bazeostower.gr* ☏ *€5* ⊗ *Closed Oct.–May.*

Kastro Apilarou

ARCHAEOLOGICAL SITE | Above the village of Sangri, you can make out the ruins of Kastro Apilarou, the castle vanquished by the Italian conquerer, Marco Sanudo. The castle was the defensive stronghold for the region and held out for two months, but locals today still say its a bit of a mystery about who the Apilarou family really was before Sanudo came and took over. If you do make the tough climb to view it up close, you'll be greeted with a fantastic view of the Naxian plains. ⊠ *Sangri* ⚜ *On Mt. Profitis Ilias.*

Temple of Demeter

ARCHAEOLOGICAL SITE | This marble Archaic temple, circa 530 BC, was lovingly restored by German archaeologists during the 1990s. Demeter was a grain goddess, and it's not hard to see what she is doing in this beautiful spot. There is also a small museum here (admission is free). ■ **TIP→ The 25-minute walk here from the village is splendid.** ⊠ *Sangri* ⚜ *Take the asphalt road right before the entrance to Sangri.*

Chalki Χαλκί

6 km (4 miles) northeast of Sangri, 17 km (10 miles) southeast of Naxos Town.

You are now entering the heart of the lush Tragaia Valley, where in spring the air is heavily scented with honeysuckle, roses, and lemon blossoms and many tiny Byzantine churches hide in the dense olive groves.

Considered one of the most charming little villages, Chalki has some of the most photographed lanes on Naxos. It doesn't take very long to walk through its bougainvillea-drenched lanes and maze of stone paths lined with gently refurbished neoclassical mansions that now serve as charming shops, galleries, and eateries.

Sights

Frangopoulos Tower
BUILDING | Chalki itself is a pretty town, known for its neoclassical houses in shades of pink, yellow, and gray, which are oddly juxtaposed with the plain but stately 17th-century Frangopoulos Tower. Like other towers erected by the Venetians on the island, it was primarily used in its heyday for defense purposes. ⊠ *Main Rd., next to Panayia Protothrone* ☉ *Hrs vary; enquire locally.*

Panagia Protothronos (*First Enthroned Virgin Church*)
RELIGIOUS SITE | With its distinct red-roof, this is one of the most important Byzantine churches. Restoration work has uncovered five layers of frescoes from the 6th through the 13th century, and the church has remained alive and functioning for 14 centuries. According to tradition it was named Protothroni because it was the first to be built on Naxos. ⊠ *Main Rd.* ☉ *Closed afternoons.*

Vallindras Distillery
WINERY/DISTILLERY | In the back of their quaint neoclassical house, the Vallindras family has supplied Naxos and Greece with *kitro* liqueur from their distillery since 1896. Before you take the free tour, sample various flavors and strengths of the Greek aperitif that is marked with a Protected Destination of Origin (PDO) status. In the distillery room, examine the more-than-100-year-old copper equipment, which continues to produce the island's strong, traditional aperitif.

⊠ *Chalki* ☎ *22850/31220* ⊕ *www.face-book.com/kitronaxouvallindras.*

Shopping

Era Products
FOOD/CANDY | Visit this little jam shop to sample natural jams and Greek fruit preserves, known as spoon sweets, handmade by Yannis Mandenakis; Mandenakis prides himself on only using three ingredients: fruit, sugar, and lemon. You may even catch sight of him through the screened kitchen door in the shop, working his magic as he mixes, cans, and packages his in-season products. ⊠ *Sakelliades Ioannis* ✛ *Off the main street in town* ☎ *22850/31009.*

★ Fish and Olive Creations
ART GALLERIES | Katherina sells her masterful ceramics and Alexander sells his sensitive jewelry—all with fish or olive motifs. A couple of doors away is their impressive little art gallery. ⊠ *Central Plateia* ☎ *22850/31771* ⊕ *www.fish-olive-creations.com.*

Handmade Textiles
TEXTILES/SEWING | Maria Maraki has been looming for decades, and if you're lucky, you may find her sitting at the wheel of her traditional silk and cotton weaving loom behind the shop window. Her creations—cotton table runners, curtains, place mats, and table covers—decorate every corner and wall of the shop. Maraki draws inspiration for her colorful designs from Greek history and her own imagination, but if she's in the shop, ask her to explain her designs. ⊠ *Sakelliades Ioannis* ☎ *22850/32938.*

Phos Gallery
ART GALLERIES | When he's not shooting for the acclaimed Greek film director Theodoros Angelopoulos, photographer Dimitris Gavalas is busy at his own gallery, which he decided to build in his father's hometown of Chalki. His work includes landscapes, panoramics, and conceptual

photography. ✉ *Chalki* ☎ *22850/31118* ⊕ *www.phosgallery.gr.*

Moni Μονή

6 km (4 miles) north of Chalki, 23 km (14 miles) east of Naxos Town.

Off the fine asphalt Chalkiou-Keramotis road, Moni ("monastery") remains high in the mountains overlooking Naxos's greenest valley and has become a popular place for a meal or coffee on a hot afternoon. Local women make embroideries for Naxos Town's shops.

◉ Sights

Panagia Drosiani

RELIGIOUS SITE | Just below Moni is one of Naxos's most important churches, Panagia Drosiani, which has faint, rare Byzantine frescoes from the 7th and 8th centuries. Its name means Our Lady of Refreshment, because once during a severe drought, when all the churches took their icons down to the sea to pray for rain, only the icon of this church got results. The fading frescoes are visible in layers: to the right when you enter are the oldest—one shows St. George the Dragon Slayer astride his horse, along with a small boy, an image one usually sees only in Cyprus and Crete. According to legend, the saint saved the child, who had fallen into a well, and there met and slew the giant dragon that had terrorized the town. Opposite him is St. Dimitrios, shown killing barbarians. The church is made up of three chapels—the middle one has a space for the faithful to worship at the altar rather than in the nave, as became common in later centuries. Next to that is a very small opening that housed a secret school during the revolution. It is open mornings and again after siesta; in deserted winter, ring the bell if it is not open. ✉ *Moni ⊕ Off of Chalki–Keramotis road* ☎ *22850/31003.*

Towering Views

The Cheimarros Pirgos (Tower of the Torrent), a cylindrical Hellenistic tower, can be reached from Filoti by a road that begins from the main road to Apeiranthos, outside town, or by a level, three-hour hike with excellent views. The walls, as tall as 45 feet, are intact, with marble blocks perfectly aligned. The tower, which also served as a lookout post for pirates, is often celebrated in the island's poetry: "O, my heart is like a bower/And Cheimarros's lofty tower!"

Filoti Φιλότι

6 km (4 miles) south of Moni, 20 km (12 miles) southeast of Naxos Town.

Filoti, a peaceful village on the lower slopes of Mt. Zas, is the interior's largest. A three-day festival celebrating the Dormition starts on August 14. In the center of town is another Venetian tower that belonged to the Barozzi and the Church of Filotissa (Filoti's Virgin Mary), with its marble iconostasis and carved bell tower. A round-trip to the summit of Mt. Zas takes around 3–4 hours on the well-marked path but your reward is a stunning panorama of all of Naxos and its neighbours—remember this is the highest point in the Cyclades. The less adventurous can head out to the 150 m deep Zas Cave.

◉ Sights

Zas Cave

CAVE | Filoti is the starting place for several walks in the countryside, including the climb up to Zas Cave where obsidian tools and pottery fragments have been found. Mt. Zas, or Zeus, is one of the god's many reputed birthplaces; on the path to the summit lies a block of unworked marble that reads *Oros Dios Milosiou*, or "Boundary of the Temple of Zeus Melosios." (Melosios, it is thought, is a word that has to do with sheep.) The islanders say that under the Turks the cave was used as a chapel, and two stalagmites are called the Priest and the Priest's Wife, who are said to have been petrified by God to save them from arrest. ⊠ *Filoti* ⊕ *Southeast of town on small dirt track.*

Apeiranthos Απείρανθος

12 km (7 miles) northeast of Filoti, 32 km (20 miles) southeast of Naxos Town.

Apeiranthos is very picturesque, with views and marble-paved streets running between the Venetian Bardani and Zevgoli towers. As you walk through the arcades and alleys, notice the unusual chimneys—no two are alike. The elders, whose ancestors came from Crete, sit on their doorsteps chatting, and their hilly home in the mountains is noticeably cooler and greener than down by the coast.

 Sights

Archaeological Museum
MUSEUM | A very small Archaeological Museum, established by a local mathematician, Michael Bardanis, displays Cycladic finds, including statues and earthen pots dug up from the east coast. The most important of the exhibits are unique dark gray marble plaques from the 3rd millennium BC with roughly hammered scenes of daily life: hunters, farmers, and sailors going about their business. ⊠ *Off main square* ☎ *22850/61725* 🎟 *€2.*

Apollonas

36 km (22 miles) northeast of Naxos Town

The route through the mountains from Apeiranthos to the north is very scenic. Apollonas is a small resort with a couple of good beaches backed by a line of tavernas and cafés. It's main attraction is the Kouros, also called the Colossus of Dionysus, an unfinished statue in an ancient quarry. The return road to Naxos Town runs along the coast and is spectacular, hugging the clifftop for most of the way.

 Sights

Kouros
MEMORIAL | Approached from a path just outside the village of Apollonas is the Kouros. Eleven meters (36 feet) long and weighing about 80 tons, it is the largest of Naxos's abandoned statues. It dates back to the 8th century BC and archaeologists are undecided as to why it remained unfinished; perhaps there was a fault in the marble, maybe they lacked the manpower to transport it, or, more prosaically, nobody wanted to pay for it. ⊠ *Apollonas.*

Milos

160 km (85 nautical miles) west of Naxos.

Wrought from volcanic eruptions and earthquakes, Milos boasts a unique geological composition that has shaped its history for millennia. Mining has long been the mainstay of the local economy, with obsidian being traded since Neolithic times. Pliny the Elder wrote of sulfur unlike elsewhere and alum to rival Egypt. Today, silver, bauxite, bentonite, and kaolin are still extracted. Moreover, it is these mineral deposits that are the reason that the beach of Sarakiniko has its eerie moonscape and why Fyriplaka has cliffs that change color from pink to bright yellow every ten metres. Add in another 70 beaches and you have the most varied landscape in the Southwest Aegean. There is an air of a place plucked from a fantastical comic rather than naturally created.

Life is concentrated mainly in the north; in the port of Adamas; in the capital of Plaka, with its Venetian castle; and in Pollonia, a lively fishing village. To the west, a large section of the island remains uninhabited as part of the Natura 2000 network. Here lie vast meadows carpeted in poppies in spring and ancient cedars on the slopes of Profitis Elias mountain.

Immortalized in history in the "Melian Dialogues," Thucydides told of how, in 416 BC, Milos refused to join with Athens in a war against Sparta. In retaliation, all of the adult males of the island were executed and the women and children sold into slavery. The island kept a low profile under Venetian and Turkish rule until 1820 when a farmer chanced upon one of the most captivating stars of Western art—the Venus de Milo—and thrust the island under the spotlight once more.

Since then, Milos has largely crept under the radar, arriving late onto the must-see scene. Tourism has never really exploded as, even today, more than half of Milos's permanent residents live off the mines. A sleeper no more, though, and increasingly positioning itself as a high-end visit, it has avoided the perils of thoughtless development. Throw in some of the best food in the islands, 128 km of coastline, stylish albeit expensive accommodation, and the most photogenic seaside villages and it all adds up to an enigmatic and unique destination unlike any other Greek island.

GETTING HERE AND AROUND
From relative obscurity, Milos has grown into a well-connected island despite being somewhat out on a limb at the southwestern end of the Cyclades. The tiny airport is 5 km south of Adamas, the port. Olympic Air connects with Athens three times a day in high season and the flight lasts 40 minutes. Buses from the airport connect with the port four times a day.

Ferries dock at the port of Adamas. Up to five boats leave Piraeus and Lavrio every day in high season, with journeys taking between 3 and 6 hours. Connections with Amorgos, Anafi, Andros, Crete, Folegandros, Karpathos, Kimolos, Koufonisi, Kythnos, Mykonos, Naxos, Paros, Rhodes, Santorini, Serifos, Sifnos, Sikinos, Syros, and Tinos are available. Fast ferries and sea jets operate on some of these lines and can save considerable time but are more expensive.

The fifth largest of the Cyclades, Milos deserves exploration outside of the three main settlements. Luckily, there is an extensive bus network that covers most needs. The main terminal is in Adamas, 100 meters from the port and fares start from €1.60. Taxis are plentiful in the urban areas and there is a stand near to the port in Adamas. If you feel confident enough to navigate the somewhat poorly surfaced roads, then there are many options to rent cars and scooters from about €20 a day. Check ⊕ *milosbuses. com* and ⊕ *miloscars.gr.*

VISITOR INFORMATION
CONTACTS Riva Travel. ⊠ *Adamas* ☎ *22870/24024* ⊕ *www.rivatravel.gr.*

Adamas

145 km (90 miles) north of Chania

Adamas, also known as Adamantas—diamond in Greek—is one of the largest natural harbors in the Aegean but remained a sleepy hamlet until it was populated by refugees from a failed rebellion in Crete in the 1820s. It lacks a well-defined historical center but the marble paved promenade is a pleasant place to stroll of an evening, and restaurants, cafés, and shops congregate at the junction of the Plaka road.

The beaches around Adamas are perfectly serviceable with **Lagada** to the east and **Papikinou** to the west—both reachable on foot. However, on an island with such a variety of coastline it pays to explore.

Sights

Mining Museum of Milos
MUSEUM | On the seafront 500 meters east of the harbor, this museum details how Milos's character, history, and wealth derive from it being born from a volcano two million years ago. A collection of mining equipment, mineral samples, and artifacts help to explain the island geology, while short films give insight into the human aspect as old miners recollect their working lives. They also have a range of Geo Walks—walking guides to the island that act as detailed introductions to the eerie landscape. ✉ *Adamas* ☎ *22870/22481* 🌐 *www.milosminingmuseum.com* 🎟 *€5.*

Restaurants

★ O! Hamos!
$$ | **GREEK** | Magic happens in the kitchens of this farm-to-table eatery. A handwritten menu in a school exercise book guides you around the local approach of the Psatha family; if they can't grow it or rear it themselves, they don't sell it. **Known for:** no reservations and big queues at busy times; no fish—everything is produced on their own farm; diners are invited to scribble messages on the furniture and walls. [$] *Average main: €18* ✉ *Papikinou Beach, Adamas* ☎ *22870/21672* 🌐 *www.ohamos-milos.gr.*

Coffee and Quick Bites

Aggeliki
$ | **FAST FOOD** | This is the favorite place on the island for satisfying sweet desires with ice cream, cakes, or waffles—the chocolate fondue is legendary. **Known for:** harborside setting is a great people-watching spot; huge range of handmade ice cream; great place for breakfast. [$] *Average main: €5* ✉ *Adamas* ☎ *6942475162.*

Hotels

Villa Notos
$ | **B&B/INN** | Laid-back and lovely, Villa Notos is just a short three-minute walk from the port of Adamas and looks over sleepy Lagada Beach. **Pros:** bird's-eye view of the beach from top rooms; traditional clean design; hospitable hosts. **Cons:** hotel is on a slope so some stairs; some rooms lack a balcony; breakfast is extra. [$] *Rooms from: €110* ✉ *Adamas* ☎ *22870/28200* 🌐 *www.villanotos.gr* 🛏 *11 rooms* 🍴 *No meals.*

Activities

Milos is an island that needs to be looked in at from the sea to best appreciate the wild blend of weird geological formations and unusual natural colors.

SEA TRIPS

★ Milos Adventures
SAILING | Sail past sea stacks as big as houses and enter Kleftiko, a pirates lair with dazzling turquoise water that looks photoshopped. Swim up to the Cave of Sykia and lie on the small beach staring at the sky through the hole in the collapsed roof. Numbers are kept small on the company catamaran and the barbecue on a pristine private beach is memorable. If the weather is right, sail on to Polyaigos, the largest uninhabited island in Greece and one of the best natural environments in the Aegean. Unless you have your own superyacht, you won't see

Milos better. ✉ *Adamas* ☎ *22870/23809* ⊕ *www.milosadventures.gr.*

Milos Fishing Trip

FISHING | Kyriakos Haldaios has been fishing the waters of Milos since his youth, and now, aided by daughter Tina, organizes angling tours of the island on their boat, *Anna Maria*. Excursions are to hidden coves where guests are equipped with rods and bait, and are taught the local fishing secrets. An on-deck meal of the day's catch is a highlight. ✉ *Adamas* ☎ *6989295087* ⊕ *www.milosfishingtrip.gr.*

★ Sea Kayak Milos

KAYAKING | Australian geologist Rod Feldt-mann came to Milos to work in a gold mine and never left. He organizes kayak tours of the island that take in caves, uninhabited isles, and stops on isolated beaches. No previous experience is need-ed and trips are planned on a day-to-day basis depending on the wind and weather. Rod is a talented leader and has a wealth of knowledge about the history and geog-raphy of the island that he loves to share. ✉ *Triovasalas, Adamas* ☎ *6946477170* ⊕ *www.seakayakgreece.com.*

Plaka

3 km (2 miles) northwest of Adamas.

North of Adamas lies the classical center of Milos. Plaka is the largest of a cluster of four villages that huddle beneath a small crag and it is the island capital. Easily the prettiest town on the island, Plaka is an unspoilt chora of whitewashed houses and warren-like streets opening up to reveal some of the best views in the southern Aegean. Dominating the town is a volcanic mound topped with chapels and the remains of the old Venetian Kastro.

A mile south, the narrow village of Tryp-iti—"perforated" from the catacombs in the cliffside nearby—runs from a windmill topped hill down to the fishing hamlet of Klima, with its string of colorful waterfront fishermen's houses.

Sights

Archaeological Museum of Milos

MUSEUM | An elegant Ernst Ziller–designed neoclassical building contains one of the better island collections. Glass cases house findings from Klima, Nyhia, and Demengaki along with a large burial jar from the 6th century BC. Many pots with sea-lilies painted on them, early Cycladic statuettes, and the famous "Lady of Phylakopi" vie for attention with Mycenaean bulls and sculptures from the Hellenistic and Roman periods.

Most visitors, though, come to see the exact copy of the Venus de Milo displayed in the main room. There is a campaign, of course, to see the original statue reunited with her island home but it has so far fallen on deaf ears. ✉ *Plaka* ☎ *22870/28026* ⊕ *odysseus.culture.gr* 🎫 *€2* 🕐 *Closed Tues.*

Catacombs

CEMETERY | Just a short walk from Trypiti, the early Christian catacombs consist of 126 vaulted graves carved into the soft volcanic rock, linked by a series of tunnels. Some 5,000 bodies were buried in the three corridors that stretch back 200m, making these the largest catacombs in Greece. The earliest known Christian site in Greece, they are thought to date from the 1st century AD, when St. Paul was shipwrecked on Milos. Look out for inscriptions left by grave robbers, intrepid visitors, and marauding pirates who etched their names into the walls over the years. ✉ *400 m from Trypiti, Plaka* ☎ *22870/21625* ⊕ *www.catacombs.gr* 🎫 *€4* 🕐 *Closed Tues.*

Roman Theatre

MEMORIAL | Dating back to the Hellenistic period in the 3rd century BC, the original site was destroyed and rebuilt in Roman times. Holding 7,000 people in its heyday, today only the first seven rows have been restored and it plays host to cultural events from time to time.

Venus de Milo

On April 8, 1820, Olivier Voutier, an ensign and keen amateur archaeologist from the French navy rowed ashore to explore the ancient theater of Milos. A farmer working in the fields nearby guided him to a recess in the wall where he saw the torso of a human figure carved in marble. Weighing 900 kilos and at 2.04 m (6 ft 7 in) tall, the Venus de Milo was reborn.

Appropriated for the Louvre, on arrival in Paris she was immediately hailed as a masterpiece by either Praxiteles or Phidias, the two great sculptors of classical Greece.

Unfortunately, early drawings of the statue show that a broken fragment of the base that mysteriously went missing in Paris bore the inscription "Alexandros of Antioch," an obscure provincial sculptor. Some critics have ungraciously claimed that the statue is an inferior work of art, observing that she would not be famous if she had stayed in Greece or wasn't brachially challenged. To many, though, the Venus de Milo is much like her sister exhibit in the Louvre, the Mona Lisa: mystical, demure, serene, and one of the great figures of Western art.

Discovered in 1735 by the wandering Jesuit monk Nicholas Sarrabat, excavations began in 1816 and famously unearthed the Venus de Milo in what is thought to have been the gymnasium. A small plaque commemorates the site of the find, and there is a plaster copy of the statue in the archaeological museum. ⊠ *Plaka* ⊹ *Downhill from the Catacombs carpark.*

Beaches

Plathenia Beach

BEACH—SIGHT | Walkable from Plaka along an old donkey path, Plathenia is quiet and lovely. The beach is sandy and faces west, offering shelter from the prevailing north winds, and the water shelves gently. Tamarisk trees offer some shade if you don't want to take advantage of the sun beds and umbrellas. The sublime sunsets are best taken from the pretty little beach bar with a drink in hand. **Amenities:** food and drink; parking; showers; toilets. **Best For:** sunset; swimming. ⊠ *Plaka.*

Restaurants

Avli-Milos

$$ | **MEDITERRANEAN** | Tables spill out onto the alley at this relaxed Plaka restaurant where the focus is on fresh flavors. Traditional recipes are refined but still recognizable. **Known for:** fills up—get there early; sheltered from the meltemi wind in summer; cute and romantic alleyway position. $ *Average main: €15* ⊠ *Plaka, Plaka* ☎ *22870/27590.*

★ Barriello

$$ | **GREEK FUSION** | Romantic and rightly popular, Barriello has an enviable position with views of the sea and the Trypiti village square. A 150-year-old mansion has been repurposed to good effect by charismatic owner Takis. **Known for:** engaging service is a cut above; well researched wine list; clever and unusual food combinations. $ *Average main: €18* ⊠ *Trypiti, Plaka* ☎ *6984218360* ⊕ *www.barriello.com.*

Coffee and Quick Bites

Remvi Cafe

$ | CAFÉ | Remvi means a dreamy, relaxed mood and it is the perfect name for this cute little café in the village of Trypiti. On the village square with a terrace looking over Milos Bay, this is the place to daydream over a healthy breakfast. **Known for:** great views; smoothie-like fruit juices; worth popping in at sunset for a sundowner. $ *Average main: €8* ⊠ *Plaka* ☎ *22870/21950.*

Hotels

★ Vaos Windmill

$$ | RENTAL | One of the most unique accommodations in the Southern Aegean, Vaos is a converted windmill in the village of Trypiti. **Pros:** five-star views; unique, historic, and atmospheric; fully equipped kitchen to prepare your own food. **Cons:** in a pedestrian area with parking 200 m away; steep stairs over three floors; the clue is in the name—it can get windy. $ *Rooms from: €190* ⊠ *Plaka* ☎ *26103/21742* ⊋ *2 bedrooms* ⍾ *No meals.*

Nightlife

Utopia

BARS/PUBS | The most famous spot on the island for cocktails and sunset views sits at the top of Plaka and looks out on a horizon peppered with isles. Front-row tables get claimed early but you can stand and enjoy the views as the sun fades into the sea. ■**TIP**➔ **If it's too busy inside, buy a can of beer from the mini-market and stand by the courtyard of the church of the Panagia Korfiatissa—the view is just as good.** ⊠ *Plaka* ☎ *22870/23678.*

Shopping

Ceramica Kymbe

CERAMICS/GLASSWARE | Inspired by the islands neolithic past, local artists Natalia and David design and create minimalist ceramics in their Plaka workshop. Japanese-like in their simplicity, these are pots for everyday use burnished in the colors of the sea and the earth. ⊠ *25 Martiou, Plaka* ☎ *22870/24113* ⊕ *www. ceramica-kymbe.com.*

MLO Souvenirs

GIFTS/SOUVENIRS | Inspired and individual keepsakes from purely Greek designers. Choose from modern bags printed with sea creatures, handmade ceramics and cosmetics, or anarchic T-shirts. It's not your average souvenir shop. ⊠ *Plaka, Plaka* ☎ *22870/22394* ⊕ *www.mlosouvenirs.gr.*

Mandraki

5 km (3 miles) north of Adamas.

As famous as neighbor Sarakiniko for its photogenic-ness, Mandraki is home to the distinctive and colorful dwellings known as *syrmata,* the two-story houses built into the soft volcanic rock right at the water's edge with the ground floor acting as a boat house. There are three theories as to why the fishermen painted their houses in such distinctive hues; they were inspired by the multi-colored rocks of the island, they were painted so that each fisherman could recognize his own home when returning by boat, or they were in defiance of a decree from Prime Minister Metaxas in the 1930s that all island houses should be painted white and blue. The fishing hamlet of Klima on the opposite coast has similar kaleidoscopic buildings and they are sometimes available to rent through Airbnb.

Beaches

★ Sarakiniko

BEACH—SIGHT | The reason that many people visit Milos, Sarakiniko is the eerily sculpted inlet whose bone-white rocks lie in the sea like vast Henry Moore abstract forms. The limestone and diatomite moonscape was on the seabed 2 million years ago and fish and shell fossils can often be seen in the rocks. Try to get there before 7 am as the sunrise is spectacular and you will be largely alone. Explore the right-hand side before settling down on the left for sunbathing, swimming, and cliff diving—past the cliffs on the right is a shipwreck half-submerged in the sea, and there are abandoned mine tunnels to explore. Beware though, there is no shade and the light reflecting from the white rocks is mesmerizing and intense. There is parking at the top that also serves as the bus stop. **Amenities**: parking. **Best For:** sunrise; sunset. ✉ *Mandraki* ✣ *4 km from Adamas.*

Restaurants

★ Medusa

$$ | **GREEK** | On a cliffside setting by the brilliantly painted huts of Mandrakia is the island's best fish taverna. The very essence of summer is to be had on the large terrace on the waterfront. **Known for:** octopus drying in the sun outside; sea-breeze and sunshine setting; only restaurant in the village. [$] *Average main: €18* ✉ *Mandraki* ☎ 🌐 *www.medusamilos.gr.*

Pollonia

10 km (6 miles) east of Adamas.

Crouching around a sheltered bay with a church at each end, Pollonia started life as a fishing village but has now developed into a low-key resort. The ferry to neighboring Kimolos leaves from here and brings visitors to the picturesque port. The beach is long and sandy with plenty of shade and is perfect for the families who use it as a base for exploring the rest of the island.

Perfect Day

Spend the morning swimming and watching the cliff-jumpers at Sarakiniko, head to Medusa for late lunch, then slump into the bean bags on the tiny beach at Firopotamos and you have a perfect Milos day!

Restaurants

Armira Milos

$$ | **MODERN GREEK** | A cut above the tavernas that cling to Pollonia's seafront, Armira harvests the local ingredients to fine effect in its take on modern Mediterranean cuisine. The roof garden is a fine place to savor the sweetest of seafood direct from the family fishing boat. **Known for:** chic courtyard; vegan and gluten-free options; venue used to be owner's grandfather's house. [$] *Average main: €18* ✉ *Pollonia* ☎ *22870/41159* 🌐 *www.armiramilos.com.*

Coffee and Quick Bites

Kivotos ton Gefseon

$ | **GREEK** | The number-one bakery of Milos is the place to stock up for your lunch essentials before a trip to the remote beaches. The name means "ark of flavors" and they come at you two by two—arrive for breakfast and you will never want to leave. **Known for:** watermelon pie is a revelation; honey from the family hives; quaint garden setting. [$] *Average main: €3* ✉ *Pollonia* ☎ *22870/41121.*

Southern Beaches

The beaches on Milos are some of the best on any island in Greece, if only for their sheer variety. The southern coast, away from the main villages, has some of the most noteworthy.

Cliffs in a striking range of pinks and yellows frame the golden sand of **Paleochori** but what goes on underground draws the crowds here. Volcanic springs warm the water and the beach, so much so that a taverna, Sirocco, cooks its food in clay pots buried in the hot geothermal sand. Umbrellas and sun beds are available but bring beach shoes as the sand and pebbles get very hot. Neighboring **Fyriplaka** has an even more dramatic rainbow-hued setting, while on the other side, **Provatas** is famous for the family of goats that live on the seashore.

Abandoned in the late 1970s, the sulfur mines of Paliorema are the backdrop to a super little beach called **Thiorichia**. Wander through the old mine works with tracks and machinery left to rust, see the old galleries and miners quarters, then step out onto the sand and pebbles, stained from the sulfur. Remote and a trek to get to, your recompense is a glimpse into the history of this fascinating island.

The journey is the reason to visit **Tsigrado** but for once the end doesn't disappoint. Accessible only by water or by a wooden ladder and rope attached to the cliffs, it is only for the intrepid but the payback is a seductive sliver of sand and some of the best snorkeling around in the caves that embrace the beach. Remember to pack light!

Hotels

★ Melian Boutique Hotel & Spa
$$$$ | **HOTEL** | Elegant but unstuffy, Melian oozes sophistication. **Pros:** simple, stylish interiors; stunning location; smart, attentive staff. **Cons:** can be a little couple-y; no direct beach access and no pool; car needed for the best beaches. [$] *Rooms from:* ✉ *Pollonia* ☎ *22870/41150* 🌐 *www.melian.gr* 🕒 *Closed Nov.–Apr.* 🛏 *15 rooms* 🍴 *Free breakfast.*

Salt Suites
$$$$ | **HOTEL** | This haven overlooks Phylakopi Bay and hosts the fashionista set when they are in town. **Pros:** elevated corner position in Pelekouda is spot on; relaxed and tranquil mood; tasteful decor and appointments. **Cons:** a distance from the rest of the island; breakfast could be improved; costly extras. [$] *Rooms from: €280* ✉ *Pollonia* ☎ *22870/41110* 🌐 *www.salt-milos.com* 🛏 *10 rooms* 🍴 *Free breakfast.*

Folegandros
Φολέγανδρος

180 km (112 miles) southeast of Piraeus harbor in Athens, 86 km (53 miles) northwest of Santorini.

If Santorini is the Hollywood leading lady of the Greek islands, Folegandros is the demure, younger sister, star of off-beat independent cinema. Built between the walls of a Venetian fort, its main town of Chora is pinch-yourself pretty, clinging to the edge of precipitous cliffs above brooding seas. An island for dedicated Cyclades lovers, small, bare Folegandros offers a pure dose of the magic essence of the Aegean. If it wasn't for the bright light shone by its sibling, Folegandros would surely be world famous.

A mere 13 km (8 miles) in length and 31 square km (12 square miles) in area, at first glance the island does not seem to have much to offer—it lacks archaeological sites and ruins, vibrant towns, verdant valleys, cultural diversions, and nightlife and it boasts of only one true road, two ATMs, and no airport. What it does have in abundance, however, are the simple authentic pleasures of Greek island life; a trio of laid-back unhurried villages, deliberately downplayed development catering to a well-heeled crowd, an array of lovely beaches, a traditional local food culture, and some of the finest cliffside scenery in the Cyclades.

Travelers to Folegandros—historians are divided over whether the name immortalizes the son of King Minos, Pholegander, or comes from the Phoenician term "iron hard" referring to the rock-strewn interior—mostly stay in Chora, the elevated main town; Karavastasi, the port; or Ano Meria, a village perched on the spine of the island that feels little changed from a century ago. Days are idled away with a walk, a swim at the beach, and a lengthy lunch; nights invariably end up in one of Chora's main squares. Out of season, Folegandros could never be described as crowded, with a mere 500 residents, but during July and August the island often appears so, mainly because the port and town are so small and struggle to cope. In truth, numbers are low compared to more popular neighbors and many are return visitors drawn by the relaxed atmosphere of this discrete little charmer.

GETTING HERE AND AROUND

For such a small, isolated island, Folegandros is suprisingly well connected. There is no airport but neighboring Santorini and Milos have flights and are within an hour's reach by fast ferry. Ferries from Piraeus and Lavrio take from 4–9 hours depending on the route and the type of boat and there are also regular connections from Amorgos, Anafi, Ios, Kea, Kimolos, Koufonisi, Kythnos, Milos, Naxos, Paros, Serifos, Sifnos, Sikinos, and Santorini. For schedules check ⊕ *ferries.gr.*

Buses meet the boats and run from the port to Chora hourly from 7:30 am until midnight. Further buses run from Chora to Aigali and from Chora to Ano Meria. The bus stop in Chora is by the post office and has a blackboard with the timetable. Tickets are from €1.60.

A taxi from the port to Chora costs about €10 (☎ *22860/41048*).

In summer, small caïques (taxi boats) run between beaches from Karavastasi.

Many agencies offer car, scooter, and ATV hire from €20 per day.

TRAVEL AGENCIES
Folegandros Travel
This agency helpfully handles most travel arrangements including ferries, accommodations, and island tours. There are offices in Chora and at the port. ⊠ *Chora* ☎ *22860/41273 (Chora) 41198 (Port)* ⊕ *www.folegandros-travel.gr.*

Sea U Diving and Private Boat Tours
Certified center offering diving, snorkeling, and private boat tours around the island. ⊠ *Chora, Chora* ☎ *22860/41624* ⊕ *www.sea-u.com.*

Chora Χώρα

42 km (26 miles) northwest of Santorini.

As the boat approaches the dusty port of Karavostasi, bare, sun-scoured rocks offer little suggestion of the glory to come. After a steep 3-mile climb, cliff-top Chora comes into view. Its sky-kissing perch out of view of the harbor was no accident, as for centuries the southern Aegean was plagued by marauding pirate raiders. Nowadays, Chora is a cozy huddle of whitewashed houses, flower-filled alleys, and brightly painted woodwork that has been lovingly preserved by the islanders. Five squares, closed to

A Water-Sports Paradise

When it comes to the Cyclades, anyone who invests in a mask, snorkel, and flippers has entry to intense, serene beauty. Yet even without underwater gear, this archipelago is a swimmer's paradise, with warm, clear, and clean waters to entice visitors.

Most of the Cycladic islands gleam with beaches, from long blond stretches of sand to tiny pebbly coves. The best beaches are probably those on the southwest coast of Naxos but every island rewards those prepared to explore off the beaten track. The strands on Santorini, though strewn with plenty of bathers, are volcanic; you can bask on sands that are strikingly red and black.

As for water sports, there are many options to entice sunseekers; water-skiing, stand-up paddleboarding (SUP), kayaking, scuba diving, and windsurfing have become ever more popular. Paros and Naxos are the islands for kitesurfing with regular, reliable winds in the channels that surround them.

vehicles, host restaurants and cafés shaded by bougainvillea and hibiscus. Some of the buildings are set into the walls of the Venetian fort, or Kastro, built by the Duke of Naxos in the 13th century. A street circles the Kastro and the precipice on which the town stands and is strikingly lined with two-story cube houses that form a wall atop the towering cliff. The glory days of Venice came to an end in 1715, when the ruling Turks sacked Folegandros and sold the captives as slaves. Folegandros joined the Greek state in 1828 and in the mid-20th century the island was used as a place of political exile due to its remoteness.

The spectacularly photogenic **Church of Komisis tis Theotkou** (or Dormition of the Mother of God) dominates the town and stands on the foundations of the ancient settlement near the top of the cliff. At Easter, an icon from the church passes through every house on the island in a three-day festival. The path that zig-zags its way to the church is quite a climb but the rewards are the enchanting views over the town and the island.

Restaurants

Blue Cuisine

$$ | MODERN GREEK | A smart and intimate garden setting plays host to outstanding flavors and presentation. This is innovative modern Greek cooking at its best, where island food goes chic. **Known for:** revisited classic tastes; super all-Greek wine list; views across to Panagia Church. $ *Average main: €15* ⌧ *Chora* ☎ *22860/41665* ⊕ *www.bluecuisine.gr* ⊘ *Closed Oct.–Apr.*

Hotels

★ Anemomilos Boutique Hotel

$$$ | HOTEL | Perched on the towering cliff overlooking the sea and set amid a series of small garden terraces, this complex with truly breathtaking vistas of sea and sky, is the best place to stay in Folegandros. **Pros:** sublime views; alluring pool; warm staff. **Cons:** always books up early; village-facing studios can be noisy; high seaon rates can be prohibitive. $ *Rooms from: €270* ⌧ *Chora* ✢ *Edge of town* ☎ *22860/41309* ⊕ *www.anemomiloshotel.com* ⊘ *Closed Oct.–May* ⇌ *17 rooms* ⍾ *Free breakfast.*

Perched at a nearly angelic height, the Church of the Dormition of the Mother of God lords it over Folegandros's main town.

Meltemi Hotel

$ | **HOTEL** | **FAMILY** | Whitewashed and spotless, these good-sized and simply furnished rooms open to verandas and are at the edge of Chora, making this little inn convenient to restaurants and the bus stop for the port, beaches, and other points on the island. **Pros:** pleasant and convenient; good basic accommodations; traditional-style rooms. **Cons:** some balconies are shared; no pool; patchy Wi-Fi. $ *Rooms from: €70* ✉ *Chora* ☎ *22860/41425* ▭ *No credit cards* ⊘ *Closed Nov.–.Apr.* ⇥ *11 rooms* ⦿ *No meals.*

Ano Meria Άνω Μεριά

5 km (3 miles) northwest of Chora.

The island's paved road runs from the port, through Chora and along the backbone of the island to Ano Meria. Terraced fields where barley was grown amid the barren rock step down to the sea, and sitting above on stone pathways is a whitewashed village seemingly from another age. A handful of tavernas and cafés make it an ideal place to stop after a day on the beach.

⊙ Sights

Ecological and Folklore Museum

MUSEUM | Exhibits reconstruct traditional farming life with remains of an olive and wine press. There are panoramic views of the island and the surrounding seas. The adjacent church of Agios Panteliemon celebrates the feast day of Saint Panteliemon on July 27, and seemingly the whole island visits. ✉ *Ano Meria* ☎ *22860/41069* ⌷ *€2.*

🍴 Restaurants

Irini

$ | **GREEK** | **FAMILY** | Part grocery store, part taverna, this step back in time is the real deal for homecooked dishes. *Matsata*, a Folegandros speciality of handmade pasta with meat sauce and traditional *soutoto* cheese, is the star.

The beaches by the port are serviceable but it is better to head out to find the finer strands on the island. Those on the north coast bear the brunt of the Meltemi winds, those on the west and south are more sheltered.

Easily reached by bus, **Agkali** is a popular sandy beach with water sports, sun beds, and a great taverna in O Psaromiligkas. There is parking and it's free.

On the south coast, named after the picturesque church above, **Agios Nikolaos Beach** has sand and pebbles with good shade and a couple of tavernas. It's good for swimming and snorkeling.

On the northwest of the island is **Ligaria**, a beautiful, tiny, sandy beach a few hundred metres before Agios Georgios. Come early and you will have it all to yourself. There are no amenities and it attracts nudists.

Just 10 minutes by boat from the port, **Katergo** is the the longest beach on the island, with tiny pebbles and sparkling azure waters. There are no facilities or shade so come prepared.

Utterly charming and special, it feels like dining in somebody's living room. **Known for:** grandma cooks and granddaughter serves; authentic, homemade, unique; dining among tins, vegetables, and bottles of oil. $ *Average main: €8* ⊠ *Ano Meria* ☎ *22860/41436*.

O Psaromiligkas

$ | **GREEK** | **FAMILY** | Perched above Agkali Beach with stunning views, this is the fish taverna you have been daydreaming of, with wooden chairs, paper tablecloths, and sea breezes to keep you cool. Super homemade food, moderate prices, and friendly service make this a must-visit on the island. **Known for:** traditional taverna atmosphere; comforting seafood dishes; prime position. $ *Average main: €10* ⊠ *Agkali Beach, Agkali Beach* ☎ *22860/41116*.

Santorini (Thira)
ΣΑΝΤΟΡΙΝΗ (ΘΗΡΑ)

235 km (146 miles) southeast of Piraeus harbor in Athens.

Undoubtedly the most extraordinary island in the Aegean, crescent-shaped Santorini remains a mandatory stop on the Cycladic tourist route—even if you must enjoy the sensational sunsets from Ia, the fascinating excavations, and the dazzling white towns with a million other travelers. Called Kallisti (the "Loveliest") as long ago as ancient times, the island has now reverted officially to its subsequent name of Thira, after the 9th-century-BC Dorian colonizer Thiras. The place is better known these days, however, as Santorini, a name derived from its patroness, St. Irene of Thessaloniki, the Byzantine empress who restored icons to Orthodoxy and died in 802.

Flying to Santorini from Athens and many other cities is the most convenient way to get here, but to enjoy a true Santorini rite of passage, opt instead for the boat trip, which provides a spectacular introduction. After the boat sails between Sikinos and Ios, your deck-side perch approaches two close islands with a passage between them. The bigger one on the left is Santorini, and the smaller on the right is Thirassia. Passing between them, you see the village of Ia adorning Santorini's northernmost cliff like a white geometric beehive. You are in the caldera (volcanic crater), one of the world's truly breathtaking sights: a crescent of cliffs rising 1,100 feet, with the white clusters of the towns of Fira and Ia perched along the top. The bay, once the high center of the island, is 1,300 feet in some places, so deep that when boats dock in Santorini's shabby little port of Athinios, they do not drop anchor (as if placed there to emphasize the depths, a sunken ocean liner lies eerily submerged beneath the surface). The encircling cliffs are the ancient rim of a still-active volcano, and you are sailing east across its flooded caldera. On your right are the Burnt Isles, the White Isle, and other volcanic remnants, all lined up as if in some outsize display in a geology museum. Hephaestus's subterranean fires smolder still—the volcano erupted in 198 BC, in about 735, and there was an earthquake in 1956.

Indeed, Santorini and its four neighboring islets are the fragmentary remains of a larger landmass that exploded about 1600 BC: the volcano's core blew sky high, and the sea rushed into the abyss to create the great bay, which measures 10 km by 7 km (6 miles by 4½ miles) and is 1,292 feet deep. The other pieces of the rim, which broke off in later eruptions, are Thirassia, where a few hundred people live, and deserted little Aspronissi ("White Isle"). In the center of the bay, black and uninhabited, two cones, the Burnt Isles of Palea Kameni and Nea Kameni, appeared between 1573 and 1925.

There has been too much speculation about the identification of Santorini with the mythical Atlantis, mentioned in Egyptian papyri and by Plato (who says it's in the Atlantic), but myths are hard to pin down. This is not true of old arguments about whether tidal waves from Santorini's cataclysmic explosion destroyed Minoan civilization on Crete, 113 km (70 miles) away. The latest carbon-dating evidence, which points to a few years before 1600 BC for the eruption, clearly indicates that the Minoans outlasted the eruption by a couple of hundred years, but most probably in a weakened state. In fact, the island still endures hardships: since antiquity, Santorini has depended on rain collected in cisterns for drinking and irrigating—the well water is often brackish—and the serious shortage is alleviated by the importation of water. Nevertheless, the volcanic soil also yields riches: small, intense tomatoes with tough skins used for tomato paste (good restaurants here serve them); the famous Santorini fava beans, which have a light, fresh taste; barley; wheat; and white-skin eggplants.

These days, unrestrained tourism has taken a heavy toll on Santorini. Fira, and now Ia, could almost be described as "a street with 40 jewelry shops"; many of the natives are completely burned out by the end of the peak season (the best times to come here are shoulder periods); and, increasingly, business and the loud ringing of cash registers have disrupted the normal flow of Greek life here. For example, if a cruise ship comes in during afternoon siesta, all shops immediately open, and you will have a difficult time walking down Fira's main street in August, so crowded is it. Still and all, if you look beneath the layers of gimcrack tourism, you'll find Greek splendor. No wonder Greece's two Nobel poets, George Seferis and Odysseus Elytis, wrote poems about this island. You, too, will be "watching the rising islands / watching the red islands sink" (Seferis) and consider, "With fire with lava with smoke / You found the great lines of your destiny" (Elytis).

GETTING HERE AND AROUND

The bay of Santorini is one of the world's great sights, and an incoming flight—45 minutes from Athens—gives a unique view of it. There are 11 daily flights, shared by Aegean Airlines, Olympic Air, Ryanair, Sky Express, and Volotea. There are also flights from Thessaloniki and from other European cities. Reservations, the earlier the better, are essential.

As many as seven daily boats from Athens's port of Piraeus ply the wine-dark Aegean to Santorini. The trip takes 4 to 10 hours, depending on route, boat, and the weather. Try to make sure your boat enters the harbor before sunset (usually an early-morning departure from Piraeus), since this is a spectacular sight, one crucial to savoring Santorini's vibe. There are also direct connections to Amorgos, Anafi, Andros, Crete, Folegandros, Halki, Ios, Karpathos, Kasos, Kea, Kimolos, Kos, Koufonisi, Kythnos, Milos, Mykonos, Naxos, Paros, Rhodes, Serifos, Sifnos, Sikinos, Symi, Syros, and Tinos. Reservations are needed in summer and at Easter, and for cars year-round. The port town, Ormos Athinios, is only that, and you must proceed by vehicle to your destination. Buses generally meet the boats, and the drive up the volcano-cut cliff is amazing.

Buses leave from the main depot in central Fira just south of the town's main square. In high season, there are hourly buses for Akrotiri and buses on the half hour for Ia, Monolithos (airport), Kamari, and Perissa. Buses also connect with the main port of Athinios (at least a half-hour ride) as well as the popular Perissa and Kamari beaches. Schedules are posted; hotel concierges should also have this info. Fares run from €1.80 to €2.40. As might be expected, Santorini's buses can be as crowded as those of rush-hour Athens, so step lively! The main taxi station is near Fira's central square on Odos 25 Martiou. Connecting Fira with the harbor port of Fira Skala is the island's famed cable-car route, with its spectacular vistas. This is a must-do, even if you're not using the port facilities—but avoid times when cruise-ship passengers are trying to get back down to their tenders and lines can be impossibly long.

CONTACTS Fira Bus Station. ✉ Near main square, Fira ☎ 22890/25404 ⊕ ktel-santorini.gr. **Fira Taxi Station.** ✉ Odos 25 Martiou, near main square, Fira ☎ 22860/22555. **Santorini Cable Car.** ✉ Town center, Fira ⊕ scc.gr. **Santorini Port Authority.** ☎ 22860/22239 ⊕ www.santorini-port.com.

TOURS

Santorini Wine Tours

SPECIAL-INTEREST | Professional sommeliers and local wine experts take you on an informative and fun tour of some of the island's leading wineries. Growers that produce a variety of wines are chosen, giving a wide-ranging introduction to many distinct varieties. The tour includes a look at the wine-making process and a drive through vineyards, but the emphasis is on tasting and lively, highly enlightening discussion. The tour includes hotel pickup in a comfortable minibus. ✉ Epar. Od Firon–Ormou Perissis, Mesaria, Fira ☎ 22860/28358 ⊕ www.santoriniwinetour.com.

Shotz Photo Tour

SPECIAL-INTEREST | For a unique and visual perspective of Santorini, and an opportunity to take great shots, too, book a half- or whole-day tour with professional photographer Judy Reinen. Reinen, a New Zealand expat, lives on the island and aims to show off what has come to be one of the most photographed destinations in the world while offering tips on taking photographs using a DSLR or an iPhone. Tours are small and intimate (up to four people who are traveling together) and can cover a range of photo-enthusiast topics. ✉ Ia ☎ 22860/83278 ⊕ www.santoriniphototours.com ✍ From €385 for 1 to 2 people.

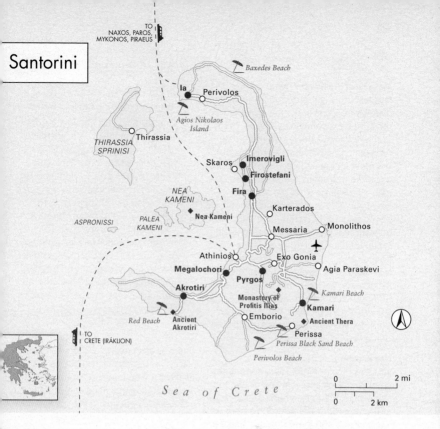

Santorini

TO
NAXOS, PAROS,
MYKONOS, PIRAEUS

Baxedes Beach

Ia
Perivolos

Agios Nikolaos
Island

THIRASSIA
SPRINISI

Thirassia

NEA
KAMENI

Skaros
Imerovigli
Firostefani

Fira

ASPRONISSI

PALEA
KAMENI

Nea Kameni

Karterados

Messaria
Monolithos

Athinios

Exo Gonia

Megalochori

Pyrgos

Agia Paraskevi

Akrotiri

Monastery of
Profitis Ilias

Kamari Beach

Kamari

Red Beach
Ancient
Akrotiri

Emborio

Ancient Thera

Perissa

TO
CRETE (IRÁKLION)

Perissa Black Sand Beach

Perivolos Beach

Sea of Crete

0   2 mi

0   2 km

TRAVEL AGENCIES

CONTACTS Nomikos Travel. ✉ *Deki-gala, Fira* ✣ *Opposite post office* ☎ *22860/23660.* **Pelican Travel.** ☎ *22860/22220* ⊕ *www.pelican.gr.*

Fira Φηρά

76 km (47 miles) southeast of Paros, 10 km (6 miles) west of the Santorini airport, 14 km (8½ miles) southeast of Ia.

Tourism is Santorini's major industry and adds more than 1 million visitors per year to a population of 15,500. As a result, Fira, the capital, midway along the west coast of the east rim, is no longer only a picturesque village but a major tourist center, overflowing with bars, shops, and restaurants. To experience life here as it was until only a couple of decades ago, walk down the much-photographed, winding staircase that descends from town to the water's edge—walk (carefully, trying to avoid the many slippery mule droppings) or take the spectacular cable car ride back up, avoiding the drivers who will try to plant you on the sagging back of one of their bedraggled-looking mules. It soon becomes clear what brings the tourists here: with its white, cubical houses clinging to the cliff hundreds of feet above the caldera, Fira is a beautiful place, an exhilarating Greek extravaganza.

Fira is also sometimes spelt Thera, not to be confused with Thira, the alternate name for the island.

👁 Sights

Museum of Prehistoric Thera
MUSEUM | This is the treasure house that displays frescoes and other artifacts from the famed excavations at Akrotiri. Many of the finds have been sent off to the Archaeological Museum in Athens, but the most charming fresco remains here: a colorful depiction of women in dresses, gathering saffron from the stamens of crocuses. Also in this small collection are fresco fragments with the famous painted swallows (the island's favorite design motif) that still flock to Santorini to roost on the cliffs. The fossilized olive leaves from 60,000 BC prove the olive to be indigenous. ✉ *Fira* ✥ *Mitropoleos, behind Orthodox Cathedral* ☎ *22860/23217* 🌐 *odysseus.culture.gr* 🎫 *€6; €15 combined ticket for archaeological sites and museum in Fira* ⏲ *Closed Tues.*

Nea Kameni
VOLCANO | To peer into a live, sometimes smoldering volcano, join one of the popular excursions to Nea Kameni, the larger of the two Burnt Isles. After disembarking, you hike 430 feet to the top and walk around the edge of the crater, wondering if the volcano is ready for its fifth eruption during the last 100 years—after all, the last was in 1956. Some tours continue on to the island of Therassia, where there is a village. Many operators on the island offer volcano tours.

Panayia Ypapantis
RELIGIOUS SITE | The modern Greek Orthodox cathedral is a major landmark. It's worth a look inside for a view of the frescoes by local artist Christoforos Asimis. You'll quickly note how the local priests, with somber faces, long beards, and black robes, look strangely out of place in summertime, tourist-jammed Fira. ✉ *Fira* ✥ *Southern part of town.*

Petros M. Nomikos Conference Center
ARTS VENUE | Upper Fira's exhibition hall, named for the famous ship owner, hosts many international conferences as well as concerts. Visitors can admire acclaimed seasonal exhibitions that reflect the culture and nature of the island through painting and sculpture. ✉ *Caldera path, just north of cable car* ☎ *22860/23017* 🌐 *www.thera-conferences.gr.*

Avoid the Mules 👁

Tourist touts still like to promote mules as a mode of transportation to take you up the zigzag cliff path to the island capital of Fira, but animal-rights groups would prefer you didn't, as would Fodor's, though the decision is ultimately up to the individual traveler. Moreover, you should be aware of another reason: the mules on Santorini are piously believed to contain souls of the dead, who are thus doing their purgatory. It is, to say the least, an arduous ascent, and best done with the funicular.

🍴 Restaurants

Naoussa
$$ | **GREEK** | Old-fashioned Greek fare, made with care and served by a friendly and accommodating staff, can be enjoyed on a breezy balcony; tables at one end get a caldera view. The decoration won't win prizes but the view will. **Known for:** traditional Greek plates; beautiful view; live music most evenings. [$] *Average main: €16* ✉ *Fira* ✥ *On caldera, near cathedral* ☎ *22860/21277.*

Nikolas Oinomagiremata
$$ | **GREEK** | This charming little taverna, all pastel colors and spindle-backed chairs, is a cozy retreat from the busy streets outside. Named after the chef and owner's grandfather, traditional hearty recipes are delivered with charm and while there

s no knockout view to distract you, the food works hard to keep you entertained. **Known for:** authentic Greek plates; third-generation family-owned business; good value. [$] *Average main: €15* ✉ *Fira* ✣ *Near the main square* ☎ *22860/36422.*

Coffee and Quick Bites

FelafeLAND

$ | **MIDDLE EASTERN** | The smart option for tasty street food in Fira—the Middle Eastern–inspired dishes are a delight here—quicky, healthy, and inexpensive. There is a small indoor dining area but the steps and benches outside are a great place to swap tips and photos with fellow travelers. **Known for:** heaven for vegans and vegetarians; bargain value; handy location near the bus station. [$] *Average main: €4* ✉ *Danezi* ☎ *22860/36359.*

Hotels

When you book a room, remember that many of Santorini's hotel cliffside balconies elbow each other out of the way for the best view and, with footpaths often running above and beside them, privacy is often hard to come by.

Everybody wants to stay in a cave-room overlooking the caldera but, unfortunately, that fantasy comes at a price—lodgings in Santorini are some of the most expensive in Greece. Consider how much time you will spend in your hotel and maybe opt for cheaper lodgings without the heart-stopping view.

Older generations would find the fascination with the caldera strange—islanders used to gather in inland places, away from the eyes of pirates. Favored daughters would get dowries of fertile inland holdings, the less-liked were given cliff-edge land where nothing would grow.

★ Aigialos Hotel

$$$$ | **HOTEL** | A former convent from the 18th century has been converted into the most comfortable and discreetly luxurious—as well as the most poetic and serenely quiet—place to stay in Fira. **Pros:** that view; quiet elegance; friendly, discreet service. **Cons:** some steps, but fewer than elsewhere; the pool is tiny; for the price, not all rooms have a fantastic view. [$] *Rooms from: €500* ✉ *Fira* ✣ *South end of cliffside walkway* ☎ *22860/25191* 🌐 *www.aigialos.gr* ⏲ *Closed Nov.–Mar.* 🛏 *16 rooms* 🍴 *Free breakfast.*

Aroma Suites

$$$ | **HOTEL** | Caldera views come at an especially good value in either small, white cave rooms with vaulted ceilings or large cave suites—all are nicely decorated, with warm touches of color and sleek marble fixtures, and share a terrace overlooking the caldera. **Pros:** attractive with nice fixtures and thoughtful touches; small and friendly; breathtaking caldera view. **Cons:** a lot of stairs; some terraces are shared; rooms are on the small side. [$] *Rooms from: €250* ✉ *Caldera walkway* ☎ *22860/24112* 🌐 *www.aromasuites.com* 🛏 *6 suites* 🍴 *No meals.*

Hotel Aressana

$$$$ | **HOTEL** | Though there's no view of the caldera, a slant of sea view is effulgently wonderful—add in the large freshwater pool, excellent service, and location in central Fira, and the sum total makes these large, bright rooms a very popular option. **Pros:** 10-second walk to popular viewing spot; stylish whitewashed design is very family-friendly; very comfortable and sparkling. **Cons:** no caldera view; some steps required to get around the hotel; no sea view from the pool. [$] *Rooms from: €325* ✉ *Fira* ✣ *South end of cliff-side walkway* ☎ *22860/23900* 🌐 *www.aressana.gr* ⏲ *Closed Nov.–Mar.* 🛏 *48 rooms* 🍴 *Free breakfast.*

Keti Hotel

$$$ | **B&B/INN** | A stay in these traditional cave rooms puts you right in the center of Fira, but well below the bustle—a climb down a staircase leads to a quiet, intimate cliffside aerie where charming vaulted rooms open to a welcoming veranda clinging to the cliff face above the old port. **Pros:** intimate and small retreat; lowest of hotels on the cliff means uninterrupted views; great rates for caldera location. **Cons:** lots of steps down to the hotel; no luxe amenities; vertigo sufferers should look elsewhere. [$] *Rooms from: €230* ✉ *Fira* ✥ *Off caldera walkway below central square* ☎ *22860/22324* 🌐 *www.hotelketi.gr* ⏲ *Closed Nov.–Mar.* 🛏 *9 rooms* 🍴 *Free breakfast.*

Panorama Boutique Hotel

$$$$ | **HOTEL** | These very pleasant rooms, in the center of Fira, combine traditional design with contemporary touches, proving that it's possible to enjoy a caldera view without breaking the bank—and without dealing with steps. **Pros:** central location in the middle of everything; elevator makes access easy; nice design. **Cons:** some rooms are quite small; over one hundred steps down to the pool; busy surroundings won't suit everybody. [$] *Rooms from: €320* ✉ *Fira* ✥ *On caldera, near central square* ☎ *22860/21760* 🌐 *www.panoramahotel.com.gr* ⏲ *Closed Dec.– Feb.* 🛏 *15 rooms* 🍴 *Free breakfast.*

Pelican Hotel

$$ | **HOTEL** | The best value lodgings in Fira are steps away from the main square, right next to the bars and restaurants, and a short walk from the bus station. **Pros:** very efficient and inexpensive; good restaurant next door; great location with no steps. **Cons:** in a busy neighborhood away from the caldera; some noise in front-facing rooms; small bathrooms. [$] *Rooms from: €135* ✉ *Fira* ✥ *On cobblestone road up from main traffic street, near town hall* ☎ *22860/23114* 🌐 *www.pelicanhotel.gr* 🛏 *18 rooms* 🍴 *Free breakfast.*

Villa Renos

$$$ | **B&B/INN** | Huge terraces, shady porticoes, and a small but dramatic cliff-hanging pool all take advantage of spectacular caldera views, while the large, elegantly furnished rooms are pleasant retreats from the madness of the crowded center of Fira, just a few steps away. **Pros:** welcome sense of quiet despite the central location; outstanding hospitality; fantastic views of the caldera. **Cons:** decor in need of refreshment in places; small pool; a lot of steep steps to negotiate. [$] *Rooms from: €240* ✉ *Fira* ✥ *Off caldera walkway, near central square* ☎ *22860/22848* 🌐 *www.villarenos.com* ⏲ *Closed Nov.–Mar.* 🛏 *9 rooms* 🍴 *Free breakfast.*

🍸 Nightlife

BARS AND PUBS

Franco's Bar

MUSIC CLUBS | Boasting a caldera view, this popular bar with a terrace plays classical music. Order a Maria Callas cocktail and listen to the diva herself heralding sunset. ✉ *Fira* ✥ *Below cliff-side walkway on steps to old port* ☎ *22860/24428.*

🎟 Performing Arts

FESTIVALS

Ifestia

SOUND/LIGHT SHOW | On the third weekend of every September, Santorini celebrates the volcanic eruption that changed the landscape of the island back in the second millennium BC. A series of concerts, exhibitions, and cultural events culminates in a spectacular fireworks show in the caldera, re-enacting the explosions and lava flow. ✉ *Fira.*

Santorini International Music Festival

FESTIVALS | Thank pianist Athena Capodistria for September's Santorini International Music Festival, which always includes internationally known musicians in a celebration of classical music ✉ *Nomikos Conference Center, Firostefani* ☎ *22860/23166.*

🛍 Shopping

Despite the proliferation of shops displaying their wares on the street that can make Fira seem like a souk, you probably will not be too tempted by the goods on offer. T-shirts and cheap trinkets are, sadly, the norm, and shops selling the fine jewelry and crafts for which the island was known in the early days of tourism are rare these days. With a little searching, however, you will come upon some treasures.

GALLERIES

AK Art Gallery

ART GALLERIES | The AK Art Gallery, in a converted flour mill, is the oldest on Santorini and was founded by internationally acclaimed artists Christoforos Asimis and his wife Eleni Kollaitou. He specializes in ethereal images from his home island of Santorini, and her work encompasses elegant jewelry, sculpture, and ceramics. Just outside town is the AK Art Foundation, an impressive space that houses exhibitions and cultural events. There is also a small sister gallery in Ia. ✉ Ypapantis walkway ☎ 22860/23041 ⊕ www.ak-galleries.com.

Mati

ART GALLERIES | There's a Greek exuberance to the work of Yorgos Kypris, accentuated in his gallery on a bright, airy perch high above the caldera. In his striking sculptural creations in glass, clay, and other natural materials, seabirds flock and fish swirl in schools; some designs are also available as jewelry and bowls. ✉ Cathedral Sq. ☎ 22860/23814 ⊕ www.matiartgallery.com.

Nikola's Art Gallery

ART GALLERIES | Objets d'art are made from highly polished semiprecious stones and glow with color and form. Pantelis and Nikola Kaloteraki can also create jewelry in the stone of your choice. Vases, sculptures, and many other distinctive pieces fill the shop, which has been a presence in Santorini for more than a quarter of a century. ✉ Fira ✛ Town center ☎ 22860/22283 ⊕ www.nikolas-santorini.com.

JEWELRY

Kostas Antoniou Jewelry

JEWELRY/ACCESSORIES | Many of Kostas's exquisite gold necklaces and bracelets take their inspiration from the art of ancient Thira and Crete. The shop also sells excellent wines from the family's Antoniou vineyards just south of Fira around Megalochori. ✉ Fira ✛ In Spiliotica shopping area, near Archaeological Museum ☎ 22860/22633 ⊕ antoniousantorini.com.

Koukla Art

JEWELRY/ACCESSORIES | Just off the main drag in a pretty square, Koukla is home to simple, modern creative jewelry from a selection of Greek designers. Nonpushy, the owners will help you select a unique memento of your trip. ✉ Fabrica shopping center ☎ 22860/28326 ⊕ www.koukla-art.com.

Firostefani Φηροστεφάνι

1 km (½ mile) northwest of Fira.

Firostefani used to be a separate village, but now it comprises the quieter, more pleasant northern end of Fira. The name derives from Fira + Stefani (meaning crown in Greek) and the 10-minute walk between central Fira and Firostefani, along the caldera, is one of Santorini's highlights. From Firostefani's single white cliffside street, walkways descend to traditional vaulted cave houses, which are fast becoming pensions. Though close to the action, Firostefani feels calm and quiet and gives a different perspective on the volcano.

🍴 Restaurants

★ Aktaion

$$ | GREEK | Since 1922, three generations of the Roussos family have offered hospitality and fine food in this tiny blue-and-white taverna. Outside tables overlook the caldera, inside murals and paintings are by the owner. **Known for:** intimate, romantic, and quaint; delicious, authentic, island food; a couple of tables at the road-side have the best views. Ⓢ *Average main: €17* ✉ *Main square* ☎ *22860/22336* ⊕ *www.aktaionsantorini.com.*

📅 Hotels

Agali Houses

$$$$ | RESORT | Agali may only be a 10-minute walk north from the center of Fira but it feels like a world apart—a village-style setting with handsomely furnished, arch-roofed houses that tumble down the cliffside on a series of dramatic terraces is a quiet enclave. **Pros:** sumptuous sea views; tranquil, traditional charm ; luxury, privacy, and comfort. **Cons:** Wi-Fi can be problematic in some rooms; many steps to get around the hotel; some balconies are shared or are common areas. Ⓢ *Rooms from: €380* ✉ *Firostefani* ⊹ *Off the main street* ☎ *22860/22811* ⊕ *www.agalihouses.gr* ☯ *Closed Nov.–Apr.* ⇶ *30 rooms* ⦿ *Free breakfast.*

Reverie Santorini Hotel

$ | B&B/INN | Only a suite and the roof terrace have caldera views, but everything about the whitewashed and tiled surroundings in this former family home makes for a charming and relaxing island getaway. **Pros:** friendly and inexpensive; small but pleasant pool; no steps and good disabled access. **Cons:** most rooms do not have sea views; standard rooms are a tight squeeze; located in what can be a noisy area of town. Ⓢ *Rooms from: €110* ✉ *Firostefani* ⊹ *Between Firostefani walkway and main traffic road* ☎ *22860/23322* ⊕ *www.reverie.gr* ☯ *Closed Nov.–Mar.* ⇶ *17 rooms* ⦿ *No meals.*

★ Tsitouras Collection Hotel

$$$$ | B&B/INN | *Architectural Digest*–worthy decor and earthy Cycladic charm blend into what is truly Santorinian splendor; think sparkling white cubes with volcanic stone trimmings surrounding an 18th-century mansion. **Pros:** beautiful design; caldera views; lots of privacy. **Cons:** noise possible from surrounding properties; not for those in search of hustle and bustle; those prices, especially during high season. Ⓢ *Rooms from: €780* ✉ *Firostefani* ⊹ *Firostefani cliff face, next to St. Mark's* ☎ *22860/23747* ⊕ *www.tsitouras.com* ☯ *Closed Nov.–Mar.* ⇶ *5 rooms* ⦿ *Free breakfast.*

Imerovigli Ημεροβίγλι

3 km (2 miles) northwest of Fira, 2 km (1 mile) northwest of Firostefani.

Set on the highest point of the caldera's rim, Imerovigli (the name means "watchtower") is quiet, traditional, and less expensive than other places on the caldera. The 25-minute walk from Fira, with incredible views, should be on everyone's itinerary. The lodgings, some of them traditional cave houses, are mostly down stairways from the cliffside walkway. The big rock backing the village was once crowned by Skaros Castle, whence Venetian overlords reigned after 1207, but it collapsed in an earthquake, leaving only the rock. A trail descending from the church of Ayios Georgios crosses the isthmus and encircles Skaros; it's only 10 minutes to the castle top. After 1 km (½ mile) it reaches the small chapel of Theoskepasti—the one with the blue dome on all the postcards—with a memorable caldera view.

🍴 Restaurants

Mezzo

$$ | **MEDITERRANEAN** | A cute wooden doorway leads to three levels of dining terraces that mean getting that all-important cliffside view is easier here than most and the international menu is no slacker either. Asian and Indian flavors mix with Mediterranean tastes to offer something a little different from your traditional taverna. **Known for:** caldera views across Skaros rock; well-chosen Greek cellar; unobtrusive service. $ *Average main: €20* ✉ *Imerovigli* ☎ *22860/21874* ⊕ *www.mezzorestaurant.gr* ⊘ *Closed Apr.–Oct.*

☕ Coffee and Quick Bites

★ Confetti Dessert Boutique

$ | **CAFÉ** | This beautifully designed patisserie offers a range of delicious bijou creations that look like works of art. Gorgeous and chic, they are the best sweet treats on the island and would not look out of place in a Parisian boutique. **Known for:** brunch menu is a treat; homemade ice creams are a delight; right next to the blue dome of Theoskepasti church and the caldera. $ *Average main: €7* ✉ *Heron Street* ☎ *22860/25167* ⊕ *www.confetti-desserts.gr.*

Hotels

★ Aenaon Villas

$$$$ | **B&B/INN** | On one of the island's highest points, these six sumptuous villas offer a 21st-century interpretation of the classic Greek-island hideaway, built in a traditional style with careful respect for Cycladic architecture, with smooth white walls standing out brilliantly against the surrounding dark volcanic stone and the deep blues of the Aegean Sea. The villas are simple in design but entirely luxurious, with a fireplace, private veranda, and modern amenities, and a private plunge pool in one. **Pros:** beautiful private setting; owners make you feel like family; lovely infinity pool with views. **Cons:** no restaurant on-site and only light snacks available; some steps, but not as many as other properties; can feel a little remote. $ *Rooms from: €600* ✉ *Imerovigli* ☎ *22860/27014* ⊕ *www.aenaonvillas.gr* ⊘ *Closed Oct.–May* ⊐ *6 villas* ⦿❘ *Free breakfast.*

Annio Furnished Flats

$ | **B&B/INN** | These cliffside apartments are attractive and simple in design and might be one of the best bargains going. **Pros:** super view of the caldera; simple, clean decor; basic kitchenette facilities. **Cons:** 45-minute walk to Fira; lots of stairs; no central pool but Jacuzzis in many rooms. $ *Rooms from: €120* ✉ *Imerovigli* ☎ *22860/24714* ⊕ *www.annioflats.gr* ⊘ *Closed Nov.–Apr.* ⊐ *11 rooms* ⦿❘ *Free breakfast.*

Astra Suites

$$$$ | **RESORT** | This intimate sanctuary is an especially magical place to stay, with terraced, vaulted-ceilinged cave houses that are sophisticated and full of character. **Pros:** small but perfectly formed spa; giant bathrooms are special; slim infinity pool with a view is a cool retreat. **Cons:** a lot of steps to reach rooms; shared terraces on ground floor lack privacy; suites are pricey. $ *Rooms from: €350* ✉ *Imerovigli* ⊹ *Below caldera walkway* ☎ *22860/23641* ⊕ *www.astrasuites.com* ⊘ *Closed Nov.–Mar.* ⊐ *26 rooms* ⦿❘ *Free breakfast.*

OMMA

$$$$ | **HOTEL** | OMMA clings to a narrow headland offering dramatic views on both sides. **Pros:** peaceful sanctuary feels private and special; artful landscaping with olive trees and volcanic rock; sincere staff are among the best. **Cons:** a little remote and away from other dining options; room service is stupidly expensive; disabled access is limited. $ *Rooms from: €420* ✉ *Imerovigli* ☎ *22860/25570* ⊕ *www.ommasantorini.com* ⊐ *30 rooms* ⦿❘ *Free breakfast.*

Activities

SAILING

Renieris Santorini Sailing Center

SAILING | This handy outfitter arranges daily yacht and speedboat trips around the island, as well as charters and runs weekly two- to three-day sailing trips in the Cyclades for groups of up to 10. ☎ *22860/21370* ⊕ *www.sailingsantorini.gr.*

la Oia

14 km (9 miles) northwest of Fira.

At the tip of the northern horn of the island sits Ia (or Oia), Santorini's second-largest town and the Aegean's most-photographed village. Ia is more tasteful than Fira (for one thing, no establishment here is allowed to play music that can be heard on the street), and the town's cubical white houses, some vaulted against earthquakes, stand out against the green-, brown-, and rust-color layers of rock, earth, and solid volcanic ash that rise from the sea. Every summer evening, travelers from all over the world congregate at the caldera's rim—sitting on whitewashed fences, staircases, beneath the town's windmill, on the old Kastro—each looking out to sea in anticipation of the performance: the Ia sunset. The three-hour rim-edge walk from Ia to Fira at this hour is unforgettable.

In the middle of the quiet caldera, the volcano smolders away eerily, adding an air of suspense to an already awe-inspiring scene. The 1956 earthquake, 7.8 on the Richter scale, left 48 people dead (thankfully, most residents were working outdoors at the time), hundreds injured, and 2,000 houses toppled. Santorini's west side—especially Ia, until then the largest town—was hard hit, and many residents decided to emigrate to Athens, Australia, and America. Although Fira, also damaged, rebuilt rapidly, Ia proceeded slowly, sticking to the traditional architectural style. In 1900, Ia had nearly

9,000 inhabitants, mostly mariners who owned 164 seafaring vessels and seven shipyards. Now there are about 500 permanent residents, and more than 100 boats. Many of these mariners use the endless flight of stairs to descend to the water and the small port of Armeni or take the road or steps to Ammoudi, where the pebble beach is home to some of the island's nicest fish tavernas and the port of embarkation for many excursion boats.

Ia is set up like the other three towns—Fira, Firostefani, and Imerovigli—that adorn the caldera's sinuous rim. There is a cliffside walkway (Nikolaos Nomikou), which is old, and a more recent road for vehicles. Shops and restaurants are all on the walkway, and hotel entrances mostly descend from it—something to check carefully if you cannot negotiate stairs easily. Short streets leading from the road to the walkway have cheaper eateries and shops. There is a parking lot at either end, and the northern one marks the end of the road and the rim. Nothing is very far from anything else.

The main walkway of Ia can be thought of as a straight river, with a delta at the northern end, where the better shops and restaurants are. Many luxurious cave-house hotels are at the southern end, and a stroll by them is part of the extended evening promenade. Although Ia is not as crowded as Fira, where the tour boats deposit their thousands of hasty shoppers, relentless publicity about the town's beauty and tastefulness—accurate enough—are making the narrow lanes impassable in August. The sunset in Ia may not really be much more spectacular than in Fira, and certainly not better than in higher Imerovigli, but somewhere along the line, the island's taxi drivers had the enterprising idea of telling their passengers that the best sunsets were in Ia, which just so happened to generate the highest fares for them as the farthest point away from the airport, Fira, or

Ia is world famous for its magnificent sunsets, which bathe the clifftop village in an ethereal light. Even if you aren't into sunset cocktails or dining with a view, Ia may convince you otherwise.

harbor. Nevertheless, there is something tribally satisfying at the sight of so many people gathering in one spot to celebrate pure beauty. Happily, the night scene isn't as frantic as Fira's—most shop owners are content to sit out front and don't cotton to the few revelers' bars in operation. In winter, Ia feels pretty uninhabited.

Sights

Domaine Sigalas

WINERY/DISTILLERY | Growing the best Greek grapes has everything to do with the land, and the oenologists at Domaine Sigalas, on the ancient plain of Ia, are happy to share their knowledge of the unique Santorini soil and over three millennia of winemaking on the island. A respected name in Greek wines, the family-run winery has opened up its lush inland vineyard at Baxes for tastings and food pairing sessions. Groups are kept small and are priced from €50 per person. ⌷ *Ia* ☎ *22860/71644* ⊕ *www.sigalas-wine.com.*

Naval Maritime Museum of Thera

MUSEUM | In an old neoclassical mansion, once destroyed in the big earthquake, the museum has an enticing collection. Pieces include ships' figureheads, seamen's chests, maritime equipment, and models that reveal the extensive nautical history of the island, Santorini's main trade until tourism took over. ⌷ *Town Center* ☎ *22860/71156* ⌷ *€5* ⊙ *Closed Tues.*

Beaches

Agios Nikolaos Island

BEACH—SIGHT | Not a beach per se, but one of the best swimming spots on the island. From Ia, walk down to Ammoudi, then follow the path past the Sunset taverna to the narrow channel that separates Santorini from little Agios Nikolaos island, so named because of the small chapel that rests on it. Intrepid adventurers swim across and rest on ledges beneath the chapel, enjoying sensational views of the cliffs and Ia perched high above. **Amenities:** none. **Best For:** swimming. ⌷ *Ia.*

Baxedes

BEACH—SIGHT | **FAMILY** | The closest sand beach to Ia is handy when you don't feel like making the trip to more famous beaches on the south end of the island. It's not that there's anything second-rate about this beautiful spot: the cliff-backed strip of sand is rarely crowded; the sea floor is sandy, too, providing nice wading for kids and a pleasant experience when splashing around in the surf; and the cliffs provide welcome shade. A downside is the summertime meltemi winds, which churn up the surf and sand. Islanders used to grow fruits and vegetables down here, and the name comes from the Turkish word for garden, *baxes*. **Amenities:** food and drink; parking (free). **Best for:** swimming. ✉ *Ia* ✥ *Near Paradissos, about 2 km (1 mile) north of Ia.*

🍴 Restaurants

Candouni

$$ | **INTERNATIONAL** | A jasmine-shaded front garden, candle-lit at night, and an antique-filled salon are the charming settings in a centuries-old sea captain's house for this traditional family taverna. All the classics are there but perhaps the best approach is to order from the sizeable meze selection, wash it down with the very palatable house white, and soak in the cozy atmosphere. **Known for:** intimate and romantic; family concern—mom cooks and son serves; live Greek music some evenings. [$] *Average main: €22* ✉ *Ia* ✥ *In back streets near bus station* ☎ *22860/71616.*

★ Red Bicycle

$$$ | **GREEK** | At the tip of Ia in a 19th-century mansion is one of Santorini's most storied eateries. A traditional white exterior and glossy painted door lead to a chic interior with Maria Callas photographs and a stupendous terrace with caldera views on all sides. **Known for:** local fine-dining favorite; beautiful terrace views are unforgettable; charming owner and staff. [$] *Average main: €28* ✉ *Ia* ✥ *Off main walkway* ☎ *22860/71918* ⏲ *Closed Nov.–Mar.*

★ Roka

$$ | **MODERN GREEK** | A pastel-yellow courtyard hidden among the sea captains' mansions is where those in the know come to eat in Ia. Elegant and delicious, these modern Greek updates on classic cooking are rays of sunshine among the more tourist-oriented fare elsewhere. **Known for:** sparkling Santorinian specialties; sea-view terrace at the rear; wood-burning stove for cozy winter evenings. [$] *Average main: €20* ✉ *Marko Mpotsari 6* ✥ *In back streets near bus station* ☎ *228/607–1896* 🌐 *www.roka.gr.*

Sphinx Wine Bar and Restaurant

$$$ | **MEDITERRANEAN** | A lovingly decorated mansion is home to the best cellar on the island with a deep and extensive international list. The food is no afterthought though; eclectic and creative magic goes on in the kitchen as a mainly Mediterranean menu is put through its paces. **Known for:** excellent wine selection—more than 400 labels; romantic and historic setting; super knowledgeable staff. [$] *Average main: €26* ✉ *Ia* ☎ *22860/71450* 🌐 *www.sphinxwinerestaurant.com.*

★ Sunset Taverna

$$ | **SEAFOOD** | The first of the Ammoudi fish houses that opened in the 1980s is still a standout among the several excellent tavernas that line the quay in this tiny fishing port just below Ia—you can walk down and take a cab back to town. Lapping waves, bobbing fishing boats, and tables so close to the water's edge that a clumsy move might add a swim to the evening's entertainment, testify to the freshness of the fish, which is simply grilled. **Known for:** beautiful waterfront harbor setting; sunset dining; excellent seafood. [$] *Average main: €25* ✉ *Waterfront* ✥ *Ammoudi* ☎ *22860/71614* 🌐 *www.sunset-ammoudi.gr.*

Coffee and Quick Bites

Skiza

$ | **BAKERY** | The balcony overlooking the caldera on top of this café-cum-bakery is a prime spot for lazing over breakfast, a coffee, or a home-baked pastry. Open all year, too, for soothing summer ice-cream or warming winter treats. **Known for:** perfect pizza; awesome Greek sweets; big blue view. *[$] Average main: €5 ✉ Ia ✣ On caldera, near church ☎ 🌐 www.skiza.gr.*

Hotels

Armeni Suites

$$$ | **HOTEL** | Armeni's whitewashed rooms, inspired by the traditional cave houses of the island, impress with a contemporary touch. **Pros:** clubby, village vibe; great views; steps away from Ia's central street and restaurants. **Cons:** there are a lot of stairs to climb; shared balconies for some rooms; breakfast is continental style and served in-room. *[$] Rooms from: €275 ✉ Ia ☎ 22860/71439 🌐 www.armenivillage.com ⏲ Closed Nov.–Mar. 🛏 15 rooms 🍴 Free breakfast.*

Canaves Oia Luxury Suites

$$$$ | **RESORT** | The Canaves Oia brand seems intent on buying up every spare property in the town, but this is the original development and still the best—a collection of beautifully furnished suites, all done in crisp whites and handsome fabrics, meticulously maintained and enjoying uninterrupted caldera views and private pools in every room. **Pros:** extremely attractive; good dining poolside and in gourmet restaurant, Petra; elevator access from street level—unheard of in Ia. **Cons:** in the busy center of town; steps in hotel section; very pricey. *[$] Rooms from: €750 ✉ Ia ✣ On caldera, center of town ☎ 22860/71453 🌐 www.canaves.com ⏲ Closed Nov.–Mar. 🛏 31 rooms 🍴 Free breakfast.*

Esperas Hotel

$$ | **HOTEL** | At this welcoming collection of sparkling white, arch-roofed cave houses that spill down the side of the caldera, homey suites and studios all have cozy sitting areas, well-equipped bathrooms, and a private, view-saturated terrace overlooking dark cliffs and turquoise seas. **Pros:** wonderful caldera location; does everything really well; quiet and private. **Cons:** lots of steps to reach the hotel, though staff help carry bags; more stairs inside to get to rooms; plain but traditional decor may not suit all. *[$] Rooms from: €220 ✉ Ia ☎ 22860/71501 🌐 www.esperas-santorini.com ⏲ Closed late Oct.–Apr. 🛏 21 rooms 🍴 Free breakfast.*

Ikies Traditional Houses

$$$$ | **RESORT** | A perch at the far eastern end of Ia provides wonderful views of the village as well as the caldera, which can be enjoyed from the private terraces of the handsomely furnished cave houses that were once used as workshops to repair and store fishing nets. **Pros:** small, off-the-beaten-track, private; modern and attractive; low-key, attentive service. **Cons:** terraces are not entirely private; the inevitable steps; no restaurant, though light snacks are available. *[$] Rooms from: €440 ✉ Ia ✣ Off eastern end of caldera path ☎ 22860/71311 🌐 www.ikies.com ⏲ Closed Nov.–Mar. 🛏 11 rooms 🍴 Free breakfast.*

Katikies

$$$$ | **RESORT** | Sumptuously furnished, this immaculate white cliffside complex layered on terraces offers ultimate luxury and sleek modern design, with Warhol wall prints, stunning fabrics, and handsome furniture—chic as the surroundings are, though, the barrel-vaulted ceilings and other architectural details also lend a traditional air to the place. **Pros:** three cliffside infinity pools; on-site dining options are superb; super location on high is dizzingly seductive. **Cons:** many stairs; pool-side areas fill up quickly; on

crowded part of caldera. $ *Rooms from: €490* ✉ *Ia* ✛ *Ia cliff face, edge of main town* ☎ *22860/72382* ⊕ *www.katikies. com* ☾ *Closed Nov.–Mar.* ⇆ *34 rooms* ☉ *Free breakfast.*

★ Perivolas

$$$$ | **RESORT** | A travel magazine favorite, Perivolas lives up to the hype and then some. **Pros:** the best infinity pool on Santorini; attentive but relaxed service; beautiful and tranquil surroundings. **Cons:** lots of steps; a walk to town; high-roller price tag. $ *Rooms from: €675* ✉ *Nomikou* ✛ *Ia cliff face, east of center* ☎ *22860/71308* ⊕ *www.perivolas. gr* ☾ *Closed Nov.–Mar.* ⇆ *20 houses* ☉ *Free breakfast.*

Nightlife

There are the usual cafés, bars, and pastry shops along the main street, but a peaceful note is struck by the fact that establishments are forbidden to play loud music.

Hassapiko

BARS/PUBS | A former butcher shop, Hassapiko is an Ia institution. Also known as MaryKay's bar, after the owner, it is open all-day for brunch and coffee but it comes alive at night when its chilled vibe attracts returning sunset-seekers and it is the ideal place for a late nightcap. ✉ *Ia* ☎ *22860/71244* ⊕ *www.hassapiko.gr.*

👜 Shopping

Ia mostly abjures the trinket madness of Fira and instead offers a variety of hand-crafted items. Since the shops are not so dependent on cruise ships, a certain sophistication reigns in the quiet streets. Art galleries, objets d'art shops, crafts shops, and icon stores set the tone.

ANTIQUES AND COLLECTIBLES
Loulaki

ANTIQUES/COLLECTIBLES | Manolis and Chara Kourtis sell antiques, ceramics, fabrics, jewelry, and clothes in a delightful shop below their Red Bicycle restaurant. Exploring their collection is a pleasure, with sea creature-painted plates a favorite. ✉ *Main St.* ☎ *22860/71856.*

BOOKS
★ Atlantis Books

BOOKS/STATIONERY | One of the great bookshops of the world is an unexpected but welcome treat in Ia. Built into a cave, it is like something from Harry Potter, with handwritten notes, painted ceilings, and books crammed onto every surface. Mostly English language books are stocked, with a great kids section and some very desirable first editions. It is a wondrous place. ■ **TIP→ Ask them to stamp your book with their famous logo for a great souvenir.** ✉ *Ia* ✛ *North end of main shopping street* ☎ *22860/72346* ⊕ *www.atlantisbooks.org.*

Activities

SAILING
Sunset Oia

SAILING | Five-hour morning and afternoon sailings from Ammoudi include stops at the hot springs around the volcano and two beaches for swimming, with stunning caldera-cliff views along the way; afternoon cruises coincide with sunset. Meals and drinks are served onboard, and relatively small groups ensure a genuinely memorable experience. Private luxury yacht charters are also available. ✉ *Ammoudi* ☎ *22860/72200* ⊕ *www. sailing-santorini.com.*

Pyrgos Πύργος

5 km (3 miles) south of Fira.

Though today Pyrgos has only 500 inhabitants, until the early 1800s it was the capital of the island. Medieval houses are stacked on top of one another and back-to-back for protection against pirates. Your reward for a climb up the picturesque streets ends at the ruined

Venetian castle, where views extend across the vineyard-studded landscape to both coasts. In Pyrgos you are really in old Santorini—hardly anything has changed.

Sights

Monastery of Profitis Ilias

RELIGIOUS SITE | Standing on the highest point on Santorini, which rises to 1,856 feet at the summit, Santorini's largest monastery offers a cinematic vista: from here you can see the surrounding islands and, on a clear day, the mountains of Crete, more than 100 km (62 miles) away. You may also be able to spot ancient Thira on the peak below Profitis Ilias.

Founded in 1711 by two monks from Pyrgos, Profitis Ilias is cherished by islanders because here, in a secret school, the Greek language and culture were taught during the dark centuries of the Turkish occupation. A museum in the monastery contains a model of the secret school in a monk's cell, another model of a traditional carpentry and blacksmith shop, and a display of ecclesiastical items. ⊠ *Pyrgos* ⚜ *At highest point on Santorini.*

 Restaurants

Metaxi Mas

$$ | **GREEK** | It seems that just about everyone in Santorini looks forward to a meal at this village taverna. Even though the name means "between us," the secret is out and the key to success appears to be to keep it simple—the kitchen sticks to traditional home-style cooking from Santorini and Crete. **Known for:** hearty delicious Greek plates; relaxed, simple home-style cooking; nice rustic views. Ⓢ *Average main: €15* ⊠ *Exo Gonia* ⚜ *Village center* ☎ *22860/31323* ⊕ *www. santorini-metaximas.gr.*

Coffee and Quick Bites

Franco's Cafe

$ | **GREEK** | The hangout that is such a caldera-side hit in Fira also has a welcoming presence in Pyrgos, where cocktails and light snacks are served on breezy terraces overlooking the village, vineyards, and the sea. This spot is especially popular at sunset, but does a brisk business throughout the day, when the bar brews great coffee. **Known for:** sunset drinks from the highest village; classical soundtrack; a hike to reach it. Ⓢ *Average main: €10* ⊠ *Pyrgos* ⚜ *Top of village near the fortress* ☎ *22860/33957.*

🛏 Hotels

Zannos Melathron

$$$$ | **HOTEL** | A delightful walled garden is the setting for this magical hideaway high above the island's medieval capital, where comfortable suites in two Cycladic-style manor houses sport stucco and stone walls, vaulted ceilings, antique furnishings, and flowery terraces that look out across the island to the sea. **Pros:** beautiful setting and surroundings; elegant yet comfortable and welcoming; surrounded by winding lanes of Pyrgos. **Cons:** pool is small and soon fills up; a climb to reach it; far from caldera views Santorini is famous for. Ⓢ *Rooms from: €375* ⊠ *Pyrgos* ⚜ *Village center* ☎ *22860/28220* ⊕ *www.zannos. gr* ⊗ *Closed Nov.–Easter* ⇋ *13 rooms* ⦿ *Free breakfast.*

Megalochori Μεγαλοχώρι

4 km (2½ miles) east of Pyrgos, 9 km (5½ miles) southwest of Fira.

Megalochori is a picturesque, half-abandoned town. Many of the village's buildings were actually *canavas,* wine-making facilities. The tiny main square is still lively in the evening.

Sights

Boutari Winery

WINERY/DISTILLERY | The first of the island's wineries to open to the public puts on a big show, with a bright, view-filled tasting room surrounded by vineyards. A distinctly Santorini experience is a taste of Kallisti, a version of the Assyrtiko variety, and the exceptional Estate Argyros Vinsanto, an international award winner. ✉ *Megalochori* ☎ *22860/81011* 🌐 *www.boutariwinerysantorini.gr* 🎟 *Tasting and tour €15* 🕒 *Closed Sun.*

Gavalas Winery

WINERY/DISTILLERY | One of the oldest vineyards, this winery has been exporting its distinguished produce since the days when mules carted wine-filled goatskins to the port in Fira. Tastings in the atmospheric old storage and pressing rooms include Voudomato, a native dry rosé, and Nykteri, a sophisticated white from the island's indigenous Assyrtiko grapes—the name means "working the night away," because the grapes have traditionally been harvested at night to avoid damage from the heat. ✉ *Megalochori* ☎ *22860/82552* 🌐 *www.gavalaswines.gr* 🎟 *Tasting from €10 for 3 wines* 🕒 *Closed Nov.–Apr.*

Hotels

Vedema

$$$$ | **RESORT** | Part of the Marriott Luxury Collection, this distant and deluxe black-lava outpost is a world unto itself, where villas have been built around a beautiful 15th-century winery. **Pros:** outdoor areas are some of the best on the island; Asian spa and fitness center; free shuttle to Black Rose Beach Club at Perissa. **Cons:** isolated from island life; no taxis in Megalochori so must be prebooked; distant sea views rather than cliffside. [$] *Rooms from: €470* ✉ *Megalochori* ☎ *22860/81796* 🌐 *www.marriott.com* 🕒 *Closed Nov.–Mar.* 🛏 *45 rooms* 🍴 *Free breakfast.*

Santorini Wine

The locals say that in Santorini there is more wine than water, and it may be true; Santorini produces more wine than any other Cyclades island. The volcanic soil, high daytime temperatures, and humidity at night are favorable to many varieties of grape, and these unique growing conditions are especially ideal for the production of Assyrtiko, a distinctive white wine. Farmers twist the vines into a basketlike shape, in which the grapes grow, protected from the wind. A highlight of any Santorini trip is a visit to one of its many wineries—log on to 🌐 *www.santorini.org/wineries* for a helpful intro.

Akrotiri Ακρωτήρι

7 km (4½ miles) west of Pyrgos, 13 km (8 miles) south of Fira.

This village is most famous for its ancient ruins, but the little collection of houses surrounded by gardens and fields is a pleasant place in its own right, a pretty slice of rural Santorini. A stay here removes you from the hustle and bustle along the caldera and puts you within easy reach of sights, wineries, and the island's best beaches.

Sights

★ Ancient Akrotiri

ARCHAEOLOGICAL SITE | If Santorini is known as the "Greek Pompeii" and is claimant to the title of the lost Atlantis, it is because of the archaeological site of Ancient Akrotiri, near the tip of the southern horn of the island. The site now has a protective roof spanning the entire enclosed area, which is in fact a whole ancient city buried under the

At Ancient Akrotiri, an archaeological site on Santorini, a whole city is buried under volcanic ashes—much of it is still waiting to be unearthed.

volcanic ashes, much of it still waiting to be unearthed—almost intact. Only one in 20 of Santorini's vistors come to the site, which is a great shame as it helps to remind of the centuries of history that the island hides beneath traveler's feet.

In the 1860s, in the course of quarrying volcanic ash for use in the Suez Canal, workmen discovered the remains of an ancient town. The town was frozen in time by ash from an eruption 3,600 years ago, long before Pompeii's disaster. In 1967 Spyridon Marinatos of the University of Athens began excavations, which continue to this day. It is thought that the 40 buildings that have been uncovered are only one-third of the huge site and that excavating the rest will probably take a century.

Marinatos's team discovered many well-preserved frescoes depicting aspects of Akrotiri life, some are now displayed in the National Archaeological Museum in Athens but many have been returned to the Museum of Prehistoric Thera in Fira. Meanwhile, postcard-size pictures of them are posted outside the houses where they were found. The antelopes, monkeys, and wildcats they portray suggest trade with Egypt.

Akrotiri was settled as early as 3000 BC, possibly as an outpost of Minoan Crete, and reached its peak after 2000 BC, when it developed trade and agriculture and settled the present town. The inhabitants cultivated olive trees and grain, and their advanced architecture—three-story frescoed houses faced with masonry (some with balconies) and public buildings of sophisticated construction—is evidence of an elaborate lifestyle. Remains of the inhabitants have never been found, possibly because they might have had advance warning of the eruptions and fled in boats—beds have been found outside the houses, suggesting the island was shaken with earthquakes that made it unwise to sleep indoors.

It is worth noting that the collection is unusually weak in jewelry, but this can probably be explained by the fact that such items are high value and easy to carry and so their owners took them with them, despite the urgency of their departure. ✉ Akrotiri ✛ South of modern Akrotiri ☎ 22860/81939 ⊕ odysseus. culture.gr 🎫 €12; €15 for combined ticket for archaeological sites and museum in Fira ⊗ Closed Nov.–Mar. and Tues.

Beaches

Red Beach

BEACH—SIGHT | A backdrop of red-and-black volcanic cliffs adds no small amount of drama to this strand of multicolored pebbles and red-hued sand, and the timelessness of the place is enhanced by the presence of nearby ancient Akrotiri. Crowds sometimes pile in during July and August, and a few too many loungers and umbrellas detract from the stunning scenery, but for the most part this is one of the quieter beaches on the south side of the island. There's a rough path from the parking area to the beach. Be warned, though, the beach is officially closed due to the danger of rocks falling, and entering is at your own risk. **Amenities:** food and drink; parking (free). **Best for:** snorkeling; swimming. ✉ Akrotiri ✛ On southwest shore below Akrotiri.

 Restaurants

The Dolphins

$$ | SEAFOOD | A jetty juts out into the sea and is a memorable setting for lunch, while on calm nights the moon playing off the water makes this quiet outpost on the southern end of the island one of the most romantic spots around. By day it's not unusual to see fish being hauled into the kitchen fresh from the docks. **Known for:** idyllic dining on the beach; simple, fresh seafood plates; a short walk from Akrotiri Museum and Red Beach. $ Average main: €20 ✉ Akrotiri ✛ On the beach ☎ 22860/81151 ⊕ www.thedolphins.gr.

Hotels

Hotel Goulielmos

$$ | HOTEL | These very simple yet comfortable rooms, many with terraces, are among the island's unsung treasures, perched on the southern side of the caldera just outside Akrotiri, enjoying spectacular views up the rim to Fira and Ia. The experience of a stay in these tile-floored rooms with plain wood furnishings is much more like what you'll find in other parts of rural Greece, not on Santorini. **Pros:** nice grounds and views; peaceful and calm; all rooms have private balconies or terraces. **Cons:** plain decor lacks luxury; few hotel amenities and services; far from caldera towns. $ Rooms from: €200 ✉ Akrotiri ✛ On caldera off road into town ⊕ www.hotel-goulielmos. gr ⊗ Closed Nov.–Mar. ➟ 27 rooms ⦿ Free breakfast.

Kamari Καμάρι

6 km (4 miles) east of Akrotiri, 6 km (4 miles) south of Fira.

Santorini's most popular beach resort is just that—a long line of hotels and tavernas strung out along a stretch of red-and-black sand on the island's southeastern coast. Tourism has all but consumed the onetime quieter pursuits of fishing and farming, though many residents still depend on both, and sun lovers descend en masse in July and August. Still, backed by fields, dramatic cliffs, and headlands, Kamari is fairly low-key and a pleasant place to hit the beach.

Sights

Ancient Thera

ARCHAEOLOGICAL SITE | A Dorian city—with 9th-century BC tombs, an engraved phallus, Hellenistic houses, and traces of Byzantine fortifications and churches—floats more than 2,100 feet above the island. At the Sanctuary of Apollo, graffiti dating to the 8th century BC records the names of some of the boys who danced naked at the god's festival (Satie's famed musical compositions, *Gymnopédies,* reimagine these). To get here, hike up from Perissa or Kamari or take a taxi up Mesa Vouno. On the summit are the scattered ruins, excavated by a German archaeology school around the turn of the 20th century; there's a fine view. ✉ *Kamari* ✣ *On a switchback up mountain, right before Kamari* ☎ *22860/23217* 🌐 *odysseus.culture.gr* 🎫 *€6 or €15 as part of 3-day combined museum ticket* 🕒 *Closed Tues.*

★ Koutsoyannopoulos Wine Museum

WINERY/DISTILLERY | Founded in 1870, the Koutsoyannopoulos Winery offers a tour of its old facility, now a multiroom museum that is picturesque, authentic, and mostly underground. Tools, techniques, and the original business office are from a world long gone—but the wines, as the ensuing tasting proves, are contemporary and refined. The *Wine Spectator* rated their Assyrtiko among the world's top 100 whites. To add your own kudos, note that this admired winery is open year-round. ✉ *Vothonas* ✣ *On the road to Kamari* ☎ *22860/31322* 🌐 *www.santorini-winemuseum.com* 🎫 *Tasting from €14.*

Beaches

Kamari Beach

BEACH—SIGHT | Santorini's most popular beach, one of several excellent stretches of sand on the southern end of the island, manages to maintain its beauty despite an onslaught of sunseekers. The black sands are backed by dramatic cliffs, including the one topped by Ancient Thira. A steep path from one end of the beach leads up to the ruins, past a refreshing and very welcome natural spring, but most beachgoers don't venture beyond their umbrella-shaded loungers or the long line of beach bars and tavernas. **Amenities:** food and drink; showers; toilets; water sports. **Best for:** snorkeling; swimming; walking. ✉ *Kamari* ✣ *8 km (5 miles) southeast of Fira.*

Perissa Beach

BEACH—SIGHT | Separated from Kamari Beach by a huge slice of rock, Mesa Vouno, Perissa is almost identical but that mountain helps to protect it from the Meltemi winds. It is a long black-sand beach that is popular with the summer crowds and where a lively beach resort town has grown to appreciate the view. **Amenities:** food and drink; showers; toilets; water sports. **Best for:** snorkeling; swimming; walking. ✉ *Kamari.*

Perivolos Beach

BEACH—SIGHT | Pretty much an extension of Perissa Beach, Perivolos features that famous volcanic black sand but with just a tad fewer restaurants, beach bars, and cafés, making it a quieter beach enclave to seek most times of the year. **Amenities:** food and drink; showers; toilets; water sports. **Best for:** snorkeling; swimming; walking. ✉ *Kamari.*

Restaurants

Forty One

$$ | **MEDITERRANEAN** | In a former historic tomato cannery off the Ayios Georgios section of Perivolos Beach, Forty One is a chic, stylish destination for fine Mediterranean dishes, with a calming sea view. Besides creatively presented favorites like regional salads, risotto, pasta, and freshly grilled seafood plates, there are a host of creative cocktails that steal the show and make a fine accompaniment to taking in the black-beach sunset. **Known for:** upmarket beach bar with bohemian atmosphere; superlative seaside sustenance; very extensive wine cellar. [$] *Average main: €24* ✉ *Kamari* ☎ *22680/82710.*

Hotels

★ Orabel Suites

$$$ | B&B/INN | This romantically designed, adults-only getaway is seemingly in the middle of nowhere—a quiet stretch of valley fronted by farmland and with a distant view of the sea—but that is part of its secluded charm. **Pros:** beautiful contemporary yet traditional design; perfect for couples and beach lovers; attentive service. **Cons:** no famous Santorini view to boast of; no on-site restaurant (but breakfast service is excellent); not within walking distance of Santorini's major sights and villages. [$] *Rooms from: €230* ✉ *Kamari* ☎ *22860/85060* 🌐 *www.orabelsuites.gr* 🕒 *Closed Nov.–Mar.* 🛏 *11 rooms* 🍴 *Free breakfast.*

Chapter 9

CRETE

Updated by
Liam McCaffrey

⊙ Sights 🍴 Restaurants 🛏 Hotels 🛍 Shopping 🍸 Nightlife
★★★★★   ★★★★☆   ★★★★☆   ★★☆☆☆   ★★☆☆☆

WELCOME TO CRETE

TOP REASONS TO GO

★ **Minoan Myths:** Explore the wonders of the 3,500-year-old civilization that flourished at Knossos.

★ **Best Beaches:** With its sandy strands and craggy coves, Crete has an array of fantastic beaches, all lapped by clean, turquoise waters.

★ **Charming Cities:** Chania, Rethymnon, and Ayios Nikolaos will seduce with their Venetian and Ottoman architecture, narrow lanes, and shady squares.

★ **The Open Outdoors:** From snowcapped peaks to deep gorges, wild Crete offers dramatic escapes for those who want to get away from it all.

★ **Luxury Living:** Live like royalty in a former Venetian palace, or indulge in the unabashed splendor of some of Greece's finest resort hotels.

Crete is long and narrow, approximately 257 km (160 miles) long and only 60 km (37 miles) at its widest. Most of the development is along the north shore; the southern coast largely remains blessedly unspoiled. The island's three major cities, Heraklion, Rethymnon, and Chania, are in the north and are connected by the island's major highway, an east–west route that traverses most of the north coast. Heraklion and Chania are served by ferry from Piraeus, and both have international airports. By car or bus, it's easy to reach other parts of the island from these gateways.

■ **Heraklion.** Crete's modern capital was the hub of island civilization 3,500 years ago.

■ **Knossos.** The most spectacular of the Minoan palaces, Knossos is also Crete's most important archaeolgoical site.

■ **Lasithi Plateau.** The plateau, rising 2,800 feet high, is breathtakingly beautiful, and ringed by small villages.

■ **Ayios Nikolaos.** Clustered on a peninsula alongside the Gulf of

Mirabello, this coastal town boasts a dramatic composition of bare mountains, islets, and deep blue sea.

■ **Elounda.** The Elounda Peninsula is the island's epicenter of luxury, where some of the world's most sumptuous resort getaways are tucked along a stunning shoreline.

Sea of Crete

DIA

Fodhele

Rethymnon

11

Arkadi   Perama

10

MOUNT IDA

1 Heraklion

2
Palace of
Knossos

CRETE

Neapolis

5 Elounda
*Gulf of
Mirabello*

6 Vai

3 *LASITHI
PLATEAU*

4 Ayios
Nikolaos

Siteia

DIKTI MOUNTAINS

Kritsa

7

Ayii Deka

Vori

8
Palace of
Phaistos

MESARA PLAIN

Ierapetra

Matala

9

CHRISI   KOUFONISI

Libyan Sea

0   15 mi

0   15 km

6 Vai. The beach at Vai is just one example of the natural beauty that abounds on the island.

7 Vori. A farming community with white-washed houses and a fine Cretan folk museum.

8 Palace of Phaistos. This palace was the center of Minoan culture in southern Crete.

9 Matala. Renowned in the 1960s as a stopover on the hippie trail, Matala today is a small, low-key beach resort that retains its flower-power vibe.

10 Arkadi. Follow a gorge inland before emerging onto the flat pastureland that surrounds a beautiful monastery.

11 Rethymnon. The charm of Crete's third-largest town perseveres in the old

quarter, dominated by a castle known as the Fortezza.

12 Vrisses. This appealing old village is famous throughout Crete for its thick, creamy yogurt—best eaten with a large spoonful of honey on top.

13 Chania. It was here that the Greek flag was raised in 1913 to mark Crete's unification with Greece.

Crete is a land of myth and imagination, where Theseus slayed the Minotaur, where Daedalus and Icarus set off on their ill-fated flight, and where Zorba danced on the sand. More than any other island, it is Greece in a nutshell—mountains, split with deep gorges and honeycombed with caves, rise in sheer walls from the sea; snowcapped peaks loom behind sandy shorelines.

It's also filled with vineyards and olive groves and delightful cities, and quaint villages front the miles of beaches that fringe the coast. It is an island blessed with natural wonders. Yet it is still the mystery surrounding Europe's first civilization and empire that draws many visitors to Crete and its world-famous Minoan palaces.

Around 1500 BC, while the rest of Europe was still in the grip of primitive barbarity, one of the most brilliant civilizations the world was ever to know approached its final climax, one that was breathtakingly uncovered through the late 19th-century excavations of Sir Arthur Evans. He determined that the Minoans, prehistoric Cretans, had founded Europe's first urban culture as far back as the 3rd millennium BC, and the island's rich legacy of art and architecture strongly influenced both mainland Greece and the Aegean islands in the Bronze Age. From around 1900 BC the Minoan palaces at Knossos (near present-day Heraklion), Malia, Phaistos, and elsewhere were centers of political power, religious authority, and economic activity—all concentrated in one sprawling complex of buildings. Their administration seems to have had much in common with contemporary cultures in Egypt and Mesopotamia. What set the Minoans apart from the rest of the Bronze Age world was their art. It was lively and naturalistic, and from the scenes illustrated on their frescoes, stone vases, seal stones, and signet rings, it is possible to build a picture of a productive, well-regulated society. Yet new research suggests that prehistoric Crete was not a peaceful place; there may have been years of warfare before Knossos became the island's dominant power, in around 1600 BC. It is now thought that political upheaval, rather than the devastating volcanic eruption on the island of Santorini, triggered the violent downfall of the palace civilization around 1450 BC.

But there are many memorable places in Crete that belong to a more recent past, one measured in centuries and not millennia. Other invaders and occupiers—Roman colonists, the Byzantines, Arab invaders, Venetian colonists, and Ottoman pashas—have all left their mark on Heraklion, Chania, Rethymnon, and other towns and villages throughout the island. Today, Crete welcomes outsiders who delight in its splendid beaches, charming Old Town quarters, and array of splendid landscapes. Openly inviting to guests who want to experience the real Greece, Cretans remain family oriented and rooted in tradition, and you'll find that one of the greatest pleasures on Crete is immersing yourself in the island's lifestyle.

Planning

When to Go

The best times to visit Crete are May, when every outcrop of rock is ablaze with brilliant wildflowers and the sea is warm enough for a brisk dip, or September and October, when the sea is still warm and the light golden and clear.

Most of Crete, outside the major cities, is really only noticeably busy from mid-July through August, when the main sights and towns on the north coast come close to overflowing with tourists. Beaches get busier, and reservations can be essential in the most popular restaurants, too. Even in the height of summer, though, you can enjoy many parts of the east, west, and south coasts without feeling oppressed by crowds.

Crete can also be a pleasure in winter, when you can visit the museums and archaeological sites and enjoy the island's delightful towns without the crush of crowds. Remember, though, that rainfall can be heavy in January and February, and note that many hotels and restaurants, especially resorts, close from late October or November through mid-April or May.

Planning Your Time

Inviting as Crete's beaches may be, there is much more to the island than lazing on the sand. Archaeological sites in Crete open at 8 or 8:30 in summer, so get an early start to wander through the ruins before the sun is blazing. You may also want to visit some of the folklife museums that pay homage to the island's traditional past, or simply head out and explore the magnificent mountain and coastal scenery. An evening should begin with a stroll around the shady squares that grace every Cretan town and village, or along a waterfront promenade—those in Chania, Ayios Nikolaos, and Sitia are especially picturesque and jammed with locals. Most evenings are spent over a long meal, almost always eaten outdoors in the warm weather.

Getting Here and Around

AIR

Olympic Air connects Athens, and other islands, with Heraklion, Chania, and Sitia. Aegean Airlines flies between Athens and Heraklion and Chania. Sky Express flies to both Heraklion and Sitia. Ryanair connects Chania to Athens, and to other European destinations. Fares on all are highest in the summer, often double that of a ferry.

The principal arrival point on Crete is Heraklion Airport, where up to 20 flights daily arrive from Athens and daily flights arrive from throughout Greece. Heraklion is also serviced directly by flights from other European cities.

There are several daily flights from Athens and, in summer, other European cities to Chania Airport, and several per week from Athens to Sitia, which is also connected to the Dodecanese islands with a few weekly flights in summer.

A bus just outside Heraklion Airport takes you to the town center. Tickets are sold from a kiosk next to the bus stop or you can pay the driver; the fare is €2. From Chania Airport, buses run hourly to the center for €2.50, but these are not running 24 hours. Tickets are available inside the airport or can be bought from the driver. Cabs line up outside all airports to meet flights; the fare into the respective towns is about €12 for Heraklion, €25 for Chania, and €5 for Sitia.

AIRPORT CONTACTS Chania Airport.

(*CHQ*) ✈ *15 km (9 miles) northeast of Chania, off the road to Sterne* ☎ *28210/83800* ⊕ *www.chq-airport. gr.* **Heraklion Airport (Kazantzakis International Airport).** (*HER*) ✈ *5 km (3 miles) east of town, off the road to Gournes* ☎ *28103/97800.* **Sitia Airport.** (*JSH*) ✈ *1 km (½ mile) northwest of town, off the main coast road* ☎ *28430/20151.*

BIKE AND MOPED

You'll find rentals in just about any town on the tourist trail. Expect to pay about €25 a day for a 50cc moped, for which you will need to present only a valid driver's license; law requires a motorcycle license to rent larger bikes. Fees usually cover insurance, but only for repairs to the bike, and usually with a deductible of at least €500. The law mandates that you wear a helmet, despite what you may think from observing the locals. Be careful—the casualty departments of hospitals are full of over-eager tourists every year.

Bicycles are available to rent in most resorts, and are offered by many hotels and car rental companies. For the more adventurous, mountain bike and road tours are available.

CONTACTS Blue Sea Rentals. ✉ *Kosmo Zoutou 5–7, Heraklion* ☎ *28102/21215* ⊕ *www.bluesearentals.com.* **Olympic Bike.** ✉ *Nikeas 48, Rethymnon* ☎ *28310/72383* ⊕ *www.olympicbike. com.*

BOAT AND FERRY

Heraklion and Souda Bay (5 km/3 miles east of Chania) are the island's main ports. Most ferries are overnight, but there are daytime ferries from Piraeus to Heraklion and Chania in the summer. Ferries also connect Crete with other islands, mostly those in the Cyclades and Dodecanese. Service includes fast-ferries between Santorini and Heraklion (cutting travel time to just under two hours) and a ferry linking Sitia with the Dodecanese islands of Kassos, Karpathos, and Rhodes. There is also a ferry linking Sitia and Heraklion. There is an irregular service from Kalamata and Gythion in the Peloponnese to Kissamos (Kastelli) in the far west of the island. Ships also sail from Heraklion to Limassol, in Cyprus, and to Haifa, Israel. On the overnight runs, you can book either a berth or an airplane-style seat, and there are usually cafeterias, dining rooms, shops, and other services onboard. The most economical berth accommodations are in four-berth cabins, which are relatively spacious and comfortable and are equipped with bathrooms.

A one-way fare from Piraeus to Heraklion or Chania without accommodations costs about €38, and from about €55 with accommodations. A small discount is given for round-trip tickets. Car fares are about €80 each way, depending on vehicle size. In July and August, a boat service around the Samaria gorge operates along the southwest coast from Hora Sfakion to Loutro, Ayia Roumeli, Souyia, Lissos, and Paleochora, the main resort on the southwest coast. Ferries also sail from Paleochora to Gavdos, the most southerly island in Europe, and from Ierapetra to Krissi, an island also to the south. Most travel agencies sell tickets for all ferries and hydrofoils. Make reservations several days in advance during the July to August high season.

Ferry routes change often, but among the lines that serve Crete are Anek (Piraeus to Heraklion and Chania), Blue

Star Ferries (Piraeus to Heraklion), Cretan Lines (Piraeus to Heraklion), Hellenic Seaways (Heraklion to Santorini, Paros, and Mykonos), and Minoan Lines (Piraeus to Heraklion). Ferry schedules are best checked at ⊕ *www.ferries.gr.*

CONTACTS Anek Lines. ✉ *Akti Konili 24, Piraeus* ☎ *21041/97470* ⊕ *www.anek.gr.*

BUS

You can find schedules and book seats in advance at bus stations, and tourist offices are also well equipped with information about service. As efficient as the bus network is, you might have a hard time getting out of Heraklion, with its confusing number of stations. You'll find the bus station for western Crete, Bus Station A, opposite the port; this also serves places on the north coast east of Heraklion, such as Hersonissos, Archanes, Sitia, Ayios Nikolaos, and the Lasithi Plateau. The station for the south, Bus Station B, is outside the Chania Gate to the right of the Archaeological Museum; this is where you get buses for such places as Matala and Phaistos. Ask someone at the tourist information office to tell you exactly where to find your bus and to show you the spot on a map. You'll need to make reservations in advance for all buses. Alternatively, travel agents offer private bus transfers to the popular sights *(see Tour Options).*

CAR

Roads on Crete are not too congested, yet the accident rate is high compared to other parts of Europe. Driving in the main towns can be nerve-racking, to say the least. Most road signs are in Greek and English, though signage is often inadequate. The Greek National Road 90 runs along the north coast from Kissamos in the west to Sitia in the east. It is mostly dual-carriageway, fast and well maintained. Gas stations are not plentiful outside the big towns, and gasoline is more expensive in Crete than it is in the United States and on par with prices elsewhere in Europe—expect to pay about €1.55 a liter (about $6.45 a gallon).

Drive defensively wherever you are, as Cretan drivers are aggressive and liable to ignore the rules of the road. Sheep and goats frequently stray onto the roads, with or without their shepherd or sheepdog. In July and August, tourists on motor scooters can be a hazard. Night driving is not advisable.

As for car rentals, you can arrange beforehand with a major agency in the United States or in Athens to pick up a car on arrival in Crete, or work through one of the many local car-rental agencies that have offices in the airports and in the cities, as well as in some resort villages. For the most part, these local agencies are extremely reliable, provide courteous service, and charge very low rates. Many, such as the excellent Kappa Car Rental, will meet your ship or plane, or come to your hotel,and drop you off again at no extra charge.

Even without advance reservations, expect to pay about €40 or less a day in high season for a medium-size car with unlimited mileage. Weekly prices are negotiable, but with unlimited mileage rentals start at about €200 in summer. At many agencies, you are responsible for a €500 deductible for any damage, regardless of your insurance coverage.

Big international agencies, including Avis, Hertz, and Sixt, are well represented on Crete *(see Car in Travel Smart for contact information).*

CONTACTS Kappa Car Rental. ✉ *Chania Airport, Chania* ☎ *28210/60120* ⊕ *www. auto-kappa.gr.*

Hotels

Some of Greece's finest resorts line the shores of Elounda Peninsula, offering sumptuous surroundings and exquisite service. Although the atmosphere at these resorts is more international than Greek, in other places you'll find authentic surroundings in the Venetian palaces and old mansions that are being sensitively restored as small hotels. Many of the better hotels on Crete offer special rates and packages through their websites, and it's always worthwhile to check out what discounts might be available during your stay—special rates often bring even a luxurious hotel into affordable range, especially outside high season. For a more rustic yet authentic experience on Crete, opt for simple, whitewashed, tile-floor rooms with rustic pine furniture in the ubiquitous "room to rent" establishments in mountain and seaside villages.

Restaurants

The Cretan diet has been the subject of much speculation recently. The reliance on fresh fruit and vegetables produced through the longest growing season in Europe, together with dairy, pulses, and mountain herbs, augmented by small amounts of fish and meat, all cooked in olive oil, has led to some of the healthiest, longest-living people on the planet. Organic is a way of life here, rather than a buzzword. Cretans are justifiably proud of their food, and you will eat well.

Of course, all the Greek classics are present, but it is worth looking out for Cretan specialties that reflect the diverse heritage of the island. *Dakos* is a staple—twice-baked barley bread topped with tomatoes, crumbled *mizithra* (a creamy soft white cheese), drizzled with olive oil, and sprinkled with oregano. Pies are ubiquitous; *boureki,* with zucchini and potato, is the classic, but fennel, greens, and *sfakianes pitas,* with cheese and honey, are always popular. The olive oil is renowned for its quality and is liberally applied. Consider taking some back home—it makes a great reminder of your journey.

Meat and fish are often simply grilled, with lamb and goat served as a stew such as *tsigariasto,* a western Crete speciality slow-cooked in olive oil. A common way to eat is to sample the *mezedes* offered—small plates to share. Like a Greek version of tapas, it is a great way to sample the island's differing delicacies. Lunch is a fairly flexible concept; often taken between 1 and 4. Similarly, dinner is a movable feast that often starts at 10:30; indeed, as the tourists are finishing their meals, locals are just preparing to go out.

Cretan wine has made great inroads recently, and the quality is ever increasing. Boutique wineries are flourishing, offering neglected indigenous varieties. The house wine, confusingly sold by the kilo, is often not a bad option; the whites tend to be more palatable. The island's main alcoholic staple, however, is *tsikouthia,* commonly known as *raki.* This local firewater is an accompaniment to every occasion from breakfast to weddings. As a gesture of hospitality, restaurants will often offer a small flask, along with a sweet or fruit, at the end of a meal.

Restaurant and hotel reviews have been shortened. For full information, visit Fodors.com.

What it Costs in euros			
$	$$	$$$	$$$$
RESTAURANTS			
under €15	€15–€25	€26–€40	over €40
HOTELS			
under €125	€125–€225	€226–€275	over €275

Tour Options

Most travel agents can arrange for personal guides.

BUS TOURS

Resort hotels and large agents organize guided tours in air-conditioned buses to the main Minoan sites; excursions to spectacular beaches such as Vai in the northeast and Elafonisi and Balos in the west; and trips to Santorini and to closer islands such as Spinalonga, a former leper colony off Ayios Nikolaos.

Crete Travel

GUIDED TOURS | Crete Travel is an excellent source for tour information, with insights into many of the island's attractions and tours, including hiking expeditions, gastronomic excursions, wine tastings, and visits to out-of-the-way monasteries, as well as the more obvious sights. Tailor-made itineraries are a specialty; if you ever wanted to make cheese in a shepherd's hut up a mountain or dreamed of skippering your own yacht, this is the place to come. ✉ Kallipoleos 11, Heraklion ☎ 28102/13445 ⊕ www. cretetravel.com.

HIKING TOURS

Crete is excellent hiking terrain, and many trails crisscross the mountains and gorges, especially in the southwest. The Greek National Tourism Organization (GNTO or EOT) is a source of information.

Alpine Travel

WALKING TOURS | This outfitter offers one-day, one-week, and two-week hiking tours throughout Crete and other islands, and arranges transportation and accommodations for individual trekkers as well. Sea kayaking and family activity holidays are also available. ✉ Chania ☎ 28210/50939 ⊕ www.alpine.gr.

Visitor Information

There are offices of the Greek National Tourism Organization (GNTO or EOT) in Ayios Nikolaos, Chania, Heraklion, and Rethymnon and they provide a wealth of information on the towns and surrounding areas.

Heraklion Ηράκλειο

175 km (109 miles) south of Piraeus harbor in Athens, 69 km (43 miles) west of Ayios Nikolaos, 78 km (49 miles) east of Rethymnon.

In Minoan times, Crete's largest city, the fifth-largest city in Greece, was a harbor for Knossos, the grandest palace and effective power center of prehistoric Crete. The Bronze Age remains were built over long ago, and now Heraklion (also known as Iraklion), with more than 150,000 inhabitants, stretches far beyond even the Venetian walls. Heraklion is not immediately appealing: it's a sprawling and untidy collection of apartment blocks and busy roadways, often cast as the ugly sister to Chania's Cinderella. Many travelers looking for Crete's more rugged pleasures bypass the island's capital altogether, but the city's renowned Archaeological Museum and the nearby Palace of Knossos make Heraklion a mandatory stop for anyone even remotely interested in ancient civilizations.

Besides, at closer look, Heraklion is not without its charms. A walk down Daidalou and the other pedestrians-only streets provides plenty of amusements, and the city has more than its share of outdoor cafés where you can sit and watch life unfold. Seaside promenades and narrow lanes that run off them can be quite animated, thanks to ongoing restoration, and the inner harbor dominated by the Koules, a sturdy Venetian fortress, is richly evocative of the island's storied past.

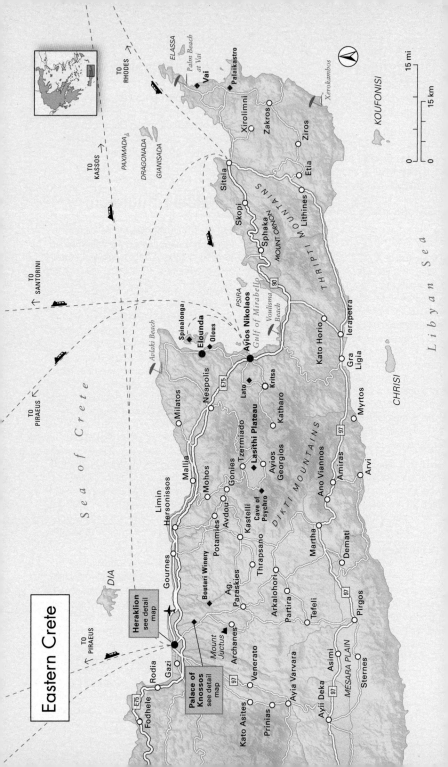

GETTING HERE AND AROUND

Heraklion is Crete's major air hub, and Kazantzakis Airport has been greatly expanded in recent years. Flights on Olympic Air and Aegean Airlines arrive almost hourly from Athens, and many flights from other European cities use the airport. The airport is only about 5 km (3 miles) east of the city.

Frequent ferries connect Heraklion to Piraeus (at least five daily, including daytime ferries from May through August), and the Cyclades (Santorini, Mykonos, and others). Operators and schedules change frequently; for the latest information, check on your route at ⊕ www.ferries.gr, or stop by one of the travel agencies that operate near all Greek ports.

Heraklion is Crete's hub for bus travel, and you can get just about anywhere on the island from any of the city's bus terminals. Service to the main towns—Ayios Nikolaos, Rethymnon, and Chania—runs hourly. Buses to all these towns arrive at and leave from the two adjacent terminals on the harbor, just east of the city center. City buses within Heraklion are blue, inter-city buses are green.

⊙ Sights

If you have just a day in Heraklion, your time will be tight. Get an early start and head for the Archaeological Museum before the crowds descend. Then, spend a couple of hours in the morning walking around the city, stepping into the churches if they're open and poking around the lively market. Nearby Knossos will easily occupy most of the afternoon. If you're staying overnight in or near Heraklion, take an evening stroll in the busy area around Ta Leontaria and Kornarou Square; half the population seems to converge here.

Heraklion's ever-improving road network is making it easier to avoid the all but impassable city center; however, if you're spending any time at all in Heraklion, it's best to wait until you are leaving the city to pick up a rental car.

Ayia Aikaterina

RELIGIOUS SITE | Nestled in the shadow of the Ayios Minas cathedral is one of Crete's most attractive small churches, named for St. Katherine and built in 1555. The church now houses a museum of icons by Cretan artists, who often traveled to Venice to study with Italian Renaissance painters. Look for six icons by Michael Damaskinos, who worked in both Byzantine and Renaissance styles during the 16th century. Crete's most famous artist, Domenikos Theotocopoulos, better known as El Greco, studied at the monastery school attached to the church in the mid-16th century. ⊠ Kyrillou Loukareos ☎ 28103/36316 ⊕ www.iakm.gr.

Ayios Markos

ARTS VENUE | This 13th-century church is named for Venice's patron saint, but, with its modern portico and narrow interior, it bears little resemblance to its grand namesake in Venice. Concerts and recitals are often staged in the afternoons. ⊠ Platia Eleftheriou Venizelou ⊗ Closed Sun.

Ayios Minas

RELIGIOUS SITE | This huge, lofty cathedral, dating from 1895, can hold up to 8,000 worshippers, but is most lively on November 11, when Heraklion celebrates the feast of Minas, a 4th-century Roman-soldier-turned-Christian. Legend has it that on Easter Sunday 1826 a ghostly Minas reappeared on horseback and dispersed a Turkish mob ready to slay the city's Orthodox faithful.

Notably, few of Heraklion's inhabitants are named after Minas, which is unusual for a city's patron saint. The reason is that many years ago babies born out of wedlock were left on the steps of the church, and were named Minas by the clergy, who took these children in and cared for them. Thus, the name Minas came to be associated with illegitimacy. ⊠ Kyrillou Loukareos.

The Koules harbor fortress is a mighty reminder of the age when Venetians ruled Crete from their outpost in Heraklion.

Ayios Titos

RELIGIOUS SITE | A chapel to the left of the entrance contains St. Tito's skull, set in a silver-and-gilt reliquary. Titus is credited with converting the islanders to Christianity in the 1st century AD on the instructions of St. Paul. Ayios Titos was founded in the 10th century, rebuilt as a mosque under Turkish rule in the 19th century, and re-dedicated as a church in the 1920s, when the minaret was removed. ⊠ *Set back from Avgoustou 25.*

★ Heraklion Archaeological Museum

MUSEUM | Standing in a class of its own, this museum guards practically all of the Minoan treasures uncovered in the legendary excavations of the Palace of Knossos as well as other monuments of Minoan civilization. These amazing artifacts, many 3,000 years old, were brought to light in 20th-century excavations by famed British archaeologist Sir Arthur Evans and are shown off in handsome modern galleries. It's best to visit the museum first thing in the morning, before the tour buses arrive, or in late afternoon, once they pull away. Top treasures include the famous seal stones, many inscribed with Linear B script, discovered and deciphered by Evans around the turn of the 20th century. The most stunning and mysterious seal stone is the so-called Phaistos Disk, found at Phaistos Palace in the south, its purpose unknown. (Linear B script is now recognized as an early form of Greek, but the earlier Linear A script that appears on clay tablets and that of the Phaistos Disk have yet to be deciphered.)

Perhaps the most arresting exhibits, though, are the sophisticated frescoes, restored fragments of which were found in Knossos. They depict broad-shouldered, slim-waisted youths, their large eyes fixed with an enigmatic expression on the Prince of the Lilies; ritual processions and scenes from the bullring, with young men and women somersaulting over the back of a charging bull; and groups of court ladies, whose flounced skirts led a French archaeologist to exclaim in surprise, "*Des Parisiennes!*," a name still applied to this striking fresco.

Even before great palaces with frescoes were being built, around 1900 BC, the prehistoric Cretans excelled at metalworking and carving stone vases, and they were also skilled at producing pottery, such as the eggshell-thin Kamares ware decorated in delicate abstract designs. Other specialties were miniature work such as the superbly crafted jewelry and the colored seal stones that are carved with lively scenes of people and animals. Though naturalism and an air of informality distinguish much Minoan art from that of contemporary Bronze Age cultures elsewhere in the eastern Mediterranean, you can also see a number of heavy rococo set pieces, such as the fruit stand with a toothed rim and the punch bowl with appliquéd flowers.

The Minoans' talents at modeling in stone, ivory, and a kind of glass paste known as faience peaked in the later palace period (1700–1450 BC). A famous rhyton, a vessel for pouring libations, carved from dark serpentine in the shape of a bull's head, has eyes made of red jasper and clear rock crystal with horns of gilded wood. An ivory acrobat—perhaps a bull-leaper—and two bare-breasted faience goddesses in flounced skirts holding wriggling snakes were among a group of treasures hidden beneath the floor of a storeroom at Knossos. Bull-leaping, whether a religious rite or a favorite sport, inspired some of the most memorable images in Minoan art. Note, also, the three vases, probably originally covered in gold leaf, from Ayia Triada that are carved with scenes of Minoan life thought to be rendered by artists from Knossos: boxing contests, a harvest-home ceremony, and a Minoan official taking delivery of a consignment of hides. The most stunning rhyton of all, from Zakros, is made of rock crystal. ⊠ *Xanthoudidou and Hatzidaki* ☎ *28102/79000* ⊕ *www.heraklionmuseum.gr* ⊠ *€12; combined ticket for museum and Palace of Knossos €16.*

★ **Historical Museum of Crete**

MUSEUM | An imposing mansion houses a varied collection of Early Christian and Byzantine sculptures, Venetian and Ottoman stonework, artifacts of war, and rustic folklife items. The museum provides a wonderful introduction to Cretan culture, and is the only place in Crete to display the work of famed native son El Greco (Domenikos Theotocopoulos), who left the island—then part of the Venetian Republic—for Italy and then Spain around 1567. His *Baptism of Christ* and *View of Mount Sinai and the Monastery of St. Catherine* hang amid frescoes, icons, and other Byzantine pieces. Upon entering, look out for the *Lion of St. Mark* sculpture, with an inscription that says in Latin "I protect the kingdom of Crete." Left of the entrance is a room stuffed with memorabilia from Crete's bloody revolutionary past: weapons, portraits of mustachioed warrior chieftains, and the flag of the short-lived independent Cretan state set up in 1898. The 19th-century banner in front of the staircase sums up the spirit of Cretan rebellion against the Turks: *eleftheria o thanatos* ("Freedom or Death"). A small section is dedicated to World War II and the German invasion of 1941. Upstairs, look in on a room arranged as the study of Crete's most famous writer, Nikos Kazantzakis (1883–1957), the author of *Zorba the Greek* and an epic poem, *The Odyssey, a Modern Sequel*; he was born in Heraklion and is buried here, just inside the section of the walls known as the Martinengo. The top floor contains a stunning collection of Cretan textiles, including the brilliant scarlet weavings typical of the island's traditional handwork, and another room arranged as a domestic interior of the early 1900s. ⊠ *Sofokli Venizelou 27* ☎ *28102/83219* ⊕ *www.historical-museum.gr* ⊠ *€5.*

Koules

MILITARY SITE | Heraklion's inner harbor, where fishing boats land their catch and yachts are moored, is dominated by this massive fortress so named by the Turks but, in fact, built by the Venetians as the

Castello del Molo in the 16th century and decorated with the three stone lions of St. Mark, the symbol of Venetian imperialism. On the east side of the fortress are the vaulted arsenal; here Venetian galleys were repaired and refitted, and timber, cheeses, and sweet malmsey wine were loaded for the three-week voyage to Venice. The view from the battlements takes in the inner as well as the outer harbor, where freighters and passenger ferries drop anchor; to the south rises Mt. Louktas and, to the west, the pointed peak of Mt. Stromboulas. ⊠ *Inner harbor* ☏ *28102/43559* ⊕ *koules. efah.gr* 🎫 *€4* ⊘ *Closed Tues.*

Loggia

BUILDING | A gathering place for the island's Venetian nobility, this open-air arcade, with a meeting hall above, was built in the early 17th century by Francesco Basilicata, an Italian architect. Restored to its original Palladian elegance, it adjoins the old Venetian Armory, now the City Hall. ⊠ *Avgoustou 25* ⊕ *www.heraklion.gr.*

Martinengo Bastion

HISTORIC SITE | Six bastions shaped like arrowheads jut out from the well-preserved Venetian walls. Martinengo is the largest, designed by Micheli Sanmicheli in the 16th century to keep out Barbary pirates and Turkish invaders. When the Turks overran Crete in 1648, the garrison at Heraklion held out for another 21 years in one of the longest sieges in European history. General Francesco Morosini finally surrendered the city to the Turkish Grand Vizier in September 1669. He was allowed to sail home to Venice with the city's archives and such precious relics as the skull of Ayios Titos—which was not returned until 1966. Literary pilgrims come to the Martinengo to visit the **burial place of writer Nikos Kazantzakis.** The grave is a plain stone slab marked by a weathered wooden cross. The inscription, from his writings, reads: "I fear nothing, I hope for nothing, I am free." ⊠ *Heraklion* ✛ *In walls south of city center, off Plastira.*

Monastery of St. Peter and St. Paul

RELIGIOUS SITE | One of Heraklion's oldest monuments, dating from the 13th century, has been been rebuilt many times over the years and has done duty as a church, monastery, mosque, and movie theater. St. Peter's is now an exhibition hall and its 15th-century frescoes, the oldest in the city, have been beautifully restored. ⊠ *Heraklion* ✛ *West of harbor along seashore road.*

Natural History Museum of Crete

MUSEUM | FAMILY | Housed in a former electricity plant, this provides a nice trip out for the whole family. Focusing on the wildlife of Crete and the wider Mediterranean, it is presented in a fun and informative manner. Four levels cover pre-history, with huge animated dinosaurs, through to modern day, with live reptiles and small mammals in glass tanks. The basement area contains a special interactive area for kids where they can discover nature hands-on, and a seismic table that recreates earthquakes from the past. ⊠ *Leof. Sofokli Venizelou* ☏ *28102/82740* ⊕ *www.nhmc.uoc.gr* 🎫 *€7.50.*

Plateia Eleftherias

PLAZA | The city's biggest square is paved in marble and dotted with fountains. The Archaeological Museum is off the north end of the square; at the west side is the beginning of Daidalou, the main thoroughfare, which follows the line of an early fortification wall and is now a pedestrian walkway lined with tavernas, boutiques, jewelers, and souvenir shops. ⊠ *Heraklion* ✛ *Southeast end of Daidalou.*

Ta Liontaria

FOUNTAIN | "The Lions," a stately marble Renaissance fountain, remains a beloved town landmark. It's the heart of Heraklion's town center—on Eleftheriou Venizelou Square, a triangular pedestrian zone filled with cafés and named after

Beaches in Crete

With hundreds of miles of dramatic coastline, Crete has an almost endless supply of beaches. Many are soft and powdery, some are action-packed with water sports, and others are blissfully untrammeled. The most celebrated bookend the island: palm-shaded Vai to the east and Elafonisi to the west.

Lovers of sand and surf quickly discover that there are really two distinct types of beaches on Crete: the highly developed strands on the north coast and the rugged getaway beaches on the south coast. Northern beaches stretch along the flat, sandy coastal plain between the island's major cities and are easily reached by the east–west national highway, as well as by an extensive bus network. Most are packed with umbrellas and sun beds and backed by hotels.

Beaches on the south coast are tucked into coves and bays, often at the end of poor roads; a rental car and a good map are essential to explore them. Strike it lucky and you will see barely a soul, even in peak season.

the Cretan statesman who united the island with Greece in 1913. The square is also known simply as Ta Liontaria or Plateia Liontarion and was the center of the colony founded in the 13th century, when Venice colonized Crete, and Heraklion became an important port of call on the trade routes to the Middle East. ✉ *Dedalou and 25 Augousto.*

🍴 Restaurants

Erganos

$ | **GREEK** | One of Heraklion's most traditional restaurants, just by Kazantzaki park, serves authentic local fare, mainly to a local crowd, far removed from the tourist havens in the center. Mouthwatering bite-sized *sfakianopita* (pies), filled with cheese and honey, are a classic true taste of Crete, and the lamb and goat are always popular, as are tremendous *keftedes* (meatballs). **Known for:** traditional Cretan cuisine; outdoor terrace for summer evenings; hospitable staff. [$] *Average main: €12* ✉ *G. Georgiadou 5* ☎ *28102/85629.*

Ippokambos

$$ | **SEAFOOD** | In a modern wood-and-glass conservatory overlooking the Koules, this Heraklion institution serves some of the best fish in town, with the waves only a stone's throw away. Ask a local for a recommendation and they will invariably mention Ippokambos. **Known for:** the freshest local fish and seafood; generous portions; seafront setting. [$] *Average main: €15* ✉ *Sofokli Venizelou 3* ☎ *28102/80240.*

★ Peskesi

$ | **MODERN GREEK** | In a restored sea captain's mansion, stone walls and arches provide the backdrop to some of the best food in Crete: traditional cuisine brought to life with modern techniques and presentation. A 60-acre farm in Harasso is dedicated to supplying the restaurant with seasonal local produce, much of it organic, and the flavors really shine through. **Known for:** atmospheric location; truly knowledgeable and interested staff; delightful purely Cretan wines. [$] *Average main: €14* ✉ *Kapetan Haralabi 6-8* ☎ *28102/88887* 🌐 *www.peskesicrete.gr.*

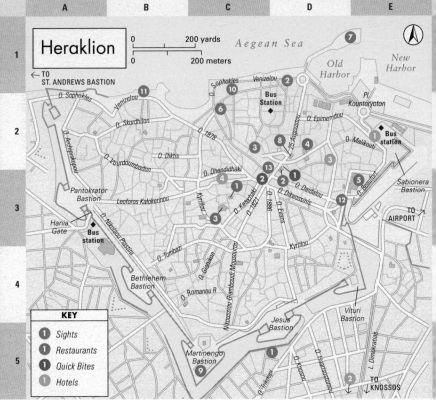

Heraklion

0 — 200 yards
0 — 200 meters

Aegean Sea

Old Harbor

New Harbor

St. Andrews Bastion

TO ST. ANDREWS BASTION

Pl. Kountoryoton

Bus Station

Bus station

Bus station

Sabionera Bastion

TO AIRPORT

Pantokrator Bastion

Hania Gate

Bethlehem Bastion

Vituri Bastion

Jesus Bastion

Martinengo Bastion

TO KNOSSOS

O. Sophokles
Venizelou
O. Skordhilon
O. Archineskopou
O. Vourdoumbadon
O. Diktis
O. 1878
O. Dhendidhaki
Leoforos Kalokerinou
O. Nikolaou Plastira
O. Tombazi
O. Giabhidaki
O. Romanou R
Nikoussiou Giambouti Moussourou
O. Katehaki
Kyrillou
O. 1821
O. 1886
O. Evans
Kyrillou
O. Daidalou
O. Dikeossinis
Sophokles
Venizelou
O. Hagussou
25 Avgoustou
O. Epimenidou
O. Malikouti
O. Beaufort
O. Irkeopi
O. Knosou
O. Hariloonnou
L. Dimikratias

KEY
- **1** Sights
- **1** Restaurants
- **1** Quick Bites
- **1** Hotels

Sights ▼
1 Ayia Aikaterina...........**C3**
2 Ayios Markos **D3**
3 Ayios Minas.............**C3**
4 Ayios Titos...............**D2**
5 Heraklion Archaeological Museum **E3**
6 Historical Museum of Crete **C2**
7 Koules...................**D1**
8 Loggia....................**D2**
9 Martinengo Bastion **C5**
10 Monastery of St. Peter and St. Paul..............**C1**
11 Natural History Museum of Crete **B1**
12 Plateia Eleftherias **D3**
13 Ta Liontaria **C2**

Restaurants ▼
1 Erganos **D5**
2 Ippokambos **D1**
3 Peskesi...................**C2**

Quick Bites ▼
1 Crumb **D2**
2 KirKor 1922 ....**C3**

Hotels ▼
1 GDM Megaron **E2**
2 Kalimera Archanes Village.....................**E5**
3 Olive Green Hotel.......**D2**
4 Veneziano Boutique Hotel.......................**C3**

Coffee and Quick Bites

Crumb

$ | **CAFÉ** | Handily placed for mid-shopping treats, Crumb serves not only great coffee but also the best healthy options in Heraklion. The shaded outside tables are an ideal place to reflect and recharge before returning to the fray. **Known for:** healthy cooking—great for vegans and vegetarians; lactose-free, gluten-free, sugar-free all available; South American coffee is some of the best in town. [$] *Average main: €5* ✉ *Kallergon square 11* ☎ *28102/28877.*

KirKor 1922

$ | **CAFÉ** | Stop into this venerable old *bougatsa* shop for an envelope of flaky pastry that's either filled with a sweet, creamy filling and dusted with cinnamon and sugar, or stuffed with soft white cheese. A portion of each, served warm with Greek coffee, is a nice treat. **Known for:** Greek pastries; Cretan-style yogurt; open early. [$] *Average main: €3* ✉ *Platia Liontarion* ☎ *28102/42705* 💳 *No credit cards.*

Hotels

GDM Megaron

$$ | **HOTEL** | A handsome building, GDM Megaron stands sentinel over the harbor front, and from its humble roots as a citrus processing enterprise in the 1930s, it has risen to be the city's luxury choice; interiors are classic and elegantly furnished, with an impressive lobby and refined air. **Pros:** central seafront location overlooking Koules; most rooms have water views; scenic rooftop restaurant. **Cons:** formal surroundings can feel a little hushed at times; rear rooms overlook the city; some noise from the nearby bus depot. [$] *Rooms from: €130* ✉ *D. Beaufort 9* ☎ *28103/05300* 🌐 *www.gdmmegaron.gr* 🔑 *58 rooms* 🍴 *Free breakfast.*

★ **Kalimera Archanes Village**

$$ | **B&B/INN** | An especially appealing base for exploring Knossos and Heraklion is the well-kept wine village of Archanes, where three 19th-century stone houses tucked into a garden are fitted out with traditional furnishings and all the modern comforts. **Pros:** highly atmospheric and very comfortable; near many sights but provides a nice dose of Greek village life; beautiful interiors and outdoor spaces. **Cons:** beaches and Heraklion are a 20-minute drive away; a pool would be the icing on the cake; own transport needed. [$] *Rooms from: €200* ✉ *Theotokopoulou, Tsikritsi, Archanes* ✣ *Off Leof. Kapetanaki, left after Likastos Taverna* ☎ *28107/52999* 🌐 *www.archanes-village.com* 🔑 *4 houses* 🍴 *Free breakfast.*

Olive Green Hotel

$ | **HOTEL** | Since opening in 2016, this city-center hotel has been shaking up the local hotel landscape with its supermodern design and facilities, allied to an eco-friendly approach. **Pros:** overlooks a tree-lined square; clean, neutral, tasteful design; supercentral location minutes from the seafront and main attractions. **Cons:** iPad control of room functions won't suit all guests; parking is a short walk around the corner and not free; strange bathroom configurations in some rooms. [$] *Rooms from: €105* ✉ *Idomeneos 22* ☎ *28103/02900* 🌐 *www.olivegreenhotel.com* 🔑 *48 rooms* 🍴 *Free breakfast.*

Veneziano Boutique Hotel

$ | **HOTEL** | A landmark building in Heraklion, with both Venetian and Ottoman heritage dating back to 1510, has been given a careful renovation, resulting in one of the city's most stylish and chic accommodations. **Pros:** beautiful, elegant building handsomely restored; a two-minute walk from the heart of town; quiet backstreet location. **Cons:** steep flight of stairs to upstairs rooms; no on-site parking; surrounding streets are a little scruffy. [$] *Rooms from: €95* ✉ *1770 and*

Sights

1 Central Court B3
2 East Bastion...... D3
3 Grand Staircase ... C3
4 North entrance.... B2
5 Queen's megaron C4
6 Royal road A2
7 South Gateway B4
8 Theatrical area A1
9 The Throne Room........ B3
10 West wing......... A3
11 Workshops........ C3

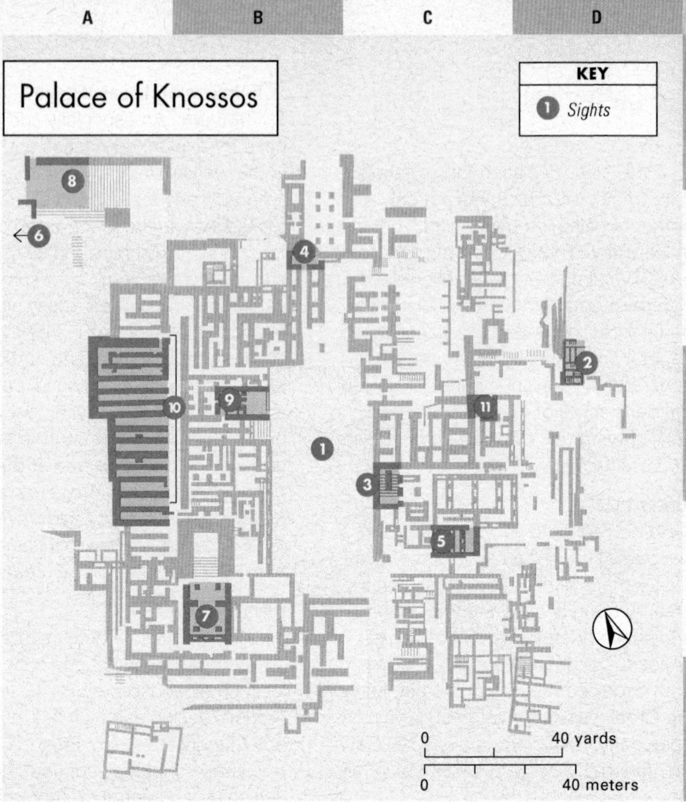

N. Kazantaki ☎ *28103/44758* ⊕ *www.veneziano.gr* *6 rooms* *Free breakfast.*

Knossos Κνωσού

5 km (3 miles) south of Heraklion.

Paintings of bull-leapers, sculptures of bare-breasted snake charmers, myths of minotaurs, and the oldest throne in Europe are just a few of the wonders that the British archaeologist Sir Arthur Evans brought up from the earth at Knossos at the close of the 19th century, to the astonishment of newspapers around the world. They provided telling evidence of the great elegance of King Minos's court (Evans chose the king's name to christen this culture), as the evocative ruins continue to do today.

GETTING HERE

Municipal bus No. 2 (€1.70) heads to the fabled Palace of Knossos every 20 minutes or so from Heraklion, where the main stops include Plateia Eleftherias.

Sights

Boutari Winery

WINERY/DISTILLERY | Established by one of the oldest wine-making families in Greece, this state-of-the-art winery marries tradition with innovation, producing more than 100,000 bottles a year. There is a modern tasting room with great views over the vines to the hills beyond, for sampling some of the estate's award-winning offerings. You can buy the wines you have tasted, along with other local delicacies. ✉ *Skalani, Heraklion* ☎ *28107/31617* ⊕ *www.boutari.gr* *€5.*

★ Palace of Knossos

ARCHAEOLOGICAL SITE | This most amazing of archaeological sites once lay hidden beneath a huge mound hemmed in by low hills. Heinrich Schliemann, father of archaeology and discoverer of Troy, knew it was here, but Turkish obstruction prevented him from exploring his last discovery. Cretan independence from the Ottoman Turks made it possible for Sir Arthur Evans, a British archaeologist, to start excavations in 1899. A forgotten and sublime civilization thus came again to light with the uncovering of the great Palace of Knossos.

The magnificent Minoans flourished on Crete from around 2700 to 1450 BC, and their palaces and cities at Knossos, Phaistos, and Gournia were centers of political power and luxury—they traded in tin, saffron, gold, and spices as far afield as Spain—when the rest of Europe was a place of primitive barbarity. They loved art, farmed bees, and worshipped many goddesses. But what caused their demise? Some say political upheaval, but others point to an eruption on Thira (Santorini), about 100 km (62 miles) north in the Aegean, that caused tsunamis and earthquakes and supposedly brought about the end of this sophisticated civilization.

The Palace of Knossos site was occupied from Neolithic times, and the population spread to the surrounding land. Around 1900 BC, the hilltop was leveled and the first palace constructed; around 1700 BC, after an earthquake destroyed the original structure, the later palace was built, surrounded by houses and other buildings. Around 1450 BC, another widespread disaster occurred, perhaps an invasion: palaces and country villas were razed by fire and abandoned, but Knossos remained inhabited even though the palace suffered some damage. But around 1380 BC the palace and its outlying buildings were destroyed by fire, and around 1100 BC the site was abandoned. Still later, Knossos became a Greek city-state.

You enter the palace from the west, passing a bust of Sir Arthur Evans, who excavated at Knossos on and off for more than 20 years. A path leads you around to the monumental **south gateway.** The **west wing** encases lines of long, narrow storerooms where the true wealth of Knossos was kept in tall clay jars: oil, wine, grains, and honey. The **central court** is about 164 feet by 82 feet long. The cool, dark **throne-room complex** has a griffin fresco and a tall, wavy-back gypsum throne, the oldest in Europe. The most spectacular piece of palace architecture is the **grand staircase,** on the east side of the court, leading to the domestic apartments. Four flights of shallow gypsum stairs survive, lighted by a deep light well. Here you get a sense of how noble Minoans lived; rooms were divided by sets of double doors, giving privacy and warmth when closed, coolness and communication when open. The **queen's megaron** (apartment or hall) is decorated with a colorful dolphin fresco and furnished with stone benches. Beside it is a bathroom, complete with a clay tub, and next door a toilet, with a drainage system that permitted flushing into a channel flowing into the Kairatos stream far below. The east side of the palace also contained **workshops.** Beside the staircase leading down to the **east bastion** is a stone water channel made up of parabolic curves and settling basins: a Minoan storm drain. Northwest of the east bastion is the **north entrance,** guarded by a relief fresco of a charging bull. Beyond is the **theatrical area,** shaded by pines and overlooking a shallow flight of steps, which lead down to the **royal road.** This, perhaps, was the ceremonial entrance to the palace.

For a complete education in Minoan architecture and civilization, consider touring Knossos and, of course, the Archaeological Museum in Heraklion (where many of the treasures from the palace are on view), then traveling south to the Palace of Phaistos, another great Minoan site that has not been reconstructed.

Although some critics claim that Sir Arthur Evans's restoration "Disneyfied" the Palace of Knossos, no one can deny the results are spectacular.

■ **TIP**→ **After a long day at the archaeological sites you may feel like you've earned a drink. Follow the signposts to one of the numerous vineyards that surround the pretty village of Archanes, 9 km (5½ miles) south of Knossos, and enjoy tasting some of the world's oldest wines.** ⊠ *Knossos* ☎ *28102/31940* ⊕ *odysseus.culture.gr* 🎫 *€15; combined ticket with Archaeological Museum in Heraklion €16.*

Lasithi Plateau
Οροπέδιο Λασιθίου

47 km (29 miles) southeast of the Palace of Knossos, 52 km (32 miles) southeast of Heraklion.

The Lasithi Plateau, 2,800 feet high and the biggest of the upland plains of Crete, lies behind a wall of barren mountains. Windmills for pumping water rise above fields of potatoes and the apple and almond orchards that are a pale haze of blossom in early spring. The plateau is remote and breathtakingly beautiful, and ringed by small villages where shops sell local weaving and embroidery.

Sights

Cave of Psychro

ARCHAEOLOGICAL SITE | This impressive, stalactite-rich cavern is one of a few places in Crete that claim to be the birthplace of Zeus, king of the gods, and where he was reared in secret, out of reach of his vengeful father, Kronos. Approach the cave, once a Minoan sanctuary and now the plateau's most popular tourist attraction, on a steep path from the large parking lot on foot. ⊠ *Lasithi* ⊕ *Near village of Psychro* ☎ *28410/22462* 🎫 *€6.*

Cretan Traditional Folklore Museum

MUSEUM | An old village house in Ayios Georgios stands as it was when generations of farmers lived here. The living quarters and stables, along with the delightful assemblage of simple furnishings, embroidery, and tools, provide a chance to see domestic life as it was, and indeed still is, for many residents of the plateau. Next door is a small exhibition devoted to the politician and statesman El Venizelos, a Crete native. ✉ *Ayios Georgios* ☎ *28440/31382* 🎫 *€3* 🕒 *Closed late Oct.–mid-Apr.*

🍴 Restaurants

Kronio

$ | **GREEK** | The promise of a meal in this cozy, family-run establishment is alone worth the trip up to the plateau. The taverna is in its fifth decade and still offering delicious pies as well as casseroles and lamb dishes, accompanied by fresh-baked bread and followed up with homemade desserts. **Known for:** authentic Cretan home-cooked dishes served with lots of personality; house wine is very palatable; can get busy with tour parties. [$] *Average main: €10* ✉ *Tzermiado* ✥ *Center of the village on the Neapolis–Hersonissos road* ☎ *28440/22375* 🌐 *www.kronio.eu* 🕒 *Closed Nov.–Mar.*

Ayios Nikolaos
Άγιος Νικόλαος

30 km (19 miles) east of the Lasithi Plateau, 69 km (43 miles) east of Heraklion.

Ayios Nikolaos is clustered on a peninsula alongside the Gulf of Mirabello, a dramatic composition of bare mountains, islets, and deep blue sea. Behind the crowded harbor lies the picturesque Lake Voulismeni, linked to the sea by a narrow channel. Hilly, with narrow, steep streets that provide sea views, the town is a welcoming and animated place, far more pleasant than Malia and the other resort centers in this part of Crete: you can stroll along waterside promenades, cafés line the lakeshore, and many streets are open only to pedestrians. Ayios Nikolaos and the nearby Elounda Peninsula provide an excellent base for exploring eastern Crete.

GETTING HERE AND AROUND

By ferry or by air, the best option is from Heraklion, less than an hour away by a bus service that runs at least every hour, and often more frequently during the day. The bus station in Ayios Nikolaos is east of the town center, on Epimenidou, and is a 15-minute walk to the lake. By car or taxi, Ayios Nikolaos is on the national highway and is easily reached from the capital. Parking in the town is difficult, and the easiest recourse is to opt for one of the inexpensive parking lots dotted around the pedestrians-only center.

VISITOR INFORMATION

CONTACTS Ayios Nikolaos Visitor Information. ✉ *Koundourou 21* ✥ *On the lake bridge corner* ☎ *28410/22357* 🌐 *www.agiosnikolaoscrete.com.*

👁 Sights

Folk Museum

MUSEUM | This interesting little museum showcases exquisite weavings and embroidered pieces, along with walking sticks, tools, and other artifacts from everyday rural life in Crete. ✉ *Kondylaki 2* ☎ *28410/25093* 🎫 *Free* 🕒 *Closed Nov.–Apr.*

Kritsa

TOWN | This delightful village on a mountainside above Ayios Nikolaos is renowned for its weaving tradition, narrow lanes wide enough for only a donkey to pass, and whitewashed houses that surround a large, shady town square filled with café tables that afford views down green valleys planted with olive trees to the sea. The woven tablecloths and other wares are hard to miss—villagers drape them over every usable surface and hang them from storefronts and even trees. The lovely Byzantine church here, **Panayia Kera,** has an unusual shape, with three naves supported by heavy triangular buttresses. Built in the early years of Venetian occupation, it contains some of the liveliest and best-preserved medieval frescoes on the island, painted in the 13th century. ✉ *Kritsa* ✥ *11 km (7 miles) west of Ayios Nikolaos* ☎ *28410/51806* 🎫 *€2* ⏲ *Closed Tues.*

Lato

ARCHAEOLOGICAL SITE | This ancient city in the hills just above Ayios Nikolaos was built by the Doric Greeks in a dip between two rocky peaks and named for the mother of Artemis and Apollo and her image appears on coins found at the site. Lato reached its peak in the 3rd century BC, but was gradually abandoned, although its port near latterday Ayios Nikolaos was in use during Roman times. Make your way over the expanse of ancient masonry to the far end of the ongoing excavations for one of the best views in Crete: on a clear day you can see Santorini, 100 km (62 miles) across the Cretan sea, as well as inland across a seemingly endless panorama of mountains and valleys. ✉ *Ayios Nikolaos* ✥ *About 10 km (6 miles) west of Ayios Nikolaos, following marked road from village of Kritsa* ☎ *28410/22462* 🌐 *odysseus.culture.gr* 🎫 *€3* ⏲ *Closed Mon.*

Beaches

You can dip into the clean waters that surround Ayios Nikolaos from several good beaches right in town. Kitroplatia and Ammos are both only about a 5- to 10-minute walk from the center. Almyros, 2 km (1 mile) away, is better and is rightly popular.

Avlaki Beach

BEACH—SIGHT | To the north of Ayios Nikalaos in the Gulf of Malia are a string of beaches clustered around the town of Sisi. A pretty little inlet with a handful of tavernas, it is a classic Greek summer resort with little else to do but swim and eat. Avlaki and Boufos beaches, separated by a cliff, are the pick of the bunch. **Amenities:** food and drink. **Best For**: swimming; snorkeling. ✉ *Malia.*

Voulisma Beach

BEACH—SIGHT | Head down the coast road to Kalo Chorio and you will pass many small inlets and strips of sand. Stop at any that take your fancy or carry on to Voulisma, an organized beach with clear, sparkling water. Often compared to a tropical shoreline, the sea is just as warm and the sand just as white. **Amenities:** food and drink; lifeguards; showers. **Best for:** swimming. ✉ *Ayios Nikolaos.*

Restaurants

Karnagio

$ | **GREEK** | Right on Lake Voulismeni, Karnagio is a riot of multi-colored tables, shouted orders, and running waiters. Proudly Cretan and proud of their local products, the grill is the center of attention here with a wide selection of meat and fish. **Known for:** the best service in town; portions fit for a king; always busy but waiting customers are offered wine. [$] *Average main: €12* ✉ *Konstantin Paleologou 24* ☎ *28410/25968.*

Migomis

$$ | **MEDITERRANEAN** | Clinging to the cliff above the lake, this restaurant offers some of the best views in town. Food is on a par, too: Mediterranean-inspired dishes accompany Greek classics, and the steaks are rightly famous. **Known for:** dramatic and very romantic cliff-top setting; well presented dishes with an Italian flavor; good international wine list. [$] *Average main: €20* ✉ *Nikou Plastira 20* ☎ *28410/24353* 🌐 *www.migomis.com* ⏲ *Closed Nov.–Mar.*

Pelagos

$$ | **SEAFOOD** | An enchanting courtyard garden and the high-ceilinged parlors of an elegant neoclassical mansion are the setting for what many consider to be the best fish tavern in Ayios Nikolaos. Simple is the keyword here: fresh catches from the fleet bobbing in the harbor just beyond are plainly grilled and accompanied by local vegetables and

Cretan wines. **Known for:** simply prepared dishes in a lovely setting; friendly service from English-speaking staff; being busy, be prepared to wait in summer. [$] *Average main: €15* ✉ *Stratigou Koraka 11* ☎ *28410/82019* ⏲ *Closed Nov.–Mar.*

Taverna Stavrakakis

$ | **GREEK** | Enhance the short trip out to Kritsa and Lato with a stop in the nearby village of Exo Lakonia to enjoy a meal at the homey *kafenion* of Manolis and Katerina Stavrakakis. Dishes are based on family recipes, and most are made from ingredients the couple grow themselves. **Known for:** authentic Cretan cooking, not tourist taverna fare; great homemade pies; the friendliest welcome. [$] *Average main: €10* ✉ *Exo Lakonia* ✥ *About 8 km (5 miles) west of Ayios Nikolaos* ☎ *28410/22478.*

Coffee and Quick Bites

Dodoni

$ | **FAST FOOD** | Airy blue-on-blue sofas and chairs look over the lake here, with a menu dreamt up by sweet-lovers. Waffles, pancakes, and toasts are offered but it is really all about the ice cream—up to 45 flavors are offered. **Known for:** lactose-free, sugar-free, and low-fat ice cream available; lakeside location perfect for an afternoon treat; family feel and welcome. [$] *Average main: €6* ✉ *Konsatantinou Palaiologou 14* ☎ *28410/25801.*

Hotels

★ **Daios Cove**

$$$$ | **RESORT** | Crashing onto the scene in 2010, this glamorous resort redefined the luxury concept with a mighty wow factor—spread over the sides of Vathi Bay (with a private sandy beach), every room has breathtaking views, and many have private terraces and pools. **Pros:** even the smallest rooms are twice the size of a regular hotel room; well-trained and friendly staff; design still feels fresh and new. **Cons:** a distance from Ayios Nikolaos and can feel a little isolated; food and drink costs are exceedingly high; seemingly hundreds of steps (but funicular to beach helps). [$] *Rooms from: €540* ✉ *Vathi* ☎ *28418/88061* 🌐 *www.daioscovecrete.com* ⏲ *Closed Nov.–Apr.* 🔑 *290 rooms* 🍴 *Free breakfast.*

Hotel Du Lac

$ | **HOTEL** | Right on the lake in the center of town, this good-value hotel has airy and spacious guest rooms that are nicely done with simple, contemporary furnishings; studios, with kitchens and large baths, are enormous and ideal for families. **Pros:** great lakeside views; good, budget option; Casa Mia apartments under same management are a nice upgrade. **Cons:** large differential in size between rooms and studios—it's worth paying the extra; no breakfast but pretty café below is handy; parking (charge payable) is a short walk away. [$] *Rooms from: €50* ✉ *28is Oktovriou 17* ☎ *28410/22711* 🌐 *www.dulachotel.gr* 🔑 *23 rooms* 🍴 *No meals.*

★ **St. Nicolas Bay**

$$$$ | **RESORT** | Lovely and luxurious, this special resort is set within immaculate, verdant gardens overlooking the Gulf of Mirabello at the edge of Ayios Nikolaos—the surroundings are magical. **Pros:** smart, generous, and indulgent atmosphere; feels intimate but never crowded; superior dining options. **Cons:** away from the town center; older rooms need an overhaul; small beach can get busy. [$] *Rooms from: €468* ✉ *Thessi Nissi* ☎ *28410/90200* 🌐 *www.stnicolasbay.gr* ⏲ *Closed Nov.–late Apr.* 🔑 *113 rooms* 🍴 *Free breakfast.*

Shopping

Bioaroma

PERFUME/COSMETICS | On the edge of town, in a trendy, pale-green, award-winning modern building, a unique interactive-experience store from a pioneering eco-cosmetics company introduces you to their range of perfumes, soaps, sun protection, and creams. All products are 100% natural, organic, vegan, and cruelty-free and harness the knowledge of the last 40 centuries. ☒ *Ayios Nikolaos - Heraklion crossroads* ☎ *28410/82293* ⊕ *www.bioaroma.gr.*

Ceramica
ANTIQUES/COLLECTIBLES | Museum-standard copies of ancient amphora, pots, and pithoi are hand-painted by supremely talented artist Nic Gabriel. ☒ *K. Palaeologou 28* ☎ *28410/24075.*

Chez Sonia
CRAFTS | An appealing array of beads, quartz and silver jewelry, woven tablecloths and scarves, carved bowls, and other handicrafts fills Chez Sonia. ☒ *28is Oktovriou 20* ☎ *28410/28475.*

Elounda Ελούντα

11 km (7 miles) north of Ayios Nikolaos, 80 km (50 miles) east of Heraklion.

From its origins as a sleepy fishing village, Elounda has transformed into the de rigueur destination for luxury resorts. The shores of the Gulf of Korfos are thronged with villas and hotels offering the last word in indulgence. Spectacular views across to Spinalonga, broodily guarding the harbor, are a constant, as are a jet-set clientele. The beaches tend to be narrow and pebbly, but the water is crystal clear, and, in truth, many guests venture no farther than their private pool. Don't come here in search of authentic Greece: expect to meet fellow international travelers. As an escape from the rigors of everyday life, though, there are few better-placed competitors.

 ## Sights

Olous
ARCHAEOLOGICAL SITE | A sunken, ancient city is visible just beneath the turquoise waters off a causeway that leads to the Spinalonga Peninsula (not to be confused with the island of the same name), an undeveloped headland. Don't imagine you are going to discover Atlantis, but the outlines of a Roman settlement on the seabed and the warm, shallow waters make for an enjoyable diversion from the hotel pool. A mosaic floor from an Early Christian basilica with a striking fish motif can also be seen about 300 feet onshore. ☒ *Elounda* ✛ *3 km (2 miles) east of Elounda.*

Spinalonga
HISTORIC SITE | The Venetians built an imposing fortress on this small island in the center of the Gulf of Mirabello in the 16th century. It withstood Turkish invasion for more than 45 years after the mainland had fallen. Nevertheless, it is more recent history that gives this isle its eerie infamy; from the beginning of the last century it became a leper colony, imprisoning the unfortunate in primitive conditions until 1957. It is a poignant and evocative place with a sense of melancholy that remains to this day. The story is brought to life in the international best-selling novel *The Island* by Victoria Hislop. Boat excursions run from Ayios Nikolaos and Elounda. Most include a swim on a deserted beach. There is also a shorter trip from Plaka, directly opposite Spinalonga. Expect to pay €12 from Elounda, €25 from Ayios Nikolaos, and €10 from Plaka. ☒ *Gulf of Mirabello, Spinalonga* ☎ *Fortress €8.*

Restaurants

Kanali

$$ | GREEK | In an impossibly picturesque position next to the sunken ancient city of Olous, and the later canal from where it takes its name, Kanali serves elegant updates of Greek staples. Wooden furniture and an old stone building dressed with bold prints and lanterns lend it a shabby-chic air that could grace the seasides of Mykonos or Santorini. **Known for:** fish baked in a salt crust theatrically opened at your table; beautifully presented modern Greek cuisine; romantic, stylish setting. $ *Average main: €20* ✉ *Elounda* ⊹ *Next to the canal by Olous* ☎ *28410/42075* ⊙ *Closed Nov.–Mar.*

Marilena

$ | GREEK | The choice among the many restaurants that cling to the harbor, this is an Elounda classic, having offered traditional Greek food for 40 years. The large rear garden decked with grapevines and the seafront-facing tables are charming places to sample the house mezedes, many with a Cypriot origin, or try some of the excellent grill dishes. **Known for:** long-serving unflustered staff; dramatic table-side flambé dishes; Cypriot twists on Greek classics. $ *Average main: €12* ✉ *Harborside, main square* ☎ *28410/41322* ⊕ *www.marilenarestaurant.gr* ⊙ *Closed Oct.–Mar.*

Hotels

Akti Olous

$ | HOTEL | Set on the edge of the gulf, with sweeping views across to the bay from its rooftop terrace pool, this hotel may be the answer to affordable accommodations in Elounda. **Pros:** seaside location within walking distance of town; same beautiful views as the fancy hotels along the bay; good value for Elounda. **Cons:** pool area is small; pricier rooms have the front sea view; adults only. $ *Rooms from: €120* ✉ *Akti Oloundos* ☎ *28410/41270* ⊕ *www.*

eloundaaktiolous.gr ⊙ *Closed Nov.–Apr.* ⇥ *70 rooms* ⦿⊙ *Free breakfast.*

★ Blue Palace Resort & Spa

$$$$ | RESORT | Overlooking the Gulf of Mirabello and Spinalonga, framed by spectacular architecture, the views from the Blue Palace are worth the price of admission alone. **Pros:** beachside spa is a treat; Isola beach club is a cool hang-out; feels intimate despite the size. **Cons:** lots of steps, though funiculars and golf buggies help; Plaka is a good walk away, Elounda is a drive; extras can get expensive. $ *Rooms from: €480* ✉ *Elounda* ☎ *28410/65500* ⊕ *www.bluepalacebeach.gr* ⊙ *Closed Nov.–Apr.* ⇥ *255 rooms* ⦿⊙ *Free breakfast.*

Elounda Beach Hotel & Villas

$$$$ | HOTEL | FAMILY | The original luxury resort hotel in Elounda, and one of Greece's most renowned, is set in 40 acres of gardens next to 1 km (½ mile) of seashore, and offers a dazzling array of delights. **Pros:** well-designed, comfortable accommodations; lovely gardens and seashore; first-class spa and kids' amenities. **Cons:** rooms in the main buildings in need of some updating; eye-wateringly expensive; very large, resort-feel, with a lot of rooms. $ *Rooms from: €550* ✉ *Elounda* ⊹ *3 km (2 miles) south of village* ☎ *28410/63000* ⊕ *www.eloundabeach.gr* ⊙ *Closed Nov.–Mar.* ⇥ *244 rooms* ⦿⊙ *Free breakfast.*

Elounda Gulf Villas and Suites

$$$$ | RESORT | For those who value privacy and comfort, this may be the ultimate Elounda destination—with less of a resort feel than its larger neighbors, it is a second home to the jet set and the bright and the beautiful. **Pros:** beautiful accommodations in an intimate setting; personal, attentive service; excellent gourmet restaurants. **Cons:** not beachfront—private beach for guests is 10-minute drive away; pricier villas have the edge on suites; 20-minute walk into the town center. $ *Rooms from: €380* ✉ *Elounda* ⊹ *3 km (2 miles)* south of village ☎ 28102/27721 ⊕ www.eloundavillas.com ⤴ 33 villas and suites ⦿ Free breakfast.

Elounda Mare

$$$$ | **HOTEL** | This Relais & Chateaux property is one of the longest established in Elounda, and it blends charm and sophistication with a comfortably relaxed atmosphere. **Pros:** gorgeous setting and meticulously maintained grounds; Old Mill restaurant acknowledged as one of the best in Crete; golf course and Six Senses Spa at sister property open to guests. **Cons:** traditional decor may not suit all guests; small beach; steep paths and many steps. Ⓢ Rooms from: €408 ✉ Elounda ✛ 3 km (2 miles) south of village ☎ 28410/68200 ⊕ www.eloundamare.gr ⏱ Closed Nov.–Apr. ⤴ 92 rooms ⦿ Free breakfast.

Vai Βάι

170 km (106 miles) east of Heraklion.

The appeal of the surrounding, fertile coastal plain was not lost on the ancient Minoans, who left behind ruins that are not as grand as those on the center of the island but are evocative nonetheless. Today, Palekastro is a sleepy village primarily known as a gateway to the superb beaches around the peninsula and as a center for watersports, as people come from all over Europe to enjoy the winds.

 Sights

Palaikastro

ARCHAEOLOGICAL SITE | A sprawling Minoan town, formerly known as Roussolakkos, is currently being excavated by archaeologists. Palaikastro is missing any Knossos-type drama; here, for instance, there is no large palace structure, but you get a strong sense of everyday life amid the stony ruins of streets, squares, and shops. ■TIP→ **Nearby, Chiona and Kouremenos beaches make for pleasant diversions**

after clambering over the excavations. ✉ Palaikastro ✛ 2 km (1 mile) outside modern Palaikastro ☎ 28410/25115 ⊕ odysseus.culture.gr ⛵ Free.

 Beaches

Palm Beach at Vai

BEACH—SIGHT | Even the classical Greeks recognized the beauty of this palm grove at the eastern end of the island, which is unique in Europe. It stood in for the Caribbean in a famous television commercial for a chocolate bar, and it's easy to see why. Indeed, the sandy stretch with nearby islets in clear turquoise water is such a stunner that many bus tours come all the way east just to show off the sand and palms, so Vai can get jammed in the summer. If the sand in front of the grove of 5,000 palms is too crowded, follow the path south over the headland to a slightly less crowded cove, Psili Ammos, or better still head north to Erimoupolis, overlooked by the ancient kastro of Poli Itanou **Amenities:** food and drink; parking (paid); showers; toilets; water sports. **Best for:** snorkeling; swimming. ✉ Vai.

Xerokambos

BEACH—SIGHT | Follow the coast south from Vai, passing through the resort of Zakros, an important harbor and commercial center of Minoan Crete, and its ruins of a palace. The drive corkscrews down to Xerokambos, less of a destination and more of a series of stunning beaches. There are a couple of tavernas, a mini-market, and not much more except idyllic white sand and nothing between yourself and Africa apart from the warm Libyan sea. **Amenities:** none. **Best for**: solitude; walking.

 **Restaurants**

★ **Hiona Seafood Restaurant**

$$ | **GREEK** | A finger of rock stretches into the sea on the edge of Chiona Beach with a handful of blue-check-clothed wooden tables. It's a magical location

with kids diving into the clearest water nearby, and fishermen tying up to the jetty to unload a fresh catch. **Known for:** kakavia (fish soup) made to order; reservations needed for those waterside tables; friendly Cretan service. [$] *Average main: €15* ✉ *Chiona Beach* ☎ *28430/61228.*

Hotels

Sitia Bay Hotel

$ | **HOTEL** | **FAMILY** | In an area not renowned for its high-quality accommodations, this apartment-hotel stands out for its easy, relaxed feel. **Pros:** great position on the beachfront; superfriendly staff know all the best places to visit in the locality; good base for exploring this forgotten part of Crete. **Cons:** beach can get busy on weekends; don't expect luxurious furnishings; reception open only 8–8. [$] *Rooms from: €100* ✉ *P. Vartholomaiou 27, Sitia* ☎ *28430/24800* 🌐 *www.sitiabay.com* 🕓 *Closed Nov.–Apr.* 🛏 *19 rooms* 🍴 *Free breakfast.*

★ **White River Cottages**

$$ | **RENTAL** | In the tranquil White Valley, 33 km (20 miles) south of Sitia, is a hamlet of restored stone cottages. **Pros:** fabulous hiking in the vicinity—the Pefki gorge is a must; super beaches all around; characterful Cretan quarters. **Cons:** remote—you need a car to get the best out of it; a lot of steps; luxury seekers should look elsewhere. [$] *Rooms from: €140* ✉ *Aspros Potamos* ☎ *28430/51120* 🌐 *www.whiterivercottages.com* 🛏 *13 rooms* 🍴 *No meals.*

Vori Βορίον

65 km (40 miles) southwest of Heraklion, 5 km (3 miles) north of Palace of Phaistos.

Vori, the closest town to Phaistos and Ayia Triada, is a pleasant farming community of whitewashed houses on narrow lanes; you might enjoy stopping here for some refreshment at one of the two cafés on the lovely main square and to visit the excellent folk museum.

Sights

Museum of Cretan Ethnology

MUSEUM | A rich collection of Cretan folk items showcases exquisite weavings and pottery, basketry, farm implements, household furnishings, and clothing, all beautifully displayed and descriptively labeled in a well-designed building. Undoubtedly, the best museum of its kind on the island. ✉ *Voroi Pirgiotissis* ✣ *Edge of village center* ☎ *28920/91110* 🌐 *www.cretanethnologymuseum.gr* 🎫 *€3* 🕓 *Closed Oct.–Apr.*

Palace of Phaistos Ανάκτορο της Φαιστού

50 km (31 miles) southwest of Heraklion, 11 km (7 miles) south of Vori.

On a steep hill overlooking olive groves and the sea on one side, and high mountain peaks on the other, the second-largest Minoan palace was the center of Minoan culture in southern Crete. Unlike Knossos, Phaistos has not been reconstructed, though the copious ruins are richly evocative. Nearby is another palace, Ayia Triada.

Sights

Ayia Triada

ARCHAEOLOGICAL SITE | Another Minoan settlement that was destroyed at the same time as Phaistos by Mycenean attackers is only a few miles away on the other side of the same hill. Ayia Triada was once thought to have been a summer palace for the rulers of Phaistos but is now believed to have consisted of a group of villas for nobility and a warehouse complex. Rooms in the villas were once paneled with gypsum slabs and decorated with frescoes: the two now hanging in the Archaeological Museum in Heraklion show a woman in a garden and a cat hunting a pheasant. Several other lovely pieces, including finely crafted vases, come from Ayia Triada and are now also on display in Heraklion, along with more Linear A tablets than at any other Minoan site. Though the complex was at one time just above the seashore, the view now looks across the extensive Messara Plain to the Lybian Sea in the distance. ✉ *Ayia Triada, Tympaki, Phaistos* ⊕ *Follow signs 3 km (2 miles) west from Phaistos* ☎ *28920/91564* ⊕ *odysseus. culture.gr* 🎫 *€4.*

★ Gortyna

ARCHAEOLOGICAL SITE | Appearing in Homeric poems, Gortyna was second only to Knossos in importance and flourished in the early centuries of Roman rule. The Gortyn Law Code, an inscription from the 5th century BC, and the earliest known written Greek law, confirms the prosperity of the city, and at its peak as many as 100,000 people may have lived nearby. It was the earliest Christian Cretan city and became the seat of Apostle Titus, the first bishop of Crete. It was later sacked by the Arabs in 824 AD

The first major monument visible is the Byzantine Basilica of Agios Titus, probably built on the remains of an older church. A soaring apse and two side chapels have been restored. Adjacent, is the Odeion, levelled by an earthquake and rebuilt by Emperor Trajan. Within the walls of the theatre are the 600 lines of the Law Code, engraved upon a wall tablet.

Crossing the road that bisects the site, the main attractions are the Praetorium, the palace of the Roman governor of Crete that dates back to the 2nd century AD, and the Nymphaeum, a public bath originally supplied by an aqueduct and adorned with statues.

Climb to the hilltop Acropolis for a view of the site; below you will see the evergreen plane tree that served as Zeus and Europa's mating-bed according to mythology. From this union, the three kings of Crete were produced: Minos, Rhadamanthus, and Sarpedon.

✉ *Agioi Deka* ☎ *28920/31144* ⊕ *odysseus.culture.gr* 🎫 *€6.*

★ Palace of Phaistos

ARCHAEOLOGICAL SITE | The Palace of Phaistos was built around 1900 BC and rebuilt after a disastrous earthquake around 1650 BC. It was burned and abandoned in the wave of destruction that swept across the island around 1450 BC, though Greeks continued to inhabit the city until the 2nd century BC, when it was eclipsed by Roman Gortyna.

You enter the site by descending a flight of steps leading into the west court, then climb a grand staircase. From here you pass through the **Propylon porch** into a light well and descend a narrow staircase into the **central court.** Much of the southern and eastern sections of the palace have eroded away. But there are large pithoi still in place in the old **storerooms.** On the north side of the court the recesses of an elaborate doorway bear a rare trace: red paint in a diamond pattern on a white ground. A passage from the doorway leads to the **north court** and the **northern domestic apartments,** now roofed and fenced off. The **Phaistos Disk** was found in 1903 in a chest made of mud brick at the northeast edge of the site and is now on display at the Archaeological Museum in Heraklion. East of the central court are the **palace workshops,** with a metalworking furnace fenced off. South of the workshops lie the **southern domestic apartments,** including a clay bath. From there, you have a memorable view across the Messara Plain. ✉ *Phaistos* ⊕ *Follow signs and ascend hill off Ayii Deka–Mires–Timbaki road* ☎ *28920/42315* ⊕ *odysseus.culture. gr* 🎫 *€8.*

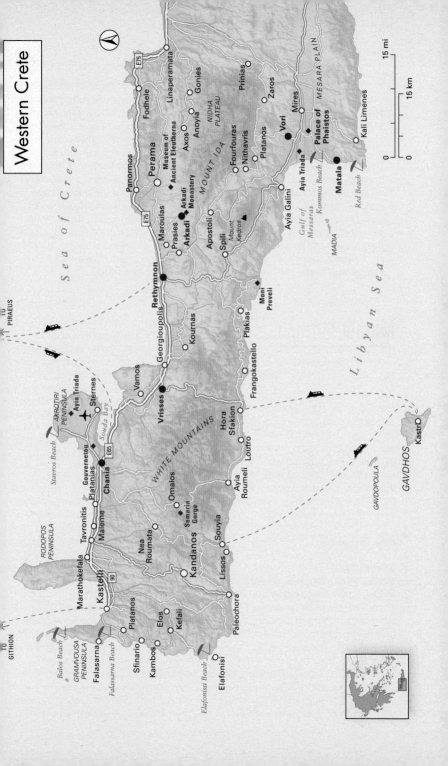

Western Crete

Sea of Crete

Libyan Sea

TO PIRAEUS

TO GITHION

Linaperamata
E75
Fodhele
Panormos
Gonies
Perama
Museum of
Ancient Eleutherna
Axos
Anoyiá
Linaperamata
Prinias
Zaros
Mires
Vori
Palace of
Phaistos
Kali Limenes
Fourfouras
Nithavris
Platanos
Ayia Triada
Matala
Kommos Beach
Red Beach
MESARA PLAIN
NIDHA PLATEAU
MOUNT IDA

Maroulas
Prasies
Arkadi
Monastery
Arkadi
Apostoli
Spili
Mount
Kedros
Ayia Galini
Gulf of
Messaras
MADIA

Rethymnon
Georgioupolis
Kournas
Plakias
Moni
Preveli
Frangokastello

Vamos
Sternes
Vrisses
AKROTIRI
PENINSULA
Ayia Triada
Souda Bay
Stavros Beach
Gouvernetou
Platanias
Chania
Omalos
WHITE MOUNTAINS
Hora
Sfakion
Loutro
Ayia
Roumeli
Samaria
Gorge
Souyia
Lissos
Paleochora
GAVDHOS
Kastro
GAVDOPOULA
GAVDOPOULA

RODOPOS
PENINSULA
Tavronitis
Marathokefala
Kastelli
90
Maleme
Nea
Roumata
Kandanos
Platanos
Elos
Kefali
Sfinario
Kambos
Elafonisi
Falasarna
GRAMVOUSA
PENINSULA
Balos Beach
Falassarna Beach
Elafonissi Beach

15 mi
15 km
0

Rural Crete Scenic Route

The quickest route from Phaistos, Matala, and other places on the Messara Plain to the north coast is Heraklion Road, a small section of which is four lanes. However, a very pleasant alternative leads northwest through Ayia Galini (the largest resort on this part of the southern coast) and the mountain town of Spili to Rethymnon. The route shows off the beauty of rural Crete as it traverses deep valleys and gorges and climbs the flanks of the interior mountain ranges. Just beyond Spili, follow signs to Moni Preveli, a stunningly located monastery perched high above the sea. A monument honors the monks here who sheltered Allied soldiers after the Battle of Crete and helped them escape the Nazi-occupied island via submarine. Below the monastery is Palm Beach, where golden sands are shaded by a palm grove watered by a mountain stream. It's lovely, but avoid this patch of paradise at midday during high season, when it is packed with day-trippers who arrive by tour boat from Ayia Galini.

Matala Μάταλα

10 km (6 miles) southwest of Vori, 70 km (42 miles) southwest of Heraklion.

Renowned in the 1960s as a stopover on the hippie trail, with Joni Mitchell immortalizing it in song, Matala today is a small, low-key beach resort that retains its flower-power vibe, although tourism is increasing. The 2nd-century AD Roman tombs cut in the cliff side, where the beatniks made their home, now attract day-trippers from Heraklion and make an impressive sight from the pleasant town beach.

Beaches

Kommos Beach

BEACH—SIGHT | Fabulous, pine-and-palm-fringed Kommos lies below the site of a Minoan harbor, once the port of Phaistos. At its far northern end lies the scrappy little resort of Kalamaki, where a few modest hotels and tavernas back the sand, but for the most part the beach is an unspoiled 2-km (1-mile) stretch of white sand washed by clear waters and backed by hills shaded with tamarisk trees. Kommos is especially popular with nudists, and it's also a nesting ground for the loggerhead sea turtle (*Caretta caretta*), so avoid taped-off areas where the females have laid their eggs. Lifeguards watch over the southern end of the beach. **Amenities:** food and drink; lifeguards; parking (free); showers; toilets. **Best for:** nudists; solitude; sunset; swimming; walking. ⊠ *Off Mires–Matala road* ⊹ *Near Pitsidia, 2 km (1 mile) from signposted turnoff.*

Red Beach

BEACH—SIGHT | This beautiful crescent of sand is accessible by a 20-minute walk across a rocky promontory on a path from Matala, or by a boat that runs from Matala in summer. The trek includes a scramble up and over a headland and some steep climbs and descents, though it is manageable with moderate exertion. Your reward is a lovely, unspoiled crescent of golden sand washed by clear waters that is especially popular with nudists. Surf in the small bay can be rough, with riptides. Shade is scarce, though a small bar sometimes rents umbrellas and offers simple snacks. At the northern edge of the beach are many carved rocks with Minoan and Egyptian figures; they are not ancient but the

;rete has some of the best beaches of any of the Greek islands.

;reation of a modern Belgian sculptor. **\menities:** food and drink (sometimes). **3est for:** nudists; solitude; swimming; valking. ✉ *Matala* ✣ *1 km (½ mile) west of town.*

Restaurants

Taverna Sigelakis

$ | **GREEK** | Residents from villages for miles around come to the town of Sivas to enjoy a meal of *stifado* (meat in a rich tomato sauce), artichokes with *avgolemono* (egg and lemon sauce), and other specialties, including delicious roasted lamb and chicken, all served on the front terrace in warm seasons or in the stone-wall, hearth-warmed dining room when the weather's cold. A meal comes with friendly service, a visit from proprietor Giorgios, and a free glass of raki and a sweet. **Known for:** true traditional Cretan cooking; authentic surroundings; hospitable owner. [$] *Average main: €10* ✉ *Sivas* ✣ *6 km (4 miles) north-east of Matala* ☎ *28920/42748* 🌐 *www.sigelakis-studios.gr.*

Hotels

Thalori

$ | **RESORT** | To enjoy a remote Cretan retreat without sacrificing comfort, it's hard to beat these beautifully renovated stone houses in an ages-old village that clings to a mountainside high above the Libyan Sea. Fireplaces, handmade wood furnishings, and embroidered carpets enhance the character-filled surroundings, while terraces, a cliff-side pool, and an outdoor summer taverna are vantage points from which to take in the mountain and sea views. **Pros:** beautiful surroundings; ideal for those who want to get away from it all and enjoy nature; very comfortable and unique. **Cons:** a half-hour drive to the nearest beach; no shop or taverna in the village; hair-raising road trip to reach the property. [$] *Rooms from: €100* ✉ *Kapetaniana* ☎ *28930/41762* 🌐 *www.thalori.com* 🛏 *20 traditional houses* 🍴 *Free breakfast.*

Arkadi

18 km (11 miles) southwest of Fodele, 30 km (19 miles) southwest of Heraklion.

As you approach Arkadi from the north, through the rolling lands at the base of Mt. Ida, one of the contenders in the dispute over the alleged Cretan birthplace of Zeus, you'll follow a gorge inland before emerging onto the flat pastureland that surrounds one of Crete's most beautiful and important monasteries. The approach is even more dramatic from the south, as you traverse the uplands of the beautiful Amari valley before dropping into the mountain plateau that the monastery and its vast holdings occupy. If you are heading east back to Heraklion, consider visiting Eleutherna, with stunning views of the local area, and pass through Fodele; a pretty village set in orange and lemon groves with a shady taverna-filled square and a small museum in the supposed birthplace of the painter El Greco.

 Sights

Arkadi Monastery

RELIGIOUS SITE | A place of pilgrimage for many Cretans, Moni Arkadi is also one of the most stunning pieces of Renaissance architecture on the island. The ornate facade, decorated with Corinthian columns and an elegant belfry above, was built in the 16th century of a local, honey-color stone. In 1866 the monastery came under siege during a major rebellion against the Turks, and Abbot Gabriel and several hundred rebels, together with their wives and children, refused to surrender. When the Turkish forces broke through the gate, the defenders set the gunpowder store afire, killing themselves together with hundreds of Turks. The monastery was again a center of resistance when the Nazis occupied Crete during World War II. ⊠ *Arkadi* ✦ *South of old Heraklion–Chania road* ☎ *28310/83135* ⊕ *www.arkadimonastery.gr* ☜ *€3.*

Museum of Ancient Eleutherna

ARCHAEOLOGICAL SITE | In the foothills of Mt. Ida, Eleutherna was founded in the 9th century BC. It was one of the most important ancient cities, even minting its own coins. At a natural crossroad between Knossos to the east and Cydonia to the northwest, it controlled the ports of Stavromenos and Panormos and was near to the sacred cave of *Idaion Andron*, another one of the alleged birthplaces of Zeus. An archaeological-site museum was opened in 2016 in a modern building and it has been designed to be updated as new discoveries and finds are made. Housing objects from prehistoric through to Byzantine eras, the current collection spans 3000 BC to AD 1300, presented in a multimedia fashion. The archaeological site itself is accessible on rough stone paths with two large canopies covering the most important excavations. The *Orthi Petra* cemetery includes a funeral pyre for a warrior from 730–710 BC, and corroborates Homer's description in *The Iliad* of a similar burial. Elsewhere, roads, villas, public buildings, baths, and cisterns are to be seen, along with magnificent views of the countryside. ⊠ *Eleutherna Mylopotamou, Rethymnon* ☎ *28340/92501* ⊕ *www.mae com.gr* ☜ *€2* ⊗ *Closed Tues.*

 Hotels

★ Kapsaliana Village Hotel

$$ | HOTEL | A 300-year-old hamlet set amid vast olive groves has been converted to one of Crete's most distinctive and relaxing lodgings, with luxurious, stylishly appointed rooms, welcoming lounges, and an excellent dining room—all fashioned out of beautiful, ancient stone houses that were once part of the Arkadi Monastery holdings. **Pros:** unique insight into a way of life that has disappeared; a welcome alternative in an outstanding setting far from anonymous resorts; low-key sophistication is very charming. **Cons:** remote location makes

a rental car a necessity; some distance from beaches; can feel a little isolated at night. **$** *Rooms from: €220* ✉ *Kapsaliana* ☎ *28310/83400* ⊕ *www.kapsalianavillage. gr* ⊐ *18 rooms* ⊙ *Free breakfast.*

Rethymnon Ρέθυμνο

25 km (15 miles) west of Arkadi Monastery, 78 km (48 miles) west of Heraklion.

Rethymnon is Crete's third-largest town, after Heraklion and Chania. The population (about 40,000) steadily increases as the town expands—a new quarter follows the coast to the east of the Old Town, where the beachfront has been developed with large hotels and other resort facilities catering to tourists on package vacations. Nevertheless, much of Rethymnon's charm perseveres in the old Venetian quarter, which is crowded onto a compact peninsula dominated by the huge, fortified Venetian castle known as the Fortezza. Wandering through the narrow alleyways, you come across handsome carved-stone Renaissance doorways belonging to vanished mansions, fountains, archways, and wooden Turkish houses with latticework screens on the balconies to protect the women of the house from prying eyes.

GETTING HERE AND AROUND

There is no direct ferry connection to Athens from Rethymnon. However, this has a habit of changing year by year; ask at local agents for availability. If a boat is not operating when you wish to make the trip, a good option is to use the ferry terminal or airport at Chania, about 45 minutes and €90 away by taxi. Rethymnon is also served by an hourly bus service from Chania and Heraklion, each about an hour away, and the fare to either is about €8 each way. Rethymnon's bus terminal is on the west side of town, on the sea near the Venetian fortress, at Atki Kefaloyianithon. Rethymnon is on Crete's national highway, which runs

along the north coast, and there is public parking on the seaside road around the Venetian fortress, next to the old harbor, and elsewhere around town.

Sights

Archaeological Museum

MUSEUM | Here's even more evidence of just how long Crete has cradled civilizations: a collection of bone tools from a Neolithic site at Gerani (west of Rethymnon); Minoan pottery; and an unfinished statue of Aphrodite, the goddess of love, from the Roman occupation (look for the ancient chisel marks). The museum is temporarily housed in the restored Venetian Chuch of St. Francisco while renovations are undertaken at the original site in the shadow of the Fortessa. ✉ *Agios Fragiskos* ☎ *28310/27506* ⊕ *www. archmuseumreth.gr* ▣ *€2* ⊙ *Closed Tues.*

Fortezza

MILITARY SITE | The west side of the peninsula on which Rethymnon sits is taken up almost entirely with this massive fortress, strategically surrounded by the sea and thick ramparts. The high, well-preserved walls enclose a vast empty space occupied by a few scattered buildings—a well-restored mosque, two churches, and abandoned barracks that once housed the town brothels—and are surrounded by fields of wildflowers in spring. After a small fortress on the site failed to thwart a 1571 attack of 40 pirate galleys, Venetians conscripted 100,000 forced laborers from the town and surrounding villages to build the huge compound. It didn't fulfill its purpose of keeping out the Turks: Rethymnon surrendered after a three-week siege in 1646. ✉ *Rethymnon* ⊹ *West end of town* ☎ *28310/28101* ⊕ *www.rethymno.gr* ▣ *€4.*

Historical and Folk Art Museum

MUSEUM | A restored Venetian palazzo almost in the shadow of the Neratze minaret houses a delightful collection of rustic furnishings, tools, weavings, and a re-creation of a traditional Cretan shopping street that provide a charming and vivid picture of what life on Crete was like until well into the 20th century. ✉ *M. Vernardou 28–30* ☎ *28310/23398* 🎫 *€4* 🕒 *Closed Sun.*

Neratze

ARTS VENUE | The most visible sign of the Turkish occupation of Rethymnon is the graceful minaret, one of the few to survive in Greece, that rises above the Neratze. This large stone structure looming over the narrow lanes of the city center was a monastery, then church, under the Venetians, and was subsequently converted to a mosque under the Ottomans before being transformed into today's concert hall. ✉ *Verna and Ethnikis Adistaseos.*

Venetian Harbor

LIGHTHOUSE | Rethymnon's small inner harbor, with its restored 19th-century lighthouse, comes to life in warm weather, when restaurant tables clutter the quayside and fishing craft and pleasure boats are crammed chockablock into the minute space. ✉ *Waterfront.*

Venetian Loggia

BUILDING | The carefully restored clubhouse of the local nobility is now enclosed in glass and houses the Archaeological Museum's shop, selling a selection of books and reproductions of artifacts from its collections. This remnant of Venetian rule is enhanced by the nearby Rimondi Fountain, just down the street at the end of Platanos Square, and is one of the town's most welcoming sights, spilling refreshing streams from several lions' heads. You'll come upon several other fountains as you wander through the labyrinth of narrow streets. ✉ *Arkadiou* ☎ *28310/53270* 🕒 *Closed weekends.*

🍴 Restaurants

★ Avli

$$ | **GREEK** | In an herb-filled multitiered courtyard that leads to a barrel-vaulted dining room, some of the finest food for miles is skillfully prepared. Refined, distinguished dishes are its calling card; sophisticated but true to their traditional roots. **Known for:** attentive, yet never overbearing service; tasting menus with matched local wines; located within a boutique hotel in a former Venetian villa. [$] *Average main: €22* ✉ *Xanthoudidou 22* ☎ *28310/26213* 🌐 *www.avli.gr.*

Kyria Maria

$ | **GREEK** | On a blink-and-you'll-miss-it small alley behind the Rimondi Fountain, under an arbor of vines, with caged birds chirping away, this homey little taverna serves some accomplished traditional dishes in an atmospheric setting. Lamb in lemon sauce, stuffed calamari, moussaka, *yemista* (stuffed vegetables)—the menu is a roll call of all the comfort food you can think of, prepared as Grandma would have made it all those years ago. **Known for:** village-style dishes; neighborhood setting on a back alley, steps from the center; friendly service, friendly prices. [$] *Average main: €10* ✉ *Moschovitou 20* ☎ *28310/29078* 🕒 *Closed Nov.–Apr.*

★ Raki Ba Raki1600

$ | **GREEK** | Opposite Avli, and part of the same stable, on one of Rethymnon's myriad pretty walkways, this is a modern reinvention of the classic Greek *rakadiko*—a place to eat small plates and drink raki. Don't assume the food is an afterthought to drinking, though, this is top-quality mezedes. **Known for:** best mezedes in town; creative Cretan flavors you won't find elsewhere; raki!—not just plain, but flavored with fruits and herbs. [$] *Average main: €8* ✉ *Arampatzoglou 17–19* ✥ *Opposite Avli* ☎ *28310/58250.*

Continued on page 484

NECTAR OF THE GODS

The roots of Greek wine run deep: Naughty Dionysus partied his way through mythology as the God of Wine and became a symbol for celebration in Greece. During the ancient festivities called Dionysia, husbands and wives alike let loose and drank themselves into a heady joy. Now that you're in the land of the god, be sure to enjoy some liquid Dionysian delights. Greece's wine is flavorful and original, so much so that some of the wines here you won't find anywhere else.

This is one reason why few can resist taking some bottles home (a bottle of excellent Greek wine will cost at least €15 to €20, but good varieties can be found for around €10). Remember to ask the clerk to pad them with bubble wrap so they won't break in your suitcase on the journey back. Following are some tips about vintners who are leading the Greek winemaking renaissance, along with a rundown of the grape varietals that Greek wineries specialize in.

Hillside vineyard, Samos Island

THE GREEK WINES TO LOOK FOR

REDS

Agiorgitiko. The name means St. George and it's mainly found in the Nemea region of the Peloponnese. Richly colored and scented, with aromas of sour cherries and pomegranate, it goes well with red meat and yellow soft cheeses.

Kotsifali. Grown mainly in Crete, it is rich and aromatic, with hints of raisins, prunes, and sage. Pair with red meat, light red sauces, and yellow cheeses.

Mandilaria. Mainly cultivated in Rhodes and Crete, it is rich and intense, with hints of pomegranate. Pair with grilled and stewed meats with spicy sauces and mild cheeses.

Mavrodaphne. Found in the Peloponnese regions of Achaia and Ilia and the Ionian Islands, it is a lovely dessert wine. Drink alone or with a light dessert.

Xinomavro. Found in Macedonia, it is rich, acidic, and bursting with aromas such as gooseberry with hints of olives and spices. Pair with grilled meats, casseroles, and yellow spicy cheeses.

WHITES

Assyrtiko. One of Greece's finest white wines and found mainly in Santorini, Attica, and Macedonia, it is rich and dry with honeysuckle and citrus aromas and an earthy aftertaste. Pair with grilled fish, poultry or pork and feta.

Athiri. An ancient variety found mainly in Santorini, Macedonia, Attica, and Rhodes, it is vibrant and fruity with tropical fruit and honey tones. Pair with poultry or pork, pasta, grilled fish, or white cheeses.

Moschofilero. Originating in the Peloponnese, it is vivid and has rich fruity and floral aromas. Pair with poultry, pasta, and seafood.

Roditis. Popular in Attica, Macedonia, Thessaly, and Peloponnese, it is light and has vibrant scents of pine apple, pear, melon, and jasmine. Pair with poultry, fish, and mild cheeses.

Rombola. Grown in the Ionian island of Cephalonia, it is scented with citrus and peach and has a lemony aftertaste. Pair with fish or poultry.

Savatiano. Grown in Attica, it is full-bodied with fruity tones of apple, pear, and peach. Pair with poultry, pork, or fish as well as soft white cheeses.

White Muscat. Cultivated on the Aegean island of Samos and in the northern Peloponnese city of Patras, it is sweet and intense. Pair with desserts and ice cream.

PICK OF THE VINE

(left) Dionysos Kantharos, God of wine; (right) a toast with Santorini wine.

Wherever you head in Greece, winemakers are perfecting the millennia-old traditions of Greek wine, with high-class estates such as Gaia, Boutari, and Porto Carras leading the way. These wineries can all be visited by appointment. A good introductory Web site is ⊕ www.allaboutgreekwine.com.

Peloponnese, Tetramythos Vineyards. While vineyards throughout the region produce Agiorgitiko, an aromatic and deeply colored red, those from Tetrmythos (⊕ www.tetramythos.com) on the northern slopes of Mt. Helmos, rising 7,775 feet above the Gulf of Corinth, are especially velvety and rich.

Cyclades, Haridimos Hatzidakis. On Santorini, his winery (⊕ www.hatzidakiswines.gr) near Pyrgos Kallistis comprises a celebrated set of organic vineyards. One of his top organic wines is the Aidani Assyritiko, a dry, fruity white.

Macedonia, Yiannis Boutaris. Up north, in Naoussa, Imathia wine lovers make a beeline to Yiannis's Ktima Kir-Yianni winery (⊕ www.kiryianni.gr). He split from his family's estate ten years ago to concentrate on producing standout dry reds.

DRINK LIKE A CRETAN

While Crete's viticultural history goes back 3,500 years, the island's wines are becoming newly popular with an emphasis on indigenous varieties. Vidiano, a complex, fruity, and full-bodied white, is quickly emerging from obscurity as a favorite of connoisseurs and has been dubbed the Greek Viognier. Vilana, a white grape with spicy aromas and notes of clementine and bananas is another native variety making waves. In the reds, Liatiko, an age-old grape, has been rescued from sweet blends to star as a perfumed, layered and nuanced wine. There are three main wine producing villages around the capital Heraklion—Archanes, Dafnes, and Peza—and there are many quality focused wineries to be found in the region. Tasting rooms here provide an intriguing introduction to Cretan wines.

☕ Coffee and Quick Bites

★ Meli Melo

$ | CAFÉ | Tucked away behind the Rimondi fountain on a pretty pedestrian street, this little gem makes the best *loukoumades*—light and fresh doughnuts. Take one of the streetside tables, order a portion with honey and cinnamon, and ask for one of their homemade lemonades.
Known for: perfect people-watching spot; great ice cream; super-fresh smoothies and juices. $ *Average main: €6* ⊠ *38 Paleologou Konstadinou* ☎ *28313/01214.*

Hotels

Avli

$$ | HOTEL | In a cluster of lovely 16th-century Venetian buildings, centered on a romantic leafy, walled yard, accommodations are split between the various properties, and characterfully decorated with sparkling chandeliers, baroque gilt frames, and antique furniture against a backdrop of rough stone and wooden beams. **Pros:** evocative, intimate abode at the heart of town; personable staff—you are always a name, never a number; romantic courtyard. **Cons:** unique old buildings means stairs to all rooms; rooms facing restaurant garden can be a little noisy; parking is a couple of streets away, but staff will come and collect your bags. $ *Rooms from: €160* ⊠ *Xanthodidou 22 and Radamanthios* ☎ *28310/58250* ⊕ *www.avli.gr* ⊷ *12 rooms* ⏲ *Free breakfast.*

Leo Hotel

$ | HOTEL | Eleni Christonaki oversees this lovely little inn that occupies the 600-year-old house in which she was raised. **Pros:** attractive, comfortable surroundings; friendly service; central location on a quiet street in the Old Town. **Cons:** steep stairs and no elevator may pose a problem for some guests; small common areas; not much in the way of amenities. $ *Rooms from: €115* ⊠ *Arkadiou and Vafe 2–4* ☎ *28310/26197* ⊕ *www.leohotel.gr* ⊷ *8 rooms* ⏲ *No meals.*

Palazzino di Corina

$ | HOTEL | Rethymnon has several hotels occupying old palaces, but Corina is one of the most handsome, with pleasant, stylish surroundings that include a nicely planted courtyard surrounding a small plunge pool. **Pros:** cool courtyard is a perfect place to relax; informal, helpful staff; attached restaurant in pretty cloister next door. **Cons:** some rooms on upper floors require a climb; street-facing rooms are the noisiest; not all rooms have balconies. $ *Rooms from: €120* ⊠ *Damvergi and Diakou* ☎ *28310/21205* ⊕ *www.corina.gr* ⊷ *29 rooms* ⏲ *Free breakfast.*

Rimondi Boutique Hotel

$$ | HOTEL | Step through the heavy 16th-century wooden door of this hotel and you are transported to an oasis of civility away from the bustle of Rethymnon's busy streets, where two buildings split by a pretty pedestrian alleyway house some of the most sumptuous rooms in town. **Pros:** loving restoration of Venetian property is full of historical detail; tranquil, quiet atmosphere; garden areas with pools are a delight. **Cons:** some split-level suites with stairs; rooms in the modern annex are less attractive; parking is a five-minute walk away. $ *Rooms from: €180* ⊠ *Xanthoudidou 21* ☎ *28310/51001* ⊕ *www.hotelsrimondi.com* ⊗ *Closed Nov.–Mar.* ⊷ *33 rooms* ⏲ *Free breakfast.*

Nightlife

Thalassographia

WINE BARS—NIGHTLIFE | The name means seascape, a poetic notion for this romantic gathering spot that spreads across a series of terraces wedged between the Fortezza and the azure waters below. Small plates are the order in this easy-going and relaxed place, with a strong selection of local wines and beers, and the best cocktails in town—the ideal spot for watching the sunset over the castle walls on a balmy summer evening. ⊠ *33 Kefalogiannidon* ☎ *28310/52569.*

Shopping

Rethymnon's narrow lanes may remind you of a Middle Eastern souk—or a tacky shopping mall, depending on your frame of mind. If you are looking for something a bit more substantial than, say, playing cards with erotic images of gods and goddesses, you can also find small shops selling some genuinely high-quality goods, whether it's Cretan olive oil or the work of island craftspeople.

Agora—Avli Raw Materials

FOOD/CANDY | This amazing shop sells many of the best herbs, spices, oils, and other ingredients that Greece offers and that flavor the cuisine served just around the corner at the restaurant. Many of the offerings are unique to the shop and give a true taste of the local area. Oil and wine tastings are given, too. ⊠ *Arampatzoglou 38–40* ☎ *28310/58250* ⊕ *www. avli.gr.*

Kalymnos

GIFTS/SOUVENIRS | For a souvenir that will be light to carry, stop in and browse shelves brimming with sponges harvested off the eponymous island and in other Greek waters. ⊠ *Arampatzoglou 26* ☎ *28310/50802.*

🏃 Activities

★ Happy Walker

HIKING/WALKING | This outfitter arranges easy day hikes in the mountains and gorges near Rethymnon, adding a welcome stop for a village lunch to each walk. The outfit also leads multiday treks through the remote regions of Crete. Walks cost from €35. ⊠ *Tombazi 56* ☎ *28310/31390* ⊕ *www.happywalker. com* 🕑 *Closed late Oct.–Mar.*

Vrisses Βρύσες

26 km (16 miles) west of Rethymnon, 105 km (65 miles) west of Heraklion.

This appealing old village is famous throughout Crete for its thick, creamy yogurt—best eaten with a large spoonful of honey on top—that is served in the cafés beneath the plane trees at the center of town. Georgioupolis, on the coast about 7 km (4½ miles) due west, is another shady, lovely old town, where the Almiros River flows into the sea. Some of the coast here is undergoing rather unattractive development, but inland walks—including one through a eucalyptus-scented valley that links Vrisses and Georgioupolis—make it easy to get away from the fray.

Chania Χανιά

52 km (32 miles) west of Vrisses, 78 km (48 miles) west of Rethymnon.

Chania surrendered its role as capital of Crete to Heraklion in 1971, but this elegant city of eucalyptus-lined avenues, miles of waterfront promenades, and shady, cobblestone alleyways lined with Venetian and Ottoman houses is still close to the heart of all Cretans. It was here that the Greek flag was raised in 1913 to mark Crete's unification with Greece, and the place is simply one of the most beautiful of all Greek cities.

GETTING HERE AND AROUND

Daily ferry service connects Chania with Pireaus, arriving at the harbor on Souda Bay every day at about 6 am and departing around 9 pm. The crossing takes roughly eight hours. During summer, ferries also provide daytime service between Pireaus and Chania, and crossings take six hours. Souda is a 20-minute taxi ride from the town center (€12), and municipal buses also run from Souda to Chania (€2.50). Chania's airport, also on Souda Bay, has daily service from Athens, as well as flights from many European cities, mostly charters, during high season. Buses run from the airport infrequently, so plan on taking a taxi or picking up your rental car at the airport. Hourly buses connect Chania with Rethymnon, about €7, and Heraklion, about €15. Less frequent bus service connects Chania with Kissamos, Paleochora, and many other places in western Crete. The well-organized bus station, with a helpful information desk, is at Kidonias 25, just off Halidon. The city center is well marked from National Road. For parking, drive to the center and make your way, following well-posted parking signs, to the west side of the Old City, where you'll find free parking near the sea. Be careful where you park, as some places are open only to residents, and violators are fined.

TRAVEL AGENTS

CONTACTS Diana's Travel. ✉ *Daskalogianni Str* ☎ *28210/33575* ⊕ *www. dianas-travel.com.* **Kyriakakis Travel.** ✉ *Chatzimichali Giannari 78* ☎ *28210/50500* ⊕ *www.kyriakakis.gr.*

 # Sights

The sizable Old Town is strung along the harbor, divided by a centuries-old seawall into outer and inner harbors, where tall Venetian houses face a pedestrians-only, taverna-lined waterside walkway, and fishing boats moor beside a long stretch of Venetian arsenals and warehouses. Well-preserved Venetian and Turkish quarters surround the harbors and a covered food-and-spice market, a remnant of Venetian trade and Turkish bazaars, is set amid a maze of narrow streets.

Archaeological Museum

MUSEUM | The former Venetian church of St. Francis, surrounding a lovely garden in the shadow of the Venetian walls, displays artifacts from all over western Crete, and the collection bears witness to the presence of Minoans, ancient Greeks, Romans, Venetians, and Ottomans. The painted Minoan clay coffins and elegant late-Minoan pottery indicate that the region was as wealthy as the center of the island under the Minoans, though no palace has yet been located. ✉ *Chalidon 25* ☎ *28210/90334* ⊕ *chaniamuseum.culture.gr* 🎫 *€4* ⊙ *Closed Tues.*

Ayia Triada

RELIGIOUS SITE | Lands at the northeast corner of the Akrotiri Peninsula, which extends into the sea from the east side of Chania, are the holdings of several monasteries, including Ayia Triada (Holy Trinity) or Tzagarolon, as it is also known. The olive groves that surround and finance the monastery yield excellent oils, and the shop is stocked with some of the island's finest. Ayia Triada is a delightful place, where you can visit the flower-filled cloisters and the ornately decorated chapel, which dates from the monastery's founding in 1611. Today, just a handful of monks remain. ✉ *Agias Triadas of Tzagarolon, Akrotiri* ✛ *16 km (10 miles) north of Chania, follow road from Chordaki* ☎ *28210/63572.*

Byzantine and Post-Byzantine Collection of Chania

MUSEUM | You'll get some insight into the Venetian occupation *and* the Christian centuries that preceded it at this small museum housed in the charming 15th-century church of San Salvadore alongside the city walls just behind the Firka. Mosaics, icons, coins, and other artifacts bring to life Cretan civilization as it was after the Roman Empire colonized the island and Christianity took root as early as the 1st century. ✉ *Theotokopoulou 78–82* ☎ *28210/96046* ⊕ *odysseus.culture.gr* 🎫 *€3* ⊙ *Closed Tues.*

Cretan House

MUSEUM | Chania's colorful folklife museum is bursting at the seams with farm equipment, tools, household items, wedding garb, and a wealth of other material reflecting the island's traditional heritage. ⊠ Chalidon 46 ✛ Off the church courtyard ☎ 28210/90816 ⌐ €2.

Etz Hayyim Synagogue

RELIGIOUS SITE | This ancient landmark is tucked away in what was once the Jewish ghetto, a warren of narrow lanes known as Evraki, just off the harbor south of the Firka. The building was formerly the Venetian church of St. Catherine, became a synagogue under the Ottomans in the 16th century, and was sorely neglected and near collapse by the end of the 20th century. Venetian Gothic arches, a mikveh (ritual bath), tombs of three rabbis, and other architectural features have been beautifully restored and are a stirring memorial to Crete's once sizable Jewish population, obliterated during World War II; many Cretan Jews drowned when a British torpedo sank the ship carrying them toward Auschwitz in 1944. ⊠ Parodos Kondylaki ☎ 28210/86286 ⊕ www.etz-hayyim-ha-nia.org ۞ Closed weekends.

★ Firka

MUSEUM | Just across the narrow channel from the lighthouse, where a chain was connected in times of peril to close the harbor, is the old Turkish prison, which now houses the **Maritime Museum of Crete.** Exhibits, more riveting than might be expected, trace the island's seafaring history from the time of the Minoans, with a reproduction of an Athenian trireme boat , amphora from Roman shipwrecks, Ottoman weaponry, and other relics. Look for the photos and mementos from the World War II Battle of Crete, when Allied forces moved across the island and, with the help of Cretans, ousted the German occupiers. Much of the fighting centered on Chania, and

great swaths of the city were destroyed during the war. Almost worth the price of admission alone is the opportunity to walk along the Firka's ramparts for bracing views of the city, sea, and mountains. ⊠ Chania ✛ Waterfront at far west end of port ☎ 28210/91875 ⊕ www.mar-mus-crete.gr ⌐ €3.

Gouvernetou

RELIGIOUS SITE | This 16th-century, Venetian-era monastery on the north end of the Akrotiri Peninsula is said to be one of the oldest and largest remaining religious communities on Crete. Delightful frescoes cover the wall of the courtyard chapel, while a path leads down the flanks of a seaside ravine past several caves used as hermitages and churches to the remote, 11th-century Katholiko, the monastery of St. John the Hermit, who pursued his solitary life in a nearby cave. Follow the path down to the sea along a riverbank for another mile or so to a secluded cove that is the perfect place for a refreshing dip, the aptly named Katholiko Beach. The return walk requires a steep uphill climb. ⊠ Stavros ✛ Northern end of Akrotiri Peninsula, 4 km (2½ miles) north of Ayia Triada; 19 km (12 miles) north of Chania, follow road north from Chordaki ☎ 28430/63319 ۞ Closed Wed. and Fri.

Janissaries Mosque

RELIGIOUS SITE | Kastelli Hill creates a backdrop to the Janissaries Mosque, the oldest Ottoman building in Crete, built at the water's edge when Turks captured the town in 1645 after a two-month siege. Its back courtyard, once home to a garden of palm trees, and its minaret were both bombed and destroyed during the Nazi occupation. You can enter the building only when the town uses it to host temporary art and trade exhibitions, but the presence of the domed structure at the edge of the shimmering sea lends Chania part of its exotic aura. ⊠ Chania ✛ East side of inner harbor.

Kastelli Hill

ARCHAEOLOGICAL SITE | The hill where the Venetians first settled rises above the east end of the harbor and it became the quarter of the local nobility. Their palaces, now partially in ruin from neglect and World War II bombings, still line the ridge above the harbor. Kastelli had been occupied much earlier; the Minoan city of Cydonia was sited here. ⊠ *Chania* ⌖ *Above harbor.*

★ Samaria Gorge

CANYON | South of Chania a deep, verdant crevice extends 16 km (10 miles) from near the village of Xyloskalo to the Libyan Sea. The landscape of forest, sheer rock faces, and running streams, inhabited by the elusive and endangered *kri-kri* (wild goat) is magnificent. The Samaria, protected as a national park, is the most traveled of the dozens of gorges that cut through Crete's mountains and emerge at the sea, but the walk through the canyon, in places only a few feet wide and almost 2,000 feet deep, is thrilling nonetheless. Reckon on five to six hours of downhill walking with a welcome reward of a swim at the end. Buses depart the central bus station in Chania at 7:30 and 8:30 am for Xyloskalo. Boats leave in the afternoon (5:30) from Ayia Roumeli, the mouth of the gorge, where it's an hour-long scenic sail to Hora Sfakion, from where buses return to Chania. Travel agents also arrange day trips to the gorge. Also from Chania, a couple of extremely scenic routes head south across the craggy White Mountains to the isolated Libyan Sea villages of **Paleochora,** the main resort of the southwest coast, and **Souyia,** a pleasant collection of whitewashed houses facing a long beach. Much of this section of the coast, including the village of **Loutro,** is accessible only by boat or by a seaside path. ⊠ *Samaria* ⌖ *35 km (22 miles) south of Chania, entrance near Omalos* ☎ ⊕ *www.samaria.gr* ⌑ *€5 entrance to National Park* ⊗ *Closed Oct. 15–May 1.*

Venetian Arsenali

HISTORIC SITE | As you follow the harbor front east from the mosque, you come to a long line of Venetian *arsenali* (warehouses) from the 16th and 17th centuries, used to store wares and repair craft. The seawalls swing around to enclose the harbor and end at the **old lighthouse** that stands at the east side of the harbor entrance; from here you get a magnificent view of the town, with the imposing White Mountains looming behind the animated harbor. ⊠ *Akti Enoseos* ⌖ *East end of old harbor.*

Beaches

A string of beaches extends west from the city center, and you can easily reach them on foot by following the sea past the old olive-oil factory just west of the walls and the Byzantine Museum. They are not idyllic, but the water is clean. Locals who want to spend a day at the beach often head out to some of the best beaches on Crete along the surrounding coastline.

Balos

BEACH—SIGHT | You already know this beach from every postcard stand in Greece. Seemingly transported from the South Seas, an islet sits dramatically amid a shallow lagoon of bright blue-and-turquoise water framed by white sand. Approach by car along the 8-km (5-mile) very rough dirt road (€1 toll) and you will be rewarded by that picture-perfect panorama. Nevertheless, a half-hour descent on foot to the beach itself, and longer return, is the price to pay. Easier on the legs is to take the boat from Kissamos, which includes a stop at the deserted island Venetian fortress of Gramvousa. Like Vai, it can get very busy here; if you are coming by car, aim to arrive in the morning before the boats, or late in the afternoon once the crowds have left. **Amenities:** food and drink; parking (free); toilets. **Best for:** snorkeling; swimming; walking.

Did You Know?

Hiking the Samaria Gorge, Europe's longest, you'll encounter wildflowers, streams (which can close the gorge in early spring), vultures, and maybe even the *kri-kri*, the Cretan wild goat.

Elafonissi

BEACH—SIGHT | A peninsula on the western end of the island, about 75 km (45 miles) west of Chania, extends into turquoise waters, with a lagoon on one side and isolated sands and coves on the other. The pink sands, rock formations, and colorful waters evoke the tropics. In places, the peninsula is broken by narrow channels, requiring beachgoers to wade through the warm, shallow waters, adding to the remote aura. The eastern, lagoon-side of the peninsula has amenities and is popular with families (the water is never more than a few feet deep) while other parts, especially the western, ocean-facing side, are relatively isolated and frequented by nudists. **Amenities:** food and drink; lifeguards; parking (free); showers; toilets. **Best for:** nudists; snorkeling; solitude (western end); sunset; swimming; walking. ✉ *Elafonissi.*

Falassarna

BEACH—SIGHT | Often cited as the best beach on the island, Falassarna stretches along the western edge of the island, about 60 km (37 miles) west of Chania. The long expanse of sand is broken into several coves and has a little bit of everything—amenities on the main section, Pacheia Ammos, plenty of isolation in other parts, and even ancient ruins behind the northern end. One small disadvantage is a steady wind from the west, which can make the water choppy (but is a boon for windsurfers). **Amenities:** food and drink; lifeguards; parking (free); showers; toilets, water sports. **Best for:** nudists; solitude; sunset; swimming; walking; windsurfing. ✉ *Falassarna.*

Stavros

BEACH—SIGHT | If this cove at the northern end of the Akrotiri Peninsula, about 15 km (9 miles) east of Chania, looks familiar, you may recognize it as the location of the 1964 movie *Zorba the Greek*. The onetime fishing village has grown a bit since then but it's still a charming place, especially with this white-sand beach on a lagoon backed by a steep mountain (it was here that Zorba did his Sirtaki dance); a slightly wilder, less crowded beach is just to the west. **Amenities:** food and drink; parking (free); showers; toilets water sports. **Best for:** snorkeling; swimming. ✉ *Stavros.*

🍴 Restaurants

Apostolis

$ | **SEAFOOD** | On the quieter end of the harbor next to the Venetian arsenals and removed from the tourist joints that surround the port, this lively taverna caters to locals and discerning tourists alike. Fresh fish and seafood are the standouts here, but also consider the stuffed aubergines, stifado, *kleftiko* (lamb), or the meats from the charcoal grill. **Known for:** the place the locals go to for the freshest fish; excellent, friendly staff; great people-watching spot right on the harbor front. [$] *Average main: €12* ✉ *Aki Enoseos 10* ☎ *28210/43470.*

★ **Dounias**

$ | **GREEK** | On a mountain perch above Chania is one of the most singular restaurants in the whole of Crete. A holistic approach is taken—this is farm-to-table eating but ramped up to the nth degree. **Known for:** drive up through the Therisso Gorge is spectacular; old recipes, old methods, new flavors; booking recommended. [$] *Average main: €12* ✉ *Drakona* ☎ *28210/65083* 🌐 *www.ntounias.gr.*

Portes

$ | **MODERN GREEK** | Relocated from the somewhat cramped alley it occupied in the city center to a pretty harborside spot in Nea Chora, Portes continues to offer some of the best cooking in Chania. Irish-born Susanna has a flare for hospitality, and the dishes on offer are always assured and pretty as a picture. **Known for:** diverse menu of Greek classics with a twist; super pies—octopus, fennel, artichoke, and asparagus are all stars;

genial, generous atmosphere. $ *Average main: €13* ✉ *Akti Papanikoli 1, Nea Chora* ☎ *28210/76261.*

Tamam

$ | **MEDITERRANEAN** | Steps away from the busy harbor, Tamam feels like a giant leap back in time—it's an ancient Turkish bath that now houses one of the most atmospheric restaurants in Chania's Old Town. Tamam means "alright" in Turkish, but the plates presented are certainly more than okay. **Known for:** atmospheric 600-year-old building; gently spiced dishes with a nod to Turkey; alleyway tables are a blessing on balmy evenings. $ *Average main: €12* ✉ *Zambeliou 49* ☎ *28210/96080* ⊕ *www.tamamrestaurant.com.*

Well of the Turk

$ | **MEDITERRANEAN** | In the old Ottoman district of Splantzia, opposite the underground church of Ayia Irene, this restaurant is somewhat difficult to find even with a map, but it is worth the endeavor. It serves a mixture of Greek and Turkish dishes with the odd trip to Northern Africa and the Middle East. **Known for:** fabulous food away from the crowds; adjoining flower-scented terrace, a nice option in summer; vegetarian moussaka—a revelation. $ *Average main: €12* ✉ *Kalinikou Sarpaki 1–3, Splantzia* ☎ *28210/54547* ⊕ *www.welloftheturk.com.*

☕ Coffee and Quick Bites

Pasteleria de Dana

$ | **CAFÉ** | On a tiny pedestrian street a block back from the harbor, sweet alchemy takes place. Extraordinary creations are offered; mini-tarts, macaroons, and eclairs that would grace the finest Parisian patisserie. **Known for:** amazing patisserie art; elegant furniture and settings; pomegranate soda is a wow. $ *Average main: €4* ✉ *Isodion Str* ☎ *28213/02801.*

Hotels

★ Ammos Hotel

$$ | **RESORT** | **FAMILY** | Quite simply, one of the best family hotels in Greece, this is the classic Greek seaside hotel brought up-to-date with a chic and funky twist, where Cycladic and Scandinavian design references throughout create an atmosphere that is both modern and timeless. **Pros:** genuinely friendly and caring service; innovative food sourced from local suppliers; fresh and fun design renovated every year. **Cons:** 5 km (3 miles) from Chania center (but on a bus route); pool can get busy; some rooms face the pretty gardens rather than the sea. $ *Rooms from: €180* ✉ *Irakli Avgoula, Glaros Beach* ☎ *28210/33003* ⊕ *www.ammoshotel.com* ⊗ *Closed Nov.–early Apr.* ⇆ *33 rooms* ⊗| *Free breakfast.*

★ Casa Delfino

$$ | **HOTEL** | If you have an ounce of romance in your body you'll love this gorgeous hotel—in 1835 Captain Delfino sailed from Genoa, only to founder on the rocks off Gramvousa, but, smitten by the beauty of Chania, he bought this Renaissance Venetian mansion as his home. **Pros:** prime position on Chania's pretty harbor, opposite the lighthouse; superb breakfast in a mosaic-pebbled courtyard with homemade specialties; stunning spa and rooftop terrace bar. **Cons:** no parking in the town center (but hotel's golf buggy will collect you); historical building means some stairs; books up early in high season. $ *Rooms from: €200* ✉ *Theofanous 9* ☎ *28210/87400* ⊕ *www.casadelfino.com* ⇆ *24 suites* ⊗| *Free breakfast.*

Doma

$$ | **HOTEL** | This 19th-century seaside mansion on the eastern edge of town, about a 20-minute walk along the waterfront from the Venetian harbor, is an outpost of old Cretan taste and refinement. **Pros:** gracious atmosphere from accommodating staff and owners;

shady rear garden; a great sense of Cretan history—this building has seen it all. **Cons:** a distance from the center in a rather nondescript area; some will find the furnishings intriguing, others will think it eccentric; busy road fronts the property. $ *Rooms from: €160* ⊠ *Eleftheriou Venizelou St. 124* ☎ *28210/51772* ⊕ *www.hotel-doma.gr* ⊙ *Closed Nov.–Mar.* ⇌ *24 rooms* ⦿ *Free breakfast.*

Porto Veneziano

$ | HOTEL | Nautical themes in blue and white make for a light, airy atmosphere in this harborside establishment, but the main draw are those views of the Venetian waterfront and the White Mountains. **Pros:** great position on the quieter end of the harbor; outside tables are a perfect breakfast spot; free bicycles to explore the delights of Chania. **Cons:** rooms at the rear overlook a pretty garden and not-so-pretty car park; rather plain common areas; standard rooms a little snug. $ *Rooms from: €120* ⊠ *Old Venetian Harbor* ☎ *28210/27100* ⊕ *www.portoveneziano.gr* ⇌ *57 rooms* ⦿ *Free breakfast.*

Samaria Hotel

$$ | HOTEL | Something of a departure from the regular offerings on the Chania hotel scene, the Samaria has the feel of a luxury business establishment, but with added personality. **Pros:** quiet, efficient service; contemporary decor is stylish and modern; city-center hotel with a pool—a rarity in Chania. **Cons:** small pool can get busy; not the prettiest of views from the balconies; some noise from the bus depot at the rear. $ *Rooms from: €140* ⊠ *Kidonias 69* ☎ *28210/38600* ⊕ *www.samariahotel.gr* ⇌ *84 rooms* ⦿ *Free breakfast.*

🛍 Shopping

The most exotic shopping experience in town is a stroll through Chania's covered market to see local merchants selling rounds of Cretan cheese, jars of golden honey, lengths of salami, salt fish, lentils, and herbs.

Carmela

CERAMICS/GLASSWARE | This enticing store just off the harbor sells the work of contemporary jewelers and other craftspeople from Crete and throughout Greece, as well as the work of owner Carmela Iatropoulou and her artist husband. ⊠ *Aggelou 7* ☎ *28210/90487.*

Top Hanak Old Cretan Blankets and Kilims

CRAFTS | Many of these antique blankets and rugs were made for dowries from homespun wool and natural dyes and they make beautiful souvenirs. ⊠ *Aggelou 3* ☎ *28210/98571.*

Chapter 10

RHODES AND THE DODECANESE

RHODES, SYMI, KOS, PATMOS

Updated by
Gareth Clark

👁 Sights   🍴 Restaurants   🏨 Hotels   🛍 Shopping   🍸 Nightlife

★★★★★   ★★★★☆   ★★★★☆   ★★☆☆☆   ★★☆☆☆

WELCOME TO
RHODES AND THE DODECANESE

TOP REASONS TO GO

★ **The Old Town of Rhodes:** The monuments built by the Knights of St. John some 700 years ago draw as many visitors to Rhodes as the beaches do; Rhodes's Old Town is a remarkably well-preserved and photogenic testimony to its Crusader past.

★ **The Asklepieion:** Kos's site of ancient healing, the Asklepieion, was the renowned medical school founded by Hippocrates, father of Western medicine.

★ **Natural wonders:** The terrain yields swarms of colorful day-flying moths (Rhodes), hot sea springs (Kos), countless coves (Patmos), and mountain paths (Symi).

★ **St. John's Patmos:** Called the "Jerusalem of the Aegean," Patmos is as peaceful as it was when the Apostle John glimpsed the Apocalypse in his cave here—the spiritual mystique of this little island is still strong.

The Dodecanese (Twelve Islands) are the eastern-most holdings of Greece and are set around the shores of Turkey and Asia Minor. Here, classic, Byzantine, and Ottoman architectures blend, and multiculturalism is an old idea. Romans, Crusaders, Turks, and Venetians have all left their marks on Rhodes, in the south of the archi-pelago—it's the busiest, most populated, and most visited of the 12 islands. Just to the north is tiny, craggy Symi, sparsely inhabited and ringed by enticing coves. Kos, with its lush fields and sandy beaches, lies between Symi and Patmos, the northern-most island of the group, where arid hillsides are occasionally clad in great stands of cypress.

1 Rhodes. Start, like the crusading Knights of St. John did, at the walled city of Rhodes's Old Town, with its monuments, shops, and restaurants. Heading south around the island, discover the moth-mecca of the Valley of the Butterflies in Petaloudes, then take the island's

mountainous western road to ancient Kameiros city and medieval Monolithos fortress. The eastern road leads to lovely, car-free Lindos and many, many beaches.

2 Symi. "Picturesque" is the word for both Yialos Harbor, with its restau-rants and shops, and Chorio, just above it. The inner island is littered with small churches. The impressive and popular Panormitis Monastery is serviced by boats.

3 Kos. The port town is an appealing blend of ancient stones and north-ern European partying teens. A short drive out of town, Asklepieion was once the greatest healing site of the ancient era. Large swathes of coast are perfect for swimming.

4 Patmos. Make your pilgrimage to Chora to see the cave where St. John is said to have seen and recorded his revelation of the Apocalypse. Towering over Chora's skyline is the imposing, fortified Monas-tery of St. John the Theologian, and far below is Skala, Patmos's pleasant main town and harbor.

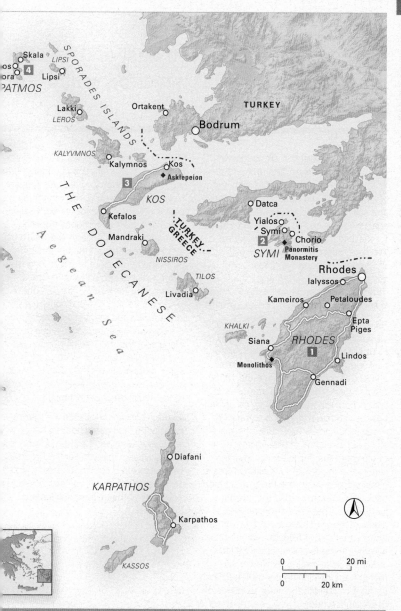

SPORADES ISLANDS

Skala
LIPSI
os 4 Lipsi
ora
PATMOS

Lakki
LEROS
Ortakent
TURKEY

Bodrum

KALYVMNOS
Kalymnos
Kos
◆ Asklepeion

3

THE *KOS*
Kefalos

Datca

Yialos
Symi
Chorio
2
SYMI ◆ Panormitis
Monastery

Mandraki

NISSIROS

THE DODECANESE

A e g e a n   S e a

TILOS
Livadia

Rhodes
Ialyssos

Kameiros Petaloudes
Epta
Piges
KHALKI
Siana *RHODES*
1
Lindos
◆ Monolithos
Gennadi

Diafani

KARPATHOS

Karpathos

KASSOS

0   20 mi

0   20 km

Wrapped enticingly around the shores of Asia Minor, the Dodecanese are Greece's easternmost island chain, edging the sunny fringes of the Aegean sea. A historic bridge between East and West, it is a location that has never been short of admirers.

Roman and Byzantine merchants grew fat off its trade routes, and to the Catholic Knights of the Order of St. John, who landed in 1309 and transformed Rhodes and Kos, they were a powerful bulwark against the spread of Islam. Even today, for that most persistent invader of all, Western tourists, the geographical oddity of Rhodes, "Europe's sunniest spot," is still a more potent lure than all the jewels of the ancient world that lie there. These islands have lived long in our imagination.

Romans, Crusaders, Persians, Turks, and Venetians have all planted their flag in the Dodecanese at some point, but it was package tourism that brought Rhodes and Kos to their knees. Since the 1960s the pair have yielded huge stretches of coastline to resorts, drawn to the golden beaches and twinkling blue waters. Yet these sands are far from lost; there are still quiet stretches of blissful shore to dip your toes. Temples, castles, and acropolises hidden among hilltop forests, ghost villages, lush vineyards, or cobbled back lanes also reward with more than just respite. These are atmospheric sights, filled with history. And for all the visitors that crowd Rhodes's Old Town in summer, there is still no other walled city in Europe as charming, while few can match Kos's healing center of Asklepieion for its glimpse into the inner workings of the ancient world.

Then there are the smaller islands: Symi and Patmos. For reasons of either culture or geography, the sting of mass tourism just hasn't taken here. The former is a pleasing warren of colorful neoclassical mansions, built with money from the sponge trade that once thrived there. Its stony shores attract little but day-trippers, and come nightfall it's among the most peaceful spots in all the Greek islands. Patmos was where St. John wrote his Book of Revelation, and it grew into a renowned monastic center during the Byzantine period. Today it is a pilgrimage spot for the Greek Orthodox faith and has little truck with resorts yet hides some fantastic shorelines. Both have few attractions but offer a welcome antidote to the addiction of mass tourism.

All the Dodecanese islands are worthy of exploration, and easily hopped on local ferries. Once there, it's often only on foot or two wheels that you can find yourself without another soul for company, and perhaps only then will you appreciate just what makes these islands so unique.

Planning

When to Go

To avoid crowds, just before and after peak seasons (May, June, and September) are good times to visit. August is the busiest season on all these islands, when hotel reservations and even spots on inter-island ferries can be hard to come by. Patmos (for its monastery) and Rhodes are popular Easter getaways for Greeks, and celebrations include candlelit processions and fireworks late Saturday around midnight; island bakeries serve *tsoureki* (sweet braided bread). From November to April, most archaeological sites remain open, but many hotels, restaurants, and shops are closed, and boat travel is limited by curtailed schedules and the weather's whims.

Planning Your Time

Rhodes and Kos are two of Greece's most popular resort islands, and for good reason: they offer not only some magnificent sandy beaches but also real historical dazzlers and rich, off-the-beach experiences. On Rhodes, cultural must-dos include visits to the Palace of the Grand Master and other sights in Rhodes's Old Town, as well as the Acropolis of Lindos. Kos's great archaeological treasure is the Asklepieion, the great healing center of antiquity. Go early to avoid the heat and crowds.

On these busy islands it's also easy to wander off the beaten path to enjoy mountainous hinterlands carpeted in pine forests, vineyards, and groves of olives and oranges. A visit to either island should include a country drive (or bus excursion) and lunch in a village taverna. Good stops are Siana and Apollona in Rhodes, and Zia on Kos. Symi and Patmos are more geared to travelers looking for low-key retreats and a glimpse of

authentic island life. It's easy to slip away to uncrowded beaches and coves on either, but also to join islanders for their time-honored ritual of an evening stroll. On Symi, you can amble around the harbor in Yialos, then walk up the Kali Strata (Good Steps) to Chorio. In Patmos, the gathering spots are the main waterfront promenade and narrow lanes of Skala, which come alive in the evening.

Getting Here and Around

AIR

Though you can get to the hubs of Rhodes or Kos in around 12 hours nowadays, on the faster ferries from Athens, if you have limited time it's best to fly to these two islands. Olympic Air (Aegean Airlines) and Sky Express both have non-stop daily flights during summer, connecting the pair to the Greek capital; flying time is about 50 minutes to either island. Less frequent direct flights also go from Thessaloniki (1¼ hours). Sky Direct runs a few flights a week between Rhodes and Kos (30 mins), though it's cheaper and less hassle to take the ferry. Finally, it's possible to fly directly to Rhodes and Kos from a number of European capitals on Aegean and several European carriers during the summer season (May.–Oct.). Neither Patmos nor Symi has an airport.

Rhodes Diogoras Airport is in Paradissi, 15 km (9 miles) southwest of Rhodes Town, and well connected by a public bus (6 am–11 pm) that reaches the Old Town (€3) in 40 minutes. Taxis cost approximately €25 for the half-hour drive. You don't have to haggle with drivers as set prices are displayed on boards at the airport taxi rank. The Old Town is inaccessible to cars, so hotels will usually arrange to have a porter meet you near one of the gates.

Kos Airport is 26 km (16 miles) southwest of Kos Town. A 45-minute bus links the airport to Kos Town (€3.20) via Mastichari, though even in summer its timings aren't always great for morning flights (the earliest service from the airport is 10 am). Expect to pay about €35 for the taxi fare to Kos Town or the beach resorts

CONTACTS Kos Airport. ☎ *22420/56000* ⊕ *www.kgs-airport.gr/en.* **Rhodes Airport.** ☎ *22410/88700* ⊕ *www.rhodes-airport.info.*

BOAT AND FERRY

In August, for good rates and an assured spot, it is essential that you book as far as possible (at least two weeks) in advance. Boats at this time can be uncomfortably crowded, with deck-class passengers claiming key spots on the floor, in the lounge areas, and even—in peak season—on the metal deck under the stars. If you're taking an overnight boat in August, book a berth so you'll be assured a comfortable place to lay your head. If you are traveling to and around the Dodecanese islands outside the summer season, you'll find that service is curtailed.

When traveling from Piraeus to Rhodes by ferry (12–18 hours), you first make several stops, including at Patmos (6–10 hours) and Kos (10–16 hours). Bringing a car aboard can quadruple costs. Of the several ferry lines serving the Dodecanese, Blue Star Ferries has the largest boats and the most frequent service, sailing several times a week out of Piraeus (Athens). The Athens–Dodecanese ferry schedule changes seasonally, and ferries to Patmos do not run daily out of season, so contact ferry lines, the Greek National Tourism Organization (GNTO or EOT) in Athens, or a travel agency for details. An excellent source for ferry schedules is the web-based tourist site, the Greek Travel Pages (GTP) ⊕ *www.gtp.gr.*

The easiest way to travel among the Dodecanese islands is by high-speed craft. Dodekanisos Seaways has the most regular services; tickets are booked online and must be picked up in advance of departure at the various offices and travel agencies listed on the site. Be sure to pay attention once on board, as the boat makes multiple stops and turnaround is

quick. Times and fares: Rhodes to/from Symi takes 50 minutes (€21); Rhodes to/from Kos takes 2¼ hours (€34); Rhodes to/from Patmos takes 5 hours (€49).

CONTACTS Blue Star Ferries. ☎ *21089/19800* ⊕ *www.bluestarferries.com/en/.* **Dodekanisos Seaways.** ✉ *Thalassini Pili, Kolona Port* ☎ *22410/70590* ⊕ *www.12ne.gr.*

BUS

There is a decent bus network on all the islands, though there are more-infrequent routes on Patmos and Symi. Buses from Rhodes Town leave from two different points on Averof Street for the island's east and west sides. Symi's and Patmos's bus stations are on the harbor. Kos Town is served by a city bus that has a stand on Dolphin Square, while KTEL buses service the rest of the island from the depot on Cleopatras Street.

CONTACTS Kos KTEL Bus Depot. ✉ *Cleopatras 7, Kos Town* ☎ *22420/22292* ⊕ *www.ktel-kos.gr.* **Rhodes East-Side Bus Depot.** ✉ *Averof, Rhodes Town* ✥ *Near the end of Platia Rimini* ☎ *22410/26300.* **Rhodes West-Side Bus Station.** ✉ *Averof, Rhodes Town* ✥ *Next to the market* ☎ *22410/26300.*

CAR

A car is useful for exploring Rhodes or Kos, or to hop between Patmos's many beaches. In Symi, with its few roads, a car is of little use, and you should opt for the vans that serve as the island buses, make use of the island taxis, or walk along the paths that connect most places on the island.

You may take a car to the Dodecanese on one of the large ferries that sail daily from Piraeus (Athens) to Rhodes and less frequently to the smaller islands. The relatively small network of roads on Rhodes is well maintained and detailed maps are available; traffic is likely to be heavy only from Rhodes Town to Lindos. In Kos, a car makes it easy to skirt the coast and make stops at the many sandy beaches, though resorts are serviced by bus. In Patmos, a car or motorbike makes it easy to tour the island, while sights and outlying restaurants are easily reached by bus or taxi, and a few beaches can be reached by either bus or boat. Symi, which has only one road suitable for cars, is best explored on foot or by bus or boat. Expect to pay at least €30–€40 a day to rent a car on one of the islands.

TAXI

Taxis are available throughout most of Rhodes, where most taxi stands have a sign listing set fares to destinations around the island. This is less common on the other islands, where taxi meters also aren't in use. Expect a delay when calling radio taxis in high season.

CONTACTS Kos Taxi. ☎ 22420/23333 ⊕ www.kosradiotaxi.gr. **Patmos Radio Taxi.** ☎ 22470/31225. **Rhodes Radio Taxi.** ☎ 22410/69800 ⊕ www.rhodes-taxi.gr.

Hotels

Rhodes has an array of resort hotels, largely scattered along the east coast, with sea views and easy access to beaches. Many old medieval houses in its Old Town have been converted to boutique hotels, some modest and others quite luxurious. Nearly all offer a quieter experience than anything else you'll find on the island. Mass tourist accommodations are also plentiful on Kos, where you'll find few boutique hotels, though a growing number of adult-only small luxury resorts balance things out. Hotels on Symi are small and usually charming, since the island never encouraged the development of mammoth caravansaries. Similarly, Patmos has attractive, high-quality lodgings that tend to be both more elegant and traditional than its resort-magnet neighbors. High season can prove extremely crowded and you may have difficulty finding a room on any of these islands if you don't book well in advance. Many hotels throughout the Dodecanese are closed from November through March.

Lodgings in water-poor Symi and Patmos may remind you to limit water use.

Restaurants

Throughout the Dodecanese, you can find sophisticated restaurants, as well as simple tavernas serving excellent food. On Rhodes and Kos, beware of many completely mediocre eateries catering to tourists with fast food—the grabby hype-men standing outside are usually a good clue. It is sometimes best to wait until after 9 pm to see where the Greeks are eating. Because Rhodes and Kos produce most of their own foodstuffs, in better restaurants you can count on fresh fruit and vegetables. Fish, of course, is readily available on all islands. Large fish goes by the kilo, so confirm the exact amount you'd like when ordering or risk huge bills. Tiny, tender Symi shrimp, found only in the waters around this island, have such soft shells they can be easily popped in the mouth whole. They are used in dozens of local dishes. Wherever you dine, ask about the specialty of the day. Rhodes produces some excellent wines that appear on tables throughout the Dodecanese, and vintages from throughout Greece also show up on wine lists. With the exception of a few very high-end spots, dress on all the islands is casual; reservations are not necessary unless specified.

Restaurant and hotel reviews have been shortened. For full information, visit Fodors.com.

What it Costs in euros			
$	$$	$$$	$$$$
RESTAURANTS			
under €15	€15–€25	€26–€40	over €40
HOTELS			
under €125	€125–€225	€226–€275	over €275

Tours

From April to October, local island boat
tours take you to area sights and may
include a picnic on a remote beach or
even a visit to the shores of Turkey.

A1 Yacht Trade Consortium

BOAT TOURS | This brokerage, rental agen-
cy, and outfitter organizes sailing tours
around the Greek islands near the Turkish
coast. ✉ *Commercial harbor, Rhodes
Town* ☎ *22410/01000* ⊕ *www.a1yachting.
com.*

Astoria Travel

BUS TOURS | On Patmos, Astoria Travel
provides day bus trips to Patmos's St.
John the Theologian Monastery and the
Monastery of the Apocalypse. ✉ *Skala
Harbor, Skala* ☎ *22270/31205* ⊕ *www.
astoriatravel.com.*

Kalodoukas Holidays

BOAT TOURS | On Symi, Kalodoukas
Holidays runs boat trips to the Monastery
of Panormitis, as well as to secluded
beaches and islets, which include walks,
swimming, and a barbecue lunch. ✉ *Harbor front, Yialos* ☎ *22460/71077* ⊕ *www.
kalodoukas.gr.*

Symi Tours

BOAT TOURS | The island's venerable tour
organizer arranges boat excursions
around the island and can help tourists
book accommodations. ✉ *Harbor front,
Yialos* ☎ *22460/71307* ⊕ *www.symitours.
com.*

Triton Holidays

BUS TOURS | Triton Holidays offers guided
bus tours around Rhodes, and can
arrange a boat tour that leaves Mandraki
Harbor, depositing you in Lindos for a
day of sightseeing and beachgoing, with
a return in the evening. ✉ *Plastira 9,
Rhodes Town* ☎ *22410/21690* ⊕ *www.
tritondmc.gr.*

Rhodes Ρόδος

Rhodes, at 1,400 square km (540 square
miles) is the fourth-largest Greek island
and, along with Sicily, Crete, and Cyprus,
is one of the great sights of the Mediterranean. It lies almost exactly halfway
between Athens and Cyprus, 18 km
(11 miles) off the coast of Turkey, and it
was long considered a bridge between
Europe and the East. Geologically similar
to the Turkish mainland, it was probably
once part of Asia Minor, separated by
one of the frequent volcanic upheavals
this volatile region has experienced.

Today Rhodes retains its role as the
center of Dodecanese trade, politics, and
culture. Rhodes Town brings together
fascinating artifacts, medieval architecture, an active nightlife, and is reputedly
the sunniest spot in all of Europe. Like a
gigantic historical pop-up book, it offers
layer upon layer of sights: Venetians,
Crusaders, and Turks all added to an array
of palaces, battlements, and churches
in exotic quarters of shady lanes and
tall houses. Head out to the island's
coasts and you'll find them blessed with
white-sand beaches, hot springs, ruined
castles, acropolises, and interspersed
with fertile valleys full of figs and olives.
Yes, resorts stitch the eastern shores,
but they're easily skipped.

The island's history unfolds as an
especially rich pageant. Rhodes saw
successive waves of settlement, including the arrival of the Dorian Greeks from
Argos and Laconia at the turn of the
1st millennium BC, who set up cities
in Ialysos, Kameiros, and Lindos. From
the 8th to the 6th century BC, the island
established settlements in Italy, France,
Spain, and Egypt and actively traded with
mainland Greece, exporting pottery, oil,
wine, and figs. Independence and expansion came to a halt when the Persians
took over at the end of the 6th century
BC and forced Rhodians to provide ships
and men for King Xerxes's failed attack

on the mainland (480 BC). A league of city-states rose under Athenian leadership. In 408 BC the united city of Rhodes was created on the site of the modern town; much of the populace moved there, and the history of the island and the town became synonymous.

In 164 BC, Rhodes came under the full hegemony of the Roman Empire, and through the years it was fabled as a beautiful city where straight roads were lined with porticoes, houses, and gardens. According to Pliny, who described the city in the 1st century AD, the town possessed some 2,000 statues, at least 100 of them of colossal scale. One of the most famous examples of its sculptural school is the world-famous *Laocöon*— probably crafted in the 1st century BC— which showed the priest who warned the Trojans to beware Greeks bearing gifts (it stands in the Vatican today). Sadly, the ancient glory of Rhodes has few visible remnants. The city was ravaged by Arab invaders in AD 654 and 807, and only with the expulsion of the Arabs and the reconquest of Rhodes by the Byzantine emperors did it begin to revive— gloriously. Rhodes was a crucial stop on the road to the Holy Land during the Crusades. It came briefly under Venetian influence, then Byzantine, then Genoese. Then, in 1309, when the Knights of the Order of St. John took the city from its Genoese masters, the island's most important modern era began.

The Knights used their wealth, plundered from the Holy Lands, to fortify Rhodes, raising 4 km (2½ miles) of fortifications around the capital and building 11 castles across the island. Such was their skill that in 1480, Rhodes Town, manned by just a few thousand, withstood a two-month seige by an Ottoman army more than 20 times their number. But in 1522 Rhodes fell to the Turks. During Turkish occupation, the island became a possession of the Grand Admiral, who collected taxes but left the Rhodians to pursue a generally peaceful and prosperous existence. They continued to build ships and trade with Greece, Constantinople (later Istanbul), Syria, and Egypt. The Greek mainland was liberated by the War of Independence in 1821, but Rhodes and the Dodecanese remained part of the Ottoman Empire until 1912, when the Italians took over. After World War II, the Dodecanese were formally united with Greece in 1947.

The last of Rhodes's great invaders are tourists; a dream set in motion by Italian dictator Benito Mussolini in the 1930s. He devised plans to turn the island into a paradise for the well-to-do, building hydrotherapy faciliaties at Kallithea as well as plush hotels. By the late 1990s, its coasts were famous among package tourists and the dawn of cheap flights saw areas such as Faliraki gain an unsavory reputation for the boozy hedonism of its visitors. This has been clamped down on by the authorities, but it didn't stop the crowds arriving. Within the walls of Rhodes's Old Town; on the beaches along the eastern coast; and amid the whitewashed walls of Lindos, their numbers can be suffocating during high summer (Jul.–early Sept.), which is best avoided. Arrive earlier or later in the season to see the island at its best, but be warned that most things shut down during winter.

GETTING HERE AND AROUND

Rhodes is well served by regularly scheduled flights from Athens and Thessaloniki as well as both scheduled and charter flights from London, Rome, and other major European cities. Two daily ferries leave from Piraeus (Athens) bound for Rhodes and the Dodecanese, a minimum 15-hour overnight trip. You will find schedules and booking information for the ferry service to and from Rhodes and other islands in the Dodecanese at ⊕ *www. ferries.gr* or ⊕ *www.gtp.gr*.

Regional ferries connect Rhodes, Kos, Symi, and Patmos. Smaller boats, including

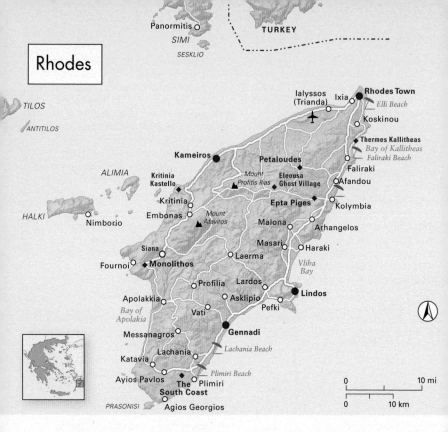

those to other islands in the Dodecanese, dock at Rhodes Town's 2,500-year-old Mandraki Harbor; the larger overnight ferries use the adjacent new harbor.

Rhodes Diogoras Airport is in Paradissi, 15 km (9 miles) southwest of Rhodes Town, and well connected by a public bus (6 am–11 pm) that reaches the Old Town (€3) in 40 minutes. Taxis cost approximately €25 for the half-hour drive.

Rhodes Town's two bus terminals are hubs for services running either side of the island—points on the western side of the island are served by buses from the West Side Station, near the shopping district of the New Town on Averof; most places on the eastern side are served from the nearby East Side Station on Platia Rimini (Rimini Square), next to the market on Mandraki Harbor. Bus service is excellent, with buses to and from Lindos running almost hourly from the East Side Station; €5.50 each way as opposed to €62 by taxi.

VISITOR INFORMATION

The central Rhodes Municipal Tourism Office, near the bus station, is open May–October, daily 7:30 am–3 pm.

CONTACTS Rhodes Municipal Tourism Office. ⊠ *Averof 3, Rhodes Town* ☎ *22410/44330* ⊕ *www.rhodes.gr.*

Rhodes Town Ρόδος (πόλη)

463 km (288 miles) east of Piraeus harbor in Athens by ferry.

Early travelers described Rhodes as a town of two parts: a castle or high town (Collachium) and a lower area (Bourgo). Today Rhodes Town—sometimes referred to as Ródos Town—is still divided: the Old Town, a UNESCO World Heritage site that incorporates the walled city, and the modern metropolis, or New Town, spreading away from the old fortifications.

The New Town is "new" only in relative terms—islanders began settling outside the walls of the Old Town with the arrival of the Turks in 1522. There is little here to hold the attention, however. Elli Beach is unconsciously crowded, and while the pedestrianized restaurant street of Niki-forou Mandilara is likeable and growing in reputation, the only other distractions are the last vestiges of Mussolini's plans to turn Rhodes into Italy's ultimate seaside retreat. The 1927-built Grande Albergo Delle Rose hotel, once a setting for the jet set, still lauds it over the eastern shore.

The Old Town is the real jewel of Rhodes, lined with Orthodox and Catholic church-es, Turkish houses, and medieval public buildings. When the Knights of St. John arrived in 1309, they built over the original Byzantine fortifications and expanded heavily. What changes the Ottomans made were mostly obliterated by the arriv-al of Italians in 1912. Fascist Italy sought to align itself with the grandiosity of the Knights' achievements and set about zeal-ously restoring and preserving their legacy during the 1930s. Walking its mostly car-less, cobbled streets today, there are few cities where you can see and feel the past quite so viscerally—though that's not as easily acheived during July and August when they fill to bursting point. Arrive later in the season (mid-Sept.–Oct.) and stay in the quieter southern corner of the old city for more peace.

 Sights

The Acropolis of Rhodes
ARCHAEOLOGICAL SITE | About 2 km (1 mile) to the west of Rhodes's town center, atop Mt. Smith, are the freely accessible ruins of the Acropolis of Rhodes, a fine example of the stately sanctuaries that

the ancient Greeks built atop many of their cities. The complex includes a theat-er that the Italians restored in the early 20th century, a stadium, three restored columns of the Temple of Apollo Pythios, the scrappy remains of the Temple of Athena Polias, a Nymphaia, and an Ode-on. For a dramatic view, make your way to the westernmost edge of the summit, which drops via a sharp and almost inaccessible cliff to the shore below, now lined with enormous hotels. ⊠ *New Town* ⊕ *www.culture.gr*.

Archaeological Museum of Rhodes
MUSEUM | The Hospital of the Knights (now the island's archaeological museum) was completed in 1489 and surrounds a Byzantine courtyard, off which are the refectory and wards where the wealthy institution once administered to the knights and townspeople. These wonderful surroundings are enhanced with findings from Rhodes's three ancient cities (Ialysos, Kameiros, and Lindos) and the nearby islands, includ-ing a magnificent collection of ceramic amphoras and *oenochoe* (wine jugs), which inevitably fell into the posses-sion of the islands' wealthy merchants. Successive rooms elegantly show the evolution of Attic pottery, from early geometric deigns to the red-on-black figures of the 5th century BC. Among its collection are also two well-known rep-resentations of Aphrodite: the *Aphrodite of Rhodes,* who, while bathing, pushes aside her hair as if she's listening; and a standing figure, known as *Aphrodite Thalassia,* or "of the sea," as she was discovered in the water off the northern city beach. There are also two 6th-cen-tury BC kouros (statues of idealized male youth) that were found in the nearby ancient city of Kameiros, and, in a beautiful 5th-century BC funerary stela, a young woman named Crito, hair cut short in mourning, gives a farewell embrace to her mother, Timarista, who is already moving outside the frame, as she leaves the world. ⊠ *Megalou Alexandrou Square*

The Colossus of Rhodes may be long gone, but the Palace of the Grand Master of the Knights of Rhodes remains a colossal landmark of the Old Town quarter.

☎ *22413/65200* 🌐 *odysseus.culture.gr* 🎫 *€6; combined museum ticket €10* ⏲ *Closed Tues. Nov.–Mar.*

Decorative Arts Collection

MUSEUM | Housed in a stone-vaulted warehouse of the Knights, this small room exhibits finely made ceramics, wooden tools and utensils, and costumes and textiles from the various regions of the Dodecanese. There's little to explain what you're seeing, but the attendant can offer some information. ✉ *Square of the Hebrew Martyrs* ☎ *22413/65200* 🌐 *odysseus.culture.gr* 🎫 *€2; combined museum ticket €10* ⏲ *Closed Tues.*

Evangelismos Church

RELIGIOUS SITE | The town's harborside cathedral is a 1920s Italian-built replica of the Knights' Church of St. John in the Old Town, which was destroyed in an accidental gunpowder explosion in the mid-1800s after the Turks began using its basement as a storage facility. The outside is drably slavish to the idea of the Gothic original, but the church interior is rather magnificent, illuminated by the Byzantine-style frescoes of the great modern Greek painter Fotis Kontoglou. ✉ *Rhodes Town* ↔ *Near Mandraki Harbor* ☎ *22410/77916.*

Fort Agios Nikolas

MILITARY SITE | This circular fortress, built by the Knights of St. John in the 15th century, guards the entrance to Mandraki Harbor, near a row of picturesque but disused windmills. ✉ *Rhodes Town* ↔ *North of Old Town walls, bordering Mandraki Harbor.*

Lady of the Castle Church (Panagia tou Kastro)

MUSEUM | Icons and frescoes from religious buildings throughout Rhodes Town (most of them long since destroyed) are displayed within this 11th-century church. The building was transformed into a mosque under Turkish rule, but later stripped of all remnants of this period

Continued on page 513

THE MARCH OF GREEK HISTORY

The 21st-century Greeks are one of the oldest peoples on the face of the earth: they have seen *everything*. While Greeks are now subjected to an annual full-scale invasion by an army of camera-toting tourists, their ancestors had to fend off far more merciless visitors over the past millennia. During this epic time span, Greece was forged, torn asunder, and remade into the vital nation it is today.

History and myth aren't always mutually exclusive in Greece. Since Hermann Schliemann's 19th-century excavations lent weight to many of the grand "tales" of the early Greek poet Homer, figures such as Agamemnon, Great King of Mycenae, and the earliest heroes of ancient Greece have moved from legend into history. Not that subsequent ages were any duller—the one epithet that is utterly unsuitable in Greece—but they lacked the master touch of the great epic poet.

However, while ancient temples still evoke Homer, Sophocles, Plato, and the rest, today's Greeks are not just the watered-down descendants of a noble people living in the ruined halls of their ancestors. From time immemorial the Greeks have been piling the present on top of the past, blithely building, layering, and overlapping their more than 30 centuries of history to create the amazing fabric that is modern Greece.

(top) The Parthenon atop the Acropolis in Athens

TIMELINE

Keroa-Syros culture
of the Cyclades

2000 First palaces
built in Crete

2300 BC   2100 BC   1900 BC   1700 BC

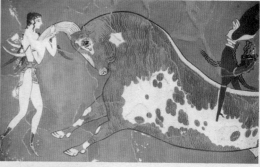

(top) Cycladic female figure; (top right) Bull fresco from Minoan ruins on Crete; (bottom) Fresco of ladies from Minoan ruins on Crete

3000 BC–1900 BC

Cycladic Origins

Greece is far older than the glory days of the Classical age—the 5th century BC—which gave us the Parthenon. Recent findings on Naxos revealed tools dating back between 13,000 and 200,000 years. One theory goes that even in the long-ago reaches of history, Greeks were sailing across the sparkling Aegean between islands and mainland shores. About the time early cultures were flourishing in Egypt and Mesopotamia, societies were emerging in the Cycladic islands, from which the first major Greek settlements, today known as the Grotta-Pelos (3,200–2,700 BC) culture, also sprang. Many of the early Cycladic people lived by the sea but, as the need for protection from invaders intensified, they moved to fortified towns in the uplands. Objects found in mass graves tell us they made tools, crockery, and jewelry. The most remarkable remnants of Cycladic civilization are flat, two-dimensional female idols, strikingly modern in appearance.

■ Sights to see: Museum of Cycladic Art (Goulandris Foundation), Athens.

2000 BC–1150 BC

Minoan Bronze Age

By 2000 BC, a great culture—Europe's oldest state (as opposed to mere tribal groupings)—had taken root on the island of Crete. What these inhabitants of Greece's southernmost island actually called themselves is not known; archaeologist Sir Arthur Evans named the civilization Minoan after Minos, the legendary king of the famous labyrinth who probably ruled from the magnificent palace of Knossos. Their warehouses were filled with spices traded throughout the Mediterranean, and royal

Presumed Minoan eruption of Thera	Hellenic tribes (Achaeans, Aeolian, Ionians, Dorians) appear		The Trojan War
1500 BC	1300 BC	1100 BC	900 BC

(top) Replica of Trojan Horse; (top, right) Lion Gate at Mycenae; (bottom) Mycenean gold funeral mask

chambers were decorated with sophisticated art—statuary, delicate rythons, and, most evocative of all, alluring frescoes depicting fanciful secular scenes as well as the goddesses who dominated the matriarchal Minoan religion. A system of writing, known as Linear A and Linear B script, appears on seal stones. The cause of the downfall of the Minoans remains a mystery—political unrest, invasions from the mainland, a volcano on nearby Santorini and subsequent earthquakes? Enter the mainland Mycenaeans.

■ Sights to see:
Palace of Knossos, Crete. Archaeological Museum, Heraklion.

1600 BC–1100 BC

The Mycenaeans

By the 14th century BC, the Mycenaeans wielded power throughout mainland Greece and much of the rest of the known world, from Sicily to Asia Minor. Their capital, Mycenae (in the Peloponnese), was one of several great cities they built around palaces filled with art and stories of the new Olympian gods and heavily fortified. As civilized as the Mycenaeans were, they were also warlike. Their exploits inspired the *Iliad* and *Odyssey*, and Agamemnon, legendary hero of the 12th-century Trojan Wars—the starting point in the endless ping-pong match between

Europe and Asia—is said to have ruled from Mycenae. For all their might, the Mycenaeans fell into decline sometime around 1100 BC. Soon the Dorians, from northern Greece, moved south, pushing the Mycenaeans into a dark age during which art and writing were lost. But Greeks who sailed across the Aegean to flee the Dorians established Ephesus, Smyrna, and other so-called Ionian cities in Asia Minor, where a rich culture soon flourished.

■ Sights to see:
Lion Gate, Mycenae, the Argolid. Cyclopean Walls, Tiryns. Nestor's Palace, Messinia.

First Pan-Hellenic
Olympics held

| 800 BC | 700 BC | 600 BC | 500 BC |

(top) Ancient vase depicting Olympic athletes; (left) Bust of Homer; (right) Statue of King Leonidas

The Age of Homer

1000 BC–800 BC

By the 8th century BC, Greeks were living in hundreds of *poleis*, city-states that usually comprised a walled city that governed the surrounding countryside. Most poleis were built around a raised acropolis and an agora (a marketplace), as well temples and often a gymnasium; limited power lay with a group of elite citizens—the first inklings of democracy. As the need for resources grew, Greeks began to establish colonies in Sicily and Gaul and on the Black Sea, and with this expansion came contact with the written word that laid the foundations of the Greek alphabet. Two essential elements of Greek culture led the new Greek renaissance that forged a nation's identity: Homeric legends began circulating, recounting the deeds of heroes and gods, and athletes showed off their strength and valor at the Olympic Games, first staged in 776 BC. Participation in these games meant support of Hellenism—the concept of a united Greece.

■ Sights to see:
Greek colonies set up in Asia Minor, Sicily (Agrigento, Syracuse), and southern Italy (Paestum).

Persian Invasions

499 BC–449 BC

The most powerful poleis, Athens and Sparta, would soon become two of history's most famous rivals—but for a brief time in the fifth century, they were allies united against a common foe, the Persians, who, in 490 BC, launched an attack against Athens. Though far outnumbered, the Athenians dealt the Persians a crippling blow on the Marathon plain. Ten years later, the Persians attacked again, this time with a massive army and navy commanded by King Xerxes. The Spartan King Leonidas and his "300"— the men of his royal guard

(top) Phoenician sailors building a pontoon bridge on the Hellespont for the Persian invasion of Greece in 480 BC; (top right) Bust of Pericles; (right) Relief sculpture fragment depicting the king of Persia; (bottom) Greek helmet

(along with an unknown number of slaves, or Helots)—sacrificed their lives to hold the Persians off at Thermopylae, allowing the Athenians time to muster ships and sink much of the Persian fleet. Xerxes returned the following year, in the summer of 479 BC, to sack Athens, but an army drawn from city-states throughout Greece and under the command of Pausanias, a Spartan general, defeated the Persians and brought the Persian Wars to an end.

■ Sights to see:
Marathon Tomb, Marathon, Attica.

460 BC–431 BC
Pericles' Golden Age

Athens thrived for much of the fifth century BC under the leadership of Pericles. The city became the center of the Hellenic world—and the cradle of Western civilization. The Parthenon was built; Socrates engaged in the dialogues that, recorded by Plato, became the basis of European philosophy; Aeschylus, Aristophanes, Euripides, and Sophocles wrote dramas; Praxiteles sculpted his masterpieces; and Herodotus became the "father of history."

■ Sights to see:
The Parthenon, Athens. Sanctuary of Apollo, Delphi.

431 BC–404 BC
Peloponnesian War

Athens was leader of the Delian League, a confederation of 140 Greek city-states, and Sparta headed the Peloponnesian League, a formidable alliance of city-states of southern and central Greece. From 431 to 404 BC these two powers engaged in battles that plunged much of Greece into bloodshed. Sparta emerged the victor after Athens suffered two devastating defeats: the destruction of a massive force sent to attack Syracuse, a Spartan ally in Sicily, and the sinking of the Athenian fleet.

■ Sights to see:
Archaeological Museum, Sparta, Laconia.

TIMELINE

Greece becomes
Roman Achala

293 Thessaloniki becomes a
capital of the Roman Empire

| 0 | 200 | 400 | 600 |

(top) Alexander the
Great listening to his
tutor Aristotle;
(top right) Byzantine
basilica; (bottom)
Alexander the Great on
horseback

Alexander the Great

338 BC– AD 323

In the years following the Peloponnesian War, Sparta, Athens, and an emerging power, Thebes, battled for control of Greece. Eventually, the victors came from the north: Macedonians led by Philip II defeated Athens in the Battle of Chaeronea in 338 BC. Philip's son, Alexander the Great, who had been tutored by Aristotle, quickly unified Greece and conquered Persia, most of the rest of the Middle East, and Egypt. In the ensuing 11 years of unparalleled triumphs he spread Greek culture from the Nile to the Indus. Alexander died in Babylon of a mysterious illness in 323 BC and the great empire he amassed soon fell asunder. Roman armies began moving toward Athens, Greece became the Roman province of Achaia in 27 BC, and for the next 300 years of peace Rome readily adapted Greek art, architecture, and thought. This cultural influence during the Pax Romana compensated for the loss of a much-abused independence.

■ Sights to see: Birthplace, Pella, Central Macedonia. Royal Tombs, Vergina, Central Macedonia. Roman Agora, Athens. Archaeological Museum, Marathon, Attica.

Byzantine Greece

324–1204

With the division of the Roman Empire into East and West, Greece came under the control of the Eastern Empire, administered from the Greek city of Byzantium (later Constantinople), where Emperor Constantine moved the capital in 324. The empire had embraced Christianity as its official religion, and Byzantium became the seat of the Eastern Orthodox Church, which led to the Great Christian Schism of 1094. Byzantium's Greek culture evolved into a distinct architectural style and religious art forms best represented by mosaics and icon paintings. For

841 Parthenon transformed
into cathedral

Fourth Crusade
invades Greece

800   1000   1200   1400

(top) Gold-leaf mosaics;
(left) Palace of the
Grand Masters, Rhodes;
(right) Portrait of
Mehmet II

centuries Byzantine Greece fended off invasions from Visigoths, Vandals, Slavs, Muslims, Bulgars, and Normans. As an ally of the empire, the Republic of Venice developed trading strongholds in Greece in the 11th century. Interested in the control of maritime routes, the Venetians built a network of fortresses and fortified towns along the Ionian coast of Greece. Venice later extended its possessions over several Aegean islands and Crete, which it held until 1669.

■ Sights to see:
Little Mitropolis, Athens.
Byzantine Museum, Rhodes.

Crusaders and Feudal Greece

1204–1453

The Byzantine Empire, and Greece with it, finally succumbed to Crusaders who pillaged Constantinople in 1204. Frankish knights created vassal feudal states in Thessalonica, the Peloponnese, and Rhodes, while other short-lived kingdoms in Epirus and on the shores of the Black Sea became the refuge of Byzantine Greek populations. Soon, however, a new threat loomed as Ottoman Turks under Sultan Mehmet II began marching into Byzantine lands, occupying most of Asia Minor, Macedonia, and Thessaly.

■ Sights to see: Palace of the Grand Masters, Rhodes.

Ottoman Age

1453–1821

Constantinople fell to the Ottomans in 1453, and by the 16th century Sultan Suleyman the Magnificent had expanded his Empire from Vienna through the Middle East. Greece was the stage of many battles between East and West. In 1687, Athens was besieged and the Parthenon heavily damaged by Venetian bombardments. Only in 1718 all of Greece was conceded to the Ottoman Empire, just in time for a resurgence of Hellenist culture in Europe, Neoclassicism in the arts, and a brand-new interest in Greek archaeology.

■ Sights to see:
Old Town, Rethymnon.

1522 Knights of St. John surrender Rhodes to the Attomans	Lord Elgin removes marbles	Olympic Games in Athens
	Greeks drive Turks out	

1600   *1800*   *2000*

(top) 2004 Olympic Stadium, Athens; (far left) Portrait of Eleftherios Venizelos; (left) Portrait of Lord Byron

A Greek Nation

1821–1935

Ottoman rulers allowed a degree of autonomy to Greece, yet uprisings became increasingly fierce. In 1821 the bloody War of Independence, which started as a successful rebellion in the Peloponnese, spread across the land. Western Europeans, including the Romantic poet Lord Byron, rushed to the Greek cause. After years of setbacks and civil wars, Britain, France, and Russia mediated with the Ottomans to establish Greece as an autonomous region. Otto of Bavaria, only 17, was named sovereign of Greece in 1831, the first of the often-unpopular monarchs who reigned intermittently until 1974. Public favor soon rested with prime ministers like Eleftherios Venizelos, who expanded Greece's borders, annexing Crete in 1908. In 1919 Venizelos, a proponent of a "Greater Greece," sought to conquer ethnic Greek regions of the new Turkish nation, but his forces were defeated and hundreds of thousands, on both sides, were massacred. The subsequent peace decreed the massive population exchange of two million people between the two countries, resulting in the complete expulsion of Greeks from Asia Minor, after 3,000 years of history.

■ Sights to see: Achilleion Palace, Corfu. National Garden, Athens.

A New Republic

1936–PRESENT

Greece emerged from the savagery of Axis occupation during World War II in the grip of civil war, with the Communist party battling right-wing forces. The right controlled the Greek government until 1963, when Georgios Papandreou became prime minister and proposed democratic reforms that were soon put down by a repressive colonels' junta led by Georgios Papadopoulos. A new republic was proclaimed in 1973, and a new constitution replaced the monarchy with an elective government—democratic ideals born in Greece more than 2,000 years earlier.

■ Sights to see: 2004 Olympic Stadium, Athens.

under Italian administration as part of a wider attempt to revive the Hospitaler character of the city. Closes at 3:30 pm. ⊠ Off Platia Mouseou ☎ 22410/38309 💻 €3; combined museum ticket €10 ⊗ Closed Tues.

Mandraki Harbor

NEIGHBORHOOD | What was once the main harbor, in use since the 5th century BC, adjoins the commercial harbor on the east side of Old Town and is home to the city's municipal buildings and an open-air bazaar. Inter-island catamarans sail from here now, but it was once said to be the site of one of the greatest acheivements of antiquity. Today, two bronze deer statues mark the spot where legend says the city's famous Colossus, a huge bronze statue of the sun god, Helios, once straddled the Mandraki Harbor entrance. Completed by the sculptor Chares of Lindos in the late 3rd century BC, the 110-foot-high figure only stood for around 50 years. In 227 BC, an earthquake razed the city and toppled the Colossus. After the calamity, the Delphic oracle advised the Rhodians to let the great Colossus remain where it had fallen. So there it lay for some eight centuries, until AD 654 when it was sold as scrap metal and carted off to Syria, allegedly by a caravan of 900 camels. ⊠ Rhodes Town.

Modern Greek Art Museum

MUSEUM | A cultural oasis amid the beach bodies of New Town. While its collection is still spread across a number of galleries in Old Town, its main building, across from 100 Palms Square, has drawn together the bulk of Greece's big art names, from Valia Semertzidis to Dimitris Koukou. ⊠ Plateia G. Xaritou, New Town ☎ 22410/36646 ⊕ www.mgamuseum.gr 💻 €3 ⊗ Closed Sat. and Sun.

Mosque of Murat Reis

MEMORIAL | The 17th-century mosque was named after Murat Reis, an Ottoman naval commander who served in Süleyman the Magnificent's navy. The shady peaceful grounds surrounding it

See More and Save

Plan on hitting all of Rhodes's Old Town attractions? Purchase a multi-site ticket (€10), which gets you admission to the Palace of the Grand Master, Archaeological Museum, Museum of Decorative Arts, and the Lady of the Castle church. It's available at any of these locations.

are a network of traditional and ornate cobblestone courtyards and a battered but proud cemetery where the marbled Ottoman grave markers remain. British expat novelist Lawrence Durrell once lived on the grounds, inspired by the tranquil beauty of the place. ⊠ Georgiou Papanikolaou 30, New Town.

Our Lady of the Bourg

ARCHAEOLOGICAL SITE | Soaring vaults are all that remains of what was once a magnificent Gothic church, completed by the Knights of St. John in 1456. The knights believed that Mary, the mother of Jesus, provided them and Rhodes special protection against the ever-present threat of a Muslim invasion; now kids play among the scattered ruins and musical events are sometimes held here. ⊠ Old Town ✛ Inside remains of walls, access through Gate of the Virgin.

★ Palace of the Grand Master of the Knights of Rhodes

CASTLE/PALACE | This grand building, with its fairy-tale towers, crenellated ramparts, and more than 150 rooms, crowns the top of the Street of Knights and is the place to begin any tour of Rhodes. Unscathed during the Turkish siege of 1522, the palace was partly destroyed in 1856 by an explosion of ammunition stored nearby in the cellars of the Church of St. John. The present structure—a Mussolini-era Italian reconstruction of the 1930s—is said to have remained fairly close to the original in its exterior, but

Thermes Kallitheas, a Moorish-style complex featuring mineral springs and mosaic-tiled baths (no longer in use), was built in 1929 by the Italians.

inside was rebuilt with all the restraint of your typical Fascist dictatorship. The building was, after all, reimagined as a holiday abode for King Vittorio Emmanuele III of Italy, and later Il Duce himself (Mussolini), whose name is still engraved at the entrance. Today the palace's collection of antiques and antiquities includes Hellenistic and Roman mosaic floors from Italian excavations in Kos, and in the permanent exhibition downstairs are extensive displays, maps, and plans showing the layout of the city that will help you get oriented before wandering through the labyrinthine Old Town. ⊠ *Ippoton, Old Town* ☎ *22413 /65270* ⊕ *odysseus.culture.gr* ✉ *€8; combined museum ticket €10* ⊘ *Closed Tue. Nov.–Mar.*

Street of Knights

HISTORIC SITE | This historic cobblestone lane, known in Greek as Ippoton, runs east from the Palace of the Grand Master to the harbor, and was once part of a longer path that wound its way to the Acropolis. During its medieval heyday it became a residential quarter. It is bordered on both sides by the seven Inns of the Tongues, auberges where visiting Knights of the Order of St. John were domiciled according to their spoken language. These were heavily renovated during the 1930s, under Italian occupation, and today mostly hold consulates and government institutions. They are nevertheless wonderfully atmospheric to wander. The most elaborate example is the **Inn of France**, whose ornately carved facade bears heraldic patterns, fleur de lis, and an inscription that dates the building to 1492 and its commission by Emery d'Ambroise. ⊠ *Ippoton, Old Town.*

★ Thermes Kallitheas

HOT SPRINGS | As you travel south along the east coast, a strange sight meets you: an assemblage of buildings that look as if they have been transplanted from Morocco. In fact, this spectacular mosaic-tile bath complex was built in 1929 by the Italians. As far back as the early 2nd century BC, the area's mineral springs were prized; the great physician Hippocrates of Kos extolled these springs

The Knights of the Order of St. John

The Knights of St. John, a Catholic order of Hospitalers, were organized during the time of the Crusades to protect and care for Christian pilgrims. By the beginning of the 12th century the order had become military in nature, and after the fall of Acre in 1291 to the Arabs, the knights fled from Palestine, withdrawing first to Cyprus and then to Rhodes. In 1312 they inherited the immense wealth of the Templars (another religious military order, which had just been outlawed by the pope) and used it to fortify Rhodes. But for all their power and the strength of their walls, moats, and artillery, the Knights could not hold back the Turks. In 1522 the Ottomans, with 300 ships and 100,000 men under Süleyman the Magnificent, began what was to be the final siege, taking the city after six months. Centuries later, Mussolini's Italy would restore many of this era's original buildings to further its own fascist agenda, and even today no one has done as much as the Knights to shape modern Rhodes.

for alleviating liver, kidney, and rheumatic ailments. Though the baths are no longer in use, the ornate rotunda has been restored (art exhibitions are often on view), as have peristyles and pergolas, and you can wander through the beautifully landscaped grounds—note the pebble mosaics, an ancient folk tradition come alive again, with mosaics of fish, deer, and other images—and have a drink or snack in the attractive café. A pretty beach rings a nearby cove. ⊠ *Rhodes Town* ✛ *10 km (6 miles) south of Rhodes Town* ☎ *22410 /65564* ⊕ *www.kallithea-springs.gr* 🎫 *€5* ⊘ *Closed Nov.–Mar.*

Turkish Library

LIBRARY | Also known as the Muslim Library, or Hafiz Ahmed Agha Library, this institution holds a rare collection of Turkish, Persian, and Arab manuscripts, including many rare Korans. Founded in 1793, this remains a striking reminder of the Ottoman presence. The collection and the adjacent Mosque of Süleyman are still used by those members of Rhodes's Turkish community who stayed here after the 1923 population exchange, a mass repatriation of Greek and Turkish migrants. ⊠ *Sokratous* ✛ *Opposite Mosque of Süleyman* ☎ ⊘ *Closed Sun.*

Walls of Rhodes

MILITARY SITE | One of the great medieval monuments in the Mediterranean, the walls of Rhodes are wonderfully restored and illustrate the engineering capabilities as well as the financial and human resources available to the Knights of St. John. For 200 years the knights strengthened the walls by thickening them, up to 40 feet in places, and curving them so as to deflect cannonballs. The moat between the inner and outer walls never contained water; it was a device to prevent invaders from constructing siege towers. You can get a sense of the enclosed city's massive scale by walking for free inside the moat; entrances can be found at the gates of St. Athanasius and Ambroise.

Part of the walkway that runs the 4 km (2½ miles) along the top of the walls is accessible through the Palace of the Grand Master ticket office; free tours are run daily between noon and 3 pm. ⊠ *Rhodes Town* ✛ *Old Town* ⊕ *odysseus. culture.gr* 🎫 *€2 for walkway* ⊘ *Closed Sat. and Sun., and Nov.–Apr.*

Beaches

Elli Beach

BEACH—SIGHT | Though the beach is pebbly rather than sandy, a handy location right at the edge of Old Town makes this seaside strip immensely popular, and it's lined with chairs and umbrellas. An offshore diving platform is a huge hit with kids and what seems to be most of the teenage population of Rhodes. What you won't find here is solitude, and what semblance of peace and quiet you might find will likely be interrupted by an endless stream of hawkers selling everything from trinkets to cold drinks. **Amenities:** food and drink; lifeguards; toilets; showers; water sports. **Best for:** swimming; walking. ⊠ *Rhodes Town* ✛ *North of Old Town, near Rhodes Yacht Club.*

Faliraki Beach

BEACH—SIGHT | Faliraki's reputation is better these days, after authorities cracked down 20 years ago on the bars that once made this the hedonistic party capital of Greece. It remains the most popular beach on Rhodes, and will be your idea of paradise or hell, depending on what you think of crowded sands backed by fun parks, supermarkets, all-inclusive resorts, and fast-food joints. Stretches of the 5 km (3 miles) of fine sand are a little less cramped than others, such as the southern end, which is officially designated as a naturist beach. Beyond its southern tip lies the beautiful Anthony Quinn Bay, named after the Mexican-American actor who loved it so much while filming *The Guns of Navarone* in 1960 that he bought the land. Years later the Greek government reclaimed it and the legal battle that ensued continued even after the actor's death. Its tiny shore fills up fast but the emerald waters here are the best for snorkeling on the island. Buses run between Rhodes Town and Faliraki throughout the day and late into the evening. **Amenities:** food and drink; lifeguards; parking (free); showers; toilets; water sports. **Best for:** nudists; partiers; swimming; walking. ⊠ *Faliraki* ✛ *14 km (8½ miles) south of Rhodes Town.*

Restaurants

Alexis 4 Seasons

$$ | **SEAFOOD** | Though known for its seafood, the handsomely decorated old rooms, beautiful walled garden, and panoramic view from the roof terrace found here are equalling enchanting. Mussels in wine, scallops in vodka sauce, shrimp risotto in an ouzo sauce, as well as simply grilled fish fill the menu. **Known for:** gourmet seafood; city-view terrace; good service. $ *Average main: €22* ⊠ *Aristotelous 33* ☎ *22410/70522* ⊕ *www.alexis4seasons.com.*

Marco Polo Cafe

$$ | **MODERN GREEK** | One of the most enchanting places to dine is the garden of this small guesthouse, where you'll want to linger amid the foliage and flowers for an entire evening. The menu features a rich lamb souvlaki and a delectable sea bass fillet with *trahanoto* (Greek-style risotto). **Known for:** romantic dining; attentive service; fantastic raised garden setting. $ *Average main: €20* ⊠ *Agiou Fanouriou 42, Old Town* ☎ *22410/25562* ⊕ *www.marcopolomansion.gr* ⊗ *Closed Nov.–Feb.*

Nireas

$$ | **SEAFOOD** | Considered by many to be the finest of the city's seafood restaurants, family-run Nireas comes with little fanfare or pushiness, just impeccable service and a peaceful, vine-draped setting apart from the hubbub of the center. Prices compare well with lesser spots in the city, especially for the quality of produce, and staff won't try to hustle you into spending big, as is the case with many seafood restaurants here where bills can suddenly rocket. **Known for:** friendly service that's eager to help; a nice setting on one of Old Town's quieter streets; excellent seafood. $ *Average main: €20* ⊠ *Sofokleous 22* ☎ *22410/21703.*

★ To Marouli

$ | **VEGETARIAN** | Vegans and vegetarians aren't well catered for in Greece, where the "fish option" is typically your only alternative to a tombstone-sized slab of fried cheese. But this ingenious restaurant from chef Mara Martinotti is the antidote, and she has a recipe book to boot. **Known for:** amazing vegan fare; a cute setting away from the hustle; best tasting menu in town. [$] *Average main: €12* ✉ *Platonos 26, Old Town* ☎ *22413/04394* 🌐 *tomaroulirodos.blogspot.com.*

To Steno

$ | **GREEK** | When Rhodians want a traditional meal, they head to this simple little taverna on a residential street south of the walled city. Dining is in a plain room and on a sparkling-white terrace in warmer months, where you can compose a meal of such delicious mezedes as *bakaliaros* (salted cod) in garlic sauce, pumpkin fritters, and zucchini flowers filled with feta cheese. **Known for:** good and simple Greek taverna food; great for vegetarians; pretty, plant-filled terrace. [$] *Average main: €8* ✉ *Agion Anargiron 29* ☎ *22410/35914.*

Coffee and Quick Bites

Mevlana

$ | **TURKISH** | This traditional Turkish coffee house claims to be the oldest of its kind in Europe, and has belonged to the same family for over 200 years. If the 14th-century setting and authentic decor doesn't hook you, the coffee will. **Known for:** Turkish coffee served the way it should be; its historic setting; a good people-watching spot. [$] *Average main: €3* ✉ *Sokratous 76* ☎ *69422/10846* 🌐 *turkish-coffee-rhodes.business.site.*

Phournariko

$ | **BAKERY** | This is a nice little Greek bakery filled with myriad honey-soaked and cheese-covered treats, ranging from baklava to bagel-style *kalouri* and pizza-like *peinirli*. It's perfect for a mid-morning snack or lunchtime treat. **Known for:** Greek snack food of the highest quality; late-night opening; good coffee. [$] *Average main: €4* ✉ *Dinokratous 1-9, Old Town* ☎ *22410/43057.*

Hotels

10GR Hotel & Wine Bar

$ | **HOTEL** | A new addition to the Old Town in 2018, this rather neat hotel makes use of vaulted stone cells dating back 600 years. **Pros:** rooms are quiet and away from the bustle below; there's nothing else quite like it in the city; great wines to choose from. **Cons:** this area can be pretty noisy; there isn't much space in the rooms; as ever, there's no parking. [$] *Rooms from: €120* ✉ *Polidorou 16, Old Town* ☎ *22410/20910* 🌐 *www.10grhotel.com* 🛏 *10 suites* 🍴 *Free breakfast.*

★ Kokkini Porta Rossa

$$$$ | **B&B/INN** | A family passion project has turned into the most beautiful small hotel on the island. **Pros:** free minibar and sumptuous terrace breakfasts; bespoke trips can be arranged with local experts; guests get a tablet loaded with maps and sights. **Cons:** with only six suites it fills up fast; minimum two-night stay; it's a longer walk than at most hotels to the center of Old Town. [$] *Rooms from: €345* ✉ *Rhodes Town* ✥ *Next to Gate of St. John* ☎ *22410/75114* 🌐 *kokkiniporta.com* 🛏 *6 suites* 🍴 *Free breakfast.*

★ Marco Polo Mansion

$$ | **HOTEL** | Entering this renovated 15th-century Ottoman mansion in the maze of the Old Town's colorful Turkish section is like stepping into another world. **Pros:** a quiet, historic retreat in the back alleys; breakfast served in the garden is a thing of joy; the courtyard restaurant is wonderful. **Cons:** rooms are reached via several sets of stairs; hotel can only be reached on foot and is tricky to find; come here to live like a pasha, not to indulge in modern amenities. [$] *Rooms from: €160* ✉ *Aghiou Fanouriou*

40–42 ☎ 22410/25562 🌐 www.marcopolomansion.gr 🕓 Closed Nov.–Apr. 🛏 10 rooms 🍴 Free breakfast.

Medieval Inn

$ | **B&B/INN** | These simple, whitewashed lodgings with bright accents are sparkling clean and surround a flowery courtyard far from the noisy tourist tracks in the northern parts of the Old Town. **Pros:** excellent location; very clean and comfortable; friendly service. **Cons:** basic comforts; some bathrooms, while private, are outside the room; can only be reached on foot. [$] *Rooms from: €85* ✉ *Timachida 9, Old Town* ☎ *22410/22469* 🌐 *www.medievalinn.com* 🕓 *Closed Nov.–Apr.* 🛏 *10 rooms* 🍴 *No meals.*

Mitsis Grand Hotel

$$$ | **RESORT** | **FAMILY** | Located steps away from Rhodes Town Beach, the Grand resort is a large complex that makes full use of its resort space, including several pools, 13 restaurants, and cozy lounge bars. **Pros:** steps away from the beach; good for families and large groups; great amenities, restaurants, and services. **Cons:** impersonal feel; extra charges apply for in-room Wi-Fi; peak season may feel crowded. [$] *Rooms from: €248* ✉ *Akti Miaouli and Papanikolaou, New Town* ☎ *22410/54700* 🌐 *www.mitsishotels.com/en/hotels/grand-hotel* 🛏 *402 rooms* 🍴 *All-inclusive.*

S. Nikolis Hotel

$$ | **HOTEL** | All the atmosphere of Rhodes's medieval Old Town is captured here at this charmingly restored 14th-century house. **Pros:** atmospheric rooms and surroundings; beautiful garden; warm hospitality. **Cons:** some rooms are small; no parking; reachable only by foot. [$] *Rooms from: €180* ✉ *Odos Ippodamou 61* ☎ *22410/34561* 🌐 *www.s-nikolis.gr* 🛏 *16 rooms* 🍴 *Free breakfast.*

Spirit of the Knights

$$$ | **HOTEL** | A restored Ottoman house on the quiet back lanes of the Old Town is one of Rhodes's most distinctive getaway, with parts of it dating back six centuries. **Pros:** lovely courtyard with Jacuzzi; you won't find a quieter spot in the city; excellent breakfast and service. **Cons:** can only be reached on foot; no elevator; no parking. [$] *Rooms from: €220* ✉ *Alexandridou 14* ☎ *22410/39765* 🌐 *www.spiritoftheknights.com* 🛏 *6 rooms* 🍴 *Free breakfast.*

Nightlife

BARS AND DISCOS

A thriving nightlife has sprung up amid the medieval buildings and flower-filled courtyards of the Old Town. Some bars and cafés here are open all day for drinks, and many—often those with beautiful medieval interiors—stay open most of the year. Nighttime-only spots in the Old Town open up around 10 pm and close around 3 or 4 am. The action centers on the clubs and bars of Hippocrates Square, where in recent times visitors have also taken to buying drinks from the wine bar tucked beneath its old stone staircase and then lining the steps above to people-watch. Alternatively, the slick cocktail bars of Arionos Square offers a far more trendy escape away from the throng.

Those wanting to venture to the New Town should avoid its infamous Orfanidou street like the plague (or an STI), unless watching shirtless meatheads try to out push-up each other is your kind of jazz. A gauntlet of catcalling prostitutes lining the grubbier western end of Nikiforou Mandilara Street makes even the approach uncomfortable. Instead, make for the central pedestrianized part of Nikiforou Mandilara and its adjoining Amarantou, where quiet cocktail bars and a few nice restaurants set a more amenable tone.

The Last Butler

BARS/PUBS | A likeable cocktail bar-cum-speakeasy that spills out onto the New Town food street of Amarantou. It's a great place to perch, all gentleman's-club-style dark woods, Victorian wallpaper, and a dizzying array of well-mixed drinks. An atmospheric spot for a nightcap. ✉ *Amarantou 45, New Town* ☎ *22410/38981.*

Macao

BARS/PUBS | A haven for grown-up lounge lizards, Macao is all about dark, moody lighting, a romantic terrace, mellow music, and worldly cocktails. ✉ *Archelaou 5* ☎ *69364/00305* ⊕ *www.macaobar.gr.*

Mozaik

BARS/PUBS | In summer, this slick open-air cocktail bar and terrace is the centerpiece of hip Arionos Square, where its DJs top the pecking order and decent sushi has been added to a light menu. ✉ *Plateia Arionos 14-15, Old Town* ☎ *69324/80006* ⊕ *www.mozaik-bar.gr.*

🛍 Shopping

In Rhodes Town you can buy good copies of Lindos ware, a delicate pottery decorated with green and red floral motifs. The Old Town's shopping area, on Sokratous, is lined with boutiques, some of which sell antiques, jewelry, and other high-ticket items.

Astero Antiques

ANTIQUES/COLLECTIBLES | Since 1970 the owner has traveled throughout Greece each winter to fill his shop with some of the most enticing goods on offer on the island, though how "antique" these items are is up for debate. ✉ *Ayiou Fanouriou 4* ⊕ *Off Sokratous* ☎ *22410/34753* ⊕ *aster-oantiquesandjewellery.business.site.*

★ George Triantafyllou

ANTIQUES/COLLECTIBLES | George is a professional iconographer, and one of a half-dozen employed to professionally paint and restore frescoes in the island's

churches. His workshop doubles as a small shop, where he sells his remarkable art, handpainted onto wood with pigment and gold, and runs workshops teaching the skills of the Byzantine fresco painters to visitors. Even if you just stop by (it's best to call ahead if visiting), he's an engaging companion and always thrilled to discuss his work. He also paints commissions. ✉ *Archiepiskopou Efthimiou, Old Town* ☎ *69748/76272* ⊙ *Call for an appointment.*

Workshop Karpetis

JEWELRY/ACCESSORIES | Lefteris Karpetis spent his early life rattling around his father's goldsmiths, whose old implements and tools scatter his current-day workshop alongside black-and-white stills of his craft. One of few old-school jewelers left in the city, his designs are unique and typically range from €15 to €5,000. ✉ *Sofokleous 8, Old Town* ☎ *22410/73280.*

Activities

Trident Diving School

DIVING/SNORKELING | A long-serving diving school that offers all levels of training in CMAS , PADI, SSI. Their boat runs daily trips from Mandraki Harbor, with all beginner dives held in Kallithea Bay. ✉ *Skevoy Zervoy 2, New Town* ☎ *22410/29160* ⊕ *www.tridentdivingschool.com.*

Epta Piges Επτά Πηγές

30 km (19 miles) south of Rhodes Town.

Sights

Epta Piges

BODY OF WATER | A deeply shaded glen watered by seven mountain springs (*epta piges* in Greek) is made all the more photogenic thanks to the imported peacocks that flaunt their plumage in the woods around the pools. The waters are channeled through a 164-yard-long tunnel, which you can walk through, emerging at the edge of a cascading dam and a small man-made lake where you can swim. Here an enterprising local shepherd began serving simple fare in 1945 and his sideline turned into the busy waterside taverna and tourist site of today. Despite its many visitors, the beauty of the springs remains unspoiled. ✉ *Archangelos* ✣ *To get here, turn right on the inland road near Kolymbia and follow signs.* ☏ *22410/56259* ⊕ *7springs.gr.*

★ Eleousa Ghost Village

GHOST TOWN | Drive west of Epta Piges and you'll come to the ghost village of **Eleousa** (formerly Campochiaro), one of many follies built under Italian rule (1912–43). The central island was useful to the Italians for its resources and agricultural potential, so villages such as the one here were created in the 1930s to accommodate workers shipped in from Northern Italy. Roads were built to link it to the capital and other pre-fab towns, and an official residence was created for the island's governor. Like everything the Italians did on Rhodes, it was a show of power designed to promote their Fascist ideology to locals. It didn't last. Under a new governor, the village became a military outpost and a prison for Greek insurrectionists. When Italy surrendered in 1943 during World War II, it lost control of the islands and the last Italian families here disappeared. In later years the town was renamed Eleousa and its abandoned buildings used as a sanitarium for tuberculosis patients, but even this fell out of use by the 1970s. Today, its eerie vision of Italian "greatness" provides a remarkable glimpse into a strange past. ✉ *Eleousa.*

Lindos Λίνδος

19 km (12 miles) southwest of Epta Piges, 48 km (30 miles) southwest of Rhodes Town.

Lindos, cradled between two harbors and dominated by its massive hilltop acropolis, is remarkably well preserved. Steep paths wind past its famous "captain's mansions," beautifully built houses of finely cut Lindos limestone decorated with elaborately arched windows and delicate *hohlaki* flooring (black-and-white pebble mosaics). Stacked alongside these are whitewashed Cycladic-style homes with square, blue-shuttered windows. It all makes for a charming, if thigh-sapping, stroll once you rise out of the maul of the covered market streets.

Before the existence of Rhodes Town, Lindos was the island's principal maritime center. By the 6th century BC, an impressive temple dominated the settlement, and after the foundation of Rhodes, the Lindians set up a *propylaia* (monumental entrance gate) on the model of that in Athens. Lindos prospered into Roman times, during the Middle Ages, and under the Knights of St. John. Only at the beginning of the 19th century did the age-old shipping activity cease, by which point its streets were lined with well-to-do mansions.

Like Rhodes Town, Lindos is enchanting in off-season but can get unbearably crowded when summertime pilgrims make the trek from Rhodes Town daily. Passage through narrow covered streets lined with shops selling clothes and trinkets slows to a snail's pace. At these times, an overnight visit allows you to enjoy the town's beauties after the day-trippers leave.

One of the most magnificent examples of Crusader-era architecture is the great fortress at Lindos.

Only pedestrians and rather sad-looking donkeys are allowed in Lindos because the town's narrow alleys are not wide enough for vehicles. If you're arriving by car, park in the lot above town, next to the bus stop, and walk the 10 minutes down (about 1,200 feet) to town.

Sights

★ Acropolis of Lindos

ARCHAEOLOGICAL SITE | FAMILY | A 15-minute climb (please don't ride a donkey), from the village center up to the Acropolis of Lindos leads past a gauntlet of Lindian women who spread out their lace and embroidery like fresh laundry over the rocks. The final approach ascends a steep flight of stairs, past a marvelous 2nd-century BC relief of the prow of a Lindian ship, carved into the rock.

The entrance takes you through the medieval castle built by the Knights of St. John, then to the Byzantine Chapel of St. John on the next level. The Romans, too, left their mark on the acropolis, with a temple dedicated to Diocletian. On the upper terraces, begun by classical Greeks around 300 BC, are the remains of elaborate porticoes and stoas, commanding an immense sweep of sea and making a powerful statement on behalf of Athena and the Lydians (who dedicated the monuments on the Acropolis to her). The lofty white columns of the temple and stoa on the summit must have presented a magnificent picture. The main portico of the stoa had 42 Doric columns, at the center of which an opening led to the staircase up to the Propylaia (or sanctuary). The Temple of Athena Lindia at the very top is surprisingly modest, given the drama of the approach. As was common in the 4th century BC, both the front and the rear are flanked by four Doric columns. Numerous inscribed statue bases were found all over the summit, attesting in many cases to the work of Lindian sculptors, who were clearly second to none. ⊠ Lindos ⊹ Above the village ☎ 22413/65200 ⊕ odysseus.culture.gr ⊴ €12 ☉ Closed Tues. Nov.–Mar.

Church of the Panagia

RELIGIOUS SITE | A graceful building with a beautiful bell tower probably antedates the Knights of St. John, though the bell tower bears the arms of Grand Master d'Aubusson with the dates 1484–90. Frescoes in the elaborate interior were painted in 1779 by Gregory of Symi, and the black-and-white *hohlaki* pebble floor is typical of the area. ⚠ **Visitors are required to dress appropriately, which means no shorts.** ✉ *Lindos* ✣ *Off main square.*

Tomb of Kleoboulos

MEMORIAL | Escape the crowds by trekking to the Tomb of Kleoboulos, which is incorrectly named after Lindos's 6th-century BC poet and sage; it's actually the final resting place of a wealthy family of the 1st and 2nd century BC. After about 3 km (2 miles), a 30-minute scenic walk on a stony path across the headland (on the north side of Lindos Bay), you encounter the small, rounded stone tomb. You can peer inside and see the candle marks, which testify to its later use as the Church of St. Emilianos, or admire the dramatic views of Lindos and Vlycha Bay all around you. ✉ *Lindos* ✣ *Look for sign at parking lot near beach above main square. Follow the dirt path along the hill on opposite side of bay from Acropolis.*

🍴 Restaurants

★ Broccolino

$$ | **ITALIAN** | Set apart from the scrummage of Lindos and buoyed by dizzying views over the bay below, this seductive Italian restaurant does everything well. The food—slow-cooked lamb, melt-in-the-mouth truffle gnocchi, juicy fillet steaks—is never less than glorious, and the house wine is great value. **Known for:** great views; a quiet spot; best Italian food on the island. [$] *Average main: €17* ✉ *Lindos* ☎ *22440/31688.*

Mavrikos

$$ | **GREEK** | With a large terrace overlooking the sea and Lindos Square, Mavrikos offers elegant simplicity through its flavorful Greek dishes, such as the chickpeas in orange zest, swordfish in caper sauce, black butter beans in carob syrup, and squid risotto. Third-generation chef Dimitris Mavrikos owns this institution along with his brother Michalis and has steadfastly maintained its stellar reputation. **Known for:** quality local dishes; open-air terrace dining; wine list has good local selection. [$] *Average main: €16* ✉ *Main square* ☎ *22440/31232* ⏲ *Closed Nov.–Mar.*

☕ Coffee and Quick Bites

Gelo Blu

$ | **CAFÉ** | The most popular hangout in town serves homemade ice cream by day and drinks day and night in the cool, blue-cushioned interior and pebbled courtyard as well as on the rooftop terrace of a sea captain's house. **Known for:** fantastic ice cream; terrace views; a cool spot for a sunset drink. [$] *Average main: €6* ✉ *Near Theotokou Church* ☎ *22440/31560.*

🛏 Hotels

Lindos Blu

$$$$ | **RESORT** | Sea views seem to fill every inch of this small, sun-drenched, adults-only resort, where many of the stylishly contemporary guest rooms and suites have their own pools tucked onto terraces. **Pros:** attentive, personalized service; resort amenities in an intimate atmosphere; all rooms have sea view. **Cons:** decor is a bit generic; not within walking distance to sights in Lindos Town; pricey in high season. [$] *Rooms from: €430* ✉ *Vlicha Lindos* ✣ *2 km (1 mile) outside village center* ☎ *22440/32110* 🌐 *www.lindosblu.gr* ⏲ *Closed Nov.–Apr.* 🛏 *70 rooms* 🍽 *Free breakfast.*

★ Melenos Lindos

$$$ | HOTEL | Overlooking Lindos Bay and set at the foot of the Acropolis, this quiet, cultured hotel has been built in the style of the old captains's houses found in the village. **Pros:** terraces with sea views; exquisite service; great restaurant and boutique shop. **Cons:** no elevator; minimum two-day stay; no parking. **$** *Rooms from: €250* ✉ *Lindos* ✛ *At edge of Lindos, on path to Acropolis* ☎ *22440/32222* ⊕ *www.melenoslindos.com* ☾ *Closed Nov.–Mar.* ⤳ *12 rooms* ❍**|** *Free breakfast.*

▼ Nightlife

Most of Lindos's bars around the main throng of the market area cater to a young, hard-drinking crowd; few are without a television showing soccer. But if you're prepared to climb, you can find plenty of quiet café-bars and tavernas with incredible views on the fringes of this old town. Many are open year-round to serve the locals.

Captain's House Bar

BARS/PUBS | This fine example of an old Lindos mariner's home, replete with intricate *hohlaki* pebble floor, has been turned into one of the most atmospheric bars in town. Owner Savvas is a lively soul and mixes a decent cocktail. ✉ *Near to Gelo Blu* ☎ *22440/31235.*

★ Rainbird

BARS/PUBS | Coffee and drinks are served all day, but the views from the romantic terrace make this spot especially popular around sunset. ✉ *Lindos* ✛ *On lane to Acropolis* ☎ *22440/32169.*

Easy as 1-2-3

Most of Lindos's mazelike streets don't have conventional names or addresses; instead, buildings are numbered, from 1 through about 500. Lower numbers are on the north side of town, higher numbers on the south.

Gennadi and the South Coast Γεννάδι και νότια παράλια

20 km (12 miles) south of Lindos, 68 km (42 miles) south of Rhodes Town.

The area south of Lindos, with fewer beaches and less fertile soil, is traditionally not as well traveled as the stretch to its north but things are changing. Development has rapidly increased, and the coast is now smothered in resorts. These and the long stretches of shoreline are the only reason to come here, though the still pretty and inexpensive coastal village of Gennadi has pensions, rooms for rent, and a handful of tavernas, nightclubs, and DJ-hosted beach parties.

⊕ Beaches

Lachania Beach

BEACH—SIGHT | Stretching uninterrupted for several miles, Lachania Beach lies below the unspoiled, whitewashed village of the same name, one of the most picturesque in Rhodes. Though stretches of the sand are lined with sun beds, it's easy to find a fairly secluded spot backed by scrub-covered dunes. **Amenities:** food and drink; water sports. **Best for:** solitude; swimming; walking. ✉ *Lachania* ✛ *9 km (5½ miles) south of Gennadi.*

Plimiri Beach

BEACH—SIGHT | A lovely bay is ringed by soft and quiet sands, where it's easy to find a relatively secluded spot. The clear, calm waters are ideal for swimming, though winds tend to pick up in the afternoon, a boon for windsurfers. A few tavernas prepare delightfully simple seafood meals. **Amenities:** food and drink. **Best for:** nudists; solitude; swimming; windsurfing.

Monolithos to Kameiros
Μονόλιθος προς Κάμειρος

28 km (17 miles) northwest of Gennadi, 74 km (46 miles) southwest of Rhodes Town.

Rhodes's west coast is more forested, with fewer notable beaches than its eastern side. But what it lacks in sun beds it more than makes up for in history. This was once home to the most powerful city on the island, founded by early Dorian Greek settlers, and in later years its coastal castles, built by the industrious Knights of St. John, saw off Ottoman Turk soldiers in their tens of thousands. They may lie in ruins now, but staring out from their scattered stones, the whip of the sea air in your ears, beats any beachside martini. Inland from these windswept snatches of the past, the landscape turns more idyllic, and if you're looking to get away from the tourist hordes, you'll find peace and quiet among the sylvan scenery and sweeping vineyards.

 Sights

Kameiros

ARCHAEOLOGICAL SITE | This is one of the three ancient cities of Rhodes, along with Lindos and Ialysos. Kameiros was for a time the most powerful of them all, and the first to cut its own currency, until earthquakes in the 2nd and 3rd centuries BC sapped the city's might. After

that, its citizens just ebbed away. It was excavated by the Italians in 1929 and lies on three levels on a slope above the sea. Most of the city—apparently never fortified—that is visible today dates to the classical period and later, and includes an acropolis, a large reservoir, a gridlike pattern of streets lined with houses and shops, and several temples. The hill hides many more ruins, yet to be unearthed. ⊠ *Rhodes Town* ⊹ *Off main Rhodes road, 23 km (14 miles) northeast of Siana; turn at sign for Ancient Kameiros* ☎ *22410/40037* ⊕ *www.culture.gr* 🎫 *€6* ⊗ *Closed Mon. Nov.–Mar.*

Kritinia Kastello

ARCHAEOLOGICAL SITE | This ruined-yet-still impressive fortress, built by the Knights of St. John in the late 15th century, rises high above the sea on the coast just north of Mt. Avrios, with good views in every direction. Above its entrance you can still make out the engraved coats of arms of two Grand Masters. ⊠ *Kritinia* ⊹ *13 km (8 miles) northeast of Siana.*

★ Monolithos

ARCHAEOLOGICAL SITE | The medieval fortress of Monolithos—so named for the jutting, 750-foot monolith on which it is constructed—was built by the Knights of St. John in 1480 and rises above a fairy-tale landscape of deep-green forests and sharp cliffs plunging into the sea. Inside the stronghold (accessible only by a steep path and series of stone steps) there is a chapel, and the ramparts provide magnificent views of Rhodes's emerald inland and the island of Halki. The small pebble beach of Fourni beneath the castle is a delightful place for a swim. ⊠ *Monolithos* ⊹ *Take western road from middle of Monolithos village; near hairpin turn there's a path up to fortress.*

Siana

TOWN | This small town perches on the wooded slopes of Mt. Acramitis above a vast, fertile valley. A popular stop on the tourist trail, Siana is known for its fragrant honey and for *souma* (a very strong, sweet wine that resembles a grape-flavor schnapps); look for stands selling both. ⊠ *Siana* ✛ *5 km (3 miles) northeast of Monolithos.*

Petaloudes Πεταλούδες και Ιαλυσός

22 km (14 miles) east of Kameiros, 25 km (15 miles) southwest of Rhodes Town.

Shady lanes and babbling brooks winding through the forested grounds of a former Venetian estate would be quite enticing even without the presence of some of Rhodes's most famous inhabitants: brown-and-red Jersey tiger moths that swarm to create a much-observed spectacle. You'll find more rustic retreats elsewhere on Rhodes, but a walk through the cooling woods can be refreshing—and especially rewarding during prime swarm times: dusk in July and August.

◉ Sights

Petaloudes
NATURE PRESERVE | FAMILY | The "Valley of the Butterflies" lives up to its name in all but one important regard. Its star attraction aren't actually butterflies. In summer the *callimorpha quadripunctaria*, a species of day-flying moth known as the Jersey tiger, cluster by the thousands around the low bushes of the pungent storax plant, which grows all over the area. In recent years numbers of the moths have diminished, partly owing to busloads of tourists clapping their hands to see the creatures fly up in dense clouds—an antic that causes the creatures to deplete their scant energy reserves and is strongly discouraged. Access to the valley involves an easy walk up an idyllic yet crowded trail through a pretty wood, past a stream and ponds. ⊠ *Rhodes Town* ✛ *Turn off*

En Route

Beyond Siana, the road continues on a high ridge through thick pine forests, which carpet the precipitous slopes dropping toward the sea. To the east looms the bare, stony massif of Mt. Ataviros, Rhodes's highest peak, at 3,986 feet. If you follow the road inland rather than continue north along the coast toward Kritinia, you'll climb the flanks of the mountains to the traditional, arbor-filled village of Embonas in Rhodes's richest wine country *(see "Nectar of the Gods" in Chapter 9).*

coastal road south and follow signs leading to the site with its own parking lot ☎ *22410/82822* ⬛ *€5* ⊗ *Closed Nov.–Mar.*

Symi ΣΥΜΗ

45 km (28 miles) north of Rhodes by ferry.

The tiny island of Symi is an enchanting place, where life centers around sparkling Yialos Harbor and a 19th-century town of neoclassical mansions, known as Chorio, which crowns the hillside above. The island has few beaches and almost no flat land, so it is not attractive to developers. As a result, quiet Symi provides a peaceful retreat for travelers, who tend to fall in love with the island on their first visit and return year after year.

Symi has especially good natural harbors, and the nearby coast of Asia Minor provided plentiful timber for the Symiotes, who were shipbuilders, fearless seafarers and sponge divers, and rich and successful merchants. Under the Ottomans their harbor was proclaimed a free port and attracted the trade of the entire region. The Symiotes's continuous travel and trade and their frequent contact with Europe led them to incorporate foreign elements in their furnishings, clothes, and cultural life. At first they lived in Chorio, high on the hillside above the port, and in the second half of the 19th century spread down to the coast at Yialos.

Proof of their prosperity exists in the neoclassical mansions that line the narrow streets of Chorio and the main harbor in Yialos. There were some 20,000 inhabitants at this acme, but under the Italian occupation at the end of the Italo-Turkish war in 1912, the island declined; the Symiotes lost their holdings in Asia Minor and were unable to convert their fleets to steam. Many emigrated to work elsewhere, leaving their mansions behind, and now there are just a few thousand inhabitants in Chorio and Yialos.

Even worse was to come during World War II, when the retreating German army set off an ammunitions blast in 1944 that destroyed many of the old houses of Chorio. Much has been done to restore the town, but you'll still come across the exposed bones of many of these old mansions, shrouded in branches, weeds, and history. It fuels the imagination for strolls among the narrow streets of the old town, though avoid entering for risk of falling masonry.

GETTING HERE AND AROUND

Little Symi is well served by boats, either on one-day excursion trips with tour operators (*see Tours*) from Mandraki Harbor in Rhodes Town or via the Dodecanese Seaways ⊕ *www.12ne.gr/en* ferry services that link the islands. The trip takes less than an hour. All boats and ferries arrive in Yialos, Symi's main harbor, while catamarans also make a stop in Panormitis or Pedi, though both are easy to reach from town once there.

From the bus stop on the south side of Yialos Harbor, the yellow city buses make the hourly trip up to Chorio and on to Pedi Bay for €1.70 one-way. The green buses go from the same stop and link Yialos and Panormitis for €4 one-way; there are just three return services a day. Hiring a car is pointless here; there is only one main road after all. Once on Symi, you'll learn that the easiest way to get around is by foot. If you are staying in Nimborio or other outlying areas that are reached via unpaved roads, make arrangements in advance for your hotel to pick you up, as most taxis, except for a few of the younger drivers, refuse to risk their cars, or will only take you part of the way.

VISITOR INFORMATION

The island does not have an official tourist office. Symi Tours ⊕ *www. symitours.com*, which has a stall across from where the ferry disembarks, is a good source of information, but as a tour operator they are hardly impartial.

Yialos Γιαλός

45 km (28 miles) north of Rhodes Town.

As the boat from Rhodes to Symi rounds the last of many rocky barren spurs, the port of Yialos, at the back of a deep, narrow harbor, comes into view. The shore is lined with mansions, their ground floors converted to cafés with waterside terraces perfect for whiling away lazy hours.

 Sights

Church of Ayhios Ioannis

RELIGIOUS SITE | This church built in 1838 incorporates in its walls fragments of ancient blocks from a temple that apparently stood on this site and is surrounded by a plaza paved in an intricate mosaic, fashioned from inlaid pebbles. ⊠ *Yialos* ✛ *Near center of Yialos Village.*

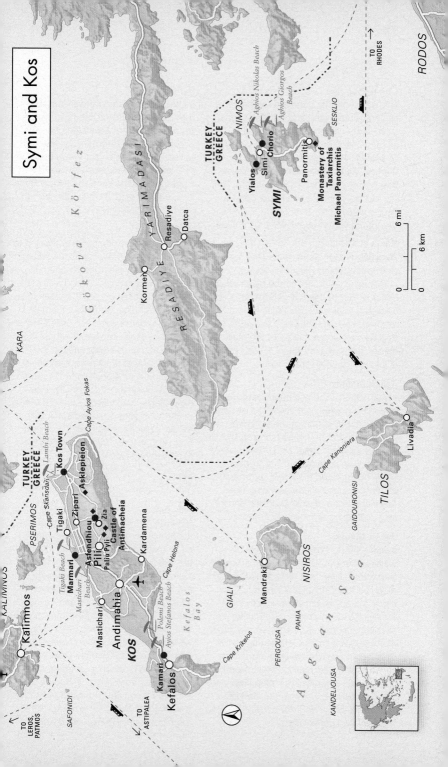

Symi and Kos

RODOS

TO RHODES

NIMOS

TURKEY
GREECE

Aghios Nikolas Beach
Aghios Giorgos Beach

SESKLIO

Yialos
Simi
Chorio

Panormitis

SYMI

Monastery of
Taxiarchis
Michael Panormitis

GÖKOVA Körfez

YARIMADASI

Resadiye
Datca

KARA

RESADIYE

Kormen

TURKEY
GREECE

Cape Ayios Fokas

PSERIMOS
Cape Skánsdari
Lambi Beach

Kos Town
Asklepieion

Tigaki
Zipari
Zia

Astendhiou
Pili
Palia Pili

Marmari
Masticbari

Castle of
Antimacheia

Kardamena

Mastichari

Cape Kanoniera

Livadia

TILOS

Tigaki Beach
Mastichari Beach

KOS

Andimahia

Cape Helona

Polemi Beach
Ayios Stefanos Beach

Kamari
Kefalos

Kefalos
Bay

GIALI

Mandraki

NISIROS

Aegean Sea

PERGOUSA

PAHIA

GAIDOURONISI

KALIMNOS

Kalimnos

TO
LEROS,
PATMOS

SAFONIDI

TO
ASTIPALEA

Cape Krikelos

KANDELIOUSA

6 mi

6 km

0   6

Beaches

One reason Symi's beaches are so pristine is that almost none are reachable by car. From the main harbor at Yialos, boats leave every half hour between 10:30 am and 1 pm for the beautiful beaches of **Aghia Marina, Aghios Nikolas, Aghios Giorgos, Agios Marathountas,** and **Nanou Bay.** Return trips run from 3 to 6 pm. The round-trips cost €10 to €14 per person depending on how many want to make the trip. In summer, there are also small boats for hire from the clock tower.

For a swim near Yialos, follow the road west out of **Yialos Harbor** for about 2 km (1 mile) and you come to the pine-shaded beach at Nimborios Bay, where there is a taverna that rents umbrellas (€5 a day). Alternatively, catch the bus to nearby **Pedi Bay**, a quieter version of the main harbor, from where Aghios Nikolas beach is just a 1km (600 yards) walk.

Aghios Giorgos
BEACH—SIGHT | The half-hour boat trip down the rugged east coast of the island from Pedi Bay is part of the pleasure of an excursion to this beautiful strip of sand, backed by sheer cliffs. The absence of amenities requires a bit of preparation—bring water, food, and an umbrella, as there are few shade-providing trees. **Amenities:** none. **Best for:** nudists; snorkeling; solitude; swimming. ✉ *Pedi Bay.*

Aghios Nikolas
BEACH—SIGHT | **FAMILY** | Accessible by water taxi from Chialos, the alternative way is to walk, taking the 1 km-long (600 yards) rough path leading east of Pedi Bay. Once there, a sandy beach slopes gently into the sea, providing shallow waters that are excellent for children; it's backed by a grove of shade-giving trees. Despite the relative isolation, the beach attracts summertime crowds and is well equipped with food vendors and other facilities. **Amenities:** food and drink; toilets; water sports. **Best for:** snorkeling; swimming. ✉ *Pedi Bay* ✥ *3 km (2 miles) east of Pedi Bay.*

Restaurants

Haritomeni
$ | **GREEK** | A ten-minute walk east of the evening bustle on the main waterfront leads to this waterside gem. The accomplished Haritomeni has a lofted terrace with spectacular views over the bay. **Known for:** fantastic views away from the crowds; good-value local Greek fare; friendly staff. [$] *Average main: €12* ✉ *Yialos* ☎ *22460/072771.*

★ Tholos
$$ | **GREEK** | A seaside perch at the end of Yialos Harbor is the picturesque setting for an excellent meal, which often begins with such traditional appetizers as stuffed zucchini or boiled greens (the taramosalata here might just be among the best in Greece) and includes fresh grilled fish and other daily home-cooked offerings. You may want to arrive early enough to enjoy sunset views of the harbor, and reserve far ahead—during peak summer season it can be booked out days in advance. **Known for:** sunset views; excellent Mediterranean dishes; polished service—not always a given on the island. [$] *Average main: €16* ✉ *Waterfront* ☎ *22460/72033* ⏲ *Closed mid-Oct.–Mar.*

Hotels

Aliki Hotel
$$ | **HOTEL** | This venerable building was the family home of George Gennimata, a crusading Greek politician during the 1980s, and is now a three-story, 19th-century mansion on the waterfront has guest rooms furnished with a tasteful mix of antiques and newer pieces—the best, of course, are those that face the water. **Pros:** lovely old house with plenty of atmosphere; waterfront location; beautiful terrace. **Cons:** rooms are reached by a climb up steep stairs; no elevator; no parking. [$] *Rooms from: €130* ✉ *Yialos waterfront* ☎ *22460/71665* 🌐 *www.hotelaliki.gr* ⏲ *Nov.–Apr.* 🛏 *15 rooms; 2 suites* 🍴 *Free breakfast.*

Did You Know?

A day trip to the magnificently frescoed Monastery of Taxiarchis Michael Panormitis is a must for any visitor to Symi, but you can also make a night of it, thanks to the 75 guest rooms (with rather spartan decor).

Emporio
$$$$ | **HOTEL** | This elegant waterside retreat, formerly a private villa, was taken over a few years ago by the people behind another Symi's property called The Old Markets. **Pros:** the dining terrace boasts fine views over the bay; an on-site masseuse is available; SUPs and inflatable canoes can be used for free. **Cons:** it's a 15-minute walk to town; due to its limited number of rooms, it fills up quickly; taxis don't like to drive to Nimborio Bay. [$] *Rooms from: €295* ✉ *Yialos* ✣ *Nimborio* ☎ *69573/02565* 🌐 *www.emporiosymi.com* ⏲ *Closed Nov.–Apr.* 🛏 *5 rooms (1 cottage)* 🍴 *Free breakfast.*

Niriides
$$ | **B&B/INN** | A small fishing village, about a mile from Yialos is the setting for a get-away-from-it-all retreat in pleasant colorful apartments surrounded by gardens. **Pros:** wonderful relaxing atmosphere; great hospitality; beautiful rural location. **Cons:** steps to get to rooms; not within close distance to major sights of Symi; bar-terrace can be a bit noisy. [$] *Rooms from: €150* ✉ *Yialos* ✣ *Nimborio* ☎ *22460/71784* 🌐 *www.niriideshotel.com* ⏲ *Closed Nov.–Apr.* 🛏 *10 rooms; 1 villa* 🍴 *Free breakfast.*

★ The Old Markets
$$$ | **HOTEL** | Symi's historic trading halls have been restored as a delightfully atmospheric inn where centuries-old surroundings are accented by stone floors and antiques. **Pros:** extremely comfortable accommodations, including a lavish suite; in-room massages can be booked; fantastic views for dinner and breakfast. **Cons:** the market rooms can be a little dark; steps to reach the hotel; no elevator. [$] *Rooms from: €240* ✉ *Kali Strata* ☎ *22460/71440* 🌐 *www.theoldmarkets.com* ⏲ *Closed Nov.–Apr.* 🛏 *10 rooms (3 suites)* 🍴 *Free breakfast.*

Nightlife

Yachta
GATHERING PLACES | A rather stylish bar-eatery from the people behind the equally excellent Pantelis seafood restaurant on the haborfront. The slightly more removed location (just a two-minute walk from its sibling) serves it well, and food is delivered with equal aplomb. But this is as much a nightspot as a diner, and a fine cocktail list does the late-evening harbor views more than justice. ✉ *Yialos Harbour* ☎ *697 72/61710.*

Chorio Χωριό

1 km (½ mile) east of Yialos.

It's a 10-minute walk from the main harbor of Yialos up to the hilltop town of Chorio, along a staircase of some 400 steps, known as Kali Strata (Good Steps). There is also a road that can be traveled in one of the island's few taxis or by bus, which makes a circuit with stops at the harbor in Yialos, Chorio, and the seaside community of Pedi. The Kali Strata are flanked by elegant neoclassical houses with elaborate stonework, lavish pediments, and intricate wrought-iron balconies. Just before the top of the stairs, a line of windmills crowns the hill of Noulia. Most of Chorio's many churches date to the 18th and 19th centuries, and many are ornamented with richly decorated iconostases and ornate bell towers. Donkeys are often used to carry materials through the narrow streets for the town's steady construction and renovation work.

Sights

Archaeological Museum of Symi
MUSEUM | The Archaeological Museum, housed amid a daze of twisting back lanes, is divided into two sections. The upper display spreads a trio of rooms depicting the history of the

island through Hellenistic and Roman sculptures and inscriptions as well as icons, costumes, and handicrafts. Below this, a museum guide takes you into a merchant's *archontiko* (manison). Built overlooking the bay to spot invaders, it offers a fascinating look at the traditional life of the wealthy family that once lived here. ⊠ *Chorio* ⊹ *Follow signs from central square to Lieni neighborhood* ☎ *22460/71114* 🖼 *€2* 🕑 *Closed Tues.*

Kastro (*Castle*)

ARCHAEOLOGICAL SITE | Incorporating fragments of an ancient acropolis within its walls, the castle was built by the Knights of St. John in a short-lived attempt to expand their holdings in Rhodes. A church and several chapels dot the sparse hillside around the remnants of its walls. The hilltop view takes in both sides of the narrow peninsula that Chorio crowns, with the villages of Yialos and Pedi (and their sparkling harbors) far below. ⊠ *Chorio* ⊹ *At top of town, in the ancient acropolis.*

🍽 Restaurants

Georgio and Maria's Taverna

$ | **GREEK** | Meals at this simple taverna, as popular with locals as it is with tourists, are served in a high-ceilinged, whitewashed dining room or on a terrace that is partially shaded by a grape arbor and affords wonderful views over the sea and surrounding hills. Fish is a specialty, and simply prepared *mezedes* (small dishes), such as roasted peppers topped with feta cheese and fried zucchini, are a great start to a meal here. **Known for:** local favorite; sea views; best place to eat in Chorio. **$** *Average main: €13* ⊠ *Chorio* ⊹ *Off the main square at top of the Kali Strata* ☎ *22460/71984.*

Zoe's Taverna

$ | **GREEK** | The steep climb up to Zoe's all but guarantees a spectacular view, though it's worth booking ahead to secure a table with front-row seats. The food is equally breathtaking, with a strong adherence to traditional Symiot cuisine: think jugged hare, *dolomades* (stuffed vine leaves) the way granny used to make them, and five-hour slow-cooked lamb and potatoes. **Known for:** fantastic views out over the coast; traditional Symiot cooking; friendly owner and service. **$** *Average main: €12* ⊠ *Kali Strata* ☎ *22460/72520.*

Hotels

Asymi Residences

$ | **HOTEL** | This rather colorful arrangement of apartments lies spread-eagled along the waterfront as you enter Pedi Bay. Rooms are all wooden floors, white walls, and green-painted beams, making it all rather folksy-meets–Laura Ashley. **Pros:** Pedi Bay is a much more peaceful waterfront than Yialos; Agios Nikolaos beach is on your doorstep; sunsets over the water are magical. **Cons:** it's a steep walk to the harbor; you're reliant on the bus; its neighboring yards are a bit scruffy. **$** *Rooms from: €110* ⊠ *Pedi Bay, Pedi Bay* ☎ *22460/72300* ⊕ *www.asymi. gr* 🕑 *Closed mid-Oct.–mid-Jun.* 🛏 *17 apartments* 🍴 *Free breakfast.*

Hotel Fiona

$ | **B&B/INN** | At this bright, cheerful perch on the hillside in Chorio, just about all the large, white-tile-floored rooms have a sea-facing balcony. **Pros:** friendly service; excellent views over the harbor far below; simple and comfortable. **Cons:** strenuous climb down and back up 400 steps to Symi Town; reached only by foot; rooms are quite basic. **$** *Rooms from: €55* ⊠ *Chorio* ⊹ *Near main square* ☎ *22460/72088* ⊕ *www.fionahotel.com* 🕑 *Closed Nov.– Apr.* 🛏 *17 rooms* 🍴 *Free breakfast.*

Nightlife

★ The Secret Garden

BARS/PUBS | This café-bar hideaway along the road from Chorio to Pedi Bay is popular among locals. It was built by hand by local owners Katja and Michael, and feels every bit the leafy escape its name suggests. The menu is tasty, traditional fare, while Friday night sees live blue bands take over. It's a true hidden delight. ⊠ Road to Pedi Bay ☎ 22460/721153.

Monastery of Taxiarchis Michael Panormitis

Μονή Ταξιάρχη Μιχαήλ Πανορμίτη

7 km (4½ miles) south of Chorio.

The tiny hamlet of Panormitis on the south end of the island is a remote and idyllic setting for this holy assemblage, a popular place of pilgrimage and a pleasure to visit simply for the scenery. A trip to the monastery can be accompanied by a refreshing swim at the designated edges of the deep-blue harbor. There's a bus service from Yialos that runs three times a day in summer, which passes through Chorio, or you can take one of the daily boats from Yialos or Rhodes. If you have a guide or map, you can make your way to the monastery via the island's old donkey tracks (about 10 km), but you won't find them otherwise; a walk along the road is your other, much longer option and takes around 3½ to 4½ hours depending on your speed. Traffic isn't busy and if you set off early, you'll beat the hot sun. Several tour companies organize day trips to the monastery, with time for a swim and a hike in the surrounding countryside, for about €25, including lunch. *(See Tours for more information.)*

Sights

★ Monastery of Taxiarchis Michael Panormitis

RELIGIOUS SITE | The main reason to venture to the atypically green, pine-covered hills surrounding the little Gulf of Panormitis is to visit this unexpectedly huge monastery dedicated to Symi's patron saint, the protector of sailors. The site's entrance is surmounted by an elaborate **bell tower,** of the multilevel wedding-cake variety on display in Yialos and Chorio. A black-and-white pebble mosaic adorns the floor of the **courtyard,** which is surrounded by a vaulted stoa. The interior of the **church,** entirely frescoed in the 18th century, contains a marvelously ornate wooden iconostasis, which is flanked by a heroic-size representation of Michael, all but his face covered with silver. There are two small **museums,** one dedicated to folk culture (closed for renovation at the time of writing) and the other to religious paraphernalia. The latter has a particularly eclectic collection, including votive offerings of wooden ship models, bottles with notes containing wishes, and, most bizarrely, stuffed crocodiles.

If a day trip isn't enough for you, the monastery rents 75 spartan rooms (from €20 per night) with kitchens and private baths. Though the price doesn't include a towel or air-conditioning and there are insects (some rather large), the spiritual aspect makes for an enriching experience. A nursing home as well as a market, bakery, restaurant, and a few other businesses make up the rest of the settlement. The monastery is at its busiest for the week leading up to November 8, Michael's feast day, an event that draws the faithful from throughout the Dodecanese and beyond. ⊹ *Symi's south side, at harbor* ☎ *22460/71581 museums, 22460/72414 rooms* ⊕ *www.imsymis.org* ▣ *Monastery free; museums €1.50.*

Hiking on Symi

Symi is well known for its hiking. It's riddled with old donkey cart tracks winding through the hills, though many of the former were dynamited in the late 1970s when the first (and only) road was built on the island. Some are marked, but the chances of stumbling across them yourself are minimal. Lance Chiltern's *Walks in Symi* book is a good independent guide, though rarely seen these days. Local tour companies **Poseidon Excursion** ⊕ *symiexcursions.com* and **Kalodoukis Holidays** ⊕ *www.kalodoukas.gr* run hiking trips from Yialos to the rugged west of the island where a boat waits at Emilianos. This tiny island has its own church and is linked to the mainland by a narrow path to take you back to the harbor. If you do go it alone, spring and autumn are the best times to hike; otherwise be sure to set off early, before the sun is at its strongest, and take plenty of water.

Kos ΚΩΣ

92 km (57 miles) north of Rhodes.

Aglow with flowering oleanders and hibiscus, the island of Kos is the third largest in the Dodecanese. It certainly remains one of the most verdant in the otherwise arid archipelago, with lush fields and tree-clad mountains, surrounded by miles of sandy beaches. Its highest peak, part of a small mountain range in the northeast, is a respectable 2,800 feet. All this beauty has not gone unnoticed, of course, and Kos undeniably suffers from the effects of mass tourism: its beaches are often crowded, most of its seaside towns have been recklessly overdeveloped, and the main town is noisy and busy between July and early September.

In Mycenaean times and during the Archaic period, the island prospered greatly. In the 6th century BC it was conquered by the Persians but later joined the Delian League, supporting Athens against Sparta in the Peloponnesian War. Kos was invaded and destroyed by the Spartan fleet, ruled by Alexander and his various successors, and was twice devastated by earthquakes. Nevertheless, the city and the economy again flourished, as did the arts and sciences. The painter Apelles, the Michelangelo of his time, came from Kos, as did Hippocrates, father of modern medicine. Under the Roman Empire, the island's Asklepieion, its renowned healing center, drew emperors and ordinary citizens alike.

The last millennium saw Kos chart a similar path to that of Rhodes, with invading Crusaders replaced by Turks, followed by Italians. But Kos was never as richly developed by the Knights of St. John as Rhodes, and fewer relics of their medieval pomp remain. What survived are ancient Roman and Hellenic sites, many discovered in the 1930s after earthquakes ravaged Kos Town. It is also the most bike-friendly of the islands, giving over a chunk of its city sprawl to large cycle lanes. The temptation to escape the crowds for pedaling the flat coast and the hilltop villages of the center is one you should most definitely give in to.

GETTING HERE AND AROUND
Kos is a major air hub, with regular service from Athens and, during high season, from many other European cities. The airport is about 25 km (15 miles) from Kos Town, about 45 minutes by bus (€3.20; tickets are sold on board) and a half-hour by taxi (€35). Keep the time and taxi cost in mind if booking an early-morning outgoing flight; the first

bus service from Kos Town leaves at 8:20 am. A single morning service also runs to the airport from Kefalos and Kardamena once a day.

Kos is well served by ferries, with at least two boats arriving from Pireaus (Athens) daily in high season, taking around 12 hours; between one and two ferries arrive from Rhodes (about 2½ hours) daily, costing from €34. Boats also arrive from Mykonos, Paros, and other islands in the Cyclades about twice a week. Schedules change all the time, so check with ⊕ www.ferries.gr, ⊕ www.gtp.gr, or with any of the many travel agencies along the waterfront in Kos Town for the latest information. Kos Harbor is adjacent to the city center, and convenient for inner-city bus connections, which can be found on Dolphin Square.

An excellent bus network serves most of the island, with all buses in Kos Town setting off from the KTEL station at 4 Cleopatras Street. As many as six services a day connect Kos Town in the north and Kefalos in the south, for example; the trip takes about an hour and costs €2.50.

VISITOR INFORMATION
CONTACTS Kos Municipal Tourism Office.
✉ *Vasileos Georgiou 1, Kos Town* ☎ *22420/360400* ⊕ *www.kos.gr.*

Kos Town Κως πόλη

92 km (57 miles) north of Rhodes.

The modern town lies on a flat plain encircling spacious Mandraki Harbor and is a pleasant assemblage of low-lying buildings and shady lanes, with a skyline pierced by minarets and palm trees. Its main waterfront, though attractive, doesn't have the best of reputations thanks to the rows of harborside bars that churn out customers deep into the small hours. Yet the area's history dates to long before a time when it had to rely on its tourist crutch, and is easily seen, in scattered ancient ruins, remnants of old

city defences draped in creepers, and an imposing medieval castle.

Platanou Square is a good place to start. It was here that Hippocrates (460–370 BC), the father of modern medicine, is supposed to have taught, in the shade of a plane tree that grows on one side. Many say this is merely legend; not least because the tree that now stands here, propped up by spidery scaffolding, is just five centuries old. Surrounding this are relics of the island's Turkish past (1523–1912), including a loggia that is actually a mosque built in 1786, and showpiece buildings erected during Fascist Italian rule (1912–43), known as the Foro Italico area. Going back further, this square was once the center of a fortified medieval city, connected to the grand castle, built by the crusading Knights of St. John, that lies across the road. Sadly, this is no longer open to the public after an earthquake in 2017 rendered it unstable, but you can still wander the city's old vine-clad fortified walls east of the harbor.

Relics of Kos's Hellenistic and Roman past can be explored everywhere, not least in the remains of an old Roman home that sits on the outskirts of town. An earthquake in 1933 allowed for proper excavations of the town center, and much of what they found is now on show in the main museum.

Sights

Agora and Harbor Ruins
ARCHAEOLOGICAL SITE | Excavations by Italian and Greek archaeologists have revealed ancient agora and harbor ruins that date from the 4th century BC through Roman times. Remnants include parts of the walls of the old city, of a Hellenistic stoa, and of temples dedicated to Aphrodite and Hercules. The ruins are not fenced and, laced with pine-shaded paths, are a pleasant retreat in the modern city. In spring the site is covered with brightly colored flowers, which nicely

frame the ancient gray-and-white marble blocks tumbled in every direction. ☒ *Kos Town ✛ Over bridge from Platia Platanou, behind Castle of the Knights.*

★ Archaeological Museum

MUSEUM | The island's archaeological museum houses Hellenistic and Roman sculpture by Koan artists, much of it unearthed by Italians during their tenure on the island in the early 20th century. Among the treasures are a renowned statue of Hippocrates—the great physician who practiced on Kos—and Asclepius, god of healing; a group of sculptures from various Roman phases, all discovered in the House of the Europa Mosaic; and a remarkable series of Hellenistic draped female statues mainly from the Sanctuary of Demeter at Kyparissi and the Odeon. ☒ *Platia Eleftherias* ☎ *22420/28326* ⊕ *www.culture.gr* ☒ *€6; €15 combo ticket (inludes the Asklepieion and Casa Romana)* ⊗ *Closed Tues.*

Casa Romana (*Roman House*)

ARCHAEOLOGICAL SITE | FAMILY | The Roman House is a lavish restoration of a 3rd-century Roman mansion, with 40 rooms grouped around three atriums. It was likely partially destroyed in the earthquake of 365 AD, though its south section continued to be inhabited until the Early Christian period. The house provides a look at what everyday life of the well-to-do residents of the Roman town might have been like and also has some beautiful frescoes and mosaics. The Greek and Roman ruins that surround the house are freely accessible, however, and are just as evocative. Last entry is 7:30 pm. ☒ *Grigoriou V Street* ☎ *22420/28326* ⊠ *www.culture.gr* ☒ *€6; €15 combo ticket (inludes the Asklepieion and Archeology Museum)* ⊗ *Closed Mon. (Apr.–Oct.); Tues. (Nov.–Mar.).*

West Excavations

ARCHAEOLOGICAL SITE | These excavations, laced through a quiet residential district, have uncovered a portion of one of the main Roman streets and many houses, including the **House of the Europa Mosaic,** and part of the **Roman baths** (near main Roman street) that was later converted into a basilica. The **gymnasium** is distinguished by its partly reconstructed colonnade, and the so-called **Nymphaion** is a lavish public latrine that has been restored. In the **Odeon,** 18 rows of stone seats remain intact. The West Excavations are always open, with free access, and significant finds are labeled. ☒ *Kos Town ✛ Southwest of agora and harbor ruins.*

⊙ Beaches

If you must get wet but can't leave Kos Town, try the narrow pebble strip of beach immediately south of the main harbor. A better bet is the nearby, kilometer-long (600-yard) sandy shore of Lambi, which is easily connected via bike lanes (15 minutes) and a slew of hourly buses from Dolphin Square. This can get very crowded in summer but is the closest major beach to the city.

Lambi Beach

BEACH—SIGHT | Flanking the northern coast above Kos Town, this long, narrow stretch of sand is guarded by a strip of resorts that run its length. Crowds ooze out from the hotels in their droves to hit the volleyball courts, bars, and sun beds, with the party continuing into the night. The further west you go, the quieter the shore becomes. A cooling breeze means this area can be rather pleasant in the fierce burn of the afternoon; it also whips up the surf nicely, making it a good spot for windsurfing . **Amenities:** food and drink; sun beds; bars; lifeguards; changing rooms; decked walkway. **Good for:** watersports; parties; clean sands. ☒ *Lambi.*

Restaurants

Ali Restaurant
$ | **GREEK** | Popular among locals, this venerable Turkish-Greek joint has a catch-all menu that hits every comfort-food high note. Zucchini flowers filled with lip-smacking Greek cheese, aubergines bursting with meat, and filling pastitsio complement a vast choice of souvlakis and kebabs. **Known for:** Turkish and Greek comfort food; fast service; a quieter setting, away from the harbor. [$] *Average main: €9* ✉ *Artemisias 23* ☎ *22420/21860* 🌐 *alirestaurantkos.gr.*

★ **Broadway Restaurant**
$ | **GREEK** | A cozy, family-run restaurant with an ambitious menu that does some very creative things with classic Greek cooking. A "krassotiri" crème brélee makes the most of the island's famous soft cheese, while mains offer an even tenderer touch, with pork cheeks nestled atop a chickpea ragout stealing the show. **Known for:** creative takes on classic Greek dishes and produce; well-located away from the busy port; good value. [$] *Average main: €13* ✉ *Alexandrou 36* ☎ *22420/27052* 🌐 *www.broadway-kos.gr* ⏲ *Closed Mon.*

Petrino
$$ | **MODERN GREEK** | The setting is the star here. Three brothers have created a calm oasis a few streets in from the hustle and bustle of Kos Harbor. **Known for:** atmospheric dining; a local favorite; a quiet garden space. [$] *Average main: €18* ✉ *Platia Ioannou Theologou* ☎ *22420/27251* 🌐 *www.petrino-kos.gr.*

Platanos
$$ | **GREEK** | Set on the shady square where Hippocrates reputedly once taught, this island institution maintains high standards for its cooking and top-notch service. Occupying an early-20th-century Italian club, the surroundings of tiled rooms and candlelit balconies are elaborate. **Known for:** romantic and historic setting; excellent dishes; a bustling spot with sea views. [$] *Average main: €19* ✉ *Platia Platanos* ☎ *22420/28991* ⏲ *Closed Nov.–Mar.*

Hotels

Aktis Art Hotel
$$$ | **HOTEL** | With a perch right on the beach at the edge of the Old Town, these modernist guest rooms seem to be afloat in the Aegean, whose azure waters fill the floor-to-ceiling windows and glass-fronted balconies. **Pros:** excellent location on the sea; relaxing and stylish decor and ambience; near all in-town attractions. **Cons:** full range of resort amenities is not available; if you want to use the pool, you have to go to its sister hotel; no local style. [$] *Rooms from: €264* ✉ *Vasileos Georgiou 7* ☎ *22420/47200* 🌐 *www.kosaktis.gr* 🛏 *42 rooms* 🍽 *Free breakfast.*

★ **Albergo Gelsomino Hotel**
$$$$ | **HOTEL** | Built in 1928, back when Kos was under the thumb of Fascist Italy, this beautiful building was originally created as a hotel for prominent military officials. **Pros:** an iconic building with a fascinating history; beachside breakfasts and good cocktails at the bar; free vintage bikes for guests to use. **Cons:** there's no pool or gym; you certainly pay for what you get; the glass "smoking booth" is a clever idea but very weird to look at. [$] *Rooms from: €280* ✉ *Vasileos Georgiou V* ☎ *22420/20200* 🌐 *www.gelsominohotel.com* 🛏 *8 rooms* 🍽 *Free breakfast.*

★ **Aqua Blu**
$$$$ | **RESORT** | Who says chic can't be supremely comfortable—as these truly exciting all-suite lodgings prove. **Pros:** small and intimate yet extremely luxurious; polished service and excellent food; free parking. **Cons:** outside town; not a full-scale resort (can be a plus); no kids allowed. [$] *Rooms from: €380* ✉ *Ephelondon Paleon Polemiston* ✥ *Lambi Beach* ☎ *22420/22440* 🌐 *www.*

aquabluhotel.gr ⏲ *Closed Nov.–Mar.* 🛏 *53 suites* 🍴 *Free breakfast.*

Hotel Afendoulis

$ | **HOTEL** | A charming, dependable standby. **Pros:** pleasant, quiet surroundings; free parking; excellent hospitality includes laundry service and homemade cakes. **Cons:** no pool; it's a ten-minute walk to the main bay area; no resort amenities. [$] *Rooms from: €40* ✉ *Evripilou 1* ☎ *22420/25321* 🌐 *www.afendoulishotel.com* ⏲ *Mid-Nov.–Mar.* 🛏 *20 rooms* 🍴 *Free breakfast.*

Nightlife

Things start cooking before 7 pm and in many cases roar on past 7 am on Akti Koundourioti, which lines the bay, and in the nearby Exarchia area that includes Nafklirou Street. Competing joints try to lure in bar-hoppers with ads for cheap beer and neon-colored drinks, and are best avoided unless your aim is to get black-out drunk. Less abrasive spots usually linger a few streets back, while a few hotel and independent bars along Georgiou V Road command their own stretch of coast.

Park

BARS/PUBS | This cute stone bar in the corner of the park on Amerikis and Psaron makes for the perfect jazz-fueled chill-out spot after dark. Laid-back music and a complete absence of noisy tourists makes it a rare gem. If you get hungry there's a good mezedes restaurant (Giameze) across the street. ✉ *Corner of Amerikis and Psaron* ☎ *22420/21268.*

Zero

BARS/PUBS | The best selection of craft beers on the island, including plenty of Greek labels, makes this ruffled-looking bar with live DJs and a quiet side-street garden worth looking up. ✉ *Megalou Alexandrou 2* ☎ *22420/20182* 🌐 *www.zerocafebar.gr.*

Activities

BIKING

Kos, particularly the area around the town, is good for bicycle riding. Ride to the Asklepieion for a picnic, or peddle the flat coast in search of quieter shores. You can rent bicycles everywhere—in Kos Town and at the more-popular resorts. Try the many shops along Eleftheriou Venizelou street in town. Renting a bike costs about €5 per day.

Asklepieion Ασκληπιείον

4 km (2½ miles) west of Kos Town.

The ruins of one of the great healing centers of antiquity still impress and fire the imagination, framed by a thick grove of cypress trees and laid out on several broad terraces connected by a monumental staircase.

Sights

★ Asklepieion

ARCHAEOLOGICAL SITE | Hippocrates began to teach the art of healing on Kos in the 5th century BC, attracting health seekers to the island almost up to the time of his death, allegedly at age 103, in 357 BC. This elaborate, multitiered complex dedicated to the god of medicine, Asklepios, was begun shortly after Hippocrates's death and flourished until the decline of the Roman Empire as the most renowned medical facility in the Western world. The lower terrace probably held the Asklepieion Festivals, famed drama and dance contests held in honor of the god of healing. On the middle terrace is an **Ionic temple,** once decorated with works by the legendary 4th-century BC painter Apelles, including his renowned depiction of Aphrodite (much celebrated in antiquity, it was said the artist used a mistress of Alexander the Great as a model). On the uppermost terrace is the **Doric Temple of Asklepios,** once

Cycling Kos

The hill country of central Kos beckons the adventurous inland, with much of it easily explored in one day if you're prepared to pedal around 40 km. Be warned that the roads here can be very steep. An e-bike or mountain bike with low gears is advised, as is starting early if you're to avoid the heat of summer. Start out on the flat coast north of town, following cycle lanes up to the crashing shores of Lambi. Hug the coastal roads west down to **Tigaki Beach**, skirting the cracked shore of **Alikes Salt Lake**, which fills with flamingos in spring, before cutting south though Marmari and its surrounding **vineyards** to the tiny village of **Pyli**. This is best known for its natural spring and as the gateway to the **ruined fortress of Old Pyli.** Follow the steep road east from the Church of Agios Georgios 3 km to the castle, where a climb on foot takes you to the **Oria Taverna**, high on the slopes, for a refreshing drink and incredible views of the hilltop ruins. Freewheeling back down, skirt east around Mount Dikaios to the pretty village of **Zia**, filled with tiny boutiques and cafés, and the **ghost town of Haihoutes**, abandoned in the 1970s due to earthquake damage. An excellent taverna here bucks its "ghost town" image and makes for a revitalizing stop. Return to the city via **Asklepieion** for a glimpse of the island's past.

surrounded by colonnaded porticoes. ✉ *Off Agiou Demetriou, Platani* ✛ *Take the local bus from Kos Town to the hamlet of Platani and walk to the ruins from there* ☎ *22420/28326* ⊕ *odysseus. culture.gr* ✇ *€8; €15 combo ticket (inludes the Casa Romana and Archeology Museum)* ◷ *Closed Tues. Nov.–Mar.*

Asfendhiou Ασφενδίου

9 km (5½ miles) west of Kos Town.

Beyond the Asklepieion, the road rises high into the central hill country of Kos, where Mount Dikiaos, the largest summit on this low-rise isle, barely scrapes 850 meters (2,788 feet). It's pure day-trip country. To the east of the mountain, vineyards sweep the foothills down to the plains; and to the south, cypress and pine trees shepherd visitors to a handful of lovely whitewashed rural villages clinging to the forested slopes of the surrounding hills, known collectively as Asfendhiou. The most popular of these is Zia, where busloads of visitors unload on its pretty craft shops and jostle in the tavernas for the fine sunset views. But the history of this area is long, and those that explore further will find excellent walking among the hills as well as ghost towns and even the ruins of a Byzantine castle. You will need a car, a bike, or very strong thighs if you want to explore the area properly.

 Sights

Haihoutes

GHOST TOWN | There was no grand reason for the abandonment of the hill village of Haihoutes; its 450 villagers just ebbed away over time, drawn to the more profitable, fertile plains below until, by the 1970s, no one remained. What was left behind crumbled due to neglect and earthquakes, then hikers discovered it and Haihoutes grew a reputation as a scenic ghost town. By 2013, a local couple had moved in and opened up an excellent taverna (closed Mon.)

among the ruins, reviving the old village *kafeneio*. They cleaned up the church and created a small museum in a renovated house that documents what the village was like here. It's rather eerie to wander the parched ruins, but life is slowly bleeding back into the village; there's even a renovated B&B here now (rented through AirBnb), so you can stay overnight. ✉ *Haihoutes, Haihoutes* ☎ *69326/37905.*

★ Palio Pyli

ARCHAEOLOGICAL SITE | The spectacular ruins of a Byzantine-era castle and the settlement that once surrounded it crown the wooded hilltop of the impossibly steep road climbing south of modern-day Pyli. It was once the capital of the island yet barely a fraction of its visitors make the effort to see it. They're missing out. The 10-minute hike from the parking lot through the thickly wooded hillside isn't too arduous, though little explains what you're seeing, or where you're going. A junction divides the route to the old village and that of the castle, where its archways and walls still stand. The former route leads past a scattering of stones to the marvellous **Taverna Oria,** which has good food and incredible views over the area and ruins. ✉ *Palio Pyli, Asfendhiou* ✚ *Take the Agios Georgios Road from Pyli and follow it for 3 km.*

Triantafyllopoulos Winery

WINERY/DISTILLERY | Just north of the Asfendhiou villages, in the eastern foothills of Mount Dikioas, lie a smattering of the island's best vineyards. The most famous of these is the Triantafyllopoulos Winery, which grows local Malagouzia, Aegean Athiri, and Asyrtiko grapes, yielding an array of impressive dry white wines. Wine tasting tours are run Monday to Saturday. ✉ *Zipari* ☎ *22420/69860* ⊕ *koswinery.gr/en/home* ⊙ *Closed Sun.*

Zia

TOWN | The busiest of the villages of the Asfendhiou area is Zia, with its appealing smattering of churches and craft shops selling local honey, weavings, and

En Route

Leaving the main road southwest of the Asklepieion (turnoff is at Zipari, 9 km [5½ miles] southwest of Kos Town), you can explore an enchanting landscape of cypress and pine trees on a route that climbs to a handful of lovely, whitewashed rural villages that cling to the craggy slopes of the island's central mountains. The busiest of them is Zia, with an appealing smattering of churches; crafts shops selling local honey, weavings, and handmade soaps; and open-air tavernas where you can enjoy the views over the surrounding forests and fields toward the sea.

handmade soaps. There is also a small nature park, which has various game and farm animals for kids to feed. Buses run here three times a day direct from Kos Town in summer, and the commercialization of the village has skyrocketed in recent years. But one thing the crowds can't take away is the views, with a handful of open-air tavernas, such as the excellent **Oromedon,** offering a fine vantage point for the village's coveted sunsets. It also makes a good base for walks in the surrounding countryside. ✉ *Zia.*

Marmari Μαρμάρι

10 km (6 miles) west of Asklepieion, 14 km (9 miles) west of Kos Town.

You won't find much that's authentically Greek in this unattractively overbuilt resort town surrounded by holiday villages. Even so, the surrounding beaches are beautiful, and this side of the island has a rather cooling breeze. Without too much effort you can find a deserted strip of sand to call your own, or go for a walk around the salt lake of nearby Alikes, which attracts a wealth of migratory birdlife in early spring, including large flocks of flamingos. The bus from Kos Town to the airport makes its only stop nearby at Mastichari.

Beaches

Mastichari Beach

BEACH—SIGHT | In this north-coast resort 32 km (20 miles) west of Kos Town, the wide sand beaches backed by shade-providing pines are much discovered, backed by tavernas, rooms for rent, and all-inclusive resorts. The beach is lined with chairs and umbrellas and the launching pad for pedal boats and jet skis. Mastichari also has a fishing pier, from where boats set sail on day trips to the uncrowded islet of Pserimos. **Amenities:** food and drink; showers; toilets; water sports. **Best for:** snorkeling; swimming; walking. ⊠ *Mastichari*.

Tigaki Beach

BEACH—SIGHT | This appealing sandy beach sits on the north coast, 13 km (8 miles) west of Kos Town. Some resort hotels line the sands, but much of the inland terrain behind the beach dunes remains rural. Beachgoers can enjoy the amenities of some of the more built-up sections. The more isolated, western edge of the beach is popular with gay men. **Amenities:** food and drink; showers; toilets; water sports. **Best for:** nudists; solitude; swimming; walking. ⊠ *Tigaki*.

Castle of Antimacheia
Κάστρο Αντιμάχειας

11 km (7 miles) southwest of Marmari, 25 km (15 miles) southwest of Kos Town.

This proud fortress standing high above the sea is not just a symbol of the former might of the Knights of St. John. These days it also reminds us that overbuilt, tourist-oriented Kos has a proud past and had

some historical clout. Plus, the cool stone interiors and views over verdant hillsides to the sparkling sea are a refreshing tonic and nice break from the beach.

Sights

Castle of Antimacheia

ARCHAEOLOGICAL SITE | The thick, well-preserved walls of this 14th-century fortress look out over the sweeping Aegean and Kos's green interior. Antimacheia was another stronghold of the Knights of St. John, a military order of crusading monks, whose coat of arms hangs above the entrance gate. After numerous fierce attacks by the Ottoman Turks in the late 15th century, the Knights eventually retreated from Kos in 1523 after the fall of Rhodes to the Turks. Within the walls, little of the original complex remains, with the exception of two stark churches; in one of them, Ayios Nikolaos, you can make out a primitive fresco of St. Christopher carrying the infant Jesus. ⊠ *Antimachia*.

Kamari Καμάρι

10 km (6 miles) south of the Castle of Antimacheia, 35 km (22 miles) southwest of Kos Town.

On Kefalos Bay, the little beach community of Kamari is pleasant and less frantic than the island's other seaside resorts though still plastered with tourist shops. On a summit above is the lovely Old Town of Kefalos, a more pleasant place to wander for its views and quintessential Greekness. Close offshore is a little rock formation holding a chapel to St. Nicholas. Opposite are the ruins of a magnificent 5th-century Christian basilica. For those who wish to escape the crowds, head to the peninsula south of here. Among the rocky bluffs and clusters of Byzantine churches, are shores that feel torn from another world entirely—windswept, remote, and crowd-free.

Beaches

yios Stefanos Beach

EACH—SIGHT | A chunk of beautiful Ayios
tefanos Beach, just north of Kefalos,
now occupied by the newly built Ikos
ria (formerly the old Club Med); the rest
elongs to beach clubs renting umbrel-
s and chairs and offering activities
at include waterskiing and jet-skiing.
xpect to pay about €45 for a waterski-
g session, €60 for jet skiing. Two early
hristian basilicas crown a promontory
c the southern end of the beach, adding
) the allure of this lovely spot. **Amenities:**
od and drink; parking (free); showers;
ater sports. **Best for:** snorkeling; swim-
ing. ⊠ Kefalos.

olemi Beach

EACH—SIGHT | This long stretch of invit-
g sand, about 10 km (6 miles) east of
efalos, is also known as Magic Beach,
d is just far enough from town to
emain wonderfully undeveloped. Backed
y scrub-covered dunes, the sands offer
:tle except some sun-bed concessions
d are washed by calm, crystal-clear
aters. The privacy afforded by this
)cation means that it has also become
omething of a enclave for naturists,
ho gather at its eastern end. **Amenities:**
arking (free). **Best for:** nudists; solitude;
vimming; walking. ⊠ Kefalos.

Hotels

otel Kokalakis Beach

| **HOTEL** | Many guests return annually
) this simple hotel to enjoy the peaceful
roximity to pebble and sand beaches
nd the hospitality of the Kokalakis
amily. **Pros:** close to beach; nice pool
rea; extremely welcoming hosts. **Cons:**
airly basic accommodations; very basic
reakfast; small rooms. $ *Rooms from:*
'47 ⊠ Kefalos ✛ *Behind waterfront*
≋ 22420/71466 ▭ *No credit cards*
) *Closed Nov.–Apr.* ➥ *32 rooms* ˚○˙ *Free*
reakfast.

Patmos ΠΑΤΜΟΣ

161 km (100 miles) north of Kos.

For better or worse, it can be difficult
to reach Patmos. For many travelers,
this lack of access is definitely for the
better, since the island retains the air of
an unspoiled retreat. Rocky and barren,
this small, 34-square-km (13-square-mile)
speck in the Aegean lies beyond the
islands of Kalymnos and Leros, northwest of Kos. Its size certainly offers little
clue to its larger influence. Here on a hillside is the Monastery of the Apocalypse,
which enshrines the cave where St. John
received his "visions" in AD 95, which
became the Book of Revelation.

The island's reputation as the "Jerusalem
of the Aegean" is not unfounded, and it
is duly popular among the faithful, who
make pilgrimages to its monasteries.
As such, the tone of the island is very
different to the rest of the Dodecanese,
even on the beaches, where signs make
the authorities' views on the matter
of nudism abundantly clear—though
the fact that these are more loosely
interpreted these days shows how things
have changed. The flip side is that admin-
istrators were also careful to contain
development, meaning Patmos remains
happily off-radar, even in the busy month
of August. Those who find their way here
tend to be a varied bunch, from vacationing Athenians to the large number
of wealthy international types that have
settled around Chora, lending this holy
island an agreeably cosmopolitan vibe.

GETTING HERE AND AROUND

Patmos has no airport, and outside of
July and August, ferries wending through
the Dodecanese from Athens call only
every other day or so. A daily inter-island
service runs in high season. The trip from
Athens takes only seven hours, but boats
arrive at the ungodly hour of 2 am. It's
much easier to fly to Kos and board one
of the daily Blue Star Ferries (⊕ *www.*

bluestarferries.com) or Dodecanese Seaways (⊕ *www.12ne.gr*) boats making the 2½-hour trip up to Patmos. A convenient way to reach beaches around the island is to board a water taxi from Skala Harbor.

The island's limited bus route provides a regular service from Skala to Chora, Kambos, and other popular spots, costing a flat rate of €2. It's easy to move around by taxi—and fairly inexpensive since distances are short.

VISITOR INFORMATION

CONTACTS Patmos Municipal Tourism Office. ⚓ *Near ferry dock* ☎ *22470/31666* ⊕ *www.patmosweb.gr.*

Skala Σκάλα

161 km (100 miles) north of Kos.

Skala, the island's small but sophisticated main town, is where almost all the shops and restaurants are located. It's a popular port of call for cruise ships, and in summer the huge liners often loom over the rooftops. There's not much to see in the town, but it is lively and very attractive. Most of the town center is closed to cars and, since strict building codes have been enforced, even new buildings have traditional architectural detail. The medieval town of Chora and the island's legendary monasteries are perched above Skala on a nearby hill. Take a 20-minute hike up to Kastelli, on a hill overlooking Skala, to see the stone remains of the city's 6th-to-4th-century BC town and acropolis.

Beaches

The small island is endowed with at least 24 beaches. Although most of them, which tend to be coarse shingle, are accessible by land, sun worshippers can sail to a few (as well as to the nearby islet cluster of Arkoi) on the caïques that make regular runs from Skala, leaving in the morning. Prices vary with the number of people making the trip (or with the boat); transportation to and from a beach for a family for a day starts around €45.

Kambos Beach

BEACH—SIGHT | FAMILY | The most popular beach on the island stretches for 1.6 km (1 mile) or so along Kambos Bay, with a gently sloping sea floor that's ideal for young waders and swimmers. Sun beds line the strand of fine pebbles and sand, and pines behind the beach provide plenty of shade. The many amenities include windsurfing, waterskiing, and pedal-boat rentals. Regular bus service connects Kambos with Skala, about 6 km (4 miles) away. **Amenities:** food and drink; parking (free); showers; water sports. **Best for:** snorkeling; swimming; windsurfing. ⊠ *Skala.*

Psili Ammos Beach

BEACH—SIGHT | It's well worth the effort required to reach the most beautiful (and remote) beach on the island, a lovely scallop of sand backed by pines and rough, goat-filled hills. Getting there requires a 45-minute caïque ride (€15) from Skala or a 20-minute walk on a footpath from Diakofti (the narrowest point on the island), where visitors can park their cars. While nudism is not officially allowed on Patmos, this is one beach where nude bathing seems to be tolerated, at the far edges. An extremely basic taverna sometimes serves light fare, but you'll want to bring water and snacks for an outing to this pristine spot. **Amenities:** food and drink;

arking (free); toilets. **Best for:** nudists; norkeling; solitude; swimming.

Restaurants

★ Benetos

$ | **MEDITERRANEAN** | A native Patmian, enetos Matthaiou, and his American vife, Susan, operate this lovely resaurant abutting a seaside garden that upplies the kitchen with fresh herbs nd vegetables. These homegrown ngredients find their way into a selection f Mediterranean-style dishes that re influenced by the couple's travels nd include house-cured sardines, the sland's freshest Greek salad, and juicy low-roasted pork atop a chickpea uree. **Known for:** good service; excellent Mediterranean dishes; homemade bread. [$] *Average main: €20* ✉ *Sapsila* ✥ *On harorside road between Skala and Grikos* ☎ *22470/33089* 🌐 *www.benetosrestaurant.com* ⏲ *Closed Mon. and mid-Oct.–May. No lunch.*

zivaeri

| **GREEK** | The excellent island cooking ere is spiced up by the sea views, which ou can savor from a seaside balcony table r right on the beach below. The mezedes nenu includes such traditional favorites as eek pie, fried eggplant, and smoked pork. **nown for:** beautiful sea views; beachside ining; live music. [$] *Average main: €10* ✉ *Harborside road* ☎ *22470/31170* 💳 *No redit cards* ⏲ *No lunch.*

Coffee and Quick Bites

elateria Marechiaro

| **CAFÉ** | This café is best known for its omemade gelato, made by its Neaolitan owner—try the dark chocolate nd orange—though it also offers fine akes on Greece's three Cs: coffee, akes, and cocktails. **Known for:** best ice ream on the island; a peaceful stop or a lunchtime sugar fix; homemade moncello. [$] *Average main: €5* ✉ *Skala* ☎ *69456/76391.*

Hotels

★ Petra Hotel & Suites

$$$$ | **HOTEL** | One of Greece's truly special retreats sits high above Grikos Bay, south of Skala, and provides a luxurious yet informal getaway, with large and sumptuous guest quarters, delightful outdoor lounges, a welcoming pool, and soothing sea views. **Pros:** wonderful outdoor spaces; superb service and hospitality; beach is just steps away. **Cons:** the hotel climbs a series of terraces reached only by steps; minimum three-night stay; not within walking distance to main sights of Patmos. [$] *Rooms from: €425* ✉ *Grigos* ☎ *22470/34020* 🌐 *www.petrahotel-patmos.com* ⏲ *Closed mid-Oct.–May* 🛏 *11 rooms* 🍴 *Free breakfast.*

Hotel Skala

$$ | **HOTEL** | Skala's best in-town option places you in the center of the action, steps from the municipal beach yet removed from the harbor noise and offers simple but comfortable guest rooms that surround a bougainvillea-filled garden. **Pros:** top location; attractive terrace and pool; elevator. **Cons:** occasionally hosts large groups; August's high-season rates are high, given simplicity of accommodations; lack of design. [$] *Rooms from: €144* ✉ *Harbor front* ☎ *22470/31343* 🌐 *www.skalahotel.gr* ⏲ *Closed Nov.–Mar.* 🛏 *78 rooms* 🍴 *Free breakfast.*

★ Porto Scoutari

$$ | **HOTEL** | It seems only fitting that Patmos should have a hotel that reflects the architectural beauty of the island while providing luxurious accommodations—and the enormous, suitelike guest rooms and a verdant garden (with a swimming pool) help it fit the bill nicely. **Pros:** beautiful grounds; near beach; excellent service. **Cons:** only ground-floor rooms are suitable for travelers with mobility issues; 5-km (3-mile) drive from Patmos Town; not within walking distance of major sights. [$] *Rooms from: €130* ✉ *Skala* ✥ *1 km (½ mile) northeast of Skala Center*

☎ 22470/33123 ⊕ www.portoscoutari. com ⊘ Closed Nov.–Mar. ⟿ 34 rooms ⏐◯⏐ Free breakfast.

Shopping

Patmos has some elegant boutiques selling jewelry and crafts, including antiques, mainly from the island.

CRAFTS
Katoi
GIFTS/SOUVENIRS | Head here to explore a wide selection of ceramics, icons, and silver jewelry of traditional design. ⊠ Skala ✛ On Skala–Chora road ☎ 22470/31487.

Selene
GIFTS/SOUVENIRS | Whether made of ceramic, glass, silver, or wood, each work—by one of 40 different Greek artists—displayed in a former boat-building shop is unique. ⊠ Harbor front ☎ 22470/31742.

Chora Χώρα

5 km (3 miles) south of Skala.

Atop a hill due south of Skala, the village of Chora, clustered around the walls of the Monastery of St. John the Theologian, has become a preserve of international wealth even as the whitewashed houses, Byzantine mansions, and quiet, twisting lanes retain a great deal of dignity and charm. Though the short distance from Skala may make walking seem attractive, a steep incline can make this challenging. A taxi ride is about €8, and there is frequent bus service (€2 from Skala and other points on the island).

⊙ Sights

Monastery of the Apocalypse
RELIGIOUS SITE | In AD 95, during the Emperor Domitian's persecution of Christians, St. John the Theologian was banished to Patmos, where he lived until his reprieve two years later. He writes that it was on Patmos that he "heard … a great voice, as of a trumpet," commanding him to write a book and "send it unto the seven churches." According to tradition, St. John wrote the text of _Revelation_ in the little cave, the Sacred Grotto, now built into the Monastery of the Apocalypse. The voice of God spoke through a threefold crack in the rock, and the saint dictated to his follower Prochorus. A slope in the wall is pointed to as the desk where Prochorus wrote, and a silver halo is set on the stone that was the apostle's pillow. The grotto is decorated with wall paintings from the 12th century and icons from the 16th.

The monastery, which is accessible via several flights of outdoor stairs, was constructed in the 17th century from architectural fragments of earlier buildings, and further embellished in later years; the complex also contains chapels to St. Artemios and St. Nicholas. ⊠ Chora ✛ 2 km (1 mile) south of Chora on Skala–Chora road ☎ 22470/31276 monastery ⛫ €2.

★ Monastery of St. John the Theologian
RELIGIOUS SITE | On its high perch at the top of Chora, the Monastery of St. John the Theologian is one of the world's best-preserved fortified medieval monastic complexes, a center of learning since the 11th century, and today recognized as a UNESCO World Heritage site. Hosios Christodoulos, a man of education, energy, devotion, and vision, established the monastery in 1088, and the complex

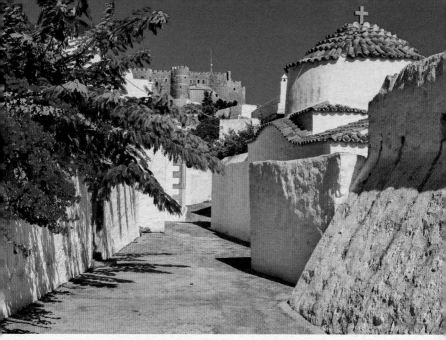

The luckiest monks on Patmos—famed for its vibrant community of monks—get to call the Monastery of St. John the Theologian (seen in the background here) home.

soon became an intellectual center, with a rich library and a tradition of teaching. Monks of education and social standing ornamented the monastery with the best sculpture, carvings, and paintings and, by the end of the 12th century, the community owned land on Leros, Limnos, Crete, and Asia Minor, as well as ships, which carried on trade exempt from taxes.

A broad staircase leads to the entrance, which is fortified by towers and buttresses.

The complex consists of buildings from a number of periods: in front of the entrance is the 17th-century **Chapel of the Holy Apostles**; the **main Church** dates from the 11th century, the time of Christodoulos (whose skull, along with that of Apostle Thomas, is encased in a silver sarcophagus here); the **Chapel of the Virgin** is from the 12th century.

The **Treasury** contains relics, icons, silver, and vestments, most dating from 1600 to 1800. An 11th-century icon of St. Nicholas is executed in fine mosaic work and encased in a silver frame. Another icon is allegedly the work of El Greco. On display, too, are some of the library's oldest codices, dating to the late 5th and the 8th centuries, such as pages from the Gospel of St. Mark and the Book of Job. For the most part, however, the **Library** is not open to the public and special permission is required to research its extensive treasures: illuminated manuscripts, approximately 1,000 codices, and more than 3,000 printed volumes. The collection was first cataloged in 1200; of the 267 works of that time, the library still has 111. The archives preserve a near-continuous record, down to the present, of the history of the monastery as well as the political and economic history of the region. ✉ *Chora* ☎ *22470/20800* ⊕ *www.patmosmonastery.gr* 🎫 *€4.*

🍴 Restaurants

Vaggelis
$$ | **GREEK** | Choose between a table on the main square (perfect for people-watching) or the raised terrace out back with stunning views of the sea. Fresh grilled fish and lemon-and-oregano-flavored goat are specialties of the traditional kitchen, and other simple dishes such as mint-flavored *dolmades* (stuffed grape leaves) and *tzatziki* (yogurt and cucumber dip) are the way to go. **Known for:** stunning sea views; excellent traditional Greek dishes; higher prices than most. [$] *Average main: €15* ✉ *Main square* ☎ *22470/31967* 💳 *No credit cards.*

🎟 Performing Arts

Patmos Festival of Sacred Music
FESTIVALS | In late August or early September, the Monastery of the Apocalypse hosts this festival, with world-class Byzantine and ecclesiastical music performances in an outdoor performance space. ✉ *Monastery of the Apocalypse* ☎ *22470/31666.*

Chapter 11

THE NORTHERN AEGEAN ISLANDS

LESVOS, CHIOS, AND SAMOS

11

Updated by
Nora Wallaya

⊙ Sights	🍴 Restaurants	🛏 Hotels	🛍 Shopping	🍸 Nightlife
★★★★☆	★★★☆☆	★★★☆☆	★☆☆☆☆	★★☆☆☆

WELCOME TO THE NORTHERN AEGEAN ISLANDS

TOP REASONS TO GO

★ **Historic stars of Samos:** Math genius Pythagoras, freedom-loving Epicurus, and the fabled Aesop were just a few of this island's brightest stars.

★ **Mesmerizing mastic villages:** Pirgi in Chios is known for the resin it produces, but with its Genoese houses patterned in black and white, it's the Escher-like landscape that's likely to draw you in.

★ **Sappho's island:** If it's poetic truth you seek, head to Skala Eresou, a popular and appealing seaside village on Lesvos and onetime home to the ancient lyric poet, who wrote much of her verse in praise of female beauty.

★ **Sailing to Byzantium:** Colorful Byzantine mosaics make Chios's 11th-century Nea Moni monastery an important piece of history—and a marvel to behold.

★ **Dizzyingly good ouzo:** Though you can get this potent potable anywhere in Greece, Lesvos's is reputedly the best—enjoy it with famed salt-baked Kalloni sardines.

About the only thing the islands of Samos, Chios, and Lesvos share is their proximity to Turkey: from their shores, reaching from Macedonia down to the Dodecanese along the coast of Asia Minor (present-day Turkey), you can see the very fields of Greece's age-old rival. No matter that these three islands may be a long haul from Athens: few parts of the Aegean have greater variety and beauty of landscape—a stunning blend of pristine shores and craggy (Homer's word) mountains.

1 Samos. This famously fertile island, in classical antiquity a center of Ionian culture and luxury, is still renowned for its fruitful land, and for the delectable Muscat wine it produces. The island attracts archaeology fanatics and lazy beach lovers alike, leaving visitors spoiled for choice among a plethora of ancient sights (such as the Temple at Heraion—once four times larger than the Parthenon) and long sandy beaches with crystal waters.

2 Lesvos. Often called Mytilini after its historic (but today somewhat boisterous) capital, Lesvos is the third-largest island in Greece. Known as the "sweet home" of lesbians from around the world, this was the land of origin of the ancient poet Sappho, whose romantic lyrical poetry was said to be addressed to women. Sapphic followers who flock to the island mostly stay in Skala Eresou, but Lesvos has something for everyone: exquisite cuisine and ouzo, beautiful beaches, medieval villages, monasteries with miraculous icons, and lush landscapes.

3 Chios. You'll find something of authentic Greece here. Go beyond the busy, almost souk-like main town to discover starkly haunting countryside and quaint village squares. The 11th-century monastery of Nea Moni is known for its Byzantine art, and for its poignant remembrance of the tragic Chios massacre of 1822. Chios is the "mastic island," producing the highly prized resin that locals add to just about everything from ice cream to hair conditioner; the most noted mastic village is Pirgi, famed for the chiseled geometric patterns on its house facades.

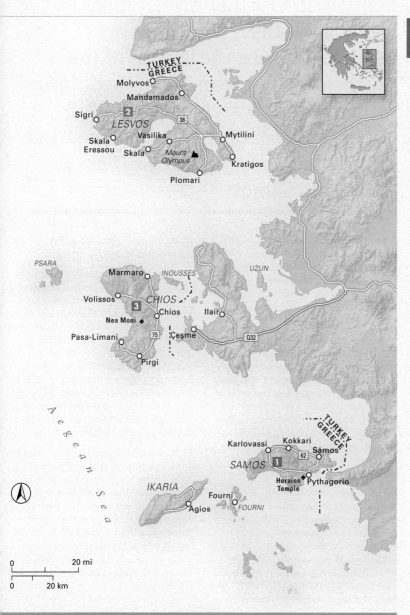

Quirky, seductive, fertile, sensual, faded, sunny, worldly, ravishing, long-suffering, hedonistic, luscious, mysterious, legendary—these adjectives only begin to describe the islands of the northeastern Aegean. This startling and rather arbitrary archipelago includes a sizable number of islands, but the three largest (and most visited) are Lesvos, Chios, and Samos.

Closer to Turkey's coast than to mainland Greece, and quite separate from one another, these islands are hilly, sometimes mountainous, with dramatic coastlines and uncrowded beaches, brilliant architecture, and unforgettable historic sites.

Lesvos, Greece's third-largest island and birthplace of legendary artists and writers, is dense with gnarled olive groves and interspersed with mineral springs. Chios, though ravaged in parts by fire in recent years, retains a raw beauty, and has fortified villages, old mansions, Byzantine monasteries, and stenciled-wall houses. Samos, the lush, mountainous land of wine and honey, whispers of the classical wonders of antiquity.

Despite their proximity to Asia Minor, the Northern Aegean islands are the essence of Greece, the result of 4,000 years of Hellenic influence. Lesvos, Chios, and Samos prospered gloriously in the ancient world as important commercial and religious centers, though their significance waned under the Ottoman Empire. They also were cultural hothouses, producing such geniuses as Pythagoras, Sappho, and (probably) Homer.

Although many young backpackers and partiers bypass the Northern Aegean, you can still carve out plenty of beach time by day and wander into lively restaurants and bars at night, but these islands reveal a deeper character, tracing histories that date back to ancient, Byzantine, and post-Byzantine times, and offer landscapes that are both serene and unspoiled. Visitors to the northern islands should come with the spirit of discovery and open themselves to opportunities to interact with rich, enduring cultures.

Many hundreds of thousands of refugees and migrants from around the world have passed through the islands in recent years. While many have moved on to Athens and beyond, thousands have remained, and have started to settle down. Their presence has not only enhanced the cosmopolitan nature of these crossroads islands, but has also shown the compassion and hospitality of the islanders.

Planning

When to Go

From early May to early June, the weather is usually sunny and warm and the sea is still a bit chilly. From mid-June until the end of August, the weather goes through quite a sweeping change and can become very hot, although the waters of the Aegean can prove sufficiently refreshing. In September the weather begins to mellow considerably, and by mid-October it's usually at its warmth limit for swimming, although sunshine can continue throughout the year on and off. Between November and March these islands can make for an enjoyable trip; unlike the holiday-oriented islands there are enough restaurants, museums, and sites open to keep visitors happy, though the weather can make ferry travel unreliable.

Planning Your Time

If you have only a week to devote to this region, try to visit two islands. Start by exploring Mytilini, the capital of Lesvos, a bustling center of commerce and learning, with its grand old mansions overlooking the harbor. From there, head to the countryside to the northern destinations: Molyvos, a medieval town sprawling under the impressive Molyvos Castle; Skala Eresou with its fine beach and bars; and the hilltop Agiassos, immersed in verdant forests. For your second stop, take a ferry to Chios, where you can enjoy the nightlife in the main town, and amble the streets of the Old Quarter. Next, go to Pirgi (admired for its unique black-and-white carved facades), and Mesta, part of the "masticohoria," or mastic villages, world-renowned for their cultivation of mastic trees, which preserve a Greece of centuries past.

If you have a little more time, take the ferry from Chios to Samos. Circle the island, stopping at its sandy beaches and at Pythagorio, the ancient capital, or the temple at Heraion, one of the Wonders of the Ancient World. Consider visiting the popular traditional fishing village of Kokkari, which has managed to keep its architectural authenticity, then head for the beaches Tsamadou and Lemonakia, where the green pine slopes meet the cobalt-blue waters of the Mediterranean. If you're drawn to the shores of Turkey, Samos makes a convenient stopover, as there's a daily ferry service to Kusadasi.

Getting Here and Around

AIR

Even if they have the time, many people avoid the 8- to 10-hour ferry ride from Athens and fly, which takes less than an hour. Sky Express, Aegean Airways, and Olympic have at least a dozen flights a week (three or four daily) from Athens to Lesvos and Chios in summer and at least four daily flights to Samos. There are several flights a week from Chios to Lesvos, Limnos, Rhodes, and Thessaloniki; and several each week from Lesvos to Chios, Limnos, and Thessaloniki. From Samos there are several weekly flights to Limnos, Rhodes, and Thessaloniki; there are also flights (usually at least one per week) between Samos and the other northern islands, some operated by Sky Express. Check in online ahead of your flight; it's not uncommon for your seat to be sold to someone else if you choose to wait and check in at the airport instead. *For airline contact information, see Air in Travel Smart.*

Lesvos Airport is 7 km (4½ miles) south of Mytilini. Chios Airport is 4½ km (3 miles) south of Chios Town. The busiest airport in the region is on Samos, 17 km (10½ miles) southwest of Samos Town, with many international charters arriving in summer.

CONTACTS Chios National Airport.
☎ 22710/81400. **Mitilini Airport.**
☎ 22510/38700. **Samos International Airport.** ☎ 22730/87800.

BOAT AND FERRY

Ferries between any of the Northern Aegean islands and Piraeus, Athens's port, take 8 to 11 hours (Piraeus–Samos, approximately €54).

There is usually one daily overnight ferry from Piraeus to Lesvos (€48, 17 hrs), which calls at Chios first (€43, 8–9 hrs).

Five to nine ferries travel each week from Piraeus to Samos, arriving in either Samos Town or Karlovassi (28 km [17 miles] northwest of Samos Town), some stopping at Syros, Mykonos, and Evdilos/Ikaria.

Ferries make a popular excursion from Samos (Pythagorio) to Patmos. At least once-a-day ferry service connects Chios with Çesme, one of Turkey's most popular resorts; the crossing takes less than a half hour. From Lesvos, a ferry runs at least once a week to and from Ayvalik, the Turkish port near the classical cities of Troy, Assos, and Pergamon; the crossing takes 1½ hours.

Service between the various Northern Aegean islands is not as frequent as one might wish, making island-hopping a bit of a challenge. There is regular service between Lesvos and Chios, costing €21 (3 hours). As many as three ferries per week run between Lesvos and Samos (5 to 7 hours, from €20) and up to three a week between Samos and Chios (3 to 4 hours, from €14). Bear in mind that you must collect your ticket from the ticket office prior to your journey. It's generally recommended to arrive at the port one hour before departure, and you must check in before you board.

CONTACTS Chios Port Authority. ☎ 22710/44433 ⊕ gtp.gr. **Mytilini Port Authority.** ☎ 22510/24115 ⊕ gtp.gr. **Piraeus Port Authority.** ☎ 21045/50000 ⊕ gtp.gr. **Samos Port Authority.** ☎ 22730/27318 in Samos Town, 22730/30888 in Karlovassi, 22730/61225 in Pythagorio ⊕ gtp.gr.

BUS

The public (KTEL) bus system on the Northern Aegean islands is generally reliable and runs to schedule. However, beyond port city limits the service is irregular and the times inconvenient, especially during the weekend. Drivers tend to be obliging—if your destination is en route but not listed, try asking for the drop-off anyway.

CAR

Lesvos, Chios, and Samos are large and public transport is limited, so a car is strongly recommended. Expect to spend about €40 to €100 per day for a compact car with insurance and unlimited mileage. An international driving permit (available at your local AAA office) is required to rent a car in Greece, although many agencies allow you to rent with your national license; however, if you are stopped by the police or get into an accident and cannot produce an international or EU license, you might have problems.

CONTACTS Aramis Rent-A-Car. ⊠ Directly across from port, Samos Town ☎ 22730/23253 ⊕ aramis.gr ⊠ Town center, opposite Commercial Bank, Kokkari ☎ 22730/92385. **Discover.** ⊠ Aristarchou 1, Mytilini ⊹ Across from port ☎ 22510/20391 ⊕ www.rentacarlesvos.gr. **Vassilakis.** ⊠ 92 El. Venizelou, Chios Town ☎ 22710/43880 ⊕ www.rentacarinchios.com.

TAXI

Due to the small number of taxis, prices are high—so always check the rates in advance. If you do spring for a ride, it's a good idea to ask for a card with the driver's number in case you need a lift later in your trip. On Lesvos, Michalis Parmakelis is a recommended driver who speaks fluent English.

CONTACTS Mike Parmakellis. ☎ 69744/63299 ⊕ lesvostaxi.gr.

Hotels

Restored mansions, village houses, sophisticated hotels, and budget accommodations are all options on the Northern Aegean islands. Reserve early for boutique hotels in high season, especially in Pythagorio on Samos and Molyvos on Lesvos. Hotels are usually small, and bar a few exceptions on Samos and Lesvos, there are few large resorts. On Lesvos, stay in Mytilini for cosmopolitan city life, in Molyvos for its dramatic medieval beauty, or in Skala Eresou for its laid-back beach style. On Chios avoid staying in the main town unless your stop is brief, as it lacks the charm of other island port cities—instead opt to stay in the outlying Kambos District or the picturesque mastic village of Mesta instead. Vathi (aka "Samos Town") is a good central option in Samos, and Pythagorio and Kokkari are more resort-like.

Restaurants

On Lesvos, sardines—traditionally left in sea salt for a few hours and eaten at a sushi-like consistency—from the Gulf of Kalloni are famous nationwide, as is the island's impressive ouzo variety. Apart from classic salads and vegetable dishes like seasonal *briam* (a kind of ratatouille), and oven-baked or stewed Greek-Turkish dishes, meat dishes may reflect more of a Turkish influence. Try *soutzoukakia* (meatballs spiced with cumin and cinnamon), or *keskek* (chopped meat mixed with wheat, served most often at festivals).

Local figs, almonds, and raisins are delicious; a Lesvos dessert incorporating one of these native treats is *baleze* (almond pudding). Besides being recognized for its mastic products, Chios is also known for mandarins—try the "mandarini" ice cream or juice in the main town. You'll also find an enormous variety of mastic-flavor sweets, as well as savory foods.

Thyme-scented honey, *yiorti* (the local version of keskek), and *revithokeftedes* (chickpea patties) are Samos's edible claims to fame.

Unless noted, reservations are unnecessary, and casual dress is always acceptable. Fresh fish tends to be expensive across the islands, €50 and up per kilo, with a typical individual portion measured at about half a kilo. The price for fish is not factored into the price categories below (and lobster is even more expensive). Many restaurants close from October to May, particularly outside of the port cities.

Restaurant and hotel reviews have been shortened. For full information, visit Fodors.com.

What it Costs in euros			
$	$$	$$$	$$$$
RESTAURANTS			
under €15	€15–€25	€26–€40	over €40
HOTELS			
under €125	€125–€225	€226–€275	over €275

Tours

Masticulture
Learn about traditional Chios life and the island's natural beauty through this travel service, which organizes activities including walking tours, cooking classes, mastic tree planting and maintenance, grape pressing, and offers unique accommodation options—an excellent option for the eclectic traveler. ☒ *Mesta ✢ On main square* ☎ *22710/76084* ⊕ *www.masticulture.com.*

Petra Tours
This action-oriented firm is located in Petra, a tiny beach town just south of Molyvos. The staff plans bird-watching, botanical, walking, and scuba-diving

excursions, and can also arrange distinctive accommodation. ⊠ *Petra* ☎ *22530/42011* ⊕ *petratours-lesvos.com.*

Rhenia Tours

Efficient staff put together informative and fun-filled tours of the classical sites on Samos and the island's natural wonders, and also arranges excursions to Ephesus in Turkey and the island of Patmos. ⊠ *15 Sofouli, Samos Town* ☎ *22730/88800* ⊕ *www.rhenia.gr.*

Visitor Information

Please see the Visitor Information listing in the pages devoted to each island for Lesvos and Chios.

Lesvos ΛΕΣΒΟΣ

The Turks called Lesvos the "garden of the empire" for its fertility: in the east and center of the island, literally millions of olive trees line the hills in seemingly endless, undulating groves, interspersed with fragrant pine forests. The western landscape is filled with oak trees, sheep pastures, rocky outcrops, and mountains. Wildflowers and fields of grain sweep the valleys, and the higher peaks are wreathed in dark green pines. Adding to the allure—and much to the delight of hedonists—are the hot, mineral-rich waters that bubble to the surface and in places are channeled into thermal baths. This third-largest island in Greece is filled with natural beauty, and its other treasures are the creative artists and thinkers it has produced and inspired through the ages, whose legacy still ripples through its towns and cities.

Lesvos was once a major cultural center known for its philosophical academy, where Epicurus and Aristotle taught. It was also the birthplace of the philosopher Theophrastus, who presided over the Academy in Athens; of the great lyric poet Sappho; of Terpander, the "father of

Greek music"; and of Arion, who influenced the later playwrights Sophocles and Alcaeus, inventors of the dithyramb (a short poem with an erratic strain). Even in modernity, artists have emerged from Lesvos: Theophilos, a poor villager who earned his ouzo by painting some of the finest native modern art Greece has produced; novelists Stratis Myrivilis and Argyris Eftaliotis; and the 1979 Nobel Prize–winning poet Odysseus Elytis.

The island's recorded history stretches back to the 6th century BC, when its two mightiest cities, Mytilini and Mythimna (also known as Molyvos), settled their squabbles under the tyrant Pittacus, considered one of Greece's Seven Sages. Thus began the creative era, but later times brought forth the same pillaging and conquest that overturned other Greek islands. In 527 BC the Persians conquered Lesvos, and the Athenians, Romans, Byzantines, Venetians, Genoese, and Turks took turns adding their influences. After the Turkish conquest, from 1462 to 1912, much of the population was sent to Turkey, and traces of past civilizations that weren't already destroyed by earthquakes were wiped out by the conquerors. Greece gained sovereignty over the island in 1923. This led to the breaking of trade ties with Asia Minor, diminishing the island's wealth, and limiting the economy to agriculture, making this one of the greener islands of Greece.

Lesvos has more inhabitants than either Corfu or Rhodes, with only a fraction of the tourists, so here you can get a good idea of real island life in Greece. Many Byzantine and post-Byzantine sites dot the island's landscape, including castles and archaeological monuments, churches, and monasteries. The traditional architecture of stone and wood, inspired by Asia Minor, adorns the mansions, tower houses, and other homes of the villages. Beach composition varies throughout the island from pebble to sand. Some of the most spectacular sandy beaches and

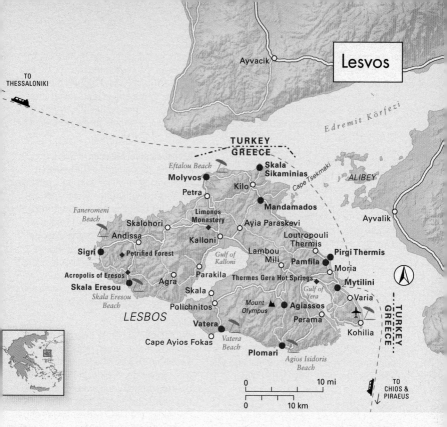

coves are in the southwest of the island, quite markedly divided into east and west at its centerpoint by the long Gulf of Kalloni.

GETTING HERE AND AROUND

From Athens there are two to four direct Aegean Airlines flights every day, which take 40 minutes and cost between €70 and €110 one-way. Mytilini Airport is 8 km (5 miles) south of town. Taxi fare into town is about €15. A bus runs between the airport and Mytilini town, though departures are infrequent.

One or two ferries leave from Piraeus for Lesvos daily in summer, a few times a week the rest of the year, take between 11 and 17 hours, and cost €48. These also stop at Chios in both directions, so there are regular links to this neighboring island (€21, 3 hours).

Lesvos's bus network is fairly extensive; there are two a day from Mytilini to Molyvos (€6.90 one way) via Kaloni, as well as service between other larger towns on the island. The local bus station is at Aghias Eirinis 2 in central Mytilini, while the bus station for destinations farther afield is located behind Agias Irinis public park, near the public library.

Mytilini Μυτιλήνη

350 km (217 miles) northeast of Piraeus by ferry.

Built on the ruins of an ancient city, Mytilini (so important through history that many call Lesvos by the port's name alone) is, like Lesvos, sculpted by two bays, one to the north and one to the south, making the town's waterfront resemble a jigsaw-puzzle piece. This busy main town and port, with stretches of grand waterfront mansions and a busy old bazaar area, was once the scene of a dramatic moment in Greek history. Early in the Peloponnesian War, Mytilini revolted against Athens but surrendered in 428 BC. As punishment, the Athens assembly decided to put to death all men in Lesvos and enslave the women and children, so a trireme set sail to issue the order. The next day a less vengeful mood prevailed in Athens and the assembly repealed its brutal decision and sent a double-manned trireme after the first one. The second trireme pulled into the harbor just as the commander of the first ship finished reading out the death sentence. Just in time, Mytilini was saved. To the south the modern town flows along the seafront into the elegant suburb and artistic enclave of Varia, once home to the modern "naive" artist Theophilos; Stratis Eleftheriadis, "Tériade," famous publisher of modern art journals; and the 20th-century poet Odysseus Elytis.

Sights

★ Agios Therapon

RELIGIOUS SITE | The enormous five-domed post-baroque church of Agios Therapon, completed in 1935, was designed by architect Argyris Adalis, an islander who studied under Ernst Ziller, the prolific architect of so many of the municipal buildings in Athens. The church is dedicated to Saint Therapon, whose name means "healer," and it's been visited by many people who came to Lesvos to recuperate from illness. It has an ornate interior, a frescoed dome, and there's a Byzantine museum in the courtyard that's filled with religious icons. ⊠ *Mytilini* ✛ *Southern waterfront* ☎ *22510/22561* 🖙 *Free.*

Ancient Theater

ARCHAEOLOGICAL SITE | This vestige of ancient Mytilini is within a pine grove and freely accessible. One of the largest theaters in ancient Greece is from the Hellenistic period and seated an estimated audience of 10,000. Pompey admired it so much that he copied it for his theater in Rome. Though the marbles are gone, the shape, carved into the mountain, remains beautifully intact. ⊠ *Mytilini* ✛ *In pine forest northeast of town, off Synoiksmos.*

Archaeological Museum of Mytilini

MUSEUM | Superseding the previous neoclassical mansion that housed the old museum, Mytilini's new archaeological museum contains finds from prehistoric Thermi, mosaics from Hellenistic houses, and reliefs of comic scenes from the 3rd-century Roman house of Menander, as well as temporary exhibits. ⊠ *8i Noemvriou* ✛ *By the junction with Papagianni* ☎ *22510/40223* ⊕ *odysseus. culture.gr* 🖙 *€4* ⊗ *Closed Tues.*

Ermou

NEIGHBORHOOD | Stroll the main bazaar street, Ermou, which goes from the port on the north side of town to the port on the south side. Walk past the fish market on the southern end, where men haul in their sardines, mullet, and octopus. Narrow lanes are filled with antiques shops and grand old mansions in varying states of romantic ruin. ⊠ *Ermou.*

★ Kastro

HISTORIC SITE | The pine-covered headland between the bays of Mytilini town supports an ancient castle and fortress, with many intact walls that seem to protect the town even today. It was built by the Byzantines on the site of an ancient acropolis possibly dating to 600 BC; the remains of a temple to Apollo and sanctuary dedicated to Demeter have been unearthed. Destroyed during battles with the Romans, it was then repaired using available materials by Francesco Gattilusio of the powerful Genoese family—note the ancient carved marble crammed here and there between stones. Finally, it fell into Ottoman hands, who expanded the castle and created new buildings including a madrasa (religious school) and Turkish hammams. Most intriguing perhaps is the temple at the center believed to be the original acropolis: it was first a sanctuary dedicated to Demeter, then repurposed as a church, then repurposed as a mosque. Look above the gates for the two-headed eagle of the Palaiologos emperors, the horseshoe arms of the Gattilusio family, and Arabic inscriptions made by Ottoman Turks. ✉ *Mytilini* ✛ *On a hill, northeast of port* ⊕ *odysseus.culture.gr* 🖃 *€2* ⊘ *Closed Tues.*

Teriade Museum

MUSEUM | The home of Stratis Eleftheriadis, better known by his French name, Teriade, houses a luminous collection of French art, much of which appeared in his highly influential Paris publications *Minotaure* and *Verve*. Among the works on display are lithographs done for the publisher/collector/critic by Picasso, Matisse, Chagall, Rouault, Giacometti, and Miró. The house is set among the olive trees of Varia and is also home to the Museum of Theophilos. ✉ *Vareia* ✛ *4 km (2½ miles) southeast of Mytilini* 🕾 *22510/23372* ⊕ *www.museumteriade. gr* 🖃 *€3* ⊘ *Closed Mon.*

Theophilos Museum

MUSEUM | Sitting amid olive groves this museum houses a large number of the eponymous artist's "naive," precise neo-Hellenic works, detailing the everyday life of local folk such as fishermen and farmers, and polytheical fantasies of another age. Theophilos lived in poverty but painted airplanes and cities he had never seen. He painted in bakeries for bread, and in cafés for ouzo, and walked around in ancient dress. For a time, he lived inside a tree that can be seen in the hamlet of Karini. ✉ *Vareia* ✛ *4 km (2½ miles) southeast of Mytilini, next to the Teriade Museum* 🕾 *22510/41644* 🖃 *€3* ⊘ *Closed weekends.*

Thermes Gera Hot Springs

HOT SPRINGS | These hot springs are just east of town on the Gulf of Gera and include both indoor and outdoor pools and tubs, a spa, and a chic outdoor café. There are delightfully warm waters that cascade from marble spouts to provide a soothing massage, but best of all, soakers can emerge from the tubs onto a beach for a refreshing dip in the waters of the gulf. ✉ *Mytilini* ✛ *On shores of Gulf of Gera off Kalloni Rd., 8 km (4 miles) west of Mytilini* 🕾 *22510/41503* 🖃 *€3.*

🍴 Restaurants

Antonis Ouzeri

$ | GREEK | This friendly spot in the hill village of Kagiani, next to Varia and just south of Mytilene, has wonderful views of Mytilene town, the Aegean, and Asia Minor beyond. Grilled octopus, fried crispy fish, and other meat favorites are served in traditional Lesvos style as small plates to accompany ouzo. **Known for:** fantastic views; delicious mezedes; friendly family-run environment. $ *Average main: €8* ✉ *Up the hill from Varia, Taxiarhes, Vareia* 🕾 *22510/61951.*

★ Kafeneion O Ermis

$ | GREEK | This centuries-old landmark on the main thoroughfare between the old and new harbors dates back to Ottoman times, and is perhaps the best place in town to sip ouzo—you'll be sat beneath a vine-shaded terrace at a wizened set of table and chairs with plenty of old-world relics to eye over while you wait. A long list of mouth-watering and excellent value mezedes are on the menu, such as *soutzoukakia,* octopus in wine sauce, long-cooked chickpeas, baked aubergines, and homemade sausages, plus traditional desserts including halva. **Known for:** old-world charm; fantastic value; authentic Greek cuisine. $ *Average main: €6* ✉ *Ermou 2, toward the north end of the street* 🕾 *22510/26232.*

Kalderimi

$ | **GREEK** | An ever-popular ouzeri and grill on shady Thassou Street in the Old Town is an almost mandatory stop while shopping along adjoining Ermou Street. Fresh grilled baby calamari and lightly fried courgette flowers stuffed with cheese are among many enticing bites that accompany the generous selection of ouzo. **Known for:** excellent seafood; rembetiko music some nights; zucchini flowers. $ *Average main: €8* ⊠ *Thassou 2* ☎ *22510/46557.*

★ Nan

$ | **INTERNATIONAL** | This not-for-profit social enterprise restaurant was founded by four Greek women seeking to integrate the refugee population into island society. Volunteer-run and offering paid employment to refugees from the Middle East, North Africa, and beyond, the refugee-chefs cook a global cuisine: you can start your meal with Syrian tabbouleh, then have an Ethiopian fava stew as a main, and an Afghan sweet for dessert. **Known for:** serving Middle Eastern and North African favorites; honorable mission statement; relaxed and friendly dining atmosphere. $ *Average main: €6* ⊠ *Komninaki 29* ☎ *22510/20250* ⊗ *Closed Sun.*

Coffee and Quick Bites

Enjoy

$ | **CAFÉ** | **FAMILY** | Creamy frozen yogurt is served with your choice of topping from a dizzying line-up of options, from Kinder Bueno to banana. Find a seat on the harbor and wolf it down as you watch the boats and marine life. **Known for:** popular with children; great value; open from morning to early hours. $ *Average main: €3* ⊠ *P. Kountourioti 63* ☎ *22510/55755.*

Hotels

Loriet Hotel

$ | **HOTEL** | Some of the island's most atmospheric digs are in an 1880s stone mansion, where high, frescoed ceilings, friezes, and antique furniture set the mood—little wonder you'll sometimes find visiting dignitaries booking the fancy suites. **Pros:** beautifully restored mansion with historic atmosphere; sophisticated pool area; convenient to airport and town. **Cons:** the long stretch of beach in front is rather unappealing; a bit run-down in places; regular rooms are small and basic. $ *Rooms from: €75* ⊠ *Vareia* ⊕ *2 km (1 mile) south of Mytilini* ☎ *22510/43111* ⊕ *www.loriet-hotel.com* ⊷ *30 rooms* ⓘⓞⓘ *Free breakfast.*

Porto Lesvos I

$ | **HOTEL** | If you want to stay in the center of Mytilini, this old, carefully renovated house a block inland from the harbor is a solid, moderately priced choice with lots of extra flair. **Pros:** excellent breakfast choices; convenient to port and town; plenty of character. **Cons:** lack of views from some rooms; some rooms can only be reached by stairs; could use some updating. $ *Rooms from: €45* ⊠ *Komninaki 21* ☎ *22510/31771* ⊕ *www.portolesvos.gr* ⊷ *12 rooms* ⓘⓞⓘ *Free breakfast.*

ⓨ Nightlife

★ Bobiras

BARS/PUBS | This effortlessly cool joint attracts an arty crowd, who fill the on-street tables in the evenings chit-chatting over cocktails. Its yellow-painted exterior, simple retro interior, and range of board games bring to mind an '80s game room. Choose the cocktails with *mastiha* liqueur from the neighboring island of Chios. A small but well put together food menu is served from 3 pm to 11 pm. ⊠ *Komninaki 22* ☎ *22510/55201.*

Bracciera
BARS/PUBS | This outdoor beach bar next to the airport has an upscale, artistic vibe and is a great place to spend time while waiting for a flight or to while away a day or evening. ✉ *Aeorodromio-Kratigos* ✥ *7 km (4½ miles) south of Mytilini, on beach past Mytilini Airport* ☎ *22510/61013.*

Shopping

Much of the best shopping is along the Ermou Street bazaar. Here you can buy a little of everything, from food (especially olive oil and ouzo) to pottery, wood carvings, and embroidery.

Veto
WINE/SPIRITS | Lesvos produces 50 brands of ouzo, and George Spentzas's shop, Veto, right on the main harbor, has made its own varietals on the premises since 1948. It also sells local food products such as olive oil, olives, dried fruit, and *hilopites* (pasta). It's open Monday through Saturday. ✉ *Aristarchou 1* ☎ *22510/24660* 🌐 *www.ouzoveto.gr.*

Pamfila Πάμφιλα

4 km (2½ miles) north of Moria, 8 km (5 miles) north of Mytilini.

In the 19th century, Pamfila's traditional tower mansions were used by wealthy families as summer homes. The views across the straits to Turkey are wonderful. Equally beautiful are the old stone factories in this area, some of which are still in use.

Pirgi Thermis Πύργοι Θερμής

8 km (5 miles) northwest of Mytilini.

Pirgi Thermis is known for its tower mansions and for its 12th-century church, Panayia Tourlot, near the outskirts of town. The town's onetime big attractions—thermal baths and a lavish spa hotel set in seaside gardens—are now closed; the latter is in a state of sad but romantic ruin.

Hotels

★ Votsala Hotel
$ | HOTEL | This alluring, Bauhaus-style retreat surrounded by peaceful gardens that run down to the water is a beloved island institution, a favorite of scores of return visitors. **Pros:** friendly, welcoming atmosphere; excellent homemade dishes at breakfast and other meals; lovely seaside grounds. **Cons:** no in-room TVs or phones, a plus for many guests; no pool but a jetty and beach for swimming; few luxuries, offset by wonderful bohemian vibes. [$] *Rooms from: €85* ✉ *Pirgi Thermis* ☎ *22510/71231* 🌐 *www.votsalahotel.com* ⏲ *Closed Nov.–Mar.* 🛏 *45 rooms* 🍴 *Free breakfast.*

Mandamados Μανταμάδος

7 km (4½ miles) northwest of Pirgi Thermis, 36 km (22½ miles) northwest of Mytilini.

Pretty Mandamados has stone houses, wood carvings, and the ruins of a medieval castle. The village is famous for its pottery, *koumari* urns (they keep water cool even in scorching heat), and an icon.

Sights

Taxiarchis Michail
RELIGIOUS SITE | The black icon of Archangel Michael is in the 17th-century monastery dedicated to the island's patron saint, Taxiarchis Michail. The gruesome legend has it that the icon was carved by a monk who used mud and the blood of his comrades, slain in an Ottoman attack, to darken it. Believers used to make a wish and press a coin to the archangel's forehead; if it stuck, the wish would be granted. Owing to wear and tear on the icon, the practice is now forbidden. ✉ *North end of village.*

Skala Sikaminias
Σκάλα Συκαμινιάς

35 km (22 miles) northwest of Mytilini.

At the northernmost point of Lesvos, past Pelopi, is the exceptionally lovely fishing port of Skala Sikaminias, a miniature gem—serene and real, with several good fish tavernas on the edge of the dock. The novelist Stratis Myrivilis used the village as the setting for his *Mermaid Madonna*. Those who have read the book will recognize the tiny chapel at the base of the jetty. The author's birthplace and childhood home are in Sikaminia, the village overlooking Skala Sikaminias—and the Turkish coast—from its perch high above the sea.

Molyvos Μόλυβος

17 km (10½ miles) southwest of Skala Sikaminias, 61 km (38 miles) west of Mytilini.

Also known by its ancient name, Mythimna, this is a place that has attracted people since antiquity. Legend says that Achilles besieged the town until the king's daughter fell for him and opened the gates; then Achilles killed her. Before 1923, Turks made up about a third of the population, living in many of the best stone houses. Today these balconied buildings are bulging with potted plants and woven together with floriferous climbing plants. Notice the red-tile roofs and cobblestone streets—they're required by law, making the village so breathtakingly picturesque that it's become a home to many artists attracted by its charms. As the sun sets, don't miss a walk down to the picture-perfect harborfront, whose bobbing boats and twinkling lights are completely enchanting.

Sights

★ Kastro
CASTLE/PALACE | A 13th-century Byzantine-Genoese fortified castle is a magnetic presence when seen from below, and a drive or walk to the hilltop landmark affords a hypnotic view down the tiers of red-tile roofs to the glittering sea. At dawn the sky begins to light up from behind the mountains of Asia Minor, casting silver streaks through the placid water as weary night fishermen come in. Wisteria vines shelter the lanes that descend from the castle and pass numerous Turkish fountains, some still in use. ⊠ *Above town* ☎ *22530/71803* 🖅 *€2* ⊘ *Closed Tues.*

Limonos Monastery
LIBRARY | This stunning 16th-century complex outside of Molyvos houses 40 chapels and an impressive collection of precious objects. Founded by St. Ignatios Agalianos on the ruins of an older Byzantine monastery, Leimonos earned its name from the "flowering meadow of souls" surrounding it. The intimate St. Ignatios church is filled with colorful frescoes and is patrolled by peacocks. A folk-art museum with historic and religious works is accompanied by a treasury of 450 Byzantine manuscripts. Women are not allowed inside the main church. ⊠ *Kalloni* ⊕ *Up a marked road 5 km (3 miles) northwest of Kalloni, 15 km (9 miles) southwest of Molyvos* ☎ *22530/22798* 🖅 *€2.*

Beaches

Eftalou
HOT SPRINGS | Just to the east of Molyvos is this empty stretch of coastline, blessed not just with a beach but with thermal mineral baths. You can soak in the enclosed tubs for a small fee or find a spot just below the old baths where the hot water bubbles into the sea. An easy walk east from there takes you past a pleasant beachside taverna to a long

Charming Molyvos, with its cobbled streets, red-tiled roofs, and 13th-century hilltop castle, attracts numerous artists and other creative types.

expanse of sand and pebbles, remote enough in parts to attract nudists. **Amenities:** food and drink, parking (no fee). **Best for:** nudists; solitude; swimming; walking. ✉ *Molyvos ✣ 3½ km (1 mile) east of Molyvos.*

🍴 Restaurants

★ The Captain's Table

$ | SEAFOOD | This harborside favorite serves seafood that's grilled to perfection including the island's famous sardines, all caught locally. It's best to enjoy the fresh fish and seafood, garden-grown vegetables, and tantalizing homemade dips as small mezedes to be shared—six are recommended for two. **Known for:** skilled at grilling seafood and vegetables; terrific harbor views; wide vegetarian and vegan selection. [$] *Average main: €9* ✉ *Molyvos ✣ Molyvos harbor* ☎ *22530/71005* ⏲ *Closed Mid-Oct.–mid-Apr. No lunch.*

Gatos

$ | GREEK | Gaze over the island and harbor from the large, wide veranda of this yellow-and-green-dressed charmer, or sit inside and watch the cooks chop and grind in the open kitchen. The beef fillet is tender, the lamb chops nicely spiced, and the salads enormous and fresh. **Known for:** grilled meats; terrace views; popular spot for coffee. [$] *Average main: €10* ✉ *Molyvos ✣ Center of old market* ☎ *22530/71661* 🌐 *www.gatos-restaurant.gr* ⏲ *Closed mid-Oct.–Mar.*

★ Kalderimi Grillhouse

$ | GREEK | FAMILY | In the quaint village of Petra, this pretty garden restaurant set amid potted plants and vine-matted pergolas specializes in grilled meats including gyros and souvlaki, though it serves traditional Greek favorites, too, and a wide selection of local cheeses. Family-owned with all the heart that goes with it, it's a popular spot for the locals who sit down to chit-chat over coffee throughout the day. **Known for:** traditional

Greek food; relaxed garden setting; large selection of local delicacies. $ *Average main: €7* ✉ *Petra* ☎ *22530/41234.*

Misirlou

$ | INTERNATIONAL | It isn't often you come by restaurants serving high-quality non-Greek food on the island of Lesvos, so for those wanting to switch things up for a night, head to this sleek, gastro-style burger and pizza restaurant perched above the harbor. **Known for:** classy, modern vibe; international menu; fabulous evening views. $ *Average main: €10* ✉ *Molyvos Harbor* ☎ *22530/72388* ⊕ *misirlou.business.site* ⊗ *No lunch.*

Hotels

Belvedere Lesvos Aeolis Hotel

$ | HOTEL | A little away from the buzz of Molyvos, this cluster of traditional red-roof buildings offers ample chance to relax, with nice grounds, pleasant beach-side rooms opening to verandas, and a swimming pool—hard to find in Molyvos. **Pros:** hotel shuttle service into town; playground and many activities for children; nice pool area with Jacuzzi. **Cons:** nearby beach is rather mediocre; unexceptional hotel decor; a somewhat generic resort feel. $ *Rooms from: €100* ✉ *Molyvos* ✛ *On road to Eftalou* ☎ *22530/71974* ⊕ *www.belvedere-lesvos.gr* ⊗ *Closed Nov.–Mar.* ⬿ *71 rooms* ⦿ *Free breakfast.*

Clara Hotel

$ | HOTEL | FAMILY | In these handsome red-roofed bungalows, soothing color palettes and lots of wood accents invite relaxation, while views from the verandas take in the sea, Petra, and Molyvos, and a small beach follows the bay beneath the L-shaped pool—all suggesting an aura of relaxed efficiency. **Pros:** great facilities and lots of activities; aesthetically pleasing architecture and decor; extremely comfortable rooms. **Cons:** hotel beach is clean but has some seaweed; no elevator and many steps; resortlike atmosphere is nice but can

seem a bit generic. $ *Rooms from: €80* ✉ *Petra* ✛ *South of Petra* ☎ *22530/41532* ⊕ *www.clarahotel.gr* ⊗ *Closed Nov.–Mar.* ⬿ *44 rooms* ⦿ *Free breakfast.*

★ Olive Press Hotel

$ | HOTEL | As the name suggests, it's a former oil-press (complete with a trademark 30-m-high chimney) that has today been renovated to an immaculate degree. **Pros:** historic and atmospheric feel; immaculate, chic furnishings; private beach area and pool. **Cons:** crashing waves could be loud for light sleepers; small depth of beach; garden a little scruffy. $ *Rooms from: €50* ✉ *Delfinia Beach* ☎ *22530/71205* ⊕ *olivepresshotel.gr* ⊗ *Closed Nov.–Apr.* ⬿ *30 rooms* ⦿ *Free breakfast.*

Sea Horse Hotel

$ | HOTEL | Most of the character-filled rooms and their balconies at this delightful stone-fronted presence on Molyvos harbor overlook the photogenic quay—the lobby even extends into a lively waterfront café that's a great place to pass the time. **Pros:** port setting; enchanting bay views; lots of character. **Cons:** despite size, hotel attracts group bookings; rooms can be noisy due to busy harbor; limited amenities. $ *Rooms from: €70* ✉ *Molyvos* ✛ *Molyvos harbor* ☎ *22530/71320* ⊕ *www.seahorse-hotel.com* ⊗ *Closed Nov.–May* ⬿ *16 rooms* ⦿ *Free breakfast.*

Nightlife

★ Congas Beach Bar

BARS/PUBS | This breezy indoor/outdoor lounge, a few steps from the waters' edge, has been a favorite hangout for some time, filling with locals and tourists alike, who come for a drink, a meal, dessert, or to dance the night away. Cool grooves, great cocktails, and colorful sunsets are the signature features. ✉ *Molyvos* ☎ *22530/72285.*

Molly's Bar
BARS/PUBS | Music to unwind to in a friendly environment is enhanced by waterside views. This popular predinner and late-night spot is open from 6 pm until the early hours. ✉ *Molyvos* ✥ *On street above harbor* ☎ *22530/71539.*

Shopping

Elleni's Workshop
CRAFTS | Stop by this shop and studio on the way to Efthalou hot springs for handmade olive wood artworks and ergonomic utensils. You'll find gifts of all shapes and sizes, for all budgets. ✉ *Molyvos* ✥ *On the road to Eftalou* ☎ *22530/72004.*

Mythos Art Gallery
JEWELRY/ACCESSORIES | Beautiful silver jewelry, statuettes, pendants, and other items fashioned by artistan Theofolis Mantzoros fill his airy, light-filled, and hospitable shop above the sea. ✉ *17 November St. 1, at Poseidon* ☎ *22530/71711* 🌐 *www.myth.gr.*

Agiassos Αγιάσος

55 km (33 miles) southeast of Molyvos, 28 km (17½ miles) southwest of Mytilini.

The prettiest hill town on Lesvos sits in an isolated valley amid thousands of olive trees, near the foot of Mt. Olympus, the highest peak. (In case you're confused, 19 mountains in the Mediterranean are named Olympus, almost all of them peaks sacred to the local sky god, who eventually became associated with Zeus.) Exempted from taxes by the Turks, the town thrived. The age-old charm of Agiassos can be seen in its gray-stone houses, cobblestone lanes, medieval castle, and local handicrafts, particularly pottery and woodwork.

Sights

Panagia Vrefokratousa
(*Madonna Holding the Infant*)
RELIGIOUS SITE | This walled compound in the village center was founded in the 12th century to house an icon of the Virgin Mary, believed to be the work of St. Luke, and it remains a popular place of pilgrimage. Built into the foundation are shops whose revenues support the church, as they have through the ages. The church museum has a little Bible from AD 500, with legible, elegant calligraphy. ✉ *Central square* 🎫 *Free.*

Restaurants

To Stavri
$ | **GREEK** | Up the hill toward the top of the village you will find this popular gathering spot with tables straddling a bridge that crosses the main thoroughfare. The menu consists of local favorites and most of the delicious produce is homegrown. **Known for:** great outdoor seating; authentic, homemade food; large portions. [$] *Average main: €8* ✉ *Agiassos* ✥ *Top of the village* ☎ *22520/22936.*

Plomari Πλωμάρι

20 km (12½ miles) south of Agiassos, 42 km (26 miles) southwest of Mytilini.

The second-largest town on Lesvos is on the southern coast, between the Gulf of Gera to the east and the Gulf of Kalloni to the west, dramatically set in a cliff face overlooking a wide harbor from where you can witness stupendous Aegean sunsets. This was once a major port, but today the town is a cheerful mix of resort and quiet fishing village, with narrow, cobbled lanes and houses spilling down to the sea. Plomari is famous throughout Greece for its ouzo, and there's a lively night scene on the harbor, where visitors gather after a long day at one of the surrounding beaches.

Beaches

Agios Isidoris

BEACH—SIGHT | FAMILY | The beach strip just east of Plomari is backed by low-key hotels and tavernas. Though the setting is hardly remote, the sea washing onto the long stretch of golden sand is sparkling clean. A bonus for swimmers and snorkelers is the bountiful sea life that flourishes on the rocky shelf just below the surface of the turquoise waters. **Amenities:** food and drink; parking (no fee); water sports. **Best for:** snorkeling; swimming; walking. ☒ *Agios Isidoris.*

Vatera Βατερά

53 km (33 miles) west of Mytilini.

This appealing place rambles along a 9-km-long (5½-mile-long) sandy strip of sparkling water, lined with tamarisk trees and framed by green hills. You can sit and enjoy the view of the cape of Agios Fokas, with its excavated Temple of Dionysus. As is often the case in succeeding cultures, the temple's marble fragments were recycled, built into the center aisle of a town basilica.

Beaches

Vatera Beach

BEACH—SIGHT | FAMILY | This long stretch of sand could in itself put Lesvos on the map for beach lovers, yet it's often easy to find a patch all to yourself—the farther east you drive or walk from the settlement of Vatera, the more remote the setting becomes. The curving, southern exposure is idyllic, and swimming is good for water enthusiasts of all ages. **Amenities:** food and drink; parking (no fee). **Best for:** solitude; swimming; walking. ☒ *Vatera.*

Skala Eresou Σκάλα Ερεσού

58 km (35 miles) southwest of Molyvos, 89 km (55 miles) west of Mytilini.

The poet Sappho, according to unreliable records, was allegedly born here circa 612 BC. She most likely presided over a finishing school for marriageable young women, and she appears to have been married herself and to have had a daughter. Dubbed the Tenth Muse by Plato because of her skill and sensitivity, Sappho wrote songs that erotically praise women and celebrate their marriages. Sappho's works—proper and popular in their time—were burned by Christians, so that mostly fragments survive; one is "and I yearn, and I desire." Sapphic meter was in great favor in Roman and medieval times; both Catullus and Gregory the Great used it, and in the 19th century, so did Tennyson. Since the 1970s, many gay women have been coming to Skala Eresou to celebrate Sappho (the word "lesbian" derives from Lesvos), although the welcoming town is also filled with plenty of heterosexual couples and other travelers who come to enjoy the delightful setting and appealing, laid-back scene.

Sights

Acropolis of Eresos

ARCHAEOLOGICAL SITE | Ancient Eresos crowned a hillside overlooking the sea, and sections of the pre-classical walls, medieval castle ruins, and the AD 5th-century church, Agios Andreas, remain from the storied and long-inhabited site. The church has a mosaic floor and a tiny adjacent museum housing local finds from tombs in the ancient cemetery. ☒ *Skala Eressou* ⊹ *1 km (½ mile) north of Skala Eresou* ☏ *22530/53037* ⊕ *odysseus.culture.gr* ☒ *Free.*

Eresos

TOWN | The old village of Eresos, separated from the coast by a large plain, was developed to protect its inhabitants from pirate raids. Along the mulberry tree–lined road leading from the beach you might encounter a villager wearing a traditional head scarf (*mandila*), plodding by on her donkey. This village of two-story, 19th-century stone and shingle houses is filled with superb architectural details. Note the huge wooden doors decorated with nails and elaborate door knockers, loophole windows in thick stone walls, elegant pediments topping imposing mansions, and fountains spilling under Gothic arches. ✉ *Skala Eressou* ✥ *11 km (7 miles) inland, north of Skala Eresou.*

Beaches

Skala Eresou Beach

BEACH—SIGHT | The 4-km-long (2½-mile-long) town beach at Skala Eresou is a wide stretch of dark sand lined with tamarisk trees. A small island is within swimming distance, and northerly winds lure windsurfers along with the swimmers and sunbathers. There are many rooms to rent within walking distance of the beach, and in the section that skirts the town, many appealing bars and cafés front the sands. **Amenities:** food and drink; parking (no fee); showers; toilets; water sports. **Best for:** partiers; snorkeling; sunset; swimming; walking; windsurfing. ✉ *Skala Eressou.*

Restaurants

Parasol Beach Bar

$ | CAFÉ | Totem poles, colored coconut lamps, and other knickknacks make this beach bar endearing in its evocation of the South Pacific, as if the setting weren't transporting enough. The owner and his wife serve omelets, fruits, yogurt, and sweet Greek coffee for breakfast, and simple dishes like pizzas, veggie spring rolls, sandwiches, and cheese platters the rest of the day. **Known for:** exotic beachside terrace; great cocktails; lively music. [$] *Average main: €10* ✉ *Skala Eresou Beach* ☎ *22530/52050* 🕓 *Closed Nov.–Apr.*

Soulatso

$ | SEAFOOD | The enormous anchor and octopi drying on a line outside are signs that you're in for some seriously good seafood. Tables set on a wooden deck are just a skipping-stone's throw from the break of the waves. **Known for:** great seafood; outdoor seaside dining; brilliant service. [$] *Average main: €10* ✉ *Skala Eresou Beach* ✥ *At beach center* ☎ *22530/52078* 🕓 *Closed Nov.–Apr.*

Hotels

★ **Heliotopos**

$ | HOTEL | FAMILY | A peaceful large garden set in olive and citrus groves behind the beach surrounds the homey and sparkling self-catering bungalows here, all with lots of outdoor space. **Pros:** peaceful setting; lush garden; delightful hominess. **Cons:** no breakfast served; not on the beach; surroundings are comfortable rather than luxurious. [$] *Rooms from: €45* ✉ *Skala Eressou* ☎ *6948/510257* 🌐 *www.heliotoposeressos.gr* 🕓 *Closed Nov.–Mar.* 🛏 *8 rooms* 🍴 *No meals.*

Sigri Σίγρι

26 km (16 miles) northwest of Skala Eresou, 93 km (58 miles) west of Mytilini.

This welcoming cluster of white houses surrounding a lovely cove is set in stark, mountainous countryside at the far western end of the island.

Sights

Natural History Museum of the Lesvos Petrified Forest

COLLEGE | FAMILY | Discover how trees in the nearby Petrified Forest became so in this museum whose exhibits are scrupulously labeled and clearly laid out. There are also unique fossils of animals like the Deinotherium, an early ancestor of the elephant, and vegetation preserved on volcanic rock that resembles delicate Zen art. ⊠ *Main Rd.* ☎ *22530/54434* ⊕ *www.petrifiedforest.gr* ⊠ *€5* ⊗ *Closed Nov.–May.*

★ Petrified Forest

FOREST | Conifer trees fossilized by volcanic ash up to 20 million years ago stand stark on a hillside above Sigri. If you're expecting a thick woods, you might be taken aback by this seemingly barren site that at first appears as a collection of stumps leaning every which way among shrubs and rock. But a walk along well-organized trails reveals delicate colors and a haunting, strange beauty. You can also study the specimens at Ipsilou, a large monastery on the highest peak in this wild, moonscape-like volcanic landscape, overlooking western Lesvos and Asia Minor across the Aegean. ⊠ *Sigri* ✢ *Between Sigri and Eresou* ☎ *22510/54434* ⊕ *www.petrifiedforest.gr* ⊠ *€2* ⊗ *Closed Nov.–Jun.*

Beaches

Faneromeni

BEACH—SIGHT | An end-of-the-world atmosphere prevails at this lovely stretch of sand at the far west of the island just north of Sigri, punctuated by a rocky outcropping and fronting a green river valley, where you're likely to see birds and turtles. **Amenities:** parking (no fee). **Best for:** nudists; solitude; sunset; swimming; walking; windsurfing. ⊠ *Sigri* ✢ *4 km (2½ miles) north of Sigri.*

Chios ΧΙΟΣ

"Craggy Chios" is what local boy Homer, the island's first publicist, so to speak, called this starkly beautiful outcropping that almost touches Turkey's coast and shares its topography. The island has suffered its share of misfortunes: the bloody Turkish massacre of 1822 during the fight for Greek independence; major earthquakes, including one in 1881 that killed almost 6,000 Chiotes; severe fires, which in recents years have burned pine forests and coveted mastic shrubs; and, through the ages, the steady stripping of forests to ax-wielding boatbuilders. Yet despite these setbacks, the island remains a wonderful destination, with friendly inhabitants, and villages so rare and captivating that just one of them alone would make this island a gem.

The name Chios comes from the Phoenician word for "mastic," the resin of the *Pistacia lentisca* evergreen shrubs that with few exceptions thrive only here, in the southern part of the island. Every August, incisions are made in the bark of the shrubs; the sap leaks out, permeating the air with a sweet fragrance, and in September the output is harvested. This aromatic resin, which brought huge revenues until the introduction of petroleum products, is still used in cosmetics, chewing gum, and mastiha liqueur sold on the island today. Pirgi, Mesta, and other villages where the mastic is grown and processed are enchanting. In these towns you can wind your way through narrow, labyrinthine Byzantine lanes protected by medieval gates and lined with homes that date back half a millennium.

Chios is also home to the elite families that control Greece's private shipping empires: Livanos, Karas, Chandris; even Onassis came here from Smyrna. The island has never seemed to need tourists or to draw them. Yet Chios intrigues, with its deep valleys, uncrowded sandy and black-pebble beaches, fields of wild tulips, Byzantine monasteries, and haunting villages—all remnants of a poignant history.

GETTING HERE AND AROUND

Aegean, Olympic Airlines, and Sky Express offer at least four flights daily between Athens and Chios (50 minutes; from €70 to €200 one-way). There are also daily flights from Thessaloniki (1 hour, around €80). Chios Airport is 4½ km (3 miles) south of Chios Town; a taxi ride runs around €6 to €10.

Daily ferries connect Chios and Piraeus in summer (between 9 and 14 hours; €40), less frequently at other times; these ferries usually go on to Lesvos (3 hours; €20). For schedule information, see ⊕ www.gtp.gr.

BUS

Buses leave the town of Chios two or three times per day for Mesta and Pirgi. The main station for local buses is in Chios Town at Leof. Egeou 14, facing the port, near the National Bank. Bus fares run €1.50 to €5. As with Lesvos bus travel, service is infrequent, though bus drivers are obliging. If your destination is en route but not listed as a stop, try asking the bus driver to make a stop for you.

VISITOR INFORMATION

CONTACTS Chios Tourist Office. ⊠ *Leof. Egeou 16, Chios Town ⊹ Next door to the main bus station* ☎ *22710/41047* ⊕ *chios. gr.*

Chios Town Χίος πόλη

285 km (177 miles) northeast of Piraeus, 55 km (34 miles) south of Mytilini.

The main port and capital, Chios Town, or Chora, is a busy commercial settlement on the east coast, across from Turkey. It lacks the historic charm of other port towns of the Northern Aegean, though the hustle and bustle of daily life here has an allure of its own—by day, the streets are clamorous with a bazaarlike atmosphere, and when the lights come on in the evening, the scene is softened by a mingling of blue hues, the cafés begin to overflow with ouzo and good cheer, and locals promenade along the bay side. The outskirts straggle into vast olive groves that stretch toward the mountains, and particularly appealing is the Kambos district, where beautiful Genoese houses are surrounded by lush gardens behind honey-colored walls.

 Sights

Bazaar District

MARKET | The capital is home to over half the island's population, and the heart of Chios life is this sprawling district behind the port. In the morning, merchants hawk everything from local mastic gum and fresh dark bread to kitchen utensils, but most stalls close in the afternoon. ⊠ *Chios Town ⊹ South and east of Vounakiou Sq. (the main square).*

Byzantine Museum

MUSEUM | The only intact mosque in this part of the Aegean, complete with a slender minaret, dates from the 19th century and houses the Byzantine Museum. The museum seems to be perpetually under renovation, but the porch and courtyard are dotted with richly inscribed Jewish, Turkish, and Armenian gravestones, including one depicting St. George slaying the dragon. Also on display are column capitals unearthed across the island and some delightful 18th-century Byzantine murals in which three sleeping girls await the miracle of St. Nicholas. ⊠ *Vounakiou Sq. ⊹ Entrance by the Vodafone shop* ☎ ⊡ *€4* ⊗ *Closed Tues.*

★ Chios Archaeological Museum

MUSEUM | Among classical pottery and sculpture is a letter carved into a stone tablet from Alexander the Great addressed to the Chiotes and dated 332 BC, along with a collection of other remarkable stone tablets that dictate the

Did You Know?

What may look like an art installation is actually a tree trunk that's been petrified—trees fossilized by volcanic ash up to 20 million years ago. To view these strange, color-rich formations up close, visit the Petrified Forest in Sigri.

local laws and regulations from antiquity. Also on display is some remarkably intact prehistoric pottery from the 14th century BC. ✉ *Michalon 10* ☎ *22710/44239* 💶 *€3* 🕑 *Closed Tues.*

Chios Maritime Museum

MUSEUM | Livanos, Karas, Chandris, Onassis: many of the world-famous shipping families were based or born on Chios. Exquisite ship models and portraits of vessels that have belonged to Chios owners over time celebrate the sea-based heritage of the island. One exhibit highlights the Liberty ships and others constructed during World War II that contributed to Greece's booming postwar shipping industry. ✉ *Stefanou Tsouri 20* ☎ *22710/44139* ⊕ *www.chiosnauticalmuseum.gr* 💶 *€2.50* 🕑 *Closed afternoons and Sun. (except Sun. in Aug.).*

Citrus Museum

FARM/RANCH | FAMILY | The Kambos district is famed as one of the most superlatively fertile orchard regions of Greece—orange and lemon groves set behind stone walls are given the status of museums and landmarks. It is only fitting that the owners of the Perleas Mansion hotel have opened this beautifully fragrant estate to showcase the history of citrus products on the island and entice visitors with a shop and delightful café selling citrus-inspired sweets. The estate buildings are gorgeous, centered on a farm where English-language placards explain the layout and workings of a historic citrus estate, and beautiful stone barns and houses are set with hunter-green window shutters. The fragrant grounds are replete with a folkloric-painted watermill, grazing animals, and an exceedingly picturesque arbor. ■TIP→ **Call in advance to check visiting hours as they can vary, sometimes dramatically.** ✉ *Artgenti St. 9–11, Kambos* ☎ *22710/31513.*

Giustiniani Museum

MUSEUM | A 15th-century palace of the Genoese, who ruled Chios until the Turks drove them out in 1566, is one of the most venerable landmarks on the island, with a loggia and external staircase. Inside are some glorious Byzantine murals of the prophets from the 13th century, as well as icons and sculptures. ✉ *Kalothetou* ✛ *At the eastern edge of the Old Quarter* ☎ *22710/22819* 💶 *€2* 🕑 *Closed Tues.*

★ Kambos District

NEIGHBORHOOD | In medieval times and later, wealthy Genoese and Greek merchants built ornate, earth-colored, three-story mansions on this fertile plain of tangerine, lemon, and orange groves south of Chios Town. On narrow lanes behind stone walls adorned with coats of arms, each estate is a world of its own, with multicolored sandstone patterns, arched doorways, and pebble-mosaic courtyards. Some houses have crumbled, but many still stand, surrounded by fragrant citrus groves and reminders of the wealth, power, and eventual downfall of an earlier time. These suburbs of Chios Town are exceptional, but the unmarked lanes can be confusing, so leave time to get lost and to peek behind the walls into another world. ✛ *4 km (2½ miles) south of Chios Town.*

Korais Library & Philip Argenti Museum

MUSEUM | The second floor above the impressive Korais Library, Greece's third largest, houses artifacts celebrating life on Chios. Meticulously designed costumes, embroideries, pastoral wood carvings, furniture from a village home, and rare books and prints are the legacy of Philip Argenti (1891–1974), a Renaissance man who studied at Oxford, was a diplomat and scholar, and for many years chronicled island history from his estate in the Kambos District. ✉ *Korais 2* ✛ *Near the cathedral* ☎ *22710/44246* ⊕ *www. koraeslibrary.gr* 💶 *€2* 🕑 *Closed Sun.*

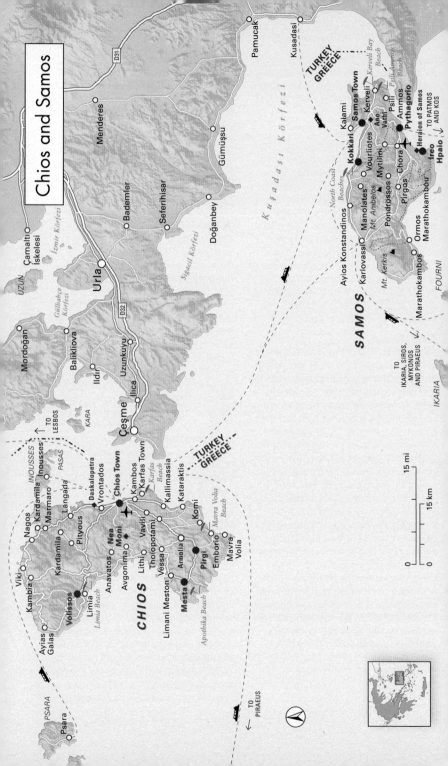

Chios and Samos

★ Old Quarter

NEIGHBORHOOD | An air of mystery pervades this old Muslim and Jewish neighborhood, full of decaying monuments, fountains, baths, and mosques, within the walls of the **Kastro** (castle) fortifications, built in the 10th century by the Byzantines and enlarged in the 14th century by the Genoese Giustiniani family. Under Turkish rule, the Greeks lived outside the wall, and the gates closed daily at sundown. Scattered among the precinct are several stone towers and, inside the old gate, the cells where the Turks jailed then hanged 75 leading Chiotes during the fight for independence in 1822, when Chios joined the rest of Greece in rebellion against occupying Turks. The revolt here on the island failed, and the sultan retaliated: the Turks killed 30,000 Chiotes and enslaved 45,000. The event was written about by Victor Hugo and depicted by Eugène Delacroix in *The Massacre of Chios.* The painting, now in the Louvre, shocked Western Europe and increased support for Greek independence. Copies hang in many places on Chios, including in the Byzantine Museum. In the quarter's Frouriou Square, look for the Turkish cemetery and the large marble tomb (with the fringed hat) of Kara Ali, chief of the Turkish flagship in 1822. ✉ *Chios Town* ✥ *Northern end of port.*

Beaches

Karfas Beach

BEACH—SIGHT | This popular and often-crowded beach fronts a shallow bay, and its golden brown sands and warm waters make it a good spot for young families. Many tavernas and hotels geared to package tours line the overbuilt shoreline, and in summer there's transportation to and from town. **Amenities:** food and drink; showers; toilets; water sports; parking (no fee). **Best for:** snorkeling; sunrise; swimming. ✥ *8 km (5 miles) south of Chios Town.*

Restaurants

★ O Hotzas

$ | **GREEK** | Family portraits and brass implements hang below a wood-beam ceiling at this spacious taverna that shows off its 19th-century origins. In addition to deep-fried dishes, there's reliably good seafood, and it's delicious with the homemade retsina or ouzo. **Known for:** old-world atmosphere; delicious home-style cooking; squid. [$] *Average main: €8* ✉ *Yioryiou Kondili 3* ☎ *22710/42787* ⏲ *Closed Sun. No lunch.*

★ The Pastards

$ | **ITALIAN** | It doesn't flaunt itself in quite the same way as the other restaurants that line the port, but the food here is far superior, and the atmosphere significantly more grown-up. Pizza, pasta, and risotto dishes feature on the menu as well as Greek favorites like salads with feta, and grilled fish and meat. **Known for:** excellent value-to-quality ratio; relaxed atmosphere amid hustle and bustle; lengthy wine menu. [$] *Average main: €10* ✉ *Michael Livanou 13* ☎ *22710/81466* ⏲ *Closed Mon.*

Coffee and Quick Bites

★ Kronos Ice Cream Parlor

$ | **CAFÉ** | A favorite stop in Chios Town is this modern, trendy ice cream shop that has been making its best-selling praline ice cream since 1930. It's open from early morning well into the wee hours. [$] *Average main:* ✉ *Philipos Argenti 2* ☎ *22710/22311* 🌐 *www.pagotakronos.gr.*

Hotels

★ Chios Chandris

$ | **HOTEL** | **FAMILY** | This icon of the Chios waterfront completed an extensive refurbishment in 2019. **Pros:** beautiful lobby and breakfast room; excellent and attentive service; sense of luxury amid humble surroundings of the town. **Cons:** pool area is in shade from the early evening; pool area can feel small in peak season; some areas of the hotel a little business-like. **$** *Rooms from: €70* ✉ *2nd Eugenia Chandris St.* ✛ *Between the port and beach* ☎ *22710/44401* ⊕ *chioschandrishotel.gr* ⤵ *148 rooms* ⦿❘ *Free breakfast.*

★ Grecian Castle Hotel

$ | **HOTEL** | With warmly appointed guest rooms, a pretty pool, and carefully landscaped grounds, this sophisticated retreat sets a high standard for Chios, as you'll see once you pass the impressive stone gateway and head up a regal, tree-lined lane into an enclave that subtly evokes a medieval castle. **Pros:** urbane ambience; professional service; lovely grounds and pool. **Cons:** a few dark and not-so-spacious rooms; beach across the road is not appealing; somewhat out-of-the-way location. **$** *Rooms from: €90* ✉ *Leoforos Enosseos* ✛ *1 km (½ mile) south of town toward the airport* ☎ *22710/44740* ⊕ *www.greciancastle.gr* ⤵ *69 rooms* ⦿❘ *Free breakfast.*

Kyma Hotel

$ | **HOTEL** | A neoclassical villa that was once the headquarters of Nikolaos Plastiras, a general in the 1920s conflicts with Turkey who later became prime minister, is these days a welcoming and character-filled waterside inn that's both quirky and comfortable. **Pros:** friendly, professional staff; good waterside location with great sea views; character-filled salons and guest rooms. **Cons:** not all rooms have a sea view; some bathrooms are small; some renovation is in order. **$** *Rooms from: €80* ✉ *Chandris 1* ☎ *22710/44500* ⊕ *hotelkyma.com* ⤵ *59 rooms* ⦿❘ *Free breakfast.*

★ Perleas Mansion

$ | **B&B/INN** | Guests soon feel like aristocrats from a lost era at this 16th-century Kambos neighborhood estate of Genoese merchants, where the lovely mansion of rough-hewn stone is surrounded by gardens fragrant with orange blossoms. **Pros:** utterly delightful surroundings; the real deal when it comes to living like gentry; fresh orange juice and homemade citrus preserves at breakfast. **Cons:** 10-minute drive from nearest beach; old-fashioned charm might not appeal to those looking for modern luxuries; no pool, but a lily pond is most soothing. **$** *Rooms from: €120* ✉ *Vitiadou 6–8* ✛ *4 km (2½ miles) south of Chios Town* ☎ *22710/32217* ⊕ *www.perleas.gr* ⤵ *8 rooms* ⦿❘ *Free breakfast.*

Nightlife

Metropolis Lounge Cafe Bar

CAFES—NIGHTLIFE | Stop by for cold coffee and chill music during the day, then return at night for exotic mixed spirits and high-tempo beats. ✉ *Aegaeou 92* ☎ *22710/43883.*

Odyssey Wine Bar

WINE BARS—NIGHTLIFE | Accompanying the generous wine list is the occasional live blues and jazz night as well as avant-garde Greek music performed by local talent. ✉ *Aigaiou 102* ☎ *22710/20585.*

★ Oz Cocktail Bar

WINE BARS—NIGHTLIFE | The mixologists reign supreme at this dark, sultry cocktail bar in the heart of Chios Town. Showcasing an eclectic drinks menu featuring new spins on old favorites as well as unique blends, this is where to go to experience a more sophisticated Chios nightlife. ✉ *Stoa Fragaki* ☎ *22710/80326* ⊕ *ozcocktailbar.gr.*

Shopping

The resinous gum made from the sap of the mastic tree is a best buy in Chios. Look out for the mastic (digestif) liqueur, *mastiha,* and *gliko koutaliou,* sugar-preserved fruit served in small portions with a spoon.

Korakis Marinos

FOOD/CANDY | Try this place for its fine array of mastiha, fruit preserves, and other sweets and spirits. ✉ *Venizelou Eleftheriou 4* ☎ *22710/23518.*

Mastic Spa

PERFUME/COSMETICS | At the elegant outlet of this local business with an international outreach, all the beauty and health products contain the local balm. ⊠ *Agoiu 84* ✛ *On the waterfront* ☏ *22710/302552.*

Volissos Βολισσός

42 km (26 miles) northwest of Chios Town.

Homer's birthplace is thought to be here at Volissos, though Smyrna, Colophon, Salamis, Rhodes, Argos, and Athens also claim this honor. Once a bustling market town, this pretty village is today half empty, with only a few hundred inhabitants. There are few services for tourists, save a casual restaurant here and there in the village and on the beach. Solid stone houses march up the mountainside to the Genoese fort, where Byzantine nobles were once exiled. At the top of the hill is an idyllic spot for sunset lovers.

Beaches

Limia

BEACH—SIGHT | Some of the best beaches on the island are in the vicinity, including Limia, with calm, turquoise waters. **Amenities:** none. **Best for:** snorkeling; solitude; sunset; swimming. ⊠ *Volissos* ✛ *2 km (1 mile) south of Volissos.*

Nea Moni Νέα Μονή

17 km (10½ miles) west of Chios Town.

👁 Sights

★ Nea Moni

RELIGIOUS SITE | Almost hidden among the olive groves, the island's most important monastery—with its finest examples of mosaic art—is the 11th-century Nea Moni. Byzantine emperor Constantine IX Monomachos ("the Dueler") ordered the monastery built where three monks found an icon of the Virgin Mary in a myrtle bush. The octagonal *katholikon* (medieval church) is the only surviving example of 11th-century court art—none survives in Constantinople. The monastery has been renovated a number of times: the dome was completely rebuilt following an earthquake in 1881, and a great deal of effort has gone into the restoration and preservation of the mosaics over the years. The distinctive three-part vaulted sanctuary has a double narthex, with no buttresses supporting the dome. This design, a single square space covered by a dome, is rarely seen in Greece. Blazing with color, the church's interior gleams with marble slabs and mosaics of Christ's life, austere yet sumptuous, with azure blue, ruby red, velvet green, and skillful applications of gold. The saints' expressiveness comes from their vigorous poses and severe gazes, with heavy shadows under the eyes. On the iconostasis hangs the icon—a small Virgin and Child facing left. Also inside the grounds are an ancient refectory, a vaulted cistern, a chapel filled with victims' bones from the massacre at Chios, and a large clock still keeping Byzantine time, with the sunrise reckoned as 12 o'clock. ⊠ *Nea Moni* ✛ *In mountains 17 km (10½ miles) west of Chios Town, beyond Karies* ☏ *22710/79391* 🖃 *Donations accepted* 🕙 *Closed daily 1–4.*

Pirgi Πυργί

25 km (15½ miles) south of Nea Moni, 25 km (15 miles) south of Chios Town.

Beginning in the 14th century, the Genoese founded 20 or so fortified inland villages in southern Chios. These villages shared a defensive design with double-thick walls, a maze of narrow streets, and a square tower, or *pyrgos,* in the middle—a last resort to hold the residents in case of pirate attack. The villages prospered on the sales of mastic gum and were spared by the Turks because of the industry. Today they depend on mastic production, unique to the island—and tourists.

Pirgi is the largest of these mastic villages, and aesthetically, the most wondrous. It could be a graphic designer's model or a set of a mad moviemaker. Many of the buildings along the tiny arched streets are adorned with *xysta* (like Italian *sgraffito*); they are coated with a mix of cement and volcanic sand from nearby beaches, then whitewashed and stenciled, often top to bottom, in patterns of animals, flowers, and geometric designs. The effect is both delicate and dazzling. This exuberant village has more than 50 churches.

Sights

Agioi Apostoli (*Holy Apostles*)
RELIGIOUS SITE | The fresco-embellished 12th-century church Ayioi Apostoli is a very small replica of the *katholikon,* or major church, at the Nea Moni Monastery. Cretan artist Antonios Domestichos created the 17th-century frescoes that completely cover the interior, and they have a distinct folk-art leaning. ⊠ *Pirgi* ✢ *Northwest of main square* ⊗ *Closed Tues.*

Armolia
TOWN | In the small mastic village of Armolia, 5 km (3 miles) north of Pirgi, pottery is a specialty. In fact, the Greek word *armolousis* ("man from Armola") is synonymous with potter. To the west, above the village, there is an impressive Byzantine castle that was built in 1446, and to the east is the wonderful 18th-century baroque-styled Vrettou Monastery. ⊠ *Armolia.*

★ The Chios Mastic Museum
LOCAL INTEREST | FAMILY | The mastic shrub has dominated Chios life, economy, culture, and destiny for centuries, and its role is explained in depth in well-designed exhibits in a stunning glass, stone, and wood pavilion overlooking a wide sweep

of mastic groves. Aside from learning about how the valuable resin is cultivated and processed, you'll see artifacts and photographs of village life and learn about the island's tumultuous history, including times when hoarding even a sliver of mastic gum was a crime punishable by death. ⊠ *Pirgi* ✢ *3 km (2 miles) south of Pirgi off Pirgi–Emborio road* ☎ *22710/72212* 💶 *€4* ⊗ *Closed Tues.*

★ Koimisis tis Theotokou
(*Dormition of the Virgin Church*)
RELIGIOUS SITE | This towering church just off the main square was built in 1694 and is embellished with a lavishly decorated portico. ⊠ *Pirgi* ✢ *Off main square.*

Beaches

★ Mavra Volia (*Black Pebbles*)
BEACH—SIGHT | Famous throughout Greece, this glittering volcanic black-pebbled beach is just next to the attractive seaside village of Emborio, where the waterfront is lined with tavernas serving seafood. The cove comprises three beaches, which are backed by jutting volcanic cliffs and fronted by calm dark-blue water colored by the deeply tinted seabed. Here, perhaps, was an inspiration for the "wine-dark sea" that Homer wrote about. **Amenities:** parking (no fee). **Best for:** solitude; sunrise; swimming; walking. ⊠ *Emborio* ✢ *8 km (5 miles) southeast of Pirgi.*

🛏 Hotels

Emporios Bay
$ | HOTEL | The closest thing Chios has to a resort is this attractive white enclave of airy and comfortable accommodations clustered around gardens and a sparkling pool at the back of a south-coast seaside village near Pirgi. **Pros:** attractive rooms and pool terrace; chance to experience village life; near the beach and southern sights. **Cons:** a bit large and generic for the village setting; some tour groups; not right on the seafront. 💲 *Rooms from:*

€40 ✉ Emborio ✣ Behind the waterfront ☎ 22710/70180 🌐 www.emporiosbay.gr 🛏 40 rooms 🍴 Free breakfast.

Shopping

Lagini

CERAMICS/GLASSWARE | At this ceramics studio and shop in the outlying village of Armolia, you can see the potter ply her trade, as well as buy traditional handmade pottery. ✉ *Armolia–Pirgi road, Armolia* ✣ *5 km (3 miles) north of Pirgi* ☎ *22710/72634.*

Mesta Μεστά

11 km (7 miles) west of Pirgi, 30 km (18½ miles) southwest of Chios Town.

Pirgi may be the most unusual of the mastic villages, but Mesta is the island's best preserved: a labyrinth of twisting vaulted streets links two-story stone-and-mortar houses that are supported by buttresses against earthquakes. The enchanted village sits inside a system of 3-foot-thick walls, and the outer row of houses also doubles as protection. In fact, the village homes were built next to each other to form a castle, reinforced with towers. Most of the narrow streets, free of cars and motorbikes, lead to blind alleys; the rest lead to the six gates. The one in the northeast retains an iron grate. Artists and craftspeople are attracted to the town, so you'll unearth art galleries and craft boutiques with a little hunting.

Sights

★ **Megalos Taxiarchis** (*Great Archangel*)

RELIGIOUS SITE | The 19th-century church that commands the main square of Mesta (and one of two churches of the same name in the town) is one of the wealthiest in Greece; its vernacular baroque is combined with the late-folk-art style of Chios. The church was built on the ruins of the central refuge tower. **■ TIP→ If the church is closed, ask at the square and someone may come and open it for you.** ✉ *Main square.*

Beaches

Apothika

BEACH—SIGHT | This remote spot, at the end of a well-marked road that leads southeast toward the coast from Mesta, is one of the best beaches on Chios. The clear waters lap against the sand and pebbles that make up this small stretch of coast. A canteen looks down upon the unspoiled beach. **Amenities:** food and drink; parking (no fee); showers; toilets; water sports. **Best for:** snorkeling; solitude; sunset; swimming; walking; windsurfing. ✉ *Mesta* ✣ *On marked road that leads from the north end of Mesta.*

Restaurants

Limenas Meston

$ | **SEAFOOD** | The fishing boats bobbing in the water only a few feet away supply the kitchen with a rich daily fish selection. Meats served at the simple taverna include homemade sausage, and lamb or beef on the spit. **Known for:** fresh seafood; harbor views; cozy wintertime ambience. [$] *Average main: €8* ✉ *Limenas* ✣ *3 km (2 miles) north of Mesta village* ☎ *22710/76389.*

Hotels

★ **Lida Mary Hotel**

$ | **HOTEL** | A lovingly restored complex set in mazelike village lanes stylishly combines modern luxuries and a mysterious medieval atmosphere with vaulted ceilings and thick stone walls. **Pros:** memorably unique experience; exciting, tasteful, and welcoming surroundings; chance to experience village like a resident. **Cons:** some steps; a walk over cobbles to reach; some rooms are a bit dark. [$] *Rooms from: €50* ✉ *Mesta* ☎ *22710/76217* 🌐 *www.lidamary.gr* 🛏 *8 rooms* 🍴 *Free breakfast.*

Nightlife

Maona

CAFES—NIGHTLIFE | The nightlife at Mesta is not exactly rocking, but this café and bar offers some relief to the restless souls who want to extend their evening. ✉ *Main square* ☎ *22710/76004*.

Activities

★ Masticulture

TOUR—SPORTS | FAMILY | The ecotourist specialists on Chios lead all kinds of tours. Trek through the mastic tree groves, where local farmers show you how they gather mastic through grooves carved into the trees' bark. Learn how wine, *souma* (a type of ouzo made from distilled figs), and olive oil are produced, and go on fascinating custom-designed walks discovering the unique flora and fauna of Chios. ✉ *Off main square* ☎ *22710/76084* ⊕ *www.masticulture. com*.

Samos ΣΑΜΟΣ

The southernmost of this group of three Northern Aegean islands lies the closest to Turkey of any Greek island, separated by only 3 km (2 miles). Samos was, in fact, a part of Asia Minor until it split off during the Ice Age. Samos means "high" in Phoenician, and the abrupt volcanic mountains soaring dramatically like huge hunched shoulders from the rock surface of the island are among the tallest in the Aegean, geologically part of the great spur that runs across western Turkey. As you approach from the west, Mt. Kerkis seems to spin out of the sea, and in the distance Mt. Ambelos guards the ter-raced vineyards that produce the famous Samian wine. The felicitous landscape has surprising twists, with lacy coasts and mountain villages perched on ravines carpeted in pink oleander, red poppy, and purple sage.

When Athens was young, in the 7th century BC, Samos was already a political, economic, and naval power. In the next century, during Polycrates's reign, it was noted for its arts and sciences and was the expanded site of the vast Temple of Hera, one of the Seven Wonders of the Ancient World. The Persian Wars led to the decline of Samos, however, which fell first under Persian rule, and then became subordinate to the expanding power of Athens. Samos was defeated by Pericles in 439 BC and forced to pay tribute to Athens.

Pirates controlled this deserted island after the fall of the Byzantine Empire, but in 1562 an Ottoman admiral repopulated Samos with expatriates and Orthodox believers. The island languished under the sun until tobacco and shipping revived the economy in the 19th century.

Small though it may be, Samos has a formidable list of great citizens stretching through the ages. The fabled Aesop, the philosopher Epicurus, and Aristarchos (first in history to place the sun at the center of the solar system) all lived on Samos. The mathematician Pythagoras was born in Samos's ancient capital in 580 BC; in his honor, the town was renamed Pythagorio in AD 1955 (it only took a couple of millennia). Plutarch wrote that in Roman times Anthony and Cleopatra took a long holiday on Samos, "giving themselves over to the feasting," and that artists came from afar to entertain them.

Since the late 1990s Samos has become popular with European package tourists, particularly in July and August. The curving terrain allows you to escape the crowds easily and feel as if you are still in an undiscovered Eden.

GETTING HERE AND AROUND

Olympic and Aegean airways operate up to four flights daily between Athens and Samos (1 hour, between €55 and €100). Olympic, Sky Express, and Hahn Air operate daily flights to Samos from Thes-saloniki (1 hour 20 mins, €55 to €120).

The spectacular north coast of Samos is lined with beautiful beaches, including Lemonakia. Though the beach itself is more pebbles than sand, the water has a gorgeous blue-green hue.

Samos Airport is 3 km (2 miles) from Pythagorio; taxis from the airport cost €20 to Samos Town (the main town, also known as Vathi) or €15 to Pythagorio.

The main port of Samos is Vathi. Ferries from Piraeus and the Cyclades usually stop at both Vathi (Samos Town) and Karlovassi (Samos's second port). During high season, there are usually two daily ferries from Pireaus (8 to 10 hours, €54); four to Chios (3 to 4 hours, €18); up to six to Mykonos (5to 6 hours, €47), with transfers available for Santorini and Naxos. Ferries arrive and depart from a facility directly across the harbor from the Vathi waterfront and *not* the docks right in town. There is usually a service most days to Patmos from Pythagorio.

BUS

Samos has reliable bus service, with frequent trips between Pythagorio, Samos Town (Vathi), and Kokkari. The island's main bus station is at Ioannou Lekati and Kanari in central Samos Town. Fares range from €1.50 to €3. Taxis can be hailed on Platia Pythagora.

TOURS

Pure Samos

GUIDED TOURS | This travel agency, created by locals, offers experiential vacations: from yoga workshops and wine tours to horseback-riding, spear-fishing, and scuba diving. ⊠ *Iras 2, Pythagorio* ☎ *22730/62760* ⊕ *www.puresamos.gr.*

Samos Town Σάμος πόλη

278 km (174 miles) east of Piraeus, 111 km (69 miles) southeast of Mytilini.

Also known as Vathi, the capital is tucked into the head of a sharply deep bay on the northeast coast. Red-tile roofs sweep around the arc of the bay and reach toward the top of red-earth hills. In the morning at the sheltered port, fishermen grapple with their nets, spreading them to dry in the sun, and in the early afternoon everything shuts down. Slow summer sunsets over the sparkling harbor match the relaxed pace of the town.

Sights

Ano Vathi

HISTORIC SITE | In the quaint 17th-century settlement just above the port, wood-and-plaster houses with pastel facades and red-tile roofs are clustered together, their balconies protruding over narrow cobbled paths. From here you can savor a beautiful view of the gulf. ⌖ *Samos Town* ✛ *Southern edge of Samos Town, beyond museum, to right.*

★ Archaeological Museum of Vathi

MUSEUM | Samian sculptures from past millennia were considered among the best in Greece, and examples here show why. The newest wing holds the impressive **kouros from Heraion,** a colossal statue of a male youth, built as an offering to the goddess Hera and the largest free-standing sculpture surviving from ancient Greece, dating from 580 BC. The work of a Samian artist, this statue was made of the typical Samian gray-and-white-band marble. Pieces of the kouros were discovered in various peculiar locations: its thigh was being used as part of a Hellenistic house wall, and its left forearm was being used as a step for a Roman cistern. The statue is so large (16½ feet tall) that the gallery had to be rebuilt specifically to house it. The museum's older section has a collection of pottery and cast-bronze griffin heads (the symbol of Samos). An exceptional collection of tributary gifts from ancient cities far and wide, including bronzes and ivory miniatures, affirms the importance of the shrine to Hera. ⌖ *Dimarhiou Sq.* ☎ *22730/27469* ⊕ *www. culture.gr* 🎫 *€4* ⊗ *Closed Tues.*

Samos Wine Museum

WINERY/DISTILLERY | Samos is famous for its (internationally awarded) wines, particularly its delectable *vin doux* liqueur and other sweet wines such as Nectar and Anthemis, and more recently its dry whites such as Phyllas, made with organic muscat grapes. All wines produced on Samos are by law made by the Union of

Vinicultural Cooperatives, who created this museum on the winery's grounds in tribute to the island's wine-making past and present, and it's the best place to dive into the island's wine culture. Start by looking at the photo exhibition of local wine-making over the last century and proceed to see the large and small tools used in production, as well as early-20th-century casks, and finally the French oak barrels used today. Then proceed to the main hall to indulge in a wine tasting of the union's wines, which are also sold at the museum shop. ⌖ *Malagari* ✛ *Opposite side of bay from port* ☎ *22730/87551* ⊕ *www.samoswine.gr* ⊗ *Closed some days in winter; call ahead.*

Visiting Turkey

From Samos Town (as well as from Pythagorio and from Ormos Marathokambos), you can easily take a ferry to Turkey. Once you're there, it's a 13-km (8-mile) taxi or bus ride from the Kusadasi port on the Turkish coast, where the boats dock, to Ephesus, one of the great archaeological sites and a major city of the ancient world. (The Temple of Artemis in Ephesus is a copy of the Temple of Hera in Heraion, which now lies in ruins.) Many travel agencies have guided round-trip full-day tours to the site (about €120), although you can take an unguided ferry trip for about €55 with same-day return.

🛆 Beaches

Kerveli Bay

BEACH—SIGHT | Calm, turquoise waters wash onto this beach of sand and pebbles that is shaded by pine trees. Time here provides a quiet escape from the beaches near the more populated centers, and getting here involves riding into a pleasurable final stretch through some of the loveliest forested parts in eastern Samos. Tavernas on the beach dish out light summer salads, fresh seafood, and heartier *magirefta* (cooked dish) of the day. **Amenities:** food and drink; parking (no fee); showers; toilets. **Best for:** snorkeling; sunrise; swimming; walking. ⊠ *Kerveli* ✛ *On the coast, 9 km (5½ miles) east of Samos Town.*

Psili Ammos

BEACH—SIGHT | One of the island's more popular beaches is pristine and sandy, protected from the wind by cliffs. There are two tavernas here, and the beach can get extremely busy during high season. **Amenities:** food and drink; parking (no fee); showers; toilets. **Best for:** sunrise; swimming. ✛ *9½ km (6 miles) southeast of Samos Town, near Mesokambos.*

Restaurants

Ta Kotopoula

$ | GREEK | Chicken is the star on the menu of this affordable grill restaurant (whose name means "the chickens" in Greek) that serves simple yet delicious seasonal dishes throughout the day in a laid-back atmosphere. **Known for:** grilled meats; shady terrace; friendly gathering spot. $ *Average main: €10* ⊠ *Vlamaris and Mykalis Sts.* ☎ *22730/28415* ▭ *No credit cards.*

Zen

$ | SEAFOOD | Sometimes it seems like everyone in town gathers at this friendly harborside spot, where the emphasis is on fresh seafood and traditional home cooking. Fresh, locally grown vegetables and Samos wines accompany the meals, which are served with care by the friendly staff. **Known for:** harbor views; nicely prepared dishes; friendly service. $ *Average main: €10* ⊠ *Kefalopoulou 6* ☎ *22730/80983.*

Coffee and Quick Bites

Solid All Day Bar

$ | CAFÉ | This "espresso bar" serves some of the town's best coffee, along with a selection of homemade cakes and pastries. Return in the evening to enjoy a cocktail in its swanky, modern setting. **Known for:** excellent coffee and cocktails; open morning to early hours; cosmopolitan atmosphere. $ *Average main: €5* ⊠ *Sofouli 43* ☎ *22730/24800.*

Hotels

Hotel Samos

$ | HOTEL | Simple but pleasant rooms are equipped with some nice amenities, including soundproof windows facing the harbor and a roof garden with a pool and hot tub. **Pros:** more luxurious than it may seem at first sight; roof garden and pool make this an in-town retreat; excellent value. **Cons:** no parking; could do with a touch-up; small bathrooms. $ *Rooms from: €75* ⊠ *Soufouli 11* ☎ *22730/28377* ⊕ *www.samoshotel.gr* ⤢ *100 rooms* ⦿| *Free breakfast.*

Ino Village Hotel

$ | HOTEL | A tranquil setting on the outskirts of Samos Town comes with a refreshing pool and nice views—enjoyed from many of the private balconies—of Samos Bay and the mountains beyond. **Pros:** some very nice rooms; pool provides a nice getaway; good dining. **Cons:** a 15-minute walk uphill from the town center (hotel will arrange transport); a car is almost necessary (parking is easy); some rooms are worn. $ *Rooms from: €65* ⊠ *Samos Town* ✛ *1 km (½ mile) north of Samos Town center* ☎ *22730/23241* ⊕ *www.inovillagehotel. com* ⤢ *65 rooms* ⦿| *Free breakfast.*

Take a walk along the pretty port area in Samos Town—in the morning you'll see local fisherman grappling with their nets.

 Nightlife

Escape Music Club

BARS/PUBS | The spacious patio just above the water is the place to party until the early hours. The music and dancing in this hip spot doesn't begin until 9 pm and lasts until 5 am. Friday is theme night and there are full-moon parties. ⊠ *Samos Town* ✣ *Past port police station, on main road out of town, near hospital* ☎ *22730/28345.*

Pythagorio Πυθαγόρειο

14 km (8½ miles) southwest of Samos Town.

Samos was a democratic state until 535 BC, when the town now called Pythagorio (formerly Tigani, or "frying pan") fell to the tyrant Polycrates (540–22 BC). Polycrates used his fleet of 100 ships to make profitable raids around the Aegean, until he was caught by the Persians and crucified in 522 BC. His rule produced what Herodotus described as "three of

the greatest building and engineering feats in the Greek world." One is the Heraion, west of Pythagorio, the largest temple ever built in Greece and one of the Seven Wonders of the Ancient World. Another is the ancient mole (stone pier) protecting the harbor on the southeast coast, on which the present 1,400-foot jetty rests. The third is the Efpalinio tunnel, built to guarantee that water flowing from mountain streams would be available even to besieged Samians. Pythagorio remains a picturesque little port, with red-tile-roof houses and a curving harbor filled with fishing boats. There are more busy restaurants and cafés here than elsewhere on the island.

 Sights

Archaeological Museum of Pythagoreion

MUSEUM | This tiny but impressive collection shows off local finds, including headless statues, grave markers with epigrams to the dead, and human and animal figurines, in addition to some notably beautiful portrait busts of the

Roman emperors Claudius, Caesar, and Augustus. ✉ *Pythagora Sq., in the municipal building* ☎ *22730/62813* ⊕ *www.culture.gr* ⌨ *€4* ⊘ *Closed Tues.*

Kastro (*castle, or fortress*)

ARCHAEOLOGICAL SITE | At the eastern corner of Pythagorio lie the crumbling ruins of the Kastro, probably built on top of the ruins of the Acropolis. Revolutionary hero Lykourgou Logotheti built this 19th-century edifice; his statue is next door, in the **courtyard** of the church built to honor the victory. He held back the Turks on Transfiguration Day, and a sign on the church announces in Greek: "Christ saved Samos 6 August 1824." On some nights the villagers light votive candles in the church cemetery, a moving sight with the ghostly silhouette of the fortress and the moonlit sea in the background. Nearby are some fragments of the wall that the ruler Polycrates built in the 6th century BC. ✉ *Pythagorio.*

Panagia Spiliani Church

RELIGIOUS SITE | Enter this spacious cave and descend 95 steps to the tiny church of Panagia Spiliani (Virgin of the Grotto). Half-church, half-cavern, this most unique landmark is also called *Kaliarmenissa* ("for good travels"), as it houses an antique icon of the Virgin Mary that, according to legend, was stolen from Samos, carried to a far-off land, and fell from a boat and broke into pieces, all of which washed ashore on Samos. A pool in the grotto, once the sanctuary of a Roman cult, is considered to contain miracle-working water. ✉ *Pythagorio* ⊹ *Above the village, near the Roman theater.*

To Efpalinio Hydragogeio
(*Tunnel of Eupalinos*)

ARCHAEOLOGICAL SITE | Considered by Herodotus as the world's Eighth Wonder, this famed underground aqueduct was completed in 524 BC with archaic tools and without measuring instruments. The ruler Polycrates, not a man who liked to leave himself vulnerable, ordered the construction of the tunnel to ensure that Samos's water supply could never be cut off during an attack. Efpalinos of Megara, a hydraulics engineer, set perhaps 1,000 slaves into two teams, one digging on each side of Mt. Kastri. Fifteen years later, they met in the middle with just a tiny difference in the elevation between the two halves. The tunnel is about 3,340 feet long, and it remained in use as an aqueduct for almost 1,000 years. More than a mile of (long-gone) ceramic water pipe once filled the space, which was later used as a hiding place during pirate raids. Today the tunnel is exclusively a tourist attraction, and though some spaces are tight and slippery, you can walk part of the length—also a wonderful way to enjoy natural coolness on swelteringly hot days. At some point, with ongoing work, it will be possible to traverse the tunnel in its entirety. On a hillside above the tunnel entrance are the scant remains of a Greek and Roman theater, and a wooden platform over the shell is occasionally used for performances. ✉ *Pythagorio* ⊹ *Just north of town* ☎ *22730/62811* ⌨ *€4* ⊘ *Closed Tues.*

🍴 Restaurants

Elia

$ | **MODERN GREEK** | A standout among the affable places along the harbor front, Elia is a little more sophisticated than its neighbors in its surroundings and, with a Swedish chef, offers a refreshingly eclectic take on Greek cuisine, with a big nod to local flavors. Prawns are sautéed in ouzo and meats are cooked with Samos wine. **Known for:** innovative takes on Greek cuisine; pleasant waterside terrace; good wine list. **$** *Average main: €12* ✉ *Pythagorio* ⊹ *Harbor front* ☎ *22730/61436* ⊕ *eliarestaurant-samos.gr.*

Maritsa

$ | **GREEK** | A regular Pythagorio clientele frequents this simple fish taverna in a garden courtyard on a quiet, tree-lined side street. You might try the shrimp souvlaki or squid garnished with garlicky *skordalia* (a thick lemony sauce with pureed potatoes, vinegar, and parsley), though the kitchen also does justice to lamb on the spit. **Known for:** fresh seafood; nice garden; lamb on the spit. [$] *Average main: €12* ✉ *Pythagorio* ✣ *Off Lykourgou Logotheti, one block from waterfront* ☎ *22730/61957.*

Hotels

Doryssa Seaside Resort
$$ | RESORT | FAMILY | A "stage set" of traditional Samian houses surrounds a rusticated main square, while beachfront accommodations are in the gigantic and plush main block; guest rooms in both are filled with elegant contemporary furnishings. **Pros:** good for families; lots of amenities; great beach. **Cons:** lots of tour groups in summer; next to the airport with associated noise; seems to be a world removed from the real Greece. [$] *Rooms from: €150* ✉ *Pythagorio Beach* ✣ *Near the airport road* ☎ *22730/88300* 🌐 *doryssa.gr* 🕓 *Closed Nov.–Mar.* 🛏 *320 rooms* 🍴 *Free breakfast.*

Fito Aqua Bleu Resort
$ | HOTEL | White bungalows glistening with terra-cotta roofs stand along winding paths lined with roses and lavender next to a sparkling pool, making it easy to settle into this friendly enclave just steps from Pythagorio Beach. **Pros:** close to beach and town; nice pool area; beautifully kept grounds. **Cons:** at end of airport runway; no sea view; no-frills rooms. [$] *Rooms from: €65* ✉ *Pythagorio Beach* ✣ *On the road to the airport* ☎ *22730/62900* 🌐 *fabresort.gr* 🕓 *Closed Oct.–Apr.* 🛏 *88 rooms* 🍴 *Free breakfast.*

★ Proteas Blu Resort
$$ | RESORT | FAMILY | Fresh, contemporary bungalows climb through Mediterranean gardens from a gorgeous pool and a beautiful, secluded beach, while airy, pastel-hued guest quarters, some with their own plunge pools, look out to sparkling sea views and purple-hued Turkish mountains from their balconies. **Pros:** great place for quiet and pampered stay; excellent meals with professional service; beautiful beach. **Cons:** not all rooms have sea views; intimate but still somewhat generic; a drive outside town. [$] *Rooms from: €220* ✉ *Pythagorio Rd.* ☎ *22730/62200* 🌐 *www.proteasbluresort.gr* 🕓 *Closed Oct.–mid-May* 🛏 *92 rooms* 🍴 *Free breakfast.*

Activities

Samosail
SAILING | Based in Pythagorio, this local yacht charter has a modern fleet of sailboats for rent for one- or two-week trips, with or without a captain. They can tailor trips to suit any needs. ✉ *Pythagorio* ☎ *22730/61739* 🌐 *www.samosail.com.*

Ireo Hpaio

6 km (4 miles) southwest of Pythagorio, 20 km (12½ miles) southwest of Samos Town.

Although Samos was a center for trade and commerce for a long time prior, it was Polycrates "the Tyrant" who really put the island on the map in the mid-6th century BC. The monumentality that he embarked on at the Heraion was a show to all—trader, pirate, ally, and would-be conqueror—that Samos's might under the watchful gaze of her patron goddess Hera was undisputable.

Sights

Heraion of Samos
ARCHAEOLOGICAL SITE | The early Samians worshipped the goddess Hera, wife of Zeus, believing she was born here beneath a bush near the stream Imbrassos. Several temples were built on the site in her honor, the earliest dating back to the 8th century BC. Polycrates rebuilt the **To Hraio**, or Temple of Hera, around 540 BC, making it four times larger than the Parthenon and the largest

The Heraion of Samos archaeological site is dedicated to the goddess of Hera, wife of Zeus.

Greek temple ever conceived, with two rows of columns (155 in all). The temple was damaged by fire in 525 BC and never completed, owing to Polycrates's untimely death. In the intervening years, masons recycled the stones to create other buildings, including a basilica (foundations remain at the site) to the Virgin Mary. Today you can only imagine the To Hraio's massive glory; of its forest of columns only one remains standing, slightly askew and only half its original height, amid acres of marble remnants in marshy ground thick with poppies.

At the ancient celebrations to honor Hera, the faithful approached from the sea along the **Sacred Road,** which is still visible at the site's northeast corner. Nearby are replicas of a 6th-century BC sculpture depicting an aristocratic family; its chiseled signature reads "Genelaos made me." The kouros from Heraion was found here, and is now in the Archaeological Museum in Samos Town. Hours may be shortened in winter. ✛ *11 km (7 miles) east of Pythagorio* ☎ *22730/95277* ⊕ *www.culture.gr* 🖂 *€6* ⊙ *Closed Tues.*

Kokkari Κοκκάρι

5 km (3 miles) southwest of Samos Town.

A spectacular stretch of coast road west of Samos Town is lined with olive groves and vineyards and ends in the fishing village of Kokkari, one of the most lively spots on the island during the summer. Until 1980, not much was here except for a few dozen houses between two headlands, and tracts of onion fields, which gave the town its name. Though now there are hotels and European tourists, you can still traipse along the rocky, windswept beach and spy fishermen mending trawling nets on the paved quay. Cross the spit to the eastern side of the headland and watch the moon rise over the lights of Samos Town (Vathi) in the next bay. East of Kokkari you pass by Malagari, the winery where farmers hawk their harvested grapes every September.

Beaches

North Coast Beaches

BEACH—SIGHT | **FAMILY** | **Lemonakia, Tsamadou,** and **Tsabou** all are just a few minutes' drive from one another, forming a continuous string of sand and pebbles separated by pine-clad headlands. They're all delightful places to lounge and swim, and well supplied with sun beds and concessions. The stretch is to be avoided when the summertime *meltemi* (northern winds) blow, unless you're a windsurfer. **Amenities:** food and drink; parking (no fee); toilets; water sports. **Best for:** swimming; walking; windsurfing. ✉ *Kokkari* ✥ *Northwest of Kokkari.*

Restaurants

Ammos Plaz

$ | **GREEK** | What many locals consider to be the best traditional Greek food in Kokkari is served in an ideal location—smack on the beach. The owner's father is a fisherman, and he brings his haul to the restaurant daily. **Known for:** beachfront setting; fresh seafood; excellent traditional food. [$] *Average main: €12* ✉ *Kokkari Promenade* ☎ *22730/92463* ⏲ *Closed Nov.–Mar.*

Hotels

★ **Armonia Bay Hotel**

$$ | **HOTEL** | Tucked away in pine trees above Tsamadou Beach, this utterly delightful villa combines sophistication and informal style and is one of the island's most special retreats, with beautiful gardens and terraces, handsomely furnished guest rooms that open to balconies and lawns, and a sparkling pool, all overlooking the sea below. **Pros:** stylish, relaxing surroundings; excellent service and food; the aura of being in a private seaside villa. **Cons:** not right on the beach; you'll want a car for convenience; parking can be tricky. [$] *Rooms from: €140* ✉ *Kokkari* ✥ *Off the coast road above Tsamadou Beach* ☎ *22730/92279* 🌐 *www.armoniahotels.com* ⏲ *Closed Nov.–Apr.* 🛏 *24 rooms* 🍴 *Free breakfast.*

Hotel Olympia Village

$$ | **HOTEL** | **FAMILY** | Surrounded by big, flowery gardens, these immaculate, comfortably furnished apartments open to wide verandas and seem a world removed from the beach scene just down the lane. **Pros:** large, well-appointed units; lovely garden hideaway; beach, shops, and restaurants are just steps away. **Cons:** sea views are limited; some noise from other units; no pool. [$] *Rooms from: €140* ✉ *Northwest beach road* ☎ *22730/92420* 🌐 *www.olympia-hotels.gr* ⏲ *Closed Nov.–Apr.* 🛏 *22 rooms* 🍴 *Free breakfast.*

Activities

Kokkari Surf and Bike Center

WINDSURFING | **FAMILY** | This professional and well-equipped windsurfing outfitter rents windsurfing equipment, sea kayaks, and mountain bikes during the summer months. They also provide windsurfing instruction for all, from absolute beginners to advanced freestyle levels, and run treks for hikers. ✉ *Kokkari* ✥ *On road to Lemonakia Beach* ☎ *22730/92102* 🌐 *www.samoswindsurfing.gr.*

ATTICA AND DELPHI

12

Updated by
Gareth Clark

👁 Sights   🍴 Restaurants   🛏 Hotels   🛍 Shopping   🍸 Nightlife
★★★★☆   ★★★☆☆   ★★★☆☆   ★☆☆☆☆   ★★☆☆☆

WELCOME TO ATTICA AND DELPHI

TOP REASONS TO GO

★ **Delphi, "Navel of the World":** Delphi's Sanctuary of Apollo invites you to imagine a time of oracles, enigmatic prophecies, and mystical emanations.

★ **Sunset at Sounion:** Perched over the water, the spectacular Temple of Poseidon still summons strong emotions in this land of seafarers.

★ **Mighty Marathon:** Dare you retrace Pheidippides's first marathon when he ran 26 hilly miles from this town to Athens in 490 BC?

★ **Cape Vouliagmeni:** Enjoy a sun-kissed day on the beach at the heart of the eternally glamorous Athens Riviera.

★ **Naval Galaxidi:** The town the shipbuilders built back in the 18th century today oozes old-world charm and quaint character.

Attica, the southeastern tip of central Greece, is much more than the home of Athens—it is also a fertile land, with fabled temples and Byzantine monasteries. A short drive from Athens to Glyfada allows travelers easy access to the famed Athens Riviera. The opposite of the slick Athens coast are the mountain towns of Delphi and Arachova. Cradled in the foothills of Mt. Parnassus, this area affords great hiking and ancient wonders.

1 Glyfada. With its palm-fringed coastal promenade lined with lavish villas, boutiques, and seaside restaurants, it's little wonder this suburb is dubbed the Hellenic Hamptons.

2 Vouliagmeni. This seaside suburb, filled with beaches and top-notch dining, is Athens's most prestigious summer address.

3 Sounion. Poised at the edge of a rugged 195-foot cliff, the Temple of Poseidon, easily viewed by boats below, is the highlight of the archaeological site at Sounion.

4 Lavrion. This industrial town's port is where many ferries depart for nearby Cycladic islands,

and an increasing number of cruise ships also stop here for easy access to Sounion.

5 Marathon & the East Coast. This region, including the fabled plain of Marathon, a man-made freshwater lake, and beautiful beaches along the coast, attracts vacationing Athenians.

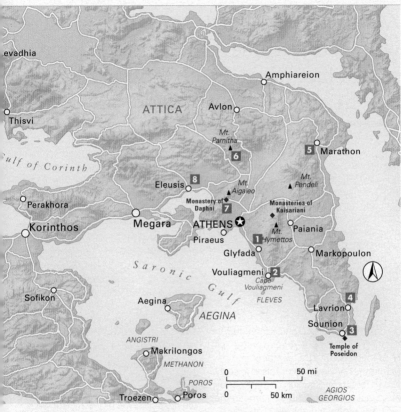

6 Mt. Parnitha. Attica's highest mountain affords stunning views of the plain of Athens.

7 Monastery of Daphni. This Orthodox monastery was likely established in the 6th century, incorporating materials of Apollo's sanctuary, though what survives now is mostly from the 11th century.

8 Eleusis. The Sanctuary of Demeter lies on an eastern slope, hardly visible amid the modern buildings of Elefsina (or Eleusis, as it was called in the ancient Greek world).

9 Osios Loukas. This monastic complex, still inhabited by a few monks, is notable for its mosaics and dramatic location, looming on a prominent rise with a sweeping view of the Elikonas peaks.

10 Arachova. This charming ski town attracts sophisticated Athenians to its slopes and restaurants.

11 Delphi. Dephi, home to an ancient oracle, was once the holiest place in all Greece.

12 Galaxidi. This former ship-building village is a hidden tourism gem.

One of the great surprises of Athens is how much there is to see around it. The mountainous region of Attica (or Attikí), which incorporates the capital, is bounded on three sides by the sea and a coastline fringed with innumerable beaches.

Inland, around the area's four great mountains, is an undulating landscape laced with vineyards and stony foothills, and by its shores remnants of an ancient past retain their power to thrill, in temples, ruined cities, and the sanctuaries of long-lost cults. Over all this hangs the famed light, the purest of lights, sharply delineating a majestic land.

The story of Attica is inextricably bound to that of Athens, the most powerful of the villages that lay scattered over the peninsula. By force and persuasion it brought these communities together, creating a unit that by the 5th century BC had become the center of an empire. Yet while relics of this era, such as the Temple of Sounion or the mysterious Eleusis, are undoubtedly among the wonders of the ancient world, its more recent history is proving just as potent a lure for those in the city.

Southwest of Athens you'll find the coastline dubbed the "Greek Riviera," a relic of a more relatable age, back in the 1950 and '60s when the wealthy and famous began to colonize this stretch of shore. It was a time when resident Jackie Onassis could be spotted bathing in the healing waters of Lake Vouliagmeni and the glare of the local paparazzi lens was fixed firmly on the area. Today, the legacy of that era is still found in the boutiques, bars, and five-star resorts that make the Riviera a popular day trip for well-to-do Athenians.

In the north of Attica, on the edge of the city, Mt. Parnitha is another slice of city life worth sampling. Its deer-strewn hills were savaged by wildfires over a decade ago, and are still recovering, but it's a beloved hike for locals taking in the weekend morning air. In its southern foothills you'll even spy the old Tatoi summer palace, left to crumble after Greece's 140-year experiment with royalty was disbanded in the 1970s. A stroll through its grounds offers a remarkable glimpse of an unusual story.

To the far northwest of Athens (around 175 km/109 miles), beyond Attica and among the Boetian mountains, is perhaps the greatest jewel of the ancient world. The sacred precinct of Delphi was the center of the universe for the ancient Greeks, home to the oracle of the god Apollo. It was here that the two eagles sent by Zeus to find the "navel of the world" met. Even today its archaeological site remains a principal place of pilgrimage and discovery, backed by a spectacular alpine setting. Similar to Attica, however, it's not just a classical playground. In winter, the slopes of nearby Mt. Parnassus, now a national park, attract Athenian skiers to the area's pretty hill towns as this ancient area fills with very modern life.

Planning

When to Go

Athens's nightlife shifts to the southern coast in the summer, typically from July through August. Après-ski town Arachova is the place to be in winter (though expensive), but it's only a stepping stone to Delphi in summer. Attica's northeastern coast is beautiful anytime, though in winter things can feel dead. In Delphi, be prepared to go head-to-head with the crowds and the heat in summer. The beaches, of course, are most enjoyable in full summer, but even chic and pricey Astir Beach gets engulfed by a rising tide of tourists. A much better time to visit is April to June, when wildflowers carpet the arid hillsides of Attica and the Marathon plain. September and October is another beautiful stretch since the sea remains warm, with temperatures that are still ideal for swimming.

Planning Your Time

A week in this region would allow plenty of time for exploring, letting you hit the major archaeological sites of Delphi and Sounion as well as traverse Marathon at less than breakneck speed. Short on time? In two to three days, you can explore Attica's coasts and visit a few key sites. The ancient Greeks believed Delphi was the center of the world, so you could do worse than making it the focus of a trip. With stunning mountain scenery, a world-famous archaeological site, and an excellent museum, touring Delphi can easily take up two days. (Note: Although it's possible to drive from Athens to Delphi and back in a day, we don't recommend it. A night in the crisp mountain air is a pleasant alternative to falling asleep behind the wheel.) If you do need to see Delphi in a day, however, be sure to leave Athens early (it's a three- to four-hour trip). A second day could be spent hiking around the mountain village of Arachova, or even skiing (in season). Or head to the pretty port town of Galaxidi.

Getting Here and Around

Athens and Attica system buses run from Athens's center to the southern and northeastern coast, and points from Marathon to Eleusis. Taking a KTEL bus to Arachova, Delphi, and Galaxidi may help you avoid road fatigue. Attica's public bus service is extensive, though can be infrequent (and frustrating); for ambitious exploring in the area, a car is invaluable. The roads to Arachova, Mt. Parnassus, and Galaxidi are decent, but include hairpin turns and can get icy in winter.

BUS

Places close to Athens can be reached with the blue city bus and metro lines. Take the metro (Line 3) to Agia Marina, then switch to bus 876 or 866 for Daphni or Elefsina. Bus A3 goes direct from Syntagma Square to Glyfada, then take either the 117 or 122 from there to Vouliagmeni. The metro (M2) also runs from Athens to nearby Elliniko, from where you can catch the 122 bus to Glyfada or Vouliagmeni. For detailed public transit information, call ☎ 11185 or go to ⊕ www.oasa.gr.

To reach other destinations in Attica, the most efficient mode of travel—if you don't rent a car—is the regional KTEL bus system in combination with taxis. KTEL buses for eastern Attica leave hourly from their main station in downtown Athens (at the corner of Mavromateon and Leoforos Alexandras), calling at Marathon and Sounion. All these fares are inexpensive and schedules can be found by calling KTEL Attikis (☎ 21088/08000 ⊕ ktelattikis.gr)

KTEL Fokidas buses servicing Delphi, Arachova, Osios Loukas, and Galaxidi depart from Terminal B (Liossion) in Athens. To Delphi, departures usually begin at 7:30 am in summer. The journey takes about three hours. Only a couple of buses a day contine on past Delphi to complete the four-hour trip to Galaxidi, usually changing at Itea. For more information on these journeys, call KTEL Fokidas (☎ 22650/29900 ⊕ www.ktel-fokidas.gr). Tickets for these buses are sold only at this terminal. *For more detailed contact information, see Bus in Travel Smart.*

CAR

Points in Attica and Delphi can be reached from the main Thessaloniki–Athens and Athens–Patras highways, with the National Road (Ethniki Odos) the most popular route, now connecting to the Athens ring road (Attiki Odos), which has a toll.

From the Peloponnese drive east via Corinth to Athens, or from Patras cross the Rion–Antirion bridge to visit Delphi. Most roads off these highways are two-lane secondary arteries. Several of these—notably from Athens to Delphi and Itea and from Athens to Sounion—are spectacularly scenic.

Local and international car rental agencies have offices in downtown Athens—most are on Syngrou Avenue—as well as at the arrivals level at Eleftherios Venizelos Athens International Airport, in Spata.

TAXI

You will find "Piatsa" taxi ranks next to all the airports, and taxis will be lined up even late at night if there is a boat or flight coming in. On the other hand, your hotel can usually arrange a taxi for you, but if you need one in the wee hours of the morning make sure you book it in advance.

Hotels

The standards are high at the hotels along Attica's much-traversed coast, and they fit roughly into three groups: those catering to families on a budget, those aimed at corporate travelers, and those servicing luxury lovers. It's no surprise why corporate moguls from all over the world often rent over-the-top bungalows at some of these resorts for the whole season, with their stunning seaside views, state-of-the-art spas, and dazzling public spaces. But no matter how many face-lifts they endure, Attica's luxury hotels cannot remove their predominant mid-20th-century "shipping tycoon" style. Conversely, in Delphi, Arachova, and Galaxidi, accommodations tend to be homey, and in some places you may even have the sensation of being part of a family, as rooms are decorated with personal heirlooms and breakfast includes homemade goodies. In Delphi and Arachova, peak demand is during ski season and Easter (many places close for summer in Arachova).

Restaurants

The cuisine of Attica resembles that of Athens, central Greece, and the Peloponnese. Local ingredients dominate, with fresh fish perhaps the greatest (and most expensive) delicacy. Since much of Attica's vegetation used to support herds of grazing sheep and the omnivorous goat, the meat of both animals is also a staple in many country tavernas. Although it is becoming increasingly difficult to find the traditional Greek taverna with large stewpots full of the day's hot meal, or big *tapsi* (pans) of *pastitsio* (layers of pasta, meat, and cheese laced with cinnamon) or *papoutsakia* (eggplant slices filled with minced meat), market towns and villages in Attica still harbor the occasional rustic haunt, offering tasty, inexpensive meals. Always ask to see the *kouzina* (kitchen) to look at the day's offerings, or even to peer inside the pots. Regional cuisine in Delphi and Arachova relies heavily on meats, including game, while in the coastal town of Galaxidi, fresh fish and seafood courses dominate. Informal dress is appropriate at all but the very fanciest of restaurants, and unless noted, reservations are not necessary.

Restaurant and hotel reviews have been shortened. For full information, visit Fodors.com.

What it Costs in euros			
$	$$	$$$	$$$$
RESTAURANTS			
under €15	€15–€25	€26–€40	over €40
HOTELS			
under €125	€125–€225	€226–€275	over €275

Tours

Taking a half-day trip from Athens to the breathtaking Temple of Poseidon at Sounion avoids the hassle of dealing with the crowded public buses or paying a great deal more for a taxi. A one-day tour to Delphi with lunch is possible, but it's a very long day; a two-day tour (with an overnight in a first-class hotel) gives you more time to explore this wonder.

RECOMMENDED OPERATORS
Dolphin Hellas
GUIDED TOURS | With headquarters within walking distance of the Acropolis, this full-service agency provides a range of services for individual and group travelers: hotel accommodations, villa rentals, ferry tickets, air tickets, organized coach tours, car rentals, fly and drive programs, and transfer and guide services. ✉ *Syngrou Ave. 16, Makriyianni* ☎ *21092/27772* ⊕ *www.dolphin-hellas.gr.*

Key Tours
EXCURSIONS | Showing travelers around Greece since 1963, this well-respected firm offers numerous scheduled excursions, including day trips to Delphi and Meteora from Athens. ✉ *Athanasiou Diakou 26, Athens* ☎ *210/923–3166, 210/923–3266* ⊕ *www.keytours.gr.*

Trekking Hellas
ADVENTURE TOURS | FAMILY | Outdoor activity company offering a number of kayaking, hiking, climbing, cycling, and historical tours around Delphi, the Athens Riviera, and Mt. Parnitha. ✉ *Dimitriou Gounari 96, Maroussi* ☎ *21033/10323* ⊕ *trekking.gr.*

Visitor Information

See the main offices listed under "Visitor Information" in the larger towns in this chapter.

Glyfada Γλυφάδα

17 km (10½ miles) southeast of Athens.

Gateway to the Athens Riviera and the Apollo Coast—which stretches from Pireaus south to Cape Sounion's famed Temple of Poseidon—Glyfada is loved for its palm-fringed coastal promenade lined with parks, beautiful villas, golf courses, shopping, dance clubs, and seaside dining spots. In the 1960s this was the place to be, back when Jackie Onassis could be seen flexing her credit card here (her villa was just to the north). Even today, it's easy to see why this busy suburb is often dubbed the Hellenic Hamptons; it's essentially where the Athenian nouveau riche come to spend their pay checks on designer wear. Most flit in and out on day trips; however, come summer, things change as the area straps on its six-inch dancing shoes and lets loose, offering its fahionistas somewhere to show off their latest purchases in a slew of in-the-know pop-up nightclubs.

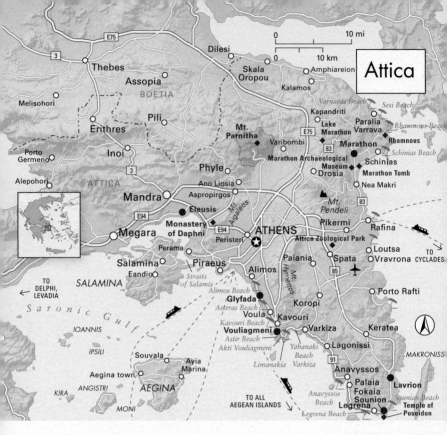

Most activity here tends to fall around the shopping streets of Kiprou and Grigoriou Lambraki, where its café-restaurant-bars provide ample opportunity to swap espressos for espresso martinis as night falls. In part, the modern reputation of the area dates back to an old U.S. air base that was built in the 1930s, just to the north. Its soldiers engendered a local fondness for Americana, from burger restaurants to drive-in movies, while their money propped up the early boutiques. The base closed in the 1990s, but even now it is still causing ripples in the area, with multi-billion-dollar plans to build a luxurious model city on the abandoned site. Given it covers an area the size of Monaco, it could transform the coast all over again, but whether such plans survive the global downturn will be seen. Certainly, the Athens Riviera is not giving up its reputation for extravagance any time soon.

GETTING HERE AND AROUND

Bus A3 leaves Athens's center (Syntagma Square) and stops at Glyfada's main square. Alternatively, take either the A2 bus or M2 (Line 2) metro to Elliniko, and take buses 122 or 171 to Glyfada from there. The A3 runs regularly (two to three an hour) in both directions until 11 pm. The ride can take an hour or more. On summer weekends only, OASA bus line 790 operates through the night (12:30 to 4:30 am) to serve clubbers who come to party and escape the Athens heat; it leaves from Glyfada Square and heads to Peristeri through the center of Athens.

The tram offers a more scenic, if often slower, route but the link between the Syntagma and Kasomouli stops closed indefinitely in 2018. The nearest metro station with a connection to the tram is Neos Kosmos on Line 2. From there you can pick up the Asklipeio Voulas tram, which stops on Poseidonos Avenue in Glyfada. Most trams run until 1 am daily, except for Friday and Saturday, when they run until 2:30 am (and a couple even later than that, but be sure to check the timetable before you depart). *For more information on Athens public transportation options, including all relevant contact information, see Getting Here and Around in Athens.*

◉ Sights

When the old international airport here closed, Glyfada became quieter and more local. Athenians come to swim, stroll, shop, and spend quiet moments gazing at the sea. On summer nights, however, the area transforms itself into a pulsing dance club scene. A large expat community seeks out the local cuisine and ample international offerings in Glyfada's center. There are also several decent hotels and, with Athens city center just a short drive away, it makes a good base for travelers who prefer being near the beach.

Sea Turtle Rescue Center

INFO CENTER | FAMILY | Since 1983, the primary objective of Archelon, the Sea Turtle Protection Society of Greece, has been to safeguard sea turtles and their habitats in Greece. At the Glyfada rescue center, housed in five disused train wagons donated by the Hellenic Railways Organization (OSE), you can watch the team of volunteers in action (caring for turtles at the last stage of rehabilitation), lend a helping hand by bringing much needed supplies, and learn about ongoing rescue efforts throughout Greece. ⊠ *3rd Marina* ☎ *21089/82600* ⊕ *www.archelon.gr.*

⊕ Beaches

Attica's southwestern coast is mainly rock, with some short, sandy stretches in Alimos, Glyfada, and Voula that have been made into public pay beaches. Along with beach bars, changing rooms,

beach umbrellas, and rental water-sport equipment for windsurfing and waterskiing, there are gardens, parking, and playgrounds. These beaches have received Blue Flags for cleanliness from the European Union despite their proximity to Athens. Most are open from 8 am to 8 pm in summer, and most charge entry fees. At some beaches, fees go up on weekends, and at others you may have to pay extra for a lounge chair or parking. In July and August, when temperatures climb past 100°F (38°C), public beaches often stay open until midnight.

Alimos Beach (*Akti tou Iliou*)

BEACH—SIGHT | The town of Alimos has the nearest developed—and clean—beach to Athens. The so-called Beach of the Sun extends over 60,000 square meters and has umbrellas and lounge chairs for rent, three beach bars, a couple of tavernas, and one minimarket. Expect it to be packed over the hot summer months. There is an entry fee (slightly higher on weekends); sun beds cost €1/€2 depending on whether it's a weekday or weekend. **Amenities:** food and drink; lifeguards; parking (fee); showers; toilets. **Best for:** swimming; walking. ⊠ *Poseidonos, (opposite no. 62), Alimos* ⊹ *10 km (6 miles) south of Athens, 5 km (3 miles) north of Glyfada* ☎ *21098/55169* ⊕ *www.aktitouiliou.gr* ⊠ *€6 weekdays; €8 weekends.*

Asteras Beach

BEACH—SIGHT | This sprawling, upmarket complex draws a hip young crowd as well as families with children, who enjoy different sides of the beach. It is built around a fine sand shore and landscaped grounds shaded by elegant pergolas, but the high-concept branding and glitz is just another attempt to glamorize (and monetize) the Riviera sands. On balance it offers a fair amount of facilities, including lounge chairs, umbrellas, pools, lockers, changing rooms, showers, trampolines, a playground, restaurants, bars, and water sports. Yet for the cost of €8 and the privilege of spending even more on

In the summer, many of Athens's trendiest clubs and restaurants relocate to be closer to Glyfada's popular beaches, many of which have received a coveted Blue Flag for cleanliness.

high-priced drinks and food, it makes you yearn for simpler pleasures. The youthful Balux poolside café-club offers a spot to cool off on abundant pillows with a chilled coffee in hand or sip a cocktail long after sundown. **Amenities:** food and drink; parking (fee); showers; toilets; water sports. **Best for:** partiers; swimming; walking; windsurfing. ✉ *Poseidonos 58* ✣ *15 km (9 miles) south of Athens* ☎ *21089/40566* 🎟 *€8.*

🍴 Restaurants

A lot of the better restaurants in Glyfada are either offshoots of successful Greek restaurants in Athens, trying their luck on the wealthy coast, or part of some mysterious "concept" dining project, usually attempting to get you to spend the whole day there—like the equivalent of fishing with a net rather than a rod. It's not a criticism; these are often impressive establishments. It also makes the dining scene here a rather polished affair, as the boat-fresh fish that arrives on its shore every day is put to ever grander use.

Ark

$$$ | **INTERNATIONAL** | Like its near neighbor, Balux Cafe, Ark is part of the Asteras Complex, an attempt to turn a stretch of sandy beach into your entire day: lounging, dinner, drinks, dancing. Ark, however, is focused on the culinary side, and under the guidance of chef Yannis Baxevanis it is a tempting affair. **Known for:** good coffee and cake; pretty waterside setting; Greek-French menu. [$] *Average main: €30* ✉ *Grigoriou Lambraki 2* ☎ *21089/48882* 🌐 *www.ark-glyfada.gr/en.*

George's Steak House

$ | **STEAKHOUSE** | This spot feels a bit like meat corner: a steakhouse opposite another steakhouse, next to a grillhouse—and, bizarrely, a krav maga dojo. But George's trumps them all. **Known for:** grilled meats; great value; juicy charcoal-grilled steaks. [$] *Average main: €12* ✉ *Konstantinoupoleos 4–6* ☎ *21089/46020* 🌐 *www.georgessteakhouse.gr* 💳 *No credit cards.*

Sardelaki

$ | SEAFOOD | There are two big rivals in the eyes of locals for the crown of best seafood in Glyfada: Barbouanki and Sardelaki. The former is fully franchised across Greece now; Sardelaki (meaning "sardine"), on the other hand, has stuck to the region where it all started, with restaurants in both Glyfada and Vouliagmeni, and feels a little more authentic because of it. **Known for:** seafood at a decent price; big portions; fresh ingredients. $ *Average main: €14* ✉ *Pandoras St. 16* ☎ *21140/21195.*

To Spiti

$$ | ITALIAN | FAMILY | This stylish Mediterranean eatery rarely disappoints, and the Glyfada branch (there's another one in Athens) feels likeably hidden away despite being on the corner of Lazaraki and Dousmani. The discreet entrance reveals a rather polished interior and a menu that does the simple stuff really well yet throws in the odd surprise, such as the octopus with caramalized onions and fava, or a prosciutto spaghetti with dill and mustard sauce. **Known for:** good pizza; stylish decor; it has a second location in Athens. $ *Average main: €15* ✉ *Lazaraki 12* ☎ *21089/80080* ⊕ *www.spiti.co.*

☕ Coffee and Quick Bites

'AVIT

$ | VEGETARIAN | A beachy vibe pervades this hip inner-city vegan café, its terrace fenced off by bamboo. The menu is entirely plant-based, with chewy mushroom gyros, buddha bowls, veggie burgers, and triple-fried potato wedges the star attractions. **Known for:** plant-based snacks; hip atmosphere; array of veggie burgers. $ *Average main: €8* ✉ *Maragkou 19, Glifada* ☎ *21089/49381* ⊗ *Closed Mon.*

Hotels

Athens Coast Hotel

$ | HOTEL | FAMILY | When it comes to budget stays in Glyfada, this new, well-placed set-up is pretty unassailable. **Pros:** good breakfasts and lobby café/bar; decent-sized pool to relax in; right in the city center and opposite bus stop. **Cons:** the walls are a bit thin; there's nearby construction; pool is closed in winter. $ *Rooms from: €40* ✉ *Grigoriou Lampraki 25* ☎ *21089/81154* ⊕ *athenscoasthotel. reserve-online.net* ⇄ *54 rooms* ⊙∣ *Free breakfast.*

Blazer Suites

$$ | HOTEL | A clublike panache, friendly and personal service, and a good location make this a solid choice for combining sightseeing with languid days by the pool or nearby beach. **Pros:** nice pool area; five-minute walk from cosmopolitan Glyfada center; spacious, comfortable guest quarters. **Cons:** located on a busy six-lane avenue, which can get noisy; surrounding area is not that attractive; geared to business travelers. $ *Rooms from: €200* ✉ *Karamanli 1, Voula* ☎ *21096/58801* ⊕ *www.blazersuites.gr* ⇄ *28 suites* ⊙∣ *Free breakfast.*

Brasil Suites

$$$$ | HOTEL | These modern, clean, minimalist suites are large (the smallest is 50 square meters/538 square feet), and all include a fully equipped kitchen. **Pros:** spacious and comfortable; good choice for families; very friendly staff. **Cons:** a bit of a journey to reach major tourist sites in downtown Athens; the neighboring building is an eyesore; expensive given location. $ *Rooms from: €300* ✉ *Eleftherias 4* ☎ *21089/42124* ⊕ *www.brasilhotel. gr* ⇄ *16 suites* ⊙∣ *Free breakfast.*

▼ Nightlife

Glyfada is the kind of place where every bar has a concept. It comes with the territory. Athens's bobo set tends to arrive for the shops in the morning, then depart by dusk. They don't stick around the suburbs come nightfall unless there's a party. The bars had to do something to keep their attention, hence the emergence of the almighty café-by-day, restaurant-club by night, of which you'll find many alongside the slick boutiques of Kiprou and the waterfront. These lure in weary shoppers desperate for a caffeine fix, then switch to mojitos after sundown as the turntables warm up. Those by the sea have more of a beach-club vibe, and the more inventive examples really are fun spots to while away the afternoon. The other side of the coin are the clubs and lively *bouzoukia* scene (raucous live shows featuring Greek pop stars that wind into the morning). Come summer, some of Athens's most popular night spots close up shop downtown and turn up here; places seem to change their name and style each season to keep up with trends, so, if that's your bag, just ask around and you'll find the latest thing. You'll discover *bouzoukia* clubs lining the coast stretching south from Athens, and if you dare, it's a night to remember—for better or worse.

★ Balux Cafe—The House Project

CAFES—NIGHTLIFE | This creative bar-café-restaurant comes in the style of an open-plan house, complete with playroom and pool area. It's the ultimate "all things to everyone" stop-by, and despite the pompous name and concept-pushing, it's great fun—albeit not cheap. By day, board games and pool tables are wheeled out in its cozy womb of a café, with a contemporary Greek menu on hand. A playground area takes care of the kids, while entrance to the beach has a fee (€8), with a private section (€12) for those who want more space to swim. Then, once the sun sets, the café becomes the perfect spot to slowly sip a cocktail on the beachfront as the evening gives way to live music (usually on Thursday) or local DJs. It's open year-round. ✉ *Asteras Seaside Complex, Poseidonos 58* ☎ *21089/83577* ⊕ *www.baluxcafe. com* 🔖 *€8 for beach area*.

Pere-Ubu

BARS/PUBS | Kiprou Street is a gauntlet of all-day café-bars these days, each morphing seamlessly from post-shopping brunch and espressos to full-on restaurant, to DJs and cocktails as the light fades. Pere-Ubu is one of the more electric; its industrial style manages to be hip without being full-on obnoxious. Excellent burgers accompany a good selection of cocktails as you segue into the evening. It's one of the busier spots in town, so book a table and be patient—service is pretty slow. ✉ *Kyprou 74* ☎ *21089/41450* ⊕ *www.pereubu.gr*.

Su Casa

BARS/PUBS | Another that comfortable fits into the café-restaurant-bar mold is Su Casa, on the corner of Kiprou and Plateia Nymfon. The main lure is its rather nicely shaded garden terrace, which offers a welcome break from the sun. But as the night winds on, the cocktail hour approaches and it comes into its own, with an array of signature drinks to accompany a vast list of speciality rums, gins, and vodkas. ✉ *Nymphs Square* ☎ *21089/85554* ⊕ *www.su-casa.gr*.

🛍 Shopping

The Greek Riviera has two speeds: people visit Vouliagmeni to relax; they go to Glyfada to shop and to dance. This is where fashion-conscious Athenians flock to blow their hard-earned cash on designer bling. On **Metaxas** you'll discover mainly high-street brands; it's on the streets of **Kiprou** and **Grigoriou Lambraki** that the bold head. The former is more cherished, filled with small designer boutiques, many unique to this area; the latter has bigger brands and malls aplenty to splash your cash.

Ensayer

CLOTHING | One of the area's better known high-end boutiques. The slick interiors are a taster for the kind of niche couture and international designers you'll find inside. Very much an encapsulation of everything Glyfada signifies to Greek shoppers. ⊠ *Kiprou 55 & Esperidon Square 2B* ☎ *21089/43043 (men's), 21089/43034 (women's)* ⊕ *www.ensayar.gr.*

Soho-Soho

CLOTHING | Not limited to Glyfada, and more of a high-end chain, this branch of the popular Soho-Soho women's boutique is no less glamorous. Discover brands such as Golden Goose, Creed, Herno, and Moncler. ⊠ *Kyprou 70* ☎ *21089/43498* ⊕ *www.sohosohoboutique.com.*

Zerteo

JEWELRY/ACCESSORIES | Founded in 2006 on Kiprou by a pair of twin brothers, Zerar and Teo, their signature "evil eye" runs across much of their designs, and they've since opened boutiques in a number of high-end hotels. Go where it all started. ⊠ *Kyprou 78* ☎ *21089/46682* ⊕ *zerteojewelry.com.*

Activities

BOATING AND SAILING

Many yacht brokers charter boats and organize scuba tours and flotilla cruises in small rented sailboats around the islands.

Vernicos Yachts

BOATING | Headquartered in a seaside suburb between Glyfada and Athens, this is the best place to go near Athens if you want to rent a boat to sail down to the islands. The company hosts crewed, weeklong cruises and also charters boats. ⊠ *Poseidonos 11, Alimos* ☎ *21098/96000* ⊕ *www.vernicosyachts.com.*

GOLF

Konstantinos Karamanlis Glyfada Golf Course

GOLF | With many distinguished politicians (including the legendary Greek politician it is named after), businessmen, and members of the diplomatic community on its roster, this green oasis of rolling hills is lovingly landscaped with tall trees and shrubbery. You need to make reservations for the weekend by Wednesday, while the greens are open Tuesday–Sunday from 7:30 am until sunset and Monday 1 pm (noon in winter) until sunset. ⊠ *Glyfada* ✛ *Off Saki Karagiorga and end of Pronois* ☎ *21089/46820* ⊕ *glyfadagolf.gr/home/* 🎫 *€60 daily, €50 for 18 holes, €30 for 9 holes* 🏌 *18 holes. 6847 yards. par 72.*

Vouliagmeni
Βουλιαγμένη

8 km (5 miles) south of Glyfada, 25 km (16 miles) south of Athens.

If Glyfada is all about credit cards and consumer bustle, Vouliagmeni showcases another side to the Athens Riviera. This classy seaside residential suburb is Athens's most prestigious summer address; and while you might buy your clothes up the road, this is where you take them off to relax. There are no shopping streets; no loud *bouzoukia* nightclubs. Restaurants and cafés double as bars later in the evening, but not until you've polished off a hundred euros' worth of boat-fresh seafood, and even then it's a laid-back, cocktail-driven affair. Vouliagmeni is all about being seen, usually on as expensive a private beach as possible, which is where the Astir Palace comes in. Back in the 1960s, just as the rest of the Riviera was taking off, the Astir complex was hosting the great, the good, and the plain filthy rich on its five-star shores. A recent takeover and multi-million-dollar rejuvenation proves little has changed, with its Laimos peninsula setting still the envy of all who visit. But you don't necessarily need oil money to enjoy this area, and great, affordable beaches and some of the best dining in Attica are a fine consolation until your penny stocks finally pay off.

GETTING HERE AND AROUND

If driving, take Highway 91 out of Athens; this drops to the west coast of Attica and runs its length all the way to Sounion. There is no direct public transport link between Athens and Vouliagmeni. Take either the A3 bus or metro (Line 2) to Elliniko and switch to bus 122 once there. Both run multiple times an hour, but only until 11 pm. From Glyfada, both the 117 and 122 buses run to Vouliagmeni. *For more information, see Bus and Tram in the Athens chapter.*

◉ Sights

Vouliagmeni is coveted for the large yacht harbor (including the exclusive Nautical Club that caters to water-sports lovers) and the scenic promontory, Laimos, which is covered with towering umbrella pines and several seaside fish tavernas as well as the upmarket restaurants of the Four Seasons Astir Palace. Vouliagmeni can serve as a convenient base from which to explore Attica, but it is far less crowded and more exclusive than Glyfada.

Vouliagmeni Lake

BEACH—SIGHT | The part-salt, part spring-fed warm waters of Vouliagmeni Lake make for a peaceful retreat. The lake is actually a subterranean cavern that collapsed and filled with water some 2,000 of years ago. Its tunnels burrow deep into the mountain, stretching for thousands of kilometers and are yet to be fully explored. Its waters are also reputed to have curative powers, and as you bathe, small fish nibble at your dead skin. As such, it's especially popular with older Greeks, though locals still bitterly recall a time when you didn't have to pay for the privilege. At the lakeshore beach, a dramatic, rocky backdrop provides one of the more exotic settings in Attica. You can rent umbrellas and sun beds, and even pay extra to recline in the absurd VIP "Prive" area, but we advise you don't. There are showers as well as a decent (if overpriced) café-restaurant. Most of the lake has a gradual slope and sandy bottom. Caution is recommended, however, as it deepens suddenly in parts. ■**TIP**➔ **Head to the northern corner of the car park and you'll find a marked route (look for the red dots). This leads to a series of interconnecting dirt roads at the top that wrap the mountains around the lake and beyond.** ✉ *Vouliagmeni* ✛ *2 km (1 mile) southeast of Vouliagmeni* ☎ *210/896–2237* ⊕ *www.limnivouliagmenis.gr* ✍ *€15 weekdays; €18 weekends.*

⬢ Beaches

Here, beaches are far quieter, and cleaner, than those found farther north toward Athens.

Akti Vouliagmeni

BEACH—SIGHT | FAMILY | A fee gives you access to elegant wooden lounge chairs, white umbrellas, and shiny beach bars. Also on-site at this public beach are basketball, volleyball, and tennis courts as well as a playground for pre- or post-swimming fun. There's also Wi-Fi and a first-aid station during the summer. **Amenities:** food and drink; lifeguards; parking (free); toilets. **Best for:** swimming; walking. ✉ *2 Poseidonos, at Apollonos* ☎ *21089/60697* ⊕ *vouliagmeni-akti.gr* ✍ *€7.*

Astir Beach

BEACH—SIGHT | This beach club on the Laimos promontory is not just a place to get a tan; it's where you go to be *seen*. Yes, it is open to the public daily from 8 am to 9 pm, but its exclusive location has always commanded a hefty entrance fee (to the indignation of locals), which means the green lawns and sandy stretch are usually not so crowded. It is also home to a slice of ancient history. The 6th-century Temple of Apollo Zoster was discovered here when a couple of young boys from a nearby orphanage—which still exists—dug it up while playing in the sand in the early part of the 20th century. If that doesn't do it for you, a range of services (including shopping, dining, water sports, and yoga on the beach) are offered at an extra cost. **Amenities:** food and drink; volleyball courts; water sports. **Best for:** swimming; relaxing in style.

■ **TIP→ If you don't fancy paying €30 to rent an umbrella, across the road is a small public beach where locals paddle in the water for free.** ⊠ *Apollonos 40* ☎ *21089/01619* ⊕ *www.astir.gr* ⌑ *€15 weekdays; €25 weekends; umbrellas from €30.*

Kavouri Beach
BEACH—SIGHT | This public beach extends north from Vouliagmeni to Voula and is one of the most easily accessible free, public beaches near the city. It has fine golden sand and is a good choice for families. There are a few modest cafés along the beach as well as some shops, while umbrellas and sun beds are available for rent. **Amenities:** food and drink; parking (free); showers; toilets. **Best for:** swimming; walking. ⊠ *Vouliagmeni* ✛ *Western shore of Vouliagmeni headland* ⌑ *Free.*

Limanakia
BEACH—SIGHT | A "limanakia" isn't so much a place as a description. It means "small cove" in Greek, and these litter the coast south of Lake Vouliagmeni. They are especially popular among young Athenians, who go to sprawl on the hot rocks, cool off in the water, and then party in the evening. One in particular has gained something of a cult following in the city, geared around a popular bar called Lefteris Canteen. This is where you'll find the beautiful people, jazzed on coffee and their own sense of youthful invulnerability. A short walk east is a nudist cove. **Amenities:** canteen; nothing but rocks. **Best for:** lazing; swimming; nudity. ⊠ *Vouliagmeni* ✛ *South of Lake Vouliagmeni, off Posidonos Rd.*

Yabanaki Beach Varkiza
BEACH—SIGHT | FAMILY | Beach-club amenities—umbrellas and sun beds for rent, water sports, bars, restaurants (including a popular *souvlaki* eatery), a children's water park, and cabins where you can change—spread across 25 acres behind a long stretch of sand. Varkiza is popular with windsurfers and waterskiers. **Amenities:** food and drink; lifeguards; parking (no fee); water sports. **Best for:** walking; windsurfing. ⊠ *Varkiza* ✛ *5 km (3 miles) east of Vouliagmeni* ☎ *21045/11888* ⊕ *www.varkizaresort.gr* ⌑ *€6 weekdays; €7.50 weekends.*

🍴 Restaurants

BlueFish
$$$ | SEAFOOD | This waterside restaurant (go through the bar Del Posto, above, to reach it) is one of the finest seafood spots in town—and there's some competition here. The dining area is level with the water, as the bay laps against the quay; you couldn't get closer to the sea without being in it. **Known for:** innovative seafood menu; perfect watery views; stylish setting. $ *Average main: €27* ⊠ *Leoforos Posidonos 4* ☎ *21096/71778.*

Garbi
$$$ | SEAFOOD | This esteemed seafood restaurant first opened here in 1924, and it's aged well. Athenians flock year-round to share a seafood platter and bottle of white wine or feast on tongue fillets stuffed with fresh shrimp, or an appetizer of scorpion-fish croquettes. **Known for:** fresh seafood; seaside terrace and views; driveable from Athens. $ *Average main: €26* ⊠ *Iliou 21 and Selinis, Patras* ✛ *3 km (2 miles) west of Vouliagmeni* ☎ *21089/63480* ⊕ *www.garbi.gr.*

Labros

$$ | **SEAFOOD** | Perched across the road from the waters of scenic Vouliagmeni Lake, this traditional fish taverna has been serving the best of Greek fishermen's catches since 1889. With wonderful views of crystalline, aquamarine waters, Labros remains legendary for its mussel rice (*mydopilafo*), its seafood pasta, and its grilled fresh fish that arrives daily from all parts of Greece. **Known for:** waterside dining; fresh fish and seafood dishes; mydopilafo (mussel rice). [$] *Average main: €22* ✉ *Poseidonos 20* ☎ *21089/60144* 🌐 *labrosrestaurant.gr/* 🕓 *Closed Mon.*

Moorings Vouliagmeni

$$$ | **MODERN GREEK** | Wonderful views over the best of the Athenian Riviera, the Vouliagmeni marina, and a small church shrine can make for an unforgettably romantic evening. The hip lounge atmosphere of this seafront café-restaurant is complemented by the Nouveau Greek menu created by chef Andreas Schoinas, with the healthy seafood and Mediterranean options standing out from the rest. **Known for:** romance-inducing views; salads and other light fare; seafood. [$] *Average main: €30* ✉ *Marina Vouliagmenis* ☎ *21096/70659* 🌐 *www.moorings.gr.*

☕ Coffee and Quick Bites

Aqua Marina

$ | **CAFÉ** | **FAMILY** | Aqua Marina is an old favorite among locals. It's hard to resist its list of sweet treats, from a huge wedge of tasty baklava to a great splodge of *galaktoboureko*, a custardy classic topped in filo pastry and sweet-scented syrup. **Known for:** a great people-watching spot; the quality coffee attracts gangs of garrulous locals; excellent sweets. [$] *Average main: €6* ✉ *Agios Panteleimonos 15* ☎ *21089/61214.*

Waffle House

$ | **CAFÉ** | **FAMILY** | The name is something of a giveaway. This local chain is beloved by families and grown-ups with a sweet tooth or a love of sorbet-based cocktails. **Known for:** waffle smothered in a topping of choice; the shakes aren't bad either; being the most improbable bar in town. [$] *Average main: €6* ✉ *Agiou Panteleimonos* ☎ *21089/61227.*

🛏 Hotels

Azur Hotel

$$ | **HOTEL** | Vouliagmeni has lacked this kind of middle-brow boutique for a while now: somewhere between the full-on luxury assault of the area's big hitters and the usual budget stays. **Pros:** quiet suburban location; nice pool area; good service. **Cons:** decoration is a little cold; it could lose some of its "art"; rooms can be a bit small. [$] *Rooms from: €200* ✉ *Dekeleias 10 and Danais* ☎ *21089/60417* 🌐 *azurhotel.gr* 🔑 *35 rooms* 🍴 *Free breakfast.*

★ **Four Seasons Astir Palace**

$$$$ | **HOTEL** | Beginning in the 1960s, the first cabanas started arriving on Vouliagmeni's wooded peninsula of Laimos and a few years later a hotel arrived—a grande dame for the golden age of the Greek Riviera, where everyone from Jackie Onassis to Frank Sinatra could be seen lounging by the pool. **Pros:** myriad facilities leave little reason to leave the peninsula; a choice of pools and (three!) private beach spots; free SUP and kayak rental. **Cons:** the price is, naturally, pretty sky-high; it's a walk back to the main town (though golf buggies are available); the guilt of just so much luxury. [$] *Rooms from: €650* ✉ *Apollonos 40* ☎ *21089/01000* 🌐 *www.fourseasons.com* 🔑 *303 rooms; 61 bungalows* 🍴 *Free breakfast.*

Grand Resort Lagonissi

$$$ | **RESORT** | **FAMILY** | With its own beaches, pools, restaurants, bars, two tennis courts, and an open-air cinema, all augmenting deluxe accommodations, you may have little need to stray from this seaside paradise. **Pros:** incredible sea

views; standard accommodations can be a relatively good value; perfect for romantic getaways. **Cons:** some suites are ridiculously expensive; food and beverages can also be pricey; some of the decor could use an update. $ *Rooms from: €292 ⊠ Km 40, Athens–Sounio Road, Lagonissi ⊕ 17 km (10 miles) southeast of Vougliameni ☎ 22910/76000 ⊕ www. lagonissiresort.gr ⊗ Closed Oct.–Mar. ⊃ 430 rooms ⦿ Free breakfast.*

★ The Margi

$$$$ | **HOTEL** | A sculptural stone fireplace in the lobby, a rich brown leather headboard in one guest room, an antique dressing table in another: no detail escapes notice at this upscale retreat whose chic, truly spectacular pool and handsome guest rooms attract young and trendy Athenians. **Pros:** romantic atmosphere; nicely decorated pool area; cool vibe. **Cons:** smallish rooms; expensive for what's on offer; the building yard next door is unfortunate. $ *Rooms from: €350 ⊠ Litous 11 ☎ 21089/29000 ⊕ www.themargi.gr ⊃ 88 rooms; 1 villa ⦿ Free breakfast.*

 Nightlife

Island

DANCE CLUBS | Claim a place at the bar of this sophisticated and pricey beachside restaurant to observe the fashionable exchange air kisses and to cast an eye around for any C-list celebs to have just staggered in, then hit the club. People come in waves, either by car or yacht: some early for drinks, some late for dancing, and some flowing from the bar to the restaurant to the dance floor. Palm trees, bamboo, flowering shrubs, and staggered terraces create an elegant and slightly exotic backdrop. Inside, the restaurant's creative Mediterranean cuisine has substance behind the flash, while the dancefloor usually displays the opposite. The mid-September end-of-summer party is *the* biggest annual event in Vouliagmeni. ⊠ *Sounio Ave., Varkiza ☎ 21096/53563*

⊕ *www.islandclubrestaurant.gr ⊗ Closed Mon. and mid-Sept.–Apr.*

Rumors

CAFES—NIGHTLIFE | Vouliagmeni is not a raging nightspot. The cafés and restaurants that run the strip along Agios Panteleimonos mostly tend to turn into drinking spots once the aperitivo hour sets in, and it's a nice area to dwell, screened from the main road by a line of trees. Rumors is the pick of the bunch, with a cozy terrace to while away the evening and an accomplished selection of cocktails. It's worth reserving a table in summer, though, as the secret is long since out. ⊠ *Agios Panteleimonos ☎ 21089/61200.*

 Activities

SCUBA DIVING

Athina Diving

SCUBA DIVING | You can take lessons or go on scheduled dives with experienced instructors. Not to be missed: the night diving available upon request, either from shore or by boat. Equipment rentals are also available. ⊠ *Km 38, Athina–Sounio road, Lagonissi ☎ 22910/25434 ⊕ www. athinadiving.gr.*

Sounion Σούνιο

50 km (31 miles) southeast of Vouliagmeni, 70 km (44 miles) southeast of Athens.

Poised at the edge of a rugged 195-foot cliff, the Temple of Poseidon hovers between sea and sky, its "marbled steep, where nothing, save the waves and I may hear our mutual murmurs sweep" unchanged in the centuries since Lord Byron penned these lines. Today the archaeological site at Sounion is one of the most photographed in Greece. The coast's raw, natural beauty has attracted affluent Athenians, whose splendid summer villas dot the shoreline around the temple. There is a tourist café-restaurant by the temple, and a few minimarts on the road, but no village proper. Arrange your visit so that you enjoy the panorama of sea and islands from this airy platform either early in the morning, before the summer haze clouds visibility and the tour groups arrive, or at dusk, when the promontory has one of the most spectacular sunset vantage points in Attica.

In antiquity, the view from the cliff was matched emotion for emotion by the sight of the cape (called the "sacred headland" by Homer) and its mighty temple when viewed from the sea—a sight that brought joy to sailors, knowing upon spotting the massive temple that they were close to home. Aegeus, the legendary king of Athens, threw himself off the cliff when he saw the approaching ship of his son, Theseus, flying a black flag. The king's death was a Greek tragedy born of misunderstanding: Theseus, returning from a mission to slay the Minotaur in Crete, had forgotten to change his ship's sails from black to white—the signal that his mission had succeeded. So the king thought his son had been killed. To honor Aegeus, the Greeks named their sea, the Aegean, after him.

GETTING HERE AND AROUND

KTEL Attikis buses leave from Aigyptou Square, off Pedion Areos park, in Athens for Sounion (also spelled Sounio). It's a two-hour journey and buses run between 8 am and 7 pm daily, hitting spots including Varkiza, Anavyssos, and Legrena. For sunset gazers, the last bus returns from the site at 9 pm (in summer). There is no straightforward local bus connection linking Glyfada or Vouliagmeni with Sounion, so if planning a visit from there either rent a car or book a tour. *For more information on Athens buses and bus stations, see Bus and Train in the Athens chapter.*

 Sights

★ Temple of Poseidon

ARCHAEOLOGICAL SITE | Although the columns at the Temple of Poseidon appear to be gleaming white from a distance in the full sun, when you get closer you can see that they are made of gray-veined marble, quarried from the Agrileza valley 2 km (1 mile) north of the cape, and have 16 flutings rather than the usual 20. Climb the rocky path that roughly follows the ancient route, and beyond the scanty remains of an ancient *propylon* (gateway), you enter the temple compound. On your left is the *temenos* (precinct) of Poseidon; on your right, a *stoa* (arcade) and rooms. The temple itself (now roped off) was commissioned by Pericles, the famous leader of Greece's golden age. It was probably designed by Ictinus, the same architect who helped design the Temple of Hephaistos in the ancient Agora of Athens, and was built between 444 and 440 BC. The people here were considered Athenian citizens, the sanctuary was Athenian, and Poseidon occupied a position second only to Athena herself. The badly preserved frieze on the temple's east side is thought to have depicted the fight between the two gods to become patron of Athens.

The temple was built on the site of an earlier cult to Poseidon. Two colossal statues of youths, carved more than a century before the temple's construction (perhaps votives to the god), were discovered in early excavations. Both now reside at the National Archaeological Museum in Athens. The 15 Doric columns that remain stand sentinel over the Aegean, visible from miles away. Lord Byron had a penchant for carving his name on ancient monuments, and you can see it and other graffiti on the right corner pillar of the portico. The view from the summit is breathtaking. In the slanting light of the late-afternoon sun, the landmasses to the west stand out in sharp profile: the bulk of Aegina backed

Did You Know?

A sighting of the Temple of Poseidon at Sounion always brought cheer to the heart of ancient Greek sailors—perched atop the southernmost cape of Attica, the temple was a sign that Athens was near.

by the mountains of the Peloponnese. To the east, on a clear day, one can spot the Cycladic islands of Kea, Kythnos, and Serifos. On the land side, the slopes of the acropolis retain traces of the fortification walls. ✉ *Cape Sounion* ☎ *22920/39363* 🌐 *odysseus.culture.gr* 🎫 *€10.*

Beaches

Anavyssos Beach

BEACH—SIGHT | **FAMILY** | The broad, sandy beach at Anavyssos is very popular with windsurfers (especially the stretch called Alykes). There's a children's playground and beach volleyball courts, as well as sun beds and umbrellas for hire. **Amenities:** food and drink; showers; toilets; water sports. **Best for:** solitude; swimming; windsurfing. ✉ *Anavyssos* ✥ *13 km (8 miles) northwest of Sounion.*

Legrena Beach

BEACH—SIGHT | On your approach to the Temple of Poseidon, there is a decent sandy beach at Legrena. The fine golden sand is reminiscent of the Cycladic islands, while an added bonus is the usual lack of crowds. A few miles before you arrive (from the west coast), look for the sight of the small island of Patroklos. It is uninhabited today, has ancient fortress ruins, and is said to belong to a wealthy Greek family. **Amenities:** food and drink. **Best for:** solitude; swimming; walking. ✉ *Legrena* ✥ *4 km (2½ miles) north of Sounion, before the turnoff for Haraka.*

Sounion Beach

BEACH—SIGHT | If you are spending the morning visiting the Temple of Poseidon, you might also want to take a swim on the free public beach just below it. Of course, this sandy strip—known locally as Kavokolones—becomes uncomfortably crowded in summer. **Amenities:** none. **Best for:** sunset; swimming. ✉ *Km 68, Athens–Sounion Ave.*

> **Full Moon**
>
> On full-moon nights in August, the Temple of Poseidon usually opens free of charge to the public.

Restaurants

Syrtaki

$$ | **GREEK** | Sit among the pines, take in the view of the sea, and snack on the traditional *pites* (homemade pastry pies, typically stuffed with cheese and spinach) before indulging in the best fresh seafood in the area. The scent of grilled fish wafts in the air, whetting the appetite. **Known for:** sea views; good choice of mezedes (small plates); great seafood. [$] *Average main: €16* ✉ *Km 69, Athens–Sounion avenue* ✥ *4 km (2½ miles) north of Sounion* ☎ *22920/39125.*

Theodoros-Eleni

$$ | **SEAFOOD** | A Greek-British husband-and-wife team build their menu around huge portions of fresh fish and seafood, like the steamed mussels with feta in wine cheese sauce or the seafood pastas. At the end of the dinner, the plate of seasonal fruit or the homemade chocolate *kormos* (log-shaped) cake is on the house. **Known for:** mussels and fresh fish; tasty seafood pastas; big portions. [$] *Average main: €18* ✉ *Legrena* ✥ *3 km (2 miles) south of Sounion, off the road into Legrena village* ☎ *22920/51936* 🕒 *Closed Nov.–Mar.*

Hotels

Aegeon Beach Hotel

$$ | **HOTEL** | Nothing can beat the location—much objected to by environmentalists and archaeologists—*on* the beach beneath the Temple of Poseidon, above the very harbor where ancient ships once navigated, and all guest rooms have balconies, most have sea views, and a

few gaze up at the temple. **Pros:** views of temple and one of the best sunsets in the world; nice beach bar; beautiful water just outside the doors. **Cons:** beach especially crowded with Athenians during summer weekends; decor is minimal and a bit dated; food is uninspired. $ *Rooms from: €150* ⊠ *Athens–Sounion Ave. Km 68* ☎ *22920/39200* ⊕ *www.aegeon-hotel.com* ☾ *Nov.–Mar.* ⇥ *45 rooms* ⏀ *Free breakfast.*

★ **Grecotel Cape Sounio**

$$$$ | **HOTEL** | **FAMILY** | One of the most elaborate hotels on the Rivera perches amid the verdant pine forest of Sounion National Park with stunning views of the Temple of Poseidon from bungalows and villas, all arranged in tiers along a hill. **Pros:** grandiose architecture; family-friendly; beautiful grounds and beach. **Cons:** decor is not as luxurious as the prices might suggest; food is good but expensive; service and maintenance are not always at five-star standards. $ *Rooms from: €383* ⊠ *Km 67, Athens–Sounion Ave.* ☎ *22920/69700* ⊕ *www.capesounio.com* ☾ *Closed Nov.–Apr.* ⇥ *153 rooms* ⏀ *Free breakfast.*

Plaza Resort Hotel

$$$ | **RESORT** | **FAMILY** | These bright rooms right next to Anavyssos Beach are sculpted in soothing white-on-white minimalist decor, and most are reasonably spacious (some are smaller than others), while outdoors is an 80-foot-long pool just a two-minute stroll away from the beach. **Pros:** impressive lobby; pleasant surroundings; private sandy beach with pool. **Cons:** nearby town a bit dull; you really need a car to stay here; high restaurant and beach bar prices. $ *Rooms from: €250* ⊠ *Km 52, Athens–Sounion Ave., Anavyssos* ✛ *13km (8 miles) northwest of Sounion* ☎ *22910/75000* ⊕ *www.plaza-resort.com* ⇥ *135 rooms* ⏀ *Free breakfast.*

 Activities

Kouros Surf Club

SURFING | This outfit on Anavyssos's Alykes Beach offers beginner and advanced windsurfing, kitesurfing, wakeboarding, stand-up paddling, and sailing lessons, a pro shop, and a relaxed beach bar-restaurant. ⊠ *Km 50, Athens–Sounion Ave., Anavyssos* ☎ *22910/40804* ⊕ *www.kourosclub.gr.*

Lavrion Λαύριο

10 km (6 miles) north of Sounion, 80 km (50 miles) southeast of Athens.

After Sounion, the road twists and turns along the coast, winding past holiday homes, before hitting a rather dreary stretch by Lavrion's boatyard, where there always seems to be marina construction work under way. There is increasing activity in the port of Lavrion during the summer, as many ferries for nearby Cycladic islands (Kythnos, Kea [Tzia], etc.) depart from here, and an increasing number of cruise ships also stop here for easy access to the Temple of Poseidon at Sounion. Lavrion, an industrial town with a few remnants of belle epoque architecture, was celebrated in antiquity for its silver mines. Several thousand ancient shafts have been discovered in the area—devoid of the riches they once yielded. The Athenian Themistocles could not have built the fleet that saved Greece from the Persians in 480 BC, nor Pericles the monuments on the Acropolis, without the area's riches. Easy access to the Athens International Airport at Spata via the Markopoulou highway has begun to attract both investment and start-ups to these sunny shores, giving the city an added buzz in recent years, but most visitors just pass through en route to the islands.

Sights

Lavrion Mineralogical Museum

MUSEUM | Even if you're just drifting through, this small mineralogical museum is worth a stop to get a gist of the history of the area. Its 700 exhibits—including several rare and beautiful specimens such as laurionite and azurite—are housed in a charming late-19th-century building once used by the French Mining Company to wash minerals. Coins made from the silver that the ancient Greeks mined around Lavrion are also on display. ✉ *Iroon Polytechniou Sq.* ☎ *22920/26270* 💶 *€2* ⏰ *Closed Mon., Tues., and Thurs.*

Marathon & the East Coast Μαραθώνας

165 km (102 miles) northwest of Sounion, 42 km (26 miles) northeast of Athens.

Athenians enter the fabled plain of Marathon to enjoy a break from the capital, visiting the freshwater lake created by the dam, or sunning at the area's beaches while enjoying views across the bay to the island of Euboia. The beauty of the region endures, despite some large-scale forest fires in recent years. When the Athenian *hoplites* (foot soldiers), assisted by the Plataians, entered the plain in 490 BC, it was to crush a numerically superior Persian force. Some 6,400 invaders were killed fleeing to their ships, while the Athenians lost 192 warriors. This, their proudest victory, became the stuff of Athenian legend; the hero Theseus was said to have appeared himself in aid of the Greeks, along with the god Pan. The Athenian commander Miltiades sent a messenger, Pheidippides, to Athens with glad tidings of the victory; it's said he ran the 42 km (26 miles) hardly taking a breath, shouted *Nenikikamen!* ("We won!"), then dropped dead of fatigue (more probably of a heart attack)—the

inspiration for the marathon race in today's Olympics. To the west of the Marathon plain are the quarries of Mt. Pendeli, the seemingly inexhaustible source for a special marble that weathers to a warm golden tint.

GETTING HERE AND AROUND

Head to the outdoors KTEL Attikis bus terminal in Aigyptou Square in Athens to check routes and plan your Marathon trip. The journey takes about 1½ hours (depending on the traffic along the busy Mesogeion and Marathonos avenues). Buses depart approximately every half hour, starting at 5:30 am. *For more information on Athens buses and bus stations, see Bus and Train in the Athens chapter.*

 Sights

Lake Marathon

SCENIC DRIVE | The huge man-made reservoir formed by the Marathon Dam (built by an American company in 1925–31) warrants a visit soley to see the only dam in the world said to be faced with real marble. At the downstream side is a marble replica of the Athenian Treasury of Delphi. This is a main source of water for Athens, supplemented with water from Parnitha and the Boeotia region. Wonderful views glimpsed from the tall front windows help make this a perfect and refreshing stop on your way back to Athens from Schinias Beach. ✉ *Marathon* ✛ *8 km (5 miles) west of Marathon, down a side road from village of Ayios Stefanos.*

Marathon Archaeological Museum

MUSEUM | Five rooms contain very well preserved objects from excavations in the area, ranging from neolithic pottery from the cave of Pan to Hellenistic and Roman inscriptions and statues (labeled in English and Greek). Eight larger-than-life sculptures came from the gates of a nearby sanctuary of the Egyptian gods and goddesses. In the center of one of the rooms stands part of the Marathon victory trophy—an ionic column that the

Athenians erected in the valley of Marathon after defeating the Persians. Next to the museum, the Middle Hellenic cemetery is well sheltered from the forces of nature and very visitor-friendly. ☒ *Plataion 114* ☩ *Approximately 6 km (4 miles) southwest of Marathon* ☎ *22940/55155* ⊕ *www.culture.gr* ☑ *€6 combined ticket with Marathon Tomb* ☉ *Closed Tues.*

Marathon Run Museum

MUSEUM | Medals, photos, and other memorablia are an homage to the Athens Marathon, run since 1896, as well as other marathons around the world. The experience of a visit seems all the more poignant since the museum is near the site where the courier Pheidipiddes is said to have set off on his impressive feat of running 26 miles to Athens to bring home the news of victory over the Persians in 490 BC. ☒ *Marathonos, at 25th Martiou St.* ☎ *22940/67617* ⊕ *www.marathonrunmuseum.com* ☑ *€2* ☉ *Closed Mon.*

Marathon Tomb

MEMORIAL | This 30-foot-high tumulus is built over graves containing the cremated remains of the 192 Athenians who died in the 490 BC battle against Persian forces. At the base, the original gravestone depicts the Soldier of Marathon, a hoplite, which has been reproduced here (the original is in the National Archaeological Museum in Athens). The battle is plotted on illustrated panels. ☒ *Marathon* ☩ *5 km (3 miles) south of Marathon* ☎ *22940/55462* ☑ *€6 combined ticket with Archaeological Museum* ☉ *Closed Tues.*

Rhamnous

ARCHAEOLOGICAL SITE | This overgrown, isolated spot on a small promontory overlooks the sea between continental Greece and the island of Euboia. It is a bit off the beaten track but if you want to escape the crowds of Athens and make it a day trip together with a swim at nearby Schinias Beach, this is definitely worth the drive (especially if you have your own vehicle). From at least the Archaic period,

Rhamnous was known for the worship of Nemesis, the great leveler, who brought down the proud and punished the arrogant. The scenic site, excavated during many years, preserves traces of temples from the 6th and 5th centuries BC. The smaller temple from the 6th century BC was dedicated to Themis, goddess of Justice. The later temple housed the cult statue of Nemesis, envisioned as a woman. Many fragments have turned up, including the head, in the British Museum. The acropolis stood on the headland, where ruins of a fortress (5th and 4th centuries BC) are visible. As you wander over the usually serene, and always evocative, site you discover at its edge little coves where you can enjoy a swim. You really need your own transport to visit, though a taxi from Marathon is pricey but worth it. ☒ *Grammatiko* ☩ *15 km (9 miles) northeast of Marathon* ☎ *22940/63477* ☑ *€4* ☉ *Closed Tues.*

🔔 Beaches

Rhamnous Beach

BEACH—SIGHT | The coves at Rhamnous, approached via a rough road about 2,000 feet before the entrance to the archaeological site, are cozy and remote. These are favorite swimming spots of nudists and free campers, although the latter is technically forbidden. Beware of spiny sea urchins when swimming off the rocks from this pebbly beach. **Amenities:** parking (free). **Best for:** nudists; solitude; walking. ☒ *Grammatiko* ☩ *15 km (9 miles) northeast of Marathon.*

★ Schinias Beach

BEACH—SIGHT | **FAMILY** | The best beach in the north of Attica, just beyond Marathon, is this long, sandy, pine-backed stretch called Schinias. It's crowded with Athenians on the weekend, has a few simple tavernas along the sand and quite a lot of beach bars, and is frequently struck by strong winds that windsurfers love in summer. A dirt-and-sand track skirts the pine groves behind the beach, providing access to some relatively remote stretches. Campers like to settle in the Schinias forest during the summer, taking care not to disturb its precious natural habitat, which is enviromentally protected. **Amenities:** food and drink; lifeguards; parking (free); showers; toilets; water sports. **Best for:** sunset; swimming; walking; windsurfing. ✉ *Schinias* ✢ *10 km (6 miles) southeast of Marathon.*

Sesi Beach

BEACH—SIGHT | The tiny Sesi Beach is about 400 meters long and has a small canteen, while the main pebble beach has crystal clear waters, a couple of tavernas, and a beach bar. There are also a few smaller stretches of sand accessible on foot that are fairly private. Bring your own sun beds and umbrellas because there's nothing for rent here. **Amenities:** food and drink. **Best for:** solitude; swimming. ✉ *Grammatiko* ✢ *6 km (4 miles) northeast of Marathon.*

Varnavas Beach

BEACH—SIGHT | This fine-pebbled beach is reached from Varnavas village, north of Marathon. There is a lifeguard here during the summer months and a few tavernas nearby where you can enjoy a post-swim snack. It's a popular spearfishing spot. **Amenities:** food and drink; lifeguards; parking (free). **Best for:** swimming; snorkeling. ✉ *Varnavas* ✢ *15 km (9 miles) northeast of Marathon.*

🍴 Restaurants

Argentina

$$ | **ARGENTINE** | While living in South America, owner Nikos Milonas learned how to carve beef, how high to fire up the grill, and exactly how to time a perfect medium-rare steak (size XXL!). The meat-loving population of Greece has been benefiting from his expertise ever since. **Known for:** incredible steaks; long waits (up to an hour) if you don't call in advance; huge portions. [$] *Average main: €25* ✉ *Bitakou 3, Vothonas* ✢ *About 1½ km (1 mile) after Marathon dam crossing* ☎ *22940/66476* ⏲ *Closed Mon.*

Isidora Fish Tavern

$$ | **SEAFOOD** | Front tables at this lively and friendly spot, a perfect stop after a day at the beach, are nearly immersed in the sea, and others are tucked into a Mediterranean garden. Family matriarch Isidora orchestrates the delicious homemade meals, many including fresh fish of the day, accompanied by rich seasonal salads and fresh village bread. **Known for:** beachside setting; fresh fish; great views. [$] *Average main: €20* ✉ *Perikleous 5* ☎ *22940/56467* 💳 *No credit cards.*

To Archontiko tou Lekka

$$ | **GREEK** | Meat is what Marathon does well. The city isn't a gastronomic gem, but it has some decent grillhouses. **Known for:** excellent meat dishes; family-run; friendly service. [$] *Average main: €15* ✉ *10 Kazantzaki* ☎ *22940/67374* 🌐 *www.archontikolekka.gr.*

🛏 Hotels

Staying in Marathon is not the most appealing prospect, as it doesn't have a huge amount of interesting accommodation. This is why it's better to make your base in the beachy suburbs to the south, which offer plusher stays. You'll need a car to get around, as public transport isn't all that prolific, but the same can be said for visiting the sights in this part of Attica, so take advantage of your freedom.

Cabo Verde

$ | **HOTEL** | A convenient spot in the seaside suburb of Mati, south of Marathon and near the airport and the port of Rafina, comes with a pool and spa that compliment spacious, comfortable guest rooms. **Pros:** relaxing views of the harbor; 20 minutes from the airport; simple but stylish rooms. **Cons:** it's a bit far from anywhere interesting; lackluster restaurant (but nice pool bar); hard to reach by public transport. [$] *Rooms from: €80* ✉ *Poseidonos 41, Mati* ✢ *7 km (4½ miles) south of Marathon*

☎ *22940/33111* 🌐 *www.caboverde.gr* 🛏 *38 rooms* 🍴 *Free breakfast.*

Marathon Beach Resort

$$ | **HOTEL** | **FAMILY** | A retro-Florida vibe permeates this sprawling, beautifully maintained mini-resort where simple but stylish rooms, decked in dazzling whites with bright accent colors, surround an enormous garden and pool terrace, all just steps from the beach. **Pros:** simple but comfortable and pleasant rooms; beautiful pool area; good choice of affordable dining options. **Cons:** no elevator; few luxuries; not all rooms have sea views. [$] *Rooms from: €140* ✉ *Poseidonos 12, Nea Makri* ☎ *22940/95022* 🌐 *www.marathonbeachresort.com* 🕓 *Closed Nov.–Apr.* 🛏 *74 rooms* 🍴 *Free breakfast.*

Activities

RUNNING

Athens Authentic Marathon

RUNNING | Usually held every year in early November (though 2020 was cancelled for obvious reasons), this route follows roughly the same course taken in 490 BC by the courier Pheidippides, when he carried to Athens the news of victory over the Persians, the 42-km (26-mile) race is open to men and women of all ages. Starting in Marathon, it finishes at the Panathenaic Stadium in Athens. In recent years, the event has been updated to include pasta parties and other events for runners. If following in all of Pheidippides's footsteps is too much for you, the 5-km (3-mile), 10-km (6-mile), or power-walking races are good options. Even if you don't have the stamina for the race, cheer on the runners at the end of the route in Athens—they represent many ages, nationalities, and physiques. Those who finish the course enter triumphantly into the marble stadium, where the first modern Olympics were held in 1896. ✉ *Marathonos, at 25th Martiou St.* ☎ *21118/77718* 🌐 *www.athensauthenticmarathon.gr.*

WATER SPORTS

Moraitis Beach Sports Center

WATER SPORTS | This part of Attica is ideal for all kinds of water sports, and accredited instructors at Moraitis specialize in windsurfing. The beach volleyball tournament is also popular with local players, while many triathletes use the center as a basis for their year-round training. ✉ *Poseidonos 210, Moraitis Beach* ☎ *22940/55965* 🌐 *www.moraitisbeach.com.*

Mt. Parnitha Πάρνηθα

62 km (38 miles) west of Marathon, 33 km (20½ miles) northwest of Downtown Athens.

The summit of Mt. Parnitha (1,413 m [4,635 feet]), Attica's highest mountain, affords splendid views of the plain of Athens. Sadly, large swaths of its protected national park, particularly on the western side, were destroyed in 2007 by wildfires; even today little more than an eighth of the 3,634 hectares lost to fire has been reforested. Yet one unexpected effect benefit to this tragedy has been a boom in wildlife. Recent years have seen a steep increase in the mountain's wild red deer population (now topping 500); these can be spotted on many of the mountain's trails and lookouts, and are profoundly ambivalent about humans, allowing you to get a close look. They are joined by wild boar, Cretan wild goats (set loose from an old wildlife reserve when the 2007 fire struck), and even wolves and jackals attracted by the abundance of prey—though sightings of predators are rare.

In April and May the forest blooms with wildflowers, red poppies, white crocuses, purple irises, and numerous species of orchid. Many Athenians come year-round, especially on Sunday, to enjoy the clean air, mountain bike trails, picnic spots, or just to take the cable car for the views. So famed was the area for its air quality that a tuberculosis sanatorium operated here until the 1960s; next to its burnt-out shell now stands the Park of Souls, an open-air gallery of sculptures in memory of those who were lost. Near the summit also stands the mountain's rather fusty casino, where the cable car finishes. At the time of writing this building was due to relocate, as new laws now allow casinos within the city limits, and its land is set to be returned to the park.

On the southeast side of the mountain is the most unsual sight of all: the abandoned royal summer palace of Tatoi. Its grounds are free to wander since royalty was abolished here in the 1970s, though legal wrangling over what to do with the estate has meant its buildings here have been sadly neglected and are off-limits to visitors. Cycling and walking tours of the park are offered by a number of local operators.

GETTING HERE AND AROUND

The easiest way to get here is to drive, taking the E75 to Kaliftaki, then turning northwest along Leof. Kimis to Thrakomakedones, where you'll find routes leading up into the mountain and the cable car station. If going by public transport, take bus 721 from Larisis Railways Station to Acharnes, where you can pick up bus 726 to Apheteria and walk from there to Thrakomakedones; it takes about one hour. To reach Tatoi, take a taxi from Thrakomakedones; it's an 8-km walk from there and public transport doesn't go the old palace. *For more information on Athens buses and bus stations, see Bus and Train in the Athens chapter.*

Sights

★ Tatoi Royal Estate

HOUSE | What was once a beautiful summer retreat for the Greek royal family is slowly being reclaimed by the wild. It's an unusual tale, even by Greek standards, and a setting that makes for a remarkable walk on the southeast slopes of Mt. Parnitha. The first piece of the estate was bought by King George I in 1871, who slowly built up the land around it and commissioned a mansion in the style of Russia's Peterhof Palace. Over the next century the estate grew and grew as vineyards, a cemetery, stables, a pool, a hotel, and various buildings were added to its 10,000 acres. Then it all came to a halt. The abolition of the monarchy in 1974 preceded a long-running dispute over the estate's ownership and saw its buildings fall sadly into neglect. Since then, clumsy attempts at restoration and plans to turn it into a museum have come to little, and today its buildings, now mostly boarded up, are off-limits to visitors. The grounds are free to roam by the public until sunset and have parking nearby to allow access. That is the extent of its facilities, however; there are no cafés, toilets, or running water inside the park. Yet the estate's fall from grace doesn't diminish what is an astonishing walk, as you wander through pine-scented forest and contemplate the fleeting nature of wealth in this "ghost palace." ✉ *Tatiou Rd., Mt Parnitha* ✣ *Southest side of Mt. Parnitha* ☎ *69759/47248* 🌐 *www.tatoi.org.*

Restaurants

★ Pappas

$ | BARBECUE | This family-run taverna at the foot of Mt. Parnitha is popular for its mountain views and cozy fireplace in the winter, as well as for its serene garden with tall plane trees providing a much needed respite from the summer heat. The menu is built around grilled meat, mostly ribs and chops, served by the kilo on heaping platters. **Known for:** homey atmosphere; refreshing garden; grilled meats. [$] *Average main: €13* ✉ *Thessalonikis 2, off Athens–Lamia road, Acharnés* ☎ *21024/31232.*

The Tatoi Palace, which has fallen into a state of neglect, was once the summer residence of the former Greek royal family.

🏃 Activities

HIKING

There are 12 marked hiking trails, with varying degrees of difficulty, on Mt. Parnitha.

Bafi Refuge

HIKING/WALKING | A 2.2-km (1.4-mile) ascent from the church of Agia Triada (takes approximately 40 minutes) leads to the Bafi Refuge, run by the EOS Hellenic Mountaineering Association of Athens, where basic board and lodging are available. The refuge has a fireplace and kitchen; water is piped in from a nearby spring. The refuge remains open all year long. Two-person rooms from €65 (breakfast included). The association is also a good source of information on trails in the area. ✉ *Parnithos Rd., Mt Parnitha* ☎ *21032/12355 EOS Hellenic Mountaineering Association* ⊕ *www. mpafi.gr.*

Church of Agios Petros

HIKING/WALKING | One of the milder, and most pleasant, hikes on Mt. Parnitha follows a marked trail from the church of Ayia Triada (Church of the Holy Trinity) through the national park to the church of Ayios Petros at Mola Forest. The path leads past the Skipiza spring, providing spectacular views of western Attica and the town of Thebes along the way. The 6-km (4-mile) walk takes about two hours, and you might spot deer darting among the trees. ✉ *Mola forest, Off Parnithos Rd., Mt Parnitha.*

Flabouri Refuge

HIKING/WALKING | From Bafi, one trail turns south, tracing the fir and pine woods along the Houni ravine, and skirting the craggy Flabouri peak—a favorite nesting place of the park's raptors. This trail intersects with another path leading to the Flabouri Refuge, a basic hikers' hut run by EOS Acharnon Hiking Club. You can stay the night or enjoy their views of Mt. Parnitha and hearty food, before exploring more trails. Beds are just mattresses placed on a wooden floor; €12 per person. ☒ *Off Parnithos Rd., Acharnés* ☎ *21024/64666* ⊕ *www.flabouri.gr.*

Monastery of Daphni
Μονή Δαφνίου

61 km (38 miles) southwest of Mt. Parnitha, 11 km (7 miles) west of Athens.

Daphni means "laurel tree," a species that was sacred to the god Apollo. The myth says that Eros made Apollo fall in love with a nymph after he mocked the God of Love's archery skills; when he finally caught her, she turned into a laurel. Apollo's sanctuary once occupied this site on the Sacred Way between Athens and Eleusis. The original temple was destroyed in AD 395 after the anti-pagan edicts of the Emperor Theodosius. The Orthodox monastery that stands here now was probably first established in the 6th century, incorporating materials of Apollo's sanctuary in the church and walls, though what survives now is mostly from the 11th century. Reoccupied by Orthodox monks some five centuries later, the Daphni complex has since been host to a barracks and a mental institution. The monastery, a UNESCO World Heritage site, is once again open to the public even though restoration work is ongoing. To reach it, take the metro (Line 3) to Agia Marina, where you can catch either the 866 or 876 bus to the monastery.

 Sights

★ Monastery of Daphni
RELIGIOUS SITE | Sacked by Crusaders, inhabited by Cistercian monks, and desecrated by Turks, this UNESCO World Heritage site remains one of the most splendid Byzantine monuments in Greece. Dating mostly from the 11th century (the golden age of Byzantine art), the church contains a series of miraculously preserved mosaics without parallel in the legacy of Byzantium: powerful portraits of figures from the Old and New Testaments, images of Christ and the Virgin Mary in the *Presentation of the Virgin,* and, in the golden dome, a stern *Pantokrator* ("ruler of all") surrounded by 16 Old Testament prophets who predicted his coming. The mosaics, made of chips of four different types of marble, are set against gold. An ongoing long-term restoration project makes it hard to see some of the mosaics, but this doesn't take away much of the awe inspired by the craftmanship of the Byzantine masters. ☒ *Peristeri* ✛ *At the end of Iera Odos, at Athinon* ☎ *21058/11558* ⊕ *www.culture. gr* ☒ *Free* ⊗ *Closed Mon. and Tues.*

Eleusis Ελευσίνα

11 km (7 miles) west of the Monastery of Daphni, 22 km (14 miles) west of Athens.

The growing city of Athens has long-since co-opted the land around what was Eleusis (now a modern city known as Elefsina), placing shipyards in the pristine gulf and steel mills and petrochemical plants along its shores. The resulting city is far from pretty, but that didn't stop it being a European Capital of Culture in 2021. The reason for this lies far more in the area's past than its industrial present, dating back to the Mycenean era. Back then there stretched in every direction fields of corn and barley sacred to the goddess Demeter, whose realm was symbolized by the sheaf and sickle, and whose cultish following spread far. Initiates were sworn to uphold their secrets on pain of death, and each year pilgrims would walk its Sacred Way in a huge festival that attracted thousands across the ancient world. What remains today is a scattering of ruins that only hints at the power this cult once held. You can reach the site, like nearby Daphni Monastery, via the metro (Line 3) and the connecting 876 bus.

Sights

Sanctuary of Demeter

MUSEUM | This once sacred place lies on an eastern slope, at the foot of the ancient acropolis protecting the settlement of Eleusis, hardly visible amid the modern buildings of the main square of Elefsina (or Eleusis, as it was called in the ancient Greek world). The legend of Demeter and her daughter Persephone explained for the ancients the cause of the seasons and the origins of agriculture.

It was to Eleusis that Demeter traveled in search of Persephone after the girl had been kidnapped by Hades, god of the underworld. Zeus himself interceded to restore her to the distraught Demeter but succeeded only partially, giving mother and daughter just half a year together.

Nevertheless, in gratitude to King Keleos of Eleusis, who had given her refuge in her time of need, Demeter presented his son Triptolemos with wheat seeds, the knowledge of agriculture, and a winged chariot so he could spread them to mankind. Keleos built a *megaron* (large hall) in Demeter's honor, the first Eleusinian sanctuary.

The worship of Demeter took the form of mysterious rites, part purification and part drama, and both the Lesser and the Greater Eleusinian rituals closely linked Athens with the sanctuary. The procession for the Greater Eleusinia began and ended there, following the route of the Sacred Way (along the avenue still called Iera Odos today).

Much of what you see now in the sanctuary is of Roman construction or repair, although physical remains on the site date back to the Mycenaean period. Follow the old Sacred Way to the great *propylaea* (gates) and continue on to the Precinct of Demeter, which was strictly off-limits on pain of death to any but the initiated. The *Telesterion* (Temple of Demeter), now a vast open space surrounded by battered tiers of seats, dates to 600 BC, when it was the hall of initiation. It had a roof supported by six rows of seven columns, presumably so the mysteries would be obscured, and it could accommodate 3,000 people.

The museum, just beyond, contains pottery and sculpture, particularly of the Roman period. Although the site is closed at night, you can see the sacred court and propylaea from a distance thanks to special lighting by Pierre Bideau, the French expert who also designed the lighting for the Acropolis in Athens. ✉ *Gkioka 1, Eleusis (Elefsina)* ☎ *21055/46019* 💶 *€6.*

Osios Loukas
Όσιος Λουκάς

150 km (93 miles) northwest of Athens.

The monastic complex at Osios Loukas, still inhabited by a few monks, is notable for its exquisite mosaics and its dramatic location, looming on a prominent rise with a sweeping view of the Elikonas peaks and the sparsely inhabited but fertile valley. The outside of the buildings is typically Byzantine, with rough stonework interspersed with an arched brick pattern. The spot is especially beautiful in February when the almond branches explode with a profusion of delicate oval pinkish-white blooms.

GETTING HERE AND AROUND

Osios Loukas is located near the town of Distomo in the Voiotia prefecture, about 160 km (99 miles) north of Athens. Driving is easiest, but there are also buses. Take one of the many KTEL Livadias buses that depart daily from bus Terminal B (Liossion) in Athens for Livadia. The one-way journey takes 2½ hours; e-tickets can be bought online at the KTEL Livadias site (🌐 *ktellivadias.gr*; in Greek). From there, you can take the local bus to

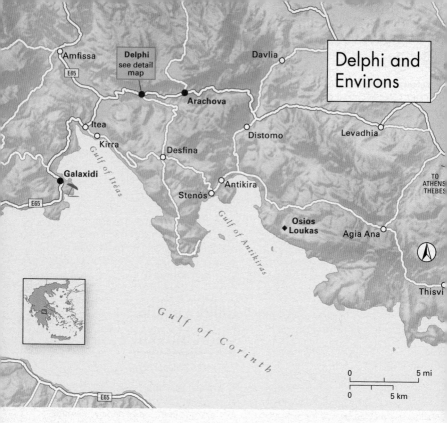

Delphi and Environs

Amfissa
Delphi
see detail
map
Davlia
E65
Arachova
Itea
Kirra
Distomo
Levadhia
Desfina
Galaxidi
Antikira
Stenós
TO ATHENS THEBES
E65
Gulf of Itéas
Osios Loukas
Agia Ana
Gulf of Antikiras
Thisvi
Gulf of Corinth
0   5 mi
0   5 km
E65

Osios Loukas, for an additional fare. *For more information on Athens buses and bus stations, see Bus and Train in the Athens chapter.*

Sights

★ Osios Loukas

RELIGIOUS SITE | Luke (Loukas) the Hermit—not the evangelist who wrote a book of the New Testament—was a medieval oracle who founded a church at this site and lived here until his death in AD 953. He was probably born in Delphi, after his family fled from Aegina during a raid of Saracen pirates. This important monastery was founded by the emperor Romanos II in AD 961, in recognition of the accuracy of Loukas's prophecy that Crete would be liberated by an emperor named Romanos. The *katholikon*, a masterpiece of Byzantine architecture,

was built in the 11th century over the tomb of Luke. It follows to perfection the Byzantine cross-in-a-square plan under a central dome and was inspired by the Ayia Sophia in Constantinople; in turn, it was used as a model for both the Monastery of Daphni and Mystra churches. Impressive mosaics in the narthex and in portions of the domed nave are set against a rich gold background and done in the somber but expressive 11th-century hieratic style by artists from Thessaloniki and Constantinople. Particularly interesting are the reactions evident on the faces of the apostles, which range from passivity to surprise as Christ washes their feet in the mosaic of *Niptir*, to the far left of the narthex.

In the second niche of the entrance is a mosaic showing Loukas sporting a helmet and beard, with his arms raised.

The engaging *Nativity, Presentation in the Temple,* and the *Baptism of Christ* mosaics are on the curved arches that support the dome. Two priceless icons from the late 16th century, *Daniel in the Lion's Den* and *Shadrach, Meshach, and Abednego in the Flames of the Furnace,* by Damaskinos, a teacher of El Greco, were stolen a few years back from the white marble iconostasis in the little apse and have been replaced with copies. The tomb of Osios Loukas is in the crypt of the katholikon; his relics, formerly in the Vatican, were moved here in 1987, making the monastery an official shrine. A highlight of the complex, evocatively clinging to a pine-scented hillside, is the Theotokos (Mother of God), a small communal church dedicated to the Virgin Mary, on the left as you enter. On the periphery are the monks' cells and a refectory, now restored, which has been used as a sculpture museum since 1993. To visit you must wear either long pants or a skirt. Bring a small flashlight to help see some of the frescoes. ✉ *On rise above valley of Mt. Elikon* ☎ *22670/22797* 💰 *€4.*

Arachova Αράχωβα

24 km (16 miles) northwest of Osios Loukas, 157 km (97 miles) northwest of Athens.

Gray-stone houses with red-tile roofs cling to the steep slopes of Mt. Parnassus, the highest mountain in Greece after Mt. Olympus, to form the small ski town of Arachova. Winter weekends bring sophisticated Athenians headed for the slopes as hotel prices soar and rooms are snapped up. During this season its cobblestone streets fill with SUVs carrying skis aloft, and the village taverns and bars get crowded after dark as people warm their weary bones before the fires. In summer, meanwhile, there are hardly any Greek tourists in Arachova and not everything may be open, which

leaves one of the best hill walking spots in the country free to roam. Surprisingly little is made of the area's incredible hiking, with the E4 walking trail running right through its heart. Hikes are best done in the cooler months of late spring and autumn. Basic hiking maps can be picked up at some hotels, but it's best to come with your own. Treks from here and neighboring Delphi yield incredible views along routes to old monasteries, wild gorges, and mountain plateaus, and include the Corycean cave, dedicated to the god Pan and linked via an ancient pilgrim's footpath. This is a town for all seasons, and not just winter.

GETTING HERE AND AROUND

KTEL Fokidas buses (⊕ *www.ktel-foki-das.gr*) servicing Arachova depart from the Terminal B (Liossion) bus station in Athens. The journey takes about three hours. It is the same regional bus that continues on to Delphi (15 minutes away) and there are typically two-to-three daily departures, beginning at 7:30 am. Taxis between Arachova and Delphi cost €15 one way. *For more information on Athens buses and bus stations, see Bus and Train in the Athens chapter.*

 Sights

Agios Georgios Church

FESTIVAL | If you're lucky enough to be in Arachova for the festival on St. George's Day—April 23 (or the Monday after Easter if April 23 falls during Lent)—you're in for the time of your life. St. George the dragon slayer, is the patron saint of Arachova, and the largest church on the top of the highest hill in town is dedicated to him. So, naturally, the festival here lasts three days and nights, starting with a procession behind the generations-old silver icon from the church, in which the villagers don the local costumes, most of them ornately embroidered silken and brocaded heirlooms that testify to the rich cultural heritage of the town. The festival is kicked off in fine form

For Byzantine splendor, look no further than the paintings covering the crypt of the great monastery at Osios Loukas.

with the race of the *yeroi*, the old men of the town, who are astonishingly agile as they clamber up the hill above the church without so much as a gasp for air. The following days are filled with athletic contests, cooking competitions, and, at night, passionate dancing in the tavernas until long after the goats go home. Visitors are welcome to partake of a feast held outside St. George (Agios Georgios) church that features Mt. Parnassus's legendary roast lamb and feta cheese and a steady flow of Arachova wine. ✉ *Arachova* ✥ *Church of Agios Georgios (off Agios Georgios St.)* ☎ 🌐 *www.panigiraki.gr.*

Folklore Museum & Clock Tower

CLOCK | This small, two-room museum has some fascinating old black-and-white shots of traditionally dressed locals and festivals as well examples of their clothing. Proceed behind the museum for access to the wonderfully moody-looking clocktower, which has been destroyed and rebuilt numerous times having been destroyed by earthquakes and Nazis alike. The view from above soars over the red-tiled roofs of this noble town and across to the spectacular gorge below. ✉ *EO Livadiass-Amfissas* ☎ *22670/31630* 🌐 *www.arachovamuseum.gr* 🎫 *Free.*

Restaurants

Dasargyres

$ | **GREEK** | Arachova's oldest taverna (more that a hundred years old) still draws gargantuan crowds—causing occasional staff surliness—simply because of the amazing food. Lamb with oregano, and beef in a red sauce are both served with *hilopites*, the thin egg noodles cut into thousands of tiny squares, for which the area is known. **Known for:** historic tavern; wine straight from the barrel; excellent food. $ *Average main: €14* ✉ *Delfon 56* ☎ *22670/31291* ▭ *No credit cards* ⏲ *Closed Aug.*

Panagiota

$$ | **GREEK** | It is well worth climbing the 263 steps leading from the main road up to the church of Agios Georgios, where the lovely smells wafting from the kitchen f this hilltop institution, from the 1930s, will prepare you for a tasty meal. Start with local specialty *opsimotyri* (tart yogurt dip) and the house salad of shredded red cabbage, carrot, and grilled mushrooms. **Known for:** homey atmosphere; traditional mountain dishes; cozy setting. $ *Average main: €18* ✉ *Ano Arachova, behind Agios Georgios* ☎ *22670/32735* ⊘ *Closed Mon.–Wed. in June–Aug.*

Taverna To Agnantio

$ | GREEK | In the winter you can warm yourself at your choice of several fireplaces in this old stone house that's been deemed a historic building by the state, and look out at the excellent views of the mountains. *Tirokafteri*, a piquant cheese spread, is the perfect accompaniment to the stone-ground country bread to start. Follow with a sampling of the large purplish Amfissa olives, *fava* (mashed yellow split peas, lemon, and raw onions), or the potent *skordalia* (garlic-mashed potato spread). **Known for:** cozy fireside dining; mountain views; hearty food. $ *Average main: €18* ✉ *Delfon* ⊕ *Next to town hall and clock tower* ☎ *22670/32114* ⊕ *www.oagnantio.gr* ⊘ *Closed Jun.–Aug.*

☕ Coffee and Quick Bites

Belleville Patisserie & Cafe

| CAFÉ | A recent makeover has elevated this old timer. Fine views from the rear terrace overlooking the rock-topped clocktower and valley accompany tasty waffles, cakes, pastries, and coffee. **Known for:** great views; waffles; recently redone. $ *Average main: €5* ✉ *Livadias Amfissas 44* ☎ *22670/31492* ⊕ *www.laxarotoparamithi.gr.*

Café Bonjour

| CAFÉ | Catch a coffee or freshly squeezed mixed-fruit juice at this popular hangout in tree-covered Lakka Square—and don't forget their croissants: the best in town! **Known for:** freshly squeezed juice; delicious croissants; good coffee. $ *Average main: €5* ✉ *Delfon, Lakka Sq.*

🛏 Hotels

★ Boutique Hotel Skamnos

$$ | HOTEL | FAMILY | This ski hotel and mountain lodge offers some of the region's best views, along with alluring, wood-ceilinged guest rooms, plus such luxurious perks as a heated indoor pool, outdoor Jacuzzi, and a spa. **Pros:** incredible mountain views, perfect for relaxation; relatively good value for the money; attractive surroundings. **Cons:** some smallish rooms; a bit of a drive to Arachova for nightlife and food; can be very busy in season. $ *Rooms from: €145* ✉ *Voiotia* ⊕ *On road between Arachova and Parnassus Ski Center* ☎ *22670/31927* ⊕ *www.skamnos.com* ⇥ *22 rooms* ⦿ *Free breakfast.*

★ Elafivolia

$$ | HOTEL | FAMILY | These half-dozen apartments, a few kilometers outside town, feel far more isolated than they are. **Pros:** incredible views and setting; great pool and BBQ area; breakfast delivered to your balcony. **Cons:** it's a 15-minute walk along a main road; you'll need a car or a taxi to get there; no amenities adjacent. $ *Rooms from: €170* ✉ *Arachova* ☎ *69482/83989* ⊕ *www.elafivolia.gr* ⇥ *6 suites* ⦿ *Free breakfast.*

Ellinon Thea

$ | HOTEL | This winter-style lodge embraces the skiing vibe with its simple wood-finished rooms and all-round cozy feel. **Pros:** cozy accomodation; the pool is small but deep; disabled facilities in ground-floor rooms. **Cons:** the rooms are a little basic; it's a walk from the main strip of restaurants; the road outside can be noisy. $ *Rooms from: €90* ✉ *Agios Georgios* ☎ *22670/32115* ⊕ *www.ellinonthea.com* ⇥ *24 rooms* ⦿ *Free breakfast.*

Nightlife

On winter weekends Arachova streets are jammed with Athenians who come almost as much for the nightlife as for the skiing. Clubs change frequently, but favorites remain.

Akouarela Restaurant Bar

BARS/PUBS | Greek music—sometimes live—sets the lively tone: drop by for a drink or tuck into a large gourmet menu of meaty offerings Friday, Saturday, and Sunday nights. In the small hours, you can still get finger food, and some center tables might be removed to make room for dancing and, even better, for some legendary "flower wars" among happy club goers. Smart dress is strongly recommended. ⊠ *Lakka Sq.* ☎ *22670/32660*.

Husky

CAFES—NIGHTLIFE | The exterior of this cozy café-bar, tucked away from the main road, is smothered in greenery, lending it a slightly fairy-tale vibe that blends with the quirky log cabin look (complete with fake animal skins and paper trophy heads) inside. The appetizing brunch menu is all cheese-slathered toasties and syrup-dripping pancakes, while in the evening it turns into a slick bar with fine cocktails and DJs. ⊠ *Platanos* ☎ *69445/23431*.

Isidora Gallery

WINE BARS—NIGHTLIFE | Don't be misled by the name: a wine bar, not a gallery (although temporary exhibitions of up-and-coming Greek artists are often shown here) combines the traditional village aura of an old mansion (built in 1760) with a monklike austerity accentuated by tall candles. A selection of excellent Greek wine is on offer, or you can opt for one of the cocktails. The cheese platters are an ideal accompaniment to your drink, while the jazzy notes in the background will not obstruct your conversation. It opens nightly at 7 pm. ⊠ *Odyssea Androutsou 297* ☎ *69444/70665*.

Shopping

Arachova was known even in pre-ski days as a place to shop for wool, with stores selling rugs and weavings lining the main street. The modern mass-produced bedspreads, *flokatis* (woolen rugs, sometime dyed vivid colors), and kilim-style carpets sold today are reasonably priced. If you poke into dark corners in the stores, you still might turn up something made of local wool; anything that claims to be antique bears a higher price. Also look for anything made of carved wood, from eating utensils to furniture, as well as local foodstuffs like the delicious Parnassus honey, the local cheese *formaella* (often served warm), and the fiery hot *rakomelo* (a combination of anise liqueur and honey), which is served in most of the bars and cafés on a cold winter's night to warm those who've been outside all day.

Pappos-Baldoumis—Snow Republic Ski Shop and Ski School

SPORTING GOODS | The biggest ski school in Greece operates a couple of well-equipped ski shops, including one in Arachova's main square and a second one in Paralia Distomou, down on the coast. ⊠ *Lakka Sq.* ☎ *22670/31552* ⊕ *www. skischool.gr*.

Activities

HIKING

Arachova and its environs are made for exploring on foot, either by simply walking a country lane to see where it leads or picking up one of the hiking trails like the E4 through Parnassus National Park or the ancient footpath down the mountain. The 8,061-foot summit of Mt. Parnassus is now easily accessible, thanks to roads opened up for the ski areas. The less hardy can drive almost up to the summit. There are few local trekking resources but tour company **Trekking Hellas** (*see Tours*) run a number of guided trips on the ancient paths around Delphi and Arachova, visiting the Corycean Cave and scaling the Parnassus summit.

SKIING

Parnassos Ski Center

SKIING/SNOWBOARDING | The center, just 40 minutes from Arachova, comprises 23 slopes, cycle and hiking trails, and thermal springs. The skiing is spread across one large area, with good restaurants, shops, ski schools, and several more-challenging runs. Perks include night ski parties. ⊠ Kelaria ✛ 25 km (17 miles) north of Arachova ☎ 22340/22700 ⊕ www.parnassos-ski.gr ☜ From €30 weekends, €15 weekdays.

Delphi Δελφοί

10 km (6 miles) west of Arachova, 189 km (118 miles) northwest of Athens.

Up in the mountains, modern Delphi is perched dramatically on the edge of a grove leading to the sea, west of an extraordinary ancient site. The hospitable people of modern Delphi take great pride in their town. They maintain a tradition of comfortable, small hotels and a main street thick with restaurants and souvenir shops. It's no secret, though. In summer, a few thousand people a day will find their way up here, to what is essentially a town made up of two main streets. They come for one thing: Ancient Delphi, the home of a famous oracle in antiquity. It's easily reached from almost any point in the central town, at most a 10-to-15-minute walk. When the archaeological site is first seen from the road, it would appear that there is hardly anything left to attest to the existence of the ancient religious city. Only the Treasury of the Athenians and a few other columns are left standing, but once you are within the precincts, ascending the slopes, the plan becomes clearer and the layout is revealed in such detail that it is possible to conjure up a vision of what the scene must have once been when Delphi was the holiest place in all Greece.

GETTING HERE AND AROUND

Despite its fame, there are no trains to Delphi, just buses. In fact, the same KTEL Fokidas buses from Athens that go to Arachova continue on to Delphi, for no additonal fare. The journey lasts 3 hours. The first KTEL bus leaves Athens Terminal B (Liossion) typically at 7:30 am or 10:30 am, depending on the day. *For more information on Athens buses and bus stations, see Bus and Train in the Athens chapter.*

◉ Sights

At first the settlement probably was sacred to Gaia, the mother goddess; toward the end of the Greek Dark Ages (circa 1100–800 BC), the site incorporated the cult of Apollo. According to Plutarch, who was a priest of Apollo at Delphi, the oracle was discovered by chance, when a shepherd noticed that his flock went into a frenzy when it came near a certain chasm in the rock. When he approached, he also came under a spell and began to utter prophecies, as did his fellow villagers. Eventually a *Pythia,* an anointed woman over 50 who lived in seclusion, was the one who sat on the three-footed stool and interpreted the prophecy.

On oracle day, the seventh of the month, the Pythia prepared herself by washing in the Castalian Fountain and undergoing a purification involving barley smoke and laurel leaves. If the male priests of Apollo determined the day was propitious for prophesying, she entered the Temple of Apollo, where she drank the Castalian water, chewed laurel leaves, and presumably sank into a trance. Questions presented to her received strange and garbled answers, which were then translated into verse by the priests. A number of the lead tablets on which questions were inscribed have been uncovered, but the official answers were inscribed only in the memories of questioners and priests. Those that have survived, from various sources, suggest the equivocal nature of these sibylline emanations: perhaps the most famous is the answer given to King Croesus of Lydia, who asked if he should attack the Persians. "Croesus, having crossed the Halys river, will destroy a great realm," said the Pythia. Thus encouraged, he crossed it, only to find his *own* empire destroyed.

During the 8th and 7th centuries BC, the oracle's advice played a significant role in the colonization of southern Italy and Sicily (Magna Graecia) by Greece's Amphictyonic League. By 582 BC the Pythian Games had become a quadrennial festival similar to those held at Olympia. Increasingly an international center, Delphi attracted supplicants from beyond the Greek mainland, including such valued clients as King Midas and King Croesus, both hailing from wealthy kingdoms in Asia Minor. During this period of prosperity, many cities built treasure houses at Delphi. The sanctuary was threatened during the Persian War but never attacked, and it continued to prosper in spite of the fact that Athens and Sparta, two of its most powerful patrons, were locked in war.

Delphi came under the influence first of Macedonia and then of the Aetolian League (290–190 BC) before yielding to the Romans in 189 BC. Although the Roman general Sulla plundered Delphi in 86 BC, there were at least 500 bronze statues left to be collected by Nero in AD 66, and the site was still full of fine works of art when Pausanias visited and described it a century later. The emperor Hadrian restored many sanctuaries in Greece, including Delphi's, but within a century or two the oracle was silent. In AD 385 Theodosius abolished the oracle. Only in the late 19th century did French excavators begin to uncover the site of Apollo.

★ Ancient Delphi

ARCHAEOLOGICAL SITE | After a square surrounded by late-Roman porticoes, pass through the main gate to Ancient Delphi and continue on to the **Sacred Way,** the approach to the Altar of Apollo. Walk between building foundations and bases for votive dedications, stripped now of ornament and statue, mere scraps of what was one of the richest collections of art and treasures in antiquity. Thanks to the 2nd-century AD writings of Pausanias, archaeologists have identified treasuries built by the Thebans, the Corinthians, the Syracusans, and others—a roster of 6th- and 5th-century BC powers. The **Treasury of the Athenians,** on your left as you turn right, was built with money from the victory over the Persians at Marathon. The **Stoa of the Athenians,** northeast of the treasury, housed, among other objects, an immense cable with which the Persian king Xerxes roped together a pontoon bridge for his army to cross the Hellespont from Asia to Europe.

The **Temple of Apollo** visible today (there were three successive temples built on the site) is from the 4th century BC. Although ancient sources speak of a chasm within, there is no trace of that opening in the earth from which emanated trance-inducing vapors. Above the temple is the well-preserved **theater,** which seated 5,000. It was built in the 4th century BC, restored in about 160 BC, and later was restored again by the Romans. From a sun-warmed seat on the last tier, you see a panoramic bird's-eye view of the sanctuary and the convulsed landscape that encloses it. Also worth the climb is the view from the **stadium** still farther up the mountain, at the highest point of the ancient town. Built and restored in various periods and cut partially from the living rock, the stadium underwent a final transformation under Herodes Atticus, the Athenian benefactor of the 2nd century AD. It lies cradled in a grove of pine trees, a quiet refuge removed from the sanctuary below and

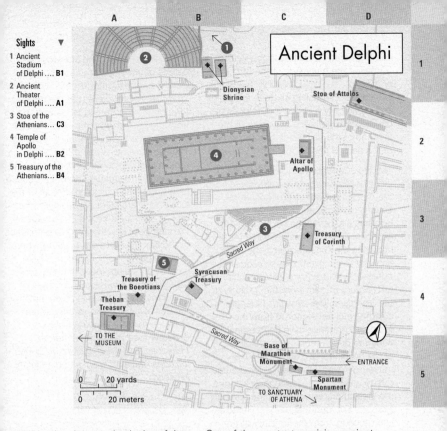

Ancient Delphi

Dionysian Shrine

Stoa of Attalos

Altar of Apollo

Treasury of Corinth

Sacred Way

Syracusan Treasury

Treasury of the Boeotians

Theban Treasury

TO THE MUSEUM

Sacred Way

Base of Marathon Monument

ENTRANCE

Spartan Monument

TO SANCTUARY OF ATHENA

0   20 yards
0   20 meters

backed by the sheer, majestic rise of the mountain. Markers for the starting line inspire many to race the length of the stadium. ⊠ *Delphi ⊹ Road to Arachova, immediately east of modern Delphi* ☎ *22650/82313* ⊕ *odysseus.culture.gr* ✉ *€12, includes the Sanctuary of Athena and Delphi Museum.*

★ **Delphi Museum**

ARCHAEOLOGICAL SITE | Visiting this museum is essential to understanding the site and sanctuary's importance to the ancient Greek world, which considered Delphi its center (literally—look for the copy of the *omphalos,* or Earth's navel, a sacred stone from the adytum of Apollo's temple). The museum is home to a wonderful collection of art and architectural sculpture, principally from the Sanctuaries of Apollo and Athena Pronoia.

One of the greatest surviving ancient bronzes on display commands a prime position in a spacious hall, set off to advantage by special lighting: the *Charioteer* is a sculpture so delicate in size (but said to be scaled to life) it is surprising when you see it in person for the first time. Created in about 470 BC, the human figure is believed to have stood on a terrace wall above the Temple of Apollo, near which it was found in 1896. It was part of a larger piece, which included a four-horse chariot. Scholars do not agree on who executed the work, although Pythagoras of Samos is sometimes mentioned as a possibility. The donor is supposed to have been a well-known patron of chariot racing, Polyzalos, the Tyrant of Gela in Sicily. Historians now believe that a sculpted likeness of Polyzalos was originally standing next to the charioteer figure. The statue commemorates a victory in the Pythian Games at the beginning of the 5th century BC. Note the eyes, inlaid with a white substance resembling enamel, the pupils consisting of two concentric onyx rings of different colors. The sculpture of the feet and of the hair clinging to the nape of the neck is perfect in detail.

Two life-size Ionian *chryselephantine* (ivory heads with gold headdresses) from the Archaic period are probably from statues of Apollo and his sister Artemis (she has a sly smirk on her face). Both gods also figure prominently in a frieze depicting the Gigantomachy, the gods' battle with the giants. These exquisitely detailed marble scenes, dated to the 6th century BC, are from the Treasury of the Siphnians. The *caryatids* (supporting columns in a female form) from the treasury's entrance have been repositioned to offer a more accurate picture of the building's size and depth. The museum's expansion also allowed curators to give more space to the *metopes*, marble sculptures depicting the feats of Greece's two greatest heroes, Heracles and Theseus, from the Treasury of the Athenians. The museum also has a pleasant outdoor café (weather permitting). ⊠ *Delphi* ⊹ *East of Ancient Delphi* ☏ *226/508–2312* ⊕ *odysseus.culture.gr* ⌧ *€12, includes Ancient Delphi and the Sanctuary of Athena.*

★ Sanctuary of Athena
ARCHAEOLOGICAL SITE | Start your tour of Old Delphi in the same way the ancients did, with a visit to the Sanctuary of Athena. Pilgrims who arrived on the shores of the Bay of Itea proceeded up to the sanctuary, where they paused before going on to the Ancient Delphi site. The most notable among the numerous remains on this terrace is the **Tholos** (Round Building), a graceful 4th-century BC ruin of Pendelic marble, the purpose and dedication of which are unknown, although round templelike buildings were almost always dedicated to a goddess. By the

2nd millennium BC, the site was already a place of worship of the earth goddess Gaia and her daughter Themis, one of the Titans. The gods expressed themselves through the murmuring of water flooding from the fault, from the rustle of leaves, and from the booming of earth tremors. The Tholos remains one of the purest and most exquisite monuments of antiquity. Theodoros, its architect, wrote a treatise on his work: an indication in itself of the exceptional architectural quality of the monument. Beneath the Phaedriades, in the cleft between the rocks, a path leads to the **Castalian Fountain,** a spring where pilgrims bathed to purify themselves before continuing. (Access to the font is prohibited because of the danger of falling rocks.) On the main road, beyond the Castalian Fountain, is the modern entrance to the sanctuary. ⊠ *Delphi* ⊹ *Below road to Arachova, before Phaedriades* ⊕ *delphi.culture.gr* ⌧ *€12, includes Ancient Delphi and the Delphi Museum.*

 **Restaurants**

Delphinios Lounge
$ | VEGETARIAN | Totter down the step bridging the streets of Apollonos and Friedrikis to discover this friendly vegetarian café-restaurant. Brightly colored tables and chairs scatter the terrace outside, with the interior potted with artwork. **Known for:** veggie food with a Greek soul; a great lunch and early dinner spot; mercurial opening hours. ⓢ *Average main: €8* ⊠ *Delphi* ⊹ *On the steps between Apollonos St. and Friedrikis St.* ☏ *22650/83236.*

Epikouros
$ | GREEK | Nothing in the simple restaurant design detracts from the view of the beautiful Itea gorge from the large, open veranda. Even in the colder months, a glass canopy protects the seating area and allows diners to look out year-round. **Known for:** views from the terrace; hearty meat dishes; a convivial atmosphere.

$] *Average main: €14* ⊠ *Vas. Pavlou and Friderikis 33* ☎ *22650/83250* ⊕ *www.epikouros.net.*

★ Taverna Vakhos

$ | GREEK | The Theorodakis family keeps watchful eye on the kitchen and on the happiness of their customers, who can choose between the spacious dining room or the large sheltered veranda with a stunning valley view. The menu is heavy on meat dishes, either grilled, boiled, or simmered in the oven, but vegetarians can put together a small feast from boiled greens and other homemade meatless Greek classics, like sweet peas in tomato sauce and stuffed cabbage leaves. **Known for:** friendly family atmosphere; homemade dishes; stunning views across to the sea. $] *Average main: €16* ⊠ *Apollonos 31* ☎ *22650/83186* ⊕ *www.vakhos.com.*

o Patriko Mas

| GREEK | A traditional stone house built in 1850 in the center of Delphi is the setting for hearty lunches and dinners. In winter, dine near the fireplace and relish hot soups, lamb chops by the kilo, and grilled local *talagani* cheeses. **Known for:** fantastic terrace views; fireside dining in winter; good local wines. $] *Average main: €14* ⊠ *Vas. Pavlou and Friderikis 69* ☎ *22650/82150* ⊕ *topatrikomas.com.*

☕ Coffee and Quick Bites

Telescope Cafe

| CAFÉ | It doesn't take an oracle to divine the reasoning behind the name of this café; two large telescopes decorate the terrace looming over the gorge below. The menu is littered with tidbits to tempt visitors, including the usual array of Greek cakes and juices, but the views are the real lure here. **Known for:** cakes to tempt—the baklava is good; great views and handy telescope; decent choice of bottled beers. $] *Average main: €4* ⊠ *Friderikis 31* ☎ *22650/83123.*

🛏 Hotels

Acropole

$ | HOTEL | Located on the lesser-strolled lower street of town, convenience, quiet, and incredible views are this simple hotel's stocks in trade. **Pros:** charming and family-run; awesome views; ample-sized rooms. **Cons:** compact bathrooms with shower only; no parking; some decor is a bit dated. $] *Rooms from: €60* ⊠ *Filellinon 13* ☎ *22650/82675* ⊕ *www.delphi.com.gr* ⤳ *35 rooms* |○| *Free breakfast.*

★ Amalia Hotel Delphi

$ | HOTEL | Clean-cut retro chic predominates at this sleek, low-lying, 1965 landmark built by well-known Greek architect Nicos Valsamakis as a part of one of the country's oldest hotel chains, with comfortable contemporary rooms and 35 acres of gardens that spread down the mountainside to olive groves and pines with, in the distance, a breathtaking vista of the Corinthian gulf. **Pros:** great vintage architecture and decoration; charming gardens and public areas; beautiful swimming pool. **Cons:** a bit farther from town center than other hotels; caters mostly to tour groups; slightly impersonal service. $] *Rooms from: €80* ⊠ *Apollonos 1* ☎ *22650/82101* ⊕ *www.amaliahoteldelphi.gr* ⤳ *180 rooms* |○| *Free breakfast.*

Fedriades Delphi Hotel

$ | B&B/INN | Certainly one of the nicer-looking spots in the center of town is accented by warm colors and a touch of Greek mountain style, while avoiding the "ancient kitsch" of several other nearby hotels. **Pros:** spic-and-span cleanliness; center-of-town location convenient to ruins; comfort at a good price. **Cons:** smallish rooms; can be noisy due to traffic on the main street; not all rooms have views. $] *Rooms from: €51* ⊠ *V. Pavlou and Friderikis 46* ☎ *22650/82370* ⊕ *www.fedriades.com* ⤳ *21 rooms; 3 suites* |○| *Free breakfast.*

 Performing Arts

FESTIVALS

⭐ **Delphi Summer Arts Festival**

FESTIVALS | Sit in the ancient stadium of Delphi or at the Frynichos theater under the stars and watch everything from the National Beijing Opera Theater's *The Bacchae* to the tragedies of Aeschylus and Euripides, and even folk and traditional music improvisations at the Summer Arts Festival, organized by the European Cultural Center of Delphi. All performances, which begin around 8:30 pm, are open to the public and charge a small fee. ✉ *Ancient Delphi site* ☎ *21033/12781* ⊕ *www.eccd.gr.*

Galaxidi Γαλαξείδι

35 km (22 miles) southwest of Delphi.

Unlike nearby Delphi, the history of Galaxidi tends more toward the modern. That's not to say it doesn't have a long past—settlements here date back to 3,000 BC—but much of it was wiped out during the War of Independence (1821–32), when the village was destroyed three times in almost as many years by the Ottomans. Galaxidi's strategic position on the coast meant its armed boats could escort Greek ships into the Corinthian Gulf, but by 1825 it had been burnt to the ground and abandoned. After the war, Galaxidi was rebuilt and it gradually began to prosper again. By 1870—thanks to shipbuilding and a thriving mercantile economy—it was launching up to 20 ships a year, and some 6,000 people lived in the area. With the invention of steamships, however, it slipped into decline, and its population dwindled with it. What remains is a remarkably intact snapshot of its 19th-century heyday, as seen in the old sea captains' homes that dot the village, often transformed into pretty boutique stays and restaurants. The Old Town is classified a historical monument and undergoes continual renovation and restoration. It all makes Galaxidi a terribly appealing destination, and one yet to be sanitized or overrun like many of the villages you'll find on the islands. It remains relatively undiscovered, except by the yacht crowd who dwell in the harbor, and a scenic base for trips to Delphi as you rise out of a flat sea of *amfissa* olive trees and up into the mountains above.

GETTING HERE AND AROUND

Only one or two buses a day make the four-hour trip from Athens to Galaxidi (€15), usually starting at 10:30 am. KTEL Fokidas buses servicing Galaxidi depart from Terminal B (Liossion) in Athens. This is the same bus that also reaches Delphi and Arachova, usually with a vehicle change in the coast town of Itea. It is a €40 taxi ride from Delphi to Galaxidi. *For more information on Athens buses and bus stations, see Bus and Tram in the Athens chapter.*

Sights

If you are a shore person rather than a mountain person, Galaxidi is a good alternative to Delphi as a base for the region. Stroll Galaxidi's narrow streets with their elegant stone mansions and squares with geraniums and palm trees, and then take a late-afternoon swim in one of the pebbly coves around the headland to the north, dine along the waterfront, and enjoy the stunning views of Galaxidi, with a mountain backdrop, reflected in the still waters.

Agios Nikolaos

RELIGIOUS SITE | The cathedral, perched atop a hill above the harbor and Old Town, is named after the patron saint of sailors and possesses a beautifully carved 19th-century altar screen. ✉ *Old Town.*

Maritime Museum of Galaxadi

MUSEUM | Housed in an 1868 neoclassical building, this small collection includes paintings with nautical themes (though some are rather undercooked sketches) and many local artifacts from Greek ships and old sea captains' houses. There's nothing jawdropping, but you'll

Did You Know?

Set along the grand
Sacred Way of Delphi—
which leads to the Altar
of Apollo—are several
beautifully preserved
treasuries, which were
built by the Athenians,
Thebans, and other
groups to store their
precious offerings to the
god.

Easter Week in Delphi

Orthodox Easter Week is the most important holiday in Greece, and Delphians celebrate it with true passion. The solemn Good Friday service in Ayios Nikolaos church and the candlelight procession following it, accompanied by the singing of haunting hymns, is one of the most moving rituals in all of Greece. By Saturday evening, the mood is one of eager anticipation as the townspeople are decked out in their nicest finery and the earnest children are carrying *lambades*, beautifully decorated white Easter candles. At midnight the lights of the cathedral are extinguished, and the priest rushes into the sanctuary shouting *Christos anesti!* (Christ is risen!). He lights one of the parishioner's candles with his own and the flame is passed on, one to the other, until the entire church is illuminated with candlelight, which is reflected in the radiant faces of the congregation. Firecrackers are set off by the village schoolboys outside to punctuate the exuberance of the moment. After the liturgy is finished, each person tries to get his or her candle home while still lighted, a sign of good luck for the following year, whereupon the sign of the cross is burned over the door. Then the Easter fast is broken, usually with *mayiritsa* (Easter soup made with lamb) and brilliantly red-dyed hard-boiled eggs. On Easter Sunday, the entire village works together to roast dozens of whole lambs on the spit. It is a joyous day, devoted to feasting with family and friends, but you are welcome and may be offered slices of roast lamb and glasses of the potent dark red local wine. In the early evening, a folk-dance performance is held in front of the town-hall square, followed by communal dancing and free food and drink.

come away with a good background of the history of the village. There is also a small archaelogical collection excavated from a series of ancient cemeteries and isolated tombs around Galaxidi on view. ✉ *Mouseiou 4* ☎ *22650/41795* 🎟 *€3.*

🍴 Restaurants

★ Absinthe

$ | **GREEK** | A relative newcomer to a local dining scene that doesn't change much over the years. This delectable Greek tapas restaurant-bar doesn't have a menu; it just serves what it has left, so don't go too late. **Known for:** great value; a good selection of tsipouros; homemade small-plate dishes. [$] *Average main: €8* ✉ *Nikolaoi Mama 33* ☎ *22650/41220* 🕒 *Closed Mon. and Tues.*

Maritsa

$$ | **SEAFOOD** | A captains' *kafeneio* (coffeehouse) from 1850 is elegantly decorated in a nautical theme with classic Chesterfield sofas and a character-filled setting in which to enjoy mussels—what Galaxidi is known for—served here in a saganaki, steamed, and in a pilaf. There's also seafood risotto and lobster pasta, as well as traditional non-seafood dishes such as homemade pies. **Known for:** many preparations of mussels; character-filled surroundings; harbor views. [$] *Average main: €18* ✉ *Akti Ianthis 34* ✣ *On the waterfront* ☎ *22650/41059.*

★ O Bebelis

$$ | **GREEK** | The wine barrel by the front door is the first hint that this cozy *ouzeri*, tucked into a side street off the harbor, is a place to sit back, relax, order the house tipple, and indulge. The dark-wood setting is truly gorgeous, and daily specials present some innovative takes on the classics; the stuffed onions and the pork with plums are especially delicious, while the six-hour slow-cooked lamb leg deserves a special mention. **Known for:** laid-back ambience; innovative dishes; beautiful old-house setting. $ *Average main: €15* ✉ *Nikolaou Mama 20–22* ✛ *Near the start of the harbor* ☎ *22650/41677.*

O Tassos

$$ | SEAFOOD | Locals and tourists pack the waterfront terrace, drawn in year-round by the quality of the seafood in this basic taverna with reasonable prices. Farm-raised crawfish (*karavides*) are simply boiled and sprinkled with lemon—a true delicacy. **Known for:** fresh seafood; harbor views; good local wine. $ *Average main: €18* ✉ *Akti Ianthis 69* ✛ *At far end of harbor on waterfront* ☎ *22650/41291.*

Taverna Porto

$$ | GREEK | Some tasteful antique decorative touches lend this portside house a quaint feeling, but in warm weather the terrace is the place to be, to watch the world pass by while enjoying a wide-ranging menu. Aside from a good choice of grilled meats and fish, there are some wonderful seafood and vegetarian pastas, along with a nice selection of salads. **Known for:** wide selection of dishes; pleasant portside terrace; vegetarian pastas. $ *Average main: €18* ✉ *Akti Oianthis* ☎ *22650/41182.*

☕ Coffee and Quick Bites

To Kaffeneio

$ | CAFÉ | This old *kaffeneio* (coffee shop) is the perfect place to sit and watch the yachts while the clack of the *tavli* (back-gammon) boards rattle around you. Come the evening—like all the cafés along the dockside—it switches from coffees to cocktails, but the easy atmosphere remains the same, and in winter the fireplace makes a welcome spot to gather

around. **Known for:** traditional decoration; coffees, waffles, and snacks; a prime yacht-watching spot. $ *Average main: €7* ✉ *Akti Oianthis 55* ☎ *22650/41315.*

Hotels

Acroploro Apartments

$ | RENTAL | FAMILY | This pair of one-bedroom houses, about 10 minutes walk from town, is a good option for families. **Pros:** good value for familes; play area for kids; near to the beach. **Cons:** road outside can be a bit noisy; you miss out on the character of Galaxidi; it's a ten-minute walk to town. $ *Rooms from: €80* ✉ *Agios Ioannos 13–15* ☎ *22650/41110* ⊕ *www.acroploro.gr* ➥ *2 apartments* ⦿ *Free breakfast.*

Archontiko Art Hotel

$ | B&B/INN | Yiannis Schizas, who established this homey and comforting adults-only hotel with his wife, Argyroula, has a knack for collecting odd items, and each guest room is decorated differently (and tastefully) with his finds—bathroom fixtures might be from ships, or a sewing machine might be used as a table in one room. **Pros:** quirky and charming; lovely home-away-from-home feeling; nice garden. **Cons:** not one for families; parking is limited; not all rooms have sea views. $ *Rooms from: €50* ✉ *Parodos, Eleftherias 80* ☎ *22650/42292* ⊕ *www.archontikoarthotel.gr* ➥ *8 rooms* ⦿ *Free breakfast.*

★ Hotel Ganimede

$ | B&B/INN | FAMILY | A 19th-century sea captain's mansion and two other houses surround a lush garden, combining welcoming outdoor spaces and homey interiors where unpretentious antiques are interspersed with weavings, small sculptures, and paintings, giving each room personality. **Pros:** home-baked breakfast served in luscious garden; gracious hospitality; welcome drinks served in the garden. **Cons:** no elevator; cooking classes are pricey; parking is on street outside. [$] *Rooms from: €70* ✉ *N. Gourgouris 20* ☎ *22650/41328* 🌐 *https://ganimede.gr* 🛏 *7 rooms; 4 apartments; 1 family apartment* 🍴 *Free breakfast.*

Hotel Miramare

$ | B&B/INN | FAMILY | Everything about this seaside house is bright, from the flower-filled garden to the huge, tile-floored rooms (all with kitchenettes) filled with light and sea views and opening to breezy terraces. **Pros:** very large rooms; bright, cheerful surroundings; lovely garden. **Cons:** no elevator; some noise from nearby bars; bathrooms are a bit basic. [$] *Rooms from: €50* ✉ *Platoni and Piniatidou* ✥ *Near the seafront* ☎ *22650/41328* ⏲ *Closed Nov.–Jan.* 🛏 *5 rooms* 🍴 *Free breakfast.*

Nostos

$ | HOTEL | Even from the outside, Nostos looks every inch the old captain's house. **Pros:** an immaculately kept historic home; beautiful garden setting; homemade breakfasts. **Cons:** not all rooms have balconies; some noise from the square; no mosquito nets on windows. [$] *Rooms from: €65* ✉ *Plateia Iroon and Papapetrou* ☎ *22650/41266* 🌐 *www.nostoshotel.info/en* 🛏 *6 rooms* 🍴 *Free breakfast.*

Performing Arts

FESTIVALS

Kathara Deftera (*Clean Monday*)

FESTIVALS | If you happen to be in Galaxidi at the start of Greek Orthodox Lent, *Kathara Deftera,* duck. Locals observe the holiday with flour fights in the town's streets, a custom dating back to the 18th century. The common baking flour is tinted with food dye and by the end of the day everyone and everything in sight—buildings, cars, shrubs—is dusted with a rainbow of colors that match spring's bright palette. The custom has pagan roots: every year the dead were thought to be allowed to leave Hades for a day and return to Earth; if they had a good time, a good crop was assured. Remember to wear your old, unwanted T-shirt and jeans for the day—nobody will ask for your permission before they throw!

Shopping

Avra Grocery

CONVENIENCE/GENERAL STORES | A traditional grocery shop on the waterfront that not only stocks all the essentials, most of them locally sourced, but also transports you back in time with its old-fashioned, romantic decor. It has been lovingly created by the family behind the Archontiko Art Hotel. ✉ *Oianthis 95* ☎ *22650/42295.*

★ **Ostria**

CERAMICS/GLASSWARE | Clearly, artists are behind the dazzling selection of gift items at Ostria. Beautifully displayed pieces include nautical objects like brass compasses and model ships, but also an array of toys, clocks, icons, and jewelry. There's also a huge selection of ceramics, some by owner Petros Skourtis. He and co-owner Katie Kapi, who is a painter, also invite customers to visit their nearby workshop, where they can even take a pottery course. ✉ *Akti Ianthis 101* ✥ *On the waterfront* ☎ *22650/41206.*

EPIRUS AND THESSALY

IOANNINA, METSOVO, AND THE METEORA MONASTERIES

Updated by
Adrian Vrettos

⊙ Sights	🍴 Restaurants	🛏 Hotels	🛍 Shopping	🍸 Nightlife
★★★★★	★★★☆☆	★★★★☆	★★☆☆☆	★★☆☆☆

WELCOME TO EPIRUS AND THESSALY

TOP REASONS TO GO

★ **Meteora monasteries:** Even more wondrous than the Meteora's soaring rock pinnacles are the medieval monasteries perched atop them—walk, climb, or drive to these still-inhabited spots where eagles once nested.

★ **Zagorohoria region:** Dotting the dramatic Vikos gorge are 46 traditional villages filled with picturesque Ottoman houses—this is some of the best hiking countryside in all of Greece.

★ **Dodona:** Visiting the ancient site of Dodona in Epirus is a must; many mystical ceremonies took place in this ancient sanctuary of Zeus.

★ **Experience Metsovo's traditions:** This mountain village has held on hard to its traditional character—discover its stone houses, customary foods, and winding alleyways (each with its own story).

★ **Haunts of Ali Pasha:** Even Lord Byron was drawn to Ioannina to trace the haunted spirit of the legendary pasha who once made Epirus his own personal potentate.

Travelers in search of wild and romantic country will be more than delighted with these two regions of northern Greece. In the markedly Balkan region of Epirus, the route east from Ioannina leads to the thriving traditional village of Metsovo and over the Katara pass on one of the most dramatic roads in Greece. Westward lies the fertile province of Thessaly, where spectacular rock-pinnacle monasteries are shadowed by the Pindos, Plion, and Olympus mountain ranges.

1 **Ioannina.** Strongly infused by the influences of Greeks, Jews, and Turks, Ioannina rests on the banks of Lake Pamvotis. Picturesquely medieval and founded by Emperor Justinian in 527, the town is shadowed by two historic mosques, which reflect the area's marked oriental character. Although it has an extensive, multicultural history, Ioannina also has a vibrant modern scene.

2 **Zagorohoria Region.** The Zagorohoria region is known for its stunning landscapes, cozy guesthouses, World Heritage–protected architecture, and sparkling rivers.

3 **Metsovo.** Studded with traditional houses filled with Epirote arts and crafts, this mountain township is famously inhabited by Vlachs who speak their distinct dialect. After visiting the noted Tositsa Museum, head to the hills for an idyllic skiing vacation, nature walks, or wine tours.

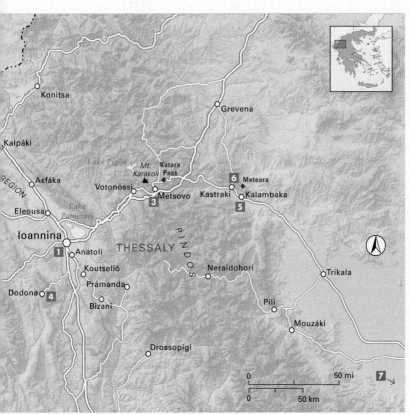

4 Dodona. Mentioned by Homer in the 10th book of the *Iliad,* the Dodona oracle once presided here, only eclipsed by Delphi in classical times. View the remains of the sanctuary of Zeus and the majestic ancient theater, which once held 17,000 spectators and is still the venue of Greek drama presentations.

5 Kalambaka. An overnight here offers a taste of everyday life in a provincial Thessalian town. It's also a jumping off point for visiting the Meteora monasteries.

6 Meteora. Looming out of the edge of Thessaly's main plain, the sky-kissing medieval monasteries of Meteora seem to float in midair, built atop bizarrely shaped pinnacles that tower over the town of Kalambaka. You can enjoy relaxed, fun nights in this "town near Meteora" on its central Dimoula Square, with the Meteora rocks as a backdrop.

7 Volos. This bustling port city derives much of its youthful energy from the student population at the University of Thessaly and from summer tourists seeking fun and sun.

As travelers journey through the provinces of northern Greece, they quickly realize that Epirus and Thessaly may have far fewer miles of drop-dead-gorgeous coastline than the south, but if visitors have brought their hiking boots as well as their bathing suits, the north's stunning mountains, folkloric villages, and lush valleys more than make up for it.

The land changes abruptly from the delicately shaded green of the idyllic olive and orange groves near the shore to the tremendous solidity of the bare mountains inland. This was the splendid massive landscape that came to cast its spell over Lord Byron, who traveled here to meet tyrant Ali Pasha (1741–1822). The Epirote capital of Ioannina still bears many vestiges of this larger-than-life figure, who seems to have stepped from the pages of *The Arabian Nights*.

Going back in time, and taking an easy trip southwest of Ioannina, you can visit Dodona, the site of the oldest oracle in Greece. North of Ioannina, in the mountainous region known as Zagorohoria, or the Zagori, dozens of tiny, unspoiled villages contain remnants of the Ottoman period, and outdoor activities such as hiking are abundant. The route east from Ioannina leads to the thriving traditional village of Metsovo, in the Pindos Mountains, and over the Katara pass on one of the most dramatic roads in Greece. It ends in the fertile province of Thessaly, where, on the edge of the plain, the Byzantine-era monasteries of Meteora seem to float in midair, built atop bizarrely shaped pinnacles that tower over

the town of Kalambaka. At this spiritual center of Orthodox Greece, the quiet contemplation of generations of monks is preserved in wondrously frescoed buildings. Nearby, spectacular mountain passes reveal shepherd villages with richly costumed women speaking the Vlach vernacular.

All in all, northwestern Greece, which stretches from the northern shore of the Gulf of Corinth to the Albanian frontier west of the Pindos range, was aroused from its centuries-old slumber several decades ago with the advent of the ferryboats from Italy. The nautical crossing from Corfu to Igoumenitsa, the westward gateway town to mainland Greece, is enchanting, with the lush green of the island slowly receding and the stark outlines of the mainland dramatically ahead. The bay is at its best in the early morning, but sunset will do, when the gray rocks likewise flame with deep pinks and violets in an unforgettable welcome. Igoumenitsa is generally unappealing as a port of entry, which means everyone quickly pushes on into the interior and discovers the often-overlooked wonders of Epirus and Thessaly.

Planning

When to Go

Ioannina is easy to visit year-round, but excursions to the countryside are best May through October, when most places are open. Winter is great for skiing and curling up by the fire, although spring, when the abundant and broadly variable natural surroundings blossom, is captivating, especially in the fabled Zagorohoria region. Metsovo can be blissfully cool even in high summer (especially at night). This helps make the town *panagyri* (saint's day festival) for Ayia Paraskevi, held July 26, quite pleasant, but the heat is oppressive elsewhere in this region at this time. The Meteora monasteries attract considerably fewer people in winter, but keep in mind the Thessalian plain can bake during summer in the vast oven formed by the surrounding high mountains. Maximum enjoyment will be obtained in the spring, especially at the Meteora monasteries. At this point, the mountains are still snow-covered and blend harmoniously with the green fields, the red poppies, and the white and pink fruit trees.

In Epirus, local tourist offices and most hotels will provide information about festivals, including the famous Ioannina International Folk Festival showcasing the region's music and dancing, which takes place in July. For those seeking the haunting traditional *klarino* (clarinet) music and graceful circle dances of Epirus such as the *pogonisios* and *beratis,* this is a fascinating event. Local groups also perform eerie polyphonic singing, another unique folk tradition rooted in the region.

Planning Your Time

Coming either from Thessaloniki, or from the northwestern port of Igoumenitsa, it's reasonable to make the lively, studenty town of Ioannina and its glittering lake your starting point. Two nights there should be enough to get a good taste of this city, leaving ample time to take in the top attractions and regional tastes on offer. From there head to the Zagorohoria villages, a unique destination that draws visitors from around the world. Two days here will offer you a good introduction to the area but will definitely leave you wanting more. The Vikos Gorge, the deepest in Europe, is a phenomenal highlight of this stunning naturally abundant area.

Metsovo is the next noteworthy destination in Epirus. A couple of nights are more than enough to enjoy this unique Vlach mountain town. From Metsovo the meandering mountain roads first wind their way up out of Epirus and then down into Thessaly and the town of Kalambaka. It's next to the breathtaking Meteora monasteries perched atop giant limestone stacks, where you should linger a couple of days.

Getting Here and Around

Volos, which has become increasingly attractive over the last decade, is the major port city of the Thessaly region, and bus, train, and boat routes often use it as a base.

AIR

Olympic Air and Aegean Airlines are the only carriers that service this region. The Ioannina airport, the primary airport in the region, is 8 km (5 miles) north of town. *For detailed information about these airlines, see Air in Travel Smart.*

CONTACTS Ioannina Airport, aka King Pyrros. ⊠ *Grammou Ave 135, Ioannina* ✛ *Km 8, Ethnikos Odos Ioanninon–Trikalon road* ☎ *26510/83600, 26510/83602.*

BUS

About seven buses a day make the 7-hour trip from Athens's Terminal A (Kifissou) to Ioannina's main Papandreou Station. One of these takes the longer route east through Kalambaka and Trikala rather than the usual southern route to the Rion–Antirion ferry over the suspension bridge, which is the largest in Europe. From Athens's dismal Terminal B (Liossion), seven buses leave daily for the 5-hour journey to Kalambaka. Most routes require you to hop on a different bus for the final leg from Trikala, but one morning bus goes direct. From Thessaloniki to Ioannina there are six buses a day, and, thanks to the Engatia highway, the trip takes a mere 3½ hours and costs €28. Thessaloniki to Kalambaka takes 2¾ hours (€19.70) with four buses leaving daily. Around four KTEL buses leave Ioannina daily for Metsovo (about 1 hour) and two buses for Kalambaka (2 hours); frequencies are the same in the opposite direction. Buses also head to Dodona. The several-times-weekly bus heading for Melingi village passes the ancient site. Other bus options drop you off 1 km (½ mile) or ½ km (¼ mile) from the site; ask for information based on the day you want to go. On Sunday, service is reduced for all towns. Regular bus service runs from Ioannina's main terminal to the towns in the Zagorohoria. There is also regular and frequent bus service from Athens to Volos (€27.40), of little interest to travelers but a major transportation hub in the region; from Volos, you can easily connect to Thessaloniki (€18.40) and other destinations in the region. *For detailed information about travel by bus, see Bus in Travel Smart.*

CONTACTS Ioannina Bus Station. ⊠ *Papandreou 45, Ioannina* ☎ *26510/25014 for Metsovo, Kalambaka, and Dodona, 26510/26286* ⊕ *www.ktelioannina.gr.* **Kalambaka Bus Station.** ⊠ *Ikonomou 9, Kalambaka* ☎ *24320/22432 in Trikala* ⊕ *www.ktel-trikala.gr.*

CAR

This region is best explored by car, and if you plan to go beyond the main sights, your own wheels are essential. Driving to Kalambaka or Ioannina from Athens takes the greater part of a day. To reach Ioannina take National Road west past Corinth in the Peloponnese, crossing the magnificent Rion–Antirion bridge. The total trip is 445 km (276 miles). For Kalambaka, take National Road north past Thebes; north of Lamia there's a turnoff for Trikala and Kalambaka (a total of 330 km [205 miles]). The drive from Thessaloniki takes around 5 hours and winds you over the mountains and river valleys of Kozani and Grevena on National Road.

The road from Ioannina to Metsovo to Kalambaka is one of the most scenic in northern Greece, but it traverses the famous Katara pass, which is curvy and can be hazardous, especially December through March (snow chains are necessary). If you are traveling with a few people, it might be more relaxing and almost as economical to hire a taxi to drive you around, at least for a day.

You can rent a car from either Avis, Budget, or Hertz at the Ioannina Airport. Avis also has an office in town. *For information about major agencies, see Car in Travel Smart.*

CONTACTS Avis Car Hire. ⊠ *Dodonis 71, Ioannina* ☎ *26510/46333* ⊕ *www.avis.gr/ greece/car-rental/ioannina_car_hire.htm.*

TAXI

If you see a cab along the street, step into the road and shout your destination. The driver will stop if he or she is going in your direction. You can ask your hotel reception desk to phone for a taxi and help you negotiate with a taxi driver, especially if you want a tour. You can find taxis at the local bus station, on the central square, and at other spots around town. Minimum tariffs are €3.60.

TRAIN

Kalambaka is reachable by train. Locals normally prefer to travel by bus, because trains generally take longer. Nevertheless, train travel makes sense on the Athens Larissis Station–Kalambaka route if you take the daily express intercity (5 hours) at 8:30 am—ironically €10 cheaper than the slow trains. It costs around the same as a bus—about €36 class A, €30 class B for the train, and €28 for the bus. Investing in a class A seat (*proti thesi*) means more room and comfort. The nonexpress train is agonizingly slow (at least 7 hours) and requires a change at Palaiofarsalo.

There are also frequent trains between Athens and Volos (a 5-hour journey that leaves six to seven times per day and costs €36–€43) via Larissa. From Volos, buses and trains connect with Thessaloniki every 2 hours (a journey lasting around 2½ hours and costing €18.40); the train trip requires a change at Larissa. Trains to Larissa leave about every hour on the 2- to 3-hour journey; tickets cost €12–€27.

For detailed information about taking the train, see Train in Travel Smart.

CONTACTS Kalambaka Train Station. ⊠ *Pindou, Kalambaka* ☎ *24320/22451.*

Hotels

Rooms are usually easy to find in Ioannina and, except at the best hotels, are simply decorated. Reservations might be necessary for Kalambaka, which is packed with tour groups to the Meteora monasteries in late spring and summer, and in Metsovo during ski season or the town's July 26 festival. In these two towns, private rooms are likely to be far cheaper than comparable hotel rooms—look for advertisements as you arrive. Off-season, prices drop drastically from those listed here, and you should always try to negotiate. Ask to see the room first, and don't assume anything; if you have special requests, such as a mountain view, a *diplo drevati* (double bed) rather than a *diklino* (twin bed); a balcony; or a bathtub, speak up. In some cases, prices will skyrocket for Greek Easter and Christmas. In Epirus, most small hotels are built in the charming and traditional style—usually recognizable by the heavy use of wood and stone, most suited to the cold winter months, when these accommodations make the perfect base for skiing, hiking, and other activities.

Restaurants

In all but the fanciest restaurants, check out what's cooking because menus change seasonally here. These regions, perhaps because of their dramatic winters, are known for some of the heartiest, rib-stickingest meals around Greece. Informal dress is usually appropriate. Metsovites are particularly known for their meat specialties, such as *kontosouvli* (lamb or pork kebab) and boiled goat, their *trahanas* soup (made from cracked wheat boiled in milk and dried then reboiled with tomatoes), and their sausages or meatballs stuffed with leeks, as well as their costly but delectable smoked Metsovone cheese. *Pites* (pies, or pita) are pastry envelopes filled with local and seasonal produce, from savory meats and vegetables to sweet dairy creams and honey. Head to the lakesides, most famously those in Ioannina, to feast on aquatic delights: frogs' legs, trout, eel, and crayfish. Wherever you head, Epirote restaurants generally offer an interesting blend of Greek, Turkish, and Jewish flavors, usually prepared with fresh local produce. Some of their tried-and-true recipes are *moschari kokkinisto* (a tomato-based veal stew with carrots, onions, and peas), lamb in lemon sauce, and *lathera* (stovetop vegetable stew made with artichoke hearts, beans, okra, and tomatoes). And the best wine to wash it all down with is Katogi red wine, pressed from French Bordeaux grapes grown locally in Metsovo.

Restaurant and hotel reviews have been shortened. For full information, visit Fodors.com

What it Costs in euros			
$	$$	$$$	$$$$
RESTAURANTS			
under €15	€15–€25	€26–€40	over €40
HOTELS			
under €125	€125–€225	€226–€275	over €275

Visitor Information

The Greek National Tourism Organization (GNTO or EOT) in Ioannina is open weekdays 7:30–2:30 and 5:30–8 and Saturday 9–1 in July and August; hours vary other months. Mornings are the best time to catch someone in. In summer a tourist information booth is usually erected on the main square of Kalambaka, but it's best to visit the town hall for information.

CONTACTS Greek National Tourism Organization. ⊠ *Dodonis 39, Ioannina* ☎ *26510/48866, 26510/41142* ⊕ *www.visitgreece.gr.* **Kalambaka Municipality.** ⊠ *Vlahava 1–3, Kalambaka* ☎ *24323/50245, 24323/50200* ⊕ *www.infotouristmeteora.gr.*

Ioannina Ιωαννινα

305 km (189 miles) northwest of Athens, 204 km (127 miles) west-southwest of Thessaloniki.

On the rocky promontory of Pamvotis Lake lies Ioannina, its fortress punctuated by mosques and minarets whose reflections, along with those of the snowy peaks of the Pindos range, appear in the calm water. The lake contains tiny Nissi, or "island," where nightingales still sing and fishermen mend their nets (and now noted as the hometown of Karolos Papoulias, a former [2005–15] president of the Greek Republic). Although on first impression parts of the city may seem noisy and undistinguished, the Old Quarter preserves a rich heritage. Outstanding examples of folk architecture remain within the castle walls and in the neighborhoods surrounding them; Ioannina's historic mansions, folk houses, seraglios, and bazaars are a reminder of the city's illustrious past. Set at a crossroads of trading, the city is sculpted by Balkan, Ottoman, and Byzantine influences. Thanks to a resident branch of the Greek national university, today the bustling provincial capital city (population 100,000) has a thriving contemporary cultural scene (and a proliferation of good restaurants and popular bars). Things get particularly lively the first two weeks of July, when the city's International Folk Festival takes place.

The name Ioannina was first documented in 1020 and may have been taken from an older monastery of St. John. Founded by Emperor Justinian in AD 527, Ioannina suffered under many rulers: it was invaded by the Normans in 1082, made a dependency of the Serbian kingdom in 1345, and conquered by the Turks in 1431. Above all, this was Ali Pasha's city, where, during its zenith, from 1788 to 1821, the despot carved a fiefdom from much of western Greece. His territory extended from the Ionian Sea to the Pindos range and from Vaona in the north to Arta in the south. The Turks ended his rule in 1821 by using deception to capture him; Ali Pasha was then shot and decapitated by Greek monks.

GETTING HERE AND AROUND

Olympic Air offers tickets from €42 to €105 one-way from Athens. Direct charter flights from any European capital to Ioannina Airport are also available.

There is no train service to Ioannina, but it is well served by bus. Ioannina KTEL bus station (⊠ *Georgiou Papandreou 45* ☎ *26510/27442*) offers routes connecting

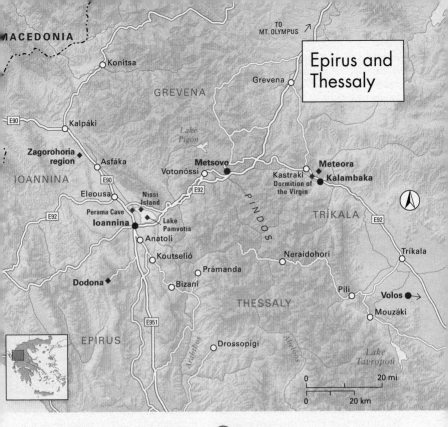

with Konitsa (2 hours), Igoumenitsa (2½ hours), Athens (6½ hours), Thessaloniki (3½ hours), and many other towns. From Athens, buses depart weekdays every four hours from 6:30 am to 10:30 pm, Sunday from 8:30 am to 10:30 pm; tickets start at €36. Buses connect with Metsovo twice a day weekdays and once a day on weekends; tickets are €5.80. Buses connect with Trikala's bus station (☎ 24310/73130), a major hub of Thessaly, twice daily; the ride takes 2½ hours and costs €12.50.

Boats depart for Nissi island in Lake Pamvotis every hour in the winter and every 45 minutes in the summer months. The boats leave from the gate of the Kastro fortress; tickets are €1.80.

Sights

Agios Nikolaos ton Filanthropinon

MUSEUM | Of Nissi's several monasteries, Agios Nikolaos ton Filanthropinon has the best frescoes. The monastery was built in the 13th century by an important Byzantine family, the Filanthropinos, and a fresco in the northern exonarthex (the outer narthex) depicts five of them kneeling before St. Nikolaos (1542). Many of the frescoes are by the Kontaris brothers, who later decorated the mighty Varlaam in Meteora. Note the similarities in the bold coloring, expressiveness, realism, and Italian influence—especially in the bloody scenes of martyrdom. Folk tradition says the corner crypts in the south chapel were the meeting places of the secret school of Hellenic culture during the Ottoman occupation. A most unusual fresco here of seven sages of antiquity, including Solon, Aristotle, and Plutarch, gives credence to this story. It is not really feasible, however, that the school would have been kept a secret from the Ottoman governors for long; more likely, the reigning Turkish pasha was one who allowed religious and cultural freedom (as long as the taxes were paid). ⊠ *Ioannina* ✛ *On Nissi, follow signs* ⊕ *odysseus. culture.gr* ✉ *Donations accepted.*

Ali Pasha Museum

MUSEUM | The main attraction on Nissi is the 16th-century Ayios Pandelimonos Monastery, now the Ali Pasha Museum. Ali Pasha was killed here in the monks' cells on January 17, 1822, after holding out for almost two years. In the final battle, Ali ran into an upstairs cell, but the soldiers shot him through its floorboards from below. (The several "bullet" holes in the floor were drilled there when the original floor had to be replaced.) A wax version of the assassination can be seen at the Pavlos Vrellis Museum of Greek History in Bizani, south of Ioannina. A happier (and significantly less dead) Ali Pasha, asleep on the lap of his wife, Vasiliki, can be seen in the museum's famous portrait. The Ali Pasha Museum also houses the crypt where Vasiliki hid, some evocative etchings and paintings of that era, an edict signed by Ali Pasha with his ring seal (he couldn't write), and his magnificent *narghile* water pipe standing on the fireplace. The community-run museum is generally open as long as boats are running; if the doors are shut, ask around to be let in. The local ticket taker will give a brief tour of the museum (supplemented by an English-language printed guide). A tour is free, but do leave a tip. ⊠ *Ioannina* ✛ *On Nissi, go left from boat landing and follow signs* ☎ *26510/81791* ⊕ *museumalipasha.gr/en/ museum* ✉ *€3.*

Archaeological Museum of Ioannina

MUSEUM | Located in the center of town, this museum is the best in the area. It houses exhibits from the greater Epirus, such as Paleolithic tools, inscriptions, statues, headstones, and a collection of coins, all presented in a contemporary exhibition space with multimedia facilities. ⊠ *25th Martiou Sq.* ☎ *26510/01089* ⊕ *www.culture.gr* ✉ *€3; €8 ticket valid for the Archaeological Museum of Ioannina, Byzantine Museum of Ioannina, Dodona* ⊙ *Closed Tues.*

Byzantine Museum

ARCHAEOLOGICAL SITE | Within the larger citadel is the fortress, called Its Kale by the Turks, where Ali Pasha built his palace; these days the former palace serves the city as the Byzantine Museum. The museum's small collection of artworks, actually almost all post-Byzantine, includes intricate silver manuscript Bible covers, wall murals from mansions, and carved wooden benediction crosses covered in lacy silver, gathered from all over the countryside of Epirus. It's carefully arranged in the front half of the museum with good English translations. The second half of the museum houses an important collection of icons and remarkable iconostases, painted by local masters and salvaged from 16th- and 17th-century monasteries. The most interesting section is devoted to silver works from Ali Pasha's treasury from the seraglio. Within the fortress grounds is a very pleasant little café—why not enjoy some light snacks and desserts as you take in the views of the lush gardens around the Byzantine Museum and the impressive old ruins? Nearby is the **Fethiye (Victory) Mosque,** which purports to contain Ali Pasha's tomb. ⊠ *Ioannina* ✛ *Eastern corner of Its Kale fortress* ☎ *26510/39580* ⊕ *odysseus.culture.gr* ✉ *€3* ⊙ *Closed Tues.*

★ Kastro (Castle)

ARCHAEOLOGICAL SITE | One of Ioannina's main attractions is the Kastro, with massive, fairly intact stone fortress walls that once dropped into the lake on three sides; Ali Pasha completely rebuilt them in 1815. The city's once-large Romaniote Jewish population, said to date from the time of Alexander the Great, lived within the walls, alongside Turks and Christians. The Jews were deported by the Nazis during World War II, to meet their deaths at extermination camps; the population of 4,000-plus around the turn of the 20th century is now fewer than 100. The area inside the walls is now a quaint residential area with a few hotels, cafés, restaurants, and stores. Outside the citadel walls, near the lake, a **monument** at Karamanli and Soutsou streets commemorates the slaughter of the Jewish community. ⊠ Ioannina ✛ Lakeside end of Odhos Averoff.

Kostas Frontzos Museum of Epirote Folk Art

MUSEUM | In a finely restored Ottoman house, this small museum has a collection of richly embroidered local costumes, rare woven textiles made by the nomadic tent-dwelling Sarakatsanis, ceramics, and cooking and farm implements. ⊠ Michail Angelou 42 ☎ 26510/23566 ✉ €2 ⊘ Closed Sat. and Sun.

Lake Pamvotis

BODY OF WATER | Despite the fact that the water level is so low (the streams that feed it are drying up) and it has become too polluted for swimming, Lake Pamvotis remains Ioannina's picturesque centerpiece. At night, youths gather with their friends to sit around the antique walls facing the lake, perhaps oblivious to the fact that it is a significant basin of biodiversity, with 170 bird species and nine amphibian species. It also has the longest rowing course in Greece—teams from all over the Balkans use it for training, while the Valkaniadia rowing championships are periodically hosted here. Legend has it that the notorious Ali Pasha drowned his son's lover (after she rejected the Pasha's advances and demands to make her his own mistress). The lake is also said to be haunted by other female victims of the tyrant, and that their spirits haunt it to this day. ⊠ Ioannina ⊕ www.lakepamvotis.gr/en/home.

Mavili Square

PLAZA | This waterfront square is lined with large, noisy cafés that fill with locals and travelers waiting for the next boat to the nearby isle of Nissi. In the evening the seawall is the place to hang out—the youth of Ioannina while away the hours here sipping turbo-charged frappé iced coffees or aperitif drinks. The volta (ritual promenade) is still a favorite way of passing the time and keeping up to date with all the action and gossip, particularly at night when the town shifts into high gear. ⊠ Ioannina.

Municipal Museum

MUSEUM | The collections in the well-preserved Aslan Mosque, now the Municipal Museum, recall the three communities (Greek, Turkish, and Jewish) that lived together inside the fortress from 1400 to 1611. The vestibule has recesses for shoes, and inscribed over the doorway is the name of Aslan Pasha and "there is only one god, allah, and muhammed is his prophet." The mosque retains its original decoration and mihrab, a niche that faces Mecca. Exhibited around the room are a walnut-and-mother-of-pearl table from Ali Pasha's period, ornate inlaid hamman (Turkish bath) shoes on tall wooden platforms, treasure chests, traditional clothing, a water pipe, and a collection of 18th- and 19th-century guns. ⊠ Al. Noutsou 18 ⊕ North end of citadel ☎ 26510/26356 ⊕ www.ioannina.gr ✉ €2.

★ Nissi Island

HISTORIC SITE | Look back at the outline of the citadel and its mosques in a wash of green as you take the 10-minute ride from the shore toward small Nissi island. The whitewashed lakeside island village was founded in the late 16th century by refugees from the Mani (in the Peloponnese). No outside recreational vehicles are allowed, and without the din of motorcycles and cars, the picturesque village seems centuries away from Ioannina. Ali Pasha once kept deer here for hunting. With its neat houses and flower-trimmed courtyards, pine-edged paths, runaway chickens, and reed-filled backwater, it's the perfect place to relax, have lunch, visit some of the monasteries (dress appropriately and carry a small flashlight to make it easier to see the magnificent frescoes), and have a pleasant dinner. Frogs' legs, eel, trout, and carp (displayed live in large tanks) take center stage, although traditional fare is also served at most tavernas here. To cap off your visit, stop by quiet Aleion Square for a relaxed coffee and a leisurely game of backgammon. ⊠ *Ioannina ✢ Ferry below citadel, near Mavili Sq.* 🛳 *Ferry €2.*

Old Bazaar

MARKET | Vestiges of 19th-century Ioannina remain in the Old Bazaar. On Anexartisias are some Turkish-era structures, such as the Liabei arcade (where cool and trendy bars and clubs now dominate), across from the bustling municipal produce market and, on Filiti, a smattering of the copper-, tin-, and silversmiths who fueled the city's economy for centuries. Some workshops still have wares for sale. ⊠ *Ioannina ✢ Around citadel's gates at Ethnikis Antistasios and Averoff.*

Pavlos Vrellis Museum of Greek History

BUILDING | **FAMILY** | Want to see a tableau of Ali Pasha's legendary murder? Head to this museum to be shocked and amused, by turns, by its collection of historical Epirote waxwork figures from the past 2,500 years, all leading players in more than 30 historical "settings," including streets, mountains, caves, churches, and more. All the figures were sculpted in wax by artist Pavlos Vrellis, a local legend who embarked on this endeavor

at the ripe age of 60. His studio is on the premises, a modern building that has stayed true to Eipirotic architectural style. ⊠ *Neo Bizani ✢ 12 km (7 miles) south of Ioannina, Ethnikos Odos Ioanninon–Athinon road* 🕾 *26510/92128* ⊕ *www.vrellis. gr* 🛳 *€6.*

Perama Cave

CAVE | The cave's passageways, discovered in the early 1940s by locals hiding from the Nazis, extend for more than 1 km (½ mile) under the hills. You learn about the high caverns and multihued limestone stalagmites during the 45-minute guided tour in English. Printed English-language information is also available. Be prepared for the many steps you must walk up on the way out. At the information center you can see some of the paleontological finds from Perama and learn more about the geology of caves. Bus No. 16 from Ioannina's clock tower gets you here. ⊠ *Ioannina ✢ E92, 4 km (2½ miles) north of Ioannina* 🕾 *26510/81521* ⊕ *spilaio-perama.gr* 🛳 *€7.*

 Restaurants

Fisa Roufa

$ | **GREEK** | This is the best place in Ioannina to enjoy Grandma's home-style cooking, such as pork and celery in a velvety egg-lemon sauce, chicken in yogurt sauce, and *patsa* (tripe) and beef in tomato sauce—simply head to the counter at the back of the charming little *magirion*, a canteen variety of taverna, and point to the dishes that strike your fancy. Beer is served cold and the wine by the kilo (or half, if you must). **Known for:** old-style Greek eatery; good value for money; warm and friendly staff. $ *Average main: €6* ⊠ *Averof 55* 🕾 *26510/26262.*

Gastra

$ | **GREEK** | For more than 30 years Mr. Vassilis has run this friendly place, where you can discover how Greek grandmothers cooked before the comforts

To assert their rule over Ioannina, the Turks built the Its Kale fortress; but it was transformed into Ali Pasha's palace in the early 19th century.

of electricity were introduced to Epirus. The *gastra* is basically a large clay or iron container placed on a fire with hot coals scattered on the iron lid over the pot. **Known for:** succulent slow-cooked meats; traditional local taverna; friendly service. $ *Average main: €11* ⊠ *Opposite the Dodonis factory, Eleousa ⊹ 7 km (4½ miles) north of Ioannina (past the airport)* ☎ *26510/61530* ⊕ *www.estiatorio-gastra. gr* ⊗ *Closed Mon.*

★ Mirovolos

$ | GREEK | One of the last in Ioannina's main and famous row of lakeside tavernas, family-run and welcoming Mirovolos serves great food. Graze while you gaze at the lovely view of the minaret of Aslan Mosque reflecting on the calm waters of Lake Pamvotis. **Known for:** al fresco lakeside dining; slightly elevated and international take on local Greek cuisine; friendly service. $ *Average main: €12* ⊠ *Strat. Papagou 28* ☎ *26510/78695.*

Stoa Louli

$ | GREEK | The old-fashioned aura created by the old stone building, the interior of which is a stoa with an arched (partly glass) ceiling and doors, is the most alluring feature of this place. Stoas are covered courtyards or walkways used in Greek architecture since ancient times and commonly created for public use, and this one is no different—except that here you can enjoy tasty and well-presented local food along with some excellent wine and an accompaniment of acoustic live music. **Known for:** great character and mood; live music; good wine list. $ *Average main: €13* ⊠ *Anexartissias 78* ☎ *26510/71322.*

☕ Coffee and Quick Bites

★ Maison

$ | MODERN GREEK | The coffee here is pretty special, but what really steals the show are the delightful desserts. Treat yourself to one of the maison speciality waffles, the honey-soaked French toast, a chocolate cheesecake, or the deconstructed banoffee pie, all with an innovotative twist inspired by pastry chef Dionisis Alertas. **Known for:** fine desserts; great coffee; lovely presentation. $ *Average main: €8* ✉ *Vlachleidi 3* ☎ *26510/27797.*

Miam Miam

$ | **ITALIAN** | **FAMILY** | A bungalow corner restaurant, with seating laid out on the wide gray flagstone pavement, Miam Miam is primarily a pasta place with 20 choices on offer. If the authentic carbonara (no cream) or the smoky bacon *amatriciana* don't tickle your fancy, try a sandwich wrap or hearty club sandwich. **Known for:** large selection of pasta dishes; good for kids; cheap well-sized portions. $ *Average main: €5* ✉ *Neomartiros Georgiou 1* ☎ *26510/65023.*

 ## Hotels

Epirus Palace

$ | **HOTEL** | **FAMILY** | Indulging oneself in the city of that sybarite Ali Pasha seems entirely fitting, and you can do so in style at this stunning and lavish hotel, which was opened in 1999 by the innovative brothers Natsis. **Pros:** special deals can make your five-star stay very affordable; good pool and poolside restaurant; high speed internet. **Cons:** 10 minutes from Ioannina by car; staff is accommodating, but it's a little disorganized for a five-star accommodations; very large hotel. $ *Rooms from: €120* ✉ *Ethnikos Odos Ioanninon–Athinon ⊕ 7 km (4½ miles) south of Ioannina* ☎ *26510/93555, 26510/91072* ⊕ *www.epiruspalace.gr* ⤴ *194 rooms* ⦿ *Free breakfast.*

Hotel Metropolis

$$ | **HOTEL** | The Hotel Metropolis is a recently renovated (2018 and upped to a five-star boutique establishment) neoclassical landmark building in the center of Ioannina. The mostly white rooms are given bold colors by the funky furniture and a mixture of antiques and modern

A Stunning Stroll

Set at the lakeside end of Odhos Averoff, tree-lined Dionyssiou Skylosofou, which circles the citadel along the lake, is ideal for a late-afternoon stroll. The street was named for a defrocked Trikala bishop who led an ill-fated uprising against the Turks in 1611 (and was flayed alive as a result). A moat, now filled, ran around the southwest landward side, and today the walls divide the Old Town—with its rose-laden pastel-color houses, overhanging balconies, cobblestone streets, and birdsong—from the new.

designs, while the beds have luxurious Coco-mat mattresses. **Pros:** excellent breakfast; great location; warm and friendly service. **Cons:** some of the rooms are small; free parking is a few minutes away from the hotel; room views are nothing to write home about. $ *Rooms from: €130* ✉ *33 Averof St.* ☎ *26510 /30004* ⊕ *www.metropolishotel.gr* ⤴ *9 rooms* ⦿ *Free breakfast.*

★ Kastro Hotel

$ | **HOTEL** | The stylish vibe of old aristocracy coupled with minimalist good taste infuses this neoclassical mansion, which features delightful wood beams, painted wooden ceilings, and fireplaces in the sitting and breakfast rooms—and it's one of the few options within the walls of the historic citadel. **Pros:** welcoming and helpful owners; beautiful antique decor throughout; historical location. **Cons:** can get booked up year-round; sometimes difficult to find parking; breakfast not always included in price, so specify this when booking. $ *Rooms from: €60* ✉ *Andronikou Paleologou 57* ☎ *26510/22866* ⊕ *hotelkastro.gr* ⤴ *7 rooms* ⦿ *No meals.*

Presiding over some of the most beautiful folkloric villages of the Zagorohoria region are grand monasteries, such as Agia Paraskevi in Monodendri.

Nightlife

Even in a relatively small city like Ioannina, the *magazia* (club-cafés) are often changing names and owners; they may close for winter and open elsewhere for summer, usually under the stars. Karamanli, adjacent to the citadel, is lined with trendy *mezedopoleia* (Greek-style tapas bars) and smart pubs, as is the area around Garivaldi Street running along the outside of the eastern wall of the citadel past Gate D.

Blue Gin Bar

BARS/PUBS | A vaulted cellar has been converted into this chic little bar-club on a trendy street next to the western wall of the Its Kale fortress. Local DJs and fun events nights make it popular with the town's students, but typically it only starts buzzing after 10 pm. It's known for great cocktails—try one with a Greek twist. ⊠ *Eth. Antistaseos 40* ☎ *6932/020361.*

Denoar

CAFES—NIGHTLIFE | In a creatively restored Ottoman-period marketplace, this cool bar-club is a mainstay of Ioannina night-life. Theme nights, imaginative drinks, and a mixture of funk, rock, and dance music keep eclectic night owls flocking in. ⊠ *Maramenou Stoa, Anexertasias 40* ☎ *26510/69945.*

★ Stoa Liabei

BARS/PUBS | This Ottoman-era arcade has been transformed into the nightlife hub of the city. Bars and clubs, all with differing styles and music, now occupy every nook and cranny, and attract Ioannina's hip and trendy crowd. One can hop from Stoa Bar, playing deep house and funky sets, to Route 66, with its alternative, soul, and funky grooves. If it's cool yuppie vibes you're after, head to trendy Montage with its breezy uptown decor. In summer the action gets combustible, as these bars merge and mingle, since most of the action is outside. In winter they become more autonomous, shutting doors and pumping up that volume.

✉ *Stoa Liabei* ✛ *Between Anexatrisias and Kannigos Sts.* ☎ *69370/23130 Route 66, 26510/33771 Montage.*

Shopping

Ioannina has long been known throughout Greece for its silver craftsmanship and for its jewelry, copper utensils, and woven items. You can find delicate jewelry on the island of Nissi, but there are also many stores selling silver on Odhos Averoff (the better place for larger items, like trays, glasses, and vases), near Neomartiros Georgiou Square. Avoid the shinier and brighter items in stores near the entrance to the citadel.

CERAMICS

Vasilis Gatzias Ergastiri Kataskevis Kosminatos

CERAMICS/GLASSWARE | On Nissi, you will find a handful of quaint little stores selling replicas of traditional objects, such as Turkish water pipes and ornate knives, silver pill boxes encrusted with semiprecious stones, ceramic vases, and jewelry. Those interested in more-original work should head here, to the only boutique that creates unique, handmade pieces. ✉ *Nissi* ☎ *26510/81878.*

CRAFTS

Center of Traditional Handcraft of Ioannina (Kepavi)

CRAFTS | A silversmiths' cooperative, Kepavii sells the silverware and jewelery produced by 44 regional workshops. Items vary in style and technique, including many traditional Epirote pieces as well as some interesting modern ones. The prices are good, and there's something to suit all pockets. ■**TIP→ You can also take a tour of some of the workshops and watch the smiths practicing their fine skills.** ✉ *Archipiskopou Makariou 11* ✛ *On the road bordering Lake Pamvotis* ☎ *26510/27650, 26510/27660* ⊕ *www. kepavi.gr* ☾ *Closed weekdays 2:30–6.*

Pagouri est. in Ioannina

CRAFTS | This is a really interesting and modern little gift shop, with handmade and painted objects like sunglasses, tote bags and clutches, painted postcards, and lighting frames of the town made by local artists. They also sell herbal olive oil soaps. ✉ *Karamanli 35* ☎ *6946/153431.*

Zagorohoria Region
Ζαγοροχόρια

40 km–60 km (25 miles–37 miles) north of Ioannina.

One of the most beguiling and untamed sections of Greece is the region of Zagorohoria (pronounced zah-go-ro- *hor-ee-ah*), also known as Zagori or Zagoria, which comprises 46 villages to the north and northwest of Ioannina. During the last decade, the famously picturesque Zagorohoria region has become popular among Greeks, and is a place mostly visited by foreigners who are "in the know." Its cultured people, stunning landscapes, cozy guesthouses, World Heritage–protected architecture, and sparkling rivers make it a unique and romantic destination.

Here you can see beautifully maintained *arhontika* (stone mansions with walls and roofs made of gray slate from surrounding mountains), winding cobblestone streets, graceful arched Turkish bridges, churches with painted interiors, *kalderimi* (old mule trails), and forests of beech, chestnut, and pine. If you have only a day to spare, rent a car or bargain with a taxi driver in Ioannina to transport you to some of the many villages connected by well-paved roads. If you opt to spend the night in one of the villages, you have the chance to truly soak up the local color, get a look at the interiors of some of the Ottoman-style living quarters, and partake of some excellent food. Wonderful hikes are another pleasure for those who choose to stay and explore awhile. Some of the villages, such as Megalo, Mikro Papingo, Monodendri, and Konitsa, are likely to be busy with travelers in July and August, particularly on weekends and major holidays. Book ahead or, better yet, stay in some of the (even) lesser-known villages, some of which have only 10 permanent residents.

Kipi, 40 km (25 miles) north of Ioannina in the central Zagori, is famous for its three-arch packhorse bridge, and the community runs a fascinating folklore museum. **Tsepelovo,** 5 km (3 miles) northeast of Kipi, is one of the most authentic villages. Perched on the slopes of Mt. Tymphai, at 3,960 feet, it was built using the gray-brown tile-like rock that makes up most of the surroundings. A must-see village, **Monodendri,** 44 km (27 miles) north of Ioannina, is a well-preserved settlement perched on the rim of a breathtaking gorge on the boundary of the Vikos–Aoos National Park. There's a stunning vista from the abandoned 15th-century monastery, Agia Paraskevi.

Papingo, 59 km (37 miles) north of Ioannina, has delightful architecture—many houses are still topped with the silvery blue slate that used to be so common throughout Epirus—varied scenery, and friendly locals, although it was among the first villages here "discovered" by wealthy Greeks. It's divided into two towns. **Megalo Papingo,** aka Big Papingo, is near the Voidomatis River, which has excellent rafting and canoeing. **Mikro Papingo,** aka Little Papingo, is 1.5 km (1 mile) up the road from Megalo Papingo, below some limestone rocks; it's really small—the population is fewer than 100—but appealing. **Dilofo** (31 km [19 miles] from Ioannina), aka Two Hills, is one of the best-preserved, quietest, and most picturesque villages in the region, and among the very few where cars can park at its entrance. Your kids (and you) can run safe and free along its cobblestone footpaths.

GETTING HERE AND AROUND

Buses, which depart from G. Papandreou Avenue 45, Ioannina, for the region's larger villages, are few and far between, going only once or twice a week: to Kipi, Monday 6 am and 1:30 pm and Thursday 5:30 am and 1:30 pm; and to Papingo, Tuesday 5:30 am and 2:30 pm. Renting a car is the ideal way to visit, or take a taxi—your hotel should be able to let you know ballpark figures for where you want to go and may arrange the taxi for you.

🛏 Hotels

Bourazani Wild Life Resort

$ | **HOTEL** | **FAMILY** | The old Bourazani hunting lodge has been revamped into this accommodating resort (more of a hotel/lodge actually), one of the few places to stay in this immediate region, which has been given over to nature; the only noises to be heard at night are the distant rustling of the river Aoos and the song of nightingales. **Pros:** owners are gold mines of info about activities; excellent river fishing nearby; great breakfast. **Cons:** access difficult without a car—and call first for detailed directions; mounted animal heads on the walls won't appeal to everyone; patchy Wi-Fi. [$] *Rooms from: €85* ✉ *Bourazani, Konitsa* ☎ *26550/61283, 26550/61320* 🌐 *www.bourazani.gr* 🛏 *20 rooms* 🍴 *Free breakfast.*

Gaia

$ | **B&B/INN** | A comfortable, elegant, and well-designed guesthouse, Gaia rose from the ruins of an 1862 mansion thanks to the efforts of devoted owners, architect Yiannis Anastasakis and his wife, Thomais, who literally built Gaia with their own hands after buying it on a passionate whim because they fell in love with the area on a trip. **Pros:** homey and comfortable; very good breakfast with homemade products; guides available for walks. **Cons:** few in-room amenities; Dilofo is a very quiet village; rooms fill fast in high season, so book early.

Ⓢ *Rooms from: €85* ✉ *Dilofo* ✛ *Off main square* ☎ *26530/22570* ⊕ *www.gaia-dilo-fo.gr* ⇆ *7 rooms* ⦶ *Free breakfast.*

Zarkada

$ | **B&B/INN** | Most of the guest rooms in this pension in the heart of the picturesque village of Monodendri have fireplaces—an essential luxury during the long and cold winter nights—and three rooms have saunas, while another seven have hot tubs. **Pros:** feel-good amenities; helpful service; central location, in one of the bigger villages of the area. **Cons:** not all the rooms have fireplaces; some bathrooms are in need of a makeover; some rooms have poor Wi-Fi signal. Ⓢ *Rooms from: €60* ✉ *Monodendri* ✛ *Off main square* ☎ *26530/71305* ⊕ *www. monodendri.gr* ⇆ *18 rooms* ⦶ *Free breakfast.*

 Activities

Hiking is one of the real pleasures of the Zagorohoria region, but trails can be challenging, not to mention dangerous. Your safest bet is to go on a guided walk; a number of outfitters schedule gorge hikes and other invigorating activities. Make sure you have proper footwear, hiking gear, food and water, and emergency supplies and provisions, and *never* hike in heavy rains or go far in groups of fewer than four. Staff at most hotels can provide basic maps and put you in touch with local guides or trekking clubs. If you want to go it alone, the Greek Alpine Club is a good source of information for a safe hike; it is also a good idea, as a precaution, to let your hotel know where you are going and when you expect to return.

If you're a physically fit hiker, you may want to hike at least part of the steep and long **Vikos gorge.** To get to the famed gorge—the deepest in the world—you follow a precipitous route from the upper limestone tablelands of Monodendri, down almost 3,300 feet to the clear, rushing waters of the Voidomatis trout stream (no swimming allowed) as it flows north into Albania. It's a strenuous but exhilarating eight-hour hike on which you are likely to see dramatic vistas, birds of prey, waterfalls, flowers and herbs, and hooded shepherds tending their flocks.

MAPS

Anavasi

WALKING TOURS | One of the best hiking maps of Zagori are by Anavasi. It's GPS compatible and includes shorter and longer walks in the area. ☎ *210/3218104* ⊕ *www.anavasi.gr.*

OUTFITTERS

★ No Limits

ADVENTURE TOURS | **FAMILY** | Specialists in the Zagorohoria region, No Limits tours are a fun way to see and explore this spectacular little corner of Europe. They offer rafting, rock climbing, river trekking, zip-lining, and hiking. ✉ *Central square, Konitsa* ☎ *6944/751418* ⊕ *www. facebook.com/nolimits.rafting* ⛴ *From €45 for a two-day excursion.*

Robinson Expeditions

ADVENTURE TOURS | This Ioannina outfitter specializes in outdoor tours and can make arrangements for single travelers or groups to hike the Vikos gorge; other programs are hang gliding, canyoning, rafting, mountain biking, kayaking, and nature study. The company also schedules rock-climbing excursions around the Meteora. ✉ *Kipi (Gardens), Zagorohoria* ☎ *26530/71850, 6944/313485* ⊕ *www. robinson-trip.com* ⛴ *From €35.*

★ Trekking Hellas

ADVENTURE TOURS | **FAMILY** | This well-established and reliable outfitter offers activities and excursions throughout Greece and uses the best local experts as guides. In Zagorohoria, activities range from a leisurely 90-minute walk from Vitsa to Kokaris bridge—ideal for families—to a full eight-day expedition in the region that includes hiking and rafting. They also lead exciting adventure tours in Meteora and Metsovo, and offer multiday guided and self-guided hikes in the area. ✉ *Spiro Lamprou 7, Zagorohoria* ☎ *26510/71703* ⊕ *www.trekking.gr* ✉ *From €52.*

Metsovo Μετσοβο

58 km (36 miles) east of Ioannina, 293 km (182 miles) northwest of Athens.

The quaintly traditional village of Metsovo cascades down a mountain at about 3,300 feet above sea level, below the 6,069-foot Katara pass, which is the highest in Greece and marks the border between Epirus and Thessaly. Even in summer, the temperatures may be in the low 20s C (70s F), and February's average highs are just above freezing. Early evening is a wonderful time to arrive. As you descend through the mist, dazzling lights twinkle in the ravine. Stone houses with gray-slate roofs and sharply projecting wooden balconies line steep, serpentine alleys. In the square, especially after the Sunday service, old men—dressed in black flat caps, dark baggy pants, and wooden shoes with pom-poms—sit on a bench, like crows on a tree branch. Should you arrive on a religious feast day, many villagers will be decked out in traditional costume. Older women often wear dark blue or black dresses with embroidered trim every day, augmenting these with brightly colored aprons, jackets, and scarves with floral embroidery on holidays. Note that there is no EOT (tourist office) in Metsovo.

GETTING HERE AND AROUND

A bus or car from Ioannina takes about 45 minutes; bus tickets are €5.80. There is no train service to Metsovo.

 Sights

Although most such villages are fading away, Metsovo, designated a traditional settlement by the Greek National Tourism Organization (GNTO or EOT), has become a prosperous, self-sufficient community with a growing population. In winter it draws skiers headed for Mt. Karakoli, and in summer it is—for better or worse—a favorite destination for tourist groups. For the most part Metsovo has preserved its character despite the souvenir shops selling inauthentic "traditional handi-crafts" and the slate roofs that have been replaced with easy-to-maintain, cheaper tile.

The natives are descendants of nomadic Vlach shepherds, once believed to have migrated from Romania but now thought to be Greeks trained by Romans to guard the Egnatia highway connecting Constantinople and the Adriatic. Metsovo became an important center of finance, commerce, handicrafts, and shepherd-ing, and the Vlachs began trading farther afield—in Constantinople, Vienna, and Venice. Ali Pasha abolished the privileges in 1795, and in 1854 the town was invad-ed by Ottoman troops led by Abdi Pasha. In 1912 Metsovo was freed from the Turks by the Greek army. Many important families lived here, including the Averoffs and Tositsas, who made their fortunes in Egyptian cotton. They contributed to the new Greek state's development and bequeathed large sums to restore Metsovo and finance small industries. For example, Foundation Baron Michalis Tositsa, begun in 1948 when a member of the prominent area family endowed it (although he was living in Switzerland), helped the local weaving industry get a start.

Agia Paraskevi

RELIGIOUS SITE | The freely accessible 18th-century church of Agia Paraskevi has a flamboyantly decorated altar screen that's worth a peek. Note that July 26 is its saint's day, entailing a big celebration in which the church's silver icon is carried around the town in a morning procession, followed by feasting and dancing. ✉ *Main square.*

★ Averoff Museum

MUSEUM | **FAMILY** | This fascinating museum of regional paintings and sculptures showcases the outstanding art collection amassed by politician and intellectual Evangelos Averoff (1910–90), whose effect on Metsovo is still lauded today. The 19th- and 20th-century paintings depict historical scenes, local landscapes, and daily activities. Most major Greek artists, such as Nikos Ghikas and Alekos Fassianos, are represented. One painting known to all Greeks is Nikiforos Litras's *Burning of the Turkish Flagship by Kanaris,* a scene from a decisive battle in Chios. Look on the second floor for Pericles Pantazis's *Street Urchin Eating Watermelon,* a captivating portrait of a young boy. Paris Prekas's *The Mosque of Aslan Pasha in Ioannina* depicts what Ioannina looked like in the Turkish period. There is also a children's art room where fidgety youngsters can create masterpieces set for the kitchen fridge. ✉ *Main Sq.* ☎ *26560/41210* ⊕ *www.averoffmuseum.gr* 💶 *€3* ⊘ *Closed Tues.*

Katogi-Averoff Winery

WINERY/DISTILLERY | Enjoy a tour around this important winery, with 1,200 oak barrels, and discover the wine-making process, animated with video projections and sound and art installations. The journey ends in the wine-tasting area, so just try leaving without a few bottles of the exquisite, full-bodied, musky red Katogi-Averoff wine. For those who can't seem to tear themselves away, booking into the four-star Katogi-Averoff Hotel is a must (pardon the pun). ✉ *Metsovo*

⊹ *Eastern edge of village, in Upper Aoos valley* ☎ *26560/31490* ⊕ *www.katogiaveroff.gr* 💶 *Free* ⊘ *Closed weekends, last tour starts at 3 pm* ☞ *Book at least one day in advance.*

★ Tossizza Museum

HOUSE | For generations the Tossizza family had been one of the most prominent in Metsovo, and to get a sense of how Metsovites lived (and endured the arduous winters in style), visit their home, a restored late-Ottoman-period stone-and-timber building that is now the Tossizza Museum of popular art and local Epirote crafts. Built in 1661 and renovated in 1954, this typical Metsovo mansion has carved woodwork, sumptuous textiles in rich colors on a black background, and handcrafted Vlach furniture. In the stable you'll see the gold-embroidered saddle used for special holidays and, unique to this area, a fanlight in the fireplace, ensuring that the hearth would always be illuminated. The goatskin bag on the wall was used to store cheese, one of the area's most noted products. Wait for the guard to open the door prior to the tour. Guides usually speak some English. ✉ *Metsovo* ⊹ *Up stone stairs to right off Tositsa (main road) as you descend to main town square* ☎ *26560/41084* 💶 *€3* ⊘ *Closed Thurs.*

🍴 Restaurants

Galaxias

$ | **GREEK** | A local classic with vintage rustic charm (crackling fireplace included), situated in the town's main square, this has been a go-to choice for quality local flavors for three decades. Try various homemade pies, a wide array of regional cheeses, *trachanas* (a Greek type of pasta crumb, served here in an extra creamy rendition with feta and butter), local *hylopytes* pasta stewed with tomato sauce in a ceramic pot, local game, and *kokoretsi* (lamb's intestines seasoned and cooked to a crisp on the spit). **Known for:** top-quality local produce; tasty traditional cuisine; great location and ambience. $ *Average main: €10* ✉ *Main Square* ☎ *26560/41202.*

★ To Koutouki Tou Nikola

$ | GREEK | *Koutouki* ("little box"), aptly named for its diminutive interior, is a good value, just one reason this place is so popular with the locals. All the taverna favorites are here, but order something made with the local cheese, or the amazing *hilopotes* (local pasta) cooked in a chicken broth, or the divine celery-leek-and-beef meatballs. **Known for:** excellent local cuisine; really good quality at a low price; warm and friendly service. $ *Average main: €9* ✉ *Aghiou Georgiou, Averof Georgiou 44200* ✛ *Next to the post office* ☎ *26560/41732* 🚫 *No credit cards.*

To Paradosiako

$ | GREEK | The name means "traditional," and that's what this comfortable spot decorated with colorful weavings and folk crafts is. Vasilis Bissas, the chef-owner, has revived many of the more esoteric regional specialties. **Known for:** hearty winter fare; good friendly service; large portions. $ *Average main: €10* ✉ *Tositsa 44* ☎ *26560/42773* 🚫 *No credit cards.*

Hotels

Apollon Hotel

$ | HOTEL | Family-run and centrally located, looking out on the Pindos mountain range, Apollon is built in traditional style, topped by picturesque coves, and offers comfortable, modern amenities along with old-world accents. **Pros:** friendly, obliging, family-run business; located right in the center of town; refurbished in 2019. **Cons:** not all rooms have good views; weak Wi-Fi signal in some rooms; small bathrooms. $ *Rooms from: €60* ✉ *Main square* ☎ *26560/41844* ⊕ *metsovohotel.gr* 🛏 *40 rooms* ❖ *Free breakfast.*

Grand Forest Metsovo

$$ | HOTEL | Your view of the verdurous and imposing nature that surrounds you is everything in this top-notch hotel, that can make for an idyllic getaway throughout the year. **Pros:** five-star amenities at an excellent price; wonderful spa and pool area; stunning mountain vistas. **Cons:** one of the floors is not serviced by an elevator; tricky to get to—you definitely need a car; 15 minutes drive from Metsovo. $ *Rooms from: €130* ✉ *Interchange 7A to Anilio* ✛ *Off Egnatia Odos Hwy.* ☎ *26560/29001, 26563/00500* ⊕ *www.grand-forest.gr* 🛏 *62 rooms* ❖ *Free breakfast.*

★ Hotel Bitouni

$ | HOTEL | FAMILY | Local craftsmen created the elegantly carved wooden ceilings in this traditional-style Metsovo mansion—at its heart a large fireplace in the main reception room nicely warms the cozy hotel. **Pros:** great breakfast with many homemade treats; excellent and helpful service; great value lodging also has free parking. **Cons:** luxury lovers, look elsewhere; only a few basic amenities in room; not all rooms have the mountain views. $ *Rooms from: €55* ✉ *Tositsa St.* ✛ *On the main street leading up from main square* ☎ *26560/41217* ⊕ *www.hotelbitouni.com* 🛏 *30 rooms* ❖ *Free breakfast.*

Katogi Averoff Hotel

$$ | HOTEL | Offering an elegant combination of cozy rural allure and modern comforts, this luxurious but not over-the-top hotel gives a sense of a prestigious country home. **Pros:** cozy, understated luxury; rooms with large, comfortable beds and elegant bathrooms; friendly, professional service. **Cons:** on the pricey side for the area; in-room Wi-Fi can be a little sketchy; a little out of town. $ *Rooms from: €130* ✉ *Metsovo* ☎ *26560/42505* ⊕ *www.katogiaveroffhotel.gr* 🛏 *15* ❖ *Free breakfast.*

🛍 Shopping

Metsovo is known for its fabrics, folk crafts, silver, and smoked cheese. Although many of the "traditional" arts and crafts here are imported low-quality imitations, with a little prowling and patience you can still make some finds, especially if you like textiles and weavings. Some are genuine antiques that cost a good deal more than the newer versions, but are far superior in quality. Everything's available on the main square.

Aris Talaris

JEWELRY/ACCESSORIES | This is actually two shops: one sells quality silver jewelry made in Talaris's own workshop, and the other displays gold pieces. The Metsovo silverwork trade is one of the oldest in the region; members of the Talaris family have been silversmiths for many generations (and now they have branched out as hoteliers, owning the hotel where their shops are). ⊠ Hotel Egnatia, Tositsa 19 ☎ 26560/41263, 26560/41900.

Divanis Gallery

ANTIQUES/COLLECTIBLES | Peruse regional collectibles and memorabilia spanning a few centuries up to the present day. Expert and enthusiast, Dimitris, has been scouring the country for over 30 years for local heirlooms, so even if you're not interested in purchasing anything, this shop is still worth a little of your time. ⊠ Tsoumaka 6 ☎ 24340/91330, 69730/11538 ⊕ www.divanisgallery.com ⊗ Closed weekdays.

Pigi

FOOD/CANDY | This colorful shop overflows with cheeses of all shapes and sizes. Metsovo is renowned for its cheese, and you will find any local variety your heart (or palate) desires, from the smoky metso-vitico ewe's and cow's milk cheese to the zingy metsovela and even a local Parmesan that rivals any from Italy. ⊠ Tositsa 17 ✛ On the left of the main road leading to the main square ☎ 26560/42163 ⊕ www.tirokomikapigi.gr/en.

🏃 Activities

Metsovo is one of the few places in Greece to offer winter skiing, when the entire region is covered in snow and the area's famed Vlach shepherds even have to move their flocks from the mountains to the lowlands around Trikala.

★ Anilio Adventure Park

SKIING/SNOWBOARDING | Until recently simply a ski resort with 12 ski runs, an ice-skating rink, and open only in the snowy months from mid-November to early March, Anilio Adventure Park, befittingly is now open year round offering a variety of lung-busting and adrenalin-enducing activities, taking full advantage of the glorious alpine locale. So now you can enjoy mountain biking, mountain running and hiking, climbing, and slacklining. The onsite chalet serves a few bites and a good variety of soothing hot drinks. ⊠ Metsovo ✛ Take the E92 and then left onto the E90 following the signs for Anilio; hotel is 6 km (4 miles) south of Metsovo ☎ 2651/200–520.

Dodona Δωδώνη

22 km (14 miles) southwest of Ioannina.

The only thing to do, or see for that matter, at the somewhat isolated Dodona, are the ancient ruins. This archaeological site, steeped in history and mystery, is worthy of the time and effort it takes to visit, and dedicating a whole day is most rewarding.

Said to be the oldest oracle in Greece, the Dodona flourished for well over a millennium, from at least the 8th century BC until the 4th century AD, when Christianity succeeded the cult of Zeus. Homer, in the *Iliad*, mentions "wintry Dodona," where Zeus's pronouncements made known through the burbling brook and the wind-rustled leaves of a sacred oak, were interpreted by priests "whose feet are unwashed and who sleep on the ground." The oak tree was central to the cult, and its image appears on the region's ancient coins. Here Odysseus sought forgiveness for slaughtering his wife's suitors, and from this oak the Argonauts took the sacred branch to mount on their ship's prow. According to one story, Apollo ordered the oracle moved here from Thessaly; Herodotus, however, writes that it was locally believed a black dove from Thebes in Egypt landed in the oak and announced, in a human voice, that the oracle of Zeus should be built.

There is a little canteen at the entrance to the site where visitors can get refreshments, but bringing a simple packed lunch—some bread, cheese, olives, and a tomato—is a pleasant alternative. You can sit and listen for whispers from long-forgotten Zeus, father of gods.

GETTING HERE AND AROUND
The most efficient way to get here from Ioannina is with a rented car or a taxi; the driver will wait an hour or so at the site. Negotiate with one of the drivers near Ioannina's clock tower or ask your hotel to call a cab. Only on Fridays are there buses from Ioannina's main bus station, G. Papandreou Ave. 45, one at 6:45 am and the other at 1 pm.

◉ Sights

★ Dodona
ARCHAEOLOGICAL SITE | Vestiges of two of ancient Greece's important cosmological and cultural institutions, divining and drama, are here—you can see the space of the ancient oracle and the superbly preserved and impressive theater. As you enter the archaeological site, you pass the **stadium** on your right, built for the Naïa games and completely overshadowed by the **theater** on your left. One of the largest and best preserved on the Greek mainland, the theater once seated 17,000; it is used for summer presentations of ancient Greek drama. Its building

in the early 3rd century BC was overseen by King Pyrrhus of Epirus. The theater was destroyed, rebuilt under Philip V of Macedon in the late 3rd century, and then converted by the Romans into an arena for gladiatorial games. Its retaining wall, reinforced by bastions, is still standing. East of the theater are the foundations of the **bouleuterion** (headquarters and council house) of the Epirote League, built by Pyrrhus, and a small rectangular temple dedicated to Aphrodite. The remains of the **acropolis** behind the theater include house foundations and a cistern that supplied water in times of siege.

The remains of the **sanctuary of Zeus Naios** include temples to Zeus, Dione (goddess of abundance), and Heracles; until the 4th century BC there was no temple. The Sacred Oak was here, surrounded by abutting cauldrons on bronze tripods. When struck, they reverberated for a long time, and the sound was interpreted by soothsayers. ✉ *On main Ioaninon–Dodonis road, signposted off E951, Dodoni* ☎ *26510/82287* ⊕ *odysseus.culture.gr* ✍ *€8, including visits to Archaeological Museum of Ioannina and Byzantine Museum of Ioannina.*

Kalambaka Καλαμπακα

71 km (44 miles) east of Metsovo, 154 km (95 miles) southwest of Thessaloniki.

Kalambaka may be dismissed as one more drab modern town, useful only as a base to explore the fabled Meteora complex north of town. Yet an overnight stay here, complete with a taverna dinner and a stroll around the main squares, offers a taste of everyday life in a provincial Thessalian town. This will prove quite a contrast to an afternoon spent at nearby Meteora, where you can get acquainted with the glorious history and architecture of the Greek Orthodox Church. Invariably, you return to modern Kalambaka and

Today the theater at Dodona—one of Greece's grandest—remains the enthralling site for summer concerts and performances.

wind up at a poolside bar to sip ouzo and contemplate the asceticism of the Meteora monks. If you'd rather stay in a more attractive place slightly closer to the monasteries, head to Kastraki, a hamlet with some pleasing folk-style houses about 2.5 km (1½ miles) north of Kalambaka.

GETTING HERE AND AROUND

The famous Meteora monasteries, set just outside Kalambaka, are easily accessible by both train and slightly more expensive bus, but, as most trips, it is by far preferable to take the bus rather than the slow and creaky trains that service the area. Buses connecting Kalambaka with Trikala take 45 minutes and leave Trikala at 5 am then hourly until 1 pm, and 2:15 then hourly until 10:15 pm; tickets are €2.10. Buses to and from Athens take 5 hours and require a change at Trikala; tickets are €29 one-way, €44 round-trip. Buses to the major port of Volos depart Kalambaka at 7 am, 11:30 am, 3 pm, and 7 pm; tickets are €15.

The Kalambaka–Ioannina bus (3 hours) departs at 8:30 am and 3 pm; tickets are €15.

There are seven trains daily from Athens to Kalambaka (€18–€38). Trains often connect with Trikala (15 minutes, €1.80–€2.60), the major transportation hub of Thessaly; there are four trains daily. Kalambaka is currently the last stop on this OSE route.

 Sights

Dormition of the Virgin

RELIGIOUS SITE | Burned by the Germans during World War II, Kalambaka has only one building of interest, the centuries-old cathedral church of the Dormition of the Virgin. Patriarchal documents in the outer narthex indicate that it was built in the first half of the 12th century by Emperor Manuel Comnenos, but some believe it was founded as early as the 7th century, on the site of a temple of Apollo (classical drums and other fragments are incorporated into the walls, and mosaics can be glimpsed under the present floor). The latter theory explains the church's paleo-Christian features, including its center-aisle *ambo* (great marble pulpit), which would usually be located to the right of the sanctuary; its rare *synthronon* (four semicircular steps where the priest sat when not officiating) east of the altar; and its Roman-basilica style, originally adapted to Christian use and unusual for the 12th century. The church has vivid 16th-century frescoes, the work of the Cretan monk Neophytos, son of the famous hagiographer Theophanes. The marble baldachin in the sanctuary, decorated with crosses and stylized grapes, probably predates the 11th century. ⊠ *Kalambaka* ✛ *North end of town, follow signs from Riga Fereou Sq.* ☎ *24320/22752* ⊕ *odysseus.culture. gr/h/2/eh251.jsp?obj_id=1703* 🎟 *€1.50.*

⊗ Restaurants

Estiatorio Meteora

$ | GREEK | At this spot on the main square, a local favorite since 1925, the Gkertsos family serves food prepared by the matriarch, Ketty. Meteora is known for hearty main courses—try Ketty's special wine-and-pepper chicken, veal, or pork *stifado* (stew)—and some specialties from Asia Minor, including *tzoutzoukakia Smyrneika*, aromatic meatballs in a red sauce laced with cumin. **Known for:** traditional local recipes; family-run service; warm surface. $ *Average main: €10* ⊠ *Ekonomou 4* ✛ *On Dimarchiou Sq.* ☎ *24320/22316* ⊕ *meteora-restaurant.gr* ▭ *No credit cards* ⊗ *Closed Dec.–Jan. Lunch only Oct.–Nov. and Mar.–May.*

Meteoron Panorama Restaurant

$ | GREEK FUSION | Come here just for the knockout views of Meteora and the Kalambaka plain below, and the food isn't bad either. Of course, to make sure you get a prime position on the veranda it's best to book in advance. **Known for:** great views of Meteora; attentive

Not So Crystal Clear

The Dodona oracle had its ups and downs. Consulted in the heroic age by Heracles, Achilles, and all the best people, it went later into a gentle decline because of its failure to equal the masterly ambiguity of Delphi.

service; traditional Greek food. $ *Average main: €10* ⊠ *Patriarchou Dimitriou 54* ☎ *24320/78128* ⊕ *www.meteoronpanorama.gr.*

★ O Kipos Tou Ilia

$ | GREEK | FAMILY | Also know as Elias's Garden restaurant, this simple taverna with a traditional Greek menu and a waterfall in the garden attracts everyone from visiting royalty to Olympic-medal winners. Kids get their own *pethika piata* (kids' plates). **Known for:** al fresco dining in a lovely shaded garden; fun, engaging, and slightly eccentric owner; great quality local meat. $ *Average main: €12* ⊠ *Trikalon 149* ✛ *At terminus of Ayia Triada, before entrance to Kalambaka* ☎ *24320/23218* ⊕ *www.gardenrestaurant.gr.*

Paradisos

$ | GREEK | When a Greek cooks with *meraki* (good taste and mood), the world does indeed find *paradissos* (paradise). Owner Kyriakoula Fassoula serves meat dishes cooked *tis oras* (to order), such as grilled pork and lamb chops. **Known for:** tasty regional cuisine; friendly service; good views of Meteora. $ *Average main: €8* ⊠ *Kastraki* ✛ *On main road to Meteora across from Spania Rooms* ☎ *24320/22723* ⊗ *Closed Nov.*

Continued on page 661

Nearer to Heaven
THE METEORA MONASTERIES

Ayia Triada

Here in the most remote corner of Greece, landscape and legend conspire to twist reality into fantasy. Soaring skyward out of dense orchards looms a different kind of forest: gigantic rock pinnacles, the loftiest of which rises 984 feet. But even more extraordinary than these stone pillars are the monasteries that perch atop the stalagmitic skyscrapers. Funded by Byzantine emperors, run by ascetic monks, and once scaled by James Bond, these saintly castles-in-air are almost literally "out of this world."

The name Meteora comes from the Greek word *meteorizome* ("to hang in midair"). These world-famous monasteries seem to do just that. The origin of these rocks, which loom up between the Pindos range and the Thessalian plain, is an enigma. Some geologists say a lake that covered the area 30 million years ago swept away the soil and softer stone as it forced its way to the sea. Others believe the inexorable flow of the Peneus River slowly carved out the towering pillars, now greatly eroded by wind and rain. Legend created, as it often does, a more colorful story: the rock needles are meteors hurled to earth by an angry god.

THE MONASTIC BUILDERS

Man first staked claim to the Meteora peaks when the inaccessible pinnacles served as refuge to pious hermits in the turbulent 14th century. As soon as the Turkish rulers of Trikkala began warring with the Byzantine emperors of Constantinople for rights to the fertile valley, these anchorite monks were forced to retreat to the heights of the impregnable rocks. In 1336 they were joined by St. Athanasios, who hailed from fabled Mt. Athos. Notwithstanding the legend that says that the saint flew up to the rocks on the back of an eagle, Athanasios began the backbreaking task of building the Megalo Meteoro (1356–72)—the biggest of the Meteora monasteries—using pulleys and ropes to haul construction materials.

By the 16th century, 13 monasteries had been established here as bastions of Christianity. During the late-Byzantine period, they are said to have helped "save" Western civilization from the inroads of Turkish domination. In the end, however, the Meteora monasteries came to poignantly epitomize both the glory and the decline of Eastern monasticism. Once the former abodes of emperors and kings, they are now largely supported by tourism.

A VISIT TODAY

For centuries, jointed ladders and descending nets were the only way to ascend the rocky peaks. Tourists who may yearn for the days when travelers made the ascent squeezed into an outsize string-bag are cured of their nostalgia after one look at the rusty windlass, especially if accompanied by the gruesome story that the rope was only ever changed "when it broke." Today, stone bridges, rock-hewn stairs, and *monopati* (old paths) guide visitors up hundreds of steps to the heavenly monasteries.

VISITING THE MAIN MONASTERIES

Set atop the Meteora's "heavenly columns" are six sky-kissing monasteries. While their dizzying perch seems attributable only to divine intervention, their architecture can be dated from the 14th to 17th centuries. Restricted by space, the buildings rise from different levels.

Monks at Megalo Meteoro use cable cars to avoid tourist crowds on the stairs

Some are whitewashed; others display the pretty Byzantine pattern of stone and brick, the multiple domes of the many churches dominating the wooden balconies that hang precariously over the frightening abysses.

NIKOLAOS ANAPAFSAS: THE ROAD LESS TRAVELED

Even though **Ayios Nikolaos Anapafsas** (Holy Monastery of St. Nicholas Anapausas) is the first monastic complex you see and is accessed by a relatively unchallenging path, many travelers hurry on to the large, Megalo Meteoro, leaving this one relatively uncrowded. Its *katholikon* (church), built 1388, faces north rather than the usual east because of the rock's peculiar shape and the rock's small area precluded the construction of a cloister, so the monks studied in the larger-than-usual narthex. While the monastery dates from the end of the 15th century, its superb frescoes are from the 16th century and the work of Theophanis Strelitzas. Though conservative, his frescoes are lively and expressive: mountains are stylized, and plants and animals are portrayed geometrically. Especially striking are the treatments of the Temptation and the scourging of Christ.

Ayios Nikolaos Anapafsas
☎ 24320/22375 ✉ €3 ⊙ Apr.–Oct., Sat.–Thurs. 9–3:30; Nov.–Mar., Sat.–Thurs. 9–1

VARLAAM: FABLED FRESCOES

The monastery closest to the Megalo Meteoro is the **Varlaam**, which sits atop a ravine and is reached by a bridge and a climb of 195 steps. Originally here were the Church of Three Hierarchs (14th century) and the cells of a hermitage started by St. Varlaam, who arrived shortly after St. Athanasios. Two brothers from the wealthy Aparas family of Ioannina rebuilt the church in 1518, incorporating it into a larger katholikon called Agii Pandes (All Saints). A church document relates how it was completed in 20 days, after the materials had been accumulated atop the rock over a period of 22 years. The church's main attraction, the 16th-century frescoes—including a disturbing Apocalypse with a yawning hell's mouth—completely covers the walls, beams, and pillars. The frescoes' realism, the sharp contrasts of light and dark, and the many-figured scenes show an Italian influence, though in the portrayal of single saints they follow the Orthodox tradition. Note the Pantocrator peering down from the

Greek icon, Meteora

dome. These are the work of Frangos Katellanos of Thebes, one of the most important 16th-century hagiographers. Set around a pretty garden, other buildings include a chapel to Sts. Cosmas and Damien. By the large storerooms is an ascent tower with a net and a winch.

Varlaam ☎ 24320/22277 💶 €3
🕙 May–Oct., Sat.–Thurs. 9–4; Nov.–Apr., Sat.–Wed. 9–3

AYIA BARBARA: GET THEE TO A NUNNERY

On the lowest rock—thought an appropriate tribute to male superiority by the early monks (who first refused to have women in the Meteora)—the compact monastery of **Ayia Barbara** (Holy Monastery of Rousanou) was the only nunnery in the complex centuries ago. With its colorful gardens in and around red- and gray-stone walls, it is a favorite for picture-taking. Set on a large mesa-like rock, the squat building was abandoned in the early 1900s and stood empty until a new order of nuns moved in some years ago and restored it. The monastery was thought to have been founded in 1288 by the monks Nicodemus and Benedict. The main church has well-preserved frescoes dating from the mid-16th century. Most depict gory scenes of mar-

tyrdom, but one shows lions licking Daniel's feet during his imprisonment. The nunnery is accessible via steps and a new bridge.

Ayiya Barbara ☎ 24320/2269 💶 €3
🕙 Apr–Oct., daily 9–6; Nov–Mar., daily 9–2

MEGALO METEORO: HIGHEST AND GRANDEST

Superlatives can be trotted out to describe the **Megalo Meteoro** (Church of the Metamorphosis [Transfiguration])—the loftiest, richest, biggest, and most popular of the monasteries. Founded by St. Athanasios, the monk from Athos, it was built of massive stones 1,361 feet above the valley floor and is reached by a stiff climb of more than 400 steps. As you walk toward the entrance, you see the chapel containing the cell where St. Athanasios once lived. This monastery, known as the Grand Meteoron, gained imperial prestige because it counted among Athanasius's disciples the Hermit-King Ioasaph of Serbia and John Cantacuzene, expelled by his joint emperor from the Byzantine throne. Dating from 1387—1388, the sanctuary of the present church was the chapel first built by St. Athanasios, later added to by St. Ioasaph. The rest of the church was erected in 1552 with an unusual transept

built on a cross-in-square plan with lateral apses topped by lofty domes, as in the Mt. Athos monasteries. To the right of the narthex are the tombs of Ioasaph and Athanasios; a fresco shows the austere saints holding a monastery in their hands. Also of interest are the gilded iconostasis, with plant and animal motifs of exceptional workmanship; the bishop's throne (1617), inlaid with mother-of-pearl and ivory; and the beautiful 15th-century icons in the sanctuary. In the narthex are frescoes of the Martyrdom of the Saints, gruesome scenes of persecution under the Romans. Note the kitchen, blackened by centuries of cooking, and the wine cellar, filled with massive wine barrels. The gift shop is noted for its icons and incense. From November to March the monastery may close early.

Megalo Meteoro ☎ 24320/22278 🎟 €3 ⏲ Apr.–Sept., Wed.–Mon. 9–4; Oct.–Mar., Thurs.–Mon. 9–3

AYIA TRIADA: FOR YOUR EYES ONLY?

The most spectacularly sited of all the Meteora monasteries, **Ayia Triada** (Monastery of the Holy Trinity) is shouldered high on a rock pinnacle isolated from surrounding cliffs; it is reached via rock tunnels and 130 stone-hewn steps (see opening photo). Primitive and remote, the monastery will also be strangely familiar: James Bond fans will recognize it from its starring role in the the 1981 movie For Your Eyes Only (the famous winch is still in place, and you may be shown it in a tour by the one monk who lives here). According to local legend, the monk Dometius was the first to arrive in 1438; the main church, dedicated to the Holy Trinity, was built in 1476, and the narthex and frescoes were added more than 200 years later. Look for the fresco with St. Sisois gazing upon the skeleton of Alexander the Great, meant to remind the viewer that power is fleeting. The apse's pseudo-trefoil window and the sawtooth decoration around it lend a measure of grace to the structure. Ayia Triada is fabled for its vistas, with Ayios Stephanos and Kalambaka in the south and Varlaam and Megalo Meteoro to the west. Conveniently, a well-traveled footpath near the entrance (red arrows) descends to Kalambaka, about 3 km (2 miles) away.

Ayia Triada ☎ 24320/22220 ☒ €3 ☾ May–Sept., Fri.–Wed. 9–5; Oct.–Apr., Fri.–Tues. 10–4

AYIOS STEPHANOS: AGING GRACEFULLY

At the far end of the eastern sector of the Meteora is **Ayios Stephanos**, the oldest monastery—a permanent bridge has replaced the movable one that once connected the monastery with the hill opposite, making this perhaps the most easily accessible, with a car road passing not far below the entrance. According to an inscription that was once on the lintel, the rock was inhabited before 1200 and was the hermitage of Jeremiah. After the Byzantine emperor Andronicus Paleologos stayed here in 1333 on his way to conquer Thessaly, he made generous gifts to the monks, which funded the building of a church in 1350. Today Ayios Stephanos is an airy convent, where the nuns spend their time painting Byzantine icons, writing, or studying music; some are involved in the community as doctors and professors. The katholikon has no murals but contains a carved wooden baldachin and an iconostasis depicting the Last Supper. You can also visit the 15th-century frescoed church of Ayios Stephanos as well as a small icon museum.

Ayios Stephanos ☎ 24320/22279 ☒ €3 ☾ Apr.–Oct., Tues–Sun. 9–1:30 and 3:30–5:30; Nov.–Mar., Tues.–Sun. 9:30–1 and 3–5

660

PLANNING YOUR METEORA VISIT

HOW MANY MONASTERIES CAN I SEE IN A DAY? All monasteries can be visited in a single journey from Kalambaka— a 21-km (13-mile) round-trip by car— but most visitors prefer to do only two or three, especially if they are hiking along the old monopati (old paths) that connect the monasteries. Most of the stairs upwards are in fine shape but some of the paths are crumbling in places and require the skill of an inordinately sure-footed goat (no heels, please!). ■TIP➔ Megalo Meteoro and Varlaam are the two most rewarding monasteries to visit if time is tight. Whatever your mode of transport, buy a map of the monasteries in Kalambaka.

WHAT IS THE GENERAL GEOGRAPHIC LAYOUT? Heading out from Kalambaka, the comfortable Patriarhou Dimitriou road serpentines past the village of Kastraki and then winds its way ingeniously through the sandstone Meteora labyrinth. The first monastery is Ayios Nikolaos Anapafsas. Beyond it lies the mammoth Megalo Meteoro and, vis-à-vis, Varlaam. Southward is Ayia Barbara and, after a major curving detour, Ayia Triada and Ayios Stephanos. Along the main road, arrowed signposts indicate the turn-offs for the various monasteries. Note, however, that you have to journey along side roads that run for at least one mile (sometimes as much as two) to get to the feet of the monasteries.

HOW CHANGEABLE ARE THE OPENING HOURS? We list official opening hours, but as these can vary depending on the season (winter hours are usually more limited), confirm the information with your hotel receptionist in Kalambaka. And leave plenty of time before setting off up the

hun-dreds of steps: if you don't, you may find the monastery door closed at the top once you get there!

IS THERE A DRESS CODE? When visiting you are expected to dress decorously: men must tuck up long hair and wear long pants, women's skirts (no pants allowed) should fall to the knee, and always cover shoulders. Some monasteries provide appropriate coverings at their entrances.

IS THERE ANYPLACE TO EAT? Once on the monastery circuit, there are just a few overpriced concession stands; if you plan to make a day of it, stock up on picnic goods in town.

CAN I GET TO THE MONASTERIES BY BUS? A bus leaves Kalambaka for Megalo Meteoro five times daily (once daily in winter); the bus returns to town in late afternoon.

Coffee and Quick Bites

O Vakis

$ | **FAST FOOD** | Best grill/souvlaki joint in town, for either a sit-down meal or take-out (they can deliver to your hotel too). The gyros, both chicken and pork, are juicy and tender. You'll need to search out this eatery as it's on a side street just off the town's main road. **Known for:** speedy service; top quality local meats; tasty Greek style fast food. [$] *Average main: €3* ✉ *Siderodromou 18* ☎ *24320/24126.*

Pub 38

$ | **AMERICAN** | English-style pub with a plethora of Greek and international beers in the heart of Kalambaka. Pop in for a sly pint (a liter here) or hang out and enjoy the predominantly rock (rather appropriate for Meteora) sounds and the easy eating, North American-inspired bar grub (burgers, hot dogs, and spicy glazed chicken wings) that they happily dish out. **Known for:** large selection of beers; warm friendly staff; tasty food. [$] *Average main: €8* ✉ *28th October St. 18* ☎ *24320/25008.*

Hotels

Amalia

$ | **HOTEL** | **FAMILY** | At this low-lying, clay-color complex just outside Kalambaka on the road to Trikala, guests can relax in the sitting room with striking antiques, floral murals, and a fireplace—you can also enjoy fireplaces in the bar and restaurant—or chill out at the poolside bar, with glistening blue tiles and rustic rafters. **Pros:** spacious, elegant public rooms; lush green garden setting; large swimming pool. **Cons:** a little outside the city; tour group stopover; somewhat unreliable Wi-Fi. [$] *Rooms from: €100* ✉ *Theopetra* ✣ *14 km (9 miles) along Ethnikos Odos Trikalon–Ioanninon road* ☎ *24320/72216* 🌐 *www.amaliahotelkalambaka.gr* 🛏 *170 rooms* 🍴 *Free breakfast.*

Dellas Boutique Hotel

$ | **HOTEL** | **FAMILY** | A good quality hotel in very close proximity to Meteora's famous rocks and the rich surrounding nature makes this a solid choice. **Pros:** free hotel parking; lovely views of the surrounding area; very helpful staff. **Cons:** weak and slow Wi-Fi; no elevator (but only two floors); small bathrooms. [$] *Rooms from: €80* ✉ *Kastraki* ✣ *On the road between Kalambaka and Kastraki* ☎ *24320/78260* 🌐 *dellasboutiquehotel.com* 🛏 *18 rooms* 🍴 *Free breakfast.*

★ **Divani Meteora Hotel**

$ | **HOTEL** | A few minutes from the center of town, this modern hotel has optimal views of the Meteora rocks from the rooms' balconies, and its large well-designed open spaces, quiet corners, and private garden encourage relaxation. **Pros:** significantly cheaper deals for booking in advance; fast and reliable service; large outdoor pool, small indoor pool and spa. **Cons:** not the prettiest building facade; tour groups regularly bused in; breakfast is rather standard. [$] *Rooms from: €110* ✉ *Ethnikos Odos Trikalon 1* ☎ *24320/23330* 🌐 *www.divanis.com* 🛏 *165 rooms* 🍴 *Free breakfast.*

★ **Doupiani House**

$ | **B&B/INN** | A stay here means residing in a traditional stone-and-wood hotel set amid vineyards in the upper reaches of the idyllic village of Kastraki, where each room—with a luxurious carved double bed, oak floors, and closets—has a balcony with panoramic views of both Meteora and Kastraki. **Pros:** excellent and helpful staff have extensive local knowledge; ideal combo of comfort and tradition; wonderful hearty breakfast. **Cons:** not all rooms have the stunning view of the monasteries; patchy Wi-Fi; a little out of the way, but close to the monasteries. [$] *Rooms from: €90* ✉ *Kastrakiou, Kastraki* ✣ *Left off main road to Meteora, near Cave Camping* ☎ *24320/75326, 24320/77555* 🌐 *www.doupianihouse.gr* 🛏 *17 rooms* 🍴 *Free breakfast.*

Pyrgos Adrachti

$$ | **HOTEL** | **FAMILY** | Immersed in greenery and directly overlooking the massive monolithic pillars of Meteora, Pyrgos Adrachti makes for a unique secret getaway. **Pros:** proximity to the monasteries makes this an ideal base for visitors; very friendly and helpful staff; free parking. **Cons:** not all rooms have the magnificent views, so request when booking; a little out of the way; the steep driveway can be tricky to navigate. [$] *Rooms from: €140* ✉ *Kastraki* ✥ *Right turn off the main road of Kastraki immediately after Hotel Gogos. 1 1/2 km (1 mile) to the end of that road.* ☎ *24320/22275* 🌐 *www.hotel-adrachti.gr* 🛏 *9 rooms* 🍴 *Free breakfast.*

Nightlife

Kalambaka isn't the most cosmopolitan town, but you may find some fun places for ice cream or coffee along the main drag, Trikalon. Dimoula Square is all abuzz on weekends, as locals descend from the surrounding villages.

Melydron Cafe

CAFES—NIGHTLIFE | If you're taking the bus up to Meteora, this busy café on the square next to the Kalambaka town hall is a good spot for that extra coffee boost, as it's right next to the bus stop. Melydron is also a decent watering hole at night. ✉ *Patriarchou Dimitriou 2* ☎ *24320/75003.*

★ Rapsodia Cafe Bar

BARS/PUBS | This is Kalambaka's hot spot, with live bands and pool tables drawing in the local youth. It's a good place to head if you need a break from the quiet austerity of monastic visits. Oh, and if you get peckish, the food here also rocks. It's typical bar fare: burgers, nachos, and the like. ✉ *Eleftheriou Venizelou 4* ☎ *24320/77741.*

Meteora Μετεωρα

3 km (2 miles) north of Kalambaka, 178 km (110 miles) southwest of Thessaloniki.

As you drive through the mighty Pindos range, strange rock formations rise ever higher from the plain. Just beyond the dramatic sheer cliff that shelters the town of Kalambaka, the legendary monasteries of Meteora—one of the wonders of the later Middle Ages—begin to appear along a circular road as it winds 6 km (4 miles) through an unearthly forest of gigantic rock pillars.

Sights

★ Meteora

HISTORIC SITE | The ancients believed the rock formations to be meteors hurled by an angry god. Ascending to 1,820 feet above sea level, these towers, in fact, owe their fantastic shapes to river erosion. But they owe their worldwide fame (and Hollywood moment of glory—remember the James Bond *For Your Eyes Only* climax?) to what perches atop six of them: the impregnable monasteries built here by pious hermits in the turbulent 14th century. ✉ *Meteora, Meteora.*

Volos

A relatively new city by Greek standards, Volos and surrounding Magnesia are steeped in history and myth, with Neolithic settlements dating to 7000 BC and tales of a visit from Jason and his Argonauts. Now a bustling port city, it derives much of its youthful energy from the student population at the University of Thessaly and from summer tourists seeking Mediterranean fun and sun.

Sights

Athanasakeion Archaeological Museum
MUSEUM | Local finds from the region's rich history are displayed in this neoclassical building from 1909. Artifacts like jewelry, pottery, clay statuettes, household utensils, and agricultural tools dating back to the neolithic period are presented in eight halls. The most popular items are entire tombs transported from nearby excavation sites, which include both skeletons and grave offerings. A few neolithic dwellings from Dimini and Sesklo have been reconstructed outside the museum. ✉ *1 Athanasaki St.* ☎ *24210/25285* 🌐 *efamagvolos.culture.gr/Mouseio_Volou* 🎫 *€4* 🕒 *Closed Tues.*

Goritsa Hill
ARCHAEOLOGICAL SITE | The east side of Volos butts up against the pine-forested Goritsa Hill, which rises about 650 feet above the town, is accessible by hiking trails, and provides panoramic views. At the top is the church of Zoodochos Pigis, erected atop of a temple on what was the summit of the ancient city's acropolis. But it's the church of Panagia Tripa di Gorista at the bottom, built inside a natural cave thought to be sacred since ancient times and once dedicated Zeus, that remains the favorite. ✉ *Volos.*

Pelion Railway
FACTORY | **FAMILY** | Industrial development in the region during the late 19th century necessitated the building of a railroad linking Volos to the picturesque Milies, 27 km (17 miles) east. Destroyed by retreating German troops and subsequent earthquakes, only the second half of the line remains open to tourists, connecting Ano Lechonia with the latter. The train itself, an old-school steam locomotive nicknamed "Moutzouris" ("smudgy," in English) chugs along at a tepid 19 km (12 miles) per hour, which is the right speed for taking in the stupendous views of Pagasitikos Bay. Trips normally take 1½ hours each way and stop for 15 minutes in Ano Gazea. ✉ *Ano Lechonia* ☎ *24210/39723* 🌐 *www.trainose.gr* 🎫 *€10.*

Restaurants

Creperie Poquito
$ | **FRENCH** | Many a late-night craving in Volos has been satisfied at this gourmet creperie near the waterfront. It's not just the sweetness or savoriness of the dishes that stimulate hunger pangs, but the inventiveness of combinations by chef and owner Konstantinos Siatras in dishes like bitter chocolate crepes with sauteed orange and cinnamon, and salmon with vegetables and pink pepper. **Known for:** crepes; creative menu; lively atmosphere. [$] *Average main: €7* ✉ *13 Skenderani* ☎ *69448/62435* 🕒 *Closed Sun. No lunch.*

★ **MeZen**
$$ | **MODERN GREEK** | One of Volos's claims to fame is its *tsipouradiko* taverns, named for the regional spirit made by distilling the residue of the grapes after pressing them to make wine. There are plenty to be found in the city's nooks and crannies, including this one, near the waterfront, which has combined the tradition with a youthful spirit that draws from modern gastro-style restaurants, with Edison lightbulbs, copper tubing, and aged raw wood. **Known for:** inventive meze dishes; upbeat environment; large selection of ouzo and tsipouro. [$] *Average main: €15* ✉ *8 Alonnisou* ☎ *24210/20844* 🌐 *www.mezen.gr* 🕒 *Closed Sun.*

To Hondro Bizeli (the Fat Pea)
$ | **GREEK** | Heartful, homemade, original and unpretentious cuisine made with love in a modern taverna ambience. Its menu, popular among students, couples, and groups of friends alike, includes saffron risotto; chicken marinated in orange juice, ginger and turmeric; green beans with garlic butter; and creamy cheese pie made with crispy angel-hair phyllo-pastry.

Known for: warm, buzzy ambience; original recipes using local and regional ingredients; friendly service. ⓢ *Average main: €7* ✉ *Aghialou 6* ☏ *24210/36989* ⊘ *Closed Sunday.*

To Katofli tis Ketis

$ | GREEK | Chef Giorgos and his mother take traditional Greek dishes and gives them a twist at this recently renovated restaurant 19 km (12 miles) from Volos in the village of Katichori. Most of the vegetables are grown in their own garden and the olive oil is produced nearby. **Known for:** fresh local cuisine; warm atmosphere; well-presented dishes. ⓢ *Average main: €14* ✉ *Volos* ☏ *24280/99108* ⊘ *Closed Tues.*

 # Hotels

Domotel Xenia Volos

$$ | RESORT | The summer residence of the gods, according to Greek myth, is now home to one of the city's top hotels. **Pros:** very good breakfast; lovely views; good facilities, spa, parking, and pool. **Cons:** public beach outside hotel stays loud into the night; pricey restaurant and bar; some wear and tear. ⓢ *Rooms from: €127* ✉ *1 Plastira St.* ☏ *24210/92700* ⊕ *domotel.gr/xenia-volos/* ⇆ *77 rooms, 2 suites* �� *Free breakfast.*

Hotel Aegli

$ | HOTEL | Although it has just three stars, the Aegli clearly has aspirations for something more—after yet another renovation in 2016, the hotel offers a suprising amount of comfort, space, and design savvy across its three floors. **Pros:** free parking is an added bonus for center of town; good value for money; waterfront location next to the port. **Cons:** rooms at the back get street noise; seaview rooms get booked quickly; limited amenities. ⓢ *Rooms from: €80* ✉ *24 Argonafton* ☏ *24210/24471, 24210/33006* ⊕ *www.aegli.gr* ⇆ *72 rooms* ⓞ *Free breakfast.*

Chapter 14

THESSALONIKI AND CENTRAL MACEDONIA

14

Updated by
Adrian Vrettos

👁 **Sights**
★★★★☆

🍴 **Restaurants**
★★★★☆

🛏 **Hotels**
★★★☆☆

🛍 **Shopping**
★☆☆☆☆

🍸 **Nightlife**
★★☆☆☆

WELCOME TO THESSALONIKI AND CENTRAL MACEDONIA

TOP REASONS TO GO

★ **Mount Olympus:** Bask in a gods'-eye view from the top of Greece's highest peak, often covered in clouds and lighting as if to prove Zeus still holds sway. Ascend skyward thanks to numerous enchanting trails.

★ **Thrilling Thessaloniki:** In this great commercial hub, the Armani suits and €5 coffees are in contrast to the ruins of the ancient city walls, Byzantine monuments, and the spirited bartering of the city's bazaar.

★ **Between heaven and earth:** Lush Mt. Athos, pinpointed with monasteries, is Greece's most solemn precinct; off-limits to women, it is an exclusive Orthodox bastion as well.

★ **Alexander the Great sites:** The fabled ancient ruler made this region the crossroads of the ancient world. Walk in his footsteps in Pella (his birthplace) and Vergina (home to the royal tomb of his father, Philip II).

At the crossroads of East and West, Macedonia bears the traces of many civilizations: Macedonian, Hellenic, Roman, Byzantine, and Ottoman. Greece's second city, cosmopolitan Thessaloniki lies in the strategic center of Macedonia, nestled gracefully in the wide but protective arms of the Thermaic Gulf and buttressed on its inland side by a low-lying mountain range around which the Axios River flows south to the Aegean. Macedonia's famed three-fingered peninsula, tipped by famed Mt. Athos monasteries, are only a few hours away by car on good highways.

1 **Thessaloniki.** Named after Alexander the Great's stepsister, this bustling, commercial center is Greece's second city and has always played a supporting role. Rather than wallow in this eternal bridesmaid status, Thessaloniki has excelled as a cultural and business center, with some of Greece's best food and nightlife (it is known as the country's Liverpool, for the jazz and rock groups that were formed here), much of which is

concentrated around its beautifully planned and architecturally rich city center.

2 **Pella.** Known as Alexander the Great's birthplace, Pella also served as the capital of the Macedonian state in the 4th century BC. On the hill to the north, one can visit the palatial complex where King Philip and Alexander once lived.

3 Vergina. It's here that Philip II, the father of Alexander the Great, was assassinated in 336 BC and where he was buried among the Royal Tombs.

4 Dion. At the this sacred site unearthed ruins of various buildings include the villa of Dionysos, public baths, a stadium, and workshops.

5 Mount Olympus. Don't miss an excursion to Greece's highest and most storied peak. Look up or down at this fabled peak and you'll understand why people settled at its foot and dreamed up the 12 Greek gods believed to live in the folds of the mountain.

6 Ouranoupolis. Meaning "heaven's city" in Greek, Ouranoupolis is an appealing village, noted for its rug and tapestry weaving. The popular holiday destination is also particularly entrancing because of the bay's aquamarine waters.

7 Mt. Athos. Called Ayion Oros (Holy Mountain) in Greek, the peninsula is prized for its monasteries, which contain priceless illuminated books and other treasures.

A land shaped by gods, warriors, and ghosts, Northern Greece sparkles with the sights, sounds, scents, and colors of its melting-pot history and epic geography. Here you will find remnants of the powerful civilizations that battled each other: temples and fortifications built by Athens and Sparta, Macedonian tombs, the arches and rotundas of imperial Rome, the domes of Byzantium, and the minarets and hammams of the Ottomans. Today, these sights rank among the most splendid sightseeing delights in Greece.

Burnished by history, the area that is often called Northern Greece borders Albania, the Former Yugoslav Republic of Macedonia (FYROM, also known as Skopje), Bulgaria, and Turkey. From north to south, this land is heritage-rich. "Even today, house-owners sometimes dream that beneath their cellars lie Turkish janissaries and Byzantine necropolises," wrote historian Mark Mazower in his 2004 book *Salonica: City of Ghosts*. "One reads stories of hidden Roman catacombs, doomed love-affairs, and the unquiet souls who haunt the decaying villas near the sea."

Around 316 BC, the Macedonian leader Cassander founded what is now the area's major city, Thessaloniki, which grew into a culturally rich and politically strategic metropolis where Christians,

Muslims, and Jews lived together for hundreds of years. Today it remains the second-largest city in Greece, is an anchor for arts and culture in the Balkans, and also brims with antiquities, old-style street markets, and old-world European flavor. Beyond Thessaloniki lies Central Macedonia, where you can explore ancient monasteries, admire the frescoed tomb of Philip II of Macedon, hike the bloom-filled trails leading to Mount Olympus, commune with farmers over grilled wild mushrooms, and enjoy some of Greece's finest beaches and seaside resorts.

The region was established as the state of Macedonia in the 8th century BC, and an illustrious monarchy was ensconced by about the 7th century BC. Philip II (382–336 BC) and his son Alexander the

Great conquered most of the rest of Greece—except Sparta—and all of Persia. After Alexander's death, his brother-in-law, Cassander, established Thessaloniki as the capital (316 BC), naming it for his new bride, Thessalonica, Alexander's half sister and daughter of the much-married Philip. (Philip had named her after his famous *nike*, or "victory," in Thessaly, where her mother had been one of the prizes.) The Romans took Macedonia as Alexander's successors squabbled, and by 146 BC, the rest of Greece had fallen under Roman rule. After the assassination of Julius Caesar, Marc Antony defeated Brutus and Cassius at the battles of Philippi in Macedonia in 42 BC. Under Pax Romana, St. Paul twice traveled through on his way to Corinth.

Greek and Macedonian culture bloomed again during the Byzantine Empire (circa AD 312–1453), when the center of Greek civilization shifted from Athens to Constantinople (modern-day Istanbul). Thessaloniki became the second-most important city in the empire, and it remained so during the Ottoman domination that lasted from the fall of Constantinople until the 1912–13 Balkan Wars. That's when Macedonia became part of Greece, and the 1923 Treaty of Lausanne established the present borders with Thrace. The collapse of Yugoslavia in the 1990s rekindled ethnic and religious animosities. Today's northern Greeks are fiercely nationalist, and they strongly oppose the Former Yugoslav Republic of Macedonia's (FYROM) insistence on calling itself "Macedonia" and using ancient Macedonian symbols such as the star of Vergina on its flag, in an attempt to create a speedy and easily identifiable post-Communist national identity. Tempers flared again in December 2006, when FYROM announced plans to name its international airport in Skopje after Alexander the Great.

Name-game squabbling aside, Northern Greece is flourishing. It's a hub for southeast European commerce and culture, and is home to Aristotle University, Greece's largest. The area is also expected to benefit from the Egnatia Odos, a 669-km (416-mile) road project that connected the Greek–Turkish border with the western port of Igoumenitsa. An influx of immigrants, many of them from Eastern Europe and the Middle East, is once again giving a multicultural flavor to Thessaloniki.

Planning

When to Go

Travel throughout Northern Greece is best from May through October. Fall is beautiful; the air is cool and clear and the forests are dressed in burnished hues of orange, red, and copper. Spring is also lovely, especially in Dion, with its blooming fields of wildflowers scenting the breeze. Winters are mild, though there's usually enough snow in the north to keep ski resorts in business. July and August are the most crowded, but best for sunning, swimming, and chatting with Northern Europeans and Greek families on holiday. In summer, Thessaloniki gets hot and humid but rarely reaches the scorching temperatures that sizzle southern Greece. As a whole, Northern Greece is rainier and cooler than the rest of Greece, especially in mountainous areas.

Autumn and winter rains, besides turning some roads to mud, do not enhance the appearance of Thessaloniki, a city designed for the sun.

Planning Your Time

Thessaloniki makes a great base for a trip to Northern Greece. Most of the city's sights are concentrated within the easily walkable center, and the city is also the main hub for regional buses and rental cars. There are wonderful museums and a great counterculture vibe. You could easily spend days exploring Greece's second-largest city, especially if you're an ecclesiastical buff (the five-aisled basilica Ayios Dimitrios is Greece's largest church) or a foodie (Thessaloniki has outstanding restaurants). From Thessaloniki, go west to Pella, the birthplace of Alexander the Great. Then go south to the town of Vergina, home of the magnificent Royal Tombs, and the ancient city of Dion, tucked into the lush foothills of Mount Olympus. You'll need at least two days to hike the great summit of the gods, including an overnight stay in the pretty village of Litochoro.

Getting Here and Around

Thessaloniki doesn't have good public transportation, but a new metro is scheduled to open in 2023. Nevertheless, getting around the city on foot is fairly easy, since most of the sights are relatively close together. Taxis are also an option, and at reasonable prices. If you choose to drive, know that the traffic here can be as bad as the gridlock in Athens. That changes once you get out of Thessaloniki. The national highway is easy to navigate, and the smaller roads in Central Macedonia are well paved. If you wish to rent a car, there are several reliable car rental agencies in Thessaloniki. There are also buses daily that go to major sites in Central Macedonia, many belonging to the giant KTEL company.

AIR

The New Thessaloniki Makedonia International Airport (SKG) is at Mikras, 13 km (8 miles) southeast of the city center on the coast; it's about a 20-minute drive. In addition to international flights from primarily European destinations, there are frequent daily flights to and from Athens; flying time is 45 minutes. Domestic carriers, including Aegean Air and its subsidiary Olympic Air, connect Thessaloniki with a number of other cities in mainland Greece as well as Mykonos, Santorini, Crete, Rhodes, Corfu, Limnos, Chios, and Lesvos.

Bus 78 to and from the airport originates at the KTEL bus terminal, stops at the train station, and makes a stop at Aristotle Square (along Egnatia). Taxis charge according to the meter, with a €3.60 surcharge from the airport; expect to pay around €25 to the Town Center (after midnight the charge doubles).

CONTACTS Thessaloniki Macedonia International Airport. ⊠ Km 16, Ethnikos Odos, Thessaloniki–Perea road, Thessaloniki ☎ ⊕ www.skg-airport.gr.

BOAT AND FERRY

Hellenic Seaways, Nel, Minoan, and other sea lines connect Thessaloniki to Chios, Lesvos, Samos, Heraklion (Crete), Kos, Rhodes, Skiathos, Skopelos, Naxos, Mykonos, Paros, and Santorini. Buy tickets at the Karacharisis Travel and Shipping Agency, Zorpidis Travel Services (Sporades and Cyclades only), Alexander Travel, or another travel agency. You can connect to Piraeus from Kavala, 136 km (85 miles) east of Thessaloniki (confirm schedules with the Kavala Port Authority). In summer, you should reserve ferries a month in advance. The Greek Travel Pages (⊕ www.gtp.gr) list ferry schedules online.

CONTACTS Choice Travel. ✉ *Zefxidos 1 and Iktinou, on Boardwalk, Thessaloniki* 🕾 *2310/237255, 2310/220104* ⊕ *www. choicetravel.gr.* **Karacharisis Travel and Shipping Agency.** ✉ *Salaminas 10, Port* 🕾 *2310/513005, 2310/524544* ⊕ *thesferry.gr.* **Kavala Port Authority.** ✉ *Averof 1, Kavala* 🕾 *2510/223691, 2510/225192* ⊕ *www.portkavala.gr.* **Zorpidis Travel Services.** ✉ *Egnatia 76, Kentro* 🕾 *2310/231170, 2310/244400* ⊕ *www. zorpidis.gr.*

BUS

The trip to Thessaloniki from Athens takes about 6 hours and costs €45 one way and €65 return (with 10 buses per day), with one rest stop. Intercity KTEL buses connect Thessaloniki with cities throughout Greece. There are small ticket-office terminals (*praktorio*) for each line and separate ticket offices and telephone numbers for each destination. You can browse the KTEL website to get an idea of timetables (it's in Greek, so use Google to translate the page), or call KTEL Thessaloniki Main Terminal, but it's best to make ticket inquiries in person. The KTEL Main Terminal is on Thessaloniki's southwestern outskirts, off National Road (Ethnikos Odos). Buses to Halkidiki leave from another KTEL terminal (⊕ *www. ktelmacedonia.gr*) every half-hour from 4 am until 10:45 pm. All of this can be confusing, so definitely confirm both the time of your bus and the terminal from which it leaves when you buy your ticket.

CONTACTS KTEL Main Terminal. ✉ *Giannitson 244, Thessaloniki* 🕾 *2310/595400 call center, 2310/595421 reservations for buses in Thessaloniki, 2310/595413 reservations for buses to Athens, 2310/595428 reservations for buses to Litochoro, 2310/595435 reservations for buses to Veria* ⊕ *ktelmacedonia.gr.*

CAR

Driving to Greece through the Former Yugoslav Republic of Macedonia is possible but often time-consuming owing to many border problems. The

Athens–Thessaloniki section of the Ethnikos Odos (National Road), the best in Greece, is 500 km (310 miles); the drive takes 5 to 7 hours. The roads in general are well maintained and constantly being improved and widened throughout the region. A good four-lane highway that begins in Athens goes to the border with Turkey. Posted speed limits are up to 120 kph (75 mph). When there's traffic, vehicles regularly use the shoulder as an extra lane, even though this is illegal. Driving in Thessaloniki is not recommended because of the congestion, frequent traffic jams, and scarcity of parking. Walking and taking a local bus or taxi are much easier on the nerves.

Having a car to get out of town and explore the smaller villages is helpful. Major car-rental agencies have offices at the Thessaloniki airport (some also have in-town locations). Aeolos is a good location option.

CONTACTS Aeolos. ✉ *Agelaki 23, Kentro* 🕾 *2312/201888* ⊕ *www.aeoloscarrentals. com.*

TRAIN

Thessaloniki is the primary entry point for train travel to Northern Greece. Of the six Athens–Thessaloniki trains that run per day, five are express (taking 5 hours 23 minutes). Make reservations in advance at Athens Larissis Station's (Stathmos Larissis) south office (far-left facing, not the main entrance ticket booths, which are for same-day tickets only), or in Thessaloniki. The fastest intercity train will set you back €55.40 for a class-A seat or €45.40 for class B, and it's worth paying the difference for the extra comfort. Other express options begin at €35.10 for class A and €25.10 class B, and take 7 hours. Thessaloniki Station also has a left-luggage office (€2 for 8 hours, €3 for 24 hours) where you can store your bags before checking into or after checking out of your hotel.

CONTACTS OSE Thessaloniki Train Station.
✉ *Monastiriou 28, West Thessaloniki*
☎ *14511 Customer Service (6 am–11 pm)*
⊕ *www.ose.gr.*

Hotels

In the past, Thessaloniki's hotels were nothing to write home about and were mostly geared to the needs of transient business travelers, with little emphasis on capturing the spirit-of-place so appealing to tourists. Today, there are some more fetching options out there with the new emergence being smaller upscale boutique hotels. The selection of hotels throughout Northern Greece varies from exclusive seaside resorts in Chalkidiki to modest family-managed hostels on the slopes of Mount Olympus to luxe outposts in Thessaloniki. Throughout the countryside, hotels are usually small, somewhat spartan affairs whose charm comes mainly from their surroundings. Note that some establishments—particularly in Chalkidiki—close for the winter (we've noted when this is the case); it is best to make arrangements ahead.

Restaurants

Thessaloniki is not only Greece's northern capital but also its culinary capital. Traditional Thracian and Macedonian cooks adapt to the seasons: in winter, rich game such as boar and venison is served; in summer, there are mussels and other seafood from the Aegean, as well as fruits and vegetables from the fertile plains. The relatively cooler climate here is reflected in rich soups like *patsas* (tripe), roast chicken, stuffed vegetables, and stewed lamb and pork. Local restaurants also reflect Jewish, French, Ottoman, and Balkan culinary traditions.

Small plates (*mezedes*) are a fundamental part of the Thessaloniki dining experience. Specialties include *midia* (mussels), which come from farms outside the bay and are served in styles that include *saganaki* (sauteed in a pan with tomatoes, peppers, and melted feta) and *achnista* (steamed in broth with herbs). Also look for *soutzoukakia* (Anatolian-style meatballs in a rich tomato sauce seasoned with cumin). *Pinerli* (an open-faced boat of bread filled with cheese and ham) is a Black Sea specialty brought here by the Pontii, Greeks who emigrated from that area. Thessaloniki's street food and indulgent sweets are also famous throughout the country.

Meals are complemented by generous amounts of wine, ouzo, and especially *tsipouro*, the local version of grappa. Try the excellent barrel or bottled local wines, especially reds under labels such as Naoussa or Porto Carras or a little bottle of Malamatina retsina, considered the best bottled version in Greece, as is the Boutari label, created by passionate wine maker and popular former mayor, Yiannis Boutaris. Throughout the city, little shops and cellars specialize in a Macedonian treat called submarine (or *ipovrihio*), a spoonful of sugary fondant often flavored with vanilla or mastic and dipped in an ice cold glass of water, or other spoon sweets such as *visino* (black) cherries in syrup. As for dinnertime, you can arrive around 8, earlier than most Greeks like to eat dinner (many places do not open before then)—but it's much more fun to come at 9 or 10 and mix with the locals until the late hours.

Restaurant and hotel reviews have been shortened. For full information, visit Fodors.com.

What it Costs in euros			
$	$$	$$$	$$$$
RESTAURANTS			
under €15	€15–€25	€26–€40	over €40
HOTELS			
under €125	€125–€225	€226–€275	over €275

Festivals

Helaxpo, the large international trade fair that is held mid-September, makes hotel reservations very difficult to come by, as does the Thessaloniki Film Festival in November.

Apokriés

FESTIVALS | Apokriés—what Greeks call their Carnival celebrations—mark the period preceding Lent and ending on the night before "Clean Monday," the beginning of Lent for Eastern Orthodox and Catholics. These costume-and-parade affairs are particularly colorful (and often bawdy) in Northern Greece. You are welcome to join in the fun in Thessaloniki and other towns. Sohos, 32 km (20 miles) northeast of Thessaloniki, hosts a festive event in which people cavort in animal hides with sheep bells around their waists and phallic headdresses. In Naoussa, 112 km (70 miles) west of Thessaloniki, some participants wear *foustanellas* (short, pleated white kilts), special masks, and chains of gold coins across their chests, which they shake to "awaken the Earth." The whole town dons costumes and takes to the streets behind brass marching bands, which have a tradition of playing New Orleans–style jazz.

Dimitria Festival

CULTURAL FESTIVALS | St. Dimitrios's feast day is celebrated on October 26. Its secular adjunct, the Dimitria Festival, has developed into a major series of cultural events that include theater, dance, art exhibits, and musical performances. They are held from September to December at venues around Thessaloniki. ✉ *Thessaloniki* ☎ *2310/228414, 2313/318222* ⊕ *www.dimitria.thessaloniki.gr.*

Nightlife

The Thessaloniki bar-and-club scene is eclectic, dynamic, and energized. Students, academics, and artists haunt the bars on Zefxidos Street near Ayia Sofia church while music lovers crowd the stages at Mylos, a former flour mill that is now Northern Greece's most coveted arts-and-entertainment complex. In summer most clubs close, as their clients flock to the beaches of Halkidiki, which functions as an outer suburb of the city. The clubs on the road to the airport go in and out of fashion and change names (and concept) from one season to the next, so ask at your hotel for the newest and best.

When you hear locals talking about Paralia, they are referring to the road that lines the city center's waterfront, Leoforos Nikis. The cafés and bars here buzz at all hours of the day and night. Walk east along Proxenou Koromila, one block up from the waterfront, to find more intimate, cool bars.

Tours

Dolphin Hellas

GUIDED TOURS | Dolphin Hellas leads organized five-day tours of Northern Greece that begin in Athens and take in the ancient archaeological sites; these are offered approximately once a month. Like other agencies, the company also arranges tailored tours and books hotels and car rental. Going through an agency often nets a cheaper rate than those quoted to individual walk-ins. ☎ *210/9227772 in Athens* ⊕ *www.dolphin-hellas.gr.*

Eat and Walk Food Day Tours

SPECIAL-INTEREST | These tours provide an excellent way to see the sights of the city while also tasting and learning about how food, which is colorfully woven into the historic and cultural tapestry of the area, has made Thessaloniki such a culinary center. Prices start at €30, for the short walks and tasting tour. ⊠ *Mitropoleos 53, Kentro* ☎ *2310/278027* ⊕ *www.eatandwalk.gr.*

The Greek Wine Experience

EXCURSIONS | Enjoy a half- or full-day tour discovering the wines of the area. Expert guides and visits to some of the best wineries in the region. ⊠ *31 Chimonidou, Kalamaria* ☎ *69749/76508* ⊕ *www.thegreekwineexperience.com.*

Thessaloniki Tourist Guide Association

GUIDED TOURS | To hire a sightseeing guide, you can contact the Thessaloniki Tourist Guide Association. Prices vary depending on the tour and the place, but count on roughly €120 for a half-day and €160 for a full-day tour in Thessaloniki itself. Note that the TTGA offices do not have regular opening hours, so leave a message or send an email and they will get back to you. ⊠ *Agiou Mina 7, Thessaloniki* ☎ *2310/546037* ✎ *guideskg@otenet.gr* ⊕ *www.touristguides-ngreece.gr/en.*

Zorpidis Travel

GUIDED TOURS | Many tours in the region leave from Halkidiki, but major tour operator Zorpidis runs half-day tours to Vergina–Pella from Thessaloniki, and even arranges honeymoon trips. ⊠ *Mitropoleos 24, Kentro* ☎ *2310/231168* ⊕ *www.zorpidis.gr.*

Visitor Information

In Thessaloniki, the Greek National Tourism Organization (GNTO or EOT) central regional office on Tsimiski is open year-round from 8:30 to 3 on weekdays, and 8:30 to 2 on Saturday. Opening hours may be longer in summer but are not guaranteed. There's also a branch at the airport.

CONTACTS Greek National Tourism Organization. *(GNTO/EOT)* ⊠ *Tsimiski 136, at Dagkli, Kentro* ☎ *2310/254839, 2310/252170* ⊕ *www.visitgreece.gr.*

Thessaloniki
ΘΕΣΣΑΛΟΝΙΚΗ

At the crossroads of East and West, where North blends into South, Thessaloniki (accent on the "ni") has seen the rise and fall of many civilizations: Macedonian, Hellenic, Roman, Byzantine, Ottoman, and that of the Jews and the modern Greeks. Each of its successive conquerors has plundered, razed, and buried much of what went before. In 1917 a great fire destroyed much of what was left, but the colorful past can still be seen and sensed. The vibrant city with close to 1.5 million inhabitants today—also known as Thessalonike, Saloniki, Salonika, or Salonica—has a spacious, orderly layout that is partly a result of French architect Ernest Hébrard, who rebuilt the city after the fire.

Though Thessaloniki has suburbanized since the 1990s, sprawling to the east and west, the old part of the city is fairly centralized and easy to get used to. Whether you're in Ano Polis (Upper City) or along the lively seaside promenade, long, leisurely walks here are well rewarded; you will come across parks, squares, old neighborhoods with narrow alleyways and gardens, courtyards draped with laundry, neoclassical mansions, and some of the more than 50 churches and 40 monasteries. Thessaloniki's Early Christian and Byzantine monuments, with their distinctive architecture and magnificent mosaics, are UNESCO World Heritage sites. The ever-changing nature of the city continues as neighborhoods like Ladadika, a former warehouse district (which got its name from the olives and olive oil or *ladi* stored here), have been recycled into pedestrian zones of restaurants and clubs. The neighborhood is filled with young and old, strolling by fountains, snapping fingers to the music in the air, and savoring mezedes and microbrews at tables spilling onto the stone squares.

One of the most alluring aspects of Greece's "second capital" is its vibrant cultural scene—annually people travel here from across the globe to attend the city's two major film festivals, the Thessaloniki International Film Festival and the International Documentary Film Festival, both of which offer numerous parallel events like exhibitions, workshops, and performances, as well as several other independent film, music, theater, dance, and gastronomy festivals throughout the year. Its intricate cultural character is also reflected in its quarters, such as the Jewish section, and the impressive museums, buildings, restaurants, and shops associated with them.

GETTING HERE AND AROUND

You can get to Thessaloniki from Athens easily by train or bus in about 6 hours (sometimes faster by express train), or you can fly. There are also international trains daily from Thessaloniki to Istanbul, Belgrade, and Bulgaria.

Buses traveling throughout the city streets of Thessaloniki are frequent, and the routes are useful. Bus 1 goes between the train station and the KTEL Main Terminal; Bus 78 goes from the KTEL Main Terminal to the train station and the airport; Bus 36 from Voulgari and Egnatia corner (in the eastern part of the city) goes to the KTEL Halkidiki Terminal (for Ouranoupolis, etc.). Tickets cost €0.80 at bus company booths and at some kiosks (*periptera*) or corner stores; or €0.90 on the bus and the ticket is reusable for any trip up to 90 minutes after the initial validation. You can also buy a 24-hour ticket for €4.

Thessaloniki's official taxis are blue with white hoods, and there are plenty cruising the streets by day, though fewer at night, and they can be hailed anywhere. The "Taxi" sign is lit up showing the availability. The minimum fare is €3.50, but make sure that the meter is on (rates double after midnight). On the whole the drivers are not only honest but also helpful, and tipping, though not essential, is the norm. Despite the heavy traffic (every hour seems to be rush hour in Thessaloniki) taking a taxi is cheap in comparison to most other places in Europe and the United States. You can also call for a pickup or use Taxibeat, a brilliant free online service that hails the taxi of your choice in the vicinity. On Taxibeat, each taxi is rated and has useful information about the driver/taxi (e.g., languages spoken, Wi-Fi on board, pet-friendly, etc.).

BUS CONTACTS O.A.S.T.H. ✉ *Papanastasiou 90, 3rd floor, West Thessaloniki* ☎ *11085, 2310/981100* ⊕ *www.oasth.gr.*

TAXI CONTACTS Taxiway. ☎ *2310/866866, 2310/214900, 18300* ⊕ *taxiway.gr.* **Makedonia.** ☎ *2310/550500.* **Beat.** ⊕ *thebeat.co.*

Kentro

The lively shopping streets, bustling markets, and cafés of the Kentro (City Center) and adjacent areas reward you with the unexpected encounters and sensual treats of a great city. A stroll along the Nea Paralia seafront promenade with its artistic installations, sitting areas and playgrounds, is also enjoyable and a good way to walk off a big lunch. Walking eastward along the promenade, the landscaped areas and lush gardens are found at the end toward the concert hall. If you're feeling sporty, then join the locals who come here for a jog. Exploring the area from the White Tower west

One of the major crossroads of Thessaloniki, Aristotelous Square is a bustling *platia* set near the sea.

along the seaside to Aristotelous Square reveals icons of the city's history: grand monuments of Emperor Galerius, artifacts from the Neolithic period through the Roman occupation housed in the Archaeological Museum, and prominent churches, as well as the city's most important landmark, the tower itself.

 Sights

Arch of Galerius

ARCHAEOLOGICAL SITE | The imposing *kamára* (arch) is one of a number of monuments built by Galerius around AD 305, during his reign as co-emperor of Diocletian's divided Roman Empire. It commemorated the Roman victory over Persia in AD 297, and you can still see scenes of those battles on the badly eroded bas-reliefs. Originally, the arch had four pediments and a dome and was intended to span not only the Via Egnatia, the ancient Roman road, but also a passageway leading north to the Rotunda. Only the large arches remain. ⊠ *Sintrivaniou Sq., Egnatia, Kentro.*

★ Archaeological Museum of Thessaloniki

MUSEUM | The unpretentious, single-story white structure gives no hint from the outside of the treasures within. A superb collection of artifacts from Neolithic times; sculptures from the Archaic, classical, and Roman eras; and remains from the Archaic temple at Thermi all reside under this roof. Objects discovered during construction of the Egnatia and Thessaloniki–Skopje highways were added in 2005 to the collection, which is displayed in eight galleries. *Thessaloniki, the Metropolis of Macedonia* traces the city's history through artifacts and a multimedia collection. *Towards the Birth of Cities* offers remains from settlements from Kastoria to Mt. Athos that date to as early as the Iron Age. ⊠ *Manoli Andronikou 6, Kentro* ☎ *2313/310201* ⊕ *www.amth.gr* ✉ *€8.*

Atatürk Museum

HOUSE | The soldier and statesman who established the Republic of Turkey and became its president, Atatürk (Mustafa Kemal) was born here in 1881. He participated in the city's Young Turk Movement, which eventually led to the collapse of the sultanate and the formation of the modern Turkish state. About eight blocks east of the Ayios Dimitrios church, the modest pink house is decorated in Ottoman style. It has been turned into a museum, with personal items and documents of Turkey's founding father. ⊠ Apostolou Pavlou 17 and Isaia St., Kentro ✛ At Ayiou Dimitriou, behind the Turkish Consulate ☎ 2310/248452 ⊗ Closed Mon.

Athonos Square

PLAZA | A warren of side streets around a tiny square with a fountain is filled with tavernas and crafts stores. The area is frequently referred to, but it rarely appears on street maps; everyone knows where it is: 200 m from the church of Ayia Sofia. ⊠ Kentro ✛ East of Aristotelous, between Gennadiou and Karolou Dil, and between Egnatia and Ermou.

Ayia Sofia

RELIGIOUS SITE | The founding date of this church, a UNESCO World Heritage site and the focal point of the city's Easter and Christmas celebrations, has been the subject of disagreements over the centuries. Ecclesiastics think it was built after the first Council of Nicea (AD 325), when Jesus was declared a manifestation of Divine Wisdom; other church historians say it was contemporaneous with the magnificent church of Ayia Sofia in Constantinople, completed in AD 537, on which it was modeled. From its architecture the church is believed to date to the late 8th century, a time of transition from the domed basilica to the cruciform plan. The rather drab interior contains two superb mosaics: one of the Ascension and the other of the Virgin Mary holding Jesus in her arms. This latter mosaic is an interesting example of the conflict in the Orthodox Church (AD 726–843) between the iconoclasts (icon smashers, which they often literally were) and the iconodules (icon venerators). At one point

in this doctrinal struggle, the Virgin Mary in the mosaic was replaced by a large cross (still partly visible), and only later, after the victory of the iconodules, was it again replaced with an image of the Virgin Mary holding baby Jesus. The front gate is a popular meeting spot. ⊠ Ermou and Ayias Sofias, Kentro ☎ 2310/270253 ⊕ www.agiasofia.info.

Ayios Dimitrios

RELIGIOUS SITE | Magnificent and covered in mosaics, this five-aisle basilica is Greece's largest church and a powerful tribute to the patron saint of Thessaloniki. It was rebuilt and restored from 1926 to 1949, with attention to preserving the details of the original; the marks left by a fire can still be seen throughout. In the 4th century, during the reign of Emperor Galerius, the young, scholarly Dimitrios was preaching Christianity in the coppersmith district, in contravention of an edict. He was arrested and jailed in a room in the old Roman baths, on the site of the present church. While he was incarcerated in AD 303, Dimitrios gave a Christian blessing to a gladiator friend named Nestor, who was about to fight Galerius's champion, Lyaios. When Nestor fought and killed Lyaios, after having made Dimitrios's blessing public, the enraged Galerius had Nestor executed on the spot and had Dimitrios speared to death in his cell. His Christian brethren were said to have buried him there. A church that was built on the ruins of this bath in the 5th century was destroyed by an earthquake in the 7th century. The church was rebuilt, and gradually the story of Dimitrios and Nestor grew to be considered apocryphal until the great 1917 fire burned down most of the 7th-century church and brought to light its true past. The process of rebuilding the church uncovered rooms beneath the apse that appear to be baths; the discovery of a reliquary containing a vial of bloodstained earth gave credence to the idea that this is where St. Dimitrios was martyred. You enter through a

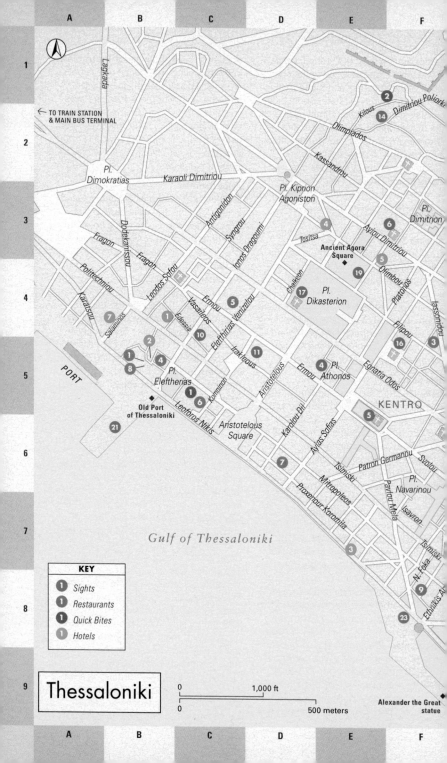

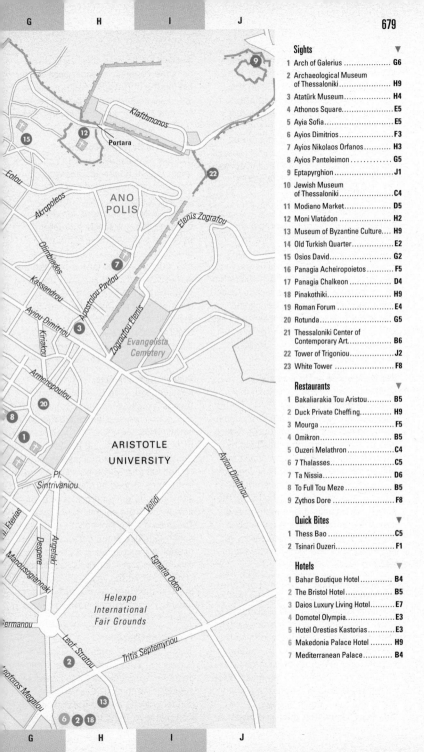

small doorway to the right of the altar. Work your way through the crypt (which tends to close a little earlier than the church itself), containing sculpture from the 3rd to 5th century AD and Byzantine artifacts. The church's interior was plastered over when the Turks turned it into a mosque, but eight original mosaics remain on either side of the altar. ⊠ *Ayiou Dimitriou 97, Kentro* ☎ *2310/270008, 2310/260915* 🖃 *Free.*

Ayios Panteleimon

RELIGIOUS SITE | A prime example of 14th-century Macedonian religious architecture, Ayios Panteleimon is an eye-catching church that draws you in to take a closer look. Restored in 1993 after an earthquake in 1978, the facade reveals the ornamental interplay of brick and stonework, and a dome displays typically strong upward motion. ⊠ *Iasonidou and Arrianou, near Egnatia, Kentro* ☎ *2310/204150.*

Jewish Museum of Thessaloniki

MUSEUM | Among the displays in this museum dedicated to the history of the local Jewish community are tombstones from the city's ancient necropolis, which was on the grounds now inhabited by Aristotle University. Also on exhibit are objects rescued from the 32 synagogues that existed around the city, some of which were destroyed by the Nazis. The neoclassical building is one of the few Jewish structures that were spared in the great fire of 1917. ⊠ *Ayiou Mina 13, Kentro* ☎ *2310/250406* ⊕ *www.jmth.gr* 🖃 *€7* ⊘ *Closed Sat.*

★ Modiano Market

BUILDING | Overhauled in 1922 by the architect Eli Modiano, this old landmark is basically a rectangular building with a glass roof and pediment facade. Inside, the rich aromas of food—fish, meats, vegetables, fruits, breads, and spices—compete with music and the noisy, colorful market characters, from the market owners to the bargain hunters. In the little tavernas nearby, ouzo and mezedes

are sold at all hours. It is worth a visit—as is the generally cheaper **open-air market** (on the north side of Ermou)—even if you have no intention of buying anything. ⊠ *Block bounded by Aristotelous, Ermou, Irakliou, and Komninon, Kentro.*

Museum of Byzantine Culture

MUSEUM | FAMILY | Much of the country's finest Byzantine art—priceless icons, frescoes, sculpted reliefs, jewelry, glasswork, manuscripts, pottery, and coins—is on exhibit here. Ten rooms contain striking treasures, notably an exquisite enamel-and-gold "woven" bracelet (Room 4), and an enormous altar with piratical skull-and-crossbones. A mezzanine (Room 7) shows how early pottery was made. Check the museum's website for the current temporary exhibitions. ⊠ *Leoforos Stratou 2, Kentro* ☎ *2313/306400* ⊕ *www.mbp.gr* 🖃 *Nov.–May €4; Apr.–Oct. €8; combined ticket with Archaeological Museum €15.*

Panagia Acheiropoietos

RELIGIOUS SITE | The name *Achiropiitos* means "made without hands" and refers to the icon representing the Virgin that miraculously appeared in this 5th-century Byzantine church during the 12th century. An early example of the basilica form, the church has marvelous arcades, monolithic columns topped by elaborate capitals, and exquisite period mosaics of birds and flowers. It is the second-oldest church in Thessaloniki and probably the oldest in continuous use in the eastern Mediterranean. An inscription in Arabic on a column states that "Sultan Murat captured Thessaloniki in the year 1430," which was the year the church was converted temporarily into a mosque. ⊠ *Ayias Sofias 56, Kentro* ☎ *2310/272820.*

Panagia Chalkeon

RELIGIOUS SITE | The name *Chalkeon* comes from the word for copper, and the beautiful "Virgin of the Copper Workers" stands in what is still the traditional copper-working area of Thessaloniki. Completed in 1028, this is one of the oldest churches in the city displaying the domed cruciform style and is filled with ceramic ornaments and glowing mosaics. Artisans and workers frequently drop by during the day to light a candle to this patron of physical laborers. Inside the sunken walls is a pretty and well-tended garden. The area around Panagia Chalkeon has many shops selling traditional copper crafts at low prices. ✉ *Chalkeon 2, Kentro* ✛ *Corner of Egnatia and Aristotelous* ☎ *2310/272910.*

Roman Forum

ARCHAEOLOGICAL SITE | The forum in the ancient agora, or market, dates back to the end of the 2nd century AD. The small amphitheater here, which hosted public celebrations and athletic and musical contests in ancient times, is now often the site of romantic concerts on balmy summer evenings. In 2011 a new museum opened here, with items from the Hellenic area through the 4th century AD. ✉ *Kentro* ✛ *Between Olimbou and Filipou, behind Dikasterion Sq.* ☎ *2310/221266, 2313/310400* ⊕ *odysseus.culture.gr* ✉ *€2; Special ticket package: Full: €15, Reduced: €8 for the site and the museum.*

Rotunda

ARCHAEOLOGICAL SITE | Also known as Ayios Giorgios, this brickwork edifice has become a layered monument to the city's rich history. Built in AD 306, it was probably intended as Roman emperor Galerius's mausoleum. When he died in Bulgaria, however, his successor refused to have the body brought back. Under Theodosius the Great, the Byzantines converted the Rotunda into a church dedicated to St. George, adding the impressive 4th-century AD mosaics of early saints. The Ottomans made it a mosque (the minaret still stands). It was restored after damage suffered in a 1978 earthquake and is still undergoing restoration at this writing. Once a month and on major holidays a liturgy is held here, as are occasional art exhibits and

All Roads Led to Thessaloniki ◉

It was during the Byzantine period that Thessaloniki came into its own as a commercial crossroads, because the Via Egnatia, which already connected the city to Rome (with the help of a short boat trip across the Adriatic), was extended east to Constantinople. Today, the avenue called Egnatia Odos virtually follows the same path; it is Thessaloniki's main commercial thoroughfare (Tsimiski, which runs parallel to it two blocks to the south, is a bit more upscale).

concerts. ✉ *Plateia Agiou Georgiou, Kentro* ☎ *2310/204868* ✉ *€2* ⊙ *Closed Tues.*

Thessaloniki Center of Contemporary Art

MUSEUM | This moody box of experimental and conceptual art, inside a remodeled warehouse on Thessaloniki's port, features a wide range of new-media art and video installations. It showcases some of the most exciting young Greek artists around and hosts cutting-edge, temporary exhibitions. ✉ *Thessaloniki Port, Warehouse B1, Kentro* ☎ *2310/593270 reception desk, 2310/546683* ⊕ *www.cact.gr* ✉ *€4* ⊙ *Closed Mon.*

★ White Tower

BUILDING | The city's most famous landmark, and a symbol of Macedonia, the White Tower is the only medieval defensive tower left standing along the seafront (the other remaining tower, the Trigoniou, is in the Upper City). Now a part of the Museum of Byzantine Culture, its six floors offer a wonderful multimedia introduction to the city's history. Much of that history occurred within these walls—for centuries this was a prison—and *on* its walls: formerly known as "Blood Tower," it got its current name in 1896 when a convict exchanged his sentence for whitewashing the entire structure (which was removed in a 1980s renovation). The displays teach you that formidable seawalls and intermittent towers encircled the medieval city and were erected in the 15th century on the site of earlier walls. In 1866, with the threat of piracy diminishing and European commerce increasingly imperative, the Ottoman Turks began demolishing them, except for the White Tower. At the top of your climb of 96 steps you are rewarded with a lovely museum café, whose rooftop setting provides sweeping vistas of the city. ✉ *Leoforos Nikis and Pavlou Melas, Kentro* ☎ *2310/267832, 2313/306400* 🌐 *www.lpth.gr* 🎫 *€6 Apr.–Oct., €3 Nov.–Mar.*

🍴 Restaurants

★ Duck Private Cheffing

$$$ | GREEK FUSION | FAMILY | A gourmet dining experience based on fresh, seasonal ingredients with an ever-changing menu, Duck offers the opportunity to sample an array of local seafood prepared in contemporary ways. You might be served fish carpaccio or shrimp *kritharoto* (barley pasta cooked risotto-style); as it should be, the duck with a fig sauce and carrot puree is exceptional. **Known for:** fresh, seasonal ingredients; a wine list with more than 50 labels; reservations-only dining. [$] *Average main: €30* ✉ *Chalkis 3, Patriarchika Pileas, Aerodromio* ✥ *Near the airport* ☎ *2315/519333* ⏲ *Closed Mon.*

★ Mourga

$ | SEAFOOD | A successful cooperative venture that has been delighting locals with their delicious seafood and veggie innovations for a few years now. Apart from the regular table seating there is a stainless steel bar in front of the open kitchen where you can watch the chefs strut their stuff up close as you chow down. **Known for:** excellent seafood; good value; great atmosphere. [$] *Average main: €10* ✉ *Christopoulou 12, Kentro* ☎ *2310/268826.*

Ouzeri Melathron

$ | MEDITERRANEAN | "Ouzo's Mansion," established as Greece's first ouzeri franchise in 1993, attracts a mainly young crowd. The chefs here are trained in a style that is essentially Mediterranean and focused on meat, with some French and Turkish influences. **Known for:** irreverently named dishes; popular and buzzy; friendly service. [$] *Average main: €10* ✉ *Karipi 21, Kentro* ✥ *In Stoa Hermion* ☎ *2310/275016.*

★ 7 Thalasses

$$ | SEAFOOD | One of the better and most creative seafood restaurants in Thessaloniki offers a menu that maintains the delicate flavors of its ingredients but also manages to add a modern twist. For instance, the marinated sea bass tartare, seasoned with fleur de sel, lemon, and olive oil, is then covered with a sprinkling of roe, bringing to mind a wave gently breaking against your tongue. **Known for:** elevated dining in a modern setting; supremely fresh seafood; good desserts. [$] *Average main: €22* ✉ *Kalapothaki 8–10 Kentro* ☎ *2310/233173* 🌐 *7thalasses.eu.*

Ta Nissia

$$ | GREEK | The food may be costly, because as the name (which means "the islands") hints, fish is king here. However, when you discover the quality, Ta Nissia doesn't seem overpriced thanks to the freshness of ingredients and artful preparations by owner-chef Yiannis Alexiou. **Known for:** offering three decades of fine dining; fish and meat with Mediterranean flavors; good wine list. [$] *Average main: €17* ✉ *Proxenou Koromila 13, Kentro* ☎ *2310/224477, 2310/285991* ⏲ *No dinner Sun. Closed Jul. and Aug.*

Zythos Dore

$$ | GREEK | Crowded and lots of fun, this café in a converted 1920s-era Viennese-style coffeehouse has a good buzz and it offers a great view of the White Tower if you choose to sit on the terrace out front. Decent Greek and international bar dishes range from mushroom orzo with Cretan gruyere and truffle oil to homemade beef, pork, and red pepper sausages. **Known for:** mini-chain in two great central locations; Greek craft beers; views from the terrace. $ *Average main: €16* ✉ *Tsiroyiannis Sq. 7, Kentro* ☎ *2310/279010* ⊕ *www.zithos.gr.*

Hotels

Stay in Kentro and all the city action will be on your doorstep, and you'll find most attractions, shopping, and good restaurants within walking distance. More important, Kentro is close enough to the waterfront that top-floor rooms may have sea views. Parking is difficult, however, and noise can be a problem, especially at cheaper hotels.

Domotel Olympia

$ | **HOTEL** | Location counts at this boutique hotel on a corner close to the flea market, copper market, Roman Forum, and Ayios Dimitrios—but there are many other pluses at this nicely stylish place, which offers quality service and an excellent, American-style breakfast. **Pros:** service is excellent; check for discounts; bicycles available for rental. **Cons:** limited parking spaces for guests; location means lower floors have traffic noise; smallish rooms and bathrooms. $ *Rooms from: €90* ✉ *Olymbou 65, at Papageorgiou, Kentro* ☎ *2310/366466* ⊕ *www.hotelolympia.gr* ⤳ *86 rooms* ⦿ *Free breakfast.*

Hotel Orestias Kastorias

$ | **HOTEL** | Blink and you may miss this circa-1920 hotel—a favorite of budget travelers—on a quiet, narrow street leading from the top corner of the Roman Forum to Ayios Dimitrios church. **Pros:** good value for those on a budget; professional and helpful service; views onto the Roman Forum. **Cons:** breakfast is not served (though there is free coffee and biscuits in the reception area); very limited parking available; no elevator. $ *Rooms from:*

Playing with Fire

On the feast day of Saints Constantine and Eleni, May 21, religious devotees in the villages of Langadha (25 km [15 miles] north of Thessaloniki) and Ayia Eleni (80 km [50 miles] northeast of Thessaloniki) take part in *pirovassia* ("fire dancing"). During the three-day rite, participants dance unharmed on a bed of hot coals while holding the saints' icons. The rite is derived from the eastern Thracian village of Kosti, where the villagers are said to have rescued the original icons from a burning church around 1250.

€60 ✉ *Agnostou Stratiotou 14, Kentro* ☎ *2310/276517* ⊕ *www.okhotel.gr* ⤳ *37 rooms* ⦿ *No meals.*

Nightlife

BARS AND CLUBS
★ Baobab

MUSIC CLUBS | Minimalist bar where the people take center stage over the decor. As the night intensifies so does the music, which morphs from easy-on-the-ear jazz, afro beat, and soul to dance-inducing electric sounds. If you're into good sounds look no further as the late-night live DJs are the bees knees. The cocktails aren't too bad either. ✉ *23 Ernestou Emprar, Kentro* ☎ *2315/538460.*

Urban

BARS/PUBS | Urban is a former art gallery–turned–glam bar for counterculture scenesters, young academics, and lifelong artists. The music is fantastic, with regular guest DJs, as is the people-watching. The music starts kicking after 9 pm. ✉ *Zefxidos 7, Kentro* ☎ *2310/272821.*

684

 Performing Arts

FILM

Alex
FILM | FAMILY | A must-do in summer, especially for film lovers, is to see a movie at an open-air cinema. There are usually two showtimes (around 8 and 11 pm, the later one usually at lower volume, depending on the neighborhood). Call ahead or check the website to see what's playing—some screen oldies and foreign art films, and others run the latest from Hollywood. Most films are subtitled, but note that animated movies are almost always dubbed. Alex is the most central theater. ✉ *Ayias Sofias and Olympou, Kentro* ☎ *2310/269403.*

★ Thessaloniki International Film Festival
FILM | Each November, the best films by new directors from around the world are screened and awarded prizes at the Thessaloniki International Film Festival. Southeast Europe's most noted cinematic festival, it attracts well-known regional talent and some internationally aclaimed stars. Films are usually subtitled, and tickets can be hard to come by. In March, there's also an international documentary film festival. ✉ *Olympion Bldg., Aristotelous Sq. 10, Kentro* ☎ *2310/378400* ⊕ *www.filmfestival.gr.*

THEATER

Kratiko Theatro (*State Theater*)
THEATER | The National Theater presents plays, ballets, and special performances of visiting artists year-round. ✉ *Ethnikis Aminis 2, Kentro* ⊹ *Opposite the White Tower* ☎ *2315/200000, 2315/200200 box office* ⊕ *www.ntng.gr.*

Shopping

CLOTHES

Axel Accessories
CLOTHING | Women in Thessaloniki are known for dressing well and this fashion outlet is one of their go-to shops. Beautiful Greek hand-made bags are what put

Shoppers' Siesta

For some shops the siesta is still observed—especially by the smaller family-owned establishments. Hours are generally from about 9 to 2:30; stores reopen at 5:30 in the evenings on Tuesday, Thursday, and Friday. Many shops close for a few weeks in August.

this place on the map, but equally luxiurious are the rest of the designer items on offer here. ✉ *Tsimiski 56, Kentro* ☎ *2310/288289* ⊕ *www.axelaccessories.com.*

GIFTS

Mastihashop
FOOD/CANDY | Mastihashop carries products containing mastic—a tree resin produced on the Aegean island of Chios that's known for its various health benefits. The broad range of cosmetics, preserves, sweets, and other items come in extremely attractive packaging. Don't miss out on the mastiha liqueur, which is to be kept in the freezer and sipped as a digestif. ✉ *Vogatsikou 12, Kentro* ⊹ *Across from the Holy Metropolis of Thessaloniki* ☎ *2310/250205* ⊕ *www.mastihashop.com.*

SWEETS

Agapitos Patisserie
FOOD/CANDY | With eight outlets in Thessaloniki, Agapitos Patisserie, which aptly translates as "loved one," is indeed one of the best loved confectionary shops in the city. Best known for chocolate-covered *tsourekia* (a sweet bread traditionally served at Easter) and the syrupy pastries from Asia Minor. ✉ *Tsimiski 10, Kentro* ☎ *2310/225950* ⊕ *www.agapitospatisserie.com.*

Hatzis

FOOD/CANDY | Thessaloniki's fabled Anatolian sweets can be sampled at central Hatzis. Specialties include the buffalo-milk cream-based *kazan dipi,* a kind of flan; *trigono,* a cream-filled triangle of phyllo; and *kataïfi* (logs of crushed and sugared walnuts wrapped in honey-drenched shredded phyllo) served with *kaïmaki* (mastic-flavored ice cream). Choose a beverage—like iced coffee, granita, or *boza* (a thick, sweet, millet-and-corn drink)—and people-watch from the pedestrian side street that faces the gardens of Panagia Chalkeon church. ✉ *Mitropoleos 24, Kentro* ☎ *2310/221655* 🌐 *www.chatzis.gr.*

Ladadika

The city's food and nightlife epicenter, with pedestrianized Katouni Street as its key thoroughfare, is the Ladadika district in central Thessaloniki, near the port. The area was named after the oil (*ladi*) vendors who moved to the area after the great fire of 1917, as this is where oil, spices, and foods were stored. Protected as a historic district from the building frenzy of the mid-1980s, the Ladadika was instead colonized by entrepreneurs who opened cheap tavernas (filling tables with inviting mezedes and carafes of ouzo) and bars in the restored turn-of-the-20th-century buildings full of storehouses. Locals thronged to the lively area, and more and more establishments opened up and spilled over into the surrounding streets and alleys. Though a bit subdued after the financial crisis, the Ladadika still has buckets of charm and still hosts many of the city's best and trendiest restaurants and drinking establishments.

🍴 Restaurants

Bakaliarakia Tou Aristou

$ | **SEAFOOD** | **FAMILY** | Serving Thessaloniki's most well known fish-and-chips since 1940, this is a classic hangout where you can get your fingers greasy as you dig into crispy fried cod and fresh-cut fries. Your fish-and-chips are always accompanied by pungent *skordalia* garlic dip and casually served on grease-proof paper. **Known for:** locally sourced fish; historical atmosphere; casual and affordable food. [$] *Average main: €7* ✉ *Katouni 3 and Fasianou 2, Ladadika* ☎ *2310/548668* 🌐 *www.mpakaliarakia-aristou.gr.*

Omikron

$ | **GREEK FUSION** | This lovely, unpretentious little restaurant in the trendy Ladadika district has become a local favorite. Delightful Greek-Mediterranean dishes are tastefully presented to reflect the chef-owner's culinary stint in France. **Known for:** popular locally; good prices for well-prepared dishes; seafood risotto. [$] *Average main: €8* ✉ *Oplopoiou 3, Ladadika* ☎ *2310/532774* 🕒 *Closed Sun.*

To Full Tou Meze

$ | **GREEK** | Ordering your meal at this establishment in the heart of the bustling Ladadika district is quite an experience. The waiters bring their own eccentric individuality to this often mundane ritual, and the menu is printed on a "newspaper" with photos from old Greek films and articles heralding the dishes you're about to munch on. **Known for:** eccentric (but somewhat erratic) waiters; tasty traditional Greek mezedes; deli-style decor. [$] *Average main: €10* ✉ *Katouni 3, Ladadika* ☎ *2310/524700* 🌐 *www.fullmeze.gr.*

☕ Coffee and Quick Bites

Thess Bao

$ | **ASIAN** | Award-winning chefs Dimitri Pamboris' and Yiannis Ziagas' new project is this street-food eatery centering around their hand-made bao buns. Pork belly, beef, and chicken fillings doused with secret sauces will tickle even the most discerning tastebuds. **Known for:** latest project from award-winning chefs; delicious bao buns; vegan options.

$ *Average main: €5* ⊠ *Kalapothaki 3, Ladadika* ☎ *2310/235225* ⊕ *www. thessbao.gr.*

 Hotels

There are only a handful of places to stay here, most in restored old buildings. These places book up quickly, so finding a room here may be a little more challenging. The neighborhood is still very central and architecturally interesting, and it's quiet in the mornings. Views, though not expansive, are engaging. But late-night noise—especially on weekends—can be a problem, and parking is almost nonexistent (the nearest parking lots are five minutes' walk away and cost at least €10/day); no hotels have parking here.

Bahar Boutique Hotel
$$ | **HOTEL** | AKA the "blue mansion," this lovingly restored 20th-century listed building has become the chic location to stay in this area. **Pros:** centrally located; early check-in, late check-out available (usually for free); excellent breakfast. **Cons:** no free hotel parking; one or two rooms are smallish; noisy area, but if you keep the double glazing widows shut it's not a problem. $ *Rooms from: €130* ⊠ *Edessis 10 and Katouni, Ladadika* ☎ *2310/553433, 2310/536881* ⊕ *www.baharboutiquehotel. com/en* ↪ *16 rooms* ❙◯❙ *Free breakfast.*

★ The Bristol Hotel
$$ | **HOTEL** | **FAMILY** | An elegant retreat with a touch of history, this exquisite boutique hotel occupies one of the few buildings that survived the great fire of 1917 untouched—during Ottoman rule the structure served as the city's post office—and, today, a mixture of handmade furniture, hand-picked antiques, and works of art makes this place special. **Pros:** small intimate hotel; excellent location; large rooms. **Cons:** no parking; patchy Wi-Fi signal; due for a touch up. $ *Rooms from: €135* ⊠ *Oplopiou 2, at Katouni, Ladadika* ☎ *2310/506500* ⊕ *www.bristol.gr* ↪ *20 rooms* ❙◯❙ *Free breakfast.*

Mediterranean Palace
$$ | **HOTEL** | From the abundance of amenities at this traditionally decorated, six-story hotel near the port and Ladadika, it's easy to see that the Mediterranean Palace caters to business travelers (there are ample meeting and conference areas), who will appreciate the consistently good service and many amenities like the spa. **Pros:** good location; top-of-the-line hotel services; free parking. **Cons:** rooms on the side of hotel can be noisy at night; no pool; only rooms on the higher floors and in the front of hotel have sea views. $ *Rooms from: €140* ⊠ *Salaminos 3, at Karatasou, Ladadika* ☎ *2311/240400* ⊕ *www.mediterranean-palace.gr* ↪ *118 rooms* ❙◯❙ *Free breakfast.*

Ano Polis

Ano Polis, where many fortified towers once bristled along the city's upper walls, is what remains of 19th-century Thessaloniki. It's filled with timber-framed houses with their upper stories overhanging the steep streets. The views of the modern city below and the Thermaic Gulf are stunning, but other than Byzantine churches, there are few specific places of historical interest. This elevated northern area of the city gained its other name, Ta Kastra (The Castles), because of the castle of Eptapyrghion and the fortified towers that once dominated the walls. The area within and just outside the remains of the walls is like a village unto itself, a pleasing jumble of the rich, the poor, and the renovated. Rustic one-story peasant houses, many still occupied by the families that built them, sit side by side with houses newly built or restored by the wealthier class. As the area continues to be upgraded, tavernas, café-bars, and restaurants spring up to serve visitors, both Greek and foreign, who flock here for a cool evening out. It's an experience in itself to navigate the steps, past gossipy women, grandfathers playing backgammon in smoky cafés, and giggling children playing tag in tiny courtyards filled with sweet-smelling flowers, stray cats, and flapping laundry.

Getting here can be a chore, as taxi drivers often try to avoid the cramped, congested streets and fear missing a fare back down. Have your hotel find a willing driver, or take a local bus. Bus 23 leaves from the terminal at Eleftherias Square (two blocks west of Aristotelous Square, on the waterfront side) every 10 to 15 minutes and follows an interesting route through the narrow streets of Ano Polis. Or you can stroll the 30 minutes north from the White Tower, along Ethnikis Aminis, to get to Ano Polis.

 Sights

Ayios Nikolaos Orfanos

RELIGIOUS SITE | Noted frescoes here include the unusual *Ayion Mandilion* in the apse, which shows Jesus superimposed on a veil sent to an Anatolian king, and the *Niptir*, also in the apse, in which Jesus is washing the disciples' feet. The artist is said to have depicted himself in the right-hand corner wearing a turban and riding a horse. The 14th-century church, which became a dependency of the Vlatádon Monastery in the 17th century, has an intriguing mix of Byzantine architectural styles and perhaps the most beautiful midnight Easter service in the city. ⊠ *Kallithea Sq. and Apostolou Pavlou, enter on Irodotou, Ano Polis* ☎ *2310/213627* ⊘ *Closed Tues.*

Eptapyrghion

BUILDING | In modern times, this Byzantine fortress—its name means "the seven towers" even though there are ten towers—was an abysmal prison, closed only in 1988. There's not much to see here except wall ruins and a small museum that documents the building's history. The area is an untended green space, not an unpleasant place to sit and survey Thessaloniki below. The surrounding

tavernas accommodate throngs of locals in the evening. ⊠ *Eptapyrghiou, Ano Polis* ☎ *2313/310400* ⊘ *Closed Tues.*

Moni Vlatádon

BUILDING | The Vlatades Monastery, shaded with pine and cypress, is a cruciform structure that displays a mixture of architectural additions, from Byzantine times to the present. It's known for its Ecumenical Foundation for Patriarchal Studies, the only one in the world. The small central church to the right of the apse has a tiny **chapel dedicated to Sts. Peter and Paul,** which is seldom open. It is believed to have been built on the spot where Paul first preached to the Thessalonians, in AD 49. Go through the gate entrance to get a panoramic view of the city of Thessaloniki. ⊠ *Eptapyrghiou 64, Ano Polis* ☎ *2310/209913, 2310/203620.*

Old Turkish Quarter

NEIGHBORHOOD | During the Ottoman occupation, this area, probably the most picturesque in the city, was considered the best place to live. In addition to the superb city views, it catches whatever breeze there is in summer. More recently, it was the home of some of the poorest families in Thessaloniki. Now the area is gentrifying, thanks to European Union development funds (which repaired the cobblestones), strict zoning and building codes, and the zeal of young couples with the money to restore the narrow old houses. The most notable houses are on Papadopolou, Kleious, and Dimitriou Poliorkitou streets. ⊠ *Ano Polis* ✛ *South of Dimitriou Poliorkitou.*

★ Osios David (*Blessed David*)

RELIGIOUS SITE | This entrancing little church with a commanding view of the city was supposedly built about AD 500 in honor of Galerius's daughter, who was secretly baptized while her father was away fighting. It was later converted into a mosque, and at some time its west wall—the traditional place of entrance (in order to look east when facing the altar)—was bricked up, so you enter

Noted for its mosaics, the Ayios Dimitrios is Greece's largest church and is the shrine of the city's patron saint.

Osios David from the south. No matter; this entirely suits the church's rather battered magic. You can still see the radiantly beautiful mosaic in the dome of the apse, which shows a rare beardless Jesus, as he seems to have been described in the vision of Ezekiel: Jesus is seen with a halo and is surrounded by the four symbols of the Evangelists—clockwise, from top left, are the angel, the eagle, the lion, and the calf. To the right is the prophet Ezekiel and, to the left, Habakuk. To save it from destruction, the mosaic was hidden under a layer of calfskin during the iconoclastic ravages of the 8th and 9th centuries. Plastered over while a mosque, it seems to have been forgotten until 1921, when an Orthodox monk in Egypt had a vision telling him to go to the church. On the day he arrived, March 25 (the day marking Greek independence from the Ottomans), an earthquake shattered the plaster, revealing the mosaic to the monk—who promptly died. ✉ *Timotheou 7, Ano Polis* ✣ *Near intersection of Dimitriou Poliorkitou and Ayias Sofias* ☎ *2310/221506.*

Tower of Trigoniou

CASTLE/PALACE | From this survivor of the city walls, you can see the city spread out below you in a graceful curve around the bay, from the suburbs in the east to the modern harbor in the west and, on a clear day, even Mount Olympus, rising near the coastline at the southwest reaches of the bay. There is, however, little of historic interest to see within the walls. ✉ *Eptapyrghiou, Ano Polis* ☎ *2313/310400* ⏲ *Closed Tues.*

☕ Coffee and Quick Bites

Tsinari Ouzeri

$ | **GREEK** | A tree shades the terrace and blue, multipaned storefront of the Tsinari Ouzeri, the last remaining Turkish-style coffeehouse (opened in 1850) and the only one to have survived the fire of 1917. During the 1920s it became the social hub for the refugees from Asia Minor who lived here. **Known for:** local meze; good ouzo; popular with groups of locals. [$] *Average main: €8* ✉ *Papadopoulou 72, at Kleious, Ano Polis* ☎ *2310/284028* 💳 *No credit cards.*

Depot

The Depot neighborhood was once where the wealthy, mainly Jewish, merchants lived in impressive 19th-century villas. Very close to the port and the city center, this area was just outside the Old City walls. Nowadays, the few remaining villas are mostly owned by foundations, and high-rise apartment blocks dominate the area.

Sights

Pinakothiki (*Municipal Art Gallery*)
HOUSE | This art gallery has a distinctive icon collection from the Byzantine and post-Byzantine periods, engravings that highlight the development of the craft of icon making in Greece, and a represent-ative collection of modern Greek art. One section shows the work of three generations of Thessalonian artists, documenting modern art in the city from the turn of the 20th century to 1967. The museum collection, once housed in the nearby Villa Mordoh, is now in Casa Bian-ca, a large three-story art nouveaux villa. ⊠ *Casa Bianca, Vasilissis Olgas 180 and Them Sofouli, Depot ⊹ East of Kentro* ☎ *2310/427555, 2310/318538* ⊕ *www. thessaloniki.gr* ⊠ *Free* ⊙ *Closed Sun. and Mon.*

Kalamaria

Performing Arts

Megaron Moussikis Thessaloniki (*Thessa-loniki Concert Hall*)
CONCERTS | The Megaron Moussikis Thes-saloniki is a large venue that hosts ballet, opera, and other high-brow musical and cultural events. Graced by international and local orchestras (including the Munic-ipal Orchestra of Thessaloniki), there are classical, folk, and jazz nights, as well as seminars and lectures. ⊠ *25 Martiou and Paralia, Kalamaria* ☎ *2310/895800* ⊕ *www.tch.gr.*

Sfageia

The nightlife district Sfageia is a short hike or cheap taxi ride southwest of the train station, along 26th Oktovriou Street. Many of the restaurants here offer live *rembetika* (Greek blues) and other Greek music.

Nightlife

★ **Mylos**
MUSIC CLUBS | Mylos, in a former mill on the southwest edge of the city, has been perhaps the best venue in Greece for jazz, folk, and pop acts, both Greek and foreign, for the last 25 years. This fabulous complex of clubs, bars, and ouzeri-tavernas, as well as art galler-ies and a concert stage, shows how a respectful architectural conversion can become a huge success. Don't miss the Xylourgeio stage, which has some of the best alternative acts around. The lively place starts to get busy as early as 11 pm. ⊠ *Andreadou Georgiou 56, Sfageia* ☎ *2310/551836* ⊕ *www.mylos.gr.*

Faliro

Faliro, a modern, residential area, is south of the city center and the White Tower. The hotels here are usually in large, high-rise buildings owned by trust-ed brands with good amenities (including swimming pools) and offering high stand-ards of service. You're still very close to the waterfront, so it's easy to get a room with a sea view, and since there's space, hotels tend to have parking and more on-site amenities. However, you'll be slightly out of the city center (20 minutes by foot), and Faliro obviously lacks the character and sparkle of the central areas.

Hotels

★ Daios Luxury Living Hotel

$$$$ | **HOTEL** | A minute's walk from the White Tower, this upscale contemporary hotel in shimmering glass stands out for all the right reasons: a prime seafront location, cool and chic interiors, and exemplary, discrete service. **Pros:** right in the heart of the city with outstanding views of the Thermaikos Gulf; free minibar in all rooms; the best luxury suites in town at good prices out of season. **Cons:** some rooms partially overlook the city to the side; expensive nightly parking fee; some road noise in the lower-floor rooms. [$] *Rooms from: €245* ✉ *Nikis 59, Faliro* ☎ *2310/250200* 🌐 *www.daioshotels.com* 🛏 *49 rooms* 🍴 *Free breakfast.*

Makedonia Palace Hotel

$$$ | **HOTEL** | **FAMILY** | You might see a rock star or the president of Albania here; it's that kind of place—just note the excellent location on the waterfront, southeast of the White Tower, with stunning views of the sunset and Mount Olympus, or the slew of amenities (mini-stereos, dual-voltage outlets, multimedia convention center) the Grecotel chain has installed behind the hotel's 1970s-era facade. **Pros:** top location right on the beachfront; discounts possible in summer; major renovations and modernizing completed in 2018. **Cons:** rooms on the lower floor might be a bit noisy from the traffic; occasional AC issues; make sure to book a room with a sea view. [$] *Rooms from: €230* ✉ *Megalou Alexandrou 2, Faliro* ☎ *2310/897197* 🌐 *makedoniapalace.com* 🛏 *276 rooms* 🍴 *Free breakfast.*

Pella Πελλα

40 km (25 miles) west of Thessaloniki.

Pella was Alexander's birthplace and the capital of the Macedonian state in the 4th century BC. The modern-day village is not the most alluring, (and there isn't anywhere to stay) and hides the fact that Pella was once a thriving city-state with the largest agora market of its time. It housed workshops, administrative buildings, shops, and much more. The city was built using the sophisticated Hippodamian grid plan—by none other than the great Hippodamos himself. On the hill to the north, one can visit the vast palatial complex where King Philip and Alexander the Great once lived.

GETTING HERE AND AROUND

If coming by train, get off at Edessa and take the KTEL bus to the site. If coming by bus, get off the Thessaloniki–Edessa KTEL bus right at the site; there are buses every hour from 6 to 6. Zorpidis Travel, among others, arranges day trips from Thessaloniki that cover both Pella and Vergina.

Sights

Pella Archaeological Site

ARCHAEOLOGICAL SITE | The ancient village ruins and its museum—both best known for their intricate, artful, and beautifully preserved floor mosaics, mainly of mythological scenes—are on either side of the main road toward Edessa (where waterfalls invite a possible further trip). It's best to first get an overview at the **Archaeological Museum,** which contains a model of the 4th-century BC dwelling that stood across the road, as well as fascinating artifacts of Neolithic, Bronze, and Iron Age settlers, some as old as the 7th century BC. Note also the unique statuette of a horned Athena (apparently influenced by Minoan Crete), the statue of Alexander sprouting the horns of Pan, and the adorable sleeping Eros (Cupid), reproductions of which can be bought at the gift shop. Descriptions are sparse, but the attendants, pointedly not experts, are happy to share what they know.

In 1914, two years after the Turks' departure, the people who lived on the land were moved to a village north of here,

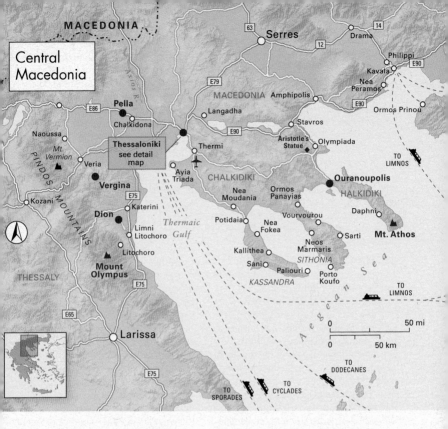

and excavations of the **archaeological site** began. These include portions of the walls; the sanctuaries of Aphrodite, Demeter, and Cybele; the marketplace; a cemetery; and several houses. In 1987, on a small rise to the north, the remains of the **palace** came to light; at present there is a restoration program at the site. ✉ Pella ✛ Off E86, Thessaloniki–Edessa road ☎ 23820/31160 ⊕ www.pella-muse-um.gr 🎫 €8 includes site and museum; €4 from Nov. 1 to Mar. 31.

Vergina Βεργίνα

40 km (25 miles) south of Pella, 135 km (84 miles) southwest of Thessaloniki.

The modern city of Vergina wasn't established in its present form until 1922, but the ancient city of Aigai, the original capital of Macedonia, was founded in the 8th century BC and was at its height in the 4th century BC. It's here that Philip II, the father of Alexander the Great, was assassinated in 336 BC and where he was buried among the Royal Tombs, which are a UNESCO World Heritage site. For years, both archaeologists and grave robbers had suspected that the large mound that stood on this site might contain something of value but, try as they might, neither of these groups was successful in penetrating its secret. Serious excavations begin in the mid-19th century, and although discoveries were made, the most important ones didn't happen for almost 100 years. Many locals still remember playing ball on the mound as children. Professor Manolis Andronikos, who discovered the tombs, theorized in his book *The Royal Tombs of Vergina* that one of Alexander's successors, wanting to protect Philip's tomb from robbers, had it covered with broken debris and tombstones to make it appear that the grave had already been plundered, and then built the tumulus so that Philip's tomb would be near the edge rather than the center. When Andronikos discovered it, on the final day of excavation, in 1977, he had been trying one of the last approaches, with little hope of finding anything—certainly not the tomb of Philip II, in as pristine condition as the day it was closed. It was the first intact Macedonian tomb ever discovered.

GETTING HERE AND AROUND

The easiest way to get to Vergina is by car. Be attentive, however, because the route is not well marked from Pella. You can also get here with public transport via Veria, 11 km (7 miles) away, using trains or buses. KTEL buses, more convenient than train services, run from Thessaloniki to Veria every hour starting early in the morning; the trip takes one hour. From Veria take a bus to Vergina (20 minutes, every other hour from 6:50 am to 8 pm). Ask to be let off at the Vergina archaeological sites. For the tombs look for a low hillock in the center of town with souvenir shops nearby. The palace and the theater are about 1 km (½ mile) southeast of the village up a low hill. Veria is also on the bus route from Athens to Naousa.

There are regular trains from Thessaloniki to Veria from 5:50 am (one hour); however, the station is 3 km (2 miles) outside of Veria, so you will need to take a taxi to the bus station in the center.

 Sights

★ Aigai Archaeological Site

ARCHAEOLOGICAL SITE | FAMILY | Some of antiquity's greatest treasures await you at the Royal Tombs of Vergina, opened to the public in 1993, 16 years after their discovery. Today the complex, including a museum, is a fitting shrine to the original capital of the kingdom of Macedonia, then known as Aigai. The entrance is appropriately stunning: you walk down a white-sandstone ramp into the partially underground structure, roofed over by a large earth-covered dome approximately the size of the original tumulus (mounded grave). Here on display are some of the legendary artifacts from the age of Philip II of Macedonia.

This was the first intact Macedonian tomb ever found—imposing and exquisite, with a huge frieze of a hunting scene, a masterpiece similar to those of the Italian Renaissance but 1,800 years older, along with a massive yet delicate fresco depicting the abduction of Persephone (a copy of which is displayed along one wall of the museum). Two of the few original works of great painting survive from antiquity. On the left are two tombs and one altar that had been looted and destroyed in varying degrees by the time Andronikos discovered them. Macedonian Tomb III, on the right, found intact in 1978, is believed to be that of the young Prince Alexander IV, Alexander the Great's son, who was at first kept alive by his "protectors" after Alexander's death and then poisoned (along with his mother) when he was 14. To the left of Tomb III is that of Philip II. He was assassinated in the nearby theater, a short drive away; his body was burned, his bones washed in wine, wrapped in royal purple, and put into the magnificent, solid-gold casket with the 16-point sun, which is displayed in the museum. His wife, Cleopatra (not the Egyptian queen), was later buried with him.

The tombs alone would be worth a special trip, but the golden objects and unusual artifacts that were buried within them are equally impressive. Among these finds, in excellent condition and displayed in dramatic dimmed light, are delicate ivory reliefs; elegantly wrought gold laurel wreaths; and Philip's crown,

Burial places for famed rulers such as Philip II and Alexander IV—the father and son of Alexander the Great—the Royal Tombs of Vergina are archaeological landmarks.

armor, and shield. Especially interesting are those items that seem most certainly Philip's: a pair of greaves (shin guards), one shorter than the other—Philip was known to have a limp. To the right of the tombs, a gift shop sells books and postcards; the official gift shop is outside the entrance gate (across from Philippion restaurant), on the same side of the road. Macedonian souvenirs available here are scarce elsewhere.

The winding road to the site of Philip's assassination goes through rolling countryside west of modern Vergina, much of it part of the vast royal burial grounds of ancient Aigai. On the way you pass three more **Macedonian tombs** of little interest, being rough-hewn stone structures in typical Macedonian style; the admission to the Royal Tombs includes these. In the field below are the remnants of the **theater,** discovered by Andronikos in 1982. It was on Philip's way here, to attend the wedding games that were to follow the marriage of his daughter to the king of Epirus, that he was murdered and where his son, Alexander the Great, was crowned. ✉ *Vergina* ✣ *Off E90, near Veria* ☎ *23310/92347* 🌐 *www.aigai.gr* 🎟 *€12; €6 from Nov. 1 to Mar. 31.*

🍴 Restaurants

★ Ap'Allou

$ | **GREEK** | With mouthwatering dishes inspired by Asia Minor and Greece, and ingredients from both the land (seasonal vegetables and quality meats) and the sea (fresh shellfish and seafood), this place is a satisfaction-guaranteed stop for lunch or dinner. The menu changes with the season, but luscious desserts, such as the delicious profiteroles and homemade ice cream are a must-try year-round. **Known for:** good prices for high-quality food; friendly service and familial ambience; excellent selection of regional wines. [$] *Average main: €10* ✉ *Patriarchi Ioakim 5* ✣ *Veroia, 15-min drive west of Vergina* ☎ *23310/20199.*

Philippion

$ | GREEK | Choose from traditional foods such as moussaka or try the highly recommended fresh local pasta. The regional vegetables are especially delicious, and fresh frozen yogurt is made with local fruits. **Known for:** quick bites before or after visit to Royal Tombs; self-service; decent Greek fare. $ *Average main: €11* ✉ *Vergina* ✛ *Immediately outside the archaeological site* ☎ *23310/92892.*

Hotels

Archontiko Dimitra

$ | B&B/INN | FAMILY | On a quiet street a five-minute walk from the ancient archaeological site at Vergina is this beautiful two-story hotel, built in 2003—you'll want to consider making this your base for area excursions, as the hotel is designed with accents of fetching wood trim and antique brass chandeliers, with each of the eight light-filled and spacious studio suites showcasing its own classic style and private balcony. **Pros:** discounts available for extended stays; free parking; good location near both the Royal Tombs and the buzzy little town. **Cons:** small, so book early; no 24-hour reception; weak Wi-Fi signal in certain rooms. $ *Rooms from: €60* ✉ *Athinas 5* ☎ *23310/92900* ⇨ *8 rooms* ❍❙ *Free breakfast.*

★ Kalaitzis Estate

$ | B&B/INN | FAMILY | Though not within Vergina itself, this countryside retreat is well worth the effort to reach and is especially delightful in the snow-covered winter months because of its plush, cozy, and sumptuous decor. **Pros:** wonderful and friendly service; tranquil coutryside retreat; the wine is a must. **Cons:** 5 to 10 minutes' drive from Vergina; only a few rooms, so do book in advance; all nightlife is in nearby Veria. $ *Rooms from: €80* ✉ *Metochi* ☎ *23310/92092* ⊕ *estate-kalaitzis.webnode.gr* ⇨ *11 rooms* ❍❙ *Free breakfast.*

Dion Διον

90 km (56 miles) south of Vergina, 87 km (54 miles) southwest of Thessaloniki.

At the foothills of Mount Olympus lies ancient Dion. Even before Zeus and the Olympian gods, the mountain was home to the Muses and Orpheus, who entranced the men of the area with his mystical music. The story says that the life-giving force of Dion came from the waters in which the murderers of Orpheus (the women of Mount Olympus, jealous for attention from their men) washed their hands on the slopes of the sacred mountain to remove the stain of their own sin. The waters entered the earth and rose, cleansed, in the holy city of Dion. (Zeus is Dias in Greek; the city was named for him.) Ancient Dion was inhabited from as early as the classical period (5th century BC) and last referred to as Dion in the 10th century AD according to the archaeological findings.

Today a feeling of tranquility prevails at Dion, at the foot of the mountain of the gods. Few people visit this vast, underrated city site. The silence is punctuated now and then by goats, their bells tinkling so melodically you expect to spy Pan in the woods at any moment. Springs bubble up where excavators dig, and scarlet poppies bloom among the cracks—this is the essence of Greece.

GETTING HERE AND AROUND

Litochoro, an hour by KTEL bus from Thessaloniki (hourly from 7 am), is the gateway to both Dion and Mount Olympus. The bus stop is in Litochoro's central *platia* (square). From Litochoro's central square, call a taxi for the 11-km (7-mile) trip, which costs €13 one-way, to the splendid archaeological park. You can also call Mr. Sakis or Mr. Zaharis, both local cabbies with good English, to come and pick you up. You take a KTEL bus from Thessaloniki to Katerini, where you can take the local "blue" bus to the Dion site

(€1.20). There are buses to Katerini from Thessaloniki every half hour.

CONTACTS Litochoro Taxi. ☎ *6937/176867 Mr. Sakis, 6987/320800 Mr. Zaharias, 23520/82333 Taxi Rank.*

Sights

★ Dion Archaeological Site
ARCHAEOLOGICAL SITE | FAMILY | Being at the base of sacred Olympus, Dion was a sacred city for the Macedonians, devoted primarily to Zeus and his daughters, the Muses. A city was built adjacent to the ancient city during the reign of Alexander. Unearthed ruins of various buildings include the villa of Dionysos, public baths, a stadium (the Macedonian Games were held here), shops, and workshops. The road from the museum divides the diggings at the archaeological site into two areas. On the left is the **ancient city** of Dion itself, with the juxtaposition of public toilets and several superb floor mosaics. On the right side are the **ancient theaters** and the **sanctuaries of Olympian Zeus, Demeter, and Isis.** In the latter, which is a vividly beautiful approximation of how it once looked, copies of the original statues, now in the museum, have been put in place. ✉ *Dion* ✥ *7 km (4½ mile) north of Litochoro, off E75/1A, Thessaloniki–Athens road* ☎ *23510/53484* 🌐 *ancientdion.org* 🎟 *€8 including museum.*

Museum of Dion
MUSEUM | FAMILY | The splendid museum is an important stop to help you get an idea of the history and importance of the city to the ancient Macedonians. Be sure to see the video (in English) prepared by the site's renowned archaeologist, Dimitris Pandermalis, which describes the excavations, the finds, and their significance. (His efforts to keep the artifacts in the place where they were found have established a trend for the decentralization of archaeological finds throughout Greece.) The second floor contains a topographical relief of the area and the oldest surviving pipe organ precursor—the 1st-century BC hydraulis. The basement learning area has an Alexander mosaic, a model of the city, and ancient carriage shock absorbers. ✉ *Dion* ✥ *Adjacent to archaeological site* ☎ *23510/53206* 🌐 *ancientdion.org* 🎟 *€8 including archaeological site.*

Restaurants

Dionysos
$ | GREEK | Excellent food and true Greek *filoxenia* (hospitality) await at the combination tourist shop, café, and three-meal-a-day restaurant. Recommended are the *loukanika* (sausages); rolled, spiced, and spit-roasted meat; and the excellent *yemista* (stuffed tomatoes and peppers) and *papoutsakia* (eggplant halves baked with cheese, spiced ground beef, and garlicy tomato sauce). **Known for:** quick, ready-made food; grilled meats; hima krasi (homemade wine) and tsipouro (Greek grappa). [$] *Average main: €11* ✉ *Village center* ✥ *Directly opposite the museum* ☎ *23510/53730.*

Hotels

Safetis
$ | RENTAL | FAMILY | The mauve-color Safeti, a most welcome addition to Dion, accommodates guests in three gorgeous, modern apartments, one of which has a hot tub (another a fireplace). **Pros:** family-run and friendly; near both Mount Olympus and the sea; next to the museum and very cose to the archaeological park. **Cons:** only for those looking to self-cater; limited number of accommodations; no breakfast. [$] *Rooms from: €80* ✉ *Opposite Museum of Dion, on main road, Olympos* ☎ *23510/46272* 🌐 *www.safetis.gr* 🛏 *3 apartments* 🍴 *No meals.*

Mount Olympus
Όρ. Όλυμπος

17 km (10 miles) southwest of Dion, 100 km (62 miles) southwest of Thessaloniki.

To understand how the mountain must have impressed the ancient Greeks and caused them to shift their allegiance from the earth-rooted deities of the Mycenaeans to those of the airy heights of Olympus, you need to see it clearly from several different perspectives. On its northern slope, the Olympus range catches clouds in a turbulent, stormy bundle, letting fly about 12 times as many thunder-and-lightning storms as anywhere else in Greece. From the south, if there is still snow on the range, it appears as a massive, flat-topped acropolis, much like the one in Athens; its vast, snowy crest hovering in the air, seemingly capable of supporting as many gods and temples as the ancients could have imagined. As you drive from the sea to Mount Olympus, the mountain appears as a conglomeration of thickly bunched summits rather than as a single peak. The truly awe-inspiring height is 9,570 feet.

Nearby, Litochoro is the lively town (population 7,000, plus a nearby army base) nestled at the foot of the mountain. It's the gateway to Mount Olympus. Souvenir shops, restaurants, local-specialty bakeries (stock up before a hike), and hotels vie for customers.

GETTING HERE AND AROUND
Trains from Athens and Thessaloniki (1 hour) stop at Litochoro, but you must then take a bus into town to catch another to the site. The train station is about 5 km (3 miles) from the town, near the seaside and motorway. It is better to take the train to Katerini or to Larissa and then a bus from there, or to simply take a bus from Litchoro *(see Dion)*. Depending on which way you decide to ascend Mount Olympus, take a taxi to Prionia, a tiny settlement 18 km (11 miles) from Litochoro.

Sights

Mount Olympus has some of the most beautiful nature trails in Europe. Hundreds of species of wildflowers and herbs bloom in spring, more than 85 of which are found only on this mountain. There are basically three routes to Zeus's mountaintop, all beginning in Litochoro. The most-traveled road is Via Prionia; the others are by Diastavrosi (literally, "crossroads") and along the Enipeos. You can climb all the way on foot or take a car or negotiate a taxi ride to the end of the road at Prionia (there's a taverna) and trek the rest of the way (six hours or so) up to snow-clad Mytikas summit— Greece's highest peak at 9,570 feet. The climb to Prionia takes about four hours; the ride, on a bumpy gravel road with no guardrails between you and breathtakingly precipitous drops, takes little less than an hour, depending on your nerves. If you can manage to take your eyes off the road, the scenery is magnificent. The trail is snow-free from about mid-May until late October.

★ Spilios Agapitos

MOUNTAIN—SIGHT | During any Mount Olympus hike, you could take a lunch break or stay overnight at Spilios Agapitos. The refuge is run by the daughter of Kostas Zolotas, a venerable climbing guru. To bunk down for the night costs €13 per person (€11 with an international mountaineering card); there are blankets but no sheets. Bring your own flashlight, towel, and soap. Campers can pitch tents for €4.20 (€3.20 with card) per person and can use the refuge's facilities (note that cooking is not permitted in the refuge). The restaurant is open all day until 9 pm. It's 6 km (4 miles), about 2½–3 hours, from Prionia to Refuge A. From here it's 5 km (3 miles), about 2½–3 hours, to the Throne of Zeus and the summit. The trail is easy going to

Skala summit (most of the way), but the last bit is scrambling and a bit hair-raising. Some people turn back. If you plan to hike up Mount Olympus, be sure to take a map; the best are produced by Anavasi. If you would prefer a guided hike up Mount Olympus, the staff at Refuge A can arrange a guide for you, and Trekking Hellas organizes treks for various-size groups. ✉ *Refuge A, Litochoro* ☎ *23520/81800* 🌐 *www.mountolympus.gr* ⏲ *Closed in winter.*

🍴 Restaurants

★ Gastrodromio En Olympo

$$ | GREEK | Self-taught and ever evolving chef Andreas Gavris creates seasonal delights fit for the gods in his justifiably popular restaurant. Standouts include the melon soup with prawns and mint; *bourani,* a rich rice dish with nettles, wild mushrooms, and a Gruyère-like cheese from Crete; and black pig of Olympus stew and mountain lamb, cooked with mushroom and wheat puree. **Known for:** tastefully elevated Greek cuisine; professional and friendly service; an extensive wine list. [$] *Average main: €19* ✉ *Agios Nikolaou 36, Litochoro* ✣ *Opposite the town hall* ☎ *23520/21300* 🌐 *www.gastrodromio.gr.*

To Pazari

$ | GREEK | This homey restaurant is known for its outstanding seafood—it's always fresh, artfully prepared, and surprisingly cheap. The grilled meats are good, too, as are the fresh bread and the dips—especially the *kopanisti* (the punchy spiced cheese dip) and the *melitzanosalata* (lovingly made from roasted eggplant and garlic). **Known for:** old-style taverna; traditional Greek fare; no-frills but well-prepared food. [$] *Average main: €8* ✉ *Martiou 25, Litochoro* ☎ *23520/82540.*

🛏 Hotels

Dion Palace Resort & Spa

$$ | RESORT | FAMILY | Enjoy excellent views of the sea or the peaks at the Dion Palace, which also offers great proximity to the beach, Mount Olympus, and the archaeological site at Dion, and let's not forget the luxury spa, as well as many activities for kids. **Pros:** enjoy the luxury of a spa while you're here; some rooms have a private pool; the restaurant has good food. **Cons:** near the National Highway so you will need a vehicle to get around; on foot, little is close by; patchy Wi-Fi. [$] *Rooms from: €150* ✉ *Limni Litochoro, Litochoro* ✣ *6 km (4 miles) northeast of Litochoro* ☎ *23520/61431* 🌐 *www.dionpalace.com* 🛏 *196 rooms* 🍴 *Free breakfast.*

★ Ktima Faki

$ | B&B/INN | FAMILY | This guesthouse, expanded and with a new swimming pool, is 700 meters (½ mile) up on the slopes of Mount Olympus, 5 km (3 miles) from Litochoro, on the road to the church of St. John (Agios Ioannis), a local landmark. **Pros:** acres of gardens for children to explore; tasteful decor; lovely swimming pool. **Cons:** a car is essential, as it is out of the way; breakfast starts late (at 8:30 am); books out especially on weekends, and some rooms can only be booked for two or more nights. [$] *Rooms from: €100* ✉ *Litochoro* ✣ *Road to the church of Agios Ioannis, 5 km (3 miles) from Litochoro* ☎ *23520/83750* 🌐 *www.ktimafaki.gr* 🛏 *21 rooms* 🍴 *Free breakfast.*

Olympus Mediterranean

$ | HOTEL | Pretty and friendly, this spa hotel—built in 2004—is a great value considering the quality of luxury and comfort on offer. **Pros:** in town and a great base for hikers visiting the mountain; indoor swimming pool and sauna; good service. **Cons:** not all rooms have great views, so make sure to ask when booking if that's important to you; patchy

Wi-Fi; tricky to find. $ *Rooms from: €121*
✉ *Dionyssou 5, Litochoro* ☎ *23520/81831*
⊕ *www.mediterraneanhotels.gr* 🛏 *23
rooms* ❖ *Free breakfast.*

Villa Pantheon

$ | **B&B/INN** | You know you're somewhere
special when you see this family-run
establishment at the trailhead for Mount
Olympus; views stretch to the sea and
the mountains—not surprisingly, given
the location and the relatively low price
for what you get here, reservations are
a must, especially on weekends and
holidays. **Pros:** only a five-minute walk
to the gorge; good value for the money;
nice vistas of the village. **Cons:** only the
suites have a fireplace; 10-minute walk
into town; poor Wi-Fi signal in some of
the rooms. $ *Rooms from: €70* ✉ *Lito-
choro* ✛ *At the end of Ayiou Dimitriou*
☎ *23520/83931, 23520/81019 after 10
pm* ⊕ *www.villapantheon.gr* 🛏 *12 rooms*
❖ *Free breakfast.*

Activities

Hellenic Alpine Club

CLIMBING/MOUNTAINEERING | The Hellenic
Alpine Club can help with information
on hiking Mount Olympus. ✉ *Spilios
Agapitos, Litochoro* ☎ *23520/81800,
210/3645904* ⊕ *www.eooa.gr.*

Olympos Trek

CLIMBING/MOUNTAINEERING | Guided treks
to the summit of Mount Olympus,
rafting, and climbing are just some of
the activities organized by this reputable
outdoor adventure agency. ✉ *Katerini*
☎ *6932/545001, 2410/921244* ⊕ *www.
olympostrek.gr* 🛏 *From €38.*

★ Personality Journeys

CLIMBING/MOUNTAINEERING | This top adven-
ture travel company will plan and arrange
your whole expedition to Mount Olympus
and other unmissable mountain destinations in Greece. From guided single-day
hikes up to full-board week-long expedi-
tions can be arranged. ☎ *2152/151629*
⊕ *www.personalityjourneys.com.*

Trekking Hellas

CLIMBING/MOUNTAINEERING | Trekking
Hellas runs hiking, rafting, mountain
biking, and other outdoor excursions in
the region, including some great trips
up the mythical Mount Olympus by foot
(or bike) from Litochoro. ✉ *Litochoro*
☎ *210/3310323 head office in Athens*
⊕ *www.trekking.gr* 🛏 *From €60.*

Ouranoupolis
Ουρανουπολη

*110 km (68 miles) east of Thessaloniki,
224 km (189 miles) north and east of
Mount Olympus.*

Meaning "heaven's city" in Greek,
Ouranoupolis (also spelled Ouranopolis)
is an appealing cul-de-sac on the final
point of land that separates the secular
world from the sacred sanctuaries of Mt.
Athos. The village, noted for its rug and
tapestry weaving, is particularly entrancing because of the bay's aquamarine
waters, and the town is full of families on
holiday in summer.—the narrow village
beaches can become overcrowded.
There are many pensions and rooms-
to-let around town, but the hotels on an
islet or slightly outside the main town are
quietest.

If you make your own way to Ouranoupolis from Thessaloniki via Route 16, stop
at Aristotle's statue in Stagira (west of
the modern village, watch for the easy-
to-miss road sign), the region of this
remarkable man's birthplace. Aristotle's
theories and inventions are re-created
in engaging hands-on exhibits (there's a
small fee) around a grassy knoll with a
surveying view.

GETTING HERE AND AROUND

Ouranoupolis is reachable by KTEL bus
from the Halkidiki terminal in Thessaloniki. There are six buses departing Thessaloniki daily (five on Sunday) with the first
heading off at 5:30 am (6:15 on Sunday)

A thrill for many is to hike up Mount Olympus, the legendary home of the ancient Greek gods—these are among Greece's most beautiful nature trails.

and the last leaving at 5:45 pm. The trip takes two hours.

Taking a taxi takes two hours but will set you back well over €100 from the Kentro or Thessaloniki airport. Renting a car may be the better option as prices tend to be reasonable here. *See Car for more information on car rentals.*

TOURS

★ Athos Sea Cruises

BOAT TOURS | FAMILY | Some travelers prefer to cruise past the area's monasteries since they are off-limits to women. Athos Sea Cruises has six separate cruises that sail here from April to October embarking at either 9:30 or 10:30 am, with an additional afternoon departure at 2 pm from May to October; tours last three hours. There is commentary in English, French, Russian, and German. Tickets can be bought from the Ouranoupolis central square. ⊠ *Ouranoupolis* ✢ *Near tower on main road* ☎ *23770/71370, 23770/71606, 23770/71071* ⊕ *www.athos-cruises.gr* 🎟 *From €20.*

Sights

Tower of Prosforion

BUILDING | Ouranoupolis was settled by refugees from Asia Minor in 1922–23, when the Greek state expropriated the land from Vatopedi Monastery on Mt. Athos. The settlement, known as Prosforion, was until then occupied by farming monks, some of whom lived in the Byzantine Tower of Prosforion, its origins dating from the 12th century. The tower subsequently became the abode of Joice and Sydney Loch, a couple who worked with Thessaloniki's noted American Farm School to help the refugees develop their rug-weaving industry. The tower was burned, altered, and restored through the centuries. Now it's a breezy and open place to take in the view on a sweltering day. ■ **TIP ➔ Take a lovely 4-mile hike to the Zygou Monastery. Now in ruins, it can be explored in its entirety and is a fine example of a Byzantine monastery unique to Mt. Athos.** ⊠ *Main Sq.* ✢ *At waterfront* ☎ *23770/71651* ⊕ *www.dimosaristoteli. gr* 🎟 *€2* ◷ *Closed in winter.*

Did You Know?

Overnight accommodations are available to men at many of the Mt. Athos monasteries, allowing them to witness some of the holy monks' twilight processions and rites.

🍴 Restaurants

★ O Kritikos

$$ | SEAFOOD | Want sublime seafood pasta or risotto? Head to a place like this one, where the owner is a local fisherman and everything served is the catch of the day. **Known for:** fresh fish and seafood; excellent service; it's busy (reservations strongly recommended). [$] *Average main: €22* ✉ *Main road, away from the tower* ☎ *23770/71222* 🌐 *www.okritikos.com.*

🛏 Hotels

Akrogiali

$ | HOTEL | Built in 1935, this was the town's first hotel, and the only one across the street from the beach—the three-story building is nothing special to look at, but the sea-view rooms are just fine for basic beach holidays. **Pros:** closest hotel to the beach; decent and clean; most rooms have great sea views. **Cons:** on a busy road; Wi-Fi signal is poor; front-facing rooms can get some street noise. [$] *Rooms from: €60* ✉ *Beach road* ☎ *23770/71201* 🌐 *www.ouranoupolis-akrogiali.gr* 🔑 *15 rooms* 🍽 *Free breakfast.*

★ Eagle's Palace

$$$$ | RESORT | FAMILY | The monastic architecture and lush gardens of this Small Luxury Hotels member is deeply inspired by the mystical Orthodox peninsula of Mt. Athos, which lies just a stone's throw away. **Pros:** endless golden-sand beaches in front of the resort; flawless service; free activities and shuttle to nearby villages. **Cons:** pack mosquito repellent; beware of hidden costs; breakfast is good but not quite up to the high standards one would expect here. [$] *Rooms from: €350* ✉ *Skala Neon Rodon* ☎ *23770/31070 reservations, 23774/40060 reservations, 23774/40050* 🌐 *www.eaglespalace.gr* 🔑 *157 rooms* 🍽 *Free breakfast.*

★ Skités

$ | B&B/INN | Find peace and privacy on a bluff off a gravel road south of town at this charming complex of garden bungalows, comprised of small and appealingly rustic, pertinently monastic, but by no means ascetic rooms, and staffed by folks who want to make you feel comfortable. **Pros:** private and peaceful; very personal service; those delicious vegetables from the owner's own plot. **Cons:** don't come here if it's buzzy nightlife you're after; the rustic bohemian style is not to everyone's taste; Wi-Fi patchy in certain areas. [$] *Rooms from: €121* ✉ *1 km (½ mile) south of town* ✣ *If you need directions, ask for the hotel of Mrs. Pola Bohn* ☎ *23770/71140, 23770/71141* 🌐 *www.skites.gr* ⏲ *Closed Nov.–late Apr.* 🔑 *25 rooms* 🍽 *Free breakfast.*

Mt. Athos Όρ. Άθως

50 km (31 miles) southeast of Ouranoupolis, 120 km (74 miles) southeast of Thessaloniki.

The third peninsula of Halkidiki, Mt. Athos is called *Ayion Oros* (Holy Mountain) in Greek, although it does not become a mountain until its southernmost point (6,667 feet). The peninsula is prized for its pristine natural beauty, seclusion, and spirituality; its monasteries contain priceless illuminated books and other treasures.

The Virgin Mary, it is said, was brought to Athos by accident from Ephesus, having been blown off course by a storm, and she decreed that it be venerated as her own special place. This story has since become the rationale for keeping it off-limits to all women but the Virgin herself. Hermits began settling here and formed the first monastery in the 10th century. By the 14th century, monasteries on the 650-square-km (250-square-mile) peninsula numbered in the hundreds. In 1924 the Greek state limited the number of monasteries, including Russian, Bulgarian, and Serbian Orthodox, to 20, but a number of hermitages and separate dependencies called *skits* also exist. The semiautonomous community falls under the religious authority of the Istanbul-based Orthodox Ecumenical Patriarch.

Only men may visit the monasteries, and the numbers are strictly limited. You must apply for a permit at the Holy Executive of the Holy Mt. Athos Pilgrims' Bureau in Thessaloniki several months in advance. Mt. Athos is a place of religious pilgrimage: proper attire is long pants and shirts with sleeves at least to midarm; wearing hats inside the monasteries is forbidden. Video cameras and tape recorders are banned from the mountain, but taking photographs is allowed.

GETTING HERE AND AROUND

From Ouranoupolis, boats leave twice daily to Daphni (the main port on the west coast of Athos). The 6:30 am boat sails direct to Daphni, but the 9:45 am boat stops at each harbor or monastery (the trip can take as long as 90 minutes). From Daphni there's a connecting service farther south to Ayias Annas. Fares vary depending on the speed of the boat. You can also take a bus to Ierissos, from where boats leave at 8:30 am (daily in summer; Thursday–Monday from September to June) for the monastery of Iviron, which is midway down the east coast here. Boats stop at each monastery en route, with the journey taking around two hours. Make sure to double-check times and travel options at the Holy Executive of the Holy Mt. Athos Pilgrims' Bureau in Thessaloniki, or inquire at the Thessaloniki bureau of the Greek National Tourism Organization for more information.

PERMITS

Holy Executive of the Holy Mt. Athos Pilgrims' Bureau

Men who want to visit Mt. Athos should contact the Holy Executive of the Holy Mt. Athos Pilgrims' Bureau (Grafio Proskyniton Ayiou Orous) four to six months in advance of arrival. ■ TIP→ **Cancellations are quite common, and you may get a pass immediately if there has been a cancellation, so it's always worth asking if you want to go but haven't made the proper arrangements in advance.** You must obtain a written permit (free) from this office, which issues 10 permits a day for non-Orthodox visitors, and 100 permits a day for Orthodox visitors (Greek or foreign). You will need to pick it up in person, presenting your passport. Enquire about making reservations for a specific monastery, which must be done in advance (some might be closed for renovations). The permits are valid for a four-day visit on specific dates, which may be extended by authorities in Karyes. When you arrive at Ouranoupolis, you also need to pick up a *diamonitirio*, or visiting permit (€30). Boats headed for the monasteries depart Ouranoupolis for Daphni on the peninsula at 6:30 am weekdays, 7 am and 11 am Saturday and Sunday respectively; it's a two-hour sail and costs €7.50. There are faster boats also that take 45 minutes; these leave at 8 am and 11:45 am daily, 8 am and 11:35 am Sunday and cost €12.50. You need to book a seat as soon as you receive your permit ⊕ *www.microathos. gr* or call ☎ *2377/071400* for boat tickets and timetables. Local transport takes you the last 13 km (8 miles) to Karyes and to monasteries beyond from there. ✉ *Egnatia 109, Thessaloniki* ☎ *2310/252578 for non-Greeks, 2310/252575 for Greeks* ⊕ *www.athosfriends.org.*

Chapter 15

THE PELOPONNESE

MONEMVASSIA, MYCENAE, NAFPLION,
THE MANI, AND OLYMPIA

Updated by
Gareth Clark

 ⊙ Sights
★★★★★

 🍴 Restaurants
★★★☆☆

🛏 Hotels
★★★☆☆

 🛍 Shopping
★★☆☆☆

 🍸 Nightlife
★★☆☆☆

WELCOME TO
THE PELOPONNESE

TOP REASONS TO GO

★ **Ancient ruins A to Z:** Some of Greece's greatest classical ruins, including Corinth, Mycenae, and Olympia, are packed into this region.

★ **Nafplion grace:** The favorite Greek city of many seasoned travelers has a magnificent setting on the Gulf of Argolis, imposing remains, an animated waterfront, and street after street of old houses, churches, and mosques.

★ **Majestic Mani:** True connoisseurs of Greece flaunt the fact that they've traveled to this far-from-the-madding-crowds peninsula, famed for its silent villages, stark coastal landscapes, and feeling of mystery.

★ **High drama:** The theater at Epidaurus, the setting for a highly acclaimed drama festival, still boasts of acoustics so perfect that every word can be heard—even from the very last of its 55 tiers.

★ **Byzantine glory:** Two remarkable strongholds, Mystras and Monemvasia, display a rich Byzantine legacy.

1 Ancient Corinth. Home to several archaeological sites.

2 Epidaurus. A pleasant village boasting the Theater at Epidaurus.

3 Nafplion. This is a pretty town on the Gulf of Argolis.

4 Tiryns. Its 3,500-year-old Mycenaean acropolis faces the water.

5 Argos. Argos is known as the economic hub of the region.

6 Mycenae. The Death Mask of Agamemnon unearthed here is now in Athens.

7 Ancient Nemea. After seeing the site, take in the vineyard views.

8 Tripoli. Due to its mountain scenery, it's nicknamed the "Switzerland of Greece."

9 Vouraikos Gorge. See the gorge's rock walls on a thrilling train ride.

10 Patras. A busy port city that offers numerous ferry connections for travelers.

11 Lousios Gorge. Marvel at the stone-built villages high above the gorge.

12 Temple of Apollo at Bassae. One of Greece's best preserved ancient monuments.

13 Olympia. Olympia was famously the site of the ancient Olympic Games.

14 Ancient Messene. The ruins of this remarkable fortified ancient city are not to be missed.

15 Pylos. The "new fortress" that dominates the town was built by the Turks in 1573.

16 Methoni. A charming fishing village with beaches and a citadel.

17 Kalamata. An excellent base for exploring the south of the peninsula.

18 Kardamyli. This getaway to the Mani is known as a hiker's paradise.

19 Areopolis. Explore Maniote tower houses–spooky sentinels amid the harsh landscape.

20 Gerolimenas. A delightful coastal village at the southern end of the Mani.

21 Gythion. A pretty town with shops, ouzeri, a busy harbor, and beaches.

22 Monemvasia. A stunning medieval town carved into the side of a massive rock.

23 Sparta. The ancient city-state Sparta is now a modern city.

24 Mystras. This town is known for its Byzantine-era churches.

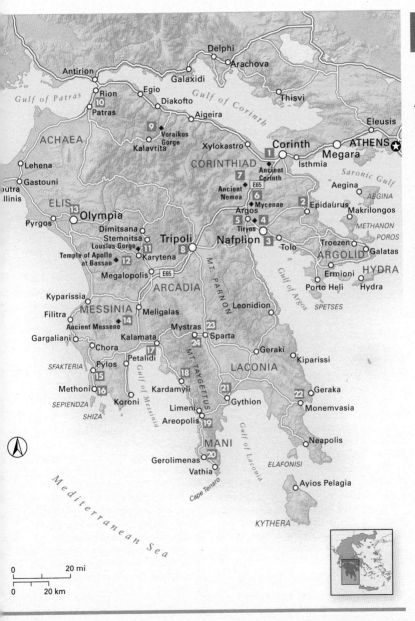

Over the millennia the rugged terrain of the Peloponnese—a vast region that hangs like a large leaf from the stem of the Corinthian isthmus—has nourished kingdoms and empires. The stony landmarks of these ancient achievers litter the ground liberally, from Epidaurus to Olympia to Ancient Messene.

This, indeed, is the fabulous Greece of history and myth: if Hercules walked the earth (some historians now believe he was an actual early king of Argos or Tiryns), his main stomping grounds were here.

Traces of these lost realms—ruined Bronze Age citadels, Greek and Roman temples and theaters, and the fortresses and settlements of the Byzantines, Franks, Venetians, and Turks—attest to this land's historical richness. Four thousand years of history are more fully illustrated in this region than nearly anywhere else in Europe. No wonder visitors who spend less than a week here wind up asking themselves why they didn't allot more time to this fascinating area of Greece, the country's most ruin-packed terrain, ground zero for anyone even remotely interested in the ancient past—with Byzantine wonders entering the mix at Monemvasia and Mystras. Plus, if you wish to forgo clamoring over ruins for a day or two, it's easy to find a mountain path or isolated stretch of sand on which to relax.

Time seems to have stood still in the smaller towns here, and even in the cities you'll encounter a lifestyle that remains more traditionally Greek than that of some of the more developed islands. The joy of exploring this region comes as much from watching life transpire in an animated town square or a remote mountain village as it does from seeing the impressive ruins, and the opportunity to discover this on foot is perhaps the greatest pleasure of all. Some of Greece's best hikes and trails wind the foothills of the Taygettus and Arcadian ranges, plunging into steep-sided gorges filled with medieval monasteries or rising up along millennia-old cobbled roads.

"Pelopónnisos" means "Island of Pelops," though only the narrow Corinth canal separates it from the mainland. Pelops was the son of the mythical Tantalos, whose tragic descendants dominate the half-legendary Mycenaean centuries. The myths and legends surrounding Pelops and his family—Atreus, Agamemnon, Orestes, and Electra, among others—provided the grist for poets and playwrights from Homer to Aeschylus and enshroud many of the region's sites to this day.

A walk through the Lion Gate into Mycenae, the citadel of Agamemnon, brings the Homeric epic to life, and the massive walls of nearby Tiryns glorify the age of might. Eastward lies Corinth, the economic superpower of the 7th and 6th centuries BC, and also Epidaurus, the sanctuary of Asklepios, god of healing, where in summer Greek dramas are re-created in the ancient theater, one of the finest and most complete to survive.

In the western side of the Peloponnese is one of Greece's greatest ancient sites, Olympia, the sanctuary of Zeus and site of the ancient Olympic Games. Ancient Messene, with its mammoth fortifications from the 4th century BC, is on the sandy cape of Messinia, in the southern part of the region.

Fast forward almost two millennia. By the 13th century the armies of the Fourth Crusade (in part egged on by Venice) had conquered the Peloponnese after capturing Constantinople in 1204. But the dominion of the Franks was brief, and Byzantine authority was restored under the Palaiologos dynasty. Soon after Constantinople fell in 1453, the Turks, taking advantage of an internal rivalry, crushed the Palaiologoi and helped themselves to the Peloponnese.

In the following centuries the struggle between the Venetians and the Ottoman Turks played out across Greece, their influence easily discerned today in cities such as Nafplion and Monemvasia, where Turkish mosques and fountains join the ruins of Venetian fortifications. Eventually, Greece would find its own voice and the modern history of the country began in the Peloponnese. Rebellion against Turkish rule ignited here. A visit to the Mani reveals the history of the clans, who rose up to the join the rebel attack on Kalamata in 1821, the first major city to fall to the Greeks. Others swiftly followed, though it wouldn't be until the end of that decade that the Turks finally withdrew. Nafplion even became the recognized capital of Greece from 1829 until the move to Athens in 1834.

Planning

When to Go

As in much of Greece, late April and May provide optimum conditions for exploration—hotels, restaurants, and sites have begun to extend their hours but the hordes of travelers have not yet arrived, and days are long. September and October are also excellent times because the weather is warm but not oppressive, the sea is at its balmiest, and the throngs of people have gone home. More touristed spots tend to operate seasonally, but in places like the upper Mani, the season tends to start earlier and finish later, running from March until November, due to the abundance of walkers arriving to explore its slopes in the cooler weather. In summer, morning and early-evening activity will avoid the worst of the heat, which can be a formidable obstacle. Mosquitoes are out in force around seaside villages, which are often surrounded by fields and groves, so bring repellent and, more important, seek out a hotel room with air-conditioning. Remember that snow renders many of the mountain regions hard to access in winter, though that's good news for those wanting to hit the slopes of Mt. Menalon.

Planning Your Time

The remains of the ancient world are what draw many visitors to the Peloponnese—Mycenae, Epidaurus, and Olympia certainly top the list of must-see sights of anyone with an interest in archaeology. Nafplion, a delightful city with Byzantine, Venetian, and Turkish roots, makes an ideal base from which to explore these well-preserved ruins of ancient Greece. After Nafplion, Ancient Olympia, a don't-miss destination, beckons the Peloponnesian traveler. Continuing southward, one enters Laconia. The rewards here include exploring the stark Mani Peninsula and ancient splendors at Messene and elsewhere, and the trip down there is easy: Highway E65 allows travelers to speed from Athens to Kalamata or Sparta and Gythion in a few hours. If driving, don't discount the much slower Route 82 between Kalamata and Sparta, which crosses the Taygettus mountain range. It has some of the hairiest mountaintop switchbacks you'll find anywhere and is prone to rockfalls (do not attempt in winter), but if you're looking for a scenic drive, the views here rival any of those found in Greece, especially at the 5,000-foot Langada Pass. Resort life is relatively low-key in the southern Peloponnese. Monemvasia, however, is a popular weekend destination for Greeks, and the narrow lanes can seem jammed; the town is much less crowded and more pleasant to visit during the week, when the medieval atmosphere regains a hold. The Mani, another favorite "remote" seaside getaway for Athenians and hikers, is rarely crowded, except on August weekends.

Getting Here and Around

Though it's possible to travel by train from Athens to the northern Peloponnese, ongoing and often delayed improvements can make this less than a magic-carpet ride, and you will have to change at Kiato. The simplest way to get around this often-rural peninsula is via the region's well-maintained and well-marked roads. The KTEL bus network between towns is excellent, though requires patience and research. Instead of one easy-to-use booking site, the Peloponnese service is broken into regions (eg. Messinia, Arcadia, Corinth, Argolid, etc.). This makes navigating the network within the Peloponnese infinitely trickier, as connections mean getting the times from two different operators, though services from Athens

are usually simple to book. In smaller towns, coffee shops, typically those next to the bus stop, often double as ticket offices. Hiring a car is the best option of all. It's easy to get to most places in the Peloponnese via the E65, a north–south highway that cuts through the region and is four lanes for much of its length, connecting Corinth, Tripoli, Sparta, and Kalamata with Athens. Tolls can mount up, though, with the Athens–Kalamata route costing around €12. Another leg, E55, branches off to the western coast near Pylos. Nafplion, about 150 km (90 miles) south of Athens, makes an excellent base for exploring the region; from here you can easily reach such ancient sites as Epidaurus and Mycenae.

AIR

The main airport in the Peloponnese is the small field 9 km (5 miles) outside Kalamata. It's not terribly well served, though Aegean Airlines offers daily one-hour flights to and from Athens, and you'll find connections to the likes of London and Amsterdam in summer.

AIRPORT CONTACTS Kalamata Airport.
⊠ *Off Hwy. E2, 9 km (5 miles) west of city center, Kalamata* ☎ *27210/63805* ⊕ *www.ypa.gr.*

BOAT AND FERRY

There are three major ferry ports in the Peloponnese. The city of Patras is the largest, with ferries to and from the southern Ionian islands of Zakynthos and Kefalonia (including connections to Lefkhada and Ithaki) operated by Levante Ferries. ANEK, Superfast, and Minoan have the most extensive international services, linking Patras with Ancona, Bari, and Venice in Italy. On the west coast, the port of Kyllini has a Levante Ferries service operating between Zakynthos and the mainland. Seajets also run a service in summer linking Gythion, in the Southern Peloponnese, with Kythera, Kissamos (Kastelli), and Crete. *For detailed information on ferry companies and port authorities, see Boat in Travel Smart.*

BUS

Bus service between Athens and the Peloponnese is excellent—so good that you might consider taking a bus to your destination and renting a car locally, saving on tolls and high fuel charges. Take advantage of the English speakers at the ticket offices; they have at their disposal a wealth of information that is otherwise hard to get. The association of regional bus companies (KTEL) has no overarching website covering Greece; instead it is broken down into several regional companies covering areas such as Messinia, Arcadia, and Corinth in the Peloponnesse. Each, frustratingly, has its own website, of varying degrees of usefulness. It's easier just to call up the ticket offices, who can explain the connections you'll need. Within the Peloponnese, you will usually find English-speaking staff behind the desk in the stations in the larger towns; in smaller towns and villages, the local coffee shop often doubles as a ticket office. The service from Athens to Corinth and Patras operates as frequently as every half hour from 6 am to late evening; it takes only an hour to Corinth and three or so to Patras. From Corinth, you can continue west or connect for services to Nafplion, from where a local network serves the nearby classical sights, and south to Tripoli and Sparta, with connections or onward service to such places as Monemvasia and the Mani. From Patras, you can make boat connections or connect to buses to Olympia and other places in the southwest Peloponnese. From Athens, direct buses also run several times daily to Gythion, Kalamata, and Tripoli and at least once a day to Monemvasia and Pylos.

CAR

For pure pleasure, traveling by car through the Peloponnese really delivers. Four wheels are not only the easiest way to get around, but a car also provides a chance to enjoy dramatic scenery and get to out-of-the-way spots. The very best driving routes? Some point to the mountain roads that lead to Stemnitsa and Demitsana—on this journey, you'll encounter thick forests, stone villages clinging to steep hillsides, and brooding Frankish castles. Others tout the road from Kalamata to Mystras: this scenic route rises from the Messinia plains onto the forested flanks of the Taygettus range and the ruined city of Mystras and modern Sparta. For some, the road down the Mani Peninsula can't be beat: setting out from Kalamata, the landscape becomes starker the farther south you travel (on a highway that is barely more than one lane in places) until you reach Cape Tenaro, the mythical entrance to the underworld.

Note that even if highways have assigned numbers, no Greek knows them by any other than their informal names, which usually refer to their destination. A well-maintained toll highway, known simply as Ethnikos Odos, or National road (officially E65), runs from Athens to the isthmus of Corinth (84 km [52 miles], 1 hour), and from there continues south to Nafplion and Kalamata (you can veer off to Sparta, Monemvasia, the Mani, and other places in the southern Peloponnese). A branch, Route 8a, heads east from Corinth toward Patras and Olympia and connects with the Rion bridge across the Gulf of Corinth. Have change ready, as a toll of about €1 to €3 is collected intermittently on parts of the system. From Corinth the trip to Patras takes about 1½ hours, and to Kalamata and Sparta around 2 hours.

Narrow roads cross mountainous terrain throughout the region, providing many a scenic route when not closed due to snow in winter. You'll need a GPS device and/or a good map to navigate the back roads, as well as a transliteration of the Greek alphabet—many signs on remote roads are in Greek only. Gas stations are few and far between in some places, so top off the tank when you have the chance.

If you're renting a car in Athens, do so at the airport and drive south from there; the E94 ring road around Athens allows you to avoid the harrowing city traffic and connects with E65 south to the Peloponnese. On the other hand, bus travel into the region is so easy that you may want to travel by bus to your destination in the Peloponnese and rent a car for local exploring. You may rent a car in Patras if you are arriving on a boat from Italy or one of the Ionian islands. *For detailed information on renting a car, see Car in Travel Smart.*

TAXI

If you have trouble reaching a site—for example, there is no public transportation to Ancient Messene—take a taxi from a town's main square, which is always near the bus station. When leaving town limits, the driver may switch his meter to the higher rate (Tarifa 2). In rural areas drivers may not speak English, though they will often find someone near the taxi stand who does to help you negotiate the ride; they also probably won't switch on the meter, so make sure you agree on the cost before getting in.

TRAIN

The good news is that train travel from Athens to the Peloponnese is improving all the time—or, at least, is scheduled to improve. The bad news is that extensive track work is ongoing on the Peloponnesian lines, service interruptions are common, and Greece's financial woes have severely curtailed improvements. There are plans for a fast network to be running from Athens to Patras, Kalamata, and other cities in the Peloponnese, but no one is counting on such a network actually being in place soon. If you are traveling from Athens to anywhere other than Corinth, you will probably find bus travel to be faster, more reliable, and in many cases your only option for public transportation. Trains run to and from Corinth (Korinth N. station) and Athens every hour between 8 and 8. The trip

takes one hour and costs €8.50 to and from Athens, €11 to and from the airport via Kato Acharnai Station. Tickets can be bought online or at stations. *For detailed information on traveling by train, see Train in Travel Smart.*

CONTACTS Greek Railways Organization (OSE). ⊕ *www.trainose.gr.*

Hotels

Hotels in Nafplion, Sparta, and other large towns and cities tend to be open year-round. Monemvasia is a year-round getaway and hotels stay open there as well. In beach resorts and areas of natural interest such as the Mani villages, and in Olympia, many hotels close in November and reopen in late March or early April. In Nafplion, many old houses have been converted to pleasant small hotels and do a brisk weekend business as a getaway for Athenians. Here you'll also be likely to find the region's more luxurious and expensive lodgings. Overall, lodging is good value in the Peloponnese, and even in high season you can usually manage to find a clean and pleasant room for two, with breakfast, for less than €100.

Restaurants

While you can enjoy elegant and nouvelle dining in some of the finer restaurants of the Peloponnese's beauty spots, such as Nafplion and Monemvasia, one of the great pleasures of traveling in this region is enjoying a meal on a square or seaside terrace in a simple village. In fact, villages here were the source of such international favorites as avgolemono soup and lamb fricassee. There are several other local specialties to watch for: in the mountain villages near Tripoli, order *stifado* (beef with pearl onions), *arni psito* (lamb on the spit), *kokoretsi* (entrails on the spit), and thick, creamy yogurt. In Sparta, look for *bardouniotiko* (a local dish of chicken stuffed with cheese, olives, and walnuts), and, around Pylos, order fresh ocean fish (priced by the kilo). In the rest of Laconia, try *loukaniko horiatiko* (village sausage), and in the Mani ask for ham, which is typically smoked.

Vegetables are almost always locally grown and fresh in this region famous for its olives and olive oil as wells as figs, tomatoes, and other produce. Seafood is plentiful, though sometimes frozen—menus will usually indicate what's frozen and what's fresh (and frozen usually hails from beyond Greece). A fresh catch is often available at seaside tavernas, and an octopus or two will usually be drying out front. Inland, many tavernas serve grilled pork from local farms, as well as chicken and roosters plucked that morning. As for wine, beyond those *varelisio* (from the barrel), there are great reds from the region around Nemea and a top light white from Mantinea. After dinner, try *mavrodaphne,* a heavy dessert wine, or *dendoura,* a clove liqueur, as a digestive. Dress is casual and reservations usually unnecessary, although you might be asked to wait for a table if you're dining at 9 pm or later.

Restaurant and hotel reviews have been shortened. For full information, visit Fodors.com.

What it Costs in euros

	$	$$	$$$	$$$$
RESTAURANTS				
	under €15	€15–€25	€26–€40	over €40
HOTELS				
	under €125	€125–€225	€226–€275	over €275

Tour Options

Many operators organize whirlwind one-day tours from Athens to Corinth, Mycenae, Epidaurus, and Nafplion; the cost is about €85. These no-frills tours, aimed at those who don't expect much handholding, can be booked at travel agencies and at larger hotels. CHAT and other operators also offer a more leisurely two-day tour of Corinth, Mycenae, and Epidaurus, with an overnight stay in Nafplion; cost is about €180. If you are in Nafplion, many local travel agencies can arrange day tours of the classical sites.

Visitor Information

The Peloponnese is woefully underserved by tourist offices. Most towns in the region do not have tourist offices of any sort. For tourist information and general help in places without tourist offices, it's best to go to the Greek National Tourism Organization website (⊕ *visitgreece.gr*).

Ancient Corinth
Αρχαια Κορινθος

81 km (50 miles) southwest of Athens.

The isthmus is where the Peloponnese begins. Were it not for this narrow neck of land less than 7 km (4½ miles) across, the waters of the Gulf of Corinth and the Saronic Gulf would meet and would make the Peloponnese an island; hence the name, which means "Pelops's island."

For the ancient Greeks the isthmus was strategically important for both trade and defense; Corinth, with harbors on either side of the isthmus, grew wealthy on the lucrative east–west trade. Ships en route from Italy and the Adriatic to the Aegean had to sail around the Peloponnese, so in the 7th century BC a paved roadway called the Diolkos was constructed across the isthmus, over which ships were hauled using rollers. You can still see remnants near the bridge at the western end of the modern canal.

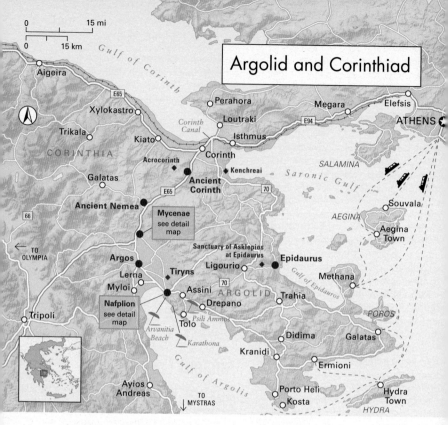

West of the isthmus, the countryside opens up into a low-lying coastal plain around the head of the Gulf of Corinth. Modern Corinth, near the coast about 8 km (5 miles) north of the turnoff for the ancient town, is a regional center of some 23,000 inhabitants. Concrete pier-and-slab is the preferred architectural style, and the city seems to be under a seismic curse: periodic earthquakes knock the buildings down before they have time to develop any character. Corinth was founded in 1858 after one of these quakes leveled the old village at the ancient site; another flattened the new town in 1928; and a third in 1981 destroyed many buildings. Most tourists tend to avoid the town altogether, visiting the ruins of Ancient Corinth and moving on.

Sights

Acrocorinth

ARCHAEOLOGICAL SITE | Looming some 540 meters (1,772 feet) above Ancient Corinth, the Acrocorinth is one of the best naturally fortified citadels in Europe. Citizens retreated in times of invasions and earthquakes, and armies could keep an eye out for approaches by land over the isthmus and by sea from the Saronic Gulf and the Gulf of Corinth. The moat and three rings of wall are largely Byzantine, Frankish, Venetian, and Turkish—but the right-hand tower of the innermost of the three gates is apparently a 4th-century BC original. Corinth's famous Temple of Aphrodite, which had 1,000 prostitutes in attendance, stood here at the summit, too. On the slope of the mountain is the Sanctuary of Demeter, which you can view but not enter. Take the road next to the ticket office in Ancient Corinth; if you don't have your own car, you can hire one of the taxis that often wait for visitors for the trip up to the tourist pavilion and café (about €5 round-trip), from which it's a 10-minute walk to Acrocorinth gate. ▣ *Corinth* ✛ *Off E94, 7 km (4½ miles) west of Corinth* ☎ *27410/31207* ⊕ *www. culture.gr* ✉ *€8 combined ticket with Ancient Corinth and Archaeological Museum.*

★ Ancient Corinth

ARCHAEOLOGICAL SITE | Excavations of one of the great cities of classical and Roman Greece have gone on since 1896, exposing ruins on the slopes of Acrocorinth and northward toward the coast. In ancient times, goods and often entire ships were hauled across the isthmus on a paved road between Corinth's two ports—Lechaion on the Gulf of Corinth and Kenchreai on the Saronic Gulf—ensuring a lively trade with colonies and empires throughout Europe and the Middle East. Most of the buildings that have been excavated are from the Roman era; only a few from before the sack of Corinth in 146 BC were rehabilitated when the city was refounded under orders of Julius Caesar.

The **Glauke Fountain** is past the parking lot on the left. According to the Greek traveler Pausanias, Glauke, Jason's second wife, also known as Creusa, threw herself into the water to obtain relief from a poisoned dress sent to her by the vengeful Medea. Beyond the fountain is the **museum,** which displays examples of the black-figure pottery—decorated with friezes of panthers, sphinxes, bulls, and warriors—for which Corinth was famous.

Seven of the original 38 columns of the **Temple of Apollo** (just above the museum) are still standing, and the structure is by far the most striking of Corinth's ancient buildings—as well as one of the oldest stone temples in Greece (mid-6th century BC). Beyond the temple are the remains of the **North Market,** a

The Isthmus Canal

Nero was the first to begin cutting a canal in AD 67, a task he then turned over to 6,000 Jewish prisoners. But the project died with Nero the following year, and the roadway was used until the 13th century. The modern canal, built 1882–93, was cut through 285 feet of rock to sea level. The impressive sight is a fleeting one if you are speeding by on the highway, so keep a sharp lookout. A turnoff leads to the tourist area, which has many restaurants (best avoided) and souvenir shops, as well as an overlook.

15

The Peloponnese ANCIENT CORINTH

colonnaded square once surrounded by many small shops, and south of the temple is the main forum of Ancient Corinth. A row of shops bounds the forum at the far western end. East of the market is a series of small temples, and beyond is the forum's main plaza. A long line of shops runs lengthwise through the forum, dividing it into an **upper (southern)** and **lower (northern) terrace,** in the center of which is the bema (large podium), perhaps the very one where in AD 52 St. Paul delivered his defense of Christianity before the Roman proconsul Gallio.

The southern boundary of the forum was the **South Stoa,** a 4th-century-BC building, perhaps erected by Philip II of Macedonia to house delegates to his Hellenic confederacy. There were originally 33 shops across the front, and the back was altered in Roman times to accommodate such civic offices as the council hall, or *bouleuterion,* in the center. The road to Kenchreai began next to the bouleuterion and headed south. Farther along the South Stoa were the entrance to the **South Basilica** and, at the far end, the **Southeast Building,** which probably was the city archive.

In the lower forum, below the Southeast Building, was the **Julian Basilica,** a former law court. Continuing to the northeast corner of the forum, you approach the facade of the **Fountain of Peirene.** Water from a spring was gathered into four reservoirs before flowing out through the arcadelike facade into a drawing basin in front. Frescoes of swimming fish from a 2nd-century Roman refurbishment can still be seen. The Lechaion road heads out of the forum to the north. A colonnaded courtyard, the **Peribolos of Apollo,** is directly to the east of the Lechaion road, and beyond it lies a **public latrine,** with toilets in place, and the remains of a **Roman-era bath,** probably the Baths of Eurykles described by Pausanias as Corinth's best known.

Along the west side of the Lechaion road is a large basilica entered from the forum through the **Captives' Facade,** named for its sculptures of captive barbarians. West of the Captives' Facade the row of **northwest shops** completes the circuit.

Northwest of the parking lot is the **odeon** (a roofed theater), cut into a natural slope, which was built during the 1st century AD, but burned around 175. Around 225 the theater was renovated and used as an arena for combats between gladiators and wild beasts. North of the odeon is the **theater** (5th century BC), one of the few Greek buildings reused by the Romans, who filled in the original seats and set in new ones at a steeper angle. By the 3rd century they had adapted it for gladiatorial contests and finally for mock naval battles.

North of the theater, inside the city wall, are the **Fountain of Lerna** and the **Asklepieion,** the sanctuary of the god of healing with a small temple (4th century BC) set in a colonnaded courtyard and a series of dining rooms in a second courtyard. Terra-cotta votive offerings representing afflicted body parts (hands, legs, breasts, genitals, and so on) were found in the excavation of the Asklepieion, and many

of them are displayed at the museum. ✉ *Corinth* ✛ *Off E94, 7 km (4½ miles) west of Corinth* ☎ *27410/31207* ⊕ *www. culture.gr* ✉ *€8 combined ticket (Ancient Corinth and Archeological Museum).*

Epidaurus Επιδαυρος

62 km (38 miles) south of the isthmus, 25 km (15 miles) east of Nafplion.

What is now a pleasant little agricultural village surrounded by orange and olive groves has been on the Greek map for millennia, and the ruins of its heyday are some of the most impressive in Greece. Epidaurus was known for its healing center and spectacular theater, which made it the envy even of Rome. Today the beautifully preserved theater, standing proud in a pine-scented glade, is a magnificent sight, and one of the most popular on the peninsula thanks to its yearly theater festival.

 Sights

★ **Sanctuary of Asklepios at Epidaurus**
ARCHAEOLOGICAL SITE | FAMILY | What was once the most famous healing center in the ancient world is today best known for the **Theater at Epidaurus,** remarkably well preserved because it was buried at some time in antiquity and remained untouched until it was uncovered in the late 19th century. Built in the 4th century BC by the architect Polykleitos the Younger, the 14,000-seat theater was never remodeled in antiquity, and because it was rather remote, the stones were never quarried for secondary building use. The extraordinary qualities of the theater were recognized even in the 2nd century AD. Pausanias of Lydia, the 2nd-century AD traveler and geographer, wrote, "The Epidaurians have a theater in their sanctuary that seems to me particularly worth a visit. The Roman theaters have gone far beyond all the others in the world … but who can begin to rival Polykleitos for the

beauty and composition of his architecture?" In addition, the acoustics are so perfect that even from the last of the 55 tiers every word can be heard. It's the setting for a highly acclaimed **summer drama festival,** with outstanding productions.

The **Sanctuary of Asklepios** is dedicated to the god of healing, the son of Apollo who was allegedly born here. The most important healing center in the ancient world drew visitors from throughout Greece and the colonies in search of a cure. The discovery of a new building in 2020 even suggest the site was in use earlier than previously thought, possibly as far back as the 6th century BC. The sanctuary is in the midst of a decades-long restoration project, but you can see the ruins of the Sleeping Hall, where clients slept in order to be visited by the gods in their dreams and told which cure to follow, as well as the enormous Guest House, with 160 rooms, and the Tholos, where serpents that were said to cure with a flick of the tongue were housed in a maze of labyrinths. Some copies of sculptures found among the ruins are in the **site museum** (the originals are in the National Archaeological Museum in Athens) along with ancient medical instruments, votives, and inscriptions expressing the gratitude of the cured. Heading south from the isthmus on Highway 70, don't take the turnoffs for Nea Epidaurus or Palaio Epidaurus; follow the signs that say "Ancient Theater of Epidaurus." ⊠ *Epidaurus* ⊕ *Off Hwy. 70, near Ligourio* ☎ *27530/22009* ⊕ *www.culture.gr* ⊠ *€12.*

🎭 Performing Arts

Athens and Epidaurus Festival

FESTIVALS | In the theater at Epidaurus, this festival offers memorable performances from late June through August, Friday and Saturday only, at 9 pm. Productions in the main theater are of ancient Greek drama in modern Greek, many presented by the national theater troupe. Actors are so expressive (or often wear ancient masks to signal the mood) that you can enjoy the performance even if you don't know a word of Greek. You can also see opera productions in the small theater. Get to the site early (and bring a picnic lunch or have a drink or a light meal at the decent Xenia Café on-site), because watching the sun set behind the mountains and fields of olives and pines is unforgettable. You can buy tickets at the Festival Box Office in Athens (at Panepistimiou 39), by phone, or online, and a short time before performance at the theater box office. Many tour operators in Athens and Nafplion offer tours that include a performance at Epidaurus. On the days of performances, four or five buses run between Nafplion and the theater, and there's service back to Nafplion after the play. Look for buses that say "Theater" or "Epidaurus," not "Nea Epidaurus" or "Archea Epidaurus." Buses also run to and from Athens on days of performances. ⊠ *Ancient theater, Epidaurus* ☎ *21092/82900 general information, 21032/72000 tickets* ⊕ *www. greekfestival.gr* ⊠ *Tickets €13–€50.*

Nafplion Ναυπλιο

65 km (40½ miles) south of Corinth, 27 km (17 miles) west of Epidaurus.

Oraia (beautiful) is the word Greeks use to describe Nafplion. The town's old section lies on a peninsula jutting into the Gulf of Argolis, and despite its colonization by boutique stores, guesthouses, and cafés, enough of the old world remains here to thrill wanderers. Greek, Venetian, and Turkish architecture still lines the cobbles and back streets, with many of its neoclassical mansions turned into eccentric stays. Narrow alleys, often just broad flights of stone stairs, lead to the hilltop fortresses of Acronafplia and Palamidi, where views sweep down to the quayside and pebble beaches, and the whole bay unravels before your eyes.

It is a singular quirk of history that Naf-plion, which long lived in the shadows of its ancient neighbors, has risen to such acclaim today. The area was believed to have been inhabited as far back as the Neolithic era, but by the time the Mycenaeans were making nearby Tiryns one of the great cities of its day (around 1400 BC), little was written about its neighbor. It had fallen off the radar again as the Classical era arrived after nearby Argos rose to prominence and destroyed Nafplion for its alliance with Sparta during the Second Messinian War. It wasn't until the Byzantines took an interest that history's gaze fell once again on the city, and come the 13th century AD it was in a tug of war between the empire and the Frankish crusaders. Yet it was arguably the Venetians who made the most lasting impression here. In the 1700s, during their second reign, they bulked up the city's existing castle defences and built a second fortress, Palamides, to safeguard its now vital port. It did little good, as the Turks once again snatched it from them, yet this era shaped much of what makes the present-day city so charming. Nafplion would finally have its day in the sun when, during the War of Independence, it became the capital (1823–1834) of the embryonic Greek state, witnessing the historic birth of a nation and even the assassination of Greece's first head of state on the steps of St. Spyridon church.

Today, Nafplion is once again just a provincial city, busy in the tourist season and on weekends when Athenians arrive to escape the city pressures. While most are content to wander the boutique stores and sip a coffee on Syntagma (Consti-tution) Square, there is some incredible dining to be found here as well as a smattering of beaches to complement the history that envelops the streets and churches. It is well worth a leisurely day of your undivided attention, and makes a good base for exploring the ruins of the nearby ancient cities who rose to greater heights yet fell so spectacularly.

GETTING HERE AND AROUND

A favorite outing for Athenians is to whisk down to Nafplion on the toll road. The trip takes two hours (less for some drivers). You may want to take a more leisurely trip and stop at the isthmus and Ancient Corinth along the way. Once in Nafplion you can usually find a space in the enormous free parking lot alongside the port next to the Old Town. From there you can walk to most Nafplion accommodations.

Travelers to Nafplion can also take advantage of the new suburban rail links between Athens and Corinth, a trip of about an hour. From there you can transfer to one of the four daily trains to Nafplion (€10 each way), for a total trip time of three to four hours, or continue to Nafplion by taxi for about €50.

Bus service, either directly from Athens or with a connection in Corinth, is good. Buses to Nafplion run about every hour, and you should allow about three hours for the trip, which costs €15 each way and often requires a change in Corinth.

◉ Sights

A full exploration of Nafplion takes an entire day; a quick tour, with some omissions, could be done in three hours, which is likely why it has become a popu-lar stop for cruise ships. You can get a good sample of the city just by following your nose through its winding streets and charming squares, beginning at Syntagma (Constitution) Square, around which are found some of the city's top sights, and finishing high atop the town's Venetian-era Palamidi fortress.

Acronafplia

CASTLE/PALACE | FAMILY | The Turks called this imposing hilltop of ruined fortifica-tions Its Kale (Inner Citadel). The heights are crowned with a series of castles: a Frankish one on the eastern end of the hill, a Byzantine one on the west, and a massive Castello del Torrione (or Toro for

Surviving nearly intact from the 4th century BC, the arena at Epidaurus remains the most famous ancient theater in the world.

short), also at the eastern end, built by the Venetians around 1480. During the second Venetian occupation, the gates were strengthened and the huge Grimani bastion was added (1706) below the Toro. The Acronafplia is accessible from the west side via the elevator next to the Nafplia Palace hotel, which sits on the ruins of the Frankish fort, and from the east via Potamianou Street, whose flights of steps ascend the hillside from St. Spyridon Square. The remains of the fortifications can be explored free of charge on overgrown sections that provide stupendous views over Nafplion and the sea. ⊠ *Nafplion*.

Agia Panagitsa

RELIGIOUS SITE | While following the seaside promenade, before you reach the very tip of the peninsula (marked by a ship's beacon), there is a little shrine at the foot of a path leading up toward the Acronafplia walls above. The tiny church of the Virgin Mary, or Agia Panagitsa, hugs the cliff on a small terrace and is decorated with icons. During the Turkish occupation the church hid one of Greece's secret schools. ⊠ *Nafplion* ⊕ *End of promenade.*

★ Arvanitia Promenade

PROMENADE | A kilometer-long seaside promenade skirts the Nafplion Peninsula, paved with flagstones and opening every so often to terraces planted with a few rosebushes and olive and cedar trees. Along the south side of the peninsula, the promenade runs midway along a cliff—it's 100 feet up to Acronafplia, 50 feet down to the sea—and leads to Arvanitia Beach, a lovely place for a dip. Here and there a flight of steps goes down to the rocky shore below. Be careful if you go swimming here, because the rocks are covered with sea urchins, which can inflict a painful wound. Directly above the beach, starting at the car park, a forested path wraps its way for 4 km (2½ miles) around the coast to the sands of Karathona, passing umpteen stretches of wild rocky shore along the way; it makes a wonderfully shaded and scenic stroll. ⊠ *Nafplion*.

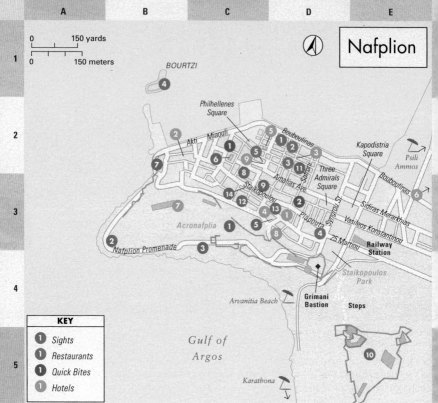

Nafplion

BOURTZI

Philhellenes Square

Akti Miaouli

Kapodistria Square

Psili Ammos

Three Admirals Square

Amalias Ave

Boubboulinas

Syngrou St.

Prapouta

Sidiras Meranthias

Vasileos Konstantinou

25 Martiou

Railway Station

Acronaflia

Staikopoulou

Staikopoulos Park

Nafplion Promenade

Arvanitia Beach

Grimani Bastion

Steps

Gulf of Argos

Karathona

KEY

- ● Sights
- ● Restaurants
- ● Quick Bites
- ● Hotels

Sights ▼

1 Acronafplia.............. **C3**
2 Agia Panagitsa.......... **B3**
3 Arvanitia Promenade.... **C3**
4 Bourtzi **B1**
5 Catholic Church of
   the Transfiguration **C3**
6 Church of Panagia...... **C2**
7 Five Brothers **B2**
8 Nafplion Archaeological
   Museum **C2**
9 Old Mosque **C3**
10 Palamidi................. **E5**
11 Peloponnesian Folklore
   Foundation Museum ... **D2**
12 Psaromachalas.......... **C3**
13 St. Spyridon Church **D3**
14 Vouleftiko **C3**

Restaurants ▼

1 Arapakos **D2**
2 Ta Fanaria **D2**
3 Taverna Byzantio **D2**
4 Taverna Noulis.......... **D3**
5 3Sixty Grill **C2**

Quick Bites ▼

1 Antica Gelateria
   di Roma **C2**
2 Kalimera **D3**

Hotels ▼

1 Aetoma.................. **D3**
2 Amphitryon **B2**
3 Amymone Suites........ **D2**
4 Byron Hotel............. **C3**
5 Hotel Latini **D2**
6 Hotel Perivoli........... **E3**
7 Nafplia Palace **B3**
8 Pension Marianna...... **D3**
9 3Sixty Hotel & Suites ... **C2**

Bourtzi

CASTLE/PALACE | Nafplion's pocket-size fortress is a captivating presence on a speck of land in the middle of the harbor generously called St. Theodore's Island. The Venetians completed a single tower in 1473, and they enlarged it with a second tower and bastion when they recaptured Nafplion in 1686. Freedom fighters captured the Bourtzi during the War of Independence in 1822 and used the island to bombard the Turks defending the town. The new Greek government retreated to the island in the unsettled times following the revolution; after 1865, the fortress was the residence of the town executioners. Boats leave on no fixed schedule from the eastern end of Akti Miaouli for €5; at the time of writing, ongoing works on the castle meant that access to the fortress continues to be partly restricted. ⊠ In harbor.

Catholic Church of the Transfiguration

RELIGIOUS SITE | In the 19th century King Otho returned this 13th-century landmark, restored and converted into a mosque under the Turks, to Nafplion's Catholics. The church is best known for the wooden arch erected inside the doorway, with the names carved on it of philhellenes (Greek admirers) who died during the War of Independence (Lord Byron is number 10). A mihrab (Muslim prayer recess) behind the altar and the amputated stub of a minaret are evidence of the church's use as a mosque. The church has a small museum and an underground crypt in which can be found sculptural work commemorating the defeat of the Turks at the hands of the Greeks and philhellenes. ⊠ Zigomala ✢ Two blocks south of St. Spyridon.

Church of Panagia

(Church of the Birth of the Virgin Mary) RELIGIOUS SITE | This post-Byzantine three-aisle basilica is by tradition linked to St. Anastasios, a Nafpliote painter. Anastasios was supposedly engaged to a local girl, but he abandoned her because she was immoral. Becoming despondent as a result of spells cast over him by her relatives, he converted to Islam. When the spell wore off, he cried out, "I was a Christian, I am a Christian, and I shall die a Christian." An Ottoman judge ordered that he be beheaded, but a Turkish mob stabbed Anastasios to death. His corpse was then allegedly hanged on an ancient olive tree that rises next to the church and that never again bore fruit. The basilica was the main Orthodox church during the Venetian occupation and has an elaborate wooden reredos carved in 1870. ⊠ Nafplion ✢ West of Syntagma Sq.

Five Brothers

MILITARY SITE | Above the harbor at the western edge of town are the ruins of a fortification known as the Five Brothers, the only remaining part of the lower wall built around Nafplion in 1502. The name comes from the five guns placed here by the Venetians around 1690; they remain in place, all bearing the winged lion of St. Mark. ⊠ Nafplion ✢ Near promontory of peninsula.

Nafplion Archaeological Museum

MUSEUM | The thick walls of this red-stone building, built in 1713 to serve as a naval storehouse for the Venetian fleet, ensure the coolest interior in town. It's more than just shelter, however. The museum houses artifacts from nearby sites Mycenae, Tiryns, Asine, and Dendra. The findings from the Mycenaean tombs are especially rich and include wonderful masks and a remarkable bronze suit of armor from the 15th century BC. ⊠ West side of Syntagma Sq. ☎ 27520/27502 ⊕ www.culture.gr ⊠ €6; €3 Nov.–Mar. ⊙ Closed Tues.

Old Mosque (Trianon)

RELIGIOUS SITE | This venerable mosque near the southeast corner of Syntagma Square has been put to various purposes since Nafplion was liberated from the Turks: as a school, a courthouse, municipal offices, and a movie theater, during the latter of which it acquired the name most still know it by: Trianon. (The writer Henry Miller, who did not care for Nafplion, felt that the use of the building as a movie theater was an example of the city's crassness.) The landmark occasionally hosts temporary exhibits and performances. It remains one of the oldest surviving examples of Ottoman architecture in Nafplion. ⊠ *Syntagma Sq.*

Palamidi

HISTORIC SITE | Whether in harsh sunlight or under floodlights at night, this mighty fortress is a beautiful sight, with red-stone bastions and flights of steps that zigzag down the 700-foot-tall cliff face. You can drive up the less-precipitous eastern slope, but if you are in reasonable shape and it isn't too hot, try climbing the stairs. Most guidebooks will tell you there are 999 of them, but 892 is closer to the mark. From the top you can look down on the Old Town, the Gulf of Argolis, and the entire Argive plain.

Built in 1711–14, the Palamidi comprises three forts and a series of freestanding and connecting defensive walls. Little good did it do them. The Palamidi fell to the Turks in 1715 after only eight days, allegedly because the Venetians assumed the fortress was impregnable and saw no need to garrison a large number of troops within the walls. In 1840, following the declaration of Greek independence, the Palamidi's Miltiadis bastion was converted by the Greeks into a fearsome prison that was used well into the 20th century. Its inmates included the revolutionary war hero Theodore Kolokotronis, on a charge of high treason that was later rescinded. His cell is indicated by a sign. ⊠ *Nafplion* ✛ *Above town* ☎ *27520/28036* €8.

★ Peloponnesian Folklore Foundation Museum

MUSEUM | This exemplary collection focuses on textiles and displays outstanding costumes, handicrafts, and household furnishings. Many of the exhibits are precious heirlooms that have been donated by Peloponnesian families, and several rooms are painstaking re-creations of 19th-century Nafplion homes. Top hats from the 1950s and contemporary fashion sandals are among items that bring the overview into the present day. The gift shop has some fascinating books and a good selection of high-quality jewelry and handicrafts, such as weavings, kilims, and collector's items such as *roka* (spindles) and wooden *koboloi* (worry beads). The shop on the ground floor stocks an appealing array of merchandise that includes jewelry, candlesticks, and handicrafts. ⊠ *Vasileos Alexandrou 1* ✛ *On block immediately north of Amalias, going up Sofroni* ☎ *27520/28379* ⊕ *www.pli.gr/en* €5.

Psaromachalas

NEIGHBORHOOD | The fishermen's quarter is a small district of narrow lanes above Staikopoulos Street, running between cramped little houses that huddle beneath the walls of Acronafplia. The old houses, painted in brownish yellow, green, and salmon red, are embellished with additions and overhangs in eclectic styles. The walk is enjoyable, though many of the houses have been turned into small pensions. Keep a low profile to respect the privacy of the locals. ⊠ *Along Kostouros.*

St. Spyridon Church

RELIGIOUS SITE | This one-aisle basilica with a dome (1702) has a special place in Greek history: it was in its doorway that the statesman Ioannis Kapodistrias, the first head of the newly independent Greek state, was assassinated in 1831 by the Mavromichalis brothers from the Mani, the outcome of a long-running vendetta. The mark of the bullet can be seen next to the Venetian portal. On the south side of the square, opposite St. Spyridon, are two of the four Turkish fountains that remain in Nafplion. A third is a short distance east on Kapodistria Street, at the steps that constitute the upper reaches of Tertsetou Street. ⊠ *St. Spirdonas Sq.*

Vouleftiko

BUILDING | This former mosque, built of carefully dressed gray stone, was where the Greek National Assembly held its first meetings, hence the name: Vouleftiko (parliament). The building dates from 1530, and legend has it that the lintel stone from the Tomb of Agamemnon was used in the construction of the large, square-domed prayer hall. Another story goes that it was built by a rich Turkish Aga in order to redeem his soul for the murder of two young men who had come to the city to find their father's treasure. The man stole the map and, years later, guiltily used the proceeds to build the mosque. Rather disappointingly, it is now used as a government conference center. ⊠ *Staikopoulou* ✛ *Next to Nafplion Archaeological Museum and behind National Bank.*

 Beaches

Arvanitia Beach

BEACH—SIGHT | This in-town swimming spot is not really a beach but a seaside perch of smooth rocks, pebbled shoreline, and concrete platforms, all backed by fragrant pines. This is a good place for a morning wake-up swim or a refreshing plunge after a day of sightseeing. At times the popular and well-maintained spot, with a pleasant beach bar, seems as sociable as the town square, so don't be surprised to hear other bathers gossiping and exchanging recipes as they bob in the delightful water. You can walk to Arvanitia by following the seaside promenade that hugs the cliffs beneath the Acronafplia south of town. **Amenities:** food and drink; parking (no fee); showers; toilets. **Best for:** swimming. ⊠ *Nafplion* ✛ *South side of town, below Acronafplia.*

Karathona

BEACH—SIGHT | FAMILY | The closest sandy beach to Nafplion, Karathona is easy to reach by road (just keep following 25 Maritou Street) or a pleasant walk first along the seaside promenade and then

a dirt track for 4 km (2½ miles). You can also get there by bus in summer. The pine-backed sands are favored by Greek families with picnic baskets, and this is an ideal spot for kids, since the waters remain shallow far out into the bay. Sun loungers and umbrellas are available for rent, though a pine grove behind the sands provides plenty of nice shady spots. Several tavernas back the beach. **Amenities:** food and drink; parking (no fee); showers; toilets; water sports. **Best for:** swimming; walking. ⊠ *Nafplion* ✛ *About 3 km (2 miles) south of town.*

Psili Ammos

BEACH—SIGHT | The resort town of Tolo, 12 km (7½ miles) south of Nafplion, is a short inexpensive bus ride from Nafplion's main station or a more expensive taxi ride; beware, though, that in the warm months the beach of fine sand is packed solid with sunburned northern Europeans and abuzz with every water sport and beach activity ever invented, from taking in the sun in the endless rows of loungers to volleyball. A long parade of bars and tavernas backs the beach, and some tables are set right on the sands. Two uninhabited islands in the bay, Romvi and Koronissi, can be reached by excursion boat. **Amenities:** food and drink; parking (fee); showers; toilets; water sports. **Best for:** partiers; swimming; walking. ⊠ *Tolo road, Tolo.*

Restaurants

The sea views of the quayside and the quaint, if rather narrow, Staikopoulou Street are a staple for visitors seeking taverna cooking and a bit of authenticity. Both offer excellent meals but the crowds to go with them. Quieter, and equally accomplished, fare can be found in and around the eastern end of Papanikolaou Street, where there's less footfall and just as much charm. However, it is a Nafplion tradition to have dessert at one of the cafés on the busy Syntagma Square or the *zacharoplasteia*

Enjoy a boat ride out to the Bourtzi fortress, built by 15th-century Venetians to protect the beautiful port town of Nafplion.

(pastry shops) on the harbor. Lingering over an elaborate ice-cream concoction or after-dinner drink is a memorable way to wrap up an evening.

Arapakos

$$ | SEAFOOD | Nafplion locals are demanding when it comes to seafood, so it's a credit to this attractive, nautical-themed taverna on the waterfront that locals pack in to enjoy expert dishes made from fresh catches. The kitchen sends out such traditional accompaniments as a memorable *taramosalata* (fish roe dip) as well as a few meat dishes, including exquisitely seasoned and grilled lamb chops. **Known for:** fresh seafood; affable service in pleasant surroundings; attracts locals. $ *Average main: €15* ⊠ *Bouboulinas 81* 🕾 *27520/27675* ⊕ *www.arapakos. gr* 🕐 *Closed Tues. in winter.*

Ta Fanaria

$ | GREEK | Staikopoulou Street is one long outdoor dining room, with dozens of pretty, tourist-oriented tavernas serving night and day. There isn't much to separate them, but this venerable stop is perhaps a nose ahead of its neighbors, and still excellent value. **Known for:** simple home-style fare; pleasant dining beneath an arbor; good value. $ *Average main: €7* ⊠ *Staikopoulou 13* 🕾 *27520/27141* ⊕ *www.fanaria.gr.*

Taverna Byzantio

$ | GREEK FUSION | Charcoal-grilled meats are the specialty in this snug, high-ceilinged old room tucked away in the backstreets off the harbor. The cuisine strays from Greece into the neighboring Balkans, with some wonderful schnitzels, cheese-filled pork roast, and other dishes that provide a nice change from a steady diet of local fare. **Known for:** grilled meats; attractive room and sidewalk terrace; Slavic influences. $ *Average main: €10* ⊠ *Alexandrou 15* 🕾 *27520/21631* ⊕ *www. taverna-byzantio.gr* ▭ *No credit cards.*

Taverna Noulis

$ | GREEK | Noulis sits on the very edge of the Old Town, stashed away like some treasured secret. It's a little pricier than the average taverna, but its small-plate menu is full of thrills. **Known for:** fiery flambe starters; a quiet spot, far from the tourist bustle; great mezedes. $ *Average main: €10* ✉ *Moutsouridou 22* ☎ *27520/25541* 🌐 *www.noulis-meze.gr/index.php/en* ⏲ *Closed Sun.*

★ 3Sixty Grill

$$ | **INTERNATIONAL** | If you tire of homespun tavernas serving up rustic menus in cobbled streets under blooming bougainvillea, 3Sixty is the rather brash grillhouse antidote. Sure, it's decoration is desperate to reassure you just how on trend it is, but after one or two excellent cocktails, you won't even mind the annoying horse photography on the walls. **Known for:** excellent wine list and cocktail menu; well-aged, grilled meats unlike anything else in Nafplion; stylish setting. $ *Average main: €20* ✉ *Vasileos Alexandrou and Ferreou* ☎ *27520/28068* 🌐 *3sixty.life.*

Coffee and Quick Bites

★ Antica Gelateria di Roma

$ | **CAFÉ** | Traditional Italian gelato (ice cream), in many flavors and dished up in colorful old surroundings, supplies a tempting excuse for a break. Try the *zuppa Inglese* (trifle) flavor, with hunks of sweet frozen sponge inside. **Known for:** traditional gelato; plenty of flavors; good prices. $ *Average main: €5* ✉ *Farmakopoulou 3* ☎ *27520/23520.*

Kalimera

$ | **CAFÉ** | A cute little breakfast and brunch spot just up from Syntagma Square. Organic produce and homemade jams and cakes make this a great little find, though it's so tiny that it can only cater to a few people. **Known for:** organic produce; homemade sides; breakfasts and brunches. $ *Average main: €9* ✉ *Plapouta 1* ☎ *27520/29061.*

Hotels

★ Aetoma

$ | **B&B/INN** | A 19th-century neoclassical mansion on a quiet square has been delightfully transformed into a petite family-run B&B with extremely comfortable guest rooms and alluring public spaces. **Pros:** friendly, attentive service; each room has a balcony; the top-floor room has a terrace; excellent breakfast. **Cons:** stairs may pose an obstacle for some travelers; parking is limited but free spots available nearby; not all rooms have views. $ *Rooms from: €75* ✉ *Spiridomas Sq.* ☎ *27520/27373* 🌐 *aetoma.gr/en* 🛏 *5 rooms* 🍴 *Free breakfast.*

Amphitryon

$$$ | **HOTEL** | Sea views fill every window in the airy, stylish, and contemporary guest rooms here, all of which open to teakwood decks—though the Old Town is just a few steps away, you may feel as if you're in the middle of the sea on a ship, and a pretty swanky one at that. **Pros:** at the edge of the Old Town and convenient to sights; comfortable rooms; sea views. **Cons:** food and drink are expensive; some complaints about maintenance; some street noise. $ *Rooms from: €258* ✉ *Spiliadou* ☎ *27520/70700* 🌐 *www.amphitryon.gr* 🛏 *45 rooms* 🍴 *Free breakfast.*

Amymone Suites

$ | **B&B/INN** | Amymone and Adiandi guesthouses have long been popular stays among the boutique-heavy B&Bs of Othonos Street. **Pros:** bespoke suites with unique designs; superb breakfasts in the Wild Duck restaurant; quayside location and sea views. **Cons:** one of the more costly guesthouses; the quayside can get very busy; some rooms might not be to your taste. $ *Rooms from: €90* ✉ *Othonos 18* ☎ *27520/22073* 🌐 *amymone-suites.gr* 🛏 *7 suites* 🍴 *Free breakfast.*

Byron Hotel

$ | **HOTEL** | A great deal of charm prevails here, with its simple but tastefully decorated rooms. **Pros:** old-fashioned atmosphere; lovely patio; tucked away in the heart of Old Town. **Cons:** some rooms are cramped; outlooks from some rooms are limited; lots of indoor and outdoor stairs could be a real hardship for guests with mobility issues. [$] *Rooms from: €50* ✉ *Platonos 16, Kapodistria Sq.* ☎ *27520/22351* 🌐 *www.byronhotel.gr* 🛏 *18 rooms* 🍴 *Free breakfast.*

★ Hotel Latini

$ | **B&B/INN** | This handsomely restored old house, just off the waterfront in the center of town, feels like a well-appointed private home, and the extremely comfortable guest rooms are graciously appointed and have sparkling bathrooms; all have views of the bay or a palm-filled square. **Pros:** convenient location in the Old Town near the port and parking; pleasing decor; comfortable, homelike atmosphere. **Cons:** no elevator; some views are limited; street noise at times. [$] *Rooms from: €50* ✉ *Othonos 47* ☎ *27520/96470* 🛏 *10 rooms* 🍴 *Free breakfast.*

★ Hotel Perivoli

$$ | **HOTEL** | **FAMILY** | Surrounded by orange groves, this hilltop retreat is just a few minutes outside Nafplion but provides a resortlike getaway, with handsome, contemporary-style rooms and large terraces overlooking a shimmering pool and, in the near distance, the Gulf of Argolis. **Pros:** attractive; attentive, friendly service; one of the few Nafplion hotels with a pool. **Cons:** reachable only by car; not near restaurants, though an evening meal is served; a drive to beaches, but the pool is beautiful. [$] *Rooms from: €130* ✉ *Pirgiotika* ✥ *8 km (5 miles) east of Nafplion* ☎ *27520/47905* 🌐 *www.hotelperivoli.com* 🛏 *12 rooms* 🍴 *Free breakfast.*

Nafplia Palace

$$ | **HOTEL** | If first impressions are everything, spare a moment for the Nafplia Palace, which is bizarrely reached via a dark, graffitied tunnel leading to a trio of battered elevators. **Pros:** beautiful setting and views; suites are the last word in luxury; superb buffet breakfast and closed parking area. **Cons:** unwelcoming public spaces; older rooms are much in need of renovation; rates and the restaurants are both very expensive. [$] *Rooms from: €200* ✉ *Acronafplia* ☎ *27520/70800* 🌐 *nafpliapalace.gr* 🛏 *51 rooms, 33 suites* 🍴 *Free breakfast.*

Pension Marianna

$ | **B&B/INN** | **FAMILY** | The 200-year-old property seems to be on top of the world, tucked away at the very top of the Old Town, just below the Acronafplia, and facing the sea from breezy balconies and gardens. **Pros:** extremely hospitable; great communal outdoor spaces; lovely perch at the top of town. **Cons:** takes a lot of stair climbing to reach; parking is not adjacent; a few of the lower rooms are a bit dark. [$] *Rooms from: €80* ✉ *Ilia Potamianou 9* ☎ *27520/24256* 🌐 *www.hotelmarianna.gr* 🛏 *21 rooms* 🍴 *Free breakfast.*

3Sixty Hotel & Suites

$$ | **HOTEL** | A jolt of modernity illuminates this late-19th-century neoclassical townhouse, bang in the center of town. **Pros:** a charmingly extravagant stay; perfect location, right in the heart of the old town; brilliant hotel restaurant and wine bar. **Cons:** the views aren't up to much; it's not to everyone's taste; it's far from any parking. [$] *Rooms from: €190* ✉ *Vasileos Alexandrou and Ferreou* ☎ *27525/00501* 🛏 *10 rooms* 🍴 *Free breakfast.*

Nightlife

Mavros Gatos (*Black Cat*)
BARS/PUBS | A slick café that turns into a humming nightlife spot after dark, with occasional live music, excellent cocktails, and a laidback air to go with the retro posters and vintage chic inside. Grab a table on the terrace and watch the world slide by. And yes, there is a rather chubby black cat in residence. ✉ *Emmanouil Sofroni* ☎ *27520/26652*.

Mediterraneo Wine & Deli
WINE BARS—NIGHTLIFE | A stylish deli and wine bar that doubles as a bottle shop during the day. Tastings (€10 per person, including tapas) are good value and the staff have excellent knowledge, with a very pourable selection of Greek wines to complement French and Italian bottles. It's small, so it gets packed fast. ✉ *Emmanouil Sofroni 11* ☎ *27520/97704*.

Shopping

Shopping in Nafplion is pleasant business, with a nice array of wares filling attractive shops tucked into old houses on shady lanes. Many shops sell clothing and decorative items geared to well-heeled Athenians who visit Nafplion for a day or weekend, while others specialize in some distinctly Greek goods.

Ef Geusis (Ευ Γεύσεις)
FOOD/CANDY | A great little food shop stuffed organic local fare, from pastas, olives, oils, local dried fruits, and herbs to homemade jam. ✉ *Plapouta 19* ☎ *27520/24082*.

Karonis
WINE/SPIRITS | This family-run business has dispensed fine wines, ouzo, and other spirits since 1869 and offers tastings and a great deal of knowledge about local vineyards. Karonis also has a distillery on the outskirts of the Old Town. ✉ *Amalias 5* ☎ *27520/24446* ⊕ *www.karonis.gr*.

Komboloi Museum Shop
LOCAL SPECIALTIES | A shop on the ground floor of this museum in an old home sells antique and new worry beads and attractive beaded key chains. The museum's exhibits of historic worry beads are fascinating and provide a little insight into the national male pastime of fiddling with a string of them. ✉ *Staikopoulou 25* ☎ *27520/21618* ⊕ *www.komboloi.gr* 🎫 *Museum €2*.

Metallagi Jewelry
JEWELRY/ACCESSORIES | Elegant handmade pieces are made on site by Greek-Australian jeweler Peter Alexopoulos in this workshop-cum-store. ✉ *3 Sofroni Emmanouil* ☎ *27520/21267* ⊕ *metallagi.gr/*.

Politimi Pottery
HOUSEHOLD ITEMS/FURNITURE | Ceramist Polytimi Biliona creates stylish lanterns, vases, and cups inspired from the Grecian sculptors of old. A worthy souvenir. ✉ *Vasilias Olgas 17* ☎ *27520/29932*.

Tiryns Τιρυνθα

5 km (3 miles) north of Nafplion.

This 3,500-year-old Mycenaean acropolis lies just north of Nafplion, facing the Gulf of Argolis.

Sights

Tiryns
ARCHAEOLOGICAL SITE | Homer describes Tiryns as "the wall-girt city." The modern writer Henry Miller was repelled by the place, as he records in *The Colossus of Maroussi*: "Tiryns is prehistoric in character. Tiryns represents a relapse. Tiryns smells of cruelty, barbarism, suspicion, isolation." Today the well-preserved site seems harmless, surrounded by citrus trees and home to a few lizards that timidly sun themselves on the stones. The citadel makes use of a long, low outcrop, on which was set the circuit wall

of gigantic limestone blocks of the type called "cyclopean" because the ancients thought they could have been handled only by the giant cyclops—the largest block is estimated at more than 15 tons. Via the **cyclopean ramp** the citadel was entered on the east side, through a gate leading to a narrow passage between the outer and inner walls. You could then turn right, toward the residential section in the **lower citadel,** or to the left toward the **upper citadel** and **palace.** The heavy **main gate** and **second gate** blocked the passage to the palace and trapped attackers caught between the walls. After the second gate, the passage opens onto a rectangular **courtyard,** whose massive left-hand wall is pierced by a **gallery of small vaulted chambers,** or casemates, opening off a **long, narrow corridor** roofed by a **corbeled arch.** (The chambers were possibly once used to stable horses, and the walls have been worn smooth by the countless generations of sheep and goats that have sheltered there.)

An elaborate entranceway leads west from the court to the upper citadel and palace, at the highest point of the acropolis. The complex included a colonnaded **court**; the great *megaron* (main hall) opened onto it and held the royal throne. Surviving fragments suggest that the floors and the walls were decorated, the walls with frescoes (now in the National Archaeological Museum in Athens) depicting a boar hunt and women riding in chariots. Beyond the megaron, a large **court** overlooks the houses in the lower citadel; from here, a long **stairway** descends to a small **postern gate** in the west wall. At the excavated part of the lower acropolis a significant discovery was made: two parallel **tunnels,** roofed in the same way as the galleries on the east and south sides, start within the acropolis and extend under the walls, leading to **subterranean cisterns** that ensured a continuous water supply. ⊠ *Tiryns ✛ Off road to Argos, 5 km (3 miles) north of Nafplion* ☎ *27520/22657* ⊕ *odysseus.culture.gr* 🎫 *€4.*

Argos Άργος

12 km (7½ miles) northwest of Nafplion, 7 km (4½ miles) northwest of Tiryns.

The city of Argos, set amid citrus groves on the western edge of the Argive plain, is the economic hub of the region, a workaday town with a long past. The fall of Mycenae and Tiryns at the close of the late Bronze Age proved favorable for Argos, and under King Pheidon in the 7th century BC, it became the chief city in the Peloponnese. In the mid-5th century BC, the city consolidated its hold on the Argive plain by eradicating Mycenae and Tiryns. But like Corinth, Argos was never powerful enough to set its own course, following in later years the leadership of Sparta, Athens, and the Macedonian kings.

Sights

Archaeological Museum

MUSEUM | A small but interesting collection of finds from the classical city and surrounding sites includes a mosaic floor representing the zodiac from a Roman villa and a squat clay statue female figure unearthed at nearby Lerna. It may have been fashioned as early as 2500 BC; it's also said to be one of the earliest known representations of the human figure to be found in Europe. ⊠ *Off main square, Ayios Petros* ☎ *27510/68819* ⊕ *www.culture.gr* 🎫 *€2* ⊙ *Closed Mon.*

Argos Kastro

CASTLE/PALACE | This Byzantine and Frankish structure incorporates remnants of classical walls and was later expanded by the Turks and Venetians. You can drive almost to the entrance, and the grounds provide an unsurpassed view of the Argive plain. ⊠ *Argos ✛ On top of hill above town* 🎫 *Free.*

Classical Argos

ARCHAEOLOGICAL SITE | Remains of the classical city are scattered throughout the modern one, and you can see in a small area the extensive ruins of the Roman bath, odeon (a roofed theater), and agora, or market. The theater is especially striking, and its well-preserved seats climb a hillside. ⊠ *Tripoleos* 🎫 *Free.*

🛍 Shopping

On Saturday morning the main square is transformed into a huge household-merchandise and produce market (dwarfing that at Nafplion). You can often find unusual household items, such as wooden stamps used to impress designs on bread loaves, at prices that haven't been inflated. Argos is also well known throughout Greece for its ouzo.

Mycenae Μυκηνες

21 km (13 miles) north of Nafplion.

The ancient citadel of Mycenae, which Homer wrote was "rich in gold and once ruled much of the Mediterranean world," stands on a low hill, wedged between sheer, lofty peaks on the edge of two deep ravines. The gloomy, stony ruins are hauntingly suggestive of what becomes of might and power.

GETTING HERE AND AROUND

Once in Nafplion, you can reach Mycenae and other nearby ancient sights via a decent local bus network; buses leave from Nafplion's Kapodistria Square for Isthmus (Corinth), passing through Argos and Fichti/Mikines, a few kilometers from the Mycenae archaeological site. The small office is often staffed by an English speaker. Times are available online on the KTEL Argolida site ⊕ *www.ktelargolida.gr/en*, which is more up to date than most regional bus services. If you're visiting more than one location, it's worth buying the combined €20 ticket, which

The Heroines of Argos

Twice in the history of Argos, women are said to have defended the city: once in 494 BC when Telesilla the poetess (who may be mere legend) armed old men, boys, and women to hold the walls against the Spartans; and again in 272 BC when Pyrrhus, king of Epirus, who was taking the city street by street, was felled from above by an old woman armed with a tile.

is valid for three days and allows entry to Mycenae, Tiryns, Asini, Palamidi, and the archaeological museums of Nafplio and Argos.

👁 Sights

★ **Mycenae**

ARCHAEOLOGICAL SITE | The gloomy, gray ruins are hardly distinguishable from the rock beneath; it's hard to believe that this kingdom was once so powerful that it ruled a large portion of the Mediterranean world, from 1500 BC to 1100 BC. The major archaeological artifacts from the dig are now in the National Archaeological Museum in Athens, so seeing those first will add to your appreciation of the ruined city. The most famous object from the treasure found here is the so-called Death Mask of Agamemnon, a golden mask that 19th-century archaeologist Heinrich Schliemann found in the last grave he excavated at Mycenae. He was ecstatic, convinced this was the mask of the king of Homeric legend who launched the Trojan War with his brother, Menelaus—but it is now known that this is impossible, since the mask dates from an earlier period. The Archaeological

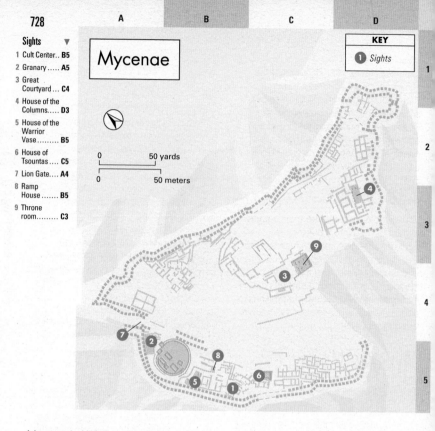

Mycenae

KEY

① *Sights*

Museum in Nafplion also houses artifacts from this once-great city.

In 1841, soon after the establishment of the Greek state, the Archaeological Society began excavations of the **ancient citadel,** and in 1874 Heinrich Schliemann began to work at the site.

Today the citadel is entered from the northwest through the famous **Lion Gate**. The triangle above the lintel depicts in relief two lions, whose heads, probably of steatite, are now missing. They stand facing each other, their forepaws resting on a high pedestal representing an altar, above which stands a pillar ending in a uniquely shaped capital and abacus. Above the abacus are four sculptured discs, interpreted as representing the ends of beams that supported a roof. The gate was closed by a double wooden door sheathed in bronze. The two halves

were secured by a wooden bar, which rested in cuttings in the jambs, still visible. The holes for the pivots on which it swung can still be seen in both sill and lintel.

Inside on the right stands the **Granary**, so named for the many *pithoi* (clay storage vessels) that were found inside the building, holding carbonized wheat grains.

Beyond the granary is the grave circle, made up of six **stone slabs**, encircled by a row of upright slabs interrupted on the northern side by the entrance. Above each grave stood a vertical stone stele. The "grave goods" buried with the dead were personal belongings including gold face masks, gold cups and jewelry, bronze swords with ivory hilts, and daggers with gold inlay, now in the National Archaeological Museum of Athens. South of the stone slabs lie the remains of the **House of the Warrior Vase,** the **Ramp House,** the **Cult Center,** and others; farther south is the **House of Tsountas** of Mycenae. The palace complex covers the summit of the hill and occupies a series of terraces; people entered through a monumental gateway in the northwest side and, proceeding to the right, beyond it, came to the **Great Courtyard** of the palace. The ground was originally covered by a plaster coating above which was a layer of painted and decorated stucco. East of the Great Courtyard is the **throne room,** which had four columns supporting the roof (the bases are still visible) and a circular hearth in the center. Remains of an **Archaic temple** and a **Hellenistic temple** can be seen north of the palace, and to the east on the right, on a lower level, are the **workshops** of the artists and craftsmen employed by the king. On the same level, adjoining the workshops to the east, is the **House of the Columns,** with a row of columns surrounding its central court. The remaining section of the east wall consists of an addition made in around 1250 BC to ensure free communication from the citadel with the subterranean reservoir cut at the same time. ⊠ *Mycenae* ⊹ *21 km (13 miles) north of Nafplion* ☎ *27510/76585* ⊕ *www.culture. gr* ✉ *Combined ticket with Treasury of Atreus and Mycenae Archaeological Museum €12.*

Mycenae Archaeological Museum

MUSEUM | Most of the great treasures of Mycenae have been removed to the National Archaeological Museum in Athens, but you'll see copies of death masks and other great artifacts in the small but well-done museum at the site. Cult offerings and other original finds are also on view. Of most interest are the model of the ancient city, helping put the ruins in context, and reconstructions of several rooms of the palace. ⊠ *Mycenae* ⊹ *Near entrance to site* ☎ *27510/76585* ✉ *Combined ticket with Mycenae and Treasury of Atreus €12.*

Treasury of Atreus

MEMORIAL | On the hill of Panagitsa, on the left along the road that runs to the citadel, lies this most imposing example of Mycenaean architecture. The construction of this huge *tholos* (or beehive tomb) took place around 1250 BC, contemporary with that of the Lion Gate, during the last century of Mycenaean prominence. Like other tholos tombs, it consists of a passageway cut into the hillside that was built of huge squared stones. The passage leads into a vast domed chamber. The facade of the entrance had applied decoration, but only small fragments have been preserved, and traces of bronze nails suggest that similar decoration once existed inside. The tomb was found empty, already robbed in antiquity, but it must at one time have contained rich and valuable grave goods. Pausanias wrote that the ancients considered this to be the Tomb of Agamemnon, and the treasury is still often referred to as such. ⊠ *Mycenae* ⊹ *Across from citadel of Mycenae* ☎ *27510/76585* ⊕ *www.culture. gr* ✉ *Combined ticket with Mycenae and Mycenae Archaeological Museum €12.*

Ancient Nemea
Αρχαια Νεμεα

18 km (11 miles) north of Mycenae.

This quiet little town, surrounded by undulating vineyards, was once as famous as Olympia, site of biennial games that attracted athletes from throughout ancient Greece.

 Sights

Ancient Nemea

ARCHAEOLOGICAL SITE | The ancient storytellers proclaimed that it was here Hercules performed the first of the Twelve Labors set by the king of Argos in penance for killing his own children—he slew the ferocious Nemean lion living

Haunted by the spirits of Agamemnon and Clytemnestra, the royal graves of Mycenae make it one of the most brooding and memorable archaeological sites in Greece.

in a nearby cave. Historians are interested in Ancient Nemea as the site of a sanctuary of Zeus and the home of the biennial Nemean games, a Panhellenic competition like those at Isthmia, Delphi, and Olympia (today there is a society dedicated to reviving the games).

The main monuments at the site are the **Temple of Zeus** (built about 330 BC to replace a 6th-century BC structure), the **stadium,** and an **early Christian basilica** of the 5th to 6th century AD. Several columns of the temple still stand. An extraordinary feature of the stadium, which dates to the last quarter of the 4th century BC, is its vaulted tunnel and entranceway. The evidence indicates that the use of the arch in building may have been brought back from India with Alexander (arches were previously believed to be a Roman invention). A spacious **museum** displays finds from the site, including pieces of athletic gear and coins of various city-states and rulers. ■ TIP→ Around Nemea, keep an eye out for roadside stands where local growers sell the famous red

Nemean wine of this region. ⊠ *Nemea* ⊕ *North of E65, near modern village of Nemea* ☎ *27460/22739* ⊕ *www.culture. gr* ✉ *Site and museum €6.*

Tripoli Τριπολη

150 km (93 miles) southwest of Athens, 70 km (43 miles) southwest of Corinth.

History, along with the practicalities of the road network in this part of Greece, makes it very likely that you'll at least pass through the outskirts of Tripoli when you're in the area. In the days of the Ottoman Empire, this crossroads was the capital of the Turkish pasha of the Peloponnese, and during the War of Independence it was the first target of Greek revolutionaries. They captured it in 1821 after a six-month siege, but the town went back and forth between the warring sides until 1827, when Ibrahim Pasha's retreating troops burned it to the ground.

Tripoli is a workaday town with few attractions to keep you here, although if you do hang around, you'll get an eyeful of Greek life. Its most attractive feature is the mountain scenery, with attendant hillside villages, that surrounds it; you will soon understand why this region is nicknamed "the Switzerland of Greece." Unless you run out of daylight, you'll probably want to move on from Tripoli quickly, but for those taking the bus in particular, there's usually a couple of hours to kill between connections and it's worth a wander into town, where the mid-19th-century marble cathedral of St. Basil (Agios Vasillos) catches the eye. By night, Platia Petrinou is a lively spot for drinks, but the impossibly vast Areos Square is the best place to people-watch.

Sights

Areos Square

PLAZA | You can observe Greek life in the center of town, especially Areos, one of the largest *platias* (central squares) in Greece and definitely the place to while away the time if you're marooned in Tripoli. At its center stands a statue of Theodoros Kolokotronis, the revered Arcadian general who helped liberate the country from the Turkish yoke. His bones are buried at its base, having been moved there from Athens in 1930. One story goes that in 1942 the invading Italian army smashed open the tomb and scattered his remains to keep the town in line. Appalled, the town's mayor and his 13-year-old son risked death to collect them up in a sugar bag, so they could be later replaced. ⊠ *Tripoli.*

War Museum of Tripoli

MUSEUM | Tripoli has a proud revolutionary history, and the War Museum is a good place to see it firsthand. Besides the many, many guns and swords here, there are fine examples of early revolutionary life, from the dashing uniforms to the sporan-like pouches used by early-19th-century fighters to stash bullets

Be Prepared ⊙

When you visit Mycenae, make sure that you are adequately protected from the sun by wearing long sleeves and a hat (there is no shade). Carry a bottle of water, and wear sturdy walking shoes. The ground is uneven and often confusing to navigate; every week paramedics carry out people who fell because they were not adequately prepared for the climb. If you have physical limitations, it's best to go only as far as the plateau by the Lion Gate and view the rest from there.

and the lard required to load them. There is even an original copper death mask of the revolutionary general Theodoros Kolokotronis. Perhaps most interesting, though, is a photo of the female fighter Peristera Kraka, the "Mulan of Greece," who became the leader of a group of guerillas who fought the Turks after her brother was killed. Visitors are shown around by museum staff. ⊠ *1 Ethnomartiron Street* ⊠ *€2* ⊙ *Closed Mon.*

🛏 Hotels

Mainalon Resort

$ | HOTEL | The refined amenities here (the best place to stay if you need to spend a night in Tripoli), include a tasteful mix of traditional and contemporary furnishings, silk fabrics in the guest rooms, and large marble bathrooms. **Pros:** in the center of things; quite comfortable; nice café on premises. **Cons:** oddly anonymous and businesslike; could use some updating; rooms in front can be noisy. $ *Rooms from: €70* ⊠ *Areos Sq.* ☎ *27102/30300* ⊕ *www.mainalonhotel.gr* ⌁ *32 rooms* ⊙ *Free breakfast.*

Vouraikos Gorge
Φαραγγι του Βουραικου

Diakofto, the coastal access point, is 81 km (49 miles) west of Corinth; Kalavrita is 25 km (15 miles) south of Diakofto.

The Vouraikos Gorge is a fantastic landscape of towering pinnacles and precipitous rock walls that you can view on an exciting train ride. In addition, a road goes directly from Diakofto, on the coast, to mountaintop Kalavrita; the spectacular 25-km (15-mile) drive negotiates the east side of the gorge.

Diakofto is a peaceful seaside settlement nestled on a fertile plain with dramatic mountains as a background; the village straggles through citrus and olive groves to the sea. If you're taking a morning train up the gorge, plan on spending the night in Diakofto, maybe enjoying a swim off one of the pebbly beaches and a meal in one of several tavernas. After dinner, take a stroll on Diakofto's main street to look at the antique train car in front of the train station, then take a seat at an outdoor table at one of the cafés surrounding the station square and enjoy a *gliko* (sweet). This is unembellished Greek small-town life.

The Kalavrita Express, a narrow-gauge train, makes a dramatic 25-km (15-mile) journey between Diakofto and Kalavrita, which is a refreshingly cool retreat in summer and a ski center in winter. Italians built the railway between 1889 and 1896 to bring ore down from Kalavrita, and these days a diminutive train—a diesel engine sandwiched between two small passenger cars—crawls upward, clinging to the steep rails with a rack and pinion, through and over 14 tunnels and bridges, rushing up and down wild mountainside terrain. Beyond the tiny hamlet of Zakhlorou, the gorge widens into a steep-sided green alpine valley that stretches the last 11 km (7 miles) to Kalavrita, a lively town of about 2,000 nestled below snowcapped Mt. Helmos. Greeks remember Kalavrita primarily as the site of the Nazis' most heinous war crime on Greek soil. On December 13, 1943, the occupying forces rounded up and executed the town's entire male population over the age of 15 (1,436 people) and then locked women and children into the school and set it on fire. They escaped, but the Nazis later returned and burned the town to the ground. The clock on the church tower is stopped at 2:34 pm, marking the time of the execution.

GETTING HERE AND AROUND

Diakofto can be reached by bus from Athens or Patras, or via train from Athens via Kiato (four hours). The Kalavrita Express makes the round-trip from Diakofto three times daily on weekdays, five times daily on weekends. Tickets, which are worth getting in advance during high season, can be bought on site or via the OSE website (⊕ *tickets.trainose.gr*) and cost €19 return; €9.50 one way. The trip takes about an hour, and the first train leaves Diakofto at 9:05 am. Comings and goings are timed so that you can do some exploring; in a day's outing, for example, you can alight at Zakhlorou, make the trek to Mega Spileo, continue on to Kalavrita, explore that town, and return to Diakofto by the last train of the day at 3:28 pm. Check with the OSE or call either station (Diakofto ☎ *26910/43206*; Kalavrita ☎ *26920/22245*) to check that the service is operating beforehand—repairs can close the line for months at a time.

VISITOR INFORMATION

Kalavrita Visitor Information
⊕ *www.ekalavrita.gr*.

Sights

Mega Spileo

RELIGIOUS SITE | This mountainside monastery, altitude 3,117 feet, was founded in the 4th century and is said to be the oldest in Greece, though it has been burned down many times, most recently in 1934. The community once had 450 monks and owned vast tracts of land in the Peloponnese, Constantinople (now Istanbul), and Macedonia, making it one of the richest in Greece. Mega Spileo sits at the base of a huge (360-foot-high) curving cliff face and incorporates a large cavern (the monastery's name means "large cave"). You can tour the monastery to see a charred black-wax-and-mastic icon of the Virgin, supposedly painted by St. Luke, found in the cave after a vision of the shepherdess Euphrosyne led some monks there in AD 362. Also on display are ornate vellum manuscripts of early gospels and the preserved heads of the founding monks. ■ TIP→ **Modest dress is required; wraps are available at the entrance.**

If you're taking the Kalavrita Express, 45 minutes into its trip you can alight at the stream-laced mountain village of Zakhlorou, from where you can hike up a steep path through evergreen oak, cypress, and fir to the monastery. This hour-long trek (one-way) along a rough donkey track gives you superb views of the Vouraikos valley and distant villages on the opposite side. The occasional sound of bells, from flocks of goats grazing on the steep slopes above, is carried on the wind. It's also possible to take a cab from the village, though they are not always available; if you're driving, the monastery is just off the road between Diakofto and Kalavrita and is well marked. ⊠ *Zakhlorou, Kalavrita* ☎ *26920/23130* 🎟 *€2.*

Tetramythos Winery

WINERY/DISTILLERY | If you're driving from Diakofto to Kalavrita, make a stop at Tetramythos. The winery attributes the high quality and refined flavor of its reds and whites to the location of its vineyards on the northern slopes of Mt. Helmos, which protects the grapes from hot winds. Tours and tastings are available year-round. ✉ *Ano Diakofto* ✥ *5 km (3 miles) south of Diakofto* ☎ *26910/97500* 🌐 *www.tetramythoswines.com* 🎟 *Free.*

🍴 Restaurants

Taverna Kostas

$ | **GREEK** | Grilled chicken is the main attraction at this *psistaria* (grill house) run by a hospitable Greek-Australian family, and regulars come from miles around to enjoy it. *Horta* (boiled wild greens), huge *horiatiki* (village, i.e., "Greek") salads with a nut-flavored feta cheese, and stuffed zucchini are other reasons to enjoy a meal on the large terrace in warm months or in the cozy dining room in winter. **Known for:** grilled meats; lively terrace dining scene; friendly service. [$] *Average main: €8* ✉ *Anapafseos 486, Diakofto* ☎ *69475/24996* 💳 *No credit cards.*

🛏 Hotels

Stavento

$ | **HOTEL** | About 4 km west of Diakofto station is the seaside village of Travese, where this pleasant set of beachside apartments and villas lies. **Pros:** a nice spot next to the beach; friendly owner and a fine restaurant; good breakfasts. **Cons:** you're a few kilometers from Diakofto; you'll need picking up to get there; the beach can get pretty windy. [$] *Rooms from: €68* ✉ *Bank 2 Pounta Beach, Diakofto* ☎ *26913/01159* 🛏 *4 rooms; 3 villas* 🍴 *Free breakfast.*

Patras Πατρα

5 km (3 miles) west of Rion, 135 km (84 miles) west of Corinth.

Like all respectable Greek cities, Patras has the kind of storied history that puts even European capitals in the shade. Off the harbor in 429 BC, Corinthian and Athenian ships once fought to a bloody standstill, while in 279 BC the city helped repel an invasion of Celtic Galatians. In between fending off attacks from Slavs and Saracens, it began to gain a name for its silk production from the 7th century, which brought renewed prosperity alongside its reputation as a major port. Like the rest of this region, it eventually fell into Turkish hands. Thomas Palaiologos, the last Byzantine to leave Patras before the Ottomans took over in 1458, carried an unusual prize with him—the skull of the apostle St. Andrew, which he gave to Pius II in exchange for an annuity. St. Andrew had been crucified in Patras and had been made the city's patron saint. In 1964 Pope Paul VI returned the head to Patras, and it now graces St. Andrew's Cathedral, seat of the Bishop of Patras.

These days the city is still a busy Greek port, though earthquakes and overdevelopment have accounted for most of the elegant European-style buildings that earned Patras the nickname "Little Paris of Greece" in the 19th and early 20th centuries. You might want to zoom right by unless you're looking to catch a ferry and you've got some time to kill, or you happen to arrive during carnival season (Jan.–Feb.), when the city turns into one big party. Having said that, the waterfront is pleasant, and as arcaded streets rise to the center, the town flattens into a series of large loungeable *platias* (squares). The tree-shaded Queen Olga Square is the nicest, and if you have time for a stroll, take Agios Nikolaos Street upward through the city until it comes to the long flight of steps leading to the Kastro, the medieval Venetian castle overlooking the harbor. The narrow lanes on the side of Agios Nikolaos are whitewashed and lined with village-style houses and the views from above are impressive.

GETTING HERE AND AROUND

Bus service between Athens and Patras is excellent, with buses running from the former's Kifissos Station about every half-hour to 45 minutes throughout the day. The bus station in Patras is near the port at Othonos-Amalias. Those transiting to the Ionian islands will be driven straight to the port; there is no wait in the city.

There is reported to be in the works a direct express-train service from Athens to Patras, which will then continue down the west coast of the Peloponnese. Until that increasingly far off day arrives, train passengers from Athens still have to change at least once, typically at Kiato. The fastest service takes around four hours and isn't the most reliable; for now, you're better off taking the bus.

Sights

Achaia Clauss

WINERY/DISTILLERY | The oldest winery in Greece was founded by the Bavarian Gustav Clauss in 1861 and continues to produce a distinctive line of wines. Mavrodaphne, a rich dessert wine, is the house specialty, and oak barrels still store vintages from Gustav's day. The winery is set on a hilltop amid fragrant pines in the village of Petroto. ⊠ *Petroto* ✛ *Exit 3 off E55, 8 km (5 miles) southwest of Patras* ☎ *26105/80100* ⊕ *www.achaiaclauss.gr.*

Archaeological Museum of Patras

MUSEUM | Stunning galleries are laden with Mycenaean-through-Roman-period finds, including tools, cups, and jewelry reflecting everyday life in the Peloponnese. More than 15 mosaics from Roman villas around Patras have been reassembled, and many items are from the ancient Roman odeon in town. A large collection of burial items includes several reconstructed tombs. ⊠ *Amerikis,*

at *Athens–Patras road* ✛ *7 km (4 miles) east of center* ☎ *26106/23820* ⊡ *€6* ⊘ *Closed Tues. (Nov.–Feb.).*

Patras Kastro

VIEWPOINT | In the evening the Frankish and Venetian citadel atop a bluff overlooking Patras draws many Greek couples seeking a spectacular view; a long flight of stone steps ascends toward the Kastro from the southern edge of the Old Town. The sight of the shimmering ships negotiating the harbor stirs even the most travel-weary. ⊠ *End of Agios Nikolaos.*

Patras Roman Odeon

ARTS VENUE | A Roman odeon remains in use in Patras, almost 2,000 years after it was built. Today the productions of Summer Arts Festival (mid-Jun.–mid-Sept.) are staged in the well-preserved theater, which was discovered in 1889 and heavily restored in 1960. ⊠ *Patras* ✛ *Off Martiou 25 Sq.*

St. Andrew's Cathedral

RELIGIOUS SITE | This is one of the largest churches in Greece, and dates from the early 20th century. It is built next to a spring that's been used for thousands of years, and during antiquity its waters were thought to have prophetic powers. St. Andrews is an important pilgrimage sight—the cavernous interior houses the head of the namesake saint, who spread Christianity throughout Greece and was crucified in Patras in AD 60. ⊠ *Patras* ✛ *At end of Trion Navarhon, at western edge of city center.*

Beaches

The closest beach to Patras is a long stretch of pebbles washed by crystal clear waters. Even so, crowds, a sea of beach umbrellas, freighter traffic, and the looming presence of the Rion suspension bridge make for a less than idyllic experience. Better shores are found further west.

Kalogria

BEACH—SIGHT | This long, sandy stretch backed by a pine forest and a grassy plain where cattle graze is much favored by Patras residents on weekends and in August. It's around 40 km (25 miles) west of the city. Bracing winds that can whip up a wild surf don't seem to deter beachgoers and are a boon for windsurfers. A river behind the beach forms estuaries that are great for bird-watching. People swim in them as well, but you may feel like Hercules if you are joined by yard-long snakes (they are nonvenomous). **Amenities:** food and drink; parking (free); showers; toilets; water sports. **Best for:** swimming; walking; windsurfing. ✉ *Kalogria* ✥ *Off E55, about 40 km (25 miles) west of Patras, near Sageika.*

🍴 Restaurants

For lighter fare or after-dinner ice cream, coffee, and pastries, choose one of the cafés along upper Gerokostopoulou Street, which is closed to traffic; in Olga Square; or in Ypsila Alonia Square—a favorite spot for locals near the Kastro, which, as a bonus, has a panoramic view of the harbor. The streets, including Papadiamatopoulou, leading through the Old Town up to the south end of the Kastro, have many small *mezedopoleia,* which serve *mezedes,* Greek-style tapas.

★ Labyrinthos

$ | **GREEK** | Labyrinthos is an old favorite of locals and visitors alike. This stonewalled setting, tucked away off the main drag, sets the perfect pace for a whistlestop tour through some classic taverna fare, from *katsikaki* (goat in olive oil) to fried anchovies, and even recognizes the region's Slavic influence with a tasty pork schnitzel. **Known for:** one of the oldest restaurants in the city; friendly service; traditional fare. [$] *Average main: €10* ✉ *Poukevil 44* ☎ *26102/26436.*

Salumeria

$ | **ITALIAN** | A likeably bobo take on modern Greek and Italian fare. A huge bar dominates the interior, wrapped in stone and with a roof of upturned glasses, reminding you this is aperitivo country. **Known for:** creative cooking that doesn't disappoint; good selection of local wines; hip setting at a good price. [$] *Average main: €14* ✉ *Pantanassis 27* ☎ *26102/25930.*

🛏 Hotels

Byzantino

$ | **HOTEL** | This neoclassical mansion in the heart of town bursts with style—thanks to stone and hardwood floors, antiques, and old kilims—and the large, high-ceilinged guest rooms have been brought efficiently up to date with good lighting and well-equipped bathrooms. **Pros:** city center location; character-filled surroundings; rooms are comfortable even if a bit outdated. **Cons:** some street noise in front rooms; bathrooms are rather basic; limited views from many rooms. [$] *Rooms from: €70* ✉ *Riga Fariou 106* ☎ *2610/243000* 🌐 *www.byzantino-hotel.gr* 🔑 *30 rooms* 🍽 *Free breakfast.*

★ The Bold Type Hotel

$ | **HOTEL** | This attractive new addition to the historic Upper City makes excellent use of the building's neoclassical mansion setting—all columns and arches. **Pros:** a refined escape well-placed to discover the city's sights; a wonderful courtyard setting for meals and drinks; five-star service. **Cons:** mimimalist style is not to all tastes; the basic rooms can be a little small; five-star prices make it a costly stay for Patras. [$] *Rooms from: €113* ✉ *Palaion Patron Germanou 10–12* ☎ *26102/20012* 🌐 *theboldtypehotel.com* 🔑 *10 rooms* 🍽 *Free breakfast.*

♈ Nightlife

BARS AND CAFÉS

On the northern side of Martiou 25 Square are the steps at the head of Gerokostopoulou Street, below the odeon. Closed to traffic along its upper reaches, this street has many cafés and music bars, making it a good choice for a relaxing evening.

🎭 Performing Arts

FESTIVALS
Patras Carnival

FESTIVALS | If you're in Patras in late January to February, you're in for a treat: the carnival, which lasts for several weeks before the start of Lent, is celebrated with masquerade balls, fireworks, and the Sunday Grand Parade competition for the best costume. Room rates can double or even triple during this time. ⊠ *Patras* ☎ *26103/90912* ⊕ *www.carnival-patras.gr.*

🛍 Shopping

Patras is a major city, and you'll find fashionable clothing, jewelry, and other products here. The big high street shops are all on Riga Fereou, Maizonas, and Korinthou streets, near Olga Square. At night in the narrow streets surrounding the Kastro, which are worth a wander, Greek craftspeople burn the midnight oil in their workshops and stores painting images of saints on wood and stone.

Lousios Gorge

40 km (25 miles) west of Tripoli, 40 km (25 miles) southwest of Olympia.

From the stone-built villages high above Lousios Gorge, a trail picks its way down to the river bed, passing medieval monasteries that dangle from the sheer limestone walls. Some are still occupied; others offer a chance to clamber their exposed bones high above the waters below. The best route in is via the five-hour trail that links the pretty villages of Dimitsana and Stemnitsa, a likeable pair of boho escapes with a distinctly alpine vibe. In winter, they draw the ski crowd destined for the slopes of nearby Mt. Menalon; the rest of the year they are given over to hikers and tour buses en route to the gorge's monasteries, their open terraces filled with excitable day-trippers huffing the mountain air.

Dimitsana is an especially pretty maze of narrow cobbled lanes with a surprisingly long history. Settlers first arrived here during the Archaic Period (650–480 BC), and ruins of a Cyclopean wall (irregular stones without mortar) and classical buildings belonging to the ancient acropolis of Teuthis can be found nearby. In revolutionary times, the town was an important center for gunpowder production during the Greek War of Independence (1821–30), and the local library is worth dropping by for its memorabilia from this tumultuous period.

Stemnitsa (aka Ipsous) is equally impressive, perched 3,444 feet above sea level amid a forest of fir and chestnut trees. For centuries this stone village was one of Greece's best-known metalworking centers, and today its minuscule school is still staffed by local artisans. Above the lively square rises the bell tower of the church of Agios Georgios, and at the top of a nearby hill is the monument to those who fought in the 1821 War of Independence against the Turks. The town even claims to have been the capital of Greece for a few weeks in 1821, when it became a base for the plotting rebels.

👁 Sights

The way into Lousios Gorge from either Dimitsana or Stemnitsa is well signed, as the path is also the beginning of the Menalon Trail (look for the "M" markers), a 72-km hike that runs across Arcadia's mountainous heart and well worth it if you have five-to-eight days to spare. This section is known for the isolated monasteries hanging from the canyon walls, and most walkers start in Stemnitsa, from where a well-marked trail tumbles down from its north side to a beautiful wooded valley and the banks of the river Lousios below. For just a taster, drive midway and walk between the monasteries of New Philosophou and Timiou Prodromou (45 minutes), or continue south and on to the site of Ancient Gortys (2 hours) and back. All of these sites can be reached by car if you don't fancy walking. In fact, the car park for New Philosophou contains a sign listing the phone numbers for local taxi companies, so you can always end your walk here and get a cab if you don't fancy the full hike back to the villages. The gift shop of the Open Air Water power Museum sells a comprehensive walking map of the area (€7.40), which is useful for multiple day treks.

Ancient Gortys

ARCHAEOLOGICAL SITE | Another way to approach the gorge walk is to start among the ruins of Ancient Gortys, 1.5 km south of Timou Prodromou Monastery. Little is known about when this city was built, but by the 4th century BC it was in its pomp, and its name was acclaimed across Arcadia. Many of the fragments of its defensive enclosures, baths, public buildings, and its temple to Asklepios date from this era. ⊠ *Stemnitsa ⊹ 4 km northeast of Atsicholos.*

Dimitsana Ecclesiastical Museum

MUSEUM | Manuscripts, a 35,000-volume library, and other artifacts here are from surrounding churches, monasteries, and the School of Greek Letters that flourished in Dimitsana in the 19th century. The school educated Germanos, a bishop of Patras, and other young men who went on to become Greek scholars and church leaders. ⊠ *Dimitsana ⊹ Off main square* ☎ *27950/31217* ☜ *€2* ⊗ *Closed Wed.–Thurs.*

New Philosophou Monastery

RELIGIOUS SITE | The "newer" of the Philosophou monasteries sits on the west side of the gorge, yet even this dates back to the 17th century. Its *katholico* (main church), dedicated to the Assumption of the Virgin Mary, has some beautiful illustrated hagiographies, though during Ottoman rule it is said their eyes were scrubbed out by the invaders. Like many of the sites in this region, the building had a part to play in the War of Independence against the Turks. It was a hideout for the Greek general Theodorous Kolokotronis and formed a meeting place for the chieftains to plot. Today, the only rebels here are the legions of cats, who bask in the shade like fallen soldiers. Exit via the black gates for an 800-meter walk to **Old Philosophou Monastery**, the bones of a 10th-century monastery dug into the walls of the gorge. It's a spectacular site, and rambling its crumbling stone remains and church, gazing out over the wild gorge, is exhilarating. It was reportedly home to one of Greece's "secret schools," where young Greeks would scrabble the ravine in the pitch darknesss in order to receive private tutoring in biblical studies, history, and the Greek language, away from the eyes of the Turkish authorities. Little evidence exists of such schools, and some historians argue they have been created as a nationalist myth. ⊠ *Dimitsana ⊹ 10km south of Dimitsana* ☎ *27950/81447.*

Open Air Water Power Museum

MUSEUM | A water mill, tannery, and gunpowder mill on the river Lousios below town provide displays and demonstrations that reveal why water power was the force behind the region's economy until the first part of the 20th century. Mills like the one here operated up and down the river and helped supply the forces who successfully fought the Turks during the War of Independence in 1821. ⊠ *Dimitsana ⊹ Off main road, south of town* ☎ *27950/31630* ⊕ *www.piop.gr* ☜ *€4* ⊗ *Closed Tues.*

A Little Night Music

Dance performances, accompanied by traditional music, are common in the region. In the *tsakonikos*, the dancers wheel tightly around each other and then swing into bizarre spirals; this dance resembles the sacred dance of Delos, first performed by Theseus to mime how he escaped from the labyrinth. The popular *kalamatianos* is a circular dance from Kalamata. The *tsamikos*, from Roumeli in central Greece, is an exclusively male dance showcasing agility. You will see your fill of dancing at local festivals to celebrate a town or village's patron saint, usually in summer. Dancing is also part of a Greek wedding, and it's not entirely unlikely that you might attend one. The guest list usually includes the entire population of a village or section of town, and if you happen to be staying there at the time of a wedding, you may well be invited.

Timou Prodromou Monastery (*Monastery of St John the Baptist*)

RELIGIOUS SITE | This is the largest of the monasteries that line the gorge, and is arguably the most spectacular. Its white frontage seemingly dangles from the rocks, lidded by the heavy brow of the stone overhang. It is home to around a dozen monks at any given time. Rules are rather strict regarding visits, and between 1 pm and 5 pm it is closed to visitors. Appropriate dress is also required, and coveralls are provided in the courtyard if you only have shorts. Parts of the building date from the 16th century, and during the War of Independence it doubled as a hospital for the revolutionaries. Inside, its tiny *katholico* (church) is filled with exquisite frescoes. It can be reached by road as well as by hiking the gorge. ⊠ *Stemnitsa*.

Hotels

Methexis Boutique Hotel

$ | **HOTEL** | Cloaked in the fir forests of the Mainalo, this stone-built boutique has more than an air of alpine magic about it. **Pros:** beautiful mountain setting; it's comfortably away from the tourist hustle of town; Jacuzzi baths in the suites. **Cons:** minimum three-night stay; you'll need a car to get around; there aren't many rooms, so it books up fast. **$** *Rooms from: €82* ⊠ *Lousios Road* ☎ *27950/31317* ⊕ *www.methexishotel. gr/* ⤳ *7 rooms* ⦿ *Free breakfast.*

Temple of Apollo at Bassae Ναος του Απολλωνα στις Βασσες

62 km (38 miles) southeast of Olympia, 90 km (55 miles) north of Kalamata.

Typically seen as part of a day trip from either Olympia or Kalamata (it's about 1½ hours from both), the winding mountain roads here morph time, turning short-distance journeys into scenic but dizzyingly long road trips, so set off early. If you're coming from Kalamata, combine this with a visit to Ancient Messene for a day of antiquity. When approaching from the north, the launching point for the drive up to the Temple of Apollo is Andritsena, a pleasant collection of stone houses that cling to the side of a deep gorge. A small library in town, found 100 yards past the town square on the main road, houses 15th-century Venetian and Vatican first editions and documents relating to the War of Independence. The hairpin roads southwest of Bassae also lead to the village of Figaleia, where gentle walks to the Neda Waterfalls, a wonderfully pretty walking and swimming spot, are well worth bringing a picnic for.

Sights

Temple of Apollo Epikourios at Bassae

ARCHAEOLOGICAL SITE | One of the great majesties of ancient Greek architecture is isolated amid craggy, uncompromising scenery. Unfortunately, these days the temple looks more like the Sydney Opera House, thanks to a modernistic shed that has cocooned the structure in an attempt to prevent further weather damage during extensive ongoing restoration. The covering destroys the sense of place that was so important to this temple, which sits in miles of empty, hilltop fields. For many years it was believed that this temple was designed by Iktinos, the Parthenon's architect. Although this theory has recently been disputed, Bassae remains one of the best-preserved classical temples in Greece, superseded in its state of preservation only by the Hephaistion in Athens. The residents of nearby Phygalia built it atop an older temple in 420 BC to thank Apollo for delivering them from an epidemic; *epikourios* means "helper." Made of local limestone, the temple has some unusual details: exceptional length compared to its width; a north–south orientation rather than the usual east–west (probably because of the slope of the ground); and Ionic half columns linked to the walls by flying buttresses. Here, too, were the first known Corinthian columns with the characteristic acanthus leaves—only the base remains now—and the earliest example of interior sculptured friezes illustrating the battles between the Greeks and Amazons (now in the British Museum). As for the restoration, it will be ongoing for some time yet, which may be a reason not to visit for some given its remoteness. ■ **TIP→ Climb to the summit northwest of the temple for a view overlooking the Nedhas River, Mt. Lykaeon, and, on a clear day, the Ionian Sea.** ✉ *Bassae* ✛ *Off Rte. 76, and then up a one-lane road* ☎ *26260/22275* ⊕ *www.culture.gr* ▭ *€6.*

Olympia Ολυμπια

112 km (69 miles) south of Patras, 85 km (53 miles) west of Stemnitsa.

Ancient Olympia, including the Sanctuary of Zeus, was famously the site of the ancient Olympic Games. Scenically located at the foot of the pine-covered Kronion Hill and set in a valley near two rivers, today the ancient ruins are among the most popular attractions in Greece. Modern Olympia, an attractive mountain town surrounded by pleasant hilly countryside, has hotels and tavernas, convenient for visitors to the ancient site.

GETTING HERE AND AROUND

From Athens, buses head to Pyrgos, via Patras, three times daily; from there you can take a bus to Olympia. The trip takes around six hours and costs €15.

At Pyrgos station ☎ *26210 20600* you can also hop aboard one of the trains that connect Katakolon, the cruise ship port, and Olympia. Trains run the whole route five times a day, but only when cruise ships are in port. The trip from Katakolon to Olympia with a stop in Pyrgos takes about 45 minutes and costs €10 round-trip. Tickets can be booked via the OSE national railway (⊕ *www.trainose.gr/en*).

You can travel directly from Athens to Olympia by car on a trip that lasts about five hours via toll roads to Corinth and Patras, then down the west coast to Olympia. Free parking is ample in Olympia, either on the street or in the lots near the entrance to the ancient site.

⊙ Sights

★ Ancient Olympia

ARCHAEOLOGICAL SITE | FAMILY | One of the most celebrated archaeological sites in Greece is located at the foot of the pine-covered Kronion Hill and set in a valley where the Kladeos and Alpheios rivers join. Just as athletes from city-states throughout ancient Greece made the journey to compete in the ancient Olympics—the first sports competition—visitors from all over the world today make their way to the small modern Arcadian town. The Olympic Games, first staged around the 8th century BC, were played here in the stadium, hippodrome, and other venues for some 1,100 years. Today, the venerable ruins of these structures attest to the majesty and importance of the first Olympiads. Modern Olympia, an attractive mountain town surrounded by pleasant hilly countryside, has hotels and tavernas, convenient for visitors to the ancient site.

As famous as the Olympic Games were—and still are—Olympia was first and foremost a sacred place, a sanctuary honoring Zeus, king of the gods, and Hera, his wife and older sister. The sacred quarter was known as the Altis, or the Sacred Grove of Zeus, and was enclosed by a wall on three sides and the Kronion hill on the other. Inside the Altis were temples, altars, and 12 treasuries of various city-states.

To honor the cult of Zeus, established at Olympia as early as the 10th century BC, altars were first constructed outdoors, among the pine forests that encroach upon the site. Around the turn of the 6th century BC, the earliest building at Olympia was constructed, the Temple of Hera, which originally honored Zeus and Hera jointly, until the Temple of Zeus was constructed around 470 BC. The latter was one of the finest temples in all of Greece: thirteen columns flanked the sides, and its interior housed the most famous work of the era—a gold and ivory statue of Zeus. Earthquakes in 551 and 552 finished off the temple.

After the Treasuries, the Bouleuterion, and the Pelopeion were built and the 5th and 4th centuries BC—the golden age of the ancient games—saw a virtual building boom. The monumental Temple of Zeus, the Prytaneion, and the Metroon went up at this time. The enormous Leonidaion was built around 300 BC, and as the games continued to thrive, the Palaestra and Gymnasion were added to the complex.

The history of the Olympic Games is long and fabled. For almost 11 centuries, free-born Greeks from the various city-states gathered to participate in the games, held every four years in August or September. These games became so much a part of the culture that the four-year interval between the games became a standard unit of time, an Olympiad. An Olympic truce—the Ekecheiria—allowed safe passage for athletes from the different city-states traveling to the games, and participation in them meant allegiance to a "Panhellenic" ideal of a united Greece. The exact date of the first games is not known, but the first recorded event is a footrace, a *stade,* run in 776 BC. A longer race, a *diaulos,* was added in 724 BC, and wrestling and a pentathlon—consisting of the long jump, the javelin throw, the discus throw, a foot race, and wrestling—in 708 BC. Boxing and chariot racing were 7th-century BC additions, as was the *pankration,* a no-holds-barred match (broken limbs were frequent and strangulation sometimes the end)—Plato, the great philosopher, was a big wrestling fan. By the 5th century BC, the games featured nine events, held over four days, with the fifth day reserved for the ceremonies. Most of the participants were professional athletes, for whom winning a laurel wreath at Olympia ensured wealth and glory from the city-states that sponsored them.

Today's tranquil pine-forested valley at Olympia, set with weathered stones of peaceful dignity, belies the sweaty drama of the first sporting festivals. Stadium foot races run in the nude; pankration wrestling was so violent that today's Ultimate Fighting matches look tame; weeklong bacchanals—serviced by an army of prostitutes—were held in the Olympic Village: little wonder this ancient event is now called the "Woodstock of its day" by modern scholars (wrestlers, boxers, and discus throwers being the rock stars of ancient Greece).

For today's sightseer, the ruins of many of Olympia's main structures are still visible. The **Altis** was the sacred quarter, also known as the Sacred Grove of Zeus. In the **Bouleuterion,** the seat of the organizers of the games, the Elean senate, athletes swore an oath of fair play. In the **Gymnasion,** athletes practiced for track and field events in an open field surrounded by porticoes. In the **Hippodrome,** horse and chariot races were run on a vast racecourse. The **House of Nero** was a lavish villa built for the emperor's visit to the games of AD 67, in which he competed. The **Leonidaion** was a luxurious hostel for distinguished visitors to the games; it later housed Roman governors. The **Metroon** was a small Doric temple dedicated to Rhea (also known as Cybele), mother of the Gods. The **Nymphaion,** a semicircular reservoir, stored water from a spring to the east that was distributed throughout the site by a network of pipes. The **Palaestra** was a section of the gymnasium complex used for athletic training; athletes bathed and socialized in rooms around the square field. The **Pelopeion,** a shrine to Pelops, legendary king of the region now known as the Peloponnese, housed an altar in a sacred grove. **Pheidias's Workshop** was the studio of the great ancient sculptor famed for his enormous statue of Zeus, sculpted for the site's Temple of Zeus. The **Prytaneion** was a banquet room where magistrates feted the winners and a perpetual flame burned in the hearth. The **Stadium** held as many as 50,000 spectators, who crowded onto earthen embankments to watch running events. The starting and finishing lines are still in place. The **Temple of Hera,** one of the earliest monumental Greek temples, was built in the 7th century BC. The **Temple of Zeus,** a great temple and fine example of Doric architecture, housed Pheidias's enormous statue of the god, one of the seven wonders of the ancient world. The famous **Treasuries** were templelike buildings that housed valuables and equipment of 12 of the most powerful of the city-states competing in the games.

You'll need at least two hours to fully see the ruins and the Archaeological Museum of Olympia (to the north of the ancient site), though three or four hours would be better. ⊠ *Off Ethnikos Odos 74 ✛ ½ km (¼ mile) outside modern Olympia)* ☎ *262/402–2517* ⊕ *odysseus. culture.gr* ✉ *€12, combined ticket with Museums, €6 Nov.–Mar.*

★ **Archaeological Museum of Olympia**

MUSEUM | Of all the sights in ancient Olympia, some say the modern archaeological museum gets the gold medal. Housed in a handsome glass and marble pavilion at the edge of the ancient site, the magnificent collections include the sculptures from the Temple of Zeus and *Hermes Carrying the Infant Dionysus,* sculpted by the great Praxiteles, which was discovered in the Temple of Hera in the place noted by Pausanias. The central gallery of the museum holds one of the greatest sculptural achievements of classical antiquity: the pedimental sculptures and metopes from the Temple of Zeus, depicting Hercules's Twelve Labors. The *Hermes* was buried under the fallen clay of the temple's upper walls and is one of the best-preserved classical statues. Also on display is the famous *Nike of Paionios.* Other treasures include notable terra-cottas of Zeus and Ganymede; the head of the cult statue of Hera; sculptures of the family and imperial patrons of Herodes Atticus; and bronzes found at the site, including votive figurines, cauldrons, and armor. Of great historical interest are a helmet dedicated by Miltiades, the Athenian general who defeated the Persians at Marathon, and a cup owned by the sculptor Pheidias, which was found in his workshop on the Olympia grounds. ✉ Off Ethnikos Odos 74 ✛ ½ km (¼ mile) outside modern Olympia ☎ 262/402–2742 ⊕ odysseus.culture. gr 🎟 €12, combined ticket with Ancient Olympia Site, €6 Nov.–Mar.

🍴 Restaurants

Aegean

$ | **GREEK** | Don't let the garish signs depicting the menu put you off: the far-ranging offerings are excellent. You can eat lightly—a gyro or pizza—but do venture into some of the more serious fare, especially such local dishes as the fish that's been oven-baked with onion, garlic, green peppers, and parsley. **Known for:** good, traditional fare; friendly atmosphere; very good for vegetarians. $ Average main: €12 ✉ Georgiou Douma 4 ☎ 26240/22540 ⊕ aegeanrestaurant. business.site.

Taverna Bacchus

$ | **GREEK** | The best restaurants in Greece are often in small villages, and this appealing family-run taverna and inn set amid fields, a favorite among Olympians, is one such example. The poolside terrace is a lovely place to spend an afternoon or evening, though locals don't start arriving until 10 pm or so for dishes that include a delicious chicken with oregano, grilled lamb, and farm-fresh vegetables that appear in such deliciously simple preparations as baked eggplant with tomatoes and feta. **Known for:** nice terrace with views; country setting just outside town; local ingredients really shine. $ Average main: €12 ✉ Ancient Pissa (Mirika) ✛ 5 km (3 miles) west of Olympia ☎ 262/402–2298 ⊕ www.bacchustavern.gr ⊗ Closed Dec.–Feb.

Taverna Thea

$ | **GREEK** | Olympians flock out to the little village of Floka, about 5 km (3 miles) west of town, at dinnertime to enjoy traditional fare in this country setting. Dining is in a homey room or on the summertime terrace with wide views across the landscape, and the specialties are the expertly grilled meats. **Known for:** village setting; grilled meats; pretty views from the terrace. $ Average main: €9 ✉ Flokas ☎ 26240/23264 ▭ No credit cards ⊗ No lunch Nov.–Apr.

Hotels

Bacchus Pension

$ | **B&B/INN** | One of the region's most popular eateries also provides attractive and character-filled guest rooms, all with balconies overlooking the countryside. **Pros:** great restaurant; beautiful pool and terrace area; pleasant, attractive rooms. **Cons:** outside town, although just a short drive to ancient site; rooms vary in size; some noise from restaurant. $ Rooms from: €85 ✉ Ancient Pissa (Mirika) ☎ 26240/22298 ⊕ www.bacchustavern.gr ⊗ Closed Dec.–Feb ⇥ 8 rooms ⊙| Free breakfast.

Grecotel Mandola Rosa

$$$$ | **RESORT** | This extremely elegant retreat, tucked into the sprawling multihotel Olympia Riviera Resort on the coast beneath the ancient city, pampers guests with handsome and comfortable suites in a luxurious Mediterranean-style villa and in lavish bungalows tucked into lush seaside gardens. **Pros:** an extremely attractive and comfortable place to stay; beautiful beach and wealth of amenities; superb and friendly service. **Cons:** the cost is as high as Mt. Olympus; part of a big resort complex; it's pretty far from the ancient site. $ Rooms from: €304 ✉ Kastro 50, Kyllini ✛ 60 km (36 miles) west of Olympia ☎ 26230/64555 ⊕ www.mandolarosa.com ⊗ Closed Nov.–Apr. ⇥ 54 suites and villas ⊙| Free breakfast.

★ Hotel Europa

$ | **HOTEL** | White stucco, pine, and red tiles are handsome accents to gracious guest rooms that are all extremely large, with queen-size beds in many, marble bathrooms, and small terraces; most have sunken sitting areas and face either the pool, which is set in an olive-shaded garden, or the countryside. **Pros:** attractive, well-maintained rooms; fine restaurants; beautiful pool and garden. **Cons:** slightly out of town center and can be reached easily only by car; can seem a bit anonymous; popular with large groups. [$] *Rooms from: €110* ✉ *Oikismou Drouba* ☎ *26240/22650* 🌐 *www.hoteleuropa.gr* 🛏 *80 rooms* 🍴 *Free breakfast.*

Hotel Pelops

$ | **HOTEL** | Suzanna and Theo Spiliopoulou and their family set the gold standard for small hotels, providing stylish and comfortable rooms that have wood floors, overlook the nearby mountains, and have small terraces. **Pros:** convenient to town and ruins; helpful hosts; attractive and welcoming. **Cons:** located in town (but in a quiet and pleasant neighborhood); no pool, but guests can use pool at Hotel Europa; simple but quite comfortable. [$] *Rooms from: €55* ✉ *Varela 2* ☎ *26240/22543* 🌐 *www.hotelpelops.gr* 🛏 *18 rooms* 🍴 *Free breakfast.*

Ancient Messene
Αρχαια Μεσσηνη

35 km (21 miles) south of Temple of Apollo at Bassae.

The ruins of this remarkable fortified ancient city, about 20 km (12 miles) north of the modern town of the same name, are set amid a lush landscape of olive groves and pine forests on the slopes of majestic Mt. Ithomi (also known as Voulkanos). It is dubbed by many as the most underrated ancient site in Greece, though at some point the sheer groundswell of collective agreement surely negates this observation. Still, far fewer visitors find their way here than to other major archaeological sites on the peninsula, such as Olympia or Epidaurus, and if you arrive late in the day (it closes at 7 pm), you can find yourself walking alone among its eerily silent Doric columns.

Dating from the 4th century BC, the city of Messene emerged later than Athens or Corinth, after the Thebans finally pried apart Sparta's iron grip on Messinia in 362 BC. Sparta had coveted its fertile lands and reduced its people to servitude. Under the Theban general Epameinondas, the city was built up into a bulwark against further Spartan encroachment, resulting in its 9 km of defensive walls. Within its protection, the Messenians prospered, becoming a cultural, religious, economic, and artistic center for the ancient world, though its golden age was short. By the 3rd century AD the city was in decline; around 360 AD it was abandoned entirely, and its survival is partly due to the fact that much of the site was never built over or cannibalized for its stone. Above it, the quiet village of **Mavromati** lines the lush slopes and it's worth a stop at one of the taverns on its main square to refuel.

Sights

Ancient Messene

ARCHAEOLOGICAL SITE | In terms of footprints, this is one of the most awe-inspiring sites of ancient Greece, thanks to its impressive walls, famed entry gates, vast theater arenas, and temples. One temple alone, the Asklepion, was thought to be an entire town by archaeologists until recently (see 🌐 *www.ancientmessene.gr* for an excellent scholarly take on the site).

The most striking aspect of the ruins is the city's **circuit wall,** a feat of defensive architecture that rises and dips across the hillsides for an astonishing 9 km (5½ miles). Four gates remain; the best preserved is the north or **Arcadian Gate,** a double set of gates separated by a round courtyard. On the ancient paving stone below the arch, grooves worn by chariot wheels are still visible. In the main site, excavations have uncovered the most important public buildings, including a **theater,** whose seats have now been restored; the **Synedrion,** a meeting hall for representatives of independent Messene; the **Sebasteion,** dedicated to worship of a Roman emperor; the **sanctuary to the god Asklepios;** and a **temple to Artemis Orthia.** One of the more unusual finds is the "**treasury,**" a rather grim crypt-like hole where the captured general Philopoemen, of the Achaean Confederacy, a collection of states that banded together against Roman control, was imprisoned and later poisoned in 183 BC. The most impressive sights are the large **stadium,** wrapped by a collar of Doric columns, and the **gymnasium** where the Messinian youth were schooled in both fighting and the arts. The site is a bit confusing, as the ruins are spread over the hillside and approached from different paths; follow the signposts indicating the theater, gates, and other major excavations. Guides hang around the entrance offering their services, though these don't come cheap and bargaining starts at around €50 for an hour, so it's better to arrange a tour beforehand. Some of the finds are held in Mavromati's's **small museum,** which is included in the ticket price. ⊠ *Mavromati ✛ From modern town of Messene, turn north at intersection of signposted road to Mavromati* ☏ *27240/51201* ⊕ *www.culture.gr* ⌱ *€10.*

Pylos

22 km (14 miles) south of Chora.

With the blue waters in its port and the bougainvillea-swathed, pristine white houses fanning up Mt. St. Nicholas, Pylos may remind you of an island town. It was built according to a plan drawn by French engineers stationed here from 1828 to 1833 and was the site of a major naval battle in the War of Independence. Ibrahim Pasha chose Sfakteria, the islet that virtually blocks Pylos Bay, as the site from which to launch his attack on the mainland. For two years Greek forces flailed under Turkish firepower until, in 1827, Britain, Russia, and France arrived to lend support to the Greek insurgents. They sent a fleet to Navarino Bay commanded by the British admiral Edward Coddington to persuade Turkey to sign a treaty. Impatient at the Turks lack of immediate response, he moved the fleet into the small bay, and at close quarters misunderstandings were inevitable. In the confusion a British ship was fired upon by the Turks, and the small fleet retaliated with devastating force. At the end of what became known as the Battle of Navarino, the allies had sunk two thirds of the Turko-Egyptian fleet without a single loss among their 27 war vessels. What had begun as a diplomatic brinkmanship became an accidental turning point in the war. The sultan was forced to renegotiate, and this paved the way for Greek independence. A column rising between a Turkish and a Venetian cannon in the town's main square, Trion Navarchon (Three Admirals) Square, commemorates the leaders of the victorious fleet.

For a closer look at the bay, take an hour-long boat tour to see various monuments on Sfakteria, some sunken Turkish ships, and the neighboring rock of Tsichli-Baba, which has a vast, much photographed natural arch, nicknamed Tripito. This former pirate hideout has 144 steps. The boats can also take you to the weed-infested 13th-century Paleokastro, one of the two fortresses guarding the channels on either side of Sfakteria, and may make a stop also at Nestor's cave. Boat trips cost about €25; walk along the dock and negotiate with the captains, or ask at the waterside kiosk (staffed only occasionally). The trip is less expensive if you go with a group, but these trips are usually prearranged for the tour buses that drop down to Pylos from Olympia.

Sights

Pylos Neokastro

CASTLE/PALACE | Neokastro, the "new fortress" that dominates the town, was built by the Turks in 1573 to control the southern—at that time, the only—entrance to Pylos Bay (an artificial embankment had drastically reduced the depth of the northern channel). Neokastro's well-preserved walls enclose the Church of the Transfiguration (a former mosque), cannons, and two anchors from the battle. The highest point of the castle is guarded by a hexagonal fort flanked by towers. A prison in the 18th and 19th centuries, the fort was more secure than most other Greek prisons because it sometimes housed convicts from the Mani, who continued their blood feuds while behind bars. Tickets include access to the archaeological museum and an excellent permanent exhibition on underwater archaeology, with relics recovered from submerged settlements around the Peloponnese. ✉ *Pylos* ✣ *Access is by trail from south side of town or off road to Methoni* ☎ *27230/22955* 🎟 *€6* 🕒 *Closed Tues.*

Hotels

Costa Navarino Resort

$$$$ | **RESORT** | **FAMILY** | This vast complex incorporates two adjoining resorts, the Westin and the slightly more upscale Romanos. **Pros:** a huge choice of dining options in 16 restaurants; beautiful sandy beach and great golf; close to Ancient Messene and other attractions. **Cons:** rather generic surroundings; removed from real Greek experience; food, drink, and other amenities can be pricey. [$] *Rooms from: €382* ✉ *Navarino Dunes* ☎ *27230/95000* 🌐 *www.costanavarino.com* 🛏 *445 rooms (Westin); 321 rooms (The Romanos)* 🍴 *All-inclusive.*

Methoni Μεθωνη

62 km (38 miles) west of Kalamata.

Methoni, a small fishing and farming village on a cape south of Pylos, has long cast a spell over visitors. It was one of the seven towns Agamemnon offered Achilles to appease him after his beloved Briseis was carried off, and few would turn it down today. According to the ancient poet Homer, Pedasos, as it was called, was "rich in vines," and one legend suggests that the town got its modern name because the *onoi* (donkeys) carrying the wine became *methoun* (drunk) from the aroma. Even to this day Methoni is still fairly intoxicating, with long beaches backed by olive groves and vineyards. It is divided into two towns: a low-key settlement huddled on the beach beneath the fortress, and, just above, an animated Old Town on the crest of a rise. The latter is a laid-back, pleasant spot to rest for a day or two, with most visitors arriving for a seaside getaway and to visit the perfectly preserved Venetian castle.

Sights

★ Methoni Fortress

CASTLE/PALACE | Methoni's principal attraction is its *kastro*, an imposing, well-kept citadel that the Venetians built when they took control of the town in 1209. The town already had a long history: after the Second Messenian War in the 7th century BC, the victorious Spartans gave Methoni to the Nafplions, who had been exiled from their homeland for their Spartan alliance. With its natural harbor, the town was an important stop on trade routes between Europe and the East during the Middle Ages. A stone bridge leads over the dry moat to the citadel; various coats of arms mark the walls, including those of Genoa and Venice's

Lion of St. Mark. A second bridge joins the kastro with the **Bourtzi**, an octagonal tower built above the crashing surf on a tiny islet during the Turkish occupation (shortly after 1500). ✉ *South end of town* 🎫 *€3* ⏲ *Closed Tues.*

🍴 Restaurants

Nikos's

$ | **GREEK** | "The only time this kitchen closes is if I'm sick," says Nikos Vile, who insists on cooking everything from *mamboulas* (a moussaka made with tomatoes) to *maridakia* (lightly fried whitebait) each day. You can sip an aperitif at the bar or hide out in the vine-covered courtyard. **Known for:** good, home-style food; warm hospitality; great seafood. [$] *Average main: €8* ✉ *Methoni* ✣ *Near entrance to fortress* ☎ *27230/31282.*

Taverna Klimataria

$ | **GREEK** | Many of the dishes that come to the table in this rustic room or on the flowery terrace are based on homegrown produce, so count on the freshest greens and succulent eggplant and zucchini appearing in moussaka and other traditional favorites. The stuffed grape leaves and stuffed zucchini flowers are excellent starters, and the lamb is grilled perfectly. **Known for:** nice garden with castle views; good vegetable dishes; friendly service. [$] *Average main: €8* ✉ *Methoni* ✣ *Near entrance to fortress* ☎ *27230/31544* 💳 *No credit cards* ⏲ *Closed Nov.–Apr.*

🛏 Hotels

Ulysses

$ | **HOTEL** | From the shady, well-manicured side garden to the attractive traditional furnishings in the spotless rooms, every part of this hotel is welcoming. **Pros:** nice village location near beach; lavish breakfast; comfortable, homey rooms. **Cons:** seasonal opening hours; rather basic bathrooms; charming without being luxurious. [$] *Rooms from: €75* ✉ *Kiprou 12* ☎ *27230/31600* 🌐 *www.ulysseshotel.com* ⏲ *Closed Nov.–Apr.* 🛏 *7 rooms* 🍽 *Free breakfast.*

Kalamata Καλαματα

91 km (56 miles) southwest of Tripoli.

Kalamata makes an excellent base for exploring the south of the peninsula—it's an hour's drive to the Mani, Messene, and Methoni, and the winding two-hour route from here to Mystras is one of Greece's most dramatic (read: hair-raising) road trips. The city has the animated air of a busy port and market town and is surrounded by an amphitheater of mountains. The beachfront promenade and a string of lively squares make for a fine evening *volta*, and the long, narrow park that drops down to the harbor doubles as a magnificent open-air railway museum. Deep into the night, you'll spot children risking their limbs by vaulting across the roofs of old train carriages as if in some pre-adolescent horse opera.

Remnants of the old city, all but leveled in a devastating earthquake in 1986, huddle beneath the 13th-century *kastro* built by Frankish knight Geoffrey de Villehardouin. Below is the Convent of Kalograion, where nuns still weave beautiful silk scarves and table linens, for sale in a shop just inside the entrance, and nearby lies the small 13th-century church Ayii Apostoli ("Holy Apostles"), which famously has two naves—one for the Roman Catholics and one for the Orthodox. Around it has grown a busy nightlife area in Martiou 23 square, which is filled with tavernas and bars that spill out onto the cobbles.

The city is built atop ancient Pharai, described by Homer as subject to the kingdom of Agamemnon. In the 8th century BC, Pharai was annexed as a province of Laconia and, like most towns in the area, was not independent again until the Battle of Leuctra ended Sparta's tyrannical rule. The city's most important hour arrived much later, however, in 1821, when it became the site of the first major battle in the War of Independence. Clans from the Mani marched north to unite with revolutionary troops under the command of Theodoros Kolokotronis and Nikitaras, aka "The Turk Eater," and liberated the city from the Ottoman yoke on March 23. It was here, in front of the Church of the Holy Apostles, that the first formal declaration of Greek independence was made.

GETTING HERE AND AROUND

Kalamata's main bus station is on Artemidos Road (☎ 27210/28581). Five-to-six buses run between Kalamata and Athens daily (€22.20), with direct (express) services usually operating twice a day and taking around three hours; other services change at Tripoli and Isthmus. Westward routes connect all the way up to Pyrgos, including stops in Methoni and Pylos. Buses to the Mani from Kalamata only reach the fringes of the Messinian side of the Peninsula, typically terminating at the fishing village of Agios Nikolaos.

If traveling by car, the E55 and E65 toll roads go all the way up to Corinth, where the No. 8 National Road can take you to Athens.

 # Sights

Agioi Apostoli

RELIGIOUS SITE | The oldest church in Kalamata is the small 13th-century Agioi Apostoli ("Holy Apostles"), dedicated to the Virgin of Kalamata ("of the good eye"), from whom the town may get its name. The Greek War of Independence was formally declared here on March 23, 1821, and a celebration is held at the church on that date every year. Even the square on which it lies, Martiou 23 (March 23rd), is named after this historic moment. ⊠ Martiou 23 Sq.

Archaeological Museum of Messina

MUSEUM | This small, well-organized collection is shown to advantage in the city's rebuilt 18th-century market hall. On display are local stone tools, proto-Geometric and Geometric pottery, and a 1st-century AD Roman mosaic floor depicting Dionysus with a panther and a satyr. ⊠ Benaki and Papazoglou, near Martiou 23 Sq. ☎ 27210 /83485 ⊕ www.archmusmes.gr ☎ €4.

Kalamata Kastro

CASTLE/PALACE | In the early 13th century William de Champlitte divided the Peloponnese into 12 baronies. He bestowed Kalamata on Frankish knight Geoffrey de Villehardouin, who built a winter kastro. Through the centuries the castle was bitterly fought over by Franks, Slavs, and Byzantines, and today it's difficult to tell what of the remains is original. From Martiou 25 Square, walk up Ipapandis past the church, take the first left at the castle gates, and climb the small hill; the views of the town, coast, and the Messinian plain are lovely. ⊠ End of Ipapandis ☎ 27210/22534 ☎ €3 ⊗ Closed Tues.

Monastery of Aghios Konstantinos & Agia Eleni (Monastery of the Kalograion)

JEWELRY/ACCESSORIES | Built in the late 18th century, this functioning nunnery houses a fraction of the 80 sisters that once lived here, but its residents are still known for their exquisite silk weaving. Silk scarves and table linens are for sale in a shop just inside the entrance; ask to step into the tranquil cloister while you're there. ⊠ Ypapanti Platia.

Restaurants

★ Kardamo

$ | GREEK | Greek comfort food is the order of the day here, albeit that does Kardamo a bit of a disservice. This isn't just fries and kebabs, but the tenets of classic Greek mezedes dishes given a creative boost. **Known for:** hearty comfort food; great people-watching spot; the meatballs are the best in Greece. [$] *Average main: €12* ✉ *Sidirodromikou Stathmou 21* ☎ *27210/98091* 🌐 *kardamo.gr.*

O Thiasos
$ | **GREEK** | A well-kept secret bandied around by expats and locals. This ebullient street-side café-ouzeri in the old town bustles of an evening under the shadow of the plane trees. **Known for:** the gournopoula (suckling pig) has the crunchiest crackling in town; an old-school vibe in a historic building; a fine selection of local liquors. [$] *Average main: €8* ✉ *Ipapantis 3* ☎ *27210/88407* ⏲ *Closed Mon.*

Coffee and Quick Bites

Blossom Owl Coffee Shop & Roastery
$ | **CAFÉ** | Greek cities live and breathe coffee, which pretty much makes Blossom Owl the lungs of Kalamata. This hugely popular café sprawls from one side of the pavement to the other, pouring cold drip coffee, pulling cappuccinos, and everything in between. **Known for:** best coffee in town; ideal for brunch; good people-watching spot. [$] *Average main: €7* ✉ *Valaoritou 7.*

Hotels

Pharae Palace Hotel
$ | **HOTEL** | Kalamata isn't blessed with an abundance of reliable city hotels, especially within the town center. **Pros:** great buffet breakfasts; the beach is outside your door; lots of facilities nearby. **Cons:** can be a little noisy in the evening; bedrooms on the rear side have poor views; no pool. [$] *Rooms from: €76* ✉ *Navarinou and Riga Feraiou* ☎ *27210/94420* 🛏 *72 rooms; 4 suites* 🍴 *Free breakfast.*

Nightlife

Luna Lounge
BARS/PUBS | This long, narrow, high-ceilinged bar is set within a 1920s arcade, and has retained an Art Deco vibe to complement its retro cocktails (around €10) and a good selection of local craft beers (Sura, Nema). ✉ *Aristomenous 23* ☎ *27210/27210* 🌐 *www.lunalounge.gr.*

Activities

Kalamata Dive Center
DIVING/SNORKELING | Swiss-Greek dive master Anthousa Papadopoulou is PADI certified and runs open-water and advanced diving courses from her shop on the harbor. Half-day boat dives (from €100) visit wrecks, caves, and walls in the local area depending on experience. ✉ *Salaminos 4* ☎ *69720/57037* 🌐 *www.kalamatadivecenter.gr.*

Kardamyli Καρδαμύλι

31 km (19 miles) southwest of Kalamata.

The gateway to the Mani on the Messenian side is Kardamyli, considered part of the outer Mani (or Exo Mani), an area less bleak and stark than the inner section, which begins at Areopolis, after which the lush vegetation of the north gives way to brown, treeless slopes and flat seas of stunted olive groves punctured only by crumbling tower houses. Here the foothills of the Taygettus range are still green, and the sun is considerably more forgiving.

This quiet and pleasant stone town has become a popular tourist stop for travelers attracted to its seaside lanes, boho boutiques, fine restaurants, and the dazzling beauty of its mountainous backdrop. It is particularly prized among hikers, who arrive en masse in the cooler months to explore the lush gorges, trails, and slopes as well as fragments of the "Royal Road," built during Roman occupation, that used to connect the town to Sparta. The old section of Kardamyli, above the modern town, lies on a pine-scented hillside dotted with small clusters of tower houses. Stone-paved paths cut through the enclave and lead to the local clan's old defensive tower, which is also the gateway for hikes into the beautiful Viros Gorge.

The area's most famous resident, and perhaps one reason for its growth in popularity in recent years, was the late Patrick Leigh Fermor, an Anglo-Irish writer who wrote extensively on the area. His old house (now a museum and seasonal hotel) lies in nearby Kalamitsi village, and battered copies of his 1958 book *Mani: Travels in the Southern Peloponnese* are still clutched by visitors eager to live his prose.

 ## Sights

★ The Leigh Fermor House

HOUSE | Celebrated travel writer Patrick "Paddy" Leigh Fermor settled in the Mani in 1964, building a beautiful house from scratch just down the road from Kardamyli, in the tiny village of Kalamitsi. Locals knew him by the name "Michalis," a nom de guerre Fermor adopted when, during the Second World War, he disguised himself as a shepherd in the mountains of Crete to help capture a German general. As a travel writer, his writings were no less courageous, and his book on the Mani is still well-thumbed by travelers to the area. His old home was donated to the Benaki Museum upon his death in 2012, and has been sensitively restored—they used old photos to place furniture and antiques in their original spots. Tours are by appointment only on Tuesdays, Thursdays, and Saturdays. Visits are limited during summer, when rooms are available to rent for 90 days a year (Jun.–Aug.), to help with the upkeep and restoration of the property. There is a three-night minimum stay. ⊠ *Kalamitsi* ☎ *21036/71090* ✉ *leighfermorhouse@ benaki.gr* ⊕ *www.benaki.org* 💳 *€10* ☞ *By appointment only.*

Mourtzinos Tower

CASTLE/PALACE | This fortified complex dates back to the 17th century, when the Troupakides clan settled in the area. In the following decades the family divided into lineages and sub-lineages, expanding outside the walls into what is now Old Kardamyli. By the time the Mourtzini, descendents of the original settlers, ruled here, the original settlement had developed into the typical fort of an 18th-century clan *kapitano* (captain). It is divided into three fortified enclosures, including a garden, olive press, smithy, and church, all overseen by a central war tower. Inside is a dinky but interesting museum depicting the history of the clans of the Mani. ⊠ *Old Kardamyli* 💳 *€3* ☾ *Closed Tues.*

 ## Beaches

Kardamyli's Ritza Beach, just north of the town, is a long stretch of sand and pebbles backed by strands of pines. In town you can also swim off the dock in the clear, deep waters of the town's small harbor. Hotel owners often attach ladders to the waterfront to allow visitors to clamber in and out. Other beaches are tucked into coves as you drive south on the main road. Stoupa, about 10 km (6 miles) south of Kardamyli, is a low-key collection of seaside tavernas and rooms for rent that stretches along a beautiful sandy beach. Neo Itilo sits on a beautiful large bay with a white-pebble beach. Enjoy a swim as you watch the fishermen fixing their nets, checking their ship hulls, and talking among themselves amid the din of their portable radios.

Did You Know?

Fiercely independent, the fortified villages of the Mani region bristle with tower houses constructed because of the incessant vendettas rife among local family clans. This medieval mini-Manhattan, Vathia, is considered the most dramatic Maniot village.

Foneas

BEACH—SIGHT | **FAMILY** | A sand-and-pebble beach rings a sparkling cove, where the languid, turquoise waters are perfect for swimming and, with offshore rocky outcroppings, a playground for snorkelers. A swim-through sea cave just off the beach is a perfect retreat in which to float and escape the sun. **Amenities:** food and drink; parking (no fee); showers; toilets. **Best for:** snorkeling; swimming. ✉ *Kardamyli* ✣ *Off Coast road, 4 km (2½ miles) south of Kardymili.*

Stoupa

BEACH—SIGHT | This long stretch of clean sand along a curving bay is undeniably the most popular beach in the Mani, though far from the quietest and most scenic spot in this rugged region. You'll share the company of frolicking young Greeks and sun-worshipping northern Europeans, but given that this is the Mani, this is a relatively low-key beach resort, and it's quite possible to find a quiet stretch. **Amenities:** food and drink; parking (free); showers; toilets; water sports. **Best for:** partiers; snorkeling; swimming; walking. ✉ *Stoupa.*

🍴 Restaurants

Elies Hotel Restaurant

$ | **GREEK** | **FAMILY** | For a lot of travelers a perfect day in Kardamyli includes lunch beneath the olive trees in the Elies garden, which stands directly across from the beach. The setting is memorable at night, too, and at any time a meal includes tasty daily preparations of lamb, chicken, and fish, infused with herbs and prepared with local olive oil. **Known for:** idyllic seaside garden setting; nice preparations of local favorites; home-grown produce. [$] *Average main: €12* ✉ *Kardamyli Beach* ✣ *On the beach road* ☎ *27210/73140* 🌐 *www.elieshotel.gr* 🕒 *Closed Nov.–Mar.*

Kastro Taverna

$ | **GREEK** | The friendly welcome of owner Petros is just the appetizer for a traditional Greek taverna where much of the produce served comes from the owner's personal farm. Gaze out from the pretty terrace over olive and lemon groves to the coast below as great juicy hunks of pork and fine stews arrive with thick wedges of potato, crispy at the tips. **Known for:** rustic Greek staples; quiet terrace setting; friendly owner. [$] *Average main: €13* ✉ *Kardamyli* ✣ *500 meters north of the river* ☎ *27210/73951* 🌐 *kastro-kardamili.gr* 🕒 *Closed Nov.–Mar.*

★ Lela's Taverna

$ | **GREEK** | The late Mrs. Lela, once housekeeper for author Patrick Leigh Fermor, was famous for her simple, old-fashioned cooking using fragrant homemade olive oil and exceedingly fresh tomatoes and herbs. Her namesake taverna is an institution in these parts, and dinner beneath the trees on the seaside terrace of an oleander-covered stone house is a high point of a visit to the Mani. **Known for:** lovely seaside terrace; nicely prepared traditional dishes; its literary connections. [$] *Average main: €9* ✉ *Kardamyli* ✣ *On the seaside, above the rocky beach near the old soap factory* ☎ *27210/73541* 🌐 *www.lelastaverna.com* 🕒 *Closed Tues. No lunch.*

Tikla Cuzina

$$ | **GREEK** | A change in ownership and a pivot away from its old wine-bar vibe to become simply a restaurant with an excellent wine list puts Tikla ahead of many of its more polished rivals along the seafront. The terrace overlooking the water is the perfect spot to indulge in feta croquettes, fresh seabass tartare, and a slew of accomplished pastas and grilled meats. **Known for:** a sumptuous seaside setting; excellent wine list; charming atmosphere. [$] *Average main: €16* ✉ *Eparchiaki Odos* ☎ *27210/74444.*

Coffee and Quick Bites

Androuvista

$ | **CAFÉ** | This old-school café is a hit among locals, who come for the homemade *karydopita* (a deliciously syrupy local walnut cake). This is best washed down with a cup of traditional Greek coffee and preceded by a delicious zucchini pie. **Known for:** local hangout; delicious walnut cake; good coffee. [$] *Average main: €5* ✉ *Kardamyli* ☎ *27210/73788.*

Hotels

★ Liakoto

$ | **HOTEL** | One of a pair of charming, family-run waterside stays (sister hotel Aniska is just a short stroll away), this largely self-catering stay puts the coast on your doorstep. **Pros:** easy access to the water and a host of fine local eateries; great pool area and free parking; well-equipped kitchenette and complementary bottle of wine on arrival. **Cons:** no restaurant; breakfast is not included and pricey; rooms are simply furnished. [$] *Rooms from: €111* ✉ *Next to the Kardamyli quayside* ☎ *27210 /73600* 🌐 *www.anniska-liakoto.com* 🕒 *Closed Dec.–Feb.* 🛏 *25* 🍴 *No meals.*

Notos Hotel

$ | **B&B/INN** | These bright, handsome stone cottages, owned by the couple behind Lela's Taverna, lie scattered across hillside gardens. **Pros:** extremely attractive and well-equipped units; friendly atmosphere; lovely views across countryside and sea. **Cons:** village is a hearty walk away; advisable to have a rental car to enjoy area; no pool, but the beach is just down the hill. [$] *Rooms from: €80* ✉ *Kardamyli* ✣ *Above the beach, about 1 km (½ mile) north of the town center* ☎ *27210/73730* 🌐 *www.notoshotel.gr* 🛏 *10 studios; 4 apartments* 🍴 *Free breakfast.*

Pierides

$ | **B&B/INN** | **FAMILY** | This collection of suites and studios, set in an old 19th-century house among the cobbled byways of the Old Town, offers a serene escape. **Pros:** well-placed for the town; there's no quieter spot in Kardamyli; rooms are wonderfully spacious. **Cons:** the decor is a little old-fashioned; breakfasts cost extra; no parking. [$] *Rooms from: €85* ✉ *Old Town* ☎ *27210 /73256* 🌐 *pierides.gr* 🕒 *Closed Nov.–Mar.* 🛏 *5 suites; 2 studios* 🍴 *No meals.*

Nightlife

1866 Beer Bar

BARS/PUBS | Decent beer is a rarity in Greece, where the grim spectre of Mythos always lingers. This cute stone bar, just up from the seafront, bucks the trend with a fair selection of international brews (think well-known Belgian ales and lots of Brewdog), good local beers (Nema, Sura), and the odd blast of live jazz. A cozy respite from the cafés blaring out live soccer on the main street. The burgers are good, too. ✉ *Eparchiaki Odos Kalamatas* ☎ *73479* 🕒 *Closed Wed.*

Activities

TOURS

2407 Outdoor Experience

BICYCLE TOURS | Named after the height (in meters) of the tallest summit of the Taygettus range, chief guide Yiannis is indefatigable, and his trips range from walks in Viros and Ridomo gorges, to hardcore hikes up Taygettus, to e-bike cultural tours of the surrounding mountain villages. They have offices in Kardamyli and Stoupa. ✉ *Kardamyli* ☎ *27210/73752* 🌐 *www.2407m.com.*

Hiking in the Mani

Kardamyli is the gateway for hikers in the upper Mani, who are spoiled for choice with trails winding up into the hills, gorges, and mountaintops. Some can be discovered yourself; others require guides to properly explore.

Kardamyli has a number of easy trails that you can wander with little preparation. The simplest is the walk to Petrovouni, a 5 km (3 mile) circular route that follows the "Royal Road," a cobbled path dating back to the 2nd century when the Roman emperor Augustus gave Kardamyli to Sparta to use as a port. The Spartans built a road to connect the two, fragments of which still exist. Follow a trail—signposted outside the Mourtzinos Tower and dotted with black-and-yellow markers—that winds forested hillsides up to Agia Sofia then loop back via Petrovouni following the red-and-white marks down cobblestone switchbacks; it should take around two hours.

A more thrilling alternative is to take the path beside Mourtzinos Tower down to the dried-up river. The rocky bed plunges deep into Viros Gorge, a spectacular route where sheer rock walls slowly envelope you. Blue-and-white markers sprayed onto the stones point to easier routes among the rocks as well as signaling side trails that rise out of the gorge up to Byzantine monasteries. Loop back via Exo Chori and Aghia Sofia for a thrilling four-to-five-hour hike.

Outside the village are a number of exciting hikes, but they require your own transport to reach. The Biliovo Trail begins 15 km (9 miles) north of Kardamyli, in the village of Sotirianki. It follows a zigzagging 3 km (5 mile) uphill route to Altomira along a 100-year-old cobbled path with more than 80 bends. Southeast of here, the village of Vorio is the gateway to the area's other great gorge hike: Ridomo. It's a straight in-and-out route and requires a lot of scrambling up rocks. Local hiking company 2407 Outdoor Experience (🌐 www.2407m.com) offers a guided trek that uses a more interesting circular route, which is advised for less experienced hikers.

Similarly, if you're thinking of attempting to hike Profitis Ilias, the highest summit of Mount Taygettus (6,715 feet), it's definitely best to use a guide. Getting to the starting point from Kardamyli requires a 4WD, and even in summer the weather can change quite dramatically at the top. Treks with 2407 typically set off at 5 am, to avoid the heat of the day, and return at 3pm. It's a steep ascent, and unthinkable without proper hiking shoes, but well worth it for the views from the top.

Areopolis Αρεόπολης

44 km (26 miles) southwest of Kardamyli.

In Areopolis, the typical Maniote tower houses begin to appear in earnest as spooky sentinels amid the harsh landscape. The town was renamed after Ares, the god of war, because of its role in kickstarting the War of Independence when local clan leader Petrobey Mavromichalis, then governor of the Mani, initiated the uprising against the Turks here. On March 17, 1821 he proclaimed a revolution and marched his men north to Kardamyli, where he met up with the other clans before joining the other Greek revolutionaries in storming

Kalamata a week later. Today his statue stands proudly in the town square.

Areopolis now enjoys protection as a historical monument by the government, but although the town seems medieval, most of the tower houses were built in the early 1800s. The Taxiarchis (Arch-angels) church, which looks as if it has 12th-century reliefs over the doors, was actually constructed in 1798. Yet it's easy to slip into a time warp as you meander dark cobblestone lanes past houses with enclosed courtyards and low-arched gateways.

Spare a moment to visit nearby Limeni, just a few kilometers north of town. The village has long been the main harbor for the area, loomed over by the ruins of Kefala Castle, a Turkish stronghold built in the 17th century to remind locals just who held sway here. These days the pretty waterfront is more likely to be filled with fishing boats than warships, and has attracted many of the best restaurants in the area. The descendants of Mavromichalis have even turned the family's seaside mansion here into a stunning small hotel.

Sights

★ Pirgos Dirou Caves
CAVE | FAMILY | Carved out of the lime-stone by the slow-moving underground river Vlychada on its way to the sea, the vast Pirgos Dirou caves—actually two main caves, Glyfada and Alepotrypa—are one of Greece's more popular natural attractions, and a visit is an entertain-ing and surreal experience. The eerie caverns, places of worship in Paleolithic and Neolithic times, were believed to be entrances to the underworld by the ancient Greeks, and served as hiding places millennia later for Resistance fighters during World War II.

Today you climb aboard a boat for a 25-minute tour of Glyfada's grottoes—with formations of luminous pink,

white, yellow, and red stalagmites and stalactites that resemble buildings and mythical beasts. The cave system is believed to be at least 70 km (43 miles) long, with more than 2,800 waterways, perhaps extending as far as Sparta, though visitors explore just 1½ km (1 mile). At the end of the tour you walk for several hundred yards before emerging on a path above the crashing surf. The close quarters in the passageways are not for the claustrophobic, and even in summer the caves are chilly. During high season you may wait up to two hours for a boat, so plan to arrive early. In low sea-son you may have to wait until enough people arrive to fill up a boat. Opening hours vary according to season. ✉ *Pirgos Dirou* ✚ *10 km (6 miles) southwest of Areopolis, 5 km (3 miles) west of Areo-polis–Vathia road* ☎ *27330/52222* 💶 *€15 (€10 if booked online).*

🍴 Restaurants

Takis
$ | SEAFOOD | The service is legendarily churlish but the fish and seafood, priced by the kilo and served at the water's edge in Limeni, are some of the freshest in the region—and best when simply grilled, usually with mountain herbs. You may end up dining next to the boat that brought in the fresh catch, or for that matter, near a crew cleaning the fish that will soon appear on your plate (it's much more charming than it sounds). **Known for:** fresh fish right off the boat; nice harborside perch; turtles floating in the water of the bay. $ *Average main: €12* ✉ *Limeni* ✚ *On Limeni waterfront, 5 km (3 miles) north of Areopolis* ☎ *27330/51327.*

Taverna Barba Petros
$ | GREEK | A simple, high-ceilinged room and terrace are the settings for the traditional meals hosted here in the oldest tavern in town. The kitchen uses only market-fresh vegetables and locally raised meat, which appear in simple

and delicious ways. **Known for:** traditional Mani dishes, including grilled meats; nice summertime terrace; a welcome taste of the old Mani. [$] *Average main: €9* ✉ *Main Street, Areopoli* ☎ *27330/51205.*

★ **Teloneio**

$$ | **GREEK** | A stately menu taking inspiration from its Mani roots makes this breezy waterside restaurant the pick of Limeni's harbor dining. Dishes hum to the tune of the region's famed smoked pork *sygklino, myzithra* cheese, and a bounty of fresh seafood, from parrotfish atop wild greens plucked from the Taygettus mountains, to its impressive Greek "sushi." **Known for:** Greek sushi—think yellowfin tuna carpaccio and anchovy ceviche; a wealth of local produce; authentic Mani food given a gastronomic kick. [$] *Average main: €17* ✉ *Limeni Bay, Limeni* ☎ *27330 /52702* 🌐 *www.teloneio-limeni.gr* ⏲ *Closed Oct.–Apr.*

Hotels

Petra & Fos Boutique Hotel & Spa

$$$ | **HOTEL** | A handful of swankier boutique stays jostle infinity pools on the northern lip of Limeni Bay, where this elegant stone-built spa and hotel cuts a dignified air. **Pros:** one of the best-looking stays in the Mani; great pool and views; excellent facilities, including a small gym. **Cons:** you'll need a car; there aren't any facilities nearby; it is one of the Mani's pricier stays. [$] *Rooms from: €240* ✉ *Oitylo, Areopoli* ☎ *27330/54050* 🌐 *www.petrafoshotel.com* 🛏 *23 rooms* 🍴 *Free breakfast.*

★ **Pirgos Mavromichali**

$$ | **B&B/INN** | The fortified, seaside stronghold of the Mavromichali clan, noted for their role in the fight for Greek independence, is now an enchanting inn with 13 character-filled rooms and suites set within the walls of a centuries-old tower building. **Pros:** panoramic, historic surroundings at the edge of the sea; extremely attentive service; an ideal base for exploring the rugged Mani landscape. **Cons:** steps may be difficult for guests with mobility issues; some rooms are a bit dark; a car is a necessity. [$] *Rooms from: €150* ✉ *Harborfront, Limeni* ✥ *5 km (3 miles) north of Areopolis* ☎ *27330/51042* 🌐 *www.pirgosmavromichali.gr* 🛏 *9 rooms* 🍴 *Free breakfast.*

Trapela

$ | **HOTEL** | In this beautiful, traditionally styled house just off the Aeropolis main square, large, stone-floored, stone-walled, wood-ceilinged rooms combine distinctive, traditional ambience with modern comforts. **Pros:** lovely terraces and a garden; pleasant decor; stylish and comfortable base for visiting the Mani. **Cons:** limited service; a distance from a beach; no elevator. [$] *Rooms from: €90* ✉ *Areopoli* ✥ *Near the center of town* ☎ *27330/52690* 🌐 *www.trapela.gr* 🛏 *9 rooms, 4 suites* 🍴 *Free breakfast.*

Gerolimenas
Γερολιμένας

22 km (14 miles) south of Areopolis.

Located at the end of a long natural harbor, Gerolimenas was an important port in the late 19th and early 20th centuries. Sleepy as it now is, it's the most tourist-friendly place in this stark part of the southernmost Mani, with several hotels, tavernas, and shops and a lively town beach. About 3 km (2 miles) north of Gerolimenas is the town of Stavri, from where you can make a memorable one-hour trek north to Tigani Castle, built by the Franks in the mid-13th century and carved into the rock face at the end of a long promontory surrounded by crashing surf.

The most photogenic sight in this part of the Mani is the picture-perfect Vathia, 10 km (6 miles) south of Gerolimenas. This old village is now virtually a ghost town. A government-sponsored plan to turn it into a sprawling hotel never came to pass, and its clusters of looming tower houses perched against the sea are one of the postcard icons of Greece. Many of the two- and three-story stone buildings have small windows and tiny openings over the doors through which boiling oil was poured on the unwelcome. The majority are in disrepair but signs of life are emerging in a handful of renovations.

The landscape becomes more rugged and even more forbidding south of Vathia, on the way to the cape at the tip of the peninsula. The road forks around the mountainsides to Porto Kayio, where a few tavernas face a lovely beach, and then to more beaches at Marmari. The alternative route leads south to barren Cape Tenaro, where the ruins of a small Roman settlement include a mosaic of the Aria's star, created in the first century, that is perilously open to the elements. A 2 km (1¼ mile) path follows a treacherously rocky route past it to the lighthouse at the peninsula's tip, where you can gaze off the southernmost edge of mainland Greece. A cave here, to which you might be able to convince a boatman to take you, is also one of several alleged entrances to the classical underworld.

Hotels

★ Citta dei Nicliani

$ | **HOTEL** | Kitta was once home to the most powerful clan in the Mani, and relics of its past scatter the horizon. **Pros:** a historic setting in an atmospheric town; excellent wine and food; incredible value for a luxury boutique. **Cons:** you need a car to get here and around; there's not much nearby within walking distance; rooms can be a little dark. [$] *Rooms from: €100* ✉ *Kitta* ☎ *27330/51827* 🌐 *www.cittadeinicliani.com* 🛏 *7 rooms* 🍴 *Free breakfast.*

★ Kyrimai Hotel

$$ | **HOTEL** | The Kyrimis family have lovingly restored a welcoming assemblage of 19th-century stone warehouses into a beautiful retreat, with comfortable guest rooms furnished with antiques and a tasteful mix of traditional and contemporary pieces; many have balconies and sleeping lofts. **Pros:** atmospheric surroundings; good swimming from hotel jetty; pleasant seaside terraces. **Cons:** some rooms are dark and do not have views; parking can be difficult; service can be hit or miss. [$] *Rooms from: €143* ✉ *Waterfront* ☎ *27330/54288* 🌐 *www.kyrimai.gr* 🛏 *26 rooms* 🍴 *Free breakfast.*

Gythion Γύθειο

79 km (49 miles) north of Vathia, 50 km (30 miles) northeast of Gerolimenas.

At the foot of the Taygettus range on the northeastern edge of the Mani, Gythion seems terribly cosmopolitan, compared to the stark countryside that surrounds it. Graceful pastel 19th-century houses march up the steep hillside and line the busy harbor, where a fishing fleet bobs alongside ouzeri and little shops. As Laconia's main port, Gythion is the region's gateway to the Mani Peninsula. It claims Hercules and Apollo as its founders, and survives today by exporting olives, oil, rice, and citrus fruits. Kranae, a tiny islet at the eastern end of the harbor, is where Paris and Helen (wife of the Mycenaean king Menelaos) allegedly consummated their love affair after escaping Sparta, provoking the Trojan War described in the *Iliad.* A causeway now joins Marathonisi to the mainland.

Monemvasia
Μονεμβασιά

140 km (85 miles) northeast of Gythion.

The eastern "finger" dangling off the southern edge of the Peloponnese is the dramatic setting for Monemvasia (meaning "single entrance"). This Byzantine town clings to the side of the 1,148-foot rock that was once a headland until in AD 375 it was separated from the mainland by an earthquake. The Laconians who settled here in the 6th century were seeking refuge against Avar and Slav raids; it proved such an effective defence that a millennia later, this became the last outpost of the Byzantine empire to hold out against the Turks.

As a port, Monemvasia prospered from the 10th century on, dominating the sea lanes from Western Europe to the Levant. Its golden age came in the 13th and 14th centuries, when wealthy Byzantine nobles settled here in the Upper Town while a thriving market flourished below, where exports of local malvasia (or "malmsey") wine, a sweet variety of Madeira prized across medieval Europe and still drunk today, made merchants filthy rich.

By the mid-14th century, the town had fallen under the control of the Despotate of Morea, a semi-autonomous Byzantine state that had spread across the Peloponnese. When the Morea finally fell to the Turks in 1460, Monemvasia turned first to the papacy for protection, then to the Venetians, who transformed the city, building fortresses and fortifications. It worked, up to a point, and the town held out for 80 more years against the relentless Ottomans.

Centuries later, Monemvasia would be the turning point in perhaps the most important war in modern Greek history,

when after a bloody four-month siege in July 1821, Greek forces stormed its walls, claiming their first major Ottoman fortress in the War of Independence. By this point, its decline was in full swing. With the town's fortifications of little modern use, the upper section was left to ruin, and the arrival of the Corinth Canal to the north rendered its port redundant.

During its heyday Monemvasia held thousands; now just ten families live here. When local tourists discovered it in the 1980s, the authorities acted swiftly to protect the city, and the rather ugly town of Gefira, at the foot of the causeway, has taken the brunt of any development. Today, the citadel is wonderfully preserved, with the Upper Town, where most of the great ruins lie, making a tingly hike through the Byzantine bones of a city, winding up to the windswept ruins of its hilltop castle. Below, houses line steep streets only wide enough for two people abreast, as visitors slip among remnants of another age—escutcheons, marble thrones, Byzantine icons. It is a delight to wander the back lanes and along the old walls, and an overnight stay here allows you to enjoy this curious relic all the better when the tour groups have departed.

 Sights

Lighthouse Trail
TRAIL | Exit the Eastern Wall gate to reach Monemvasia Lighthouse, a clean-cut innocuous building erected in the late-19th-century. The beacon contains a small museum (free; open daily) about its history; it is also the start of a 2 km (1.2 mile) rocky path that skirts the northern rim of the island (follow the red trail marks) back to the car park next to To Kastro café. It's a testing scramble in parts, and one best avoided on a windy or wet day. ⊠ *Monemvasia.*

Main Square (Lower Town)
RELIGIOUS SITE | On the main square stands the town's 13th-century **Church of Elkomenos Christos**, reputedly the largest medieval church in southern Greece. Carved peacocks on its portal are symbolic of the Byzantine era; the detached bell tower—like those of Italian cathedrals—is a sign of Venetian rebuilding in the 17th century. Sculptures from the church, together with other interesting finds from excavations around the island, are held across the square in the town's **Archaeological Collection** (€3; closed Tues.), a small, interesting museum housed within an 16th-century former mosque. Outside, a canon dominates the square, typically forming a backdrop to the many selfie-ing couples. ✉ *Tzamiou Sq., along main street.*

Portelo
BEACH—SIGHT | A small gate in the southern walls of the castle leads to a rocky outcrop that was once an unloading dock for goods traded in and out of the city. Today it is a small bathing area where paddlers can bob in the shadow of the great walls, protected from the strong northerly winds. ✉ *Monemvasia.*

Upper Town
RELIGIOUS SITE | For solitude and a dizzying view, pass through the upper town's wooden entrance gates, complete with the original iron reinforcement. Up the hill is a rare example of a domed octagonal church, **Agia Sofia,** founded in the 13th century by Emperor Andronicus II and patterned after Dafni Monastery in Athens. Under Venetian rule the Byzantine complex served as a convent. Follow the path to the highest point on the rock for a breathtaking view of the coast. ✉ *Monemvasia* ✣ *At top of mountain.*

Beaches

Some people swim off the rocks at the base of the Old Town and along the road leading to the main gate, but the pebble beach in the New Town is safer and more appealing. For the most rewarding beach experience, head to the sandy strands at Pori, about 5 km (3 miles) northwest of Monemvasia.

Restaurants

Marianthi
$ | GREEK | You'll feel as if you're dropping into someone's home at dinner here: family photos of stern, mustachioed ancestors hang on the walls along with local memorabilia, and the service, at tables on the street in good weather, is just as welcoming (perhaps too much so, as cats can be as numerous as diners). A memorable meal makes the most of local ingredients—wild mountain greens, any of the fish but especially the fresh red mullet, the addictive potato salad (you may have to order two plates), and the marinated octopus sprinkled with oregano. **Known for:** character-filled surroundings; excellent small plates; cash only. [$] *Average main: €9* ✉ *Main street* ☎ *27320/61371* 💳 *No credit cards* ⏲ *Closed Sat.*

To Kanoni
$ | GREEK | Kanoni is known for its fine breakfasts, served on a rooftop terrace that gazes down to the square's cannon and across the old battlements to sea. Choose from omelets, ham and eggs, or thick, creamy yogurt and honey, then come back at lunch or dinner for a nicely varied menu that offers some sumptuous seafood alongside old Greek standbys of moussaka, lamb *kleftiko*, and *stamna*. **Known for:** nice view-filled terrace; wide-ranging menu; a pleasant lunch spot. [$] *Average main: €10* ✉ *Main Sq.* ✣ *Old Town* ☎ *27320/61387* 🌐 *tokanoni.com.*

★ Voltes

$ | GREEK | While it lacks the pretty terrace setting of the other restaurants along Monemvasia's main street, Voltes more than makes up for it with culinary wit. Imaginative takes on the staples of Greek mezedes yields traditional cheese pies raised to new heights with a dash of sweet tomato jam, or local-style stir fry *kototigania* spiced with ample chillies, tart mollasses, and sweet caramelized onions. **Known for:** exciting small plate menu; great local wine; atmsopheric stone cellar setting. **$** *Average main: €12* ✉ *Next to the main gate of Monemvasia* ☎ *27320/61919.*

Hotels

Byzantino

$ | B&B/INN | Like many stays in Monemvasia, Byzantino is spread across a half-dozen of old stone buildings in the Old Town. **Pros:** character-filled accommodation in medieval houses; some units have nice terraces and sea views; warm hospitality. **Cons:** steep streets and stairs to reach some rooms; ask about accessibility when booking; rooms vary greatly, so ask to see a few if available; noise from nearby bars in some rooms. **$** *Rooms from: €90* ✉ *Monemvasia* ✛ *The hotel office is on the main street near the town entrance gate* ☎ *27320/61351* ⊕ *www.hotelbyzantino. com* ⇌ *25 rooms* ⦿| *Free breakfast.*

Eumelia

$$ | B&B/INN | FAMILY | A working farm near a village 45 minutes outside of Sparta provides a rare chance to experience rural Greece, while enjoying handsome bunglow accommodations, homecooked organic meals, yoga sessions, and easy excursions to Monemvasia and other places of interest in the southeastern Peloponnese. **Pros:** well designed and attractive; a chance to see how a farm is run; genial, English-speaking host. **Cons:** remote location not suitable for everyone; not on the coast (though beaches are within easy driving distance); may be a bit too laid-back for some guests. **$** *Rooms from: €160* ✉ *Gouvai* ☎ *69471/51400* ⊕ *www.eumelia.com* ⇌ *5 bungalows* ⦿| *Free breakfast.*

Kellia

$ | B&B/INN | Accommodations in this old monastery (*kellia* means "cells") are fairly simple, but they are extremely appealing and face an airy square above the sea. **Pros:** beautiful seaside location, tucked away from the busy main street and squares; atmospheric surroundings; friendly hosts. **Cons:** a long walk from the west entrance; a steep climb to steps in some rooms; some rooms are a bit dark. **$** *Rooms from: €75* ✉ *Monemvasia* ✛ *On the lower square, opposite the Church of Panagia Chrissafitissa* ☎ *27320/61520* ⊕ *www.keliamonemvasia.com* ⇌ *9 rooms* ⦿| *Free breakfast.*

★ Kinsterna Hotel and Spa

$$$ | HOTEL | A countryside Ottoman estate has been brought back to life as one of Greece's most distinctive hotels, where courtyards, terraces, domes, vaulted ceilings, arches, stone work, fireplaces, and other architectural elements are put to dazzling effect. **Pros:** excellent choice of fine dining restaurants; beautifully furnished and well-equipped rooms and suites; attractive pool, spa, vineyards, and a private beach. **Cons:** countryside setting that can only be reached by car (ask for directions or you will get lost); food can be expensive; rooms vary in character. **$** *Rooms from: €250* ✉ *Agios Stefanos* ☎ *27320/66300* ⊕ *www.kinsternahotel.gr* ⇌ *27 rooms* ⦿| *Free breakfast.*

Malvasia Traditional Hotel

$ | B&B/INN | A complex of restored buildings at the far edge of the Old Town (reached on a trek over sometimes steep and uneven pavement) provides atmospheric and comfortable lodgings tucked into nooks and crannies under cane-and-wood or vaulted brick ceiling. **Pros:** appealing and nicely designed bright rooms with character; many private terraces and sea views; pleasant public indoor and outdoor spaces. **Cons:** reached via a trek through town on rough streets; reserve well in advance for July and August; steps to reach some rooms. $ *Rooms from: €70* ✉ *Monemvasia* ✛ *End of Old Town* ☎ *27320/61323* ⊕ *www.malvasiahotel-traditional.gr* ↴ *16 rooms* ❍❙ *Free breakfast.*

Moni Emvasis

$$$ | HOTEL | The conversion of this 500-year-old building is a thing of beauty. **Pros:** views from the rooms and terrace bar are magnificent; luggage is portered from the gate; superb breakfasts made with local produce. **Cons:** it doesn't come cheap; there are stairs to climb and no disabled access; inside can be a little dark. $ *Rooms from: €250* ✉ *Monemvasia* ✛ *Take the steps opposite Enetiko Cafe* ☎ *27320/62122* ⊕ *moniemvasis.gr* ↴ *3 rooms* ❍❙ *Free breakfast.*

 ## Nightlife

Byron's Wine Tasting Bar

WINE BARS—NIGHTLIFE | An excellent spot, tucked into the alleyways south of the main square, and a welcome opportunity to acquaint yourself with the famous wines of the area. Owner Byron is a knowledgable, charismatic source; tastings (including three mezze) start at €20. ✉ *Main Portello bathing access path* ☎ *69743/70964* ⊕ *byrons-wine-tasting-bar.business.site.*

Enetiko

BARS/PUBS | A trio of cocktail bars-cum-cafés dot the main street, but the brightest and largest is this slick affair. Inside, its cool, wooden interior offers respite from the heat, but it's the large terrace that catches the eye, affording fine views over the water and an agreeable spot to sip its signature Skyfall cocktail. ✉ *Monemvasia* ☎ *27320/61352* ⊕ *enetiko.olympicbiz.com.*

Sparta Σπαρτη

96 km (60 miles) northwest of Monemvasia.

For those who have read about ancient Sparta, the bellicose city-state that once dominated the Greek world, the modern city on the broad Eurotas River might be a disappointment, since ruins are few and far between. Given the area's earthquakes and the Spartans' tendency to live more like an army camp than a city-state, no elaborate ruins remain, a fact that so disconcerted Otto, Greece's first king, that in 1835 he ordered the modern city built on the ancient site. The modern town that lies here now is not terribly attractive, but it's pleasant enough, with a lively pedestrian-only city center. It's perhaps best used as a pit stop en route to Monemvasia or the Laconian part of the Mani, or as a metropolitan base for visits to Mystras.

GETTING HERE AND AROUND

Sparta is a useful hub for buses connecting the north and deep south of the peninsula. Several buses a day connect Athens and Sparta, a trip of about four hours that costs about €18 each way. From Sparta's bus station (☎ *27310/26441*), located downtown at the junction of Lykourgou and Dafnou, you can catch one of six daily buses to Monemvasia (about 2 hours, €5) andor also continue onsouth to the Mani region via (service several times a day daily services to Gythion and Aeropolis) and other places in the southern Peloponnese.

By car, follow the toll highway south from Athens through Corinth and Tripoli to a well-marked exit onto Highway 70 for Sparta. The trip from Athens takes about three hours of reasonable driving.

The Spartan Ethic

The Spartans' relentless militarism set them apart from other Greeks in the ancient world. They were expected to emerge victorious from a battle or not at all, and for most of its existence Sparta was without a wall, because according to Lykourgos, who wrote Sparta's constitution sometime around 600 BC, "chests, not walls, make a city." The government was an oligarchy, with two kings who also served as military leaders. Spartan society had three classes: a privileged elite involved with warfare and government; farmers, traders, and craftspeople, who paid taxes; and the numerous Helots, a serf class with few rights.

Selected boys in the reigning warrior class were taken from their parents at the age of seven and submitted to a training regimen without parallel in history for its ruthlessness. Their diet involved mostly herbs, roots, and the famous black broth, which included pork, the blood of the pig, and vinegar. Rich foods were thought to stunt growth. Forbidden to work, boys and young men trained for combat and practiced stealing, an acceptable skill—it was believed to teach caution and cunning—unless one was caught. One legend describes a Spartan youth who let a concealed fox chew out his bowels rather than reveal his theft. Girls also trained rigorously in the belief they would bear healthier offspring; for the same reason, newlyweds were forbidden to make love frequently.

The kingdom's iron coinage was not accepted outside Sparta's borders, creating a contempt for wealth and luxury (and, in turn, rapacious kings and generals). Sparta's warrior caste subjugated the native Achaean inhabitants of the region. Today all that remains of this realm founded on martial superiority is dust.

◉ Sights

Museum of the Olive and Greek Olive Oil

MUSEUM | FAMILY | Olives are thick on the ground in these parts, so it's only fitting that Sparta is home to a quirky and appealing collection of apparatus and culture related to the staple of Greek economy since ancient times, housed in a stunning renovation of the city's first electricity works. ⊠ *Othonos-Amalias 129* ☎ *27310/89315* 🎫 *€4* ⏰ *Closed Tues.*

Sparta Acropolis

ARCHAEOLOGICAL SITE | What little remains of Ancient Sparta's acropolis is now part archaeological site, part park. Locals can be seen here strolling, along with many young couples stealing a romantic moment amid the fallen limestone and shady trees. The sparse ruins include a **theater,** a **stadium,** and a **sanctuary to Athena.** ⊠ *Sparta* ✛ *North end of town.*

Sparta Archaeological Museum

MUSEUM | This eclectic collection reflects Laconia's turbulent history and is worth an hour to see Neolithic pottery; jewels and tools excavated from the Alepotrypa cave; Mycenaean tomb finds; bright 4th- and 5th-century Roman mosaics; and objects from Sparta. Most characteristic of the relatively few pieces of Spartan art that have survived are the bas-reliefs with deities and heroes; note the one depicting a seated couple bearing gifts who are framed by a snake (540 BC). ⊠ *Agios Nikonos, between Dafnou and Evangelistria* ☎ *27310/28575* ⊕ *www. culture.gr* 🎫 *€2.*

Statue of Leonidas

PUBLIC ART | Stop a moment and contemplate the statue of the stern Spartan leader. During the Second Persian War in the 5th century BC, with 30,000 Persians advancing on his army of 8,000, Leonidas, ordered to surrender his weapons, was said to have jeered, "Come and get them." For two days he held off the enemy, until a traitor named Efialtes (the word has since come to mean "nightmare" in Greek) showed the Persians a way to attack from the rear. When forced to retreat to a wooded knoll, Leonidas is said to have commented, "So much the better, we will fight in the shade." His entire troop was slaughtered and an icon was born. Today his likeness adorns everything from wines to T-shirts, to the tattooed arms of young Greek men. ✉ *End of Konstantinou.*

Temple of Artemis Orthia

ARCHAEOLOGICAL SITE | At this temple outside town, young Spartan men underwent *krypteia* (initiations) that entailed severe public floggings. The altar had to be splashed with blood before the goddess was satisfied. Traces of two such altars are among sparse vestiges of the 6th-century BC temple. The larger ruins are the remains of a grandstand built in the 3rd century AD by the Romans, who revived the flogging tradition as a public spectacle. ✉ *Tripoli Rd.* ✥ *Down path to Eurotas River.*

🍴 Restaurants

Diethnes

$ | **GREEK** | Locals claim this is one of Sparta's best restaurants, but then again, most head out to village tavernas for a big meal and leave this place to the tour-bus crowd. Even so, the food is reliably good. **Known for:** shady rear garden; traditional dishes; handy central location. [$] *Average main: €9* ✉ *Paleologou 105* ☎ *27310/28636.*

★ En Chatipi

$ | **GREEK** | A ten-minute walk south of the center takes you across the river and into the suburbs, where you'll find this friendly, unselfconsciously retro neighborhood taverna. Inside, jazz music echoes the vintage ad posters for 1950s Greek cigarettes and long-gone liquors, while the menu is a treasure trove of hearty classics, from Spartan dishes like pork with olives and orange, to the lightest of moussakas. **Known for:** peaceful shaded terrace; friendly neighborhood vibe; bargain prices. [$] *Average main: €8* ✉ *Panagioti Chrysikou 27* ☎ *27310/26677* ⏲ *Closed Sun.*

🛏 Hotels

Maniatis Hotel

$ | **HOTEL** | The sleek style here begins in the modern marble lobby and extends through fittingly spartan yet handsome guest rooms, with their contemporary, light-wood furnishings and soft, soothing colors. **Pros:** attractive accommodations; good in-house restaurant; central location. **Cons:** small rooms and bathrooms; relatively few luxuries; some street noise. [$] *Rooms from: €60* ✉ *Paleologou 72* ☎ *27310/22665* 🌐 *www.maniatishotel.gr* 🔑 *80 rooms* 🍴 *Free breakfast.*

Menelaion Hotel

$ | **HOTEL** | The pool sparkling in the leafy courtyard is a welcome sight after a hot day of exploring the ruins of nearby Mystras, and the well-equipped guest rooms have a degree of business chic about them. **Pros:** attractive public areas; good in-house restaurant and bar; courtyard with pool. **Cons:** rooms are stylish but lack a little character; street noise in front-facing rooms; no garage and difficult parking. [$] *Rooms from: €100* ✉ *Paleologou 91* ☎ *27310/22161* 🌐 *www.menelaion.com* 🔑 *30 rooms* 🍴 *Free breakfast.*

Magnificently redolent of the Byzantine era, Mystras is a town filled with churches and monasteries, many adorned with 12th-century paintings.

Mystras Μυστράς

8 km (5 miles) west of Sparta, 64 km (40 miles) southwest of Tripoli.

While little remains to attest to Spartan power and might, residents of the Byzantine capital just to the west left behind a treasure trove of architectural splendors. A visit to Sparta requires a fertile imagination; in Mystras all you need is a good pair of walking shoes and some water as you scramble amid the copious remnants of the last days of the Byzantine Empire.

In spring Mystras is resplendent with wildflowers and butterflies, but it can be oppressively hot in summer, so get an early start to avoid exploring the site in the midday sun. That said, it's easy to spend half a day here, so wear sunscreen, a hat, and sturdy shoes for traction on slippery rocks. If pushed for time, you can cut your visit in half by parking at the upper entrance, from where it's only a 10-minute ascent to the castle atop the hill. Do watch out for the occasional snake on the way up.

Sights

★ Mystras Archaeological Site

ARCHAEOLOGICAL SITE | FAMILY | In this Byzantine city, abandoned gold-and-stone palaces, churches, and monasteries line serpentine paths; the scent of herbs and wildflowers permeates the air; goat bells tinkle; and walnut, fig, and lime trees scatter the ground with their fruit. An intellectual and cultural center where philosophers like Chrysoloras, "the sage of Byzantium," held forth on the good and the beautiful, Mystras seems an appropriate place for the last hurrah of the Byzantine emperors. Today the splendid ruins are a UNESCO World Heritage site and one of the most impressive sights in the Peloponnese. A pleasant modern town adjoins the ruins.

In 1249 William Geoffrey de Villehardouin built the castle in Mystras in an attempt to control Laconia and establish Frankish supremacy over the Peloponnese. He held court here with his Greek wife, Anna Comnena, surrounded by knights of Champagne, Burgundy, and Flanders, but in 1259 he was defeated by the Byzantines. As part of the Despotate of Morea, a semi-autonomous state within the empire, it became the capital of Morea, and a palace and numerous churches (whose frescoes exemplified several periods of painting) were built. A town gradually grew down the slope and the city thrived, enjoying a golden age even as the rest of the Byzantine Empire crumbled around it.

Surrender to the Turks in 1460 signaled a long decline. For a couple of centuries Mystras survived because of its silk industry, flourishing once again under brief occupation by the Venetians in the late 17th century. Following reoccupation by the Turks, Russian and Albanian invasions razed the city in 1770 and 1780, but it was the troops of Pasha Ibrahim that spelt its final demise. His Egyptian army marked one last throw of the dice by the Ottomans in the 1821–1830 War of Independence, and when they marched on Mystras in 1825, his troops burnt and looted the city beyond repair.

Among the most important buildings in the lower town (Kato Chora) is **Agios Demetrios,** the *mitropolis* (cathedral) founded in 1291. Set in its floor is a stone with the two-headed Byzantine eagle marking the spot where Constantine XII, the last emperor of Byzantium, was consecrated. The cathedral's brilliant frescoes include a vivid depiction of the Virgin and the infant Jesus on the central apse and a wall painting in the narthex of the Second Coming, its two red-and-turquoise-winged angels sorrowful as they open the records of Good and Evil. One wing of the church houses a **museum** that holds fragments of Byzantine sculptures, later Byzantine icons, decorative metalwork, and coins.

In the Vrontokion monastery are **Agios Theodoros** (AD 1295), the oldest church in Mystras, and the 14th-century **Church of Panagia Odegetria,** or **Afendiko,** which is decorated with remarkable murals. These include, in the narthex, scenes of the miracles of Christ: *The Healing of the Blind Man, The Samaritan at the Well,* and *The Marriage of Cana.* The fluidity of the brushstrokes, the subtle but complicated coloring, and the resonant expressions suggest the work of extremely skilled hands.

The **Pantanassa monastery** is a visual feast of intricate tiling, rosette-festooned loops, and myriad arches. It is the only inhabited building in Mystras; the hospitable nuns still produce embroidery that you can purchase. Step out onto the east portico for a view of the Eurotas River valley below.

Every inch of the tiny **Perivleptos monastery,** meaning "attracting attention from all sides," is covered with exceptional 14th-century illustrations from the New Testament, including *The Birth of the Virgin,* in a lush palette of reds, yellows, and oranges; *The Dormition of the Virgin* above the entrance (with Christ holding his mother's soul represented as a baby); and, immediately to the left of the entrance, the famous fresco the *Divine Liturgy.*

In the upper town (Ano Chora), where most aristocrats lived, stands a Byzantine civic building, the **Palace of Despots,** home of the last emperor and rather over-zealously restored. The older, northeastern wing contains a guardroom, a kitchen, and the residence. The three-story northwest wing contains an immense reception hall on its top floor, lighted by eight Gothic windows and heated by eight huge chimneys; the throne probably stood in the shallow alcove that's in the center of a wall.

In the palace's **Agia Sofia chapel,** the Italian wives of emperors Constantine and Theodore Palaiologos are buried. Note the polychromatic marble floor and the frescoes that were preserved for years under whitewash, applied by the Turks when they transformed this into a mosque. Climb to the **castle** and look down into the gullies of Mt. Taygettus, where it's said the Spartans, who hated weakness, hurled their malformed babies. ⊠ *Ano Chora* ☎ *27310/23315* ⊕ *odysseus.culture.gr* 🖼 *€12.*

Hotels

Pyrgos of Mystras

$$ | B&B/INN | A stone mansion set in a fragrant garden at the edge of the modern town is the setting for this stylish country retreat, where luxurious rooms, all decorated with rich colors and fabrics, overlook orange groves and Mt. Taygettus. **Pros:** beautiful decor; extremely comfortable; pleasant terrace. **Cons:** not a full-service hotel; a bit fussy for country setting; no pool. $ *Rooms from: €220* ⊠ *Manousaki 3* ☎ *27310/20870* ⊕ *www. pyrgosmystra.gr* ⇄ *7 rooms* ⊚l *Free breakfast.*

Index

Photo Credits

Front Cover: Funkystock - www.agefotostock.com [Description: The circular Delphi Tholos temple with Doric columns, 380 BC, Sanctuary of Athena Pronaia, Delphi Archaeological Site, Greece.]. **Back cover, from left to right:** Anilah | Dreamstime.com, elgreko / Shutterstock, cheng (c) Ianwool | Dreamstime.com. **Spine:** ivanmateev/iStockphoto. **Interior, from left to right:** Cristian Mircea Balate/Shutterstock (1). Kite_rin/Shutterstock (2). Ralf Siemieniec/Shutterstock (5). **Chapter 1: Experience Greece:** Aetherial Images/Shutterstock (8-9). Little_Desire/Shutterstock (10). Milosk50 | Dreamstime.com (11). Chubykin Arkady / Shutterstock (11). Elgreko74 | Dreamstime.com (12). Leonid Andronov / Shutterstock (12). Aetherial | Dreamstime.com (12). Vassilis | Dreamstime.com (12). Eng101 | Dreamstime.com (13). elgreko / Shutterstock (13). Heracles Kritikos / Shutterstock (13). EQRoy/Shutterstock (13). Pitk/Shutterstock (14). Rangpl | Dreamstime.com (14). Mdfotori | Dreamstime.com (14). Ellobo1 | Dreamstime.com (14). Katsyka | Dreamstime.com (15). Giuseppemasci | Dreamstime.com (16). Bennymarty | Dreamstime.com (16). Pat@xs4all.nl | Dreamstime.com (16) Milangonda | Dreamstime.com (16). Freesurf69 | Dreamstime.com (17). Samot / Shutterstock (17). Eugen3B/Shutterstock (24). Freesurf69 | Dreamstime.com (25). Dglavinova | Dreamstime.com (26). Rawf88 | Dreamstime.com (26). Nina Firsova/Shutterstock (26). Kev Vincent Photography/Shutterstock (27). Pedjamilosavljevic | Dreamstime.com (27). ian woolcock/96393822 (28). pkazmierczak/iStockphoto (28). Joaquin Ossorio Castillo/Shutterstock (28). Sven Hansche/Shutterstock (28). Aerial-motion/Shutterstock (29). vivooo/Shutterstock (29). KOSTAS TSEK/Shutterstock (29). Georgios Alexandris/96393822 (29). Joe Khup/Shutterstock (30). JordeAngjelovik/96393822 (30). Freeartist (30). zoom-zoom/iStockphoto (30). Lev Levin/Shutterstock (31). Gatsi/iStockphoto (31). Calin Stan/Shutterstock (31). sssanchez//iStockphoto (31). **Chapter 3: Athens:** Elgreko74 | Dreamstime.com (87). Remzi1977 | Dreamstime.com (106-107). Vidler (108). Kord.com (109). Juha-Pekka Kervinen/Shutterstock (112). Green Bear/Shutterstock (113). Alvaro Leiva / age fotostock (124). George Kavallierakis / age fotostock (128). Milangonda | Dreamstime.com (132). P. Narayan / age fotostock (137). Bobthenavigator (149). Sanga Park/iStockphoto (158). vittorio sciosia (165). Elpis Ioannidis/Shutterstock (166). Bridget McGill/iStockphoto (166). Charles Stirling (Travel) / Alamy (166). Inger Anne Hulbækdal/Shutterstock (167). Rene Mattes (167). Amal Sajdak/iStockphoto (167). **Chapter 4: The Saronic Gulf Islands:** Andreas Karelias / Alamy (181). ivan bastien/Shutterstock (192). Natalia Pavlova/iStockphoto (197). vlas2000/Shutterstock (203). franco pizzochero (204). LOOK Die Bildagentur der Fotografen GmbH / Alamy (204). Alvaro Leiva (205). KatarinaPalenikova/Shutterstock (205). IML Image Group Ltd / Alamy (206). Liv friis-larsen/Shutterstock (206). foodfolio / Alamy (206). imagebroker / Alamy (206). Bratwustle | Dreamstime.com (206). IML Image Group Ltd / Alamy (207). Alanesspe | Dreamstime.com (207). Christopher Leggett (207). MihiScholl/Flickr, [CC BY 2.0] (207). Apostolis Giontzis/Shutterstock (217). IML Image Group Ltd / Alamy (221). **Chapter 5: The Sporades, Skiathos, Skopelos, and Skyros:** Aetherial | Dreamstime.com (233). Alanesspe | Dreamstime.com (233). Constantinos Iliopoulos/Shutterstock (242). Robert Harding Produc / age fotostock (245). Georgios Tschlis/shutterstock (248). Genetzakis/IML / age fotostock (255). **Chapter 6: Ionian Islands, Corfu, Kefalonia, Zakynthos:** Adisa/Shutterstock (257). Ellen Rooney / age fotostock (273). Werner Otto / age fotostock (278). Ljupco Smokovski/Shutterstock (287). Georgios Tsichlis/shutterstock (293). Andronos Haris/Shutterstock (299). Igor Tichonow/Shutterstock (303). PavelJiranek/shutterstock (310). Aerial-motion/Shutterstock (314-315). Mikhail Leonov/Shutterstock (317). **Chapter 7: Northern Cyclades, Tinos, Syros, Mykonos, Delos:** Milan Gonda/shutterstock (319). Milangonda | Dreamstime.com (330). Jenifoto406 | Dreamstime.com (353). San Rostro / age fotostock (356). Sddbb (368). Marco Simoni / age fotostock (371). volk65/Shutterstock (373). Danilo Ascione/Shutterstock (376). **Chapter 8: Southern Cyclades, Paros, Antiparos, Naxos, Milos, Folegandros, Santorini:** Svetlana Ryajentseva/Shutterstock (379). Spyropoulos/IML / age fotostock (388). Cheryl Jenkins (401). leoks/Shutterstock (406). Constantineas/IML / age fotostock (425). Josefskacel | Dreamstime.com (437). R. Lemieszek/Shutterstock (443). **Chapter 9: Crete:** Dbyjuhfl | Dreamstime.com (447). Olgacov | Dreamstime.com (458). Yiannis Papadimitriou/Shutterstock (466). Avatavat | Dreamstime.com (477). Jon Arnold Images Ltd / Alamy Stock Photo (481). liv friis-larsen/iStockphoto (482). Jastrow/wikipedia.org (483). Okssi68 | Dreamstime.com (483). blickwinkel / Alamy (483). Dziewul/Shutterstock (489). **Chapter 10: Rhodes and the Dodecanese, Rhodes, Symi, Kos, Patmos:** Philippos Philippou/Shutterstock (493). saiko3p/Shutterstock (504). Parispho | Dreamstime.com (505). Walter Bibikow (506). Public Domain (506). SLATER Eliott (506). Terence Waeland / Alamy (507). giulio andreini (507). Image Asset Managemen (507). Rene Mattes (508). ACE STOCK LIMITED / Alamy (508). Public Domain (508). Keith Binns/iStockphoto (509). Peter Horree / Alamy (509). Peter Horree / Alamy (509). Classic Image / Alamy Stock Photo (509). Public Domain (510). Image Asset Managemen (510). T. Papageorgiou (510). Public Domain (511). ALIKI SAPOUNTZI / aliki image library / Alamy (511). terry harris just greece photo library / Alamy (511). Public Domain (512). Public Domain (512). Public Domain (512). Lubos K/Shutterstock (514). Jakub Rutkiewicz/Shutterstock (521). Jon Arnold Images Ltd / Alamy (529). Freesurf69 | Dreamstime.com (545). **Chapter 11: The Northern Aegean Islands, Lesvos, Chios, and Samos:** Nejdet Duzen/Shutterstock (547). Freesurf69 | Dreamstime.com (561). Diverroy | Dreamstime.com (568). Freesurf69 | Dreamstime.com (577). Ctppix | Dreamstime.com (580). Mangojuicy | Dreamstime.com (583). **Chapter 12: Attica and Delphi:** Krishna.Wu / Shutterstock (585). Hercules Milas / Alamy (594). stefano lunardi / age fotostock (603). Aerial-motion/shutterstock (611). Wojtek Buss / age fotostock (616). Wojtek Buss / age fotostock (625). **Chapter 13: Epirus and Thessaly, Ioannina, Metsovo, and the Meteora Monasteries:** kostasgr/Shutterstock (629). Kostas1gr | Dreamstime.com (641). giulio andreini / age fotostock (643). DEA PICTURE LIBRARY / age fotostock (654). R. Matina/agefotostock (654). Ralf Siemieniec/Shutterstock (656). cod_gabriel/Flickr, [CC BY 2.0] (656). Petr Svarc / Alamy (657). R. Matina/aefotostock (657). Jose Fuste Raga/agefotostock (658). Ciprian Dumitrescu/iStockphoto (659). Walter Zerla/agefotostock (660). **Chapter 14: Thessaloniki and Central Macedonia:** Lambroskazan | Dreamstime.com (665). Ververidis | Dreamstime.com (676). giulio andreini / age fotostock (688). DEA / G DAGLI ORTI / age fotostock (693). MONTICO Lionel - www.agefotostock.com (699). Hapsis/IML / age fotostock (700). **Chapter 15: The Peloponnese, Monemvassia, Mycenae, Nafplion, the Mani, and Olympia:** Nikolais | Dreamstime.com (703). Tuul / age fotostock (717). Greece / Alamy (722). DEA / A VERGANI / age fotostock (730). Richard Bowden/Shutterstock (752-753). J.D. Dallet / age fotostock (766). **About Our Writers:** All photos are courtesy of the writers.

Every effort has been made to trace the copyright holders, and we apologize in advance for any accidental errors. We would be happy to apply the corrections in the following edition of this publication.

Notes

Fodor's ESSENTIAL GREECE

Publisher: Stephen Horowitz, *General Manager*

Editorial: Douglas Stallings, *Editorial Director*; Jill Fergus, Amanda Sadlowski, *Senior Editors*; Kayla Becker, Alexis Kelly, *Editors*

Design: Tina Malaney, *Director of Design and Production*; Jessica Gonzalez, *Graphic Designer*; Mariana Tabares, *Design & Production Intern*

Production: Jennifer DePrima, *Editorial Production Manager*; Elyse Rozelle, *Senior Production Editor*; Monica White, *Production Editor*

Maps: Rebecca Baer, *Senior Map Editor*; Mark Stroud and Henry Colomb (Moon Street Cartography), David Lindroth, *Cartographers*

Photography: Viviane Teles, *Senior Photo Editor*; Namrata Aggarwal, Ashok Kumar, *Photo Editors*; Rebecca Rimmer, *Photo Intern*

Business & Operations: Chuck Hoover, *Chief Marketing Officer*; Robert Ames, *Group General Manager*; Devin Duckworth, *Director of Print Publishing*; Victor Bernal, *Business Analyst*

Public Relations and Marketing: Joe Ewaskiw, *Senior Director Communications & Public Relations*; Esther Su, *Senior Marketing Manager*

Fodors.com: Jeremy Tarr, *Editorial Director*; Rachael Levitt, *Managing Editor*

Technology: Jon Atkinson, *Director of Technology*; Rudresh Teotia, *Lead Developer*; Jacob Ashpis, *Content Operations Manager*

Writers: Alexia Amvrazi, Stephen Brewer, Gareth Clark, Liam McCaffrey, Hilary Whitton Paipeti, Adrian Vrettos, Nora Wallaya

Editor: Jill Fergus

Production Editor: Elyse Rozelle

Copyright © 2021 by Fodor's Travel, a division of MH Sub I, LLC, dba Internet Brands.

Fodor's is a registered trademark of Internet Brands, Inc. All rights reserved. Published in the United States by Fodor's Travel, a division of Internet Brands, Inc. No maps, illustrations, or other portions of this book may be reproduced in any form without written permission from the publisher.

2nd edition

ISBN 978-1-64097-369-5

ISSN 2574–349X

All details in this book are based on information supplied to us at press time. Always confirm information when it matters, especially if you're making a detour to visit a specific place. Fodor's expressly disclaims any liability, loss, or risk, personal or otherwise, that is incurred as a consequence of the use of any of the contents of this book.

SPECIAL SALES

This book is available at special discounts for bulk purchases for sales promotions or premiums. For more information, e-mail SpecialMarkets@fodors.com.

PRINTED IN THE UNITED STATES OF AMERICA

10 9 8 7 6 5 4 3 2 1

About Our Writers

Alexia Amvrazi has been writing and presenting about Greece for global and local media for 20+ years and is the author of the book *111 Places in Athens That You Shouldn't Miss.* She is also the editor of the lifestyle website "InSights Greece." Raised in Rome, Cairo, and Athens she's passionate about holistic wellness, gastronomy, and travel. In this edition she has updated the Athens chapter. You can follow her on Instagram @alexia_amvrazi and check out her blog, imverywellthankyou.com and the website www.insightsgreece.com.

Stephen Brewer has been exploring the Greek islands and mainland for more than 30 years. He admits to being partial to the south of Crete, where he spends part of every year, but he never tires of island-hopping or exploring mainland mountains, and he continues to find the experience of stepping onto any patch of stony ground or clamoring over any ruin transporting. He writes about his experiences in Greece frequently for Fodor's and magazines. For this edition, he updated the Experience and Travel Smart chapters.

Since venturing cautiously from his native Northeast England, **Gareth Clark** has worked in publishing across the world, editing *Time Out* magazines in the UAE and China before returning to the UK to work on long-running travel magazine *Wanderlust.* Along the way, he has updated guidebooks for Fodor's and Time Out on China, the UAE, Malta, Belgium, and Greece including the Peloponnese, Rhodes and the Dodecanese, Attica and Delphi, and the Ionian Islands (Zakynthos and Kefalonia) chapters of this edition.

Liam McCaffrey first came to Greece in the 1980s and has spent the intervening years traveling all over the country. After a career in publishing, as well as stints as a restaurateur and hotelier, he finally took the plunge and moved to Athens in 2012. He works in a forest school, teaches English to reluctant teenagers, and writes extensively as a freelancer for the international press. Happiest sharing a meal by the sea with friends, he is still looking for the perfect Greek island but is enjoying the search. Liam updated the Northern Cyclades, Southern Cyclades, and Crete chapters.

Hilary Whitton Paipeti is an English-born publisher, journalist, author, and hiking guru who lives in the beautiful depths of rural Corfu. She shares her large garden with two rescue dogs that accompany her everywhere on her many mountain walks, either by herself or with hiking groups she leads during weekends. Her books include *The Corfu Book of Walks* and *In the Footsteps of Lawrence Durrell and Gerald Durrell in Corfu (1935–1939),* and nine hiking and non-hiking guides to Corfu, now available through *www.corfuwalks.com.* Along the way, her treks prompted her to create "The Corfu Trail," a now-celebrated island-long trekking route (*www.thecorfutrail.com*). She updated Corfu for this edition.

About Our Writers

 Adrian Vrettos first traveled to Greece from London two decades ago to work as a field archaeologist on prehistoric and classical excavations throughout the country. He now works as a freelance travel writer, journalist, and editor in Athens. Adrian updated Epirus and Thessaly; Thessaloniki and Central Macedonia; and the Saronic Gulf Islands.

 Nora Wallaya is a London-based travel writer and editor with a deep interest in nature, history, and culture. She has written for publications including *National Geographic Traveller*, *London Evening Standard*, Atlas Obscura, *Wanderlust Travel Magazine*, *BBC Gardeners' World Magazine*, and *The Telegraph*, covering destinations in Europe, Asia, and Africa. Nora is currently working on her debut novel, a piece of adventure fiction based upon her childhood experiences in Sudan. You can follow her on Instagram @nora.wallaya. Nora updated the Sporades and Northern Aegean chapters.